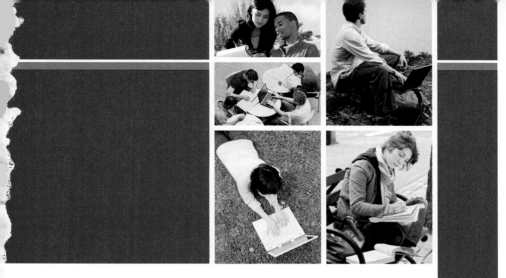

The Little, Brown Handbook

Instructor's Annotated Edition

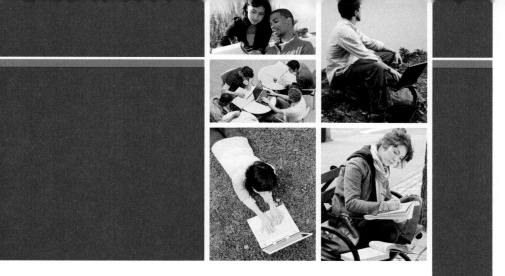

The Little, Brown Handbook

H. Ramsey Fowler
St. Edward's University

Jane E. Aaron

Cynthia K. Marshall
Wright State University

Instructor's
Annotated
Edition

Longman

New York   San Francisco   Boston
London   Toronto   Sydney   Tokyo   Singapore   Madrid
Mexico City   Munich   Paris   Cape Town   Hong Kong   Montreal

Publisher: Joseph Opiela
Senior Development Editor: Anne Brunell Ehrenworth
Senior Supplements Editor: Donna Campion
Senior Media Producer: Stefanie Liebman
Senior Marketing Manager: Susan Stoudt
Production Manager: Bob Ginsberg
Project Coordination, Text Design, and Electronic Page Makeup:
    Nesbitt Graphics, Inc.
Cover Design Manager: John Callahan
Cover Designer: Kay Petronio
Cover Photos: (*clockwise from top*): Anderson Ross/Blend Images/Getty
    Images, Inc.; Stone/Getty; David Fischer/Digital Vision/Getty Images,
    Inc.; Janie Grill/Iconica/Getty Images, Inc.; Image Source/Getty
Photo Researcher: Rebecca Karamehmedovic
Senior Manufacturing Buyer: Roy L. Pickering, Jr.
Printer and Binder: RR Donnelley & Sons Company/Crawfordsville
Cover Printer: Phoenix Color Corporation

Longman
is an imprint of

12345678910—DOC—12 11 10 09
ISBN-13: 978-0-205-67311-7
ISBN-10:   0-205-67311-2

www.pearsonhighered.com

Designing and Teaching Composition Courses

These chapters appear only in this *Instructor's Annotated Edition*

1 Teaching Writing as a Process   *IAE-2*

Writing as a *how* ■ Writing as an expressive process ■ Writing as a cognitive process ■ Writing as a social process ■ Resources for teaching writing

2 Using *The Little, Brown Handbook*   *IAE-8*

Assumptions shaping *The Little, Brown Handbook* ■ New features of the eleventh edition ■ Familiarizing students with the handbook ■ Organizing a composition course ■ Using the handbook with other texts ■ Tutoring with the handbook ■ Sample syllabi ■ Resources for designing a writing course

3 Working with Student Writing   *IAE-21*

The roles of response ■ Commenting on papers ■ Making sure students understand your comments ■ Evaluating essays for a grade ■ Evaluating for revision ■ Coping with the paper load ■ Evaluation *cans* and *can'ts* ■ Resources for response and evaluation

4 Using Collaborative Learning with the Handbook   *IAE-35*

Forming groups for collaboration ■ Developing skills in collaboration ■ Customizing collaborative materials ■ Resources for collaborative learning and peer criticism

5 Using Computers to Teach Writing   *IAE-47*

Possibilities for teaching with technology ■ Computer technology in and out of the classroom ■ *The Little, Brown Handbook* in the computer-assisted classroom ■ Sample schedule for a first-year composition course ■ Resources for using computers to teach writing

6 Teaching Writing to ESL Students   *IAE-62*

Profile of ESL students ■ Cross-cultural issues ■ Issues in working with ESL writing ■ Sentence-level errors in ESL writing ■ Conclusion ■ Resources for teaching ESL students

Brief Contents of the Student Edition

The complete student edition of *The Little, Brown Handbook*, Eleventh Edition, with its detailed table of contents, follows the six chapters appearing only in this instructor's edition. The annotations in the margins of this instructor's edition—which include answers to the exercises and tips for presenting the material—do not appear in the student edition.

1 The Writing Process *1*

1 Assessing the Writing Situation *2*
2 Developing and Shaping Ideas *16*
3 Drafting and Revising *46*
4 Writing and Revising Paragraphs *72*
5 Designing Documents *112*

2 Reading and Writing in College *127*

6 Developing Academic Skills *128*
7 Forming a Critical Perspective *138*
8 Writing in Academic Situations *162*
9 Reading Arguments Critically *176*
10 Writing an Argument *196*
11 Reading and Using Visual Arguments *216*

3 Grammatical Sentences *229*

12 Understanding Sentence Grammar *230*
13 Case of Nouns and Pronouns *264*
14 Verbs *272*
15 Agreement *301*
16 Adjectives and Adverbs *315*

4 Clear Sentences *329*

17 Sentence Fragments *330*
18 Comma Splices and Fused Sentences *338*
19 Pronoun Reference *345*
20 Shifts *352*
21 Misplaced and Dangling Modifiers *359*
22 Mixed and Incomplete Sentences *369*

5 Effective Sentences *377*

23 Emphasizing Ideas *378*
24 Using Coordination and Subordination *388*
25 Using Parallelism *398*
26 Achieving Variety *405*

6 Punctuation *415*

27 End Punctuation *418*
28 The Comma *422*
29 The Semicolon *443*
30 The Apostrophe *451*
31 Quotation Marks *459*
32 Other Punctuation Marks *467*

7 Mechanics *481*

33 Capitals *482*
34 Italics or Underlining *488*
35 Abbreviations *492*
36 Numbers *496*

8 Effective Words *501*

37 Using Appropriate Language *502*
38 Using Exact Language *511*
39 Writing Concisely *523*
40 Spelling and the Hyphen *531*

9 Research Writing *547*

41 Planning a Research Project *548*
42 Finding Sources *561*
43 Working with Sources *589*
44 Avoiding Plagiarism and Documenting Sources *626*
45 Writing the Paper *635*
46 Using MLA Documentation and Format *644*
47 Two Research Papers in MLA Style *691*

10 Writing in the Academic Disciplines *727*

48 Working with the Goals and Requirements of the Disciplines *728*
49 Reading and Writing About Literature *731*
50 Writing in Other Humanities *755*
51 Writing in the Social Sciences *774*
52 Writing in the Natural and Applied Sciences *805*

11 Special Writing Situations *821*

53 Essay Examinations *822*
54 Writing Online *828*
55 Public Writing *840*
56 Oral Presentations *856*
Glossary of Usage 865
Glossary of Terms 882
Index 907

Designing and Teaching Composition Courses

1

Teaching Writing as a Process

■ Writing as a *how*

Drawing on the results of three decades of research into the composing processes of writers, most writing instructors now emphasize the *how* of writing. Although theorists such as Lester Faigley and Susan Miller have pointed out the limitations of trying to define systematically what happens when a writer sits down to compose a work, most writing teachers and their students have effectively adapted a focus on the processes through which students generate and revise their writing, rather than concentrating solely on a final product. This book is designed to support that focus on the *hows* of writing.

Most writers agree that at least three components contribute to the processes they use most of the time: *prewriting*, the finding and exploring of ideas and the construction of plans for expressing them (in classical terminology, *invention*); *drafting*, getting the ideas down on paper and generating sentences about them; and *revising*, reconsidering the ideas, the treatment they receive, the plans for expressing them, and the ways they are expressed (in classical terminology, *arrangement, style*, and to some extent, *delivery*).

Theories about the writing process have focused on the ways in which writers do the following:

- perceive and explore themselves and their worlds through the medium of language;
- consider their subject matter as the occasion for interpretive analysis and as the testing ground for ideas and hypotheses;
- respond to, understand, and to some degree, invent their audiences; and
- position themselves in relation to writerly conventions, to institutional restraints, and to communities within and outside of the classroom.

These assumptions are based on the theories outlined below.

■ Writing as an expressive process

Many theories of the writing process from the 1960s and 1970s focused on its expressive content, the attempts of writers to use language to capture and articulate the unique vision of the writer. For instance, D. Gordon Rohman and Albert O. Wlecke argue that techniques such as meditative exercises, journal keeping, and the composition of analogies (called "existential sentences") help writers find a personal truth in even the most abstract of subjects. They argue that such "prewriting" techniques lead in a smooth and linear fashion to drafting and revision as writers refine the expression of the truth they tell. This privileging of self-discovery, what is sometimes called the *expressionistic* or *romantic* view of composing, is also held by Peter Elbow, Ken Macrorie, William Coles, and Donald Murray, to name a few of its most influential proponents. Elbow argues for the efficacy of freewriting and drafting in helping writers explore ideas before worrying about structure and presentation. Macrorie encourages students to use "case histories" of past experiences and to work from direct observation in order to go beyond the obvious clichés, which he calls "Engfish" (because they stink of insincerity). Coles values prewriting because it allows students to explore multiple relationships to readers and subjects (what he calls "plural I's"). Murray emphasizes aspects of prewriting that cultivate surprise, originality, and new combinations of ideas which lead to personal discovery.

The expressionistic theory gives discovery of ideas primacy in the writing process and sees the writer's personal vision as more important than conventions and codes;

its emphasis on pre- and freewriting is an attempt to give writers the power to control or even exploit conventions and expectations to convey an original vision. These beliefs have thus attracted criticism from those who believe that the teacher's responsibility is to show writers how to become part of a community, not how to put themselves outside it. However, the expressionists' contributions to our understanding of the formative stages of prewriting and drafting and their respect for students as writing colleagues have benefited many teachers and theorists. Ann Berthoff's work is an interesting example of that influence; she draws on the expressionistic emphasis by stressing the power of the imagination to create relationships between ideas, but in "Recognition, Representation and Revision" she also develops an understanding of revision as a nonlinear part of the composing process, an ongoing reconsideration of those relationships. Where many expressionists might insist that pre-writing generates the ideas, that revision is the process of getting them right, and that editing is the radically separate task of adjusting the etiquette of presentation (spelling, punctuation, and the like), Berthoff and others view revision as a recursive process, as the meaningful reconsideration and development of ideas articulated through the grammar of the paragraph and the sentence.

▪ Writing as a cognitive process

A second school of theories about the writing process is deeply rooted in psychology, particularly in studies of cognition. For such *cognitive* theorists, "protocols" (detailed descriptions of how a document is produced) and draft analyses play a key role. One of the earliest such cognitive studies is Janet Emig's *The Composing Process of Twelfth Graders* (1971), where she studies writing behaviors: how student writers find and develop their ideas. Drawing on James Britton's terminology, she finds that these processes differ with the audience: if students write for themselves (expressively), they are concerned with the presentation of ideas, but if students write for teachers (transactionally), they are concerned (even obsessed) with mechanical correctness. Emig's technique of asking writers to compose out loud has also been used by Sondra Perl in her studies of unskilled writers and by Carol Berkenkotter in her study of a professional writer's composing processes. Nancy Sommers's comparisons of

student and experienced adult writers show that experienced writers come to value the development of ideas far more than mechanical correctness, whereas student writers' concern with correctness and with the demands of the writing situation often impedes the development of ideas.

Richard Young, Alton Becker, and Kenneth Pike also developed a cognitive theory of the writing process; however, theirs depends on the writer's knowledge not of the audience but of the subject. Their "tagmemics" theory models cognitive efforts to know a subject; it focuses on how writers perceive a subject's individuality, variability, and place in a larger system. These cognitive efforts should help writers find and develop new combinations of ideas. Like the romantic theories, tagmemics emphasizes prewriting and only discusses drafting or revision as it manifests writers' developing understanding of their subject matter.

The cognitivist position has been most fully expanded by Linda Flower, John Hayes, and their graduate students and colleagues at Carnegie-Mellon University. They view the composing process as a series of decision-making strategies: planning texts, translating those plans into sentences, and revising the texts produced to bring them in line with the original (or reshaped) plans. Although Emig first suggested it, Flower and Hayes and their collaborators have done a great deal to demonstrate the recursive and hierarchical levels of writing processes, especially in the planning and revising stages of writing activities.

Cognitivists find linear expressionist models too simplistic; they argue that writers continually move back and forth between stages to adjust their plans. Like the expressionists, the cognitivists value personal expression highly, claiming it represents most validly an individual's way of thinking. Cognitivists spend little time discussing the finished forms writing may take; it's rare to see an entire piece of discourse reproduced in their discussions. More recently, they have been giving slightly more emphasis to the audience's role in the cognitive workings of writers. But for cognitivists, the writer's "brain work" and reflections on it remain paramount. This position has been challenged as an attempt to systematize the complex cognitive processes of writers and their varying situations. However, cognitive studies have arguably helped teachers to become more attentive to the varied composing processes of individuals and better able to respond to the particular challenges faced by student writers.

■ Writing as a social process

Most recently, as theorists have focused on the social functions of and constraints on writing, studies of the writing process have broadened to examine the contexts in which writing occurs, to define the discourse communities in which particular writing processes participate. This composition theory draws heavily from cultural studies practices by foregrounding issues of ethnicity, class, gender, and ability in the writing classroom. The changing demographics of college populations have also influenced this perspective. As more and more nontraditional students—older or returning, working class, of non-European origin, international—have entered the academy, teachers have been forced to change their expectations about the kinds of knowledge students bring with them. No longer can a teacher take for granted that students know what an essay looks like, or what "thesis and support" are, or how academics think. (Indeed, research conducted by Robert Connors and Andrea Lunsford suggests that an unfamiliarity with the look of the printed page may be responsible for many student "errors.")

Because of the traditional link between writing programs and English departments, one response to this situation has been to teach students the kinds of discourse that scholars trained in literature and its criticism value: journals, poetry, fiction, and literary analysis. But the "social-epistemic" theorists, as James Berlin called them, have argued that the role of writing programs is to prepare students to read and respond to the various specialized languages—academic, legal, governmental—that they might encounter.

The social theories of the writing process have two current focuses. According to the political focus, represented by David Bartholomae and Anthony Petrosky, Patricia Bizzell, and others influenced to some extent by the Brazilian theorist Paolo Freire, awareness of the constraints of a discourse community is politically liberating, potentially enabling, and revolutionary. If students can understand the constraints of that community and master them, they can come to control and change the community through their own discourse. For theorists who believe this, discovery of the contexts in which students write and the constraints that govern those contexts comes before any other part of the writing process. In terms of classroom practice such theories emphasize a problem-solving format in which students often work with discursive academic prose in peer-group settings and use revision and rereading to establish articulate positions within and against those discourses. Critics of liberatory pedagogy like Maxine Hairston (see Richard Fulkerson for a more recent critique) charge that this overtly political approach amounts to indoctrinating students; proponents of the activist pedagogy contend that all pedagogies, even apparently neutral ones, are in fact political.

Another socially focused theory sees writing as a fundamental tool for learning in all communities and at all curricular levels and attempts to foster the teaching of writing beyond the limits of traditional writing programs. In particular, this focus is apparent in "writing-across-the-curriculum" (WAC) and "writing-across-the-disciplines" movements, which have achieved increasing success in the colleges where they have been implemented. Toby Fulwiler and Barbara Walvoord, two noted proponents of the movement, have both argued convincingly for the benefits of writing instruction beyond the first-year courses. Some WAC supporters (Joseph Petraglia and David Smit, for example) favor abolishing general composition altogether. Related "social construction" theories make the case that knowledge is achieved as a consensus among communities rather than as a hierarchical transfer of information from teacher to student. In *Collaborative Learning: Higher Education, Interdependence, and the Authority of Knowledge*, Kenneth Bruffee argues for collaborative student learning as the process through which students become members in their college communities and in communities of knowledge. While social constructionism has been critiqued for its goal of consensus on the grounds that it erases vital differences and competing discourses within communities, collaborative work has become an invaluable part of most classrooms (see for instance the works of Stewart and Sullivan). Other classroom applications of social theories include incorporating service learning (see Deans and Feldman) and using new technologies in writing courses. Specifically, the proliferation of new media, such as Web sites, instant messages, and blogs, is viewed as an opportunity for students to explore new genres (see Wysocki et al.) and to end the academy's privileging of print (see Yancey). For more information on technology in the classroom, see Chapter 5, "Using Computers to Teach Writing."

Ultimately, teachers generally adapt the theories and methods that make the most sense given the needs of their students and the shape of their institutional setting. The key effort of this book is to support a range of pedagogical emphases on the composing processes of writers and to help students understand rhetorical forms as flexible frameworks rather than as rigid formulas—as essential parts of a creative composing process.

■ Resources for teaching writing

Bartholomae, David. "A Conversation with Peter Elbow." *College Composition and Communication* 46.1 (1995): 62–71. Print.

---. "Inventing the University." *When a Writer Can't Write: Studies in Writer's Block and Other Composing Process Problems.* Ed. Mike Rose. New York: Guilford, 1985. 134–65. Print.

---. *Writing on the Margins: Essays on Composition and Teaching.* New York: Bedford/St. Martin's, 2005. Print.

Berkenkotter, Carol. "Decisions and Revisions: The Planning Strategies of a Publishing Writer and Response of a Laboratory Rat: Or, Being Protocoled." *College Composition and Communication,* 34.2 (1983), 156–72. Print.

Berlin, James. "Rhetoric and Ideology in the Writing Class." *College English* 50.5 (1988): 477–94. Print.

Berthoff, Ann. *The Making of Meaning: Metaphors, Models, and Maxims for Writing Teachers.* Upper Montclair: Boynton/Cook, 1981. Print.

---. *Reclaiming the Imagination: Philosophical Perspectives for Writers and Teachers of Writing.* Upper Montclair: Boynton/Cook, 1984. Print.

---. "Recognition, Representation and Revision." *Rhetoric and Composition.* Ed. Richard L. Graves. Upper Montclair: Boynton/Cook, 1984. 27–38. Print.

Bizzell, Patricia. *Academic Discourse and Critical Consciousness.* Pittsburgh: U of Pittsburgh P, 1992. Print.

Bloom, Lynn Z., Donald A. Daiker, and Edward M. White, eds. *Composition Studies in the New Millennium: Rereading the Past, Rewriting the Future.* Carbondale: Southern Illinois UP, 2003. Print.

Britton, James. "Theories of the Disciplines and a Learning Theory." *Writing, Teaching, and Learning in the Disciplines.* Ed. Anne Herrington and Charles Moran. New York: MLA, 1992. 47–60. Print.

Bruffee, Kenneth. *Collaborative Learning: Higher Education, Interdependence, and the Authority of Knowledge.* 2nd ed. Baltimore: Johns Hopkins UP, 1998. Print.

Coles, William E., Jr. *The Plural I: The Teaching of Writing.* New York: Holt, 1978. Print.

Connors, Robert J., and Andrea A. Lunsford. "Frequency of Formal Errors in Current College Writing, or Ma and Pa Kettle Do Research." *College Composition and Communication* 39.4 (1988): 395–409. Print.

Corbett, Edward P. J., et al., eds. *The Writing Teacher's Sourcebook.* 4th ed. New York: Oxford UP, 2000. Print.

Deans, Thomas. *Writing Partnerships: Service-Learning in Composition.* Urbana: NCTE, 2000. Print.

Dejoy, Nancy. *Process This: Undergraduate Writing in Composition Studies.* Logan: Utah State UP, 2004. Print.

Downs, Douglas, and Elizabeth Wardle. "Teaching about Writing, Righting Misconceptions: (Re)Envisioning 'First-Year Composition' as 'Introduction to Writing Studies.'" *College Composition and Communication* 58.4 (2007): 552–84. Print.

Elbow, Peter. "Reflections on Academic Discourse: How It Relates to Freshmen and Colleagues." *College English* 53.2 (1991): 135–55. Print.

Emig, Janet. *The Composing Processes of Twelfth Graders.* Urbana: NCTE, 1971. Print.

---. *The Web of Meaning.* Upper Montclair: Boynton/ Cook, 1983. Print.

Faigley, Lester. *Fragments of Rationality: Postmodernity and the Subject of Composition.* Pittsburgh: U of Pittsburgh P, 1992. Print.

Feldman, Ann M. *Making Writing Matter: Composition in the Engaged University.* Albany: State U of New York P, 2008. Print.

Flower, Linda. *The Construction of Negotiated Meaning: A Social Cognitive Theory of Writing.* Carbondale: Southern Illinois UP, 1994. Print.

---. "The Construction of Purpose in Writing and Reading." *College English* 50.5 (1988): 528–50. Print.

Flower, Linda, and John R. Hayes. "A Cognitive Process Theory of Writing." *College Composition and Communication* 32.4 (1981): 365–87. Print.

Fulkerson, Richard. "Composition at the Turn of the Twenty-First Century." *College Composition and Communication* 56.4 (2005): 654–87. Print.

Fulwiler, Toby, and Art Young, eds. *Language Connections: Writing and Reading Across the Curriculum.* Urbana: NCTE, 1978. Print.

---. *Programs That Work: Models and Methods for Writing Across the Curriculum*. Portsmouth: Boynton/Cook (Heinemann), 1990. Print.

Hairston, Maxine. "Different Products, Different Processes: A Theory About Writing." *College Composition and Communication* 37.4 (1986): 442–52. Print.

---. "Diversity, Ideology, and Teaching Writing." *College Composition and Communication* 43.2 (1992): 179–93. Print.

Hayes, John R., and Linda S. Flower. "Writing Research and the Writer." *American Psychologist* 41.10 (1986): 1106–13. Print.

Jarratt, Susan C., and Lynn Worsham, eds. *Feminism and Composition Studies: In Other Words*. New York: MLA, 1998. Print.

Kent, Thomas, ed. *Post-Process Theory: Beyond the Writing-Process Paradigm*. Carbondale: Southern Illinois UP, 1999. Print.

Lindquist, Julie. "Class Ethos and the Politics of Inquiry: What the Barroom Can Teach Us about the Classroom." *College Composition and Communication* 51.2 (1999): 225–47. Print.

Macrorie, Ken. *Searching Writing*. Upper Montclair: Boynton/ Cook, 1980. Print.

McComiskey, Bruce. *Teaching Composition as a Social Process*. Logan: Utah State UP, 2000. Print.

Miller, Susan. *Textual Carnivals: The Politics of Composition*. Carbondale: Southern Illinois UP, 1991. Print.

---. "Writing Theory: Theory Writing." *Methods and Methodology in Composition Research*. Ed. Gesa Kirsch and Patrick A. Sullivan. Carbondale: Southern Illinois UP, 1992. 62–83. Print.

Moffett, James. *Teaching the Universe of Discourse*. Boston: Houghton, 1968. Print.

Murray, Donald M. *The Craft of Revision*. New York: Harcourt, 1991. Print.

---. *Expecting the Unexpected: Teaching Myself— and Others—to Read and Write*. Portsmouth: Heinemann, 1989. Print.

Newkirk, Thomas. *The Performance of Self in Student Writing*. Portsmouth: Boynton/Cook (Heinemann), 1997. Print.

Perl, Sondra. "The Composing Process of Unskilled College Writers." *Research in the Teaching of English* 13.4 (1979): 317–36. Print.

Perelman, Les. "The Context of Classroom Writing." *College English* 48.5 (1986): 471–79. Print.

Petraglia, Joseph, ed. *Reconceiving Writing, Rethinking Writing Instruction*. Mahwah: Erlbaum, 1995. Print.

Reither, James A. "Writing and Knowing: Toward Redefining the Writing Process." *College English* 47.6 (1985): 620–28. Print.

Roberts-Miller, Patricia. "Post-Contemporary Composition: Social Constructivism and Its Alternatives." *Composition Studies* 30.1 (2002): 97–115. Print.

Rohman, D. Gordon, and Alberto O. Wlecke. *Pre-Writing: The Construction and Application of Models for Concept-Formation in Writing*. USOE Cooperative Research Project No. 2174. East Lansing: Michigan State UP, 1964. Print.

Rose, Mike. "Rigid Rules, Inflexible Plans, and the Stifling of Language: A Cognitivist Analysis of Writer's Block." *College Composition and Communication* 31.4 (1980): 389–401. Print.

Russell, David P. *Writing in the Academic Disciplines: A Curricular History*. Carbondale: Southern Illinois UP, 1991. Print.

Smit, David W. *The End of Composition Studies*. Carbondale: Southern Illinois UP, 2004. Print.

Sommers, Nancy. "Across the Drafts." *College Composition and Communication* 58.2 (2006): 248–57. Print.

---. "Revision Strategies of Student Writers and Experienced Adult Writers." *College Composition and Communication* 31.4 (1980): 378–88. Print.

Sternglass, Marilyn. *Time to Know Them: A Longitudinal Study of Writing and Learning at the College Level*. Mahwah: Erlbaum, 1997. Print.

Stewart, Donald. "Collaborative Learning and Composition: Boon or Bane?" *Rhetoric Review* 7.1 (1988): 58–83. Print.

Sullivan, Patricia A. "Social Constructionism and Literacy Studies." *College English* 57.8 (1995): 950–59. Print.

Vandenberg, Peter, Sue Hum, and Jennifer Clary-Lemon, eds. *Relations, Locations, Positions: Composition Theory for Writing Teachers*. Urbana: NCTE, 2006. Print.

Villanueva, Victor, ed. *Cross-Talk in Comp Theory: A Reader*. 2nd ed. Urbana: NCTE, 2003. Print.

Walvoord, Barbara E. "The Future of WAC." *College English* 58.1 (1996): 58–79. Print.

Wolff, Janice M., ed. *Professing in the Contact Zone: Bringing Theory and Practice Together*. Urbana: NCTE, 2002. Print.

Wysocki, Anne, Johndan Johnson-Eilola, Cynthia Selfe, and Geoffrey Sirc. *Writing New Media: Theory and Applications for Expanding the Teaching of Composition*. Logan: Utah State UP, 2004. Print.

Yancey, Kathleen Blake. "Made Not Only in Words: Composition in a New Key." *College Composition and Communication* 56.2 (2004): 297–328. Print.

Young, Richard E., Alton L. Becker and Kenneth L. Pike. *Rhetoric: Discovery and Change*. New York: Harcourt, 1970. Print.

2

Using *The Little, Brown Handbook*

In many writing courses, the writing done by the students in that class serves as the core. The text or texts the instructor chooses should serve as resources to encourage and improve that writing. And the instructor's choice should be based on a clear understanding of the assumptions on which each text is founded.

■ Assumptions shaping *The Little, Brown Handbook*

It would be foolish to suggest that all composition instructors who emphasize the composing process are in agreement over specific teaching strategies—or that they ought to be. Two teachers who share a belief in the importance of revision or who encourage students to discover ideas and information through freewriting may also disagree strongly about the purposes for writing. Yet it is possible to identify some generally agreed-upon elements of a process paradigm.

The process paradigm of *The Little, Brown Handbook* is based on the following assumptions:

■ Writing consists of a variety of activities including *developing* (exploring, gathering, focusing, organizing); *drafting* (finding and expressing meaning, establishing relationships); and *revising* (rethinking, rewriting, editing, proofreading).

■ The activities that make up the writing process are recursive, not fixed in order. For example, revising often includes the discovery of fresh insights, and the drafting of one part of a paper may occur at the same time the writer is gathering materials for another part.

■ Writing often is a process of discovering ideas, arriving at knowledge of the self, and selecting effective ways to present concepts and information.

■ Knowledge of the conventions of expression and of stylistic options is an important part of the writer's repertoire, but a premature striving for correctness and for grace and clarity often can impede the free flow of ideas and the discovery of appropriate form. Thus, activities such as editing and proofreading, which pay considerable attention to style, grammar, and mechanics, are generally best left until relatively late in the composing of an essay.

■ Skilled writers (in contrast to unskilled writers) are characterized by the range of strategies they know and employ in developing, drafting, and revising—strategies that can be both taught and learned.

■ Effective writing is the product of interaction among the four elements of the writing situation: author, subject, language, and audience.

These assumptions shape the advice offered throughout *The Little, Brown Handbook*, not only in the discussions of the writing process (Part 1) and of reading and writing in college (Part 2), but also in treatments of research writing (Part 9), writing in the academic disciplines (Part 10), special writing situations (Part 11), strategies for clear and effective sentences (Parts 4 and 5), and diction (Part 8). Even the discussions of grammatical sentences (Part 3), punctuation (Part 6), and mechanics (Part 7) mix firm and relatively conservative advice with an awareness of the demands of various audiences and of the difference between an early draft and a final, carefully edited draft.

At the same time, discussions in the handbook point out that different writing situations may call for different composing processes and that the knowledge of forms for expression—the *what* of writing—is an important companion to an awareness of the *how*. In this the handbook agrees with the work of theorists and teachers such as Maxine Hairston, James Reither, Patricia Bizzell, and Arthur Applebee. These writers share a belief that the process paradigm needs to be augmented by:

- an awareness of the ways the writing process varies according to the writer's purpose and the social context;
- a recognition of the important roles knowledge of form and convention can play in guiding the composing process; and
- an acknowledgment of the extent to which communities of readers and writers are bound together by specific expectations governing the form and content of discourse.

The handbook recognizes that the processes of composing are "strategies that writers employ for particular purposes" (Applebee 106) and emphasizes this perspective in:

- the writing process (Chapters 1–5)
- reading and writing in college (Chapters 6–11)
- discussions of specialized forms of writing:

   research writing (Chapters 41–47)
   writing in the academic disciplines (Chapters 48–52)
   online writing (Chapter 54)
   public writing (Chapter 55)
   oral presentations (Chapter 56)

The emphasis throughout is on seeing the forms as the shared expectations of readers and writers and using these expectations to guide the discovery and expression of ideas so as not to constrain creativity.

■ New features of the eleventh edition

The eleventh edition of *The Little, Brown Handbook* has been revised to meet the needs of today's students, providing a solid foundation in the goals and requirements of college writing and research. Listed below are highlights of the new edition.

- A reorganized Part 2, on reading and writing in college, proceeds through a chapter each on academic skills in general (Chapter 6); critical thinking and reading (Chapter 7); and academic writing, which now provides a discussion of using synthesis when

writing in response to texts and two sample critiques (Chapter 8). The part concludes with three chapters on arguments—reading them, writing them, and using visual arguments (Chapters 9-11). A greater stress on opposing views in argument includes discussion of Rogerian approaches (Chapter 10). New visuals include graphs, a Web site, advertisements, and a photograph (Chapters 7 and 11).

- Research writing, covered in Part 9, continues to emphasize using the library as a Web gateway while keeping pace with the methods and challenges of research in an electronic environment. Coverage includes new discussions of research sources—blogs, wikis, and multimedia as well as first-hand observations and surveys (Chapter 42); an expanded discussion of evaluating sources with critical criteria applied to sample articles, Web documents, and a blog (Chapter 43); and more help with recognizing plagiarism and examples of plagiarized and unplagiarized sources (Chapter 43). A new research-paper-in-progress on green consumerism culminates in an annotated paper documented in MLA style (Chapters 41–45 and 47). Updated source lists in Part 10 provide reliable starting points for research in every discipline (Chapters 49–52).

- The extensive coverage of documentation in four styles—MLA, Chicago, APA, and CSE—reflects each style's latest version and includes many examples of electronic sources: MLA style is expanded and completely updated to reflect the 2008 *MLA Style Manual and Guide to Scholarly Publishing*, Third Edition (Chapter 46); APA style is updated to reflect the 2007 supplement *APA Style Guide to Electronic References* (Chapter 51); and CSE style is updated to reflect the 2006 *Scientific Style and Format: The CSE Manual for Authors, Editors, and Publishers*, Seventh Edition (Chapter 52). Annotated samples of key source types show students how to find the bibliographical information needed to cite each type (Chapters 46 and 51). And for all styles, color highlighting makes authors, titles, dates, and other citation elements easy to grasp.

- In Part 1, on the writing process, a new work-in-progress paper on globalization and outsourcing illustrates the many stages of the writing process (Chapters 2 and 3), new discussions of voice help students inject themselves into their academic writing

(Chapters 1 and 2), expanded coverage of thesis development now includes thesis questions and examples of explanatory and argumentative thesis statements (Chapter 2), and new diagrams visually reinforce the recursiveness of the writing process (Chapters 1–3).

- The handbook's core reference chapters include seven added boxes on helping verbs (Chapter 14), sentence fragments (Chapter 17), comma splices and fused sentences (Chapter 18), misplaced modifiers (Chapter 21), appropriate language (Chapter 37), word choice (Chapter 38), and spelling (Chapter 40), while color highlighting in many boxes throughout Parts 3 through 8 stresses and distinguishes sentence elements for quick reference. New advice on avoiding the informalities common to online communication targets nonstandard grammar, punctuation, abbreviations, and spelling (Chapter 37).

For more information about the revisions to the eleventh edition, see "Preface for Instructors" on pp. vii–xiii.

■ Familiarizing students with the handbook

Many students have little experience with a comprehensive handbook like *The Little, Brown Handbook,* so it is well worth the time to review where they can find material, how the book is organized, and how they might use it. Encourage students to personalize the book by marking sections that are particularly useful to them and by keeping an ongoing list of the sections they find themselves returning to for reference or that correspond to their identified patterns of error. The Editing Checklist (pp. 60–61) is a useful place to begin discussions about recognizing common errors, and it also provides a touchstone for your responses to student papers. It is equally important to make handbook usage part of the continuing conversation of the classroom, with frequent, in-class index and content searches, so that the handbook becomes a familiar resource. Such exercises can be a useful accompaniment to group or class-wide revision work on student papers.

Several users of previous editions of this handbook have successfully used a quiz as a means of orienting students to the material it contains. We offer this one with thanks to George Meese of Eckerd College, Florida.

Quiz for handbook users

Your goal is to show me that you can find answers to common writing questions by using your handbook. For instance, if the question is how to paraphrase material from a book in your research paper, you would need to turn to 43d (pp. 611–20). For each question below, list the page or section you would consult to answer this question. For extra credit, answer the question itself.

1. You need to cite an article in the *New York Times* using the MLA system of citations.
2. You can't decide whether to use *that* or *which* in a sentence.
3. You need pointers for writing the introduction for your essay.
4. You can't decide whether to use *rise* or *raise* as the verb in your sentence.
5. You need to know how to write a business letter.
6. You're confused about the difference between *affect* and *effect*.
7. You need to know whether to put a comma before *and* in the phrase *environment, politics and society*.
8. You need to know if the period goes before or after the quotation marks at the end of a direct quotation.
9. You have trouble narrowing the topic for your essay.
10. You need to know how to fix a comma splice in your essay.

■ Organizing a composition course

Organizing a composition course means choosing to emphasize those aspects of writing or kinds of texts that the instructor or the department considers most important and that meet the students' needs. Each institution will set its own goals and standards for what students are expected to achieve in a required writing course, and your class must help students meet those goals. This discussion may be particularly useful for inexperienced teachers who are planning a course for the first time.

In recent years, composition teaching has followed several general patterns for organizing a course, including emphasis on:

- patterns of expression and thought,
- the writing process,

- content and ideas, and
- academic writing (writing across the curriculum).

Each approach can be successful if it meets the needs of a particular group of students and if the instructor pays some attention to all aspects of composing.

Emphasis on patterns of expression and thought

Many instructors believe that a composition course ought to give students a chance to understand and practice basic patterns of expression and thought. Such courses may vary widely in the patterns they emphasize:

- rhetorical and logical patterns, such as classification, comparison-contrast, and deduction;
- general essay structures, such as thesis and support or general to specific;
- types of essays, such as informative and argumentative;
- patterns of paragraph development;
- sentence patterns.

Courses designed in this fashion are often used as basic writing courses, designed to meet the needs of students who enter college with limited experience in reading and writing. These courses emphasize the writing skills and patterns of thought essential to success in college courses. Although courses of this kind have their roots in "current-traditional rhetoric," an approach that tended to emphasize product over process, they can be adapted to take students' composing processes into consideration. The course might begin with sentence and paragraph construction, moving to longer essay forms as students become more comfortable with different kinds of paragraphs. A process approach would vary the focus from sentence-level constructions to considerations of the student's overall project in the paragraph and in the essay in order to emphasize their interrelated functions.

Organizing the course

In organizing a skills course, you might begin with a unit on sentence structure, drawing on Chapters 12–16 of the handbook ("Grammatical Sentences"), and you might stress an understanding of phrases, clauses, basic sentence types, and verb forms and tenses. Along with this, you might require paragraph-length writing that helps students to understand the functions of those sentence structures, and make use of the extensive discussion in Chapter 4 ("Writing and Revising Paragraphs"). Paragraph- and essay-length writing can continue through the semester, accompanied by work in Chapters 17–22 ("Clear Sentences") and 23–26 ("Effective Sentences"). Chapters on punctuation, mechanics, diction, and usage can be assigned whenever they meet the needs of the class or of individual students. Students might also use the Editing Checklist to keep track of the patterns of error that recur in their writing. In-class sessions can reinforce this practice by focusing on identifying errors in order to create meaningful revisions.

Teaching suggestions

Have students start writing paragraphs as early in the semester as possible to give them a sense of accomplishment and a chance to put into practice what they are learning in the sentence units. Also early on, you can incorporate essay-length writings into the course by requiring students to keep a writing journal with a specific number of pages to be devoted to a single topic at least once a week. You can integrate the journals into the class work by having them serve as topics for the students' paragraph and sentence constructions. This helps students to understand the relationship between the function of individual sentences and paragraphs and the overall purpose of an essay.

Other considerations

Although an effective basic course, often planned for developmental students, can focus on sentence, paragraph, and essay patterns, it also needs to pay attention to the writing process and to audience (see Chapters 1, 2, and 3 in the handbook). Students who have trouble mastering the basic forms of expression are also likely to underestimate the importance of planning and revising and to have difficulty shaping their writing to the needs of an audience. Collaborative revision work can help by providing students with immediate feedback from an identified audience of their peers. These matters can also be reinforced throughout the course with assignments that require planning, drafting, and revising and also create realistic audiences and situations for students to address in their writing. For example, the exercises in sections 1d and 1e on purpose and audience can be developed into group projects on which students work collaboratively to create directed appeals to the campus newspaper, to local government, or to a defined public organization.

Emphasis on patterns of development

Rhetorically oriented courses use standard essay types or patterns of development (for instance, comparison-contrast or process analysis) as a means of probing subjects and developing and organizing essays. Instructors who use such approaches share the belief that helping students understand these patterns and practice them in their writing will enable them to use the patterns in a variety of writing tasks. Most of these instructors would also agree that each pattern of development directs attention to a different aspect of a subject and thus the patterns can be seen as shaping the way we think about a subject and as affecting a reader's attitudes. Instructors of rhetorically oriented courses often rely on a reader or rhetoric to provide examples of essay types and patterns of development.

Organizing the course

If you wish to give your course a rhetorical orientation, you may want to begin with Parts 1 and 2 ("The Writing Process" and "Reading and Writing in College") to show students how to develop, write, revise, and edit an essay and to adapt it to an audience. Later in the course, you may want to return to this material to remind students how important the stages of the writing process are, particularly planning and revising. You can also point out that Chapters 2 and 4 treat the rhetorical patterns as answers to questions about aspects of a topic as well as ways of organizing and developing essays and paragraphs. You might include a unit on essay types or patterns of essay and paragraph development (Chapters 1–4) with assignments that give students a chance to use the forms. The chapters on sentence emphasis, coordination and subordination, parallelism, and variety (Chapters 23–26, "Effective Sentences") can be introduced later in the course to add variety and style to students' writing. The Editing Checklist and the chapters on common sentence errors, punctuation, mechanics, diction, and usage can be assigned according to the needs of individuals or of the class and may also be used for reference. The course might culminate in a research paper (Chapters 41–45) or oral presentations (Chapter 56) or business and community-based writing projects (Chapter 55).

Teaching suggestions

The risk in a rhetorically oriented course is that students will come to regard the various forms as ends in themselves and ignore the role they play in viewing experience and in shaping communication to an audience or situation. For this reason, many instructors emphasize throughout the course the process of exploring subjects and revising the plan for an essay, and they encourage students to create specific audiences and situations to address in their writing. Collaborative work in which students debate topics in class and/or through a Web site can be enormously useful in helping students to work toward particular audiences and purposes. These activities help students learn that the different forums—online writing, face-to-face discussion, and the resulting revised essays, which can be shared with the class in small groups or electronically—powerfully affect the choices they make as writers.

Emphasis on the writing process

Some instructors choose to organize their courses around an exploration of the writing process, so that students become aware of the range of strategies and choices available to them as writers and become confident in their ability to respond to future writing tasks. In such courses,

- students are taught to respond to writing situations with a full awareness of the importance of discovering, focusing, planning, drafting, revising, and editing;
- students are given the opportunity to adapt the process to the demands of different kinds of writing;
- forms of expression are presented as strategies best learned in the context of a particular writing task; and
- grammar, punctuation, and mechanics are introduced when necessary for effective communication in an essay.

Organizing the course

In organizing a course that emphasizes the writing process, you might begin by having students look over the discussion of the process in the handbook (Chapter 1, "Assessing the Writing Situation," Chapter 2, "Developing and Shaping Ideas," Chapter 3, "Drafting and Revising," Chapter 7, "Forming a Critical Perspective," and Chapter 8, "Writing in Academic Situations"). You will have to review briefly the writing process as part of each assignment, both to remind students that each of the elements of composing is important and to show how the kinds of planning and revising a writer must do will vary slightly depending on the subject, the aim of the writing task, and the audience for the essay. You may wish to include personal writing as a way to enhance students' awareness of the range of approaches and personas available to them as writers. When you move to more public kinds of writing, however, section 10f ("Reaching Your Readers") will help alert students to the need to take their readers into account as they shape what they have to say and decide how to say it.

Teaching suggestions

Assignments in a process-oriented course should stress planning and revising in all writing tasks and also suggest a range of writing strategies that students can use to deal with a subject and meet the needs of a reader.

If the assigned essay requires particular attention to paragraphing—a persuasive paper, for example—then students might be required to look at Chapter 4 ("Writing and Revising Paragraphs"). Chapters 23–26 ("Effective Sentences") will also help introduce students to useful strategies, and Chapters 41–45 ("Research Writing") and Chapters 53–56 ("Special Writing Situations") can be good resources when students are asked to write for a business or professional audience or to prepare oral presentations. Coverage of matters of grammar, punctuation, diction, and usage will depend on the needs of the class and of individual students.

Since many problems in student writing stem from a lack of effective planning or revising, a composition course that emphasizes process can have a significant effect on student writing. But students need to be aware that word choice, sentence structure, paragraph development, and essay organization also contribute to the effectiveness of writing. Therefore a course that emphasizes the writing process needs to introduce students to the options made possible by formal proficiency (the flexibility that semicolon usage can add to a writer's repertoire, for example—see Chapter 29). Collaborative peer-group revision work supported by the handbook can help student writers to understand the usefulness of formal strategies in communicating the purpose of an essay to an audience.

Emphasis on content and ideas (thematic courses)

In some courses, the writing grows out of the students' strong need to communicate about significant ideas and issues. Such courses focus on ideas and issues, whether personal (family life, education, social relationships) or public policy (healthcare, the American legal system). The source for content may be an anthology, a lecture series, films, or the students' own research and experience. Although the handbook uses many examples that are thematically organized around the subject of the environment, students working with this or any other thematic content could be encouraged to draw examples from their own writing to consider in conjunction with those offered by the handbook. Instructors looking for a theme around which to organize their own courses may wish to add to the environment-oriented examples in the handbook with a supplemental collection of readings on the environment, or with other locally available material, so that students get more exposure to extended pieces of discourse on this topic. Because students may be unused to working interpretively with discursive prose, exercises that encourage them to practice responding to quotations, individually and in groups, will be particularly useful. See Exercises 43.5 and 43.10 in Chapter 43, especially sections c and d, for exercises that help students to position themselves in relation to other authors. Depending on the kinds of material that students are reading, the chapters in Part 10 ("Writing in the Academic Disciplines") encourage students to recognize relationships between formal, discipline-based strategies and thematic content. The chapters in Part 2 ("Reading and Writing in College") help students to read and write in academic situations.

Organizing the course

Since instructors who teach such courses generally value the content of a piece of writing most, they cover the forms of writing and the writing process primarily to help students communicate ideas and feelings clearly and effectively. If you choose to emphasize the content of essays in your composition course, you may wish to begin by introducing students to the writing process and the basic forms of the essay with Chapters 1–5 ("The Writing Process"). These chapters suggest ways students can develop their ideas and organize them into paragraphs and whole essays. Chapters 6–11 on academic skills; critical thinking, reading, and writing; academic writing; and reading and writing text-based and visual arguments can also help students to analyze the strategies of the writers they are reading and to respond effectively.

Teaching suggestions

As students struggle to express their ideas, you may wish to assign Chapters 37–40 ("Effective Words") to help them communicate more precisely and Chapters 23–26 ("Effective Sentences") to help them add variety, clarity, and style to their writing. The Editing Checklist can be a useful touchstone in helping students to identify patterns of error that recur in their work; students can often use the recognized error (such as comma splices, fused sentences, ambiguous pronoun references) as the occasion for substantive revision. Chapters on punctuation, mechanics, grammar, and usage can be assigned to the class or to individual students according to need. Whether or not students are required to use research in their writing, the discussion of differences among summary, paraphrase, and analysis in Chapter 43 ("Working with Sources") can help students to work effectively with their quoted sources.

Emphasis on writing about literature

Writing about literature in a writing course

In a writing class that includes literature, many sections of *The Little, Brown Handbook* will be relevant. Students can begin by reviewing the chapters in Part 2 on critical thinking, reading, and writing; and academic writing; argument, as well as the material in Part 1 about beginning a writing project, and then move on to Chapter 49, "Reading and Writing About Literature," which shows how those general skills translate into questions and strategies for reading and writing about fiction, poetry, and drama. Thorough coverage of MLA documentation in Chapter 46 will also be useful, as will the strategies for conducting research in Chapters 41–44. And the high standards of editing usually found in literary texts can profitably be tied to the discussions of sentence-construction problems in Chapters 17–22 and to matters of punctuation in Chapters 27–32.

Writing about literature in literature courses

Many college and university literature courses now stress writing as well as reading, and *The Little, Brown Handbook* can play a vital role in such courses. The guide to writing about literature in Chapter 49 stresses the interplay of critical thinking, reading, and writing as discussed in Part 2, and it shows students how to transfer those skills to the literature classroom. The thorough coverage of style (Chapters 23–26 on fluid and effective sentences, Chapters 37–40 on diction) can be used not only to help students analyze the works of literature they read but also to help them write more effectively about those works. And the material in Chapter 49 on drafting, writing, and revising a literary analysis, along with the sample student paper and thorough coverage of MLA documentation, will prove invaluable to students and teachers in any literature course.

Teaching suggestions

Because of the pressure to cover content thoroughly, many literature classes underemphasize the role of drafting and revision. Assignments that foreground these processes, such as prewriting in response to quotes, in-class work with student drafts, and group revisions of selected paragraphs and single sentences by student writers, will help students to develop and gain confidence in their writing skills.

Emphasis on academic writing

Writing across the curriculum in a writing course

Chapters 48–52 ("Writing in the Academic Disciplines") cover much of the territory appropriate for a course emphasizing writing across the curriculum. Such a course may ask students to write papers in each of the areas covered by these chapters—literature, the humanities, the social sciences, and the natural and applied sciences—and may ask students to become acquainted with the research tools in each area (also discussed in detail in the chapters). The treatment of the writing process in Chapters 1–3; of paragraphing in Chapter 4; of critical thinking, academic writing, and argument in Chapters 6–11; and of the functions of sentence structure in Chapters 23–26 can also be important elements of a course built around the varieties of academic writing.

Writing across the curriculum in the disciplines

In many writing-across-the-curriculum programs, writing instruction is part of content courses, employed both as a tool for learning and as a way of sharing knowledge in forms appropriate to a discipline. Because it is designed as a reference tool and therefore does not impose a particular design on a course, the handbook can be a useful resource for content courses emphasizing writing. It provides discussions of the writing process and of research and documentation in specific disciplines as well as resources for editing style, grammar, and mechanics. Whatever the particular uses of writing in a course, the handbook's advice about the process of writing (Chapters 1–3) is likely to prove valuable.

■ Using the handbook with other texts

Although the handbook can be used as the only text in a course, many instructors also adopt a reader, a rhetoric, or a workbook such as *The Little, Brown Workbook*. Each kind of text enables you to emphasize different elements of the course and also provides activities to help students develop their writing.

Readers

There are generally three kinds of readers: rhetorical, thematic, or cross-curricular.

Rhetorical readers

Rhetorical readers illustrate different aims and patterns of writing with selections by professional authors and sometimes by students. Readers of this type frequently begin with writing patterns that students find most accessible—narration, description, exemplification—and move on to patterns that students find more difficult to use—classification, comparison-contrast, inductive and deductive argument. Many readers provide extensive introductions to the rhetorical patterns, discussing their uses in writing and the aspects of a subject that they focus on. Some recent rhetorical readers go beyond the basic rhetorical patterns to discuss common forms of nonfiction writing—such as the problem-solution report, the personal essay, the evaluation, and the proposal—that combine the basic patterns in a number of ways. The questions accompanying the essays in most rhetorical readers direct students' attention to the most important features of the models and suggest ways students can incorporate such features into their own writing.

Thematic readers

Thematic readers illustrate and explore a number of themes, such as the stages of personal growth or family relationships, or topics of general interest, such as capital punishment or the impact of technology. The readings may include fiction or poetry as well as essays. If the main purpose for using the reader is to provide subject matter for essays, a thematic reader may be preferable because, as a rule, they provide several perspectives on a subject and more background information to get class discussion started and give students material to use in their writing.

Some readers are both rhetorical and thematic in organization and coverage, providing a table of contents for each emphasis. Both types of readers can be used to generate class discussion and topics for student writing. Some readers even provide questions to stimulate discussion and include lists of possible topics for papers, as well as bibliographies for further reading and research.

Cross-curricular readers

Cross-curricular readers typically provide examples of writing in a variety of disciplines and cover a range of topics. Some include essays directed to general readers as well as to specialists. Others focus on the kinds of writing expected from students or professionals in a discipline. Readers of this kind often emphasize writing as a social process and are designed to help students participate actively within specialized discourse communities. While the primary aim of readers of this type is to provide models of academic and professional prose, some also arrange readings in thematic clusters designed to encourage discussion and suggest subjects for students to pursue in their own writing. Instructors often choose a problem-posing approach to the readings by encouraging students to work on an essay individually and in groups, identifying difficult passages and terms and creating interpretive responses. Classroom practice focuses on student responses to texts, and particularly on the revision process as the means to create meaningful positions in relation to those readings.

Integrating *The Little, Brown Handbook* with a reader

Instructors who adopt a reader typically make discussion of its essays a major activity in the course, yet they also tend to make significant use of a handbook. If the reader chosen for a course does not provide a rhetorical framework for students' essays or a thorough coverage of writing and reasoning processes, instructors using *The Little, Brown Handbook* may wish to direct students to the coverage of these matters in Chapters 1–3 and 6–11. As students begin working with quotation and citation, Chapter 43 on working with sources can become a useful resource, even outside of the research context. The handbook provides explanations and examples of other matters frequently not covered in readers, such as the revision and editing checklists (Chapter 3); paragraphing (Chapter 4); sentence structure, grammar, and style (Chapters 12–26); diction and usage (Chapters 37–40 and the Glossary of Usage); research writing (Chapters 41–47); and writing in the disciplines (Chapters 48–52). In addition, the handbook can be used as a reference guide for punctuation and mechanics, as an aid in marking student papers, and as a guide for revision. Some instructors who use a reader like to devote one period each week to subjects covered in the handbook; others like to set aside part of each day.

Rhetorics

Rhetorics and handbooks

Rhetorics cover many of the same topics as handbooks—discovering, planning, drafting, revising, rhetorical patterns, and paragraphing—but do so in greater depth, at the same time giving less coverage to grammar, punctuation, mechanics, and usage. A rhetoric usually embodies a particular perspective toward writing and the teaching of writing—a theoretical bias, perhaps, or an emphasis on thesis-and-support essays, personal writing, academic writing, argumentation, critical thinking, or tone and style. Since a rhetoric helps determine the emphasis within a course, it provides less flexibility for the teacher than the handbook does, especially if the rhetoric has been chosen by a department rather than by the instructor.

Integrating *The Little, Brown Handbook* with a rhetoric

Because rhetorics provide full coverage in some areas at the expense of others, instructors frequently adopt a handbook as a supplement. Used in this way, *The Little, Brown Handbook* can provide treatment of sentence style (Chapters 23–26), research writing (Chapters 41–47), and writing in the disciplines (Chapters 48–52) for rhetorics that give only brief attention to these matters. It can also provide discussion and exercises for sentence structure and grammar (Chapters 12–22), punctuation and mechanics (Chapters 27–36), and diction and usage (Chapters 37–40 and the Glossary of Usage). The discussions of the writing process, paragraphs, academic writing skills,

critical thinking, and argument (Chapters 1–11) can supplement the material in a rhetoric and provide useful exercises.

When the handbook is used with a rhetoric, instructors often assign its chapters and exercises along with those in the rhetoric, and they devote class time to discussing both texts and reviewing the exercises. They also use the handbook as a reference for students, as an aid to grading papers, and as a guide for revision.

The handbook's ancillary publications

The Little, Brown Handbook comes with an instructional package that will meet the needs of many classes.

- The new Web site *MyCompLab* (*mycomplab.com*) integrates instruction, multimedia tutorials, and exercises for writing, grammar, and research with an online composing space and assessment tools. This seamless, flexible environment comes from extensive research in partnership with composition faculty and students across the country. It provides help for writers in the context of their writing, with functions for instructors' and peers' commentary. Special features include an e-portfolio, a bibliography tool, tutoring services, an assignment builder, and a gradebook and course-management organization created specifically for writing classes. In addition, an e-book of *The Little, Brown Handbook* integrates the many resources of *MyCompLab* into the text.

- Students can subscribe to *The Little, Brown Handbook* as a *CourseSmart* e-textbook (*coursesmart.com*). The site includes all of the handbook's content in a format that enables students to search the text, bookmark passages, integrate their notes, and print reading assignments that incorporate lecture notes. For more information, or to subscribe to the *CourseSmart* e-textbook, visit *coursesmart.com*.

- *The Instructor's Resource Manual* includes all the teaching material and exercise answers from the book you are holding.

- *The Little, Brown Handbook Answer Key* provides answers to the handbook's exercises.

- *The Little, Brown Workbook*, by Donna Gorrell, parallels the handbook's organization but provides many more exercises and briefer instructional text. A separate answer key is available.

- *VangoNotes* are study guides in MP3 format that enable students to download handbook information into their own players and then listen to it whenever and wherever they wish. The notes include "need to know" tips for each handbook chapter, practice tests, audio flash cards for learning key concepts and terms, and a rapid review for exams. For more information, visit *VangoNotes.com*.
- *Diagnostic and Editing Tests and Exercises* are cross-referenced to *The Little, Brown Handbook* and are available both in print and online.

Sentence combining with the handbook

During the past decade, extensive research has shown that having students work with the elements of sentences—manipulating, combining, and altering—leads not only to a greater understanding of sentence structure but also to a greater willingness to experiment stylistically, leading to more flexible, expressive syntax characteristic of mature writing. However, teachers and students can get carried away with sentence combining. Doing exercises with someone else's prose can be fun; students seem to enjoy the activities, but they are no substitute for the students' writing their own sentences and applying the techniques to them as part of a larger writing assignment.

What sentence combining is

Sentence combining arose from applications of transformational-generative grammar principles to classroom practices. Researchers such as Kellogg Hunt and Frank O'Hare determined that encouraging students to expand sentences by coordinating (adding on), deleting (eliminating repeated words), and embedding (inserting new information into a main clause) enables them to write complex, fluent sentences without having to master elaborate grammatical terminology. They recommend giving students a base sentence and several other sentences of information to incorporate into it; then, students experiment with various ways to combine the information.

In most sentence-combining instruction, students learn various kinds of combinations, starting with relatively simple coordination and subordination using conjunctions. Then they progress to removing repeated elements and embedding information such as adjectives

and phrases, culminating in "advanced" structures such as adverbials and absolutes. After they control the structures, they are introduced to the punctuation conventions the new sentences require. Students are encouraged to practice not only on the words of other writers but also on their own sentences in their drafts as they master new stylistic patterns.

A sequence for sentence combining

Chapter 12 introduces students to basic sentence structures, and Chapters 21 and 28 introduce modifying clauses and phrases along with their primary focus on grammar and punctuation. Chapters 28 and 29 present strategies of coordination as well as of punctuation, and Chapters 24 and 25 introduce progressively more sophisticated sentence strategies. In Chapters 23 and 26 students encounter sentence patterns characteristic of mature writing, and in Chapter 4 they get a chance to combine all the strategies in paragraphs.

The handbook exercises you might stress in teaching sentence combining are these:

Chapter 4, Exercises 4.4, 4.11
Chapter 12, Exercises 12.8, 12.10, 12.12, 12.13, 12.15, 12.16, 12.17, 12.21
Chapter 13, Exercise 13.4
Chapter 18, Exercise 18.3
Chapter 21, Exercise 21.7
Chapter 23, Exercises 23.2, 23.6
Chapter 24, Exercises 24.1, 24.3, 24.6
Chapter 25, Exercises 25.3, 25.4
Chapter 26, Exercises 26.1, 26.2, 26.3, 26.6
Chapter 28, Exercises 28.2, 28.4, 28.6
Chapter 29, Exercises 29.2, 29.4

■ Tutoring with the handbook

Writing centers and tutoring programs can make good use of the handbook to set common goals and to develop a common language that will sustain the diverse relationships among students, tutors, and teachers. For example, if teachers' responses to papers refer to the handbook, then students can use those handbook references to focus tutoring sessions on identified problem areas in specific assignments and on overall patterns of error. Students are also able to refer to explanations and exercises in the tutor's absence, to keep a journal of their error patterns and sample revisions, and to refer to the handbook to reinforce what they have learned in tutoring sessions. The handbook can also become a primary reference for the tutoring center or lab by providing advice and practice exercises for targeted areas. Tutors should encourage students to bring the handbook along with their work-in-progress. Once tutor and student together have identified revision areas or targeted patterns of error, they might review the relevant sections of the handbook together; the tutor might then give the student a chance to apply the reviewed information from the handbook to a selected section of the student's own work. As a resource tool for the lab or tutoring center, the handbook can help resolve conflicts over points of grammar and usage, becoming a primary reference or arbiter in debates. It can be a training manual for new tutors, providing simple and clear explanations of problems they will encounter every day. In particular, the revision worksheets included in the chapter on collaborative learning (pp. IAE-35 to IAE-46) can guide tutorial sessions. And the handbook can be a reference for students who are working on a paper in the writing center without direct supervision by a tutor.

The Little, Brown Workbook and the *ESL Worksheets* can provide the "raw material" of tutoring—sample sentences, exercises, and brief explanations—to be used in discussion with the student or for independent work. The workbook can be particularly effective for tutoring if students are taking a composition course that uses the handbook, because the language, rules, and exercises encountered in tutoring will be consistent with those encountered in the classroom.

■ Sample syllabi

Syllabus for a ten-week course with four graded papers:

Week	Goals
1	Introduction and course description; diagnostic writing sample. Begin discussion of essay development (Chapter 1); assign first essay. Academic writing (Chapter 8) and critical thinking, reading, and writing (Chapter 7).
2	Developing ideas (Chapter 2), drafting and revising essays (Chapter 3); first peer-response workshop. Preparing a manuscript (Chapter 5).
3	Writing and revising paragraphs (Chapter 4); conferences with students to discuss drafts and journals. Review common errors seen in drafts (Parts 4–6).
4	First essay due. Assign second essay. Repeat emphasis on prewriting (Chapters 1 and 2); discuss correction symbols and grading.
5	Return first essay; discuss clear sentences (Part 4). Peer-response workshop for second paper.
6	Effective words (Part 8); conferences to discuss drafts and journals. If needed, discuss with the class common errors or problems.
7	Second essay due; assign third essay. Work on invention strategies in small groups.
8	Return second essay; peer-group workshop in class; work on effective sentences (Part 5). Introduce basics of argument (Chapters 9–11).
9	Third essay due; assign last essay, which may be a revision of an earlier piece of writing, an essay from another course, or an essay exam. Peer-group activities. If students are keeping portfolios (pp. IAE-31 to IAE-32), final copies of first two papers are due this week. Journals due.
10	Return third essay. Final essay due; individual conferences and course evaluations; last two papers for portfolio due.

Syllabus for a fifteen-week course with five graded papers, including a research paper:

Week	Goals
1	Course introduction and requirements; writing sample. Discuss Chapters 1 and 2. Introduce journals.
2	Assign first paper. Begin draft work. Peer-response session for first paper. Review Chapter 54 if appropriate. Discuss Chapter 3 and Part 4.
3	Conferences about drafts. Discuss Chapter 4.
4	Take up journals. Second peer-response session for first paper. Review Chapter 5. Discuss Chapters 28 and 29.
5	First paper due. Assign second paper. Discuss Chapter 3 again; discuss Chapters 24 and 25.
6	Return first paper. Discuss evaluation criteria and correction symbols. If appropriate, dis-

cuss Chapter 55. Draft work on second paper. Peer-response session for second paper.

7   Discuss Chapter 37. Discuss Chapters 23 and 26. Second peer-response session for second paper.

8   Second paper due. Assign third paper. Take up journals. Reemphasize developing the essay (Chapter 2) and conduct microclinics on problem areas with small groups of students. Conferences to discuss drafts and journals.

9   Return second paper. Assign fourth paper (research paper). Discuss Chapter 41. Peer-response session for third paper. Assign each student an appropriate chapter from Part 10.

10   Research week. Library tour (if available). Chapter 42.

11   Return third paper. Documentation week. Chapters 43–47, and appropriate sections of the chapters in Part 10. Miniconferences to address specific research problems.

12   Fourth paper due. Discuss Chapter 48 and appropriate sections of the chapters in Part 10. Discuss Chapter 5.

13   Return fourth paper. Assign fifth paper. Discuss Chapters 9–11. Journals due.

14   Draft work for fifth paper. If students are keeping portfolios (pp. IAE-31 to IAE-32), edited copies of first four papers are submitted this week.

15   Finished copy of fifth paper due. Individual conferences and course evaluations.

■ Resources for designing a writing course

Applebee, Arthur N. "Problems in Process Approaches: Toward a Reconceptualization of Process Instruction." *The Teaching of Writing*. Ed. Anthony Petrosky and David Bartholomae. Chicago: National Society for the Study of Education, 1986. 95–113. Print.

Bartholomae, David, and Anthony Petrosky. *Facts, Counterfacts, Artifacts: Theory and Method for a Reading and Writing Course*. Upper Montclair: Boynton/Cook, 1986. Print.

Dawkins, John. "Teaching Punctuation as a Rhetorical Tool." *College Composition and Communication* 46.4 (1995): 533–48. Print.

DeLuca, Geraldine, ed. *Dialogue on Writing: Rethinking ESL, Basic Writing, and First-Year Composition*. Mahwah: Erlbaum, 2001. Print.

Dixon, Chris Jennings, ed. *Lesson Plans for Teaching Writing*. Urbana: NCTE, 2007. Print.

Eble, Kenneth E. *The Craft of Teaching: A Guide to Mastering the Professor's Art*. 2nd ed. San Francisco: Jossey-Bass, 1988. Print.

Fishman, Stephen M., and Lucille McCarthy. *John Dewey and the Challenge of Classroom Practice*. New York: Teachers College P, 1998. Print.

Fontaine, Sheryl I. "Teaching with the Beginner's Mind: Notes from My Karate Journal." *College Composition and Communication* 54.2 (2002): 208–21. Print.

Foster, David. *A Primer for Writing Teachers: Theories, Theorists, Issues, Problems*. 2nd ed. Portsmouth: Boynton/Cook, 1993. Print.

Gardner, Traci. *Designing Writing Assignments*. Urbana: NCTE, 2008. Print.

George, Diana. "Who Teaches the Teacher? A Note on the Craft of Teaching College Composition." *College English* 51.4 (1989): 418–23. Print.

Graves, Richard L., ed. *Rhetoric and Composition: A Sourcebook for Teachers and Writers*. 3rd ed. Portsmouth: Boynton/Cook, 1990. Print.

Herzberg, Bruce. "Composition and the Politics of the Curriculum." *The Politics of Writing Instruction: Postsecondary*. Ed. Richard Bullock and John Trimbur. Portsmouth: Boynton/Cook (Heinemann), 1991. 97–118. Print.

Hunt, Kellogg. *Grammatical Structures Written at Three Grade Levels*. Urbana: NCTE, 1965. Print.

Irmscher, William. *Teaching Expository Writing*. New York: Holt, 1979. Print.

Lee, Amy. *Composing Critical Pedagogies: Teaching Writing as Revision*. Urbana: NCTE, 2000. Print.

Lindemann, Erika. *A Rhetoric for Writing Teachers*. 4th ed. New York: Oxford UP, 2001. Print.

---. "Teaching as a Rhetorical Art." *CEA Forum* 15.2 (1985): 9–12. Print.

Lindemann, Erika, and Gary Tate, eds. *An Introduction to Composition Studies*. New York: Oxford UP, 1991. Print.

McCrary, Donald. "Womanist Theology and Its Efficacy for the Writing Classroom." *College Composition and Communication* 52.4 (2001): 521–52. Print.

McCrimmon, Miles. "Across the Great Divide: Anxieties of Acculturation in College English." *College English* 69.2 (2006): 117–26. Print.

O'Hare, Frank. *Sentence Combining: Improving Student Writing Without Formal Grammar Instruction.* Urbana: NCTE, 1973. Print.

Passmore, John. *The Philosophy of Teaching.* London: Duckworth, 1980. Print.

Ponsot, Marie, and Rosemary Deen. *Beat Not the Poor Desk! Writing: What to Teach, How to Teach It, and Why.* Upper Montclair: Boynton/Cook, 1982. Print.

Rankin, Elizabeth. "From Simple to Complex: Ideas of Order in Assignment Sequences." *Journal of Advanced Composition* 10.1 (1990): 126–35. Print.

Roen, Duane, et al., eds. *Strategies for Teaching First-Year Composition.* Urbana: NCTE, 2002. Print.

Ronald, Kate, and Hephzibah Roskelly. *Reason to Believe: Romanticism, Pragmatism, and the Possibility of Teaching.* Albany: State U of New York P, 1998. Print.

Shaughnessy, Mina. *Errors and Expectations: A Guide for the Teacher of Basic Writing.* New York: Oxford UP, 1977. Print.

Sommers, Nancy, and Laura Saltz. "The Novice as Expert: Writing the Freshman Year." *College Composition and Communication* 56.1 (2004): 124–49. Print.

Strong, William. *Sentence Combining: A Composing Book.* 3rd ed. New York: McGraw-Hill, 1994. Print.

Tobin, Lad. "Reading Students, Reading Ourselves: Revising the Teacher's Role in the Writing Class." *College English* 53.3 (1991): 333–48. Print.

Yancey, Kathleen Blake, ed. *Delivering College Composition: The Fifth Canon.* Portsmouth: Boynton/Cook, 2006. Print.

3

Working with Student Writing

Nothing we do as composition teachers—not lecturing, setting up peer critique groups, leading discussions, or preparing activities—has as much potential for helping students improve their writing as do our efforts to respond as sensitive and thorough readers. Moreover, as readers we can play several roles, some of them simultaneously. We can respond to a work in progress, acting as editors and critics with suggestions for revision or as ordinary readers whose reactions students can take into account as they shape the final product. Or we can be judges of a finished work, justifying a grade (as evaluators) or pointing out strengths and weaknesses (as teachers), encouraging students to build on one and avoid the other.

At some time, of course, all the work that you and students put into the course has to be judged—and in the final analysis, you'll be the one who has to make the judgments and assign the grade. This is one of the hardest parts of your job as a writing teacher, yet it's also one of the most essential. But you needn't go it alone; students can collaboratively do a good deal of the preliminary work for you and set standards that will allow fair assignment of grades.

■ The roles of response

It takes more than an efficient correction system to bring about improvement in writing. How we respond and when are most important. In addition, the correction system we choose needs to be consistent with our purposes for responding and the roles we play as readers.

Responses to papers in progress

Responses directed toward a paper in progress often need to focus as much on the way the writer approaches the task as on the evolving text. On the one hand, it makes little sense to comment on detailed matters of punctuation in a draft full of helter-skelter ideas, thereby drawing attention away from advice about strategies the writer can employ to develop focus and discover purpose. On the other hand, helpful comments on agreement or mechanics coming at later stages in the writing of an essay can enable students to understand the importance of editing and can provide knowledge for later use.

Responses to a paper in progress ought to focus to a considerable extent on the writer's behaviors. Novice writers generally need to pay as much attention to learning how to discover ideas or draft an entire paper as to using topic sentences and effective patterns of paragraph development. Much of the advice in the handbook, especially in Chapters 1, 2, and 3, is directed toward strategies for writing. Other discussions, such as the treatment of paragraphs in Chapter 4, pay more attention to the specific features of essays, though they do not ignore the process of composition.

In commenting on drafts of an essay, we can assume the role of a general reader, noting points of interest or confusion, expressing an interest in more information or requesting stronger support, sharing feelings of pleasure and surprise—but always recognizing that at this point a paper belongs primarily to the writer. When a draft of an essay has a clear purpose and structure, however, we can read as editors or critics, identifying particular options for paragraphing or expression the writer might consider during revision or suggesting areas of grammar and style that need attention.

Responses to final drafts

Response to a final draft ought to provide a clear evaluation and the justification for it yet at the same time look toward future efforts. Student writers need to recognize their successes; they also need to understand what steps they can take in later essays. The essentially supportive tone of explanations in the handbook can help create this kind of understanding even when comments or the number-and-letter codes are used to identify outright errors.

When as evaluators we comment on a graded final draft, we need to provide a clear justification for the judgment on one or more of the following grounds:

- the paper's success in achieving its goals
- the requirements set by the assignment
- the standards established for the course

Comments that refer students to a particular section of the handbook, perhaps to specific sets of exercises, can provide a bridge to future writing efforts.

Composing comments: praise

Most students will give you an honest effort. They will use the strategies they know to complete an assignment well and to win your approval in the form of a high grade. But effort notwithstanding, students will have differing degrees of success with an assignment. And your reactions will have to differ accordingly.

Any writing effort will have strengths, even if they are few and sometimes hard to find. It's essential to identify them; not only do they show what goals have been attained, but also they help the students see which competencies they can apply to different situations. Even when you praise a very minor feature or an insight that could be developed more, the student has something to start from in a revision or in the next paper. It is also important to remember that critique can be either ego-crushing or empowering for the writer. Encouragement through praise can help keep your students, especially those with the weakest skills, from despairing about their capacity for improving their writing. Of course, the strengths sometimes outweigh the weaknesses; then the only problem is deciding what to praise. No matter what the level of skill in the paper, however, your goal is to help each student recognize and learn to capitalize on her strengths in future papers. The role of encouragement is often underestimated, seen as the "positive spin" tacked onto the "real" message of critique. Instead, it should be seen as an integral part of critique and a powerful tool for improvement. Students need to know when they have

revised even one paragraph effectively, when they have gained control over a single pattern of error, when they have successfully used a quotation, even if their overall argument fell apart in the process. You may want to review your comments on a set of papers before handing them back to your students, in order to make sure that you have included some positive commentary on each paper.

Composing comments: critique

What about the weaknesses? The weaknesses are what most of us first see when we read a student paper. We feel compelled to alert our students to these problems so that their writing can improve. But the method of identifying such weaknesses must be constructive and goal-oriented. Ideally, students will be able to read our responses and focus on the one substantive issue or skill that will move their writing forward. As Nancy Sommers discovered in her research on teachers' responses, many teachers try to mark every error (often idiosyncratically and elliptically), leaving students with the confused sense that the paper is "all wrong" but with no sense of revision priorities. The effect of such comments is to superimpose the grid of an "ideal" paper against the actual project that the student writer was trying to accomplish. Sommers proposes instead a carefully selected and focused comment that enters into the student's own project and suggests a way to move it forward. The teacher might also identify a single pattern of error, mark several instances, ask the student to find several more instances and then to hand in revised versions of all those sentences. In some cases, the pattern of error and the substantive comment are linked, as for example a pattern of fused sentences manifesting the writer's tendency to rush cryptically through ideas rather than slowing down to think them through. In those cases, recognition of the error can lead the student to the points in the paper that are most rushed and become the basis for an effective revision (see Richard Straub's useful review article for a discussion of Sommers, Brannon/Knoblauch, and styles of teacher response).

Mina Shaughnessy, in her book *Errors and Expectations*, did all of us a great service by reminding us that the intentionality of student texts is quite different from that of literary works. In a literary work the writer is in control; he or she adheres to or violates conventions based on deliberate decisions. But when students violate the etiquette of syntax or spelling or punctuation, Shaughnessy reminds us, we assume that they did so with the same kind of artistic control experience that writers wield (or with a studied carelessness). And this is not the case. Students rarely if ever make deliberate errors; they are trying to succeed. Often, however, they attempt syntactic structures or make linguistic choices over which they have imperfect control. And so we must not regard their errors and weaknesses as intentions to fail; rather, we must determine at what they were trying to succeed. We must not just identify and criticize their errors; we must analyze them and try to help students fulfill their true intentions.

David Bartholomae, applying some of Shaughnessy's observations to basic writers, argues that such error analysis can be a valuable diagnostic technique for instructors. "By investigating and interpreting the patterns of error in [students'] writing, we can help them begin to see those errors as evidence of hypotheses or strategies they have formed and, as a consequence, put them in a position to change, experiment, imagine other strategies. Studying their own writing puts students in a position to see themselves as language users, rather than as victims of a language that uses them" (258).

Many times, in fact, errors and weaknesses signal growth. Often student papers submitted after sentence-combining practices are plagued with comma splices, as students struggle to master new syntactic patterns. The students are courageously trying new techniques; penalizing them for failing at their first attempt to master the punctuation required may defeat your efforts to help them grow. Sometimes, of course, there will be careless errors: a word transposed or omitted in copying, the phonetic mishearing of a term (such as Freud's "edible complex"), an embarrassing or amusing typo (such as "Shakespeare's play of love and punishment, *Romeo and Joliet*"). These represent failures of editing skills, language performance rather than language competence, and can be treated as such.

Finally, remember that exposing their work to the critique of others can make writers feel intensely vulnerable. It is essential to be delicate in your tone when you identify weaknesses so as not to arouse feelings of shame in your students. Especially when you are trying to move through a stack of papers efficiently, you may find yourself falling into a kind of terseness in your comments that may seem harsh to your students. Try drafting your comments in pencil and then reviewing them before handing the papers back to your students; in this way you can fine-tune any comments whose tone is too negative.

■ Commenting on papers

Composition instructors have developed innovative and useful ways of evaluating student writing, including conferences, recorded and electronic commentary, and peer evaluation. The handbook can be a useful aid for all these approaches, particularly peer evaluation (see "Using Collaborative Learning with the Handbook," pp. IAE-35 to IAE-46). Many teachers, however, still prefer to respond to student essays through marginal and summary comments. These responses take three general forms: a correction code, correction symbols, and written comments. Each method has advantages and disadvantages; some teachers combine them to draw on the strengths of each while others feel that correction codes and symbols undercut students' individualized projects. Some teachers use a correction code method accompanied by student conferences in which they give more personalized feedback; other teachers use written comments and establish feedback sessions, during which students respond to those comments and outline a revision plan or a goal for the next paper. The important thing is that your students understand your method and are able to work productively from your comments.

Using the correction code

To use the correction code, an instructor simply writes in the margin of a paper the number and letter of the section of the handbook a student should consult for help with a particular problem or error, for example, 15b (pronoun and antecedent agreement), 18a (comma splice), or 2b (problem with thesis). The code for each section of the handbook is listed inside the front cover; after a short time, most instructors find they have memorized the codes for common problems and seldom have to consult the list. Here is a section of a student paper marked using the correction code:

Parents have become more lenient with regard to television

(17) watching. For example, allowing their children to watch

(39c) cartoons in the early morning before school. As soon as they

come home from school they sit before the set again,

(28b) completely ingrossed with (40a) a soap opera or a talk show. Some

(38c) parents actually allow their children to watch television while

(21b) (they) are at the supper table. (19a) Of course, the latter part of the

evening, the prime time, is solely set aside for the purpose of

watching a special show or a favorite series. In some ways,

parents are using the television as a substitute for personal

(28c) communication with the child. The days then, remain a

(40d) never ending chain of program after program.

When students get their graded papers back, they need only turn to the front of the handbook to understand what the instructor's notations mean and then refer to the appropriate section of the text for a full explanation (the code for each section appears in colored boxes at the sides of the pages). Students, too, quickly learn to recognize the notations for common errors and problems. An important follow-up to this method is to ask students to identify several more instances of one kind of error and to revise those sentences using the handbook. The goal is to help students identify the kinds of errors that commonly occur in their writing so that they can look for those errors on the next draft. As a helpful accompaniment to this method you might ask students to keep a list or journal of the errors that you have marked and that they have revised as a resource for future revisions. That journal can also become the basis for an individual conference, in which you and the student discuss a pattern of error and its significance for revision (a pattern of vague pronoun references that manifests the student's difficulty in defining and working with key terms, for instance).

Using the correction symbols

Correction symbols work in much the same way as the number-and-letter code. An instructor locates the appropriate symbol in the list inside the back cover of the handbook (e.g., *dev, log, agr, coh*) and writes it in the margin of the essay, often drawing a line to indicate the location and extent of the problem. Students reverse the

procedure, looking up symbols on the list, which also gives the name of the problem and a reference to the appropriate section of the text: for example, *dm*—Dangling modifier, 21h. Here is the passage from above marked in this way:

Parents have become more lenient with regard to television

frag
watching. For example, allowing their children to watch

rep
cartoons in the early morning before school. As soon as they

come home from school, they sit before the set again,

sp   *ww*
completely ingrossed with a soap opera or a talk show. Some

parents actually allow their children to watch television while

ref
they are at the supper table. Of course, the latter part of the

mm
evening, the prime time, is solely set aside for the purpose of

watching a special show or a favorite series. In some ways,

parents are using the television as a substitute for personal

communication with the child. The days then, remain a

p
never ending chain of program after program.

hyph

Because correction symbols are easier to remember than the number-and-letter code, both students and teachers can spend less time turning away from a paper to consult the list of symbols than they might do with the code. Yet symbols are less specific than the code; *shift*, for instance, covers a variety of problems—20a (person and number), 20b (tense and mood), and 20c (subject and voice). Moreover, instead of being able to turn directly from the paper to a discussion in the handbook, students may need to consult the list of symbols to find the appropriate section of the text. Most of the symbols, however, also appear in the colored boxes in the margins of the pages. It becomes increasingly important, then, to augment the symbol method with comments or conferences that help students create revision priorities. For instance, you might write a marginal comment next to the first instance of a sentence fragment, then put the symbol (*frag*) next to three other occasions of the same error. An end comment or conference would direct the student to Chapter 17 of the handbook, ask the student to locate several more instances of the error in the paper, and request revisions. Once students understand that the fragment is often an undeveloped thought, they are able to use their recognition of the error to create substantive revisions, not only of sentences but of paragraphs and papers as well.

Using written comments

Written comments can appear in two places: in the margins and at the paper's end. Each does a different job, and students need to learn what those jobs are. Marginal comments generally note specific areas of strength or weakness in student papers. As Nancy Sommers reminds us, marginal comments focus a student's attention on a particular draft, often causing the student to ignore the possibilities of revision and moving on in new drafts. Students sometimes become so overwhelmed by marginal comments that they want only to "fix" what's "wrong" with a particular draft. Sparing use of marginal comments may make students look to the end comments for your directions. Carefully phrased marginal comments can also direct students to revise. Often in such a system, the marginal comments that identify weaknesses are questions or statements that lead students to examine the text more carefully: "Can you give a more precise description of the hotel than 'nice' and 'rad'?" "What's your evidence for this claim?" "Does your reader know what a 'buydown mortgage' is?" Or they can describe your reaction as a reader ("I can't see the connection between these two ideas. Did you leave a step out?"). Occasionally you may want to refer the student to a particular reference source ("Your citations should be in MLA format; see Chapter 46").

Checks in the margin can direct a student's attention to mechanical, grammatical, or stylistic weaknesses. Such individual problems should be summed up as part of your end comment: "Often you provide a quotation to support your assertions, but you rarely analyze the quotations to show how they fit into your argument. Where you do this, as on p. 3, it really strengthens your argument. Where you leave it out, your argument is less persuasive—you make your readers guess the connections you see." "A lot of the check marks have to do with where commas go in complex sentences. Review Chapter 28 to correct these problems."

The second kind of comment, usually at the end of the paper, should direct students to new writing goals. Whether you rely on a single method or a combination of methods to mark students' papers, it is usually important to provide students with a comment at the end of their papers to explain the grade and to tie together the marginal commentary, emphasizing the key points. This is also a good place to assign exercises in the handbook and to remind students what they need to do in future essays. The discussion "Evaluating Essays for a Grade" later in this chapter contains several examples of summary comments. Your end comments need to give clear rhetorical response and guidance to your students: "Your careful examination of King's religious language gives your paper a great deal of credibility. In your subsequent papers you can use this sensitivity to language to support your own assertions." Every writer likes to know he or she has succeeded; tell your students what competencies they show, and give them goals to strive for. Your end comment needs a context just like the student papers do; don't neglect it.

Establishing priorities for the students

When commenting on students' papers, try to be selective about the issues you address. Two, or at most three, weaknesses are enough for a student to focus on for the next paper. Focus on the largest issues first; if the writer can't address an audience or formulate a thesis, spelling and colon placement are trivial problems. And often, as in the cases discussed above, the weaknesses are signs of growth. Even if a student has not yet learned to analyze evidence, he's learned to provide it; even if a student continues to make comma splices, she's learning to write more complex sentences. Your comments can be phrased to reflect these tentative steps of growth: "I'm glad you tried some of the sentence combining we practiced. Now that you've learned the patterns, take a close look at where the punctuation goes so that you can use those elaborate sentences to their best effect." "You've picked really sharp quotations to back up your points. Next time follow up each of those quotes with a sentence or two of comment to help your audience see how they fit into your argument."

Finally, your response should help the writer set and reach new goals. These will usually involve mastering skills that were not used effectively in the current text or moving on to apply those skills in new contexts. Here is where the critical teaching in comments takes place: you want the student to move to a new level of achievement. The goals should be clearly expressed: "Now that you've mastered simple and compound sentences, it's time to move to complex ones." "It's clear you can persuade an audience that basically agrees with you. Next time why don't you aim to persuade a mildly hostile audience?" And your comments should suggest clear strategies for achieving those goals: "Try brainstorming and using the journalist's questions to generate more details about your subject. Then you can choose which ones you want to use." "Write down all the arguments opposed to your position that you can think of, and try to find reasonable answers to those objections." You may even need to offer a small reward to encourage timorous students to take risks: "Try to write some different kinds of sentence patterns; I won't 'mark off' if you don't quite master the punctuation next time." Your response can also encourage students to reconsider their writing processes: "The drafts of this paper show you just changed a few words; you didn't revise much. Next time, once you've got your ideas down, allow yourself to move paragraphs around, change sentences, scratch out! Revision is the chance to improve the problems mentioned above; make your organization clearer, smooth sentences, add details. Let your drafts be messy."

In sum, your end comments should encourage the student not only to go back into this paper but to move forward to the next. If you keep the tripartite structure in mind—praise strengths, identify weaknesses, set goals—you'll find it relatively easy to write a coherent, goal-oriented end comment. Encourage students to discuss those comments with you before they submit their next paper; often a word or two of reinforcement or clarification can lead to quantum leaps in writing performance.

■ Making sure students understand your comments

Dealing with codes and symbols

Perhaps the most common reason students fail to understand our comments is that they do not understand the symbols or terms we use. If you were to ask a class what a fused sentence is, some students might answer in this vein: "a sentence where everything seems to run together and gets confused or awkward." Such terms as *reference, development,* and *parallelism* are also likely to draw puzzled or incorrect responses, though a few students might be able to give general explanations. Asking students the meaning of such common symbols as *pass, cs, dm,* and *[agr]* will produce similar results.

Telling students to look up correction marks on the front or back endpapers of the handbook can help, as can directing them to the Glossary of Grammatical Terms or handing out a list of terms you plan to use in written comments. A lot of students, however, are likely to put off learning the symbols or terms until they absolutely have to, perhaps several papers into the semester, when they realize how much help they need to improve their writing. One technique that can speed the process is to foreground student papers in group work and in revision exercises with the entire class. For example, you might hand out a paper that has two sentence fragments and a comma splice in a key paragraph. After asking students to use the Editing Checklist and the relevant sections from the handbook to identify and "correct" the errors, have them work in groups to revise the errors substantively and in doing so to develop the content of the paragraph. In a follow-up class you might hand out the revised paragraphs created in the groups and ask students to compare the different analytical and grammatical choices that were made. Such exercises help students to understand the reasons for seemingly arbitrary codes.

Discussing a graded paper

Another good way to help students understand your comments is to discuss a graded paper with them. Chapter 3 of the handbook (pp. 57–59 and 66–68) contains two student papers that you may wish to "grade" and then use as the basis of class discussion. In addition, the paragraphs presented earlier in this chapter contain many errors of the kind likely to turn up on student papers. The paragraphs can be distributed in class with either or both of the marking systems or with some other system you prefer. If you choose to distribute the paragraphs without markings, you can ask the students to work with you in identifying errors and choosing appropriate symbols or comments.

■ Evaluating essays for a grade

A grade can carry several messages: it can describe the overall quality of a paper; it can indicate how close the essay comes to achieving the goals for writing set forth in the course; and it can help tell a student writer what elements to work on in the next assignment. But unless grading standards are clear, the grades we assign will have little value for teaching beyond establishing a final grade for the course.

To help establish clear evaluation standards, many instructors discuss grading criteria with students and distribute sample papers, either already graded or to be graded in class. Another method is to attach to each paper a comment sheet reflecting the goals for the assignment. Preparing a comment sheet for each assignment can be taxing, however, so many instructors prepare a sheet that can be used for all assignments. Here is a sample:

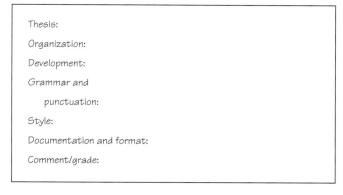

If you do not like to use comment sheets, you may prefer to hand out grading criteria at the beginning of the course. Sometimes a department or program provides its own set of criteria for grading papers; if yours does not, you may wish to adapt for your own use the following set that reflects the major areas of emphasis in the handbook:

- **A** (superior). An A paper meets the standards in all these areas and excels in one or more of them:

  The *paper as a whole* presents a fresh subject or main idea or treats it in an interesting or original manner, displaying unusual insight and taking appropriate account of the audience. The *paragraphs* are fully developed with detail that supports the main idea; sentences within the paragraphs are clearly linked, forming an appropriate pattern; transitions are effective. *Sentences* are varied and imaginative in style, concise and creative in wording. The paper contains few errors in *grammar and punctuation* or errors only in sophisticated matters, and few *spelling* errors.

- **B** (strong). A B paper meets the standards in all these areas:

  The *paper as a whole* presents an interesting subject or main idea and approaches it in a consistent and careful manner, displaying good insight, though without the freshness or originality characteristic of the *A* paper. The writing makes use of consistent rhetorical strategies and a tone appropriate to the audience. *Paragraphs* are, with only a few exceptions, adequately developed and generally successful in supporting the main idea; transitions are clear, and sentences within the paragraphs are, for the most part, clearly related. *Sentences* are generally clear and correct in structure and style and are not excessively wordy. Word choice is usually appropriate. *Grammar, punctuation,* and *spelling* follow accepted conventions, except for a few minor errors.

- **C** (adequate). A C paper is deficient in one of these areas:

  The *paper as a whole* presents a clearly defined subject or main idea, but the treatment may be trivial, uninteresting, or too general and the insight adequate but not marked by independent thought. The plan and purpose are clear but inconsistently or incompletely carried out; tone may be inconsistent. Some paragraphs may lack adequate supporting detail or may be only loosely linked to the main idea. Sentences within paragraphs may be only loosely related, and some transitions may be missing. *Sentences* are generally correct in structure but may be excessively wordy, vague, or, at times, even incorrect. Style and word choice may be flat, inconsistent, or not entirely appropriate to the audience. The paper may display isolated serious errors in *grammar and punctuation* or frequent minor errors that do not interfere substantially with meaning or that do not greatly distract the reader; the paper may contain occasional *misspellings*.

- *D* (weak). A D paper is seriously deficient in any one of these areas:

   The *paper as a whole* presents a poorly defined or inconsistently treated subject or central idea and displays little insight or development. The tone is inappropriate to the audience. *Paragraphs* contain little supporting detail. Sentences within paragraphs are often unrelated to the main idea and transitions are lacking. *Sentences* are frequently incorrect in structure, vague, wordy, and distracting. Style and word choice are inappropriate, incorrect, or inconsistent. The paper may contain serious and distracting errors in *grammar and punctuation* as well as numerous irritating minor errors and frequent *misspellings*.

- *F* (unacceptable/no credit). An F paper is unacceptable in any one of these areas:

   The *paper as a whole* does not have a clear subject or main idea and has no apparent purpose or plan; or the subject and main idea are defined and treated in a way that clearly does not meet the requirements of the assignment. *Paragraphs* are not related to the main idea; sentences within paragraphs are unrelated, and transitions are missing. *Sentences* are so faulty in structure and style that the essay is not readable. Frequent serious errors in *grammar, punctuation,* and *spelling* indicate an inability to handle the written conventions; there are excessive minor errors or misspellings.

These criteria need to be adapted to the level of students in a particular course or institution and to the goals set for the course. For example, admirable organization or style may differ markedly for a student in a two-year technical program and a student in a four-year school that stresses the arts and humanities.

■ Evaluating for revision

Revision in composition teaching

In recent years the process of revision has come to be viewed as increasingly important in composition instruction. Instructors who make revision a regular part of their composition classes argue that writers should be judged not (or not only) on the early version of an essay but on what they are able to make of the essay after they have had a chance to revise it and, perhaps, to take into account the comments of readers.

Composition instructors have long viewed revision as an important process for student writers to learn. What is new is the extent to which revision is being made a regular part of instruction, an emphasis reflected in the extensive treatment of both revision and editing in Chapter 3 of the handbook. In addition, many instructors have begun structuring their classes around collaborative learning groups that provide audiences for papers in progress and advice for revision. This method is reinforced in Chapter 3, which contains checklists for students' giving and receiving criticism. The chapter "Using Collaborative Learning with the Handbook," which follows this discussion, contains suggestions for handouts to help students analyze their peers' work. Furthermore, students' increasing access to computers and the availability of computer classrooms have made possible a range of new approaches to the revision process (see Daniel Anderson's chapter on pp. IAE-47 to IAE-61).

Commenting on drafts for revision

The distinction made in Chapter 3 of the handbook between revision and editing is important for instructors to keep in mind when responding to a student paper in progress. For essays whose perspective, form, and content are well enough developed to require only editing, your role may be simply to call attention to errors or to suggest ways to polish sentences and paragraphs. Many of the techniques already discussed for commenting on papers can be used to aid editing, particularly those that refer students to sections of the handbook for advice on improving a passage or correcting a problem. In addition, you may wish to refer students to the editing checklist in Chapter 3 (pp. 54–55).

Evaluation for revision, however, is more likely to suggest extensive changes in a paper, often encouraging the writer to adopt a different perspective on a topic. Since revision may and often should involve substantial changes in the direction of an essay, however, you should be wary of comments that impose your view of what a paper should do or how it should be accomplished. Instead, try to identify a problem clearly and offer some possible solutions but at the same time leave the student writers free to make their own choices. Such comments as "Your thesis statement needs to focus more sharply on the specific government toxic-waste regulations to which you object" may be helpful in cases where the student's intentions and the direction of a paper are quite clear. But when a writer is still struggling with subject and intention, such statements may limit the process of revision rather than encourage it. A comment like the following, however, leaves the eventual direction of the essay up to the student:

> I'm not sure which specific regulations you object to most. Is this a place in the essay where you want to focus your concerns sharply for readers? From the detailed evidence you present later about the struggles of small businesses to pay for state-of-the-art pollution equipment, I suspect that one of your main purposes is to have readers understand the hard times these ordinary people are facing. What do you care most about in this subject, and what do you most want your audience to understand and feel?

In commenting on papers for revision, you should call attention to any serious errors. At the same time, however, keep in mind this maxim: "Don't spend time improving a sentence that ought to be dropped from the paper." Remember, too, that awkward and confused sentences are often signs of confusion about the overall direction of an essay, and problems at the sentence level may disappear as the writer resolves the larger problems.

> You shift pronouns often in this passage, sometimes addressing the reader as "you," sometimes using "one" or "we." I think the root of the problem is that you are not sure of your relation to your readers. Since you are talking about a situation that you face along with most readers, you might choose "we" and stick to it.

In addition, most students need more than advice about what sections of a paper need to be revised; they need advice about the process of revision itself. By focusing your comments on how to go about revising rather than solely on the direction of possible changes, you can avoid doing the students' work for them and can instead help them develop an effective writing/revising process.

■ Coping with the paper load

At this point you may well be asking, "How am I supposed to do all these things—run groups, intervene in processes, hold conferences, analyze errors, write long comments—and remain sane?" That's a good question, probably the most vexing one writing teachers face. You can't avoid it: grading papers takes time, lots of it, time that you'd often rather spend reading or working on your own scholarship or having a personal life or just enjoying fresh air and natural light. The best way to speed up the grading process, then, is to reduce the amount of grading you have to do. Several techniques will help you achieve this goal.

Grading the paper

Evaluating student papers can be time-consuming: instructors often report spending fifteen to twenty minutes on each paper, making marginal notes, writing summary comments, and deciding on a grade. Many set aside hours of office time for individual conferences. To help make the job of marking papers somewhat easier and quicker, *The Little, Brown Handbook* provides a number of aids:

- a list of correction symbols keyed to discussions in the text;
- a number-and-letter correction code that refers students to appropriate sections of the handbook; and
- a thorough index and glossary of terms directing students to explanations of grammatical and rhetorical terms used in an instructor's written comments.

Some practical tips will help you speed up the grading process:

1. Start with carefully designed assignments and give students enough time to complete the assignment successfully. The clearer the assignment, the fewer variables will be left for you to cope with; the more adequate the time, the fewer hasty or careless errors you should have to contend with.

2. Be realistic when telling students when they'll get papers back. Many authorities insist that teachers return papers at the first class meeting after the assignments are submitted. Two class meetings—or a week—is more realistic. The students also need at least one class meeting to review your comments and suggestions on one paper before submitting their next effort—and more time is helpful if they need a conference to discuss those comments with you. Schedule papers far enough apart so you can grade them carefully, and don't make promises you can't keep.

3. Not all papers must be new assignments. Students often profit from revising and reshaping an earlier paper, either one of their own choosing or one that you suggest they revise. Such assignments teach students the crucial importance of revising while giving you time to hold conferences, attend to individual problems, and design subsequent assignments.

4. Set a schedule for your grading and keep it. If you must grade fifty papers in five days, that's ten a day. At half an hour for each paper (a good beginner's rate), that's five hours of grading a day (you'll need a break or two to maintain your concentration).

5. Set reasonable time limits. Buy a timer and be ruthless about paying attention to it. Allow yourself a maximum time per paper—as a beginner, twenty-five or thirty minutes for an average (500–700 word) paper; as you get more experienced, fifteen to twenty minutes. Read the paper through once in its entirety before you mark anything, even minor mechanical errors. This allows you to assess the biggest strengths and weaknesses, to target your attention. Reread the paper, making your minimal marks and marginal comments. Then skim it one more time and compose your end comments. Sometimes the end comments written by beginning teachers are a page or longer; you'll learn to control this with experience. Again, using the three-part formula—strengths, a few weaknesses, and goals and strategies—can help you compose a response quickly.

Although you may find yourself calling on stock phrases to compose your end comments, it will help to refer to specific marginal comments and moments in the paper as well. For example, you might say, "One of the strongest things about this paper is your use of quotations to support your opinions. On p. 2, for example, I've noted a particularly well-chosen quote and suggested ways that you might further develop your response to it." The relationship that you develop between your marginal comments and your end comment can be particularly helpful in guiding students from their global priorities for revision to local examples of where they might begin (or may already have begun) to develop the paper further.

6. Write a good end comment. If you have clear grading standards, put a letter grade on the paper after you've written your end comment; if not, sort all the papers into roughly defined piles—the good ones, the okay ones, the problem ones—and go back to assign grades later. If your time runs out, finish your note immediately and move on; you're probably asking the student to address too many issues. If you finish early, take a quick stretch and keep going; you'll want that time later. If a paper is very weak, set it aside; you'll want time to write a thoughtful note later. Don't turn the end comment into a justification or apology for a low grade; use it as a chance to teach the student ways to improve. If you think that assigning a very low grade would be detrimental to the student's progress, you can always mark the paper "No grade pending conference," discuss the paper with the student, and grade it after the student has revised it further. This solution works best when used sparingly and privately; otherwise you'll have B+ students clamoring for a chance to rewrite papers to get an A. (You can choose to allow such students to do so, of course, but be prepared to fight accusations of grade inflation.)

7. Keep good records. Don't just put the grade on the paper; record it in your grade book or progress folder immediately. If you're keeping a progress chart in the student's folder, make a few sketchy notes now; you can go back and elaborate later if necessary. If you forget to record grades now, you'll eventually find yourself in the position of returning a set of papers without having recorded the grades; then you have to go through all sorts of contortions to get the papers back to record the grades. Such a time-consuming annoyance can be avoided by keeping records carefully from the beginning.

Portfolios

You can reduce the number of assignments you actually give letter grades by allowing students to select some of their papers to submit as a portfolio for the class. Usually students submit drafts at an early point in the semester for your comments, then revise them and choose which ones to submit for their final grade in the course. Such an approach grants them more autonomy and may heighten their desire to achieve. Portfolios also encourage students to see writing as a process, enabling their growth as writers; for this reason, many colleges and universities are using portfolios not only in first-year writing but throughout a student's academic career; these portfolios become substantially more than just an evaluation method. Electronic portfolios are becoming increasingly popular as students can publish their work to various audiences. And because electronic portfolios are easily revisable and portable, students may use them throughout college and even in the workplace.

Portfolio grading, at its best, empowers students and spurs revision; thus it has drawn a great deal of attention in recent years as programs struggle with the question of evaluation. Several fine collections of perspectives on the portfolio question include *Portfolios: Process and Product*, edited by Pat Belanoff and Marcia Dickson; *Situating Portfolios: Four Perspectives*, edited by Kathleen Blake Yancey and Irwin Weiser; and *Portfolios in the Writing Classroom: An Introduction*, edited by Kathleen Blake Yancey. (See also Glazer; Gill; Gilbert; and Black.)

If you decide to use portfolios in your classes, you'll need to make choices about scheduling them, grading them, and selecting what should go in them. You may want to experiment with the following options before settling on the arrangements you think work best for you and your students:

- Structuring portfolio assignments over the course of the semester takes some logistical planning. One issue is the pace of your own workload. Consider: if you have four classes of 25 students each, and each student turns in a portfolio of four papers at the end of the term, you'll have 400 papers to grade all at once. Students too may have difficulty managing an unbalanced workload. Moreover, students benefit most from getting feedback throughout the semester—your comments on

one paper may help them not only with the revision of that paper but with the first draft of their next paper. To balance the workload for yourself and your students, you may want to require that some of the portfolio revisions be turned in for comments midway through the semester. Alternatively, you can make sure to give back first drafts well enough in advance of the portfolio due date that students will have ample time to work on revisions. Another option is to give very thorough critiques on first drafts and minimal comments on the revisions in the portfolio. If you choose the latter option, you may want to have your students write you a memo about each revised paper, or even annotate the paper, to show what changes they made from the first draft, so that you will have a focus for your comments. Or you could have them resubmit the first draft of each paper along with the revised version; in this way you can review your comments on the draft and more quickly evaluate the success of the revision.

- You'll need to give some thought to developing a grading system for portfolios in your courses. You may want to give only comments (no grades) on first drafts, and then give a grade for each revised paper and another for the portfolio as a whole. Alternatively, you can give grades on individual first drafts and then one overall grade for the portfolio. You can give all papers equal weight in determining the overall grade or allow students to choose which papers they'd like to have weighed more heavily. You may want to give credit for degree of improvement, but if you do so you'll need to take care not to end up with inflated grades.

- Students should decide for themselves what to include in the portfolio, but it can be very productive for them to discuss their decisions with you and/or their classmates. You can meet with students to discuss which papers they think they'd like to revise and why. You may want to ask your students to prepare for these conferences by filling out self-assessment forms identifying the strengths and weaknesses of each paper and setting goals for revision. Or have students work in small groups to help one another select which papers should be revised. If you have all your students bring their portfolios to class and pass them around, so that each student looks at fifteen or more, they will quickly get a feeling for what makes a good portfolio.

Conference

You can also work individually with students on the development of their papers, looking at rough drafts of either portions or complete versions of their texts. You could "evaluate" some papers in one-to-one conferences, assigning verbal grades of "excellent," "very good," "fair," and the like. Since these grades will likely be high, reflecting your evaluation of the project at many stages, you might then assign letter grades only to papers students produce independently, alternating conference and independent papers. This strategy reduces by half the number of written comments you must produce; its drawback is the amount of time such conference teaching requires. Some teachers address the time issue by meeting with selected groups of students for intensive revision discussions focused on those students' particular needs. An additional advantage of conferences is that you can work through relevant sections of the handbook with students, so that they have specific places to look for information as they revise their papers. A good rule of thumb in planning conferences is to set a defined agenda in advance so that students come to the conference with a particular piece of writing, a list of questions, or a revision plan, as well as a mutually understood goal for the session.

Collaborating

A different kind of workload reduction can be achieved by letting your students do some of the work for you collaboratively. When students work effectively in small and large groups, they can identify writing problems at the draft stage and help their fellow students remedy weaknesses. Group proofreading sessions likewise can find and solve many mechanical problems before they reach your desk. If you train the groups to look for the kinds of problems students are having, they can do a great deal of the diagnostic work for each other. You'll occasionally have to correct a faulty diagnosis, but you will save yourself a little time while promoting students' independent revision and editing skills. If all students have access to computer facilities, they can use e-mail, instant messaging, or online course management software (like *WebCT* or *Blackboard*) to share their work with one another in pairs or small groups. They can also form chat groups using the course Web site or other instant messaging programs to assist one another with writing and editing concerns they encounter outside class meetings.

Student-set standards

You can also encourage students to set the standard for achievement in the class, perhaps using a model such as the description of letter grades given above. Or, using that model as a starting point, you might ask students to derive a more specific set of criteria from a particular assignment. Such an exercise might ask: "What kinds of things does this assignment ask for? What might be a minimal (C-level) response to this assignment? What kinds of strategies might an excellent (B- to A-level paper) adopt in responding to this assignment?" Or, early in the semester, you can have students develop sets of criteria that characterize above-average, average, and below-average writing; then hold them to these criteria in assigning grades. Distribute the criteria to the class members; use them to develop goals for assignments, to develop heuristics for group work, and to support your comments.

■ Evaluation *cans* and *can'ts*

Some teachers, particularly beginning ones, have an extremely idealistic view of evaluation: they see it as a cure-all for all the writer's problems. To gain these results, they write comments that may approach (or exceed) the original paper in length. The overwhelmed student may try to respond but is usually daunted by all the advice and suggestions—and subsequent papers sometimes are disasters. It's crucial to remember that students rarely learn a new skill or learn to recognize and correct even a single pattern of error overnight. It takes an enormous amount of practice and consideration for a student to locate sentence fragments in his or her own writing—about as much time as it takes to create well-developed paragraphs. Although it can be frustrating to see recurring errors of exactly the same type that you have carefully marked in previous papers, those errors are rarely a sign of carelessness; more often they suggest that the student needs more personalized support (a conference, a tutoring session, an assigned task using the handbook).

Evaluating individual written products is a matter of seeing how well students have reached intermediate goals in the course. It can't be done on the bell curve; writing progress is too individual a process for that. While you'll want to apply the same standards to all students, you'll probably have to allow some leeway in measuring achievement. Students who quickly master narrow competencies (such as mechanics or syntactic variety) should receive credit for these successes but should probably be judged more on how well they master more open matters—audience manipulation, voice, development, and so on. Students who have a great deal of difficulty mastering the narrow skills—those who come from particularly weak backgrounds or who have dialect interference problems, for example—may have excellent ideas but difficulty in presenting them. They should be rewarded for the content of their papers but encouraged to master the conventions of academic discourse as well. Make it clear to students that you're not evaluating how well they compete against other students—or against your ideals—but how much progress they're making in achieving the goals set for all students.

Likewise, you may be tempted to reward a student's effort on a paper rather than the product he or she actually produces ("This just doesn't hold together, but he worked so hard; look at all these drafts!"); such sympathy may be human, but it's not going to help the student. Giving good grades for effort rather than for results provides students with false assessments of their achievements. It's dishonest. Better in such cases to withhold a grade pending a conference and revision than to inflate students' expectations artificially.

■ Resources for response and evaluation

Bartholomae, David. "Released into Error: Errors, Expectations and the Legacy of Mina Shaughnessy." *The Territory of Language*. Ed. Donald A. McQuade. Carbondale: Southern Illinois UP, 1986. 65–88. Print.

---. "The Study of Error." *College Composition and Communication* 31.3 (1980): 253–69. Print.

Belanoff, Pat, and Marcia Dickson, eds. *Portfolios: Process and Product*. Portsmouth: Boynton/Cook, 1991. Print.

Black, Laurel Johnson. *Between Talk and Teaching: Reconsidering the Writing Conference*. Logan: Utah State UP, 1998. Print.

Black, Laurel, et al., eds. *New Directions in Portfolio Assessment: Reflective Practice, Critical Theory, and Large-Scale Scoring*. Portsmouth: Boynton/Cook, 1994. Print.

Brannon, Lil, and C. H. Knoblauch. "On Students' Rights to Their Own Texts: A Model of Teacher Response." *College Composition and Communication* 33.2 (1982): 157–66. Print.

Broad, Bob. *What We Really Value: Beyond Rubrics in Teaching and Assessing Writing*. Logan: Utah State UP, 2003. Print.

Conners, Robert J., and Andrea Lunsford. "Teachers' Rhetorical Comments on Student Papers." *College Composition and Communication* 44.2 (1993): 200–23. Print.

Cooper, Charles R., and Lee Odell, eds. *Evaluating Writing: Describing, Measuring, Judging*. Urbana: NCTE, 1977. Print.

Fife, Jane Mathison, and Peggy O'Neill. "Moving beyond the Written Comment: Narrowing the Gap between Response Practice and Research." *College Composition and Communication* 53.2 (2001): 300–21. Print.

Freedman, Sarah Warshauer. *Responses to Student Writing*. Urbana: NCTE, 1987. Print.

Freedman, Sarah Warshauer, and Melanie Sperling. "Teacher–Student Interaction in the Writing Conference: Response and Teaching." *The Acquisition of Written Language: Response and Revision*. Ed. Sarah Warshauer Freedman. Norwood: Ablex, 1985. 106–30. Print.

Garrison, Roger. *One-to-One: Making Writing Instruction Effective*. Instructor's Manual to Accompany Garrison's *How a Writer Works*. New York: Harper & Row, 1981. Print.

Gere, Ann Ruggles, and Robert Stevens. "The Language of Writing Groups: How Oral Response Shapes Revision." *The Acquisition of Written Language: Response and Revision*. Ed. Sarah Warshauer Freedman. Norwood: Ablex, 1985. 85–105. Print.

Gilbert, Judith C. *Portfolio Resource Guide: Creating and Using Portfolios in the Classroom*. Ottawa: The Writing Conference, 1993. Print.

Gill, Ken, and the Committee on Classroom Practices, eds. *Process and Portfolios in Writing Instruction*. Urbana: NCTE, 1993. Print.

Glazer, Susan Mandel, and Carol Smullen Brown. *Portfolios and Beyond: Collaborative Assessments in Reading and Writing*. Norwood: Christopher-Gordon, 1993. Print.

Golub, Jeffrey N., ed. *More Ways to Handle the Paper Load: On Paper and Online*. Urbana: NCTE, 2006. Print.

Harris, Muriel. *Teaching One-to-One: The Writing Conference*. Urbana: NCTE, 1986. Print.

Hillocks, George. "The Interaction of Instruction, Teacher Comment, and Revision in Teaching the Composing Process." *Research in the Teaching of English* 16.3 (1982): 261–78. Print.

Huot, Brian. *(Re)Articulating Writing Assessment*. Logan: Utah State UP, 2002. Print.

Larson, Bruce, Susan Stern Ryan, and Ross Winterowd, eds. *Encountering Student Texts: Interpretive Issues in Reading Student Writing*. Urbana: NCTE, 1990. Print.

McDonald, W. U., Jr. "The Revising Process and the Marking of Student Papers." *College Composition and Communication* 29.2 (1978): 167–70. Print.

Rutz, Carol. "Recovering the Conversation: A Response to 'Responding to Student Writing' via 'Across the Drafts.'" *College Composition and Communication* 58.2 (2006): 257–61. Print.

Shaughnessy, Mina. *Errors and Expectations: A Guide for the Teacher of Basic Writing*. New York: Oxford UP, 1977. Print.

Shaw, Margaret L. "What Students Don't Say: An Approach to the Student Text." *College Composition and Communication* 42.1 (1991): 45–54. Print.

Sommers, Jeffrey. "The Effects of Tape-Recorded Commentary on Student Revision: A Case Study." *Journal of Teaching Writing* 8.2 (1989): 49–75. Print.

Sommers, Nancy. "Responding to Student Writing." *College Composition and Communication* 33.2 (1982): 148–56. Print.

Speck, Bruce. *Grading Student Writing: An Annotated Bibliography*. Westport: Greenwood, 1998. Print.

Straub, Richard. "The Concept of Control in Teacher Response: Defining the Varieties of 'Directive' and 'Facilitative' Commentary." *College Composition and Communication* 47.2 (1996): 223–51. Print.

---. "Reading and Responding to Student Writing: A Heuristic for Reflective Practice." *Composition Studies* 30.1 (2002): 15–60. Print.

White, Edward M. "The Scoring of Writing Portfolios: Phase 2." *College Composition and Communication* 56.4 (2005): 581–600. Print.

Yancey, Kathleen Blake. "Postmodernism, Palimpsest, and Portfolios: Theoretical Issues in the Representation of Student Work." *College Composition and Communication* 55.4 (2004): 738–61. Print.

Yancey, Katherine Blake, ed. *Portfolios in the Writing Classroom: An Introduction*. Urbana: NCTE, 1992. Print.

Yancey, Kathleen Blake, and Irwin Weiser, eds. *Situating Portfolios: Four Perspectives*. Logan: Utah State UP, 1997. Print.

Zak, Frances, and Christopher C. Weaver, eds. *The Theory and Practice of Grading Writing*. Albany: State U of New York P, 1998. Print.

4

Using Collaborative Learning with the Handbook

Collaborative learning activities provide effective ways to get students to write to a tangible audience of their peers, to practice their revision skills in a supportive, non-intimidating environment, and to experience alternative perspectives and approaches to writing and to the course readings. Group work also shifts classroom learning to an ongoing conversation among students rather than constantly deferring to the teacher's greater authority. Kenneth Bruffee, a key proponent of collaborative learning, argues that because knowledge itself is the result of consensus among members of a community, and is produced by collaborative activity, "interdependent" student groups offer the ideal learning tool (3). They become "transition communities or support groups that students can rely on as they go through the risky process of becoming new members of the knowledge communities" (4). While Bruffee argues for a long history of informal cooperation and support systems among students as the natural basis for collaborative classroom assignments, others have pointed to the difficulty of grafting collaborative procedures into institutions that base their standards on individual performance and reward individual excellence (Gergits and Schramer, Heller). Still others have countered Bruffee's model of consensus as one that overlooks or erases the powerful differences between groups and individuals, differences that are the basis for continual collaborative negotiation (Trimbur and Spellmeyer, for example).

As these theoretical models suggest, it is important to be aware of potentially contradictory messages when setting up collaborative activities. For instance, students may not readily embrace a collaborative revision exercise if the grading system for the class, the teacher's responses on papers, and other classroom practices are all focused on individual performance. Conversely, the more collaborative work that students do, and the more that work is supported by other classroom practices, the more students will understand the goals of group activities and feel confident in negotiating group dynamics. It also helps to remember that collaborative groups are part of a complex social process; as students work to overcome the social awkwardness of organizing and starting the task, they are also finding some common ground, acquiring the ability to communicate across (sometimes) enormous ideological and conceptual differences (see *Singular Texts/Plural Authors*, Andrea Lunsford and Lisa Ede).

■ Forming groups for collaboration

Teachers who are considering collaborative activities may find the following suggestions useful. Collaborative groups can vary in size and configuration depending on the activity—from pairs to groups of four or five. For example, if the task is to choose a passage from the reading and come up with an interpretive response to present to the class, a larger group is useful in producing energetic debates (especially if each student is responsible for presenting some of the material). If you are having students work with the handbook to identify and revise particular problems, groups of three allow for both a range of skills and attention to individual difficulties. Students might begin with the revision checklist (pp. 54–55) or the editing checklist (pp. 60–61) to identify recurrent problem patterns in each other's work, then revise using the relevant sections from the handbook. If your revision groups of three or four are becoming careless in their suggestions for each other's papers, you might pair students in groups of two and ask them to respond in writing and at length to another student's paper.

Some teachers always allow students to choose their own groups; the advantage here is that students generally establish a working dynamic and continue to choose the same group throughout the course. Other teachers select groups in order to mix or isolate skill levels or to create productive environments for silent or outspoken students. Again, you might make this decision based on the particular task and on group dynamics. If the task you have assigned is to revise a sentence or a paragraph in a student essay, you might streamline the process by asking students to work with the person next to them. If you notice a larger revision group veering into discussions of movies or a sociology exam, you might sit in with them for that session to listen to the group dynamic, then make an effort to reorganize groups for the next session (see Brook, Mirtz, and Evans for further discussion of small group dynamics).

One way to reinforce the significance of collaborative work in a course in which grades depend upon individual performance is to incorporate peer-review suggestions into your final comments on each student's paper. After reading the student's paper and scanning the peer-review worksheets or marked drafts, you might say, for example, "You have effectively made use of Jeffrey D's suggestion about developing paragraphs 5–8. Audrey F's question about your transitions on pages 4 and 5 might have led you to strengthen your argument—look out for those transitional movements next time!" Another way to reinforce those goals is to assign one or two collaboratively written and graded projects.

Many instructors assign students in pairs or small teams to collaborate on papers; for certain kinds of writing, especially research writing, such strategies can be very effective and will prepare students well for the kinds of writing they may do in their careers. Many of the exercises in Chapters 41–46 can be adapted for collaborative projects. Such projects can be combined with individually produced and evaluated papers as well. For example, you might have students work in pairs to write out the different sides of a debate, then ask each student to produce an individually written paper that takes the other student's perspective into account. "Collaborative Learning" exercises in Chapters 7–11 suggest various ways for students to produce arguments and to analyze each other's claims.

■ Developing skills in collaboration

As with any other process, collaborative work is a slowly developed skill. New teachers will sometimes report that they tried it once and it "didn't work" so they're hesitant to try it again. Remember that groups might not seem highly productive at first; students can be unsure of their revision skills, hesitant about sharing their work, and dependent on the teacher's greater authority. One way to make group work more productive is to give students shorter, highly directed tasks at first; for example, each group might read and discuss Chapter 4, section c, on developing paragraphs, then work together to revise a student writer's paragraph. It also helps to model the assigned activity with the class as a whole before moving to smaller groups. For example, you might bring in a sample student paper, have each student come up with a revision suggestion or practice revising a sample sentence, then share the results with the class. Then, when students undertake a similar activity in smaller groups, you can refer back to the previous class-wide activity. Also, in many cases in which group work appears to "fail," students are simply confused about the assigned activity. It helps to be extremely clear about what you want each group to accomplish—even to provide a written handout or worksheet (sample worksheets follow this discussion). It's also important that students recognize the relationship between the group activity and their personal goals as writers; many teachers preface group work with a discussion of those goals in relation to the group task.

The crucial thing to remember is that working in revision or writing groups is as much a skill to be demonstrated and learned as any other. In working with a sample paper, for example, you might start with basic questions that help students to look globally at the writing as a teacher (evaluator) would look at it. "What's the point of this paper? Who are the readers supposed to be? What are some things this writer does well?" Then you might ask students to look more specifically at the construction of the paper: the places where assertions are backed up by evidence and the places where more evidence is needed; the indications of strong organizational control and the places where the text seems choppy and disorganized; the clear definition with supporting examples and the terms of the essay that need further clarification and development. The sample worksheets that accompany this chapter can be modified to guide students through particular tasks. For example, you might ask each student writer to create a self-evaluation of the paper (Form G), then compare it to her or his group's suggestions (Forms A, B, or C). If students seem to be supplying vague responses to larger questions about audience and argument, Forms D, E, and F suggest ways to focus the groups on specific areas of the essay.

In addition to identifying strengths and problem areas, collaborative groups can go on to help each writer begin the work of revision. If, for instance, the text seems choppy or disorganized, they can experiment with organizational tools (using Exercise 2.12 in 2c, for example) or look for transition problems (using Exercise 4.10, 4b). If the thesis is underdeveloped, they might apply the questions in 10i, Exercise 10.11, to suggest places where new examples or analysis would help. Or, if the essay seems to lack a directed purpose, Exercises 1.6 and 1.11 in 1d and 1e offer specific and effective practice in thinking about audience and purpose. Many of the other exercises in *The Little, Brown Handbook* are well suited to such collaborative work.

■ Customizing collaborative materials

Many teachers like to modify the worksheets and exercises to suit a particular class. For instance, worksheet questions can be adapted to focus on a particular reading or essay assignment. Some teachers begin the course with detailed revision worksheets, then gradually taper off as group members become familiar with each other and confident about their revision skills. Teachers working in a computer classroom can supplement these exercises by creating networked revision groups, using e-mail or chat groups and by publishing student work online, allowing a wider audience to read and respond to

the writers' work (see Barrett; Moxley and Meehan; and Strenski, Feagin, and Singer, for example). Also see Daniel Anderson's chapter, IAE Chapter 5.

Some teachers are active participants in group activities, whereas other teachers try not to intervene directly in groups unless students have questions or have ceased to address the task (for more on this topic see "A Conversation About Small Groups" in Brook et al.). The teacher's primary role in a collaborative classroom is to design effective group tasks that take the varying needs of students into account. For example, highly skilled students may not always trust their peers to give them revision advice. For those students it is important to emphasize that learning to critique another writer's work in a way that encourages productive revision hones their own revision skills as well. Conversely, less skilled writers occasionally feel overwhelmed by the group's advice and may seek to deflect attention from the paper by protesting that it's not a real draft or that it's not ready to be read. Here it helps to emphasize that active revision can begin from a sketchy paragraph or from notes. In some cases, the most effective task for a group might be to help the writer pinpoint useful passages in the readings, or to ask the writer to describe verbally where he or she intends to go with the project. In this sense, collaborative work can be flexibly attuned to the needs of various writers at different stages of a project. In a process-oriented class, this emphasis on the way different writers work can be a useful focus for class-wide discussions—and a way to encourage students to take themselves and each other seriously as writers. (See Brammer and Rees and Grimm for more on understanding students' reservations and making peer review more productive.)

Since students may profit from having specific guidelines for collaboration, we've prepared the following worksheets that will help you guide collaborative activities in your classroom.

Worksheets for collaborative activities

FORM A

General Guidelines for Peer Readers Commenting Directly on a Writer's Work

Author: _____   Reader: _____

As a reader, you are going to comment directly on a photocopy of a classmate's paper. Read the paper through carefully before making any comments. Then follow the guidelines below. If the writer has submitted a self-evaluation sheet, read it after answering question 1.

1. Consider the thesis, purpose, and audience for the paper. Are they indicated clearly? Are they consistent? If not, ask the writer questions to help clarify these essential elements of writing.

2. Skim the paper to see how it is organized. Are there any breaks in the organization? If so, try to explain why you feel that a gap exists. Whenever possible, phrase your comments as questions, not judgments. If you think that the organization needs to be revised significantly, skip to question 7 after answering this question.

3. Now go back and look at each paragraph. Is it unified, coherent, and developed? If not, ask the writer a question to help focus or complete the paragraph.

4. Are the paragraphs connected to one another smoothly and logically? If there are any logical gaps between the paragraphs, ask the writer how one paragraph is linked to the next. If you think that most of the paragraphs need to be revised significantly, skip to question 7 after answering this question.

5. Now look at sentences. Do any sentences confuse you? If so, try to describe your confusion or ask the writer a question about the sentence.

6. Are there any mechanical or grammatical problems in the paper? If so, point them out to the writer, but do not correct them.

7. Decide what the paper's two most important strengths are. Point them out to the writer.

FORM B

Reader Response Sheet for a Descriptive Critique

Author: _____   Reader: _____

Answer the questions below, being as specific as possible.

1. Read the first paragraph and then pause. Write down what you expect will be the topic, purpose, and audience of the paper.

2. Now finish reading the paper. Were your expectations for the paper's topic, purpose, and audience fulfilled? If not, what do you now think the topic, purpose, and audience are?

3. What do you think the main idea, or thesis, of the paper is?

4. What sort of evidence is used to develop or support this main idea?

5. Summarize the paper, devoting one sentence to each paragraph.

FORM C

Reader Response Sheet for an Evaluative Critique

Author: _____   Reader: _____

Answer the questions below, being as specific as possible. If the author has included a self-evaluation sheet, do not read it until you have answered questions 1 through 6.

1. Read the first paragraph and then pause. Write down what you expect will be the topic, purpose, and audience of the paper.

2. Now finish reading the paper. Were your expectations for the paper's topic, purpose, and audience fulfilled? If not, what do you now think the topic, purpose, and audience are?

3. What do you think the main idea, or thesis, of the paper is?

4. What sort of evidence is used to develop or support this main idea?

5. Summarize the paper, devoting one sentence to each paragraph.

6. What did you like best about the paper?

7. Did anything in the paper surprise you?

8. What two features of the paper most need improvement?

9. Please respond to the author's questions on the back of this sheet.

_____

To the author: Before giving this sheet to your reader, list on the back the three questions that you would like your reader to answer about this paper.

FORM D

Reader Response Sheet for a Thorough Critique

Author: _____   Reader: _____

Answer the questions below, being as specific as possible. If the author has included a self-evaluation sheet, do not read it until you have answered questions 1 through 3.

1. Read the first paragraph and then pause. Write down what you expect will be the topic, purpose, and audience of the paper.

2. Now finish reading the paper. Were your expectations for the paper's topic, purpose, and audience fulfilled? If not, what do you now think the topic, purpose, and audience are?

3. Summarize the paper, devoting one sentence to each paragraph.

4. What do you think the main idea, or thesis, of the paper is? Do you agree with this thesis? Why or why not? What is your position on this topic?

5. What sort of evidence is used to develop or support this main idea? Is this evidence appropriate? Is there sufficient evidence? If not, what sort of evidence should the writer consider?

6. Does the author take into account different points of view about the thesis of the paper? Does the author consider counterarguments?

7. Are there counterarguments that the author does not consider, but should?

8. What did you like best about this paper?

9. What two features of the paper most need improvement?

10. Please respond to the author's questions on the back of this sheet.

To the author: Before giving this sheet to your reader, list on the back the three questions that you would like your reader to answer about this paper.

FORM E

Author's and Reader's Responses in the Second Round
of a Thorough Critique

Author: _____   Reader: _____

Author's section. Please attach a revision of your original paper to this form and answer the following questions.

1. What do you think is your reader's point of view on this subject? Do you share that point of view?

2. What assumptions does your reader make about the topic? Do you agree with these assumptions? Why or why not?

3. What two comments by the reader were the most useful? Why were they helpful?

4. What are the two most important changes that you have made in this revision?

5. What do you like best about the essay?

6. What two questions would you like your reader to answer about this revision?

Reader's section. Please respond to the questions below.

1. Please summarize the author's revision, devoting one sentence to each paragraph.

2. How do you think that the author has improved the essay?

3. Has the author changed your feeling about the topic?

4. What is the strongest argument against the writer's thesis?

5. What two features most need improvement?

6. Respond to the author's questions.

FORM F

Reader Response Sheet for an Essay Assignment Stressing Paragraphing
(Handbook, Chapter 4)

Author: _____   Reader: _____

Answer the questions below, being as specific as possible. If the author has included a self-evaluation sheet, do not read it until you have answered questions 1 through 6.

1. Read the first paragraph and then pause. Write down what you expect will be the topic, purpose, and audience of the paper.

2. Now finish reading the paper. Were your expectations for the paper's topic, purpose, and audience fulfilled? If not, what do you now think the topic, purpose, and audience are?

3. What do you think the main idea, or thesis, of the paper is?

4. What sort of evidence is used to develop or support this main idea?

5. Number the paragraphs. Are the author's paragraphs unified, coherent, and developed? If so, note them. Also indicate any that confuse you, and explain why.

6. Do the paragraphs follow a logical order? Describe how the argument does or does not flow from the first to the second, from the second to the third, and so on.

7. What did you like best about the paper?

8. What two features of the paper most need improvement?

FORM G

Self-Evaluation Sheet to Accompany an Essay for Peer Response or Instructor's Evaluation

Author: In order to help your instructor or peer reader evaluate this essay, you should explain where you are in the writing process. Be as specific as possible in answering the following questions.

1. What are you trying to say in this paper? What is your main idea?

2. Who might be interested in reading this paper?

3. What do you like best in the paper?

4. What do you like least in the paper?

5. What would you work on if you had twenty-four hours more to spend on the project?

6. What three questions would you like to ask your reader? How can your reader help you develop the paper further?

■ Resources for collaborative learning and peer criticism

Barrett, Edward. "Collaboration in the Electronic Classroom." *Technology Review* 96.2 (1993): 51–55. Print.

Bishop, Wendy. "Helping Peer Writing Groups Succeed." *Teaching English in the Two-Year College* 15.2 (1988): 120–25. Print.

Bizzaro, Patrick, and Stuart Werner. "Collaboration of Teacher and Counselor in Basic Writing." *College Composition and Communication* 38.4 (1987): 458–61. Print.

Brammer, Charlotte, and Mary Rees. "Peer Review from the Students' Perspective: Invaluable or Invalid?" *Composition Studies* 35.2 (2007): 71–86. Print.

Brook, Robert, Ruth Mirtz, and Rick Evans, eds. *Small Groups in Writing Workshops*. Urbana: NCTE, 1994. Print.

Bruffee, Kenneth. *Collaborative Learning: Higher Education, Interdependence, and the Authority of Knowledge*. Baltimore: Johns Hopkins UP, 1993. Print.

Clark, Beverly Lyon. *Talking About Writing: A Guide for Tutor and Teacher Conferences*. Ann Arbor: U of Michigan P, 1985. Print.

Clark, Irene L. "Portfolio Evaluations, Collaboration, and Writing Centers." *College Composition and Communication* 44.4 (1993): 515–24. Print.

Corder, Jim W. "Tribes and Displaced Persons: Some Observations on Collaboration." *Theory and Practice in the Teaching of Writing: Rethinking the Discipline*. Ed. Lee Odell. Carbondale: Southern Illinois UP, 1993. 271–88. Print.

Elbow, Peter, and Pat Belanoff. *Sharing and Responding*. 3rd ed. Boston: McGraw-Hill, 2000. Print.

Forman, Janis, ed. *New Visions of Collaborative Writing*. Portsmouth: Boynton/Cook, 1992. Print.

Gergits, Julia M., and James J. Schramer. "The Collaborative Classroom as the Site of Difference." *Journal of Advanced Composition* 14.1 (1994): 187–202. Print.

George, Diana. "Working with Peer Groups in the Composition Classroom." *College Composition and Communication* 35.3 (1984): 320–26. Print.

Gere, Anne Ruggles. *Writing Groups: History, Theory, and Implications*. Carbondale: Southern Illinois UP, 1987. Print.

---. and Robert D. Abbott. "Talking About Writing: The Language of Writing Groups." *Research in the Teaching of English* 19.4 (1985): 362–86. Print.

---. and Ralph Stevens. "The Language of Writing Groups: How Oral Response Shapes Revision." *The Acquisition of Written Language: Response and Revision*. Ed. Sarah Warshauer Freedman. Norwood: Ablex, 1985. 85–105. Print.

Golub, Jeff, and the Committee on Classroom Practices, eds. *Focus on Collaborative Learning*. Urbana: NCTE, 1988. Print.

Gonzalez, Casey. "Building Trust While Building Skills in a Peer Writing Group." *Journal of Teaching Writing* 18.1-2 (2000): 56–69. Print.

Grimm, Nancy. "Improving Students' Responses to Their Peers' Essays." *College Composition and Communication* 37.1 (1986): 91–3. Print.

Haring-Smith, Tori. *Writing Together: Collaborative Learning in the Classroom*. New York: HarperCollins, 1994. Print.

Harris, Joseph. "The Idea of Community in the Study of Writing." *College Composition and Communication* 40.1 (1989): 11–22. Print.

Harris, Muriel. "Collaboration Is Not Collaboration Is Not Collaboration: Writing Center Tutorials vs. Peer-Response Groups." *College Composition and Communication* 43.3 (1992): 369–83. Print.

Heller, Rafael. "Questionable Categories and the Case for Collaborative Writing." *Rhetoric Review* 22.3 (2003): 300–17. Print.

Hillocks, George. "Environments for Active Learning." *Theory and Practice in the Teaching of Writing: Rethinking the Discipline*. Ed. Lee Odell. Carbondale: Southern Illinois UP, 1993. 244–70. Print.

Kail, Harvey. "Collaborative Learning in Context: The Problem with Peer Tutoring." *College English* 45.6 (1983): 594–99. Print.

Leonard, James S., Christine E. Wharton, Robert Murray Davis, and Jeanette Harris, eds. *Author-ity and Textuality: Current Views of Collaborative Writing*. West Cornwall: Locust Hill P, 1994. Print.

Lunsford, Andrea, and Lisa Ede. *Singular Texts/Plural Authors: Perspectives on Collaborative Writing*. Carbondale: Southern Illinois UP, 1992. Print.

Madden-Simpson, Janet. "A Collaborative Approach to the Research Paper." *Teaching English in the Two-Year College* 16.2 (1989): 113–15. Print.

Moss, Beverly, Nels P. Highberg, and Melissa Nicholas, eds. *Writing Groups Inside and Outside the Classroom*. Mahwah: Erlbaum, 2004. Print.

Moxley, Joe, and Ryan Meehan. "Collaboration, Literacy, Authorship: Using Social Networking Tools to Engage the Wisdom of Teachers." *Kairos* 12.1 (2007): n.pag. Web. 10 Oct. 2008.

Reither, James A., and Douglas Vipond. "Writing as Collaboration." *College English* 51.8 (1989): 855–67. Print.

Roskelly, Hephzibah. *Breaking (into) the Circle: Group Work for Change in the English Classroom*. Portsmouth: Boynton/Cook, 2002. Print.

---. "The Risky Business of Group Work." *The Writing Teacher's Sourcebook*. 4th ed. Ed. Edward P. J. Corbett et al. New York: Oxford UP, 2000. 123–28. Print.

Smit, David W. "Some Difficulties with Collaborative Learning." *Journal of Advanced Composition* 9.1-2 (1989): 45–58. Print.

Spear, Karen. *Sharing Writing: Peer Response Groups in English Classes*. Portsmouth: Heinemann, 1988. Print.

Speck, Bruce, et al., eds. *Collaborative Writing: An Annotated Bibliography*. Westport: Greenwood, 1999. Print.

Spellmeyer, Kurt. "On Conventions and Collaboration: The Open Road and the Iron Cage." *Writing Theory and Critical Theory*. Ed. John Clifford and John Schilb. New York: MLA, 1994. 73–95. Print.

Spiegelman, Candace. *Across Property Lines: Textual Ownership in Writing Groups*. Carbondale: Southern Illinois UP, 2000. Print.

Stewart, Donald. "Collaborative Learning and Composition: Boon or Bane?" *Rhetoric Review* 7.1 (1988): 58–85. Print.

Strenski, Ellen, Caley O'Dwyer Feagin, and Jonathan A. Singer. "E-mail Small Group Peer Review Revisited." *Computers and Composition* 22.2 (2005): 191–208. Print.

Stygall, Gail. "Women and Language in the Collaborative Writing Classroom." *Feminism and Composition Studies: In Other Words*. Ed. Susan C. Jarratt and Lynn Worsham. New York: MLA, 1998. 252–75. Print.

Trimbur, John. "Collaborative Learning and Teaching Writing." *Perspectives on Research and Scholarship in Composition*. Ed. Ben W. McClelland and Timothy R. Donovan. New York: MLA, 1985. 87–109. Print.

---. "Consensus and Difference in Collaborative Learning." *College English* 51.6 (1989): 602–16. Print.

Tobin, Lad. *Writing Relationships: What Really Happens in the Composition Class*. Portsmouth: Boynton/Cook, 1993. Print.

Wiener, Harvey S. "Collaborative Learning in the Classroom: A Guide to Evaluation." *College English* 48.1 (1986): 52–61. Print.

Yancey, Kathleen Blake, and Michael Spooner. "A Single Good Mind: Collaboration, Cooperation, and the Writing Self." *College Composition and Communication* 49.1 (1998): 45–62. Print.

York, Lorraine. *Rethinking Women's Collaborative Writing: Power, Difference, Property*. Toronto: U Toronto P, 2002. Print.

5

Using Computers to Teach Writing

By Daniel Anderson

Information technologies continue to make dramatic alterations in the educational landscape, and many writing teachers wish to use technological tools in their teaching. Administrators may ask that curricula adapt to serve the changing demands of constituents. Students may arrive at school either already equipped with information skills or insistent that these skills be included as part of their learning. The chapter provides an overview of some of the opportunities made possible by information technology, discusses concerns likely to arise as teachers adapt information technologies to teaching, and offers practical advice for using instructional technologies critically. (*The Little, Brown Handbook* also serves to illuminate the use of information technologies. Chapter 3 offers advice on managing files, using spelling and grammar checkers, and other computer skills in the context of revising and editing; Chapter 5 discusses document design; Chapters 42–44 offer specific information about electronic research; and Chapter 54 focuses on the rhetorical issues of writing online, including e-mail, collaboration, and Web composition; and computer tips appear throughout the text.)

■ Possibilities for teaching with technology

Information technologies offer new modes of learning and avenues for research and collaboration. Word processors and basic computing skills help students enhance and strengthen their writing process. Electronic discussions enable them to converse with one another as they explore issues and ideas about writing. File-sharing functions and collaboration programs allow students to work together on projects. Course management software allows students to accomplish many of these tasks in a centralized electronic location using any Internet-connected computer. Using this software as an electronic classroom allows some writing courses to be taught fully online, with students never meeting face-to-face in a classroom; some writing courses are offered as "hybrids," combining traditional classroom time with online activities and interaction in place of some class meetings. Electronic library resources provide students with extended opportunities for research. And students who compose Web pages and other electronic documents can develop and sharpen their writing skills as they participate in emergent forms of communication and literacy.

What makes this range of possibilities exciting for writing instructors is the way all of these activities build upon what we know to be useful methodologies for helping students to become better writers. Here are some ideas about the pedagogical uses of computers:

■ You can use computers to foreground the process-oriented nature of successful writing. The fluid nature of electronic text and the capacity to write multiple drafts and revisions can help convey an understanding of the ongoing and evolving nature of successful writing. You can teach your students the difference between surface-level revision and deep or structural revision by having them use word-processing features to track the changes they make to documents. You can also help them master the elements of format and document design.

■ Electronic discussion tools can stimulate thinking and provide a space in which students can practice writing. You can create opportunities for students to express their ideas freely in writing using e-mail, wikis, blogs, or chat, and you can coordinate discussion activities with class readings or projects. You can further authorize student ideas by making public the transcripts of conversations or encouraging the citation of peer comments in formal class documents. If you appoint discussion moderators or provide credit for productive participation in any of these conversations, you will be enabling your students to take charge of their learning. These activities can also help your students evaluate the ways that conventions and media affect communication, and they can promote writing within a social context by showing students how to interact conversationally with groups outside of the classroom.

- Computers can promote collaboration and student-centered learning in numerous ways. You might employ file-sharing or set up a wiki to simplify the logistics of group projects and peer review. You can teach students to use the comment and change-tracking functions of word processors to amplify their ability to conduct peer reviews. Web-based collaboration options can be used to create work spaces for small groups and to conduct peer-to-peer activities. You can even capitalize upon the different levels of computer literacy among your students, allowing the more skilled to mentor their peers about information technologies.

- Students can develop their research skills and information literacy by using computers. When you give research assignments to your students, you have an opportunity to help them learn to think and use resources critically. You can emphasize the ways that library and Internet research complement one another. At the same time, you can ask students to consider the relative advantages and disadvantages of print and electronic resources, and to evaluate electronic resources for credibility. You can show students how to find, manage, and document electronic research. You can learn to supplement your own courses by finding and providing appropriate learning resources for students (the most exciting of which may be related to ways of conducting primary research using Internet communications).

- One of the greatest advantages of information technologies is that they promote new forms of literacy. You'll need to teach your students to read electronic compositions critically and to look at elements of interactivity and design in terms of purpose and audience. You might conduct some comparisons between print and electronic compositions to explore the larger rhetorical issues addressed by each. You might also assign Web or other multimedia compositions to allow students to practice working with visual and hypertextual rhetoric, or you could craft Web composition assignments that ask students to manage and tap into selected Web resources. If you assign some Web projects, you can highlight the importance of audience and issues of publication as they relate to writing.

■ Computer technology in and out of the classroom

For many years the only practical way of integrating technology-related activities into your classes was through full or part-time use of a computer-assisted classroom. Today you may have a number of options when it comes to integrating technology into teaching, including the use of supplemental Internet resources, the use of a companion course Web site, wiki, or blog, or the use of a computer-assisted classroom or lab.

The key to choosing the best option for integrating computer technology into your teaching is to investigate the resources already available at your institution and to identify others that might be feasible to develop. Begin by talking with your colleagues in technology support. Ideally, your institution will offer support in the form of technical infrastructure and instructional planning and design. Once you have established a good working relationship with people knowledgeable about the resources at your school, you can consider and choose among the numerous opportunities to adapt information technologies to the teaching of writing. Before leaping into the breach, however, you should acquaint yourself with some of the challenges associated with using instructional technologies and develop strategies that can make your efforts more successful.

The following list details some of those challenges and offers suggestions for how to address them.

Access

You may find that your school has no computer-assisted lab or classroom facilities—or that the equipment in these facilities is outdated. Students may also have inadequate access to technology outside of class. Some students may own the latest computers, others may have three-year-old machines, and still others will have to use the computers in a lab or library. You may not be able to improve or equalize your students' access, but you can work to adapt to whatever level of access they have. If you will be working in a computer-assisted classroom, investigate the capabilities of the environment. If you will be asking students to do Internet work or to interact with a course Web site outside of class, check to make sure your students will have adequate access and make clear to them what your expectations for participation are. It can be difficult to anticipate every contingency, but you should try to find out ahead of time what access problems are likely to arise and plan accordingly.

Skills and training

Once you've made sure that your students have access to adequate technological resources, the next step is to make sure that they have the skills necessary to accomplish technology-related work. Again, you'll need to investigate the options available to you and your students. Many institutions offer workshop training courses in computer basics and other aspects of technology. There are also many resources available online that can provide advice for learning about computer technologies. You could even make learning about technology a central focus of your course, something that you and your students do together. Allow knowledgeable students to take the lead in helping others learn computer-related tasks: by "deputizing" them, you will not only relieve yourself of the burden of having to solve every technical problem, but you'll also foster collaborative work in your classroom.

Time demands

It is a cruel misconception that technology makes teaching and learning more efficient. If anything, you will find that using information technologies places heavy demands on your time. Not only must you devote yourself to learning new skills, but also you must invest energy into reconceiving the ways that you teach. The best strategy for protecting your time as you integrate new technologies into your teaching is to take small bites. Don't try to implement every option available to you for every class. In fact, you can build a highly successful semester around exploring a single computer-assisted activity. Additionally, rather than conducting or monitoring all computer-related work yourself, you can allow students to take charge of some of the class activities, appointing them to moderate class e-mail discussions or to spearhead class research expeditions.

Distractions

One of the most powerful aspects of instructional technology is its capacity to enable student-centered activities. There are some drawbacks, however. You may find that the computers become a distraction when you are trying to conduct a face-to-face discussion or present information to your class, or you may notice students drifting away from the task at hand or behaving inappropriately when interacting in electronic forums. A good way to address these potential distractions is to develop rules of decorum as a class. Early in the semester, talk over these concerns and decide upon conventions that you will follow during class activities. You may also want to build those rules right into your course requirements. For problems related to computers in the classroom, ask students to turn off their monitors or close the lids of their laptops when distractions become overwhelming.

Institutional culture

Not only does instructional technology place new demands on your time and energy, but it also prompts you to work in ways that may not be familiar to your colleagues or fit in with traditional categories used for promotion and reward. A related problem some teachers have is that they are isolated from other colleagues in the department who may not actively be pursuing instructional technologies. Again, explore the context at your school as you consider how the technology-related work you do will fit in with your institution's culture. Ask administrators about their expectations for and ways of evaluating computer-related work. It may also help to establish contact with other members of your institution who use computers in their teaching and/or with Internet communities devoted to technology-based pedagogies (see the links at the end of this chapter).

■ *The Little, Brown Handbook* in the computer-assisted classroom

Many instructors wonder how textbooks fit into the computer-assisted learning environment. At present, it is impossible to predict how soon, or if, the dominant medium for instructional publishing will shift from the bound book to an electronic medium. Remembering that access to computers may vary greatly, the eleventh edition of *The Little, Brown Handbook* and its ancillaries provide resources for teaching all phases of the writing process for instructors working in both electronic and traditional classroom environments. Additionally, the book design facilitates quick reference while working online through checklists and other emphasized material set aside in quickly identifiable tinted boxes, a list of which appears in the endpapers. Throughout the handbook are specific strategies for working with computers.

Basic computer skills for writers

Basic computer skills for writers—organizing with a word processor, revising on screen versus on paper, and so on—are covered throughout Part 1 on the writing process. In addition, Chapter 3 emphasizes how computers can help break down the boundaries between prewriting and drafting and support collaborative work. Chapter 3 includes discussions of how students can use file management techniques to work on multiple drafts of papers, which will help them develop the understanding that successful writing results from an evolving and recursive process of prewriting, drafting, and revision. Students can also use file management and naming conventions to share and review one another's papers more easily; this will enable them to strengthen their writing based upon feedback and interaction with their peers. Chapter 3 also instructs students in the use of advanced word-processing features, such as Comment and Track Changes. Teaching students to use just one or two of these advanced functions is an easy way to promote process-oriented writing in a collaborative context.

Later in the book, Chapter 54 discusses options for using computers in the service of collaboration. Students are shown how to collaborate with classmates using e-mail and the Web (including Web-based courseware such as *Blackboard*, *WebCT*, or a blog log). The coverage includes strategies for interacting in class discussions, sharing files, and using online collaboration tools.

Editing and other sentence-level activities

Teaching grammar, mechanics, punctuation, and other sentence-level concerns with computers is a double-edged sword. Although functions like spelling and style checkers offer powerful assistance in many situations, they can also lull a student into a false sense of security when it comes to editing her work. Furthermore, they can prove distracting, focusing undeserved attention on surface errors at times when deeper revision or drafting deserves the writer's full

attention. Chapter 3 discusses these concerns in detail in order to help students develop a critical understanding of the value of spelling and grammar functions. It also offers instruction in how to customize spelling and grammar functions to maximize their usefulness.

Opportunities for using spelling and style checkers are noted throughout the handbook. These notations also warn students about problems that may arise from uncritical reliance on computer-based editing tools.

Research-based writing

The research chapters cover the use of computers in the research process. Beginning with Chapter 41, "Planning a Research Project," the handbook distinguishes between online and print sources and explains how to find bibliographic information for online sources. Chapter 42, "Finding Sources," emphasizes using the library as Web gateway and includes coverage of keyword searches for both library and Internet sources, as well as how to use electronic catalogs, indexes, abstracts, and subscription services. Chapters 43 and 44, "Working with Sources" and "Avoiding Plagiarism and Documenting Sources," discuss ways of evaluating and managing electronic materials, warn about online plagiarism, and explain how plagiarism can be detected by online tools. In addition, the four documentation sections—MLA, Chicago, APA, and CSE—provide the most up-to-date models for citing electronic sources in each style.

Document design

Chapter 5 shows students how to use computers to design academic papers and also provides guidance in the principles of electronic document design (including the role of flow, spacing, emphasis, color, fonts, and illustrations). Chapter 5 also includes guidelines on designing for readers with disabilities.

Online communication and electronic documents

Chapters 54–56 cover a range of opportunities for writing and communicating online. Chapter 54, "Writing Online," focuses on the rhetorical issues of writing e-mail, working in online collaborative writing environments, and composing online papers and original Web sites. Chapter 55, "Public Writing," contains guidelines for preparing an electronic, scannable résumé and a student sample. Chapter 56, "Oral Presentations," provides tips for working with PowerPoint and sample slides from a student presentation.

■ The new Web site *MyCompLab* (*mycomplab.com*) integrates instruction, multimedia tutorials, and exercises for writing, grammar, and research with an online composing space and assessment tools (see p. IAE-16). An e-book of *The Little, Brown Handbook* is also available in *MyCompLab*.

■ Students can subscribe to *The Little, Brown Handbook* as a *CourseSmart* e-textbook (*coursesmart.com*). The site includes all of the handbook's content in a format that enables students to search the text, bookmark passages, integrate their notes, and print reading assignments that incorporate lecture notes. For more information, or to subscribe to the *CourseSmart* e-textbook, visit *coursesmart.com*.

■ *VangoNotes* are study guides in MP3 format that enable students to download handbook information into their own players and then listen to it whenever and wherever they wish. The notes include "need to know" tips for each handbook chapter, practice tests, audio flash cards for learning key concepts and terms, and a rapid review for exams. For more information, visit *VangoNotes.com*.

Grammar software programs

Applications devoted to issues of grammar, mechanics, and punctuation generally fall into one of two categories—tutorials or style checkers. Tutorials contain sets of questions (multiple choice, true/false, short answer) on various topics. They may also contain various levels of description and explanation of the topics covered, as well as diagnostic or proficiency tests. Tutorials currently available on the market include *Understanding and Using English Grammar Interactive*, *EasyWriter*, and *The Grammar Key*. Grammar/style checkers examine writing for potential grammatical problems. *Microsoft Word* and *WordPerfect* include style checkers, and others available include *WhiteSmoke*, *StyleWriter*, and *LanguageTool* (open source). Though occasionally useful in helping students spot specific flaws in their work, these applications should never be viewed as a substitute for careful and thorough editing. (For more information on using word-processor grammar and style checkers, see Chapter 3.)

1 Assessing the Writing Situation

Instruction
- Speaking to Your Audience
- Researching Possible Topic
- Planning
- General Writing Guides and Grammar Links
- Checking Voice
- Link to E-book

Multimedia
- Video

Exercises
- Text Exercises

2 Developing and Shaping Ideas

Instruction
- Prewriting
- Planning
- Developing a Working Thesis
- Organizing Main Points
- Link to E-book

Multimedia
- Video

Exercises
- Text Exercises

3 Drafting and Revising

Instruction
- Writing Introductions
- Writing Body Paragraphs
- Writing Conclusions
- Improving Sentence Flow
- Editing Symbols Guide
- Link to E-book

Multimedia
- Videos

Exercises
- Text Exercises

4 Writing and Revising Paragraphs

Instruction
- Working with Transitions
- Improving Focus and Structure
- Sharpening Your Paragraphs
- Link to E-book

Multimedia
- Video

Exercises
- Text Exercises

5 Designing Documents

Instruction
- Designing Your Document
- Link to E-book

Multimedia
- Videos

Exercises
- Text Exercises

6 Developing Academic Skills

Instruction
- Link to E-book

Multimedia
- Audio Lesson

7 Forming a Critical Perspective

Instruction
- Writing to Analyze
- Writing to Evaluate
- Link to E-book

Multimedia
- Sample Paper
- Audio Lesson
- Interactive Documents
- Videos

Exercises
- Text Exercises
- Image Exercises
- Video Exercises
- Web Exercises

8 Writing in Academic Situations

Instruction
- Writing to Analyze
- Writing to Evaluate
- Writing to Argue
- Writing to Discuss
- Writing to Inform
- Checking Voice
- Link to E-book

Multimedia
- Audio Lesson
- Sample Paper
- Interactive Documents
- Videos

Exercises
- Text Exercises
- Image Exercises
- Video Exercises
- Web Exercises

9 Reading Arguments Critically

Instruction
- Link to E-book

Multimedia
- Videos
- Sample Paper
- Interactive Documents

Exercises
- Text Exercises
- Image Exercises
- Video Exercises
- Web Exercises

10 Writing an Argument

Instruction
- Writing to Argue
- Link to E-book

Multimedia
- Videos
- Sample Paper
- Interactive Documents

Exercises
- Text Exercises
- Image Exercises
- Video Exercises
- Web Exercises

11 Reading and Using Visual Arguments

Instruction
- Analyzing a Visual Text
- Reading Visual Arguments
- Link to E-book

Multimedia
- Videos
- Interactive Documents

Exercises
- Text Exercises
- Web Exercises

12 Understanding Sentence Grammar

Instruction
- Participles
- Subordinating Conjunctions
- Link to E-book

Multimedia
- Videos

Exercises
- Text Exercises

13 Case of Nouns and Pronouns

Instruction
- Pronoun Case
- Plurals and Possessives
- *Who* and *Whom*
- Pronoun Case in Compound Structures
- Pronoun Case with *Than* or *As*
- Link to E-book

Multimedia
- Videos

Exercises
- Text Exercises

14 Verbs

Instruction
- Using *Lie/Lay, Sit/Set,* and *Rise/Raise*
- Using Perfect Tenses
- Adjusting Tense Sequence
- The Subjunctive
- Forming the Subjunctive
- Participles
- Distinguishing Active and Passive Voice
- Link to E-book

Multimedia
- Videos

Exercises
- Text Exercises

15 Agreement

Instruction
- Basic Pronoun Agreement
- Agreement with Words Between the Subject and Verb
- Agreement with Compound Subjects
- Agreement with Indefinite Pronouns as Subjects
- Agreement with Collective Nouns
- Agreement When the Subject Follows the Verb
- Agreement with Linking Verbs
- Pronoun Agreement with Indefinite Pronouns
- Agreement with Plural Forms that Have Singular Meaning
- Pronoun Agreement with Compound Antecedents
- Pronoun Agreement with Collective Nouns
- Link to E-book

Multimedia
- Videos

Exercises
- Text Exercises

16 Adjectives and Adverbs

Instruction
- Comparative and Superlative Forms
- Negative Expressions

- Articles
- Link to E-book

Multimedia
- Videos

Exercises
- Text Exercises

17 Sentence Fragments

Instruction
- Correcting Fragments
- Link to E-book

Multimedia
- Videos

Exercises
- Text Exercises

18 Comma Splices and Fused Sentences

Instruction
- Commas and Comma Splices
- Correcting Run-On Sentences
- Link to E-book

Multimedia
- Videos

Exercises
- Text Exercises

19 Pronoun Reference

Instruction
- Correcting Ambiguous Pronoun References
- Correcting Problems with *This, That, Which,* and *It*
- Making Antecedents Clear
- Link to E-book

Multimedia
- Videos

Exercises
- Text Exercises

20 Shifts

Instruction
- Correcting Pronoun Shifts
- Correcting Tense Shifts
- Link to E-book

Multimedia
- Video

Exercises
- Text Exercises

21 Misplaced and Dangling Modifiers

Instruction
- Correcting Misplaced Modifiers
- Correcting Placement of Limiting Modifiers
- Correcting Dangling Modifiers
- Link to E-book

Multimedia
- Video

Exercises
- Text Exercises

22 Mixed and Incomplete Sentences

Instruction
- Correcting Mixed Sentences
- Link to E-book

Multimedia
- Video

23 Emphasizing Ideas

Instruction
- Achieving Parallelism
- Coordinating Conjunctions
- Clarifying Sentences
- Link to E-book

Exercises
- Text Exercises

24 Using Coordination and Subordination

Instruction
- Correcting Faulty Coordination
- Correcting Illogical Subordination
- Subordinating Conjunctions
- Link to E-book

Exercises
- Text Exercises

25 Using Parallelism

Instruction
- Achieving Parallelism
- Link to E-book

Multimedia
- Video

Exercises
- Text Exercises

26 Achieving Variety

Instruction
- Link to E-book

Exercises
- Text Exercises

27 End Punctuation

Instruction
- End Punctuation
- Link to E-book

Exercises
- Text Exercises

28 The Comma

Instruction
- Commas with Introductory Elements
- Commas with Restrictive and Nonrestrictive (Essential and Nonessential) Clauses
- Commas with Items in a Series
- Commas with Some Adjectives
- Commas with Expressions
- Commas in Special Cases
- Link to E-book

Multimedia
- Videos

Exercises
- Text Exercises

29 The Semicolon

Instruction
- Semicolons with Conjunctive Adverbs
- Semicolons to Separate Main Clauses
- Semicolons with Items in a Series
- Link to E-book

Exercises
- Text Exercises

30 The Apostrophe

Instruction
- Apostrophes with Possessive Nouns
- Apostrophes with Contractions
- Plurals and Possessives
- Link to E-book

Multimedia
- Videos

Exercises
- Text Exercises

31 Quotation Marks

Instruction
- Capitalizing in Direct Quotations
- Punctuation with Quotation Marks
- Quotation Marks in Special Cases
- Quotation Marks with Other Punctuation
- Link to E-book

Exercises
- Text Exercises

32 Other Punctuation Marks

Instruction
- Dashes
- Parentheses and Brackets
- Link to E-book

Exercises
- Text Exercises

33 Capitals

Instruction
- Link to E-book

Multimedia
- Video

Exercises
- Text Exercises

34 Italics or Underlining

Instruction
- Link to E-book

Exercises
- Text Exercises

35 Abbreviations

Instruction
- Appropriate Abbreviations
- Link E-book

Exercises
- Text Exercises

36 Numbers

Instruction
- Numbers in Writing
- Link to E-book

Exercises
- Text Exercises

37 Using Appropriate Language

Instruction
- Using Standard American English
- Avoiding Slang and Jargon
- Avoiding Pretentious Writing
- Revising Sexist Language
- Link to E-book

Multimedia
- Video

Exercises
- Text Exercises

38 Using Exact Language

Instruction
- Avoiding Trite Expressions
- Link to E-book

Multimedia
- Video

39 Writing Concisely

Instruction
- Link to E-book

Multimedia
- Videos

Exercises
- Text Exercises

40 Spelling and the Hyphen

Instruction
- Correcting Omitted -*s* or -*ed* Endings
- Spelling
- Using Commonly Confused Words Correctly
- Link to E-book

Multimedia
- Videos

Exercises
- Text Exercises

41 Planning a Research Project

Instruction
- Understanding a Research Assignment
- Finding a Topic
- Selecting a Mix of Primary and Secondary Sources
- Creating Effective Notes
- Research Paper Paradigms
- Link to E-book

Exercises
- Text Exercises

42 Finding Sources

Instruction
- Understanding and Finding Source Material
- Using the Library
- Using Print and Electronic Sources
- Reading All or Part of a Source
- Link to E-book

Multimedia
- Interactive Documents
- Videos

Exercises
- Text Exercises

43 Working with Sources

Instruction
- Guidelines for Evaluating Online Sources
- Responding to Sources
- Quoting Sources
- Paraphrasing
- Summarizing
- Blending Reference Material into Your Writing
- Link to E-book

Multimedia
- Videos

Exercises
- Web Exercises
- Text Exercises

44 Avoiding Plagiarism and Documenting Sources

Instruction
- Introduction
- When to Document
- Seven Rules for Avoiding Plagiarism
- Rule #1: Attribution
- Rule #2: Citation
- Rule #3: Citation for Images
- Rule #4: Loyalty to Source
- Rule #5: Paraphrase
- Rule #6: Quotation Marks
- Rule #7: Works Cited
- Seven Rules Wrap-Up
- Link to E-book

Multimedia
- Videos

Exercises
- Web Exercises
- Text Exercises

45 Writing the Paper

Instruction
- Drafting a Paper in an Academic Style
- Writing the Introduction of the Paper
- Writing the Body of the Paper
- Writing the Conclusion of the Paper
- Revising and Proofreading
- Formatting the Paper
- Link to E-book

Multimedia
- Videos

Exercises
- Text Exercises

46 Using MLA Documentation and Format

Instruction
- Using MLA Style
- Link to E-book

Multimedia
- Videos

Exercises
- Text Exercises

47 Two Research Papers in MLA Style

Instruction
- Link to E-book

Multimedia
- Sample Papers

Exercises
- Text Exercises

48 Working with the Goals and Requirements of the Disciplines

Instruction
- Link to E-book

Multimedia
- Sample Papers
- Videos

Exercises
- Text Exercises
- Web Exercises
- Image Exercises
- Video Exercises

49 Reading and Writing About Literature

Instruction
- Link to E-book

Multimedia
- Sample Paper

Exercises
- Text Exercises

50 Writing in Other Humanities

Instruction
- Link to E-book

Multimedia
- Sample Papers

51 Writing in the Social Sciences

Instruction
- Using APA Style
- Link to E-book

Multimedia
- Sample Papers
- Videos

Exercises
- Text Exercises

52 Writing in the Natural and Applied Sciences

Instruction
- Link to E-book

Multimedia
- Sample Papers

53 Essay Examinations

Instruction
- Link to E-book

Exercises
- Text Exercises

54 Writing Online

Instruction
- Link to E-book

Exercises
- Web Exercises

55 Public Writing

Instruction
- Link to E-book

Multimedia
- Sample Papers

Exercises
- Text Exercises
- Web Exercises

56 Oral Presentations

Instruction
- Link to E-book

Exercises
- Text Exercises

■ Sample schedule for a first-year composition course

The following schedule represents one possible way of structuring a composition course using *The Little, Brown Handbook* and relying on computer-assisted activities. The schedule assumes that you use a course Web site, blog, or e-mail to supplement class activities and that your students have access to computers and support resources. Students will complete four major projects during the course; these may either be graded individually or collectively in a portfolio, depending on your institution's requirements.

In the objectives-and-requirements portion of your syllabus, be sure to explain fully any requirements involving technology as you would any others. For example:

- Require that students back up all their work. Make it known that technical difficulties such as lost or damaged files are unacceptable excuses for not turning in assignments.

- Clarify requirements for participation in online components of the course, while taking into account that some students may need to participate as "lurkers" for a week or two before involving themselves in conversations.
- If you expect students to attend computer-related workshops or complete computer-related tasks such as obtaining e-mail accounts, provide them with handouts and schedules that will help them do so.

Week 1

General course introduction, including objectives; discussion of requirements—assignments, participation, attendance. Complete writing sample, if desired. Introduction to course Web site. Make sure students have e-mail accounts and can check them regularly. Make sure students have access to computers for class activities. Establish conventions for online behavior. Assign Chapter 1.

Week 2

Discussions of purpose and audience in writing, using various examples from online and printed sources. Assign first essay. Discuss invention techniques and have students apply to first assignment. Have students begin using online class discussion e-mail list for brainstorming or to discuss class readings. Assign Chapters 2–4.

Week 3

Draft of first essay due. Discuss and model peer response techniques. Have students review each other's work. Review drafts yourself, focusing on scope and suitability to objectives of the assignment. Establish small groups for semester activities. Conduct peer responses using the Comment and Track Changes functions on a word processor or embedded comments in e-mail or forum postings of papers. Review peer responses, focusing on attention to deepest levels of revision. Continue online discussion exchanges to brainstorm topics or discuss revision strategies.

Week 4

Discuss problem areas individually or in small groups with students, or e-mail suggestions on drafts, focusing on larger organization and meaning problems and one or two sentence-level concerns, and referring students to appropriate handbook chapters. Assign Chapter 5. Continue online discussions to brainstorm topics, discuss class readings, or plan final revision strategies. First essay due.

Week 5

Assign second essay. Employ small groups for pre-writing and invention work using e-mail or class Web tools. Assign Chapter 54. Begin drafting essays. Continue Web forum or class e-mail exchanges to brainstorm topics, discuss class readings, or converse about issues of collaboration.

Week 6

Model successful peer responses using samples from the first essay. Conduct peer response exercise using word-processing Comment and Track Changes functions, embedded comments in e-mail, or forum postings of papers. Revise drafts.

Week 7

Second essay due. Assign third essay (research-based). Assign Chapters 41–43. In-class introduction to research techniques. Continue online discussions to brainstorm topics, discuss class readings, or converse about research issues and strategies.

Week 8

Online discussions of research projects: work in class to compile working bibliography of online and print sources. Discuss bibliographic tools and conventions. Browse discussion-group archives to explore topics. Continue online discussions to brainstorm topics, explore class readings, or discuss assignment.

Week 9

Assign Chapters 44–46. Continue browsing discussion-group archives. Working bibliography due. Begin drafting essay. Continue online discussions to brainstorm topics, explore class readings, or discuss assignment.

Week 10

Individual conferences during class with students on their projects. Model successful integration of quotation, paraphrase, and summary. Continue online discussions to brainstorm topics, explore class readings, or discuss research assignment.

Week 11

Peer response to research projects. Final revisions. Research projects due. Continue online discussions to brainstorm topics, explore class readings, or discuss research assignment.

Week 12

Assign fourth project—a problem/solution proposal, based on research essay, for students not in computer-assisted classrooms, or a Web site exploring the research topic for students in computer-assisted classrooms. Assign Chapter 54 for Web projects. Continue online discussions to brainstorm topics, explore class readings, or discuss final assignment.

Week 13

Web-building workshop for Web project. Additional research and modeling of formats for proposal project. Continue online discussions to brainstorm topics, explore class readings, or discuss research assignment.

Week 14

Drafts due. Discuss and implement uploading of Web projects. Peer reviews in small groups. Continue online discussions to brainstorm topics, explore class readings, or discuss research assignment.

Week 15

In-class editing. Final drafts due. Course evaluations. Final online discussions to evaluate course and assignments.

■ Resources for using computers to teach writing

Books

Alexander, Jonathan, and Marcia Dickson, eds. *Distance Learning and the Teaching of Writing*. Cresskill: Hampton P, 2006. Print.

Bolter, Jay David, and Richard Grusin. *Remediation: Understanding New Media*. Cambridge: MIT, 1999. Print.

Breuch, Lee-Ann Kastman. *Virtual Peer Review: Teaching and Learning about Writing in Online Environments*. Albany: State U of New York P, 2004. Print.

Coogan, David. *Electronic Writing Centers: Computing the Field of Composition*. Stamford: Ablex, 1999. Print.

Crow, Angela. *Aging Literacies*. Cresskill: Hampton P, 2006. Print.

Hawisher, Gail, and Cynthia Selfe, eds. *Passions, Pedagogies and 21st Century Technologies*. Logan: Utah State UP, 1999. Print.

Hobson, Eric. *Wiring the Writing Center*. Logan: Utah State UP, 1998. Print.

Hocks, Mary E. "Understanding Visual Rhetoric in Digital Writing Environments." *College Composition and Communication* 54.4 (2003): 629–56. Print.

Inman, James. *Computers and Writing: The Cyborg Era*. Mahwah: Erlbaum, 2004. Print.

Kalmbach, James R. *The Computer and the Page: Publishing, Technology, and the Classroom*. Norwood: Ablex, 1997. Print.

Landow, George. *Hypertext 3.0: Critical Theory and New Media in an Era of Globalization*. Baltimore: Johns Hopkins, 2006. Print.

Penrod, Diane. *Composition in Convergence: The Impact of New Media on Writing Assessment*. Mahwah: Erlbaum, 2005. Print.

Porter, James E., and Patricia Sullivan. *Opening Spaces: Writing Technologies and Critical Research*. Norwood: Ablex, 1997. Print.

Reiss, Donna, Dickie Self, and Art Young, eds. *Electronic Communication Across the Curriculum*. Urbana: NCTE, 1998. Print.

Selber, Stuart. *Multiliteracies for a Digital Age*. Carbondale: Southern Illinois UP, 2004. Print.

Sidler, Michelle, Richard Morris, and Elizabeth Overman Smith, eds. *Computers in the Composition Classroom: A Critical Sourcebook*. Boston: Bedford/St. Martin's, 2008. Print.

Snyder, Ilana, ed. *Silicon Literacies: Communication, Innovation and Education in the Electronic Age*. New York: Routledge, 2002. Print.

Snyder, Ilana, and Catherine Beavis, eds. *Doing Literacy Online: Teaching, Learning, and Playing in an Electronic World*. Cresskill: Hampton P, 2004. Print.

Takayoshi, Pamela, and Brian A. Huot, eds. *Teaching Writing with Computers: An Introduction*. 3rd ed. Boston: Houghton, 2002. Print.

Taylor, Todd W., and Irene Ward, eds. *Literacy Theory in the Age of the Internet.* New York: Columbia UP, 1998. Print.

Westbrook, Steve. "Visual Rhetoric in a Culture of Fear: Impediments to Multimedia Production." *College English* 68.5 (2006): 457–80. Print.

Wysocki, Anne, Johndan Johnson-Eilola, Cynthia Selfe, and Geoffrey Sirc. *Writing New Media: Theory and Applications for Expanding the Teaching of Composition.* Logan: Utah State UP, 2004. Print.

Journals

CCC
College English
Computers and Composition
Currents in Electronic Literacy
JAC (formerly *Journal of Advanced Composition*)
Kairos
  (english.ttu.edu/Kairos)

Blogs

Kairos Blog
  Includes a listing of blogs by composition and rhetoric teachers and scholars
  kairosnews.org
PeerCentered
  Blog for peer writing tutors and those interested in writing center issues
  www.peercentered.org

EFLBlogs
  Has a searchable listing of many ESL/EFL blogs
  eflblogs.com
ESL Trail
  Includes links to other resources
  esltrail.com

Web sites

Writing@CSU: For Teachers
  writing.colostate.edu
MyCompLab
  mycomplab.com
Computer Writing and Research Lab
  www.cwrl.utexas.edu
CourseCompass
  coursecompass.com
Purdue University's *Online Writing Lab*'s Online Resources
  owl.english.purdue.edu/internet/resources
Studio for Instructional Technology in English Studies (*SITES*) Instructional Tool Resources
  sites.unc.edu/tools
SITES Main Page
  siteslab.org
Traci's Lists of Ten
  tengrrl.com/tens
The World Lecture Hall
  web.austin.utexas.edu/wlh

6

Teaching Writing to ESL Students

By Dawn Schmid and Jocelyn Steer

The composition instructor's reaction to having ESL students included in a class of native speakers can be a mixture of pleasure and apprehension. On the one hand, students using English as a second language can introduce a fresh perspective both in class discussions and in their written work. Competing with this positive response to the richness of cultural diversity, however, may be a feeling of trepidation at entering into the syntactical and lexical labyrinth of the ESL student's written world. There is no question about it: ESL writers struggle with a number of language problems that do not trouble native speakers and for which writing instructors may not have quick solutions. However, encouraging ESL writers to become outspoken members of the class and shaping the overall goals of the class to include ESL students' needs provides benefits for native and nonnative speakers alike.

This chapter is intended to help instructors find their way within that ESL labyrinth. It presents a profile of ESL students, an overview of how culture shapes their notions about learning and composing, a description of effective approaches to teaching writing to ESL students, and some guidelines for evaluating their writing. A cursory look at the most common grammatical errors found in ESL writing and a list of print and online resources for teaching ESL students are also included.

■ Profile of ESL students

The ESL label indicates that a student's first language is not English, but it says nothing about the student's country of origin or reasons for being at college, and very little about specific language problems. In fact, ESL students are a remarkably heterogeneous group, and thus it is often difficult to make any generalizations about them.

One of the first and most important distinctions to make is between international and permanent resident students.

International students

Generally speaking, international students (also referred to as foreign students) reside permanently in another country and obtain student (F-1) visas in order to study at a school in the United States. Their stay in the United States is usually funded by their families, their place of employment, their government, or their own savings. Their countries of origin vary; they come to the United States in waves, affected by global political and economic events.

Most likely these international students have had previous formal English language instruction either in their home countries or in the United States. Students trained in their home countries have probably had heavy doses of grammar, vocabulary, and reading, with some translation. Although they may be proficient readers and possess good theoretical knowledge of grammar, they may lack ease and confidence in speaking up in class. Their written work may be mechanically accurate but lack fluency and appropriate organization. International students who have learned English at a language institute in this country will have a higher degree of oral fluency and some basic notions about the conventions of academic writing in the United States.

Permanent residents

Unlike international students, permanent residents usually do not plan to return to their home country. Their reasons for staying in the United States are varied and may include the need for political asylum, the desire for economic advancement, or family ties.

Most students admitted to the United States with refugee status have come for political, not economic, reasons. Refugee students have come from places such as Cambodia, Vietnam, Laos, Eastern Europe, the Middle East, Latin America, Haiti, Ethiopia, and Somalia. Many came to the United States as children and went through the public school system here; others are adults who have decided to return to school to get a better job. Students who graduate from a high school in the United States and who are permanent residents are usually admitted to universities and colleges without submitting a Test of English as a Foreign Language (TOEFL) score, which is required of international students.

Not all permanent residents are refugees seeking political asylum. Many have come to the United States for family or employment reasons. Immigrants are given a resident alien card (a "green card"), which does not grant them citizenship but allows them to reside permanently in the United States and to work here legally. After a number of years, green card holders may apply for citizenship and become naturalized citizens. Immigrants are given permanent resident status for many reasons; for example, they may have married a U.S. citizen or may have been sponsored by a family member. Immigrant students usually acquire English informally, so their spoken English is quite fluent, but their written English requires more formal instruction to achieve the same fluency and accuracy.

Generation 1.5

One group of students whose written work exhibits traits of ESL writing has been termed "Generation 1.5." These students either arrived in the United States at a young age or were born here, but they speak another language at home. Although they are conversationally bilingual or multilingual, they may not be able to read or write in their home language. In addition, because they have learned English primarily through verbal interaction, they generally are fluent in conversational English but not in academic English (Roberge). They will not self-identify as ESL students because of this conversational fluency, but their writing may exhibit traits characteristic of ESL students, such as omitting -s from third-person singular verbs (because native speakers tend not to clearly articulate these word endings in spoken English).

Obviously, ESL students have varying degrees of language ability in speaking, reading, and writing. You can also expect to see wide gaps in socioeconomic status among ESL students in the same class, even among those from the same country, and such differences may create friction. ESL students may also hold varying attitudes toward the United States, ranging from open anti-American hostility to a Pollyanna-like view of the United States as the epitome of freedom and opportunity. This range of attitudes can provide an interesting basis for in-class discussions by including a variety of perspectives and stimulating native speakers to rethink their cultural assumptions.

■ Cross-cultural issues

Some ESL students will freely admit to being in a mild state of confusion much of the time during their academic experience. Clearly, a large portion of this confusion may be attributed to having to read and write at a very sophisticated level in a language that they have not yet mastered. There are also cultural factors less visible to the student and the instructor: the unwritten, but well-entrenched, conventions of the academy. These range from the acceptable forms of compiling a research paper to the appropriate ways of addressing an instructor. Because of their prior experience and training, native speakers may be somewhat familiar with these academic conventions, whereas ESL students may not even know that they exist. However, one advantage in having ESL writers as active participants in a class is that their questions can propel the class as a whole to discover the reasons for conventions that often seem puzzlingly arbitrary. For example, in some cases ESL students know the "rules" of grammar far better than the native speakers and can be called upon to share that expert knowledge.

Ideas about learning

ESL students may approach the learning situation from a schema formed largely by their experiences in their first culture. For example, many Latin cultures foster more cooperative learning, whereas Japan adheres to a hierarchical, teacher-dominated model. Although these cultural generalities cannot be presumed to apply to individual students, they can be useful in sensitizing us to our own cultural assumptions. The situation in a college classroom may well shock ESL students—the informality of instructors who sit on the desk, or classmates who openly disagree with or interrupt their professors. Such students are not comfortable with the open discussion format in which American students feel free to express their opinions, regardless of whether their opinions align with those of the professor. Instructors may view their more quiet ESL students as resistant or unprepared, when in fact these students are showing respect by remaining silent.

In some cultures, professors are expected to mentor and guide students to a greater extent than they do in the United States. Thus, many ESL students may feel that their professors do not do enough for them. It is not unusual for an ESL student to bring in a piece of writing for another class and ask the composition instructor to correct it. Or some students may attempt to negotiate grades because they "need" that grade for a scholarship or admission to a school, and they may be visibly disappointed when an instructor refuses to change a grade. A teacher in the United States may interpret such behavior as impertinent, whereas the student may view it as a chance for the instructor to use his or her power to further the student's career. And while ESL students may find the informality of the classroom surprising, many find constant testing, penalties for absences, and general surveillance on the part of the instructor to be offensive to their sense of maturity. Many ESL students have attended foreign universities that do not monitor student behavior so closely.

Cross-cultural discussions in which students trace how basic assumptions result in varying styles of learning behavior may be useful for both ESL students and native English speakers. Many ESL students benefit from such discussions because they wish to conform to the conventions of their school in order to enjoy academic success. Similarly, such explorations can help native English speakers develop sensitivity to these cross-cultural issues.

Contrastive rhetoric

Cross-cultural analyses of ESL student writing can also be fruitful. Cultures express ideas using different organizational patterns and types of support, and the written and unwritten rules governing what is considered appropriate writing in the culture are transmitted to children in school. It is not surprising, therefore, that ESL students use these first-language writing strategies when they compose in English. The result may be a grammatically correct piece of writing with an idiosyncratic development.

Instructors need to apply the principles of contrastive rhetoric cautiously. Although it is not necessary to undertake an extensive study of the rhetorical conventions of all languages, it is important to recognize how a culture shapes its members' expectations of good writing. An instructional approach that places too much emphasis on contrastive rhetoric, on the other hand, is reductionistic. Such an approach would fail to account for a specific writer's process, potentially misinterpreting a writer's lack of experience as interference from first-language writing strategies. (For a detailed discussion of contrastive rhetoric, consult Ilona Leki's *Understanding ESL Writers: A Guide for Teachers.*)

Levels of support and specificity

One important feature of ESL writing that varies among cultures is the level of support and specificity required for assertions. It is not always obvious to ESL writers that facts and statistics are considered to be the strongest method of support in English and that when a student makes an assertion, it must be supported with specific examples or quantifiable measures. Other cultures may rely on the hierarchical, rather than the scientific, model of proof. It is not unusual, for example, to have ESL students use quotes from religious books or statements made by a political leader as evidence for their assertions. Students will need practice in identifying and supplying the kinds of support expected in academic writing in English.

Another central issue in cross-cultural analyses of texts is the level of explicitness expected in academic writing. English is a "writer-responsible" language: the onus is on the writer to present ideas clearly and succinctly. If the reader has difficulty with a text, the blame usually rests with the writer and not the reader. We expect to have the main points stated directly and clearly in a piece of writing; this may help to explain some of our frustration at reading a piece of writing by an ESL student who does not share the same expectation. In fact, ESL writers may consider such direct statements of main points to be childish or insulting.

This distinction is especially pertinent to native writers of Japanese and Chinese, which are "reader-responsible" languages. Japanese and Chinese readers do not expect the writer to link information and draw conclusions; they expect to do that as readers (Cowie). A Japanese student explained this when asked why she used transitions so sparingly and never seemed to tie up her examples with a general statement: she said that doing so would be insulting to Japanese readers, who are expected to be informed and sensitive enough to be able to make those inferences on their own.

Attitudes toward plagiarism

American students who commit plagiarism usually have a sense that it is an academic offense. ESL students, however, may come from countries where plagiarism, although not completely ethical, is more easily overlooked or accepted. Research and writing in the United States is prized for its originality, but this is not the case in all cultures. Some ESL students may have been taught to incorporate great writing from their culture into their own work out of respect for those scholars (McDonnell). For some students, plagiarism may also be a way of coping with their uncertainty about their own lexical abilities (Currie). Other students may be too modest to believe that they can paraphrase the writing of a respected author.

Of course, many ESL students copy for the same reasons American students do—because it's easier, faster, and sure to be more fluent. Whether or not your students are guilty, they need to be warned that plagiarism is unacceptable in a college in the United States. Be sure to discuss the issue of plagiarism early in the semester and invite students to share their understanding of the differences among quoting, paraphrasing, and plagiarizing. Students will benefit from explicit classroom discussion of different cultural attitudes toward what constitutes plagiarism, instruction in how to distinguish between borrowing of words and borrowing of ideas, and plenty of practice with paraphrasing, summarizing, and citing sources. Chapter 44 can be particularly useful here in showing students examples of unacceptable writing with plagiarized sections.

Topic selection

Topics that seem to be extremely pertinent to the lives of your native English speakers may be inappropriate or difficult for ESL writers. An essay on breaking away from family or living on one's own, for example, may have no meaning for those ESL students who expect to live with their families until they get married. In fact, you may find that your ESL students are more comfortable writing about impersonal subjects than those designed to facilitate self-discovery. Other topics such as living together before marriage, gay rights, and evolution may offend certain groups of students because of their religious beliefs. We once assigned what seemed to be an innocuous topic—"superstitions in my culture"—only to find out that the Islamic religion does not tolerate superstitions. At the same time, some topics will be more appealing to ESL students, who are often better informed about and more interested in topics dealing with global issues than are American students.

■ Issues in working with ESL writing

The above discussion of cross-cultural differences in organization, style, and topic selection underscores the need to provide ESL students with guidelines and models of academic writing so that they can function smoothly and successfully in the college culture. Yet there is a danger—as there is in any acculturation process—of placing too great a value on the expected and accepted form of the writing and too little value on the writer's discovery of voice.

Process versus product approach to writing

This dilemma between emphasizing the product over the process of writing is not a new one, but it takes on a slightly different slant when applied to teaching writing to ESL students. An approach that emphasizes the conventions of academic discourse provides ESL students with models of discipline-specific writing that they can emulate, along with guidelines for operating within that discipline. It has been our experience that ESL students welcome this type of instruction. Since they lack the cultural and linguistic schema of native speakers, they benefit from explicit instruction in how to complete academic tasks. Essay-test prompts are an excellent example of this: native speakers have a better notion than ESL students of what is meant by "discuss," for example. By the same token, when ESL students feel free to raise questions about the wording of assignments, the whole class often benefits from the discussion. Assignments that allow students to practice writing essay exams, critical reviews, laboratory reports, or case reports will also help to equip students with the necessary tools for their academic careers.

If students rely more on the imposed model of academic communication than on their own voice and expression, the result may be mimicry rather than inspiration. This is especially true for ESL students who enter the writing process haltingly. An approach that emphasizes the process of brainstorming, sharing ideas, and collaborating on a topic nurtures ESL students' wavering self-confidence as writers in a second language. By engaging students in the discovery of ideas, this approach also distracts them from ruminating over potential surface errors.

Since a process approach to writing does not outline a single "accepted" product, it encourages students to identify their own personal style first before reconciling it with the models of writing endorsed by the academic community. Yet we would be remiss if we failed to provide our ESL students with those models. Clearly, a combination of the two approaches, without overreliance on product or neglect of process, will serve your ESL students best. As with any student it is important to focus on the strengths of an ESL writer's work and to suggest one or two issues for revision rather than to view the paper as a profusion of errors.

Attitudes toward errors

Although research indicates that ESL students need more work with actual composing than with language development (Zamel, "Composing"), it may be difficult to explain this to them. They may believe that good writing means producing grammatically correct sentences. They see errors as obstacles to good writing, and, unlike many native speakers, they do not perceive them as symbols of personal failure. They expect to make mistakes since they are learning a second language, and they expect those errors to be corrected. Leki's survey on student perceptions of teacher feedback supports what any ESL teacher might have predicted: students believe that error correction is important. Out of 100 ESL college students surveyed, 91 percent believed that it was very important to have as few errors as possible in their writing, and 93 percent stated that it was important to have teachers correct the errors.

It was once thought that errors in a second language were the result of interference from the first language. For example, if writers had problems with word order in English, it was because they were applying first-language rules of word order to the second language. Now, however, it is largely believed that most ESL errors are the result of an "interlanguage," a system for communicating in the second language that the student has developed based on what he or she knows about the second language.

Theoretically, this interlanguage is constantly changing as the learner mentally reorganizes what is known about the language. This is an important point and a major distinction between native English and ESL writers. During the course of a semester, your ESL students will probably make a great deal of progress in English because their language-acquisition process is still activated. Their improvement will result not only from your class but also from exposure to other sources of language input. The more that students write, the more likely they are to improve their writing. According to Cowie, the act of writing and revising itself is key to improving student writing at both surface and global levels.

Viewing ESL errors as temporary edifices supporting an ESL writer's ideas lends credence to the argument against correcting every single error in an ESL composition. These errors will disappear as students gain more control over the second language. Errors that seem to be careless mistakes to the reader may not be that at all. They may be the student's individual system for organizing English structure, which will change as the student acquires more language. Nor is it uncommon for advanced ESL students to regress temporarily in their language accuracy as they struggle with new forms and constructions.

You may have some students in your class who have been in the United States for quite some time and who, for some reason, may have reached a plateau; second-language researchers say that these students' errors are "fossilized." It is not clear why fossilization occurs, but it is clear that working with fossilized errors can be difficult. Distinguishing between errors that occur as the result of fossilization and those that occur because of interlanguage is important; unlike interlanguage errors, which diminish spontaneously with increased exposure to the language, fossilized errors require more explicit and direct treatment.

Techniques for responding to ESL writing

As an experienced composition instructor, you have probably developed a variety of techniques and strategies for providing effective feedback to your students. (In this manual, "Working with Student Writing" on pp. IAE-21to

IAE-34 provides guidelines for responding to student work.) Below are some suggested techniques and strategies that may be especially helpful in providing feedback to your ESL students.

Sometimes students are confused about what to do with feedback. Research (Conrad and Goldstein) suggests that students have difficulty revising when asked to develop their points by being more explicit, explaining, or analyzing. Providing students with training in how to respond to feedback will enable them to produce better revisions (Conrad and Goldstein; Currie). Moreover, if you use peer feedback in your class, you may find that students from cultures where the teacher is considered the source of knowledge and truth do not take into account their peers' feedback when revising. In this case, it is important to train students in how to give effective peer feedback as well as how to receive it (Cowie; Nelson and Carson).

In general, it is best to provide feedback on grammar, punctuation, and spelling in earlier drafts so that students can incorporate those corrections into subsequent drafts. Students are not as likely to benefit from feedback that is offered on a final draft; they will often look at the grade, read the comments quickly, and file the paper away. However, you can encourage attention to final drafts by asking for localized revisions of a particular pattern of error or of a paragraph. Students can also be encouraged to make note of their common patterns of error and to keep revised examples as a resource for the next paper.

There is no one method for drawing students' attention to sentence-level errors, but generally it is best to locate the error for the student and have the student correct the error on a subsequent draft. Leki's survey found that students like to be given a clue regarding the nature of the error. A numbering system for the most basic errors (for example, verb tense, number agreement, word order, spelling, punctuation, and word form) works well because students seem to respond better to numbers than to abbreviations or words (for example, *sp, awk*), and they become familiar with the errors they tend to make often. The correction code in the handbook is easy to use; it includes a number-and-letter system that directs students to the appropriate section in the handbook that deals with the error. (See pp. IAE-23 to IAE-24 for a more detailed description of the correction code.) It is most useful to identify one or two significant patterns of error (subject-verb

problems and misused articles, for example) rather than correct every example of error.

Some errors—often those pertaining to sentence boundaries, clause structure, and choice of words—cannot be identified by circling and numbering. When the meaning of a sentence is unclear, avoid the temptation to rewrite it for the student. You may find your interpretation is quite different from what the student intended. It's best to ask the student to rewrite the passage.

A concern that continues to surface when dealing with ESL writing is knowing what and how much to correct. As noted earlier, students make many errors; some of them may be careless mistakes, but more likely the sentences were carefully constructed using the students' still-developing knowledge of English structure and vocabulary. Correcting ESL work seems to be more an art than a science because the instructor needs to gauge the particular student's threshold for error correction and identify the errors that the student will benefit from knowing about.

We have also found that students are very receptive to and benefit a great deal from immediate, oral feedback, especially when they solicit it. Students often ask for help with grammar and vocabulary during in-class writing, and they almost always incorporate those revisions into their writing.

Some teachers and students find it helpful to keep track of repeated errors. Using a numbering system such as the one mentioned above can facilitate this process. (See p. 62 in the handbook for a model that can be used to track errors.) In any case, it is very important to recommend or require that students consult the handbook. Not only will it help clarify a confusing grammatical point, but also it will teach students to edit their work independently, an extremely important skill for the ESL student.

Evaluation

The question of evaluation is a thorny one in composition classes comprising both native and nonnative speakers. Some of the questions that come up are: How do I compare the two? Will I need to lower my standards? Should I expect error-free writing from my ESL students? Should I give a grade to each draft? How many revisions should I allow before assigning a grade?

Keep a few points in mind when deciding how to evaluate ESL writers. First, the ESL student is writing in a second (or third or fourth) language. It is next to impossible to achieve native fluency and accuracy in a second language, especially when the learner began acquisition as an adult. Thus, we need to consider whether it is realistic to expect ESL students to produce error-free writing.

Research (Santos) has indicated that college professors in disciplines other than English tend to be more forgiving of ESL speakers' errors than of native speakers' errors, which they regard as careless. In addition, although ESL students may not always produce fluent English, their prior training and knowledge in their field of study may far exceed that of their native-speaker classmates. Professors may be delighted to have their input, both in writing and in class discussions, because of the value of their comments and diverse points of view for the class. In such cases, the standards of these professors and their discipline may be less stringent than those maintained in the composition class.

When assigning grades to ESL students, consider a few guidelines that may make the situation more equitable for ESL writers. If at all possible, allow students the opportunity to write multiple drafts that are not graded. This will permit ESL writers the opportunity to refine a piece of writing to their satisfaction. A split grade for the content (for example, organization, development, exemplification) and form (for example, the grammar, spelling, and punctuation) sometimes proves beneficial, especially when ESL students have many good ideas but still struggle with expression. Such a grading system helps students focus on the specific areas in which their writing needs improvement (Song and Caruso). Other solutions include assigning a satisfactory/unsatisfactory grade for work done during the semester and requiring a portfolio of the student's best work at the end of the class. (See p. IAE-31 for a discussion of portfolios.) The final grade is based on the final portfolio and not the individual assignments.

A final, very important consideration is the time it takes for ESL students to complete written work. It may seem obvious that ESL writers need more time to complete their assignments, but even after many years of teaching ESL students, we are still surprised at the amount of time they actually do need. All writers need help getting started, but ESL writers seem more frightened of that first sentence than native speakers do. As Ann Raimes has said, "The first sentence restricts them before they have begun to develop their ideas" (261). This need

for more time also has implications for in-class and timed writing assignments. Research (Polio, Fleck, and Leder) has shown that ESL students can self-correct their papers when given extra time, even without feedback from the teacher. If at all possible, allow students a flexible schedule of deadlines.

■ Sentence-level errors in ESL writing

English composition instructors know a great deal about grammar and punctuation, but many who have not worked extensively with ESL students are puzzled by the errors such students make. Below are a few areas of grammar that are especially troublesome to many ESL students. All these trouble spots are discussed and illustrated in *The Little, Brown Handbook*. For more detailed explanations, consult Marianne Celce-Murcia and Diane Larsen-Freeman's *Grammar Book*, 2nd ed., a specialized ESL reference grammar for the instructor; Jocelyn Steer and Karen Carlisi's *Advanced Grammar Book*, 2nd ed., an ESL grammar textbook with an accompanying workbook by Jocelyn Steer and Dawn Schmid; or *Teaching English as a Second or Foreign Language*, 3rd ed., edited by Marianne Celce-Murcia.

Verb tenses

ESL students have difficulty with verb tenses and forms of helping verbs. Some tenses in English are straightforward and usually have a direct translation in most languages. These include the past tense, the future tense, and in some cases the present tense. However, other tenses (for example, present progressive and the present perfect) do not have equivalent forms in some languages. (See handbook section 14g.)

Helping verbs

Students often have difficulty choosing the appropriate form of the helping verb in a sentence. You may encounter sentences like *He should has been gone* rather than *He should have gone*. (See handbook section 14d.)

Verb endings

ESL students often leave off the *-ed* endings on verbs used in the passive (*It was return*) and in the past perfect tense (*I had return it*). One explanation may be that they do not hear the *-ed* ending in spoken English. (See handbook sections 14c and 14d.) They also often forget to add the *-s* or *-es* ending on present-tense verbs in the third-person singular (*He go; it don't work*) but can correct this error immediately when it is pointed out. It is a good idea to have your ESL students check their papers for subject-verb agreement before handing them in to you. (See handbook section 15a.)

Verbs with gerunds or infinitives

One particularly difficult area for ESL students to master is the use of a gerund or an infinitive after a verb. Some English verbs may be followed by a gerund (*He recommended going*). Others may be followed by an infinitive (*I want to go*). Some may be followed by either a gerund or an infinitive with no change in meaning (*I continued eating; I continued to eat*). Finally, some verbs may be followed by either form, but with a change in meaning (*I stopped smoking yesterday; I stopped to smoke*). (See handbook section 14e.)

Count and noncount nouns

The distinction between count and noncount nouns in English is especially troublesome for ESL students because correct choice of article or quantifier and agreement with the verb depend on these distinctions. When ESL students first learn about count and noncount nouns, they are told that count nouns (*book/books; girl/girls*) are easily divided and counted, whereas noncount nouns are not. This rule is fine for the clear-cut examples such as *water, cheese,* or *love.* However, when students learn that *money* is a noncount noun, the rule seems to fall apart: Who hasn't counted money easily and successfully? (See handbook section 16h.)

Articles

Choosing an appropriate article is extremely trying for ESL students, especially students whose native language does not have articles (e.g., Japanese, Chinese). It is equally trying for ESL teachers to explain why a definite article is used instead of an indefinite one. Once again, students learn rules to guide them in their choices. (See handbook section 16h.)

Verbs with particles

Students often complain about prepositions in English. These combinations of verbs and so-called particles (some of them adverbs) are particularly confusing: what may seem to be a simple construction of two (or three) words has a specific meaning that cannot be discerned from the individual meanings of the specific verb and preposition. There are literally hundreds of these idiomatic constructions. (See handbook section 14f.)

■ Conclusion

Initially, you may feel overwhelmed by the number of errors your ESL students make, and you may even wish that you did not have to spend so much time correcting them. In such cases, it is important to remember that these students are still learning the language as well as writing skills. Don't feel compelled to correct every single mistake. Help students instead to develop and organize their ideas. And keep in mind that it may take your ESL students a long time before they write without making a large number of errors.

As you can see, ESL students—regardless of the cultural or socioeconomic group they may be from—confront a number of obstacles in their daily college lives. Most of these students spend an enormous amount of energy simply listening to lectures and trying to understand both the language and the cultural content of what the instructor is saying. Anyone who has lived in a foreign country and listened to a foreign language continuously knows how exhausting negotiating simple tasks in the foreign culture can be. As their instructor, you have a chance to assist your students in this process of acculturation to the academic community and to give them the encouragement they need to succeed in their academic endeavors.

■ Resources for teaching ESL students

Print resources

Braine, George. "ESL Students in First-Year Writing Courses: ESL Versus Mainstream Classes." *Journal of Second Language Writing* 5.2 (1996): 91–107. Print. Includes examples of rubrics for evaluating compositions.

Celce-Murcia, Marianne, and Diane Larsen-Freeman. *The Grammar Book.* 2nd ed. Boston: Heinle and Heinle, 1999. Print. An excellent reference book on ESL grammar for instructors.

Connor, Ulla. *Contrastive Rhetoric: Cross-Cultural Aspects of Second-Language Writing*. New York: Cambridge UP, 1996. Print.

Conrad, Susan M., and Lynn M. Goldstein. "ESL Student Revision after Teacher-Written Comments: Text, Contexts, and Individuals." *Journal of Second Language Writing* 8.2 (1999): 147–79. Print.

Cowie, Neil. "Students of Process Writing Need Appropriate and Timely Feedback on Their Work, and in Addition, Training in Dealing With That Feedback." *Saitama University Review* 31.1 (1995): 181–94. *ERIC*. Web. 17 Nov. 2008. Includes a summary of the research and practical suggestions for giving effective feedback on student papers.

Currie, Pat. "Staying Out of Trouble: Apparent Plagiarism and Academic Survival." *Journal of Second Language Writing* 7.1 (1998): 1–18. Print.

Hyland, Ken, and Fiona Hyland, eds. *Feedback in Second Language Writing: Contexts and Issues*. New York: Cambridge UP, 2006. Print. A collection of articles by distinguished researchers in second-language writing.

Leki, Ilona. "The Preferences of ESL Students for Error Correction in College Level Writing Classes." *Foreign Language Annals* 24.3 (1991): 203–14. Print.

---. *Understanding ESL Writers: A Guide for Teachers*. Portsmouth: Boynton/Cook/Greenwood-Heinemann, 1992. Print. An often-cited text.

Matsuda, Paul. "Composition Studies and ESL Writing: A Disciplinary Division of Labor." *College Composition and Communication* 50.4 (1999): 699–721. Print. A history of the development of ESL instruction as a profession separate from composition instruction; includes a helpful listing of titles of several second-language and composition-study journals.

Mlynarczyk, Rebecca Williams. *Conversations of the Mind: The Uses of Journal Writing for Second-Language Learners*. Mahwah: Erlbaum, 1998. Print.

Nelson, Gayle L., and Joan G. Carson. "ESL Students' Perceptions of Effectiveness in Peer Response Groups." *Journal of Second Language Writing* 7.2 (1998): 113–31. Print.

Polio, Charlene, Catherine Fleck, and Nevin Leder. "If Only I Had More Time: ESL Learners' Changes in Linguistic Accuracy on Essay Revisions." *Journal of Second Language Writing* 7.1 (1998): 43–68. Print.

Raimes, Ann. "Anguish as a Second Language? Remedies for Composition Teachers." *Composing in a Second Language*. Ed. Sandra McKay. Rowley: Newbury, 1984. 81–96. Print.

---. "Out of the Woods: Emerging Traditions in the Teaching of Writing." *TESOL Quarterly* 25.3 (1991): 407–30. Print.

Reid, Joy M., ed. *Writing Myths: Applying Second Language Research to Classroom Teaching*. Ann Arbor: U of Michigan P, 2008. Print. Practicing teachers address myths and research regarding writing and ESL students.

Roberge, Mark. "Generation 1.5 Immigrant Students: What Special Experiences, Characteristics and Educational Needs Do They Bring to Our English Classes?" *The CATESOL Journal* 14.1 (2003): 107–30. Print.

Santos, Tony. "Professors' Reactions to the Academic Writing of Nonnative-Speaking Students." *TESOL Quarterly* 22.1 (1988): 69–90. Print.

Song, Bailin, and Isabella Caruso. "Do English and ESL Faculty Differ in Evaluating the Essays of Native English-Speaking and ESL Students?" *Journal of Second Language Writing* 5.2 (1996): 163–82. Print. Includes a sample writing assessment test, evaluation scale, and analytic assessment sheet for rating ten essay components.

Steer, Jocelyn, and Karen Carlisi. *The Advanced Grammar Book*. 2nd ed. Boston: Heinle and Heinle, 1998. Print. Presents grammar principles in context for ESL students.

Steer, Jocelyn, and Dawn Schmid. *The Advanced Grammar Book. 2nd ed. Workbook*. Boston: Heinle and Heinle, 1998. Print. Highly contextualized practice of grammar principles for ESL students.

Zamel, Vivian "The Composing Process of Advanced ESL Students: Six Case Studies," *TESOL Quarterly* 17.2 (1983): 165–87. Print.

---. "Strangers in Academia: The Experiences of Faculty and ESL Students Across the Curriculum." *The Writing Teacher's Sourcebook*. 4th ed. Ed. Edward P. J. Corbett et al. New York: Oxford UP, 2000. 100–12. Print.

Online resources

Dave's ESL Cafe

> *eslcafe.com*
>
> A collection of ESL resources for students and teachers. Includes chat rooms and discussion forums, mailing lists, and an ESL quiz center with questions on current news, grammar, idioms and slang, reading comprehension, writing, and world culture. Includes phrasal verbs arranged in a complete list, sorted by meanings and examples, and by random phrasal verbs from the collection. Contains a FAQ section.

The Internet TESL Journal Links

> *iteslj.org/links/*
>
> Access to articles, lessons, techniques, writing topics and exercises, and links to related sites. Updated regularly to eliminate dead links.

McDonnell, Kathryn E. "Academic Plagiarism Rules and ESL Learning—Mutually Exclusive Concepts?" *AU TESOL Working Papers 2*. American University Department of Language and Foreign Studies. 18 Jan. 2007. Web. 16 Oct. 2008. *american.edu/tesol/wpmcdonnell.pdf.*

> A comprehensive review of the literature regarding plagiarism and ESL students, with results of a survey of composition professors about handling plagiarism by ESL students.

Purdue University Writing Lab

> *owl.english.purdue.edu/handouts/esl/eslstudent.html*
>
> A directory of Web sites about ESL resources for students, compiled by the Purdue University Writing Lab. Includes links to information about online courses, grammar, vocabulary, quizzes, listservs, and games.

Why do you need this new edition?

This edition of *The Little, Brown Handbook* differs from the previous edition in countless ways. Here are six that make the book indispensable:

1 More help with college reading and writing ▪ A chapter on **academic writing** explains the key academic skill of synthesizing your own and others' views as you write in response to texts and images. ▪ A chapter on **academic skills** emphasizes the habits you need to succeed in college.

2 More help with research writing ▪ Material on **finding and evaluating library and Web sources** covers all kinds of print and electronic resources and shows you how to tell the difference between reliable and unreliable sources. ▪ A **research-paper-in-progress** on the environment follows one student's research and writing process, making it easy to see what's expected of you.

3 Up-to-date, more accessible help with citing sources ▪ Detailed explanations and highlighted examples present the **most recent revisions of MLA, APA,** and **CSE documentation styles** and show how to document a wide range of print and electronic sources. A fourth style, **Chicago,** includes models for citing new media. ▪ **Annotated sample sources** show you how to find and format bibliographic information in articles, books, and Web sites.

4 New help with the writing process ▪ **Four diagrams** and a **student work-in-progress** on globalization and jobs illustrate how the writing process can serve you in college work. ▪ Discussions of **voice in writing** help you maintain a strong presence in everything you write.

5 Current, more accessible help with grammar and usage ▪ Material on **text-message and e-mail shortcuts** gives tips for spotting and editing them in your academic writing. ▪ **Checklist and summary boxes** on grammar, style, and punctuation—all with **color highlighting**—offer quick reference help with crafting clear and correct sentences.

6 Access to *MyCompLab* ▪ *The Little, Brown Handbook* is even more useful when you combine it with *MyCompLab,* a Web gateway to resources on grammar, writing, and research developed specifically for writers.

PEARSON
mycomplab

Become a better writer and researcher—and get better grades in all your courses—with *MyCompLab*!

Writing, grammar, and research help are at your fingertips as you draft and revise.

Composing. This dynamic space for composing, revising, and editing is easy to use and built to function like the most popular word-processing programs.

- Use the Writer's Toolkit to search for answers to your writing questions.
- View instructor, peer, and tutor comments on your work in one place.
- Store and manage all your work in one place.
- Access paper review help from experienced tutors through Pearson Tutor Services.

Access instruction, multimedia tutorials, and exercises in the Resources area to help you master skills and get a better grade.

Share e-portfolios of your work with instructors, classmates, and friends.

Portfolio. With this tool, it's easy to create, publish, manage, and share your portfolio. Continue adding material through your college career and beyond!

Manage all your written work and assignments online, in one easy-to-use place.

To Do. This area captures assignments and due dates from your instructor along with the personal writing you've done in *MyCompLab*.

Gradebook. This area shows writing and exercise scores. You can see how you are progressing toward a better grade!

Access an e-book version of your handbook

E-book. Access a searchable electronic version of your handbook anywhere you have an Internet connection.

Register for *MyCompLab* today!

Questions? Go to www.mycomplab.com/help.html and click "Student Support."

If this book did not come packaged with an access code to *MyCompLab*, you can purchase access online at **www.mycomplab.com/buy-access.html** or ask your bookstore to order an access card for you.

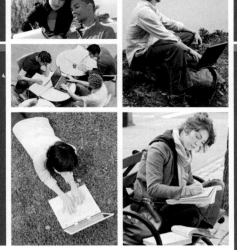

ELEVENTH EDITION

The Little, Brown Handbook

H. Ramsey Fowler
St. Edward's University

Jane E. Aaron

Longman

New York   San Francisco   Boston
London   Toronto   Sydney   Tokyo   Singapore   Madrid
Mexico City   Munich   Paris   Cape Town   Hong Kong   Montreal

Publisher: Joseph Opiela
Senior Development Editor: Anne Brunell Ehrenworth
Senior Supplements Editor: Donna Campion
Senior Media Producer: Stefanie Liebman
Senior Marketing Manager: Susan Stoudt
Production Manager: Bob Ginsberg
Project Coordination, Text Design, and Electronic Page Makeup:
    Nesbitt Graphics, Inc.
Cover Design Manager: John Callahan
Cover Designer: Kay Petronio
Cover Photos: *(clockwise from top):* Anderson Ross/Blend Images/Getty Im-
    ages, Inc.; Stone/Getty; David Fischer/Digital Vision/Getty Images, Inc.;
    Jamie Grill/Iconica/Getty Images, Inc.; Image Source/Getty
Photo Researcher: Rebecca Karamehmedovic
Senior Manufacturing Buyer: Roy L. Pickering, Jr.
Printer and Binder: RR Donnelley & Sons Company/Crawfordsville
Cover Printer: Phoenix Color Corporation

The authors and publisher are grateful to the many students who allowed
their work to be reprinted here and to the copyright holders who are listed
on pp. 905–06, which are hereby made part of this copyright page.

Library of Congress Cataloging-in-Publication Data

Fowler, H. Ramsey (Henry Ramsey)
  The Little, Brown handbook / H. Ramsey Fowler, Jane E. Aaron. --
11th ed.
    p. cm.
  ISBN-13: 978-0-205-65171-9
  ISBN-10: 0-205-65171-2
  1. English language--Grammar--Handbooks, manuals, etc. 2. English
language--Rhetoric--Handbooks, manuals, etc. 3. Report writing--
Handbooks, manuals, etc. I. Aaron, Jane E. II. Title.
  PE1112.F64 2009
  808'.042--dc22
                                    2008049608

Longman
is an imprint of

1 2 3 4 5 6 7 8 9 10—DOC—12 11 10 09

ISBN-13: 978-0-205-65171-9
ISBN-10:   0-205-65171-2

www. pearsonhighered. com

Preface for Students: Using This Book

The Little, Brown Handbook is a basic resource that will answer almost any question you have about writing. Here you can find how to get ideas, develop paragraphs, punctuate quotations, search the Internet, cite sources, or write a résumé. The handbook can help you not only in writing courses but also in other courses and outside of school.

Don't let the size of the handbook put you off. You need not read the whole book to get something out of it, and no one expects you to know everything included. Primarily a reference tool, the handbook is written and arranged to help you find the answers you need when you need them, quickly and easily.

Using this book will not by itself make you a good writer; for that, you need to care about your work at every level, from finding a subject to spelling words. But learning how to use the handbook and its information can give you the means to write *what* you want in the *way* you want.

Reference aids

You have many ways to find what you need in the handbook:

- **Use the directory.** "Plan of the Book," inside the front cover, displays the book's entire contents.
- **Use a glossary.** "Glossary of Usage" (pp. 865–81) clarifies more than 275 words that are commonly confused and misused. "Glossary of Terms" (pp. 882–904) defines more than 350 words used in discussing writing.
- **Use the index.** Beginning on page 907, the extensive index includes every term, concept, and problem word or expression mentioned in the book.
- **Use a list.** Three helpful aids fall inside the book's back cover: (1) "CULTURE LANGUAGE Guide" pulls together all the book's material for students using standard American English as a second language or a second dialect. (2) "Editing Symbols" explains abbreviations often used to comment on papers. And (3) "Useful Lists and Summaries" indexes topics that students frequently ask about.
- **Use the elements of the page.** As shown in the illustration on the next page, the handbook constantly tells you where you are and what you can find there.

The handbook's page elements

Running head (header) and page tab showing the topic being discussed on this page, its section code (**19a**), and its editing symbol (**ref**)

ref
19 a   347

Summary or checklist box providing key information in accessible form

Principal causes of unclear pronoun reference

▦ More than one possible antecedent   (below):

Confusing   To keep birds from eating seeds, soak them in blue food coloring.

Clear   To keep birds from eating seeds, soak the seeds in blue food coloring.

▦ Antecedent too far away   (facing page):

Confusing   Employees should consult with their supervisor who require personal time.

Clear   Employees who require personal time should consult with their super visor.

▦ Antecedent only implied   (p. 349):

Confusing   Many children begin reading on their own by watching television, but this should probably be discounted in government policy .

Clear   Many children begin reading on their own by watching television, but such self-instruction should probably be discounted in government policy .

See also pages 350–51.

Section heading, a main convention or topic labeled with the section code, **19a:** chapter number (**19**) and section letter (**a**)

19a   Make a pronoun refer clearly to one antecedent.

When either of two nouns can be a pronoun' s antecedent, the reference will not be clear:

Examples, always indented, with underlining and annotations highlighting sentence elements and revisions

Confusing   Emily Dickinson is sometimes compared with Jane Austen, but she was quite different.

Revise such a sentence in one of two ways:

▦ Replace the pronoun with the appropriate noun:

Clear   Emily Dickinson is sometimes compared with Jane Austen, but Dickinson [or Austen] was quite different.

▦ Avoid repetition by rewriting the sentence. If you use the pronoun, make sure it has only one possible antecedent:

Clear   Despite occasional comparison, Emily Dickinson and Jane Austen were quite different.

Web box linking to *MyCompLab*

mycomplab

Visit mycomplab.com for more resour ces and exer cises on pronoun reference.

CULTURE LANGUAGE   An English pronoun does need a clear antecedent nearby, but don't use both a pronoun and its antecedent as the subject of the same sentence or clause: Jim [not Jim he] told Mark to go alone.   (See also pp. 370–71.)

Culture-language connection, a pointer for students using standard American English as a second language or a second dialect

Exer cise 19.3   Revising: Pronoun reference

Revise the following paragraph so that each pronoun refers clearly to a single specific and appropriate antecedent.

In Charlotte Brontë's Jane Eyre, she is a shy young woman that takes a job as governess. Her employer is a rude, brooding man named Rochester. He lives in a mysterious mansion on the English moors, which contributes an eerie quality to Jane's experience. Eerier still are the fires, strange noises, and other unexplained happenings in the house; but Rochester refuses to discuss this. Eventually, they fall in love. On the day

Exercise providing opportunity for practice

Content and organization

An overview of the handbook's contents appears inside the front cover. Briefly, the book divides into the following sections:

- **Chapters 1–5:** The big picture, including the writing process, paragraphs, and document design.
- **Chapters 6–11:** Reading and writing in college, with chapters on academic skills, critical reading and writing, academic writing, reading arguments, writing arguments, and reading and using visual arguments.
- **Chapters 12–26:** Sentence basics, including the conventions of English grammar, errors that affect clarity, and techniques of effective sentences.
- **Chapters 27–36:** Punctuation and mechanics (capital letters, italics, and the like).
- **Chapters 37–40:** Words—how to use them appropriately and precisely, how to edit them for conciseness, how to spell them.
- **Chapters 41–47:** Research writing, from planning through revising, with detailed help on finding and evaluating electronic sources, a complete guide to citing sources, and two sample papers.
- **Chapters 48–52:** Writing in the academic disciplines, including concepts, tools, and source citations in literature, other humanities, the social sciences, and the natural and applied sciences.
- **Chapters 53–56:** Practical information about essay exams, on-line writing, business and other public writing, and oral presentations.

Recommended usage

The conventions described and illustrated in this handbook are those of standard American English—the label given the dialect used in higher education, business, and the professions. (See also pp. 168–70.) The handbook stresses written standard English, which is more conservative than the spoken dialect in matters of grammar and usage. A great many words and constructions that are widely spoken remain unaccepted in careful writing.

When clear distinctions exist between the language of conversation and that of careful writing, the handbook provides examples of each and labels them *spoken* and *written*. When usage in writing itself varies with the level of formality intended, the handbook labels examples *formal* and *informal*. When usage is mixed or currently changing, the handbook recommends that you choose the more conservative usage because it will be accepted by all readers.

Preface for Instructors

The Little, Brown Handbook always aims to address both the current and the recurrent needs of writing students and teachers. This eleventh edition is no exception. Writing and its teaching change continuously, and the handbook has changed in response. At the same time, much about writing does not change, and the handbook remains a comprehensive, clear, and accessible guide to a host of writing situations and challenges.

The Little, Brown Handbook is actually many books in one, and each is stronger in this edition. The revisions—highlighted below with **New**—affect most pages.

A guide to academic writing

The handbook gives students a solid foundation in the goals and requirements of college writing.

- **New** A reorganized Part 2 ("Reading and Writing in College") proceeds through a chapter each on academic skills in general, critical thinking and reading, and academic writing. The part concludes with three chapters on arguments—reading them, writing them, and using visual arguments.
- **New** The revised chapter on academic skills emphasizes time management, reading for comprehension, the basics of academic writing, and preparing for exams.
- **New** The reconceived chapter on academic writing shows students how to write in response to texts. The chapter concludes with two sample critiques—a response to a text and a new paper analyzing an advertisement.
- **New** Synthesis receives special emphasis wherever students might need help balancing their own and others' views, such as in responding to texts.
- **New** Expanded advice on avoiding plagiarism shows students at every turn how to acknowledge borrowed material.
- **New** A greater stress on acknowledging opposing views in argument includes discussion of Rogerian approaches.
- Parts 9 and 10 give students a solid foundation in research writing, writing about literature, and writing in other humanities, the social sciences, and the natural and applied sciences. Extensive, specially highlighted sections on documentation and format cover the most recent updates of MLA, Chicago, APA, and CSE styles.

A guide to research writing

With detailed advice and two sample MLA papers, the handbook always attends closely to research writing. The discussion stresses using the library as Web gateway, managing information, evaluating and synthesizing sources, integrating source material, and avoiding plagiarism.

- **New** A research-paper-in-progress on green consumerism follows a student through the research process and culminates in an annotated paper documented in MLA style.
- **New** An expanded discussion of evaluating sources shows the application of critical criteria to sample articles, sample Web documents, and a sample blog.
- **New** Many kinds of electronic resources—blogs, wikis, and multimedia as well as Web documents—receive attention as possible sources that require careful evaluation and documentation.
- **New** The advice for generating primary sources now covers conducting observations and surveys as well as interviews.
- **New** Paired examples of summaries, paraphrases, and quotations compare plagiarized and unplagiarized versions.
- **New** Updated source lists in Part 10 provide reliable starting points for research in every discipline.

A guide to documenting sources

The extensive coverage of documentation in four styles—MLA, Chicago, APA, and CSE—reflects each style's latest version and includes many examples of electronic sources.

- **New** MLA style is expanded and completely updated to reflect the 2008 *MLA Style Manual and Guide to Scholarly Publishing,* Third Edition.
- **New** APA style is updated to reflect the 2007 supplement *APA Style Guide to Electronic References.*
- **New** CSE style is updated to reflect the 2006 *Scientific Style and Format: The CSE Manual for Authors, Editors, and Publishers,* Seventh Edition.
- **New** Annotated samples of key source types illustrate MLA and APA documentation, showing students how to find the bibliographical information needed to cite each type.
- **New** For all styles, color highlighting makes authors, titles, dates, and other citation elements easy to grasp.

A guide to the writing process

The handbook takes a practical approach to assessing the writing situation, generating ideas, developing the thesis statement, revising, and other elements of the writing process.

- **New** A student's work-in-progress on globalization and outsourcing illustrates the stages of the writing process.
- **New** Diagrams visually reinforce the recursiveness of the writing process.
- **New** A discussion of voice helps students inject themselves into their academic writing.
- **New** Expanded coverage of thesis development now includes examples of explanatory and argumentative thesis questions and statements.
- An extensive chapter on paragraphs provides nearly fifty annotated examples.
- An extensive chapter on document design includes help with using illustrations and a section on designing for readers with vision loss.

A guide to usage, grammar, and punctuation

The handbook's core reference material reliably and concisely explains basic concepts and common errors, provides hundreds of annotated examples from across the curriculum, and offers frequent exercises in connected discourse (including end-of-part exercises that combine several kinds of problems).

- **New** Seven added boxes cover helping verbs, sentence fragments, comma splices and fused sentences, misplaced modifiers, appropriate language, word choice, and spelling.
- **New** Color highlighting in boxes stresses and distinguishes sentence elements for quick reference.
- **New** Advice on avoiding the informalities common to online communication targets nonstandard grammar, punctuation, abbreviations, and spelling.

A guide for culturally and linguistically diverse writers

At notes and sections labeled ⟨CULTURE LANGUAGE⟩, the handbook provides extensive rhetorical and grammatical help for writers whose first language or dialect is not standard American English.

- Fully integrated coverage, instead of a separate section, means that students can find what they need without having to know which problems they do and don't share with native SAE speakers.
- "⟨CULTURE LANGUAGE⟩ Guide," inside the back cover, orients students with advice on mastering SAE and pulls all the integrated coverage together in one place.

A guide to visual literacy

The handbook helps students process visual information and use it effectively in their writing.

- ■ **New** The discussion of viewing images critically uses fresh and diverse examples to demonstrate identifying and analyzing visual elements.
- ■ **New** A student work-in-progress illustrates the process of analyzing an advertisement and culminates in a sample critique.
- ■ **New** The chapter on reading and using visual arguments includes new graphs and advertisements and a new photograph for analysis.
- ■ Detailed help with preparing or finding illustrations appears in the discussions of document design, research writing, and Web composition.
- ■ Illustrations in many of the handbook's student papers show various ways to support written ideas with visual information.

An accessible reference guide

The handbook is designed to be easy to use.

- ■ **New** A clean, uncluttered page design uses color and type clearly to distinguish parts of the book and elements of the pages.
- ■ **New** Color highlighting in boxes and on documentation models distinguishes important elements.
- ■ Annotations on both visual and verbal examples connect principles and illustrations.
- ■ Dictionary-style headers in the index make it easy to find entries.
- ■ Helpful endpapers offer several paths to the book's content.
- ■ More than 160 boxes provide summaries and checklists of key information.
- ■ A preface just for students outlines the book's contents, details reference aids, and explains the page layout.

A reference for college and beyond

With chapters on document design, academic skills and academic writing, cross-curricular writing, essay exams, online writing, public writing, and oral presentations, the handbook is a resource that students keep. With a hard cover and sturdy binding, it is a book that lasts.

Supplements

Pearson offers a variety of support materials to make teaching easier and to help students improve as writers. The following resources are geared specifically to *The Little, Brown Handbook*. For more information on these and scores of additional supplements, visit *pearsonhighered.com* or contact your local Pearson sales representative.

- **New** mycomplab The Web site *MyCompLab* (*mycomplab.com*) integrates instruction, multimedia tutorials, and exercises for writing, grammar, and research with an online composing space and assessment tools. This seamless, flexible environment comes from extensive research in partnership with composition faculty and students across the country. It provides help for writers in the context of their writing, with functions for instructors' and peers' commentary. Special features include an e-portfolio, a bibliography tool, tutoring services, an assignment builder, and a gradebook and course-management organization created specifically for writing classes. In addition, an e-book version of *The Little Brown Handbook* integrates the many resources of *MyCompLab* into the text.

- **New** Students can subscribe to *The Little, Brown Handbook* as a *CourseSmart* e-textbook. The site includes all of the handbook's content in a format that enables students to search the text, bookmark passages, integrate their notes, and print reading assignments that incorporate lecture notes. For more information or to subscribe to the *CourseSmart* e-textbook, visit *coursesmart.com*.

- The *Instructor's Annotated Edition* of *The Little, Brown Handbook* has been thoroughly revised by Cynthia Marshall, Wright State University. It provides a complete teaching system in one book. Integrated with the student text are essays on teaching, updated reading suggestions, specific tips for class discussions and activities, and answers to the handbook's exercises.

- The *Instructor's Resource Manual* includes all the teaching material and exercise answers from the *Instructor's Annotated Edition*.

- *The Little, Brown Handbook Answer Key* provides answers to the handbook's exercises.

- *The Little, Brown Workbook,* by Donna Gorrell, parallels the handbook's organization but provides many more exercises and briefer instructional text. A separate answer key is available.

- *Diagnostic and Editing Tests and Exercises* are cross-referenced to *The Little, Brown Handbook* and are available both in print and online.

- vango notes *VangoNotes* are study guides in MP3 format that enable students to download handbook information into their own players and then listen to it whenever and wherever they wish. The notes include "need to know" tips for each handbook chapter, practice tests, audio flash cards for learning key concepts and terms, and a rapid review for exams. For more information, visit *VangoNotes.com*.

Acknowledgments

The Little, Brown Handbook stays fresh and useful because instructors talk with Pearson's sales representatives and editors, answer questionnaires, write detailed reviews, and send us personal notes.

For the eleventh edition, we are especially grateful to the many instructors who communicated with us directly or through reviews, drawing on their rich experience to offer insights into the handbook and suggestions for its improvement: Paula Berggren, Baruch College, City University of New York; Sandra Cooper, Central Florida Community College; Lori Rios Doddy, Texas Woman's University; Hilary Englert, New Jersey City University; Holly French, Bossier Parish Community College; Richard F. Gaspar, Hillsborough Community College; Diana Gatz, St. Petersburg College; Mickey Hall, Volunteer State Community College; Barbara Hanna, East Mississippi Community College; Daryl Y. Holmes, Nicholls State University; Melissa Joarder, Delaware County Community College; Kathleen Keating, Greensboro College; Joselle LaGuerre, Miami Dade College, Homestead; Jaquelyn S. Lyman, Anne Arundel Community College; Gladys Jane McClain, University of West Georgia; John Schaffer, Blinn College; Nancy M. Staub, Lamar University; and Mary Wright, Christopher Newport University.

In responding to the ideas of these thoughtful critics, we had the help of several creative people. Caroline Crouse, George Washington University, guided us through the labyrinth of the contemporary library. Nanette Tamer, Villa Julie College, provided helpful suggestions to improve many exercises. Sylvan Barnet, Tufts University, continued to lend his expertise in the chapter "Reading and Writing About Literature," which is adapted from his *Short Guide to Writing About Literature* and *Introduction to Literature* (with William Burto and William E. Cain). Ellen Kuhl provided creative, meticulous, and invaluable help with the material on research writing. And Carol Hollar-Zwick, sine qua non, served brilliantly as originator, sounding board, critic, coordinator, researcher, producer, and friend.

A superb publishing team helped us make this book. At Longman, our editors, Joe Opiela and Anne Brunell Ehrenworth, offered perceptive insights into instructors' and students' needs, while the production editor, Bob Ginsberg, helped us resolve sometimes competing production goals in favor of quality and accuracy. At Nesbitt Graphics, Jerilyn Bockorick created the striking new design, and Susan McIntyre performed her usual calm (and calming) miracles of scheduling and management to produce the book. We are grateful to all these collaborators.

Contents

Preface for Students: Using This Book vii
Preface for Instructors x

PART 1   The Writing Process *1*

1 Assessing the Writing Situation *2*

- **a** Understanding how writing happens *2*
- **b** Analyzing the writing situation *4*
- **c** Discovering and limiting a subject *6*
- **d** Defining a purpose *9*
- **e** Considering the audience *12*

2 Developing and Shaping Ideas *16*

- **a** Discovering ideas *16*
- **b** Developing a thesis *27*
- **c** Organizing ideas *33*
  - SAMPLE ESSAY *43*

3 Drafting and Revising *46*

- **a** Writing the first draft *46*
- **b** Revising the first draft *50*
- **c** Examining a sample revision *56*
- **d** Editing the revised draft *59*
- **e** Preparing and proofreading the final draft *65*
- **f** SAMPLE FINAL DRAFT *66*
- **g** Giving and receiving comments *68*
- **h** Preparing a writing portfolio *71*

4 Writing and Revising Paragraphs *72*

- **a** Maintaining paragraph unity *74*
- **b** Achieving paragraph coherence *79*
- **c** Developing the paragraph *92*
- **d** Writing special kinds of paragraphs *103*
- **e** Linking paragraphs in the essay *111*

5 Designing Documents *112*

- **a** Designing academic papers and other documents *112*
- **b** Considering principles of design *113*

c Using the elements of design *117*
d Using illustrations *121*
e Considering readers with vision loss *126*

PART 2 Reading and Writing in College *127*

6 Developing Academic Skills *128*

a Managing your time *129*
b Listening and taking notes in class *130*
c Reading for comprehension *131*
d Becoming an academic writer *135*
e Preparing for exams *136*

7 Forming a Critical Perspective *138*

a Using techniques of critical reading *140*
b Developing a critical response *146*
c Viewing images critically *153*

8 Writing in Academic Situations *162*

a Writing in response to texts *162*
b Determining purpose *165*
c Analyzing audience *166*
d Choosing structure and content *167*
e Using academic language *168*
f Examining sample critical responses *171*
    SAMPLE CRITIQUE OF A TEXT *171*
    SAMPLE CRITIQUE OF AN IMAGE *174*

9 Reading Arguments Critically *176*

a Recognizing the elements of argument *177*
b Testing claims *178*
c Weighing evidence *181*
d Discovering assumptions *185*
e Watching language, hearing tone *186*
f Judging reasonableness *187*
g Recognizing fallacies *190*

10 Writing an Argument *196*

a Finding a subject *196*
b Conceiving a thesis statement *198*
c Analyzing your purpose and your audience *198*
d Using reason *199*
e Using evidence *204*

f Reaching your readers *205*
g Organizing your argument *209*
h Revising your argument *210*
i SAMPLE ARGUMENT *211*

11 Reading and Using Visual Arguments *216*

a Reading visual arguments critically *216*
b Using visual arguments effectively *223*

PART 3   Grammatical Sentences *229*

12 Understanding Sentence Grammar *230*

a Understanding the basic sentence *231*
b Expanding the basic sentence with single words *239*
c Expanding the basic sentence with word groups *242*
d Compounding words, phrases, and clauses *256*
e Changing the usual word order *260*
f Classifying sentences *262*

13 Case of Nouns and Pronouns *264*

a Compound subjects and complements *266*
b Compound objects *267*
c *We* or *us* with a noun *267*
d Appositives *267*
e Pronoun after *than* or *as* in a comparison *268*
f Subjects and objects of infinitives *268*
g *Who* vs. *whom* *269*
h Case before a gerund *271*

14 Verbs *272*

Verb Forms *272*
a Regular and irregular verbs *275*
b *Sit* and *set; lie* and *lay; rise* and *raise* *278*
c Omitted *-s* and *-ed* endings *279*
d Helping verbs *280*
e Verb plus gerund or infinitive *285*
f Verb plus particle *287*

Tense *289*
g Appropriate tense for meaning *290*
h Sequence of tenses *292*

Mood *296*
i Subjunctive verb forms *296*

Voice *298*
j Active vs. passive voice *299*

15 **Agreement** *301*

a Agreement between subject and verb *301*
b Agreement between pronoun and antecedent *309*

16 **Adjectives and Adverbs** *315*

a Adjectives only with nouns and pronouns *316*
b Adjectives after linking verbs *317*
c Adjectives with objects; adverbs with verbs *317*
d Comparative and superlative forms *318*
e Double negatives *320*
f Overuse of nouns as modifiers *321*
g Present and past participles as adjectives *321*
h *A, an, the*, and other determiners *322*

PART 4   Clear Sentences *329*

17 **Sentence Fragments** *330*

a Tests for sentence completeness, revision of fragments *330*
b Subordinate clause *334*
c Verbal or prepositional phrase *334*
d Other fragments *335*
e Acceptable uses of incomplete sentences *337*

18 **Comma Splices and Fused Sentences** *338*

Comma Splices *340*
a Main clauses not joined by coordinating conjunction *340*
b Main clauses related by a conjunctive adverb or transitional expression *342*

Fused Sentences *343*
c Main clauses with no conjunction or punctuation *343*

19 **Pronoun Reference** *345*

a Clear reference to one antecedent *346*
b Clear placement of pronoun and antecedent *347*
c Reference to specific antecedent *348*
d Indefinite use of *you* *350*
e Clear use of *it* *350*
f Appropriate *who, which, that* *350*

20 **Shifts** *352*

a Person and number *353*
b Tense and mood *355*

c Subject and voice 356
d Indirect and direct quotations and questions 357

21 Misplaced and Dangling Modifiers 359

Misplaced Modifiers 359
a Clear placement of modifiers 359
b Limiting modifiers 361
c Squinting modifiers 361
d Separation of subjects, verbs, and objects 362
e Separation of parts of infinitives or verb phrases 362
f Position of adverbs 364
g Order of adjectives 365

Dangling Modifiers 366
h Dangling modifiers 366

22 Mixed and Incomplete Sentences 369

Mixed Sentences 369
a Mixed grammar 369
b Mixed meaning (faulty predication) 371

Incomplete Sentences 373
c Compound constructions 373
d Comparisons 374
e Careless omissions 374

PART 5   Effective Sentences 377

23 Emphasizing Ideas 378

a Using subjects and verbs effectively 378
b Using sentence beginnings and endings 380
c Arranging parallel elements effectively 383
d Repeating ideas 384
e Separating ideas 385
f Being concise 386

24 Using Coordination and Subordination 388

a Coordinating to relate equal ideas 388
b Subordinating to distinguish main ideas 391
c Choosing clear connectors 397

25 Using Parallelism 398

a Using parallelism for coordinate elements 399
b Using parallelism to increase coherence 403

26 **Achieving Variety** *405*

  a Varying sentence length and structure *406*
  b Varying sentence beginnings *408*
  c Inverting the normal word order *411*
  d Mixing types of sentences *411*

PART 6   Punctuation *415*

    Chart *416*

27 **End Punctuation** *418*

  a The period *418*
  b The question mark *419*
  c The exclamation point *420*

28 **The Comma** *422*

  a Main clauses linked by coordinating conjunctions *422*
  b Introductory elements *425*
  c Nonessential elements *427*
  d Absolute phrases *432*
  e Phrases expressing contrast *432*
  f Series and coordinate adjectives *433*
  g Dates, addresses, place names, long numbers *435*
  h With quotations *436*
  i To prevent misreading *438*
  j Misuse and overuse *439*

29 **The Semicolon** *443*

  a Main clauses not joined by a coordinating conjunction *445*
  b Main clauses related by a conjunctive adverb or transitional expression *446*
  c Main clauses that are long or contain commas *448*
  d Series items that are long or contain commas *448*
  e Misuse and overuse *449*

30 **The Apostrophe** *451*

  a Possession *453*
  b Misuses with noun plurals, verbs, and personal pronouns *455*
  c Contractions *456*
  d Plurals of abbreviations, dates, and words or characters named as words *458*

31 Quotation Marks *459*

    Chart *460*
a Direct quotations *459*
b Quotation within a quotation *461*
c Dialog *462*
d Titles of songs, short stories, etc. *463*
e Words used in a special sense *464*
f Overuse *464*
g Placement with other punctuation marks *465*

32 Other Punctuation Marks *467*

a The colon *467*
b The dash *470*
c Parentheses *472*
d Brackets *474*
e The ellipsis mark *475*
f The slash *478*

PART 7   Mechanics *481*

33 Capitals *482*

a First word of a sentence *482*
b Titles of works *483*
c Pronoun *I* and interjection *O* *484*
d Proper nouns and adjectives *484*
e Titles before proper names *486*
f Misuses of capitals *486*

34 Italics or Underlining *488*

a Titles of books and periodicals *488*
b Names of ships, aircraft, spacecraft, trains *490*
c Foreign words and phrases *490*
d Words, letters, and numbers named as words *490*
e For emphasis *490*
f In online communication *491*

35 Abbreviations *492*

a Titles before and after proper names *492*
b Familiar abbreviations and acronyms *493*
c *BC, BCE, AD, CE, AM, PM, no.,* and *$* *493*
d Latin abbreviations *494*
e *Inc., Bros., Co.,* and *&* *494*

f Misuse with units of measurement, geographical names, and so on *494*

36 Numbers *496*

   a Numerals vs. words *496*
   b For dates, addresses, etc. *497*
   c Beginning sentences *498*

PART 8   Effective Words *501*

37 Using Appropriate Language *502*

   a Revising nonstandard dialect *503*
   b Revising shortcuts of online communication *504*
   c Using slang only when appropriate *504*
   d Using colloquial language only when appropriate *505*
   e Using regionalisms only when appropriate *506*
   f Revising neologisms *506*
   g Using technical words with care *506*
   h Revising indirect or pretentious writing *506*
   i Revising sexist and other biased language *507*

38 Using Exact Language *511*

   a Using a dictionary and a thesaurus *512*
   b Using the right word for your meaning *514*
   c Balancing the abstract and concrete, the general and specific *516*
   d Using idioms *518*
   e Using figurative language *520*
   f Using fresh expressions *522*

39 Writing Concisely *523*

   a Focusing on subject and verb *524*
   b Cutting or shortening empty words and phrases *525*
   c Cutting unnecessary repetition *527*
   d Reducing clauses to phrases, phrases to single words *528*
   e Revising *there is, here is,* and *it is* constructions *529*
   f Combining sentences *529*
   g Rewriting jargon *529*

40 Spelling and the Hyphen *531*

   a Recognizing typical spelling problems *531*
   b Following spelling rules *534*
   c Developing spelling skills *538*
   d Using the hyphen to form or divide words *544*

PART 9   Research Writing *547*

41 Planning a Research Project *548*

a Starting out *549*
b Finding a researchable subject and question *550*
c Developing a research strategy *554*
d Making a working, annotated bibliography *557*

42 Finding Sources *561*

a Starting with your library's Web site *561*
b Searching electronically *563*
c Finding reference works *565*
d Finding books *569*
e Finding periodicals *571*
f Finding sources on the Web *578*
g Finding other online sources *581*
h Finding government publications *583*
i Finding images, audio, and video *584*
j Generating your own sources *586*

43 Working with Sources *589*

a Evaluating sources *590*
b Synthesizing sources *604*
c Mining and interacting with sources *607*
d Using summary, paraphrase, and quotation *611*
e Integrating sources into your text *620*

44 Avoiding Plagiarism and Documenting Sources *626*

a Committing and detecting plagiarism on the Internet *628*
b Knowing what you need not acknowledge *628*
c Knowing what you *must* acknowledge *629*
d Acknowledging online sources *632*
e Documenting sources *634*

45 Writing the Paper *635*

a Developing a thesis statement *636*
b Creating a structure *637*
c Drafting the paper *640*
d Revising and editing the paper *641*
e Preparing and proofreading the final draft *643*

46 Using MLA Documentation and Format *644*

a USING MLA IN-TEXT CITATIONS *644*
b PREPARING THE MLA LIST OF WORKS CITED *653*
c USING MLA DOCUMENT FORMAT *689*

47 Two Research Papers in MLA Style *691*

"THE FALSE PROMISE OF GREEN CONSUMERISM" *692*

"ANNIE DILLARD'S HEALING VISION" *720*

PART 10 Writing in the Academic Disciplines *727*

48 Working with the Goals and Requirements of the Disciplines *728*

a Using methods and evidence *728*
b Understanding writing assignments *729*
c Using tools and language *729*
d Following styles for source citations and document format *730*

49 Reading and Writing About Literature *731*

a Using the methods and evidence of literary analysis *731*
b Understanding writing assignments in literature *739*
c Using the tools and language of literary analysis *740*
d Citing sources and formatting documents in writing about literature *741*
e Drafting and revising a literary analysis *742*
SAMPLE ANALYSIS OF A SHORT STORY *746*
f Writing about fiction, poetry, and drama *747*
SAMPLE ANALYSIS OF A POEM *750*
SAMPLE ANALYSIS OF A PLAY *752*

50 Writing in Other Humanities *755*

a Using the methods and evidence of the humanities *755*
b Understanding writing assignments in the humanities *756*
c Using the tools and language of the humanities *756*
d CITING SOURCES IN CHICAGO STYLE *760*
e FORMATTING DOCUMENTS IN CHICAGO STYLE *771*

51 Writing in the Social Sciences *774*

a Using the methods and evidence of the social sciences *774*
b Understanding writing assignments in the social sciences *775*
c Using the tools and language of the social sciences *776*
d CITING SOURCES IN APA STYLE *779*
e FORMATTING DOCUMENTS IN APA STYLE *799*
f SAMPLE SOCIAL SCIENCE PAPER *802*

52 Writing in the Natural and Applied Sciences *805*

a Using the methods and evidence of the sciences *806*
b Understanding writing assignments in the sciences *806*

c Using the tools and language of the sciences *807*
d CITING SOURCES IN CSE STYLE *811*
e FORMATTING DOCUMENTS IN CSE STYLE *817*
f SAMPLE SCIENCE PAPER *818*

PART 11 Special Writing Situations *821*

53 Essay Examinations *822*

a Preparing for an essay examination *822*
b Planning your time and your answer *823*
c Starting the essay *825*
d Developing the essay *825*
   SAMPLE ESSAY EXAMS *826*
e Rereading the essay *828*

54 Writing Online *828*

a Writing effective e-mail *829*
b Collaborating online *831*
c Creating effective Web compositions *834*

55 Public Writing *840*

a Writing business letters and memos *841*
   SAMPLE LETTER AND MEMO *842, 845*
b Writing a job application *847*
   SAMPLE LETTER AND RÉSUMÉS *847, 849–50*
c Writing business reports and proposals *849*
   SAMPLE REPORT AND PROPOSAL *851, 852*
d Writing for community work *852*
   SAMPLE FLYER, NEWSLETTER, AND BROCHURE *853–55*

56 Oral Presentations *856*

a Writing and speaking *856*
b Considering purpose and audience *856*
c Organizing the presentation *858*
d Delivering the presentation *859*

Glossary of Usage *865*

Glossary of Terms *882*

Index *907*

PART 1

The Writing Process

1 Assessing the Writing Situation

2 Developing and Shaping Ideas

3 Drafting and Revising

4 Writing and Revising Paragraphs

5 Designing Documents

HIGHLIGHTS

Teachers know that writing is *not* easy, but students, especially beginning writers, often have the misconception that writing comes easily to experienced writers and is hard only for the untalented or inexperienced. This chapter begins by recognizing the difficulties faced by all writers, experienced and inexperienced alike. Next, the chapter alerts students to the various elements of the writing situation and the writing process and discusses ways to discover and limit subjects. The concluding sections explore flexible strategies for defining a purpose and considering audience for writing. Special features of this chapter are the attention paid to purpose and audience throughout the composition process, the list of "Questions About Audience" (p. 13), and the discussion of voice.

Although Chapters 1 and 2 look at activities typical of the early stages of composing and Chapter 3 treats drafting and revising, the text does not endorse a strictly linear view of the composing process. Instead, all three chapters emphasize the writer's many options and the flexibility of the composing process. They point out that writing is a way of thinking and discovering: that in the middle of drafting an essay a writer may recognize the need to develop new supporting ideas, to make major changes in the organization, or to shift the purpose of the essay and modify the thesis.

1

Assessing the Writing Situation

"Writing is easy," snarled the late sportswriter Red Smith. "All you do is sit down at the typewriter and open a vein." Most writers would smile in agreement, and so might you. Like anything worthwhile, writing well takes hard work. This chapter and the next two will show you some techniques that successful writers use to ease the discomfort of writing and produce effective compositions.

1a | Understanding how writing happens

Every time you sit down to write, you embark on a **writing process**—the term for all the activities, mental and physical, that go into creating what eventually becomes a finished piece of work. Even for experienced writers the process is usually messy, which is one reason that it is sometimes difficult. Though we may get a sense of ease and orderliness from a published magazine article, we can safely assume that the writer had to work hard to achieve those qualities, struggling to express half-formed thoughts, shaping and reshaping paragraphs to make a point convincingly.

There is no *one* writing process; no two writers proceed in the same way, and even an individual writer adapts his or her process to the task at hand. Still, most writers experience writing as a **recursive** process in which the following stages overlap and influence one another:

- **Analyzing the writing situation:** considering subject, purpose, audience, and other elements of the project (pp. 4–15).
- **Developing or planning:** gathering information, focusing on a central theme, and organizing material (pp. 16–44).
- **Drafting:** expressing and connecting ideas (pp. 46–50).
- **Revising and editing:** rethinking and improving structure, content, style, and presentation (pp. 50–68).

mycomp|lab

Visit *mycomplab.com* for more resources and exercises on the writing situation and the writing process.

The writing process

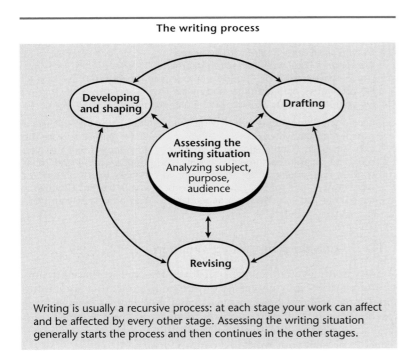

Writing is usually a recursive process: at each stage your work can affect and be affected by every other stage. Assessing the writing situation generally starts the process and then continues in the other stages.

With experience, as you complete varied assignments and try the varied techniques described in this book, you will develop your own basic writing process.

Note Like many others, you may believe that writing is only, or even mainly, a matter of correctness. True, any written message will find a more receptive audience if it is correct in grammar, spelling, and similar matters. But these concerns should come late in the writing process, after you've allowed yourself to discover what you want to say, freeing yourself to make mistakes along the way. As one writer put it, you need to get the clay on the potter's wheel before you can shape it into a bowl, and you need to shape the bowl before you can perfect it. So get your clay on the wheel, and work with it until it looks like a bowl. Then worry about correctness.

Exercise 1.1   Starting a writing journal

Recall several writing experiences that you have had—a letter you had difficulty composing, an essay you enjoyed writing, an all-nighter spent happily or miserably on a term paper, a posting to a blog that received a surprising response. What do these experiences reveal to you about

COLLABORATIVE LEARNING

INDIVIDUALS' WRITING PROCESSES

Ask students to discuss their individual writing processes in small groups. When confronted with a writing task, what steps do they take? How do they gather ideas? Do they prefer to dive right in or to spend some time gathering ideas? Do they compose on a computer or on paper? Do they prefer to discuss their ideas with others? Do they prefer to write in silence or with music on? At what time of day do they like to write? By sharing their answers with one another, students can begin to see the diversity of individualized responses to the writing process. Also, you might want to encourage students to try different approaches, like composing on the computer if they normally write longhand.

AT EASE

Students often bring their apprehensions about writing (and writing instructors) with them to class. To create a positive atmosphere for your course, you may wish to establish a setting in which students feel at ease about acknowledging and sharing their apprehensions. One way to do this is to ask them to *list* what they dislike (and like) about writing without worrying about the form or correctness of entries in their lists. Voluntary sharing of the entries can help reduce the isolation many students feel and help you (and them) set priorities for instruction.

ANSWERS: EXERCISE 1.1

Individual response.

RESOURCES AND IDEAS

Ball, Kevin, and Amy Goodburn. "Composition Studies and Service Learning: Appealing to Communities?" *Composition Studies* 28.1 (2000): 79–94. Print. The authors, critical of service learning pedagogy, offer suggestions for writing assignments that include the perspectives of community participants.

Bartholomae, David. "Inventing the University." *When a Writer Can't Write: Studies in Writer's Block and Other Composing Process Problems.* Ed. Mike Rose. New York: Guilford, 1985. 134–65. Print. Argues that student writers need to be taught explicitly the discourse standards of an academic community in order to write successfully for it.

Berlin, James A. "Contemporary Composition: The Major Pedagogical Theories." *College English* 44.8 (1982): 765–77. Print. Berlin points out that various process approaches have consequences instructors must consider.

Blakeslee, Ann M. "Bridging the Workplace and the Academy: Teaching Professional Genres Through Classroom-Workplace Collaborations." *Technical Communication* 10.2 (2001): 169–92. Print. Using case studies, Blakeslee shows how student writing improves when students work on projects provided by professionals in business and industry.

Bloom, Lynn Z., Donald A. Daiker, and Edward M. White, eds. *Composition Studies in the New Millennium: Rereading the Past, Rewriting the Future.* Carbondale: Southern Illinois UP, 2003. Print. This collection addresses significant issues in composition studies: how, where, and by whom composition will be taught, how students will respond, and how outside cultural forces will influence the teaching of composition.

Flower, Linda, and John R. Hayes. "A Cognitive Process Theory of Writing." *College Composition and Communication* 32.4 (1981): 365–87. Print. This classic article contains what is probably the best-known and most widely accepted discussion of the components of the writing process, though its model is more theoretical than practical.

writing, particularly your successes and problems with it? Consider the following questions:

Do you like to experiment with language?
Are some kinds of writing easier than others?
Do you have trouble getting ideas or expressing them?
Do you worry about grammar and spelling?
Do your readers usually understand what you mean?

Record your thoughts as part of continuing journal entries that track your experiences as a writer. (See pp. 19–21 on keeping a journal, and see the exercises titled "Considering your past work" in Chapters 1–4.) As you complete writing assignments for your composition course and other courses, keep adding to the journal, noting especially which procedures seem most helpful to you. Your aim is to discover your feelings about writing so that you can develop a dependable writing process of your own.

1b Analyzing the writing situation

Any writing you do for others occurs in a context that both limits and clarifies your choices. You are communicating something about a particular subject to a particular audience of readers for a specific reason. You may need to conduct research. You'll be up against a length requirement and a deadline. And you may be expected to present your work in a certain format.

These are the elements of the **writing situation,** and analyzing them at the very start of a project can tell you much about how to proceed. (For more information about these elements, refer to the page numbers given in parentheses.)

Context
- **What is your writing for?** A course in school? Work? Something else? What do you know of the requirements for writing in this context?
- **Will you present your writing on paper, online, or orally?** What does the presentation method require in preparation time, special skills, and use of technology?
- **How much leeway do you have for this writing?** What does the stated or implied assignment tell you?

Subject (pp. 6–9)
- **What does your writing assignment require you to write about?** If you don't have a specific assignment, what subjects might be appropriate for this situation?
- **What interests you about the subject?** What do you already know about it? What questions do you have about it?
- **What does the assignment require you to do with the subject?**

Purpose (pp. 9–11)

- **What aim does your assignment specify?** For instance, does it ask you to explain something or argue a point?
- **Why are you writing?**
- **What do you want your work to accomplish?** What effect do you intend it to have on readers?
- **How can you best achieve your purpose?**

Audience (pp. 12–15)

- **Who will read your writing?**
- **What do your readers already know and think about your subject?** What characteristics—such as education or political views—might influence their response?
- **How should you project yourself in your writing?** What role should you play in relation to your readers, and what information should you provide? How informal or formal should your writing be?
- **What do you want readers to do or think after they read your writing?**

Research (pp. 548–635)

- **What kinds of evidence will best suit your subject, purpose, and audience?** What combination of facts, examples, and expert opinions will support your ideas?
- **Does your assignment require research?** Will you need to consult sources or conduct interviews, surveys, or experiments?
- **Even if research is not required, what information do you need to develop your subject?** How will you obtain it?
- **What documentation style should you use to cite your sources?** (See pp. 634–35 on source documentation in the academic disciplines.)

Deadline and length

- **When is the assignment due?** How will you apportion the work you have to do in the time available?
- **How long should your writing be?** If no length is assigned, what seems appropriate for your subject, purpose, and audience?

Document design

- **What organization and format does the assignment require?** (See pp. 112–13 on format in the academic disciplines and pp. 840–55 on format in public writing.)
- **How might you use margins, headings, and other elements to achieve your purpose?** (See pp. 117–21.)
- **How might you use graphs, photographs, or other images to support ideas and engage readers?** (See pp. 121–25, 223–26.)

Fulkerson, Richard. "Composition at the Turn of the Twenty-First Century." *College Composition and Communication* 56.4 (2005): 654–87. Print. Fulkerson addresses the fragmentation in the composition community, in particular, the influence of "critical/cultural studies," which has led to politicization of composition pedagogy.

Lindemann, Erika. "Three Views of English 101." *College English* 57.8 (1995): 287–302. Print. This article lays out the opposing claims and assumptions of the "process," "product," and "system of social action" approaches.

McComiskey, Bruce. *Teaching Composition as a Social Process.* Logan: Utah State UP, 2000. Print. McComiskey extends composition theory beyond a discussion of the writing process, re-examining the product in the context of cultural theory as a cycle of production, distribution, and consumption.

Tobin, Lad, and Thomas Newkirk, eds. *Taking Stock: The Writing Process Movement in the '90's.* Portsmouth: Boynton, 1994. Print. This collection of essays analyzes the goals of the writing process movement, its application in particular institutions, and the ways in which a focus on the writing process can be adapted for the classrooms of the future.

Yagelski, Robert P. *Literacy Matters: Writing and Reading the Social Self.* New York: Teachers College Press, 2000. Print. Yagelski supports changes to writing curricula to account for the seminal influence of social context on the production and composition of written texts.

COMPUTER ACTIVITY

WEB MODELS

Ask students to locate articles or other material on the World Wide Web that can serve as effective models (having clear subjects, audiences, and purposes) or as negative models (having unclear subjects, purposes, or audiences). Students can e-mail their findings to their classmates.

COLLABORATIVE LEARNING

GROUP ANALYSIS

Break students into small groups and ask them to work together to analyze a writing situation using the questions on pp. 5–6 as a guideline.

ANSWERS: EXERCISE 1.2

The assignment specifies the subject (the combinations of client, therapist, and theory that tend to make psychotherapy successful), the audience (the instructor and a "discussion group" of classmates), and the purpose (to explain and support a conclusion about the subject). It requires research into studies of psychotherapy. It specifies a length range and a deadline. It does not specify a format, but APA format could be assumed because the course is in psychology.

RESOURCES AND IDEAS

Brooke, Rupert, Ruth Mirtz, and Rick Evans, eds. *Small Groups in Writing Workshops: Invitations to a Writer's Life.* Urbana: NCTE, 1994. Print. This collection of essays offers many strategies for using collaborative group work to create an active learning situation.

Flower, Linda S., and John R. Hayes. "The Cognition of Discovery: Defining a Rhetorical Problem." *College Composition and Communication* 31.1 (1980): 21–32. Print. This article reports on a detailed study of how good writers and poor writers conceive of writing tasks as they begin to compose.

Goldfine, Ruth. "Making Word Processing More Effective in the Composition Classroom." *Teaching English in the Two-Year College* 28.3 (2001): 307–15. Print. Goldfine identifies problems with using word processing in the classroom and shares solutions to help students learn with computers at each stage of the writing process.

Golub, Jeff. *Activities for an Interactive Classroom.* Urbana: NCTE, 1994. Print. Golub provides a number of hands-on suggestions for creating an effective workshop environment.

Hillocks, George, Jr. "Environments for Active Learning." *Theory and Practice in the Teaching of Writing: Rethinking the Discipline.* Ed. Lee Odell. Carbondale: Southern Illinois UP, 1993. 244–70. Print. Hillocks' essay is part case study and part analysis of a classroom structure based on student interactions with each other and with texts.

Exercise 1.2 Analyzing a writing situation

The following assignment was given in a survey course in psychology. What does the assignment specify about the elements of the writing situation? What does it imply? Given this assignment, how would you answer the questions on the previous two pages?

When is psychotherapy most likely to work? That is, what combinations of client, therapist, and theory tend to achieve good results? In your paper, cite studies supporting your conclusions. Length: 1500 to 1800 words. Post your paper online to me and to your discussion group by March 30.

1c | Discovering and limiting a subject

For most college and public writing, you will write in response to an assignment. The assignment may specify your subject, or it may leave the choice to you. (If you're stuck, you can use the discovery techniques on pp. 16–26 to think of subjects.) Whether the subject is assigned or not, it will probably need some thought if it is to achieve these aims:

- **The subject should be suitable for the assignment.**
- It should be **neither too general nor too limited** for the length of the project and the deadline assigned.
- It should be **something you are willing to learn more about, even something you care about.**

1 | Responding to a specific assignment

Many assignments will set boundaries for your subject. For instance, you might be asked to discuss what makes psychotherapy effective, to prepare a lab report on a physics experiment, or to analyze a character in a short story.

Such assignments may seem to leave little room for you to move around, but in fact you'll have several questions to answer:

- **What's wanted from you?** Writing assignments often contain words such as *discuss, describe, analyze, report, interpret, explain, define, argue,* and *evaluate.* These words specify the way you are to approach your subject, what kind of thinking is expected of you, and what your general purpose is. (See pp. 9–11 for more on purpose.)
- **For whom are you writing?** Many assignments will specify or imply your readers, but sometimes you will have to figure out for yourself who your audience is and what it expects from you. (For more on analyzing audience, see pp. 12–15.)

■ **What kind of research is required?** Sometimes an assignment specifies the kinds of sources you are expected to consult, and you can use such information to choose your subject. (If you are unsure whether research is required, check with your instructor.)

■ **How can you narrow the assigned subject to do it justice in the length and time required?** (See below.)

2 Responding to a general assignment

Some assignments specify features such as length and amount of research, but they leave the choice of subject entirely to you. Others are somewhat more focused—for instance, "Respond to a reading assigned in this course" or "Discuss a proposal for solving a local social problem"—but still give you much leeway in choosing a particular reading or a particular proposal. To find your approach, consider your own experiences, interests, or curiosities:

■ **What subject do you already know something about or have you been wondering about?** Athletic scholarships? Unemployment in your town?

■ **Have you recently disagreed with someone over a substantial issue?** The change in relations between men and women? The methods being used to fight terrorism?

■ **What have you read or seen lately?** A shocking book? A violent or funny movie? An effective television commercial?

■ **What topic in the reading or class discussion for a course has intrigued you?** An economic issue such as taxes? A psychological problem such as depression?

■ **What makes you especially happy or especially angry?** A hobby? The behavior of your neighbors?

■ **Which of your own or others' dislikes and preferences would you like to understand better?** The demand for hybrid cars? The decision to become a vegetarian?

Once you have a subject, you'll also need to answer the questions in the bulleted list opposite.

3 Narrowing a subject to a question

Let's say you've decided to write about social-networking sites on the Internet or about a particular character in a short story. You've got a subject, but it's still broad, worthy of a lengthy article if not a whole book. For a relatively brief paper, you'll need a narrow focus in order to provide the specific details that make writing significant and interesting—all within the length and deadline specified by the assignment.

Spiegelman, Candace. *Personally Speaking: Experience as Evidence in Academic Discourse.* Urbana: NCTE, 2004. Print. Spiegelman argues for the inclusion of personal experience as evidence in academic writing and offers examples of successful student use of personal experience.

Tedlock, David. "The Case Approach to Composition." *College Composition and Communication* 32.3 (1981): 253–61. Print. Tedlock argues for the use of cases—detailed, self-contained descriptions of a writing situation—as a basis for assignments and instructions.

COMPUTER ACTIVITY

NARROWING SUBJECTS USING A SEARCH ENGINE

Have students search for a broad term such as *environment* using a search engine like *Google* or *Yahoo!* Ask them to examine how they can narrow their search using the list of related searches. Then, have students follow some of the links to find more specific key terms they could then use as search terms, like *global warming* or *green living*. Ask students to discuss which terms have the most promise as essay topics, and to explain why they think so.

NARROWING SUBJECTS TO TOPICS

Clustering (2a-6) and asking the journalist's questions (2a-7) can also help students narrow subjects to topics. For example, the broad subject "Islam" can be the center point of a cluster, and students can write related topic ideas such as "theology of Islam," "Western attitudes toward Muslims and Islam," and "women in Islam" in branches radiating from the center. "Islam" can also be narrowed by asking such questions as "*Who* are major figures in Islam?", "*What* do Muslims believe?", "*How* are Muslims and Islam viewed in the United States?", "*Where* is Islam practiced?", and "*How* and *Why* are women and men treated differently in Islamic tradition?"

Other good subject areas that give students practice in narrowing topics are movies, cars, television programs, and academic fields (for example, sociology, geology).

RESOURCES AND IDEAS

Seabury, Marcia Bundy. "The Abstraction Ladder in Freshman Composition." *College Composition and Communication* 40.1 (1989): 89–92. Print. Seabury has found that teaching S. I. Hayakawa's abstraction ladder can benefit first-year composition students in their thinking through and writing about their topics.

Shipka, Jody. "A Multimodal Task-Based Framework for Composing." *College Composition and Communication* 57.2 (2005): 277–306. Print. Shipka argues that students should write in various modes, moving beyond even simply incorporating visual literacy or multimedia. She advocates allowing students to define the context for these multimodal projects while still meeting the goals of the assignment.

Taylor, Tim N. "The Research Paper as an Act of Citizenship: Possibilities and Pragmatism." *Teaching English in the Two-Year College* 33.1 (2005): 50–61. Print. Taylor argues that students should focus on local issues as a form of civic engagement.

Wallace, David. "From Intentions to Text: Articulating Initial Intentions for Writing." *Research in the Teaching of English* 30.2 (1996): 182–219. Print. This essay explores the relationship between the planning and composing stages of writing. Wallace's study found that students who were most able to articulate their initial intentions for a writing task were also most able to complete the task effectively.

On limiting subjects

Coe, Richard M. "If Not to Narrow, Then How to Focus: Two Techniques for Focusing." *College Composition and Communication* 32.3 (1981): 272–77. Print. Coe describes ways to get students to focus on a particular aspect of a topic as an alternative to the usual approach of narrowing a topic.

Tucker, Amy. *Decoding ESL: International Students in the American College Classroom.* Portsmouth: Boynton, 1995. Print. This book explores the larger issues of how to read and respond to ESL writers, and includes (particularly in Chapter 8) strategies for using readings as the prompts for writing assignments.

One helpful technique for narrowing a subject is to ask focused questions about it, seeking one that seems appropriate for your assignment and that promises to sustain your interest through the writing process. The following examples illustrate how questioning can scale down broad subjects to specific subjects that are limited and manageable:

Broad subjects	Specific subjects
Social-networking sites	What draws people to these sites? How do the sites alter the ways people interact? What privacy protections should the sites provide for users?
Mrs. Mallard in Kate Chopin's "The Story of an Hour"	What changes does Mrs. Mallard undergo? Why does Mrs. Mallard respond as she does to news of her husband's death? What does the story's irony contribute to the character of Mrs. Mallard?
Lincoln's weaknesses as President	What was Lincoln's most significant error as commander-in-chief of the Union army? Why did Lincoln delay emancipating the slaves? Why did Lincoln have difficulties controlling his cabinet?
Federal aid to college students	Which students should be entitled to federal aid? How adequate are the kinds of federal aid available to college students? Why should the federal government aid college students?

As these examples illustrate, your questions should not lend themselves to yes-or-no answers but should require further thinking.

Here are some guidelines for posing questions:

- **Reread the assignment.** Consider what it tells you about purpose, audience, sources, length, and deadline.
- **Pursue your interests.** If questions don't come easily, try freewriting or brainstorming (pp. 21–23) or use a tree diagram (pp. 35–36).
- **Ask as many questions as you can think of.**
- **Test the question that seems most interesting and appropriate by roughly sketching out the main ideas.** Consider how many paragraphs or pages of specific facts, examples, and other details you would need to pin those ideas down. This thinking should give you at least a vague idea of how much work you'd have to do and how long the resulting paper might be.
- **Break a too-broad question down further, and repeat the previous step.**

The Internet can also help you limit a general subject. On the Web, browse a directory such as *BUBL LINK* (*bubl.ac.uk*). As you pursue increasingly narrow categories, you may find a suitably limited topic.

Don't be discouraged if the perfect question does not come easily or early. You may find that you need to do some planning and writing, exploring different facets of the general subject and pursuing your specific interests, before you hit on the best question. And the question you select may require further narrowing or may shift subtly or even dramatically as you move through the writing process.

Exercise 1.3   Narrowing subjects

Following are some general writing assignments. Use the given information and your own interests to pose specific questions for three of these assignments.

1. For a writing course, consider how Web sites such as *YouTube* are altering the experience of popular culture. Length: three pages. Deadline: one week.
2. For a course in sociology, research and analyze the dynamics of a particular group of people. Length: unspecified. Deadline: four weeks.
3. For a writing course, read and respond to an essay in a text you are using. Length: three pages. Deadline: two weeks.
4. For a government course, consider possible restrictions on legislators. Length: five pages. Deadline: two weeks.
5. For a letter to the editor of the town newspaper, describe the effects of immigration on your community. Length: two pages. Deadline: unspecified.

Exercise 1.4   Considering your past work: Discovering and limiting a subject

Think of something you've recently written—perhaps an application essay, a business report, or a term paper. How did your subject evolve from beginning to end? In retrospect, was it appropriate for your writing situation? How, if at all, might it have been modified?

Exercise 1.5   Finding and narrowing a subject for your essay

As the first step in developing a three- to four-page essay for the instructor and the other students in your writing course, choose a subject and narrow it. Use the guidelines in the previous section to come up with a question that is suitably interesting, appropriate, and specific.

1d   Defining a purpose

When you write, your **purpose** is your chief reason for communicating something about a topic to a particular audience. Purpose thus links both the specific situation in which you are working and

---

Have students work in groups to find specific topics for the assignments in Exercise 1.3, and then share their conclusions with the class. Students benefit from realizing the numerous and varied options for narrowing a broad subject.

ANSWERS: EXERCISE 1.3

Possible answers

1. How has the availability of video on Web sites such as *YouTube* affected how people form opinions about public figures?
2. How does slang help to bind members of the college community?
3. How does X's theory about math anxiety apply to me?
4. How might term limits affect the House of Representatives?
5. How has immigration affected food choices?

SHARING PAST WRITING

Sharing past work can help students connect the writing they are doing in your class to their broader experience as writers, a connection that helps them to gain greater awareness of their own progress as writers. Have students bring in a piece of previous work and present it to their group, describing the context in which that piece was written, their purpose in writing it, what they learned from writing it, and how it differs from other kinds of writing they have done. Ask groups to report on the interesting or unexpected moments that occurred in the group presentations.

ANSWERS: EXERCISE 1.4

Individual response.

ANSWERS: EXERCISE 1.5

Individual response.

As part of the process of developing their topics for Exercise 1.5, have students verbally articulate their ideas in small groups and receive suggestions for further development and focus.

IDENTIFYING PURPOSE

Use paragraphs drawn from magazine articles, essays in a reader, or student papers as the basis for class discussion of the purposes of writing. You may ask students to work individually or in groups to compare the aims of individual paragraphs with the overall purpose of the essay from which they are taken and to decide what role the paragraphs play within the essay.

COMPUTER ACTIVITY

Give your students a series of Web pages to look at and ask them to evaluate what they find on each page in terms of purpose.

AUDIENCE INVENTORY

Ask students to choose a possible topic for an essay and to list the kinds of people who might be interested in the topic. Tell students that if they wish they may employ the "Questions About Audience" on page 13. (In theory, the lists might be very long. In practice, students soon run out of ideas, but not until they have begun to visualize the audience for their essays.) To extend the exercise, ask students what part of the potential audience they would most like to address or what kinds of people would be most interested in the topic. Then ask them to list either (1) what the restricted audience probably already knows about the topic and what it needs to know or (2) what its attitudes are and what kinds of arguments will be needed to change them.

the goal you hope to achieve. It is your answer to a potential reader's question, "So what?"

The general purposes for writing

- To entertain readers
- To express your feelings or ideas
- To explain something to readers (exposition)
- To persuade readers to accept or act on your opinion (argument)

1 Defining a general purpose

Your purpose may fall into one of four general categories: entertainment, self-expression, explanation, or persuasion. These purposes may overlap in a single piece of writing, but usually one predominates. And the dominant purpose will influence your particular slant on your topic, the supporting details you choose, even the words you use.

In college or public writing, by far the most common purposes are explanation and persuasion:

- **Writing that is mainly explanatory is often called** *exposition* (from a Latin word meaning "to explain or set forth"). Using examples, facts, and other evidence, you present an idea about your subject so that readers understand it as you do. Almost any subject is suitable for exposition: how to pitch a knuckleball, why you want to major in business, the implications of a new discovery in computer science, the interpretation of a short story, the causes of an economic slump. Exposition is the kind of writing encountered most often in newspapers, magazines, and textbooks.
- **Writing that is primarily persuasive is often called** *argument*. Using examples, facts, and other evidence, you support your position on a debatable subject so that readers will at least consider your view and perhaps agree with it or act on it. A newspaper editorial favoring city council reform, a business proposal for a new personnel policy, a student paper recommending more required courses or defending a theory about human psychological development—all these are arguments. (Chapters 9–11 discuss argument in some detail and provide examples.)

2 Defining a specific purpose

Purpose can be conceived more specifically, too, in a way that incorporates your particular subject and the outcome you intend—

what you want readers to do or think as a result of reading your writing. Here are some examples of specific purposes:

> To explain how Annie Dillard's "Total Eclipse" builds to its climax so that readers appreciate the author's skill

> To explain the methods and results of an engineering experiment so that readers understand and accept your conclusions

> To explain why the county has been unable to attract new businesses so that readers better understand the local economic slump

> To persuade readers to support the college administration's plan for more required courses

> To argue against additional regulation of health-maintenance organizations so that readers perceive the disadvantages for themselves

> To argue for additional gun licensing so that readers agree on its necessity

Often, a writing assignment will specify or imply both a general and a specific purpose. Say, for instance, that a psychology teacher assigns a review of the research on infants' perception of color. You know that the purpose is generally to explain, more specifically to summarize and analyze the established findings on the subject. You want readers to come away understanding the current state of the investigation into the subject. In addition, you want your instructor to see that you can competently read others' work and write about it. (See p. 165 for more on purpose in academic writing.)

With any writing assignment, try to define your specific purpose as soon as you have formed a question about your subject. Don't worry, though, if you feel uncertain of your purpose at the start. Sometimes you may not discover your purpose until you begin drafting, or you may find that your initial sense of purpose changes as you move through the writing process.

Exercise 1.6   Finding purpose in assignments
For each of your questions from Exercise 1.3 (p. 9), suggest a likely general purpose (entertainment, self-expression, explanation, persuasion) and try to define a specific purpose as well.

Exercise 1.7   Considering your past work: Defining a purpose
Look over two or three things you've written in the past year or so. What was your specific purpose in each one? How did the purpose influence your writing? Did you achieve your purpose?

Exercise 1.8   Defining a purpose for your essay
For your essay-in-progress, use your thinking so far about your subject (Exercise 1.5, p. 9) to define a general and specific purpose for your writing.

Ask students to develop their responses to Exercise 1.6 in groups, paying particular attention to places where the purposes of a given topic could differ. This discussion will help students to explore ways in which a topic might lend itself to various purposes.

ANSWERS: EXERCISE 1.6

Possible answers

1. *How has the availability of video on Web sites such as* YouTube *affected how people form opinions about public figures?* Explain how the ability to view video clips of public figures on the Web results in viewers' gaining information to use in forming their own opinions.
2. *How does slang help to bind members of the college community?* Explain how the community's unique slang contributes to a sense of belonging.
3. *How does X's theory about math anxiety apply to me?* Explain the way X's theory reflects your own experience.
4. *How might term limits affect the House of Representatives?* Argue against term limits for legislators.
5. *How has immigration affected food choices?* Explain how immigrants have vastly increased the variety of foods available. Help readers appreciate this benefit of immigration.

ANSWERS: EXERCISE 1.7

Individual response.

ANSWERS: EXERCISE 1.8

Individual response.

RESOURCES AND IDEAS

Bacon, Nora. "Building a Swan's Nest for Instruction in Rhetoric." *College Composition and Communication* 51.4 (2000): 589–609. Print. Bacon shows how community-based writing assignments help students understand how purpose and style must change as a result of rhetorical context.

Elbow, Peter. "Reconsiderations: Voice in Writing Again: Embracing Contraries." *College English* 70.2 (2007): 168–88. Print. Elbow encourages scholars to take up the topic of "voice" again, as the term is still used by many composition teachers; he provides many reasons for and against "attending to voice" in writing.

Ong, Walter J., S. J. "The Writer's Audience Is Always a Fiction," *PMLA* 90.1 (1975): 9–21. Print. Ong argues that writers must construct audiences in their imaginations as an essential part of the act of writing and that readers must play the role defined for them by the writer's act of imagination. Of course, students are probably aware that in many writing circumstances, such as writing for a professor or a manager at work, the audience is real, not fictional. It's worth discussing how a writer's task can be shaped by his or her knowledge of actual readers.

COLLABORATIVE LEARNING

AUDIENCE INVENTORY

Ask students to compare the lists they developed for the audience inventory and suggest changes, additions, or deletions.

AUDIENCE ASSESSMENT

Distribute to your class an article from a special interest magazine, a newspaper feature or editorial, an article from the Internet, or another brief essay whose appeal to a particular audience students will be able to recognize fairly easily. Ask students to read the essay and then to work together to identify the characteristics and attitudes of the intended audience as they think the author viewed it. Ask them also to identify the tone of the essay and to decide whether or not it is appropriate to the subject, the intended audience, and the publication in which the essay appeared. Tell them to be ready to point out what evidence in the essay they used to identify the in-

---

1e Considering the audience

- **Who are my readers?**
- **Why will they read my writing?**
- **What will they need from me?**
- **How do I want them to perceive me?**
- **What do I want them to think or do after they read my writing?**

These questions are central to any writing project, and they will crop up again and again. Except in writing meant only for yourself, you are always trying to communicate with readers—something about a particular subject, for a particular purpose.

Your audience will often be specified or implied in a writing assignment. When you write an editorial for the student newspaper, your audience consists of fellow students. When you write a report on a physics experiment, your audience consists of your physics instructor and perhaps other physicists or your classmates. (See p. 166 for more on audience in academic writing.) Whatever the audience, considering its needs and expectations can help you form or focus a question about your subject, gather answers to the question, and ultimately decide what to say and how to say it.

1 Knowing what readers need

As a reader yourself, you know what readers need:

- **Context:** a link between what they read and their own knowledge and experiences.
- **Predictability:** an understanding of the writer's purpose and how it is being achieved.
- **Information:** the specific facts, examples, and other details that make the subject clear, interesting, and convincing.
- **Respect:** a sense that the writer respects their values and beliefs, their backgrounds, and their intelligence.
- **Voice:** a sense that the writer is a real person whose mind and values are expressed in the writing (see p. 14).
- **Clarity and correctness:** writing free of unnecessary stumbling blocks and mistakes.

For much academic and public writing, readers have definite needs and expectations. Thus Chapter 8 discusses academic writing in general, Chapters 48–52 discuss writing in various disciplines, and Chapter 55 discusses public writing. Even in these areas, you must make many choices based on audience. In other areas where the conventions of structure and presentation are vaguer, the choices are even more numerous. The box below contains questions that can help you define and make these choices.

Questions about audience

Identity and expectations

- Who *are* my readers?
- **What are my readers' expectations for the kind of writing I'm doing?** Do readers expect features such as a particular organization and format, distinctive kinds of evidence, or a certain style of documenting sources?
- **What do I want readers to know or do after reading my work?** How should I make that clear to them?
- **How should I project myself to readers?** How formal or informal will they expect me to be? What role and tone should I assume?

Characteristics, knowledge, and attitudes

- **What characteristics of readers are relevant for my subject and purpose?** For instance:

    Age and sex
    Occupation: students, professional colleagues, etc.
    Social or economic role: subject-matter experts, voters, car buyers, potential employers, etc.
    Economic or educational background
    Ethnic background
    Political, religious, or moral beliefs and values
    Hobbies or activities

- **How will the characteristics of readers influence their attitudes toward my subject?**
- **What do readers already know and *not* know about my subject?** How much do I have to tell them?
- **How should I handle any specialized terms?** Will readers know them? If not, should I define them or avoid them?
- **What ideas, arguments, or information might surprise, excite, or offend readers?** How should I handle these points?
- **What misconceptions might readers have of my subject and/or my approach to it?** How can I dispel these misconceptions?

Uses and format

- **What will readers do with my writing?** Should I expect them to read every word from the top, to scan for information, to look for conclusions? Can I help by providing a summary, headings, illustrations, or other aids? (See pp. 112–26 on document design.)

---

tended audience and the tone. Rather than bring articles to class yourself, ask students either individually or as teams to bring in a variety of essays or writings aimed at particular audiences. Some potential target audiences include consumers, sports fans, parents, businesspeople, patients, and health-care workers.

COLLABORATIVE LEARNING

SPECIFIC VERSUS NONSPECIFIC AUDIENCE

Have students work in small groups or pairs to compose a short paragraph about a class-related policy directed to a nonspecific audience. For example, ask students to explain the goals of the course or your policy on attendance. They will need to include sufficient information for this general audience and to write in a level tone. Then, ask students to write a revised paragraph summarizing the same information for an audience of their peers. What information can be omitted because of the change in audience? Is there any additional information (like the consequence for one's GPA of failing the course for nonattendance, for example) that should be included? What role do students assume when addressing other students as equals in this revised paragraph? What common knowledge can they assume the student audience has that the nonspecific audience may not share? Are there course- or school-specific terms that they need to define for the nonspecific audience? How does their tone differ when addressing other students versus writing for the nonspecific audience?

RESOURCES AND IDEAS

Ede, Lisa, and Andrea Lunsford. "Audience Addressed/Audience Invoked: The Role of Audience in Composition Theory and Pedagogy." *College Composition and Communication* 35.2 (1984): 155–71. Print. The authors suggest a negotiated balance between the writer's desires and the audience's needs. See also their "Representing Audience: 'Successful' Discourse and Disciplinary Critique" in *College Composition and Communication* 47.2 (1996): 167–79. Print.

Kirsch, Gesa, and Duane H. Roen. *A Sense of Audience in Written Communication.* Newbury Park: Sage, 1990. Print. Sixteen interdisciplinary essays on audience treat the subject from a number of critical perspectives.

Park, Douglas B. "Analyzing Audiences." *College Composition and Communication* 37.4 (1986): 478–88. Print. Understanding the social context of a writing act helps students define their audiences.

Simmons, Jay, and Timothy McLaughlin. "Longer, Deeper, Better." *Teaching English in the Two-Year College* 30.4 (2003): 416–27. Print. The authors discuss assignments that require students to publish their work to both their classmates and other readers at a different grade level. This awareness of audience, in part, seems to help students to take more time and care with their writing.

Tichenor, Stuart. "Using Niche-Market Magazines to Teach Audience." *Teaching English in the Two-Year College* 33.4 (2006): 455–61. Print. Tichenor discusses two exercises he used with technical writing students in which they must analyze the content of magazines targeting readers with specific interests or of a particular gender.

Trimbur, John. "Composition and the Circulation of Writing." *College Composition and Communication* 52.2 (2000): 188–219. Print. Trimbur suggests that teachers should enrich composition instruction by alerting students to the effects a broader circulation of students' work would have on the manner of its composition.

Wells, Susan. "Rogue Cops and Health Care: What Do We Want from Public Writing?" *College Composition and Communication* 47.3 (1996): 325–41. Print. Wells explores the problems of addressing a "general public" audience in student assignments.

COLLABORATIVE LEARNING

Have students work in groups to critique and revise one of their paragraph-length responses to Exercise 1.9. In networked classrooms, students can "publish" the revised paragraphs for the class.

ANSWERS: EXERCISE 1.9

Possible answers

1. *For elementary school students:* physical effects in simple terms; statistics in simple figures; difficulty of quitting once addicted; importance of resisting peer pressure.

2 **Expressing your voice**

Your sense of your audience will influence three key elements of what you write:

- **The specific information you use to gain and keep the attention of readers and to guide them to accept your conclusions.** This information may consist of concrete details, facts, examples, or other evidence that makes your ideas clear, supports your assertions, and suits your readers' needs. The evidence may come from your experience or from outside sources.
- **The role you choose to play in relation to your readers.** Depending on your purpose and your attitude toward your topic, you will want readers to perceive you in a certain way. The possible roles are many and varied—for instance, scholar, storyteller, lecturer, guide, reporter, advocate, inspirer.
- **The tone you use.** Tone in writing is like tone of voice in speaking: words and sentence structures on the page convey some of the same information as pitch and volume in the voice. Depending on your aims and what you think your readers will expect and respond to, your tone may be formal or informal. The attitude you convey may be serious or light, forceful or calm, irritated or cheerful.

These three elements contribute to what's often called **voice:** your projection of yourself into the writing. Your voice conveys your sense of the world as it applies to the particular writing situation: this subject, this purpose, this audience. Thus voice can vary quite a bit from one writing situation to another, as the following memos illustrate. Both were written by a student who worked part-time in a small company and wanted to get the company to conserve paper. But the two memos address different readers.

To coworkers

Ever notice how much paper collects in your trash basket every day? Well, most of it can be recycled with little effort, I promise. Basically, all you need to do is set a bag or box near your desk and deposit wastepaper in it. I know, space is cramped in these little cubicles. But can't we all accept a little more crowding when the earth's at stake? . . .

Voice: a peer who is thoughtful, cheerful, and sympathetic

Information: how employees could handle recycling; no mention of costs

Role: colleague

Tone: informal, personal (*Ever notice; Well; you; I know, space is cramped*)

To management

In my four months here, I have observed that all of us throw out baskets of potentially recyclable

Voice: a subordinate who is thoughtful, responsible, and serious paper every day. Considering the drain on our forest resources and the pressure on landfills that paper causes, we could make a valuable contribution to the environmental movement by helping to recycle the paper we use. At the company where I worked before, employees separate clean wastepaper from other trash at their desks. The maintenance staff collects trash in two receptacles, and the trash hauler (the same one we use here) makes separate pickups. I do not know what the hauler charges for handling recyclable material. . . .

> **Information:** specific reasons; view of company as a whole; reference to another company; problem of cost

> **Role:** employee

> **Tone:** formal, serious (*Considering the drain; forest resources; valuable contribution; no you*)

Typically for business writing, the voice grows more professional as the readers increase in rank.

Projecting your writing voice can be challenging when you are responding to another's work or drawing on multiple sources for evidence. Especially if you feel unconfident about your subject, you may be tempted to let the other writers do the talking for you. You can find advice on pages 162–65 and 604–06 for maintaining your voice by using synthesis.

Exercise 1.9 Considering audience

Choose one of the following subjects and, for each audience specified, ask the questions on page 13. Decide on four points you would make, the role you would assume, and the tone you would adopt for each audience. Then write a paragraph for each based on your decisions.

1. The effects of smoking: for elementary school students and for adult smokers
2. Your opposition to a proposed law requiring adult bicyclists to wear helmets: for cyclists who oppose the law and for people who favor it
3. Why your neighbors should remove the wrecked truck from their front yard: for your neighbors and for your town zoning board

Exercise 1.10 Considering your past work: Writing for a specific audience

How did audience figure in a piece of writing you've done in the recent past—perhaps an essay for an application or a paper for a course? Who were your readers? How did your awareness of them influence your voice? At what point in the writing process did you find it most productive to consider your readers consciously?

Exercise 1.11 Analyzing the audience for your essay

Use the questions on page 13 to determine as much as you can about the probable readers of your essay-in-progress (see Exercises 1.5 and 1.8). What might be an appropriate voice for your writing? What specific information will your readers need? What role do you want to assume? What tone will best convey your attitude toward your topic?

Role: combined teacher and parent. Tone: warm, slightly admonitory.

For adult smokers: graphic depiction of physical effects; detailed statistics; influence on children; effect on smoker's appearance, odor, breath.

Role: combined friend and lecturer. Tone: no-nonsense.

2. *For cyclists who oppose the law:* status of law; reasons for opposition; need for action; suggested actions.

Role: peer, motivator. Tone: informal, urgent.

For people who favor the law: acknowledgment of pro-law position; disadvantages of helmets; lack of proven need; infringement of cyclists' rights.

Role: fellow citizen. Tone: informative, reasonable, appealing to shared values.

3. *For your neighbors:* feelings of neighborhood residents; dangers to children and pets; lowered property values; threat of petition to zoning board.

Role: peer. Tone: direct, a bit angry.

For the zoning board: violation of zoning regulations; length of time the wrecked truck has been present; number of unsuccessful appeals to neighbors; dangers to children and pets.

Role: plaintiff. Tone: serious, reasonable.

ANSWERS: EXERCISE 1.10

Individual response.

COLLABORATIVE LEARNING

Students can often experience difficulty in identifying the implied readers of their own work. Have students work in small groups to compare their responses to Exercise 1.11, to help one another identify the probable readers of their essays-in-progress, and to note places in each essay where too much or too little information is supplied.

ANSWERS: EXERCISE 1.11

Individual response.

2 Developing and Shaping Ideas

Once you have assessed your writing situation, or even while you're assessing it, you'll begin answering the question you posed about your subject (pp. 7–8). As you generate ideas and information, they in turn may cause you to rephrase your lead question, which will open up new areas to explore. Throughout this discovery process, you'll also be bringing order to your thoughts, eventually focusing and organizing them so that readers will respond as you intend.

2a Discovering ideas

For some writing projects, you may have little difficulty finding what you have to say about your subject: possible answers to your starting question will tumble forth as ideas on paper or screen. But when you're stuck for what to say, you'll have to coax answers out. Instead of waiting around for inspiration to strike, use a technique to get your mind working. Anything is appropriate: if you like to make drawings or take pictures, for instance, then try that.

The following pages describe techniques for discovering ideas. These techniques are to be selected from, not followed in sequence: some may help you during early stages of the writing process, even before you're sure of your topic; others may help you later on; and one or two may not help at all. Give yourself ample time with the techniques, experimenting to discover which ones work best for you.

Note Whatever techniques you use, do your work in writing, not just in your head. Your work will be retrievable, and the act of writing will help you concentrate and lead you to fresh, sometimes surprising, insights.

mycomplab

Visit *mycomplab.com* for more resources and exercises on discovering and shaping ideas.

Developing and shaping ideas

Developing ideas and shaping them may occur at any point in the writing process, from the initial choice of subject through drafting and revision.

CULTURE & LANGUAGE The discovery process encouraged here rewards rapid writing without a lot of thinking beforehand about what you will write or how. If your first language is not standard American English, you may find it helpful initially to do this exploratory writing in your native language or dialect and then to translate the worthwhile material for use in your drafts. This process can be productive, but it is extra work. You may want to try it at first and gradually move to composing in standard American English.

Techniques for developing a subject

- Read (p. 18).
- Keep a journal (p. 19).
- Observe your surroundings (p. 21).
- Freewrite (p. 21).
- Brainstorm (p. 22).
- Cluster (p. 23).
- Use the journalist's questions (p. 24).
- Use the patterns of development (p. 25).

ing their horizons. (These other media will have to be submitted separately if you have students hand their journals in.)

It's important to make the journal a productive tool, not just make-work. Encourage students to plumb their journals for essay topics and samples of strategies they might use in more formal pieces of writing. You can also make journals productive by encouraging students to write journal entries as letters to you or to classmates, and then incorporate your or their classmates' answers into the journal as well.

Most instructors react to issues raised or comment on attempts to try new strategies without actually grading the journal. Students will often include very personal material in their journals, so they should be encouraged to fold over, staple, or secure (but not remove) personal material before they show it to you; they must trust that you will respect their confidentiality.

COMPUTER JOURNALS

If your students keep their journals on their computers, the Cut-and-Paste function will make it easy for them to mine their journal entries for appropriate material to copy to the document in which they are drafting their paper.

USING JOURNALING TO SPARK CLASS DISCUSSION

In-class journaling can be helpful before a class discussion, as it allows students to gather their initial thoughts. Providing a specific prompt on the reading assignment or other topics to be discussed can focus students' attention without putting them on the spot. After writing for 5–10 minutes on the topic, students are better prepared to participate in class discussion. In-class journaling also helps students develop greater fluency and practice on-demand writing without the pressure for correctness and formality they might feel writing a graded essay.

RESOURCES AND IDEAS

On keeping journals

Fulwiler, Toby, and Susan Gardner. *The Journal Book for Teachers of At-Risk College Writers*. Portsmouth: Boynton/Cook, 1999. Print. Building on the ideas presented in their *The Journal Book* (Portsmouth: Boynton/Cook, 1987), Fulwiler and Gardner address how journaling can also benefit students with learning disabilities, basic writers, and nontraditional students.

Gannett, Cinthia. *Gender and the Journal: Diaries and Academic Discourse*. Albany: State U of New York P, 1992. Print. Gannett discusses the development of the genre and how it has been "feminized," with consideration of the pedagogical implications of this history.

White, Fred D. "Releasing the Self: Teaching Journal-Writing to Freshmen." *The Writing Instructor* 1 (1982): 147–54. Print. White offers practical advice on the use of journals: kinds of journals and entries, professional samples, exercises, and a summary of supporting research.

Whitehill, Sharon. "Using the Journal for Discovery: Two Devices." *College Composition and Communication* 38.4 (1987): 472–74. Print. Whitehill argues that journal assignments calling for lists and for imaginary dialogues can help generate ideas and alleviate writing blocks, and she provides detailed examples of each strategy.

1 **Reading**

Many assignments require you to respond to reading or to consult texts as sources for your writing. But even when reading is not required, it can help you locate or develop a subject by introducing you to ideas you didn't know or by expanding on what you do know.

For example, say you were writing in favor of amateur athletics, a subject to which you had given a lot of thought. You might be inclined to proceed entirely on your own, drawing on facts, examples, and opinions already in your head. But a little digging in sources might open up more ideas. For instance, an article in *Time* magazine could introduce you to an old rule for amateur status, or a comment on a blog could suggest an argument in favor of amateurism that hadn't occurred to you. Remember: whenever you use the information or ideas of others in your writing, you must acknowledge your sources in order to avoid the serious offense of plagiarism. (See Chapter 44.)

Often you will be given an assignment that asks you to use a text or texts in your writing. In a composition course, Katy Moreno's instructor distributed "It's a Flat World, After All," an essay by Thomas L. Friedman about globalization and the job market. The instructor then gave the following assignment, calling for a response to reading:

> In "It's a Flat World, After All," Thomas L. Friedman describes today's global job market, focusing not on manufacturing jobs that have been "outsourced" to overseas workers but on jobs that require a college degree and are no longer immune to outsourcing. Friedman argues that keeping jobs in the United States requires that US students, parents, and educators improve math and science education. As a college student, how do you respond to this analysis of the global market for jobs? Does anything Friedman says cause you to rethink how you will spend your college years or what your major will be?

To respond to Friedman's essay, Moreno had to digest its argument. On first reading the essay, she had found it convincing because Friedman's description of the job market matched her family's experience: her mother had lost her job when it was outsourced to India. After rereading the essay, however, Moreno was not persuaded that more math and science would necessarily improve students' opportunities and preserve their future jobs. She compared Friedman's advice with details she recalled from her mother's experience, and she began to develop a response by writing in her journal:

> Friedman is certainly right that more jobs than we realize are going overseas—that's what happened to Mom's job and we were shocked! But he gives only one way for students like me to compete—take more math and science. At first I thought he's totally right. But then I thought that what he said didn't

really explain what happened to Mom—she had lots of math + science + tons of experience, but it was her salary, not better training, that caused her job to be outsourced. An overseas worker would do her job for less money. So she lost her job because of money + because she wasn't a manager. Caught in the middle. I want to major in computer science, but I don't think it's smart to try for the kind of job Mom had—at least not as long as it's so much cheaper for companies to hire workers overseas.

When you read for ideas, you need to be active, probing the text and illustrations with your mind, nurturing any sparks they set off. Always write while you read, taking notes on content and—just as important—on what the content makes you *think*. If you read passively, absorbing content like a sponge and not interacting with it, you won't have much to say about it. (See pp. 131–33 for specific tips on active reading.)

2 Keeping a journal

A **journal** is a place to record your responses, thoughts, and observations about what you read, see, hear, or experience. It can also be a good source of ideas for writing. It is a kind of diary, but one more concerned with ideas than with day-to-day events. *Journal* comes from the Latin for "daily," and many journal keepers do write faithfully every day; others make entries less regularly, when the mood strikes or an insight occurs or they have a problem to work out.

Advantages of a journal

Writing in a journal, you are writing to yourself. That means you don't have to worry about main ideas, organization, correct grammar and spelling, or any of the other requirements of writing for others. You can work out your ideas and feelings without the pressure of an audience "out there" who will evaluate your thinking and expression. The freedom and flexibility of a journal can be liberating. Like many others, you may find writing easier, more fun, and more rewarding than you thought possible.

You can keep a journal either on paper (such as a notebook) or on a computer. If you write in the journal every day, or almost, even just for a few minutes, the routine will loosen up your writing muscles and improve your confidence. Indeed, journal keepers often become dependent on the process for the writing practice it gives them, the concentrated thought it encourages, and the connection it fosters between personal, private experience and public information and events.

Usually for the same reasons, teachers of writing and other subjects sometimes require students to keep journals. The teachers may even collect students' journals to monitor progress, but they

ACTIVITIES THAT SUGGEST TOPICS AND IDEAS

1. Ask students to take a notebook with them to some place likely to be filled with activity and vivid sense impressions—a shopping mall, the center of the campus, a busy restaurant. They can record their impressions of the scene in the notebook, later turning those impressions into a structured description or using the material in some other form of writing.

2. Ask students to look at a variety of magazines and to bring in a list of the topics covered in the articles. These topics may in turn suggest topics for student essays. The exercise can be extended by asking students to summarize the contents of one or more of the articles and to indicate how the content might appeal to a particular audience.

3. Check with your media center or a film rental service for short films that deal with values or controversies. The films or the ensuing discussions can become the basis of student papers.

4. Set up class presentations or debates on an issue in order to provide information and sharpen the focus for papers dealing with the issue or related topics.

5. Ask students to consider the many communities to which they belong: campus organizations, community or church groups, their hometown, and their state. Then, have them list issues that affect them as members of these communities. For example, is a student organization to which they belong having difficulty obtaining funding or finding good leadership? Is there a divide between students who commute to campus and those who live in campus housing? Is there an ongoing debate about certain chain stores moving into their hometown? Topics that affect students personally make more compelling papers.

PLACES TO WRITE

To help students discover interesting topics and ideas through freewriting, you might give them some places to begin. For essays focusing on events:

> sports, contests, camping, accidents, storms, childhood experiences, giving a speech, getting lost in a department store, robberies, fires

For writing about a scene or character:

> outdoors—woods, seashore, mountains, fields, city streets, parks
> indoors—dorm rooms, laundromats
> scenes—family gatherings, football games, funerals, a snowy morning
> people—parents, grandparents, uncles, aunts, childhood friends, people in a public place, teachers, unpleasant people, cartoon characters

For informative or explanatory writing:

> hobbies, jobs, investments, fields of study, recent scientific discoveries, places to visit, ways to save money, fishing, gardening, study habits, car repair, canoeing, audio equipment, magazines

For persuasive writing:

> campus issues, environmental concerns, automobile or airline safety, support for education, cost of medical care, regulation of new drugs, specialized education versus liberal arts education, rights of minorities and women, gun control, divorce and child rearing, school prayer, censorship, proposals to improve campus or local services, ways of dealing with a social problem

read the journals with an understanding of purpose (in other words, they do not evaluate work that was not written to be evaluated), and they usually just credit rather than grade the work.

CULTURE LANGUAGE A journal can be especially helpful if your first language is not standard American English. You can practice writing to improve your fluency, try out sentence patterns, and experiment with vocabulary words. Equally important, you can experiment with applying what you know from experience to what you read and observe.

Uses of a journal

Two uses of a journal are discussed elsewhere in this book: a reading journal, in which you think critically (in writing) about what you read (pp. 141, 732–33); and a research journal, in which you record your activities and ideas while you pursue a research project (p. 549). But you can use a journal for other purposes as well. Here are just a few:

- **Prepare for or respond to a course you're taking** by puzzling over a reading or a class discussion.
- **Build ideas for specific writing assignments.**
- **Sketch possible designs for a Web composition.**
- **Explore your reactions to events, trends, or the media.**
- **Confide your hopes.**
- **Write about your own history:** an event in your family's past, a troubling incident in your life, a change you've seen.
- **Analyze a relationship that disturbs you.**
- **Practice various forms or styles of writing**—for instance, poems or songs, reviews of movies, or reports for TV news.

The writing you produce in your journal will help you learn and grow, and even the personal and seemingly nonacademic entries can supply ideas when you are seeking a subject to write about or are developing an essay. A thought you recorded months ago about a chemistry lab may provide direction for a research paper on the history of science. Two entries about arguments with your brother may suggest what you need to anchor a psychology paper on sibling relations. If you keep your journal on a computer, you can even copy passages from it directly into your drafts.

On pages 18–19 we saw Katy Moreno's journal response to an essay she read. The next two student samples give a taste of journal writing for different purposes. In the first, Charlie Gabnes tries to work out a personal problem with his child:

> Will's tantrums are getting worse—more often, more intense. Beginning to realize it's affecting my feelings for him. I feel resentment sometimes, and it's not as easy for me to cool off afterward as for him. Also I'm afraid of him

sometimes for fear a tantrum will start, so treat him with kid gloves. How do we break this cycle?

In the second example Megan Polanyis ponders something she learned from her biology textbook:

> *Ecology* and *economics* have the same root—Greek word for house. Economy = managing the house. Ecology = studying the house. In ecology the house is all of nature, ourselves, the other animals, the plants, the earth, the air, the whole environment. Ecology has a lot to do with economy: study the house in order to manage it.

3 | Observing your surroundings

Sometimes you can find a good subject or good ideas by looking around you, not in the half-conscious way most of us move from place to place in our daily lives but deliberately, all senses alert. On a bus, for instance, are there certain types of passengers? What seems to be on the driver's mind? On campus, which buildings stand out? Are bicyclists and pedestrians at peace with each other?

To get the most from observation, you should have a handheld computer or a notepad and pen handy for taking notes and making sketches. If you have a camera, you may find that the lens sees things your unaided eyes do not notice. (When observing or photographing people, though, keep some distance, take photographs quickly, and avoid staring. Otherwise your subjects will feel uneasy.) Back at your desk, study your notes, sketches, or photographs for oddities or patterns that you'd like to explore further.

In some academic writing, you'll be expected to formalize observation with surveys, interviews, or experiments. See pages 586–88.

4 | Freewriting

Writing into a subject

Many writers find subjects or discover ideas by **freewriting**: writing without stopping for a certain amount of time (say, ten minutes) or to a certain length (say, one page). The goal of freewriting is to generate ideas and information from *within* yourself by going around the part of your mind that doesn't want to write or can't think of anything to write. You let words themselves suggest other words. *What* you write is not important; that you *keep* writing is. Don't stop, even if that means repeating the same words until new words come. Don't go back to reread, don't censor ideas that seem dumb or repetitious, and above all don't stop to edit: grammar, punctuation, vocabulary, spelling, and the like are irrelevant at this stage.

COLLABORATIVE LEARNING

TEAMED FREEWRITING

A good variation on freewriting is to make it collaborative: have students write freely for five or ten minutes, then pass their freewriting to the students sitting next to them. Students should read the freewriting, then reflect on it in another freewriting session. This encourages not only more perspectives on a topic but the notion that writing is a dialogue between writer and reader—and it teaches the value of feedback and audience awareness in writing as well.

COMPUTER ACTIVITY

FREEWRITING ONLINE

Have students freewrite on the computer using the "invisible writing" technique if desired. During the next class period ask students to revise their freewriting into a paragraph, then e-mail that paragraph to another student in the class for a further critique and for revision suggestions. After a final revision, students might "publish" the resulting paragraphs on the network or hand them in for the teacher's evaluation.

RESOURCES AND IDEAS

On generative strategies

Flower, Linda S., and John R. Hayes. "Problem-Solving Strategies and the Writing Process." *College English* 39.4 (1977): 449–61. Print. Flower and Hayes describe techniques for discovering and developing ideas, including cue words, nutshelling, idea trees, and brainstorming.

Hunter, Susan. "Oral Negotiations in a Textual Community: A Case for Pedagogy and Theory." *Writing Instructor* 8.3 (1989): 105–10. Print. Hunter states that validating oral communication during the composing process is theoretically sound and helpful in generalizing successful oral communication to successful written communication.

Lackey, Kris. "Amongst the Awful Subtexts: Scholes, *The Daily Planet*, and Freshman Composition." *College Composition and Communication* 38.1 (1987): 88–93. Print. In this thought-provoking piece, Lackey suggests encouraging and enabling students to tease out the binary oppositions in texts as a way of discovering various subtexts that suggest topics for students' own writing.

Perrin, Robert. "10:00 and 2:00: A Ten-Paragraph Defense of the Five-Paragraph Theme." *Teaching English in the Two-Year College* 27.3 (2000): 312–14. Print. Perrin defends assigning the infamous five-paragraph essay, showing that it does not necessarily stifle creativity.

Qualley, Donna. *Turns of Thought: Teaching Composition as Reflexive Inquiry*. Portsmouth: Boynton/Cook (Heinemann), 1997. Print. Qualley advocates "essayism"—a mode of writing in which students reflect upon and reconsider their own claims in response to an encounter with a new idea or text.

Rice, Jeff. "The 1963 Hip-Hop Machine: Hip-Hop Pedagogy As Composition." *College Composition and Communication* 54.3 (2003): 453–71. Print. Rice proposes a "hip-hop pedagogy" of invention for argumentative writing based on the techniques of digital sampling in music.

Wesley, Kimberly. "The Ill Effects of the Five-Paragraph Theme." *English Journal* 90.1 (2000): 57–60. Print. Wesley argues that students' ability to think critically is stifled when a writing assignment is too prescribed.

COLLABORATIVE LEARNING

TOPIC CLUSTERS

The topic cluster we show in 2a-6 is very well developed; students need to know it's acceptable to develop smaller or messier clusters. You might ask students to work on topic clusters in groups. If your classroom permits, you might also want to try doing clusters on overhead transparencies or the blackboard, so that students can add to and change their contents more easily.

The physical act of freewriting may give you access to ideas you were unaware of. For example, the following freewriting by a student, Robert Benday, drew him into the subject of writing as a disguise:

> Write to write. Seems pretty obvious, also weird. What to gain by writing? never anything before. Writing seems always—always—Getting corrected for trying too hard to please the teacher, getting corrected for not trying hard enuf. Frustration, nail biting, sometimes getting carried away making sentences to tell stories, not even true stories, *esp.* not true stories, *that* feels like creating something. Writing just pulls the story out of me. The story lets me be someone else, gives me a disguise.

(A later phase of Benday's writing appears on p. 24.)

If you write on a computer, try this technique for moving forward while freewriting: turn off your computer's monitor, or turn its brightness control all the way down so that the screen is dark. The computer will record what you type but keep it from you and thus prevent you from tinkering with your prose. This **invisible writing** may feel uncomfortable at first, but it can free the mind for very creative results. When you've finished freewriting, simply turn the monitor on or turn up the brightness control to read what you've written, and then save or revise it as appropriate. Later you may be able to transfer some of your freewriting directly into your draft.

〈 CULTURE LANGUAGE 〉 Invisible writing can be especially helpful if you are uneasy writing in standard American English and you tend to worry about errors while writing. The blank computer screen leaves you no choice but to explore ideas without giving attention to the way you are expressing them. If you choose to write with the monitor on, concentrate on *what* you want to say, not *how* you are saying it.

Focused freewriting

Focused freewriting is more concentrated: you start with your question about your subject and answer it without stopping for, say, fifteen minutes or one full page. As in all freewriting, you push to bypass mental blocks and self-consciousness, not debating what to say or editing what you've written. With focused freewriting, though, you let the physical act of writing take you into and around your subject.

An example of focused freewriting can be found in Katy Moreno's journal response to Thomas L. Friedman's "It's a Flat World, After All" (pp. 18–19). Since she already had an idea about Friedman's essay, Moreno was able to start there and expand on the idea.

5 Brainstorming

In **brainstorming**, you focus intently on your subject for a fixed amount of time (say, fifteen minutes), pushing yourself to list every idea and detail that comes to mind. Like freewriting, brainstorming requires turning off your internal editor so that you keep moving ahead instead of looping back over what you have already written to correct it. It makes no difference whether the ideas and details are expressed in phrases or complete sentences. It makes no difference if they seem silly or irrelevant. Just keep pushing. If you are working on a computer, the technique of invisible writing, described opposite, can help you move forward.

Here is an example of brainstorming by a student, Johanna Abrams, responding to the question *What can a summer job teach?*

> summer work teaches—
>
>>   how to look busy while doing nothing
>>   how to avoid the sun in summer
>>   seriously: discipline, budgeting money, value of money
>
> which job? Burger King cashier? baby-sitter? mail-room clerk?
> mail room: how to sort mail into boxes: this is learning??
> how to survive getting fired—humiliation, outrage
> Mrs. King! the mail-room queen as learning experience
> the shock of getting fired: what to tell parents, friends?
> Mrs. K was so rigid—dumb procedures
> Mrs. K's anger, resentment: the disadvantages of being smarter than your boss
> The odd thing about working in an office: a world with its own rules for how
>>   to act
> what Mr. D said about the pecking order—big chick (Mrs. K) pecks on little
>>   chick (me)
> probably lots of Mrs. Ks in offices all over—offices are all barnyards
> Mrs. K a sad person, really—just trying to hold on to her job, preserve her
>>   self-esteem
> a job can beat you down—destroy self-esteem, make you desperate enough to
>>   be mean to other people
> how to preserve/gain self-esteem from work??
> if I'd known about the pecking order, I would have been less show-offy, not so
>>   arrogant

(A later phase of Abrams's writing appears on pp. 35–36.)

When you think you've exhausted the ideas on your topic, you can edit and shape the list into a preliminary outline of your paper (see pp. 34–35). Working on a computer makes this step fairly easy: you can delete weak ideas, expand strong ones, and rearrange items with a few keystrokes. You can also freewrite from the list if you think some items are especially promising and deserve more exploration.

6 | Clustering

Like freewriting and list making, **clustering** draws on free association and rapid, unedited work. But it also emphasizes the *relations* between ideas by combining writing and nonlinear drawing. When clustering, you radiate outward from a center point—your

USING QUESTIONS AND PATTERNS

To help students discover the power of sets of questions or the patterns of development for exploring topics, begin by giving them a list of general subjects—music, sports, guns, multiculturalism, the environment—and then ask them to explore each, looking for limited aspects that might make good topics for essays. Do not encourage students to use either the questions or the patterns in probing the topics. Class discussion can focus on how to limit the topics and can indicate how an audience might respond to them.

Following the discussion, ask students to explore the same topics using either the journalist's questions (2a-7) or the patterns of development (2a-8). Ask students to direct their attention to as many different aspects of the topic as they can and at the same time to suggest ways of developing it and organizing an essay around it. Discussion should focus on differences between the "guided" and "unguided" approaches to developing a topic.

RESOURCES AND IDEAS

On freewriting

Blackburn-Brockman, Elizabeth. "Prewriting, Planning, and Professional Communication." *English Journal* 91.2 (2001): 51–53. Print. Blackburn-Brockman discusses the extensive prewriting strategies of one professional writer and suggests using some of those prewriting activities with students, including analyzing texts and talking informally through ideas, to widen their understanding of prewriting.

Dunn, Patricia. *Talking, Sketching, Moving: Multiple Literacies in the Teaching of Writing.* Portsmouth: Boyton/Cook, 2001. Print. Dunn encourages us to motivate students to write and improve their attitude to writing through pre-writing assignments that include oral and visual presentations.

Elbow, Peter. *Everyone Can Write: Essays Toward a Hopeful Theory of Writing and Teaching Writing.* New York: Oxford UP, 1999. Print. Elbow elaborates on and theorizes about his prominent expressivist ideas, including freewriting.

---. *Writing Without Teachers.* New York: Oxford UP, 1973. Print. In this classic work, Elbow discusses freewriting and other techniques for tapping imagination and creativity during the writing process.

Price, Gayle B. "A Case for a Modern Commonplace Book." *College Composition and Communication* 31.2 (1980): 175–82. Print. This article reviews freewriting and other techniques for helping students generate ideas and tells how students can use a notebook to record ideas.

Reynolds, Mark. "Make Free Writing More Productive." *College Composition and Communication* 39.1 (1988): 81–82. Print. Reynolds offers twenty "questions, activities, and guidelines" for drawing useful ideas and promising topics from the often jumbled material provided by freewriting.

On clustering

Frye, Bob. "Artful Compositions, Corder's 'Laws of Composition,' and the Weekly Letter: Two Approaches to Teaching Invention and Arrangement in Freshman English." *Journal of Teaching Writing* 8 (1989): 1–14. Print. Frye argues that having students write replies to the instructor's weekly letters allows them to experience genuine rhetorical invention rather than experiencing closure, often the product of structure.

Rico, Gabriele Lusser. *Writing the Natural Way.* Los Angeles: Tarcher, 1983. Print. Rico draws on research about brain functions as the basis for advice about strategies—especially clustering—that encourage creativity in expression.

topic. When an idea occurs, you pursue related ideas in a branching structure until they seem exhausted. Then you do the same with other ideas, staying open to connections, continuously branching out or drawing arrows.

The example of clustering below shows how Robert Benday used the technique for ten minutes to expand on the topic of creative writing as a means of disguise, an idea he arrived at through freewriting (see p. 22). Though he ventured into one dead end, Benday also circled into the interesting possibility (at the bottom) that the fiction writer is like a god who forgives himself by creating characters that represent his good and bad qualities.

Clustering

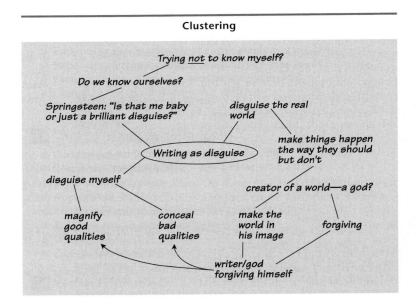

7 | Using the journalist's questions

Asking yourself a set of questions about your subject—and writing out the answers—can help you look at the subject objectively and see fresh possibilities in it. Asking questions can also provide some structure to the development of ideas.

One such set of questions is that posed by a journalist with a story to report:

- Who was involved?
- What happened and what were the results?
- When did it happen?
- Where did it happen?

- Why did it happen?
- How did it happen?

These questions can also be useful in probing an essay subject, especially if you are telling a story or examining causes and effects. (See also the next page.)

8 | Using the patterns of development

The **patterns of development**—such as narration, definition, comparison and contrast, and classification—are ways we think about and understand a vast range of subjects, from our own daily experiences to the most complex scientific theories. They also serve as strategies and patterns for writing about these subjects, as illustrated by the discussions and paragraph-length examples on pages 93–101. You may want to refer to those pages for more information about each pattern.

To see your subject from many angles and open up ideas about it, you can ask the following questions based on the patterns of development. Not all these questions will be productive, but at least a few should open up new possibilities.

How did it happen?

In **narration** you develop the subject as a story, with important events usually arranged chronologically (as they occurred in time): for instance, an exciting basketball game or the steps leading to a war.

How does it look, sound, feel, smell, taste?

In **description** you use sensory details to give a clear impression of a person, place, thing, or feeling, such as a species of animal, a machine, a friend, a building, or an experience.

What are examples of it or reasons for it?

The pattern of **illustration** or **support** suggests development with one or more examples of the subject (one couple's efforts to adopt a child, say, or three states that outlaw Internet gambling) or with the reasons for believing or doing something (three reasons for majoring in English, four reasons for increasing federal aid to college students).

What is it? What does it encompass, and what does it exclude?

These questions lead to **definition:** specifying what the subject is and is not to give a precise sense of its meaning. Abstract terms—such as *justice, friendship,* and *art*—especially need defining (see p. 181).

What are its parts or characteristics?

Using the pattern of **division** or **analysis,** you separate a subject such as a bicycle or a short story into its elements and examine the relations between elements. The first step in critical thinking, analysis is also discussed on pages 147–48.

On heuristics

Kneupper, Charles W. "Revising the Tagmemic Heuristic: Theoretical and Pedagogical Considerations." *College Composition and Communication* 31.2 (1980): 160–68. Print. Kneupper offers a simplified version of the powerful question system introduced by Young, Becker, and Pike in their text, *Rhetoric: Discovery and Change* (New York: Harcourt, 1970).

Washington, Eugene. "WH-Questions in Teaching Composition." *College Composition and Communication* 28.1 (1977): 54–56. Print. Washington suggests using *what, why, where,* and *how* questions to increase density of information in essays and clarify structure.

On patterns of development

D'Angelo, Frank J. *A Conceptual Theory of Rhetoric.* Cambridge: Winthrop, 1975. Print. D'Angelo argues that rhetorical patterns of organization (e.g., analysis, classification, and description) are also patterns of thought and invention and can be used to probe experience as part of the composing process. See also D'Angelo's "Topoi and Form in Composition," *The Territory of Language.* Ed. Donald A. McQuade. Carbondale: Southern Illinois UP, 1986. 114–22. Print.

Hecker, Linda. "Walking, Tinkertoys, and Legos: Using Movement and Manipulatives to Help Students Write." *English Journal* 86.6 (1997): 46–52. Print. Hecker discusses how physical movement and manipulatives can engage students with learning disabilities, helping them to understand language structures and organize their work.

Podis, Leonard A. "Teaching Arrangement: Defining a More Practical Approach." *College Composition and Communication* 31.1 (1980): 197–204. Print. Podis describes a teaching sequence designed to make students aware of the basic principles of organization, and he reviews some standard patterns of arrangement useful for academic and professional writing.

Wilcox, Lance. "Time Lines in the Composing of Narratives: A Graphic Aid to Organization." *The Writing Instructor* 6 (1987): 162–73. Print. Wilcox describes in detail the use of time lines to help develop and organize narrative essays.

EXPLORING THE PATTERNS OF DEVELOPMENT

Divide the class into ten groups. Assign each group one of the patterns of development. Then, provide a single general topic (reality television, action movies, or college students) to the class. Each group must apply their pattern to the topic. Groups should report their findings to the whole class, so students can see how the patterns resulted in varying approaches to one topic.

ROLE-PLAYING

Students often don't know how to respond to readings; role-playing exercises that ask them to pose as book reviewers or participants on a political talk show may help them find an angle to start responding to a reading.

EDITORIAL RESPONSES

Ask students to bring in journal or newspaper articles on controversial topics and work individually or in groups to compose letters of response "to the editor." Students should consult with their groups to determine the appropriate tone and implied journal or newspaper audience for each response.

ANSWERS: EXERCISE 2.1

Individual response.

ANSWERS: EXERCISE 2.2

Individual response.

Exercise 2.3 can be readily transferred to the computer classroom to encourage students to practice generating material on the computer. At the end of the exercise you might ask students to read through their material to develop ideas and to highlight ideas for future revision, but to avoid deleting material. As a take-home assignment or in the following class, students can revise and delete more extensively; they might then present the resulting material to their groups.

What groups or categories can it be sorted into?

Classification involves separating a large group (such as cars) into smaller groups (subcompact, compact, and so on) based on the characteristics of the individual items (the sizes of the cars). Another example: academic, business, personal, literary, and other types of writing.

How is it like, or different from, other things?

With **comparison and contrast** you point out the similarities and differences between ideas, objects, people, places, and so on: the differences between two similar computer systems, for instance, or the similarities between two opposing political candidates.

Is it comparable to something that is in a different class but more familiar to readers?

This question leads to **analogy,** an extended comparison of unlike subjects. Analogy is often used to explain a topic that may be unfamiliar to readers (for instance, the relation of atoms in a molecule) by reference to a familiar topic (two people dancing close together).

Why did it happen, or what results did it have?

With **cause-and-effect analysis,** you explain why something happened or what its consequences were or will be, or both: the causes of cerebral palsy, the effects of a Supreme Court decision, the causes and effects of a gradual change in the climate.

How do you do it, or how does it work?

In **process analysis** you explain how the subject happens (how a plant grows, how a robot works) or how to accomplish it (how to write an essay).

Exercise 2.1 Considering your past work: Developing a topic

In the past how have you generated the ideas for writing? Have you used any of the techniques described on the preceding pages? Have you found the process especially enjoyable or difficult? If some writing tasks were easier than others, what do you think made the difference?

Exercise 2.2 Keeping a journal

If you haven't already started a journal on your own or in response to Exercise 1.1 (pp. 3–4), try to do so now. Every day for at least a week, write for at least fifteen minutes about anything on your mind—or consult the list on page 20 for ideas of what to write about. At the end of the week, write about your experience. What did you like about journal writing? What didn't you like? What did you learn about yourself or the world from the writing? How can you use this knowledge?

Exercise 2.3 Using freewriting, brainstorming, or clustering

If you haven't tried any of them before, experiment with freewriting, brainstorming, or clustering. Continue with the subject you selected in Exercise 1.5 (p. 9), or begin with a new subject. Write or draw for at least ten minutes without stopping to reread and edit. (Try using invisible writing as described on p. 22 if you're freewriting or brainstorming on a computer.) When you finish your experiment, examine what you have written for ideas and relationships that could help you develop the subject. What do you think of the technique you tried? Did you have any difficulties with it? Did it help you loosen up and generate ideas?

Exercise 2.4   Sending an online query

When you have spent some time developing your subject, consider any doubts you may have or any information you still need. Send an online message to your classmates posing your questions and asking for their advice and insights.

Exercise 2.5   Developing your subject

Use at least two of the discovery techniques discussed on the preceding pages to develop the subject you selected in Exercise 1.5 (p. 9). (If you completed Exercise 2.3 above, then use one additional technique.) Later exercises for your essay-in-progress will be based on the ideas you generate in this exercise.

2b   Developing a thesis

Your readers will expect an essay you write to be focused on a central idea, or **thesis,** to which all the essay's paragraphs, all its general statements and specific information, relate. The thesis is the controlling idea, the main point, the conclusion you have drawn about the evidence you have accumulated. It is the answer to the question you have been posing about your subject.

1   Conceiving a thesis statement

A thesis is an idea. Spelling out the idea in a **thesis statement** gives you something concrete to work with. Such a statement, or even the thesis idea itself, probably will not leap fully formed into your head. You may begin with an idea you want to communicate, but you will need to refine that idea to fit the realities of the paper you write. Often you will have to write and rewrite before you come to a conclusion about what you have. For this reason, you may prefer to delay conceiving a thesis statement until you are well into drafting. Instead, you can proceed with a **thesis question** that begins when you try to narrow your subject (pp. 7–9) and sharpens as you discover ideas and information. Either a tentative thesis statement or a thesis question can help you organize your ideas, start drafting, and stay focused when changes inevitably occur during drafting and revision.

ANSWERS: EXERCISE 2.3

Individual response.

ANSWERS: EXERCISE 2.4

Individual response.

ANSWERS: EXERCISE 2.5

Individual response.

As an expression of the thesis, the thesis statement serves four crucial functions and one optional one.

Functions of the thesis statement

- The thesis statement **narrows your subject** to a single, central idea that you want readers to gain from your essay.
- It **claims something specific and significant** about your subject, a claim that requires support.
- It **conveys your purpose**—usually explanation or argument in college writing.
- It **establishes your voice,** suggesting your attitude toward your subject and the role you assume with readers.
- It often concisely **previews the arrangement of ideas,** in which case it can also help you organize your essay.

Here are some examples of thesis questions and answering thesis statements. As assertions, the thesis statements each consist of a topic (usually naming the general subject) and a claim about the topic. Notice how each statement also expresses purpose. Statements 1–3 are **explanatory:** the writers mainly want to explain something to readers, such as how a company survived a scandal. Statements 4–6 are **argumentative:** the authors mainly want to convince readers of something, such as that drivers' use of cell phones should be outlawed. Most of the thesis statements you write in college papers will be either explanatory or argumentative.

Thesis question	Explanatory thesis statement
1. How did Home Inc. survive the scandal over its hiring practices?	After Home Inc.'s hiring practices were exposed in the media, the company avoided a scandal with policy changes and a well-publicized outreach to employees and consumers. [**Topic:** the company. **Claim:** avoided a scandal in two ways.]
2. Why did Abraham Lincoln delay in emancipating the slaves?	Lincoln delayed emancipating any slaves until 1863 because his primary goal was to restore and preserve the Union, with or without slavery. [**Topic:** Lincoln's delay. **Claim:** was caused by his goal of preserving the Union.]
3. What steps can prevent juvenile crime?	Juveniles can be diverted from crime by active learning programs, full-time sports, and intervention by mentors and role models. [**Topic:** juveniles. **Claim:** can be diverted from crime in three ways.]

IMPLICIT THESIS VERSUS EXPLICIT THESIS

Students need to understand that all good writing has a controlling idea (an implied thesis) but that some good writing doesn't have an explicit thesis. Asking students to look for theses in various kinds of writing (from textbooks to novels to travel articles to junk mail) is one way of showing them that a writer must decide whether to use an explicit thesis based on his or her purpose and audience.

Thesis question	Argumentative thesis statement
4. Why should drivers' use of cell phones be banned?	Drivers' use of cell phones should be outlawed because people who talk and drive at the same time cause accidents. [**Topic:** drivers' use of cell phones. **Claim:** should be outlawed because it causes accidents.]
5. Which college students should be entitled to federal aid?	As an investment in its own economy, the federal government should provide a tuition grant to any college student who qualifies academically. [**Topic:** federal aid. **Claim:** should be provided to any college student who qualifies academically.]
6. Why should strip-mining be controlled?	Strip-mining should be tightly controlled in this region to reduce its pollution of water resources, its destruction of the land, and its devastating effects on people's lives. [**Topic:** strip-mining. **Claim:** should be tightly controlled for three reasons.]

Often the thesis statement predicts the organization of the essay that will follow, as statements 1, 3, and 6 do. For example, the essay that followed from statement 3 had three main points: active learning programs, full-time sports, and mentors and role models. Many students prefer this type of thesis statement because it helps them organize their writing and keep on track during drafting.

CULTURE · LANGUAGE In some cultures it is considered rude or unnecessary for a writer to state his or her main idea outright or to state it near the beginning. When writing in American schools or workplaces, you can assume that your readers expect a clear and early idea of what you think.

2 Drafting and revising a thesis statement

To draft a thesis statement, read over your notes and mark words, phrases, or sentences that stand out as central. Consider your question about your subject. If you have sharpened the question as you generated ideas and information, answering it can get you started.

Question	Why did Lincoln delay in emancipating the slaves?
Answer	Lincoln's goal was primarily to restore and preserve the Union.
Question	To what extent do I agree or disagree with Friedman's argument that students today need better technical training to compete in the global job market?
Answer	Based on my mother's experience of having her job outsourced, I disagree with Friedman that better technical training will necessarily give students the skills they need to compete.

ORAL PROGRESS REPORTS

Have students report orally to the class or to their peer writing groups on topics and thesis statements for a coming paper. Giving an oral presentation forces students to focus their ideas and adopt a stance. As they speak, moreover, students may sense difficulties with the topic or thesis. Comments and questions from classmates can help identify strengths and weaknesses and suggest an appropriate tone for the essay.

CONDENSING THE ARGUMENT

Often the exercise of condensing the main ideas of a paper in a separate forum can help writers recognize and articulate their thesis. Ask students to set their paper-in-progress aside and write a short (three sentences to one paragraph) abstract summarizing its central argument.

STUDENT MODELS

You may wish to copy effective thesis statements from student papers to use in class discussion or small-group work. The statements will provide positive models and may suggest topics for future essays. You can vary this exercise by copying ineffective statements and discussing how they may be revised. Be sure to keep the discussion of ineffective statements positive in tone, however.

SUPPLYING AN OMITTED THESIS STATEMENT

Ask students to read their papers to the class or to a peer group, deliberately leaving out the thesis statement. Ask the other students to supply a thesis for the essay. If the original thesis and the one supplied by the students match, fine. If not, the thesis a student has chosen may be inappropriate for the paper and the discussion that follows can suggest possible revisions.

COLLABORATIVE LEARNING

AGREEMENT ON THESIS

Ask students to read an essay from a collection or a fellow student's paper and then to state its thesis in their own words. Divide students into small groups and ask the group members to come up with a thesis statement together. Next have the groups try to identify a thesis statement in the essay. If the essay has an explicit thesis statement, ask if they consider it effective or if the thesis statement they produced would be more effective. If the thesis is implicit, ask students whether or not the essay would benefit from an explicit thesis statement.

The next step is to spell out the answer in a sentence that names the topic and makes a claim about it. Creating this sentence may require several drafts.

Katy Moreno went through a common process in developing her thesis statement on the global job market. She first answered her starting question, as shown in the second pair of examples on the previous page. Then she tried a statement derived from her answer:

> The outsourcing of my mother's job proves that Thomas L. Friedman's advice to improve students' technical training is too narrow.

This statement gave Moreno a sense of direction, and she used it in her first draft (p. 49). At that point, however, she saw that the statement put too little emphasis on her starting topic (*technical training*) and overstated her disagreement with Friedman (*proves . . . is too narrow*). In addition, a reader's comment showed Moreno that her claim wasn't specific: *too narrow* for what? In her first revision, Moreno tried to emphasize her intended subject:

> Technical training by itself . . .

Then she worked on her claim:

> . . . can be too narrow to produce the communicators and problem solvers needed by contemporary businesses.

This statement clarified the claim (*can be too narrow to produce . . .*) and said why the subject was significant (. . . *communicators and problem solvers needed by contemporary businesses*). However, Moreno had dropped her mother's experience of losing her job to outsourcing, which was a key point in her response to Friedman's essay. Moreno tried again, adding her mother's experience:

> My mother's experience of having her job outsourced showed that technical training by itself can be too narrow to produce the communicators and problem solvers needed by contemporary businesses.

For her final revision, Moreno responded to another reader's suggestion that she state her point of disagreement with Friedman more clearly:

> My mother's experience of having her job outsourced taught a lesson that Thomas L. Friedman overlooks: technical training by itself can be too narrow to produce the communicators and problem solvers needed by contemporary businesses.

Often you must deliberately consider your audience as you draft a thesis statement. One student, Ben Nelson, was writing an argument for more student parking on campus. He arrived fairly easily at his initial claim:

Most students who commute to campus must drive to school, and they need more places to park.

However, to persuade school administrators to take action, Nelson realized that he needed to focus on them as his audience and strengthen his voice:

The school must provide enough parking spaces to accommodate the many students who drive to school and to protect all students from otherwise dangerous traffic congestion.

As you draft and revise your thesis statement over the course of the writing process, test it with the following questions:

Checklist for revising the thesis statement

- How well does the **subject** of your statement capture the subject of your paper?
- What **claim** does your statement make about your subject?
- What is the **significance** of the claim? How does it answer "So what?" and convey your purpose?
- How can the claim be **limited** or made more **specific**? Does it state a single idea and clarify the boundaries of the idea?
- How **unified** is the statement? How does each word and phrase contribute to a single idea?
- How well does the statement convey your **voice**?

Here are other examples of thesis statements revised to meet these requirements:

Original	Revised
Seat belts can save lives, but now carmakers are installing air bags. [Not unified: how do the two parts of the sentence relate?]	If drivers had used lifesaving seat belts more often, carmakers might not have needed to install air bags.
This new product brought in over $300,000 last year. [A statement of fact, not a claim about the product: what is significant about the product's success?]	This new product succeeded because of its innovative marketing campaign, including widespread press coverage, in-store entertainment, and a consumer newsletter.
People should not go on fad diets. [A vague statement that needs limiting with one or more reasons: what's wrong with fad diets?]	Fad diets can be dangerous when they deprive the body of essential nutrients or rely excessively on potentially harmful foods.

ANSWERS: EXERCISE 2.6

1. The statement lacks unity because the two halves do not seem to relate to each other.
 Possible revision: We should channel our natural feelings of aggression toward constructive rather than destructive ends.
2. The statement needs to be more specific and significant: How is Islam misunderstood? So what?
 Possible revision: Americans' misconceptions about Islam—especially that it is fanatical and oppressive—contribute to global instability.
3. The statement needs to be more specific: How do manners work as "social glue"?
 Possible revision: Manners are a kind of social glue, binding people together by regulating the interactions of acquaintances and strangers alike.
4. Good thesis statement: significant, specific, and unified.
5. The statement simply states a fact.
 Possible revision: The poem depicts motherhood as a saintly calling.

ANSWERS: EXERCISE 2.7

Individual response.

ANSWERS: EXERCISE 2.8

Individual response.

RESOURCES AND IDEAS

Liszka, Thomas R. "Formulating a Thesis for Essays Employing Comparison." *College Composition and Communication* 38.4 (1987): 474–77. Print. Liszka offers a method that helps students to generate theses and guides them in organizing and developing their essays; the method appears to be adaptable to various kinds of essays.

Original	Revised
Televised sports are different from live sports. [A general statement: how are they different, and why is the difference significant?]	Although television cannot transmit all the excitement of a live game, its close-ups and slow-motion replays reveal much about the players and the strategy of the game.
Television viewing can reduce loneliness, cause laughter, and teach children. [Lacks voice: what is the writer's attitude toward the subject?]	Despite its many faults, television has at least one strong virtue: it provides replacement voices that can ease loneliness, spark healthful laughter, and even educate young children.

Note You may sometimes need more than one sentence for your thesis statement, particularly if it requires some buildup:

> Modern English, especially written English, is full of bad habits that interfere with clear thinking. Getting rid of these habits is a first step to political regeneration. —Adapted from George Orwell, "Politics and the English Language"

However, don't use this leeway to produce a wordy, general, or disunified statement. The two (or more) sentences must build on each other, and the final sentence must present the key assertion of your paper.

Exercise 2.6 Evaluating thesis statements
Evaluate the following thesis statements, considering whether each one is sufficiently significant, specific, and unified. Rewrite the statements as necessary to meet these goals.

1. Aggression usually leads to violence, injury, and even death, and we should use it constructively.
2. The religion of Islam is widely misunderstood in the United States.
3. Manners are a kind of social glue.
4. One episode of a radio talk show amply illustrates both the appeal of such shows and their silliness.
5. The poem is about motherhood.

Exercise 2.7 Considering your past work: Developing a thesis
Have you been aware in the past of focusing your essays on a central idea, or thesis? Have you found it more efficient to try to pin down your idea early or to let it evolve during drafting? To what extent has a thesis helped or hindered you in shaping your draft?

Exercise 2.8 Drafting and revising your own thesis statement
Continuing from Exercise 2.5 (p. 27), write a thesis statement for your essay-in-progress. As much as possible at this point, your statement should be significant, specific, and unified, and it should convey your attitude toward your subject.

2c | Organizing ideas

An effective essay has a recognizable shape—an arrangement of parts that guides readers, helping them see how ideas and details relate to each other and contribute to the whole. You may sometimes let an effective organization emerge over one or more drafts. But many writers find that organizing ideas to some extent before drafting can provide a helpful sense of direction, as a map can help a driver negotiate a half-familiar system of roads. If you feel uncertain about the course your essay should follow or have a complicated topic with many parts, devising a shape for your material can clarify your options.

Before you begin organizing your material, look over all the writing you've done so far—freewriting, notes from reading, whatever. Either on paper or on a computer, pull together a master list of all the ideas and details you think you might want to include. You can add to or subtract from the list as you think about shape.

1 | Distinguishing the general and the specific

To organize material for an essay, you need to distinguish general and specific ideas and see the relations between ideas. **General** and **specific** refer to the number of instances or objects included in a group signified by a word. The "ladder" below illustrates a general-to-specific hierarchy.

Most general

life form
plant
flowering plant
rose
American Beauty rose
Uncle Dan's prize-winning American Beauty rose

Most specific

Here are some tips for arranging the ideas in your preliminary writing:

- **Underline, boldface, or circle the most general ideas.** These are the ideas that offer the main support for your thesis statement. They will be more general than the evidence that in turn supports them.
- **Make connections between each general idea and the more specific details that support it.** On paper, start with a fresh sheet, write each general idea down with space beneath it, and add specific information in the appropriate spaces. On a

computer, rearrange supporting information under more general points. Your word processor may include a Comment function that allows you to add notes about connections.

- **Respect the meanings of ideas.** Think through the implications of ideas as you sort them. Otherwise, your hierarchies could become jumbled, with *rose*, for instance, illogically subordinated to *animal*, or *life form* somehow subordinated to *rose*.
- **Remove information that doesn't fit.** If you worry about losing deleted information, transfer the notes to a separate sheet of paper or word-processing file.
- **Fill holes where support seems skimpy.** If you recognize a hole but don't know what to fill it with, try using a discovery technique such as freewriting or clustering, or go back to your research sources.
- **Experiment with various arrangements of general ideas and supporting information.** Seek an order that presents your material clearly and logically. On paper, you can cut the master list apart and paste or tape each general idea and its support on a separate piece of paper. Then try different orders for the pages. On a computer, first save the master list and duplicate it. To move material around, select a block of text and either copy and then paste it where you want it or (a little quicker) drag the selected text to where you want it.

2 | Choosing an organizing tool

Some writers view outlines as chores and straitjackets, but they need not be dull or confining. There are different kinds of outlines, some more flexible than others. All of them can enlarge and clarify your thinking, showing you patterns of general and specific, suggesting proportions, and highlighting gaps or overlaps in coverage.

Many writers use outlines not only before but also after drafting—to check the underlying structure of the draft when revising it (see p. 52). No matter when it's made, though, an outline can be changed to reflect changes in your thinking. View any outline you make as a tentative sketch, not as a fixed paint-by-numbers diagram.

A scratch or informal outline

For many essays, especially those with a fairly straightforward structure, a simple listing of ideas and perhaps their support may provide adequate direction for your writing.

A **scratch outline** lists the key points of the paper in the order they will be covered. Here is Katy Moreno's scratch outline for her essay on the global job market:

Thesis statement

My mother's experience of having her job outsourced taught a lesson that Thomas L. Friedman overlooks: technical training by itself can be too narrow to produce the communicators and problem solvers needed by contemporary businesses.

Scratch outline

Mom's outsourcing experience
  Excellent tech skills
  Salary too high compared to overseas tech workers
  Lack of planning + communication skills, unlike managers who kept jobs

Well-rounded education to protect vs. outsourcing
  Tech training, as Friedman says
  Also, experience in communication, problem solving, other management
    skills

Moreno put more into this outline than its simplicity might imply, not only working out an order for her ideas but also sketching their implications.

An **informal outline** is usually more detailed than a scratch outline, including key general points and the specific evidence for them. A student's informal outline appears below.

Thesis statement

After Home Inc.'s hiring practices were exposed in the media, the company avoided a scandal with policy changes and a well-publicized outreach to employees and consumers.

Informal outline

Background on scandal
  Previous hiring practices
  Media exposure and public response (brief)

Policy changes
  Application forms
  Interviewing procedures
  Training of personnel

Outreach to employees
  Signs and letters
  Meetings and workshops

Outreach to consumers
  Press conference
  Store signs
  Advertising—print and radio

A tree diagram

In a **tree diagram,** ideas and details branch out in increasing specificity. Like any outline, the diagram can warn of gaps, overlaps, and digressions. But unlike more linear outlines, it can be supplemented and extended indefinitely, so it is easy to alter for new ideas and arrangements discovered during drafting and revision.

Below is a tree diagram by Johanna Abrams, based on her earlier brainstorming about a summer job (p. 23) and the following thesis statement:

Thesis statement

Two months working in a large government agency taught me that an office's pecking order should be respected.

Tree diagram

Each main part of the four-part diagram represents a different general idea about the summer-job experience. Within each part, information grows more specific as it branches downward.

A tree diagram or other visual map can be especially useful for planning a project for the Web. The diagram can help you lay out the organization of your project and its links and later can serve as a site map for your readers. (For more on composing for the Web, see pp. 834–40.)

A formal outline

For complex topics requiring complex arrangements of ideas and support, you may want or be required to construct a **formal outline.** More rigidly arranged and more detailed than other outlines, a formal outline not only lays out main ideas and their support but also shows the relative importance of all the essay's elements and how they connect with one another.

Note Because of its structure, a formal outline can be an excellent tool for planning a revision. For instance, you might use an outline to check that your organization is logical or to see how a new section might fit in. Katy Moreno created the following formal outline to plan expansions and other changes that were suggested by readers of her first draft.

Thesis statement

My mother's experience of having her job outsourced taught a lesson that Thomas L. Friedman overlooks: technical training by itself can be too narrow to produce the communicators and problem solvers needed by contemporary businesses.

Formal outline

I. Summary of Friedman's article
   A. Reasons for outsourcing
      1. Improved technology and access
      2. Well-educated workers
      3. Productive workers
      4. Lower wages
   B. Need for improved technical training in US
II. Mother's experience
   A. Outsourcing of job
      1. Mother's education, experience, performance
      2. Employer's cost savings
   B. Retention of managers' jobs
      1. Planning skills
      2. Communication skills
III. Conclusions about ideal education
   A. Needs of US businesses
      1. Technical skills
      2. Management skills
         a. Communication
         b. Problem solving
         c. Versatility
   B. Personal goals
      1. Technical training
      2. English and history courses for management skills

Moreno's outline illustrates several principles of outlining that can help ensure completeness, balance, and clear relationships. (These principles largely depend on distinguishing between the general and the specific. See pp. 33–34.)

- **All the outline's parts are systematically indented and labeled.** Roman numerals (I, II) label primary divisions of the essay, followed by capital letters (A, B) for secondary divisions, Arabic numerals (1, 2) for principal supporting points, and

PURPOSE OUTLINES

Some students have trouble maintaining unity of purpose and coherent organization even after they have outlined an essay because the outline describes the content of the essay but does not indicate the function of each part. To help students overcome this problem, ask them to add a statement of purpose to each major section of their outlines and to indicate how the section will carry out the purpose of the paper, as in this example:

> In this section I plan to explain how much money industries lose by failing to treat industrial waste to recover precious metals like chromium, gold, silver, and platinum. This will be the second of the three little-known costs of pollution that my thesis statement promises the paper will discuss.

Statements of purpose can alert students to potential problems in the organization or unity of an essay, and they can provide instructors with a quick way to spot the problems. Some instructors even ask students to submit "purpose outlines" in place of formal outlines:

> In this section of the paper, I plan to show that there is a real need for this university to provide more funds for the library. To support my point, I plan to explore three serious effects of underfunding—lack of basic reference materials, lack of staff to shelve books properly and check for missing volumes, and poor maintenance of the library building.

USING VISUAL CUES

Some students find it handy to write their purpose statement or thesis on squares of stick-on paper and post these on their drafts, over their desks, or on the monitor of their computers in order to keep these ideas clearly in mind.

Principles of the formal outline

- Labels and indentions indicate order and relative importance.
- Sections and subsections reflect logical relationships.
- Topics of equal generality appear in parallel headings.
- Each subdivision has at least two parts.
- Headings are expressed in parallel grammatical form.
- The introduction and conclusion may be omitted (though not, of course, from the essay).

small letters (a, b) for details. Each succeeding level contains more specific information than the one before it.

- **The outline divides the material into several groups.** A list like the one following needs tighter, more logical groups to show the relationships between A and B and between C and D. (Compare this example with part III of Moreno's actual outline.)

  III. Conclusions about ideal education
     A. Business needs for technical skills
     B. Needs for management skills such as communication and problem solving
     C. Personal goal of technical training
     D. Additional courses for management skills

- **Within each part of the outline, distinct topics of equal generality appear in parallel headings,** with the same indention and numbering or lettering. In the following example, points 3, 4, and 5 are more specific than point 2, not equally general, so they should appear as subheadings a, b, and c under it. (See section III.A of Moreno's outline.)

  A. Needs of US businesses
     1. Technical skills
     2. Management skills
     3. Communication
     4. Problem solving
     5. Versatility

- **All subdivided headings in the outline break into at least two parts** because a topic cannot logically be divided into only one part. The following example violates this principle:

  B. Personal goals
     1. Technical training along with other courses for management skills

Any single subdivision should be matched with another subdivision (as in section III.B of Moreno's actual outline), combined with the heading above it, or rechecked for its relevance to the heading above it.

- **All headings are expressed in parallel grammatical form** (see pp. 398–402 on parallelism). Moreno's is a **topic outline,** in which the headings consist of a noun (*summary, reasons, technology and access,* and the like) with modifiers (*of Friedman's essay, improved, well-educated,* and the like). In a **sentence outline** all headings are expressed as full sentences, as in the following rewrite of part III.A of Moreno's outline.

> III. Friedman's article and my mother's experience lead me to conclusions about the ideal education.
>   A. US businesses have dual needs for the jobs they keep here.
>   1. They need employees with technical training.
>   2. They need employees with management skills.

See pages 694–95 for a complete sentence outline.

- **The outline covers only the body of the essay, omitting the introduction and the conclusion.** The beginning and the ending are important in the essay itself, but you need not include them in the outline unless you are required to do so or you anticipate special problems with their organization.

3 | Choosing a structure

Introduction, body, and conclusion

Most essays share a basic shape:

- **The** *introduction,* **usually a paragraph or two, draws readers into the world of the essay.** At a minimum, it announces and clarifies the topic. Often it ends with the thesis statement, making a commitment that the rest of the essay delivers on. (See pp. 104–07 for more on introductions.)

- **The** *body* **of the essay develops the thesis and thus fulfills the commitment of the introduction.** The paragraphs in the body develop the general points that support the thesis—the items that would be labeled with Roman numerals and capital letters in a formal outline like the one on page 37. These general points are like the legs of a table supporting the top, the thesis. Each general point may take a paragraph or more, with the bulk of the content providing the details, examples, and reasons (the wood of the table) to support the general point and thus the thesis.

- **The** *conclusion* **gives readers something to take away from the essay**—a summary of ideas, for instance, or a suggested course of action. (See pp. 107–09 for more on conclusions.)

CULTURE LANGUAGE

WRITING PATTERNS

In some cultures, expository writing patterns are circular rather than linear: students will repeat or restate the topic sentence before going on to the next topic. As a result, students seem to be "writing in circles" when they are simply following the pattern they have been taught. Explain to students that in American expository writing development is linear; that transitions, not restated topics, link ideas together in a paper; and that the conclusion is the point at which ideas are restated or summarized.

> I. Introduction with thesis
>   A. Idea 1
>   1. Support
>   B. Idea 2 (with transition)
>   1. Support
> II. Conclusion
>   A. Summarize ideas
>   B. Restate thesis in a fresh way

COMPUTER ACTIVITY

IDENTIFYING PATTERNS OF ORGANIZATION

Find several Web sites that convey information using different patterns of organization, such as a timeline describing a historical event or a site that teaches readers how to accomplish a specific task. Have students review the sites and discuss how the pattern of organization supports the purpose, audience, and thesis of the work. How might the emphasis of the piece been different if another pattern of organization had been used? You could even ask students to rearrange the pieces to fit another pattern of organization, such as changing the chronological historical piece into a spatial or increasing importance organizational pattern. How does the new organizational pattern affect the purpose, audience, or thesis?

This basic shape applies mainly to traditional essays. A composition for the Web probably will have a more flexible structure and will lack a formal conclusion. See pages 834–40 for more on composing for the Web.

CULTURE LANGUAGE If you are not used to reading and writing American academic prose, its pattern of introduction-body-conclusion and the particular schemes discussed below may seem unfamiliar. For instance, instead of introductions that focus quickly on the topic and thesis, you may be used to openings that establish personal connections with readers or that approach the thesis indirectly. And instead of body paragraphs that first emphasize general points and then support those points with specific evidence, you may be used to general statements without support (because writers can assume that readers will supply the evidence themselves) or to evidence without explanation (because writers can assume that readers will infer the general points themselves). When writing American academic prose, you need to take into account readers' expectations for directness and for the statement and support of general points.

Organizing the body by space or time

Two organizational schemes—spatial and chronological—grow naturally out of the topic. A **spatial organization** is especially appropriate for essays that describe a place, an object, or a person. Following the way people normally survey something, you move through space from a chosen starting point to other features of the subject. Describing a building, for instance, you might begin with an impression of the whole, then scan exterior details from top to bottom, and then describe interior spaces.

A **chronological organization** reports events as they occurred in time, usually from first to last. This pattern, like spatial organization, corresponds to readers' own experiences and expectations. It suits an essay in which you do one of the following:

- **Recount a sequence of events,** such as a championship baseball game or the Battle of Gettysburg.
- **Explain a process from beginning to end**—for instance, how to run a marathon or how a tree converts carbon dioxide to oxygen.
- **Explain the causes that led to an effect,** such as the lobbying that helped to push a bill through the legislature. Alternatively, explain how a cause, such as a flood or a book, had multiple effects.
- **Tell a story about yourself or someone else.**
- **Provide background**—for instance, the making of a film you are analyzing or the procedure used in an experiment you are reporting.

Schemes for organizing ideas in an essay

- Space
- Time
- Emphasis

General to specific	Increasing importance (climax)
Specific to general	Decreasing familiarity
Problem-solution	Increasing complexity

Organizing the body for emphasis

Some organizational schemes must be imposed on ideas and information to aid readers' understanding and achieve a desired emphasis.

General to specific

Two ways of organizing essays depend on the distinction between the general and the specific, discussed on pages 33–34. The **general-to-specific scheme** is common in expository and argumentative essays that start with a general discussion of the main points and then proceed to specific examples, facts, or other evidence. The following thesis statement forecasts a general-to-specific organization:

> As an investment in its own economy, the United States should provide a tuition grant to any college student who qualifies academically.

The body of the essay might first elaborate on the basic argument and then provide the supporting data.

Specific to general

Sometimes you may anticipate that readers will not appreciate or agree with your general ideas before they see the support for them—for instance, in an expository essay that presents a unique way of looking at common experience, or in an argumentative essay that takes an unpopular view. In these cases a **specific-to-general scheme** can arouse readers' interest in specific examples or other evidence, letting the evidence build to statements of more general ideas. The following thesis statement could be developed in this way:

> Although most of us are unaware of the public relations campaigns directed at us, they can significantly affect the way we think and live.

The writer might devote most of the essay to a single specific example of a public relations campaign and then explain more generally how the example typifies public relations campaigns.

RESOURCES AND IDEAS

On organizational strategies

Elbow, Peter. "The Music of Form: Rethinking Organization in Writing." *College Composition and Communication* 57.4 (2006): 620–66. Print. Elbow argues that traditional organizational methods implicitly privilege space over time, and he suggests new methods of organizing that consider time and space differently.

Lotto, Edward. "Utterance and Text in Freshman English." *College English* 51.7 (1989): 677–87. Print. Lotto analyzes the differences between spoken and written language as they relate to the difficulties students have in supporting generalizations with concrete examples. He makes suggestions for helping students become aware of text and concrete expression.

Perdue, Virginia. "The Politics of Teaching Detail." *Rhetoric Review* 8.2 (1990): 280–88. Print. Perdue provides methods for using detail to arrive at broader thoughts in the composing process.

Walvoord, Barbara, Virginia Johnson Anderson, John R. Breihan, Lucille Parkinson McCarthy, Susan Miller Robinson, and A. Kimbrough Sherman. "Functions of Outlining Among College Students in Four Disciplines." *Research in the Teaching of English* 29.4 (1995): 390–421. Print. The authors demonstrate the varying functions served by outlining across the disciplines and explore the strategies that students use in different situations.

On unity and coherence

Duncan, Mike. "Whatever Happened to the Paragraph?" *College English* 69.5 (2007): 470–95. Print. Duncan traces the rise and decline of paragraph theory in composition studies. He calls for compositionists to return to studying the paragraph to provide new terminology for teachers and to perform empirical research on the teaching of paragraphs.

Sloan, Gary. "The Frequency of Transitional Markers in Discursive Prose." *College English* 46.2 (1984): 158–79. Print. Sloan shows how infrequently explicit transition markers are used by either professional or student writers.

Smith, Rochelle. "Paragraphing for Coherence: Writing as Implied Dialogue." *College*

Problem-solution

Many arguments use a **problem-solution scheme:** first outline a problem that needs solving; then propose a solution. (If the solution involves steps toward a goal, it may be arranged chronologically.) The following thesis statement announces a problem-solution paper:

> To improve response time and quality, the customer service department should add one part-time staffer and retrain three others in the new systems.

Climax

A common scheme in both explanations and arguments is the **climactic organization,** in which ideas unfold in order of increasing drama or importance to a climax. For example, the following thesis statement lists three effects of strip-mining in order of their increasing severity, and the essay would cover them in the same order:

> Strip-mining should be tightly controlled in this region to reduce its pollution of water resources, its destruction of the land, and its devastating effects on people's lives.

As this example suggests, the climactic organization works well in arguments because it leaves readers with the most important point freshest in their minds. In exposition such an arrangement can create suspense and thus hold readers' attention.

Familiarity or complexity

Expository essays can also be arranged to take account of readers' knowledge of the subject. An essay on the effects of air pollution might proceed from **most familiar to least familiar**—from effects readers are likely to know to ones they may not know. Similarly, an explanation of animals' nervous systems might proceed from **simplest to most complex,** so that the explanation of each nervous system provides a basis for readers to understand the more difficult one following.

4 | Checking for unity and coherence

In conceiving your organization and writing your essay, you should be aware of two qualities of effective writing that relate to organization: unity and coherence. When you perceive that someone's writing "flows well," you are probably appreciating these two qualities. An essay has **unity** if all its parts relate to and support the thesis statement. Check for unity with these questions:

- Is each main section relevant to the main idea (thesis) of the essay?

■ Within main sections, does each example or detail support the principal idea of that section?

An essay has **coherence** if readers can see the relations among parts and move easily from one thought to the next. Check for coherence with these questions:

■ Do the ideas follow in a clear sequence?
■ Are the parts of the essay logically connected?
■ Are the connections clear and smooth?

A unified and coherent outline will not necessarily guide you to a unified and coherent essay because so much can change during drafting. Thus you shouldn't be too hard on your outline, in case a seemingly wayward idea proves useful. But do cut obvious digressions and rearrange material that clearly needs moving.

Sample essay

The following essay illustrates some ways of achieving unity and coherence (highlighted in the annotations).

A Picture of Hyperactivity

A hyperactive committee member can contribute to efficiency. A hyperactive salesperson can contribute to profits. When children are hyperactive, though, people—even parents—may wish they had never been born. A collage of those who must cope with hyperactivity in children is a picture of frustration, anger, and loss.

> Introduction establishing subject of essay

> Thesis statement

The first part of the collage is the doctors. In their terminology, the word *hyperactivity* has been replaced by *ADHD*, attention-deficit hyperactivity disorder. They apply the term to children who are abnormally or excessively busy. But doctors do not fully understand the problem and thus differ over how to treat it. Some recommend a special diet, others recommend behavior-modifying drugs, and still others, who do not consider ADHD a medical problem, recommend psychotherapy. The result is a merry-go-round of tests, confusion, and frustration for the children and their parents.

> Paragraph idea, linked to thesis statement

> Paragraph developed with evidence supporting its idea

As the mother of an ADHD child, I can say what the disorder means to the parents who form the second part of the collage. It means worry that is deep and enduring. It means despair that is a constant companion. It means a mixture of frustration, guilt, and anger. And finally, since there are times when parents' anger goes out of control and threatens the children, it means self-loathing.

> Paragraph idea, linked to thesis statement

> Paragraph developed with evidence supporting its idea

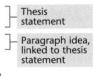

English 46.1 (1984): 8–21. Print. Smith uses reader-response theory and the notion of author-reader dialogue to improve paragraph cohesion.

Witte, Stephen P., and Lester Faigley. "Coherence, Cohesion, and Writing Quality." *College Composition and Communication* 32.2 (1981): 189–204. Print. Students need to learn the features of coherence that extend across sentence boundaries; the article stresses ways to make them aware of coherence strategies.

MODELS OF STUDENT WRITING

While "A Picture of Hyperactivity" is included here for its ways of achieving unity and coherence, its argument and tone are also worthy of consideration. If your students have had any experience with ADHD themselves, they may have a lot to say about the argument of this essay. If they knew nothing about ADHD before reading Linda Devereaux's essay, they might want to do additional research about learning disabilities. You might also want to ask your students to discuss how well the emotional tone of the piece advances its argument, and this might lead to a more general discussion of how to write about emotionally laden topics.

ANSWERS: EXERCISES 2.9 & 2.10

Possible answer

I. In the past, professional soccer could not get a foothold in the United States because of poor TV coverage and lack of financial backing.

  A. Professional soccer tried but could not get a foothold in the United States. [new general idea]

    1. Isolated events such as the US's hosting of the World Cup in 1994 greatly increased American interest in soccer.

    2. Past American interest in soccer quickly died down.

  B. In the United States the success of a sport depends largely on its ability to attract huge TV audiences.

    1. Soccer was not often presented on US television.

    2. Potential fans did not have a chance to see soccer games.

  C. Failures like that of the start-up North American Soccer League made potential backers wary of new ventures.

II. Recently, the outlook for professional soccer has changed dramatically.

  A. Professional soccer has attracted both TV audiences and financial backing. [new general idea]

    1. The US television audience for soccer's 2007 World Cup final was larger than the average US television audience for baseball's World Series the same year.

    2. Investors have poured hundreds of millions of dollars into Major League Soccer, the top US professional league.

    3. Many of Major League Soccer's games are well attended, and some of its teams are making a profit.

  B. The growing Hispanic population in the United States could help soccer grow as well.

    1. In the countries of South and Latin America, soccer is the favorite sport.

    2. In 2007 soccer's World Cup final was broadcast on ABC and on Spanish-language Univision.

Transition

Paragraph idea, linked to thesis statement

Paragraph developed with evidence supporting its idea

The weight of ADHD, however, does not rest on the doctors and parents. The darkest part of the collage belongs to the children. From early childhood they may be dragged from doctor to doctor, attached to machines, medicated until they feel numb, and tested or discussed by physicians, teachers, neighbors, and strangers on the street. They may be highly intelligent, but they'll still do poorly in school because of their short attention spans. Their playmates dislike them because of their temper and their unwillingness to follow rules. Even their pets mistrust them because of their erratic behavior. As time goes on, the children see their parents more and more in tears and anger, and they know they are the cause.

Conclusion echoing thesis statement, summarizing, and looking ahead

The collage is complete, and it is dark and somber. *ADHD,* as applied to children, is a term with uncertain, unattractive, and bitter associations. The picture does have one bright spot, however, for inside every ADHD child is a lovely, trusting, calm person waiting to be recognized.

—Linda Devereaux (student)

Unity and coherence within paragraphs

The unity and coherence of writing begin in its paragraphs, so the two concepts are treated in greater detail in Chapter 4. You may want to consult several sections in particular before you begin drafting:

- **The topic sentence and unity** (pp. 74–77)
- **Transitions and coherence** (pp. 79–90, 109–10)
- **Linking paragraphs in the essay** (p. 111)

Unity and coherence on the Web

Unity and coherence may seem unimportant in compositions for the Web, in which entire documents are linked to each other so that it's easy to move among them. However, precisely because the Web is such a fluid medium, you risk losing or confusing your readers if you don't consider unity and coherence. Your project should have a clear purpose and clear ideas relating to that purpose, and the connections between ideas should be spelled out to orient readers. (For more on composing for the Web, see pp. 834–40.)

Exercise 2.9　Organizing ideas

The following list of ideas was extracted by a student from freewriting he did for a brief paper on soccer in the United States. Using his thesis statement as a guide, pick out the general ideas and arrange the relevant specific points under them. In some cases you may have to infer general ideas to cover specific points in the list.

Thesis statement

Although its growth in the United States has been slow and halting, professional soccer may finally be poised to become a major American sport.

List of ideas

In countries of South and Latin America, soccer is the favorite sport.

In the United States the success of a sport depends largely on its ability to attract huge TV audiences.

Soccer was not often presented on US television.

In 2007 soccer's World Cup final was broadcast on ABC and on Spanish-language Univision.

In the past, professional soccer could not get a foothold in the United States because of poor TV coverage and lack of financial backing.

The growing Hispanic population in the United States could help soccer grow as well.

Investors have poured hundreds of millions of dollars into Major League Soccer, the top US professional league.

Potential fans did not have a chance to see soccer games.

Failures like that of the start-up North American Soccer League made potential backers wary of new ventures.

Recently, the outlook for professional soccer has changed dramatically.

Isolated events such as the US's hosting of the World Cup in 1994 greatly increased American interest in soccer.

The US television audience for soccer's 2007 World Cup final was larger than the average US television audience for baseball's World Series the same year.

Past American interest in soccer quickly died down.

Many of Major League Soccer's games are well attended, and some of its teams are making a profit.

Exercise 2.10 Creating a formal outline

Use your arrangement of general ideas and specific points from Exercise 2.9 as the basis for a formal topic or sentence outline. Follow the principles given on pages 37–39.

Exercise 2.11 Considering your past work: Organizing ideas

What has been your experience with organizing your writing? Many writers find it difficult. If you do, too, can you say why? What kinds of outlines or other organizing tools have you used? Which have been helpful and which have not?

Exercise 2.12 Organizing your own essay

Continuing from Exercise 2.8 (p. 32), choose an appropriate organization for your essay-in-progress. Then experiment with organizing tools by preparing a tree diagram or other visual map or a scratch, informal, or formal outline.

COMPUTER ACTIVITY

CUT-AND-PASTE OUTLINES

The flexibility of a computer's Cut-and-Paste feature allows students to arrange ideas in various order and then to consider the result. As a follow-up to Exercises 2.9 and 2.10, pose a thesis statement (such as one of the revised examples from Exercise 2.6); then have students brainstorm on the computer to come up with a related list of ideas and organize them into several possible outlines.

COLLABORATIVE LEARNING

Ask students to compare their responses to Exercise 2.9 and then to work in pairs to create the formal outline described in Exercise 2.10. The discussions necessitated by this collaborative project encourage students to think through and articulate an organizational logic.

ANSWERS: EXERCISE 2.11

Individual response.

ANSWERS: EXERCISE 2.12

Individual response.

HIGHLIGHTS

This chapter continues the exploration, begun in Chapters 1 and 2, of writing as a flexible process and looks in detail at strategies for drafting, revising, editing, and proofreading. The journey from initial draft to finished essay may involve many decisions and changes of direction for which there are no firm rules. To alert student writers to the options available to them, the chapter provides lists of strategies for drafting an essay and checklists for revising (pp. 54–55) and editing (pp. 60–61). It also provides concrete advice for the stages of composing that many writers find the most difficult: getting started and completing the initial draft.

Students who view revision as an expendable stage in the writing process may benefit from following, draft by draft, the development of Katy Moreno's essay (begun in Chapter 2) on the global job market. Like most initial efforts, Moreno's early draft can benefit from revisions in organization, content, tone, and approach to clarify the essay's purpose and the relationships among its ideas and also to make it easier for readers to share Moreno's perspective. The revised draft, in turn, needs editing for clarity, style, and correction of errors in grammar, usage, punctuation, and spelling—changes that appear in the final version of the essay. Moreno's paper can provide material for small-group discussion and evaluation, and the section on benefiting from criticism (3g) can help students learn to work effectively in peer critique groups. "Commenting on others' writing" and "Benefiting from comments on your writing" on pages 69–70 and 70–71 clarify peer review in a helpful list format.

A WRITER'S PERSPECTIVE

> *I've never thought of myself as a good writer; anyone who wants reassurance of that should read one of my first drafts. But I'm one of the world's great rewriters.*
>
> —JAMES MICHENER

> *How can I know what I think until I see what I say?*
>
> —E. M. FORSTER

3

Drafting and Revising

The separation of drafting and revising from the planning and development discussed in Chapters 1 and 2 is somewhat artificial because the stages almost always overlap during the writing process. Indeed, if you compose on a computer, you may not experience any boundaries between stages at all. Still, your primary goal during the writing process will usually shift from gathering and shaping information to forming connected sentences and paragraphs in a draft and then restructuring and rewriting the draft.

3a Writing the first draft

The only correct drafting style is the one that works for you. Generally, though, the freer and more fluid you are, the better. Some writers draft and revise at the same time, but most let themselves go during drafting and *especially* do not worry about errors. Drafting is the occasion to find and convey meaning through the act of writing. If you fear making mistakes while drafting, that fear will choke your ideas. You draft only for yourself, so errors do not matter. Write freely until you have worked out what you want to say; *then* focus on any mistakes you may have made.

Starting to draft sometimes takes courage, even for seasoned professionals. Students and pros alike find easy ways to procrastinate—checking e-mail, meeting for coffee, napping. Such procrastination may actually help you if you let ideas for writing simmer at the same time. At some point, though, enough is enough: the deadline looms; you've got to get started. If the blankness still stares back at you, then try one of the following techniques for unblocking.

Ways to start drafting

- **Read over what you've already written**—notes, outlines, and so on. Immediately start your draft with whatever comes to mind.

mycomplab

Visit *mycomplab.com* for more resources and exercises on drafting, revising, editing, and collaborating.

- **Freewrite** (see p. 21).
- **Write scribbles or type nonsense** until words you can use start coming.
- **Pretend you're writing to a friend about your subject.**
- **Describe an image that represents your subject**—a physical object, a facial expression, two people arguing over something, a giant machine gouging the earth for a mine, whatever.
- **Write a paragraph.** Explain what you think your essay will be about when you finish it.
- **Skip the opening and start in the middle.** Or write the conclusion.
- **Start writing the part that you understand best or feel most strongly about.** Using your outline, divide your essay into chunks—say, one for the introduction, another for the first point, and so on. One of these chunks may call out to be written.

Drafting

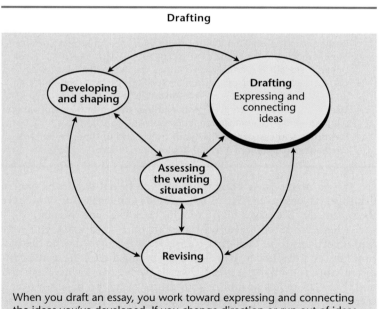

When you draft an essay, you work toward expressing and connecting the ideas you've developed. If you change direction or run out of ideas during drafting, you can always circle back to renew your purpose, discover new ideas, or rethink your thesis.

You should find some momentum once you've started writing. If not, however, or if your energy flags, try one or more of the following techniques to keep moving ahead.

OVERCOMING WRITING BLOCKS

Many students have a hard time writing first drafts because they try to get everything right the first time. They end up writing sentences and then crossing out what they have written so often that they have no time left to revise their thoughts in a second draft. Sometimes the pressure of perfection is so great that students become blocked writers, unable to finish even a single draft before the deadline. Here are four ways to help students get started and to help them develop flexibility and self-confidence in their approach to the task:

1. Show them copies of your own first and final drafts to indicate that you were not afraid to make mistakes in the initial draft because you had a chance to correct them in the later versions.

2. Give students a time limit for the first draft, perhaps an hour and a half or two hours, depending on the length of the assignment. Require them to hand in the draft with the final paper so that you can see how they approached the task of writing.

3. Have students start writing in class, where you can encourage them to get ideas down on paper before they try to perfect the wording.

4. Require students to spend some time either jotting down ideas and phrases or freewriting so that they will be loosened up before tackling the initial draft.

COMPUTER ACTIVITY

KEEPING TRACK OF IDEAS

Writers can often become anxious about adding in or losing track of ideas that don't seem to fit as they write out a rough draft. Students who are composing on the computer might keep a notebook nearby to scrawl down extra ideas that occur as they write. Students who draft on the computer should keep open a second blank document for alternative ideas that may not fit into the first draft. They might also use the "Comment" feature in Word to jot down these ideas without cluttering the main text.

RESOURCES AND IDEAS

On writer's block

Bartholomae, David. "Inventing the University." *When a Writer Can't Write: Studies in Writer's Block and Other Composing Process Problems.* Ed. Mike Rose. New York: Guilford, 1985. 134–65. Print. Bartholomae points out that one of the factors causing blocks or writing anxiety may be an unfamiliarity with the community for which the writer is writing, and he suggests ways to familiarize writers with the discourse expectations of academic writing.

Bloom, Lynn Z. "Research on Writing Blocks, Writing Anxiety, and Writing Apprehension." *Research in Composition and Rhetoric.* Ed. Michael G. Moran and Ronald F. Lunsford. Westport: Greenwood, 1984. 71–91. Print. Bloom surveys research on the fears and blocks that many writers encounter and examines strategies, similar to those presented in this chapter, for overcoming the difficulties.

Flaherty, Alice. *The Midnight Disease: The Drive to Write, Writer's Block, and the Creative Brain.* New York: Houghton Mifflin, 2004. Print. Flaherty uses neuroscience to describe how the brain processes both the urge to write and the inability to do so.

Rose, Mike. *Writer's Block: The Cognitive Dimension.* Carbondale: Southern Illinois UP, 1984. Print. The case studies of student writers that Rose discusses demonstrate that blocked writers often follow rigid, absolute rules about the forms and process of writing, whereas fluent writers use flexible, enabling strategies.

---. "Writing Around Rules." *Patterns in Action,* 2nd ed. Ed. Robert A. Schwegler. Glenview: Scott, 1988. 473–80. Print. As an illustration of the kinds of rules that block writing and the kinds of strategies that enable it, Rose tells of the difficulties he encountered in titling a poem.

Ways to *keep* drafting

- **Set aside enough time for yourself.** For a brief essay, a first draft is likely to take at least an hour or two.
- **Work in a quiet place.**
- **Make yourself comfortable.**
- **If you must stop working, write down what you expect to do next.** Then you can pick up where you stopped with minimal disruption.
- **Be as fluid as possible, and don't worry about mistakes.** Spontaneity will allow your attitudes toward your subject to surface naturally in your sentences, and it will also make you receptive to ideas and relations you haven't seen before. Mistakes will be easier to find and correct later, when you're not also trying to create.
- **Keep going.** Skip over sticky spots; leave a blank if you can't find the right word; put alternative ideas or phrasings in brackets so that you can consider them later. If an idea pops out of nowhere but doesn't seem to fit in, quickly write it into the draft and bracket or boldface it for later attention. Use an asterisk (*) or some other symbol to mark places where you feel blocked or uncertain.
- **Resist self-criticism.** Don't worry about your style, grammar, spelling, punctuation, and the like. Don't worry about what your readers will think. These are very important matters, but save them for revision. On a computer, turn off automatic spelling- or grammar-checking functions if they distract you, or try invisible writing (p. 22).
- **Use your thesis statement and outline** to remind you of your planned purpose, organization, and content.
- **But don't feel constrained by your thesis and outline.** If your writing leads you in a more interesting direction, follow.

If you write on a computer, frequently save the text you're drafting—at least every five or ten minutes and every time you leave the computer. See pages 55–56 for tips on saving documents.

Whether you compose on paper or on a computer, you may find it difficult to tell whether a first draft is finished. The distinction between drafts can be significant because creating text is different from rethinking it and because your instructor may ask you and your classmates to submit your drafts, either on paper or over a computer network, so that others can give you feedback on them. For your own revision or others' feedback, you might consider a draft finished for any number of reasons: perhaps you've reached the assigned length and have run out of ideas; perhaps you find yourself writing the conclusion; perhaps you've stopped adding content and are just tinkering with words.

Sample first draft

Following is Katy Moreno's first-draft response to Thomas L. Friedman's "It's a Flat World, After All." As part of her assignment,

Moreno showed the draft to four classmates, whose suggestions for revision appear in the margin of this draft. They used the Comment function of *Microsoft Word*, which allows users to add comments without inserting words into the document's text. (Notice that the classmates ignore errors in grammar and punctuation, concentrating instead on larger issues such as thesis, clarity of ideas, and unity.)

Title?

In "It's a Flat World, After All," Thomas L. Friedman argues that, most US students are not preparing themselves as well as they should to compete in today's economy. Not like students in India, China, and other countries are. The outsourcing of my mother's job proves that Thomas L. Friedman's advice to improve students' technical training is too narrow.

> **Comment [Jared]:** Your mother's job being outsourced is interesting, but your introduction seems rushed.

> **Comment [Rabia]:** The end of your thesis statement is a little unclear—too narrow for what?

Friedman describes a "flat" world where recent technology like the Internet and wireless communication make it possible for college graduates all over the globe, in particular in India and China, to get jobs that once were gotten by graduates of US colleges and universities. He argues that US students need more math and science in order to compete.

> **Comment [Erin]:** Can you include the reasons Friedman gives for overseas students' success?

I came to college with first-hand knowledge of globalization and outsourcing. My mother, who worked for sixteen years in the field of information technology (IT), was laid off six months ago when the company she worked for decided to outsource much of its IT work to a company based in India. My mother majored in computer science, had sixteen years of experience, and her bosses always gave her good reviews. She never expected to be laid off and was surprised when she was. She wasn't laid off because of her background and performance. In fact, my mother had a very strong background in math and science and years of training and job experience. The reason was because her salary and benefits cost the company more than outsourcing her job did. Which hurt my family financially, as you can imagine.

> **Comment [Nathaniel]:** Tighten this paragraph to avoid repetition? Also, how does your mother's experience relate to Friedman and your thesis?

A number of well-paid people in the IT department where my mother worked, namely IT managers, were not laid off. As my mother explained at the time, they kept their jobs because they were better at planning and they communicated better, they were better writers and speakers than my mother.

> **Comment [Erin]:** What were the managers better at planning for?

MODELS OF STUDENT WRITING

Katy Moreno's essay

Katy Moreno's essay is the first of several models of student writing that appear throughout *The Little, Brown Handbook*. Reading these examples of student writing may give your students a better idea of what you expect from their writing. Even when your students are not yet able to produce papers as strong as these sample papers, they may find it helpful to have concrete examples to emulate.

The inclusion of multiple drafts of Katy Moreno's essay is intended to help students understand the process by which a paper is formulated, developed, and polished. Several of this chapter's exercises ask students to evaluate drafts of the paper; you might want to supplement these exercises by asking your students what they think about the final draft. If your students are well versed in the five-paragraph essay, they may be particularly interested to see how Moreno's essay departs from that structure while still maintaining a coherent organization and a measure of fluidity.

You may also find the topic of this essay and its argument about education and the global economy to be very interesting to students. The essay might be a springboard for class debate on the topic; you could ask students to compose a rebuttal to Moreno's essay, or you could allow them to use it to begin to formulate their own research projects.

Like my mother, I am more comfortable in front of a computer than I am in front of a group of people. I planned to major in computer science. Since my mother lost her job, though, I have decided to take courses in English and history too, where the classes will require me to do different kinds of work. When I enter the job market, my well-rounded education will make me a more attractive job candidate, and, will help me to be a versatile, productive employee.

Comment [Nathaniel]: Can you be more specific about the kinds of work you'll need to do?

Comment [Rabia]: Can you work this point into your thesis?

We know from our history that Americans have been innovative, hard-working people. We students have educational opportunities to compete in the global economy, but we must use our time in college wisely. As Thomas L. Friedman says, my classmates and I need to be ready for a rapidly changing future. We will have to work hard each day, which means being prepared for class, getting the best grades we can, and making the most of each class. Our futures depend on the decisions we make today.

Comment [Jared]: Conclusion seems to go off in a new direction. Friedman mentions hard work, but it hasn't been your focus before.

Comment [Rabia]: Don't forget your works cited.

ANSWERS: EXERCISE 3.1

Possible Answers

Some significant differences between Moreno's scratch outline and her first draft:

- Moreno gives a detailed summary of Friedman's essay in paragraphs 1 and 2.
- In paragraph 3, Moreno gives work experience and education as evidence of her mother's excellent technical skills.
- In paragraph 5, Moreno explains the kinds of classes she plans to take to obtain a well-rounded education
- In the conclusion, Moreno addresses a new topic, hard work, which was not part of her scratch outline.

ANSWERS: EXERCISE 3.2

Individual response.

ANSWERS: EXERCISE 3.3

Individual response.

COLLABORATIVE LEARNING

Ask students to work in groups to complete Exercise 3.1 and to use that exercise as the occa-

Exercise 3.1 Analyzing a first draft

Compare Moreno's draft with the previous step in her planning (her scratch outline) on page 35. List the places in the draft where the act of drafting led Moreno to rearrange her information, add or delete material, or explore new ideas. Mark Moreno's thesis statement and each key idea developing the thesis. Note places where you think the ideas could be clearer or better supported.

Exercise 3.2 Considering your past work: Drafting

Think back over a recent writing experience. At what point in the writing process did you begin drafting? How did drafting go—smoothly, haltingly, painfully, painlessly? If you had difficulties, what were they? If you didn't, why do you think not?

Exercise 3.3 Drafting your essay

Prepare a draft of the essay you began in Chapters 1 and 2. Use your thesis statement and your outline as guides, but don't be unduly constrained by them. Concentrate on opening up options, not on closing them down. Do not, above all, worry about mistakes.

3b Revising the first draft

Revision literally means "re-seeing"—looking anew at ideas and details, their relationships and arrangement, the degree to which they work or don't work for the thesis. While drafting, you focus inwardly, concentrating on pulling your topic out of yourself. In revising, you

Revising

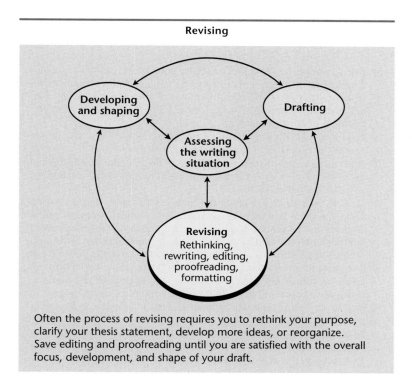

Often the process of revising requires you to rethink your purpose, clarify your thesis statement, develop more ideas, or reorganize. Save editing and proofreading until you are satisfied with the overall focus, development, and shape of your draft.

look out to your readers, trying to anticipate how they will see your work. You adopt a critical perspective toward your work, examining it as a pole-vaulter or dancer would examine a video of his or her performance. (Writing teachers often ask students to read each other's drafts partly to develop this critical perspective. See p. 68 for more on such collaboration.)

1 | Gaining distance from your work

Reading your own work critically can be difficult. Changing or even deleting material that you've worked hard to express can be still more difficult. The key is to gain some objectivity toward your writing. The following techniques may help.

Ways to gain distance from your work

■ **Take a break after finishing the draft.** A few hours may be enough; a whole night or day is preferable. The break will clear your mind, relax you, and give you some objectivity.

(continued)

sion to discuss their own drafting processes (Exercise 3.2). Students can benefit a great deal both from articulating their habits, choices, and difficulties throughout the writing process and hearing how other writers work.

REVISION ACTIVITIES

Here are a few revision activities for students working on their own or in groups:

Making out an inventory. After students have written an initial draft, ask them to complete a brief version of the audience inventory described in Chapter 1 (p. 13). Their completed inventory can help guide the choices they make during revision. Students may wish to share drafts and inventories with other students.

Using dialog. For narrative writing, ask students to circle every use of "He said that" and "She thought that" or similar phrases in their own or someone else's paper. Then ask them to consider replacing the indirect discourse with dialogue and direct quotations to make the writing more vivid and realistic.

Using the senses. For narrative and descriptive writing, ask students to check how many of the senses they have drawn on; then ask them to consider making use of the other senses.

Adding other arguments. For argumentative essays, have students list all the arguments they could use but have not yet included in the paper; they may wish to turn to other students for advice about including these arguments.

Soliciting class suggestions. For argument essays, ask students to summarize their theses and supporting arguments for their classmates. Then ask the other students to suggest more supporting arguments and opposing arguments the writer might consider during revision.

Answering more questions. For expository essays, ask students to answer these questions for their own or someone else's paper: What five things do you know about this topic that are not included in the draft? Which ones could be put into the essay without harming its unity or coherence? What three things are readers most likely to find interesting, useful, or surprising about this topic? Could these three things be given more emphasis without disrupting the organization or clarity of the essay?

QUESTIONING TABOOS

A good way to emphasize the distinction between revising and editing is to ask students to brainstorm a list of the taboos they've been taught about writing: "Don't begin sentences with I"; "Don't end sentences with prepositions"; "Never use contractions"; and so on. Then discuss the possible reasons for these rules and the occasions when they would apply. Once students understand the reasons for the rules they are much more able to check for usage errors in the editing process and to avoid allowing such taboos to hamper their revision processes.

ENCOURAGING REVISION

The only way to get students to revise regularly is to require it. You may need some ingenuity; one strategy that works is to require students to revise each graded essay and return it to you. Only when the essay is revised do you formally record a grade. Then students who don't revise won't get credit for their papers. Another method for encouraging revision efforts is to focus your written comments on the areas that students have revised effectively or failed to revise. Later in the semester it can also be useful to ask students to choose one of their own earlier papers to revise in the light of further reading or increased skills. This practice helps students to gain confidence in their own revision skills.

REWRITING TO REVISE

To reinforce to students how revision should be a "re-seeing" of their text, ask them to use Toby Fulwiler's suggestion, discussed extensively in *College Writing: A Personal Approach to Academic Writing*, of rewriting to revise. For a narrative essay, ask students to rewrite a scene entirely in dialogue or to select a particular moment and expand it. Even for an argumentative essay, students might also try rewriting the work, in whole or in part, in some new genre, such as a newspaper article, a song or poem, a screenplay, or a journal entry. Although these rewrites may or may not make it into the final draft of the work, the act of rewriting can get students to see revision as a more extensive process than just making changes to the existing text.

Ways to gain distance from your work
(continued)

- **Ask someone to read and react to your draft.** Many writing instructors ask their students to submit their first drafts so that the instructor and, often, the other members of the class can serve as an audience to help guide revision. (See also pp. 70–71 on receiving and benefiting from comments.)
- **Type a handwritten draft.** The act of transcription can reveal gaps in content or problems in structure.
- **Print out a word-processed draft.** You'll be able to view all pages of the draft at once, and the different medium can reveal weaknesses you didn't see on screen.
- **Outline your draft.** Highlight the main points supporting the thesis, and write these sentences down separately in outline form. (If you're working on a computer, you can copy and paste the sentences.) Then examine the outline you've made for logical order, gaps, and digressions. A formal outline can be especially illuminating because of its careful structure. (See pp. 34–39 for a discussion of outlining.)
- **Listen to your draft.** Read the draft out loud to yourself or a friend or classmate, record and listen to it, or have someone read the draft to you. Experiencing your words with ears instead of eyes can alter your perceptions.
- **Ease the pressure.** Don't try to re-see everything in your draft at once. Use a checklist like the one on pp. 54–55, making a separate pass through the draft for each item.

2 | Revising, then editing

Strictly speaking, revision includes editing—refining the manner of expression to improve clarity or style or to correct errors. In this chapter, though, revision and editing are treated separately to stress their differences: in revision you deal with the underlying meaning and structure of your essay; in editing you deal with its surface. By making separate drafts beyond the first—a revised one and then an edited one—you'll be less likely to waste time tinkering with sentences that you end up cutting, and you'll avoid the temptation to substitute editing for more substantial revision.

The temptation to edit while revising can be especially attractive on a computer because it's easy to alter copy. Indeed, writers sometimes find themselves editing compulsively, spinning their wheels with changes that cease to have any marked effect on meaning or clarity and that may in fact sap the writing of energy. Planning to revise and then to edit encourages you to look beyond the confines of the screen so that deeper issues of meaning and structure aren't lost to surface matters such as word choice and sentence arrangement.

3 | Titling your essay

The revision stage is a good time to consider a title. After drafting, you have a clearer sense of your direction, and the attempt to sum up your essay in a title phrase can help you focus sharply on your topic, purpose, and audience.

Here are suggestions for titling an essay:

- *A descriptive title* **is almost always appropriate and is often expected for academic writing.** It announces the topic clearly, accurately, and as briefly as possible. The final title of Katy Moreno's essay is an example: "Can We Compete? College Education for the Global Economy." Other examples include "Images of Lost Identity in *North by Northwest,*" "An Experiment in Small-Group Dynamics," "Why Lincoln Delayed Emancipating the Slaves," and "Food Poisoning Involving *E. coli* Bacteria: A Review of the Literature."

- *A suggestive title*—**the kind often found in popular magazines—may be appropriate for more informal writing.** Examples include "Making Peace" (for an essay on the Peace Corps) and Thomas L. Friedman's "It's a Flat World, After All" (on the global job market). For a more suggestive title, Moreno might have chosen "Training for the New World" or "Education for a Flat World" (echoing Friedman's title). A suggestive title conveys the writer's attitude and main concerns but not the precise topic, thereby pulling readers into the essay to learn more. A source for such a title may be a familiar phrase, a fresh image, or a significant expression from the essay itself.

- **A title tells readers how big the topic is.** For Moreno's essay, the title "Globalization and Jobs" or "Competing in Today's Job Market" would have been too broad, whereas "Outsourcing Our Jobs" or "The Importance of a Broad Education" would have been too narrow because each deals with only part of the paper's content.

- **A title should not restate the assignment or the thesis statement,** as in "The Trouble with Thomas L. Friedman's View of the Global Job Market" or "What I Think About Technical Training and Today's Job Market."

For more information on essay titles, see pages 349–50 (avoiding reference to the title in the opening of the paper), 483 (capitalizing words in a title), and 690 (formatting a title in the final paper).

RESOURCES AND IDEAS

On revision generally

Allal, Linda, Lucile Chanquoi, and Pierre Largy, eds. *Revision: Cognitive and Instructional Processes*. Norwell: Kluwer, 2004. Print. This collection reviews previous studies and presents current research on revision as a cognitive process; the second half addresses the impact of instruction on revision processes.

Bishop, Wendy, ed. *Elements of Alternate Style: Essays on Writing and Revision*. Portsmouth: Boynton/Cook (Heinemann), 1997. Print. A collection of essays offering hands-on approaches to recovering play and joy in the writing and revision processes.

Elbow, Peter. *Writing with Power: Techniques for Mastering the Writing Process*. New York: Oxford UP, 1981. Print. Elbow's book offers detailed, practical, and often innovative advice on drafting, revising, shaping for an audience, and making use of feedback, including several chapters on revising ("Quick Revising," "Thorough Revising," "Revising with Feedback," and "Cut and Paste Revising and the Collage").

Fulwiler, Toby. *College Writing: A Personal Approach to Academic Writing*. 3rd ed. Portsmouth: Boynton/Cook, 2002. Print. To encourage more extensive and creative revision, the chapter "Options for Revision" suggests that students rewrite parts or all of an existing text in some new way rather than simply making changes to the existing essay.

Harris, Joseph. *Revision: How to Do Things with Texts*. Logan: Utah State UP, 2006. Print. Harris models how students can work with their academic writing to make it more lively and less static.

Harris, Muriel. "Composing Behaviors of One- and Multi-Draft Writers." *College English* 51.2 (1989): 174–91. Print. Harris emphasizes the differences in revision techniques and success of student writers.

Sommers, Nancy. "Revision Strategies of Student Writers and Experienced Adult Writers." *College Composition and Communication* 31.4 (1980): 378–88. Print. According to Sommers, students see revision as changes in small units—words and sentences. Experienced

4 Using a revision checklist

Set aside at least as much time to revise your essay as you took to draft it. Plan on going through the draft several times to answer the questions in the checklist below and to resolve any problems. (If you need additional information on any of the topics in the checklist, refer to the page numbers given in parentheses.) Note that the checklist can also help you if you have been asked to comment on another writer's draft (see pp. 69–70).

Checklist for revision

See also specific revision checklists for arguments (p. 211), research papers (p. 642), and literary analyses (p. 745).

Purpose
What is the essay's purpose? Does that purpose conform to the assignment? Is it consistent throughout the paper? (See pp. 9–11.)

Thesis
What is the thesis of the essay? Where does it become clear? How well do thesis and paper match: Does the paper stray from the thesis? Does it fulfill the commitment of the thesis? (See pp. 27–32.)

Structure
What are the main points of the paper? (List them.) How well does each support the thesis? How effective is their arrangement for the paper's purpose? (See pp. 33–34, 39–43.)

Development
How well do details, examples, and other evidence support each main point? Where, if at all, might readers find support skimpy or have trouble understanding the content? (See pp. 16–26, 92–93.)

Voice
How clearly can readers hear your writer's voice? What role will they see you as playing? What tone will they hear? How appropriate is your voice for your subject, purpose, and audience? (See pp. 14–15.)

Unity
What does each sentence and paragraph contribute to the thesis? Where, if at all, do digressions occur? Should they be cut, or can they be rewritten to support the thesis? (See pp. 42–44, 74–77.)

Coherence
How clearly and smoothly does the paper flow? Where does it seem rough or awkward? Can any transitions be improved? (See pp. 42–44, 79–81.)

Title, introduction, conclusion
How accurately and interestingly does the title reflect the essay's content? (See p. 53.)
How well does the introduction engage and focus readers' attention? (See pp. 104–07.)
How effective is the conclusion in providing a sense of completion? (See pp. 107–09.)

5 | Revising on a computer

Word processors have removed the mechanical drudgery of revising by hand or on a typewriter, but they have also complicated the process: you must conscientiously save your changes and manage the files you create, both discussed below. At the same time, like the more cumbersome revision methods, word processors allow you to display changes as you make them.

Saving changes

Computers malfunction frequently. You can avoid losing your work by taking two precautions:

- **Save your work every five to ten minutes.** Most word processors have an Auto Save function that will save your work automatically as you type, at the interval you specify. Still, get in the habit of saving manually whenever you make major changes.
- **After doing any major work on a project, create a backup version of the file.** Use a second hard drive, a removable disk, or a removable flash drive. If you need to share files but have difficulty e-mailing them, or if you need to save large multimedia files, you can also store backups on a drive accessed through the Internet. *Xdrive*, for example, offers storage space for a reasonable price (*xdrive.com*).

Managing files

You can organize your work for a course or the drafts of a paper by giving each file a name that indicates the content, the date, and (if you're sharing work with others) the author. The screen shot on the next page shows Katy Moreno saving a document she named *Katy_Friedman_response_D1_10-17-08.doc* in a new folder titled *English110*. In addition to her name and the date, the file name includes an identifier for the paper (*Friedman_response*) and the draft number (*D1*).

writers see it as a recursive process directed at larger units of the text and the meaning it conveys.

Welch, Nancy. *Getting Restless: Rethinking Revision in Writing Instruction*. Portsmouth, NH: Boynton/Cook (Heinemann), 1997. Print. Welch looks at what student writers have to say about their own attempts at revision. She concludes that revision engages the domain of the emotional/personal, a domain which makes most academics uncomfortable.

On computers and the revision process

Many writers find that the computer facilitates their composing and revision processes without realizing the extent to which the medium has changed the way we think and write. In "The Metaphor of Collage: Beyond Computer Composition," Russel Wiebe and Robert S. Dornsife, Jr., argue that computers are not simply an addition to the classroom; rather, they revolutionize the way we and our students write and think about texts. The authors use the metaphor of a multimedia collage to describe the best pedagogical approach to these changes (*Journal of Advanced Composition* 15.1 (1995): 131–37). See also Cynthia Selfe and Susan Hilligoss, *Literacy and Computers: the Complications of Teaching and Learning with Technology* (New York: MLA, 1994), and Michelle Sidler, Elizabeth Smith Overman, and Richard Morris, eds. *Computers in the Composition Classroom: A Critical Sourcebook*. Boston: Bedford/St. Martin's, 2008. Print.

On collaborative revision

Peer editing and collaborative learning have become regular features of many composition courses over the past two decades, and these approaches are particularly well suited to drafting and revising activities. Section 3g coaches students in giving and receiving criticism. And the chapter "Using Collaborative Learning with the Handbook" on pages IAE 35–46 offers detailed advice about designing collaborative activities and preparing students to work in groups. It also provides sample reader response forms, which you may wish to copy and use in your class.

Much has been written recently about collaborative learning and peer writing groups. See, for example, the *Journal of Advanced Composition* 14:1 (1994); the entire issue is devoted to issues of collaboration. The following works offer good starting points for someone interested in examining both the opportunities offered by this approach and the controversies that it has created:

Ede, Lisa, and Andrea Lunsford. *Singular Texts/ Plural Authors: Perspectives on Collaborative Writing.* Carbondale: Southern Illinois UP, 1990. Print. Longtime collaborators themselves, Ede and Lunsford study the theory and history of collaborative writing and argue that collaborative work, a necessity in current society, should be encouraged in institutions and valued as equal to individual endeavors.

Gere, Anne Ruggles. *Writing Groups: History, Theory, and Implications.* Carbondale: Southern Illinois UP, 1987. Print. Gere reviews the history, theory, and practice of writing groups and collaborative learning; she also provides a useful annotated bibliography of research and pedagogy.

Trimbur, John. "Collaborative Learning and Teaching Writing." *Perspectives on Research and Scholarship in Composition.* Ed. Ben W. McClelland and Timothy R. Donovan. New York: MLA, 1985. 87–109. Print. Trimbur offers a compact survey of the history and theories behind collaborative learning and raises important questions about the roles of response and evaluation in a student- (rather than teacher-) centered classroom.

On independent revision

Even though you encourage students to revise and offer them detailed advice about what and when to revise, you may still find that their revisions are limited to superficial changes. Part of the problem may be that students have not yet become good enough readers of their own texts to identify features that might be altered or dropped and to identify places where something might be added. Here are some resources for helping students to become active readers and writers, aware of what they have written and how it might be changed:

Beck, James P. "Asking Students to Annotate Their Own Papers." *College Composition and Communication* 33.3 (1982): 322–26. Print. Beck asks students to identify specific techniques they have used in their writing (including features of structure, detail, argument, and style) and to evaluate how well they have used those techniques.

Save As screen

Save As copies an existing document.

Save the file in an existing folder if it relates to others already in the folder.

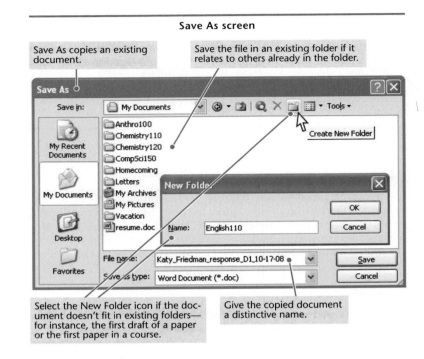

Select the New Folder icon if the document doesn't fit in existing folders—for instance, the first draft of a paper or the first paper in a course.

Give the copied document a distinctive name.

Displaying changes

You can keep track of the revisions you make in a document with an option often called Track Changes and usually found under the Tools or File menu. The function highlights additions and deletions so they're easy to spot (see Katy Moreno's revised draft on the facing page). Tracking changes may encourage you to revise more freely because you can always revert to your original text. You can weigh the original and revised versions as you view them side by side. You can also evaluate the kinds of changes you are making. For instance, if during revision you see only minor surface alterations (word substitutions, added punctuation, and the like), then you might consider whether and where to read more deeply for more fundamental changes.

3c Examining a sample revision

Katy Moreno was satisfied with her first draft: she had her ideas down, and the arrangement seemed logical. Still, from the revision checklist she knew the draft needed work, and her classmates' comments (pp. 49–50) highlighted what she needed to focus on. The following revised draft shows Moreno's changes in response to these comments. Moreno used the Track Changes function on her word processor, so that deletions are crossed out and additions are in blue.

Can We Compete?
College Education for the Global Economy
~~Title?~~

Today's students cannot miss news stories about globalization of the economy and outsourcing of jobs, but are students aware of how these trends are affecting the job market? In "It's a Flat World, After All," Thomas L. Friedman argues that most US students are not preparing themselves as well as ~~they should to compete in today's economy. Not like~~ students in India, China, and other countries ~~are.~~ to compete in today's economy, which requires hard-working, productive scientists and engineers. Friedman's argument speaks to me me because my mother recently lost her job when it was outsourced to India. But her experience taught a lesson that Friedman overlooks: technical training by itself can be too narrow to produce the communicators and problem solvers needed by contemporary businesses. ~~The outsourcing of my mother's job proves that Thomas L. Friedman's advice to improve students' technical training is too narrow.~~

Friedman describes a "flat" world where recent technology like the Internet and wireless communication makes it possible for college graduates all over the globe~~, in particular~~ to compete for high paying jobs that once belonged to graduates of US colleges and universities. He focuses on workers **in India and China**~~,~~ who graduate from college with excellent educations in math and science, who are eager for new opportunities, and who are willing to work exceptionally hard, often harder than their American counterparts and, for less money. ~~to get jobs that once were gotten by graduates of US colleges and universities.~~ **He** Friedman **argues that US stu-**dents must be better prepared academically, especially in ~~need more~~ **math and science**, so that they can get and keep jobs that will otherwise go overseas. ~~in order to compete.~~

~~I came to college with first hand knowledge of globalization and outsourcing. My mother, who worked for sixteen years in the field of information technology (IT), was laid off six months ago when the company she worked for decided to outsource much of its IT work to a company based in India. My mother~~ At first glance, my mother's experience of losing her job might seem to support the argument of Friedman that better training in math and science is the key to competing in the global job market.

Descriptive title names topic and forecasts approach.

Expanded introduction draws readers into Moreno's topic, clarifies her point of agreement with Friedman, and states her revised thesis.

Expanded summary of Friedman's article specifies qualities of overseas workers.

New opening sentences connect to introduction and thesis statement, restating points of agreement and disagreement with Friedman.

Berzsenyi, Christyne A. "Comments to Comments: Teachers and Students in Written Dialogue about Critical Revision." *Composition Studies* 29.2 (2001): 71–92. Print. Berzsenyi details a system of commenting on student papers that requires students to transcribe and respond to instructor comments, creating a dialogue between teacher and student about revision.

Mellen, Cheryl, and Jeff Sommers. "Audiotaped Response and the Two-Year-Campus Writing Classroom: The Two-Sided Desk, the 'Guy with the Ax,' and the Chirping Birds." *Teaching English in the Two-Year College* 31.1 (2003): 25–39. Print. Mellen and Sommers provide an overview of work on response and argues for the efficacy of audiotaped commentary on student work.

Sommers, Nancy. "Across the Drafts." *College Composition and Communication* 58.2 (2006): 248–57. Print. Sommers revises the conclusions of her influential article, "Responding to Student Writing" (*College Composition and Communication* 33.2 [1982]: 148–56. Print.). Specifically, she disputes her initial assertion "We do not know in any definitive way what constitutes thoughtful commentary or what effect, if any, our comments have on helping our students become more effective writers" (148). In "Across the Drafts," Sommers relates study results that illustrate the significant impact of instructor comments on undergraduate students' development as writers.

Straub, Richard. "The Concept of Control in Teacher Response: Defining the Varieties of 'Directive' and 'Facilitative' Commentary." *College Composition and Communication* 47.2 (1996): 223–51. Print. Straub reviews the influential studies on teacher response in an effort to identify the kinds of comments that encourage students to produce effective independent revisions.

COMPUTER ACTIVITY

AN ARCHIVE FOR REJECTED PASSAGES

Having labored so hard to produce a first draft, writers are sometimes reluctant to cut passages when revising their drafts. Your students may find it easier to make cuts if they paste the cut passages into a blank document, saving that document as part of their own personal writing archive. They can choose to replace the cut passages later or use them for a different piece of writing altogether.

Revisions condense long example of mother's experience.

Concluding sentences reinforce the point of the paragraph and connect to thesis statement.

Numbered point (second) connects this paragraph to the previous one.

New examples support general point.

Concluding sentences connect paragraph to thesis.

New examples add specificity.

Expanded sentence connects to thesis statement.

Her experience, however, adds dimensions to the globalization story, which Friedman misses. First my mother had the kind of strong background in math and science that Friedman says, today's workers need. She majored in computer science, rose within the information technology (IT) department of a large company, ~~had sixteen years of experience,~~ and her bosses always gave her good performance reviews. Still, when her employer decided to outsource most of its IT work, my mother lost her job. ~~She never expected to be laid off and was surprised when she was. She wasn't laid off because of her background and performance. In fact, my mother had a very strong background in math and science and years of training and job experience.~~ The reason wasn't because her technical skills were inadequate. Instead, her salary and benefits cost the company more than outsourcing her job did. Until wages rise around the globe, jobs like my mother's will be vulnerable. No matter how well you are trained. ~~Which hurt my family financially, as you can imagine.~~

The second dimension that Friedman misses is that ~~A~~ a number of well-paid people in ~~the~~ my mother's IT department ~~where my mother worked~~, namely IT managers, were not laid off. As my mother explained at the time, they kept their jobs because they were experienced at figuring out the company's IT needs, planning for changes and, researching and proposing solutions. They also communicated better and were better at writing and speaking than my mother was. ~~were better at planning and, they communicated better, they were better writers and speakers than my mother.~~ Friedman misses these skills by focusing only on technical training. Without the ability to solve problems creatively and to communicate, people with technical expertise alone may not have enough to save their jobs. It wasn't enough to save my mother's.

Like my mother, I am more comfortable in front of a computer than I am in front of a group of people, and I had planned to major in computer science. Since my mother lost her job, ~~though~~ however, I have decided to take courses in English and history too, where the classes will require me to ~~do different kinds of work~~ read broadly, think critically, research, and communicate ideas in writing—skills that make managers. When I enter the job market, my well-rounded education will make me a more attractive job candidate, and, will help me ~~be a versatile, productive employee~~ become the kind of forward-thinking manager that US companies will always need to employ here in the US.

~~We know from our history that Americans have been innovative, hard working people. We students have educational opportunities to compete in~~

~~the global economy, but we must use our time in college wisely. As Thomas L. Friedman says,~~ Many jobs that require a college degree are indeed going overseas, as Thomas L. Friedman says, and my classmates and I need to be ready for a rapidly changing future. But rather than focus only on math and science, we need to broaden our academic experiences so that the skills we develop make us not only employable, but also indispensable. ~~We will have to work hard each day, which means being prepared for class, getting the best grades we can, and making the most of each class. Our futures depend on the decisions we make today.~~

> New conclusion recaps Friedman's points and Moreno's thesis and points to the future.

Work Cited

Friedman, Thomas L. "It's a Flat World, After All." *New York Times Magazine* 3 Apr. 2005: 32-37. Print.

> New work-cited entry. (See p. 653 on MLA style.)

Exercise 3.4 Analyzing a revised draft

Can you see the reasons for most of the changes Moreno made in her revised draft? Where would you suggest further revisions, and why?

Exercise 3.5 Considering your past work: Revising

In the past, have you usually revised your drafts extensively? Do you think your writing would benefit from more revision of the sort described in this chapter? Why or why not? Many students who don't revise much explain that they lack the time. Is time a problem for you? Can you think of ways to resolve the problem?

Exercise 3.6 Revising your own draft

Revise your own first draft from Exercise 3.3 (p. 50). Use the checklist for revision on pages 54–55 as a guide. Concentrate on purpose, content, and organization, leaving smaller problems such as sentence structure, word choice, and grammar for the next draft.

3d Editing the revised draft

Editing for style, clarity, and correctness may come second to more fundamental revision, but it is still very important. A carefully developed essay will fall flat with readers if you overlook awkwardness and errors.

1 Discovering what needs editing

After you've read and reread a draft to revise it, finding awkwardness and errors can be difficult. Try the following approaches to spot possible flaws in your revised draft:

COLLABORATIVE LEARNING

Exercise 3.4 works well as a small-group project. Encourage students to discuss their differing ideas for further revisions and then have each group present their conclusions to the class.

DEFINING REVISION

Using Exercise 3.5, "Considering your past work: Revising" as a starting point, ask small groups or pairs of students to create a working definition of revision. How have they understood revision in the past? How could they redefine their concept of "revision" now, using the sort of revision described in this chapter? How would they explain revision, as they now understand it, to a new group of students taking this course next semester? What advice might they give those students in terms of time management? As a class, compare each group's responses to discover the variety of perceptions among students.

ANSWERS: EXERCISE 3.4

Individual response.

ANSWERS: EXERCISE 3.5

Individual response.

ANSWERS: EXERCISE 3.6

Individual response.

Ways to find what needs editing

- **Take a break,** even fifteen or twenty minutes, to clear your head.
- **Read the draft** *slowly,* **and read what you** *actually see.* Otherwise, you're likely to read what you intended to write but didn't. (If you have trouble slowing down, try reading your draft from back to front, sentence by sentence.)
- **Read as if you are encountering the draft for the first time.** Put yourself in the reader's place.
- **Have a classmate, friend, or relative read your work.** Make sure you understand and consider the reader's suggestions, even if eventually you decide not to take them.
- **Read the draft aloud or, even better, record it.** Listen for awkward rhythms, repetitive sentence patterns, and missing or clumsy transitions.
- **Learn from your own experience.** Keep a record of the problems that others have pointed out in your writing. (See p. 62 for a suggested format.) When editing, check your work against this record.

In your editing, work first for clear and effective sentences that flow smoothly from one to the next. Then check your sentences for correctness. Use the questions in the following checklist to guide your editing, referring to the page numbers in parentheses as needed.

Checklist for editing

Are my sentences clear?

Do my words and sentences mean what I intend them to mean? Is anything confusing? Check especially for these:

Exact language (pp. 511–22)
Parallelism (pp. 398–404)
Clear modifiers (pp. 359–67)
Clear reference of pronouns (pp. 345–51)
Complete sentences (pp. 330–37)
Sentences separated correctly (pp. 338–44)

Are my sentences effective?

How well do words and sentences engage and hold readers' attention? How appropriate and effective is the voice created by words and sentences? Where does the writing seem wordy, choppy, or dull? Check especially for these:

Expression of voice (pp. 14–15)
Emphasis of main ideas (pp. 378–86)

Smooth and informative transitions (pp. 87–89, 109–10)
Variety in sentence length and structure (pp. 405–12)
Appropriate language (pp. 502–10)
Concise sentences (pp. 523–30)

Do my sentences contain errors?
Where do surface errors interfere with the clarity and effectiveness of my sentences? Check especially for these:

- **Spelling errors** (pp. 531–34)
- **Sentence fragments** (pp. 330–37)
- **Comma splices** (pp. 338–43)
- **Verb errors**

  Verb forms, especially -*s* and -*ed* endings, correct forms of irregular verbs, and appropriate helping verbs (pp. 272–88)
  Verb tenses, especially consistency (pp. 289–95, 355)
  Agreement between subjects and verbs, especially when words come between them or the subject is *each, everyone,* or a similar word (pp. 301–08)

- **Pronoun errors**

  Pronoun forms, especially subjective (*he, she, they, who*) vs. objective (*him, her, them, whom*) (pp. 264–71)
  Agreement between pronouns and antecedents, especially when the antecedent contains *or* or the antecedent is *each, everyone, person,* or a similar word (pp. 309–13)

- **Punctuation errors**

  Commas, especially with comma splices (pp. 338–43), with *and* or *but* (422–24), with introductory elements (425–26), with nonessential elements (427–29), and with series (443)
  Apostrophes in possessives but not plural nouns (*Dave's/witches*) and in contractions but not possessive personal pronouns (*it's/its*) (pp. 452–57)

The third paragraph of Katy Moreno's edited draft appears below. Among other changes, she tightened wording, improved parallelism (with *consistently received*), corrected several comma errors, and repaired the final sentence fragment.

> At first glance, my mother's experience of losing her job might seem to support ~~the~~ Friedman's argument ~~of Friedman~~ that better training in math and science is the key to competing in the global job market. However, ~~Hh~~er experience~~, however,~~ adds dimensions to the globalization story~~, which~~ that Friedman misses. First, my mother had the kind of strong

INDIVIDUALIZED CHECKLISTS

Since most students' work demonstrates patterns of repeated error, have them keep ongoing lists of their recurring editing errors and stylistic problems. Ask them to bring their lists to class for in-class revision and editing sessions and to have their revision group help them look particularly for those errors.

COMPUTER ACTIVITIES

EDITING VEHICLES

To help students explore how editing on a computer may produce different results from editing hard copy, ask half of the students to edit a sample paper on the computer and the other half by hand. Then, in small groups, have them compare their edits and discuss the differences.

HUMAN VERSUS MACHINE

Have a contest between student proofreaders and the spell check or grammar check program of their word processing software, to see which method produces the cleanest copy.

background in math and science that Friedman says, today's workers need. She majored in computer science, rose within the information technology (IT) department of a large company, and consistently received her bosses always gave her good performance reviews. Still, when her employer decided to outsource most of its IT work, my mother lost her job. The reason wasn't because that her technical skills were inadequate. Instead, her salary and benefits cost the company more than outsourcing her job did. Until wages rise around the globe, jobs like my mother's will be vulnerable,. Nno matter how well you are a person is trained.

2 Tracking your errors

You won't make all the errors described in this book; instead, you may make the same three or four kinds of errors in each essay you write. The key to correcting such errors is recognizing them, keeping track of them, and checking for them each time you edit your writing.

To track your errors, try making a chart like the one below, with a vertical column for each assignment (or draft) and a horizontal row for each error or weakness that you or others have noted in your writing. Check marks indicate how often the problem occurs in every essay. The chart also provides a convenient place to keep track of words you misspell so that you can master their spellings. When you edit, check your work against the list so that you learn to see—and correct—the errors that you typically make.

Record of errors

Weaknesses	Assignment		
	1	2	3
not enough details for readers	✓	✓	✓
unity—wanders away from thesis	✓		
subject-verb agreement	✓		✓
comma splice	✓✓	✓	✓
misspellings	among deceive	rebel seize	omission cruelty

3 Editing on a computer

When you write on a word processor, consider these additional approaches to editing:

- **Don't rely on a spelling or grammar/style checker to find what needs editing.** See the discussion of these checkers below.
- **If possible, work on a double-spaced paper copy.** Most people find it much harder to spot errors on a computer screen than on paper.
- **Use the Find command to locate and correct your common problems**—certain misspellings, wordy phrases such as *the fact that,* overuse of *there is,* and so on.
- **Resist overediting.** The ease of editing on a computer can lead to rewriting sentences over and over, stealing the life from your prose. If your grammar/style checker contributes to the temptation, consider turning it off.
- **Take special care with additions and omissions.** Make sure you haven't omitted needed words or left in unneeded words.

4 Working with spelling and grammar/style checkers

A spelling checker and a grammar/style checker can be helpful *if* you work within their limitations. The programs miss many problems and may even flag items that are actually correct. Further, they know nothing of your purpose and your audience, so they cannot make important decisions about your writing. Always use these tools critically:

- **Read your work yourself to ensure that it's clear and error-free.**
- **Consider a checker's suggestions carefully, weighing each one against your intentions.** If you aren't sure whether to accept a checker's suggestion, consult a dictionary, writing handbook, or other source. Your version may be fine.

Using a spelling checker

Your word processor's spelling checker can be a great ally: it will flag words that are spelled incorrectly and will usually suggest alternative spellings that resemble what you've typed. However, this ally also has the potential to undermine you because of its limitations:

- **The checker may flag a word that you've spelled correctly** just because the word does not appear in its dictionary.
- **The checker may suggest incorrect alternatives.** In providing a list of alternative spellings for your word, the checker may highlight the one it considers most likely to be correct.

For example, if you misspell *definitely* by typing *definately,* your checker may highlight *defiantly* as the correct option. You need to verify that the alternative suggested by the checker is actually what you intend before selecting it. Consult an online or printed dictionary when you aren't sure about the checker's recommendations.

■ **Most important, a spelling checker will not flag words that appear in its dictionary but you have misused.** The jingle in the following screen shot has circulated widely as a warning about spelling checkers (we found it in the *Bulletin of the Missouri Council of Teachers of Mathematics*).

Spelling checker

A spelling checker failed to catch any of the thirteen errors in this jingle. Can you spot them?

Document 1—Microsoft Word

I have a spelling checker,
It came with my PC;
It plainly marks four my revue
Mistakes I cannot sea.
I've run this poem threw it,
I'm sure your please too no.
Its letter perfect in it's weigh,
My checker tolled me sew.

Using a grammar/style checker

Grammar/style checkers can flag incorrect grammar or punctuation and wordy or awkward sentences. However, these programs can call your attention only to passages that *may* be faulty. They miss many errors because they are not capable of analyzing language in all its complexity. (For instance, they can't accurately distinguish a word's part of speech when there are different possibilities, as *light* can be a noun, a verb, or an adjective.) The checkers can't detect problems involving relationships between ideas, so they usually miss errors such as faulty parallelism, inconsistent verb tenses, and problems with adjectives or adverbs. And they often question passages that don't need editing, such as an appropriate passive verb or a deliberate and emphatic use of repetition. The screen shot on the facing page illustrates the limitations.

You can customize a grammar and style checker to suit your needs and habits as a writer. (Select Options under the Tools menu.) Most checkers allow you to specify whether to check grammar only or grammar and style. Some style checkers can be set to the level of writing you intend, such as formal, standard, and informal. (For academic writing choose formal.) You can also instruct the checker to flag specific grammar and style problems that tend to occur in

Grammar/style checker

your writing, such as mismatched subjects and verbs, apostrophes in plural nouns, overused passive voice, or a confusion between *its* and *it's*.

Exercise 3.7 Considering your past work: Editing

How do you find what needs editing in your drafts? What kinds of changes do you make most often? Have you tried focusing on particular kinds of changes, such as correcting mistakes you made in previous writing? If your readers often comment on editing concerns in your work, what can you do to reduce such comments?

Exercise 3.8 Editing your own draft

Use the checklist for editing (pp. 60–61) and your own sense of your essay's needs to edit the revised draft of your essay-in-progress.

3e Preparing and proofreading the final draft

After editing your essay, retype or print it once more for submission to your instructor. You may be required to use one of the following formats: MLA (pp. 689–91), Chicago (pp. 771–73), APA (pp. 799–802), or CSE (pp. 817–18). If no format is specified, consult the document-design guidelines in Chapter 5. If you've composed on a word processor, use the Print Preview function under the File menu to check for formatting problems that may not otherwise show up on your screen.

Be sure to proofread the final essay several times to spot and correct errors. To increase the accuracy of your proofreading, you may need to find ways to keep yourself from relaxing into the rhythm and the content of your prose. The following box gives a few tricks, including some used by professional proofreaders:

Have students respond individually to the questions in Exercise 3.7 and then return to those questions as they work through drafts in their revision groups. Especially if students are working regularly with a particular group, they can be extremely helpful in pointing to one another's recurring strengths and problems.

ANSWERS: EXERCISE 3.7

Individual response.

ANSWERS: EXERCISE 3.8

Individual response.

NAMING THE PROBLEM, USING THE HANDBOOK

Using their individualized editing checklists or their responses to Exercise 3.7 "Considering your past work: Editing," have students start familiarizing themselves with the handbook portion of the text. Help students assign the proper names to the problem, such as "fragments" and define the problem. If they have listed a very general problem, like "commas," have them find examples in their work and name the problem. Ask them to look up that issue in the handbook and note the appropriate pages and section numbers. Students will become more familiar and comfortable with the handbook, while also learning how to name and correct their specific problems.

INDIVIDUALIZED PROOFREADING LISTS

Students often struggle to recognize common proofreading errors in their own work. Ask students to keep an ongoing list of the misspellings, typos, and minor grammatical errors that occur frequently in their own work and use that list for proofreading.

Techniques for proofreading

- **Read printed copy,** even if you will eventually submit the paper electronically. Most people proofread more accurately when reading type on paper than when reading it on a computer screen. (At the same time, don't view the printed copy as necessarily error-free just because it's clean. Clean-looking copy may still harbor errors.)
- **Read the paper aloud.** Slowly and distinctly pronounce exactly what you see.
- **Place a ruler under each line as you read it.**
- **Read "against copy."** Compare your final draft one sentence at a time against the edited draft you copied it from.
- **Ignore content.** To keep the content of your writing from distracting you while you proofread, read the essay backward, end to beginning, examining each sentence as a separate unit. Or, taking advantage of a computer, isolate each paragraph from its context by printing it on a separate page. (Of course, reassemble the paragraphs before submitting the paper.)

3f Examining a final draft

Katy Moreno's final essay begins below, typed in MLA format except for page breaks and numbers. Comments in the margins point out key features of the essay's content.

Katy Moreno

Professor Lacourse

English 110

14 Nov. 2008

Descriptive title

Can We Compete?

College Education for the Global Economy

Introduction

Today's students cannot miss news stories about globalization of the economy and outsourcing of jobs, but are students aware of how these trends are affecting the job market? In "It's a Flat World, After All," Thomas L. Friedman argues that most US students are not preparing themselves as well as students in India, China, and other countries to compete in today's economy, which requires hard-working, productive scientists and engineers. Friedman's argument speaks to me because my mother lost her

Thesis statement: basic disagreement with Friedman

job when it was outsourced to India. But her experience taught a lesson that Friedman overlooks: technical training by itself can be too narrow to produce the communicators and problem solvers needed by contemporary businesses.

Friedman describes a "flat" world where recent technology like the Internet and wireless communication makes it possible for college graduates all over the globe to compete for high-paying jobs that once belonged to graduates of US colleges and universities. He focuses on workers in India and China who graduate from college with excellent educations in math and science, who are eager for new opportunities, and who are willing to work exceptionally hard, often harder than their American counterparts, and for less money. Friedman argues that US students must be better prepared academically, especially in math and science, so that they can get and keep jobs that will otherwise go overseas.

> Summary of Friedman's article
>
> No source citation for Friedman because paragraph summarizes entire article and mentions Friedman's name

At first glance, my mother's experience of losing her job might seem to support Friedman's argument that better training in math and science is the key to competing in the global job market. However, her experience adds dimensions to the globalization story that Friedman misses. First, my mother had the kind of strong background in math and science that Friedman says today's workers need. She majored in computer science, rose within the information technology (IT) department of a large company, and consistently received good performance reviews. Still, when her employer decided to outsource most of its IT work, my mother lost her job. The reason wasn't that her technical skills were inadequate; instead, her salary and benefits cost the company more than outsourcing her job did. Until wages rise around the globe, jobs like my mother's will be vulnerable, no matter how well a person is trained.

> Transition to disagreements with Friedman
>
> First disagreement with Friedman
>
> Examples to support first disagreement
>
> Example to qualify first disagreement
>
> Clarification of first disagreement

The second dimension that Friedman misses is that a number of well-paid people in my mother's IT department, namely IT managers, were not laid off. As my mother explained at the time, they kept their jobs because they were experienced at figuring out the company's IT needs, planning for changes, researching and proposing solutions, and communicating in writing and speech—skills that her more narrow training and experience had missed. Friedman misses these skills by focusing only on technical training. Without the ability to solve problems creatively and to communicate, people with technical expertise alone may not have enough to save their jobs, as my mother learned.

> Second disagreement with Friedman
>
> Explanation of second disagreement
>
> Conclusion summarizing both disagreements with Friedman

Like my mother, I am more comfortable in front of a computer than I am in front of a group of people, and I had planned to major in computer science. Since my mother lost her job, however, I have decided to take courses in English and history as well. Classes in these subjects will require me to read broadly, think critically, research, and communicate ideas in writing—in short, to develop skills that make managers. When I enter the

> Final point: business needs and author's personal goals

COLLABORATIVE LEARNING

Exercises 3.9 and 3.10 can be productive collaborative projects. Ask students to revise the sample paragraph together and then to proofread each other's work.

RESOURCES AND IDEAS

Cook, Devan. "Revising Editing." *Teaching English in the Two-Year College* 29.2 (2001): 154–61. Print. Cook demonstrates how an activity that is editing for punctuation can also lead to revision.

Harrington, Jane. "Editing: the Last Step in the Process." *Nuts and Bolts: A Practical Guide to Teaching.* Ed. Thomas Newkirk. Portsmouth: Boynton, 1993. 151–78. Print. Harrington defines the editing process and provides practical suggestions for making editing a familiar part of classroom practice.

Harris, Jeanette. "Proofreading: A Reading/Writing Skill." *College Composition and Communication* 38 (1987): 464–66. Print. Harris argues that proofreading is a reading skill, a process of looking at each word and punctuation mark rather than of paying attention to the meaning of the text; and she suggests teaching students strategies like those outlined in this chapter— using a pointer (finger, pencil), reading aloud, reading in reverse order, and letting time elapse between writing and proofreading—in order to develop the specialized skill of proofreading.

Horner, Bruce. "Rethinking the 'Sociality' of Error: Teaching Editing as Negotiation." *Rhetoric Review* 11 (1992): 172–99. Print. Horner argues for a consideration of editing as a process of social exchange best supported by peer groups and one-on-one conferences.

Kearns, Edward A. "Encouraging Editing." *Strategies for Teaching First-Year Composition.* Ed. Duane Roen, Veronica Pantoja, Lauren Yena, Susan K. Miller, and Eric Waggoner. Urbana: NCTE, 2002. 566–68. Print. Kearns discusses marking essays to encourage students to edit more independently.

ANSWER: EXERCISE 3.9

An environmental group, Natural Resources Defense Council, has estimated that 5,500 to 6,200 children who are <u>in</u> preschool today may contract cancer dur<u>ing</u> <u>their</u> lives bec<u>au</u>se of the pesticides they consume in <u>their</u> food<u>.</u> In addition, these children will be at greater risk for kidney damage, problems with immunity, and other serious impair<u>ments</u>. The government bases <u>its</u> pesticide-safety standards on adults, but child<u>ren</u> consume many more <u>of</u> the fruits and fruit products likely <u>to</u> contain pesticides.

ANSWERS: EXERCISE 3.10

Individual response.

CONSTRUCTIVE CRITICISM

Students sometimes initially think of "criticizing" as a negative activity rather than a supportive practice. These "suggestions for commenting" on each other's writing can help set a supportive tone for collaborative revision groups. Criticism that is given in a helpful and careful manner is perhaps the easiest kind of criticism to benefit from. You can also encourage student writers to take an active role by bringing in questions and concerns about their own papers and by probing their peers' comments for specific examples and explanations: "Can you show me the places where my organization starts to break down?" See the chapter "Using Collaborative Learning with the Handbook" on pages IAE 34–45 for a detailed discussion on preparing students to provide and receive peer criticism. You may wish to draw on this discussion as a way of helping your students understand how to benefit from criticism and learn how to offer their classmates advice that can lead to real improvements in expression.

Explanation of final point

job market, my well-rounded education will make me a more attractive job candidate and will help me to become the kind of forward-thinking manager that US companies will always need to employ here in the US.

Conclusion recapping points of agreement and disagreement with Friedman and summarizing essay

Many jobs that require a college degree are indeed going overseas, as Thomas L. Friedman says, and my classmates and I need to be ready for a rapidly changing future. But rather than focus only on math and science, we need to broaden our academic experiences so that the skills we develop make us not only employable but also indispensable.

Work cited in MLA style (see p. 653)

Work Cited

Friedman, Thomas L. "It's a Flat World, After All." *New York Times Magazine* 3 Apr. 2005: 32-37. Print.

Exercise 3.9   Proofreading

Proofread the following passage, using any of the techniques listed on page 66 to bring errors into the foreground. There are thirteen errors in the passage: missing and misspelled words, typographical errors, and the like. If you are in doubt about any spellings, consult a dictionary.

An envirnmental group, Natural Resources Defense Council, has estimated that 5500 to 6200 children who are preschool today may contract cancer durng there lives becuase of the pesticides they consume in there food In addition, these children will be at greater risk for kidney damage, problems with immunity, and other serious imparments. The government bases it's pesticide-safety standards on adults, but childen consume many more the fruits and fruit products likely too contain pestcides.

Exercise 3.10   Preparing your final draft

Prepare the final draft of the essay you have been working on throughout Chapters 1–3. Proofread carefully and correct all errors before submitting your essay for review.

 Giving and receiving comments

1 **Working collaboratively**

Almost all the writing you do in college will generate responses from an instructor. In courses that stress writing, you may submit early drafts as well as your final paper, and your readers may include your classmates as well as your instructor. Like Katy Moreno's, such courses may feature **collaborative learning,** in which students work together on writing, from completing exercises to commenting on each other's work to producing whole papers. (At more and more schools this group work occurs over a computer network. See pp. 831–34.)

Whether you participate as a writer or as a writing "coach," collaboration can give you experience in reading written work and in reaching readers through writing. You may at first be anxious about criticizing others' work or sharing your own rough drafts, but you'll soon grow to appreciate the interaction and the confidence it gives you in your own reading and writing.

CULTURE LANGUAGE In some cultures writers do not expect criticism from readers, or readers do not expect to think critically about what they read. If critical responses are uncommon in your native culture, collaboration may at first be uncomfortable for you. As a writer, consider that readers are responding to your draft or even your final paper more as an exploration of ideas than as the last word on your subject; then you may be more receptive to readers' suggestions. As a reader, allow yourself to approach a text skeptically, and know that your tactful questions and suggestions will usually be considered appropriate.

2 Responding to the writing of others

When you are the reader of someone else's writing, keep the following principles in mind:

Commenting on others' writing

- **Be sure you know what the writer is saying.** If necessary, summarize the paper to understand its content. (See pp. 134–35.)
- **Address only your most significant concerns with the work.** Use the revision checklist on pp. 54–55 as a guide to what is significant. Unless you have other instructions, ignore mistakes in grammar, punctuation, spelling, and the like. (The temptation to focus on such errors may be especially strong if the writer is less experienced than you are with standard American English.) Emphasizing mistakes will contribute little to the writer's revision.
- **Remember that you are the reader, not the writer.** Don't edit sentences, add details, or otherwise assume responsibility for the paper.
- **Phrase your comments carefully.** Avoid misunderstandings by making sure comments are both clear and respectful. If you are responding on paper or online, not face to face with the writer, remember that the writer has nothing but your written words to go on. He or she can't ask you for immediate clarification and can't infer your attitudes from gestures, facial expressions, and tone of voice.
- **Be specific.** If something confuses you, say *why.* If you disagree with a conclusion, say *why.*

(continued)

CREATING A PEER REVIEW CONTRACT

To ensure that students benefit from the peer review process, ask them to discuss their previous experiences with peer reviews. Ask them to identify any problems they encountered with the process. Discuss what they have found helpful about it. Then, as a class, create a set of peer review guidelines for the class to follow. For example, many students are reluctant to criticize their peers, so discuss how asking questions or praising good parts of a draft can neutralize such fears. Also, the class could create a set of expectations for both the writers and the responders to follow. For example, responders will provide honest and specific feedback, and writers will not get defensive when receiving constructive feedback.

COMPUTER ACTIVITY
ELECTRONIC FEEDBACK

If students have easy access, it's possible to post drafts or sample essays to a course Web site to receive comments and feedback. See Daniel Anderson's essay on "Using Computers to Teach Writing" on pages IAE 47–61 for more information on working in a computer classroom.

MAKING PEER REVIEW COUNT

Sometimes, despite your best efforts, students might not take peer review as seriously as they should. To combat student lethargy, make specific demands of the responders. For instance, you might require them to complete a form. (See IAE Chapter 4, "Using Collaborative Learning with the Handbook" for samples.) Or you might require a specific amount of feedback (250 words or one-typed page). If you are counting peer reviews for credit, you might also evaluate responses for their specificity and quality, rather than simply requiring a certain quantity of feedback.

RESOURCES AND IDEAS

Breuch, Lee-Ann Kastman. *Virtual Peer Review: Teaching and Learning about Writing in Online Environments.* Albany: State U of New York P, 2004. Print. Breuch explores how technology affects the peer review process and discusses theoretical implications of the interaction of composition and technology.

Crow, Angela. "What's Age Got to Do with It? Teaching Older Students in Computer-Aided Classrooms." *Teaching English in the Two-Year College* 27.4 (2000): 400–06. Print. Crow offers suggestions for helping returning college students succeed: expect those students to learn more slowly, don't overload them with information, and scaffold assignments to reinforce new skills.

Grimm, Nancy. "Constructing Ideas of the Social Self." *Journal of Teaching Writing* 8.1 (Spring 1989): 11–20. Print. Social pressures, social rules, and social values are at work in the composition classroom and may interfere in collaborative learning, particularly in classes made up of a culturally diverse student population. The classroom composition must be considered when instructors expect students to think critically and to question dominant cultural values.

Kim, Loel. "Online Technologies for Teaching Writing: Students React to Teacher Response in Voice and Written Modalities." *Research in the Teaching of English* 38.3 (2004): 304–37. Print. Loel reports that students in online courses described varied reactions to written and vocal teacher responses. Although it was anticipated that students would prefer the voice modality, their preferences were split.

Kuhne, Michael, and Gill Creel. "Student Evaluation and an Introduction to Academic Discourse: 'I didn't like it, and I don't know how to improve it, because it works.'" *Teaching English in the Two-Year College* 33.3 (2006): 279–94. Print. Michael Kuhne and Gill Creel apply the theories of Paulo Freire and Ira Shor, among others, to peer review, discussing how it can be a democratic and dialogic process for students.

Johnson, T. R. "School Sucks." *College Composition and Communication* 52.4 (2001): 620–630. Print. Johnson explains why so many students dislike writing classes and provides advice on improving students' attitudes.

Sirc, Geoffrey, and Tom Reynolds. "The Face of Collaboration in the Networked Writing Classroom." *Computers and Composition* 7.3 (1990): 53–70. Print. Sirc and Reynolds discuss the use of networked classrooms in peer response to compositions.

Commenting on others' writing
(continued)

- **Be supportive as well as honest.** Tell the writer what you like about the paper. Word comments positively: instead of *This paragraph doesn't interest me,* say *You have an interesting detail here that I almost missed.* Comment in a way that emphasizes the effect of the work on you, the reader: *This paragraph confuses me because. . . .* And avoid measuring the work against a set of external standards: *This essay is poorly organized. Your thesis statement is inadequate.*

- **While reading, make your comments in writing.** Even if you will be delivering your comments in person later on, the written record will help you recall what you thought.

- **Link comments to specific parts of a paper.** Especially if you are reading the paper on a computer, be clear about what part of the paper each comment relates to. You can embed your comments directly into the paper, distinguishing them with highlighting or color. Or you can use the Comment function of a word processor (see below).

If you are reviewing others' drafts on a word processor, its Comment function will allow you to add comments without inserting words into the document's text. Usually found on the Insert menu, the function creates marginal annotations (such as those on Katy Moreno's first draft, pp. 49–50) or creates pop-ups that appear when readers move their cursors across words you have highlighted.

3 | Responding to comments on your own writing

When you *receive* comments from others, whether your classmates or your instructor, you will get more out of the process if you follow the guidelines below.

Benefiting from comments on your writing

- **Think of your readers as counselors or coaches.** They can help you see the virtues and flaws in your work and sharpen your awareness of readers' needs.
- **Read or listen to comments closely.**
- **Know what the critic is saying.** If you need more information, ask for it, or consult the appropriate section of this handbook.
- **Don't become defensive.** Letting comments offend you will only erect a barrier to improvement in your writing. As one writing teacher advises, "Leave your ego at the door."

- **Revise your work in response to appropriate comments.** Whether or not you are required to act on comments, you will learn more from actually revising than from just thinking about it.
- **Remember that you are the final authority on your work.** You should be open to suggestions, but you are free to decline advice when you think it is inappropriate.
- **Keep track of both the strengths and the weaknesses others identify.** Then in later assignments you can build on your successes and give special attention to problem areas.

As the last item in the preceding box indicates, you'll gain the most from collaboration if you carry your learning from one assignment into the next. To keep track of things to work on, try a chart like the one on page 62.

3h | Preparing a writing portfolio

Your writing teacher may ask you to assemble samples of your writing into a portfolio, or folder, once or more during the course. Such a portfolio gives you a chance to consider all your writing over a period and to showcase your best work.

Teachers' requirements for portfolios vary. For instance, some teachers ask students to choose their five or so best papers and to submit final drafts only. Others ask for final papers illustrating certain kinds of writing—say, one narrative, one critique, one argument, one research paper, and so on. Still others ask for notes and drafts along with selected papers in order to see students' writing processes. If your class is using online writing tools, your work may be archived as part of the course site and you may be asked to submit your portfolio electronically.

Just as teachers' requirements differ, so do their purposes. But most are looking for a range of writing that demonstrates your progress and strengths as a writer. You, in turn, see how you have advanced from one assignment to the next, as you've had time for new knowledge to sink in and time for practice. Teachers often allow students to revise papers before placing them in the portfolio, even if the papers were submitted earlier. In that case, every paper in the portfolio can benefit from all your learning.

An assignment to assemble a writing portfolio will probably also provide guidelines for what to include, how the portfolio will be evaluated, and how (or whether) it will be weighted for a grade. Be sure you understand the purpose of the portfolio and who will

Sperling, Melanie. "Constructing the Perspective of Teacher as Reader: A Framework for Studying Response to Student Writing." *Research in the Teaching of English* 28.2 (1994): 175–223. Print. This article studies one teacher's responses to student papers in order to evaluate the impact of teacher comments on student writing.

Weissberg, Bob. "Speaking of Writing: Some Functions of Talk in the ESL Composition Class." *Journal of Second Language Writing* 3.2 (1994): 1121–39. Print. This essay examines class discussion and peer input as learning factors, particularly in the ESL context.

Welch, Nancy. "Sideshadowing Teacher Response." *College English* 60.4 (1998): 374–95. Print. Welch suggests the technique of "sideshadowing," in which students make marginal comments on their own drafts.

White, Edward M. "The Scoring of Writing Portfolios: Phase 2." *College Composition and Communication* 56.4 (2005): 581–600. Print. White discusses the problems of holistic evaluation with portfolios and proposes a new system of scoring portfolios developed from portfolio theory rather than from essay theory. He argues for the importance of students' reflective writing in scoring portfolios.

Yancey, Kathleen Blake. "Postmodernism, Palimpsest, and Portfolios: Theoretical Issues in the Representation of Student Work." *College Composition and Communication* 55.4 (2004): 738–61. Print. Yancey compares differing possibilities presented by print and electronic portfolios. She advises instructors to consider how each differently represents students' intellectual work.

Yancey, Kathleen Blake and Irwin Weiser, eds. *Situating Portfolios: Four Perspectives.* Logan: Utah State UP, 1997. Print. This collection of essays explores the issues of power and authority in portfolio evaluation.

COLLABORATIVE LEARNING

PORTFOLIO PRESENTATION

Ask students to prepare to hand in their portfolios by making an oral presentation to their regular revision group. Each student can briefly describe the pieces she has chosen to include in her portfolio and explain how each piece has contributed to her progress. Revision group members can often remind writers of noticeable overall strengths that they might have overlooked.

HIGHLIGHTS

The writing some American high school students do is no more than a paragraph in length, and even older or nontraditional students may have had little writing experience. So learning to think of paragraphs as units in larger pieces of discourse may be a challenge for your students. If they have written longer essays, these probably have been in the familiar "five-paragraph theme" pattern of introduction, three paragraphs of development, and conclusion. ESL students may conceptualize and shape paragraphs differently or may not be used to writing in paragraphs at all. Don't be surprised, then, if learning to use paragraphs in different ways presents a challenge for your students.

Here we present a strategy of developing paragraphs as mini-essays, each with a generalization (topic sentence) supported by limitations and evidence. Practicing these essays-in-miniature can help students develop longer essays as they gain more skill. Of course, not all paragraphs in

read it. For instance, if your composition teacher will be the only reader and her guidelines urge you to show evidence of progress, you might include a paper that took big risks but never entirely succeeded. In contrast, if a committee of teachers will read your work and the guidelines urge you to demonstrate your competence as a writer, you might include only papers that did succeed.

Unless the guidelines specify otherwise, provide error-free copies of your final drafts, label all your samples with your name, and assemble them all in a folder. Add a cover letter or memo that lists the samples, explains why you've included each one, and evaluates your progress as a writer. The self-evaluation involved should be a learning experience for you and will help your teacher assess your development as a writer.

4

Writing and Revising Paragraphs

A **paragraph** is a group of related sentences set off by a beginning indention or, sometimes, by extra space. For you and your readers, paragraphs provide breathers from long stretches of text and indicate key changes in the development of your thesis. They help to organize and clarify ideas.

In the body of an essay, you may use paragraphs for any of these purposes:

- **To introduce and give evidence for a main point supporting your essay's central idea (its thesis).** See pages 27–32 for a discussion of an essay's thesis.
- **Within a group of paragraphs centering on one main point, to develop a key example or other important evidence.**

mycomplab

Visit *mycomplab.com* for more resources and exercises on paragraphs.

- **To shift approach**—for instance, from pros to cons, from problem to solution, from questions to answers.
- **To mark movement in a sequence,** such as from one reason or step to another.

In addition, you will use paragraphs for special purposes:

- **To introduce or to conclude an essay.** See pages 104 and 107.
- **To emphasize an important point or to mark a significant transition between points.** See pages 109–10.
- **In dialog, to indicate that a new person has begun speaking.** See page 110.

The following paragraph illustrates simply how an effective body paragraph works to help both writer and reader. The thesis of the essay in which this paragraph appears is that a Texas chili championship gives undue attention to an unpleasant food.

> Some people really like chili, apparently, but nobody can agree how the stuff should be made. C. V. Wood, twice winner at Terlingua, uses flank steak, pork chops, chicken, and green chilis. My friend Hughes Rudd of CBS News, who imported five hundred pounds of chili powder into Russia as a condition of accepting employment as Moscow correspondent, favors coarse-ground beef. Isadore Bleckman, the cameraman I must live with on the road, insists upon one-inch cubes of stew beef and puts garlic in his chili, an Illinois affectation. An Indian of my acquaintance, Mr. Fulton Batisse, who eats chili for breakfast when he can, uses buffalo meat and plays an Indian drum while it's cooking. I ask you.
>
> —Charles Kuralt, *Dateline America*

General statement relating to thesis: announces topic of paragraph

Four specific examples, all providing evidence for general statement

While you are drafting, conscious attention to the requirements of the paragraph may sometimes help pull ideas out of you or help you forge relationships. But don't expect effective paragraphs like Kuralt's to flow from your fingertips while you are grappling with what you want to say. Instead, use the checklist on the next page to guide your revision of paragraphs so that they work to your and your readers' advantage.

Note On the Web the paragraphing conventions described here do not always apply. Web readers sometimes skim text instead of reading word for word, and they are accustomed to embedded links that may take them from the paragraph to another page. Writing for the Web, you may want to write shorter paragraphs than you would in printed documents, and save embedded links for the ends

professional writing conform in length, structure, or purpose to the models this chapter provides.

The chapter reviews strategies for improving paragraph unity, achieving paragraph coherence, developing paragraph content, and writing special-purpose paragraphs. It concludes by showing how paragraphs can be linked within the larger context of the essay. Helping students learn and practice the standard paragraphing strategies elaborated in this chapter can be a good way to help them improve their writing. The annotations provided for sample paragraphs help students see the strategies explained in the chapter "in practice."

A WRITER'S PERSPECTIVE

> *The purpose of paragraphing is to give the reader a rest. The writer is saying . . . : "Have you got that? If so, I'll go on."*
>
> —H. W. Fowler

COMPUTER ACTIVITY

Have students print out Web pages and bring them into class. Individually or as a class, they can evaluate the paragraphs for unity, coherence, and development. Students can make suggestions for how to revise each page's paragraphs and for where to position links to other pages.

RESOURCES AND IDEAS

Rhetorical scholarship is split on a number of the "givens" of paragraphing: whether paragraphs are self-contained units or building blocks of larger discourses, whether topic sentences are needed, and so on. These references offer you a fairly mainstream view of research into paragraphing.

Duncan, Mike. "Whatever Happened to the Paragraph?" *College English* 69.5 (2007): 470–95. Print. Duncan traces the rise and decline of paragraph theory in composition studies. He calls for compositionists to return to studying the paragraph to provide new terminology for teachers and to perform empirical research on the teaching of paragraphs.

Knoblauch, C. H. "The Rhetoric of the Paragraph." *Journal of Advanced Composition* 2.1/2 (1981): 53–61. Print.

Stern, Arthur A. "When Is a Paragraph?" *College Composition and Communication* 27.3 (1976): 253–57. Print. Stern argues for the rhetorical flexibility of paragraphs as development devices.

HIGHLIGHTS

Section 4a of this chapter addresses the need for a paragraph to focus on a topic and to make the focus clear to the reader through an explicit statement in the form of a topic sentence. It introduces the basic form of the expository paragraph—topic sentence, illustrations, and details—and indicates how this pattern can be varied to suit a writer's purpose and to fit within the context created by the surrounding paragraphs.

The concept of a clearly stated and variously placed topic sentence that controls the shape of a paragraph is an oversimplification. But it appears to help students a great deal to think of the paragraph as a unit dominated and controlled by an expressly stated generalization. Students can see the topic sentence as a commitment they make to the reader, with the rest of the paragraph following through on the commitment. Seeing the obvious parallel between the paragraph's topic sentence and the essay's thesis statement is also helpful to many students. Finally, stating a central point in a single sentence and marshaling support for it enables students to see more clearly what is required for unity.

Checklist for revising paragraphs

- **Is the paragraph unified?** Does it adhere to one general idea that is either stated in a topic sentence or otherwise apparent? (See below.)
- **Is the paragraph coherent?** Do the sentences follow a clear sequence? Are the sentences linked as needed by parallelism, repetition or restatement, pronouns, consistency, and transitional expressions? (See p. 79.)
- **Is the paragraph developed?** Is the general idea of the paragraph well supported with specific evidence such as details, facts, examples, and reasons? (See p. 92.)

of paragraphs lest readers miss important information. (For more on composing for the Web, see pp. 834–40.)

CULTURE LANGUAGE Not all cultures share the paragraphing conventions of American academic writing. The conventions are not universal even among users of standard American English: for instance, US newspaper writers compose very short paragraphs that will break up text in narrow columns. In some other languages, writing moves differently from English—not from left to right, but from right to left or down rows from top to bottom. Even in languages that move as English does, writers may not use paragraphs at all. Or they may use paragraphs but not state the central ideas or provide transitional expressions to show readers how sentences relate. If your native language is not English and you have difficulty with paragraphs, don't worry about paragraphing during drafting. Instead, during a separate step of revision, divide your text into parts that develop your main points. Mark those parts with indentions.

4a Maintaining paragraph unity

Readers generally expect a paragraph to explore a single idea. They will be alert for that idea and will patiently follow its development. In other words, they will seek and appreciate paragraph **unity:** clear identification and clear elaboration of one idea and of that idea only.

In an essay the thesis statement often asserts the main idea as a commitment to readers (see p. 27). In a paragraph a **topic sentence** often alerts readers to the essence of the paragraph by asserting the central idea and expressing the writer's attitude toward it. In a brief essay each body paragraph will likely treat one main point supporting the essay's thesis statement; the topic sentences simply elaborate on parts of the thesis. In longer essays paragraphs tend to work in groups, each group treating one main point. Then the topic sentences will tie into that main point, and all the points together will support the thesis.

1 Focusing on the central idea

Like the thesis sentence, the topic sentence is a commitment to readers, and the rest of the paragraph delivers on that commitment. Look again at Kuralt's paragraph on chili on page 73: the opening statement conveys the author's promise that he will describe various ways to make chili, and the following sentences keep the promise. But what if Kuralt had written this paragraph instead?

> Some people really like chili, apparently, but nobody can agree how the stuff should be made. C. V. Wood, twice winner at Terlingua, uses flank steak, pork chops, chicken, and green chilis. My friend Hughes Rudd, who imported five hundred pounds of chili powder into Russia as a condition of accepting employment as Moscow correspondent, favors coarse-ground beef. He had some trouble finding the beef in Moscow, though. He sometimes had to scour all the markets and wait in long lines. For any American used to overstocked supermarkets and department stores, Russia can be quite a shock.

Topic sentence: general statement

Two examples supporting statement

Digression

By wandering off from chili ingredients to consumer deprivation in Russia, the paragraph fails to deliver on the commitment of its topic sentence.

You should expect digressions while you are drafting: if you allow yourself to explore ideas, as you should, then of course every paragraph will not be tightly woven, perfectly unified. But spare your readers the challenge and frustration of repeatedly shifting focus to follow your rough explorations: revise each paragraph so that it develops a single idea.

While revising your paragraphs for unity, you may want to highlight the central idea of each paragraph to be sure it's stated and then focus on it. On paper you can bracket or circle the idea. On a computer you can format the idea in color or highlight it with a color background. Just be sure to remove the color or highlighting before printing the final draft.

2 Placing the topic sentence

The topic sentence of a paragraph and its supporting details may be arranged variously, depending on how you want to direct

The exercises for this section ask students to identify the central idea in unified paragraphs, to revise paragraphs, to build a paragraph by combining and revising kernel sentences, and to write their own paragraphs. These exercises can be easily adapted to small-group work: in coming to understand how others view paragraphs, students may more readily understand the influence of paragraph structure and unity on readers.

USING STUDENT WRITING

Ask students to choose key paragraphs from their work-in-progress and read them aloud to their groups. The listeners should take notes on the effectiveness of the various unity strategies they hear in each paragraph. If students have trouble responding without seeing a written text, you can have them work in pairs to critique and revise the unity of each other's paragraphs.

COLORING PARAGRAPHS

Bring in copies of sample paragraphs and felt-tipped pens or pencils in two colors. Split the class into groups and ask each group to underline topic sentences in one color and examples and details in another color. Students should then be able to discover the arrangement of each paragraph, the placement of the topic sentence, and the way the parts fit together to form a unified whole. Students working in a computer classroom can use the Bold feature and designated fonts instead of pens to identify each of these elements.

USING STUDENT WRITING

Ask students to bring in paragraphs from writings in other classes or other disciplines to use in the "coloring paragraphs" activity. They will find it instructive to note how different writers decide to place, emphasize, or omit topic sentences. They can also perform this exercise on the paragraphs in their drafts.

SEEING PARAGRAPHS

Visually, students may find it easier to understand topic sentence placement and paragraph arrangement by using these diagrams as guides:

Topic sentence at the beginning:	△
Topic sentence at the beginning and in the middle:	△ △
Topic sentence at the end:	▽
Topic sentence at the beginning and the end:	◇

readers' attention and how complex your central idea is. In the most common arrangements, the topic sentence comes at the beginning of the paragraph, comes at the end, or is not stated at all but is nonetheless apparent. The advantages of each approach are described on these two pages. If you write on a computer, you can easily experiment with the position of the topic sentence by moving the sentence around (or deleting it) to see the effect. (The sentence will probably take some editing to work smoothly into various positions.)

Topic sentence at the beginning

When you place the topic sentence first in a paragraph, it can help you select the details that follow. For readers, the topic-first model establishes an initial context in which all the supporting details can be understood. Reading Kuralt's paragraph on page 73, we easily relate each detail or example back to the point made in the first sentence.

The topic-first model is common not only in expository paragraphs, such as Kuralt's, but also in argument paragraphs, such as the one following:

> It is a misunderstanding of the American retail store to think we go there necessarily to buy. Some of us shop. There's a difference. Shopping has many purposes, the least interesting of which is to acquire new articles. We shop to cheer ourselves up. We shop to practice decision-making. We shop to be useful and productive members of our class and society. We shop to remind ourselves how much is available to us. We shop to remind ourselves how much is to be striven for. We shop to assert our superiority to the material objects that spread themselves before us.
>
> —Phyllis Rose, "Shopping and Other Spiritual Adventures"

Topic sentence: statement of misconception

Correction of misconception

Topic sentence at the end

In some paragraphs the central idea may be stated at the end, after supporting sentences have made a case for the general statement. Since this model leads the reader to a conclusion by presenting all the evidence first, it can prove effective in argument. And because the point of the paragraph is withheld until the end, this model can be dramatic in exposition, too, as illustrated by the following example from an essay about William Tecumseh Sherman, a Union general during the US Civil War:

Sherman is considered by some to be the inventor of "total war": the first general in human history to carry the logic of war to its ultimate extreme, the first to scorch the earth, the first to consciously demoralize the hostile civilian population in order to subdue its army, the first to wreck an economy in order to starve its soldiers. He has been called our first "merchant of terror" and seen as the spiritual father of our Vietnam War concepts of "search and destroy," "pacification," "strategic hamlets," and "free-fire zones." As such, he remains a cardboard figure of our history: a monstrous arch-villain to unreconstructed Southerners, and an embarrassment to Northerners.
— Adapted from James Reston, Jr.,
"You Cannot Refine It"

Information supporting and building to topic sentence

Topic sentence

Expressing the central idea at the end of the paragraph does not eliminate the need to unify the paragraph. The idea in the topic sentence must still govern the selection of all the preceding details.

Central idea not stated

Occasionally, a paragraph's central idea will be stated in the previous paragraph or will be so obvious that it need not be stated at all. The following is from an essay on the actor Humphrey Bogart:

Usually he wore the trench coat unbuttoned, just tied with the belt, and a slouch hat, rarely tilted. Sometimes it was a captain's cap and a yachting jacket. Almost always his trousers were held up by a cowboy belt. You know the kind: one an Easterner waiting for a plane out of Phoenix buys just as a joke and then takes a liking to. Occasionally, he'd hitch up his slacks with it, and he often jabbed his thumbs behind it, his hands ready for a fight or a dame.
— Peter Bogdanovich,
"Bogie in Excelsis"

Details adding up to the unstated idea that Bogart's character could be seen in his clothing

Paragraphs in descriptive writing (like the one above) and in narrative writing (relating a sequence of events) often lack stated topic sentences. But a paragraph without a topic sentence still should have a central idea, and its details should develop that idea.

Exercise 4.1 Finding the central idea

What is the central idea of each of the following paragraphs? In what sentence or sentences is it expressed?

TOPIC SENTENCE OMISSION

Some research suggests that the necessity of a topic sentence is determined by the author's relation to his or her readers; a writer writing to less expert or more expert readers is more likely to use a topic sentence than one writing for peers, for instance. Ask students to work in groups to collect examples of topic sentence use and omission, then analyze the different author-reader relationships implied in each example. Encourage students to collect samples from their own journals and papers, but also from various kinds of published writing, to get the best results from this survey.

PRACTICE SUPPLYING TOPIC SENTENCES

Bring in two or three paragraphs from magazine or newspaper articles or Web sites that use clear topic sentences. Provide copies of the paragraphs to each group with the topic sentences removed. Ask each group to read the paragraph and write an appropriate topic sentence for each paragraph. As a class, have each group share their sentences. How do the new sentences compare both to one another and to the original topic sentence?

COMPUTER ACTIVITY

REORGANIZING PARAGRAPHS

For students working on computers, the reorganization of paragraphs is particularly easy. Encourage students to select one or two paragraphs from their drafts and reorganize them with the controlling idea at the end, as Reston does. Then ask them to judge whether they gain any rhetorical advantage from such a rearrangement. Leonard A. Podis suggests some other exercises of this nature in "Teaching Arrangement: Defining a More Practical Approach," *College Composition and Communication* 31.2 (1980): 197–204 (Print.), and JoAnne M. Podis and Leonard A. Podis present more exercises in "Identifying and Teaching Rhetorical Plans for Arrangement," *College Composition and Communication* 41.4 (1990): 430–42. Print.

COLLABORATIVE LEARNING

Have students work in groups to complete Exercise 4.1. Ask each group to discuss what effect the particular placement of each topic sentence has, and then report back to the class on the sentences that best express the central idea of each paragraph.

ANSWERS: EXERCISE 4.1

1. The central idea is sentence 8: The black bourgeoisie feel a sense of shame about their own identity.
2. The central idea is sentence 1: Scientists know something about the song of the humpback whale.

COLLABORATIVE LEARNING

Have students work in groups to complete Exercise 4.2. Ask groups to consider how they might revise and expand the deleted material to include it in a follow-up paragraph.

ANSWERS: EXERCISE 4.2

The topic sentence is sentence 1. Unrelated are sentences 4 and 7.

ANSWERS: EXERCISE 4.3

Individual response.

1.   Today many black Americans enjoy a measure of economic security [1] beyond any we have known in the history of black America. But if they [2] remain in a nasty blue funk, it's because their very existence seems an affront to the swelling ranks of the poor. Nor have black intellectuals ever [3] quite made peace with the concept of the black bourgeoisie, a group that is typically seen as devoid of cultural authenticity, doomed to mimicry and pallid assimilation. I once gave a talk before an audience of black [4] academics and educators, in the course of which I referred to black middle-class culture. Afterward, one of the academics in the audience, deeply [5] affronted, had a question for me. "Professor Gates," he asked rhetorically, [6] his voice dripping with sarcasm, "what *is* black middle-class culture?" I [7] suggested that if he really wanted to know, he need only look around the room. But perhaps I should just have handed him a mirror: for just as [8] nothing is more American than anti-Americanism, nothing is more characteristic of the black bourgeoisie than the sense of shame and denial that the identity inspires.
    —Henry Louis Gates, Jr., "Two Nations . . . Both Black"

2.   Though they do not know why the humpback whale sings, scientists [1] do know something about the song itself. They have measured the length [2] of a whale's song: from a few minutes to over half an hour. They have [3] recorded and studied the variety and complex arrangements of low moans, high squeaks, and sliding squeals that make up the song. And they [4] have learned that each whale sings in its own unique pattern.
    —Janet Lieber (student), "Whales' Songs"

Exercise 4.2   Revising a paragraph for unity

The following paragraph contains ideas or details that do not support its central idea. Identify the topic sentence in the paragraph and delete the unrelated material.

In the southern part of the state, some people still live much as they did a century ago. They use coal- or wood-burning stoves for heating and cooking. Their homes do not have electricity or indoor bathrooms or running water. The towns they live in don't receive adequate funding from the state and federal governments, so the schools are poor and in bad shape. Beside most homes there is a garden where fresh vegetables are gathered for canning. Small pastures nearby support livestock, including cattle, pigs, horses, and chickens. Most of the people have cars or trucks, but the vehicles are old and beat-up from traveling on unpaved roads.

Exercise 4.3   Considering your past work: Paragraph unity

For a continuing exercise in this chapter, choose a paper you've written in the past year. Examine the body paragraphs for unity. Do they have clear topic sentences? If not, are the paragraphs' central ideas still clear? Are the paragraphs unified around their central ideas? Should any details be deleted for unity? Should other, more relevant details be added in their stead?

Exercise 4.4 Writing a unified paragraph

Develop the following topic sentence into a unified paragraph by using the relevant information in the supporting statements. Delete each statement that does not relate directly to the topic, and then rewrite and combine sentences as appropriate. Place the topic sentence in the position that seems most effective to you.

Topic sentence

Mozart's accomplishments in music seem remarkable even today.

Supporting information

Wolfgang Amadeus Mozart was born in 1756 in Salzburg, Austria.
He began composing music at the age of five.
He lived most of his life in Salzburg and Vienna.
His first concert tour of Europe was at the age of six.
On his first tour he played harpsichord, organ, and violin.
He published numerous compositions before reaching adolescence.
He married in 1782.
Mozart and his wife were both poor managers of money.
They were plagued by debts.
Mozart composed over six hundred musical compositions.
His most notable works are his operas, symphonies, quartets, and piano concertos.
He died at the age of thirty-five.

Exercise 4.5 Turning topic sentences into unified paragraphs

Develop three of the following topic sentences into detailed and unified paragraphs.

1. Men and women are different in at least one important respect.
2. The best Web search engine is [*name*].
3. Fans of _____ music [*country, classical, rock, rap, jazz, or another kind*] come in [*number*] varieties.
4. Professional sports have [*or have not*] been helped by extending the regular season with championship play-offs.
5. Working for good grades can interfere with learning.

4b Achieving paragraph coherence

A paragraph is unified if it holds together—if all its details and examples support the central idea. A paragraph is **coherent** if readers can see *how* the paragraph holds together—how the sentences relate to each other—without having to stop and reread.

Incoherence gives readers the feeling of being yanked around, as the following example shows.

ANSWERS: EXERCISE 4.4

Delete statements not pertaining to Mozart's accomplishments: when he was born, where he lived, when he married, his debts. Possible paragraph:

Mozart's accomplishments in music seem remarkable even today. At the age of six he made his first concert tour of Europe, playing harpsichord, organ, and violin. He had begun composing music at the age of five, and by adolescence he had published numerous musical compositions. When he died at thirty-five, his work included over six hundred compositions, most notably operas, symphonies, quartets, and piano concertos.

COMPUTER ACTIVITY

REARRANGING PARAGRAPHS

Exercises 4.4 and 4.5 work well in a computer classroom because students have the flexibility to rearrange sentences multiple times without retyping them. Students can print out the results in order to compare their differing responses in groups. Students might also e-mail their responses to a partner in the class, or you could post several volunteer responses on the class Web site for the whole class to read and discuss.

ANSWERS: EXERCISE 4.5

Individual response.

RESOURCES AND IDEAS

Becker, A. L. "A Tagmemic Approach to Paragraph Analysis." *College Composition and Communication* 16.5 (1965): 237–42. Print. Becker observes that expository paragraphs generally follow a variation of one of two patterns: topic-restriction-illustration (TRI) or problem-solution (PS).

Wiener, Harvey S. "The Single Narrative Paragraph and College Remediation." *College English* 33.6 (1972): 660–69. Print. Wiener suggests using paragraph-length narrative themes to help students develop both paragraph and essay skills.

HIGHLIGHTS

This section of the chapter deals with paragraph coherence, addressing it from the reader's perspective as well as the writer's. Students are shown how the devices they use to achieve paragraph coherence help readers to follow the arguments or information being presented.

The discussion emphasizes the need to maintain a clear organizational pattern as one of the principal ways to ensure coherence, and it presents examples of two basic ways of organizing paragraphs: organizing by space or time and organizing for emphasis. Students who have difficulty organizing their own writing can usually see the pattern of organization in a well-made example from another writer's work.

Following the discussion of patterns, the section takes up and illustrates other methods of achieving coherence: parallelism; repetition of words; careful use of pronouns; consistency in person, tense, and number; and transitional expressions. Analysis of paragraphs can help students understand these explicit and implicit means by which individual sentences are held together so that the reader effortlessly follows the flow of ideas and information. As in the preceding section, the exercises move from analysis to revision to production and are useful in small-group activities as well as in individual work.

Ways to achieve paragraph coherence

- Organize effectively (p. 81).
- Repeat or restate key words and word groups (p. 85).
- Use parallel structures (p. 85).
- Use pronouns (p. 86).
- Be consistent in nouns, pronouns, and verbs (p. 86).
- Use transitional expressions (p. 87).

The ancient Egyptians were masters of preserving dead people's bodies by making mummies of them. — **Topic sentence**

Mummies several thousand years old have been discovered nearly intact. The skin, hair, teeth, finger- and toenails, and facial features of the mummies were evident. One can diagnose the diseases they suffered in life, such as smallpox, arthritis, and nutritional deficiencies. The process was remarkably effective. Sometimes apparent were the fatal afflictions of the dead people: a middle-aged king died from a blow on the head, and polio killed a child king. Mummification consisted of removing the internal organs, applying natural preservatives inside and out, and then wrapping the body in layers of bandages. — **Sentences related to topic sentence but disconnected from each other**

The paragraph as it was actually written appears below. It is much clearer because the writer arranged information differently and also built links into his sentences so that they would flow smoothly:

- After stating the central idea in a topic sentence, the writer moves to two more specific explanations and illustrates the second with four sentences of examples.
- (Circled) words repeat or restate key terms or concepts.
- Boxed words link sentences and clarify relationships.
- Underlined phrases are in parallel grammatical form to reflect their parallel content.

The ancient Egyptians were masters of preserving dead people's bodies by (making mummies) of them. — **Topic sentence**

Basically, (mummification) consisted of removing the internal organs, applying natural preservatives inside and out, and then wrapping the body in layers of bandages. And (the process) was remarkably effective. — **Explanation 1: What mummification is**

Indeed, mummies several thousand years old have been discovered nearly intact. Their skin, hair, teeth, finger- and toenails, and facial features are still evident. Their diseases in life, such as smallpox, arthritis, and nutritional deficiencies, are still diagnosable. Even their fatal afflictions are still apparent: a middle-aged king died from a blow on the head; a child king died from polio.

> Explanation 2: Why the Egyptians were masters

> Specific examples of explanation 2

—Mitchell Rosenbaum (student), "Lost Arts of the Egyptians"

Though some of the connections in this paragraph were added in revision, the writer attended to them while drafting as well. Not only superficial coherence but also an underlying clarity of relationships can be achieved by tying each sentence to the one before—generalizing from it, clarifying it, qualifying it, adding to it, illustrating it. Each sentence in a paragraph creates an expectation of some sort in the mind of the reader, a question such as "How was a mummy made?" or "How intact are the mummies?" or "What's another example?" When you recognize these expectations and try to fulfill them, readers are likely to understand relationships without struggle.

1 Organizing the paragraph

The paragraphs on mummies illustrate an essential element of coherence: information must be arranged in an order that readers can follow easily and that corresponds to their expectations. The common organizations for paragraphs correspond to those for entire essays: by space, by time, and for emphasis. (In addition, the patterns of development also suggest certain arrangements. See pp. 93–101.)

Note On a computer you can experiment with different paragraph organizations and emphases. Copy a paragraph, paste the copy into your document, and then try moving sentences around. To evaluate the versions, you'll need to edit each one so that sentences flow smoothly, attending to repetition, parallelism, transitions, and the other techniques for achieving coherence.

Organizing by space or time

A paragraph organized **spatially** focuses readers' attention on one point and scans a person, object, or scene from that point. The movement usually parallels the way people actually look at things, from top to bottom, from side to side, from near to far. Virginia Woolf follows the last pattern in the following paragraph:

PARAGRAPH PATTERNS II

Write a paragraph following one of the basic organizational schemes discussed in 4b-1. Leave the subject and content of the paragraph up to the individual student. If they wish, students may make up information, as long as they keep it plausible. Students can compare results in groups, then work together to revise one of those responses into a paragraph to be "published" on the class Web site or printed out and distributed.

EXTRA EXAMPLES

The following examples illustrate the specific-to-general pattern in a sentence and may be extended to short sample paragraphs:

(specific) + good study habits
(specific) + consistent effort
(specific) + curiosity
(general) = good grades

Good study habits, consistent effort, and intellectual curiosity will result in good grades.

(specific) + seeds
(specific) + soil
(specific) + sunlight
(specific) + water
(general) = good vegetable crop

A combination of fresh seeds, well-balanced soil, and adequate sunlight and water results in a good vegetable crop.

Spatial organization

The sun struck straight upon the house, making the white walls glare between the dark windows. Their panes, woven thickly with green branches, held circles of impenetrable darkness. Sharp-edged wedges of light lay upon the window-sill and showed inside the room plates with blue rings, cups with curved handles, the bulge of a great bowl, the criss-cross pattern in the rug, and the formidable corners and lines of cabinets and bookcases. Behind their conglomeration hung a zone of shadow in which might be a further shape to be disencumbered of shadow or still denser depths of darkness.

—Virginia Woolf, *The Waves*

> Description moving from outside (closer) to inside (farther)

> Unstated central idea: Sunlight barely penetrated the house's secrets.

Another familiar way of organizing the elements of a paragraph is **chronologically**—that is, in order of their occurrence in time. In a chronological paragraph, as in experience, the earliest events come first, followed by more recent ones.

Chronological organization

In early spring, millions of monarch butterflies that have spent the winter months in Mexico begin an annual migration north to the monarch's summer habitats. After covering about fifty miles a day, most make their first stop in Texas, where they lay their eggs on milkweed and die soon after. Their offspring continue the flight to the northern United States and Canada, laying the eggs of the next generation of monarchs along the way. By late spring, these offspring or their offspring reach their summer homes. In August, the third or fourth generation of the original monarchs begins the long return migration south. They do not reproduce in the north but return to where their ancestors wintered and hibernate there. The following spring they start the cycle over by flying north to Texas.

—Ben Kampe (student), "The Monarch Trail"

> Topic sentence

> Details in order of their occurrence

Organizing for emphasis

Some organizational schemes are imposed on paragraphs to achieve a certain emphasis. The most common is the **general-to-specific** scheme, in which the topic sentence often comes first and then the following sentences become increasingly specific. The paragraph on mummies (pp. 80–81) illustrates this organization: each sentence is either more specific than the one before it or at the same level of generality. Here is another illustration:

General-to-specific organization

Perhaps the simplest fact about sleep is that individual needs for it vary widely. ⟶ Topic sentence

Most adults sleep between seven and nine hours, but occasionally people turn up who need twelve hours or so, while some rare types can get by on three or four. Rarest of all are those legendary types who require almost no sleep at all; respected researchers have recently studied three such people. One of them—a healthy, happy woman in her seventies—sleeps about an hour every two or three days. The other two are men in early middle age, who get by on a few minutes a night. One of them complains about the daily fifteen minutes or so he's forced to "waste" in sleeping. ⟶ Supporting examples, increasingly specific

—Lawrence A. Mayer,
"The Confounding Enemy of Sleep"

In the less common **specific-to-general** organization, the elements of the paragraph build to a general conclusion:

Specific-to-general organization

It's disconcerting that so many college women, when asked how their children will be cared for if they themselves work, refer with vague confidence to "the day care center" as though there were some great amorphous kiddie watcher out there that the state provides. ⟶ Common belief

But such places, adequately funded, well run, and available to all, are still scarce in this country, particularly for middle-class women. And figures show that when she takes time off for family-connected reasons (births, child care), a woman's chances for career advancement plummet. In a job market that's steadily tightening and getting more competitive, these obstacles bode the kind of danger ahead that can shatter not only professions, but egos. ⟶ Actual situation

A hard reality is that there's not much more support for our daughters who have family-plus-career goals than there was for us; there's simply a great deal more self and societal pressure. ⟶ General conclusion: topic sentence

—Judith Wax,
Starting in the Middle

As its name implies, the **problem-solution** arrangement introduces a problem and then proposes or explains a solution. The next paragraph explains how to gain from Internet newsgroups despite their limitations:

PARAGRAPH SCRAMBLES

These activities are suitable for students working individually; when assigned to small groups, however, the activities work even better by encouraging considerable discussion and discovery.

1. Take a good paragraph, by either a student or a professional, and rearrange the sentences. Then ask students to unscramble the sentences and make a clear, coherent paragraph. This exercise will make students aware of the flow of a coherent paragraph and will alert them to the number of examples and details found in a well-developed paragraph.

2. Choose a paragraph that lacks coherence and rearrange the sentences. Tell students to unscramble the sentences to form a coherent paragraph. Indicate that students are free to add any transitions, sentences, illustrations, or details they feel are necessary to make the paragraph both coherent and well developed. Students will quickly spot any coherence problems in the original paragraph, and unless the topic of the paragraph is quite unusual, they will be able to add any necessary content.

DRAMATIC EXAMPLES

Climactic order is a form of structuring that moves from least to most important. To help explain this strategy you may wish to draw examples from drama, particularly from the structure of tragedy. Othello provides an obvious example of structuring that moves from least dramatic/tension-filled to most dramatic/tension-filled.

Least dramatic—Othello marries Desdemona
More dramatic—Othello suspects Desdemona
  of infidelity
More dramatic—Desdemona defends her chastity and argues for her life
Most dramatic (climax)—Othello kills Desdemona and then realizes that she has been faithful to him

Problem-solution organization

Even when you do find a newsgroup with apparently useful material, you have no assurance of a correspondent's authority because of e-mail's inherent anonymity. Many people don't cite their credentials. Besides, anyone can pose as an expert. The best information you can get } — Topic sentence and clarification: statement of the problem

initially is apt to be a reference to something of which you were not aware but can then investigate for yourself. Internet newsgroups can be valuable for that alone. I have been directed to software-problem solutions, owners of out-of-print books, and important people who know nothing about communicating through electronic communities. It is best to start with the assumption that you are conversing with peers, people who know things that you don't, while you probably know things that they don't. Gradually, by trading information, you develop some virtual relationships and can assess the relative validity of your sources. Meanwhile, you will probably have learned a few things along the way. — Solution to the problem

—Adapted from John A. Butler,
Cybersearch

When your details vary in significance, you can arrange them in a **climactic** order, from least to most important or dramatic:

Climactic organization

Nature has put many strange tongues into the heads of her creatures. There is the frog's } — Topic sentence

tongue, rooted at the front of the mouth so it can be protruded an extra distance for nabbing prey. } — Least dramatic example

There is the gecko lizard's tongue, so long and agile that the lizard uses it to wash its eyes. But the ultimate lingual whopper has been achieved in the anteater. The anteater's head, long as it is, is not long enough to contain the tremendous tongue which licks deep into ant-hills. Its tongue is not rooted in the mouth or throat: it is fastened to the breastbone. — Most dramatic example

—Alan Devoe, "Nature's Utmost"

In other paragraph organizations, you can arrange details according to how you think readers are likely to understand them. In discussing the virtues of public television, for instance, you might proceed from **most familiar to least familiar,** from a well-known program your readers have probably seen to less well-known programs they may not have seen. Or in defending the right of government employees to strike, you might arrange your reasons from **simplest to most complex,** from the employees' need to be able to redress grievances to the more subtle consequences for relations between employers and employees.

2 Repeating or restating key words

Repeating or restating the important words in a paragraph binds the sentences together and keeps the paragraph's topic uppermost in readers' minds. In the next example, notice how the circled words relate the sentences and stress the important ideas of the paragraph:

> Having listened to both Chinese and English, I also tend to be suspicious of any comparisons between the two languages. Typically, one language—that of the person doing the comparing—is often used as the standard, the benchmark for a logical form of expression. And so the language being compared is always in danger of being judged deficient or superfluous, simplistic or unnecessarily complex, melodious or cacophonous. English speakers point out that Chinese is extremely difficult because it relies on variations in tone barely discernible to the human ear. By the same token, Chinese speakers tell me English is extremely difficult because it is inconsistent, a language of too many broken rules, of Mickey Mice and Donald Ducks.
>
> —Amy Tan, "The Language of Discretion"

This paragraph links sentences through their structure, too, because the subject of each one picks up on key words used earlier:

Sentence 1: Having listened to both Chinese and English, I tend to be suspicious of any comparisons between the two languages.

Sentence 2: Typically, one language . . .

Sentence 3: And so the language . . .

Sentence 4: English speakers . . .

Sentence 5: Chinese speakers . . .

In many incoherent paragraphs, such as the one on mummification on page 80, each sentence subject introduces a topic new to the paragraph so that readers have trouble following the thread. (See pp. 380–82 for more on linking sentences through their subjects.)

3 Using parallel structures

Another way to achieve coherence is through **parallelism,** the use of similar grammatical structures for similar elements of meaning

---

LISTENING TO THE MUSIC

To recognize the power of repetition, students need only turn to rock music. Have them begin by listing the titles of popular songs whose lyrics they know by heart. Then ask them to identify words and phrases that they remember best from the songs or that they learned first. Chances are that they will identify the chorus because it is the element of the song most often repeated. You might point out that choruses help unify songs. Students may also note that the considerable amount of repetition in many songs makes them easy to remember and helps create a unified effect. This exercise may also be used to point out the difference between effective use of repetition and overuse.

RESOURCES AND IDEAS

These two sources draw on current linguistic and rhetorical theory to provide frameworks for describing patterns of coherence and development in paragraphs:

Coe, Richard M. *Toward a Grammar of Passages.* Carbondale: Southern Illinois UP, 1988. Print.

Markels, Robin Bell. *A New Perspective on Cohesion in Expository Paragraphs.* Carbondale: Southern Illinois UP, 1984. Print.

Other good readings on paragraph coherence include the following:

Brostoff, Anita. "Coherence: 'Next to' Is Not 'Connected to.'" *College Composition and Communication* 32.3 (1981): 278–94. Print. Brostoff discusses the causes of lack of coherence in writing and describes a program for helping students achieve coherence.

Sloan, Gary. "The Frequency of Transitional Markers in Discursive Prose." *College English* 46.2 (1984): 158–79. Print. Sloan shows how infrequently explicit transition markers are used by either professional or student writers.

Smith, Rochelle. "Paragraphing for Coherence: Writing as Implied Dialogue." *College English*

46.1 (1984): 8–21. Print. Smith uses reader-response theory and the notion of author-reader dialogue to improve paragraph cohesion.

Witte, Stephen, and Lester Faigley. "Coherence, Cohesion, and Writing Quality." *College Composition and Communication* 32.2 (1981): 189–204. Print. Students need to learn the features of coherence that extend across sentence boundaries; the article stresses ways to make them aware of coherence strategies.

Winterowd, W. Ross. "The Grammar of Coherence." *College English* 31.8 (1971): 828–35. Print. This article describes the kinds of relations that link sentence to sentence and paragraph to paragraph.

HE'S ON SECOND

To illustrate the importance of clear pronoun reference in paragraphs, try to locate a recording or transcript of the famous Abbott and Costello skit, "Who's on First." While humorous, this skit demonstrates the frustration a reader can feel when encountering a series of pronouns with unclear antecedents. Keep in mind that students' use of unclear pronoun antecedents may signal a larger difficulty in defining or expanding on their subject matter.

within a sentence or among sentences. (See Chapter 25 for a detailed discussion of parallelism.) Parallel structures help tie together the last three sentences in the paragraph on mummies (p. 81). In the following paragraph, underlining highlights the parallel structures linking sentences. Aphra Behn (lived 1640–89) was the first Englishwoman to write professionally.

> In addition to her busy career as a writer, Aphra Behn also found time to briefly marry and spend a little while in debtor's prison. She found time to take up a career as a spy for the English in their war against the Dutch. She made the long and difficult voyage to Suriname [in South America] and became involved in a slave rebellion there. She plunged into political debate at Will's Coffee House and defended her position from the stage of the Drury Lane Theater. She actively argued for women's rights to be educated and to marry whom they pleased, or not at all. She defied the seventeenth-century dictum that ladies must be "modest" and wrote freely about sex.
> —Angeline Goreau, "Aphra Behn"

Note Though planned repetition can be effective, careless or excessive repetition weakens prose (see pp. 527–28).

4 | Using pronouns

Pronouns such as *she, he, it, they,* and *who* refer to and function as nouns (see p. 235). Thus pronouns naturally help relate sentences to one another. In the following paragraph the pronouns and the nouns they refer to are circled:

> After dark, on the warrenlike streets of Brooklyn where Ⓘ live, Ⓘ often see ⓦomen who fear the worst from ⓜe. Ⓣhey seem to have set ⓣheir faces on neutral, and with ⓣheir purse straps strung across ⓣheir chests bandolier-style, ⓣhey forge ahead as though bracing ⓣhemselves against being tackled. Ⓘ understand, of course, that the danger ⓣhey perceive is not a hallucination. Ⓦomen are particularly vulnerable to street violence, and young black males are drastically overrepresented among the perpetrators of that violence. Yet these truths are no solace against the kind of alienation that comes of being ever the ⓢuspect, a fearsome entity with ⓦhom pedestrians avoid making eye contact.
> —Brent Staples, "Black Men and Public Space"

5 | Being consistent

Being consistent is the most subtle way to achieve paragraph coherence because readers are aware of consistency only when it is absent. Consistency (or the lack of it) occurs primarily in the tense of verbs and in the number and person of nouns and pronouns (see Chapter 20). Although some shifts will be necessary to reflect your meaning, inappropriate shifts, as in the following passages, will interfere with a reader's ability to follow the development of ideas.

Shifts in tense

In the Hopi religion, water is the driving force. Since the Hopi lived in the Arizona desert, they needed water urgently for drinking, cooking, and irrigating crops. Their complex beliefs are focused in part on gaining the assistance of supernatural forces in obtaining water. Many of the Hopi kachinas, or spirit essences, were directly concerned with clouds, rain, and snow.

Shifts in number

Kachinas represent the things and events of the real world, such as clouds, mischief, cornmeal, and even death. A kachina is not worshiped as a god but regarded as an interested friend. They visit the Hopi from December through July in the form of men who dress in kachina costumes and perform dances and other rituals.

Shifts in person

Unlike the man, the Hopi woman does not keep contact with kachinas through costumes and dancing. Instead, one receives a small likeness of a kachina, called a *tihu*, from the man impersonating the kachina. You are more likely to receive a tihu as a girl approaching marriage, though a child or older woman sometimes receives one, too.

Grammar checkers Grammar checkers cannot help you locate shifts in tense, number, or person among sentences. Shifts are sometimes necessary (as when tenses change to reflect actual differences in time). Furthermore, a passage with needless shifts may still consist of sentences that are grammatically correct, as all the sentences are in the preceding examples. The only way to achieve consistency in your writing is to review it yourself.

6 | Using transitional expressions

Specific words and word groups, called **transitional expressions,** can connect sentences whose relationships may not be instantly clear to readers. Notice the difference in the following two versions of the same paragraph:

Medical science has succeeded in identifying the hundreds of viruses that can cause the common cold. It has discovered the most effective means of prevention. One person transmits the cold viruses to another most often by hand. An infected person covers his mouth to cough. He picks up the telephone. His daughter picks up the telephone. She rubs her eyes. She has a cold.

Paragraph is choppy and hard to follow

READING ALOUD

Often students can spot a lack of transitions in their own writing if they read their papers aloud. If you ask students to read one another's papers aloud, the student writers will often be able to recognize missing or unclear transitions at those points where the readers stumble over a passage or have to stop to figure out the meaning.

It spreads. To avoid colds, people should wash their hands often and keep their hands away from their faces.

Medical science has thus succeeded in identifying the hundreds of viruses that can cause the common cold. It has also discovered the most effective means of prevention. One person transmits the cold viruses to another most often by hand. For instance, an infected person covers his mouth to cough. Then he picks up the telephone. Half an hour later, his daughter picks up the same telephone. Immediately afterward, she rubs her eyes. Within a few days, she, too, has a cold. And thus it spreads. To avoid colds, therefore, people should wash their hands often and keep their hands away from their faces.

—Kathleen LaFrank (student),
"Colds: Myth and Science"

> Transitional expressions (boxed) remove choppiness and spell out relationships

There are scores of transitional expressions on which to draw. The box below shows many common ones, arranged according to the relationships they convey.

Transitional expressions

To add or show sequence
again, also, and, and then, besides, equally important, finally, first, further, furthermore, in addition, in the first place, last, moreover, next, second, still, too

To compare
also, in the same way, likewise, similarly

To contrast
although, and yet, but, but at the same time, despite, even so, even though, for all that, however, in contrast, in spite of, nevertheless, notwithstanding, on the contrary, on the other hand, regardless, still, though, yet

To give examples or intensify
after all, an illustration of, even, for example, for instance, indeed, in fact, it is true, of course, specifically, that is, to illustrate, truly

To indicate place

above, adjacent to, below, elsewhere, farther on, here, near, nearby, on the other side, opposite to, there, to the east, to the left

To indicate time

after a while, afterward, as long as, as soon as, at last, at length, at that time, before, earlier, formerly, immediately, in the meantime, in the past, lately, later, meanwhile, now, presently, shortly, simultaneously, since, so far, soon, subsequently, then, thereafter, until, when

To repeat, summarize, or conclude

all in all, altogether, as has been said, in brief, in conclusion, in other words, in particular, in short, in simpler terms, in summary, on the whole, that is, therefore, to put it differently, to summarize

To show cause or effect

accordingly, as a result, because, consequently, for this purpose, hence, otherwise, since, then, therefore, thereupon, thus, to this end, with this object

Note Draw carefully on the preceding list of transitional expressions because the ones in each group are not interchangeable. For instance, *besides, finally,* and *second* may all be used to add information, but each has its own distinct meaning.

To see where transitional expressions might be needed in your paragraphs, examine the movement from each sentence to the next. (On a computer or on paper, you can highlight the transitional expressions already present and then review the sentences that lack them.) Abrupt changes are most likely to need a transition: a shift from cause to effect, a contradiction, a contrast. You can smooth and clarify transitions *between* paragraphs, too. See pages 110 and 111.

CULTURE LANGUAGE If transitional expressions are not common in your native language, you may be tempted to compensate when writing in English by adding them to the beginnings of most sentences. But such explicit transitions aren't needed everywhere, and in fact too many can be intrusive and awkward. When inserting transitional expressions, consider the reader's need for a signal: often the connection from sentence to sentence is already clear from the context, or it can be made clear by relating the content of sentences more closely (see pp. 85–86). When you do need transitional expressions, try varying their positions in your sentences, as shown in the sample paragraph on the facing page.

CULTURE LANGUAGE

CROSS-CULTURAL COMMUNICATION

Pan-cultural examples lend themselves to collaborative discussion; students might collect and discuss examples of mistranslations from other languages to English or from English to other languages. For instance, the Chevy Nova was a failure when it was introduced in Puerto Rico because *No va* means "It doesn't run" in Spanish. Students for whom English is a second language can contribute many examples of idioms that give them trouble.

COMPUTER ACTIVITY

SCRAMBLING SENTENCES

The computer makes scrambling exercises particularly viable. Ask each student to scramble the sentence order deliberately in one of their own paragraphs and then present that exercise in "unscrambling" to their group. It can be very useful for each writer to hear their own coherence "clues" being analyzed and debated.

ANALYZING FOR COHERENCE

Exercise 4.6 works well as a group exercise because students have more opportunity to debate and explore options. Have each group report back to the class on the different methods each writer uses to achieve coherence.

ANSWERS: EXERCISE 4.6

1. Lieber paragraph (p. 78): Organization: general to specific. Parallelism after first sentence: *They have measured . . . recorded and studied . . . learned.* Repetition: *whale, sings, song.* Pronoun: *they.* Transitional expression: *And.*
2. Begas paragraph (p. 93): Organization: chronological. Parallelism: *They persuaded . . . they deprived; Jill became . . . she dropped out.* Repetition: *lonely, college/school.* Pronouns: *Jill/she; men and women/they.* Transitional expressions: *Between . . . , increasingly, Before long, too.*
3. Dyson paragraph (p. 95): Organization: climactic. Parallelism and repetition: *reason is the need . . . reason is the need . . . reason is our spiritual need.* Further repetition: *space, earth/this planet.* Pronouns: *we, our, us.* Transitional expressions: *first, second, third.*

ANSWERS: EXERCISE 4.7

The coherent order is 1, 2, 5, 3, 6, 4.

ANSWERS: EXERCISE 4.8

The Hopi tihu, or kachina likeness, is often called a "doll," but its owner, usually a girl or woman, does not regard it as a plaything. Instead, <u>she treats it</u> as a valued possession and <u>hangs it</u> out of the way on a wall. For its owner the tihu represents a connection with the kachina's spirit. <u>It is</u> considered part of the kachina, carrying a portion of the kachina's power.

Punctuating transitional expressions

A transitional expression is usually set off by a comma or commas from the rest of the sentence:

<u>Immediately afterward,</u> she rubs her eyes. <u>Within a few days,</u> she, too, has a cold.

See page 430 for more on this convention and its exceptions.

7 | Combining devices to achieve coherence

The devices for achieving coherence rarely appear in isolation in effective paragraphs. As any example in this chapter shows, writers usually combine sensible organization, parallelism, repetition, pronouns, consistency, and transitional expressions to help readers follow the development of ideas.

Exercise 4.6 Analyzing paragraphs for coherence

Study the paragraphs by Janet Lieber (p. 78), Hillary Begas (p. 93), and Freeman Dyson (p. 95) for the authors' use of various devices to achieve coherence. Look especially for organization, parallel structures and ideas, repetition and restatement, pronouns, and transitional expressions.

Exercise 4.7 Arranging sentences coherently

After the topic sentence (sentence 1), the sentences in the student paragraph below have been deliberately scrambled to make the paragraph incoherent. Using the topic sentence and other clues as guides, rearrange the sentences in the paragraph to form a well-organized, coherent unit.

> We hear complaints about the Postal Service all the time, but we [1] should not forget what it does *right*. The total volume of mail delivered [2] by the Postal Service each year makes up almost half the total delivered in all the world. Its 70,000 employees handle 140,000,000,000 pieces of [3] mail each year. And when was the last time they failed to deliver yours? [4] In fact, on any given day the Postal Service delivers almost as much mail [5] as the rest of the world combined. That huge number means over [6] 2,000,000 pieces per employee and over 560 pieces per man, woman, and child in the country.

Exercise 4.8 Eliminating inconsistencies

The following paragraph is incoherent because of inconsistencies in person, number, or tense. Identify the inconsistencies and revise the paragraph to give it coherence. For further exercises in eliminating inconsistencies, see pages 354, 356–57, and 358.

> The Hopi tihu, or kachina likeness, is often called a "doll," but its owner, usually a girl or woman, does not regard them as a plaything. Instead, you treated them as a valued possession and hung them out of

the way on a wall. For its owner the tihu represents a connection with the kachina's spirit. They are considered part of the kachina, carrying a portion of the kachina's power.

Exercise 4.9 Using transitional expressions

Transitional expressions have been removed from the following paragraph at the numbered blanks. Fill in each blank with an appropriate transitional expression (1) to contrast, (2) to intensify, and (3) to show effect. Consult the list on pages 88–89 if necessary.

All over the country, people are swimming, jogging, weightlifting, dancing, walking, playing tennis—doing anything to keep fit. ___(1)___ this school has consistently refused to construct and equip a fitness center. The school has ___(2)___ refused to open existing athletic facilities to all students, not just those playing organized sports. ___(3)___ students have no place to exercise except in their rooms and on dangerous public roads.

Exercise 4.10 Considering your past work: Paragraph coherence

Continuing from Exercise 4.3 (p. 78), examine the body paragraphs of your essay to see how coherent they are and how their coherence could be improved. Do the paragraphs have a clear organization? Do you use repetition and restatement, parallelism, pronouns, and transitional expressions to signal relationships? Are the paragraphs consistent in person, number, and tense? Revise two or three paragraphs in ways you think will improve their coherence.

Exercise 4.11 Writing a coherent paragraph

Write a coherent paragraph from the following information, combining and rewriting sentences as necessary. First, begin the paragraph with the topic sentence given and arrange the supporting sentences in a climactic order. Then combine and rewrite the supporting sentences, helping the reader see connections by introducing repetition and restatement, parallelism, pronouns, consistency, and transitional expressions.

Topic sentence

Hypnosis is far superior to drugs for relieving tension.

Supporting information

Hypnosis has none of the dangerous side effects of the drugs that relieve tension.

Tension-relieving drugs can cause weight loss or gain, illness, or even death.

Hypnosis is nonaddicting.

Most of the drugs that relieve tension do foster addiction.

Tension-relieving drugs are expensive.

Hypnosis is inexpensive even for people who have not mastered self-hypnosis.

ANSWERS: EXERCISE 4.9

Possible answers

1. *Yet, However, Even so,* or *Nevertheless*
2. *even, also,* or *further*
3. *As a result, Consequently,* or *Therefore*

TRANSITIONAL EXPRESSIONS

Ask students to compare answers to Exercise 4.9 and discuss the effects of each student's choices on the meaning of the sentences and of the paragraph.

ANSWERS: EXERCISE 4.10

Individual response.

ANSWERS: EXERCISE 4.11

Possible paragraph

Hypnosis is far superior to drugs for relieving tension. It is inexpensive even for people who have not mastered self-hypnosis, whereas drugs are expensive. It is nonaddictive, whereas drugs foster addiction. And most important, hypnosis has none of the dangerous side effects of drugs, such as weight loss or gain, illness, and even death.

COMPUTER ACTIVITY

REARRANGING SENTENCES

Exercise 4.11 is particularly feasible on the computer since students can rearrange the information in multiple ways without retyping.

COHERENT PARAGRAPHS

The kind of coherence achieved in Exercises 4.11 and 4.12 will depend a great deal on each individual's choice of connective strategies. When students compare their responses to Exercises 4.11 and 4.12 in groups, it is beneficial for them to note the results of other writers' differing choices.

HIGHLIGHTS

Section 4c looks at ways to convey the central idea of a paragraph fully and convincingly to the reader. Developing paragraphs and essays fully is often difficult for students. One of the important differences between casual conversation and formal writing is the degree to which ideas must be concretely developed in writing. Because students are more experienced in conversation than in writing, they find generalizations much easier to come by than the details, examples, and reasons to support them.

All of us must grapple with the student essay or single paragraph that is largely a succession of generalizations without support or explanation. Part of the solution to such problem paragraphs is to make students aware of readers as a special kind of audience for ideas. Another part is to make them aware of different strategies for developing paragraphs or essays.

The ways to develop ideas are infinite, but this section focuses on a limited number. The initial emphasis falls on the use of details, examples, and reasons, which are essential to any more specific method of development. Students are encouraged to follow the standard methods or patterns of development by posing questions about an idea, event, or object in order to uncover concrete information about it.

You may wish to ask students to spend time in class or in groups working with sample topics to discover how the methods of development can be used to probe a topic and how the questions reveal different aspects of a topic. This discussion may help students see how the process of development can be an act of discovery. You will

Exercise 4.12 Turning topic sentences into coherent paragraphs

Develop three of the following topic sentences into coherent paragraphs. Organize your information by space, by time, or for emphasis, as seems most appropriate. Use repetition and restatement, parallelism, pronouns, consistency, and transitional expressions to link sentences.

1. The most interesting character in the book [or movie] was _____.
2. Of all my courses, _____ is the one that I think will serve me best throughout life.
3. Although we in the United States face many problems, the one we should concentrate on solving first is _____.
4. The most dramatic building in town is the _____.
5. Children should not have to worry about the future.

4c Developing the paragraph

In an essay that's understandable and interesting to readers, you will provide plenty of solid information to support your general statements. You work that information into the essay through the paragraph, as you build up each point relating to the thesis.

A paragraph may be unified and coherent but still be inadequate if you skimp on details. Take this example:

> Untruths can serve as a kind of social oil when they smooth connections between people. In preventing confrontation and injured feelings, they allow everyone to go on as before.

 General statements needing examples to be clear and convincing

This paragraph lacks **development**, completeness. It does not provide enough information for us to evaluate or even care about the writer's assertions.

1 Using specific information

If they are sound, the general statements you make in any writing will be based on what you have experienced, observed, read, and thought. Readers will assume as much and will expect you to provide the evidence for your statements—sensory details, facts, statistics, examples, quotations, reasons. Whatever helps you form your views you need, in turn, to share with readers.

Here is the actual version of the preceding sample paragraph. With examples, the paragraph is more interesting and convincing.

> Untruths can serve as a kind of social oil when they smooth connections between people. Assuring a worried friend that his haircut is flattering, claiming an appointment to avoid an

aunt's dinner invitation, pretending interest in an acquaintance's children—these lies may protect the liar, but they also protect the person lied to. In preventing confrontation and injured feelings, the lies allow everyone to go on as before.

Examples specifying kinds of lies and consequences

> —Joan Lar (student), "The Truth of Lies"

If your readers often comment that your writing needs more specifics, you should focus on that improvement in your revisions. Try listing the general statements of each paragraph on lines by themselves with space underneath. Then use one of the discovery techniques discussed on pages 16–26 (freewriting, brainstorming, and so on) to find the details to support each sentence. Write these into your draft. If you write on a computer, you can do this revision directly on your draft. First create a duplicate of your draft, and then, working on the copy, separate the sentences and explore their support. Rewrite the supporting details into sentences, reassemble the paragraph, and edit it for coherence.

2 Using a pattern of development

If you have difficulty developing an idea or shaping your information, try asking yourself questions derived from the patterns of development. (The same patterns can help with essay development, too. See pp. 25–26.)

How did it happen? (Narration)

Narration retells a significant sequence of events, usually in the order of their occurrence (that is, chronologically):

> Jill's story is typical for "recruits" to religious cults. She was very lonely in college and appreciated the attention of the nice young men and women who lived in a house near campus. They persuaded her to share their meals and then to move in with them. Between intense bombardments of "love," they deprived her of sleep and sometimes threatened to throw her out. Jill became increasingly confused and dependent, losing touch with any reality besides the one in the group. She dropped out of school and refused to see or communicate with her family. Before long she, too, was preying on lonely college students.
>
> —Hillary Begas (student),
> "The Love Bombers"

Important events in chronological order

As this paragraph illustrates, a narrator is concerned not just with the sequence of events but also with their consequence, their importance to the whole. Thus a narrative rarely corresponds to

probably want to stress, however, that the methods of development covered in the handbook are not the only ones writers can use and that most paragraphs use more than a single method.

The exercises for this section range from analyzing paragraphs to producing them, and whether used in groups or by students working individually, they encourage students to treat the patterns of development as different ways of viewing a topic.

WHAT AND WHY

Students from non-Western cultures may be unaccustomed to analysis that involves critical thinking. They may know how to describe an item or text by listing component parts, for instance, but they may not be accustomed to including discussion of why the thing or text is important. A quick way to help these students learn to distinguish between "what" a thing is and "why" it is important is to ask them the following series of questions about a flag:

What is the object attached to the tall pole in the quad? (Describe its appearance, give its name, discuss the component colors and shapes.)

How does the object work? (How is it attached? How is it raised and lowered? When is it raised and lowered?)

Why does it get flown? (This question will lead students into a discussion of the symbolism and meaning of the flag and of its being flown on campus.)

real time; instead, it collapses transitional or background events and focuses on events of particular interest. In addition, writers sometimes rearrange events, as when they simulate the workings of memory by flashing back to an earlier time.

How does it look, sound, feel, smell, taste? (Description)

Description details the sensory qualities of a person, place, thing, or feeling. You use concrete and specific words to convey a dominant mood, to illustrate an idea, or to achieve some other purpose. Some description is **subjective**: the writer filters the subject through his or her biases and emotions. In the subjective description by Virginia Woolf on page 82, the *glare* of the walls, the *impenetrable darkness*, the *bulge of a great bowl*, and the *formidable corners and lines* all indicate the feelings of the author about what she describes.

In contrast to subjective description, journalists and scientists usually strive for description that is **objective**, conveying the subject without bias or emotion:

> The two toddlers, both boys, sat together for half an hour in a ten-foot-square room with yellow walls (one with a two-way mirror for observation) and a brown carpet. The room was unfurnished except for two small chairs and about two dozen toys. The boys' interaction was generally tense. They often struggled physically and verbally over several toys, especially a large red beach ball and a small wooden fire engine. The larger of the two boys often pushed the smaller away or pried his hands from the desired object. This larger boy never spoke, but he did make grunting sounds when he was engaging the other. In turn, the smaller boy twice uttered piercing screams of "No!" and once shouted "Stop that!" When he was left alone, he hummed and muttered to himself.
>
> —Ray Mattison (student),
> "Case Study: Play Patterns of Toddlers"

Objective description: specific record of sensory data without interpretation

What are examples of it or reasons for it? (Illustration or support)

Some ideas can be developed simply by **illustration or support** —supplying detailed examples or reasons. The writer of the paragraph on lying (pp. 92–93) developed her idea with several specific examples of her general statements. You can also supply a single extended example:

> The language problem that I was attacking loomed larger and larger as I began to learn more. When I would describe in English certain ⌐

THE SUBJECT-OBJECT BOUNDARY

Students may find that the subjective-objective boundary is sometimes fuzzy. Even the objective paragraph has judgmental language like "piercing" in it. Perhaps a way of solving this dilemma is to say that in *subjective* description, the writer's intention is to interpret experience for readers, while in *objective* description, the writer's intention is to allow the audience to interpret the reported experiences themselves.

concepts and objects enmeshed in Korean emotion and imagination, I became slowly aware of nuances, of differences between two languages even in simple expression. The remark "Kim entered the house" seems to be simple enough, yet, unless a reader has a clear visual image of a Korean house, his understanding of the sentence is not complete. When a Korean says he is "in the house," he may be in his courtyard, or on his porch, or in his small room! If I wanted to give a specific picture of entering the house in the Western sense, I had to say "room" instead of house— sometimes. I say "sometimes" because many Koreans entertain their guests on their porches and still are considered to be hospitable, and in the Korean sense, going into the "room" may be a more intimate act than it would be in the English sense. Such problems!

— Kim Yong Ik, "A Book-Writing Venture"

> Topic sentence (assertion to be illustrated)

> Single detailed example

Sometimes you can develop a paragraph by providing your reasons for stating a general idea:

There are three reasons, quite apart from scientific considerations, that mankind needs to travel in space. The first reason is the need for garbage disposal: we need to transfer industrial processes into space, so that the earth may remain a green and pleasant place for our grandchildren to live in. The second reason is the need to escape material impoverishment: the resources of this planet are finite, and we shall not forgo forever the abundant solar energy and minerals and living space that are spread out all around us. The third reason is our spiritual need for an open frontier: the ultimate purpose of space travel is to bring to humanity not only scientific discoveries and an occasional spectacular show on television but a real expansion of our spirit.

— Freeman Dyson, "Disturbing the Universe"

> Topic sentence

> Three reasons arranged in order of increasing drama and importance

What is it? What does it encompass, and what does it exclude? (Definition)

A **definition** says what something is and is not, specifying the characteristics that distinguish the subject from the other members of its class. You can easily define concrete, noncontroversial terms in a single sentence: *A knife is a cutting instrument* (its class) *with a sharp blade set in a handle* (the characteristics that set it off from, say, scissors or a razor blade). But defining a complicated or controversial topic often requires extended explanation, and you may need to devote a whole paragraph or even an essay to it. Such a definition

PARAGRAPH COHERENCE

Students sometimes have the idea that "next to" means "connected to" as far as coherence goes; this is emphatically not the case. Take a paragraph like this one and have students mark the coherence devices used; or sabotage a paragraph by removing or disguising the coherence devices, and ask students to put them back in.

EXTRA EXAMPLE

Division: Face

Eyes	*Nose*	*Mouth*
Pupil	Nostrils	Lips
Iris	Bridge	Tongue
Cornea		Teeth

Teeth
Molars
Incisors
Bicuspids

may provide examples to identify the subject's characteristics. It may also involve other methods of development discussed here, such as classification or comparison and contrast.

The following definition of the word *quality* comes from an essay asserting that "quality in product and effort has become a vanishing element of current civilization":

> In the hope of possibly reducing the hail of censure which is certain to greet this essay (I am thinking of going to Alaska or possibly Patagonia in the week it is published), let me say that quality, as I understand it, means investment of the best skill and effort possible to produce the finest and most admirable result possible. — *General definition*
>
> Its presence or absence in some degree characterizes every man-made object, service, skilled or unskilled labor— laying bricks, painting a picture, ironing shirts, practicing medicine, shoemaking, scholarship, writing a book. — *Activities in which quality may figure*
>
> You do it well or you do it half-well. Materials are sound and durable or they are sleazy; method is painstaking or whatever is easiest. Quality is achieving or reaching for the highest standard as against being satisfied with the sloppy or fraudulent. It is honesty of purpose as against catering to cheap or sensational sentiment. It does not allow compromise with the second-rate. — *Contrast between quality and nonquality*
>
> —Barbara Tuchman,
> "The Decline of Quality"

What are its parts or characteristics? (Division or analysis)

Division and **analysis** both involve separating something into its elements, the better to understand it. Here is a simple example:

> A typical daily newspaper compresses considerable information into the top of the first page, above the headlines. — *The subject being divided*
>
> The most prominent feature of this space, the newspaper's name, is called the *logo* or *nameplate*. Under the logo and set off by rules is a line of small type called the *folio line*, which contains the date of the issue, the volume and issue numbers, copyright information, and the price. To the right of the logo is a block of small type called a *weather ear*, a summary of the day's forecast. And above the logo is a *skyline*, a kind of advertisement in which the paper's editors highlight a special feature of the issue. — *Elements of the subject, arranged spatially*
>
> —Kansha Stone (student),
> "Anatomy of a Paper"

Generally, analysis goes beyond simply identifying elements. Often used as a synonym for *critical thinking,* analysis also involves interpreting the elements' meaning, significance, and relationships. You identify and interpret elements according to your particular interest in the subject. (See pp. 146–52 for more on critical thinking and analysis.)

The following paragraph comes from an essay about soap operas. The analytical focus of the whole essay is the way soap operas provide viewers with a sense of community missing from their own lives. The paragraph itself has a narrower focus related to the broader one.

> The surface realism of the soap opera conjures up an illusion of "liveness." The domestic settings and easygoing rhythms encourage the viewer to believe that the drama, however ridiculous, is simply an extension of daily life. The conversation is so slow that some have called it "radio with pictures." (Advertisers have always assumed that busy housewives would listen, rather than watch.) Conversation is casual and colloquial, as though one were eavesdropping on neighbors. There is plenty of time to "read" the character's face; close-ups establish intimacy. The sets are comfortably familiar: well-lit interiors of living rooms, restaurants, offices, and hospitals. Daytime soaps have little of the glamour of their prime-time relations. The viewer easily imagines that the conversation is taking place in real time.
> —Ruth Rosen, "Search for Yesterday"

Topic and focus: how "liveness" seems an extension of daily life

Elements:
Slow conversation

Casual conversation

Intimate close-ups

Familiar sets

Absence of glamour
Appearance of real time

What groups or categories can it be sorted into? (Classification)

Classification involves sorting many things into groups based on their similarities. Using the pattern, we scan a large group composed of many members that share at least one characteristic—workers, say—and we assign the members to smaller groups on the basis of some principle—salary, perhaps, or dependence on computers. Here is an example:

> In my experience, the parents who hire daytime sitters for their school-age children tend to fall into one of three groups. The first group includes parents who work and want someone to be at home when the children return from school. These parents are looking for an extension of themselves, someone who will give the care they would give if they were at home. The second group includes parents who may be home all day themselves but are too disorganized or too frazzled by their children's demands to handle child care alone. They are looking for an organizer and helpmate. The third and final group includes parents who do not want to be

Topic sentence

Three groups:
Alike in one way (all hire sitters)
No overlap in groups (each has a different attitude)

Classes arranged in order of increasing drama

CLASSIFICATION PRACTICE

Other topics to be classified might include car models, job categories, types of music, and local restaurants. (You might want to bring in the Yellow Pages for the last topic.)

EXTRA EXAMPLE

Classification:

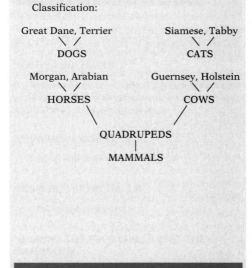

Great Dane, Terrier   Siamese, Tabby
          DOGS   CATS

Morgan, Arabian   Guernsey, Holstein
       HORSES   COWS

               QUADRUPEDS
                     |
                 MAMMALS

COLLABORATIVE LEARNING

TEAM CLASSIFICATION

Ask teams of students to compile the group of sentences or facts from an area they know well (for instance, sports, business, entertainment, social groups, or activities). Have the groups exchange sets of sentences and then attempt to assemble them into paragraphs. When the paragraphs are written, the "expert" collectors should critique the perspective each offers.

bothered by their children, whether they are home all day or not. Unlike the parents in the first two groups, who care for their children whenever and however they can, these parents are looking for a permanent substitute for themselves.

—Nancy Whittle (student),
"Modern Parenting"

How is it like, or different from, other things? (Comparison and contrast)

Asking about similarities and differences leads to **comparison and contrast:** comparison focuses on similarities, whereas contrast focuses on differences. The two may be used separately or together to develop an idea or to relate two or more things. Commonly, comparisons are organized in one of two ways. In the first, **subject by subject,** the two subjects are discussed separately, one at a time:

Consider the differences also in the behavior of rock and classical music audiences. At a rock concert, the audience members yell, whistle, sing along, and stamp their feet. They may even stand during the entire performance. The better the music, the more active they'll be. At a classical concert, in contrast, the better the performance, the more *still* the audience is. Members of the classical audience are so highly disciplined that they refrain from even clearing their throats or coughing. No matter what effect the powerful music has on their intellects and feelings, they sit on their hands.

— *Subjects: rock and classical audiences*
— *Rock audience*
— *Classical audience*

—Tony Nahm (student),
"Rock and Roll Is Here to Stay"

In the second comparative organization, **point by point,** the two subjects are discussed side by side and matched feature for feature:

Arguing is often equated with fighting, but there are key differences between the two. Participants in an argument approach the subject to find common ground, or points on which both sides agree, while people engaged in a fight usually approach the subject with an "us-versus-them" attitude. Participants in an argument are careful to use respectful, polite language, in contrast to the insults and worse that people in a fight use to get the better of their opponents. Finally, participants in an argument commonly have the goal of reaching a new understanding or larger truth about the subject they're debating, while those in a fight have winning as their only goal.

— *Subjects: arguing and fighting*
— *Approach to subject: argument, fight*
— *Language: argument, fight*
— *Goal: argument, fight*

—Erica Ito (student),
"Is an Argument Always a Fight?"

The following examples show the two organizing schemes in outline form. The one on the left corresponds to the point-by-point paragraph about the differences between arguing and fighting. The one on the right uses the same information but reorganizes it to cover the two subjects separately: first one, then the other.

Point by Point	**Subject by Subject**
I. Approach to subject	I. Argument
A. Argument	A. Approach to subject
B. Fight	B. Language
II. Language	C. Goal
A. Argument	II. Fight
B. Fight	A. Approach to subject
III. Goal	B. Language
A. Argument	C. Goal
B. Fight	

Is it comparable to something that is in a different class but more familiar to readers? (Analogy)

Whereas we draw comparisons and contrasts between elements in the same general class (audiences, disputes), we link elements in different classes with a special kind of comparison called **analogy.** Most often in analogy we illuminate or explain an unfamiliar, abstract class of things with a familiar and concrete class of things:

> We might eventually obtain some sort of bedrock understanding of cosmic structure, but we will never understand the universe in detail; it is just too big and varied for that. If we possessed an atlas of our galaxy that devoted but a single page to each star system in the Milky Way (so that the sun and all its planets were crammed on one page), that atlas would run to more than ten million volumes of ten thousand pages each. It would take a library the size of Harvard's to house the atlas, and merely to flip through it, at the rate of a page per second, would require over ten thousand years.
>
> —Timothy Ferris,
> *Coming of Age in the Milky Way*

Abstract subject: the universe, specifically the Milky Way

Concrete subject: an atlas

Why did it happen, or what results did it have? (Cause-and-effect analysis)

When you use analysis to explain why something happened or what is likely to happen, then you are determining causes and effects. **Cause-and-effect analysis** is especially useful in writing about social, economic, or political events or problems. In the next paragraph the author looks at the causes of Japanese collectivism, which he elsewhere contrasts with American individualism:

COMBINING FOR EMPHASIS

Put together a group of sentences or bits of information about a topic, perhaps drawing the material from an essay in a reader or a magazine article. Ask students, working individually or in groups, to combine the material into a paragraph that has a distinct point of view. You might, for example, provide information about a recent controversial incident and ask for a paragraph emphasizing one perspective toward the incident or one perspective on its causes and effects.

PRACTICAL INSTRUCTIONS

The most hilarious process exercise is one of the oldest: bring the ingredients for peanut butter and jelly sandwiches to class. Have each group write instructions for making a peanut butter and jelly sandwich. Then have the groups exchange instructions and make the sandwich exactly according to instructions they receive. (Typically, students' instructions will omit using a knife to spread the fillings, or putting together the sides with fillings.) The results are usually hilarious—and messy—but prove the point that process paragraphs must be complete to be effective.

The *shinkansen* or "bullet train" speeds across the rural areas of Japan giving a quick view of cluster after cluster of farmhouses surrounded by rice paddies. [**Effect: pattern of Japanese farming**] This particular pattern did not develop purely by chance, but as a consequence of the technology peculiar to the growing of rice, the staple of the Japanese diet. The growing of rice requires the construction and maintenance of an irrigation system, something that takes many hands to build. More importantly, the planting and the harvesting of rice can only be done efficiently with the cooperation of twenty or more people. The "bottom line" is that a single family working alone cannot produce enough rice to survive, but a dozen families working together can produce a surplus. [**Causes: Japanese dependence on rice, which requires collective effort**] Thus the Japanese have had to develop the capacity to work together in harmony, no matter what the forces of disagreement or social disintegration, in order to survive. [**Effect: working in harmony**]
—William Ouchi, *Theory Z*

Cause-and-effect paragraphs tend to focus either on causes, as Ouchi's does, or on effects, as this paragraph does:

At each step, with every graduation from one level of education to the next, the refrain from bystanders was strangely the same: "Your parents must be so proud of you." [**Cause: education**] I suppose that my parents were proud, although I suspect, too, that they felt more than pride alone as they watched me advance through my education. They seemed to know that my education was separating us from one another, making it difficult to resume familiar intimacies. Mixed with the instincts of parental pride, a certain hurt also communicated itself—too private ever to be adequately expressed in words, but real nonetheless. [**Effects: Pride / Separation / Loss of intimacies / Hurt**]
—Richard Rodriguez, "Going Home Again"

How does one do it, or how does it work? (Process analysis)

When you analyze how to do something or how something works, you explain the steps in a **process**. Paragraphs developed by process analysis are usually organized chronologically, as the steps in the process occur. Some process analyses tell the reader how to do a task:

As a car owner, you waste money when you pay a mechanic to change the engine oil. The job is not difficult, even if you know little about cars. All you need is a wrench to remove the drain [**Process: changing oil**]

plug, a large, flat pan to collect the draining oil, plastic bottles to dispose of the used oil, and fresh oil. First, warm up the car's engine so that the oil will flow more easily. When the engine is warm, shut it off and remove its oil-filler cap (the owner's manual shows where this cap is). Then locate the drain plug under the engine (again consulting the owner's manual for its location) and place the flat pan under the plug. Remove the plug with the wrench, letting the oil flow into the pan. When the oil stops flowing, replace the plug and, at the engine's filler hole, add the amount and kind of fresh oil specified by the owner's manual. Pour the used oil into the plastic bottles and take it to a waste-oil collector, which any garage mechanic can recommend.

— Anthony Andreas (student),
"Do-It-Yourself Car Care"

Equipment needed

Steps in process

Other process analyses explain how processes are done or how they work in nature. Annie Dillard's paragraph on mangrove islands (p. 82) is one example. Here is another:

What used to be called "laying on of hands" is now practiced seriously by nurses and doctors. Studies have shown that therapeutic touch, as it is now known, can aid relaxation and ease pain, two effects that may in turn cause healing. A "healer" must first concentrate on helping the patient. Then, hands held a few inches from the patient's body, the healer moves from head to foot. Healers claim that they can detect energy disturbances in the patient that indicate tension, pain, or sickness. With further hand movements, the healer tries to redirect the energy. Patients report feeling heat from the healer's hands, perhaps indicating an energy transfer between healer and patient.

— Lisa Kuklinski (student),
"Old Ways to Noninvasive Medicine"

Process: therapeutic touch

Benefits

Steps in process

How process works

Diagrams, photographs, and other figures can do much to clarify process analyses. See pages 121–25 for guidelines on creating and clearly labeling figures.

Combining patterns of development

Whatever pattern you choose as the basis for developing a paragraph, other patterns may also prove helpful. Combined patterns have appeared often in this section: Dyson analyzes causes and effects in presenting reasons (p. 95); Tuchman uses contrast to define *quality* (p. 96); Nahm uses description to compare (p. 98); Ouchi uses process analysis to explain causes (p. 100).

IMITATING PARAGRAPHS

Choose a successful paragraph (student or professional) with a clear pattern, and discuss it in class. Then ask students to write paragraphs imitating the pattern but not the content of the model paragraph.

DEVELOPING PARAGRAPHS

Take underdeveloped paragraphs on subjects likely to be familiar to students and ask them to develop the paragraphs fully by drawing on their own knowledge. Student paragraphs often provide good material for this exercise. Students can work collaboratively in groups of two or three to develop each person's paragraph. Alternatively, groups can supply a list of questions for each paragraph based on the questions provided in this chapter. Then each student can brainstorm responses to the questions and use that material to revise his or her own paragraph.

ANALYZING PARAGRAPHS

When students work together to analyze the paragraphs in Exercise 4.13 they benefit by discovering a broader range of interpretive responses. Those discoveries can be put to work in revising the underdeveloped paragraphs in Exercise 4.14 either individually or in groups.

ANSWERS: EXERCISE 4.13

1. Gates paragraph (p. 78): Patterns of development: cause-and-effect analysis and illustration. Supporting information: mainly the example in sentences 4–8.
2. Wax paragraph (p. 83): Pattern of development: cause-and-effect analysis. Supporting information: first three sentences.

ANSWERS: EXERCISE 4.14

Possible answers

1. Sentence 1 requires some expansion to explain *quality of communication*. Each of the next two sentences needs to be supported with specific examples of the two qualities named.
2. Sentences 2, 3, and 4 should each be followed by at least two specific examples of gestures to make the writer's meaning concrete.
3. Sentences 2 and especially 3 require specific support: examples of easy changes, advantages of trying out different versions, and clarification of *the hard work of revising*. What does it involve? Why is it *hard*? Why is it different from what a word processor can do?

ANSWERS: EXERCISE 4.15

Individual response.

3 | Checking length

The average paragraph contains between 100 and 150 words, or between four and eight sentences. The actual length of a paragraph depends on the complexity of its topic, the role it plays in developing the thesis of the essay, and its position in the essay. Nevertheless, very short paragraphs are often inadequately developed; they may leave readers with a sense of incompleteness. And very long paragraphs often contain irrelevant details or develop two or more topics; readers may have difficulty following, sorting out, or remembering ideas.

When you are revising your essay, reread the paragraphs that seem very long or very short, checking them especially for unity and adequate development. If the paragraph wanders, cut everything from it that does not support your main idea (such as sentences that you might begin with *By the way*). If it is underdeveloped, supply the specific details, examples, or reasons needed, or try one of the methods of development we have discussed here.

Exercise 4.13   Analyzing paragraph development

Examine the paragraphs by Henry Louis Gates, Jr. (p. 78), and Judith Wax (p. 83) to discover how the authors achieve paragraph development. What pattern or patterns of development does each author use? Where does each author support general statements with specific evidence?

Exercise 4.14   Analyzing and revising skimpy paragraphs

The following paragraphs are not well developed. Analyze them, looking especially for general statements that lack support or leave questions in your mind. Then rewrite one into a well-developed paragraph, supplying your own concrete details or examples.

1.   One big difference between successful and unsuccessful teachers is the quality of communication. A successful teacher is sensitive to students' needs and excited by the course subject. In contrast, an unsuccessful teacher seems uninterested in students and bored by the subject.

2.   Gestures are one of our most important means of communication. We use them instead of speech. We use them to supplement the words we speak. And we use them to communicate some feelings or meanings that words cannot adequately express.

3.   I've discovered that a word processor can do much—but not everything—to help me improve my writing. I can easily make changes and try out different versions of a paper. But I still must do the hard work of revising.

Exercise 4.15   Considering your past work: Paragraph development

Continuing from Exercises 4.3 (p. 78) and 4.10 (p. 91), examine the development of the body paragraphs in your writing. Where does specific information seem adequate to support your general statements? Where does support seem skimpy? Revise the paragraphs as necessary to make your ideas clearer and more interesting. It may help you to pose the questions on pages 93–100.

Exercise 4.16 Writing with the patterns of development

Write at least three unified, coherent, and well-developed paragraphs, each one developed with a different pattern. Draw on the topics provided here, or choose your own topics.

1. **Narration**
   An experience of public speaking
   A disappointment
   Leaving home
   Waking up
2. **Description (objective or subjective)**
   Your room
   A crowded or deserted place
   A food
   An intimidating person
3. **Illustration or support**
   Why study
   Having a headache
   The best sports event
   Usefulness or uselessness of a self-help book
4. **Definition**
   Humor
   An adult
   Fear
   Authority
5. **Division or analysis**
   A television news show
   A barn
   A Web site
   A piece of music
6. **Classification**
   Factions in a dispute
   Styles of playing poker
   Types of Web sites
   Kinds of teachers
7. **Comparison and contrast**
   Surfing the Web and watching TV
   AM and FM radio DJs
   High school and college football
   Movies on TV and in a theater
8. **Analogy**
   Paying taxes and giving blood
   The US Constitution and a building's foundation
   Graduating from high school and being released from prison
9. **Cause-and-effect analysis**
   Connection between tension and anger
   Causes of failing or acing a course
   Connection between credit cards and debt
   Causes of a serious accident
10. **Process analysis**
    Preparing for a job interview
    Setting up a blog
    Protecting your home from burglars
    Making a jump shot

ANSWERS: EXERCISE 4.16

Individual response.

COLLABORATIVE LEARNING

DEVELOPING PARAGRAPHS

In exercises like 4.15 and 4.16, where students may find it difficult to develop their own paragraphs, they can work initially with their revision groups to pinpoint unsupported statements, highlight unclear claims, and create a list of specific questions to aid each writer in a further revision.

RESOURCES AND IDEAS

Cohan, Carol. "Writing Effective Paragraphs." *College Composition and Communication* 27.4 (1976): 363–65. Print. Cohan suggests encouraging paragraph development by treating topic sentences as questions to be answered by the paragraph that follows.

Eden, Rick, and Ruth Mitchell. "Paragraphing for the Reader." *College Composition and Communication* 37.4 (1986): 416–30. Print. The authors suggest that judgments about length and paragraph decisions should be made with the readers in mind.

Lanham, Richard. *Analyzing Prose.* 2nd ed. London: Continuum, 2003. Print. Lanham offers extensive advice on revising paragraphs for stylistic effect.

Witte, Stephen, and Lester Faigley. "Coherence, Cohesion, and Writing Quality." *College Composition and Communication* 32.2 (1981): 189–204. Print. Students need to learn the features of coherence that extend across sentence boundaries; the article stresses ways to make them aware of coherence strategies.

4d Writing special kinds of paragraphs

Several kinds of paragraphs do not always follow the guidelines for unity, coherence, development, and length because they serve special functions. These are the essay introduction, the essay conclusion, the transitional or emphatic paragraph, and the paragraph of spoken dialog.

HIGHLIGHTS

This section addresses introductory and concluding paragraphs, the occasionally useful transitional and short emphatic paragraphs, and the conventions of paragraphing in dialogue. The emphasis you give to introductory and concluding paragraphs may vary with the experience of your students. For some, writing a straightforward introductory paragraph that simply sets the stage for the essay and presents a thesis statement will be an accomplishment. Others will benefit from experimenting with some of the variations illustrated. Most, however, will appreciate the list of don'ts for introductory paragraphs.

Because concluding paragraphs often present a special problem, you may wish to highlight the common inept endings that trap students and then suggest satisfactory alternatives.

USING JOURNALS

Encourage students to collect a repertoire of introduction strategies in their journals. They can draw these strategies from class readings, other courses, and their outside reading. They might also make a log of the ways television news or tabloid shows introduce various subjects, and add them to this repertoire. This strategy can also be applied to conclusions.

1 Opening an essay

Most of your essays will open with a paragraph that draws readers from their world into your world. A good opening paragraph usually satisfies several requirements:

- **It focuses readers' attention on your subject and arouses their curiosity about what you have to say.**
- **It specifies what your topic is and implies your attitude.**
- **Often it provides your thesis statement.**
- **It is concise and sincere.**

The box on the facing page provides a range of options for achieving these goals.

Note If you are composing on the Web, you'll want to consider the expectations of Web readers. Your opening page may take the place of a conventional introduction, providing concise text indicating your site's subject and purpose, a menu of its contents, and links to other pages. (See pp. 834–40 for more on composing for the Web.)

CULTURE LANGUAGE The requirements and options for essay introductions may not be what you are used to if your native language is not English. In other cultures, readers may seek familiarity or reassurance from an author's introduction, or they may prefer an indirect approach to the subject. In academic and business English, however, writers and readers prefer concise, direct expression.

The funnel introduction

One reliably effective introduction forms a kind of funnel:

Funnel introduction

Statement or question about the subject, a hook that relates to readers' experience or knowledge

One or more sentences that clarify or narrow the subject

Thesis statement (pp. 27–29)

Some strategies for opening paragraphs

- Ask a question.
- Relate an incident.
- Use a vivid quotation.
- Offer a surprising statistic or other fact.
- State an opinion related to your thesis.
- Outline the argument your thesis refutes.
- Provide background.

- Create a visual image that represents your subject.
- Make a historical comparison or contrast.
- Outline a problem or dilemma.
- Define a word central to your subject.
- In some business or technical writing, summarize your paper.

Here are two examples of the funnel introduction:

Can your home or office computer make you sterile? Can it strike you blind or dumb? The answer is: probably not. Nevertheless, reports of side effects relating to computer use should be examined, especially in the area of birth defects, eye complaints, and postural difficulties. Although little conclusive evidence exists to establish a causal link between computer use and problems of this sort, the circumstantial evidence can be disturbing.
—Thomas Hartmann,
"How Dangerous Is Your Computer?"

> Questions about subject
>
> Clarification of subject: bridge to thesis statement
>
> Thesis statement

The Declaration of Independence is so widely regarded as a statement of American ideals that its origins in practical politics tend to be forgotten. Thomas Jefferson's draft was intensely debated and then revised in the Continental Congress. Jefferson was disappointed with the result. However, a close reading of both the historical context and the revisions themselves indicates that the Congress improved the document for its intended purpose.
—Ann Weiss (student), "The Editing of the Declaration of Independence"

> Statement about subject
>
> Clarification of subject: bridge to thesis statement
>
> Thesis statement

Other effective introductions

Several other types of introduction can be equally effective, though they are sometimes harder to invent and control.

Quotation leading into the thesis statement

"It is difficult to speak adequately or justly of London," wrote Henry James in 1881. "It is not a

MAGAZINE MODELS

Magazines like *Time, Glamour, Outdoor Life, Ebony,* and *Self* contain a variety of informative articles. The authors of these articles and students writing expository essays face a similar problem—how to get readers interested enough to keep reading. Have students collect effective openings and bring them to class for discussion. Students can also comb editorials and magazine articles for openings of argumentative essays.

LEARNING STRATEGIES

To help students learn effective strategies for writing opening paragraphs, give the class outlines of well-known essays and ask students to construct opening paragraphs based on the information provided. Compare students' opening paragraphs with those of the essays. This exercise will expose students to the numerous possibilities for creating good opening paragraphs and will promote discussion of the relative merits of different techniques for a specific subject, essay, or audience.

IMITATING OPENINGS AND CLOSINGS

When experienced writers have trouble beginning or ending essays, they usually turn to strategies that have been successful on other occasions. To help student writers develop similar resources, distribute opening and closing paragraphs that demonstrate particularly effective strategies and ask students to write their own paragraphs using the same strategies but containing different content.

IF THE INTRODUCTION IMPEDES WRITING

If some students have difficulty starting to write because they can't compose a "perfect" introduction, advise them to leave the introduction for last. They might instead begin the paper with only their tentative thesis statement as a placeholder for the introduction. Once they have composed the remaining paragraphs, they can try some of the strategies provided to write an opening paragraph that truly reflects the rest of the essay.

pleasant place; it is not agreeable, or cheerful, or easy, or exempt from reproach. It is only magnificent." — Quotation

Were he alive today, James, a connoisseur of cities, might easily say the same thing about New York or Paris or Tokyo, for the great city is one of the paradoxes of history. — Bridge to thesis statement

In countless different ways, it has almost always been an unpleasant, disagreeable, cheerless, uneasy and reproachful place; in the end, it can only be described as magnificent. — Thesis statement

—*Time*

Incident or image setting up the thesis statement

Canada is pink. I knew that from the map I owned when I was six. On it, New York was green and brown, which was true as far as I could see, so there was no reason to distrust the map maker's portrayal of Canada. When my parents took me across the border and we entered the immigration booth, I looked excitedly for the pink earth. Slowly it dawned on me: this foreign, "different" place was not so different. — Incident from writer's experience

I discovered that the world in my head and the world at my feet were not the same. — Thesis statement

—Robert Ornstein, *Human Nature*

Startling opinion or question

Caesar was right. Thin people need watching. I've been watching them for most of my adult life, and I don't like what I see. When these narrow fellows spring at me, I quiver to my toes. Thin people come in all personalities, most of them menacing. You've got your "together" thin person, your mechanical thin person, your condescending thin person, your tsk-tsk thin person. — Opinion

All of them are dangerous. — Thesis statement

—Suzanne Britt,
"That Lean and Hungry Look"

Background, such as a historical comparison

Throughout the first half of this century, the American Medical Association, the largest and most powerful medical organization in the world, battled relentlessly to rid the country of quack potions and cure-alls; and it is the AMA that is generally credited with being the single most powerful force behind the enactment of the early pure food and drug laws. — Historical background

Today, however, medicine's guardian seems to have done a complete about-face and become one of the pharmaceuti- — Thesis statement

cal industry's staunchest allies—often at the public's peril and expense.
　　　　　—Mac Jeffery, "Does Rx Spell Rip-off?"

An effective introductory paragraph need not be long, as the following opener shows:

> I've often wondered what goes into a hot dog. Now I know and I
> wish I didn't.
> 　　　　　—William Zinsser, *The Lunacy Boom*

Ineffective introductions

When writing and revising an introductory paragraph, avoid
the following approaches that are likely to bore readers or make
them question your sincerity or control:

Openings to avoid

- **A vague generality or truth.** Don't extend your reach too wide with
  a line such as *Throughout human history . . .* or *In today's world. . . .*
  Readers can do without the warm-up.
- **A flat announcement.** Don't start with *The purpose of this essay is . . . ,*
  In this essay I will . . . , or any similar presentation of your intention or
  topic.
- **A reference to the essay's title.** Don't refer to the title of the essay in
  the first sentence—for example, *This is a big problem* or *This book is
  about the history of the guitar.*
- ***According to Webster.* . . .** Don't start by citing a dictionary definition. A definition can be an effective springboard to an essay, but this
  kind of lead-in has become dull with overuse.
- **An apology.** Don't fault your opinion or your knowledge with *I'm not
  sure if I'm right, but . . . ; I don't know much about this, but . . . ;* or a
  similar line.

---

2 Closing an essay

Most of your compositions will end with a closing statement or
conclusion, a signal to readers that you have not simply stopped
writing but have actually finished. The conclusion completes an
essay, bringing it to a climax while assuring readers that they have
understood your intention.

Note Compositions for the Web usually do not provide the
kind of closure featured in essays. In fact, you'll need to ensure that
your Web pages don't dead-end, leaving the reader stranded without options for moving backward or forward through your material.
(For more on Web composition, see pp. 834–40.)

RESOURCES AND IDEAS

Fulkerson, Richard. "Composition at the Turn of
the Twenty-First Century." *College Composition and Communication* 56.1 (2005): 654–87.
Print. Fulkerson provides an excellent introduction to current key issues in composition
theory and pedagogy, including the influence
on curriculum of critical/cultural studies and
genre analysis and the continuing popularity
of expressive approaches to teaching writing.

McClish, Glen. "Of Attention-Getting Openers
and Contracts: A Reassessment of an Introductory Dilemma." *Journal of Teaching Writing* 13.1 (1996): 197–207. Print. McClish discusses the metaphor of the "contract" as a
way to teach students about the rhetorical
impact of introductions without prompting
clichés.

Platz, Judith. "Revision and Process: 'Round
Robin' Group Writing." *Teaching English in
the Two Year College* 27.3 (2000): 342. Print.
Platz shows how a collaborative writing activity can improve the structure and content of
student writing.

COMPARING CLOSINGS

Using the same essays gathered for the preceding activity, ask students to read all but the
conclusions. Then have them underline the thesis
statement and the main ideas of each paragraph.
Finally, have students write their own conclusions. This exercise will help students to recognize the structure, effectiveness, and importance
of concluding paragraphs and will provide diverse examples of how key information may be
arranged for variety and emphasis.

Effective conclusions

An essay conclusion may consist of a single sentence or a group of sentences, usually set off in a separate paragraph. The conclusion may take one or more of the following approaches:

Some strategies for closing paragraphs

- Recommend a course of action.
- Summarize the paper.
- Echo the approach of the introduction.
- Restate your thesis and reflect on its implications.
- Strike a note of hope or despair.
- Give a symbolic or powerful fact or other detail.
- Give an especially compelling example.
- Create an image that represents your subject.
- Use a quotation.

The following paragraph concludes the essay on the Declaration of Independence (the introduction appears on p. 105):

> The Declaration of Independence has come to be a statement of this nation's political philosophy, but that was not its purpose in 1776. Jefferson's passionate expression had to bow to the goals of the Congress as a whole to forge unity among the colonies and to win the support of foreign nations.
>
> —Ann Weiss (student), "The Editing of the Declaration of Independence"

Echo of introduction: contrast between past and present

Restatement and elaboration of thesis

Maxine Hong Kingston uses a different technique—a vivid image—to conclude an essay about an aunt who committed suicide by drowning:

> My aunt haunts me—her ghost drawn to me because now, after fifty years of neglect, I alone devote pages of paper to her, though not origamied into houses and clothes. I do not think she always means me well. I am telling on her, and she was a spite suicide, drowning herself in the drinking water. The Chinese are always very frightened of the drowned one, whose weeping ghost, wet hair hanging and skin bloated, waits silently by the water to pull down a substitute.
>
> —Maxine Hong Kingston, "No Name Woman"

Summary

Image

In the next paragraph the author concludes an essay on environmental protection with a call for action:

Until we get the answers, I think we had better keep on building power plants and growing food with the help of fertilizers and such insect-controlling chemicals as we now have. The risks are well known, thanks to the environmentalists. If they had not created a widespread public awareness of the ecological crisis, we wouldn't stand a chance. But such awareness by itself is not enough. Flaming manifestos and prophecies of doom are no longer much help, and a search for scapegoats can only make matters worse. The time for sensations and manifestos is about over. Now we need rigorous analysis, united effort and very hard work.

— Summary and opinion

— Call for action

—Peter F. Drucker, "How Best to Protect the Environment"

Ineffective conclusions

The preceding examples illustrate ways of avoiding several pitfalls of conclusions:

Closings to avoid

- **A repeat of the introduction.** Don't simply replay your introduction. The conclusion should capture what the paragraphs of the body have added to the introduction.
- **A new direction.** Don't introduce a subject different from the one your essay has been about. If you arrive at a new idea, this may be a signal to start fresh with that idea as your thesis.
- **A sweeping generalization.** Don't conclude more than you reasonably can from the evidence you have given. If your essay is about your frustrating experience trying to clear a parking ticket, you cannot reasonably conclude that *all* local police forces are tied up in red tape.
- **An apology.** Don't cast doubt on your essay. Don't say, *Even though I'm no expert* or *This may not be convincing, but I believe it's true* or anything similar. Rather, to win your readers' confidence, display confidence.

---

3 | Using short emphatic or transitional paragraphs

A short emphatic paragraph can give unusual stress to an important idea, in effect asking the reader to pause and consider before moving on.

In short, all those who might have taken responsibility ducked it, and catastrophe was inevitable.

A transitional paragraph, because it is longer than a word or phrase and is set off by itself, moves a discussion from one point to another more slowly or more completely than does a single transitional expression or even a transitional sentence attached to a larger paragraph.

> These, then, are the causes of the current contraction in hospital facilities. But how does this contraction affect the medical costs of the government, private insurers, and individuals?

> So the debates were noisy and emotion-packed. But what did they accomplish? Historians have identified at least three direct results.

Use transitional paragraphs only to shift readers' attention when your essay makes a significant turn. A paragraph like the following one betrays a writer who is stalling:

> Now that we have examined these facts, we can look at some others that are equally central to an examination of this important issue.

4 Writing dialog

When recording a conversation between two or more people, start a new paragraph for each person's speech. The paragraphing establishes for the reader the point at which one speaker stops talking and another begins.

> The dark shape was indistinguishable. But once I'd flooded him with light, there he stood, blinking.
> "Well," he said eventually, "you're a sight for sore eyes. Should I stand here or are you going to let me in?"
> "Come in," I said. And in he came.
> —Louise Erdrich, *The Beet Queen*

Though dialog appears most often in fiction writing (the source of the preceding example), it may occasionally freshen or enliven narrative or expository essays. (For guidance in using quotation marks and other punctuation in passages of dialog, see pp. 436–38 and 462.)

> **Exercise 4.17   Analyzing an introduction and conclusion**
> Analyze the introductory and concluding paragraphs in the first and final drafts of the student essay in Chapter 3, pages 49–50 and 66–68. What is wrong with the first-draft paragraphs? Why are the final-draft paragraphs better? Could they be improved still further?

> **Exercise 4.18   Considering your past work: Introductions and conclusions**
> Examine the opening and closing paragraphs of the essay you've been analyzing in Exercises 4.3, 4.10, and 4.15. Do the paragraphs fulfill the requirements and avoid the pitfalls outlined on pages 104–09? Revise them as needed for clarity, conciseness, focus, and interest.

ANSWERS: EXERCISE 4.17

Possible answer

The introduction in the first draft rushes to a short summary of Friedman's essay without first securing the reader's interest, and it moves to the thesis statement without carefully connecting the essay to the thesis. In contrast, the final introduction opens with an engaging question and a provocative answer that leads smoothly into Moreno's thesis.

The conclusion in the first draft goes in a new direction by introducing the importance of working hard in college, which is not addressed elsewhere in the essay. In the final draft, the conclusion restates Moreno's points of agreement and disagreement with Friedman (her thesis) and finishes by looking toward the future.

ANSWERS: EXERCISE 4.18

Individual response.

4e Linking paragraphs in the essay

Your paragraphs do not stand alone: each one is a key unit of a larger piece of writing. Though you may draft paragraphs or groups of paragraphs almost as mini-essays, you will eventually need to stitch them together into a unified, coherent, well-developed whole. The techniques parallel those for linking sentences in paragraphs:

- **Make sure each paragraph contributes to your thesis.**
- **Arrange the paragraphs in a clear, logical order.** See pages 33–44 for advice on essay organization.
- **Create links between paragraphs.** Use repetition and restatement to stress and connect key terms, and use transitional expressions and transitional sentences to indicate sequence, direction, contrast, and other relationships.

The essay "A Picture of Hyperactivity" on pages 43–44 illustrates the first two of these techniques. The following passages from the essay illustrate the third technique, with (circled) repetitions and restatements, [boxed] transitional expressions, and transitional sentences noted in annotations.

A (hyperactive) committee member can contribute to efficiency. A hyperactive salesperson can contribute to profits. When (children) are hyperactive, though, people—even parents—may wish they had never been born. A (collage) of those who must cope with hyperactivity in children is a picture of frustration, anger, and loss.

> Introduction establishing subject and stating thesis
>
> Thesis statement

The [first] part of the (collage) is the (doctors.) In their terminology, the word (hyperactivity) has been replaced by (ADHD,) attention-deficit hyperactivity disorder. They apply the term to (children) who are abnormally or excessively busy. . . .

> Transitional topic sentence relating to thesis statement

As the mother of an (ADHD) (child,) I can say what the disorder means to the (parents) who form the [second] part of the (collage.) . . .

> Transitional topic sentence relating to thesis statement

The weight of (ADHD,) [however,] does not rest on the (doctors) and (parents.) The darkest part of the (collage) belongs to the (children.) . . .

> Transitional sentence
>
> Topic sentence relating to thesis statement

The (collage) is complete, and it is dark and somber. (ADHD,) as applied to (children,) is a term with uncertain, unattractive, and bitter associations. The (picture) does have one bright spot, [however,] for inside every (ADHD) (child) is a lovely, trusting, calm person waiting to be recognized.

> Transitional sentence into conclusion, restating thesis statement

ANSWERS: EXERCISE 4.19

Possible answer

Throughout the essay, Moreno repeats or restates key terms: *outsourcing/globalization, education/academic experience, communication/ communicate/writing/communicators, technical training/technical expertise/technical skills, problem solver/proposing solutions.* For each main point, the opening sentence connects specifically to the thesis statement. The pronouns *I/me, she/her,* and *they/their* appear consistently. Transitional expressions (*At first glance, however, First, Still, Also*) and many others link sentences and paragraphs. (Further analysis of this essay appears in Chapter 3 of the handbook and in the answers to Exercise 4.17.)

ANSWERS: EXERCISE 4.20

Individual response.

HIGHLIGHTS

Document design is increasingly important to the creation of written documents, as technology gives the individual computer user access to increasingly powerful design tools. If the courses you teach include diverse forms of writing, or if you teach journalism, technical writing, or business writing, you may wish to ask your students to put together a smart-looking newsletter, report, or brochure, and they will need to know how to design their projects. Even if you are teaching a course strictly focused on argument and academic prose, your students can benefit from understanding how to design their documents.

The chapter begins by covering various academic formatting styles that will probably be useful to your students. Section 5b explains the principles of good document design: creating flow, using good spacing techniques, grouping related elements, emphasizing important elements, and standardizing the appearance of elements. Section 5c covers application of design principles using specific tools and features, including print quality, margins, text, lists, headings, tables, figures, charts, graphs, images, and color. Section 5d discusses using illustrations, with examples of tables, figures, charts, graphs, and photographic or other images. Section 5e which considers readers who have vision loss, ends the chapter.

Exercise 4.19   Analyzing paragraphs in an essay

Analyze the ways in which paragraphs combine in the student essay in Chapter 3, pages 66–68. What techniques does the writer use to link paragraphs to the thesis statement and to each other? Where, if at all, does the writer seem to stray from the thesis or fail to show how paragraphs relate to it? How would you revise the essay to solve any problems it exhibits?

Exercise 4.20   Considering your past work: Paragraphs in the essay

Examine the overall effect of the essay you've been analyzing in Exercises 4.3, 4.10, 4.15, and 4.18. Do all the paragraphs relate to your thesis? Are they arranged clearly and logically? How do repetition and restatement, transitional expressions, or transitional sentences connect the paragraphs? Can you see ways to improve the essay's unity, coherence, and development?

5

Designing Documents

Imaginehowharditwouldbetoreadandwriteiftextlookedlikethis. To make reading and writing easier, we place a space between words. This convention and many others—such as page margins, page numbers, and paragraph breaks—have evolved over time to help writers communicate clearly with readers.

5a   Designing academic papers and other documents

The design guidelines offered in this chapter apply to all types of documents, including academic papers, Web sites, business reports, flyers, and newsletters. Each type has specific requirements as well, covered elsewhere in this book.

mycomplab

Visit *mycomplab.com* for more resources as well as exercises on document design.

1 Designing academic papers

Many academic disciplines prefer specific formats for students' papers. This book details four such formats:

- **MLA,** used in English, foreign languages, and some other humanities (pp. 689–91).
- **Chicago,** used in history, art history, religion, and some other humanities (pp. 771–73).
- **APA,** used in the social sciences (pp. 799–802).
- **CSE,** used in some natural and applied sciences (pp. 817–18).

Other academic formats can be found in the style guides listed on pages 760, 779–80, and 811.

The design guidelines in this chapter extend the range of elements and options covered by most academic styles. Your instructors may want you to adhere strictly to a particular style or may allow some latitude in design. Ask them for their preferences.

2 Writing online

In and out of school, you are likely to do a lot of online writing—certainly e-mail and possibly blogs and other Web sites. The purposes and audiences for online writing vary widely, and so do readers' expectations for its design. Chapter 54 details the approaches you can take in different online writing situations.

3 Designing business documents and other public writing

When you write outside your college courses, your audience will have certain expectations for how your documents should look and read. Guidelines for such writing appear in the following chapters:

- **Chapter 55 on public writing:** letters, job applications, reports, proposals, flyers, newsletters, brochures.
- **Chapter 56 on oral presentations:** *PowerPoint* slides and other visual aids.

5b Considering principles of design

Most of the principles of design respond to the ways we read. White space, for instance, relieves our eyes and helps to lead us through a document. Groupings or lists help to show relationships. Type sizes, images, and color add variety and help to emphasize important elements.

The sample documents on the following pages illustrate quite different ways of presenting a report for a marketing course. Even at

---

A WRITER'S PERSPECTIVE _____

[After revising,] nothing should then remain that offends the eye.

—ROBERT GRAVES

RESOURCES AND IDEAS

Connors, Robert J. "Actio: A Rhetoric of Manuscripts." *Rhetoric Review* 2.1 (1983): 64–73. Print. Connors discusses the rhetorical effect of typefaces, paper, and format on readers.

Flammia, Madelyn. "Avoiding Desktop Disasters: Why Technical Communication Students Should Learn About Mechanical Paste Up Techniques." *Journal of Technical Writing and Communication* 23.3 (1993): 287–95. Print. Flammia discusses a group of assignments intended to make students more aware of the principles of page design and layout.

George, Diana. "From Analysis to Design: Visual Communication in the Teaching of Writing." *College Composition Communication* 54.1 (2002): 11–39. Print. George argues for a broader definition of composition that incorporates more visual aspects.

Henry, Matthew. "Advertising and Interpretive Analysis: Developing Reading, Thinking, and Writing Skills in the Composition Course." *Teaching English in the Two-Year College* 29.4 (2002): 355–66. Print. Henry explains how he helps students develop critical thinking, writing, and reading skills by having them analyze advertisements.

Madraso, Jan. "Proofreading: The Skill We've Neglected to Teach." *English Journal* 82.2 (1993): 32–41. Print. Madroso suggests ways to make this activity more productive for students.

Norton, Robert. "Commentary: Graphic Excellence for the Technical Communicator." *Journal of Technical Writing and Communication* 23.1 (1993): 1–6. Print. Norton reminds students how good visuals can contribute to a better understanding of difficult concepts.

Penrod, Diane. *Composition in Convergence: The Impact of New Media on Writing Assessment.* Mahwah: Lawrence Erlbaum, 2005. Print. Penrod discusses how technological innovations in the composition classroom affect not just the texts created but also the process of assessment. She argues that instructors must look beyond surface correctness to assess the underlying purposes of new media texts.

PACKAGING SELLS

Students who have written résumés probably understand how important formatting is to a résumé (both because of the multilayered nature of résumé text and because hiring decisions are at stake), but they may not be used to thinking about college papers as having comparable requirements. A moment's reflection will probably produce the realization that almost all of the written material they encounter in their daily lives, from cereal-box blurbs to the newspaper, is formatted in some way.

PREVIOUS WORK

Students who have already written papers using one of the academic formats can send their old papers as e-mail attachments to the rest of the class. Ask them to write a cover note explaining why the document format standards are useful within the discipline.

NEWSLETTER CRITIQUE

If any student organization on your campus produces a newsletter, bring in copies of one issue and ask the class to critique it from a document design standpoint.

Original design

Runs title and subtitle together. Does not distinguish title from text.

Crowds the page with minimal margins.

Downplays paragraph breaks with small indentions.

Buries statistics in a paragraph. Obscures relationships with non-parallel wording.

Does not introduce the figure, leaving readers to infer its meaning and purpose.

Overemphasizes the figure with large size and excessive white space.

Presents the figure undynamically, flat on.

Does not caption the figure to explain what it shows, offering only a figure number and a partial text explanation.

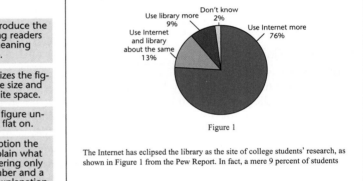

Generation Online: College Students and the Internet

College life once meant classrooms of students listening to teachers or groups of students talking over lunch in the union. But the reality today is more complex: students interact with their peers and professors by computer as much as face to face. As these students graduate and enter the workforce, all of society will be affected by their experience.

According to the Pew Internet Research Center (2008), today's college students are practiced computer and Internet users. The Pew Center reports that 24 percent of students in college today started using computers between ages five and eight. By age eighteen all students were using computers. Almost all college students, 92 percent, rely on the Internet, with 66 percent of students using more than one e-mail address. Computer ownership among this group is also very high: 85 percent have purchased or have been given at least one computer.

Students are eager to tap into the Internet's benefits and convenience.

Figure 1

The Internet has eclipsed the library as the site of college students' research, as shown in Figure 1 from the Pew Report. In fact, a mere 9 percent of students

---

a glance, the revised document is easier to scan and read. It makes better use of white space, groups similar elements, uses bullets and fonts for emphasis, and successfully integrates and explains the chart.

As you design your own documents, think about your purpose, the expectations of your readers, and how readers will move through your document. Also consider the following general principles of design, noting how they overlap and support each other.

1 | Creating flow

Many of the other design principles work in concert with the larger goal of conducting the reader through a document by establishing flow, a pattern for the eye to follow. In text-heavy documents like that on the facing page, flow may be achieved mainly with headings,

Revised design

Generation Online:
College Students and the Internet

College life once meant classrooms of students listening to teachers or groups of students talking over lunch in the union. But the reality today is more complex: students interact with their peers and professors by computer as much as face to face. As these students graduate and enter the workforce, all of society will be affected by their experience.

According to the Pew Internet Research Center (2008), today's college students are practiced computer users and Internet users.

- They started young: 24 percent were using computers between ages five and eight, and all were using them by age eighteen.
- They rely on the Internet: 92 percent have used the network, and 66 percent use more than one e-mail address.
- They own computers: 85 percent have purchased or have been given at least one computer.

Students are eager to tap into the Internet's benefits and convenience. Figure 1, from the Pew Report, shows that the Internet has eclipsed the library as the site of college students' research. In fact, a mere 9 percent of students reported using the library more than the Internet as a starting point for research.

- 9% 2% 76%
- 13%
- ■ Use Internet more
- ■ Use Internet and library about the same
- ■ Use library more
- □ Don't know

Figure 1. College students' use of the Internet and the library for research

Distinguishes title from subtitle and both from text.

Provides adequate margins.

Emphasizes paragraph breaks with white space.

Groups statistics in a bulleted list set off with white space. Uses parallel wording for parallel information.

Introduces the figure to indicate its meaning and purpose.

Reduces white space around the figure.

Presents the figure to emphasize the most significant segment.

Captions the figure so that it can be read independently from the text.

lists, and illustrations. In more visual documents, flow will come as well from the arrangement and spacing of information.

2 Spacing

The white space on a page eases crowding and focuses readers' attention. On an otherwise full page, just the space indicating paragraphs (an indention or a line of extra space) gives readers a break and reassures them that ideas are divided into manageable chunks.

In papers, reports, and other formal documents, spacing appears mainly in paragraph breaks, in margins, and around headings and lists. In publicity documents such as flyers and brochures, spacing is usually more generous between elements and helps boxes, headings, and the like pop off the page.

APPLYING THE PRINCIPLES OF DESIGN

Demonstrate to students the effect of different arrangements and presentations of the same text. Comparing formats in this way teaches them the importance of good manuscript presentation. Take the text of a well-designed letter, Web site, or advertisement, and provide the text only, with no formatting. Ask students in small groups to revise the document to apply the principles of document design. Then, as a class, compare the group revisions to the original. How does the original document apply those principles?

DESIGN ANALYSIS

Have students bring to class a brochure, advertisement, or announcement. In small groups, ask them to discuss each document and evaluate it for flow, spacing, grouping, emphasis, and standardization of elements. Each group might also write up a report of their analysis and present it to the class.

CAMPUS FLYER SERVICE I

Set up a flyer designing service for your campus, perhaps located at the college writing center. Campus groups that need a flyer designed for an event can bring content and ideas to your students, the designers. As a first step, have teams of students use the "Principles of document design" list on p. 116 to plan the flyer they will be designing.

REVISING DESIGN

Have students locate a brochure, ad, or announcement that they think has an ineffective design. On their computers, they can redesign the document, using the comment function of their word processing software to insert notes about what they changed and why.

STANDARDIZING AND EMPHASIZING

Provide students with the text of a document that has no standardization to its design and uses too many fonts, sizes, and types of highlighting (bold, capital letters, italics, and so on). Discuss how those problems make the document hard to read and impede meaning. Then, ask students to revise the document to apply the principles of design to standardize and emphasize appropriately.

Principles of document design

- **Create flow** to conduct the reader through the document.
- **Space elements** to give the reader's eye a rest and to focus the reader's attention.
- **Group related elements** in lists or under similar headings.
- **Standardize elements** to match appearance with content and to minimize variations.
- **Emphasize important elements.**

---

3 Grouping

Grouping information shows relationships visually, reinforcing the sense of the text itself. Here in this discussion, we group the various principles of design under visually identical headings to emphasize them and their similar importance. In the revised design on the previous page, the bulleted list details statistics about students' computer use. The list uses similar wording for each item to reinforce the similarities in the data. Thinking of likely groups as you write can help you organize your material so that it makes sense to you and your readers.

4 Standardizing

As we read a document, the design of its elements quickly creates expectations in us. We assume, for instance, that headings in the same size and color signal information of the same importance or that a list contains items of parallel content. Just as the design creates expectations, so it should fulfill them, treating similar elements similarly. Anticipating design standards as you write a document can help you treat its elements consistently and emphasize the elements you want to draw attention to.

Standardizing also creates clear, uncluttered documents. Even if they are used consistently, too many variations in type fonts and sizes, colors, indentions, and the like overwhelm readers as they try to determine the significance of the parts. Most formal documents, such as papers and reports, need no more than a single type font for text and headings, with type size and highlighting (such as CAPITAL LETTERS, **boldface,** or *italics*) distinguishing the levels of headings. Publicity documents, such as flyers and brochures, generally employ more variation to attract readers' attention.

5 Emphasizing

Part of a critical reader's task is to analyze and interpret the meaning of a document, and design helps the reader by stressing what's important. Type fonts and sizes, headings, indentions, color, boxes, white space—all of these elements establish hierarchies of information, so that the reader almost instinctively grasps what is crucial, what is less so, and what is merely supplementary. In this book, for example, the importance of headings is clear from their size and from the use of decorative elements, such as the box around 5c below; and boxes like the one opposite clearly mark summaries and other key information. As you design a document, considering where and how to emphasize elements can help you determine your document's priorities.

5c Using the elements of design

Applying the preceding principles involves margins, text, lists, headings, color, and illustrations. You won't use all these elements for every project, and in many writing situations you will be required to follow a prescribed format (see pp. 112–13). If you are addressing readers who have vision loss, consider as well the points discussed on page 126.

Note Your word processor may provide wizards or templates for many kinds of documents, such as letters, memos, reports, agendas, résumés, and brochures. **Wizards** guide you through setting up and writing complicated documents. **Templates** are preset forms to which you add your own text, headings, and other elements. Wizards and templates can be helpful, but not if they lead you to create cookie-cutter documents no matter what the writing situation. Always keep in mind that a document should be appropriate for your subject, audience, and purpose.

1 Setting margins

Margins at the top, bottom, and sides of a page help to prevent pages from overwhelming readers with unpleasant crowding. Most academic and business documents use a minimum one-inch margin on all sides. Publicity documents, such as flyers and brochures, often use narrower margins, compensating with white space between elements.

2 Creating readable text

A document must be readable. You can make text readable by choosing appropriate line spacing, type fonts and sizes, highlighting, word spacing, and line breaks.

Line spacing

Most academic documents are double-spaced, with an initial indention for paragraphs, while most business documents are single-spaced, with an extra line of space between paragraphs. Double or triple spacing sets off headings in both. Web sites and publicity documents, such as flyers and brochures, tend to use more line spacing to separate and group distinct parts of the content.

Type fonts and sizes

The readability of text also derives from the type fonts (or faces) and their sizes. For academic and business documents, generally choose a type size of 10 or 12 points, as in these samples:

10-point Courier	10-point Times New Roman
12-point Courier	12-point Times New Roman

Fonts like these and the one you're reading have **serifs**—the small lines finishing the letters, such as the downward strokes on the top of this T. Serif fonts are appropriate for formal writing and are easier for most people to read on paper. **Sans serif** fonts (*sans* means "without" in French) include this one found on many word processors:

10-point Arial	12-point Arial

Sans serif fonts are usually easier to read on a computer screen and are clearer on paper for readers with some vision loss (see p. 126).

Your word processor probably offers many decorative fonts as well:

10-point Bodega Sans	10-point Tekton
10-POINT STENCIL	10-point Ruzicka Freehand
10-point Lucida Sans	10-point Park Avenue

Decorative fonts are generally inappropriate in academic and business writing, where letter forms should be conventional and regular. But on some Web sites and in publicity documents, decorative fonts can attract attention, create motion, and reinforce a theme.

Note The point size of a type font is often an unreliable guide to its actual size, as the decorative fonts above illustrate: all the samples are 10 points, but they vary considerably. Before you use a font, print out a sample to be sure it is the size you want.

Highlighting

Within a document's text, underlined, *italic*, **boldface**, or even color type can emphasize key words or sentences. Underlining is rarest these days, having been replaced by italics. Both academic and business writing sometimes use boldface to give strong emphasis—for instance, to a term being defined—and publicity documents often rely extensively on boldface to draw the reader's eye. Neither academic nor business writing generally uses color within passages of text. In Web and publicity documents, however, color may be effective if the color is dark enough to be readable. (See p. 121 for more on color in document design.)

No matter what your writing situation, use highlighting selectively to complement your meaning, not merely to decorate your work. Many readers consider type embellishments to be distracting.

Word spacing

In most writing situations, follow these guidelines for spacing within and between words:

- **Leave one space between words.**
- **Leave one space after all punctuation, with these exceptions:**

Dash (two hyphens or the so-called em dash on a computer)	book--its book—its
Hyphen	one-half
Apostrophe within a word	book's
Two or more adjacent marks	book.")
Opening quotation mark, parenthesis, or bracket	("book [book

- **Leave one space before and after an ellipsis mark.** In the examples below, ellipsis marks indicate omissions within a sentence and at the end of a sentence. See pages 475–76 for additional examples.

book . . . in   book. . . . The

Line breaks

Your word processor will generally insert appropriate breaks between lines of continuous text: it will not, for instance, automatically begin a line with a comma or period, and it will not end a line with an opening parenthesis or bracket. However, you will have to prevent it from breaking a two-hyphen dash or a three-dot ellipsis mark by spacing to push the beginning of each mark to the next line.

When you instruct it to do so (usually under the Tools menu), your word processor will also automatically hyphenate words to prevent very short lines. If you must decide yourself where to break words, follow the guidelines on page 545.

? asks Cheryl

3 | Using lists

Lists give visual reinforcement to the relations between like items—for example, the steps in a process or the elements of a proposal. A list is easier to read than a paragraph and adds white space.

When wording a list, work for parallelism among items—for instance, all complete sentences or all phrases (see also pp. 401–02). Set the list with space above and below. Number the items, or mark them with bullets: centered dots or other devices, such as the squares used in the list above about word spacing. On most word processors you can use the Format menu to create a list automatically.

LISTING THE REASONS

The occasional student may submit a paper entirely in list form, not understanding that a list is an inappropriate format for an academic paper. To illustrate this point, you might give them two versions of a sample paragraph, one with the evidence in list form and the other written conventionally, and discuss how the list affects the flow of the paragraph. Students should also identify any information the list leaves out such as transitions or logical connections.

4 | Using headings

Headings are signposts: they direct the reader's attention by focusing the eye on a document's most significant content. In Web and publicity documents, headings may be decorative as well as functional, capturing the reader's attention with large sizes, lots of white space, and unconventional fonts. In academic and much business writing, however, headings are more purely functional. They break the text into discrete parts, create emphasis, and orient the reader.

When you use headings in academic and business writing, follow these guidelines:

- **Use one, two, or three levels of headings** depending on the needs of your material and the length of your document. Some level of heading every two or so pages will help keep readers on track. (A three-page paper probably will not need headings.)
- **Create an outline of your document to plan** where headings should go. Reserve the first level of heading for the main points (and sections). Use a second and perhaps a third level of heading to mark subsections of supporting information.
- **Keep headings as short as possible** while making them specific about the material that follows.
- **Word headings consistently**—for instance, all questions (*What Is the Scientific Method?*), all phrases with *-ing* words (*Understanding the Scientific Method*), or all phrases with nouns (*The Scientific Method*).
- **Indicate the relative importance of headings** with type size, positioning, and highlighting, such as capital letters or boldface.

First-Level Heading

Second-Level Heading

Third-Level Heading

Generally, you can use the same type font and size for headings as for the text.

- **Don't break a page immediately after a heading.** Push the heading to the next page.

Note Document format in psychology and some other social sciences requires a particular treatment of headings. See page 801.

5 | Using color

With a computer and color printer, you can produce documents that use color for bullets, headings, illustrations, and other elements. Web and publicity documents almost always use color, whereas academic and business documents may not need color at all. (Ask your instructor or supervisor for his or her preferences.) If you do use color in an academic document, follow these guidelines:

- Print text in black, not red, blue, or another color.
- Make sure that color headings are dark enough to be readable.
- Stick to the same color for all headings at the same level—for instance, red for primary headings, black for secondary headings.
- Use color for bullets, lines, and other nontext elements. But use no more than a few colors to keep pages clean.
- Use color to distinguish the parts of illustrations. Use only as many colors as you need to make your illustration clear. (See below.)

See also page 126 on the use of color for readers who have vision loss.

EXERCISE 5.1 Redesigning a paper

Save a duplicate copy of a recent paper or one you are currently working on. Then format the duplicate using appropriate elements of design, such as type fonts, lists, and headings. (For a new paper, be sure your instructor will accept your new design.) When you have finished the redesign, share the work with your instructor.

5d Using illustrations

An illustration can often make a point for you more efficiently than words can. Tables present data. Figures (such as graphs and charts) usually recast data in visual form. Diagrams, drawings, and photographs can explain processes, represent what something looks like, or add emphasis.

Note The Web is an excellent resource for photographs (see pp. 584–85), and you can edit the images with a program such as *Adobe Photoshop*. Your computer may include a program for creating tables, graphs, and other illustrations, or you can work with specialized software such as *Excel* (for graphs and charts) or *Adobe Illustrator* (for diagrams, maps, and the like). Use *PowerPoint* or a similar program for visuals in oral presentations (see pp. 861–62).

1 Using illustrations appropriately for the writing situation

Academic and many business documents tend to use illustrations differently from publicity documents. In the latter, illustrations generally attract attention or emphasize. In academic and business writing, however, illustrations directly reinforce and amplify the text. Follow these guidelines for academic and most business writing:

- Focus on a purpose for each illustration—a reason for including it and a point you want it to make. Otherwise, readers may find it irrelevant or confusing.
- Provide a source note whenever the data or the entire illustration is someone else's independent material (see pp. 629–30).

INSTRUCTIONS FOR MAKING A HOT FUDGE SUNDAE

Have students create an instructional document on how to "build" a hot fudge sundae (or other dessert of their choice). They should apply elements of design appropriately and create the document on their computer. They can include illustrations, color, highlighting, numbered lists, or other elements they think will make for a well-designed document. The goal is for the document to be visually appealing and easy to read.

Each discipline has a slightly different style for such source notes: those in the illustrations below and on the next three pages reflect MLA style. See also Chapters 46 and 50–52.

- **Number figures, photographs, and other images together**, and label them as figures: Fig. 1, Fig. 2, and so on.
- **Number and label tables separately:** Table 1, Table 2, and so on.
- **Refer to each illustration in your text**—for instance, "See fig. 2." Place the reference at the point(s) in the text where readers will benefit by consulting the illustration.
- **Determine the placement of illustrations.** The social sciences and some other disciplines require each illustration to fall on a page by itself immediately after the text reference to it (see p. 802). You may want to follow this rule in other situations as well if you have a large number of illustrations. Otherwise, you can embed them in your text pages just after you refer to them.

2 Using tables

Tables usually present raw data, making complex information accessible to readers. The data may show how variables relate to one another or how two or more groups contrast, as in the example below. Some tables use rows and columns to present related textual information rather than data. See page 824 for an example.

Table

| A self-explanatory title falls above the table. | The layout of rows and columns is clear: headings align with their data, and numbers align vertically down columns. |
| Self-explanatory headings label horizontal rows and vertical columns. | |

Table 1

Public- and private-school enrollment of US students age five and older, 2006

	Number of students	Percentage in public school	Percentage in private school
All students	74,220,937	83.2	16.8
Kindergarten	4,012,680	86.0	14.0
Grades 1-4	15,758,734	88.8	11.2
Grades 5-8	16,498,217	89.4	10.6
Grades 9-12	17,500,473	90.5	9.5
College (undergraduate)	17,063,732	77.0	23.0
Graduate and professional school	3,387,101	59.8	40.2

Source: Data from *2006 American Community Survey*; US Census Bureau, n.d.; Web; 10 Oct. 2008; table S1404.

EXCELLING AT TABLES

Most word processors and spreadsheet programs contain different options for creating tables and charts from data. Your students can experiment with different presentations of the same data to see which conveys the information best or to emphasize different aspects of the data.

3 Using figures

Figures represent data or show concepts visually. They include charts, graphs, diagrams, and photographs.

Pie charts

Pie charts show the relations among the parts of a whole. The whole totals 100 percent, and each pie slice is proportional in size to its share of the whole. Use a pie chart when shares, not the underlying data, are your focus.

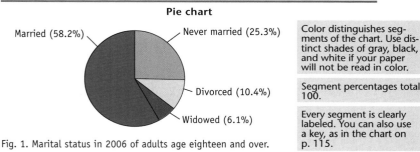

Pie chart

Married (58.2%)   Never married (25.3%)

Divorced (10.4%)

Widowed (6.1%)

Color distinguishes segments of the chart. Use distinct shades of gray, black, and white if your paper will not be read in color.

Segment percentages total 100.

Every segment is clearly labeled. You can also use a key, as in the chart on p. 115.

Self-explanatory caption falls below the chart.

Fig. 1. Marital status in 2006 of adults age eighteen and over. Data from *Statistical Abstract of the United States: 2008*; US Census Bureau, 27 Mar. 2007; Web; 10 Oct. 2008.

Bar charts

Bar charts compare groups or time periods on a measure such as quantity or frequency. Use a bar chart when relative size is your focus. Be sure to start with a zero point in the lower left corner so that the values on the vertical axis are clear.

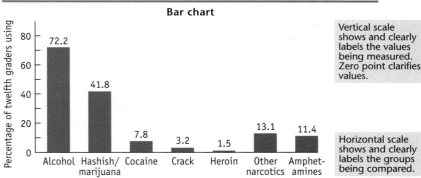

Bar chart

Percentage of twelfth graders using

80
72.2
60
41.8
40
20
7.8   3.2   1.5   13.1   11.4
0

Alcohol   Hashish/   Cocaine   Crack   Heroin   Other   Amphet-
          marijuana   narcotics amines

Vertical scale shows and clearly labels the values being measured. Zero point clarifies values.

Horizontal scale shows and clearly labels the groups being compared.

Self-explanatory caption falls below the chart.

Fig. 2. Lifetime prevalence of use of alcohol and other drugs among twelfth graders in 2007. Data from *Monitoring the Future: A Continuing Study of American Youth*; U of Michigan, 11 Dec. 2007; Web; 10 Aug. 2008.

Line graphs

Line graphs show change over time in one or more subjects. They are an economical and highly visual way to compare many points of data. Be sure to start with a zero point in the lower left corner so that the values on the vertical axis are clear.

Line graph

Vertical scale shows and clearly labels the values being measured. Zero point clarifies values.

Color and labels distinguish the subjects being compared. Use dotted and dashed black lines if your paper will not be read in color.

Horizontal scale shows and clearly labels the range of dates.

Self-explanatory caption falls below the graph.

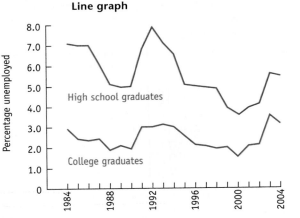

Fig. 3. Unemployment rates of high school graduates and college graduates, 1984-2004. Data from Antony Davies; *The Economics of College Tuition*; Mercatus Center, George Mason U, 3 Mar. 2005; Web; 26 June 2008.

Diagrams

Diagrams show concepts visually, such as the structure of an organization, the way something works or looks, or the relations among subjects. (See the example on the facing page.) Often, diagrams show what can't be described economically in words. For other examples of diagrams, see pages 3, 104, and 835.

Photographs and other images

Sometimes you may focus an entire paper on analyzing an image such as a photograph, painting, or advertisement (see pp. 173–75). But most commonly you'll use images to add substance to ideas or to enliven them. You might clarify an astronomy paper with a photograph of Saturn (see opposite), add information to an analysis of a novel with a drawing of the author, or capture the theme of a brochure with a cartoon. Images grab readers' attention, so use them carefully to explain, reinforce, or enhance your writing.

Diagram

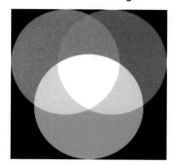

Diagram makes concept comprehensible.

Fig. 4. RGB color theory, applied to televisions and computer monitors, in which all possible colors and white are created from red, green, and blue. From "Color Theory"; *Wikipedia*; Wikimedia, 15 Mar. 2005; Web; 13 May 2008.

Self-explanatory caption falls below the diagram.

Note When using an image prepared by someone else—for instance, a photograph downloaded from the Web—you must verify that the source permits reproduction of the image before you use it. In most documents, but especially in academic papers, you must also fully cite the source of any borrowed image. See pages 632–34 on copyright issues with Internet sources.

Photograph

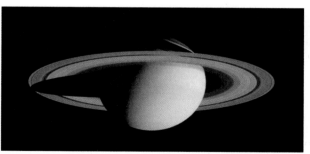

Photograph shows subject more economically and dramatically than words could.

Fig. 5. View of Saturn from the *Cassini* spacecraft, showing the planet and its rings. From *Cassini-Huygens: Mission to Saturn and Titan*; US Natl. Atmospheric and Space Administration, Jet Propulsion Laboratory, 24 Feb. 2005; Web; 26 Apr. 2008.

Self-explanatory caption falls below the image.

RESOURCES AND IDEAS

Draga, Sam and Van Doss. "Cruel Pies: The Inhumanity of Technical Illustrations." *Technical Communication* 48.3 (2001): 265–74. Print. The authors' review of the research on the ethics of visual communication suggests that visual information is not always presented accurately and honestly; they suggest ways of correcting the problem.

Williams, Robin. *The Non-Designer's Design Book*, 3rd ed. Berkeley: Peachpit, 2008. Print. This is an accessible beginner's guide to modern document design.

5e   Considering readers with vision loss

Your audience may include readers who have low vision, problems with color perception, or difficulties processing visual information. If so, consider adapting your design to meet these readers' needs. Here are a few pointers:

- **Use large type fonts.** Most guidelines call for 14 points or larger.
- **Use standard type fonts.** Many people with low vision find it easier to read sans serif fonts such as Arial than serif fonts (see p. 118). Avoid decorative fonts with unusual flourishes, even in headings.
- **Avoid words in all-capital letters.**
- **Avoid relying on color alone to distinguish elements.** Label elements, and distinguish them by position or size.
- **Use red and green selectively.** To readers who are red-green colorblind, these colors will appear in shades of gray, yellow, or blue.
- **Use contrasting colors.** To make colors distinct, choose them from opposite sides of the color spectrum—violet and yellow, for instance, or orange and blue.
- **Use only light colors for tints behind type.** Make the type itself black or a very dark color.

PART 2

Reading and Writing in College

6 Developing Academic Skills

7 Forming a Critical Perspective

8 Writing in Academic Situations

9 Reading Arguments Critically

10 Writing an Argument

11 Reading and Using Visual Arguments

HIGHLIGHTS
Chapter 6 covers key academic skills. It opens with practical discussions of time management (6a) and listening and taking notes in class (6b). Section 6c covers reading for comprehension and includes such topics as writing while reading, previewing, reading in depth, and summarizing. Section 6d introduces academic writing, reviewing key concepts from Part 1 (the writing situation, organization, revising, and editing) and discussing synthesis and acknowledgment of sources. The chapter concludes with how to prepare for exams (6e).

6

Developing Academic Skills

When you take college courses, you enter an academic discipline—a community of teachers and students who are studying a particular subject and whose basic goal is to build knowledge about that subject, whether it is English, history, engineering, or something else. You participate in a discipline community first by studying a subject, acquiring its vocabulary, and learning to express yourself in its ways. As you gain experience and knowledge, you contribute to the community by asking questions and communicating your answers in writing. This active, involved learning is the core of academic work. It may seem beyond you at first, as you try to grasp the content of assigned reading and identify important ideas. But the transition will be easier if you follow the advice in this chapter for managing your time, getting the most from your classes, understanding assigned reading, being an academic writer, and preparing for exams.

Developing your academic skills

- **Learn the key procedures on your campus.** Make sure you know how to register for classes, drop or add a class, declare or change your major, request a transcript, and pay tuition bills.
- **Manage your time.** College coursework often takes more time than students anticipate. The tips in the next section will help you schedule regular time for study, organize your workload, and use your study time wisely.
- **Study the syllabus for each course.** This outline specifies the instructor's expectations as well as the course topics, assignments, and deadlines.
- **Attend and participate in class.** Make class attendance a priority, whether or not the instructor checks the roll. Listen carefully,

mycomplab

Visit *mycomplab.com* for more resources as well as exercises on academic skills.

take notes (see p. 131 for tips), ask questions, and participate in discussions.

- **Do the assigned reading.** You'll gain experience with the language and ideas used in each of your classes, and you'll become familiar with the kinds of writing expected of you. See pages 131–33 for help with reading.
- **Understand each writing assignment.** Knowing the writing situation posed by each assignment—the audience, purpose, options for subjects, and other elements of the situation—will help you meet its expectations. Use the advice on pages 135–36 and in Chapter 8 to understand writing in academic situations.
- **Prepare for exams.** See pages 136–38 in this chapter on study skills and page 822 in Chapter 53 on taking essay exams.
- **Get help when you need it.** Most instructors post weekly office hours, and many hold online office hours. In addition, most schools provide advisers and counselors, writing centers, tutoring centers, computer assistance, library tours, and other services.

6a Managing your time

Like many students, you may find that college demands more time and energy than you anticipated. You can minimize the stress of college work by setting priorities and by planning and pacing your schoolwork and other activities.

1 Surveying your activities

How do you spend your days? For a week, keep track of all your activities and the time they absorb. How many of the week's 168 hours do you spend eating, sleeping, watching television, talking on the phone, reading e-mail, attending classes, studying, working at a job, attending religious services, exercising, commuting, caring for children, doing laundry, socializing, and so on? How much time can you realistically devote to studying? What activities, if any, do you need to limit so that you have adequate time for studying?

2 Scheduling your time

One way to organize your time is to use a calendar that divides each day into waking hours. Block out your activities that occur regularly and at specific times, such as commuting, attending classes, and working. Then fill in the other activities (such as exercise, eating, and studying) that do not necessarily occur at fixed times. Be sure to leave time for relaxing: an unrealistic schedule that assigns all available time to studying will quickly prove too difficult to live by. If you use a

ADD & TIME MANAGEMENT

Students with attention deficit disorder often have difficulty with time management. For these students, time management strategies (alarm clocks or other external cueing devices, planners, and study schedules) are essential. Most campuses have a learning center or academic assistance office that can provide additional support to these students.

WRITING CHUNKS

Remind your students that paper-writing usually requires multiple sessions, with time for incubating thoughts in between. So when they are planning their weekly work schedule, they will do best to break a paper assignment into chunks, such as brainstorming, outlining, drafting, and revising. Chunks can be spread out over several days or longer.

DIFFERENTIATED INSTRUCTION TECHNIQUES

Students who are visual or global learners may have difficulty taking notes from an oral class lecture without supplementary materials. To help reach students with these learning styles, you might pass out a written version of lecture notes or post notes on your class Web site so that students can review them later.

computer regularly, consider keeping your schedule online using a calendar program. Set it to remind you of important due dates.

3 | Organizing your workload

Use the syllabuses for your courses to estimate the amount of weekly study time required for each course. Generally, plan on two hours of studying for each hour in class—that is, about six hours for a typical course. Block out study periods using these guidelines:

- **Schedule study time close to class time.** You'll study more productively if you review notes, read assigned material, or work on projects shortly after each class period.
- **Pace assignments.** Plan to start early and work regularly on projects requiring extensive time, such as research papers, so that you will not be overwhelmed near the deadline. (See pp. 549–50 for advice on scheduling research projects.)
- **Adjust the weekly plan as needed to accommodate changes in your workload.** Before each week begins, examine its schedule to be sure you've built in enough time to study for an exam, finish a paper, or meet other deadlines and commitments.

4 | Making the most of study time

When you sit down to study, use your time efficiently:

- **Set realistic study goals.** Divide your study sessions into small chunks, each with a short-term goal, such as previewing a textbook chapter or drafting three paragraphs of a paper. Plan breaks, too, so that you can clear your mind, stretch, and refocus on your goals.
- **Tackle difficult homework first.** Resist any urge to put off demanding jobs, such as working on papers, reading textbooks, and doing math problems. Save easy tasks for when you're less alert.
- **Evaluate how you use your study time.** At the end of each week, ask yourself whether you were as productive as you needed to be. If not, what changes can you make to accomplish your goals for the coming week?

6b | Listening and taking notes in class

When you begin each class meeting, push aside other concerns so that you can focus and listen. Either on paper or on a computer, record what you hear as completely as possible while sorting out the main ideas from the secondary and supporting ones. (See the box below.) Such active note taking will help you understand the instructor's approach to the course and provide you with complete material for later study.

Tips for taking class notes

- **Use your own words.** You will understand and retain the material better if you rephrase it. But use the speaker's words if necessary to catch everything.
- **Leave space in your notes if you miss something.** Instructors usually welcome questions about content but not requests for simple repetition, and it's not fair to distract fellow students during class. Ask someone for the missing information as soon as possible after the class ends.
- **Include any reading content mentioned by your instructor.** Use your notes to integrate all the components of the course—your instructor's views, your own thoughts, and the assigned reading, even if you've already read it.
- **Review your notes shortly after class.** Reinforce your new knowledge when it is fresh by underlining key words and ideas, adding headings and comments in the margins, converting your notes to questions, or outlining the lecture based on your notes. If you don't understand something in the notes, consult a classmate for his or her version.

6c Reading for comprehension

The assigned reading you do for college courses—such as textbooks, journal articles, essays, and works of literature—requires a greater focus on understanding and retention than does the reading you do for entertainment or for practical information. The process discussed here may seem time consuming, but with practice you'll become efficient at it.

Note The following process stresses ways of understanding what you read. In critical reading, covered in the next chapter, you extend this process to analyze and evaluate what you read and see.

1 Writing while reading

Reading for comprehension is an *active* process. Students often believe they are reading actively when they roll a highlighter over the important ideas in a text, but truly engaged reading requires more than that. If you take notes while reading, you "translate" the work into your own words and reconstruct it for yourself.

The substance of your reading notes will change as you preview, read, and summarize. At first, you may jot quick, short notes

READING NOTES

Have students read a short article in class and take reading notes on it. Then ask them to use their reading notes to discuss the article in small groups.

PRACTICE PREVIEWING

Give your students practice in previewing techniques by bringing a collection of books to class (one per student) and asking them each to preview one. Then ask them to present the book to the rest of the class.

A WRITER'S PERSPECTIVE _____

Those who fail to reread are obliged to read the same story everywhere.
                                    —ROLAND BARTHES

in the margins, on separate pages, or on a computer. (Use the last two for material you don't own or are reading online.) As you delve into the work, the notes should become more detailed, restating important points, asking questions, connecting ideas. (See p. 143 for an example of a text annotated in this way by a student.) For in-depth critical reading, you may want to keep a reading journal that records both what the work says and what you think about it. (See p. 143.)

2 Previewing

For most course reading, you should **skim** before reading word for word. Skimming gives you an overview of the material that will help you understand any part of it. Your goal is not to comprehend all the details or even the structure of the author's argument. Rather, working as outlined below, aim for a general sense of the length and difficulty of the material, its organization, and its principal ideas.

- **Gauge length and level.** Is the material brief and straightforward enough to read in one sitting, or do you need more time?
- **Examine the title and introduction.** The title and first couple of paragraphs will give you a sense of the topic, the author's approach, and the main ideas. As you read them, ask yourself what you already know about the subject so that you can integrate new information with old.
- **Move from heading to heading or paragraph to paragraph.** Viewing headings as signposts or as the levels of an outline will give you a feeling for which ideas the author sees as primary and which subordinate. In a text without headings, reading the first sentence of each paragraph will give you a sense of the author's important ideas.
- **Note highlighted words.** You will likely need to learn the meanings of terms in **bold**, *italic*, or color.
- **Slow down for pictures, diagrams, tables, graphs, and other illustrations.** They often contain concentrated information.
- **Read the summary or conclusion.** These paragraphs often recap the main ideas.
- **Think over what you've skimmed.** Try to recall the central idea, or thesis, and the sequence of ideas.

3 Reading

After previewing a text, you can settle into it to learn what it has to say.

First reading

The first time through new material, read as steadily and smoothly as possible, trying to get the gist of what the author is saying.

■ **Read in a place where you can concentrate.** Choose a quiet environment away from distractions such as music or talking.

■ **Give yourself time.** Rushing yourself or worrying about something else you have to do will prevent you from grasping what you read.

■ **Try to enjoy the work.** Seek connections between it and what you already know. Appreciate new information, interesting relationships, forceful writing, humor, good examples.

■ **Make notes sparingly during this first reading.** Mark major stumbling blocks—such as a paragraph you don't understand—so that you can try to resolve them before rereading.

(CULTURE LANGUAGE) If English is not your first language and you come across unfamiliar words, don't stop and look up every one. You will lose more in concentration than you will gain in understanding. Instead, try to guess the meanings of unfamiliar words from their contexts, circle them, and look them up later.

Rereading

After the first reading, plan on at least one other. This time read *slowly.* Your main concern should be to grasp the content and how it is constructed. That means rereading a paragraph if you didn't get the point or using a dictionary to look up words you don't know.

Use your pen, pencil, or keyboard freely to highlight and distill the text:

■ **Distinguish main ideas from supporting ideas.** Look for the central idea, or thesis, for the main idea of each paragraph or section, and for the evidence supporting ideas.

■ **Learn key terms.** Understand both their meanings and their applications.

■ **Discern the connections among ideas.** Be sure you see why the author moves from point A to point B to point C and how those points work together to support the central idea. It often helps to outline the text or summarize it (see the next page).

■ **Add your own comments.** In the margins or separately, note links to other readings or to class discussions, questions to explore further, possible topics for your writing, points you find especially strong or weak. (This last category will occupy much of your time when you are expected to read critically. See pp. 146–52.)

READING GOALS

Reading with a goal in mind can help students focus their reading process. You could give students a list of study questions before they read to help them focus their reading to extract key ideas. Alternatively, you could ask each student to bring to class one discussion question based on the reading.

DEMONSTRATE ANNOTATING A TEXT

To help students learn to follow the reading guidelines and annotate their text while reading, you might share a brief newspaper editorial on the overhead projector and annotate the piece together as a class, showing students how to skim and then read. Then, together, reread to identify the thesis, main ideas, and supporting ideas; note key terms and learn their definitions, if needed; find connections among the ideas; and finally, add your own questions, comments, and responses.

SUMMARY ASSIGNMENTS

A summary can make a good short writing assignment, especially for beginning writers. Students can focus on comprehending another writer's argument without the additional task of making their own argument in a written assignment.

SUMMARY CONTEST

Ask students to submit summaries anonymously to your class Web page and then have the class vote on which summary is the best. Follow up with a discussion of why the winning summary was successful.

4 | Summarizing

A good way to master the content of a text is to **summarize** it: reduce it to its main points, in your own words. Some assignments call for brief summaries, as when you summarize the plot in a critical essay about a novel (p. 743). Summary is also an essential tool in research papers and other writing that draws on sources (pp. 611–12). Here, though, we're concerned with summarizing for yourself—for your own enlightenment.

A summary should state in as few words as possible the main ideas of a passage. When you need to summarize a few paragraphs or a brief article, your summary should not exceed one-fifth the length of the original. For longer works, such as chapters of books or whole books, your summary should be quite a bit shorter in proportion to the original. A procedure for drafting a summary appears in the following box.

Writing a summary

- **Understand the meaning.** Look up words or concepts you don't know so that you understand the author's sentences and how they relate to one another.
- **Understand the organization.** Work through the text to identify its sections—single paragraphs or groups of paragraphs focused on a single topic. To understand how parts of a work relate to one another, try drawing a tree diagram or creating an outline (pp. 34–39).
- **Distill each section.** Write a one- or two-sentence summary of each section you identify. Focus on the main point of the section, omitting examples, facts, and other supporting evidence.
- **State the main idea.** Write a sentence or two capturing the author's central idea.
- **Support the main idea.** Write a full paragraph (or more, if needed) that begins with the central idea and supports it with the sentences that summarize sections of the work. The paragraph should concisely and accurately state the thrust of the entire work.
- *Use your own words.* By writing, you re-create the meaning of the work in a way that makes sense for you.

Summarizing even a passage of text can be tricky. The facing page shows one attempt to summarize the following material from an introductory biology textbook.

Original text

As astronomers study newly discovered planets orbiting distant stars, they hope to find evidence of water on these far-off celestial bodies, for water is the substance that makes possible life as we know it here on Earth. All organisms familiar to us are made mostly of water and live in an environment dominated by water. They require water more than any other substance. Human beings, for example, can survive for quite a few weeks without food, but only a week or so without water. Molecules of water participate in many chemical reactions necessary to sustain life. Most cells are surrounded by water, and cells themselves are about 70–95% water. Three-quarters of Earth's surface is submerged in water. Although most of this water is in liquid form, water is also present on Earth as ice and vapor. Water is the only common substance to exist in the natural environment in all three physical states of matter: solid, liquid, and gas.

—Neil A. Campbell and Jane B. Reece, *Biology*

Draft summary

Astronomers look for water in outer space because life depends on it. It is the most common substance on Earth and in living cells, and it can be a liquid, a solid (ice), or a gas (vapor).

This summary accurately restates ideas in the original, but it does not pare the passage to its essence. The work of astronomers and the three physical states of water add color and texture to the original, but they are asides to the key concept that water sustains life because of its role in life. The following revision narrows the summary to this concept:

Revised summary

Water is the most essential support for life—the dominant substance on Earth and in living cells and a component of life-sustaining chemical processes.

Note Do not count on the AutoSummarize function on your word processor for summarizing texts that you may have copied onto your computer. The summaries are rarely accurate, and you will not gain the experience of interacting with the texts on your own.

6d Becoming an academic writer

As a member of an academic community, you will communicate with other members mainly through writing. Each discipline has its own conventions for writing, but in all disciplines you will be expected to do the following:

■ **Know the writing situation posed in each assignment.** Most assignments will at least suggest possible subjects and imply a purpose and an audience. In that context, you refine your subject, your purpose, and your sense of audience as you proceed through the writing process. For a review of assessing the writing situation, see pages 4–5.

- **Develop and organize your writing.** Most academic papers center on a main point, or thesis, and support the thesis with evidence. For more on developing a thesis and organizing a paper, see pages 27–44.
- **Synthesize your own and others' ideas.** Academic writing often involves interacting with the works of other writers—responding to them, comparing them, using them to answer questions. Such interaction requires you to read critically (the subject of the next chapter) and to **synthesize,** or integrate, others' ideas into your own. For more on synthesis, see pages 162–65.
- **Revise and edit your writing.** Academic writing is careful writing. Allow yourself enough time to revise and edit so that readers can see your main ideas, follow your train of thought, and make sense of your sentences. Consult this book's revision and editing checklists on pages 54–55 and 60–61.
- **Acknowledge your sources.** Academic writers build on the work of others by fully crediting borrowed ideas and information. Always record the publication information of any source you consult so that you can cite it if you decide to use it later in your writing. See the discussion of avoiding plagiarism on pages 626–34 and the guides to specific documentation styles on pages 644–88 (MLA style for English and some other humanities), 760–71 (Chicago style for history, philosophy, and some other humanities), 779–99 (APA style for the social sciences), and 811–17 (CSE style for the natural and applied sciences).

Note Chapter 8 provides a detailed introduction to academic writing, and Chapters 48–52 treat writing in specific disciplines.

6e Preparing for exams

Examinations give you a chance to demonstrate what you have learned from listening, reading, and writing. Studying for an exam involves three main steps, each requiring about a third of the preparation time: reviewing the material, organizing summaries of the material, and testing yourself. Your main goals are to strengthen your understanding of the subject, making both its ideas and its details more memorable, and to increase the flexibility of your new knowledge so that you can apply it in new contexts.

The procedure outlined here works for any exam, no matter how much time you have, what material you're studying, or what kind of test you'll be taking. Because an essay exam requires a distinctive approach during the exam itself, it receives special attention in Chapter 53, pages 822–28.

Note Cramming for an exam is about the least effective way of preparing for one. It takes longer to learn under stress, and the learning is shallower, more difficult to apply, and more quickly forgotten. Information learned under stress is even harder to apply in stressful situations such as taking an exam. And the lack of sleep that usually accompanies cramming makes a good performance even more unlikely. If you must cram for a test, face the fact that you can't learn everything. Spend your time reviewing main concepts and facts.

1 Reviewing and memorizing the material

Divide your class notes and reading assignments into manageable units. Reread the material, recite or write out the main ideas and selected supporting ideas and examples, and then skim for an overview. Proceed in this way through all the units of the course, returning to earlier ones as needed to refresh your memory or to relate ideas.

During this stage you should be memorizing what you don't already know by heart. Try these strategies for strengthening your memory:

- **Link new and known information.** For instance, to remember a sequence of four dates in twentieth-century African history, link the dates to simultaneous and more familiar events in the United States.
- **Create groups of ideas or facts that make sense to you.** For instance, memorize French vocabulary words in related groups, such as words for parts of the body or parts of a house. Keep the groups small: research has shown that we can easily memorize about seven items at a time but have trouble with more.
- **Create narratives and visual images.** You may recall a story or a picture more easily than words. For instance, to remember how the economic laws of supply and demand affect the market for rental housing, you could tie the principles to a narrative about the aftermath of the 1906 San Francisco earthquake, when half the population was suddenly homeless. Or you could visualize a person who has dollar signs for eyes and is converting a spare room into a high-priced rental unit, as many did after the earthquake to meet the new demand for housing.
- **Use _mnemonic devices_, or tricks for remembering.** Say the history dates you want to remember are separated by five years, then four, then nine. By memorizing the first date and recalling $5 + 4 = 9$, you'll have command of all four dates.

2 Organizing summaries of the material

Allow time to reorganize the material in your own way, creating categories that will help you apply the information in various contexts.

AURAL AND KINESTHETIC MEMORY

Repeating facts out loud may work for some students. They may retain an aural memory of the sound of the words, or a kinesthetic memory of how their mouth feels shaping the words.

For instance, in studying for a biology exam, work to understand a process, such as how a plant develops or how photosynthesis occurs. Or in studying for an American government test, explain the structures of the local, state, and federal levels of government. Other useful categories include causes/effects and advantages/disadvantages. Such analytical thinking will improve your mastery of the course material and may even prepare you directly for specific essay questions.

3 Testing yourself

Convert each heading in your lecture notes and course reading into a question. Answer in writing, going back to the course material to fill in what you don't yet know. Be sure you can define and explain all key terms. For subjects that require solving problems (such as mathematics, statistics, and physics), work out a difficult problem for every type on which you will be tested. For all subjects, focus on the main themes and questions of the course. In a psychology course, for example, be certain you understand principal theories and their implications. In a literature course, test your knowledge of literary movements and genres or the relations among specific works.

When you are satisfied with your preparation, stop studying. If your exam is the next day, get as much sleep as your schedule allows. You will be able to think more clearly on exam day if you are rested.

7 Forming a Critical Perspective

Throughout college and beyond, you will be expected to think, read, and write critically. **Critical** here means "skeptical," "exacting," "creative." When you operate critically, you question, test, and

mycomplab

Visit *mycomplab.com* for more resources and exercises on critical thinking and reading.

build on what others say and what you yourself think. The word *critical* does not mean "negative" in this context: you can think critically about something you like, don't like, or just view neutrally.

You already operate critically every day of your life, as when you probe a friendship ("What did she mean by that?"), discuss a movie you just saw ("Don't you think the bad guy was too obvious?"), or attempt to solve a problem ("How can I help my study group make progress on our project?"). Such questioning helps you figure out why things happen to you, what your experiences mean, and how you can create a needed change.

This chapter introduces more formal methods of critical thinking: preparing to read critically (next page), developing a critical response (p. 146), and viewing images critically (p. 153). Learning and applying these methods will both engage you in and prepare you for school courses, career, and life in a democratic society:

- **Teachers and employers will expect you to think critically.** In every field, you will need to assess what you read, see, and hear and to make a good case for your own ideas.
- **Critical thinking helps you understand and express yourself.** With it, you gain insight into your actions and ideas, can weigh them against opposing views, and can persuasively articulate your reasoning and motivations.
- **Critical thinking improves your problem-solving skills.** Seeing academic and real-life problems from multiple angles can open your mind to creative solutions.
- **Your very independence and freedom depend on your ability to think, read, and write critically.** An open democracy allows as much play for stupid and false claims as for sound ones, and the claims that seem sound often conflict with each other. Critical thinking empowers you to decide rationally for yourself what's useful, fair, and wise—and what's not.

There's no denying that critical thinking, reading, and writing require discipline and hard work. Besides channeling your curiosity, paying attention, and probing, you will often need to consult experts, interpreting and evaluating their ideas. Such an approach also requires a healthy tolerance for doubt or uncertainty—that feeling you may have when the old rules don't seem to apply or when a change is frightening but still attractive. Out of uncertainty, though, comes creativity—the capacity to organize and generate knowledge, to explain, resolve, illuminate, play. Compared to passive, rote learning, creative work is more involving, more productive, and more enjoyable.

constructing a critical response with the use of analysis, interpretation, synthesis, and evaluation.

The section on "Viewing images critically" discusses writing while reading an image; previewing, interpreting, analyzing, and evaluating an image; and synthesizing ideas about an image. Several illustrations provide examples for this section.

THE MEANING OF *CRITICAL*

One of the greatest difficulties in teaching critical strategies is the problems students have with the negative connotations of the word *critical*. Brainstorm all the meanings and uses of the word they know; beyond those implying value judgments, some students will come up with "critical temperature," "critical mass," "critical condition," "critical point of the game," and so on. By showing how these terms connect to discernment, or important stages of development, you can demonstrate that the word need not always have negative overtones and thus help students to study these techniques with a better attitude.

MATTHIESSEN'S MISTAKE

One good anecdote to share with students concerns F. O. Matthiessen's classic work of literary criticism, *American Renaissance*. When it first appeared in 1941, it contained a passage praising the irony in Herman Melville's metaphor "the soiled fish of the sea" (describing an eel). When readers rushed to read the Melville passage in question, however, they found that "soiled" was actually a typographical error; the correct reading was "coiled." Matthiessen's brilliant critique of Melville's irony was founded on a typesetter's mistake. Students find it comforting to know that great critics can make mistakes, too; you can point out that it was, in fact, people employing critical reading who found Matthiessen's misreading!

CULTURE LANGUAGE

CHALLENGING TEXTS

Critical activities may provide an additional hurdle for students whose first language is not English or who come from cultures outside the United States. In many cultures, students are taught not to challenge ideas in print; such questions may be considered disrespectful by some who see print as an indication of authority and value. (This is especially true if the text refers to religious beliefs.) Other students, especially those who grew up in nondemocratic societies, may know from experience how dangerous it can be to challenge the "party line" espoused in school. And depending on the area of the United States you teach in, you may find students who believe in the "inerrancy of the word," even if the text is not biblical. Discuss the students' right to ask questions about, respond to, and challenge printed works, whether in published texts or in personal manuscripts.

7a Using techniques of critical reading

In college much of your critical thinking will focus on written texts (a short story, a journal article, a blog) or on visual objects (a photograph, a chart, a film). Like all subjects worthy of critical consideration, such works operate on at least three levels: (1) what the creator actually says or shows, (2) what the creator does not say or show but builds into the work (intentionally or not), and (3) what you think. Discovering the first of these levels—reading for comprehension—is discussed in the preceding chapter as part of academic skills (see pp. 131–33). This chapter builds on that material to help you discover the other two levels. The box below summarizes the reading techniques involved.

Techniques of critical reading

For reading a work of literature, which requires a somewhat different approach, see pp. 731–39.

- **Writing:** making notes on your reading throughout the process (next page)
- **Previewing:** getting background; skimming (p. 142)
- **Reading:** interacting with and absorbing the text (pp. 142–44)
- **Summarizing:** distilling and understanding content (pp. 145–46)
- **Forming your critical response** (pp. 146–52)

  Analyzing: separating into parts
  Interpreting: inferring meaning and assumptions
  Synthesizing: reassembling parts; making connections
  Evaluating: judging quality and value

The techniques of critical reading are not steps in a firm sequence. You will not use all of them for all the reading you do. On some occasions, even when a close, critical reading is required, you may simply lack the time to preview, read, and reread. (But if your reading time is continually squeezed by your schedule, you may need to rethink your schedule.) On other occasions your reason for reading (your purpose) will determine which techniques you use.

Even a publication like *People* magazine is open to different methods of reading for different purposes:

Purpose	Learn some gossip while filling time in the dentist's office.
Kind of reading	Quick, uncritical

| Purpose | Examine *People* as an artifact of our popular culture that reflects and perhaps even molds contemporary values. |
| Kind of reading | Close, critical |

Course assignments, too, differ in their requirements. A book report may require writing, previewing, reading, and summarizing but not intense critical reading. An evaluation of a journal article, in contrast, requires all the techniques discussed here.

(CULTURE LANGUAGE) The idea of reading critically may require you to make some adjustments if readers in your native culture tend to seek understanding or agreement more than engagement from what they read. Readers of English use texts for all kinds of reasons, including pleasure, reinforcement, information, and many others. But they also read skeptically, critically, to see the author's motives, test their own ideas, and arrive at new knowledge.

1 Writing while reading

Reading a work for comprehension and then for a critical approach is an *active* process. Making notes on what you read involves you by helping you understand how the text works, why, and what you think about it. The notes help you bring to the work your own experiences, knowledge, and questions.

If you own the material you're reading (a book, a photocopy, or a printout), you can make notes in the margins (see p. 143 for an example). If you don't own the material or if your notes won't fit in the margins, make notes separately using pen and paper or your computer. Many readers keep a **reading journal** in which they regularly work out questions and thoughts about what they read. One technique for keeping such a journal is to divide a page or computer screen into two vertical columns, the left side for the work itself, such as summary and questions, and the right side for what the work makes you think, such as agreements or doubts based on your own experiences, comparisons with other works, and ideas for writing. A two-column journal can encourage you to go beyond summarizing what you read to interacting critically with it because the blank right column will beckon you to respond. See page 143 for an example of this technique.

Note Whenever you photocopy or download a document or take notes separately from the text you're reading, be sure to record all necessary information about the text's location so that you can find it again and cite it fully if you use it. See page 559 for a list of information to record.

CONSIDER THE WRITER'S PERSPECTIVE

Discuss critical reading from the writers' perspective: writers make choices about their work in terms of overall organization, as well as at the paragraph, sentence, and word levels to create a particular impact on readers. Students are sometimes surprised to learn that so much thought and strategy goes into a piece of writing. Simply realizing that writers compose with intent can help students understand that there is truly a method behind the features they're discovering during critical reading; it can also help them connect the act of critical reading to the act of writing.

COLLABORATIVE LEARNING

GROUP PRACTICE

Even after they work through the materials in this chapter, students will need to practice critical reading until it becomes a familiar process. Having students work in groups to answer previewing questions or to create questions for rereading can make the critical approach to reading more accessible, and it will result in a broader range of interpretive responses.

COMPLEX TEXTS

Choose a relatively complex essay from your reader or another published collection. Ask students to work through various sections of the essay in small groups, then present their findings to the class. After those presentations, students might reread the essay and write an interpretive response to a short passage from it, which they again can share and critique in groups. Students can also use the essay as the basis for the appropriate exercises in this chapter. This will give them further confidence in their critical skills.

2 Previewing the material

When you're reading a work of literature, such as a story or a poem, it's often best to plunge right in (see pp. 732–33). But for critical reading of other works, it's worthwhile to skim before reading word for word, forming expectations and even preliminary questions. The preview will make your reading more informed and fruitful.

Use the questions in the box below as a guide to previewing a text.

Questions for previewing a text

- **What is the work's subject and structure?** Following the steps outlined on page 132, gauge length and level, read the title and introduction for clues to the topic and main ideas, read the headings, note highlighted words (defined terms), examine illustrations, and read the summary or conclusion.
- **What are the facts of publication?** Does the date of publication suggest currency or datedness? Does the publisher or publication specialize in a particular kind of material—scholarly articles, say, or popular books? For a Web document, who or what sponsors the site: an individual? a nonprofit organization? an academic institution? a corporation? a government body? (See pp. 673, 681, and 682 on locating the authors of online sources.)
- **What do you know about the author?** Does a biography tell you about the author's publications, interests, biases, and reputation in the field? For an online source, which may be posted by an unfamiliar or anonymous author, what can you gather about the author from his or her words? If possible, trace unfamiliar authors to learn more about them.
- **What is your preliminary response?** What do you already know about the author's subject? What questions do you have about either the subject or the author's approach to it? What biases of your own might influence your reception of the work—for instance, curiosity, boredom, or an outlook similar or opposed to the author's?

---

3 Reading

Reading is itself more than a one-step process. You want to understand the first level on which the text operates—what the author actually says—and begin to form your impressions.

A procedure for this stage appears in the preceding chapter (pp. 132–33). To recap: Read once through fairly smoothly, trying to appreciate the work and keeping your notes to a minimum. Then read again more carefully, this time making detailed notes, to grasp the ideas and their connections and to pose questions.

Following are examples of active reading from a student, Charlene Robinson. She was responding to Thomas Sowell's "Student Loans," reprinted on the next two pages. First Robinson annotated a photocopy of the essay (the first four annotated paragraphs appear below):

> The first lesson of economics is scarcity: There is never enough of anything to fully satisfy all those who want it.
>
> The first lesson of politics is to disregard the first lesson of economics. When politicians discover some group that is being vocal about not having as much as they want, the "solution" is to give them more. Where do politicians get this "more"? They rob Peter to pay Paul.
>
> After a while, of course, they discover that Peter doesn't have enough. Bursting with compassion, politicians rush to the rescue. Needless to say, they do not admit that robbing Peter to pay Paul was a dumb idea in the first place. On the contrary, they now rob Tom, Dick, and Harry to help Peter.
>
> The latest chapter in this long-running saga is that politicians have now suddenly discovered that many college students graduate heavily in debt. To politicians it follows, as the night follows the day, that the government should come to their rescue with the taxpayers' money.

Annotations (right margin):
- *Basic contradiction between economics and politics*
- ← *biblical reference?*
- *ironic and dismissive language*
- *politicians = fools? or irresponsible*

After reading the text, Robinson wrote about it in the journal she kept on her computer. She divided the journal into two columns, one each for the text and her responses. Here is the portion pertaining to the paragraphs above:

Text	Responses
Economics teaches lessons (1), and politics (politicians) and economics are at odds	Is economics truer or more reliable than politics? More scientific?
Politicians don't accept econ. limits—always trying to satisfy "vocal" voters by giving them what they want (2)	Politicians do spend a lot of our money. Is that what they're elected to do, or do they go too far?
"Robbing Peter to pay Paul" (2)— from the Bible (the Apostles)?	
Politicians support student loan program with taxpayer funds bec. of "vocal" voters (2-4): another ex. of not accepting econ. limits	I support the loan program, too. Are politicians being irresponsible when they do? (Dismissive language underlined on copy.)

You should try to answer the questions about meaning that you raise in your annotations and your journal, and that may take another reading or some digging in other sources, such as dictionaries and

COLLABORATIVE LEARNING

Since students in your class will have different abilities as well as different levels of experience with texts like Sowell's, their responses to Exercise 7.1 may be widely different. Having students discuss their responses in small groups lets them see a variety of reading and understanding strategies at work; students who had difficulty with the passage should be encouraged to talk about the part(s) that gave them trouble and ask for suggestions on how to tackle similar readings in the future. You might ask each group to create a list of key quotes, questions, and comments, which they can later summarize for the class.

If possible, avoid giving students a "correct" response (usually one you've written) to this exercise and the other exercises in this chapter, since it subconsciously but powerfully reinforces the mistaken stereotype that there is one right way to read an essay—the teacher's.

ANSWERS: EXERCISE 7.1

Individual response.

encyclopedias. Recording in your journal what you think the author means will help you build an understanding of the text, and a focused attempt to summarize will help even more (see pp. 134–35 and opposite). Such efforts will resolve any confusion you feel, or they will give you the confidence to say that your confusion is the fault of the author, not the reader.

Exercise 7.1   Reading

Below is an essay on the US student-loan program by Thomas Sowell, an economist who writes on economics, politics, and education. The essay was first published in the 1990s, but the debate over student loans has never subsided.

Read this essay at least twice, until you think you understand what the author is saying. Either on these pages or separately, note your questions and reactions in writing.

Student Loans

The first lesson of economics is scarcity: There is never enough of anything to fully satisfy all those who want it.   1

The first lesson of politics is to disregard the first lesson of economics. When politicians discover some group that is being vocal about not having as much as they want, the "solution" is to give them more. Where do politicians get this "more"? They rob Peter to pay Paul.   2

After a while, of course, they discover that Peter doesn't have enough. Bursting with compassion, politicians rush to the rescue. Needless to say, they do not admit that robbing Peter to pay Paul was a dumb idea in the first place. On the contrary, they now rob Tom, Dick, and Harry to help Peter.   3

The latest chapter in this long-running saga is that politicians have now suddenly discovered that many college students graduate heavily in debt. To politicians it follows, as the night follows the day, that the government should come to their rescue with the taxpayers' money.   4

How big is this crushing burden of college students' debt that we hear so much about from politicians and media deep thinkers? For those students who graduate from public colleges owing money, the debt averages a little under $7,000. For those who graduate from private colleges owing money, the average debt is a little under $9,000.   5

Buying a very modestly priced automobile involves more debt than that. And a car loan has to be paid off faster than the ten years that college graduates get to repay their student loans. Moreover, you have to keep buying cars every several years, while one college education lasts a lifetime.   6

College graduates of course earn higher incomes than other people. Why, then, should we panic at the thought that they have to repay loans for the education which gave them their opportunities? Even graduates with relatively modest incomes pay less than 10 percent of their annual salary on the loan the first year—with declining percentages in future years, as their pay increases.   7

Political hysteria and media hype may focus on the low-income stu- 8 dent with a huge debt. That is where you get your heart-rending stories—even if they are not at all typical. In reality, the soaring student loans of the past decade have resulted from allowing high-income people to borrow under government programs.

Before 1978, college loans were available through government pro- 9 grams only to students whose family income was below some cut-off level. That cut-off level was about double the national average income, but at least it kept out the Rockefellers and the Vanderbilts. But, in an era of "compassion," Congress took off even those limits.

That opened the floodgates. No matter how rich you were, it still 10 paid to borrow money through the government at low interest rates. The money you had set aside for your children's education could be invested somewhere else, at higher interest rates. Then, when the student loan became due, parents could pay it off with the money they had set aside—pocketing the difference in interest rates.

To politicians and the media, however, the rapidly growing loans 11 showed what a great "need" there was. The fact that many students welshed when time came to repay their loans showed how "crushing" their burden of debt must be. In reality, those who welsh typically have smaller loans, but have dropped out of college before finishing. People who are irresponsible in one way are often irresponsible in other ways.

No small amount of the deterioration of college standards has been 12 due to the increasingly easy availability of college to people who are not very serious about getting an education. College is not a bad place to hang out for a few years, if you have nothing better to do, and if someone else is paying for it. Its costs are staggering, but the taxpayers carry much of that burden, not only for state universities and city colleges, but also to an increasing extent even for "private" institutions.

Numerous government subsidies and loan programs make it possi- 13 ble for many people to use vast amounts of society's resources at low cost to themselves. Whether in money terms or in real terms, federal aid to higher education has increased several hundred percent since 1970. That has enabled colleges to raise their tuition by leaps and bounds and enabled professors to be paid more and more for doing less and less teaching.

Naturally all these beneficiaries are going to create hype and hys- 14 teria to keep more of the taxpayers' money coming in. But we would be fools to keep on writing blank checks for them.

When you weigh the cost of things, in economics that's called 15 "trade-offs." In politics, it's called "mean-spirited." Apparently, if we just took a different attitude, scarcity would go away.

—Thomas Sowell

4 Summarizing

Summarizing a text—distilling it to its essential ideas, in your own words—is an important step for comprehending the text before approaching it critically. Summary is discussed in detail in the previous chapter (pp. 134–35). Here, we'll look at how Charlene

WEARING THE FILM CRITIC'S HAT

To help students understand the concept of "misreading," try the "movie critic" exercise: a movie critic writes that a film is "one of the really great awful films of the decade." An ad for the film that claims "Critic So-and-So calls this 'one of the really great . . . films of the decade'" is a deliberate misreading. Ask students to construct deliberate misreadings of reviews or critiques as a way of teaching them what *not* to do in their own summaries.

COLLABORATIVE LEARNING

COMPARING SUMMARIES

Ask students to compare their summaries in groups and list points that are similar and different among the summaries in their group. Then, as a way of deciding how much information is needed to create an effective summary, have each student defend the places where his or her summary differs from the group consensus.

SUMMARY STRATEGIES

Students learning standard American English may find synonyms for some key words in the sentences that express the main points of a source, but they may feel insecure about using other sentence structures. Encourage students to change the sentence structure as well as the vocabulary of the original in writing summaries. Working collaboratively on summaries helps students see alternative ways to express ideas; in addition, stronger students (and native speakers) can help the weaker students and, in so doing, reinforce their own writing skills. Alice Oshima and Ann Hogue, in *Writing Academic English*, 4th ed. (New York: Longman, 2006, Print.), include useful exercises for students who need additional practice in summarizing.

RESOURCES AND IDEAS

On approaches to teaching critical thinking

Anson, Chris M., ed. *Writing and Response: Theory, Practice, and Research.* Urbana: NCTE, 1989. Print. This collection of essays explores the practical and theoretical issues involved in reading and commenting on student texts.

Brookfield, Stephen D. *Developing Critical Thinkers.* San Francisco: Jossey-Bass, 1987. Print. Brookfield encourages connections between critical skills developed in school and their applications in daily life.

Buffamanti, Suzanne, Denise David, and Robert Morris. "Imposed Upon: Using Authentic Assessment of Critical Thinking at a Community College." *Teaching English in the Two-Year College* 34.1 (2006): 70–83. Print. The authors discuss the process of developing tools to assess critical thinking in their first-year course on writing about literature, and they discuss the implications of assessing critical thinking in other courses. They include both their original and revised rubrics for evaluating critical thinking in student essays. *(continued on page 147)*

COLLABORATIVE LEARNING

Make Exercise 7.2 collaborative by asking each group of students to write a collective summary; then switch summaries among groups and have the readers decide how effective the other group's effort is in conveying the essential information in Sowell.

ANSWERS: EXERCISE 7.2

Possible answer

As their support of the government's student loan program illustrates, politicians ignore the economic reality that using resources to benefit one group (students in debt) involves taking the resources from another group (taxpayers). Students' average debt is not even that high, and college graduates can afford to pay it off. The greatest attention is paid to the graduate with a large debt, but the law also allows affluent students to borrow, even if their parents profit and the students drop out of school or waste time there. Funded by taxpayers, the loan program has contributed to declining educational standards, rising tuitions, and rising professors' salaries. Taxpayers should balk at funding the program further.

Robinson summarized paragraphs 1–4 of Thomas Sowell's "Student Loans." She first drafted this sentence:

Draft summary

As much as politicians would like to satisfy voters by giving them everything they ask for, the government cannot afford a student loan program.

Rereading the sentence and Sowell's paragraph, Robinson saw that this draft misread the text by asserting that the government cannot afford student loans. She realized that Sowell's point is more complicated than that and rewrote her summary:

Revised summary

As their support of the government's student loan program illustrates, politicians ignore the economic reality that using resources to benefit one group (students in debt) involves taking the resources from another group (taxpayers).

Note Using your own words when writing a summary not only helps you understand the meaning but also constitutes the first step in avoiding plagiarism. The second step is to cite the source when you use it in something written for others. See Chapter 44.

Exercise 7.2 Summarizing

Start where Robinson's summary of Thomas Sowell's essay ends (at paragraph 5) to summarize the entire essay. Your summary, in your own words, should not exceed one paragraph. For additional exercises in summarizing, see pages 619–20.

7b Developing a critical response

Once you've grasped the content of what you're reading—what the author says—then you can turn to understanding what the author does not say outright but suggests or implies or even lets slip. At this stage you are concerned with the purpose or intention of the author and with how he or she carries it out. Depending on what you are reading and why, you may examine evidence, organization, attitude, use of language, and other elements of the text.

Critical thinking and reading consist of four operations: analyzing, interpreting, synthesizing, and (often) evaluating. Although we'll look at them one by one, these operations interrelate and overlap. Indeed, the first three are often combined under the general label *analysis,* and evaluation is sometimes taken for granted as a result of the process.

In the following pages, we use two quite different examples to show how critical reading can work: *People* magazine and Sowell's "Student Loans."

Guidelines for analysis, interpretation, and synthesis

- **What is the purpose of your reading?**
- **What questions do you have about the work,** given your purpose?
- **What elements does the most interesting question highlight?** What elements might you ignore as a result?
- **How do you interpret the meaning and significance of the elements?** What are your assumptions about the work? What do you infer about the author's assumptions?
- **What patterns can you see in (or synthesize from) the elements?** How do the elements relate? How does this whole work relate to other works?
- **What do you conclude about the work?** What does this conclusion add to the work?

1 Analyzing

Analysis is the separation of something into its parts or elements, the better to understand it. To see these elements in what you are reading, begin with a question that reflects your purpose in analyzing the text: why you're curious about it or what you're trying to make out of it. This question will serve as a kind of lens that highlights some features and not others.

Here are some questions you might ask about *People* magazine, listed along with the elements of the magazine that each question highlights:

Questions for analysis	Elements
Does *People* challenge or perpetuate stereotypes?	Stereotypes: explicit and implicit stereotypes or challenges in the magazine
Does the magazine offer positive role models for its readers?	Role models: text and photographs presenting positive or negative role models
Does the magazine's editorial material (articles and accompanying photographs) encourage readers to consume goods and entertainment?	Encouragement of consumption: references to goods and entertainment, focus on consumers, equation of consumption with happiness or success

As these examples show, a question for analysis concentrates your attention on relevant features and eliminates irrelevant features. To answer the question in the preceding list about *People*'s encouragement of consumption, you would focus on items that feature consumption and the products consumed: photographs of designer clothes and celebrities' well-appointed homes, articles on

---

MAGAZINE COLLECTION

Encourage students to bring magazines of various kinds to class. Have students work in groups to brainstorm lists similar to the one shown here for each magazine they collected. Each group might present their most surprising or revealing findings to the class.

RESOURCES AND IDEAS
(continued)

Chambers, Marilyn J. "Text Cues and Strategies Successful Readers Use to Construct the Gist of Lengthy Written Arguments." *Reading Research Quarterly* 30.4 (1995): 778–807. Print. Chambers examines students' strategies for identifying argument structure, claim, and evidence in lengthy texts.

Elbow, Peter. "Ranking, Evaluating, and Liking: Sorting Out Three Forms of Judgment." *College English* 55.2 (1993): 187–206. Print. Elbow's essay is largely concerned with these three activities as part of teacher assessment of student writing, but it gives many ideas that can be translated into classroom practice.

Fiske, John. *Introduction to Communication Studies.* New York: Routledge, 1990. Print. Fiske provides a general overview (for students and teachers) of the methods of cultural criticism, with explicit connections to the teaching of writing.

Golub, Jeff, and the NCTE Committee on Classroom Practices, eds. *Activities to Promote Critical Thinking.* Urbana: NCTE, 1986. Print. The authors have compiled a collection of essays focusing on practical advice and teaching strategies.

Jenseth, Richard. "Understanding Hiroshima: An Assignment Sequence for Freshman English." *College Composition and Communication* 40.2 (1989): 215–19. Print. Jenseth describes a course in which students focus on one work (or theme) for an entire semester, considering and reconsidering issues from various critical perspectives.

Johnson, J. Paul. "Critical Reading and Response: Experimenting with Anonymity in Draft Workshops." *Practice in Context*. Ed. Cynthia Moore and Peggy O'Neill. Urbana: NCTE, 2002. Print. Johnson recommends that students conduct peer reviews anonymously to help them focus on the act of critical reading rather than the socializing aspects of the activity.

Jones, Libby Falk. "Exploring Beliefs Through Dialectical Thinking." *The Critical Writing Workshop: Designing Writing Assignments to Foster Critical Thinking*. Ed. Toni-lee Capossella. Portsmouth: Boynton, 1993. 17–34. Print. This essay and the collection as a whole offer general discussion and practical examples of how to structure thought-provoking assignments.

(continued on page 149)

COMPUTER ACTIVITIES

WEB THREADS

Have students visit an online discussion group or chat room and follow a "thread" of conversation. Ask them to list some of the assumptions made by individual writers, make inferences about those writers' beliefs, and then evaluate whether or not most of the participants seem to share those beliefs.

NETWORKED INFERENCES

Having students summarize and draw inferences from one another's work can be a useful exercise for both reader and writer. Have students work in pairs (either on the computer or on printed copy) to summarize, then practice making both reasonable and deliberately faulty inferences of passages from each other's work. In each case, the writer of the passage can argue for his or her intention in writing the passage and evaluate the effectiveness of the summary, while the reader can point to evidence or lack of evidence for the inference. Particularly in a wired classroom, each student pair can send two passages with attached summary and inferences to another group for evaluation, and/or the instructor can post one or two examples for the entire class.

the authors of best-selling books and the stars of new movies. At the same time, you would skip over items that have little or no relevance to consumption, such as uplifting stories about families or the physically challenged.

Analyzing Thomas Sowell's "Student Loans" (pp. 144–45), you might ask these questions:

Questions for analysis	Elements
What is Sowell's attitude toward politicians?	References to politicians: content, words, tone
How does Sowell support his assertions about the loan program's costs?	Support: evidence, such as statistics and examples

A difference in the kinds of questions asked is a key distinction among academic disciplines. A sociologist neatly outlined three disciplines' approaches to poverty:

> Political science does a wonderful job looking at poverty as a policy issue. Economics does an equally wonderful job looking at it from an income-distribution perspective. But sociology asks how people in poverty live and what they aspire to.

Even within disciplines, approaches may differ. The sociologist quoted above may focus on how people in poverty live, but another may be more interested in the effects of poverty on cities or the changes in the poor population over the last fifty years. (See Chapters 49–52 for more on the disciplines' analytical questions.)

2 Interpreting

Identifying the elements of something is of course only the beginning: you also need to interpret the meaning or significance of the elements and of the whole. Interpretation usually requires you to infer the author's **assumptions,** opinions or beliefs about what is or what could or should be. (**Infer** means to draw a conclusion based on evidence.)

The word *assumption* here has a more specific meaning than it does in everyday usage, where it may stand for expectation (*I assume you'll pay*), speculation (*It was a mere assumption*), or error (*The report was riddled with assumptions*). Defined more strictly as what a person *supposes* to be true, assumptions are unavoidable. We all adhere to certain values and beliefs; we all form opinions. We live our lives by such assumptions.

Though pervasive, assumptions are not always stated outright. Speakers and writers may judge that their audience already understands and accepts their assumptions; they may not even be aware of their assumptions; or they may deliberately refrain from stating their assumptions for fear that the audience will disagree. That is why your job as a critical thinker is to interpret what the assumptions are.

Reasonable inferences

Like an author deciding what to say in an article, the publishers of *People* magazine make assumptions that guide their selection of content for the magazine. One set of assumptions, perhaps the most important, concerns what readers want to see: as a for-profit enterprise, the magazine naturally aims to maintain and even expand its readership (currently about 3.4 million each week). If your analysis of the magazine's editorial material reveals that much of it features consumer products, you might infer the following:

> **Reasonable** The publishers of *People* assume that the magazine's readers are consumers who want to see and hear about goods and entertainment.

Nowhere in *People* will you find a statement of this assumption, but the evidence implies it.

Similarly, Thomas Sowell's "Student Loans" (pp. 144–45) is based on certain assumptions, some obvious, some not so obvious. If you were analyzing Sowell's attitude toward politicians, as suggested earlier, you would focus on his statements about them. Sowell says that they "disregard the first lesson of economics" (paragraph 2), which implies that they ignore important principles (knowing that Sowell is an economist himself makes this a reasonable assumption on your part). Sowell also says that politicians "rob Peter to pay Paul," are "[b]ursting with compassion," "do not admit . . . a dumb idea," are characters in a "long-running saga," and arrive at the solution of spending taxes "as the night follows the day"—that is, inevitably (paragraphs 2–4). From these statements and others, you can infer the following:

> **Reasonable** Sowell assumes that politicians become compassionate when a cause is loud and popular, not necessarily just, and they act irresponsibly by trying to solve the problem with other people's (taxpayers') money.

Unreasonable inferences

Interpreting assumptions gives you greater insight into an author's intentions. But it's crucial that inferences fit the evidence of the text, as those above about *People* and Sowell's essay do. Sometimes it's tempting to read too much into the text, as in the next examples:

> **Faulty** *People*'s publishers deliberately skew the magazine's editorial material to promote products on which they receive kickbacks. [The inference is far-fetched, even absurd. It would be reasonable only if there were hard evidence of kickbacks.]

RESOURCES AND IDEAS
(continued)

Kline, Nancy. "Intertextual Trips: Teaching the Essay in the Composition Class." *Journal of Teaching Writing* 8.2 (1989): 15–37. Print. Kline describes an "active and playful" strategy used by writers of essays and suggests ways to help students detect and appreciate it.

Marzano, Robert J. *Cultivating Thinking in English: The Language Arts.* Urbana: NCTE, 1991. Print. Marzano explores strategies for enhancing student learning, emphasizing ways in which students can analyze their own values and responses to class texts and discussions.

McLeod, Susan H. "Cultural Literacy, Curricular Reform, and Freshman Composition." *Rhetoric Review* 8.2 (1990): 270–78. Print. McLeod argues that students can move beyond personal experience in writing essays by reading scholarly materials and responding to them.

Mirskin, Jerry. "Writing as a Process of Valuing." *College Composition and Communication* 46.3 (1995): 387–410. Print. Mirskin argues that because values shape meaning, teachers must learn to recognize students' systems of value in order to best help them make meaningful connections within an academic environment.

Odell, Lee. "Strategy and Surprise in the Making of Meaning." *Theory and Practice in the Teaching of Writing: Rethinking the Discipline.* Ed. Lee Odell. Carbondale: Southern Illinois UP, 1993. 213–43. Print. This essay explores the debates over fostering spontaneity and intuitive insights in the teaching of writing as opposed to teaching conscious control, and identifies several approaches that work to do both.

Qualley, Donna. "Using Reading in the Writing Classroom." *Nuts and Bolts: A Practical Guide to Teaching College Composition.* Ed. Thomas Newkirk. Portsmouth: Boynton, 1993. Print. Qualley lays out strategies for integrating critical reading and writing using journals, reading conferences, and small group discussions.

Robertson, Julie Fisher, and Donna Rane Szotstak. "Using Dialogues to Develop Critical Thinking Skills: A Practical Approach." *Journal of Adolescent and Adult Literacy* 39.7 (1996): 552–56. Print. Robertson and Szotstak describe how students can write, analyze, and perform dialogues in order to develop critical thinking skills.

Shaughnessy, Mina. *Errors and Expectations: A Guide for the Teacher of Basic Writing.* New York: Oxford UP, 1977. Print. This groundbreaking study of the challenges faced by basic writers reveals the connections between student error and issues of critical thinking.

Shor, Ira. *Empowering Education: Critical Teaching for Social Change.* Chicago: U of Chicago P, 1992. Print. Shor promotes critical thinking as a part of a pedagogy designed to empower students and citizens.

Tierney, Robert J., John E. Readence, and Ernest K. Dishner, eds. *Reading Strategies and Practices: A Compendium,* 6th ed. Boston: Allyn and Bacon, 2005. Print. This textbook approach to reading offers a number of exercises and work-sheets that help to focus students on particular aspects of the reading process.

Toulmin, Stephen, Richard Rieke, and Allan Janik. *An Introduction to Reasoning,* 2nd ed. New York: Macmillan, 1984. Print. Toulmin et al. detail the reasoning processes involved in making claims, supplying evidential backing, and preparing for rebuttal.

Tripp, Ellen L. "Speak, Listen, Analyze, Respond: Problem-Solving Conferences." *Teaching English in the Two-Year College* 17.3 (1990): 183–86. Print. Tripp suggests collaborative and individual activities to be completed before students write final papers proposing solutions.

On writing and critical reading

Berthoff, Ann E. "A Curious Triangle and the Double-Entry Notebook: Or, How Theory Can Help Us Teach Reading and Writing." *The Making of Meaning: Metaphors, Models, and Maxims for Writing Teachers.* Upper Montclair: Boynton/Cook, 1981. Print. Berthoff shows how use of a double-entry journal can help students improve critical reading skills.

Emig, Janet. "Writing as a Mode of Learning." *College Composition and Communication* 28.2 (1977): 122–28. Print. A seminal analysis of the ways in which writing facilitates mental processes like intuition, reformulation, and the construction of meaningful relationships between ideas.

| Faulty | Sowell thinks that politicians should not be entrusted with running the country. [The inference misreads Sowell. Although he does not outline a solution for politicians' irresponsibility, there's no evidence that he would overhaul our democratic political system.] |

Faulty inferences like these are often based on the reader's *own* assumptions about the text or its subject. When thinking and reading critically, you need to look hard at *your* ideas, too.

3 Synthesizing

If you stopped at analysis and interpretation, critical thinking and reading might leave you with a pile of elements and possible meanings but no vision of the whole. With **synthesis** you make connections among parts *or* among wholes. You use your perspective—your knowledge and beliefs—to create a new whole by drawing conclusions about relationships and implications.

A key component of academic reading and writing, synthesis receives attention in the next chapter (pp. 162–65) and then in the context of research writing (pp. 604–06). Sometimes you'll respond directly to a text, as in the following two conclusions. The first pulls together the earlier analysis of *People* magazine's editorial content and the interpretation of the publisher's assumptions about readers:

| Conclusion | *People* magazine appeals to its readers' urge to consume by displaying, discussing, and glamorizing consumer goods. |

The next statement, about Thomas Sowell's essay "Student Loans," connects Sowell's assumptions about politicians to a larger idea also implied by the essay:

| Conclusion | Sowell's view that politicians are irresponsible with taxpayers' money reflects his overall opinion that the laws of economics, not politics, should drive government. |

Often synthesis will take you outside the text to its surroundings. The following questions can help you investigate the context of a work:

- **How does the work compare with works by others?** For instance, how does *People*'s juxtaposition of articles and advertisements compare with that in similar magazines, such as *Us Weekly, Entertainment Weekly,* and *Interview*? Or how have other writers responded to Sowell's views on student loans?

- **How does the work fit into the context of other works by the same author or group?** What distinguishes *People* from the many other magazines published by Time Inc., such as *Time, Sports Illustrated, Family Circle,* and *Fortune*? How do Sowell's views on student loans typify, or not, the author's other writings on political and economic issues?

■ **What cultural, economic, or political forces influence the work?** Why, for instance, are *People* and other celebrity magazines increasingly popular with readers? What other examples might Sowell have given to illustrate his view that economics, not politics, should determine government spending?

■ **What historical forces influence the work?** How does *People* reflect changes in the ways readers choose magazines? How has the indebtedness of college students changed over the past four decades?

To create links among the elements of a work or between a work and its context, it helps (again) to write while reading and thinking. The active reading recommended earlier is the place to start, as you note your questions and opinions about the text. You can also create connections with a combination of writing and drawing: start with your notes, expand them as needed to take account of context, and draw connections between related thoughts with lines and arrows. (On a word processor you can use the Highlight function or different colors to link related ideas, or use the Comment function to annotate connections.) You want to open up your thinking, so experiment freely.

With synthesis, you create something different from what you started with. To the supermarket shopper reading *People* while standing in line, the magazine may be entertaining and inconsequential. To you—after a critical reading in which you analyze, interpret, and synthesize—the magazine is (at least in part) a significant vehicle of our consumer culture. The difference depends entirely on the critical reading.

4 Evaluating

Many critical reading and writing assignments end at analysis, interpretation, and synthesis: you explain your understanding of what the author says and doesn't say. Only if you are expected to evaluate the work will you state and defend the judgments you've made about its quality and its significance.

You'll inevitably form judgments while reading the work: *What a striking series of images* or *That just isn't enough evidence*. In evaluating, you collect your judgments, determine that they are generally applicable and are themselves not trivial, and turn them into assertions: *The poet creates fresh, intensely vivid images. The author does not summon the evidence to support his case.* And you support these statements with citations from the text.

Evaluation takes a certain amount of confidence. You may think that you lack the expertise to cast judgment on another's

Greene, Stuart, and John M. Ackerman. "Expanding the Constructivist Metaphor: A Rhetorical Perspective on Literacy Research and Practice." *Review of Educational Research* 65.4 (1995): 383–420. Print. This review essay evaluates a number of constructivist explanations of the relationship between reading and writing as a learning model.

Price, Gayle B. "A Case for a Modern Commonplace Book." *College Composition and Communication* 31.2 (1980): 175–82. Print. Price suggests using classic techniques for commonplace books in conjunction with other journal activities.

Snair, Scott. "Are Your Students Critically Reading an Opinion Piece? Have them RATTKISS it!" *English Journal* 97.3 (2008): 52–55. Print. Snair suggests using the mnemonic device RATTKISS to help students remember how to analyze a brief opinion piece: *R* stands for the "'riter's" background, *A* for analyze, *T* for tone, *T* for topic, *KI* "kontrolling" idea, *S* for synthesize, and *S* for scrutinize.

Stewart, Ruth. "Teaching Critical Thinking in First-Year Composition: Sometimes More Is More." *Teaching English in the Two-Year College* 29.2 (2001): 162–71. Print. Stewart argues that students sometimes need to be challenged by material that is more complex than textbook information, and she uses primary documents regarding a historical incident to challenge her students in this way.

Walsh, John A. "Circle Diagrams for Narrative Essays." *Journal of Reading* 32.4 (1989): 366–68. Print. Use of a graphic technique of concentric circles (similar to Venn diagrams) helps students comprehend and analyze narrative events, relationships, and significance.

On discourse communities

Carter, Duncan. "Critical Thinking for Writers: Transferable Skills or Discipline-Specific Strategies?" *Composition Studies: Freshman English News* 21.1 (1993): 86–93. Print. Carter explores the question of whether critical thinking skills are transferable across discourse communities.

Dejoy, Nancy. *Process This: Undergraduate Writing in Composition Studies*. Logan: Utah State UP, 2004. Print. Dejoy argues that despite recent developments in composition theory, composition practices at the classroom level

(continued on page 155)

When students have completed Exercises 7.3, 7.4, and 7.5 individually, it is beneficial to have them share their analyses in small groups so that they are able to note and discuss the differing conclusions that each student may have reached. In a wired classroom, this sharing can take place by e-mail, which encourages dialogue and helps students deepen their critical analyses.

ANSWERS: EXERCISE 7.3
Possible answers

1. *Analysis:* What is the basis for the author's comparison of print and televised journalism? The key phrases are *demand reading, not just viewing.*

   Interpretation: Are better ... than implies a value judgment. *Demand reading, not just viewing* reveals the author's assumption that viewing is somehow less worthy than reading, perhaps because viewing is more passive.

   Synthesis: This author prefers print journalism and disparages television journalism because of the different activities needed to partake of them.

   Evaluation: This statement shows the author's bias in favor of written news and implies some contempt for TV news. The author's reasons for preferring reading over viewing are not evident and require explanation. Some other questions: Are people who get their news from TV less well informed than those who get it from reading? Even if television news is inferior, isn't it better than no news at all (for those who won't or can't read)? Might television news be preferable for its immediacy?

2. *Analysis:* What is the author's purpose? The key words and phrases are *true, democratic, giving voice to,* and *people of all persuasions.*

   Interpretation: Democratic means "of or for the people." *True democratic forum* means that there are competing, perhaps misleading, forums. *Giving voice to people* appeals to a sense of fair play and belief in free speech, while *all persuasions* implies open-mindedness. The author assumes that people need a public forum where they can voice their opinions. Because it is immediate, radio gives people the freedom to say what they want. Other forums may censor or restrict who can say what.

writing, especially if the text is difficult or the author well known. True, the more informed you are, the better a critical reader you are. But conscientious reading and analysis will give you the internal authority to judge a work *as it stands* and *as it seems to you,* against your own unique bundle of experiences, observations, and attitudes.

The box below gives questions that can help you evaluate many kinds of works. There's more on evaluation (including evaluation of online sources) on pages 590–603. For arguments and in academic disciplines, you'll require additional, more specific criteria. See Chapters 9, 11, and 48–52.

Guidelines for evaluation

- **What are your reactions to the work?** What in the work are you responding to?
- **How sound are the work's central idea and evidence?**
- **How well does the author achieve his or her purpose?** How worthwhile is the purpose?
- **How authoritative, trustworthy, and sincere is the author?**
- **How unified and coherent is the work?** Do its parts all support a central idea and clearly relate to one another?
- **What do color, graphics, or (online) sound or video contribute to the work?** Do such elements add meaning or merely decoration?
- **What is the overall quality and significance of the work?**
- **Do you agree or disagree with the work?** Can you support, refute, or extend it?

Exercise 7.3 Thinking critically

Following are some statements about the communications media. Use systematic critical thinking to understand not only what each statement says but also why its author might have said it. As in the example, do your thinking in writing: the act of writing will help you think, and your notes will help you discuss your ideas with your classmates.

Example:

Statement: Every year sees the disappearance of more book publishers because the larger companies gobble up the smaller ones.

Analysis: Why did the author make this statement? Certain words reveal the author's purpose: *disappearance of more book publishers; because; larger companies gobble up smaller ones.*

Interpretation: *More* book publishers means others have disappeared. *Because* specifies cause. *Gobble up* implies consumption, predator to prey. Author's assumptions: Large publishers behave like predators. The predatory behavior of large companies causes the disappearance of small companies. The more publishing companies there are, the better.

Synthesis: The author objects to the predatory behavior of large publishing companies, which he or she holds responsible for eliminating small companies and reducing the total number of companies.

Evaluation: This biased statement against large publishers holds them responsible for the shrinking number of book publishers. But are the large companies solely responsible? Do they offer value in return? And why is the shrinking necessarily bad?

1. Newspapers and newsmagazines are better news sources than television because they demand reading, not just viewing.
2. Radio call-in shows are the true democratic forum, giving voice to people of all persuasions.
3. Participation in online communities threatens to undermine our ability to interact face to face.

Exercise 7.4 Reading an essay critically

Reread Thomas Sowell's "Student Loans" (pp. 144–45) in order to form your own critical response to it. Follow the guidelines for analysis, interpretation, synthesis, and evaluation in the boxes on pages 147 and 152. Focus on any elements suggested by your question about the text: possibilities are assumptions, evidence, organization, use of language, tone, authority, vision of education or students. Be sure to write while reading and thinking; your notes will help your analysis and enhance your creativity, and they will be essential for writing about the selection (Exercise 8.5, p. 176).

Exercise 7.5 Reading a magazine critically

Do your own critical reading of *People* or another magazine. What do you see beyond the obvious? What questions does your reading raise? Let the guidelines on pages 147 and 152 direct your response, and do your work in writing.

7c Viewing images critically

Every day we are bombarded with images—pictures on billboards, commercials on television, graphs and charts in newspapers and textbooks, to name just a few examples. Most images slide by without our noticing them, or so we think. But images, sometimes even more than text, can influence us covertly. Their creators have purposes, some worthy, some not, and understanding those purposes requires critical reading. The method parallels that in the previous sections for reading text critically: write while reading, preview, read for comprehension, analyze, interpret, synthesize, and (often) evaluate.

1 Writing while reading an image

Writing as you read an image helps you view it deliberately and allows you to record your impressions precisely. If possible, print a copy of the image or scan it into your reading journal, and write your

Synthesis: The writer values radio call-in shows for affording all kinds of people a chance to express themselves without censorship.

Evaluation: This writer evidently believes that radio is somehow freer than other places for people to speak their minds. What other forums for free speech are there? Does radio censor or alter the opinions expressed? (What about the time delays for excluding objectionable language?) Are "people of all persuasions" really calling such shows, or just some kinds of people? Are unedited, inexpert opinions a democratic necessity?

3. *Analysis:* What is the author's attitude toward participation in online communities? The key words and phrases are *threaten, undermine, ability,* and *interact face to face.*

Interpretation: Threaten and *undermine* imply danger; *ability* and *interact face to face* imply that face-to-face communication is a kind of skill or talent. Together the words imply that the skill or talent is vulnerable, subject to some kind of destruction. The author's assumptions: Online and face-to-face interaction are different. Face-to-face interaction has an intrinsic value. Online interaction does not have this value. Interacting online diminishes this value.

Synthesis: The author believes that something valuable will be lost to online interaction.

Evaluation: This statement indicates a preference for face-to-face interaction over online interaction and a concern about the latter overwhelming the former. But what exactly is special about face-to-face interaction? What does it provide that online communities don't? Won't people continue to meet face to face even if they also interact online? Will online communities necessarily undermine face-to-face interaction? Might online communities also contribute something positive of their own, adding to rather than subtracting from the ways people interact?

ANSWERS: EXERCISE 7.4

Individual response.

ANSWERS: EXERCISE 7.5

Individual response.

THE ONION

It may help students to understand previewing if they think of an onion. Their job in looking at the image is to work their way from the outside (the most striking elements of the image, the publication and authorship information, and their first response) to deeper, internal layers of meaning.

COLLABORATIVE LEARNING

SUMMARIZING AN IMAGE

Before they begin to "read" an image, it can be helpful for students to take time to describe it. Bring in ads from magazines or a list of Web sites, if groups have access to the Internet. Ask each group to describe carefully its image in writing. Ask group members to consider what organizational strategy to use, possibly moving left to right or top to bottom. Students should also describe which parts of the image are most dominant and which are part of the background. As a class, ask each group to share its summary with the rest of the class, and then share the image (on the overhead, if possible). Have other groups critique the summaries. What do the summaries leave out? Do they over- or underemphasize certain aspects?

LIST OF READING QUESTIONS

Students may want to use the questions on this page and the next about purpose, audience, words and symbols, subject, and form as a guideline to help them in their notetaking. These questions would also be helpful if students are creating annotated lists of images.

CHANGE THE CAPTION

To help students understand how images and words work together, ask them to write some alternative captions for the Kody ad. The class can then discuss how the new captions help influence the meaning of the visual image.

comments in the image margins or separately. The example on the next page shows how one student annotated an image he was reading.

2 Previewing an image

Your first step in exploring an image is to form initial impressions of the work's origin and purpose and to note distinctive features. This previewing process is like the one for previewing a text (p. 142):

Questions for previewing an image

- **What do you see?** What is most striking about the image? What is its subject? What is the gist of any text or symbols? What is the overall effect of the image?
- **What are the facts of publication?** Where did you first see the image? Do you think the image was created especially for that location or for others as well? What can you tell about when the image was created?
- **What do you know about the person or group that created the image?** For instance, was the creator an artist, scholar, news organization, or corporation? What seems to have been the creator's purpose?
- **What is your preliminary response?** What about the image interests, confuses, or disturbs you? Are the form, style, and subject familiar or unfamiliar? How might your knowledge, experiences, and values influence your reception of the image?

---

3 Reading an image

Reading an image requires the same level of concentration as reading a text. Plan to spend more than one session working with the image to absorb its meaning and purpose and then to analyze and maybe challenge its message.

Try to answer the following questions about the image. If some answers aren't clear at this point, skip the question until later.

- **What is the purpose of the image?** Is it mainly explanatory, conveying information, or is it argumentative, trying to convince readers of something or to persuade them to act? What information or point of view does it seem to want to get across?
- **Who is the intended audience for the image?** What does the source of the image, including its publication facts, tell about the image creator's expectations for readers' knowledge, interests, and attitudes? What do the features of the image itself add to your impression?
- **What do any words or symbols add to the image?** Whether located on the image or outside it (such as in a caption), do words or symbols add information, focus your attention, or alter your impression of the image?

- **What people, places, things, or action does the image show?** Does the image tell a story? Do its characters or other features tap into your knowledge, or are they unfamiliar?
- **What is the form of the image?** Is it a photograph, advertisement, painting, graph, diagram, cartoon, or something else? How do its content and apparent purpose and audience relate to its form?

The following notes by a student, Matthew Greene, illustrate the results of asking questions like these. Greene first saw this advertisement on a bus shelter and then found it online so that he could examine it more closely. He annotated a copy of the image and filled out his ideas in his reading journal.

Annotation of an image

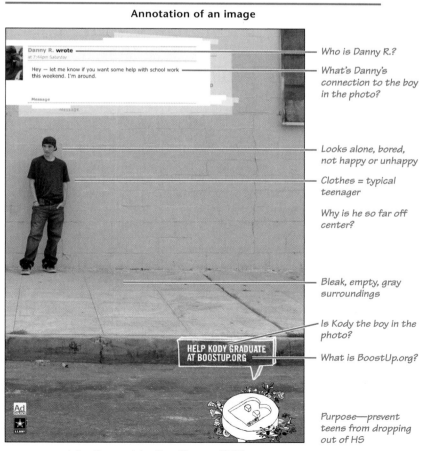

Danny R. wrote
at 7:44pm Saturday —— Who is Danny R.?

Hey — let me know if you want some help with school work —— What's Danny's
this weekend. I'm around. connection to the boy
in the photo?

Message

—— Looks alone, bored,
not happy or unhappy

—— Clothes = typical
teenager

Why is he so far off
center?

—— Bleak, empty, gray
surroundings

—— Is Kody the boy in the
photo?

HELP KODY GRADUATE
AT BOOSTUP.ORG —— What is BoostUp.org?

Purpose—prevent
teens from dropping
out of HS

Advertisement for *BoostUp.org,* 2007

RESOURCES AND IDEAS

(*continued from page 151*)

remain essentially unchanged. She advocates moving student discourse outside the classroom and offers specific advice for reshaping classroom practices and composition curriculum.

Feldman, Ann M. *Making Writing Matter: Composition in the Engaged University.* Albany: State U of New York P, 2008. Print. Feldman argues that by engaging with the community in service-learning writing projects, students and universities benefit from participating in these "communities of practice."

Killingsworth, M. Jimmie. "Discourse Communities—Global and Local." *Rhetoric Review* 11.1 (1992): 110–22. Print. Killingsworth makes readers aware that they are members of both kinds of communities, and he suggests ways to negotiate the bridge(s) between the two.

Williams, James D., David Huntley, and Christine Hanks. *The Interdisciplinary Reader: A Collection of Student Writing.* New York: Harper-Collins, 1992. Print. The editors provide a collection of student essays from various disciplines, accompanied by critiques of their effectiveness in writing critically for particular discourse communities.

On summaries

Hartman, Kathleen A., and Thomas Stewart. "It's a Wrap: Writing, Reading, and Art Projects for Developmental College Students." *Research and Teaching in Developmental Education* 18.1 (2001): 79–83. Print. Hartman and Stewart discuss how to use visual arts to teach aspects of writing, including making felt "wraps" to demonstrate writing summaries.

Lambert, Judith R. "Summaries: A Focus for Basic Writers." *Journal of Developmental Education* 8.2 (1984): 10+. Print. Lambert reviews advantages of teaching students to summarize.

Sherrard, Carol. "Summary Writing: A Topographical Study." *Written Communication* 3.3 (1986): 324–43. Print. Sherrard shows that assigning longer summaries forces students to use their own words instead of copying from the source.

SUGGESTED READINGS

George, Diana. "From Analysis to Design: Visual Communication in the Teaching of Writing." *College Composition and Communication* 54.1 (2002): 11–39. Print. This is an excellent explanation of how instruction in visual literacy can inform the composition curriculum.

Soleil, Naome. "Reflective Reading: A Study in (Tele)literacy." *Journal of College Reading and Learning* 30.1 (Fall 1999): 5–16. Print. Soleil shows how a reflective reading of television texts can provide a bridge to link oracy and literacy.

Spalter, Anne Morgan, and Andries van Dam. "Digital Visual Literacy." *Theory into Practice* 47.2 (2008): 99–101. Print. The authors discuss the importance of digital visual literacy, which they define as the ability to create and understand works made on a computer. They discuss potential problems and ways to incorporate digital visual literacy into courses.

Wickliff, Greg, and Kathleen Blake Yancey. "The Perils of Creating a Class Web Site: It Was the Best of Times, It Was the . . . ." *Computers and Composition* 18.2 (2001): 177–86. Print. The authors discuss how college junior honors students who were highly proficient with print performed like basic writing students when confronted with the demands of new technologies and visual literacy. The authors conclude that an illustrated essay assignment allows students to bridge their print writing competence to the new media they are learning.

Wysocki, Anne, Johndan Johnson-Eilola, Cynthia Selfe, and Geoffrey Sirc. *Writing New Media: Theory and Applications for Expanding the Teaching of Composition*. Logan: Utah State UP, 2004. Print. The authors discuss new media both in terms of composition theory and practical applications in the classroom. They offer extensive guidance on specific assignments.

Image details	Responses
Gray background: street, sidewalk, wall, blocked-up window	The grim landscape conveys a feeling of emptiness, hopelessness.
Teen dressed in T-shirt, jeans, and a backward baseball cap, standing off to the side with hands in pockets	The clothing seems typical for an urban high school student. Positioned at the edge of the photo, he looks to be on his own, even isolated.
Message from "Danny R." taped to the top of the photo with another message underneath	The message is an offer of help, probably directed at the boy. Danny R. looks to be a friend—is he trying to help the boy stay in school? Is the message underneath also from Danny R.? Taped messages break up the gray = hope for the boy.
Logo at lower right and words "Help Kody graduate at BoostUp.org."	The boy in the picture must be Kody. This is a direct appeal to readers to find out more. What is *BoostUp.org*? How can I or other readers help Kody graduate?

4 Analyzing an image

Elements for analysis

As when analyzing a written work, you analyze an image by identifying its elements. The image elements you might consider appear in the box below. Keep in mind that an image is a visual *composition* whose every element likely reflects a deliberate effort to communicate. Still, few images include all the elements, and you can narrow the list further by posing a question about the image you are reading, as illustrated on the next page.

Elements of images

- **Emphasis:** Most images pull your eyes to certain features: a graph line moving sharply upward, a provocative figure, bright color, thick lines, light against shadow, and so on. The cropping of a photograph or, say, the date range in a chart will also reflect what the image creator considers most important.
- **Narration:** Most images tell stories, whether in a sequence (a TV commercial or a graph showing changes over time) or at a single moment (a photograph, a painting, or a pie chart). Sometimes dialog or a title or caption contributes to the story.
- **Point of view:** The image creator influences responses by taking account of both the viewer's physical relation to the image subject— for instance, whether it is seen head-on or from above—and the viewer's assumed attitude toward the subject.

- **Arrangement:** Patterns among colors or forms, figures in the foreground and background, and elements that are juxtaposed or set apart contribute to the image's meaning and effect.
- **Color:** An image's colors can direct the viewer's attention and convey the creator's attitude toward the subject. Color may also suggest a mood, an era, a cultural connection, or another frame for viewing the image.
- **Characterization:** The figures and objects in an image have certain qualities—sympathetic or not, desirable or not, and so on. Their characteristics reflect the roles they play in the image's story.
- **Context:** The source of an image or the background in an image affects its meaning, whether it is a graph from a scholarly journal or a photo of a car on a sunny beach.
- **Tension:** Images often communicate a problem or seize attention with features that seem wrong, such as misspelled or misaligned words, distorted figures, or controversial relations between characters.
- **Allusions:** An **allusion** is a reference to something the audience is likely to recognize and respond to. Examples include a cultural symbol such as a dollar sign, a mythological figure such as a unicorn, or a familiar movie character such as Darth Vader from *Star Wars*.

Question for analysis

As discussed on pages 147–48, you can focus your analysis of elements by framing your main interest in the image as a question. Matthew Greene concentrated his analysis of the *BoostUp.org* ad by asking the question *Does the ad move readers to learn more about* BoostUp.org *and how they can help teens to graduate?* The question led Greene to focus on certain elements of the ad and to ignore others, as seen in the following entry from his reading journal:

Image elements	Responses
Emphasis	The ad's grayness and placement of Kody at the far left puts primary emphasis on the boy's isolation. Danny R.'s message, breaking up the gray, receives secondary emphasis.
Narration	The taped-on message suggests a story and connection between Kody and Danny R. Danny R. might be a friend, relative, or mentor. Based on the direct appeal in the word bubble, it appears that Danny R. is trying to help Kody graduate by offering to help him with schoolwork.
Arrangement	The ad places Danny R. and Kody together on the left side of the page, with Danny's message a bright spot on the dull landscape. The appeal to help Kody graduate is subtle and set on its own—the last thing readers look at. It also pulls the elements together so that the ad makes sense.

COMPARING IMAGES

To give students practice in analyzing elements of images, give them several images and ask them to compare a single element in all the images. By focusing on one element at a time, you can help students develop their ability to analyze that element. You could also ask them to find examples of images that have a distinctive use of an element, such as an image with an unusual point of view, a compelling narration, or a good use of tension or allusion.

POSTER IMAGES

Posters often abound on college campuses, and they provide legitimate fodder for image analysis. Ask students to bring in one of their favorite posters and have them work in small groups to analyze the elements.

Image elements	Responses
Color	The lack of color in most of the photo emphasizes Kody's isolation. The whiteness of Danny R.'s message relieves the grayness, like a ray of hope.

Sample images for analysis

The following images give you a chance to analyze selective elements in two kinds of images, a photograph and Web pages. Questions in the annotations can help to open up your thinking.

Elements in a photograph

Emphasis: What is the focus of the photograph? What are your eyes drawn to?

Arrangement: What is interesting about the arrangement of elements?

Characterization: What does the man seem to be feeling? Consider especially his mouth and eyes.

Color: What does the black-and-white presentation contribute to the image? How might the image differ in full color?

Narration: What story or stories might the photograph tell?

Allusion: What symbol do you see? What meaning does it give to the photograph?

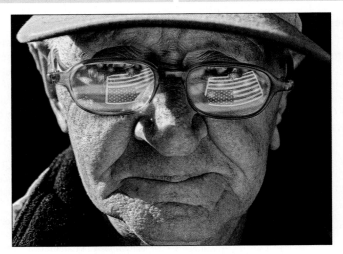

Photograph by Steve Simon

The screen shots opposite are from *AIDS Clock,* an interactive Web site sponsored by the United Nations Population Fund (*www.unfpa.org/aids_clock*). The top image is the home page, displaying a traditional world map. The bottom image appears when viewers click on "Resize the map": now each country's size reflects

Elements of Web pages

Emphasis and color: What elements on these pages draw your attention? How does color distinguish and emphasize elements?

Narration: What story do the two Web pages tell? What does each map contribute to the story? What does the red number contribute? (Notice that the number changes from the first screen to the second.)

Arrangement: What does the arrangement of elements on the pages contribute to the story being told?

Tension: How do you respond to the distorted map in the second image? What does the distortion contribute to your view of the Web site's effectiveness?

Context: How does knowing the Web site's sponsoring organization, the United Nations Population Fund, affect your response to these images?

AIDS Clock Web pages, 2008

COMPUTER ACTIVITIES

VIEWS OF THE WEB

The Web, so abundant in visual images, is an ideal place to practice critical viewing. You can create a guided tour for your students through some choice Web pages. As they follow the links in order, students can answer worksheet questions or just record their interpretations of the images they see.

PERSONAL WEB PAGES

Some of your students may have their own Web pages with graphics or other visual images. Ask for volunteers to have their Web pages viewed and evaluated by the rest of the class. Alternatively, if your students are building their own Web pages, you can ask them to experiment with images and try them out on their classmates.

the number of its people who live with HIV, the virus that causes AIDS. (For example, South Africa grows while the United States shrinks.) The large red number in the upper right changes every fifteen seconds. The "Wake up video" to its left scrolls through photos of people along with text urging viewers to join the World AIDS Campaign.

5 Interpreting an image

The strategies for interpreting an image parallel those for interpreting a written text (pp. 148–50). In this process you look more deeply at the elements, considering them in relation to the image creator's likely assumptions and intentions. You aim to draw reasonable inferences about *why* the image looks as it does. Here's a reasonable inference about the *BoostUp.org* advertisement on page 155:

Reasonable The creators of the *BoostUp.org* ad assume that readers want teens to graduate from high school.

This inference is supported by the ad's text: the word bubble connecting to the *BoostUp.org* logo specifically says, "Help Kody graduate at BoostUp.org." In contrast, the next inference is *not* reasonable because it leaps to a conclusion that is not supported by the ad:

Faulty The creators of the *BoostUp.org* ad want readers to help improve the quality of education in the United States.

The ad implies that readers believe education is important, but it does not suggest that readers should take steps to change the educational system.

6 Synthesizing ideas about an image

As discussed on pages 150–51, with synthesis you take analysis and interpretation a step further to consider how a work's elements and underlying assumptions mesh: How do the elements and assumptions relate to one another? What is the overall message of the image? You may also expand your synthesis to view the whole image in a larger context: How does the work compare with works by others? How does the work fit into the context of other works by the same author or group? What cultural, economic, political, or historical forces influence the work?

Placing an image in its context often requires research. For instance, to learn more about the assumptions underlying the *BoostUp.org* advertisement and the goals of the larger ad campaign, Matthew Greene visited the Web sites of *BoostUp.org* and the Ad Council, one of the ad's sponsors. The following entry from his reading journal synthesizes this research and his own ideas about the ad:

> The *BoostUp.org* magazine ad that features Kody is part of a larger campaign designed to raise public awareness about high school dropouts and encourage pubic support to help teens stay in school. Sponsored by the US Army and the nonprofit Ad Council, *BoostUp.org* profiles high school seniors who are at risk of dropping out and asks individuals to write the students personal messages of support. Ads like "Kody" are the first point of contact between the public and the teens, but they don't by themselves actually help the teens. For that, readers need to visit *BoostUp.org*. Thus the ad's elements work together like pieces of a puzzle, with the solution to be found only on the Web site.

7 Evaluating an image

If your critical reading moves on to evaluation, you'll form judgments about the quality and significance of the image. Questions to ask for evaluation appear in the box on page 152. Briefly: Is the message of the image accurate and fair, or is it distorted and biased? Can you support, refute, or extend the message? Does the image achieve its apparent purpose, and is the purpose worthwhile? How does the image affect you?

See Matthew Greene's paper on pages 174–75 for an evaluation of the *BoostUp.org* advertisement.

Exercise 7.6   Viewing an image critically

Review the list of visual elements on pages 156–67 and then take another close look at the *BoostUp.org* advertisement on page 152. Using the guidelines on the preceding pages, draw your own conclusions about the ad. Write while reading and thinking to help yourself concentrate and develop ideas. A writing suggestion based on this activity appears in Exercise 8.6, page 176.

Exercise 7.7   Viewing an image critically

Select either the photograph on page 158 or the Web pages on page 159 to examine in more detail. Using the guidelines on the preceding pages, read the image(s) methodically and critically. Write down your ideas. A writing suggestion based on this activity appears in Exercise 8.7, page 176.

Exercise 7.8   Comparing images critically

Two images in this section—the advertisement and the photograph—use people as subjects to reinforce their messages. The other images—two Web pages—center on maps and statistics. Using the guidelines on the preceding pages, compare these images, focusing on each one's emphasis. How effective are these emphases? Write down your responses. A writing suggestion based on this activity appears in Exercise 8.8, page 176.

RESOURCES AND IDEAS

Zeller, Robert. "Developing the Inferential Reasoning of Basic Writers." *College Composition and Communication* 38.3 (1987): 343–46. Print. Zeller suggests that asking students to make connections between visual prompts like photographs and writing helps their critical thinking skills.

COLLABORATIVE LEARNING

IMAGE AUCTION

Have your students imagine they are the auctioneer for an estate sale of images (you provide the collection of images). Ask them each to select an image they think is excellent in quality and/or high in significance, and to write a blurb for the auction program in which they describe the image and try to "sell" their classmates on its value and significance. You can put the images online and the class members can work together to create an online auction program including each of their entries.

Exercise 7.6 can work well as a group activity. Have students discuss the *Sports Illustrated* advertisement in small groups, using the list of visual elements, to develop alternative interpretations.

ANSWERS: EXERCISE 7.6

Individual response.

ANSWERS: EXERCISE 7.7

Individual response.

COLLABORATIVE LEARNING

Exercise 7.8 can work well as a group exercise. Each group member can supply one image, and then the group can perform the analysis together.

ANSWERS: EXERCISE 7.8

Individual response.

8

Writing in Academic Situations

The academic disciplines differ widely in their subjects and approaches, but they all share the common goal of building knowledge through questioning, research, and communication. The differences among disciplines lie mainly in the kinds of questions asked, the kinds of research done to find the answers, and the **genres**, or types of writing, used to communicate the answers, such as case studies, research reports, literary analyses, and reviews of others' writings.

Both a discipline's concerns and the kind of writing create an academic writing situation, which in turn shapes a writer's choice of subject, conception of audience, definition of purpose, choice of structure and content, and even choice of language. This chapter introduces academic writing situations in general. Chapters 49–52 detail the particular goals and expectations for writing about literature and in other humanities, the social sciences, and the natural and applied sciences.

8a Writing in response to texts

Academic knowledge building depends on reading, analyzing, and expanding on the work of others. Thus many academic writing assignments require you to respond to one or more texts—not only written products such as short stories and journal articles but also visual communications such as images, charts, films, and advertisements. As you form a response to a text, you will integrate, or synthesize, its ideas and information with yours to come to your own conclusions.

Note A common academic assignment, the research paper, expects you to consult and respond to multiple texts in order to support and extend your ideas (see Chapters 41–46). This section focuses on

---

my**comp**lab

Visit *mycomplab.com* for more resources and exercises on academic writing.

responding directly to a single text, but the skills involved apply to research writing as well.

1 Deciding how to respond

When an assignment asks you to respond directly to a text, you might take one of the following approaches. (Note that the word *author* refers to a photographer, painter, or other creator as well as to a writer.)

- **Agree with and extend the author's ideas,** exploring related ideas and providing additional examples.
- **Agree with the author on some points but disagree on others.**
- **Disagree with the author on one or more main points.**
- **Explain how the author achieves a particular effect,** such as evoking a historical period or balancing opposing views.
- **Analyze the overall effectiveness of a text**—for example, how well a writer supports a thesis with convincing evidence or whether an advertisement succeeds in its unstated purpose.

2 Forming a response

You will likely have an immediate response to at least some of the texts you analyze: you may agree or disagree strongly with what the author is saying. But for some other responses, you may need time and thought to determine what the author is saying and what you think about it.

Whatever your assignment, your first task is to examine the text or texts thoroughly so that you're sure you understand what the author says outright and also assumes or implies. You can use the process of critical reading described in the previous chapter to take notes on the text, summarize it, and develop a critical response. Then, as you write, you can use the tips in the following box to convey your response to readers.

Responding to a text

- **Make sure your writing has a point**—a central idea, or thesis, that focuses your response. (For more on developing a thesis, see pp. 27–32.)
- **Include a very brief summary if readers may be unfamiliar with your subject.** But remember that your job is not just to report what the text says or what an image shows; it is to *respond* to the work from your own critical perspective. (For more on summary, see pp. 134–35.)
- **Center each paragraph on an idea of your own that supports your thesis.** Generally, state the idea outright, in your own voice.

(continued)

---

authors show how focused, critical reading can benefit student writing.

CONTEXTS FOR RESPONDING TO TEXTS

Ask groups to brainstorm for situations in which they might need to respond to a text. For example, a history assignment might require students to respond to a primary historical document; an employer might request a response to a client's proposal. As a class, compile a list of such scenarios to demonstrate how fundamental these skills are both for school and beyond.

INITIAL RESPONSE

Particularly with charged political and social topics, students may have a strong emotional reaction to a text. Encourage them to journal about their initial response. Expressing these initial reactions without fear of being wrong can then clear the way for students to write a more reasoned, logical response.

BRIEF RESPONSE

Provide a paragraph from an article to each group. Ask students to collaborate on a short response to the text, using the "Responding to a text" box on p. 163 as a guide. Students should produce a response that includes a central thesis, brief summary, textual evidence, and interpretation on the paragraph. Then, each group should share their response with the class for feedback.

Responding to a text

(continued)

- **Support the paragraph idea with evidence from the text**—quotations, paraphrases, details, and examples.
- **Conclude each paragraph with your interpretation of the evidence.** As a general rule, avoid ending paragraphs with source evidence; instead, end with at least a sentence that explains what the evidence shows.

3 | Emphasizing synthesis in your response

Following the suggestions in the preceding box will lead you to show readers the synthesis you achieved by thinking critically about the text. That is, you integrate your perspective with that of the author in order to support a conclusion of your own about the work.

A key to synthesis is deciding how to present evidence from your reading and observation in your writing. Especially when you are writing about a relatively unfamiliar subject, you may be tempted to let a text or other source do the talking for you through extensive summary or quotations. However, your voice is crucial in academic writing, where readers expect to see you managing ideas and information to make your points. A typical paragraph of text-based writing follows the pattern outlined in the box above: the writer's own idea, evidence from the text, and the writer's interpretation of the evidence. You can see this pattern in the following paragraph from an essay that appears later in this chapter (p. 172):

Sowell's portrait of student-loan recipients is questionable. It is based on averages, some statistical and some not, but averages are often deceptive. For example, Sowell cites college graduates' low average debt of $7,000 to $9,000 (131) without acknowledging the fact that many students' debt is much higher or giving the full range of statistics. Similarly, Sowell dismisses "heart-rending stories" of "the low-income student with a huge debt" as "not at all typical" (132), yet he invents his own exaggerated version of the typical loan recipient: an affluent slacker ("Rockefellers" and "Vanderbilts") for whom college is a "place to hang out for a few years" sponging off the government, while his or her parents clear a profit from making use of the loan program (132). Although such students (and parents) may well exist, are they really typical? Sowell does not offer any data one way or the other—

Writer's idea

Evidence and interpretation

for instance, how many loan recipients come from each income group, what percentage of loan funds go to each group, how many loan recipients receive significant help from their parents, and how many receive none. Together, Sowell's statements and omissions cast doubt on the argument that students don't need or deserve the loans.

Writer's conclusion

—Charlene Robinson, "Weighing the Costs"

This example meets an important goal of synthesis in academic writing: Robinson finds **balance** in her own and Sowell's claims so that her claims are reasonable and believable. Disagreeing with Sowell, Robinson might simply have dismissed his claims about loan recipients as "ridiculous" and moved on. Instead, she takes a more serious and impartial approach by giving Sowell's claims a fair hearing, explaining clearly why she faults them, and detailing the omissions she sees. Thus she gives readers a chance to evaluate Sowell's and her own claims for themselves.

Note Effective synthesis requires careful handling of evidence from the text (quotations, paraphrases, and summaries) so that the evidence meshes smoothly into your sentences and yet is clearly distinct from your own ideas. See pages 620–25 on integrating borrowed material.

8b Determining purpose

For most academic writing, your general purpose will be mainly explanatory or mainly argumentative. That is, you will aim to explain your subject so that readers understand it as you do, or you will aim to gain readers' agreement with a debatable idea about the subject. (See p. 10 for more on general purposes and Chapters 9–11 for more on argument.) Although the general purpose for writing may not be stated outright in an assignment, it will probably be implied, as you can see in these two abbreviated assignments:

Explanation
Compare the depiction of war in two films viewed this semester, considering plots, characters, dialog, battle scenes, production designs, and other elements of the films.

Argument
What ideology do you see informing the movies of director Steven Spielberg? What beliefs about the world do his choices convey, whether explicitly or implicitly, intentionally or unintentionally? Support your claim with evidence from at least four of Spielberg's movies, considering plots, characters, dialog, production designs, and other elements.

COMPUTER ACTIVITY

INTERPRETING ASSIGNMENTS

Post a number of sample assignments from several disciplines on your class Web site. You can either create your own, hunt for samples online, or ask your colleagues if they will provide a sample assignment for this purpose. Ask students to post on the Web site their interpretations of purpose as implied by each sample assignment.

CROSSOVER WRITERS

Many academic professionals write successfully for different audiences. Stephen Jay Gould, Carl Sagan, and Deborah Tannen are well known for their crossover writings, but there are many others as well. Show your students two samples of a single author's writing on the same subject for different audiences, to help them see the differences.

CLASSROOM AUDIENCES

The members of your classroom, including the students and you, constitute an educated or academic audience (albeit less specialized or sophisticated than an audience composed of academic professionals). Asking students to read their papers aloud in class, standing at the front of the class or a podium, can be a way to establish a more formal atmosphere. The experience of making a formal oral presentation may help them get a better feeling for the formal qualities of academic writing.

Your specific purpose—including your subject and how you hope readers will respond—depends on the kind of writing you're doing. For instance, in a literature review for a biology class, you want readers to understand the research area you're covering, the recent contributions made by researchers, the issues needing further research, and the sources you consulted. Not coincidentally, these topics correspond to the major sections of a literature review. In following the standard format, you both help to define your purpose and begin to meet the discipline's (and thus your instructor's) expectations.

Your specific purpose will be more complex as well. You take a course to learn about a subject and the ways experts think about it. Your writing, in return, contributes to the discipline through the knowledge you uncover and the lens of your perspective. At the same time, as a student you want to demonstrate your competence with research, evidence, format, and other requirements of the discipline.

8c Analyzing audience

Many academic writing assignments will specify or assume an educated audience or an academic audience. Such readers look for writing that is clear, balanced, well-organized, and well-reasoned, among other qualities discussed on the opposite page. Other assignments will specify or assume an audience of experts on your subject, readers who look in addition for writing that meets the subject's requirements for claims and evidence, organization, language, format, and other qualities discussed in Chapters 48–52.

Of course, much of your academic writing will have only one reader besides you: the instructor of the course for which you are writing. Instructors fill two main roles as readers:

- **They represent the audience you are addressing.** They may actually be members of the audience, as when you address academic readers or subject experts. Or they may imagine themselves as members of your audience—reading, for instance, as if they sat on the city council. In either case, they're interested in how effectively you write for the audience.
- **They serve as coaches,** guiding you toward achieving the goals of the course and, more broadly, toward the academic aims of building and communicating knowledge.

Like everyone else, instructors have preferences and peeves, but you'll waste time and energy trying to anticipate them. Do attend to written and spoken directions for assignments, of course. But otherwise view your instructors as representatives of the community you are writing for. Their responses will be guided by the community's aims and expectations and by a desire to teach you about them.

8d Choosing structure and content

Many academic writing assignments will at least imply how you should organize your paper and even how you should develop your ideas. Like the literature review mentioned earlier, the type of paper required will suggest discrete parts, each with its own requirements for content. Even a direct response to a text, whose content depends on the text and the response, still implies certain requirements: you are asked to make a claim and to support the claim with specific evidence. Sometimes you may also be expected to show that you understand what others think about the text.

No matter what type of paper an assignment specifies, the broad academic aims of building and exchanging knowledge determine features that are common across disciplines. Follow these general guidelines for your academic writing, supplementing them as indicated with others elsewhere in this book:

- **Develop a thesis**—a central idea or claim to which everything in the paper clearly relates. Usually, state your thesis near the beginning of the paper. For more on theses, see pages 27–32.
- **Support the thesis with evidence,** drawn usually from reading and sometimes from your own experience. The kinds of evidence will depend on the discipline you're writing in and the type of paper you're doing. For more on evidence in the disciplines, see pages 739 (literature), 755–56 (other humanities), 774–75 (social sciences), and 806 (natural and applied sciences).
- **Synthesize.** Put your sources to work for you by thinking critically about them. Integrate them into your own perspective in your own voice. For more on synthesis, see pages 162–65 in this chapter and pages 604–06 in the discussion of research writing.
- **Acknowledge sources fully, including online sources.** *Not* acknowledging sources undermines the knowledge-sharing foundation of academic writing and opens you to charges of plagiarism, which can be punishable. See pages 626–34 on plagiarism and the following pages for details on source-citation styles: 644–88 (MLA style for English and some other humanities), 760–71 (Chicago style for history, philosophy, and some other humanities), 779–99 (APA style for the social sciences), and 811–17 (CSE style for the natural and applied sciences).
- **Organize clearly within the framework of the type of writing you're doing.** Develop your ideas as simply and directly as your purpose and content allow. Clearly relate sentences, paragraphs, and sections so that readers always know where they are in the paper's development.

DISCIPLINARY DIFFERENCES

Give students samples of discipline-specific academic writing. In small groups, they can compare the samples, locating differences in structure and content conventions. They can use this section's bulleted list of guidelines to help them evaluate the samples.

CULTURALLY SPECIFIC CONVENTIONS

If you have international students in your course, you might invite them to bring in samples of writing they produced for teachers in their home country, and to explain to the rest of the class any structure or content conventions in their culture that differ from U.S. conventions.

WEB SITE PROSE/ACADEMIC PROSE

Ask students to bring to class a paragraph taken from a Web site of their choice. Then ask them to evaluate the degree to which the excerpt adheres to, or departs from, academic conventions of content, structure, and language.

CULTURE LANGUAGE These features are far from universal. In other cultures, academic writers may be indirect, may expect readers to discover the thesis, or may assume that readers do not require acknowledgment of well-known sources. Recognizing such differences between practices in your native culture and in the United States can help you adapt to US academic writing.

8e   Using academic language

American academic writing relies on a dialect called standard American English. The dialect is also used in business, government, the media, and other sites of social and economic power where people of diverse backgrounds must communicate with one another. It is "standard" not because it is better than other forms of English, but because it is accepted as the common language, much as the dollar bill is accepted as the common currency.

You'll recognize standard American English as the dialect used in this handbook, in magazines and newspapers, and on television news. But you might also notice that the dialect varies a great deal, from the formal English of a President's State of the Union address through the middle formality of this handbook to the informal chitchat between anchors on morning TV. Even in academic writing, standard American English allows much room for the writer's own voice, as these passages on the same topic show:

More formal

Using the technique of "color engineering," manufacturers and advertisers can heighten the interest of consumers in a product by adding color that does not contribute to the utility of the product but appeals more to emotions. In one example from the 1920s, manufacturers of fountain pens, which had previously been made of hard black rubber, dramatically increased sales simply by producing the pens in bright colors.

> Two complicated sentences, one explaining the technique and one giving the example

> Drawn-out phrasing, such as *interest of consumers* instead of *consumers' interest*

> Formal vocabulary, such as *heighten, contribute,* and *utility*

Less formal

A touch of "color engineering" can sharpen the emotional appeal of a product or its ad. New color can boost sales even when the color serves no other use. In the 1920s, for example, fountain pen makers introduced brightly colored pens along with the familiar ones of hard black rubber. Sales shot up.

> Four sentences, two each explaining the technique and giving the example

> More informal phrasing, such as *Sales shot up*

> More informal vocabulary, such as *boost* and *ad*

As different as they are, both examples illustrate several common features of academic language:

- **Its formality varies depending on the writer's voice and audience.** For instance, the first passage might reflect the writer's preference for more formal language and also an audience of experts in the field who expect a serious, measured approach. Addressing peers instead of experts, the same writer might still sound more formal than the second writer does—perhaps retaining the formal vocabulary—but might also shorten sentences and tighten phrasing.

- **It follows the conventions of standard American English for grammar and usage.** These conventions are detailed in guides to the dialect, such as this handbook. Note that standard American English excludes many forms that are encouraged by rapid communication in e-mail and in text or instant messaging, such as incomplete sentences, no capital letters, and abbreviations and shortened spellings (*u* for "you," *b4* for "before," *thru* for "through," *imo* for "in my opinion," and so on). See page 504 for more on these forms.

- **It uses a standard vocabulary,** not one that only some groups understand, such as slang, an ethnic or regional dialect, or another language. See pages 502–03 for more on specialized vocabularies.

- **It creates some distance between writer and reader with the third person** (*he, she, it, they*). The first person (*I, we*) is sometimes appropriate to express personal opinions or invite readers to think along, but not with a strongly explanatory purpose (*I discovered that "color engineering" can heighten. . .*). The second person (*you*) is appropriate only in addressing readers directly (as in this handbook), and even then it may seem condescending or too chummy (*You should know that "color engineering" can heighten . . .*).

- **It is authoritative and neutral.** In the examples on the facing page, the writers express themselves confidently, not timidly (as in *One possible example of color engineering that might be considered in this case is . . .*). They also refrain from hostility (*Advertisers will stop at nothing to achieve their goals*) and enthusiasm (*Color engineering is genius at work*).

At first, the diverse demands of academic writing may leave you groping for an appropriate voice. In an effort to sound fresh and confident, you may write too casually:

Too casual

"Color engineering" is a great way to get at consumers' feelings. . . . When the guys jazzed up the color, sales shot through the roof.

In an effort to sound "academic," you may produce wordy and awkward sentences:

Wordy and awkward

The emotions of consumers can be made more engaged by the technique known as "color engineering." . . . A very large increase in the sales of fountain pens was achieved by the manufacturers of the pens as a result of this color enhancement technique. [The passive voice in this example, such as *increase . . . was achieved* instead of *the manufacturers achieved,* adds to its wordiness and indirection. See pp. 298–300 for more on verb voice.]

A cure for writing too informally or too stiffly is to read academic writing so that the language and style become familiar and to edit your writing (see pp. 59–61). With experience and practice, you will develop a voice that is sufficiently formal but still authentic and natural, as in the examples on page 168.

CULTURE LANGUAGE If your first language is not English or is an English dialect besides standard American, you know well the power of communicating with others who share your language. Learning to write standard American English in no way requires you to abandon your first language. Like most multilingual people, you are probably already adept at switching between languages as the situation demands—speaking one way with your relatives, say, and another way with an employer. As you practice academic writing, you'll develop the same flexibility with it.

Exercise 8.1 Using academic language
Revise the following paragraph to make the language more academic while keeping the factual information the same.

If you buy into the stereotype of girls chatting away on their cell phones, you should think again. One of the major wireless companies surveyed 1021 cell phone owners for a period of five years and—surprise!—reported that guys talk on cell phones more than girls do. In fact, guys were way ahead of girls, using an average of 571 minutes a month compared to 424 for girls. That's 35 percent more time on the phone! The survey also asked about conversations on home phones, and while girls still beat the field, the guys are catching up.

Exercise 8.2 Considering your past work: Writing in academic situations
Look back at a paper you wrote for a course in high school or college. To what extent does it share the features of academic writing discussed in this chapter? How does it differ? Write a revision plan for making the paper more academic.

Exercise 8.3 Considering your native language or dialect
What main similarities and differences do you notice between writing in your native language or dialect and writing for US college courses? Consider especially audience, purpose, content, structure, and the expression

of ideas. Which differences do you think are easiest to bridge? Which are most difficult? Why?

8f Examining sample critical responses

A critical response to a text or an image, often called a **critique,** is a common academic assignment. The specifics depend on the discipline, but the principles illustrated here apply across disciplines.

Note Critical writing is *not* summarizing. You might summarize to clarify a text or an image for yourself, and you may briefly summarize a work in your larger piece of writing. But in critical writing you go further to bring your perspective to the work.

1 Writing critically about a text

The following essay by the student Charlene Robinson responds to Thomas Sowell's essay "Student Loans" (pp. 144–45). Robinson arrived at her response, an argument, through the process of critical reading outlined in the previous chapter and then by gathering and organizing her ideas, developing a thesis about Sowell's text that synthesized his ideas and hers, and drafting and revising until she believed she had supported her thesis with sufficient evidence from her own experience and from Sowell's text.

Robinson did not assume that her readers would see the same things in Sowell's essay or share her views, so her essay offers evidence of Sowell's ideas in the form of direct quotations, summaries, and paraphrases (restatements in her own words). Robinson documents these borrowings from Sowell using the style of the Modern Language Association (MLA): the numbers in parentheses are page numbers in the book containing Sowell's essay, listed at the end as a "work cited." (See Chapter 46 for more on MLA style.)

Weighing the Costs

In the essay "Student Loans," the economist Thomas Sowell challenges the US government's student-loan program for three main reasons: a scarce resource (taxpayers' money) goes to many undeserving students, a high number of recipients fail to repay their loans, and the easy availability of money has led to both lower academic standards and higher college tuitions. Sowell wants his readers to "weigh the costs of things" (133) in order to see, as he does, that the loan program should not receive so much government funding. But does he provide the evidence of cost and other problems to lead the reader to agree with him? The answer is no, because hard evidence is less common than debatable and unsupported assumptions about students, scarcity, and the value of education.

[margin labels: Introduction | Summary of Sowell's essay | Robinson's critical question | Thesis statement]

First main point

Evidence for first point: paraphrases and quotations from Sowell's text

Evidence for first point: Sowell's omissions

Conclusion of first point: Robinson's interpretation

Transition to second main point

Second main point

Evidence for second point: Sowell's omissions

Conclusion of second point: Robinson's interpretation

Third main point

Evidence for third point: paraphrases and quotations from Sowell's text

Sowell's portrait of student-loan recipients is questionable. It is based on averages, some statistical and some not, but averages are often deceptive. For example, Sowell cites college graduates' low average debt of $7,000 to $9,000 (131) without acknowledging the fact that many students' debt is much higher or giving the full range of statistics. Similarly, Sowell dismisses "heart-rending stories" of "the low-income student with a huge debt" as "not at all typical" (132), yet he invents his own exaggerated version of the typical loan recipient: an affluent slacker ("Rockefellers" and "Vanderbilts") for whom college is a "place to hang out for a few years" sponging off the government, while his or her parents clear a profit from making use of the loan program (132). Although such students (and parents) may well exist, are they really typical? Sowell does not offer any data one way or the other—for instance, how many loan recipients come from each income group, what percentage of loan funds go to each group, how many loan recipients receive significant help from their parents, and how many receive none. Together, Sowell's statements and omissions cast doubt on the argument that students don't need or deserve the loans.

Another set of assumptions in the essay has to do with "scarcity": "There is never enough of anything to fully satisfy all those who want it," Sowell says (131). This statement appeals to readers' common sense, but the "lesson" of scarcity does not necessarily apply to the student-loan program. Sowell omits many important figures needed to prove that the nation's resources are too scarce to support the program, such as the total cost of the program, its percentage of the total education budget and the total federal budget, and its cost compared to the cost of defense, Medicare, and other expensive programs. Moreover, Sowell does not mention the interest paid by loan recipients, even though the interest must offset some of the costs of running the program and covering unpaid loans. Thus his argument that there isn't enough money to run the student loan program is unconvincing.

The most fundamental and most debatable assumption underlying Sowell's essay is that higher education is a kind of commodity that not everyone is entitled to. In order to diminish the importance of graduates' average debt from education loans, Sowell claims that a car loan will probably be higher (131). This comparison between education and an automobile implies that the two are somehow equal as products and that an affordable higher education is no more a right than a new car is. Sowell also condemns the "irresponsible" students who drop out of school and

"the increasingly easy availability of college to people who are not very serious about getting an education" (132). But he overlooks the value of encouraging education, including the education of those who don't finish
college or who aren't scholars. For many in the United States, education has
a greater value than that of a mere commodity like a car. And even from an
economic perspective such as Sowell's, the cost to society of an uneducated
public needs to be taken into account. By failing to give education its
due, Sowell undermines his argument at its core.

Evidence for third point: Sowell's omissions

Conclusion of third point: Robinson's interpretation

Sowell writes with conviction, and his concerns are valid: high
taxes, waste, unfairness, declining educational standards, obtrusive
government. However, the essay's flaws make it unlikely that Sowell
could convince readers who do not already agree with him. He does
not support his portrait of the typical loan recipient, he fails to
demonstrate a lack of resources for the loan program, and he neglects
the special nature of education compared to other services and products. Sowell may have the evidence to back up his assumptions, but by
omitting it he himself does not truly weigh the costs of the loan program.

Conclusion

Acknowledgment of Sowell's concerns

Summary of three main points

Return to theme of introduction: weighing costs

Work Cited

Sowell, Thomas. "Student Loans." *Is Reality Optional? and Other Essays.*
    Stanford: Hoover, 1993. 131-33. Print.

Work cited in MLA style (p. 653)

—Charlene Robinson (student)

2 | Writing critically about an image

The following essay, by the student Matthew Greene, responds
to the *BoostUp.org* advertisement on page 155. As we saw in the previous chapter, Greene examined the image over several stages, each
time discovering more in it and gradually developing his own ideas.
In his paper Greene takes pains to be sure that readers will see the
image as he does: he reproduces the ad, captions it, and clearly describes its features. He cites his sources using MLA style (Chapter 46).
(All but one of Greene's text citations lack page numbers because
the sources themselves are not numbered.)

Note An image is a source just as a written work is, and like a
written source it must be acknowledged. Greene cites the *BoostUp.org*
ad in the image caption. (MLA style does not require him to cite it
again in his list of works cited.) If Greene published his paper online, he would also need to seek the copyright owner's permission to
use the image. See pages 629–31 for more about acknowledging
sources and pages 632–34 for more about permissions for online
publication.

RESOURCES AND IDEAS

Cheville, Julie. "Automated Scoring Technologies and the Rising Influence of Error." *English Journal* 93.4 (2004): 47–52. Print. Cheville cautions that automated assessment can shape a writing curriculum that may benefit private industry but is at odds with current composition theory and research.

Herrington, Anne, and Charles Moran. "What Happens When Machines Read Our Students' Writing?" *College English* 63.4 (2001) 480–99: Print. The authors are highly critical of software programs that claim they can grade students' essays accurately for both style and content.

Jones, Billie J. "Learning with, through and about Computers: Students' Best Friend or Worst Nightmare?" *Teaching English in the Two-Year College* 30.3 (2003): 286–95. Print. The author reports on students' responses to her computer-based writing class, noting that some students were intimidated by computers while others thrived.

Koerber, Amy. "Toward a Feminist Rhetoric of Technology." *Journal of Business and Technical Communication* 14.1 (2000): 58–73. Print. Koerber argues that the rhetoric of technology must evolve to account for feminist concerns, including the gender inequities that technology fosters.

Lent, Robin. "'I Can Relate to That . . .': Reading and Responding in the Writing Classroom." *College Composition and Communication* 44.2 (1993): 232–40. Print. Lent demonstrates how using short, informal response papers can deepen students' interpretations of assigned readings.

Moran, Charles. "Computers and Composition 1983–2002: What We Have Hoped For." *Computers and Composition* 20.4 (2003): 343–58. Print. Moran provides a practical and comprehensive review of the literature on the question: Do computers improve student writing?

Salvatori, Mariolina. "Conversations with Texts: Reading in the Teaching of Composition." *College English* 58.4 (1996): 440–54. Print. Salvatori examines the theoretical basis for

Giving a Boost

Introduction

Description of image

How many commuters paused, as I did, to puzzle over a bus shelter advertisement that shows a teenage boy standing in a sea of gray street, sidewalk, and wall? (See fig. 1.) Were other readers curious about the message from "Danny R.," taped to the top of the photograph, that reads, "Hey—let me know if you want some help with school work this weekend. I'm around"? Did they follow the ad's instruction: "HELP KODY GRADUATE AT BOOSTUP.ORG"? If they did, they probably appreciated how effective the ad

Thesis statement

is. Through its photograph, taped-on message, and direct appeal, it encourages readers to find out how they can help students stay in high school.

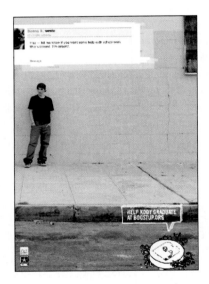

Caption giving the ad's main idea and source

Fig. 1. An advertisement for *BoostUp.org* encourages viewers to visit its Web site and support students who are at risk of dropping out of high school. From "High School Dropout Prevention"; *Ad Council*; Ad Council, 2007; Web; 10 Apr. 2008.

Background information on the ad campaign

The *BoostUp.org* campaign is sponsored by the nonprofit Ad Council and the US Army. It aims to raise public awareness about high school dropouts and encourage public support to help teens stay in school ("High School"). When people visit *BoostUp.org*, they can learn about particular at-risk seniors and offer them "boost" through e-mail or text messages; users of *YouTube*, *Facebook*, and *MySpace* can send support through those sites ("What"). First, though, people have to visit the site, and that's where "Kody" and similar ads come in. They are very effective at making people curious enough to go to the site and concerned enough to participate in the campaign.

The main image in the *BoostUp.org* ad—the photograph of a teenager wearing a T-shirt, baggy jeans, and a backward baseball cap—presents the boy as especially isolated. The cropping of the photograph pushes him to one side and makes him seem small amid hard gray surfaces. His off-center stance, hands in pockets, and glance to the side all heighten the sense that he is alone, vulnerable, and in need of a friend or help. At the same time, nothing in the photograph suggests that the boy is causing trouble or planning it. He's just very much by himself.

The second major element in the ad, Danny R.'s message in the upper left corner, counters the photograph in two ways. First, with the offer to help with school work over the weekend, Danny R. shows that he is someone who knows and cares about the person he's writing to. It isn't immediately clear who this person is, but if it's the boy in the photograph then he isn't as alone as he first seems. Second, Danny R.'s message is literally taped on the photo, over another message that can't be read. This covered message implies that Danny R. is not the only support the boy has. Together, the messages break up the bleak grayness that the photograph depicts as the boy's world, offering hope that the boy has friends who want to help him.

The third important element in the ad—the word bubble in the lower right—pulls together the other two elements. The word bubble is a direct appeal to readers to get involved. It is less prominent than the other two elements, so it is probably the final place readers look when scanning the ad. It suggests that the boy is named Kody and that he is at risk of not graduating. Yet the text still does not say what *BoostUp.org* is or how readers can help Kody there. Some mystery remains to attract readers to the Web site.

The creators of this advertisement seem to assume that readers see dropping out as a negative step for high school students. Thus the ad is designed to draw readers in by showing Kody's world, providing an example of an encouraging message, and inviting visits to *BoostUp.org*. Once there, readers may be moved, as I was, to offer a "boost" of their own to Kody and his classmates.

Works Cited

"High School Dropout Prevention." *Ad Council*. Ad Council, 2007. Web. 18 Apr. 2008.

"What Is Boost?" *BoostUp.org*. US Army and Ad Council, 2007. Web. 15 Apr. 2008.

—Matthew Greene (student)

[Margin annotations:]
- First main point
- Evidence for first point: analysis of photograph
- Conclusion of first point: Greene's interpretation
- Second main point
- Evidence for second point: analysis of message
- Conclusion of second point: Greene's interpretation
- Third main point
- Evidence for third point: analysis of word bubble
- Conclusion of third point: Greene's interpretation
- Conclusion
- Works cited in MLA style
- No works-cited entry for advertisement because the caption provides complete source information

---

the argument that critical reading and writing are linked learning activities.

Tuzi, Frank. "The Impact of E-feedback on the Revisions of L2 Writers in an Academic Writing Course." *Computers and Composition* 21.2 (2004): 217–35. Print. Tuzi's study suggests that ESL students benefit more from electronic feedback than oral feedback.

Wilson, Smokey. "When Computers Come to English Class." *Teaching English in the Two-Year College* 27.4 (2000): 387–99. Print. Wilson's study shows that students who took English in computer-based classrooms were more likely to pass the course and less likely to drop out compared to students in non–computer-based classrooms.

COLLABORATIVE LEARNING

Have students discuss the questions for Exercise 8.4 and come up with a number of responses to each question. Then ask each student to revise those responses individually into a brief essay. When students exchange the completed essays in their group, they are often surprised by the varying interpretations developed by the individual essays.

You might also put students into groups to compare their answers to these questions. Encourage students to focus not only on points on which they agree but on their disagreements. Such differences of opinion indicate where their analytical frameworks and assumptions vary, even though they may consider themselves all part of the same "audience."

ANSWERS: EXERCISE 8.4 (next page)

Individual response.

ANSWERS: EXERCISE 8.5 (next page)

Individual response.

ANSWERS: EXERCISE 8.6 (next page)

Individual response.

ANSWERS: EXERCISE 8.7

Individual response.

ANSWERS: EXERCISE 8.8

Individual response.

HIGHLIGHTS

This chapter presents a discussion of reading arguments critically. The first section describes the elements of arguments: assertions, evidence, and assumptions (9a). The next section offers techniques for testing assertions; for identifying fact, opinion, belief, and prejudice; and for looking at a writer's definition of terms, use of evidence, and appeals to beliefs or needs (9b). Discussions of weighing evidence, analyzing underlying assumptions, attending to language and tone, and judging reasonableness round out the first part of this chapter. Ways for students to recognize logical fallacies—various kinds of evasions and oversimplifications—constitute the second half of this chapter.

Exercise 8.4 Responding to critiques

Read Charlene Robinson's and Matthew Greene's essays carefully. Do you think the authors' critiques are accurate and fair? Are they perceptive? Do the authors provide enough evidence to convince you of their points? Do they miss anything you would have mentioned? Write your responses to one of the essays in a brief critique of your own.

Exercise 8.5 Writing critically about a text

Write an essay based on your own critical reading of Thomas Sowell's "Student Loans" (Exercise 7.4, p. 153). Your critique may be entirely different from Charlene Robinson's, or you may have developed some of the same points. If there are similarities, they should be expressed and supported in your own way, in the context of your own critical perspective.

Exercise 8.6 Writing critically about an image

Write an essay based on your own critical reading of the *BoostUp.org* advertisement (Exercise 7.6, p. 161). Your critique may be entirely different from Matthew Greene's, or you may have developed some of the same points. If there are similarities, they should be expressed and supported in your own way, in the context of your own critical perspective.

Exercise 8.7 Writing critically about an image

Write an essay based on your own critical reading of the photograph on page 158 or the Web pages on page 159 (Exercise 7.7, p. 161).

Exercise 8.8 Writing critically about several images

Write an essay based on your critical reading and comparison of the three images in the previous chapter (Exercise 7.8, p. 161)

9

Reading Arguments Critically

Argument is writing that attempts to open readers' minds to an opinion, change readers' own opinions, or move readers to action. A

mycomplab

Visit *mycomplab.com* for more resources and exercises on reading arguments critically.

good argument is neither a cold exercise in logic nor an attempt to beat others into submission. It is a work of negotiation and problem solving in which both writer and reader search for the knowledge that will create common ground between them.

Of course, not all arguments are "good." Whether deliberately or not, some are unclear, incomplete, misleading, or downright false. The negotiation fails; the problem remains unsolved. This chapter will help you read written arguments critically, and the next chapter will help you write effective arguments. After that, in Chapter 11, you'll see how to read and use visual arguments.

CULTURE LANGUAGE The ways of reading and writing arguments described in this chapter and the next may be uncomfortable to you if your native culture approaches such writing differently. In some cultures, for example, a writer is expected to begin indirectly, to avoid asserting his or her opinion outright, or to establish a compromise rather than argue a position. In American academic and business settings, readers and writers look or aim for a well-articulated opinion, evidence gathered from many sources, and a direct and concise argument for the opinion.

9a Recognizing the elements of argument

Few arguments are an easy read. Most demand the attentive critical reading discussed in Chapter 7. (If you haven't read pp. 140–52, you should do so before continuing.) As a reader of argument, your purpose will almost always be the same: you'll want to know whether you should be convinced by the argument. This purpose focuses your attention on the elements that make an argument convincing, or not.

In a scheme adapted from the work of the British philosopher Stephen Toulmin, an argument has three main elements:

- **Claims:** positive statements that require support. In a written argument the central claim is stated outright in a **thesis statement** (see p. 27). This central claim is what the argument is about. For instance:

  In both its space and its equipment, the college's chemistry laboratory is outdated.

  Several minor claims, such as that the present equipment is inadequate, will contribute to the central assertion.

- **Evidence:** the facts, examples, expert opinions, and other information that support the claims. (Toulmin calls evidence *data* or

The need to read arguments critically is becoming ever more important as argumentation proliferates online. Web sites and blogs are breeding grounds for arguments based on poor evidence, prejudice, or false authority. Exercises and teaching tips offer suggestions for helping students become more critical users of cyberspace.

This chapter assumes that students have read Chapter 7, "Forming a Critical Perspective," and are familiar with its terminology and research.

A WRITER'S PERSPECTIVE

A great many people think they are thinking when they are merely rearranging their prejudices.

—WILLIAM JAMES

COMPUTER ACTIVITIES

HIGHLIGHTING THE ELEMENTS

Create an electronic version of an assigned reading, or ask students to find an argument-based text of their own. Using the shading function of their word processor, students can highlight the elements of argument in the text, using different colors for claims, evidence, and assumptions.

MISSING ELEMENTS

On your class Web site or via e-mail, post an essay from which you have deleted necessary evidence. Then ask your students to insert comments into their copy of the essay where they think evidence is necessary, and send their commented versions back to you.

RESOURCES AND IDEAS

Brent, Doug. "Young, Becker, and Pike's 'Rogerian' Rhetoric: A Twenty-Year Reassessment." *College English* 53.4 (1991): 452–66. Print. Brent reassesses the usefulness of argument based on common views and values in a culturally diverse world.

Brunk-Chavez, Beth L. "What's So Funny about Stephen Toulmin?: Using Cartoons to Teach the Toulmin Analysis." *Teaching English in the Two-Year College* 32.2 (2004): 179–85. Print. Brunk-Chavez details how she uses cartoons to demonstrate the six parts of Toulmin's model of argument. She finds that cartoons are particularly useful in helping students understand warrants.

Ferris, Dana R. "Rhetorical Strategies in Student Persuasive Writing: Differences Between Native and Non-native Speakers." *Research in the Teaching of English* 28.1 (1994): 45–65. Print. Ferris analyzes sixty persuasive essays by first-year composition students to show the particular difficulties that nonnative speakers can encounter in formulating claims, using data, and anticipating counterarguments.

Katula, Richard A., and Richard W. Roth. "A Stock-Issues Approach to Writing Arguments." *College Composition and Communication* 31.2 (1980): 183–96. Print. The authors use problem-solving strategies as ways to build arguments.

Maxley, John M. "Reinventing the Wheel or Teaching the Basics: College Writers' Knowledge of Argumentation." *Composition Studies: Freshman English News* 21.2 (1993): 3–15. Print. Maxley reviews various approaches to teaching argument, including the "Toulmin model," in an effort to identify the most effective strategies.

Rapkins, Angela A. "The Uses of Logic in the College Freshman English Classroom." *Activities to Promote Critical Thinking: Classroom Practices in Teaching English.* Urbana: NCTE, 1986. Print. Rapkins argues that students should be introduced to logic early in the semester, even if writing arguments comes later.

Roberts-Miller, Patricia. *Deliberate Conflict: Argument, Political Theory, and Composition Classes.* Carbondale: Southern Illinois UP, 2004. Print. Roberts-Miller argues that the transformative power of argument makes it a powerful force in the composition classroom, if instructors understand the many theories and models of argument available.

Schultz, Marcia. "Analyzing Argumentative Strategies." *Teaching English in the Two-Year College* 31.1 (2003): 77–80. Print. Schultz

grounds, terms that indicate both its specificity and its work as an argument's foundation.) Evidence to support the preceding claim might include the following:

The present lab's age and square feet
An inventory of equipment
The testimony of chemistry professors

Like the claims, the evidence is always stated outright.

- **Assumptions:** the writer's underlying (and often unstated) beliefs, opinions, principles, or inferences that tie the evidence to the claims. (Toulmin calls these assumptions *warrants:* they justify making the claims on the basis of the evidence provided.) For instance, the following assumption might connect the evidence of professors' testimony with the claim that a new lab is needed:

Chemistry professors are the persons most capable of evaluating the present lab's quality.

In the following pages, we'll examine each of these elements along with several others: tone and language, reasonableness, and common errors in reasoning. Charlene Robinson's "Weighing the Costs" in the previous chapter (pp. 171–73) provides a good example of critically reading an argument for its claims, evidence, and assumptions.

Questions for critically reading an argument

- What **claims** does the writer make?
- What kinds and quality of **evidence** does the writer provide to support the claims?
- What **assumptions** underlie the argument, connecting evidence to claims? Are they clear and believable?
- What is the writer's **tone?** How does the writer use **language?**
- Is the writer **reasonable?**
- Is the argument **logical?** Does it contain any **fallacies?**
- Are you convinced? Why or why not?

9b Testing claims

The claims or assertions in an argument will likely be statements of opinion, fact, belief, or prejudice. It's important to distinguish between the kinds of statements and to analyze the definitions of terms.

1 Recognizing opinions

An **opinion** is a judgment based on facts and arguable on the basis of facts. Reasonable people could and probably do disagree over opinions, and they are potentially changeable: with more facts, a writer might change opinions partly or wholly.

The thesis statement of an effective argument is an opinion, often one of the following:

- **A claim about past or present reality:**

  In both its space and its equipment, the college's chemistry laboratory is outdated.

  Academic cheating increases with students' economic insecurity.

- **A claim of value:**

  The new room fees are unjustified given the condition of the dormitories.

  Computer music pirates undermine the system that encourages the very creation of music.

- **A recommendation for a course of action,** often a solution to a perceived problem:

  The college's outdated chemistry laboratory should be replaced incrementally over the next five years.

  Schools and businesses can help to resolve the region's traffic congestion by implementing car pools and rewarding participants.

The backbone of an argument consists of specific claims that support the thesis statement. These may be statements of opinion, too, or they may state facts or beliefs.

Opinions do not make arguments by themselves. As a critical reader, you must satisfy yourself that the writer has specified the evidence for the opinions and that the assumptions linking claims and evidence are clear and believable.

2 Recognizing facts

A **fact** may be a verifiable statement—that is, one that can be proved as true:

Last year tuition increased 16 percent.

Or it may be an inference from verifiable facts:

Over their lifetimes, four-year college graduates earn almost twice as much as high school graduates.

A claim of fact does not work as the thesis of an argument. Although people often dispute facts, they are not fundamentally

discusses how she uses accounts of well-known trials to help students understand argument techniques and critique them, and then helps students incorporate those techniques into their own writing.

Toulmin, Stephen, Richard Rieke, and Allan Janik. *An Introduction to Reasoning.* New York: Macmillan, 1979. Print. This is a classic textbook exposition of reasoning.

"STUMP THE CLASS" GAME SHOW

Students can benefit from lots of practice in distinguishing between facts, opinions, beliefs, and prejudices. Divide your class into two teams and give each team a set of statements. The team members have to decide on whether the statement is a fact, opinion, belief, or prejudice. The team that gets the most right answers in the shortest amount of time wins.

WEB CLAIMS

Ask students to locate and visit a blog on an assigned topic (environmentalism, for instance) and follow a thread of conversation. Have them make a list of claims they find and then evaluate whether each claim is one of fact, opinion, belief, or prejudice. Students may find that opinion statements rely upon facts presented in earlier entries by other thread participants, so they should make sure to look beyond a single entry or writer for facts.

DEFINING ARGUMENT

Some students may need instruction on the technical meaning of *argument*, since their view of this rhetorical mode may include only vehement disagreement. Ask students to look up *argument* in various dictionaries and bring a number of definitions of this word to share with their group. Have them discuss how all of the definitions come into play in persuasive writing.

COLLABORATIVE LEARNING

CUT AND PASTE

Ask groups of students to identify an issue, collect newspaper or magazine articles on it, and bring the articles to class (in photocopied form, if possible). Then ask them to work in groups to identify what the articles say on the different sides of the issue and to cut out the assertions and paste them in columns (or simply write them out) according to the particular perspective on the argument they represent.

ANALYZING ISSUES

Break students into groups to discuss a campus issue such as residential policies, parking arrangements, or library or computer services. The goal of students' discussion should be to identify the assertions and supporting evidence on each side of the argument. As each group reports back on their findings, list the assertions and evidence on the board so that students can distinguish fact from opinion and identify terms that need defining. If students know enough about issues of public policy (such as gun control, capital punishment, or nuclear disarmament), these topics, too, can be used for discussion.

arguable because ultimately they can be verified. Facts have another important role in argument, providing crucial evidence for other claims (see p. 182).

3 Recognizing beliefs

A **belief** is a conviction based on cultural or personal faith, morality, or values:

> Abortion is legalized murder.
>
> Capital punishment is legalized murder.
>
> The primary goal of government should be to provide equality of opportunity for all.

Such statements are often called opinions because they express viewpoints, but unlike opinions they are not based on facts and other evidence. Since they cannot be disproved by facts or even contested on the basis of facts, they cannot serve as the central or supporting claims of an argument. However, beliefs can play a significant role in argument. Appeals to readers' beliefs can serve as a kind of evidence by tapping into emotions (see pp. 183 and 205–06), and beliefs often form the assumptions that link claims and evidence (see pp. 183 and 185–86).

4 Recognizing prejudices

One kind of assertion that has no place in argument is a **prejudice,** an opinion based on insufficient or unexamined evidence:

> Women are bad drivers.
> Fat people are jolly.
> Teenagers are irresponsible.
> Athletes are unintelligent.
> People who use wheelchairs have cognitive disabilities.

Unlike a belief, a prejudice is testable: it can be contested and disproved on the basis of facts. Very often, however, we form prejudices or accept them from others—parents, friends, the communications media—without questioning their meaning or testing their truth. Writers who display prejudice do not deserve your confidence and agreement.

When reading arguments that appear online, you should be especially vigilant for claims of belief or prejudice that pose as considered opinions. Anyone with a computer and an Internet connection can post anything on the Internet, without passing it through an editorial screening like that undergone by books and by articles in journals and magazines. The filtering of such material is entirely up to the reader.

5 | Looking for defined terms

In any argument, but especially in arguments about abstract ideas, the clear and consistent definition of terms is essential. In the following claim, the writer is not clear about what she means by the crucial term *justice:*

> Over the past few decades, justice has deteriorated so badly that it almost does not exist anymore.

The word *justice* is **abstract:** it does not refer to anything specific or concrete and in fact has varied meanings. (The five definitions in *The American Heritage Dictionary* include "the principle of moral rightness" and "the administration and procedure of law.") When the writer specifies her meaning, her assertion is much clearer:

> If by *justice* we mean treating people fairly, punishing those who commit crimes, and protecting the victims of those crimes, then justice has deteriorated badly over the past few decades.

Writers who use highly abstract words such as *justice, equality, success,* and *maturity* have a responsibility to define them. If the word is important to the argument, such a definition may take an entire paragraph. As a reader you have the obligation to evaluate the writer's definitions before you accept his or her assertions. (See pp. 95–96 for more on definition and a paragraph defining the abstract word *quality.*)

9c | Weighing evidence

In argument, evidence demonstrates the validity of the writer's claims. If the evidence is inadequate or questionable, the claims are at best doubtful.

1 | Recognizing kinds of evidence

Writers draw on several kinds of evidence to support their claims.

Evidence for argument

- **Facts:** verifiable statements
- **Statistics:** facts expressed in numbers
- **Examples:** specific cases
- **Expert opinions:** the judgments of authorities
- **Appeals to readers' beliefs or needs**

REASSEMBLING AN ARGUMENT

Select a short text that contains claims and evidence. Put each claim or item of evidence on a separate slip of paper and shuffle them. Give a set of randomized slips to each small group of students and ask them to sort the slips into two piles: one pile of claims and another of evidence. If they like, they can then try to match each claim with its appropriate supporting evidence.

PEER REVIEW FOR UNDEFINED TERMS

Ask students to work with their peer review partner to identify abstract terms in their own essays. They can work collaboratively on creating or revising definitions for those terms.

COMPUTER ACTIVITY

TERMS NEEDING DEFINITIONS

Ask students to go online to locate op-ed articles that contain abstract terms. If the author has provided the definition, the student can highlight the definition and insert a comment evaluating the usefulness of the definition. If the author has not defined the term, the student can propose a definition they think would be appropriate in context.

Facts

Facts are statements whose truth can be verified or inferred (see p. 179). Facts employing numbers are **statistics:**

> Of those polled, 62 percent stated a preference for a flat tax.
>
> In 2005 there were 1,370,237 men and women on active duty in the US armed forces.
>
> The average American household consists of 2.58 persons.

Numbers may be implied:

> Earth is closer to the sun than Saturn is.
> The cost of medical care is rising.

Or a fact may involve no numbers at all:

> The city council adjourned without taking a vote.
> The President vetoed the bill.

Examples

Examples are specific instances of the point being made, including historical precedents and personal experiences. The passage below uses a personal narrative as partial support for the claim in the first sentence:

> Besides broadening students' knowledge, required courses can also introduce students to possible careers that they otherwise would have known nothing about. Somewhat reluctantly, I enrolled in a psychology course to satisfy the requirement for work in social science. But what I learned in the course about human behavior has led me to consider becoming a clinical psychologist instead of an engineer.

Expert opinions

Expert opinions are the judgments formed by authorities on the basis of their own examination of the facts. In the following passage the writer cites the opinion of an expert to support the claim in the first sentence:

> Despite the fact that affirmative action places some individuals at a disadvantage, it remains necessary to right the wrongs inflicted historically on whole groups of people. Howard Glickstein, a past director of the US Commission on Civil Rights, maintains that "it simply is not possible to achieve equality and fairness" unless the previous grounds for discrimination (such as sex, race, and national origin) are now considered as grounds for admission to schools and jobs (26).

As this passage illustrates, a citation of expert opinion should always refer you to the source, here indicated by the author's name, Glickstein, and the page number in parentheses, "(26)." Such a citation is also generally accompanied by a reference to the expert's credentials. See pages 623–24 and 634–35.

CULTURE LANGUAGE — In some cultures a person with high standing in government, society, or organized religion may be considered an authority on many different subjects. In American academic and business settings, authority tends to derive from study, learning, and experience: the more knowledge a person can demonstrate about a subject, the more authority he or she has. See the next page on relevant evidence.

Appeals to beliefs or needs

A writer's **appeal to beliefs or needs** asks you to accept an assertion in part because you already accept it as true without evidence or because it coincides with your needs. Each of the following examples combines such an appeal (second sentence) with a summary of factual evidence (first sentence).

> Thus the chemistry laboratory is outdated in its equipment. In addition, its shabby, antiquated appearance shames the school, making it seem a second-rate institution. [Appeals to readers' belief that their school is or should be first-rate.]

> That police foot patrollers reduce crime has already been demonstrated. Such officers might also restore our sense that our neighborhoods are orderly, stable places. [Appeals to readers' need for order and stability.]

(For more on beliefs, see p. 180. For more on appeals to emotion, see pp. 205–06.)

2 Judging the reliability of evidence

To be convinced by evidence, you should see it as reliable. The test of reliability for an appeal to beliefs or needs is specific to the situation: whether it is appropriate for the argument and correctly gauges how you, the reader, actually feel (see p. 206). With the other kinds of evidence, the standards are more general, applying to any argument.

Criteria for weighing evidence

- Is it **accurate**: trustworthy, exact, undistorted?
- Is it **relevant**: authoritative, pertinent, current?
- Is it **representative**: true to context?
- Is it **adequate**: plentiful, specific?

Accuracy

Accurate evidence is true:

- It is drawn from trustworthy sources.
- It is quoted exactly.
- It is presented with the original meaning undistorted.

RESOURCES AND IDEAS

Chambers, Marilyn J. "Text Cues and Strategies Successful Readers Use to Construct the Gist of Lengthy Written Arguments." *Reading Research Quarterly* 30.4 (1995): 778–807. Print. Chambers examines students' strategies for comprehending the argument structure, claims, and evidence in lengthy texts.

McCormick, Kathleen. "Teaching Critical Thinking and Writing." *The Writing Instructor* 2 (1983): 137–44. Print. McCormick suggests having students develop critical and analytical skills by critiquing flawed essays, and she describes several units in a course employing this strategy.

Pederson, Don. "Question and Answer: Reading Nonfiction To Develop the Persuasive Essay." *English Journal* 91.4 (2002): 59–63. Print. Pederson discusses how he has incorporated nonfiction readings into his classes to help students learn to read critically and use that information in their persuasive writing.

Wu, Su-Yueh, and Donald L. Rubin. "Evaluating the Impact of Collectivism and Individualism on Argumentative Writing by Chinese and North American College Students." *Research in the Teaching of English* 35.2 (2000): 148–78. Print. The authors compare features of argumentative writing including indirectness, use of proverbs, and assertiveness from two groups of students: a group from Taiwan, who have a collectivist orientation, and a group from the United States, who have an individualist orientation.

Reading an argument in favor of gun control, you might expect the writer to cite some procontrol sources, which are undoubtedly biased. But you should also look for anticontrol sources (representing the opposite bias) and neutral sources (attempting to be unbiased). If the writer quotes an expert, the quotation should present the expert's true meaning, not just a few words that appear to support the writer's argument. (As a reader you may have difficulty judging the accuracy of quotations if you are not familiar with the expert's opinions.)

Not just opinions but also facts and examples may be misinterpreted or distorted. Suppose you were reading an argument for extending a three-year-old law allowing the police to stop vehicles randomly as a means of apprehending drunk drivers. If the author cited statistics showing that the number of drunk-driving accidents dropped in the first two years of the law but failed to note that the number rose back to the previous level in the third year, then the evidence would be distorted and thus inaccurate. You or any reader would be justified in questioning the entire argument, no matter how accurate the rest seemed.

Relevance

Relevant evidence pertains to the argument:

- **It comes from sources with authority on the subject.**
- **It relates directly to the point the writer is making.**
- **It is current.**

If you are reading an argument against a method of hazardous-waste disposal and the writer offers his church minister's opinion as evidence, you should accept the evidence only if the minister is an authority on the subject and her expertise is up-to-date. If she is an authority on Method A and not Method B, you should accept her authority only about Method A. If the writer relates his own experience of living near a hazardous-waste site, you should accept the story as relevant only if it pertains to his thesis. His authority in this case is that of a close observer and a citizen. (See also p. 192 on the fallacy of false authority.)

Representativeness

Representative evidence is true to its context:

- **It reflects the full range of the sample from which it is said to be drawn.**
- **It does not overrepresent any element of the sample.**

In an essay arguing that dormitories should stay open during school holidays, a writer might say that "the majority of the school's students favor leaving the dormitories open." But that writer would mislead you and other readers if the claim were based only on a poll of her roommates and dormitory neighbors. A few dormitory residents could not be said to represent the entire student body, particularly the nonresident students. To be representative, the poll would have to take in many more students in proportions that reflect the numbers of resident and nonresident students on campus.

Adequacy

Adequate evidence is sufficient:

- It is plentiful enough to support the writer's assertions.
- It is specific enough to support the writer's assertions.

A writer arguing against animal abuse should not hope to win you over solely with statements about her personal experiences and claims of her opinions. Her experience may indeed be relevant evidence if, say, she has worked with animals or witnessed animal abuse. And her opinions are indeed important to the argument, so that you know what she thinks. But even together her experiences and opinions are not adequate evidence: they cannot substitute entirely for facts, nonpersonal examples, and the opinions of experts to demonstrate abuse and describe the scope of the problem.

9d | Discovering assumptions

Assumptions connect evidence to claims: they are the opinions or beliefs that explain why a particular piece of evidence is relevant to a particular claim. As noted in Chapter 7 on critical thinking, assumptions are not flaws in arguments but necessities: we all acquire beliefs and opinions that shape our view of the world. Here are examples of beliefs that you, or people you know, may hold:

> Criminals should be punished.
> Hard work is virtuous.
> Teachers' salaries are too low.

Assumptions are inevitable in argument, but they aren't neutral. For one thing, an assumption can weaken an argument. Say that a writer claims that real estate development should be prevented in your town. As evidence for this claim, the writer offers facts about past developments that have replaced older buildings. But the evidence is relevant to the claim only if you accept the writer's extreme assumptions that old buildings are always worthy and new development is always bad.

In such a case, the writer's bias may not even be stated. Hence a second problem: in arguments both sound and unsound, assumptions are not always explicit. Following are a claim and evidence forming a reasonable argument. What is the unstated assumption?

Claim

The town should create a plan to manage building preservation and new development.

Evidence

Examples of how such plans work; expert opinions on how and why both preservation and development are needed.

In this instance the assumption is that neither uncontrolled development nor zero development is healthy for the town. If you can accept this assumption, you should be able to accept the writer's claim (though you might still disagree over particulars).

Here are tips for dealing with assumptions:

Guidelines for analyzing assumptions

- **What are the assumptions underlying the argument?** How does the writer connect claims with evidence?
- **Are the assumptions believable?** Do they express your values? Do they seem true in your experience?
- **Are the assumptions consistent with one another?** Is the argument's foundation solid, not slippery?

9e Watching language, hearing tone

Tone is the expression of the writer's attitudes toward himself or herself, toward the subject, and toward the reader (see p. 14 for a discussion). Tone can tell you quite a bit about the writer's intentions, biases, and trustworthiness. For example:

> Some women cite personal growth as a reason for pursuing careers while raising children. Of course, they are equally concerned with the personal growth of the children they relegate to "child-care specialists" while they work.

In the second sentence this writer is being **ironic,** saying one thing while meaning another. The word *relegate* and the quotation marks with *child-care specialists* betray the writer's belief that working mothers may selfishly neglect their children for their own needs. Irony can sometimes be effective in argument, but here it marks the author as insincere in dealing with the complex issues of working parents and child care.

When reading arguments, you should be alert to the author's language. Look for words that **connote,** or suggest, certain attitudes and evoke certain responses in readers. (Notice your own responses to these word pairs with related meanings but different connotations: *daring/foolhardy, dislike/detest, glad/joyous, angry/rabid, freedom/license.*) Connotative language is no failure in argument; indeed, the

---

ADVERTISING TONE

People who have something to sell provide examples of subtle or not-so-subtle tone. Have students evaluate print advertisements, commercial Web sites, television ads, even junk mail. How does each solicitor try to persuade the reader to buy/use/subscribe to his or her product?

COLLABORATIVE LEARNING

EUPHEMISM HUNTING

Have students work in small groups to find examples of euphemisms common in public discourse. They can mine the newspaper or other current events organs; speeches made by politicians or government officials; the nightly newscast; or even sources closer to home such as documents produced on campus by student groups. See which group can collect the most examples.

strongest arguments use it skillfully to appeal to readers' hearts as well as their minds (see pp. 205–06). But be suspicious if the language runs counter to the substance of the argument.

Look also for evasive words. **Euphemisms,** such as *attack of a sexual nature* for "rape" or *peace-keeping force* for a war-making army, are supposedly inoffensive substitutes for words that may frighten or offend readers (see pp. 506–07). In argument, though, they are sometimes used to hide or twist the truth. An honest, forthright arguer will avoid them.

Finally, watch carefully for sexist, racist, and other biased language that reveals deep ignorance or, worse, entrenched prejudice on the part of the writer. Obvious examples are *broad* for woman and *fag* for homosexual. (See pp. 507–10 for more on such language.)

9f | Judging reasonableness

The **reasonableness** of an argument is the sense you get as a reader that the author is fair and sincere. The reasonable writer does not conceal or distort facts, hide prejudices, mask belief as opinion, manipulate you with language, or resort to any of dozens of devices used unconsciously by those who don't know better and deliberately by those who do.

Reasonableness involves all the elements of argument examined so far: claims, evidence, assumptions, and language. In addition, the fair, sincere argument always avoids so-called fallacies (covered in the next section), and it acknowledges the opposition.

Judging whether a writer deals adequately with his or her opposition is a fairly simple matter for the reader of argument. By definition, an arguable issue has more than one side. Even if you have no preconceptions about a subject, you will know that another side exists. If the writer pretends otherwise or dismisses the opposition too quickly, you are justified in questioning the honesty and fairness of the argument. (For the more complicated business of *writing* an acknowledgment of opposing views, see pp. 207–08.)

Exercise 9.1   Reading arguments critically

Following are two brief arguments. Though not directly opposed, the two arguments do represent different stances on environmental issues. Read each argument critically, following the process outlined in Chapter 7 (pp. 140–52) and answering the questions in the box on page 178 (questions about claims, evidence, assumptions, and the other elements of argument). Develop your responses in writing so that you can refer to them for later exercises and class discussion.

The Environmental Crisis Is Not Our Fault

I am as responsible as most eco-citizens: I bike everywhere; I don't [1] own a car; I recycle newspapers, bottles, cans, and plastics; I have a

The ecological crisis requires a *drastic overhaul of this civilization*, not individual *life-style solutions* (3). Such solutions divert individuals from the hard truths and hard choices of truly changing consciousness (4).

Evidence: Statistics and other facts: 2–5. Examples: 1, 3–5. Appeals to beliefs or needs: mainly, we should do what's necessary to solve the ecological crisis (throughout).

Assumptions: Notably: There is an environmental crisis. It must be solved. Ozone depletion and rain forest destruction are *corporate crimes* (2). Industry and government are powerful and self-protective. They will not respond appropriately to the ecological crisis unless forced to do so by the people. The people are unwilling to make more than life-style changes to solve the crisis.

Tone: No-nonsense (*I don't . . . believe that I am saving the planet*), unrestrained (*patently corporate crimes; truly pernicious*), sardonic ("*all of us*"; "*our*" *control; life-style solutions; write-your-congressperson solutions*).

Reasonableness: Sale is obviously biased, so his reasonableness will probably reside in the eye of the beholder. He does offer evidence for his key assertion about the environmental responsibility of industry and government, and his examples show him to be familiar with the mentality of most recyclers (a group he even includes himself in). He acknowledges the opposition most clearly in paragraph 5, where he rebuts the claim that the individualistic approach is at least a start on consciousness raising.

Fallacies: See the answer to Exercise 9.4.

Evaluation: Answers will vary.

Oil corporation advertisement

Claims: Thesis (paragraphs 2, 6, 10, 13): Myths about oil exploration, waste, and conservation do not address America's true energy needs. Supporting claims: Offshore drilling is necessary and does not unduly pollute (4). Though heavy, America's energy use is appropriate for the nation's size and productivity (7, 9). Favoring conservation over exploration would increase oil imports or stop economic growth (12).

Evidence: Statistics and other facts: 3–4, 7–9, 12. Examples: 3. Appeals to beliefs or needs: Mainly, America is a strong country whose economic health is crucial for all (throughout).

vegetable garden in the summer; I buy organic products; and I put all vegetable waste into my backyard compost bin, probably the only one in all of Greenwich Village. But I don't at the same time believe that I am saving the planet, or in fact doing anything of much consequence about the various eco-crises around us. What's more, I don't even believe that if "all of us" as individuals started doing the same it would make any but the slightest difference.

Leave aside ozone depletion and rain forest destruction—those are patently corporate crimes that no individual actions can remedy to any degree. Take, instead, energy consumption in this country. In the most recent figures, residential consumption was 7.2 percent of the total, commercial 5.5 percent, and industrial 23.3 percent; of the remainder, 27.8 percent was transportation (about one-third of it by private car) and 36.3 percent was electric generation (about one-third for residential use). Individual energy use, in sum, was something like 28 percent of total consumption. Although you and I cutting down on energy consumption would have some small effect (and should be done), it is surely the energy consumption of industry and other large institutions such as government and agribusiness that needs to be addressed first. And it is industry and government that must be forced to explain what their consumption is for, what is produced by it, how necessary it is, and how it can be drastically reduced. [2]

The point is that the ecological crisis is essentially beyond "our" control, as citizens or householders or consumers or even voters. It is not something that can be halted by recycling or double-pane insulation. It is the inevitable by-product of our modern industrial civilization, dominated by capitalist production and consumption and serviced and protected by various institutions of government, federal to local. It cannot possibly be altered or reversed by simple individual actions, even by the actions of the millions who take part in Earth Day—even if they all go home and fix their refrigerators and from then on walk to work. Nothing less than a drastic overhaul of this civilization and an abandonment of its ingrained gods—progress, growth, exploitation, technology, materialism, anthropocentricity, and power—will do anything substantial to halt our path to environmental destruction, and it's hard to see how life-style solutions will have an effect on that. [3]

What I find truly pernicious about such solutions is that they get people thinking they are actually making a difference and doing their part to halt the destruction of the earth: "There, I've taken all the bottles to the recycling center and used my string bag at the grocery store; I guess that'll take care of global warming." It is the kind of thing that diverts people from the hard truths and hard choices and hard actions, from the recognition that they have to take on the larger forces of society—corporate and governmental—where true power, and true destructiveness, lie. [4]

And to the argument that, well, you have to start somewhere to raise people's consciousness, I would reply that this individualistic approach does not in fact raise consciousness. It does not move people beyond their old familiar liberal perceptions of the world, it does nothing to challenge the belief in technofix or write-your-Congressperson solutions, and it does not begin to provide them with the new vocabulary [5] and modes of thought necessary for a true change of consciousness. We need, for example, to think of recycling centers not as the answer to our waste problems, but as a confession that the system of packaging and production in this society is out of control. Recycling centers are like hospitals; they are the institutions at the end of the cycle that take care of problems that would never exist if ecological criteria had operated at the beginning of the cycle. Until we have those kinds of understandings, we will not do anything with consciousness except reinforce it with the same misguided ideas that created the crisis.

—Kirkpatrick Sale

Myths We Wouldn't Miss

There are tall tales and legends. There are fables and apocryphal 1 stories. And there are myths—a number of which we would like to see disappear. Here are some myths that would not be missed:

MYTH: Offshore drilling would be an ecological disaster.   2

Truth is, there hasn't been a serious spill in US waters resulting from 3 offshore drilling operations in decades—and even that one, in Santa Barbara Channel in 1969, caused no permanent damage to the environment.

This is why we always have such a problem with the reasoning of 4 those who call for moratoriums or outright bans on such activity while the nation continues to import foreign oil. The fact is, oil industry offshore drilling operations cause less pollution than urban runoff, atmospheric phenomena, municipal discharges or natural seeps.

Why this nation would choose *not* to drill for oil and *not* to provide 5 the jobs, profits and taxes such activity would mean for the American economy when there are no better alternatives is a mystery we hope puzzles others as much as it does us.

MYTH: America is a profligate waster of energy.   6

The myth makers like to throw around numbers that read like this: 7 with only 5 percent of the world's population, the US uses about 25 percent of the world's energy. But ours is a big country—three thousand miles from one ocean to the next. Transportation accounts for more than 60 percent of US oil use. We could probably cut down if we moved everybody into one corner of the country, but where is the waste?

It certainly isn't the automobiles that are inefficient. They are twice 8 as efficient as the ones we used thirty years ago. If American drivers use more gasoline than their counterparts in Europe and Japan, it may just have something to do with the country's size.

In fact, proof of the country's size may be in our economic output— 9 and may also hold a clue as to why we use the energy we do. Despite having only 5 percent of the world's population, America may indeed use 25 percent of the world's energy. However, according to the latest statistics, we also produce about 25 percent of the world's goods and services. Again, where's the waste?

MYTH: Conservation is *the answer* to America's energy problems.   10

No doubt about it, we all need to be careful of the amount of 11 energy we use. But as long as this nation's economy needs to grow, we are going to need energy to fuel that growth.

For the foreseeable future, there are no viable alternatives to petro- 12 leum as the major source of energy, especially for transportation fuels.

Assumptions: Notably: Policy needs to be guided by truths, not myths. Importing foreign oil is undesirable. Some pollution is inevitable and acceptable. America is justified in using energy proportionate to its size and productivity. Conservation is desirable. Economic growth is essential.

Tone: Sincere (*a mystery we hope puzzles others as much as it does us; We probably can—and should—do more*), candid (*Truth is; The fact is; In fact; Let's face it; No doubt about it*), perplexed (*We always have such a problem; where is the waste*).

Reasonableness: Like Sale's essay, the ad is strongly biased, but the statistics and other facts and the sincere tone contribute to a sense of reasonableness. So do the several bows to the opposition, including the statements of the objectionable myths themselves and the support for con-servation.

Fallacies: See the answer to Exercise 9.4.

Evaluation: Answers will vary.

Let's face it. Over the past thirty years we *have* learned to conserve—in our factories, our homes, our cars. We probably can—and should—do more. But conservation and new exploration should not be mutually exclusive, because even without an increase in energy consumption, we are using up domestic reserves of oil and gas and must replace them. For the good of the economy, those reserves should be replaced with new domestic production, to the extent economically possible. Otherwise, the only solutions would be additional imports or no growth. And stifling growth would be a gross disservice to the people for whom such growth would provide the opportunity for a better life.

Simply put, America is going to need more energy for all its people. 13
And that is no myth. 14

—Oil corporation advertisement

9g Recognizing fallacies

Fallacies—errors in argument—fall into two groups. Some evade the issue of the argument. Others treat the argument as if it were much simpler than it is.

1 Recognizing evasions

The central claim of an argument defines an issue or question: Should real estate development be controlled? Should drug testing be mandatory in the workplace? An effective argument faces the central issue squarely with relevant opinions, beliefs, and evidence. An ineffective argument dodges the issue.

Begging the question

A writer **begs the question** by treating an opinion that is open to question as if it were already proved or disproved. In essence, the writer begs readers to accept his or her ideas from the start.

The college library's expenses should be reduced by cutting subscriptions to useless periodicals. [Begged questions: Are some of the library's periodicals useless? Useless to whom?]

The fact is that political campaign financing is too corrupt to be reformed. [Begged questions: How corrupt is campaign financing? Does corruption, even if extensive, put campaign financing beyond reform?]

Non sequitur

A **non sequitur** occurs when no logical relation exists between two or more connected ideas. In Latin *non sequitur* means "it does not follow." In the sentences below, the second thought does not follow from the first:

She uses a wheelchair, so she must be unhappy. [The second clause does not follow from the first.]

NAMING FALLACIES

Many students are put off by the terminology used to classify fallacies. Let them know that the fallacies sometimes overlap and that it is more important for them to recognize and avoid oversimplifications and evasions than to know the correct terms for them.

COMPUTER ACTIVITIES

FALLACY HUNTING

To sharpen student sensitivity to fallacies, tell your students to go "fallacy hunting" on the Web. Each student should try to collect at least one example of each fallacy on the checklist. You can prepare a "dictionary of fallacies" to be posted on your class Web site.

WATCHING FALLACIES IN ACTION

On *YouTube* or a similar site, find clips of politicians giving speeches. (Stump speeches can work well for this purpose.) If possible, find two or three clips from politicians of various persuasions. Then, show the clips to students and ask them to point out and name any fallacies used. It can be helpful for students to see that many political speeches use fallacies, and that fallacies are not specific to a particular politician or party. If you want to extend the activity, ask students to find their own clips online and analyze them for fallacies.

Checklist of fallacies

Evasions

- **Begging the question:** treating an opinion that is open to question as if it were already proved or disproved.
- **Non sequitur** ("it does not follow"): drawing a conclusion from irrelevant evidence.
- **Red herring:** introducing an irrelevant issue to distract readers.
- **False authority:** citing as expert opinion the views of a person who is not an expert.
- **Inappropriate appeals:**

  Appealing to readers' fear or pity.
  Snob appeal: appealing to readers' wish to be like those who are more intelligent, famous, rich, and so on.
  Bandwagon: appealing to readers' wish to be part of the group.
  Flattery: appealing to readers' intelligence, taste, and so on.
  Argument ad populum ("to the people"): appealing to readers' general values, such as patriotism or love of family.
  Argument ad hominem ("to the man"): attacking the opponent rather than the opponent's argument.

Oversimplifications

- **Hasty generalization (jumping to a conclusion):** asserting an opinion based on too little evidence.
- **Sweeping generalization:** asserting an opinion as applying to all instances when it may apply to some, or to none. **Absolute statements** and **stereotypes** are variations.
- **Reductive fallacy:** generally, oversimplifying causes and effects.
- **Post hoc fallacy:** assuming that *A* caused *B* because *A* preceded *B*.
- **Either/or fallacy (false dilemma):** reducing a complicated question to two alternatives.
- **False analogy:** exaggerating the similarities in an analogy or ignoring key differences.

Kathleen Newsome has my vote for mayor because she has the best-run campaign organization. [Shouldn't one's vote be based on the candidate's qualities, not the campaign's organization?]

Red herring

A **red herring** is literally a kind of fish that might be drawn across a path to distract a bloodhound from a scent it's following. In argument, a red herring is an irrelevant issue intended to distract readers from the relevant issues. The writer changes the subject rather than pursue the argument.

A campus speech code is essential to protect students, who already have enough problems coping with rising tuition. [Tuition costs and speech codes are different subjects. What protections do students need that a speech code will provide?]

Instead of developing a campus speech code that will infringe on students' First Amendment rights, administrators should be figuring out how to prevent another tuition increase. [Again, tuition costs and speech codes are different subjects. How would the code infringe on rights?]

False authority

Arguments often cite as evidence the opinions of people who are experts on the subject (see pp. 182–83). But writers use **false authority** when they cite as an expert someone whose expertise is doubtful or nonexistent.

Jason Bing, a recognized expert in corporate finance, maintains that pharmaceutical companies do not test their products thoroughly enough. [Bing's expertise in corporate finance bears no apparent relation to the testing of pharmaceuticals.]

According to Helen Liebowitz, the Food and Drug Administration has approved sixty dangerous drugs in the last two years alone. [Who is Helen Liebowitz? On what authority does she make this claim?]

Inappropriate appeals

Appeals to readers' emotions are common in effective arguments. But such appeals must be relevant and must supplement rather than substitute for facts, examples, and other evidence.

Writers sometimes ignore the question with **appeals to readers' fear or pity.**

By electing Susan Clark to the city council, you will prevent the city's economic collapse. [Trades on people's fears. Can Clark singlehandedly prevent economic collapse? Is collapse even likely?]

She should not have to pay taxes because she is an aged widow with no friends or relatives. [Appeals to people's pity. Should age and loneliness, rather than income, determine a person's tax obligation?]

Sometimes writers ignore the question by appealing to readers' sense of what other people believe or do. One approach is **snob appeal,** inviting readers to accept an assertion in order to be identified with others they admire.

As any literate person knows, James Joyce is the best twentieth-century novelist. [But what qualities of Joyce's writing make him a superior novelist?]

Tiger Woods has an account at Big City Bank, and so should you. [A celebrity's endorsement does not guarantee the worth of a product, a service, an idea, or anything else.]

A similar tactic invites readers to accept an assertion because everybody else does. This is the **bandwagon approach.**

As everyone knows, marijuana use leads to heroin addiction. [What is the evidence?]

Yet another diversion involves **flattery** of readers, in a way inviting them to join in a conspiracy.

We all understand campus problems well enough to see the disadvantages of such a policy. [What are the disadvantages of the policy?]

The **argument ad populum** ("argument to the people") asks readers to accept a conclusion based on shared values or even prejudices and nothing else.

Any truly patriotic American will support the President's action. [But why is the action worth taking?]

One final and very common kind of inappropriate emotional appeal addresses *not* the pros and cons of the issue itself but the real or imagined negative qualities of the people who hold the opposing view. This kind of argument is called **ad hominem**, Latin for "to the man."

One of the scientists has been treated for emotional problems, so his pessimism about nuclear waste merits no attention. [Do the scientist's previous emotional problems invalidate his current views?]

2 Recognizing oversimplifications

To **oversimplify** is to conceal or ignore complexities in a vain attempt to create a neater, more convincing argument than reality allows.

Hasty generalization

A **hasty generalization**, also called **jumping to a conclusion**, is a claim based on too little evidence or on evidence that is unrepresentative. (See also pp. 184–85.)

It is disturbing that several of the youths who shot up schools were users of violent video games. Obviously, these games can breed violence, and they should be banned. [A few cases do not establish the relation between the games and violent behavior. Most youths who play violent video games do not behave violently.]

From the way it handled this complaint, we can assume that the consumer protection office has little intention of protecting consumers. [One experience with the office does not demonstrate its intention or overall performance.]

Sweeping generalization

Whereas a hasty generalization comes from inadequate evidence, a **sweeping generalization** probably is not supportable at all.

RESOURCES AND IDEAS

Moore, Vincent. "Using Role Playing in Argument Papers to Deconstruct Stereotypes." *Teaching English in the Two-Year College* 22.3 (1995): 190–96. Print. Moore argues for the efficacy of role-playing to help students gain flexibility in seeing multiple perspectives when developing an argument.

Rapkins, Angela A. "The Uses of Logic in the College Freshman English Curriculum." *Activities to Promote Critical Thinking.* Ed. Jeff Golub. Urbana: NCTE, 1986. 130–35. Print. Rapkins suggests emphasizing logic in all the papers in a course and describes in detail the use of ads in a final argumentation unit, a strategy that expands awareness of the logical fallacies students have been developing throughout the course.

Have students work in groups to list and analyze the fallacies found in Exercise 9.2. Ask each group to present the advertisement with the most blatant or surprising fallacy to the class.

Ask students to work in groups on Exercise 9.4. After completing the exercise, each group might go on to compose an advertisement in which the argument for the product contains each of these fallacies.

ANSWERS: EXERCISE 9.2

Individual response.

ANSWERS: EXERCISE 9.3

Possible answers

1. Begged question, argument ad populum, and false analogy.

   A revision: The fact that individuals in the United States cannot legally sell nuclear technology to nonnuclear nations, which the government can, points up a disturbing limit on individual rights.

One kind of sweeping generalization is the **absolute statement** involving words such as *all, always, never,* and *no one* that allow no exceptions. Rarely can evidence support such terms. Moderate words such as *some, sometimes, rarely,* and *few* are more reasonable.

Another common sweeping generalization is the **stereotype,** a conventional and oversimplified characterization of a group of people.

> People who live in cities are unfriendly.
> Californians are fad-crazy.
> Women are emotional.
> Men can't express their feelings.

(See also pp. 507–10 on sexist and other biased language.)

Reductive fallacy

The **reductive fallacy** oversimplifies (or reduces) the relation between causes and their effects. The fallacy (sometimes called **oversimplification**) often involves linking two events as if one caused the other directly, whereas the causes may be more complex or the relation may not exist at all. For example:

> Poverty causes crime. [If so, then why do people who are not poor commit crimes? And why aren't all poor people criminals?]

> The better a school's athletic facilities are, the worse its academic programs are. [The sentence assumes a direct cause-and-effect link between athletics and scholarship.]

Post hoc fallacy

Related to the reductive fallacy is the assumption that because *A* preceded *B*, then *A* must have caused *B*. This fallacy is called in Latin *post hoc, ergo propter hoc,* meaning "after this, therefore because of this," or the **post hoc fallacy** for short.

> In the two months since he took office, Mayor Holcomb has allowed crime in the city to increase 12 percent. [The increase in crime is probably attributable to conditions existing before Holcomb took office.]

> The town council erred in permitting the adult bookstore to open, for shortly afterward two women were assaulted. [It cannot be assumed without evidence that the women's assailants visited or were influenced by the bookstore.]

Either/or fallacy

In the **either/or fallacy** (also called **false dilemma**), the writer assumes that a complicated question has only two answers, one good and one bad, both bad, or both good.

> City police officers are either brutal or corrupt. [Most city police officers are neither.]

Either we permit mandatory drug testing in the workplace or productivity will continue to decline. [Productivity is not necessarily dependent on drug testing.]

False analogy

An **analogy** is a comparison between two essentially unlike things for the purpose of definition or illustration. In arguing by analogy, a writer draws a likeness between things on the basis of a single shared feature and then extends the likeness to other features. For instance, the "war on drugs" equates a battle against a foe with a program to eradicate (or at least reduce) sales and use of illegal drugs. Both involve an enemy, a strategy of overpowering the enemy, a desired goal, officials in uniform, and other similarities.

Analogy can only illustrate a point, never prove it: just because things are similar in one respect, they are not *necessarily* alike in other respects. In the fallacy called **false analogy**, the writer assumes such a complete likeness. Here is the analogy of the war on drugs taken to its false extreme:

> To win the war on drugs, we must wage more of a military-style operation. Prisoners of war are locked up without the benefit of a trial by jury, and drug dealers should be, too. Soldiers shoot their enemy on sight, and officials who encounter big drug operators should be allowed to shoot them, too. Military traitors may be executed, and corrupt law enforcers could be, too.

Exercise 9.2   Analyzing advertisements

Leaf through a magazine or watch commercial television for half an hour, looking for advertisements that attempt to sell a product not on the basis of its worth but by snob appeal, flattery, or other inappropriate appeals to emotions. Be prepared to discuss the advertisers' techniques. (See Chapter 11, pp. 225–26, if you need help analyzing the appeals in images.)

Exercise 9.3   Identifying and revising fallacies

Fallacies tend to appear together, as each of the following sentences illustrates. Identify at least one fallacy in each sentence. Then revise the sentences to make them more reasonable.

1. The American government can sell nuclear technology to nonnuclear nations, so why can't individuals, who after all have a God-given right to earn a living as they see fit?
2. A successful marriage demands a maturity that no one under twenty-five possesses.
3. Students' persistent complaints about the grading system prove that it is unfair.
4. People watch television because they are too lazy to talk or read or because they want mindless escape from their lives.
5. Racial tension is bound to occur when people with different backgrounds are forced to live side by side.

2. Sweeping generalization and begged question.
   A revision: A successful marriage demands a degree of maturity.
3. Hasty generalization and non sequitur.
   A revision: Students' persistent complaints about the unfairness of the grading system should be investigated.
4. Either/or fallacy and hasty generalization.
   A revision: People watch television for many reasons, but some watch because they are too lazy to talk or read or because they want mindless escape from their lives.
5. Reductive fallacy and begged question.
   A revision: Racial tension may occur when people with different backgrounds live side by side.

ANSWERS: EXERCISE 9.4 (next page)
Possible answers

Though free of the most egregious appeals, the Sale essay and the advertisement both demonstrate several basic fallacies. Most notably:

Kirkpatrick Sale essay

Either/or: Either we achieve a *drastic overhaul of our civilization* or the environment will be destroyed (paragraph 3).

Begged question: The individualistic approach to environmental problems does not *challenge the belief in technofix or write-your-Congressperson solutions* [Do these not work?] or achieve an essential, fundamental change in thinking [Is the change essential?] (5).

False analogy: The analogy between recycling centers and hospitals (5) implies that a preventive approach (*ecological criteria* for packaging and production; preventive medicine) would eliminate the need for the institution. This isn't true of hospitals (people would still get sick), so how is it true of recycling centers?

Oil corporation advertisement

Begged question: The fact is, oil industry offshore drilling operations cause less pollution than other sources of pollution (4). [But how much pollution do the drilling operations cause?]

Either/or: Either we move everyone to one place or we continue to use a disproportionate amount of the world's energy (7).

(continued from page 195)

Either/or: Either we find more energy or the economy will not grow; either we find more energy or we will have to increase imports (2).

Begged question: Despite good conservation efforts, we still need petroleum exploration (12). [But why can't conservation be improved to eliminate the need for risky exploration?]

ANSWERS: EXERCISE 9.5

Individual response.

HIGHLIGHTS

This chapter introduces students to the process of conceiving their own written arguments. Discussions of subject, thesis, purpose, and audience are considered before the chapter turns to the concepts of inductive and deductive argumentation. As they construct their own arguments, students will consider their own use of evidence, the most effective kinds of appeals to readers, how to deal with opposing views, how to organize their arguments, and how to revise their arguments. A helpful checklist for revising an argument appears on p. 211. The chapter concludes with an annotated sample argument written by a student.

The Internet can be particularly useful for the novice argument-builder. A series of exercises in this chapter's annotations asks students to work with blogs: to evaluate subjects, theses, purposes, and audience. You could create an extended project in which students mine blogs for the elements of argument and then construct one of their own.

LISTING PRIORITIES AND VALUES

Ask groups of students first to list the five (or ten) issues they consider most worth arguing about and then to record their different opinions about the top two or three.

Exercise 9.4 Identifying fallacies in arguments

Analyze the two arguments on pages 187–90 for fallacies. To what extent do any fallacies weaken either argument? Explain.

Exercise 9.5 Identifying fallacies online

At *blogsearch.google.com* or *groups.yahoo.com*, find a conversation about drug testing in the workplace, environmental pollution, violence in the media, or any other subject that interests you and that is debatable. Read through the arguments made in the conversation, noting the fallacies you see. List the fallacious statements as well as the types of fallacies they illustrate, keeping in mind that a given statement may illustrate more than a single type.

10

Writing an Argument

In composing an argument, you try to clarify an issue or solve a problem by finding the common ground between you and your readers. Using critical thinking, you develop and test your own ideas. Using a variety of techniques, you engage readers in an attempt to narrow the distance between your views and theirs.

This chapter introduces the process and techniques of composing a written argument. The next chapter discusses the use of images, such as photographs and charts, as effective tools for argument.

10a Finding a subject

An argument subject must be arguable—that is, reasonable people will disagree over it and be able to support their positions with evidence. This sentence implies the *do*s and *don't*s listed in the box on the facing page.

mycomplab

Visit *mycomplab.com* for more resources as well as exercises on writing arguments.

Tests for an argument subject

A good subject:

- Concerns a matter of opinion—a conclusion drawn from evidence.
- Can be disputed: others might take a different position.
- *Will* be disputed: it is controversial.
- Is something you care about and know about or want to research.
- Is narrow enough to argue in the space and time available.

A bad subject:

- Cannot be disputed because it concerns a fact, such as the distance to Saturn or the functions of the human liver.
- Cannot be disputed because it concerns a personal preference or belief, such as a liking for a certain vacation spot or a moral commitment to vegetarianism.
- *Will not* be disputed because few if any disagree over it—the virtues of a secure home, for instance.

Additional help on subjects for writing appears earlier in this book:

- **Working with a specific assignment,** pages 6–7.
- **Working with a general assignment,** page 7.
- **Narrowing a subject to a question,** pages 7–9.

CULTURE LANGUAGE Choosing a subject for argument may seem difficult if you're not familiar with what people in the United States find debatable. One way to find a subject is to scout online discussion groups, such as those listed at *groups.yahoo.com,* for subjects on which there is a range of opinion. Another approach is to read a newspaper every day for at least a week, looking for issues that involve or interest you. Following the development of the issues in articles, editorials, and letters to the editor will give you a sense of how controversial they are, what the positions are, and what your position might be.

Exercise 10.1 Finding a subject for argument
Explain why each subject below is or is not appropriate for argument. Refer to the box above if you need help.

1. Granting of athletic scholarships
2. Care of automobile tires
3. Censoring the Web sites of hate groups
4. History of the town park
5. Housing for the homeless
6. Billboards in urban residential areas or in rural areas
7. Animal testing for cosmetics research

RESTRICTED LISTS

Ask students to prepare lists as above, but to restrict the list to a specific area, such as sports, the economy, or drugs. In so doing, you will create a situation in which students will need to go beyond obvious issues and opinions to complete their lists.

COLLABORATIVE LEARNING

THE ART OF LAMPOON

In the course of your work on what makes a good topic for argument, you might ask your students to come up with a subject that is ridiculous but nonetheless is technically possible to argue. (Give them a copy of Jonathan Swift's "A Modest Proposal" as an example.) Ask them to work with partners to write an argument based upon their subject and then to read it aloud to the class. The results can be hilarious.

COMPUTER ACTIVITY

INTERNET DEBATES

Blogs are prime sites for argumentation, both the elegant and the sophomoric. Have your students explore some hotly debated topics on their favorite Web sites and compile a list of the best and worst subjects for argument.

COLLABORATIVE LEARNING

Have students work on Exercise 10.1 in groups and then share their group's findings with those of the rest of the class.

ANSWERS: EXERCISE 10.1
Possible answers

Topics that are not appropriate for argument:

2. A matter of facts, and few people would disagree.
4. A matter of facts, and few people would disagree.
8. A matter of personal preference.
9. A matter of facts.
10. A matter of personal belief.

INTERNET THESES

As a follow-up to the "Internet debates" exercise suggested in 10a (see above), ask your students to find examples of good thesis statements among the blogs they have been shadowing.

THESIS POSTING

If you are working in a wired classroom, you might post the list of potential subjects to your Web site and ask students to add thesis statements with analyses of purpose and audience.

TELEVISED ARGUMENTS

Ask small groups of students to gather outside of class to watch C-Span, or find political speeches online on *YouTube*. Ask them to see if they can agree on what the thesis statement is for each speech they watch, and keep a class collection of those thesis statements.

For Exercise 10.2, encourage groups to come up with more than one possible thesis for each appropriate topic and then have each group present their most compelling thesis statements.

ANSWERS: EXERCISE 10.2

Possible answers

Thesis statements for appropriate topics in Exercise 10.1:

1. An athletic scholarship should be what the term implies: an award to one who is both a superior athlete and a superior scholar.
3. Although censoring the Web sites of hate groups might offer some protection to persecuted groups or individuals, such censorship would be far too costly to free speech.
5. Until the city can construct private housing for the homeless, it must do more to make public shelters safe and clean.
6. Billboards help to destabilize urban neighborhoods by creating the impression that the neighborhoods are mere roadways.
7. Humane testing methods are adequate enough that cosmetics companies do not have to abuse animals in testing.

8. Cats versus dogs as pets
9. Ten steps in recycling wastepaper
10. Benefits of being a parent

 10b Conceiving a thesis statement

The **thesis** is the main idea of your paper (see pp. 27–32). In an argument the **thesis statement** makes the claim that you want your readers to accept or act on. Here are two thesis statements on the same subject:

> The new room fees are unjustified given the condition of the dormitories.

> The administration should postpone the new room fees at least until conditions in the dormitories are improved.

Your thesis statement must satisfy the same requirements as your subject (see the box on the previous page). But it must also specify the basis for your claim. In both thesis statements above, the basis for protesting the room fees is that the dorms are in poor condition.

Note that the writer of either of these arguments must clarify the definition of *condition(s)* if the argument is to be clear and reasonable. Always take pains to define abstract and general terms that are central to your argument, preferably in or just after the thesis statement. (See p. 181.)

Exercise 10.2 Conceiving a thesis statement

For each subject in Exercise 10.1 that you deemed arguable, draft a tentative thesis statement that specifies the basis for an argument. If you prefer, choose five arguable subjects of your own and draft a thesis statement for each one. One thesis statement should interest you enough to develop into a complete argument in later exercises.

10c Analyzing your purpose and your audience

Your purpose in argument is, broadly, to engage readers in order to convince them of your position or persuade them to act. But arguments have more specific purposes as well, such as the following:

> To strengthen the commitment of existing supporters
> To win new supporters from the undecided or uninformed
> To get the opposition to reconsider
> To inspire supporters to act
> To deter the undecided from acting

It's no accident that each of these purposes characterizes the audience (*existing supporters, the undecided,* and so on). In argument, even more than in other kinds of writing, achieving your purpose depends on the response of your readers, so you need a sense of who they are and where they stand. The "Questions About Audience" on page 13 can help you identify readers' knowledge, beliefs, and other pertinent information. In addition, you need to know how readers stand on your subject—not only whether they agree or disagree generally, but also which specific assertions they will find more or less convincing.

Your purpose can help you fill in this information. If you decide to address supporters or opponents, you essentially select readers with certain inclinations and ignore other readers who may tune in. If you decide to win new supporters from those who are undecided on your topic, you'll have to imagine skeptical readers who will be convinced only by an argument that is detailed, logical, and fair. Like you when you read an argument critically, these skeptical readers seek to be reasoned with, not manipulated into a position or hammered over the head.

> **Exercise 10.3   Analyzing purpose and audience**
> Specify a purpose and a likely audience for the thesis statement you chose to develop in Exercise 10.2. What do purpose and audience suggest about the way you should develop the argument?

10d Using reason

As a reader of argument, you seek evidence for the writer's claims and clear reasoning about the relationship of evidence to claims. As a writer of argument, you seek to provide what the reader needs in a way that furthers your case.

The thesis of your argument is a conclusion you reach by reasoning about evidence. Two common processes of reasoning are induction and deduction—methods of thinking that you use all the time even if you don't know their names. You can think of induction and deduction as two different ways of moving among claims, evidence, and assumptions—the elements of argument derived from Stephen Toulmin's work (pp. 177–78).

1 Reasoning inductively

When you're about to buy a used car, you consult friends, relatives, and consumer guides before deciding what kind of car to buy. Using **inductive reasoning,** you make specific observations about cars (your evidence) and you induce, or infer, a **generalization** (or claim) that Model X is the most reliable. Writing a paper on the effectiveness of print advertising, you might also use inductive reasoning:

COLLABORATIVE LEARNING

AUDIENCE APPEALS

Have the class select two or three broad subjects; then, in small groups, have them decide what more focused purposes they could have in writing about such subjects and what evidence and appeals they would choose in writing for different audiences. If the topic is "censorship," for instance, you might have groups arguing for or against certain kinds of censorship for audiences ranging from the library trustees to the city council to the manager at a local DVD rental store.

COMPUTER ACTIVITY

INTERNET PURPOSES AND AUDIENCES

As a follow-up to the "Internet debates" and "Internet theses" exercises suggested for 10a and 10b, ask your students to describe the purpose and intended audience of each thesis statement they collect from the blogs they have been shadowing.

Inductive reasoning

First analyze statistics on advertising in print and in other media (evidence).
Then read comments by advertisers and publishers (more evidence).
Finally, form a conclusion that print is the most cost-effective advertising medium (generalization).

This reasoning builds from the evidence to the claim, with assumptions connecting evidence to claim. By predicting something about the unknown based on what you know, you create new knowledge out of old.

The more evidence you accumulate, the more probable it is that your generalization is true. Note, however, that absolute certainty is not possible. At some point you must *assume* that your evidence justifies your generalization, for yourself and your readers. Most errors in inductive reasoning involve oversimplifying either the evidence or the generalization. See pages 190–95 on fallacies.

2 | Reasoning deductively

You use **deductive reasoning** when you proceed from your generalization that Model X is the most reliable used car to your own specific circumstances (you want to buy a used car) to the conclusion (or claim) that you should buy a Model X car. Like induction, deduction uses the elements of argument—claims, evidence, and assumptions—but with it you apply old information to new.

Deductive reasoning

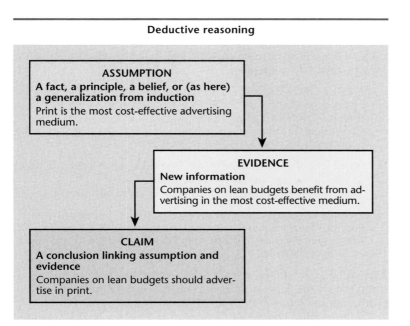

ASSUMPTION
A fact, a principle, a belief, or (as here) a generalization from induction
Print is the most cost-effective advertising medium.

EVIDENCE
New information
Companies on lean budgets benefit from advertising in the most cost-effective medium.

CLAIM
A conclusion linking assumption and evidence
Companies on lean budgets should advertise in print.

Lynch, Dennis A., Diana George, and Marilyn M. Cooper. "Moments of Argument: Agonistic Inquiry and Confrontational Cooperation." *College Composition and Communication* 48.1 (1997): 61–85. Print. The authors propose a concept of argument that contains elements of both the nonconfrontational argument advocated by Lamb and Lunsford, and Ede, and the more antagonistic argument advocated by Bizzell, Jarratt, and others.

The deductive syllogism

The conventional way of displaying a deductive argument is in a **syllogism**:

Premise: All human beings are mortal. [A generalization, fact, principle, or belief that you assume to be true.]
Premise: I am a human being. [New information: a specific case of the first premise.]
Conclusion: Therefore, I am mortal.

As long as the premises of a syllogism are true, the conclusion derives logically and certainly from them. If you want the school administration to postpone new room fees for one dormitory, your deductive argument might be expressed in this syllogism:

Premise: The administration should not raise fees on dorm rooms in poor condition.
Premise: The rooms in Polk Hall are in poor condition.
Conclusion: Therefore, the administration should not raise fees on the rooms in Polk Hall.

The force of deductive reasoning depends on the reliability of the premises and the care taken to apply them in drawing conclusions. The reasoning process is **valid** if the premises lead logically to the conclusion. It is **true** if the premises are believable.

COMPUTER TEMPLATES AND OUTLINE TOOLS

Outlining tools of word-processing programs can help students work through inductive or deductive schema. Students can make templates in their word-processing programs, with categories for evidence, assumptions, and assertions (induction) and for premises and conclusions (deduction). Then they can use the templates to plug in data to build specific logical arguments.

INTERNET LOGIC

As a follow-up to the "Internet debates," "Internet theses," and "Internet purposes and audiences" exercises suggested for 10a, 10b, and 10d, ask your students to find good examples of inductive and deductive reasoning in the blogs they have been shadowing.

Problems with syllogisms

Sometimes the reasoning in a deductive argument is true because the premises are believable, but it is *not* valid because the conclusion doesn't derive logically from the premises:

> **Premise:** The administration should not raise fees on dorm rooms in poor condition.
> **Premise:** Tyler Hall is a dormitory.
> **Conclusion:** Therefore, the administration should not raise fees on the rooms in Tyler Hall.

Both premises may be true, but the first does not *necessarily* apply to the second, so the conclusion is invalid.

Sometimes, too, deductive reasoning is valid but *not* true:

> **Premise:** All college administrations are indifferent to students' needs.
> **Premise:** The administration of Central State is a college administration.
> **Conclusion:** Therefore, the administration of Central State is indifferent to students' needs.

This syllogism is valid but useless: the first premise is an untrue assumption, so the entire argument is untrue. Invalid and untrue syllogisms underlie many of the fallacies discussed on pages 190–95.

A particular hazard of deductive reasoning is the **unstated premise:** the basic assumption linking evidence and conclusion is not stated but implied. Here the unstated premise is believable and the argument is reasonable:

> Ms. Stein has worked with drug addicts for fifteen years, so she knows a great deal about their problems. [Unstated premise: Anyone who has worked fifteen years with drug addicts knows about their problems.]

But when the unstated premise is wrong or unfounded, the argument is false. For example:

> Since Jane Lightbow is a senator, she must receive money illegally from lobbyists. [Unstated premise: All senators receive money illegally from lobbyists.]

To avoid such false conclusions, you may be tempted to make your claims sound more reasonable. But even a conclusion that sounds reasonable must be supportable. For instance, changing *must* to *might* modifies the unstated assumption about Senator Lightbow:

> Since Jane Lightbow is a senator, she might receive money illegally from lobbyists. [Unstated premise: *Some* senators receive money illegally from lobbyists.]

But it does not necessarily follow that Senator Lightbow is one of the "some." The sentence, though logical, is not truly reasonable unless evidence demonstrates that Senator Lightbow should be linked with illegal activities.

Tests for inductive and deductive reasoning

Induction

- Have you stated your evidence clearly?
- Is your evidence complete enough and good enough to justify your claim? What is the assumption that connects evidence and claim? Is it believable?
- Have you avoided fallacies?

Deduction

- What are the premises leading to your conclusion? Look especially for unstated premises.
- What does the first premise assume? Is the assumption believable?
- Does the first premise necessarily apply to the second premise?
- Is the second premise believable?
- Have you avoided fallacies?

Exercise 10.4 Reasoning inductively

Study the facts below and then evaluate each of the numbered conclusions following them. Which of the generalizations are reasonable given the evidence, and which are not? Why?

In 2006–07 each American household viewed an average of 57 hours and 12 minutes of television, DVDs, or videos weekly.

Each individual viewed an average of 16 hours and 23 minutes every week.

Those viewing the most television per week (36 hours and 58 minutes) were women over age 55.

Those viewing the least television per week (23 hours and 34 minutes) were teens, ages 12–17.

Households earning under $30,000 a year watched an average of 59 hours and 55 minutes a week.

Households earning more than $60,000 a year watched an average of 55 hours and 7 minutes a week.

1. Households with incomes under $30,000 tend to watch more television than average.
2. Women watch more television than men.
3. Nonaffluent people watch less television than affluent people.
4. Women over age 55 tend to watch more television than average.
5. Teens watch less television than critics generally assume.

Exercise 10.5 Reasoning deductively

Convert each of the following statements into a syllogism. (You may have to state unstated assumptions.) Use the syllogism to evaluate both the validity and the truth of the statement.

Students can work effectively together on Exercises 10.4 and 10.5. To foster a more active discussion of likely inferences and deductions, ask each group to note places where individuals disagree and to pose those cases to the class as a whole.

ANSWERS: EXERCISE 10.4

The unreasonable generalizations from the given evidence are statements 2 (can't be inferred from the facts), 3 (contradicted by the facts), and 5 (can't be inferred from the facts).

ANSWERS: EXERCISE 10.5
Possible answers

1. *Premise:* Anyone who has opposed pollution controls may continue to do so.
   Premise: The mayor has opposed pollution controls.
   Conclusion: The mayor may continue to do so.
   The statement is valid and true.
2. *Premise:* Corporate Web sites are sponsored by for-profit entities.
   Premise: Information from for-profit entities is unreliable.
   Conclusion: Information on corporate Web sites is unreliable.
   The statement is untrue because the second premise is untrue.
3. *Premise:* Many good artists trained at Parsons.
   Premise: Schroeder trained at Parsons.
   Conclusion: Schroeder is a good artist.
   The statement is invalid because the first premise does not necessarily apply to the second.
4. *Premise:* Those who use their resources to help others deserve our particular appreciation.
   Premise: Some wealthy athletes use their resources to help others.
   Conclusion: Some wealthy athletes deserve our particular appreciation.
   The statement is valid and, if the first premise is accepted, true.
5. *Premise:* Any employer who has hired only one woman is sexist.
   Premise: Jimson is an employer who has hired only one woman.
   Conclusion: Jimson is sexist.
   The statement is untrue because the first premise is not true: there may be other reasons besides sexism for hiring only one woman.

RESOURCES AND IDEAS

Corrigan, Dagmar Stuehrk, and Chidsley Dickson. "Ezines and Freshman Composition." *Kairos* 7.2 (2002): n. pag. Web. 4 Nov. 2008. <http://english.ttu.edu/kairos7.2sectiontwo/corrigan/description.html>. The authors show how course content is enriched with the addition of assignments that ask students to contribute to electronic magazines.

Dickson, Randi. "Developing 'Real-World Intelligence': Teaching Argumentative Writing through Debate." *English Journal* 94.1 (2004): 7. Print. For auditory learners, Dickson's method of combining argumentative essay writing with debate can reinforce their understanding.

Gage, John T. "Teaching the Enthymeme: Invention and Arrangement." *Rhetoric Review* 2.1 (1983): 38–50. Print. Gage argues that students can gain awareness and control over the context, logic, and structure of their arguments by stating their reasoning in enthymemic fashion, as a sentence containing an assertion and a because clause.

Geisler, Cheryl, et al. "Itext: Future Directions for Research on the Relationship between Information Technology and Writing." *Journal of Business and Technical Communication* 15.3 (2001): 269–309. Print. The authors argue that Itexts such as e-mail are altering the nature of written communication and recommend a variety of ways to monitor such changes and to assess their social impact.

George, Diana. "From Analysis to Design: Visual Communication in the Teaching of Writing." *College Composition and Communication* 54.1 (2002): 11–39. Print. In this review of current theory and research and the pedagogical history of visual literacy, George provides an excellent introduction for writing teachers who want to include instruction in visual literacy in their curricula.

Porter, Jeffrey. "The Reasonable Reader: Knowledge and Inquiry in Freshman English." *College English* 49.3 (1987): 332–44. Print. Porter argues that enthymemes organize readers' "participation in the text."

Walker, Jeffrey. "The Body of Persuasion: A Theory of the Enthymeme." *College English* 56.1 (1994): 46–65. Print. Walker redefines the concept of enthymeme and discusses its current relevance using examples from Martin Luther King, Jr. and Roland Barthes.

Example:

DiSantis is a banker, so he does not care about the poor.

Premise: Bankers do not care about the poor.
Premise: DiSantis is a banker.
Conclusion: Therefore, DiSantis does not care about the poor.

The statement is untrue because the first premise is untrue.

1. The mayor opposed pollution controls when he was president of a manufacturing company, so he may not support new controls or vigorously enforce existing ones.
2. Information on corporate Web sites is unreliable because the sites are sponsored by for-profit entities.
3. Schroeder is a good artist because she trained at Parsons, like many other good artists.
4. Wealthy athletes who use their resources to help others deserve our particular appreciation.
5. Jimson is clearly a sexist because she has hired only one woman.

10e   Using evidence

Whether your argument is reasonable or not depends heavily on the evidence you marshal to support it. The kinds of evidence and the criteria for evaluating evidence are discussed in detail on pages 181–85. Finding evidence is discussed under research writing on pages 565–88. Evaluating sources of evidence, including online sources, is discussed under research writing on pages 590–603.

The kind and quantity of evidence you use should be determined by your purpose, your subject, and the needs of your audience. Some arguments, such as an appeal for volunteer help in a soup kitchen, will rely most heavily on examples (including perhaps a narrative of your own experience) and on appeals to readers' beliefs. Other arguments, such as a proposal for mandatory side air bags in cars, will rely much more on statistics and expert opinions. Most arguments, including these, will mingle facts, examples, expert opinions, and appeals to readers' beliefs and needs.

In using evidence for argument, you'll need to be especially wary of certain traps that carelessness or zeal can lure you into. These traps are listed in the following box.

Responsible use of evidence

■ **Don't distort.** You mislead readers when you twist evidence to suit your argument—for instance, when you claim that crime in your city occurs five times more often than it did in 1955, without mentioning that the population is also seven times larger.

- **Don't stack the deck.** Ignoring damning evidence is like cheating at cards. You must deal forthrightly with the opposition. (See pp. 207–08.)
- **Don't exaggerate.** Watch your language. Don't attempt to manipulate readers by characterizing your own evidence as *pure* and *rock-solid* and the opposition's as *ridiculous* and *half-baked*. Make the evidence speak for itself.
- **Don't oversimplify.** Avoid forcing the evidence to support more than it can. (See also pp. 193–95.)
- **Don't misquote.** When you cite experts, quote them accurately and fairly.

Exercise 10.6   Using reason and evidence in your argument

Develop the structure and evidence for the argument you began in Exercises 10.2 and 10.3 (pp. 198 and 199). (You may want to begin drafting at this stage.) Is your argument mainly inductive or mainly deductive? Use the box on page 203 to test the reasoning of the argument. Use the boxes on page 183 and above to test your evidence.

10f   Reaching your readers

To reach your readers in argument, you appeal directly to their reason and emotions, you present yourself as someone worth heeding, and you account for views opposing your own.

1   Appealing to readers

In forming convictions about arguable issues, we generally interpret the factual evidence through the filter of our values, beliefs, tastes, desires, and feelings. You may object to placing the new town dump in a particular wooded area because the facts suggest that the site is not large enough and that prevailing winds will blow odors back through the town. But you may also have fond memories of playing in the wooded area as a child, feelings that color your interpretation of the facts and strengthen your conviction that the dump should be placed elsewhere. Your conviction is partly rational, because it is based on evidence, and partly emotional, because it is also based on feelings.

Rational and emotional appeals

In most arguments you will combine **rational appeals** to readers' capacities for reasoning logically between evidence and claims with **emotional appeals** to readers' beliefs and feelings. The following passages, all arguing the same view on the same subject, illustrate

COMPUTER ACTIVITIES

POLLING THE ONLINE AUDIENCE

The Web offers access to audiences beyond the classroom community, which can help students learn how to assess the needs of audiences as they build arguments. Students whose personal Web sites include arguments or claims can solicit responses from their audiences which will help them evaluate the effectiveness of their audience appeals. They can survey visitors to their Web site to find out whether they have targeted their audience accurately and to find out how visitors respond to the appeals made on the Web site. Composing the survey is the first component of this exercise; collecting and interpreting the information is the second; revising the Web site to use more effective appeals is the third.

INTERNET APPEALS

As a follow-up to the "Internet debates," "Internet theses," "Internet purposes and audiences," "Internet logic," and "Internet evidence" exercises suggested for 10a, 10b, 10c, 10d, and 10e, ask your students to find examples of rational and emotional appeals in the blogs they have been shadowing.

how either a primarily rational or a primarily emotional appeal may be weaker than an approach that uses both:

> **Rational appeal**
> Advertising should show more physically challenged people. The millions of Americans with disabilities have considerable buying power, yet so far advertisers have made no attempt to tap that power. [Appeals to the logic of financial gain.]
>
> **Emotional appeal**
> Advertising should show more physically challenged people. By keeping people with disabilities out of the mainstream depicted in ads, advertisers encourage widespread prejudice against disability, prejudice that frightens and demeans those who hold it. [Appeals to a sense of fairness and open-mindedness.]
>
> **Rational and emotional appeals**
> Advertising should show more physically challenged people. The millions of Americans with disabilities have considerable buying power, yet so far advertisers have made no attempt to tap that power. Further, by keeping people with disabilities out of the mainstream depicted in ads, advertisers encourage widespread prejudice against disability, prejudice that frightens and demeans those who hold it.

The third passage, in combining both kinds of appeal, gives readers both rational and emotional bases for agreeing with the writer.

For an emotional appeal to be successful, it must be appropriate for the audience and the argument:

- **It must not misjudge readers' actual feelings.**
- **It must not raise emotional issues that are irrelevant to the claims and the evidence.** See pages 192–93 for a discussion of specific inappropriate appeals, such as the bandwagon approach.

One further caution: Photographs and other images can reinforce your claims with a strong emotional appeal, but they must be relevant to your claims, and you must explain their relevance in your text and captions. See pages 225–26 for more on the appeals in images.

Ethical appeal

A third kind of approach to readers, the **ethical appeal,** is the sense you give of being a competent, fair, trustworthy person. A sound argument backed by ample evidence—a rational appeal—will convince readers of your knowledge and reasonableness. (So will your acknowledging the opposition. See the next page.) Appropriate emotional appeals will demonstrate that you share readers' beliefs and needs. An argument that is concisely written and correct in grammar, spelling, and other matters will underscore your competence. In addition, a sincere and even tone will assure readers that you are a balanced person who wants to reason with them.

A sincere and even tone need not exclude language with emotional appeal—words such as *frightens* and *demeans* at the end of the third example on the previous page. But avoid certain forms of expression that will mark you as unfair:

■ **Insulting words,** such as *idiotic* or *fascist.*
■ **Biased language,** such as *rednecks* or *fags.* (See pp. 507–10.)
■ **Sarcasm**—for instance, using the phrase *What a brilliant idea* to indicate contempt for the idea and its originator.
■ **Exclamation points!** They'll make you sound shrill!

See also pages 186–87 on tone.

2 | Responding to opposing views

A good test of your fairness in argument is how you handle possible objections. Assuming your thesis is indeed arguable, then others can marshal their own evidence to support a different view or views. By dealing squarely with these opposing views, you show yourself to be honest and fair. You strengthen your ethical appeal and thus your entire argument.

Before or while you draft your essay, list for yourself all the opposing views you can think of. You'll find them in your research, by talking to friends and classmates, and by critically thinking about your own ideas. You can also look for a range of views in an online discussion that deals with your subject. Two places to start are the *Yahoo!* archive of discussion groups at *groups.yahoo.com* and the *Google* blog directory at *blogsearch.google.com.*

Rebutting opposing views

A common way to handle opposing views is to state them, refute those you can, grant the validity of others, and demonstrate why, despite their validity, the opposing views are less compelling than your own. The following paragraph illustrates this approach:

> For Springfield to become a first-rate academic institution, it will need to reduce its funding of intercollegiate sports in favor of academic programs. The athletic director argues against a reduction on the grounds that the team programs more than pay for themselves. ⎤ *Statement of opposing view* It is true that the surpluses from the team programs have gone into the general university fund. ⎤ *Concession that opposing view is partly valid* However, this argument misses the point that the team programs demand too many resources to begin with for an institution whose main priorities should be academic. ⎤ *Demonstration that opposing view is irrelevant* Some members of the athletic department have acknowledged that intercollegiate sports could manage with budget cuts of 20 percent. ⎤ *Evidence for author's claim*

ANTICIPATING OPPOSITION

A good strategy for teaching students to anticipate opposition is to have them generate "yes, but" lists. Ask them to list all the strong points supporting their argument, then think of a counterargument for each point. (Sometimes they will be able to overcome these counterarguments; at other times they may have to concede the point.) For instance, if their thesis is "Raising the tuition at Golden College will reduce enrollment," they might produce a "yes, but" list like this:

SUPPORTING POINT	"YES, BUT" OBJECTION
Tuition rose 3 percent last year, and enrollment dropped by 2 percent.	Yes, but the recession and the lack of financial aid may also have contributed to lower enrollment.
There are cheaper schools in the area.	Yes, but Golden College is rated in the top ten of small schools in the area.
Students can't afford higher tuition costs.	Yes, but they seem to afford all the clothes, cars, and CDs they want to buy. Where are their priorities?

COLLABORATIVE LEARNING

DEVIL'S ADVOCATE

Group work is particularly useful in helping students to anticipate opposition to an argument. Ask the groups to play devil's advocate in order to test each writer's reasoning processes and use of evidence. To ensure that this is a supportive experience, remind groups to frame their questions about each writer's argument as a series of productive revision suggestions.

RESOURCES AND IDEAS

Johnson, Cheryl, and Jayne Moneysmith. *Multiple Genres, Multiple Voices: Teaching Argument in Composition and Literature.* Portsmouth: Boynton/Cook, 2005. Print. Johnson and Moneysmith offer advice for teaching argument using the "multi-voiced argument" assignment to offer an alternative to the traditional research paper that helps students engage with the work and improve their critical thinking skills.

Winder, Barbara E. "The Delineation of Values in Persuasive Writing." *College Composition and Communication* 29.1 (1978): 55–58. Print. Winder asks writers to spell out both sides of an argument to make them sensitive to both their own values and those of their readers.

COLLABORATIVE LEARNING

Ask students to work in small groups to identify the emotional, rational, and ethical appeals of the passages in Exercise 10.7, and then to identify similar grounds for appeal in their own arguments (as specified in Exercise 10.8).

ANSWERS: EXERCISE 10.7

Possible answers

1. Primarily emotional appeal. Ethical appeal: knowledgeable, concerned, reasonable (at least in the two uses of *may*), slightly sarcastic (*most essential of skills*).
2. Primarily rational appeal. Ethical appeal: knowledgeable, reasonable.
3. Primarily rational appeal. Ethical appeal: knowledgeable, fair, willing to acknowledge opposing views.
4. Primarily emotional appeal. Ethical appeal: sympathetic toward animals (but perhaps unfair to *so-called scientists*).
5. Primarily rational appeal. Ethical appeal: knowledgeable, fair, willing to acknowledge opposing views.

Committing the savings to academic programs would establish a more appropriate balance between the competing goals of athletic power and academic strength. — Author's claim

Finding common ground

A somewhat different approach to addressing opposing views, developed by the psychologist Carl Rogers, emphasizes the search for common ground. A **Rogerian argument** can be especially helpful when you expect readers to resist your claims. You start by showing that you understand readers' views and by establishing points on which you and readers agree and disagree. Creating a connection in this way can encourage readers to hear you out as you argue your own claims. Recast as a Rogerian argument, the preceding example might read as follows:

The Springfield community thus seems united in the goal of making the university a first-rate academic institution, but it differs over whether to help pay for the needed improvements by reducing funds for intercollegiate sports. Most of us who support this step do value the sports, and we appreciate the athletic director's point that the team programs more than pay for themselves, contributing surpluses to the general university fund. We certainly do not propose that the university abandon the sports altogether or even dramatically cut their funding. However, some members of the athletic department have acknowledged that intercollegiate sports could manage with budget cuts of 20 percent. Thus we seek this manageable reduction so that Springfield can continue as a sports power while also putting more resources to work for academic excellence. — Focus on points of agreement / Rejection of more extreme solutions / Evidence for author's claim / Author's claim

Exercise 10.7 Identifying appeals

Identify each passage below as primarily a rational appeal or primarily an emotional appeal. Which passages make a strong ethical appeal as well?

1. Use of the Web may contribute to the global tendency toward breadth rather than depth of knowledge. Relying on those most essential skills—pointing and clicking—our brightest minds may now never encounter, much less read, the works of Plato and Shakespeare.
2. Thus the data collected by these researchers indicate that a mandatory sentence for illegal possession of handguns may lead to a reduction in handgun purchases.
3. Most broadcasters worry that further government regulation of television programming could breed censorship—certainly, an undesirable outcome. Yet most broadcasters also accept that children's television is a fair target for regulation.

4. Anyone who cherishes life in all its diversity could not help being appalled by the mistreatment of laboratory animals. The so-called scientists who run the labs are misguided.
5. Many experts in constitutional law have warned that the rule violates the right to free speech. Yet other experts have viewed the rule, however regretfully, as necessary for the good of the community as a whole.

Exercise 10.8 Reaching your readers

Continuing your argument-in-progress from Exercise 10.6 (p. 205), analyze whether your claims are rational or emotional and whether the mix is appropriate for your audience and argument. Analyze your ethical appeal, too, considering whether it can be strengthened. Then make a list of possible opposing views. Think freely at first, not stopping to censor views that seem far-fetched or irrational. When your list is complete, decide which views must be taken seriously and why, and develop a response to each one.

10g Organizing your argument

All arguments include the same parts, but depending on the type of argument the organization can vary:

- **Introduction:** Commonly, the introduction establishes the significance of the subject or the scope of the problem, provides the background, and usually includes the thesis statement. However, if you think your readers may have difficulty accepting your thesis statement before they see at least some support for it, then it may come later in the paper. In a Rogerian argument, you might use the introduction to emphasize the common ground between you and readers and delay stating the thesis until the conclusion.

- **Body:** The body paragraphs state and develop the claims supporting the thesis, using clearly relevant evidence. The arrangement of the claims can vary widely, as can their position relative to the response to opposing views. See the next page.

- **Response to opposing views:** The response to opposing views details and addresses those views, finding common ground, demonstrating the arguments' greater strengths, or conceding the opponent's points. For some arguments, readers will be satisfied to see opposing views dealt with at the end. For others, each claim will invite its own objections, and those opposing views will need to be addressed claim by claim. When readers' resistance may be very strong, the Rogerian approach of discussing and conceding opposing views right away can establish a common understanding that opens readers to the argument's claims.

- **Conclusion:** The conclusion completes the argument. Often it restates the thesis, summarizes the supporting claims, and

COLLABORATIVE LEARNING

Ask students to complete Exercise 10.8. Have group members exchange their lists of opposing views to identify any additional ones that should be added. Once each writer reviews the list and has identified the opposing views he or she deems should be taken seriously, have group members note the views they believe should be addressed in the essay. Students might benefit from others' perspectives to help them generate opposing views and determine which ones might be most important to respond to in the argument.

ORGANIZING TOGETHER

Many students have difficulty organizing their papers. Allow them to work in pairs on organizing each of their papers in turn. Ask them to pay special attention to anticipating opposing views.

ELECTRONIC ORGANIZING TOOLS

Students may want to use the outlining function of their word-processing software to organize the introduction, body, and conclusion of their papers, to outline a traditional or problem-solution scheme, and to cut and paste supporting claims and evidence to find the optimum arrangement.

makes a final appeal to readers. In a Rogerian argument, the conclusion often states the thesis as a solution, giving ground and inviting the audience to do the same.

For more on introductions and conclusions, see pages 103–10.

You may want to experiment with various organizations—for instance, trying out your strongest claims first or last in the body, stating claims outright or letting the evidence build to them, answering the opposition near the beginning or near the end or claim by claim. You can do this experimentation on paper, of course, but it's easier on a computer. Try rearranging your outline as described on page 37. Or try rearranging your draft (work with a copy) by cutting and pasting parts of it for different emphases.

Organizing an argument's body and response to opposing views

A common scheme
Claim 1 and evidence
Claim 2 and evidence
Claim X and evidence
Response to opposing views

A variation
Claim 1 and evidence
Response to opposing views
Claim 2 and evidence
Response to opposing views
Claim X and evidence
Response to opposing views

The Rogerian scheme
Common ground and concession to opposing views
Claim 1 and evidence
Claim 2 and evidence
Claim X and evidence

The problem-solution scheme
The problem: claims and evidence
The solution: claims and evidence
Response to opposing views

ANSWERS: EXERCISE 10.9

Individual response.

PEER OUTLINING

Making an outline of a draft of a paper is challenging to do, but is a very powerful tool for revision. To make it easier for students, have them work with a partner to construct an outline of the draft. Then, the writer can revise the outline before writing the next draft.

Exercise 10.9 Organizing your argument
Continuing from Exercise 10.8 (p. 209), develop a structure for your argument. Consider especially how you will introduce it, how you will arrange your claims, where you will place your responses to opposing views, and how you will conclude.

10h Revising your argument

When you revise your argument, do it in at least two stages—revising underlying meaning and structure, and editing more superficial elements. The checklists on pages 54–55 and 60–61 can be a guide. Supplement them with the checklist opposite, which encourages you to think critically about your own argument.

Checklist for revising an argument

Thesis
- What is your thesis? Where is it stated?
- In what ways is your thesis statement an arguable claim?

Reasoning
- If your thesis derives from induction, where have you related the evidence to your generalization?
- If your thesis derives from deduction, is your syllogism both true and valid?
- Have you avoided fallacies in reasoning?

Evidence
- Where have you provided the evidence readers need?
- Where might your evidence not be accurate, relevant, representative, or adequate? (Answer this question from the point of view of a neutral or even skeptical reader.)

Appeals
- Where have you considered readers' probable beliefs and values?
- How are your rational appeals and emotional appeals appropriate for your readers?
- What is your ethical appeal? How can you improve it?

Opposing views
- What opposing views have you answered?
- How successfully have you refuted opposing views? (Again, consider the neutral or skeptical reader.)

Organization
- How clearly does your argument move from one point to the next?
- How appropriate is your organization given your readers' likely views?

Exercise 10.10   Writing and revising your argument

Draft and revise the argument you have developed in the exercises in this chapter. Use the revision checklists on pages 54–55 and above to review your work.

ANSWERS: EXERCISE 10.10

Individual response.

10i | Examining a sample argument

The following essay by the student Craig Holbrook illustrates the principles discussed in this chapter. As you read the essay, notice especially the organization, the relation of claims and supporting evidence (including illustrations), the kinds of appeals Holbrook makes, and the ways he responds to opposing views.

MODELS OF STUDENT WRITING

Craig Holbrook's essay "TV Can Be Good for You" is a strong example of student writing featuring an introductory hook, a tight structure (with topic sentence claims at the ends of some paragraphs), extensive research, and effective appeals to reason. It may serve as a model of writing as engagement in reasoned debate, especially for students whose own writing overuses emotional appeals. It may also serve as a model of writing that goes against the grain of received wisdom, and does so persuasively.

To help your students formulate their own responses to the paper (especially in Exercise 10.11, questions 6 and 7), you might begin with classroom discussion or debate on the topic of television's effects on viewers. Students generally love to talk about television, although they may have an emotional stake in believing that their own viewing habits are not harmful. You might compile some anecdotal data about class members and their families, and then discuss whether the evidence provided by the class seems to confirm or refute Holbrook's findings. On the basis of this discussion, you might also introduce the concept of evidence gathered in controlled studies versus anecdotal evidence.

Introduction	
Identification and modification of prevailing view	
Thesis statement: three claims for TV	
Background for claim 1: effects of loneliness	
Evidence for effects of loneliness	
Evidence for effects of television on loneliness	
Statement of claim 1	
Illustration supporting claim 1	
Background for claim 2: effects of laughter	

TV Can Be Good for You

Television wastes time, pollutes minds, destroys brain cells, and turns some viewers into murderers. Thus runs the prevailing talk about the medium, supported by serious research as well as simple belief. But television has at least one strong virtue, too, which helps to explain its endurance as a cultural force. It provides replacement voices that ease loneliness, spark healthful laughter, and even educate young children.

Most people who have lived alone understand the curse of silence, when the only sound is the buzz of unhappiness or anxiety inside one's own head. Although people of all ages who live alone can experience intense loneliness, the elderly are especially vulnerable to solitude. For example, they may suffer increased confusion or depression when left alone for long periods but then rebound when they have steady companionship (Bondevik and Skogstad 329-30).

A study of elderly men and women in New Zealand found that television can actually serve as a companion by assuming "the role of social contact with the wider world," reducing "feelings of isolation and loneliness because it directs viewers' attention away from themselves" ("Television Programming"). (See fig. 1.) Thus television's replacement voices can provide comfort because they distract from a focus on being alone.

Fig. 1. Television can be a source of companionship for people whose living situations and limited mobility leave them lonely. Photograph by Jean Michel Foujols; *Corbis*; Corbis, 2005; Web; 13 Oct. 2008.

The absence of real voices can be most damaging when it means a lack of laughter. Here, too, research shows that television can have a positive effect on health. Laughter is one of the most powerful calming forces available to human beings, proven in many studies to reduce heart rate, lower blood pressure, and ease other stress-related ailments (Burroughs, Mahoney, and Lippman 172; Griffiths 18). (See fig. 2.) Television offers plenty of laughter: the recent listings for a single Friday night included more than twenty comedy programs running on the networks and on basic cable.

Evidence for effects of laughter

Evidence for comedy on television

Fig. 2. According to the Society for Neuroscience, the process of understanding and being amused by something funny stimulates at least three main areas of the brain. The society makes no recommendation about TV watching, but other studies show the healthful effects of the activity. Illustration by Lydia Kibiuk from *Brain Briefings*; Soc. for Neuroscience, Dec. 2001; Web; 12 Oct. 2008.

Illustration supporting healthful effects of laughter

A study reported in a health magazine found that laughter inspired by television and video is as healthful as the laughter generated by live comedy. Volunteers laughing at a video comedy routine "showed significant improvements in several immune functions, such as natural killer-cell activity" (Laliberte 78). Further, the effects of the comedy were so profound that "merely anticipating watching a funny video improved mood, depression, and anger as much as two days beforehand" (Laliberte 79). Even for people with plenty of companionship, television's replacement voices can have healthful effects by causing laughter.

Evidence for effects of laughter in response to television

Television also provides information about the world. This service can be helpful to everyone but especially to children, whose natural curiosity can exhaust the knowledge and patience of their parents and caretakers. While the TV may be baby-sitting children, it can also enrich them. For example, educational programs such as those on the Discovery Channel, the Disney Channel, and PBS offer a steady stream of information at various

Statement of claim 2

Background for claim 3: educational effects

Evidence for educational programming on television

cognitive levels. (See fig. 3.) Even many cartoons, which are generally dismissed as mindless or worse, familiarize children with the material of literature, including strong characters enacting classic narratives.

Illustration supporting claim 3

Fig. 3. Educational television programs such as *Sesame Street* are an important source of learning for children. Characters such as Elmo (shown here) pro-mote reading, learning, and healthy behaviors. Photograph from *The State of the World's Children*; United Nations Children's Fund, 2002; Web; 12 Oct. 2008.

Evidence for educational effects of television on children

Three researchers conducting a review of studies involving children and television found that TV can inspire imaginative play, which psychologists describe as important for children's cognitive development (Thakkar, Garrison, and Christakis 2028). In the studies reviewed, children who watched *Mister Rogers' Neighborhood*, a show that emphasized make-believe, demonstrated significant increases in imaginative play (2029). Thus high-quality educational programming can both inform young viewers and improve their cognitive development.

Statement of claim 3

Anticipation of objection: harm of television

The value of these replacement voices should not be oversold. Almost everyone agrees that too much TV does no one any good and may cause much harm. Many studies show that excessive TV watching increases violent behavior, especially in children, and can cause, rather than ease, other antisocial behaviors (Reeks 114; Walsh 34). In addition, human beings require the give and take of actual interaction. Steven Pinker, an expert in children's language acquisition, warns that children cannot develop language properly by watching television. They need to interact with actual speakers who respond directly to their needs (282). Replacement voices are not real voices and in the end can do only limited good.

Anticipation of objection: need for actual interaction

Response to objections: qualification of claims

Conclusion

But even limited good is something, especially for those who are lonely or neglected. Television is not an entirely positive force, but neither is it an entirely negative one. Its voices stand by to provide company, laughter, and information whenever they're needed.

Works Cited

Bondevik, Margareth, and Anders Skogstad. "The Oldest Old, ADL, Social
     Network, and Loneliness." *Western Journal of Nursing Research* 20.3
     (1998): 325-43. Print.

Burroughs, W. Jeffrey, Diana L. Mahoney, and Louis G. Lippman. "Attributes
     of Health-Promoting Laughter: Cross-Generational Comparison."
     Journal of Psychology 136.2 (2004): 171-81. Print.

Griffiths, Joan. "The Mirthful Brain." *Omni* Aug. 1996: 18-19. Print.

Laliberte, Richard W. "The Benefits of Laughter." *Shape* Sept. 2003: 78-79.
     Print.

Pinker, Steven. *The Language Instinct: How the Mind Creates Language.* New
     York: Harper, 1994. Print.

Reeks, Anne. "Kids and TV: A Guide." *Parenting* Apr. 2005: 110-15. Print.

"Television Programming for Older People: Summary Research Report." *NZ
     on Air.* NZ on Air, 25 July 2004. Web. 15 Oct. 2008.

Thakkar, Rupin R., Michelle M. Garrison, and Dimitri A. Christakis. "A
     Systematic Review for the Effects of Television Viewing by Infants and
     Preschoolers." *Pediatrics* 18.5 (2006): 2025-31. Web. 12 Oct. 2008.

Walsh, Teri. "Too Much TV Linked to Depression." *Prevention* Feb. 2001:
     34-36. Print.

—Craig Holbrook (student)

Works cited in MLA style

No works-cited entries for illustrations because captions provide complete source information

Exercise 10.11   Critically reading an argument

Analyze the construction and effectiveness of the preceding essay by answering the following questions.

1. Where does Holbrook make claims related to his thesis statement, and where does he provide evidence to support the claims?
2. Where does Holbrook appeal primarily to reason, and where does he appeal primarily to emotion? What specific beliefs and values of readers does he appeal to?
3. How would you characterize Holbrook's ethical appeal?
4. How effective do you find the illustrations as support for Holbrook's claims? What appeals do they make? (For an analysis of Holbrook's first illustration, see p. 226.)
5. What objections to his argument does Holbrook anticipate? How does he respond to them?
6. How effective do you find this argument? To what extent does Holbrook convince you that television has virtues? Do some claims seem stronger or weaker than others? Does Holbrook respond adequately to objections?
7. Write a critical evaluation of "TV Can Be Good for You." First summarize Holbrook's views. Then respond to those views by answering the questions posed in number 6 above.

ANSWERS: EXERCISE 10.11

Possible answers

1. *Claims* related to the thesis statement: the last sentences of paragraphs 3, 5, and 7; the first and last sentences of paragraph 8; and the conclusion. *Evidence:* studies cited in paragraphs 2, 3, 4, 5, 7, and 9; evidence gathered by the author in paragraphs 4 (comedy programming) and 6 (educational programming).
2. *Appeals to reason:* mainly, the use of studies as evidence (pars. 2, 3, 4 5, 7), the tempered claim (pars. 8, 9), and the deductive argument (replacement voices can be helpful; television provides replacement voices; therefore, television can be helpful). *Appeals to emotion:* sympathy for the lonely (par. 2), appreciation of children (par. 6). The argument is mainly rational.
3. The ethical appeal is that of a fair-minded, reasonable person.
4. *Appeals made by the illustrations:* Responses about the effectiveness of the illustrations will vary. Some of the appeals:

   Fig. 1 backs up the claim that TV can ease loneliness (rational appeal), shows the man enjoying himself (emotional appeal), and conveys the writer's competence in choosing an appropriate image (ethical appeal).

   Fig. 2 strengthens the claim that laughter is healthful with information from a reliable source (rational appeal), arouses curiosity with an unusual combination of photograph and diagram (emotional appeal), and proves the writer trustworthy and fair with the caption's acknowledgment that the source does not mention TV watching (ethical appeal).

   Fig. 3 supports the claim that TV can educate children by showing children with a character from a respected educational program (rational appeal), depicts a familiar, comfortable character and cute, smiling children (emotional appeal), and shows sensitivity to readers' probable knowledge as well as seriousness.
5. The objections are raised and answered in paragraph 8: too much TV is harmful, and replacement voices are not enough. Both objections are accepted as valid.
6. Individual response.
7. Individual response.

HIGHLIGHTS

This chapter's coverage of visual argument should be very timely for students who are bombarded with visual images on television, in the print media, and online. The first half of the chapter teaches students how to read images for their underlying claims; how to evaluate the kinds of evidence used by a visual argument; how to identify the underlying assumptions upon which the image's claims are based; and how to recognize fallacies in visual arguments. The chapter's second half focuses on to how to use visual arguments to optimum effect. Students are shown how to choose images, how to use them as evidence, and how to evaluate their appeal to readers. Throughout the chapter, examples of visual arguments are provided as concrete illustrations of the concepts presented in each section.

IMAGE CAPTIONING

Collect a group of magazine ads that make claims visually. Cover the captions or text of each image so only the image is visible. Then have your students try to guess what the caption is by looking at the image alone. This exercise might produce hilarious results, and you can use it to help students understand how text and picture work together.

11

Reading and Using Visual Arguments

Visual arguments use images to engage and convince readers. Advertisements often provide the most vivid and memorable examples, but writers in almost every field—from astronomy to music to physiology—support their claims with images. In this chapter you'll learn how to read visual arguments critically (below) and how to use images to strengthen your own arguments (p. 223).

Note This chapter builds on Chapters 7 and 9–10, which discuss forming a critical perspective (including viewing images critically), reading an argument critically, and writing an argument. If you haven't already done so, read those chapters before this one.

11a Reading visual arguments critically

Chapter 9 explains the three main elements of any argument: claims, evidence, and assumptions. To read visual arguments critically, you'll analyze all three elements.

1 Testing claims

Claims are positive statements that require support (see pp. 177, 178–81). In a visual argument, claims may be made by composition as well as by content, with or without accompanying words. Here are a few examples of visual claims:

Image	A magnetic sticker shaped like a ribbon and decorated with the colors and symbols of the American flag, positioned prominently on a car.
Claim	I support American troops overseas, and you should, too.
Image	A photograph framing hundreds of chickens crammed into small cages, resembling familiar images of World War II concentration camps.

Claim   Commercial poultry-raising practices are cruel and unethical.

Image   A chart with dramatically contrasting bars that represent the optimism, stress, and weight reported by people before and after they participated in a program of daily walking.

Claim   Daily exercise leads to a healthier and happier life.

Image   A cartoon featuring affluent-looking young adults on an affluent-looking college campus, conversing and frowning sadly as they gaze downhill at rough-looking teens in a dilapidated schoolyard. The caption reads, "Yes, it's sad what's happening to schools today. But everyone knows that throwing money at the problem isn't the solution."

Claim   Better funding makes for better schools.

The following image is one of a series of advertisements featuring well-known people as milk drinkers. The celebrity here is Serena Williams, a tennis champion. The advertisement makes several claims both in the photograph and in the text.

Claims in an image

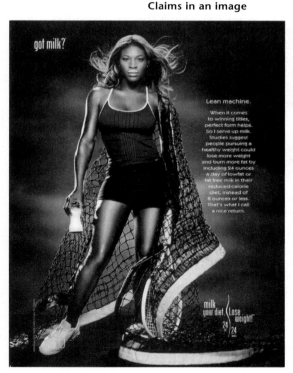

Image claim: Strong, shapely women drink milk.

Image claim: Attractive people drink milk.

Image claim: Athletes drink milk.

Text claim: Milk can help dieters reduce to a healthy weight.

Advertisement by the Milk Processor
Education Program

FASHION DESIGN EXAMPLES

If your students are interested in fashion, you could ask them to bring in flyers or catalogs from their favorite designers or stores. Photographic examples of clothing can be compared from designer to designer or store to store.

PSEUDO-EXPERTS

Students are often very savvy about advertising claims. Ask them to locate an image using an expert opinion that they find suspect, and to explain to the rest of the class why they think the "expert" may not be credible.

COMPUTER ACTIVITY

GALLERY OF APPEALS

Ask students to look around on the Web and collect visual appeals that reinforce readers' values. They can provide links to the Web site and a brief analysis on your class Web site of the values to which the images appeal.

COLLABORATIVE LEARNING

RIIS'S IMAGES

Jacob Riis, the famous photojournalist, provides an excellent example of using visual images to advance an argument in his classic text *How the Other Half Lives* (New York: Charles Scribner's Sons, 1890. Have students work together to evaluate selected images and the accompanying data and text.

---

2 | **Weighing evidence**

The kinds of evidence provided in images parallel those found in written arguments (see pp. 181–83):

- **Facts** can be verified by observation or research. In visual arguments they may be data, as in a graph showing a five-year rise in oil prices. Or they may be inferences drawn from data, as in the statement in the preceding ad that milk can help dieters "lose more weight and burn more fat." Sometimes images serve as facts themselves, objects that are analyzed in accompanying writing, as the milk ad is examined by this text or as the *BoostUp.org* ad is examined by Matthew Greene in the essay on pages 174–75.

- **Examples** illustrate and reinforce a point. Visual arguments often focus on an instance of the argument's claims, as the milk ad does on Serena Williams. Another ad might feature multiple images as examples: a Sizzler TV commercial, for instance, shows a sequence of luscious-looking foods to be had at the restaurant. An image might also illustrate a claim made in accompanying writing, as the milk ad does in this text.

- **Expert opinions** are the findings of subject-matter authorities based on their research and experience. A visual argument might present a chart from an expert showing a trend in, say, unemployment among high school graduates. The familiar TV ad that features a doctor recommending a particular medicine to a patient offers the doctor as an expert.

- **Appeals to beliefs or needs** reinforce readers' values or truths. Many visual arguments make such appeals by depicting how things clearly ought to be (an antidrug ad featuring a teenager who is confidently refusing peer pressure) or, in contrast, by showing how things clearly should not be (a Web site for an antihunger campaign featuring images of emaciated children).

The evidence in a visual argument should be judged by the same criteria used to judge a written argument (pp. 183–85):

- **Is the evidence accurate?** Images can be manipulated just as words can, and like words they should be analyzed for their fairness, precision, and trustworthiness. For example, a graph claiming to show changes in college living expenses between 1998 and 2008 should identify the source and purpose of the research, supply data for all the years, and clarify the definition of *living expenses* (the cost of room and board only, or transportation, recreation, and other expenses as well?).

- **Is the evidence relevant and adequate?** An image should pertain to the claims made in the larger argument and should sufficiently demonstrate its own claims. In an article on eating disorders, for instance, relevant and adequate images might include a medical diagram showing the liver damage from malnutrition and a photograph of a frail-bodied person suffering from anorexia. However, a photograph of a skinny model or actor would be neither relevant nor adequate, merely sensationalistic, unless the subject had publicly confirmed that his or her low weight resulted from an eating disorder.

■ **Does the evidence represent the context?** Representative visual evidence reflects the full range of the sample it's drawn from and does not overrepresent or hide important elements of the subject. For example, a photographic essay claiming to document the poor working conditions of migrant farm workers might reasonably include images of one worker's scarred hands and another worker suffering from heat prostration. But to be representative, the essay would also need to illustrate the full range of migrant workers' experiences.

The annotations on the graph below demonstrate one way of analyzing visual evidence for this claim: *The teen birthrate has dropped steadily since 1990.* The data come from the Centers for Disease Control and Prevention (CDC), a US agency and a reputable source. But the data are incomplete, so the graph is misleading.

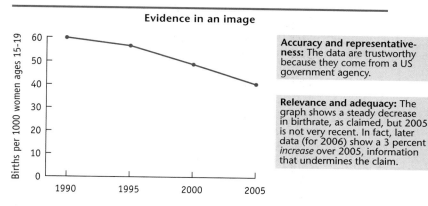

Evidence in an image

Accuracy and representativeness: The data are trustworthy because they come from a US government agency.

Relevance and adequacy: The graph shows a steady decrease in birthrate, as claimed, but 2005 is not very recent. In fact, later data (for 2006) show a 3 percent *increase* over 2005, information that undermines the claim.

Fig. 1. Decrease in birthrate among women ages 15 to 19 in the United States, 1990-2005. Data from Stephanie J. Ventura et al.; *National Vital Statistics Reports*; US Dept. of Health and Human Services, Centers for Disease Control and Prevention, 22 Apr. 2007; Web; 10 July 2008.

3 Discovering assumptions

Like a written argument, a visual argument is based on **assumptions**—the creator's ideas, often unstated, about why the evidence relates to the claims (see pp. 185–87). In visual arguments many assumptions involve the creator's beliefs about the audience,

COLLABORATIVE LEARNING

RIIS'S IMAGES II

As a follow-up to the previous exercise, have student groups evaluate Riis's assumptions about who his readers are, what they know about his subject, and how readily they will be persuaded by the images by presents.

THE DINNER PARTY

Locate images from artist Judy Chicago's famous installation *The Dinner Party*, and show them to students. A virtual online tour of the exhibit is available at *brooklynmuseum.org/exhibitions/dinner_party*. Chicago's triangular table, with place settings for famous women from history, is an excellent example of visual art used for persuasion and social commentary. Lead a class discussion about who Chicago's audience was, how sympathetic they were likely to be to her claims, and what kinds of images appealed to them. You can also talk about the way she uses an unfamiliar format to provoke interest and response from her viewers.

ECONOMIC TRENDS

Economists often use graphs or charts showing changes in tax spending over time, budget deficit projections, cost of living changes over time, or other financial trends affecting the populace. However, some images may be misleading. If your course focuses on economics, you may want to spend some time looking at competing visual evidence from different economic think tanks (liberal and conservative).

as detailed below. The examples analyze the milk ad on page 217, featuring the tennis player Serena Williams.

- **Who readers are and where they will see the argument.** The Williams ad first appeared in sports magazines, so the advertiser could assume readers who are interested in sports and athletes.
- **What readers already know about the subject.** To sports fans, Williams would be a familiar subject. The advertiser presumably considers readers less familiar with the benefits of milk or with its appeal to celebrities like Williams.
- **How familiar readers are with the purpose, format, and style of the argument.** With more than two hundred print and TV ads since 1994, the milk-mustache campaign has become a fixture of US popular culture. Each new ad fits into the framework established by its predecessors.
- **Whether readers are likely to lean toward the argument's claims.** The advertiser clearly assumes that the endorsement of a sports star like Williams will influence readers who are interested in healthy weight loss. At the same time, it seems to assume that the benefits of milk still need selling to readers.
- **What kinds of information, ideas, and images readers will find persuasive.** The advertiser seems to assume that a strictly factual claim about the health benefits of milk would not be persuasive enough to readers, so it shows that attractive and talented people like Williams consume milk. The photograph of Williams emphasizes qualities that the advertiser presumably thinks will appeal to readers: strength, shapeliness, beauty, even glamour.

4 | Recognizing fallacies

Fallacies, or errors in argument, are sometimes accidental, but they are often used deliberately to manipulate readers' responses. All the fallacies of written arguments discussed on pages 190–95 may appear in visual arguments as well. Here we'll focus on examples of the two main categories.

Evasions

Evasions attempt to deflect the reader from the central claim of the argument. One evasion is **snob appeal,** inviting readers to think or be like someone they admire. Look again at the Williams milk ad on page 217. Like all celebrity ads in the milk-mustache campaign, this one appeals to the reader's wish to emulate a famous person. If you drink milk, the ad says subtly, you too may become strong, beautiful, and fearless (notice that Williams looks unguardedly into the camera). The ad does have some substance in its specific and verifiable claim that drinking "24 ounces a day of lowfat or fat free milk" could help people reduce to a healthy weight, but Williams herself, with her milk mustache, makes a stronger claim.

Oversimplifications

Oversimplifications imply that subjects are less complex than they are. An example is the **hasty generalization,** a claim that is based on too little evidence or that misrepresents the facts. This fallacy appears in the following graph, which is intended to support this claim: *After a steep decline over the preceding five years, the teen birthrate shot up in 2006.* At first, the graph appears to demonstrate the claim, but a close look reveals that it badly misrepresents the data.

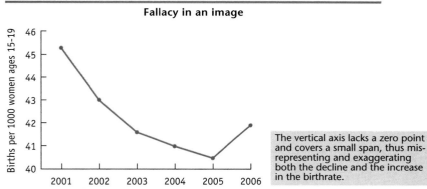

Fallacy in an image

The vertical axis lacks a zero point and covers a small span, thus misrepresenting and exaggerating both the decline and the increase in the birthrate.

Fig. 2. Steep decline and sharp increase in the birthrate among women ages 15 to 19 in the United States, 2001-06. Data from Brady E. Hamilton et al.; *National Vital Statistics Reports*; US Dept. of Health and Human Services, Centers for Disease Control and Prevention, 1 May 2008; Web; 10 July 2008.

The corrected graph below uses exactly the same data, but they tell a different story because they are presented without manipulation.

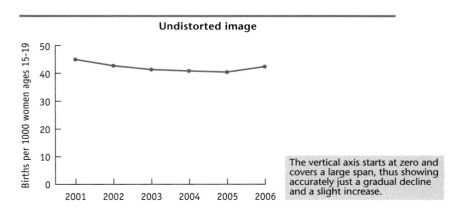

Undistorted image

The vertical axis starts at zero and covers a large span, thus showing accurately just a gradual decline and a slight increase.

ANSWERS: EXERCISE 11.1

Possible answers

1. The audience seems to be people who are serving or might serve as Big Brothers or Big Sisters (primarily the latter since the people depicted are female). The happiness and togetherness of the subjects would reinforce the commitment of current volunteers and invite the participation of others.
2. The organization fosters pairings of adults and children and emphasizes togetherness and having fun.
3. The main claim is in the large text: "Time spent with you is like a day at the beach." In other words, the relationship of volunteer and child is carefree, invigorating, fun.
4. The photograph provides the evidence for the claim: the beach is inviting, the subjects are happy, lively, and affectionate.
5. Some assumptions: Happy, affectionate relationships are good for adults and children. The smiling subjects are in fact a volunteer and her "little sister." A day at the beach is an appealing prospect and a desirable parallel for a relationship.
6. The most noticeable elements of the image are the subjects' feet, the subjects' smiles and windblown hair, and the bright background, all conveying beach fun. The foregrounded bare feet, especially, emphasize freedom and playfulness. The large type across the woman's feet further focuses attention on them.
7. Individual response.

ANSWERS: EXERCISE 11.2

Individual response.

Exercise 11.1 Reading a visual argument critically

The image below is an e-card found on the Web site of Big Brothers Big Sisters of America, a community organization that brings children and mentors together. The organization invites site visitors to send its cards "to encourage friends and family members to support Big Brothers Big Sisters." Examine the card's visual argument closely, and jot down your answers to the following questions.

1. Who appears to be the intended audience? What aspects of the text and photograph seem best suited to that audience?
2. What can you tell about Big Brothers Big Sisters from this e-card?
3. What claims does the image make?
4. What evidence supports the claims? How effective is it?
5. What assumptions underlie the argument, connecting evidence to claims?
6. How does the visual organization (cropping of the photograph, placement of the text) make the argument more or less effective?
7. Is the argument persuasive to you? Why or why not?

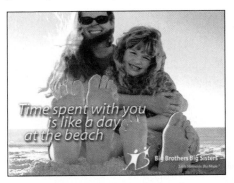

E-card from the Web site of
Big Brothers Big Sisters of America

Exercise 11.2 Identifying fallacies in visual arguments

Locate a current or historical source with extreme views on a subject, such as the Web site of an outspoken political commentator, a sensationalist tabloid newspaper, or a collection of wartime propaganda (from any nation or era). Photocopy or print an image that seems especially rife with fallacies and, referring to the complete list of fallacies on page 191, find as many as possible in the image. The following sites can help you begin your search:

Political commentators

Keith Olbermann: *msn.com/id/3036677*
Rush Limbaugh: *rushlimbaugh.com/home/today.guest.html*

Tabloids

National Enquirer (US): *nationalenquirer.com*
Daily Mail (Great Britain): *www.dailymail.co.uk/home/index.html*

World War II propaganda

Northwestern University (American images): *www.library.northwestern.edu/ govinfo/collections/wwii-posters*

Calvin College (German images): *www.calvin.edu/academic/cas/gpa*

11b Using visual arguments effectively

Visual images can make strong arguments. Sometimes they work by themselves, as a painting might, to convince viewers of an idea. More often in academic situations, they serve as evidence for verbal claims.

Note Any visual you include in a paper requires the same detailed citation as a written source. If you plan to publish your argument online, you will also need to seek permission from the author. See pages 632–34 for more on acknowledging sources and obtaining permissions.

1 Choosing images

You can wait until you've drafted an argument before concentrating on what images to include. This approach keeps your focus on the research and writing needed to craft the best argument from sources. But you can also begin thinking visually at the beginning of a project, as you might if your initial interest in the subject was sparked by a compelling image. Either way, ask yourself some basic questions as you consider visual options:

- **Which parts of your argument require visual evidence or can use visual reinforcement?** Do readers need a visual to understand your argument? Can a claim be explained better visually than verbally? Can a graph or chart present data compactly and interestingly? Can a photograph appeal effectively to readers' beliefs and values?
- **What are the limitations or requirements of your writing situation?** What do the type of writing you're doing and its format allow? Look through examples of similar writing to gauge the kinds of illustrations readers will expect. And consider the medium you're writing in: a short animation sequence might be terrific in a *PowerPoint* presentation or on the Web, but a printed document requires photographs, drawings, and other static means of explanation.
- **What kinds of visuals are readily available on your subject?** As you researched your subject, what images seemed especially effective? What sources have you not yet explored? Tips for locating images, whether printed or online, appear on pages 584–85.

CONTEMPORARY PROPAGANDA

The propaganda sources listed in Exercise 11.2 are for World War II, but propaganda has arguably been used by the United States in more recent wars (Vietnam, Persian Gulf, Iraq). The validity of these wars and the US role in them are matters highly contested by the American public. Students may hold strong opinions that impair their ability to evaluate US documents about these wars or to entertain the notion that the US might have engaged in propaganda activities. However, if your students are able to handle such controversial issues, it could be productive to bring in some examples of government-produced images about these wars.

OVERRELIANCE UPON THE VISUAL

Caution your students that a visual image is not usually an adequate substitute for verbal argument, and that they should be careful not to rely upon images to convey what they find difficult to say in words. Images should always be tied closely into the argument with captioning or prose.

COLLABORATIVE LEARNING

SELECTING THE BEST IMAGES

Ask students to locate four or more images related to an argument in progress or a topic they are interested in writing about. In their groups, ask students to evaluate the appropriateness of other group members' images for their topic using the questions in the "Choosing images" section. Do the writers agree with other group members' assessments? Why or why not?

TESTING IMAGES ON PEERS

Peer groups can function as test audiences for student authors using images. Have each student bring to class an image he or she plans to use in a paper and show the image to the members of their peer group (who will already have read their paper draft). The peer group can help to evaluate the usefulness of the image and how the author has linked it to the paper's argument.

SEARCHING FOR VISUALS

Some search engines, such as *Google,* allow users to limit a search to images only, which can help students search more efficiently.

SUGGESTED READINGS

Hocks, Mary E. "Understanding Visual Rhetoric in Digital Writing Environments." *College Composition and Communication* 54.4 (2003): 629–56. Print. Hocks discusses visual rhetoric in two works created for the Web and argues for teaching design as part of writing pedagogy.

Hocks, Mary E., and Michelle R. Kendrick, eds. *Eloquent Images: Word and Image in the Age of New Media.* Cambridge: MIT Press, 2003. Print. This collection discusses historical and current use of images and text, and explores the complex relationships between them.

Langrehr, Don. "From a Semiotic Perspective: Inference Formation and the Critical Comprehension of Television Advertising." *Reading Online* 6.9 (2003). Print. Langrehr illustrates the difficulty students have "reading" television advertisements and offers advice on improving this dimension of visual literacy.

Sellen, Mary. "Information Literacy in the General Education: A New Requirement for the 21st Century." *Journal of General Education* 51.2 (2002): 115–26. Print. Sellen suggests that there is a need for instruction in multimedia literacy because students can now incorporate visual and aural information into their texts.

Stroupe, Craig. "Visualizing English: Recognizing the Hybrid Literacy of Visual and Verbal Authorship on the Web." *College English* 62.5 (2000): 607–32. Print. Stroupe presents a method for combining verbal and nonverbal features in student texts, made possible by the advances in visual digitality.

Westbrook, Steve. "Visual Rhetoric in a Culture of Fear: Impediments to Multimedia Production." *College English* 68.5 (2006): 457–80. Print. Westbrook discusses how institutional forces, including copyright laws, can limit the distribution of multimedia student work.

■ **Should you create original images tailored to your argument?** Instead of searching for existing images, would your time be better spent taking your own photographs or using computer software to compose visual explanations, such as diagrams, charts, and graphs? Tips for creating images appear on pages 121–25.

2 Using images as evidence

An image can attract readers' attention, but if it stops there it will amount to mere decoration or, worse, it will distract readers from the substance of your argument. When you use images as *evidence* for your argument, you engage readers both intellectually and visually.

Images can work in various ways as evidence. In an evaluation of an advertisement, the ad itself would support the claim. In a paper arguing for earthquake preparedness, a photograph could provide a visual record of earthquake damage and a chart could show levels of current preparedness. The two images here supported an argument with this thesis: *Despite proof that the depiction of smoking in movies encourages children and teens to smoke, studios continue to release youth-oriented movies that show stars smoking.*

To make an image work hard as evidence, ensure that it relates directly to a point in your argument, adds to that point, and gives

---

Image as evidence

Photograph of an actress smoking in a PG-13 movie —a visual example of the claim that youth-oriented movies depict smoking

Caption explaining the image, tying it to the text of the paper and providing source information

Fig. 1. The actress Kate Hudson in *Raising Helen,* one of many PG-13 movies released each year in which characters smoke. Photograph by Peggy Storm; *gettyimages.com*; Getty Images, 2003; Web; 21 Apr. 2008.

Image as evidence

[One in a Series]

Eighty percent of this year's nominated movies feature smoking. And the winner is

the global tobacco industry. It gains at least $4 billion in lifetime sales revenue, in the U.S. alone, from the new teen smokers recruited to smoke by films each year. In 2007, two-thirds of new U.S. releases featured smoking: 39% of G/PG movies, 66% of PG-13 films, 84% of R-rated films. Together, these movies delivered **6.6 billion tobacco impressions** to North American theater audiences. R-rating smoking is reasonable, responsible—and inevitable. You'll still be able to include smoking in any film, just like this year's R-rated nominees for Best Picture. Yet by keeping smoking out of the G/PG/PG-13 films that kids see most, you'll save 60,000 lives a year. So who's trying to stop the "R"? Must be somebody with a lot to lose.

SMOKE FREE MOVIES

SmokeFreeMovies.ucsf.edu

Advertisement by a reputable research and advocacy group, reinforcing the thesis and providing data about depictions of smoking in movies

Fig. 2. Advertisement by the research and advocacy group Smoke Free Movies, providing data on the depiction of smoking in movies and linking the tobacco industry to the practice. From "Our Ads"; *Smoke Free Movies*; U of California, San Francisco, Cardiovascular Research Inst., 2008; Web; 23 Apr. 2008.

Caption interpreting the ad and providing source information

readers something to think about. Always include a caption that explicitly ties the image to your text, so that readers don't have to puzzle out your intentions, and that provides source information. Number images in sequence (Fig. 1, Fig. 2, and so on), and refer to them by number at the appropriate points in your text. (See Chapter 5, pp. 121–25, for more on captioning and numbering illustrations.)

3 Considering images' appeals to readers

Images can help to strengthen your argument's appeals to readers. The appeals are discussed in detail on pages 205–07. The following summary suggests how they apply to images:

- **Rational appeals target readers' capacity for reasoning logically.** Images can strengthen the evidence for an argument if they come from reliable sources, present information fairly and accurately, and relate clearly to the paper's claims.

- **Emotional appeals tap into readers' beliefs and feelings.** Images can appeal to a host of ideas and emotions, including patriotism, curiosity, moral values, sympathy, and anger. Any such appeal should correctly gauge readers' beliefs and feelings and should be clearly relevant to the argument.
- **Ethical appeals show readers that you are a competent, fair, and trustworthy source of information.** Images make ethical appeals largely by making appropriate rational and emotional appeals. In addition, they can show awareness of readers' knowledge, prove your seriousness, and demonstrate your neutrality.

To see how all three appeals can work in images, look again at a photograph used in the sample argument paper on pages 212–15. This image illustrates the writer's claim that television can ease loneliness.

COLLABORATIVE LEARNING

CONTEST OF IMAGES

After students have completed Exercise 11.3, have each group find or create an image to go with each of the five argument subjects. Hold a class contest to choose the best image for each argument subject.

ANSWERS: EXERCISE 11.3

Possible answers

1. Images helpful: photographs of seniors and their pets; graph relating pet care and life improvement.
2. Images somewhat helpful; photographs of people gathered in building entrances or other places where smokers congregate, emphasizing variety of people and obvious interactions.
3. Images essential: Military recruitment ads targeted to certain kinds of people.
4. Images helpful: photograph of solid-waste landfill; chart showing current and proposed volume of campus waste; diagram showing proposed recycling process.
5. Images not helpful unless data demonstrate a relationship between music listening and information retention.

Appeals in an image

Rational appeal: Backs up the writer's claim that TV can ease loneliness: the man appears to live alone (only one chair is visible) and is interacting enthusiastically with the TV

Emotional appeal: Reinforces the benefits of TV watching: the man's isolation may be disturbing, but his excitement is pleasing

Ethical appeal: Conveys the writer's competence through the appropriateness of the image for the point being made

Fig. 1. Television can be a source of companionship for people whose living situations and limited mobility leave them lonely. Photograph by Jean Michel Foujols; *Corbis*; Corbis, 2005; Web; 13 Oct. 2008.

Exercise 11.3 Brainstorming images for a visual argument

Working on your own or with others in a small group, apply the four questions for choosing images (pp. 223–24) to the following argument subjects. Which subject would most likely benefit from images? Which would be most difficult to illustrate? Why?

1. A program to help senior citizens adopt and care for a pet would improve seniors' lives and benefit the community.
2. Smoking cigarettes is a good way to meet interesting people.
3. Today's military-recruitment advertising targets certain kinds of people more than others.
4. Our campus needs a better recycling program.
5. Listening to music while studying helps one retain information.

Exercise 11.4   Filling gaps in a visual argument

Take another look at the photograph and the advertisement on pages 224–25, taken from a paper claiming that movie studios continue to release youth-oriented movies that show stars smoking despite proof that showing smoking in movies encourages children and teens to smoke. What additional images might bolster the argument? Consider especially how you might supplement the data in the ad to connect the number of movies that depict smoking with the number of children and teens who start smoking.

Exercise 11.5   Creating a deliberately bad visual argument

Purposely breaking the rules of argument can be fun and illuminating, building your knowledge about what works best and why. Using one of the topics listed in Exercise 11.3 or a new one, create a visual argument and an accompanying paragraph of text that deliberately antagonize readers instead of appealing to them. Do your best to do your worst: instead of demonstrating logic, use flawed reasoning or confusing examples; instead of appealing to readers' values and emotions, let your argument be boring or hostile; instead of communicating your credibility and expertise, display ignorance or ineptness.

Exercise 11.6   Revising an ineffective visual argument

Locate an ineffective visual argument, and use the guidelines on pages 225–26 to improve its likely appeal to readers. If your classmates completed Exercise 11.5, you could revise another student's deliberately bad argument.

ANSWERS: EXERCISE 11.4

Additional images might include a graph showing the correlation between the number of children and adolescents who view movies in which stars smoke and the number of children and adolescents who start smoking, or a graph showing the average number of instances children will be exposed to smoking in movies by age 12. Other images might include photographs of actors who are popular with children smoking in movies rated PG or PG-13 to supplement the photograph of Kate Hudson.

COMPUTER ACTIVITY

USING IMAGES TO SUPPORT OPPOSING VIEWPOINTS

Have students complete Exercise 11.4 and discuss their responses. Then, ask them to consider what kinds of images could be used to back an argument supporting an opposing position against giving an R rating to films featuring smoking. Use *Google* Image Search or a similar search engine to find additional images to support both positions on the argument. Compare the images for and against giving films showing smoking an R rating, and discuss how the images are similar and different. What will the explanatory text need to say to connect the images sufficiently to the respective arguments? Could the images in support of the opposing argument also be used to illustrate a counterargument?

ANSWERS: EXERCISE 11.5

Individual response.

ANSWERS: EXERCISE 11.6

Individual response.

COLLABORATIVE LEARNING

DAILY SHOWS

Television comedians like Jon Stewart often use visual images in a deliberately bad way to expose ironies and poke fun at public figures. As a follow-up to Exercise 11.5, have your class create and perform its own daily news spoof show, juxtaposing images and text for satirical effect.

PART 3

Grammatical Sentences

12 Understanding Sentence Grammar

13 Case of Nouns and Pronouns

14 Verbs

15 Agreement

16 Adjectives and Adverbs

12

Understanding Sentence Grammar

Grammar describes how language works. Following the rules of standard English grammar is what allows you to communicate with others across barriers of personality, region, class, or ethnic origin. If you are a native English speaker, you follow these rules mostly unconsciously. But when you're trying to improve your communication, making the rules conscious and learning the language for them can help.

Grammar reveals a lot about a sentence, even if you don't know the meanings of all the words:

The rumfrums prattly biggled the pooba.

You don't know what this sentence means, but you can infer that some things called *rumfrums* did something to a *pooba*. They *biggled* it, whatever that means, in a *prattly* way. Two grammatical cues, especially, make this sentence like *The students easily passed the test:*

- **Word forms.** The ending *-s* means more than one *rumfrum.* The ending *-ed* means that *biggled* is an action that happened in the past. The ending *-ly* means that *prattly* probably describes *how* the rumfrums biggled.
- **Word order.** *Rumfrums biggled pooba* resembles a common sequence in English: something (*rumfrums*) performed some action (*biggled*) to or on something else (*pooba*). Since *prattly* comes right before the action, it probably describes the action.

This chapter explains how such structures work and shows how practicing with them can help you communicate more effectively.

Grammar checkers A grammar checker can both offer assistance and cause problems as you compose sentences. Look for the cautions and tips for using a checker in this and the next five parts

mycomplab

Visit *mycomplab.com* for more resources and exercises on sentence grammar.

of this book. For more information about grammar checkers, see pages 64–65.

Understanding the basic sentence

The **sentence** is the basic unit of thought. Its grammar consists of words with specific forms and functions arranged in specific ways.

1 Identifying subjects and predicates

Most sentences make statements. First the **subject** names something; then the **predicate** makes an assertion about the subject or describes an action by the subject.

Subject	Predicate
Art	thrives.

The **simple subject** consists of one or more nouns or pronouns, whereas the **complete subject** also includes any modifiers. The **simple predicate** consists of one or more verbs, whereas the **complete predicate** adds any words needed to complete the meaning of the verb plus any modifiers.

Sometimes, as in the short example *Art thrives,* the simple and complete subject and predicate are the same. More often, they are different:

In the second example, the simple subject and simple predicate are both **compound:** in each, two words joined by *and* serve the same function.

Note If a sentence contains a word group such as *that makes it into established museums* or *because viewers finally agree about its quality,* you may be tempted to mark the subject and verb in the word group as the subject and verb of the sentence. But these word groups are subordinate clauses, made into modifiers by the words they begin with: *that* and *because.* See pages 250–51 for more on subordinate clauses.

CULTURE LANGUAGE The subject of an English sentence may be a noun (*art*) or a pronoun that refers to the noun (*it*), but not both. (See p. 233.)

| Faulty | Some <u>art</u> it stirs controversy. |
| Revised | Some <u>art</u> stirs controversy. |

to gain greater control of subordination and emphasis within their sentences. This process will take place only if students get a chance to put knowledge into action through exercises that ask them to manipulate and create sentences. In this regard, the sentence-combining exercises in the chapter can be coordinated with those in other chapters of the text to create a program of sentence combining designed to complement instruction in essay and paragraph writing.

RESOURCES AND IDEAS

Grammar instruction

Does grammar instruction help? The effectiveness of grammar instruction in improving writing and in helping students achieve correctness in their prose is still a hotly debated issue. The essays in *The Place of Grammar in Writing Instruction: Past, Present, Future,* edited by Susan Hunter and Ray Wallace, explore the various possibilities for integrating grammar into writing instruction, including Eric H. Hobson's "Taking Computer-Assisted Grammar Instruction to New Frontiers" (Portsmouth: Boynton, 1995). A recent issue of *English Journal* (92.3, January 2003) was dedicated to the topic "Revitalizing Grammar."

Other useful works on grammar instruction include the following:

Blaauw-Hara, Mark. "Why Our Students Need Instruction in Grammar, and How We Should Go about It." *Teaching English in the Two-Year College* 34.2 (2006): 165–178 Print. Blaauw-Hara provides an overview of major ideas regarding the teaching of grammar. He asserts the importance of grammar correctness beyond first-year composition and offers several suggestions for helping students learn grammar, including working on errors in the context of the students' own writing, using minimal marking techniques, and asking students to maintain a "fix-it page" that logs both patterns of errors and resources to correct those mistakes.

Connors, Robert, J. "The Erasure of the Sentence." *College Composition and Communication* 52.1 (2001): 96–128. Print. Connors suggests that sentence combining and imitation exercises, which fell out of favor after the paradigm shift in composition theory, remain useful for improving student writing.

Enos, Teresa, ed. *A Sourcebook for Basic Writing Teachers.* New York: Random, 1987. Print. This collection of essays explores the debates over the efficacy of grammar instruction for standard speakers as well as for nonstandard dialect speakers. The collection includes Sarah D'Eloia's "The Uses—and Limits—of Grammar," which suggests ways to integrate instruction in writing and grammar, including dictation, paraphrase and conversion, imitation, follow-ups to writing assignments, and exercises that ask students to "discover" a rule from examples of it in operation (373–416).

Myers, Sharon A. "ReMembering the Sentence." *College Composition and Communication* 54.4 (2003): 610–28. Print. Myers echoes Robert Connors's call for a return to sentence-based methods of instruction. She answers critics of sentence combining by providing both theoretical and pedagogical perspectives on sentence-based instruction.

Newman, Michael. "Correctness and Its Conceptions: The Meaning of Language Form for Basic Writers." *Journal of Basic Writing* 15.1 (1996): 23–38. Print. Newman discusses changing views on "correctness" and "error" since Mina Shaughnessy's pathbreaking *Errors and Expectations.*

Noguchi, Rei. R. *Grammar and the Teaching of Writing: Limits and Possibilities.* Urbana: NCTE, 1991. Print. Noguchi has made an important contribution in helping teachers conceive of grammar instruction as a conceptual issue, and of student errors as an inseparable part of the larger concerns with meaning-making in writing instruction.

Online Writing Center of the University of Wisconsin at Madison. Web. *wisc.edu/writing.* This site is especially helpful to students with grammar problems.

The Purdue Online Writing Lab (OWL). Web. *owl.english.purdue.edu.* This is one of our profession's most respected OWLs.

Sams, Lynn. "How to Teach Grammar, Analytical Thinking, and Writing: A Method That Works." *English Journal* 92.3 (2003): 57–65. Sams rejects instruction in prescriptive grammar and in-context grammar instruction in favor of a sequenced approach to grammar instruction designed to build students' competence gradually.

Tests to find subjects and predicates

The tests below use the following example:

> Art that makes it into museums has often survived controversy.

Identify the subject.

- **Ask *who* or *what* is acting or being described in the sentence.**

Complete subject	art that makes it into museums

- **Isolate the simple subject by deleting modifiers**—words or word groups that don't name the actor of the sentence but give information about it. In the example, the word group *that makes it into museums* does not name the actor but modifies it.

Simple subject	art

Identify the predicate.

- **Ask what the sentence asserts about the subject:** what is its action, or what state is it in? In the example, the assertion about *art* is that it *has often survived controversy.*

Complete predicate	has often survived controversy

- **Isolate the verb, the simple predicate, by changing the time of the subject's action.** The simple predicate is the word or words that change as a result.

Example	Art . . . has often survived controversy.
Present	Art . . . often survives controversy.
Future	Art . . . will often survive controversy.
Simple predicate	has survived

2 Identifying the basic words: Nouns and verbs

The following five simple sentences consist almost entirely of two quite different kinds of words:

Subject	Predicate
The earth	trembled.
The earthquake	destroyed the city.
The result	was chaos.
The government	sent the city aid.
The citizens	considered the earthquake a disaster.

The words in the subject position name things, such as *earth, earthquake,* and *government.* In contrast, the words in the predicate position express states or actions, such as *trembled, destroyed,* and *sent.*

These two groups of words work in different ways. *Citizen* can become *citizens,* but not *citizened. Destroyed* can become *destroys,* but not *destroyeds.* Grammar reflects such differences by identifying

The parts of speech

Nouns name persons, places, things, ideas, or qualities: *Roosevelt, girl, Kip River, coastline, Koran, table, strife, happiness.* (See below.)

Pronouns usually substitute for nouns and function as nouns: *I, you, he, she, it, we, they, myself, this, that, who, which, everyone.* (See p. 235.)

Verbs express actions, occurrences, or states of being: *run, bunt, inflate, become, be.* (See the next page.)

Adjectives describe or modify nouns or pronouns: *gentle, small, helpful.* (See p. 240.)

Adverbs describe or modify verbs, adjectives, other adverbs, or whole groups of words: *gently, helpfully, almost, really, someday.* (See p. 240.)

Prepositions relate nouns or pronouns to other words in a sentence: *about, at, down, for, of, with.* (See pp. 242–43.)

Conjunctions link words, phrases, and clauses. **Coordinating conjunctions** and **correlative conjunctions** link words, phrases, or clauses of equal importance: *and, but, or, nor; both . . . and, not only . . . but also, either . . . or.* (See pp. 256–57.) **Subordinating conjunctions** introduce subordinate clauses and link them to main clauses: *although, because, if, whenever.* (See p. 251.)

Interjections express feeling or command attention, either alone or in a sentence: *hey, oh, darn, wow.*

the **parts of speech** or **word classes** shown in the box above. Except for *the* and *a*, which simply point to and help identify the words after them, the five sentences about the earthquake consist entirely of nouns and verbs.

Nouns

Meaning

Nouns name. They may name a person (*Angelina Jolie, Jesse Jackson, astronaut*), a thing (*chair, book, Mt. Rainier*), a quality (*pain, mystery, simplicity*), a place (*city, Washington, ocean, Red Sea*), or an idea (*reality, peace, success*).

Form

Most nouns form the **possessive** to indicate ownership or source. Singular nouns usually add an apostrophe plus *-s* (*Auden's poems*); plural nouns usually add just an apostrophe (*citizens' rights*).

Nouns also change form to distinguish between singular (one) and plural (more than one). Most nouns add *-s* or *-es* for the plural: *earthquake, earthquakes; city, cities.* Some nouns have irregular plurals: *woman, women; child, children.*

(CULTURE LANGUAGE) Some useful rules for forming noun plurals appear on pages 537–38. The irregular plurals must be memorized. Note that some nouns (noncount nouns) do not form

RESOURCES AND IDEAS

Bartholomae, David. "The Study of Error." *College Composition and Communication* 31.3 (1980): 253–69. Print. Bartholomae suggests that asking basic writers to read their papers aloud helps identify sources of error and can contribute to improvement in writing.

Beason, Larry. "Ethos and Error: How Business People React to Errors." *College Composition and Communication* 53.1 (2001): 33–64. Print. Beason conducts research to determine the impact of errors on nonacademic readers. His research demonstrates that errors bother readers because "errors create misunderstandings of the text's *meaning*, and they harm the *image* of the writer."

Horner, Bruce. "Discoursing Basic Writing." *College Composition and Communication* 47.2 (1996): 199–222. Print. Horner discusses the larger trends in the basic writing movement since the 1970s, including changing approaches to error.

Shaughnessy, Mina P. *Errors and Expectations: A Guide for the Teacher of Basic Writing.* New York: Oxford UP, 1977. Print. This valuable book focuses on basic writing but is also an important work for teachers of writing at all levels. It provides a detailed analysis of the causes of student errors as well as useful strategies for dealing with writing problems.

Viera, Carroll. "Helping Students to Help Themselves: An Approach to Grammar." *College Composition and Communication* 37.1 (1986): 94–96. Print. Viera suggests having students analyze their own grammatical problems, do research in their handbooks, and present mini-lessons in small groups.

DICTATION

Read to your class the words in the list below (or in a similar one) and then go through the list again, giving students a minute or two to write sentences using the words in as many different roles (parts of speech) as they can. The word *good*, for example, can be an adjective or a noun.

well	post	set
bill	that	needle
while	bit	turn

CULTURE
LANGUAGE

ARTICLES AND LANGUAGES

Students who are native speakers of such languages as Russian, Korean, and Japanese may have difficulty understanding the concept of the article, and you may need to work on this basic concept before moving on to the distinction between definite and indefinite articles. Students who are native speakers of Spanish or Italian may have difficulty hearing the difference between "this" and "these" because of the way "i" is pronounced in those languages.

plurals in English—for instance, *equality, anger, oxygen, equipment.* (See p. 323.)

Nouns with *the, a,* and *an*

Nouns are often preceded by *the* or *a* (*an* before a vowel sound: *an apple*). These words are usually called **articles** or **determiners** and always indicate that a noun follows.

CULTURE
LANGUAGE
See pages 322–25 for the rules governing the use of *the, a/an,* or no article at all before a noun.

Verbs

Meaning

Verbs express an action (*bring, change, grow*), an occurrence (*become, happen*), or a state of being (*be, seem*).

Form

Most verbs can be recognized by two changes in form:

- Most verbs add *-d* or *-ed* to indicate a difference between present and past time: *They play today. They played yesterday.* Some verbs indicate past time irregularly: *eat, ate; begin, began* (see pp. 275–77).
- Most present-time verbs add *-s* or *-es* with subjects that are singular nouns: *The bear escapes. It runs. The woman begins. She sings.* The exceptions are *be* and *have*, which change to *is* and *has.*

(See Chapter 14, pp. 272–88, for more on verb forms.)

Helping verbs

Certain forms of all verbs can combine with other words such as *do, have, can, might, will,* and *must.* These other words are called **helping verbs** or **auxiliary verbs.** In phrases such as *could run, will be running,* and *has escaped,* they help to convey time and other attributes. (See Chapter 14, pp. 274, 283–87.)

A note on form and function

In different sentences an English word may serve different functions, take correspondingly different forms, and belong to different word classes. For example:

The government sent the city aid. [*Aid* functions as a noun.]
Governments aid citizens. [*Aid* functions as a verb.]

Because words can function in different ways, we must always determine how a particular word works in a sentence before we can identify what part of speech it is. **The *function* of a word in a sentence always determines its part of speech in that sentence.**

Pronouns

Most **pronouns** substitute for nouns and function in sentences as nouns do. In the following sentence all three pronouns—*who, they, their*—refer to *nurses:*

> Some nurses <u>who</u> have families prefer the night shift because <u>they</u> have more time with <u>their</u> children.

The most common pronouns are the **personal pronouns** (*I, you, he, she, it, we, they*) and the **relative pronouns** (*who, whoever, which, that*). Most of them change form to indicate their function in the sentence—for instance, *He called <u>me</u>. <u>I</u> called <u>him</u> back.* (See Chapter 13 for a discussion of these form changes.)

Exercise 12.1   Identifying subjects and predicates

In the following sentences, insert a vertical line between the complete subject and the complete predicate. Underline each simple subject once and each simple predicate twice. Then use each sentence as a model to create a sentence of your own.

Example:

The <u>pony</u>, the light <u>horse</u>, and the draft <u>horse</u> | <u>are</u> three types of domestic horses.

Sample imitation: Toyota, Honda, and Nissan are three brands of Japanese cars.

1. The leaves fell.
2. October ends soon.
3. The orchard owners made apple cider.
4. They examined each apple carefully for quality.
5. Over a hundred people will buy cider at the roadside stand.

Exercise 12.2   Identifying nouns, verbs, and pronouns

In the following sentences identify all words functioning as nouns with *N*, all words functioning as verbs with *V*, and all pronouns with *P*.

Example:

   P   V   N   N
<u>They</u> <u>took</u> the <u>tour</u> through the <u>museum</u>.

1. The trees died.
2. They caught a disease.
3. The disease was a fungus.
4. It ruined a special grove.
5. Our great-grandfather planted the grove in the last century.

Exercise 12.3   Using nouns and verbs

Identify each of the following words as a noun, as a verb, or as both. Then create sentences of your own, using each word in each possible function.

ANSWERS: EXERCISE 12.1

      SUBJECT|PREDICATE
1. The leaves|fell.
   Sample imitation: The kite soared.
      SUBJECT|PREDICATE
2. October|ends soon.
   Sample imitation: My class begins soon.
        SUBJECT|PREDICATE
3. The orchard owners|made apple cider.
   Sample imitation: The couple grew summer squash.
   SUBJECT|PREDICATE
4. They|examined each apple carefully for quality.
   Sample imitation: They inspected each egg for cracks.
         SUBJECT|PREDICATE
5. Over a hundred people|will buy cider at the roadside stand.
   Sample imitation: Few pool owners will swim at the public beach.

ANSWERS: EXERCISE 12.2

      N   V
1. The <u>trees</u> <u>died</u>.
   P   V   N
2. <u>They</u> <u>caught</u> a <u>disease</u>.
      N   V   N
3. The <u>disease</u> <u>was</u> a <u>fungus</u>.
   P   V   N
4. <u>It</u> <u>ruined</u> a special <u>grove</u>.
   P   N   V   N
5. <u>Our</u> <u>great-grandfather</u> <u>planted</u> the <u>grove</u> in
            N
   the last <u>century</u>.

ANSWERS: EXERCISE 12.3

Possible answers

1. Noun and verb.
   Blow out the candles and make a <u>wish</u>. [Noun.] The child <u>wished</u> for a new bicycle. [Verb.]
2. Noun and verb.
   Many people purchase <u>ties</u> as Father's Day presents. [Noun.] <u>Tie</u> the rope into a square knot. [Verb.]
3. Noun and verb.
   The <u>swing</u> hung from a large oak tree. [Noun.] Ted picked up his niece and <u>swung</u> her around and around. [Verb.]
4. Noun and verb.
   The <u>mail</u> does not come on national holidays. [Noun.] <u>Mail</u> the package to her home address. [Verb.]
5. Verb.
   He <u>spends</u> his free time doing volunteer work.
6. Noun and verb.
   The <u>label</u> bore a poison warning. [Noun.] The companies must <u>label</u> their products. [Verb.]
7. Noun.
   The <u>door</u> flew open by itself.
8. Noun.
   My younger sister was good <u>company</u>.
9. Noun and verb.
   The <u>whistle</u> released us from work. [Noun.] We <u>whistle</u> all the way home. [Verb.]
10. Noun and verb.
    The <u>glue</u> stuck to my hands. [Noun.] We <u>glue</u> our models together. [Verb.]

Example:

fly
Noun and verb.
The <u>fly</u> sat on the meat loaf. [Noun.] The planes <u>fly</u> low. [Verb.]

1. wish	6. label
2. tie	7. door
3. swing	8. company
4. mail	9. whistle
5. spend	10. glue

3 **Forming sentence patterns with nouns and verbs**

English builds all sentences on the five basic patterns shown in the box on the facing page. As the diagrams indicate, the patterns differ in their predicates because the relation between the verb and the remaining words is different.

CULTURE LANGUAGE Word order in English sentences may not correspond to word order in the sentences of your native language. English, for instance, strongly prefers subject first, then verb, then any other words, whereas some other languages prefer the verb first. The main exceptions to the word patterns discussed here appear on pages 260–61. See also pages 359–65 on positioning modifiers in sentences.

Pattern 1: The earth trembled.

In the simplest pattern the predicate consists only of the verb. Verbs in this pattern do not require following words to complete their meaning and thus are called **intransitive** (from Latin words meaning "not passing over").

Subject	Predicate
	Intransitive verb
The earth	trembled.
The hospital	may close.

Pattern 2: The earthquake destroyed the city.

In pattern 2 the predicate consists of a verb followed by a noun that identifies who or what receives the action of the verb. This noun is a **direct object.** Verbs that require direct objects to complete their meaning are called **transitive** ("passing over"): the verb transfers the action from subject to object.

Subject	Predicate	
	Transitive verb	*Direct object*
The earthquake	destroyed	the city.
Education	opens	doors.

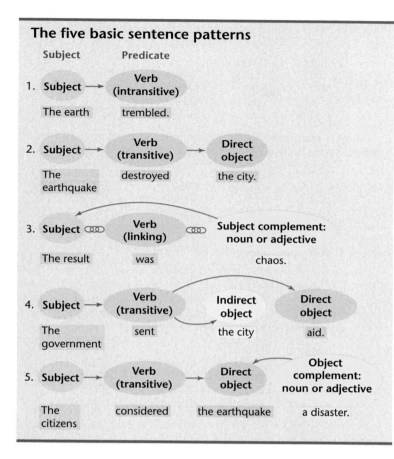

The five basic sentence patterns

Subject   Predicate

1. **Subject** → **Verb (intransitive)**

   The earth   trembled.

2. **Subject** → **Verb (transitive)** → **Direct object**

   The earthquake   destroyed   the city.

3. **Subject** ⚬ **Verb (linking)** ⚬ **Subject complement: noun or adjective**

   The result   was   chaos.

4. **Subject** → **Verb (transitive)** → **Indirect object** → **Direct object**

   The government   sent   the city   aid.

5. **Subject** → **Verb (transitive)** → **Direct object** → **Object complement: noun or adjective**

   The citizens   considered   the earthquake   a disaster.

〈CULTURE LANGUAGE〉 The distinction between transitive verbs and intransitive verbs like those in pattern 1 is important because only transitive verbs may be used in the passive voice (*The city was destroyed*). (See pp. 298–99.) Your dictionary says whether a verb is transitive or intransitive. Some verbs (*begin, learn, read, write,* and others) are both.

Pattern 3: The result was chaos.

In pattern 3 the predicate also consists of a verb followed by a noun, but here the noun renames or describes the subject. We could write the sentence *The result = chaos*. The verb serving as an equal sign is a **linking verb** because it links the subject and the following description. The linking verbs include *be, seem, appear, become, grow, remain, stay, prove, feel, look, smell, sound,* and *taste*. The word

〈CULTURE LANGUAGE〉

TRANSITIVE AND INTRANSITIVE VERBS

Remind students that intransitive verbs *cannot* be followed by a direct object. Transitive verbs, in contrast, *must* have a direct object to complete the meaning of a sentence. Some transitive verbs can have both a direct object and an indirect object. For students who need additional practice with transitive and intransitive verbs and passive voice, Jocelyn Steer and Karen Carlisi include useful exercises in Chapters 5 and 11 of *The Advanced Grammar Book* (Boston: Heinle, 1991).

that describes the subject is called a **subject complement** (it complements, or completes, the subject).

Subject	Predicate	
	Linking verb	*Subject complement*
The result	was	chaos.
The man	became	an accountant.

Subject complements in this sentence pattern may also be adjectives, words such as *tall* and *hopeful* (see p. 240):

Subject	Predicate	
	Linking verb	*Subject complement*
The result	was	chaotic.
The apartments	seem	expensive.

Pattern 4: The government sent the city aid.

In pattern 4 the predicate consists of a verb followed by two nouns. The second noun, *aid,* is a direct object (see pattern 2). But the first noun, *city,* is an **indirect object,** identifying to or for whom the action of the verb is performed. The direct object and indirect object refer to different things, people, or places.

Subject	Predicate		
	Transitive verb	*Indirect object*	*Direct object*
The government	sent	the city	aid.
One company	offered	its employees	bonuses.

A number of verbs can take indirect objects, including those above and *allow, bring, buy, deny, find, get, leave, make, pay, read, sell, show, teach,* and *write.*

(CULTURE LANGUAGE) With some verbs that express action done to or for someone, the indirect object must be turned into a phrase beginning with *to* or *for.* These verbs include *admit, announce, demonstrate, explain, introduce, mention, prove, recommend, say,* and *suggest.* The *to* or *for* phrase then falls after the direct object.

Faulty	The manual explains <u>workers</u> the new procedure.
Revised	The manual explains the new procedure <u>to workers</u>.

Pattern 5: The citizens considered the earthquake a disaster.

In pattern 5, as in pattern 4, the predicate consists of a verb followed by two nouns. But in pattern 5 the first noun is a direct object and the second noun renames or describes it. Here the second noun is an **object complement** (it complements, or completes, the object):

***TO BE* TEST**

Advise students that one way to determine whether a sentence fits into pattern 5 is to insert the words *to be* between the first noun and the following noun or adjective: *The citizens considered the earthquake to be a disaster.*

Subject	Predicate		
	Transitive verb	*Direct object*	*Object complement*
The citizens	considered	the earthquake	a disaster.
The class	elected	Joan O'Day	president.

Like a subject complement (pattern 3), an object complement may be a noun or an adjective, as below:

Subject	Predicate		
	Transitive verb	*Direct object*	*Object complement*
The citizens	considered	the earthquake	disastrous.
Success	makes	some people	nervous.

Exercise 12.4　Identifying sentence patterns

In the following sentences, identify each verb as intransitive, transitive, or linking. Then identify each direct object (DO), indirect object (IO), subject complement (SC), and object complement (OC).

Example:

　　　　　transitive
　　　　　verb　　　　IO　　　　　DO　　　　　　DO
Children give their parents both headaches and pleasures.

1. Many people find New York City exciting.
2. Tourists flock to New York each year.
3. Often they visit Times Square first.
4. The square's lights are astounding.
5. The flashing signs sell visitors everything from TVs to underwear.

Exercise 12.5　Creating sentences

Create sentences by using each of the following verbs in the pattern indicated. (For the meanings of the abbreviations, see the directions for Exercise 12.4.) You may want to change the form of the verb.

Example:

give (S-V-IO-DO)
Sam gave his brother a birthday card.

1. laugh (S-V)
2. elect (S-V-DO-OC)
3. steal (S-V-DO)
4. catch (S-V-DO)
5. bring (S-V-IO-DO)
6. seem (S-V-SC)
7. call (S-V-DO-OC)
8. become (S-V-SC)
9. buy (S-V-IO-DO)
10. study (S-V)

12b　Expanding the basic sentence with single words

Most of the sentences we read, write, or speak are more complex and also more informative and interesting than those examined

ANSWERS: EXERCISE 12.4

1. Find is transitive.
　　　　　　　　　　　　　　DO　　　　OC
　Many people find New York City exciting.
2. Flock is intransitive.
　No objects or complements.
3. Visit is transitive.
　　　　　　　　　　　　　　DO
　Often they visit Times Square first.
4. Are is linking.
　　　　　　　　　　　　　　SC
　The square's lights are astounding.
5. Sell is transitive.
　　　　　　　　　　　　　IO　　　　DO
　The flashing signs sell visitors everything

　from TVs to underwear.

ANSWERS: EXERCISE 12.5
Possible answers

1. The audience laughed.
2. The town elected Flynn mayor.
3. Pip stole the pie.
4. Josie caught the ball.
5. My uncle brought me a cake.
6. Marilou seems unhappy.
7. One candidate called the other a crook.
8. We became reckless.
9. We bought ourselves a television set.
10. No one studied.

so far. Most sentences contain one or more of the following: (1) modifying words (discussed here); (2) word groups, called phrases and clauses (p. 242); and (3) combinations of two or more words or word groups of the same kind (p. 256).

1 Using adjectives and adverbs

The simplest expansion of sentences occurs when we add modifying words to describe or limit the nouns and verbs. Modifying words add details:

> <u>Recently</u>, the earth trembled.
> The earthquake <u>nearly</u> destroyed the <u>old</u> city.
> The <u>federal</u> government <u>soon</u> sent the <u>city</u> aid.
> The grant was a <u>very generous</u> one but disappeared <u>too quickly</u>.

The underlined words represent two different parts of speech:

- **Adjectives** describe or modify nouns and pronouns. They specify which one, what quality, or how many.

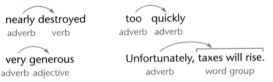

| old city | generous one | two pears |
| adjective noun | adjective pronoun | adjective noun |

- **Adverbs** describe or modify verbs, adjectives, other adverbs, and whole groups of words. They specify when, where, how, and to what extent.

> nearly destroyed   too quickly
> adverb   verb   adverb adverb
>
> very generous   Unfortunately, taxes will rise.
> adverb adjective   adverb   word group

An *-ly* ending often signals an adverb, but not always: *friendly* is an adjective; *never, not,* and *always* are adverbs. The only way to tell whether a word is an adjective or an adverb is to determine what it modifies.

Adjectives and adverbs appear in three forms:

- The **positive** form is the basic form, the one listed in the dictionary: *good, green, angry; badly, quickly, angrily.*
- The **comparative** form indicates a greater degree of the quality named by the word: *better, greener, angrier; worse, more quickly, more angrily.*
- The **superlative** form indicates the greatest degree of the quality named: *best, greenest, angriest; worst, most quickly, most angrily.*

(For further discussion of these forms, see p. 318.)

2 Using other words as modifiers

Nouns and special forms of verbs may sometimes serve as modifiers of other nouns. In combinations such as *office buildings*, *Thanksgiving prayer*, and *shock hazard*, the first noun modifies the second. In combinations such as *singing birds*, *corrected papers*, and *broken finger*, the first word is a verb form modifying the following noun. (These modifying verb forms are discussed in more detail on pp. 245–47.) Again, the part of speech to which we assign a word always depends on its function in a sentence.

Exercise 12.6 Identifying and using adjectives and adverbs

Identify the adjectives and adverbs in the following sentences. Then use each sentence as a model for creating a sentence of your own.

> *Example:*
>
>   adjective   adverb   adjective
> The red barn sat uncomfortably among modern buildings.
>
> *Sample imitation:* The little girl complained loudly to her busy mother.

1. The blue water glistened in the hot afternoon sunlight.
2. Happily, children dipped their toes in the cool lake.
3. Excitedly, some of the children hopped into the water.
4. Cautious parents watched from their shady porches.
5. The children played contentedly until the day finally ended.

Exercise 12.7 Using verb forms as modifiers

Use each of the following verb forms to modify a noun in a sentence of your own.

> *Example:*
>
> smoking
> Only a smoking cigar remained.

1. scrambled
2. twitching
3. rambling
4. typed
5. painted
6. written
7. charging
8. ripened
9. known
10. driven

Exercise 12.8 Sentence combining: Single-word modifiers

To practice expanding the basic sentence patterns with single-word modifiers, combine each group of sentences below into one sentence. You will have to delete and rearrange words.

> *Example:*
>
> Paris offers tourists food. Paris offers food proudly. The food is delicious.
>
> Paris proudly offers tourists delicious food.

ANSWERS: EXERCISE 12.6

1. The blue [ADJ] water glistened in the hot [ADJ] afternoon [ADJ] sunlight.
   Sample imitation: The blue bird perched on a thin leafy branch.
2. Happily [ADV], children dipped their toes in the cool [ADJ] lake.
   Sample imitation: Quietly, we peeked into the silent cathedral.
3. Excitedly [ADV], some of the children hopped into the water.
   Sample imitation: Impatiently, two of the children howled for the candy.
4. Cautious [ADJ] parents watched from their shady [ADV] porches.
   Sample imitation: Ambitious runners train for every marathon.
5. The children played contentedly [ADV] until the day finally [ADV] ended.
   Sample imitation: The babies lay still while the singer quietly crooned.

ANSWERS: EXERCISE 12.7

Possible answers

1. Jack woke up craving scrambled eggs.
2. The twitching limb relaxed when the sedative took effect.
3. The treasurer's rambling speech covered more topics than I can remember.
4. The typed manuscript contained many errors.
5. Painted birds decorate the window.
6. He wanted to know the origins of the written word.
7. The man escaped the charging animal.
8. We picked the ripened fruit.
9. All the known facts contradict his theory.
10. Driven people may have hypertension.

ANSWERS: EXERCISE 12.8

Possible answers

1. The turn of the twentieth century ushered in improved technology and new materials.
2. A sturdy steel skeleton made the construction of skyscrapers possible.
3. By 1913 the towering Woolworth Building, with its Gothic ornaments, stood 760 feet (55 stories).
4. At 1450 feet the Sears Tower in Chicago now doubles the relatively puny height of the Woolworth Building.
5. Skyscrapers became practical in 1857 when Elisha Graves Otis built the first safe passenger elevator.

RESOURCES AND IDEAS

Bushman, Donald, and Elizabeth Ervin. "Rhetorical Contexts of Grammar: Some Views from Writing Emphasis Instructors." *The Place of Grammar in Writing Instruction: Past, Present, Future.* Ed. Susan Hunter and Ray Wallace. Portsmouth: Boynton, 1995. 136–58. Print. This essay explains strategies for teaching grammar in cross-disciplinary rhetorical contexts.

Hashimoto, I. "Sentence Variety: Where Theory and Practice Meet and Lose." *Composition Studies: Freshman English News* 21.1 (1993): 66–77. Print. Hashimoto explores the contradictions between the common injunctions to students about sentence variation and stylistic choices of professional writers.

Herriman, Jennifer, and Aimo Seppänen. "What is an Indirect Object?" *English Studies* 77.5 (1996): 484–500. Print. This essay contrasts the consensus on defining and teaching the "direct object" with the vaguer approaches to the indirect object.

Herrington, Anne J. "Grammar Recharted: Sentence Analysis for Writing." *Writing Exercises from "Exercise Exchange."* Ed. Charles R. Duke. Vol. 2. Urbana: NCTE, 1984. 276–87.

1. The turn of the century ushered in technology and materials. The century was the twentieth. The technology was improved. The materials were new.
2. A skeleton made the construction of skyscrapers possible. The skeleton was sturdy. It was made of steel.
3. By 1913 the Woolworth Building, with its ornaments, stood 760 feet (55 stories). The building was towering. The ornaments were Gothic.
4. At 1450 feet the Sears Tower in Chicago doubles the height of the Woolworth Building. The doubling is now. The Woolworth height is puny. The puniness is relative.
5. Skyscrapers became practical in 1857 when Elisha Graves Otis built the elevator. It was the first elevator. The elevator was safe. It served passengers.

12c Expanding the basic sentence with word groups

Most sentences we read or write contain word groups that serve as nouns and modifiers. Such word groups enable us to combine several bits of information into one sentence and to make the relations among them clear, as in the following sentence:

When the experiment succeeded, the researchers, excited by the results, expanded the study to enroll more patients.

Attached to *researchers expanded the study*, the skeleton of this sentence, are three groups of words that add related information: *When the experiment succeeded, excited by the results, to enroll more patients.* These constructions are phrases and clauses:

- A *phrase* is a group of related words that lacks either a subject or a predicate or both: *excited by the results, to enroll more patients.*
- A *clause* contains both a subject and a predicate: *When the experiment succeeded* and *the researchers expanded the study* are both clauses, though only the second can stand alone as a sentence.

1 Using prepositional phrases

Prepositions are connecting words. Unlike nouns, verbs, and modifiers, which may change form, prepositions never change form. As the box opposite shows, many prepositions signal relationships of time or space; others signal relationships such as addition, comparison or contrast, cause or effect, concession, condition, opposition, possession, and source. Notice that some prepositions consist of more than one word.

A preposition connects a noun or pronoun to another word in

Common prepositions

Time or space (position or direction)			Other relationships (addition, comparison, etc.)	
about	by	out of	according to	in spite of
above	down	outside	as	instead of
across	during	over	as for	like
after	for	past	aside from	of
against	from	since	because of	on account of
along	in	through	concerning	regarding
along with	inside	throughout	despite	regardless of
among	inside of	till	except	unlike
around	into	to	except for	with
at	near	toward	excepting	without
before	next to	under	in addition to	
behind	off	underneath		
below	on	until		
beneath	onto	up		
beside	on top of	upon		
between	out	within		
beyond				

the sentence: *Robins nest in trees.* The noun or pronoun so connected (*trees*) is the **object of the preposition.** The preposition plus its object and any modifiers is a **prepositional phrase:**

Preposition	Object
on	the surface
upon	entering the room
from	where you are standing
except for	ten employees

Prepositional phrases function as adjectives (modifying nouns) or as adverbs (modifying verbs, adjectives, or other adverbs). As modifiers, they add details that make sentences clearer and more interesting for readers.

Life on a raft was an opportunity for adventure.
adjective phrase   adjective phrase

Huck Finn rode the raft by choice.
adverb phrase

 The meanings and idiomatic uses of English prepositions can be difficult to master; most must be memorized or looked up in a dictionary. (A list of dictionaries for English as a second language appears on p. 513.) See pages 287–88 for the uses of prepositions in two-word verbs such as *look after* and pages 518–19 for the uses of prepositions in idioms.

Print. Herrington suggests using a five-column chart to analyze sentence patterns and help make students aware of syntax. The five columns in the chart—Preceding Subject, Subject, Between Subject and Verb, Verb, and Following Verb—allow the system to account for both relatively simple sentences and those to which considerable information has been added. The columns can be layered as well to account for compound sentences.

Johnson, Walter H. "The Sentence-Structure Dilemma." *English Journal* 95.3 (2006): 14–15. Print. The author laments the policy at the community college where he teaches that severely penalizes students for sentence-level writing errors.

Pettersen, Nancy-Laurel. "Grammar Instruction in the Land of Curiosity and Delight." *Teaching English in the Two-Year College* 33.4 (2006): 388–391. Print. Petterson offers strategies for teaching grammar that require students to analyze language conventions.

Thomas, Katherine M., and Marlisa Austin. "Instructional Note: Fun with Fundamentals–Games and Electronic Activities to Reinforce Grammar in the College Writing Classroom." *Teaching English in the Two-Year College* 33.1 (2005): 62–69. Print. Thomas and Austin advocate the use of games and electronic activities to reinforce grammar skills, including interactive Web sites and software programs. They view these tools as interactive and fun, as well as individualized for the student and useful to instructors for assessment.

Weaver, Constance. *Teaching Grammar in Context.* Portsmouth: Boynton/Cook, 1996. Print. Weaver discusses the research indicating that grammar cannot be taught successfully in isolated drills, and she offers practical examples of how students can learn grammar in the context of their own work.

CULTURE LANGUAGE

PREPOSITIONS AND DIALECTS

Regional and social dialects may contribute to prepositional confusion; for instance, students may become sick *in, on,* or *to* their stomachs. In parts of the Northeast, people stand *on,* not *in,* line. Prepositions and idioms are given detailed coverage in 38d.

PREPOSITION PROBLEMS

Prepositions follow few specific rules, and, because of idiomatic usage, often cannot be translated directly into students' first languages. As a result, even advanced ESL students find prepositions difficult. Refer students who need additional practice to Alan Meyers, *Writing with Confidence* (9th ed., New York: Longman, 2009).

Punctuating prepositional phrases

Since a prepositional phrase lacks a subject and a predicate, it should not be punctuated as a complete sentence. If it is, the result is a **sentence fragment** (Chapter 17):

Fragment   Toward the sun.

The phrase must be attached to another group of words containing both a subject and a predicate:

Revised   The plane turned <u>toward the sun</u>.

A prepositional phrase that introduces a sentence is set off with punctuation, usually a comma, unless it is short (see p. 425):

<u>According to the newspaper and other sources</u>, the governor has reluctantly decided to veto the bill.

<u>In 1865</u> the Civil War finally ended.

A prepositional phrase that interrupts or concludes a sentence is *not* set off with punctuation when it is essential to the meaning of the word or words it modifies (see p. 429):

The announcement <u>of a tuition increase</u> surprised no one.

Students expected new fees <u>for the coming year</u>.

When an interrupting or concluding prepositional phrase is *not* essential to meaning, but merely adds information to the sentence, then it *is* set off with punctuation, usually a comma or commas (see p. 428):

The governor, <u>according to the newspaper and other sources</u>, has reluctantly decided to veto the bill.

As all the preceding examples illustrate, a preposition and its object are not separated by a comma.

Exercise 12.9   Identifying prepositional phrases

Identify the prepositional phrases in the following passage. Indicate whether each phrase functions as an adjective or as an adverb, and underline the word that the phrase modifies.

Example:

┌── adverb ──┐   ┌── adverb ──┐ ┌── adjective ──┐
After an hour I finally <u>arrived</u> at the <u>home</u> of my professor.

On July 3, 1863, at Gettysburg, Pennsylvania, General Robert E. Lee gambled unsuccessfully for a Confederate victory in the American Civil War. The battle of Pickett's Charge was one of the most disastrous conflicts of the war. Confederate and Union forces faced each other on parallel ridges separated by almost a mile of open fields. After an artillery bombardment of the Union position, nearly 12,000 Confederate infantry marched toward the Union ridge. The Union guns had been silent but suddenly roared against the approaching Confederates. Within an hour, perhaps half of the Confederate soldiers lay wounded or dead.

Exercise 12.10   Sentence combining: Prepositional phrases

To practice writing sentences with prepositional phrases, combine each group of sentences below into one sentence that includes one or two prepositional phrases. You will have to add, delete, and rearrange words. Some items have more than one possible answer.

> *Example:*
> I will start working. The new job will pay the minimum wage.
> I will start working <u>at a new job</u> <u>for the minimum wage.</u>

1. The slow loris protects itself well. Its habitat is Southeast Asia. It possesses a poisonous chemical.
2. The loris frightens predators when it exudes this chemical. The chemical comes from a gland. The gland is on the loris's upper arm.
3. The loris's chemical is highly toxic. The chemical is not like a skunk's spray. Even small quantities of the chemical are toxic.
4. A tiny dose can affect a human. The dose would get in the mouth. The human would be sent into shock.
5. Predators probably can sense the toxin. They detect it at a distance. They use their nasal organs.

2 Using verbals and verbal phrases

Verbals are special verb forms such as *smoking* or *hidden* or *to win* that can function as nouns (*smoking is dangerous*) or as modifiers (*the hidden money, the urge to win*).

Note A verbal *cannot* stand alone as the complete verb in the predicate of a sentence. For example, *The man smoking* and *The money hidden* are not sentences but sentence fragments (see p. 330). Any verbal must combine with a helping verb to serve as the predicate of a sentence: *The man was smoking. The money is hidden.*

Because verbals cannot serve alone as sentence predicates, they are sometimes called **nonfinite verbs** (in essence, they are "unfinished"). **Finite verbs,** in contrast, can make an assertion or express a state of being without a helping verb (they are "finished"). Either of the following two tests can distinguish finite and nonfinite verbs.

Tests for finite and nonfinite verbs (verbals)

Test 1 Does the word require a change in form when a third-person subject changes from singular to plural?

Yes   Finite verb: *It sings. They sing.*

No   Nonfinite verb (verbal): *bird singing, birds singing*

(continued)

ANSWERS: EXERCISE 12.9

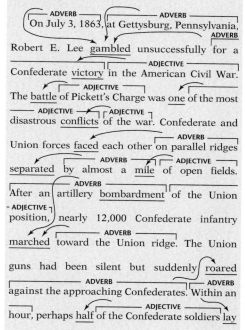

ANSWERS: EXERCISE 12.10

Possible answers

1. The slow loris of Southeast Asia protects itself well with a poisonous chemical.
2. The loris frightens predators when it exudes this chemical from a gland on its upper arm.
3. Unlike a skunk's spray, the loris's chemical is highly toxic even in small quantities.
4. A tiny dose in the mouth can send a human into shock.
5. Predators probably can sense the toxin at a distance with their nasal organs.

Tests for finite and nonfinite verbs (verbals)

(continued)

Test 2 Does the word require a change in form to show the difference in present, past, and future?

Yes   Finite verb: *It sings. It sang. It will sing.*

No   Nonfinite verb (verbal):   *The bird singing is a robin.*
                                        The bird singing was a robin.
                                        The bird singing will be a robin.

There are three kinds of verbals: participles, gerunds, and infinitives.

Participles

All verbs have two participle forms, a present and a past. The **present participle** consists of the dictionary form of the verb plus the ending *-ing: beginning, completing, hiding.* The **past participle** of most verbs consists of the dictionary form plus *-d* or *-ed: believed, completed.* Some common verbs have an irregular past participle, such as *begun* or *hidden.* (See pp. 275–77.)

Both present and past participles function as adjectives to modify nouns and pronouns:

Shopping malls sometimes frustrate shoppers.

Shoppers may feel trapped.

> **CULTURE LANGUAGE**   For English verbs expressing feeling, the present and past participles have different meanings: *It was a boring lecture. The bored students slept.* See pages 322–23.

Gerunds

Gerund is the name given to the *-ing* form of the verb when it serves as a noun:

subject
Strolling through stores can exhaust the hardiest shopper.

object
Many children learn to hate shopping.

Present participles and gerunds can be distinguished *only* by their function in a sentence. When the *-ing* form functions as an adjective (*a teaching degree*), it is a present participle. When the *-ing* form functions as a noun (*Teaching is difficult*), it is a gerund.

> **CULTURE LANGUAGE**   In English, always use a gerund, not any other verb form, as the object of a preposition: *Diners are prohibited from smoking.* See also the culture-language note opposite.

GRAMMAR TERMS

Terminology like *gerund* is one reason many students are convinced they can't "do" grammar, despite the fact that they construct sophisticated sentences every day. You may want to use a synonym like *verbal noun* or *-ing noun* to help students become more comfortable with this term.

Infinitives

The **infinitive** is the *to* form of the verb, the dictionary form preceded by the infinitive marker *to: to begin, to hide, to run*. Infinitives may function as adjectives, nouns, or adverbs:

adjective
The question to answer is why shoppers endure mall fatigue.

noun
The solution for mall fatigue is to leave.

adverb
Still, shoppers find it difficult to quit.

CULTURE LANGUAGE Infinitives and gerunds may follow some English verbs and not others and may differ in meaning after a verb: *The cowboy stopped to sing. The cowboy stopped singing*. (See pp. 285–86.)

Verbal phrases

Participles, gerunds, and infinitives—like other verb forms—may take subjects, objects, or complements, and they may be modified by adverbs. The verbal and all the words immediately related to it make up a **verbal phrase**. With verbal phrases, we can create concise sentences packed with information.

Like participles, **participial phrases** always serve as adjectives, modifying nouns or pronouns:

Buying things, most shoppers feel themselves in control.

They make selections determined by personal taste.

Gerund phrases, like gerunds, always serve as nouns:

subject
Shopping for clothing and other items satisfies personal needs.

object of preposition
Malls are good at creating such needs.

Infinitive phrases may serve as nouns, adverbs, or adjectives:

sentence subject   subject complement
To design a mall is to create an artificial environment.
noun phrase   noun phrase

Malls are designed to make shoppers feel safe.
adverb phrase

The environment supports the impulse to shop for oneself.
adjective phrase

Note When an infinitive or infinitive phrase serves as a noun after verbs such as *hear, help, let, make, see,* and *watch,* the infinitive marker *to* is omitted: *We all heard her tell* [not *to tell*] *the story.*

Punctuating verbals and verbal phrases

Verbal phrases punctuated as complete sentences are sentence fragments (Chapter 17). A complete sentence must contain a subject and a finite verb (p. 245):

| Fragment | <u>Treating</u> the patients kindly. |
| Revised | <u>She treats</u> the patients kindly. |

A verbal or verbal phrase serving as a modifier is almost always set off with a comma when it introduces a sentence (see p. 425):

<u>To pay tuition,</u> some students work at two jobs.

A modifying verbal or verbal phrase that interrupts or concludes a sentence is *not* set off with punctuation when it is essential to the meaning of the word or words it modifies (see p. 428):

Jobs <u>paying well</u> are hard to find.

When an interrupting or concluding verbal modifier is *not* essential to meaning but merely adds information to the sentence, it *is* set off with punctuation, usually a comma or commas (see p. 428):

One good job, <u>paying twelve dollars an hour,</u> was filled in fifteen minutes.

Exercise 12.11 Identifying verbals and verbal phrases

The following sentences contain participles, gerunds, and infinitives as well as participial, gerund, and infinitive phrases. First underline each verbal or verbal phrase. Then indicate whether it is used as an adjective, an adverb, or a noun.

Example:

adjective   adverb

<u>Laughing</u>, the talk-show host prodded her guest <u>to speak</u>.

1. Written in 1850 by Nathaniel Hawthorne, *The Scarlet Letter* tells the story of Hester Prynne.
2. Shunned by the community, Hester endures her loneliness.
3. Hester is humble enough to withstand her Puritan neighbors' cutting remarks.
4. Enduring the cruel treatment, the determined young woman refuses to leave her home.
5. By living a life of patience and unselfishness, Hester eventually becomes the community's angel.

Exercise 12.12 Sentence combining: Verbals and verbal phrases

To practice writing sentences with verbals and verbal phrases, combine each of the following pairs of sentences into one sentence. You will have to add, delete, change, and rearrange words. Each item has more than one possible answer.

Example:

My father took pleasure in mean pranks. For instance, he hid the neighbor's cat.

My father took pleasure in mean pranks such as <u>hiding the neighbor's cat</u>.

1. Air pollution is a health problem. It affects millions of Americans.
2. The air has been polluted mainly by industries and automobiles. It contains toxic chemicals.
3. Environmentalists pressure politicians. They think politicians should pass stricter laws.
4. Many politicians waver. They are not necessarily against environmentalism.
5. The problems are too complex. They cannot be solved easily.

3 Using absolute phrases

Absolute phrases consist of a noun or pronoun and a participle, plus any modifiers:

```
            ┌────── absolute phrase ──────┐
Many ethnic groups, their own place established, are making way for
new arrivals.
```

```
┌──── absolute phrase ────┐ ┌───── absolute phrase ─────┐
Their native lands left behind, an uncertain future looming, immi-
grants face many obstacles.
```

These phrases are called *absolute* (from a Latin word meaning "free") because they have no specific grammatical connection to a noun, verb, or any other word in the rest of the sentence. Instead, they modify the entire rest of the sentence, adding information.

Notice that absolute phrases, unlike participial phrases, always contain a subject. Compare the following sentences:

```
        ┌─participial phrase─┐
For many immigrants learning English, the language introduces Ameri-
can culture.
```

```
┌────── absolute phrase ──────┐
The immigrants having learned English, their opportunities widen.
```

We often omit the participle from an absolute phrase when it is some form of *be,* such as *being* or *having been:*

```
┌────── absolute phrase ──────┐
Two languages [being] at hand, bilingual citizens in fact have many
cultural and occupational advantages.
```

Punctuating absolute phrases

Absolute phrases are always set off from the rest of the sentence with punctuation, usually a comma or commas (see also p. 432):

<u>Their future more secure</u>, these citizens will make room for new arrivals.
These citizens, <u>their future more secure</u>, will make room for new arrivals.

COLLABORATIVE LEARNING

Students can work productively in pairs or small groups to combine the sentences in Exercise 12.13. The collaborative effort and consequent discussion can be useful for students who are having difficulty with absolute phrases.

ANSWERS: EXERCISE 12.13

Possible answers

1. Her face beaming, Geraldine Ferraro enjoyed the crowd's cheers after her nomination for Vice President.
2. A vacancy having occurred, Sandra Day O'Connor was appointed the first female Supreme Court justice.
3. Her appointment confirmed, Condoleezza Rice became the first female national security advisor.
4. The midterm elections over, Nancy Pelosi was elected the first female minority leader of the House of Representatives.
5. The election won, Elizabeth Dole was the first woman to become a US senator from North Carolina.

CREATE YOUR OWN

Divide the class into groups. Ask each group to create its own set of sentence-combining exercises following the pattern of the exercises in the handbook. Then ask the groups to trade exercises, work on them, and return them to the authors with both answers and constructive feedback.

Exercise 12.13   Sentence combining: Absolute phrases

To practice writing sentences with absolute phrases, combine each pair of sentences below into one sentence that contains an absolute phrase. You will have to add, delete, change, and rearrange words.

> *Example:*
> The flower's petals wilted. It looked pathetic.
> <u>Its petals wilted</u>, the flower looked pathetic.

1. Geraldine Ferraro's face beamed. She enjoyed the crowd's cheers after her nomination for Vice President.
2. A vacancy had occurred. Sandra Day O'Connor was appointed the first female Supreme Court justice.
3. Her appointment was confirmed. Condoleezza Rice became the first female national security adviser.
4. The midterm elections were over. Nancy Pelosi was elected the first female minority leader of the House of Representatives.
5. The election was won. Elizabeth Dole was the first woman to become a US senator from North Carolina.

4 Using subordinate clauses

A **clause** is any group of words that contains both a subject and a predicate. There are two kinds of clauses, and the distinction between them is important:

- A *main* or *independent clause* makes a complete statement and can stand alone as a sentence: *The sky darkened.*
- A *subordinate* or *dependent clause* is just like a main clause except that it begins with a subordinating word: *when the sky darkened; because he wants it; whoever calls.* The subordinating word reduces the clause to a single part of speech—an adjective, an adverb, or a noun—that supports the idea in a main clause. Because it only modifies or names something, a subordinate clause cannot stand alone as a sentence (see the discussion of punctuation on p. 253). (The word *subordinate* means "secondary" or "controlled by another." It comes from the Latin *sub*, "under," and *ordo*, "order.")

The following examples show the differences between main and subordinate clauses:

┌──────main clause──────┬─main clause─┐
The school teaches parents. It is unusual.

┌──────subordinate clause──────┬─main clause─┐
Because the school teaches parents, it is unusual.

┌──────main clause──────┬──────main clause──────┐
Some parents avoid their children's schools. They are often illiterate.

┌──────main clause──────┐
Parents who are illiterate often avoid their children's schools.
     └subordinate clause┘

Two kinds of subordinating words introduce subordinate clauses: subordinating conjunctions and relative pronouns.

Subordinating conjunctions

Subordinating conjunctions, like prepositions, never change form in any way. In the following box they are arranged by the relationships they signal. (Some fit in more than one group.)

Common subordinating conjunctions

Cause or effect	Condition	Comparison or contrast	Space or time
as	even if	as	after
because	if	as if	as long as
in order that	if only	as though	before
since	provided	rather than	now that
so that	since	than	once
	unless	whereas	since
Concession	when	whether	till
although	whenever	while	until
as if	whether		when
even if		**Purpose**	whenever
even though		in order that	where
though		so that	wherever
		that	while

CULTURE LANGUAGE   Subordinating conjunctions convey their meaning without help from other function words, such as the coordinating conjunctions *and, but, for,* and *so* (p. 257).

Faulty <u>Even though</u> the parents are illiterate, but their children may read well. [*Even though* and *but* have the same meaning, so both are not needed.]

Revised <u>Even though</u> the parents are illiterate, their children may read well.

Relative pronouns

Unlike subordinating conjunctions, **relative pronouns** usually act as subjects or objects in their own clauses, and two of them (*who* and *whoever*) change form accordingly (see pp. 269–70).

Relative pronouns

which	what	who (whose, whom)
that	whatever	whoever (whomever)

Subordinate clauses

Subordinate clauses function as adjectives, adverbs, or nouns.

Adjective clauses

Adjective clauses modify nouns and pronouns. They usually begin with the relative pronoun *who, whom, whose, which,* or *that,* although a few adjective clauses begin with *when* or *where* (standing for *in which, on which,* or *at which*). The pronoun is the subject or object of the clause it begins. The clause ordinarily falls immediately after the noun or pronoun it modifies:

Parents who are illiterate often have bad memories of school.

Schools that involve parents are more successful with children.

One school, which is open year-round, helps parents learn to read.

The school is in a city where the illiteracy rate is high.

Adverb clauses

Like adverbs, **adverb clauses** modify verbs, adjectives, other adverbs, and whole groups of words. They usually tell how, why, when, where, under what conditions, or with what result. They always begin with subordinating conjunctions.

The school began teaching parents when adult illiteracy gained national attention.

At first the program was not as successful as its founders had hoped.

Because it was directed at people who could not read, advertising had to be inventive.

Noun clauses

Noun clauses function as subjects, objects, and complements in sentences. They begin with *that, what, whatever, who, whom, whoever, whomever, when, where, whether, why,* or *how.* Unlike adjective and adverb clauses, noun clauses *replace* a word (a noun) within a clause; therefore, they can be difficult to identify.

———————— sentence subject ————————
Whether the program would succeed depended on door-to-door advertising.

———————— object of verb ————————
Teachers explained in person how the program would work.

———————— object of preposition ————————
A few parents were anxious about what their children would think.

Elliptical clauses

A subordinate clause that is grammatically incomplete but clear in meaning is an **elliptical clause** (*ellipsis* means "omission"). The meaning of the clause is clear because the missing element can be supplied from the context. Most often the elements omitted are the pronouns *that, which,* and *whom* or the predicate from the second part of a comparison.

> Skepticism and fear were among the feelings [that] the parents voiced.
>
> The parents knew their children could read better than they [could read].

Punctuating subordinate clauses

Subordinate clauses punctuated as complete sentences are sentence fragments (Chapter 17). Though a subordinate clause contains a subject and a predicate and thus resembles a complete sentence, it also begins with a subordinating word that makes it into an adjective, adverb, or noun. A single part of speech cannot stand alone as a complete sentence.

> **Fragment**   Because a door was ajar.
>
> **Revised**   A door was ajar.
>
> **Revised**   The secret leaked because a door was ajar.

A subordinate clause serving as an adverb is almost always set off with a comma when it introduces a sentence (see p. 425):

> Although the project was almost completed, it lost its funding.

A modifying subordinate clause that interrupts or concludes a main clause is *not* set off with punctuation when it is essential to the meaning of the word or words it modifies (see p. 429):

> The woman who directed the project lost her job.
>
> The project lost its funding because it was not completed on time.

When an interrupting or concluding subordinate clause is *not* essential to meaning, but merely adds information to the sentence, it *is* set off with punctuation, usually a comma or commas (see pp. 428–29):

> The project lost its funding, although it was almost completed.
>
> The director, who holds a PhD, sought new funding.

Exercise 12.14   Identifying subordinate clauses

Identify the subordinate clauses in the following sentences. Then indicate whether each is used as an adjective, an adverb, or a noun. If the clause is a noun, indicate what function it performs in the sentence.

CULTURE LANGUAGE

CLAUSE CONNECTORS

ESL students may try unsuccessfully to use ellipsis in writing. Remind students that generally, in formal writing, clause connectors such as *that* and the relative pronouns *that, which,* and *whom* are not omitted. Students *will not* go wrong if they keep the clause connectors in their writing, but they *may* be wrong if they omit them.

COLLABORATIVE LEARNING

Exercises 12.14 and 12.15 work well as collaborative projects. In particular, students with varying grammatical skills have the opportunity to discuss the parts of speech and their relative functions.

ANSWERS: EXERCISE 12.14

1. Scientists <u>who want to catch the slightest signals from space</u> [ADJ] use extremely sensitive receivers.
2. <u>Even though they have had to fight for funding</u> [ADV], these scientists have persisted in their research.
3. The research is called SETI, <u>which stands for Search for Extraterrestrial Intelligence</u> [ADJ].
4. The theory is <u>that intelligent beings in space are trying to get in touch with us</u> [N (SUBJECT COMPLEMENT)].
5. Scientists do not yet know <u>what frequency these beings would use to send signals</u> [N (DIRECT OBJECT)].

ANSWERS: EXERCISE 12.15

Possible answers

1. Moviegoers expect <u>that movie sequels should be as exciting as the original films</u>.
2. <u>Although a few sequels are good films</u>, most are poor imitations of the originals.
3. <u>Whenever a sequel to a blockbuster film arrives in the theater</u>, crowds quickly line up to see it.
4. Viewers pay to see the same villains and heroes <u>whom they remember fondly</u>.
5. Afterward, viewers often grumble about filmmakers <u>who rehash tired plots and characters</u>.

EXPECTING PROBLEMS

As students begin using appositives, you may find more comma splices and fragments in their essays. Warn students to expect these errors, so that they will proofread more carefully. Be understanding as you evaluate student papers in which the students are practicing these strategies for the first time. If you focus on grammar faults, they may lose the incentive to take stylistic risks.

Example:

The article explained <u>how one could build an underground house</u> [noun]. [Object of *explained*.]

1. Scientists who want to catch the slightest signals from space use extremely sensitive receivers.
2. Even though they have had to fight for funding, these scientists have persisted in their research.
3. The research is called SETI, which stands for Search for Extraterrestrial Intelligence.
4. The theory is that intelligent beings in space are trying to get in touch with us.
5. Scientists do not yet know what frequency these beings would use to send signals.

Exercise 12.15   Sentence combining: Subordinate clauses

To practice writing sentences with subordinate clauses, combine each pair of main clauses into one sentence. Use either subordinating conjunctions or relative pronouns as appropriate, referring to the lists on page 251 if necessary. You will have to add, delete, and rearrange words. Each item has more than one possible answer.

Example:

She did not have her tire irons with her. She could not change her bicycle tire.

<u>Because she did not have her tire irons with her</u>, she could not change her bicycle tire.

1. Moviegoers expect something. Movie sequels should be as exciting as the original films.
2. A few sequels are good films. Most sequels are poor imitations of the originals.
3. A sequel to a blockbuster film arrives in the theater. Crowds quickly line up to see it.
4. Viewers pay to see the same villains and heroes. They remember these characters fondly.
5. Afterward, viewers often grumble about filmmakers. The filmmakers rehash tired plots and characters.

5 | Using appositives

An **appositive** is usually a noun that renames another noun nearby, most often the noun just before the appositive. (The word *appositive* derives from a Latin word that means "placed near to" or "applied to.") An **appositive phrase** includes modifiers as well.

Bizen ware, a dark stoneware, has been produced in Japan since the fourteenth century.

The name Bizen comes from the location of the kilns used to fire the pottery.

All appositives can replace the words they refer to: *A dark stoneware has been produced in Japan.*

Appositives are often introduced by words and phrases such as *or, that is, such as, for example,* and *in other words:*

> Bizen ware is used in the Japanese tea ceremony, that is, the Zen Buddhist observance that links meditation and art.

Appositives are economical alternatives to adjective clauses containing a form of *be*, as shown in the next example.

> Bizen ware, [which is] a dark stoneware, has been produced in Japan since the fourteenth century.

Although most appositives are nouns that rename other nouns, they may also be and rename other parts of speech, such as the verb *thrown* in the sentence below:

> The pottery is thrown, or formed on a potter's wheel.

Punctuating appositives

Appositives punctuated as complete sentences are sentence fragments (see Chapter 17). To correct such fragments, you can usually connect the appositive to the main clause containing the word referred to:

> **Fragment** An exceedingly tall man with narrow shoulders.
>
> **Revised** He stood next to a basketball player, an exceedingly tall man with narrow shoulders.

An appositive is *not* set off with punctuation when it is essential to the meaning of the word it refers to (see p. 429):

> The verb *howl* comes from the Old English verb *houlen.*

When an appositive is *not* essential to the meaning of the word it refers to, it *is* set off with punctuation, usually a comma or commas (see p. 429):

> An aged elm, the tree was struck by lightning.
> The tree, an aged elm, was struck by lightning.
> Lightning struck the tree, an aged elm.

A nonessential appositive is sometimes set off with a dash or dashes, especially when it contains commas (see p. 471):

> Three people—Will, Erica, and Alex—object to the new procedure.

A concluding appositive is sometimes set off with a colon (see p. 469):

> Two principles guide the judge's decisions: justice and mercy.

RESOURCES AND IDEAS

Sentence combining: Background and suggestions

Many of the exercises in this chapter can be used as the basis for a sequence of sentence-combining activities. The appropriate exercises are 8, 10, 12, 13, 15, 16, 17, 21.

Exercises in other chapters that can be part of a sentence-combining sequence are listed in the discussion "A Sequence for Sentence Combining" in the chapter "Using *The Little, Brown Handbook*," page IAE-7 of this instructor's edition.

Much has been written about sentence combining over the past two decades. The twenty-three essays in *Sentence Combining: A Rhetorical Perspective*, ed. Donald A. Daiker, Andrew Kerek, and Max Morenberg (Carbondale: Southern Illinois UP, 1985) provide excellent perspectives on the strengths and weaknesses of sentence combining as a way of improving the quality of writing and of developing an understanding of language and style.

The following works are also useful resources:

Daiker, Donald, Andrew Kerek, and Max Morenberg. "Sentence-Combining and Syntactic Maturity in Freshman English." *College Composition and Communication* 29.1 (1978): 36–41. Print. The authors discuss the results of an experiment demonstrating the effectiveness of sentence combining over fifteen weeks of intensive instruction.

Johnson, Karen E. "Cognitive Strategies and Second Language Writers: A Re-evaluation of Sentence Combining." *Journal of Second Language Writing* 1.1 (1992): 61–75. Print. This essay reviews debates over the effectiveness of sentence combining in the context of ESL writers.

Larsen, Richard B. "Sentence Patterning." *College Composition and Communication* 37.1 (1986): 103–04. Print. Larsen describes a sequence in which students are introduced to a variety of sentence patterns and then asked to use the patterns in their writing, including paragraph-length compositions.

Solomon, Martha. "Teaching the Nominative Absolute." *College Composition and Communication* 26.4 (1975): 356–61. Print. Solomon offers advice on analyzing and teaching the absolute.

Strong, William. *Sentence Combining*. 3rd ed. New York: McGraw-Hill, 1994. Print. Strong divides the exercises combining sentences into three different levels of difficulty and provides examples from the work of well-known writers.

ANSWERS: EXERCISE 12.16

1. Some people, <u>geniuses from birth</u>, perform amazing feats when they are very young.
2. John Stuart Mill, <u>a British philosopher</u>, had written a history of Rome by age seven.
3. Paul Klee and Gustav Mahler, <u>two great artists</u>, began their work at age four.
4. Mahler, <u>a Bohemian composer of intensely emotional</u> works, was also the child of a brutal father.
5. As a child the Swiss painter <u>Paul Klee</u> was frightened by his own drawings of devils.

Exercise 12.16   **Sentence combining: Appositives**

To practice writing sentences with appositives, combine each pair of sentences into one sentence that contains an appositive. You will have to delete and rearrange words. Some items have more than one possible answer.

Example:

The largest land animal is the elephant. The elephant is also one of the most intelligent animals.

The largest land animal, <u>the elephant</u>, is also one of the most intelligent animals.

1. Some people perform amazing feats when they are very young. These people are geniuses from birth.
2. John Stuart Mill was a British philosopher. He had written a history of Rome by age seven.
3. Two great artists began their work at age four. They were Paul Klee and Gustav Mahler.
4. Mahler was a Bohemian composer of intensely emotional works. He was also the child of a brutal father.
5. Paul Klee was a Swiss painter. As a child he was frightened by his own drawings of devils.

12d Compounding words, phrases, and clauses

A **compound construction** combines words that are closely related and equally important. It makes writing clearer and more economical because it pulls together linked information.

Headaches can be controlled by biofeedback. Heart rate can be controlled by biofeedback.

┌──— compound subject ——┐
Headaches and heart rate can be controlled by biofeedback.

Without medication, biofeedback cures headaches. It steadies heart rate. It lowers blood pressure. It relaxes muscles.

┌───— compound predicate ———┐
Without medication, biofeedback cures headaches, steadies heart rate, lowers blood pressure, and relaxes muscles.

1 Using coordinating conjunctions and correlative conjunctions

Two kinds of words create compound constructions: coordinating and correlative conjunctions. **Coordinating conjunctions** are few and do not change form. In the following box the relationship that each conjunction signals appears in parentheses.

Coordinating conjunctions

and (*addition*)	nor (*alternative*)	for (*cause*)	yet (*contrast*)
but (*contrast*)	or (*alternative*)	so (*effect*)	

To remember the coordinating conjunctions, use the word *fanboys: for, and, nor, but, or, yet, so.*

The coordinating conjunctions *and, but, nor,* and *or* always connect words or word groups of the same kind—that is, two or more nouns, verbs, adjectives, adverbs, phrases, subordinate clauses, or main clauses:

> Biofeedback or simple relaxation can relieve headaches.
> Biofeedback is effective but costly.
> Relaxation also works well, and it is inexpensive.

The conjunctions *for* and *so* connect only main clauses. *For* indicates cause; *so* indicates effect.

> Biofeedback can be costly, for the training involves technical equipment and specialists.
>
> Relaxation can be difficult to learn alone, so some people do seek help from specialists.

Some coordinating conjunctions pair up with other words to form **correlative conjunctions**. In the following box the relationship each conjunction signals appears in parentheses.

Common correlative conjunctions

both . . . and (*addition*)	neither . . . nor (*negation*)
not only . . . but also (*addition*)	whether . . . or (*alternative*)
not . . . but (*substitution*)	as . . . as (*comparison*)
either . . . or (*alternative*)	

> Both biofeedback and relaxation can relieve headaches.
>
> The techniques require neither psychotherapy nor medication.
>
> The headache sufferer learns not only to recognize the causes of headaches but also to control those causes.

Punctuating compounded words, phrases, and clauses

Two words, phrases, or subordinate clauses that are connected by a coordinating conjunction are *not* separated by a comma (see pp. 439–40):

The library needs <u>renovation and rebuilding</u>.
The work will begin <u>after spring term but before fall term</u>.

When two *main* clauses are joined into one sentence with a coordinating conjunction, a comma precedes the conjunction (see p. 422):

The project will be lengthy, <u>and</u> everyone will suffer some inconvenience.

When two main clauses are joined *without* a coordinating conjunction, they must be separated with a semicolon to avoid the error called a comma splice (see p. 338):

The work cannot be delayed; it's already overdue.

In a series of three or more items, commas separate the items, with *and* usually preceding the last item (see p. 433):

The renovated library will feature <u>new study carrels, new shelving, and a larger reference section</u>.

Semicolons sometimes separate the items in a series if they are long or contain commas (see p. 448).

A comma also separates two or more adjectives when they modify a noun equally and are not joined by a coordinating conjunction (see p. 433):

<u>Cracked, crumbling</u> walls will be repaired.

The comma does *not* separate adjectives when the one nearer the noun is more closely related to it in meaning (see p. 434):

<u>New reading</u> lounges will replace the old ones.

2 Using conjunctive adverbs

One other kind of connecting word, called a **conjunctive adverb,** relates only main clauses, not words, phrases, or subordinate clauses. In the box opposite, the conjunctive adverbs are arranged by the relationships they signal.

It's important to distinguish between conjunctive adverbs and conjunctions (coordinating and subordinating) because they demand different punctuation (see the next page). Conjunctive adverbs are *adverbs:* they describe the relation of ideas in two clauses, and, like most adverbs, they can move around in their clause:

Relaxation techniques have improved; <u>however</u>, few people know them.
Relaxation techniques have improved; few people know them, <u>however</u>.

In contrast, conjunctions bind two clauses into a single grammatical unit, and they cannot be moved.

Common conjunctive adverbs

Addition	Emphasis	Comparison or contrast	Cause or effect	Time
also	certainly	however	accordingly	finally
besides	indeed	in comparison	as a result	meanwhile
further	in fact	in contrast	consequently	next
furthermore	still	instead	hence	now
in addition	undoubtedly	likewise	similarly	then
incidentally		nevertheless	therefore	thereafter
moreover		nonetheless	thus	
		otherwise		
		rather		

<u>Although</u> few people know them, relaxation techniques have improved. [The subordinating conjunction can't be moved: *Few people know them although, relaxation techniques have improved.*]

Relaxation techniques have improved, <u>but</u> few people know them. [The coordinating conjunction can't be moved: *Relaxation techniques have improved, few people know them <u>but</u>.*]

Note Some connecting words have more than one use. *After, until,* and some other words may be either prepositions or subordinating conjunctions. Some prepositions, such as *behind* and *in,* can serve also as adverbs, as in *He trailed <u>behind</u>.* And some conjunctive adverbs, particularly *however,* may also serve simply as adverbs in sentences such as *<u>However</u> much the books cost, we must have them for our classes.* Again, the part of speech of a word depends on its function in a sentence.

Punctuating sentences containing conjunctive adverbs

Because the two main clauses related by a conjunctive adverb remain independent units, they must be separated by a semicolon. If they are separated by a comma, the result is a comma splice (Chapter 18):

Comma splice	Interest rates rose, <u>therefore</u>, real estate prices declined.
Revised	Interest rates rose; <u>therefore</u>, real estate prices declined.

A conjunctive adverb is almost always set off from its clause with a comma or commas (see p. 430):

The decline was small; <u>however</u>, some home owners suffered unexpected losses.

The decline was small; some home owners, <u>however</u>, suffered unexpected losses.

GRAMMAR TERMS

Terminology like *conjunctive adverb* is another reason that many students are convinced they can't "do" grammar, despite the fact that they construct sophisticated sentences every day. You may want to use a synonym like *movable adverb* or *floating adverb* to help students become more comfortable with this term.

MAKING CONNECTIONS BETWEEN GRAMMAR AND CONTENT

Because conjunctive adverbs are often used to signal transitions, you might consider discussing transitions at this time (see Ch. 4, "Paragraphs") or reviewing these ideas. Using a returned paragraph or essay, have students identify conjunctive adverbs and how they function in their writing.

COLLABORATIVE LEARNING

Students can work effectively in groups on Exercise 12.17. Have each group try the effect of different conjunctive adverbs and coordinating and correlative conjunctions from the lists on pages 257 and 259 and discuss the effect that each change has on the meaning of the sentence.

ANSWERS: EXERCISE 12.17

Possible answers

1. All too often people assume that old age is not a productive time; however, many people in their nineties have had great achievements.
2. In his nineties the philosopher Bertrand Russell spoke vigorously for both international peace and nuclear disarmament.
3. Grandma Moses did not retire to an easy chair; instead, she began painting at age seventy-six and was still going at one hundred.
4. The British general George Higginson and the British archaeologist Margaret Murray published their memoirs after they were ninety.
5. The architect Frank Lloyd Wright designed his first building at age twenty and his last at age ninety.

RESOURCES AND IDEAS

Gorrell, Donna. "Controlled Composition for Basic Writers." *College Composition and Communication* 32.3 (1981): 308–16. Print. Gorrell suggests having students manipulate and alter previously written material to develop basic skills.

Exercise 12.17 Sentence combining: Compound constructions

To practice compounding words, phrases, and clauses, combine each of the following pairs of sentences into one sentence that is as short as possible without altering meaning. Use an appropriate connecting word of the type specified in parentheses, referring to the lists on pages 257 and 259 as necessary. You will have to add and delete words, and you may have to change or add punctuation.

> *Example:*
> The encyclopedia had some information. It was not detailed enough. (*Conjunctive adverb.*)
>
> The encyclopedia had some information; however, it was not detailed enough.

1. All too often people assume that old age is not a productive time. Many people in their nineties have had great achievements. (*Conjunctive adverb.*)
2. In his nineties the philosopher Bertrand Russell spoke vigorously for international peace. He spoke for nuclear disarmament. (*Correlative conjunction.*)
3. Grandma Moses did not retire to an easy chair. She began painting at age seventy-six and was still going at one hundred. (*Conjunctive adverb.*)
4. The British general George Higginson published his memoirs after he was ninety. The British archaeologist Margaret Murray published her memoirs after she was ninety. (*Coordinating conjunction.*)
5. The architect Frank Lloyd Wright designed his first building at age twenty. He designed his last building at age ninety. (*Coordinating conjunction.*)

12e Changing the usual word order

So far, all the examples of basic sentence structure have been similar: the subject of the sentence comes first, naming the performer of the predicate's action, and the predicate comes second. This arrangement describes most English sentences, but four kinds of sentences change the order.

Questions

In most questions the predicate verb or a part of it precedes the subject:

verb   subject ⌐— verb —⌐
Have interest rates been rising?

verb subject verb
Did rates rise?

      verb subject verb
Why did rates rise today?

subject verb
What is the answer? [Normal subject-verb order.]

Commands

In commands the subject *you* is omitted:

verb
Think of the options.

verb
Watch the news.

Passive sentences

Generally, the subject performs the action of a verb in the **active voice.** But sometimes the subject *receives* the action of a verb in the **passive voice:**

subject verb
Active   Kyong wrote the paper.

subject —— verb ——
Passive   The paper was written by Kyong.

See pages 298–99 for more on forming the passive voice, and see pages 299–300 on overuse of the passive voice.

Sentences with postponed subjects

The subject follows the predicate in two sentence patterns. The normal order may be reversed for emphasis:

Henry comes here. [Normal order.]
Here comes Henry. [Reversed order.]

Or the word *there, here,* or *it* may postpone the subject:

verb   subject
There will be eighteen people attending the meeting.

verb   ———— subject ————
It was surprising that Marinetti was nominated.

verb   subject
Here are the reasons why.

There, it, and *here* in such sentences are called **expletives.** Expletive sentences have their uses, but they can also be wordy and unemphatic (see p. 529).

When you use an expletive construction, be careful to include *there, here,* or *it.* Only commands and some questions can begin with verbs.

Faulty   No one predicted the nomination. Were no polls showing Marinetti ahead.

Revised   No one predicted the nomination. There were no polls show-ing Marinetti ahead.

Exercise 12.18   Forming questions and commands

Form a question and a command from the following noun and verb pairs.

Example:
wood, split
Did you split all this wood? Split the wood for our fire.

EXPLETIVES

Remind students that because English is a subject-verb-object language, something must fill the subject position when the subject is delayed. *There* and *it* fulfill this requirement by acting as dummy subjects.

ANSWERS: EXERCISE 12.18
Possible answers

1. Will the water boil?
   Boil the water, please.
2. Did the music stop?
   Stop the music.
3. Have you set the table?
   Set the table.
4. Have you rolled the dice yet?
   Roll the dice.
5. Who can use the telephone?
   Use the telephone.

1. water, boil
2. music, stop
3. table, set
4. dice, roll
5. telephone, use

ANSWERS: EXERCISE 12.19

1. <u>Milo Addica and Will Rokos cowrote</u> the screenplay for *Monster's Ball*.
2. <u>Marc Foster directed</u> the film.
3. <u>Only one performance in the movie received</u> an Academy Award.
4. <u>Halle Berry won</u> the award for best actress.
5. <u>The press congratulated</u> Berry for being the first African American to win the award.

COLLABORATIVE LEARNING

DECODING THE SENTENCE

Divide the class into small groups and have each group write a set of nonsense sentences that conform to English syntax and punctuation. Students should be sure to include nonsense prepositional phrases, verbals, appositives, absolutes, and subordinate and coordinate structures. Warn students to punctuate the sentences carefully. Students can use the nonsense sentence at the beginning of Chapter 12 as a model.

COLLABORATIVE LEARNING

PARTS OF SPEECH

Once the sentences are written, have groups exchange sentences or write them on the board and try to identify the part of speech for each nonsense word. If the creators of the sentences have made errors in punctuation, the puzzle-solvers should be prepared to correct them. This exercise should help students see how grammar and punctuation work together to define a word's role in a sentence and to create different kinds of sentences.

A WRITER'S PERSPECTIVE

Prose is architecture, and the Baroque is over.
—ERNEST HEMINGWAY

---

1. water, boil
2. music, stop
3. table, set
4. dice, roll
5. telephone, use

Exercise 12.19 Rewriting passives and expletives

Rewrite each passive sentence below as active, and rewrite each expletive construction to restore normal subject-predicate order. (For additional exercises with the passive voice and with expletives, see pp. 300, 380, and 530.)

Example:
All the trees in the park were planted by the city.
<u>The city planted</u> all the trees in the park.

1. The screenplay for *Monster's Ball* was cowritten by Milo Addica and Will Rokos.
2. The film was directed by Marc Foster.
3. There was only one performance in the movie that received an Academy Award.
4. It was Halle Berry who won the award for best actress.
5. Berry was congratulated by the press for being the first African American to win the award.

12f Classifying sentences

We describe and classify sentences in two different ways: by function (statement, question, command, exclamation, and so on) or by structure. Four basic sentence structures are possible: simple, compound, complex, and compound-complex. Each structure gives different emphasis to the sentence's main idea or ideas and to any supporting information.

1 Writing simple sentences

A **simple sentence** consists of a single main clause and no subordinate clause:

——— main clause ———
Last summer was unusually hot.

——————— main clause ———————
The summer made many farmers leave the area for good or reduced them to bare existence.

2 Writing compound sentences

A **compound sentence** consists of two or more main clauses and no subordinate clause. The clauses may be joined by a coordinating conjunction and a comma, by a semicolon alone, or by a conjunctive adverb and a semicolon.

┌────── main clause ──────┐   ┌────── main clause ──────┐
Last July was hot, but August was even hotter.

┌───────── main clause ─────────┐ ┌───────── main clause ─────────┐
The hot sun scorched the earth; the lack of rain killed many crops.

3 Writing complex sentences

A **complex sentence** contains one main clause and one or more subordinate clauses:

┌──── main clause ────┐ ┌────── subordinate clause ──────┐
Rain finally came, although many had left the area by then.

┌──────── main clause ────────┐ ┌─── subordinate clause ───
Those who remained were able to start anew because the government

subordinate clause
came to their aid.

Notice that length does not determine whether a sentence is complex or simple; both kinds can be short or long.

4 Writing compound-complex sentences

A **compound-complex sentence** has the characteristics of both the compound sentence (two or more main clauses) and the complex sentence (at least one subordinate clause):

┌───── subordinate clause ─────┐ ┌────── main clause ──────┐
When government aid finally came, many people had already been re-

┌────── main clause ──────┐
duced to poverty and others had been forced to move.

Exercise 12.20 Identifying sentence structures

Mark the main clauses and subordinate clauses in the following sentences. Identify each sentence as simple, compound, complex, or compound-complex.

Example:

┌────── main clause ──────┐ ┌─── subordinate clause ───
The police began patrolling more often when crime in the neighborhood increased. [Complex sentence.]

1. Joseph Pulitzer endowed the Pulitzer Prizes.
2. Pulitzer, incidentally, was the publisher of the New York newspaper *The World.*
3. Although the first prizes were for journalism and letters only, Pulitzers are now awarded in music and other areas.
4. For example, Berke Breathed won for his *Bloom County* comic strip, and Roger Reynolds won for his musical composition *Whispers Out of Time.*
5. Although only one prize is usually awarded in each category, in 1989 Taylor Branch's *Parting the Waters* won a history prize, and it shared the honor with James M. McPherson's *Battle Cry of Freedom.*

(student text continues on p. 264)

RESOURCES AND IDEAS

Dawkins, John. "Teaching Punctuation as a Rhetorical Tool." *College Composition and Communication* 46.4 (1995): 533–48. Print. Dawkins makes a case for teaching the rhetorical thinking processes that accompany decisions about punctuation marks.

Herrington, Anne J. "Grammar Recharted: Sentence Analysis for Writing." *Writing Exercises from "Exercise Exchange."* Vol. 2. Urbana: NCTE, 1984. 276–87. Print. Herrington offers a number of useful classroom activities.

COLLABORATIVE LEARNING

Exercises 12.20 and 12.21 work well as group projects. Students might begin by working individually on Exercise 12.20, then compare responses in small groups and work together on Exercise 12.21.

ANSWERS: EXERCISE 12.20

┌──────── MAIN ────────┐
1. *Simple:* Joseph Pulitzer endowed the Pulitzer Prizes.

┌──────── MAIN ────────┐
2. *Simple:* Pulitzer, incidentally, was the publisher of the New York newspaper *The World.*

┌──── SUBORDINATE ────┐
3. *Complex:* Although the first prizes were for
┌──── MAIN ────┐
journalism and letters only, Pulitzers are now awarded in music and other areas.

┌──── MAIN ────┐
4. *Compound:* For example, Berke Breathed won for his *Bloom County* comic strip, and
┌──── MAIN ────┐
Roger Reynolds won for his musical composition *Whispers Out of Time.*

┌──── SUBORDINATE ────┐
5. *Compound-complex:* Although only one prize is usually awarded in each category, in 1989
┌──── MAIN ────┐
Taylor Branch's *Parting the Waters* won a history prize, and
┌──── MAIN ────┐
it shared the honor with James M. McPherson's *Battle Cry of Freedom.*

SUMMARY GUIDES

The guides on this and the next five pages appear only in the *Instructor's Annotated Edition*. They are included here for use in conferences and labs. Each guide collects all the descriptions and conventions for a different element: nouns, pronouns, verbs and verbals, and modifiers. Thus the guides provide convenient indexes or texts for students having difficulty with, say, identifying and placing modifiers or distinguishing verbs and verbals. The listings under "Conventions" in each guide contain at least one example showing correct or preferred usage. For additional examples or detailed explanations, consult the sections given in parentheses.

Guide to nouns

Summary and index of information in the student text (consult sections or pages in parentheses).

Description of nouns

Nouns as sentence subjects (12a-1, 12a-2)

Nouns as direct and indirect objects (12a-3), object complements (12a-3), objects of prepositions (12c-1), appositives (12c-5), modifiers (16f)

Classes of nouns: proper, common, collective, count, mass, concrete, abstract (12a-2)

Forms of nouns: subjective and objective case (13a, 13b), possessive case (30a), and plural (30b)

Other structures serving as nouns: gerunds and gerund phrases (12c-2), infinitives and infinitive phrases (12c-2), subordinate clauses (12c-4)

Conventions regarding nouns

Forms of nouns

Possessive forms: *boy's* vs. *boys'*; *Park's* vs. *Parks's* vs. *Parkses'* (30a)

Possessives before gerunds: *Nguyen's writing is clear.* (13h)

Plurals of nouns and compound nouns: *dish, dishes; child, children; mother-in-law, mothers-in-law* (40b-6)

Nouns and other sentence parts

Agreement of subjects and verbs: *The towel was wet. The towels were wet.* (15a)

Agreement of antecedents and pronouns: *The children surrounded their father.* (15b)

Grammatical fit between subjects and predicates (avoiding mixed grammar): In the supervision of others is the best preparation for a management career.→The supervision of others is the best preparation for a management career. (22a)

Fit in meaning of subjects and predicates (avoiding faulty predication): The use of the airwaves is the ideal medium for campaigning. →The airwaves are the ideal medium for campaigning. (22b)

Clarity and effectiveness

Nouns as modifiers (avoiding overuse): adult education grants workshop→workshop on grants for adult education (16f)

Consistency in subjects and the voice of verbs: Tony woke suddenly, but his eyes were kept shut.→Tony woke suddenly, but he kept his eyes shut. (20c)

Guide to pronouns

Summary and index of information in the student text (consult sections or pages in parentheses).

Description of pronouns

Pronouns as substitutes for nouns (12a-2; 15b)

Pronouns as subjects, objects, complements, appositives, modifiers (Chapter 13)

Case forms of pronouns: subjective, objective, possessive (Chapter 13)

Person, number, and gender of personal pronouns (12a-2; 15b)

Conventions regarding pronouns

Forms of pronouns

Subjective case for subjects and subject complements: *You and I can talk. It was she.* (13a)

Objective case for objects: *Ken gave me a dog. He gave her to me.* (13b)

We or us with nouns: *We drivers like highways. Many of us drivers like highways.* (13c)

Case in appositives: *Two drivers, she and Nell, won the award. The state rewarded two drivers, her and Nell.* (13d)

Case after than or as: *Nell likes Buddy more than [she likes] him. Nell likes Buddy more than he [likes Buddy].* (13e)

Objective case for subjects and objects of infinitives: *We invited him to meet her.* (13f)

Who vs. *whom*: *Who can predict whom he will ask?* (13g)

Possessives before gerunds: *his working* (13h)

Possessive forms of personal pronouns: *hers (not her's); theirs (not their's)* (30b)

Possessive pronouns vs. contractions: *its* vs. *it's; your* vs. *you're; their* vs. *they're* (30c)

Pronouns and other sentence parts

Agreement of pronoun subjects and verbs: *Neither he nor they are late. Everybody is finished.* (15a)

Agreement of pronouns and antecedents: *Everybody finished his or her paper. Lisa or Maria left her notebook.* (15b)

Reference of pronouns to antecedents (avoiding unclear or remote reference): *The first act of the play seemed weak, but then it improved.→The first act of the play started weakly but then improved.* Or: *Though the first act was weak, the play then improved.* (19a–19f)

NOTE

This page does not appear in the students' edition.

Guide to verbs and verbals

Summary and index of information in the student text (consult sections or pages in parentheses).

Description of verbs and verbals

Verb as sentence predicate (12a-1, 12a-2, 12a-3)

Transitive, intransitive, and linking verbs (12a-3)

Forms of verbs: infinitive, past tense, past participle, present participle, -s form (pp. 272–89)

Regular vs. irregular verbs (14a)

Finite vs. nonfinite verbs (12c-2)

Helping (auxiliary) verbs (14d)

Tense of verbs: present, past, future, etc. (pp. 289–95)

Mood of verbs: indicative, imperative, subjunctive (pp. 296–98)

Voice of verbs: active and passive (pp. 298–301)

Verbals and verbal phrases: participles, gerunds, infinitives (12c-2)

Conventions regarding verbs and verbals

Forms and tenses of verbs

Principal parts of common irregular verbs: e.g., *begin, began, begun; run, ran, run* (14a)

Sit vs. *set, lie* vs. *lay,* and *rise* vs. *raise* (14b)

Needed -*s* and -*ed* endings: *He asks/asked too much.* (14c)

Needed helping verbs: *He is asking too much.* (14d)

Present tense (*runs*) and perfect tenses (*has/had/will have run*) (14g)

Sequence of tenses: e.g., *We would like to have gone* vs. *We would have liked to go.* (14h)

Subjunctive mood: *I wish I were there.* (14i)

Verbs and other sentence parts

Agreement of verbs and subjects: *The guests are here. Nobody is missing.* (15a)

Unseparated verb phrases and infinitives: *They had before long agreed to voluntarily surrender.→Before long they had agreed to surrender voluntarily.* (21e)

Grammatical fit between subjects and predicates (avoiding mixed grammar): *By saving is how they could buy a car.→By saving, they could buy a car.* (22a)

Fit in meaning of subjects and predicates (avoiding faulty predication): *The reason is because they were frugal.→The reason is that they were frugal.* (22b)

Problems with verbals

Verbs required in complete sentences (avoiding sentence fragments with verbals): *Rain falling silently.→Rain* <u>*fell*</u> *silently.* (17a, 17c)

Clear and logical modifiers (avoiding dangling modifiers): *Flying home, her thoughts remained behind.→*<u>*As she flew*</u> *home, her thoughts remained behind.* (21h)

Punctuation with verbals

Commas after introductory verbal modifiers: <u>*Struggling for air*</u>*, the climbers reached the summit.* (28b)

Commas to set off nonessential verbal modifiers: *The climbers,* <u>*struggling for air,*</u> *reached the summit.* (28c)

Clarity and effectiveness

Active rather than passive voice: *Hands were raised by the students.→*<u>*The students*</u> *raised their hands.* (14j)

Consistency in voice: *Before you tighten the bolts, the car should be lowered to the ground.→Before you tighten the bolts,* <u>*you should lower*</u> *the car to the ground.* (20c)

Consistency in tense: *The hero escapes, but he was captured.→The hero escapes, but he* <u>*is*</u> *captured.* (20b)

Consistency in mood: *Unscrew the bolts, and then you remove the wheel.→Unscrew the bolts and* <u>*then remove*</u> *the wheel.* (20b)

Strong rather than weak verbs (avoiding wordiness): *The book is a depiction of family strife.→The book* <u>*depicts*</u> *family strife.* (23a, 39a)

NOTE

This page does not appear in the students' edition.

NOTE

This page does not appear in the students' edition.

Guide to modifiers

Summary and index of information in the student text (consult sections or pages in parentheses).

Description of modifiers

Functions of adjectives: modifying nouns and pronouns (p. 315–17)

Functions of adverbs: modifying verbs, adjectives, other adverbs, phrases, and clauses (pp. 315–20)

Forms of adjectives and adverbs: positive, comparative, superlative (16d)

Irregular adjectives and adverbs (16d-1)

Classes of adjectives: descriptive, limiting, proper, attributive, predicate (pp. 882–83)

Classes of adverbs: modifiers of verbs, adjectives, and other adverbs (pp. 315–17); transitional and parenthetical expressions (28b); conjunctive adverbs (12d-2)

Other structures serving as modifiers: nouns (16f); prepositional phrases (12c-1); participles and participial phrases (12c-2); infinitives and infinitive phrases (12c-2); subordinate clauses (12c-4)

Conventions regarding modifiers

Distinctions between adjectives and adverbs

Adverbs (not adjectives) to modify verbs, adjectives, adverbs: *Susan writes well* [not *good*]. (16a)

Adjectives after linking verbs, adverbs to modify other verbs: *I feel bad. She sings badly.* (16b)

Adjectives to modify objects, adverbs to modify verbs: *We believed him honest. We treated him honestly.* (16c)

Forms of adjectives and adverbs

Comparatives and superlatives: *steady, steadier/more steady, steadiest/most steady; good/well, better, best* (16d-1); *most steadiest→ most steady* (16d-2); *the bigger of two and the biggest of three* (16d-3); *most unique→unique* (16d-4)

Modifiers and other sentence parts

Clear placement of modifiers: *We waited for the rain to stop in a doorway.→We waited in a doorway for the rain to stop.* (21a–21g)

Clear and logical modifiers (avoiding dangling modifiers): *Watching the rain, our hands and feet froze.→As we watched the rain, our hands and feet froze.* (21h)

Punctuation and mechanics with modifiers

Commas after most introductory modifiers: *Happily, we have friends.* (28b)

Commas to set off nonessential modifiers: *Ellen, who is our best friend, checks in every day.* (28c)

Commas to set off absolute phrases: *Her workday finished, she calls us.* (28d)

Commas for coordinate adjectives: *She is a steady, reliable friend.* (28f-2)

Commas with conjunctive adverbs and transitional and parenthetical expressions: *Traffic was bad; we left, however, before it could get worse.* (28c-3, 29b)

Semicolons between clauses related by conjunctive adverbs: *We did not leave right away; instead, we waited for Ellen.* (18b, 29b)

Capital letters for proper adjectives: *Indian tea; Buddhist chant* (33d)

Figure vs. words for numbers: *327* vs. *twenty-three* (36a)

Hyphens in compound adjectives and numbers: *well-spoken words* vs. *words well spoken* (40d-1); *thirty-two minutes* (40d-2)

Clarity and effectiveness

Clear negation (avoiding double negatives): *They don't want no interruptions.→They don't want any interruptions.* Or: *They want no interruptions.* (16e)

Nouns as modifiers (avoiding overuse): *business managers spreadsheet analysis seminar→seminar in spreadsheet analysis for business managers* (16f)

Complete and logical comparisons: *The value of friendship is greater than money.→The value of friendship is greater than the value of* [or *that of*] *money.* (22d)

NOTE

This page does not appear in the students' edition.

ANSWERS: EXERCISE 12.21

Possible answers

1. Recycling takes time, but it reduces garbage in landfills.
2. After people begin to recycle, they generate much less trash.
3. Although white tissues and paper towels biodegrade more easily than dyed ones, people still buy dyed papers.
4. Aluminum cans bring recyclers good money.
5. Environmentalists hope that more communities will recycle newspaper and glass, but many citizens refuse to participate.

Exercise 12.21   Sentence combining: Sentence structures

Combine each set of simple sentences below to produce the kind of sentence specified in parentheses. You will have to add, delete, change, and rearrange words.

Example:
The traffic passed the house. It never stopped. (*Complex.*)
The traffic that passed the house never stopped.

1. Recycling takes time. It reduces garbage in landfills. (*Compound.*)
2. People begin to recycle. They generate much less trash. (*Complex.*)
3. White tissues and paper towels biodegrade more easily than dyed ones. People still buy dyed papers. (*Complex.*)
4. The cans are aluminum. They bring recyclers good money. (*Simple.*)
5. Environmentalists have hope. Perhaps more communities will recycle newspaper and glass. Many citizens refuse to participate. (*Compound-complex.*)

HIGHLIGHTS

The forms that nouns and pronouns take according to their role in a sentence are relatively few in English when compared with some other languages. Nonetheless, most students are likely to find compound subjects and objects or questions of *who* and *whom* occasionally troublesome. Others may need to review pronoun forms more extensively to gain control over this part of their writing.

This chapter opens with a review of the functions a pronoun can perform, functions that determine the form, or case, of the pronoun. In addition to the familiar list of forms of the personal pronouns, the chapter provides sentences illustrating the wide variety of uses for pronouns. Following this are brief discussions of the proper case for pronouns in contexts that usually cause difficulty for student writers, including compound subjects and objects, appositives, comparisons using *than* or *as*, possessive case with gerunds, and the different uses of *who* and *whom*.

The exercises ask students to select the appropriate forms of pronouns in the troublesome contexts treated in the discussion, to correct any case errors in a paragraph, and to combine sentences so as to use *who* or *whom* in relative clauses.

13

Case of Nouns and Pronouns

Case is the form of a noun or pronoun that shows the reader how it functions in a sentence—that is, whether it functions as a subject, as an object, or in some other way. As shown in the box on the next page, only *I, we, he, she, they,* and *who* change form for each case. Thus these pronouns are the focus of this chapter.

The **subjective case** generally indicates that the word is a subject or a subject complement. (See pp. 231 and 237–38.)

subject
She and Novick discussed the proposal.

subject
The proposal ignores many who need help.

subject complement
The disgruntled planners were she and Novick.

mycomplab

Visit *mycomplab.com* for more resources and exercises on noun and pronoun case.

Case forms of nouns and pronouns

	Subjective	Objective	Possessive
Nouns	boy	boy	boy's
	Jessie	Jessie	Jessie's
Personal pronouns			
Singular			
1st person	I	me	my, mine
2nd person	you	you	your, yours
3rd person	he	him	his
	she	her	her, hers
	it	it	its
Plural			
1st person	we	us	our, ours
2nd person	you	you	your, yours
3rd person	they	them	their, theirs
Relative and interrogative pronouns			
	who	whom	whose
	whoever	whomever	—
	which, that, what	which, that, what	—
Indefinite pronouns	everybody	everybody	everybody's

RESOURCES AND IDEAS

Redfern, Richard K. "Pronouns Are Highly Personal." *English Journal* 85.7 (1996): 80–81. Print. Redfern presents further strategies for teaching pronoun usage.

THE CHART

Students may be tempted to skip over this chart, which gives the case forms of nouns and pronouns. Get them to pay attention by asking them to fill out the whole chart in class—without looking at the text. The act of remembering the forms or figuring them out will be more valuable than listening to an explanation. Students who have trouble completing the chart probably need to spend time reviewing the chapter.

The **objective case** generally indicates that the word is the object of a verb or preposition. (See pp. 236–39 and 242–43.)

object of verb

The proposal disappointed her and Novick.

object   object
of verb   of verb

A colleague whom they respected let them down.

object of
preposition

Their opinion of him suffered.

The **possessive case** generally indicates ownership or source:

Her counterproposal is in preparation.
Theirs is the more defensible position.
The problem is not his.

Do not use an apostrophe to form the possessive of personal pronouns: *yours* (not *your's*); *theirs* (not *their's*). (See p. 456. See also p. 452 for the possessive forms of nouns, which do use apostrophes.)

Grammar checkers A grammar checker may flag some problems with pronoun case, but it will also miss a lot. For instance, one checker spotted the error in *We asked whom would come* (should

NOUN-NOUN POSSESSIVES

Students who are nonnative speakers of English learn that people and animals go in possessive case ("Phoebe's phone," "the ferret's fur") but that inanimate objects take "of" formations ("the end of the line"). Students may be confused by the exceptions to this rule ("table top," "car engine.") Have your students keep a list of exceptions to this rule and see how long the list grows by the end of your course.

BACK TO NOUNS

Distribute copies of a paragraph taken from a magazine article, an essay in a reader, or a student paper. Ask students to rewrite it, substituting the appropriate noun for each pronoun. This exercise will help students to understand the role of pronouns and see the relationship between the case of a pronoun and the function of the noun it stands for.

be *who would come*), but it overlooked *We dreaded them coming* (should be *their coming*).

 In standard American English, *-self* pronouns do not change form to show function. Their only forms are *myself, yourself, himself, herself, itself, ourselves, yourselves, themselves.* Avoid nonstandard forms such as *hisself, ourself,* and *theirselves.*

13a Use the subjective case for compound subjects and for subject complements.

In compound subjects use the same pronoun form you would use if the pronoun stood alone as a subject:

      subject
She and Novick will persist.

              subject
The others may lend their support when she and Novick get a hearing.

If you are in doubt about the correct form, try the test in the box below.

After a linking verb, such as a form of *be,* a pronoun renaming the subject (a subject complement) should be in the subjective case:

         subject complement
The ones who care most are she and Novick.

   subject
   complement
It was they whom the mayor appointed.

If this construction sounds stilted to you, use the more natural order: *She and Novick are the ones who care most. The mayor appointed them.*

A test for case forms in compound constructions

1. **Identify a compound construction** (one connected by *and, but, or, nor*).

   [He, Him] and [I, me] won the prize.
   The prize went to [he, him] and [I, me].

2. **Write a separate sentence for each part of the compound.**

   [He, Him] won the prize. [I, Me] won the prize.
   The prize went to [he, him]. The prize went to [I, me].

3. **Choose the pronouns that sound correct.**

   He won the prize. I won the prize. [Subjective.]
   The prize went to him. The prize went to me. [Objective.]

4. **Put the separate sentences back together.**

   He and I won the prize.
   The prize went to him and me.

13b Use the objective case for compound objects.

In compound objects use the same pronoun form you would use if the pronoun stood alone as an object:

direct object
The mayor nominated <u>Zhu and him</u>.

indirect object
The mayor gave <u>Zhu and him</u> awards.

object of preposition
Credit goes equally to <u>them and the mayor</u>.

If you are in doubt about the correct form, try the test in the box opposite.

> **Exercise 13.1** **Choosing between subjective and objective pronouns**
>
> From the pairs in brackets, select the appropriate subjective or objective pronoun(s) for each of the following sentences.
>
> *Example:*
>
> "Between you and [I, me]," the seller said, "this deal is a steal."
> "Between you and <u>me</u>," the seller said, "this deal is a steal."
>
> 1. Lisa and [I, me] were competing for places on the relay team.
> 2. The fastest runners at our school were [she, her] and [I, me], so [we, us] expected to make the team.
> 3. [She, Her] and [I, me] were friends but also intense rivals.
> 4. The time trials went badly, excluding both [she, her] and [I, me] from the team.
> 5. Next season we are determined to earn at least one place between [she, her] and [I, me].

13c Use the appropriate case when the plural pronoun *we* or *us* occurs with a noun.

Whether to use *we* or *us* with a noun depends on the use of the noun:

object of preposition
Freezing weather is welcomed by <u>us</u> skaters.

subject
<u>We</u> skaters welcome freezing weather.

13d In appositives the case of a pronoun depends on the function of the word described or identified.

object of verb   appositive identifies object
The class elected two representatives, DeShawn and <u>me</u>.

PAYING ATTENTION TO PRONOUN USE

Ask students to spend a day or two paying close attention to people's pronoun use, particularly subjective and objective case. Newscasters and advertising copy writers, in particular, will use the subjective case *I* when they should use the objective case *me*. What other mix-ups do students note?

ANSWERS: EXERCISE 13.1

1. I
2. she, I, we
3. She, I
4. her, me
5. her, me

US THE PEOPLE

If students try out pronoun forms in sentences, they can often "hear" the contrast between correct and incorrect forms by relying on their implicit understanding of the language or by using familiar phrases as touchstones:

Us the people.
Us are the world.
Are you going with *we*?
Take *we* to the movies.

This approach will not work with students for whom standard English is a second language or a second dialect.

subject | appositive identifies subject

Two representatives, DeShawn and I, were elected.

If you are in doubt about case in an appositive, try the sentence without the word the appositive identifies: *The class elected De-Shawn and me. DeShawn and I were elected.*

Exercise 13.2 Choosing between subjective and objective pronouns

From the pairs in brackets, select the appropriate subjective or objective pronoun for each of the following sentences.

Example:

Convincing [we, us] veterans to vote yes will be difficult.
Convincing us veterans to vote yes will be difficult.

1. Obtaining enough protein is important to [we, us] vegetarians.
2. Instead of obtaining protein from meat, [we, us] vegetarians get our protein from other sources.
3. Jeff claims to know only two vegetarians, Helena and [he, him], who avoid all animal products, including milk.
4. Some of [we, us] vegetarians eat fish, which is a good source of protein.
5. [We, Us] vegetarians in my family, my parents and [I, me], drink milk and eat fish.

 13e **The case of a pronoun after *than* or *as* in a comparison depends on the meaning.**

When a pronoun follows *than* or *as* in a comparison, the case of the pronoun indicates what words may have been omitted. When the pronoun is subjective, it must serve as the subject of an omitted verb:

subject

Some critics like Glass more than he [does].

When the pronoun is objective, it must serve as the object of an omitted verb:

object

Some critics like Glass more than [they like] him.

13f **Use the objective case for pronouns that are subjects or objects of infinitives.**

subject of infinitive

The school asked him to speak.

object of infinitive

Students chose to invite him.

ANSWERS: EXERCISE 13.2

1. us
2. we
3. him
4. us
5. we, I

MAKE UP YOUR OWN TEST

Give students time in class to write out five to ten sentences in quiz form. The easiest way for students to do this is to pattern their questions after the exercises and sample sentences in the handbook:

Most of [we, us] college students realize that finding a good job isn't easy.
There is a five-hundred-dollar reward for [whomever, whoever] finds the missing stock certificates.

Students can use the handbook in preparing the questions, and as long as they know that one of the possible answers they have provided must be right, they need not be sure which one it is.

When the tests are completed, students should exchange them and fill them out. Correcting the tests is best done in small groups so that students can help one another or turn to the instructor for any information necessary to provide answers to the toughest questions.

13g Use *who* or *whom* depending on function.

To choose between *who* and *whom*, *whoever* and *whomever*, you need to figure out whether the word serves as a subject or as an object. Use *who* where you would use *he* or *she*—all ending in vowels. Use *whom* where you would use *him* or *her*—all ending in consonants.

1 At the beginning of a question, use *who* for a subject and *whom* for an object.

subject→
Who wrote the policy?

object ←
Whom does it affect?

A test for *who* versus *whom* in questions

1. **Pose the question.**

   [Who, Whom] makes that decision?
   [Who, Whom] does one ask?

2. **Answer the question, using a personal pronoun.** Choose the pronoun that sounds correct, and note its case.

   [She, Her] makes that decision. She makes that decision. [Subjective.]
   One asks [she, her]. One asks her. [Objective.]

3. **Use the same case (*who* or *whom*) in the question.**

   Who makes that decision? [Subjective.]
   Whom does one ask? [Objective.]

Note In speech the subjective case *who* is commonly used whenever it is the first word of a question, regardless of whether it is a subject or an object. But formal writing requires a distinction between the forms:

Spoken Who should we credit?

Written object ←
Whom should we credit?

2 In a subordinate clause, use *who* or *whoever* for the subject, *whom* or *whomever* for an object.

The case of a pronoun in a subordinate clause depends on its function in the clause, regardless of whether the clause itself functions as a subject, an object, or a modifier:

subject →
Credit whoever wrote the policy.

object ←———
Research should reveal <u>whom</u> to credit.

Note Don't let expressions such as *I think* and *she says* confuse you when they come between the subject *who* and its verb:

subject ————
He is the one <u>who</u> the polls say will win.

To choose between *who* and *whom* in such constructions, delete the interrupting phrase: *He is the one <u>who</u> will win.*

A test for *who* versus *whom* in subordinate clauses

1. **Locate the subordinate clause.**

   Few people know [who, whom] they should ask.
   They are unsure [who, whom] makes the decision.

2. **Rewrite the subordinate clause as a separate sentence, substituting a personal pronoun for *who, whom*.** Choose the pronoun that sounds correct, and note its case.

   They should ask [she, her]. They should ask her. [Objective.]
   [She, Her] makes the decision. She makes the decision. [Subjective.]

3. **Use the same case (*who* or *whom*) in the subordinate clause.**

   Few people know whom they should ask. [Objective.]
   They are unsure who makes the decision. [Subjective.]

COLLABORATIVE LEARNING

Students might complete Exercise 13.3 independently, then compare answers and work on Exercise 13.4 in pairs or in small groups. Ask each group to create several sentences of their own using *who* and *whom*, and based on the models provided in Exercise 13.4. Each group might present some of their most inventive responses to the class by writing them on the chalkboard, making transparencies, or posting them on the class Web site.

ANSWERS: EXERCISE 13.3

1. whom
2. who
3. whoever
4. Who
5. Whom

Exercise 13.3 Choosing between *who* and *whom*

From the pairs in brackets, select the appropriate form of the pronoun in each of the following sentences.

Example:
My mother asked me [who, whom] I was going out with.
My mother asked me <u>whom</u> I was going out with.

1. The judges awarded first prize to Inez, [who, whom] they believed gave the best performance.
2. Inez beat the other contestants [who, whom] competed against her.
3. She is a consummate performer, singing to [whoever, whomever] would listen.
4. [Who, Whom] in the school has not heard Inez sing?
5. [Who, Whom] has she not performed for?

Exercise 13.4 Sentence combining: *Who* versus *whom*

Combine each of the following pairs of sentences into one sentence that contains a clause beginning with *who* or *whom*. Be sure to use the appropriate case form. You will have to add, delete, and rearrange words. Each item may have more than one possible answer.

Example:

David is the candidate. We think David deserves to win.
David is the candidate <u>who</u> we think deserves to win.

1. Some children have undetected hearing problems. These children may do poorly in school.
2. They may not hear important instructions and information from teachers. Teachers may speak softly.
3. Classmates may not be audible. The teacher calls on those classmates.
4. Some hearing-impaired children may work harder to overcome their disability. These children get a lot of encouragement at home.
5. Some hearing-impaired children may take refuge in fantasy friends. They can rely on these friends not to criticize or laugh.

13h Ordinarily, use a possessive pronoun or noun immediately before a gerund.

A **gerund** is the *-ing* form of a verb (*running, sleeping*) used as a noun (p. 246). Like nouns, gerunds are commonly preceded by possessive nouns and pronouns: *our vote* (noun), *our voting* (gerund).

The coach disapproved of their lifting weights.

The coach's disapproving was a surprise.

A noun or pronoun before an *-ing* verb form is not always possessive. Sometimes the *-ing* form will be a present participle modifying the preceding word:

Everyone had noticed him weightlifting. [Emphasis on *him*.]
  objective participle
  pronoun

Everyone had noticed his weightlifting. [Emphasis on the activity.]
  possessive gerund
  pronoun

Note that a gerund usually is not preceded by the possessive when the possessive would create an awkward construction:

Awkward	A rumor spread about <u>everybody's</u> on the team wanting to quit.
Less awkward	A rumor spread about <u>everybody</u> on the team wanting to quit.
Better	A rumor spread <u>that everybody</u> on the team <u>wanted</u> to quit.

Exercise 13.5 Revising: Case

Revise all inappropriate case forms in the following paragraph, and explain the function of each case form.

ANSWERS: EXERCISE 13.4

Possible answers

1. Some children <u>who have undetected hearing problems</u> may <u>do</u> poorly in school.
2. They may not hear important instructions and information from teachers <u>who speak softly</u>.
3. Classmates <u>whom the teacher calls on</u> may not be audible.
4. Some hearing-impaired children <u>who get a lot of encouragement at home</u> may work harder to overcome their handicap.
5. Some hearing-impaired children may take refuge in fantasy friends <u>whom they can rely on not to criticize or laugh</u>.

COLLABORATIVE LEARNING

CREATE A STORY

On the board, write a sentence or two that introduces as many people's names as possible. For example, you might write,

Bob went to a party last night, and there he saw his first-grade teacher, Mrs. West; his neighbor George; his old girlfriend Sarah; and her children Susan and Jason. In the middle of the party, Bob's dog Bowser came racing into the living room.

Divide the class into small groups and ask each group to write a one-paragraph story that grows out of the sentences on the board. (In the example above, students would probably describe what happened after the dog's entrance.) In writing their story, students should try to use as many pronouns as possible without introducing any ambiguity into the tale.

Groups should then read their stories aloud or write them on the board so that other students can try to understand the stories and verify that all the pronoun cases are accurate.

ANSWERS: EXERCISE 13.5

Written four thousand years ago, *The Epic of Gilgamesh* tells of the friendship of Gilgamesh and Enkidu. Gilgamesh was a bored king whose people thought he was too harsh. Then he met Enkidu, a wild man <u>who</u> had lived with the animals in the mountains. Immediately, <u>he</u> and Gilgamesh wrestled to see <u>who</u> was more powerful. After hours of struggle, Enkidu admitted that Gilgamesh was stronger than <u>he</u>. Now the friends needed adventures worthy of the two strongest men on earth. Gilgamesh said, "Between you and <u>me</u>, mighty deeds will be accomplished, and our fame will be everlasting." Among their acts, Enkidu and <u>he</u> defeated a giant bull, Humbaba, and cut down the bull's cedar forests. <u>Their</u> bringing back cedar logs to Gilgamesh's treeless land won great praise from the people. When Enkidu died, Gilgamesh mourned his death, realizing that no one had been a better friend than <u>he</u>. When Gilgamesh himself died many years later, his people raised a monument praising Enkidu and <u>him</u> for their friendship and their mighty deeds of courage.

HIGHLIGHTS

Verbs can cause trouble for writers regardless of their level of skill. For some writers, choosing the correct tense or form of a verb can be a formidable challenge. In addition, certain regional and social dialects of English have different patterns for marking verb tenses and forms, which may add to the confusion. Even experienced writers may occasionally stumble over the choice between *sit* and *set* or struggle to maintain the correct sequence of tenses in a complex sentence.

For all these needs (and many others as well) this chapter can be useful, although it must be supplemented to provide the more sustained support and practice some students may require. Students whose first language is not English may benefit from the ESL coverage and the worksheets by Jocelyn Steer and Dawn Schmid. If your campus is fortunate enough to have a writing center, your students may benefit from the extra support it can provide.

Students looking for help with verb *forms* will benefit from the chapter's thorough explanations, list of the principal parts of frequently used irregular verbs, discussion of the troublesome pairs *sit/set* and *lie/lay*, and treatment of two problems often associated with dialect interfer-

Written four thousand years ago, *The Epic of Gilgamesh* tells of the friendship of Gilgamesh and Enkidu. Gilgamesh was a bored king who his people thought was too harsh. Then he met Enkidu, a wild man whom had lived with the animals in the mountains. Immediately, him and Gilgamesh wrestled to see whom was more powerful. After hours of struggle, Enkidu admitted that Gilgamesh was stronger than him. Now the friends needed adventures worthy of the two strongest men on earth. Gilgamesh said, "Between you and I, mighty deeds will be accomplished, and our fame will be everlasting." Among their acts, Enkidu and him defeated a giant bull, Humbaba, and cut down the bull's cedar forests. Them bringing back cedar logs to Gilgamesh's treeless land won great praise from the people. When Enkidu died, Gilgamesh mourned his death, realizing that no one had been a better friend than him. When Gilgamesh himself died many years later, his people raised a monument praising Enkidu and he for their friendship and their mighty deeds of courage.

Note See page 327 for an exercise involving case along with other aspects of grammar.

Verbs

The verb is the most complicated part of speech in English, changing form to express a wide range of information.

Verb Forms

All verbs except *be* have five basic forms. The first three are the verb's **principal parts.**

■ The *plain form* is the dictionary form of the verb. When the subject is a plural noun or the pronoun *I*, *we*, *you*, or *they*, the plain form indicates action that occurs in the present, occurs habitually, or is generally true.

mycomplab

Visit *mycomplab.com* for more resources and exercises on verb forms.

Terms used to describe verbs

Tense

The time of the verb's action—for instance, present (*kick*), past (*kicked*), future (***will** kick*). (See p. 289.)

Mood

The attitude of the verb's speaker or writer—the difference, for example, in *I kick the ball, Kick the ball,* and *I suggested that she kick the ball.* (See p. 296.)

Voice

The distinction between the **active**, in which the subject performs the verb's action (*I kick the ball*), and the **passive**, in which the subject is acted upon (*The ball is kicked by me*). (See p. 298.)

Person

The verb form that reflects whether the subject is speaking (*I/we kick the ball*), spoken to (*You kick the ball*), or spoken about (*She kicks the ball*). (See p. 302.)

Number

The verb form that reflects whether the subject is singular (*The girl kicks the ball*) or plural (*Girls kick the ball*). (See p. 302.)

A few artists <u>live</u> in town today.
They <u>hold</u> classes downtown.

■ The *past-tense form* indicates that the action of the verb occurred before now. It usually adds *-d* or *-ed* to the plain form, although some irregular verbs form it in other ways (see p. 275).

Many artists <u>lived</u> in town before this year.
They <u>held</u> classes downtown. [Irregular verb.]

■ The *past participle* is the same as the past-tense form, except in most irregular verbs. It combines with forms of *have* or *be* (*has <u>climbed</u>, was <u>created</u>*), or by itself it modifies nouns and pronouns (*the <u>sliced</u> apples*).

Artists have <u>lived</u> in town for decades.
They have <u>held</u> classes downtown. [Irregular verb.]

■ The *present participle* adds *-ing* to the verb's plain form. It combines with forms of *be* (*is <u>buying</u>*), modifies nouns and pronouns (*the <u>boiling</u> water*), or functions as a noun (*<u>Running</u> exhausts me*).

A few artists are <u>living</u> in town today.
They are <u>holding</u> classes downtown.

ence: omitted *-s* and *-ed* endings and omitted helping verbs.

Students looking for help with verb *tense* can make use of the chapter's discussion of the major tenses and of appropriate sequences of tenses. Tense sequence becomes increasingly important as students begin to write ambitious narratives and expository or argumentative essays.

RESOURCES AND IDEAS

Yoder, Rhoda Byler. "Of Fake Verbs and Kid Words: Developing a Useful Grammar." *English Journal* 85.7 (1996): 82–7. Print. The author discusses developing a simplified language for teaching students the functions of verbs and verbals.

ONE-FORM PARAGRAPHS

Choose groups of three to five verbs and have students create paragraphs using only one form of the verbs. Then have students rewrite the paragraphs using a different verb form. This exercise will reinforce consistent use of form and may make students more aware of the element of time in verb usage. Following are student-written examples that use the past-participle form of the verbs *break, bring, burst, buy,* and *catch.*

> *Because his bubble had burst and she had broken his heart, he had caught the next train home and had brought his mother some flowers.*
> —JENNIFER HAAS

> *We had brought the dishes out to the table to set it. When we looked we realized that we had broken some of them. We had burst out laughing, but it wasn't too funny when we realized that my mother had caught us.*
> —NICOLE HANNA

> *He had broken the vase that she had brought. She had burst into tears. If only he had caught it.*
> —JIM ROSEN

■ **The -s form ends in -s or -es.** When the subject is a singular noun, a pronoun such as *everyone,* or the personal pronoun *he, she,* or *it,* the *-s* form indicates action that occurs in the present, occurs habitually, or is generally true.

The artist lives in town today.
She holds classes downtown.

The verb *be* has eight forms rather than the five forms of most other verbs:

Plain form	be		
Present participle	being		
Past participle	been		
	I	*he, she, it*	*we, you, they*
Present tense	am	is	are
Past tense	was	was	were

 If standard American English is not your native language or dialect, you may have difficulty with verbs' *-s* forms (including those for *be: is, was*) or with the forms that indicate time (such as the past-tense form). See pages 279–80 and 290–92, respectively, for more on these forms.

Helping verbs

Helping verbs, also called **auxiliary verbs,** combine with some verb forms to indicate time and other kinds of meaning, as in *can run, was sleeping, had been eaten.* These combinations are **verb phrases.** Since the plain form, present participle, or past participle in any verb phrase always carries the principal meaning, it is sometimes called the **main verb.**

	Verb phrase	
Helping	*Main*
Artists can	train others to draw.
The techniques have	changed little.

These are the most common helping verbs:

Forms of *be:* be, am, is, are, was, were, been, being
Forms of *have:* have, has, had, having
Forms of *do:* do, does, did

be able to	had better	must	used to
be supposed to	have to	ought to	will
can	may	shall	would
could	might	should	

 The helping verbs of standard American English may be problematic if you are used to speaking another language or dialect. See pages 280–84 for more on helping verbs.

14a Use the correct forms of regular and irregular verbs.

Most verbs are **regular;** that is, they form their past tense and past participle by adding *-d* or *-ed* to the plain form.

Plain form	Past tense	Past participle
live	lived	lived
act	acted	acted

Since the past tense and past participle are the same, the forms of regular verbs do not often cause problems (but see pp. 279–80).

About two hundred English verbs are **irregular;** that is, they form their past tense and past participle in some irregular way.

Plain form	Past tense	Past participle
begin	began	begun
break	broke	broken
sleep	slept	slept

You can see the difference between a regular and an irregular verb in these examples:

Plain form	Today the birds twitter. Today the birds sing.
Past tense	Yesterday the birds twittered. Yesterday the birds sang.
Past participle	In the past the birds have twittered. In the past the birds have sung.

The box on the next two pages lists the forms of many irregular verbs. Check this box or a dictionary if you have any doubt about a verb's principal parts. If a dictionary lists only the plain form, the verb is regular: both the past tense and the past participle add *-d* or *-ed* to the plain form. If the verb is irregular, the dictionary will list the plain form, the past tense, and the past participle in that order (*go, went, gone*). If the dictionary gives only two forms (as in *think, thought*), then the past tense and the past participle are the same.

Grammar checkers A grammar checker may flag incorrect forms of irregular verbs, but it may also fail to do so. For example, a checker did not flag *The runner had steal second base* (*stolen* is correct). When in doubt about the forms of irregular verbs, refer to the box on the next page or consult a dictionary.

(CULTURE · LANGUAGE) Some English dialects use distinctive verb forms that differ from those of standard American English: for instance, *drug* for *dragged, growed* for *grew, come* for *came,* or *went* for *gone.* In situations requiring standard American English, use the forms in the list on the next page or in a dictionary.

THE ORIGIN OF IRREGULAR VERBS

Irregular verbs are antiques reflecting the history of English well before the Norman Conquest of England in 1066. In the first few centuries AD, speakers of the Germanic languages that evolved into English used changes in the internal vowel structure of words to show tense. Thus, verbs like *drink, throw,* and especially *be* preserve a little of the linguistic history of our ancestors. A very readable account of this period is found in Joseph Williams, *Origins of the English Language* (New York: Free Press, 1975).

HYPOTHETICAL VERBS

A good game to play to show students how well they intuitively understand how irregular verbs are formed is to invent some (e.g., *flink*) and ask students to decide what their other forms would be (*flink, flank, flunk* or *flink, flought, flought*). A variation is to take a more regular verb and pretend it's irregular: *The light should not blink. The light hasn't blunk.*

Principal parts of common irregular verbs

Plain form	Past tense	Past participle
arise	arose	arisen
be	was, were	been
become	became	become
begin	began	begun
bid	bid	bid
bite	bit	bitten, bit
blow	blew	blown
break	broke	broken
bring	brought	brought
burst	burst	burst
buy	bought	bought
catch	caught	caught
choose	chose	chosen
come	came	come
cut	cut	cut
dive	dived, dove	dived
do	did	done
draw	drew	drawn
dream	dreamed, dreamt	dreamed, dreamt
drink	drank	drunk
drive	drove	driven
eat	ate	eaten
fall	fell	fallen
find	found	found
flee	fled	fled
fly	flew	flown
forget	forgot	forgotten, forgot
freeze	froze	frozen
get	got	got, gotten
give	gave	given
go	went	gone
grow	grew	grown
hang (suspend)	hung	hung
hang (execute)	hanged	hanged
have	had	had
hear	heard	heard
hide	hid	hidden
hold	held	held
keep	kept	kept
know	knew	known
lay	laid	laid
lead	led	led
leave	left	left
lend	lent	lent
let	let	let
lie	lay	lain

Plain form	Past tense	Past participle
lose	lost	lost
pay	paid	paid
prove	proved	proved, proven
ride	rode	ridden
ring	rang	rung
rise	rose	risen
run	ran	run
say	said	said
see	saw	seen
set	set	set
shake	shook	shaken
shrink	shrank, shrunk	shrunk, shrunken
sing	sang, sung	sung
sink	sank, sunk	sunk
sit	sat	sat
sleep	slept	slept
slide	slid	slid
speak	spoke	spoken
spring	sprang, sprung	sprung
stand	stood	stood
steal	stole	stolen
swim	swam	swum
swing	swung	swung
take	took	taken
teach	taught	taught
tear	tore	torn
throw	threw	thrown
wear	wore	worn
write	wrote	written

Exercise 14.1 Using irregular verbs

For each irregular verb in brackets, give either the past tense or the past participle, as appropriate, and identify the form you used.

Example:

Though we had [hide] the cash box, it was [steal].

Though we had <u>hidden</u> the cash box, it was <u>stolen</u>. [Two past participles.]

1. The world population has [grow] by two-thirds of a billion people in less than a decade.
2. In 2000 it [break] the 6 billion mark.
3. Experts have [draw] pictures of a crowded future.
4. They predict that the world population may have [slide] up to as much as 10 billion by the year 2050.
5. Though the food supply [rise] in the last decade, the share to each person [fall].

CREATING AN IRREGULAR VERB "FIX-IT" LIST

Ask students to review the list of common irregular verbs. Which ones from the list do they routinely forget or confuse? For example, *set*, *go*, *lie*, and *lay* errors are frequently heard in conversation. From this list, ask students to create a customized list of problem verbs, their correct forms, and the corresponding textbook page numbers. When they edit their work, remind them to consult their fix-it lists!

ANSWERS: EXERCISE 14.1

1. The world population has <u>grown</u> by two-thirds of a billion people in less than a decade. (Past participle.)
2. In 2000 it <u>broke</u> the 6 billion mark. (Past tense.)
3. Experts have <u>drawn</u> pictures of a crowded future. (Past participle.)
4. They predict that the world population may have <u>slid</u> up to as much as 10 billion by the year 2050. (Past participle.)
5. Though the food supply <u>rose</u> in the last decade, the share to each person <u>fell</u>. (Both past tense.)

IRREGULAR VERBS AND THE DICTIONARY

The need to learn the uses of *sit* and *set*, *rise* and *raise*, and *lie* and *lay* makes a great excuse to introduce students to the wonders of the *Oxford English Dictionary*, in either its first or its second edition. Your campus library may subscribe to the *OED Online* as well. The entries for these words, among the longest in the *OED*, will show students the number of meanings words can have and the reasons all writers find these particular words so difficult.

14b Distinguish between *sit* and *set*, *lie* and *lay*, and *rise* and *raise*.

The forms of *sit* and *set*, *lie* and *lay*, and *rise* and *raise* are easy to confuse:

Plain form	Past tense	Past participle
sit	sat	sat
set	set	set
lie	lay	lain
lay	laid	laid
rise	rose	risen
raise	raised	raised

In each of these confusing pairs, one verb is **intransitive** (it does not take an object) and one is **transitive** (it does take an object). (See pp. 236–39 for more on this distinction.)

Intransitive

The patients lie in their beds. [*Lie* means "recline" and takes no object.]

Visitors sit with them. [*Sit* means "be seated" or "be located" and takes no object.]

Patients' temperatures rise. [*Rise* means "increase" or "get up" and takes no object.]

Transitive

Orderlies lay the dinner trays on tables. [*Lay* means "place" and takes an object, here *trays*.]

Orderlies set the trays down. [*Set* means "place" and takes an object, here *trays*.]

Nursing aides raise the shades. [*Raise* means "lift" or "bring up" and takes an object, here *shades*.]

ANSWERS: EXERCISE 14.2

1. Yesterday afternoon the child lay down for a nap.
2. The child has been raised by her grandparents.
3. Most days her grandfather has sat with her, reading her stories.
4. She has risen at dawn most mornings.
5. Her toys were laid out on the floor.

Exercise 14.2 Distinguishing *sit/set, lie/lay, rise/raise*

Choose the correct verb from the pair given in brackets. Then supply the past tense or past participle, as appropriate.

Example:
After I washed all the windows, I [lie, lay] down the squeegee and then I [sit, set] the table.

After I washed all the windows, I laid down the squeegee and then I set the table.

1. Yesterday afternoon the child [lie, lay] down for a nap.
2. The child has been [rise, raise] by her grandparents.
3. Most days her grandfather has [sit, set] with her, reading her stories.
4. She has [rise, raise] at dawn most mornings.
5. Her toys were [lie, lay] out on the floor.

14c Use the -s and -ed forms of the verb when they are required.

Speakers of some English dialects and nonnative speakers of English sometimes omit the *-s* and *-ed* verb endings when they are required in standard American English.

Grammar checkers A grammar checker will flag many omitted *-s* and *-ed* endings from verbs, such as in *he ask* and *was ask.* But it will miss many omissions, too.

Required -s ending

Use the *-s* form of a verb when *both* of these situations hold:

- **The subject is a singular noun (*boy*), an indefinite pronoun (*everyone*), or *he, she,* or *it.*** These subjects are **third person,** used when someone or something is being spoken about.
- **The verb's action occurs in the present.**

The letter asks [not ask] for a quick response.
Delay costs [not cost] money.

Be especially careful with the *-s* forms of *be* (*is*), *have* (*has*), and *do* (*does, doesn't*). These forms should always be used to indicate present time with third-person singular subjects.

The company is [not be] late in responding.
It has [not have] problems.
It doesn't [not don't] have the needed data.
The contract does [not do] depend on the response.

In addition, *be* has an *-s* form in the past tense with *I* and with third-person singular subjects:

The company was [not were] in trouble before.

I, you, and plural subjects do *not* take the *-s* form of verbs:

I am [not is] a student.
You are [not is] also a student.
They are [not is] students, too.

Required -ed or -d ending

The *-ed* or *-d* verb form is required in *any* of these situations:

- **The verb's action occurred in the past:**

Yesterday the company asked [not ask] for more time.

- **The verb form functions as a modifier:**

The data concerned [not concern] should be retrievable.

CULTURE LANGUAGE

Speakers of Black English Vernacular may tend to use the verb forms of this dialect in their writing rather than those of standard written English, particularly by dropping *-s* and *-ed* endings. Becoming aware of the verb system of standard written English and the differences between it and the verb system of Black English Vernacular is an important step for students seeking control over their writing. But as Marcia Farr and Harvey Daniels point out in *Language Diversity and Writing Instruction* (New York: ERIC Clearing House on Urban Education and Urbana: NCTE, 1986), awareness of and practice in identifying and using the verb forms are useful only if they take place in a context that includes a wide range of reading and writing experiences; substantial practice in writing; collaborative activities; sentence combining or similar activities; and flexible, sensitive feedback from the instructor. Farr and Daniels also offer a detailed discussion of dialects and language variations, along with concrete suggestions for teaching.

Other helpful resources on dialect include:

Heath, Shirley Brice. *Ways with Words: Language, Life, and Work in Communities and Classrooms.* New York: Cambridge UP, 1983. Print.

Lyman, Huntington, and Margo A. Figgins. "Democracy, Dialect, and the Power of Every Voice." *English Journal* 94.5 (2005): 40–47. Print.

Smitherman, Geneva. *Talkin and Testifyin: The Language of Black America.* Detroit: Wayne State UP, 1977. Print.

■ **The verb form combines with a form of *be* or *have*:**

> The company is <u>supposed</u> [not <u>suppose</u>] to be the best.
> It has <u>developed</u> [not <u>develop</u>] an excellent reputation.

Watch especially for a needed *-ed* or *-d* ending when it isn't pronounced clearly in speech, as in *asked, discussed, mixed, supposed, walked,* and *used.*

Exercise 14.3 Using *-s* and *-ed* verb endings

Supply the correct form of each verb in brackets. Be careful to include *-s* and *-ed* (or *-d*) endings where they are needed for standard English.

> A teacher sometimes [ask] too much of a student. In high school I was once [punish] for being sick. I had [miss] some school, and I [realize] that I would fail a test unless I had a chance to make up the classwork. I [discuss] the problem with the teacher, but he said I was [suppose] to make up the work while I was sick. At that I [walk] out of the class. I [receive] a failing grade then, but it did not change my attitude. Today I still balk when a teacher [make] unreasonable demands or [expect] miracles.

ANSWERS: EXERCISE 14.3

A teacher sometimes <u>asks</u> too much of a student. In high school I was once <u>punished</u> for being sick. I had <u>missed</u> some school, and I <u>realized</u> that I would fail a test unless I had a chance to make up the classwork. I <u>discussed</u> the problem with the teacher, but he said I was <u>supposed</u> to make up the work while I was sick. At that I <u>walked</u> out of the class. I <u>received</u> a failing grade then, but it did not change my attitude. Today I still balk when a teacher <u>makes</u> unreasonable demands or <u>expects</u> miracles.

 14d **Use helping verbs with main verbs appropriately.**

Helping verbs combine with main verbs to form verb phrases (see p. 274).

Common helping verbs

Forms of *be:* be, am, is, are, was, were, been, being
Forms of *have:* have, has, had, having
Forms of *do:* do, does, did

be able to	had better	must	used to
be supposed to	have to	ought to	will
can	may	shall	would
could	might	should	

Grammar checkers A grammar checker often spots omitted helping verbs and incorrect main verbs with helping verbs, but sometimes it does not. A checker flagged *Many been fortunate* and *She working* but overlooked other examples on the following pages.

1 **Use helping verbs when they are required.**

Standard American English requires helping verbs in certain situations:

■ **The main verb ends in** *-ing:*

Researchers <u>are</u> conducting fieldwork all over the world. [Not <u>Researchers</u> <u>conducting</u>. . . .]

■ **The main verb is** *been* **or** *be:*

Many <u>have</u> been fortunate in their discoveries. [Not <u>Many been</u>. . . .]
Some <u>could</u> be real-life Indiana Joneses. [Not <u>Some be</u>. . . .]

■ **The main verb is a past participle, such as** *talked, begun,* **or** *thrown.*

Their discoveries <u>were</u> covered in newspapers and magazines. [Not <u>Their</u> <u>discoveries covered</u>. . . .]

Often the researchers <u>have</u> done TV interviews. [Not <u>the researchers</u> <u>done</u>. . . .]

In every example above, omitting the helping verb would create an incomplete sentence, or **sentence fragment** (see Chapter 17). In a complete sentence, some part of the verb (helping or main) must be capable of changing form to show changes in time: *I <u>run</u>, I <u>ran</u>; you <u>are running</u>, you <u>were running</u>* (see p. 330). But a present participle (*conducting*), an irregular past participle (*been*), and the infinitive *be* cannot change form in this way. They need helping verbs to work as sentence verbs.

2 **Combine helping verbs and main verbs appropriately for your meaning.**

Helping verbs and main verbs combine into verb phrases in specific ways.

Note The main verb in a verb phrase (the one carrying the main meaning) does not change to show a change in subject or time: *she has <u>studied</u>, you had <u>studied</u>.* Only the helping verb may change.

Form of *be* **+ present participle**

The **progressive tenses** indicate action in progress (see p. 292). Create them with *be, am, is, are, was, were,* or *been* followed by the main verb's present participle:

She <u>is working</u> on a new book.

Be and *been* always require additional helping verbs to form the progressive tenses:

can	might	should		have	
could	must	will	} be working	has	} been working
may	shall	would		had	

When forming the progressive tenses, be sure to use the *-ing* form of the main verb:

Faulty   Her ideas are <u>grow</u> more complex. She is <u>developed</u> a new approach to ethics.

Revised   Her ideas are <u>growing</u> more complex. She is <u>developing</u> a new approach to ethics.

Form of *be* + past participle

The **passive voice** of the verb indicates that the subject *receives* the action of the verb (see p. 298). Create the passive voice with *be, am, is, are, was, were, being,* or *been* followed by the main verb's past participle:

Her latest book <u>was completed</u> in four months.

Be, being, and *been* always require additional helping verbs to form the passive voice:

| have
has
had | } | <u>been</u> completed | am
is
are | was
were | } | <u>being</u> completed |

will <u>be</u> completed

Be sure to use the main verb's past participle for the passive voice:

Faulty   Her next book will be <u>publish</u> soon.

Revised   Her next book will be <u>published</u> soon.

Note Only transitive verbs may form the passive voice:

Faulty   A philosophy conference <u>will be occurred</u> in the same week. [*Occur* is not a transitive verb.]

Revised   A philosophy conference <u>will occur</u> in the same week.

See pages 299–300 for advice on when to use and when to avoid the passive voice.

Forms of *have*

Four forms of *have* serve as helping verbs: *have, has, had, having.* One of these forms plus the main verb's past participle creates one of the **perfect tenses,** those expressing action completed before another specific time or action (see p. 291):

Some students <u>have complained</u> about the laboratory.
Others <u>had complained</u> before.

Will and other helping verbs sometimes accompany forms of *have* in the perfect tenses:

Several more students <u>will have complained</u> by the end of the week.

Forms of *do*

Do, does, and *did* have three uses as helping verbs, always with the plain form of the main verb:

- **To pose a question:** *How did the trial end?*
- **To emphasize the main verb:** *It did end eventually.*
- **To negate the main verb, along with** *not* or *never:* The judge *did not withdraw*.

Be sure to use the main verb's plain form with any form of *do:*

Faulty	The judge did remained in court.
Revised	The judge did remain in court.

Modals

The modal helping verbs include *can, could, may,* and *might,* along with several two- and three-word combinations, such as *have to* and *be able to*. (See p. 280 for a list of helping verbs.) Use the plain form of the main verb with a modal unless the modal combines with another helping verb (usually *have*):

Faulty	The equipment can detects small vibrations. It should have detect the change.
Revised	The equipment can detect small vibrations. It should have detected the change.

Modals convey various meanings, with these being most common:

- **Ability:** *can, could, be able to*

The equipment can detect small vibrations. [Present.]

The equipment could detect small vibrations. [Past.]

The equipment is able to detect small vibrations. [Present. Past: was able to. Future: will be able to.]

- **Possibility:** *could, may, might; could/may/might have* + past participle

The equipment could fail. [Present.]
The equipment may fail. [Present or future.]
The equipment might fail. [Present or future.]
The equipment may have failed. [Past.]

- **Necessity or obligation:** *must, have to, be supposed to*

The lab must purchase a backup. [Present or future.]
The lab has to purchase a backup. [Present or future. Past: had to.]
The lab will have to purchase a backup. [Future.]
The lab is supposed to purchase a backup. [Present. Past: was supposed to.]

■ **Permission:** *may, can, could*

The lab <u>may spend</u> the money. [Present or future.]
The lab <u>can spend</u> the money. [Present or future.]
The lab <u>could spend</u> the money. [Present or future, more tentative.]
With budget approval, the lab <u>could have spent</u> the money. [Past.]

■ **Intention:** *will, shall, would*

The lab <u>will spend</u> the money. [Future.]

<u>Shall</u> we <u>offer</u> advice? [Future. Use *shall* for questions requesting opinion or consent.]

We <u>would have offered</u> advice. [Past.]

■ **Request:** *could, can, would*

<u>Could</u> [or <u>Can</u> or <u>Would</u>] you please <u>obtain</u> a bid? [Present or future.]

■ **Advisability:** *should, had better, ought to; should have* + past participle

You <u>should obtain</u> three bids. [Present or future.]
You <u>had better obtain</u> three bids. [Present or future.]
You <u>ought to obtain</u> three bids. [Present or future.]
You <u>should have obtained</u> three bids. [Past.]

■ **Past habit:** *would, used to*

In years past we <u>would obtain</u> five bids.
We <u>used to obtain</u> five bids.

Exercise 14.4   Using helping verbs   (CULTURE LANGUAGE)

Add helping verbs in the following sentences where they are needed for standard English.

> *Example:*
> The story been told for many years.
> The story <u>has</u> been told for many years.

1. Each year thousands of new readers been discovering Agatha Christie's mysteries.
2. The books written by a prim woman who had worked as a nurse during World War I.
3. Christie never expected that her play *The Mousetrap* be performed for decades.
4. During her life Christie always complaining about movie versions of her stories.
5. Readers of her stories been delighted to be baffled by her.

Exercise 14.5   Revising: Helping verbs plus main verbs   (CULTURE LANGUAGE)

Revise the following sentences so that helping verbs and main verbs are used correctly. Mark the number preceding any sentence that is already correct.

ANSWERS: EXERCISE 14.4

1. Each year thousands of new readers <u>have</u> been discovering Agatha Christie's mysteries.
2. The books <u>were</u> written by a prim woman who had worked as a nurse during World War I.
3. Christie never expected that her play *The Mousetrap* <u>would</u> be performed for decades.
4. During her life Christie <u>was</u> always complaining about movie versions of her stories.
5. Readers of her stories have <u>been</u> delighted to be baffled by her.

Example:

The college testing service has test as many as five hundred students at one time.

The college testing service has <u>tested</u> as many as five hundred students at one time.

1. A report from the Bureau of the Census has confirm a widening gap between rich and poor.
2. As suspected, the percentage of people below the poverty level did increased over the last decade.
3. More than 17 percent of the population is make 5 percent of all the income.
4. About 1 percent of the population will keeping an average of $500,000 apiece after taxes.
5. The other 99 percent all together will retain about $300,000.

 14e | Use a gerund or an infinitive after a verb as appropriate.

Nonnative speakers of English sometimes stumble over using a gerund or an infinitive after a verb. A **gerund** is the *-ing* form of a verb used as a noun (*opening*). An **infinitive** is the plain form of a verb preceded by *to* (*to open*). (See pp. 246–47 for more on these forms.)

Gerunds and infinitives may follow certain verbs but not others. And sometimes the use of a gerund or infinitive with the same verb changes the meaning.

Grammar checkers A grammar checker will spot some but not all errors in matching gerunds or infinitives with verbs. For example, a checker failed to flag *I practice <u>to swim</u>* and *I promise <u>helping out</u>*. Use the lists given here and a dictionary of English as a second language to determine whether an infinitive or a gerund is appropriate. (See p. 513 for a list of ESL dictionaries.)

Either gerund or infinitive

A gerund or an infinitive may follow these verbs with no significant difference in meaning:

begin	hate	love
can't bear	hesitate	prefer
can't stand	intend	start
continue	like	

The pump began <u>working</u>.
The pump began <u>to work</u>.

Meaning change with gerund or infinitive

With four verbs, a gerund has quite a different meaning from an infinitive:

CULTURE LANGUAGE

CHOOSING BETWEEN GERUNDS AND INFINITIVES

ESL students generally find gerunds more problematic than infinitives, perhaps because gerunds occur less frequently; as a result, students may use infinitives where gerunds are required. According to Marianne Celce-Murcia and Diane Larsen-Freeman in *The Grammar Book*, 2nd ed. (Boston: Heinle, 1999), gerunds tend to express "fulfilled action," whereas infinitives tend to express "unfulfilled action":

I *enjoyed meeting* your brother at the party. (The action, the meeting, was fulfilled.)
I *hoped to meet* your brother at the party. (The action, the hoped-for meeting, was unfulfilled.)
I'll always *remember calling* my son when he was overseas. (The action, calling, was fulfilled before the remembering.)
I *remembered to call* my son on his birthday. (The action, calling, was unfulfilled until after the remembering.)

Refer students who need additional practice distinguishing gerunds and infinitives to Chapter 14 of Jocelyn Steer and Karen Carlisi, *The Advanced Grammar Book*, 2nd ed. (Boston: Heinle, 1998) and Raymond Murphy, "-ing and the Infinitive" in *Grammar in Use Intermediate*, 2nd ed., (Cambridge UP, 2000).

forget   stop
remember   try

The engineer stopped eating. [He no longer ate.]
The engineer stopped to eat. [He stopped in order to eat.]

Gerund, not infinitive

Do not use an infinitive after these verbs:

admit	discuss	mind	recollect
adore	dislike	miss	resent
appreciate	enjoy	postpone	resist
avoid	escape	practice	risk
consider	finish	put off	suggest
deny	imagine	quit	tolerate
detest	keep	recall	understand

Faulty   He finished to eat lunch.
Revised   He finished eating lunch.

Infinitive, not gerund

Do not use a gerund after these verbs:

agree	decide	mean	refuse
appear	expect	offer	say
ask	have	plan	wait
assent	hope	pretend	want
beg	manage	promise	wish
claim			

Faulty   He decided checking the pump.
Revised   He decided to check the pump.

Noun or pronoun + infinitive

Some verbs may be followed by an infinitive alone or by a noun or pronoun and an infinitive. The presence of a noun or pronoun changes the meaning.

ask	dare	need	wish
beg	expect	promise	would like
choose	help	want	

He expected to watch.
He expected his workers to watch.

Some verbs *must* be followed by a noun or pronoun before an infinitive:

admonish	allow	challenge	convince
advise	cause	command	encourage

forbid	oblige	remind	tell
force	order	request	train
hire	permit	require	urge
instruct	persuade	teach	warn
invite			

He instructed <u>his workers to watch</u>.

Do not use *to* before the infinitive when it follows one of these verbs and a noun or pronoun:

feel	make ("force")
have	see
hear	watch
let	

He let his workers <u>learn</u> by observation.

Exercise 14.6   Revising: Verbs plus gerunds or infinitives

Revise the following sentences so that gerunds or infinitives are used correctly with verbs. Mark the number preceding any sentence that is already correct.

Example:
A politician cannot avoid to alienate some voters.
A politician cannot avoid <u>alienating</u> some voters.

1. A program called HELP Wanted tries to encourage citizens take action on behalf of American competitiveness.
2. Officials working on this program hope improving education for work.
3. American businesses find that their workers need learning to read.
4. In the next ten years the United States expects facing a shortage of 350,000 scientists.
5. HELP Wanted suggests creating a media campaign.

14f Use the appropriate particles with two-word verbs. CULTURE LANGUAGE

Standard American English includes some verbs that consist of two words: the verb itself and a **particle**, a preposition or adverb that affects the meaning of the verb. For example:

<u>Look up</u> the answer. [Research the answer.]
<u>Look over</u> the answer. [Examine the answer.]

The meanings of these two-word verbs are often quite different from the meanings of the individual words that make them up. (There are some three-word verbs, too, such as *put up with* and *run out of*.)

A dictionary of English as a second language will define two-word verbs and say whether the verb may be separated in a sentence, as explained below. (See p. 513 for a list of ESL dictionaries.) A grammar checker will rarely recognize misused two-word verbs.

Note Many two-word verbs are more common in speech than in more formal academic or business writing. For formal writing, consider using *research* instead of *look up, examine* or *inspect* instead of *look over.*

Inseparable two-word verbs

Verbs and particles that may not be separated by any other words include the following:

call on	go out with	run across	stay away
catch on	go over	run into	stay up
come across	grow up	run out of	take care of
get along	keep on	speak up	turn out
get up	look for	speak with	turn up at
give in	look into	stand up	work for
go on	play around		

Faulty   Children <u>grow</u> quickly <u>up</u>.
Revised   Children <u>grow up</u> quickly.

Separable two-word verbs

Most two-word verbs that take direct objects may be separated by the object:

Parents <u>help out</u> their children.
Parents <u>help</u> their children <u>out</u>.

If the direct object is a pronoun, the pronoun *must* separate the verb from the particle:

Faulty   Parents <u>help out</u> them.
Revised   Parents <u>help</u> them <u>out</u>.

The separable two-word verbs include the following:

bring up	give back	make up	throw out
call off	hand in	point out	try on
call up	hand out	put away	try out
drop off	help out	put back	turn down
fill out	leave out	put off	turn on
fill up	look over	take out	wrap up
give away	look up	take over	

Exercise 14.7   Revising: Verbs plus particles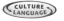

The two- and three-word verbs in the following sentences are underlined. Some are correct as given, and some are not because they should or should not be separated by other words. Revise the verbs and other words that are incorrect. Consult the lists on the preceding page or an ESL dictionary if necessary to determine whether verbs are separable.

Example:

Hollywood producers never seem to <u>come up with</u> entirely new plots, but they also never <u>run</u> new ways <u>out of</u> to present old ones.

Hollywood producers never seem to come up with [correct] entirely new plots, but they also never <u>run out of</u> new ways to present old ones.

1. American movies treat everything from <u>going out with</u> someone to <u>making up</u> an ethnic identity, but few people <u>look</u> their significance <u>into</u>.
2. While some viewers <u>stay away from</u> topical films, others <u>turn</u> at the theater <u>up</u> simply because a movie has sparked debate.
3. Some movies attracted rowdy spectators, and the theaters had to <u>throw out</u> them.
4. Filmmakers have always been eager to <u>point</u> their influence <u>out</u> to the public.
5. Everyone agrees that filmmakers will <u>keep</u> creating controversy <u>on</u>, if only because it can <u>fill up</u> theaters.

ANSWERS: EXERCISE 14.7

1. American movies treat everything from going out with [correct] someone to making up [correct] an ethnic identity, but few people <u>look into</u> their significance.
2. While some viewers stay away from [correct] topical films, others <u>turn up at the theater</u> simply because a movie has sparked debate.
3. Some movies attracted rowdy spectators, and the theaters had to <u>throw them out</u>.
4. Filmmakers have always been eager to point their influence out [correct; *or* <u>point out their influence</u>] to the public.
5. Everyone agrees that filmmakers will <u>keep on creating controversy</u>, if only because it can fill up [correct] theaters.

Tense

Tense shows the time of a verb's action. The box on the next page defines and illustrates the tense forms for a regular verb in the active voice. (See pp. 275 and 298 on regular verbs and voice.)

Grammar checkers A grammar checker can provide little help with incorrect verb tenses and tense sequences because correctness usually depends on meaning. You'll have to proofread carefully yourself to catch errors in tense or tense sequence.

CULTURE LANGUAGE In standard American English, a verb conveys time and sequence through its form. In some other languages and English dialects, various markers besides verb form may indicate the time of a verb. For instance, in African American dialect *I be attending class on Wednesday* means that the speaker attends class every Wednesday. To a speaker of standard American English, however, the sentence may be unclear: last Wednesday? this Wednesday? every Wednesday? The intended meaning must be indicated by verb tense: *I* <u>attended</u> *class on Wednesday. I* <u>will attend</u> *class on Wednesday. I* <u>attend</u> *class on Wednesday.*

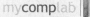
my**comp**lab

Visit *mycomplab.com* for more resources and exercises on verb tense.

Tenses of a regular verb (active voice)

Present Action that is occurring now, occurs habitually, or is generally true

Simple present Plain form or -s form

I walk.
You/we/they walk.
He/she/it walks.

Present progressive *Am, is,* or *are* plus *-ing* form

I am walking.
You/we/they are walking.
He/she/it is walking.

Past Action that occurred before now

Simple past Past-tense form (-*d* or -*ed*)

I/he/she/it walked.
You/we/they walked.

Past progressive *Was* or *were* plus *-ing* form

I/he/she/it was walking.
You/we/they were walking.

Future Action that will occur in the future

Simple future Plain form plus *will*

I/you/he/she/it/we/they will walk.

Future progressive *Will be* plus *-ing* form

I/you/he/she/it/we/they will be walking.

Present perfect Action that began in the past and is linked to the present

Present perfect *Have* or *has* plus past participle (-*d* or -*ed*)

I/you/we/they have walked.
He/she/it has walked.

Present perfect progressive *Have been* or *has been* plus *-ing* form

I/you/we/they have been walking.
He/she/it has been walking.

Past perfect Action that was completed before another past action

Past perfect *Had* plus past participle (-*d* or -*ed*)

I/you/he/she/it/we/they had walked.

Past perfect progressive *Had been* plus *-ing* form

I/you/he/she/it/we/they had been walking.

Future perfect Action that will be completed before another future action

Future perfect *Will have* plus past participle (-*d* or -*ed*)

I/you/he/she/it/we/they will have walked.

Future perfect progressive *Will have been* plus *-ing* form

I/you/he/she/it/we/they will have been walking.

 14g ## Use the appropriate tense to express your meaning.

Many errors in verb tense are actually errors in verb form like those discussed earlier. Still, the present tense, the perfect tenses, and the progressive tenses can cause problems.

1 Observe the special uses of the present tense.

The present tense has several distinctive uses:

Action occurring now

She <u>understands</u> the problem.
We <u>define</u> the problem differently.

Habitual or recurring action

Banks regularly <u>undergo</u> audits.
The audits <u>monitor</u> the banks' activities.

A general truth

The mills of the gods <u>grind</u> slowly.
The earth <u>is</u> round.

Discussion of literature, film, and so on (see also p. 740)

Huckleberry Finn <u>has</u> adventures we all envy.
In that article, the author <u>examines</u> several causes of crime.

Future time

Next week we <u>draft</u> a new budget.
Funding <u>ends</u> in less than a year.

(In the last two examples, time is really indicated by *Next week* and *in less than a year.*)

2 Observe the uses of the perfect tenses.

The perfect tenses generally indicate action completed before another specific time or action. (The term *perfect* derives from the Latin *perfectus*, "completed.") The present perfect tense also indicates action begun in the past and continued into the present. The perfect tenses consist of a form of *have* plus the verb's past participle.

present perfect
The dancer <u>has performed</u> here only once. [The action is completed at the time of the statement.]

present perfect
Critics <u>have written</u> about the performance ever since. [The action began in the past and continues now.]

past perfect
The dancer <u>had trained</u> in Asia before his performance. [The action was completed before another past action.]

future perfect
He <u>will have danced</u> here again by the end of the year. [The action begins now or in the future and will be completed by a specified time in the future.]

 With the present perfect tense, the words *since* and *for* are followed by different information. After *since*, give a specific point in time: *The United States has been a*

THE USE OF PROGRESSIVE TENSES

Some languages (for example, Arabic) use progressive tenses to express habitual activities, whereas English uses simple tenses. Explain to students that in English, the progressive tenses emphasize the *duration* or *continuous nature* of an action. Perfect progressive tenses are also used for ongoing action that is intersected by another action.

EXCEPTIONS

As the text notes, verbs that express mental states or activities are generally not used in the progressive tenses. However, there are some exceptions:

> *see* = date or consult: *Marsha isn't seeing John any more. Gina is seeing a doctor about her allergies.*
> *think* = consider: *I'm thinking about taking a literature course next term.*
> *cumulative effects: I'm understanding English better and better as I go through this course.*

COLLABORATIVE LEARNING

IMAGINARY REPORTING

A good activity is to ask students, either individually or in groups, to construct some imaginary event (an episode from a TV show, a football game, a newscast) and recount its chronology using the correct sequence of tenses. Students can work together to revise their reported events, and volunteer groups might read their responses to the class or post them on the network.

---

member of the United Nations since 1945. After *for*, give a span of time: *The United States has been a member of the United Nations for many decades.*

3 Observe the uses of the progressive tenses.

The progressive tenses indicate continuing (therefore progressive) action. In standard American English the progressive tenses consist of a form of *be* plus the verb's *-ing* form (present participle). (The words *be* and *been* must be combined with other helping verbs. See pp. 281–82.)

present progressive
The economy is improving.

past progressive
Last year the economy was stagnating.

future progressive
Economists will be watching for signs of growth.

present perfect progressive
The government has been expecting an upturn.

past perfect progressive
Various indicators had been suggesting improvement.

future perfect progressive
By the end of this month, investors will have been pushing the markets up for half a year.

Note Verbs that express unchanging states (especially mental states) rather than physical actions do not usually appear in the progressive tenses. These verbs include *adore, appear, believe, belong, care, doubt, hate, have, hear, imagine, know, like, love, mean, need, own, prefer, realize, remember, see, sound, taste, think, understand,* and *want.*

Faulty   She is wanting to study ethics.
Revised She wants to study ethics.

14h Use the appropriate sequence of verb tenses.

The term **sequence of tenses** refers to the relation between the verb tense in a main clause and the verb tense in a subordinate clause or phrase. The tenses should change when necessary to reflect changes in actual or relative time. (For a discussion of tense shifts—changes *not* required by meaning—see p. 355.)

1 Use the appropriate tense sequence with infinitives.

The **present infinitive** is the verb's plain form preceded by *to*. It indicates action *at the same time* as or *later* than that of the verb:

She would have liked to see [not to have seen] change before now.

verb: present perfect | *infinitive: present*

The verb's **perfect infinitive** consists of *to have* followed by the past participle, as in *to have talked, to have won.* It indicates action *earlier* than that of the verb:

Other researchers would like [not would have liked] to have seen change as well.

verb: present | *infinitive: perfect*

2 Use the appropriate tense sequence with participles.

The present participle shows action occurring *at the same time* as that of the verb:

Testing a large group, the researcher had posed multiple-choice questions.

participle: present | *verb: past perfect*

The past participle and the present perfect participle show action occurring *earlier* than that of the verb:

Prepared by earlier failures, she knew not to ask open questions.

participle: past | *verb: past*

Having tested many people, she understood the process.

participle: present perfect | *verb: past*

3 Use the appropriate tense sequence with the past or past perfect tense.

When the verb in the main clause is in the past or past perfect tense, the verb in the subordinate clause must also be past or past perfect:

The researchers discovered that people varied widely in their knowledge of public events.

main clause: past | *subordinate clause: past*

The variation occurred because respondents had been born in different decades.

main clause: past | *subordinate clause: past perfect*

None of them had been born when Warren G. Harding was President.

main clause: past perfect | *subordinate clause: past*

Exception Always use the present tense for a general truth, such as *The earth is round:*

Most understood that popular Presidents are not necessarily good Presidents.

main clause: past | *subordinate clause: present*

CREATING A STORY

Write on the board a sentence containing one or more characters and an action. Here are some examples:

> As he rounded the corner, John heard a loud noise, somewhere between a crash and a bang.
>
> As he came into the classroom, Jim noticed that Carolyn was already there reviewing her notes.

Ask students to form groups, and then require the groups to write paragraph-length (seven to eight sentences) stories. The stories should begin with the sentence you have provided, and individual members of the group should add sentences to the narrative one by one until it is complete. The final story should maintain a correct sequence of tenses, contain proper verb forms, and use a variety of action verbs. Students may wish to use ideas or episodes from their journals in completing this exercise.

DISCUSSION STORY

Put a lead sentence (as in "Creating a story," above) on the board and ask the class as a whole to decide on the events that follow it. Summarize the events briefly; then ask groups of students to write out the story as in the preceding activity, making it as vivid as they can. This entire exercise will provide both oral and written practice with verb tense and sequence.

COMPUTER ACTIVITY

Both the "Creating a story" and the "Discussion story" work well as electronic exercises. In each case, the teacher posts the opening prompt for the story then asks students to work collaboratively or individually on their responses. Periodically, the teacher might post the entire story (or one group's version of the story) for the whole class to read and discuss. For related activities, see Daniel Anderson's chapter on "Using Computers to Teach Writing," beginning on page IAE-47.

4 **Use the appropriate tense sequence in conditional sentences.**

A conditional sentence states a factual relation between cause and effect, makes a prediction, or speculates about what might happen. Such a sentence usually contains a subordinate clause beginning with *if, when,* or *unless* along with a main clause stating the result. The three kinds of conditional sentences use distinctive verbs.

Factual relation

Statements linking factual causes and effects use matched tenses in the subordinate and main clauses:

subordinate clause: *present*   main clause: *present*
When a voter <u>casts</u> a ballot, he or she <u>has</u> complete privacy.

subordinate clause: *past*   main clause: *past*
When voters <u>registered</u> in some states, they <u>had</u> to pay a poll tax.

Prediction

Predictions generally use the present tense in the subordinate clause and the future tense in the main clause:

subordinate clause: *present*   main clause: *future*
Unless citizens <u>regain</u> faith in politics, they <u>will</u> not <u>vote</u>.

Sometimes the verb in the main clause consists of *may, can, should,* or *might* plus the verb's plain form: *If citizens regain faith, they may vote.*

Speculation

The verbs in speculations depend on whether the linked events are possible or impossible. For possible events in the present, use the past tense in the subordinate clause and *would, could,* or *might* plus the verb's plain form in the main clause:

subordinate clause: *past*   main clause: *would* + plain form
If voters <u>had</u> more confidence, they <u>would vote</u> more often.

Use *were* instead of *was* in the subordinate clause, even when the subject is *I, he, she, it* or a singular noun. (See p. 297 for more on this distinctive verb form.)

subordinate clause: *past*   main clause: *would* + plain form
If the voter <u>were</u> more confident, he or she <u>would vote</u> more often.

For impossible events in the present—events that are contrary to fact—use the same forms as above (including the distinctive *were* when applicable):

subordinate clause: *past*   main clause: *might* + plain form
If Lincoln <u>were</u> alive, he <u>might inspire</u> confidence.

For impossible events in the past, use the past perfect tense in the subordinate clause and *would, could,* or *might* plus the present perfect tense in the main clause:

subordinate clause:
past perfect

main clause:
might + present perfect

If Lincoln had lived past the Civil War, he might have helped stabilize the country.

Exercise 14.8 Adjusting tense sequence: Past or past perfect tense

The tenses in each sentence below are in correct sequence. Change the tense of one verb as instructed. Then change the tense of infinitives, participles, and other verbs to restore correct sequence. Some items have more than one possible answer.

Example:

Delgado will call when he reaches his destination. (Change *will call* to *called*.)

Delgado called when he reached [or had reached] his destination.

1. Diaries that Adolf Hitler is supposed to have written have surfaced in Germany. (*Change have surfaced to had surfaced.*)
2. Many people believe that the diaries are authentic because a well-known historian has declared them so. (*Change believe to believed.*)
3. However, the historian's evaluation has been questioned by other authorities, who call the diaries forgeries. (*Change has been questioned to was questioned.*)
4. They claim, among other things, that the paper is not old enough to have been used by Hitler. (*Change claim to claimed.*)
5. Eventually, the doubters will win the debate because they have the best evidence. (*Change will win to won.*)

Exercise 14.9 Revising: Tense sequence with conditional sentences

Supply the appropriate tense for each verb in brackets below.

Example:

If Babe Ruth or Jim Thorpe [be] athletes today, they [remind] us that even sports heroes must contend with a harsh reality.

If Babe Ruth or Jim Thorpe were athletes today, they might [or could or would] remind us that even sports heroes must contend with a harsh reality.

1. When an athlete [turn] professional, he or she [commit] to a grueling regimen of mental and physical training.
2. If athletes [be] less committed, they [disappoint] teammates, fans, and themselves.
3. If professional athletes [be] very lucky, they [play] until age forty.
4. Unless an athlete [achieve] celebrity status, he or she [have] few employment choices after retirement.
5. If professional sports [be] less risky, athletes [have] longer careers and more choices after retirement.

ANSWERS: EXERCISE 14.8

1. Diaries that Adolf Hitler was supposed to have written had surfaced in Germany.
2. Many people believed that the diaries were authentic because a well-known historian had declared them so.
3. However, the historian's evaluation was questioned by other authorities who called the diaries forgeries.
4. They claimed, among other things, that the paper was not old enough to have been used by Hitler.
5. Eventually, the doubters won the debate because they had the best evidence.

ANSWERS: EXERCISE 14.9

1. When an athlete turns professional, he or she commits to a grueling regimen of mental and physical training.
2. If athletes were less committed, they would disappoint teammates, fans, and themselves.
3. If professional athletes are very lucky, they may play until age forty.
4. Unless an athlete achieves celebrity status, he or she will have few employment choices after retirement.
5. If professional sports were less risky, athletes would have longer careers and more choices after retirement.

Mood

Mood in grammar is a verb form that indicates the writer's or speaker's attitude toward what he or she is saying. The **indicative mood** states a fact or opinion or asks a question:

> The theater needs help. [Opinion.]
> The ceiling is falling. [Fact.]
> Will you contribute to the theater? [Question.]

The **imperative mood** expresses a command or gives a direction. It omits the subject of the sentence, *you:*

> Help the theater. [Command.]
> Send contributions to the theater. [Direction.]

The **subjunctive mood** expresses a suggestion, a requirement, or a desire, or it states a condition that is contrary to fact (that is, imaginary or hypothetical). The subjunctive mood uses distinctive verb forms.

- **Suggestion or requirement:** plain form with all subjects.

  > The manager asked that he donate money. [Suggestion.]
  > Rules require that every donation be mailed. [Requirement.]

- **Desire or present condition contrary to fact:** past tense; for *be,* the past tense *were* for all subjects, singular as well as plural.

  > We wish that the theater had more money. [Desire.]
  > It would be in better shape if it were better funded. [Present condition contrary to fact.]

- **Past condition contrary to fact:** past perfect.

  > The theater could have been better funded if it had been better managed.

Note that with conditions contrary to fact, the verb in the main clause also expresses the imaginary or hypothetical with the helping verb *could, would,* or *might.* (See also p. 294.)

For a discussion of keeping mood consistent within and among sentences, see page 355.

14i Use the subjunctive verb forms appropriately.

Contemporary English uses distinctive subjunctive verb forms in only a few constructions and idioms. (For the sequence of tenses in many subjunctive sentences, see pp. 294–95.)

Grammar checkers A grammar checker may spot some simple errors in the subjunctive mood, but it may miss others. For example, a checker flagged *I wish I was home* (should be *were home*) but not *If I had a hammer, I will hammer in the morning* (should be *would hammer*).

1 **Use the subjunctive in contrary-to-fact clauses beginning with *if* or expressing desire.**

If the theater were saved, the town would benefit.
We all wish the theater were not so decrepit.
I wish I were able to donate money.

Note The indicative form *was* (*We all wish the theater was not so decrepit*) is common in speech and in some informal writing, but the subjunctive *were* is usual in formal English.

Not all clauses beginning with *if* express conditions contrary to fact. In the sentence *If Joe is out of town, he hasn't heard the news,* the verb *is* is correct because the clause refers to a condition presumed to exist.

2 **Use *would, could,* or *might* only in the main clause of a conditional statement.**

The helping verb *would, could,* or *might* appears in the main clause of a sentence expressing a condition contrary to fact. The helping verb does not appear in the subordinate clause beginning with *if*:

Not   Many people would have helped if they would have known.
But   Many people would have helped if they had known.

3 **Use the subjunctive in *that* clauses following verbs that demand, request, or recommend.**

Verbs such as *ask, demand, insist, mandate, recommend, request, require, suggest,* and *urge* indicate demand or suggestion. They often precede subordinate clauses beginning with *that* and containing the substance of the demand or suggestion. The verb in such a *that* clause should be in the subjunctive mood:

The board urged that everyone contribute.
The members insisted that they themselves be donors.
They suggested that each donate both time and money.

Note These constructions have widely used alternative forms that do not require the subjunctive, such as *The board urged everyone to contribute* and *The members insisted on donating.*

COLLABORATIVE LEARNING

If students are struggling with the subjunctive mood, have them work in small groups on Exercise 14.10, then ask each group to compose three additional sentences in the subjunctive mood.

ANSWERS: EXERCISE 14.10

1. If John Hawkins <u>had known</u> of the danger-ous side effects of smoking tobacco, would he have introduced the dried plant to Eng-land in 1565?
2. Hawkins noted that if a Florida Indian <u>were</u> to travel for several days, he <u>would smoke</u> to-bacco to satisfy his hunger and thirst.
3. Early tobacco growers feared that their product would not gain acceptance unless it <u>were</u> perceived as healthful.
4. To prevent fires, in 1646 the General Court of Massachusetts passed a law requiring that colonists <u>smoke</u> tobacco only if they were five miles from any town.
5. To prevent decadence, in 1647 Connecticut passed a law mandating that one's smoking of tobacco <u>be</u> limited to once a day in one's own home.

PASSIVE SENTENCES—COUNT THE WORDS

Write on the board a number of sentences in the active voice, the sentences ranging from sim-ple to relatively complex. Ask students to change the sentences into the passive voice and then to count the number of words in each version. Fi-nally, ask students to read some of the passive sentences aloud and comment on their effective-ness. This exercise will allow you to check stu-dents' understanding of the passive voice and at the same time demonstrate its wordiness.

RESOURCES AND IDEAS

Robinson, William S. "Sentence Focus, Cohesion, and the Active and Passive Voice." *Teaching English in the Two-Year College* 27.4 (2000): 440–45. Print. Robinson discusses three uses of the passive voice and advocates that teach-ing sentence focus, "keeping the topic of the sentence in the subject position," will help stu-dents learn how to use both active and passive voice correctly.

Exercise 14.10 Revising: Subjunctive mood

Revise the following sentences with appropriate subjunctive verb forms.

Example:
I would help the old man if I was able to reach him.
I would help the old man if I <u>were</u> able to reach him.

1. If John Hawkins would have known of the dangerous side effects of smoking tobacco, would he have introduced the dried plant to Eng-land in 1565?
2. Hawkins noted that if a Florida Indian was to travel for several days, he would have smoked tobacco to satisfy his hunger and thirst.
3. Early tobacco growers feared that their product would not gain ac-ceptance unless it was perceived as healthful.
4. To prevent fires, in 1646 the General Court of Massachusetts passed a law requiring that colonists smoked tobacco only if they were five miles from any town.
5. To prevent decadence, in 1647 Connecticut passed a law mandating that one's smoking of tobacco was limited to once a day in one's own home.

─── **Voice** ───

The **voice** of a verb tells whether the subject of the sentence performs the action (**active voice**) or is acted upon (**passive voice**). In the passive voice, the actual actor may be named in a preposi-tional phrase (such as *by the city*) or may be omitted.

CULTURE LANGUAGE A passive verb always consists of a form of *be* plus the past participle of the main verb: *rents are con-trolled*. Other helping verbs must also be used with *be, being, and been: rents have been controlled*. Only a transitive verb (one that takes an object) may be used in the passive voice. (See p. 282.)

Converting passive to active

To change a passive verb to active, name the verb's actor as the subject, use an active verb form, and convert the old subject into an object:

	subject	passive verb	
Passive	Tenants	are protected	by leases.
	new subject	active verb	old subject = object
Active	Leases	protect	tenants.

mycomplab

Visit *mycomplab.com* for more resources and exercises on verb voice.

Active and passive voice

Active voice   The subject acts.

Subject = actor	→	Transitive verb in active voice	→	Direct object
The city		controls		rents.

Passive voice   The subject is acted upon.

Subject = object of action	←	Transitive verb in passive voice		(optional) by actor
Rents		are controlled		by the city.
Rents		are controlled.		

Converting active to passive

To change a transitive verb from active to passive voice, convert either an indirect object or a direct object into the subject of the sentence, and use the passive verb form:

	subject	transitive verb	indirect object	direct object
Active	The city	gives	tenants	leases.

	new subject	passive verb	direct object	
Passive	Tenants	are given	leases.	

	new subject	passive verb	old indirect object	old subject
	Leases	are given	to tenants	by the city.

 14j   **Generally, prefer the active voice. Use the passive voice when the actor is unknown or unimportant.**

Because the passive omits or de-emphasizes the actor (the performer of the verb's action), it can deprive writing of vigor and is often vague or confusing. The active voice is usually stronger, clearer, and more forthright.

Weak passive	The <u>library is used</u> by students and teachers for studying and research, and the <u>plan</u> to expand it <u>has been praised</u> by many.
Strong active	<u>Students and teachers</u> <u>use</u> the library for studying and research, and <u>many</u> <u>have praised</u> the plan to expand it.

PROBLEMS WITH THE PAST PARTICIPLE

Not all languages include a passive voice. As a result, ESL students are not always certain about when passive voice is appropriate. Also, because ESL students do not always hear the past-participle *-ed* ending, particularly when *-ed* sounds like *t*, they may omit *-ed* in writing passive voice. Encourage students to listen for the use of the passive voice *-ed* ending in political speeches or in news programs or documentaries. Chapter 11 of Jocelyn Steer and Karen Carlisi, *The Advanced Grammar Book*, 2nd ed. (Boston: Heinle, 1998), includes useful exercises both in writing and in determining when to use passive voice.

COLLABORATIVE LEARNING

PASSIVE SENTENCES—FINDING PASSAGES

Have students, working in groups, locate passive sentences in an essay from a reader or a similar source. Ask them to decide if the passive voice provides emphasis appropriate for the essay or if the active voice would be better. Tell them to be ready to defend their choice of the passive or to offer a revision of the sentence in the active voice. Have each group present its most hotly debated case to the class.

SCIENTIFIC STYLE

Many editors of scientific journals now recommend that authors use first person pronouns and active verbs where possible instead of relying on the passive. They recommend that authors use the passive when the performer of the action is unknown or unimportant or when emphasis should be placed on the recipient of the action. Students writing in science courses should check with their instructors to see what stylistic guide they should follow; see also Chapters 51 and 52.

COLLABORATIVE LEARNING

ACTIVE/PASSIVE

Ask students to work on Exercise 14.11 in small groups; then ask each group to compose additional examples of active- and passive-voiced sentences.

ANSWERS: EXERCISE 14.11

Possible answers

1. When <u>engineers built</u> the Eiffel Tower in 1889, the <u>French thought</u> it was ugly.
2. At that time industrial <u>technology was</u> still resisted <u>by</u> many people.
3. This <u>technology was epitomized</u> by the tower's naked steel construction.
4. <u>People expected</u> beautiful ornament to grace fine buildings.
5. Further, <u>people could not even call</u> the tower a building because it had no solid walls.

ANSWERS: EXERCISE 14.12

For centuries the natives of Melanesia, a group of islands (lying) northeast of Australia, (have practiced) an unusual religion. It (began) in the eighteenth century when European explorers first (visited) the islands. The natives (were fascinated) by the rich goods or "cargo" (possessed) by the explorers. They (saw) the wealth as treasures of the gods, and cargo cults eventually (arose) among them. Over the centuries some Melanesians (turned) to Christianity in the belief that the white man's religion (would bring) them the white man's trea-

---

The passive voice is useful in two situations: when the actor is unknown and when the actor is unimportant or less important than the object of the action.

> The Internet <u>was established</u> in 1969 by the US Department of Defense. The network <u>has been extended</u> internationally to governments, foundations, corporations, educational institutions, and private individuals. [In the first sentence the writer wishes to stress the Internet rather than the Department of Defense. In the second sentence the actor is unknown or too complicated to name.]

> After the solution <u>had been cooled</u> to 10°C, the acid <u>was added</u>. [The person who cooled and added, perhaps the writer, is less important than the facts that the solution was cooled and acid was added. Passive sentences are common in scientific writing. See p. 808.]

Except in such situations, however, you should prefer the active voice in your writing.

Grammar checkers Most grammar checkers can be set to spot the passive voice. (See pp. 64–65.) But the checkers will flag appropriate passives as well, such as when the actor is unknown.

Exercise 14.11 Converting between active and passive voices

To practice using the two voices of the verb, convert the following sentences from active to passive or from passive to active. (In converting from passive to active, you may have to add a subject for the new sentence.) Which version of each sentence seems more effective, and why? For additional exercises with the passive voice, see pages 262 and 380.

Example:
The aspiring actor was discovered in a nightclub.
A <u>talent scout</u> <u>discovered</u> the aspiring actor in a nightclub.

1. When the Eiffel Tower was built in 1889, it was thought by the French to be ugly.
2. At that time many people still resisted industrial technology.
3. The tower's naked steel construction epitomized this technology.
4. Beautiful ornament was expected to grace fine buildings.
5. Further, the tower could not even be called a building because it had no solid walls.

Exercise 14.12 Revising: Verb forms, tense, mood

Mark all the verbs and verbals in the following paragraph and correct their form, tense, or mood if necessary.

For centuries the natives of Melanesia, a group of islands laying northeast of Australia, have practice an unusual religion. It began in the eighteenth century when European explorers first have visited the islands. The natives were fascinated by the rich goods or "cargo" possessed by the explorers. They saw the wealth as treasures of the gods, and cargo cults eventually had arisen among them. Over the centuries some Melanesians turned to Christianity in the belief that the white man's religion will bring them the white man's treasures. During World War II, US soldiers, having arrived by boat and airplane to have occupied some of the islands, introduced new and even more wonderful cargo. Even today some leaders of the cargo cults insist that the airplane is worship as a vehicle of the Melanesians' future salvation.

Note See page 327 for an exercise involving verbs along with other aspects of grammar.

15

Agreement

Agreement helps readers understand the relations between elements in a sentence. Subjects and verbs agree in number and person:

More Japanese Americans live in Hawaii and California than elsewhere.
　　　　subject　　　　　verb

Daniel Inouye was the first Japanese American in Congress.
　　subject　　verb

Pronouns and their **antecedents**—the words they refer to—agree in person, number, and gender:

Inouye makes his home in Hawaii.
antecedent　　pronoun

Hawaiians value his work for them.
antecedent　　　　　　　pronoun

15a Make subjects and verbs agree in number.

Most subject-verb agreement problems arise when endings are omitted from subjects or verbs or when the relation between sentence parts is uncertain.

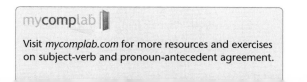
Visit *mycomplab.com* for more resources and exercises on subject-verb and pronoun-antecedent agreement.

sures. During World War II, US soldiers, hav-(ing arrived by) boat and airplane (to occupy) some of the islands, (introduced) new and even more wonderful cargo. Even today some leaders of the cargo cults (insist) that the airplane (be worshipped) as a vehicle of the Melanesians' future salvation.

in English, subjects that are singular in form, like *audience* or *the faculty*, may be plural in meaning. In speech, even educated speakers sometimes treat indefinite pronouns like *anybody* and *everybody* as plural: "Everybody ought to pay attention to their own business." This change in part reflects a desire to avoid the generic *he*, a form of usage many people regard as sexist. The discussions present alternatives designed to avoid sexist language, while at the same time making clear the need to treat *everybody, someone,* and the like as singular, at least in the more conservative written medium.

THE RULE OF ONE -S

Remind students that this is "the rule of one -s"—in the present tense, English sentences require one -s in the third person:

Singular noun + verb + s
Noun + s (plural noun) + verb

Refer students who need additional practice to Unit 3 of Len Fox, *Focus on Editing: A Grammar Workbook for Advanced Writers* (White Plains: Longman, 1992), and to Alan Meyers, *Writing with Confidence* (7th ed., New York: Longman, 2002).

Person and number in subject-verb agreement

Person	Number	
	Singular	Plural
First	I eat.	We eat.
Second	You eat.	You eat.
Third	He/she/it eats.	They eat.
	The bird eats.	Birds eat.

Grammar checkers A grammar checker will catch many simple errors in subject-verb agreement, such as *Addie and John is late*, and some more complicated errors, such as *Is Margaret and Tom going with us?* (should be *are* in both cases). But a checker failed to flag *The old group has gone their separate ways* (should be *have*) and offered a wrong correction for *The old group have gone their separate ways*, which is already correct.

1 The *-s* and *-es* endings work differently for nouns and verbs.

An *-s* or *-es* ending does opposite things to nouns and verbs: it usually makes a noun *plural*, but it always makes a present-tense verb *singular*. Thus a singular noun as subject will not end in *-s*, but its verb will. A plural noun as subject will end in *-s*, but its verb will not. **Between them, subject and verb use only one *-s* ending.**

Singular	Plural
The boy plays.	The boys play.
The bird soars.	The birds soar.

The only exceptions to these rules involve the nouns that form irregular plurals, such as *child/children, woman/women*. The irregular plural still requires a plural verb: The *children play*.

If your first language or dialect is not standard American English, subject-verb agreement may be problematic, especially for these reasons:

■ **Some English dialects follow different rules for subject-verb agreement,** such as omitting the *-s* ending for singular verbs or using the *-s* ending for plural verbs.

Nonstandard	The voter resist change.
Standard	The voter resists change.
Standard	The voters resist change.

The verb *be* changes spelling for singular and plural in both present and past tenses. (See also p. 274.)

Nonstandard	Taxes is high. They was raised just last year.
Standard	Taxes are high. They were raised just last year.

Summary of subject-verb agreement

- **Basic subject-verb agreement** (opposite):

  singular singular
  subject verb

  The kite flies.

  plural plural
  subject verb

  The kites fly.

- **Words between subject and verb** (p. 304):

  The kite with two tails flies badly. The tails of the kite compete.

- **Subjects joined by** *and* (p. 304):

  The kite and the bird are almost indistinguishable.

- **Subjects joined by** *or* or *nor* (p. 305):

  The kite or the bird dives. Kites or birds fill the sky.

- **Indefinite pronoun as subject** (p. 305):

  No one knows. All the spectators wonder.

- **Collective noun as subject** (p. 306):

  A flock appears. The flock disperse.

- **Verb preceding subject** (p. 307):

  Is the kite or the bird blue? Are the kite and the bird both blue?

- **Linking verb** (p. 307):

  The kite is a flier and a dipper.

- ***Who, which, that* as subject** (p. 307):

  The kite that flies longest wins. Kites that fall lose.

- **Subject with plural form and singular meaning** (p. 308):

  Aeronautics plays a role in kite flying.

- **Title or word named as word** (p. 308):

  Kite Dynamics is one title. *Vectors* is a key word.

Have also has a distinctive *-s* form, *has*:

Nonstandard   The new tax have little chance of passing.

Standard   The new tax has little chance of passing.

- **Some other languages change all parts of verb phrases to match their subjects.** In English verb phrases, however, only

WIDELY SEPARATED SUBJECTS AND VERBS

Ask students (working individually or in groups and using the handbook as a guide) to identify the sentence strategies that often result in widely separated subjects and verbs. Then ask them to write in their own words a description of these strategies (i.e., the grammatical rules governing them). Finally, ask students to write sentences using the strategies and containing proper subject-verb agreement. (This exercise can also be used with compound subjects, collective nouns, inverted word order, or other strategies that frequently lead to agreement problems.)

TRUE COMPLEXITY

Sometimes the sample sentences we offer to students to illustrate a point of grammar or style seem a bit artificial or a bit too simple. Writers such as Charles Dickens and Henry James offer sentences with considerable variety and flair in structure that can be used either as models themselves or as patterns for sentences with a more contemporary content and cast. The following sentence, from James's preface to *The Princess Casamassima*, illustrates tight control of subject-verb and pronoun-antecedent agreement:

> The troubled life mostly at the center of our subject—whatever our subject, for the artistic hour, happens to be—embraces them [fools] and deals with them for its amusement and its anguish: they are apt largely indeed, on a near view, to be all the cause of its trouble.

Although students often produce grammatically complex sentences, particularly in response to readings, it can be fun and enlightening for them to practice different kinds of complexity. Copy a sentence like this one on the board, on a transparency, or on the course Web site, and ask students to compose sentences that mimic, even parody, its complex structure.

Ask students to speculate about why James might craft such a complicated sentence. As they compare their own complex sentences, ask them to discuss the effect of such a sentence on readers. Is the point clear? Will readers understand or be confused? Remind students that complexity, while admirable, is not necessarily preferable—even in college-level writing—to the clarity that attends simplicity.

the helping verbs *be, have,* and *do* change for different subjects. The modal helping verbs—*can, may, should, will,* and others—do not change:

| Nonstandard | The tax mays pass next year. |
| Standard | The tax may pass next year. |

The main verb in a verb phrase also does not change for different subjects:

| Nonstandard | The tax may passes next year. |
| Standard | The tax may pass next year. |

2 Subject and verb should agree even when other words come between them.

When the subject and verb are interrupted by other words, make sure the verb agrees with the subject:

A catalog of courses and requirements often baffles [not baffle] students.

The requirements stated in the catalog are [not is] unclear.

Note Phrases beginning with *as well as, together with, along with,* and *in addition to* do not change the number of the subject:

The president, as well as the deans, has [not have] agreed to revise the catalog.

If you really mean *and* in such a sentence, use it. Then the subject is compound, and the verb should be plural: *The president and the deans have agreed to revise the catalog.*

3 Subjects joined by *and* usually take plural verbs.

Two or more subjects joined by *and* usually take a plural verb, whether one or all of the subjects are singular:

Frost and Roethke were contemporaries.

Frost, Roethke, Stevens, and Pound are among the great American poets.

Exceptions When the parts of the subject form a single idea or refer to a single person or thing, they take a singular verb:

Avocado and bean sprouts is a California sandwich.

When a compound subject is preceded by the adjective *each* or *every,* the verb is usually singular:

Each man, woman, and child has a right to be heard.

But a compound subject *followed* by *each* takes a plural verb:

The man and the woman each have different problems.

4 When parts of a subject are joined by *or* or *nor,* the verb agrees with the nearer part.

When all parts of a subject joined by *or* or *nor* are singular, the verb is singular; when all parts are plural, the verb is plural.

Either the painter or the carpenter knows the cost.

The cabinets or the bookcases are too costly.

When one part of the subject is singular and the other plural, avoid awkwardness by placing the plural part closer to the verb so that the verb is plural:

Awkward   Neither the owners nor the contractor agrees.

Revised   Neither the contractor nor the owners agree.

When the subject consists of nouns and pronouns of different person requiring different verb forms, the verb agrees with the nearer part of the subject. Reword if this construction is awkward:

Awkward   Either Juarez or I am responsible.

Revised   Either Juarez is responsible, or I am.

5 With an indefinite pronoun such as *anybody* or *all,* use a singular or plural verb as appropriate.

An **indefinite pronoun** is one that does not refer to a specific person or thing. Most indefinite pronouns take a singular verb, but some take a plural verb and some take a singular *or* a plural verb.

Common indefinite pronouns

Singular			Singular or plural	Plural
anybody	everyone	no one	all	both
anyone	everything	nothing	any	few
anything	much	one	more	many
each	neither	somebody	most	several
either	nobody	someone	some	
everybody	none	something		

ARE EVERYONE READY?

   Though many students will not, at first, hear anything wrong with sentences like *Everyone ought to pay attention to their own business* (a pattern that has wide acceptance in speech), almost all will find sentences like these unacceptable: *Are everyone ready for lunch? Do everybody have enough money to buy tickets for the rides?* Anyone who finds the latter sentences acceptable is probably having trouble recognizing the singular and plural forms of verbs. Sample sentences can, therefore, help you identify the real source of a student's problems with agreement.

The singular indefinite pronouns refer to a single unspecified person or thing, and they take a singular verb:

Something smells.   Neither is right.

The plural indefinite pronouns refer to more than one unspecified thing, and they take a plural verb:

Both are correct.   Several were invited.

The other indefinite pronouns take a singular or a plural verb depending on whether the word they refer to is singular or plural. The word may be stated in the sentence:

All of the money is reserved for emergencies.

All of the funds are reserved for emergencies.

The word referred to by the pronoun may also be implied:

All are planning to attend. [*All* implies "all the people."]

All is lost. [*All* implies "everything."]

> **CULTURE LANGUAGE** See page 326 for the distinction between *few* ("not many") and *a few* ("some").

6 **Collective nouns such as *group* take singular or plural verbs depending on meaning.**

A **collective noun** has singular form but names a group of individuals or things—for example, *army, audience, committee, crowd, family, group, team.* As a subject, a collective noun may take a singular or plural verb, depending on the context. When the group acts as one unit, use a singular verb:

The group agrees that action is necessary.

But when considering the group's members as individuals who act separately, use the plural form of the verb:

The old group have gone their separate ways.

The collective noun *number* may be singular or plural. Preceded by *a*, it is plural; preceded by *the*, it is singular.

A number of people are in debt.

The number of people in debt is very large.

> **CULTURE LANGUAGE** In English some noncount nouns (nouns that don't form plurals) are collective nouns because they

---

> **CULTURE LANGUAGE**
>
> **SEPARATED BY A COMMON LANGUAGE?**
>
> In British usage, collective nouns are treated as plurals; students educated in British usage (such as those from countries formerly under British dominion) may use constructions like *The team were ready for the game.* Such constructions also appear in the works of British authors.

name groups: for instance, *furniture, clothing, mail.* These noncount nouns usually take singular verbs: *Mail arrives daily.* But some of these nouns take plural verbs, including *clergy, military, people, police,* and any collective noun that comes from an adjective, such as *the poor, the rich, the young, the elderly.* If you mean one representative of the group, use a singular noun such as *police officer* or *poor person.*

7 The verb agrees with the subject even when it precedes the subject.

The verb precedes the subject mainly in questions and in constructions beginning with *there* or *here* and a form of *be:*

Is voting a right or a privilege?

Are a right and a privilege the same thing?

There are differences between them.

In constructions beginning with *there* or *here,* you may use *is* before a compound subject when the first element in the subject is singular:

Here lies both the problem and its solution.

Word order may sometimes be reversed for emphasis. The verb still agrees with its subject:

From the mountains comes an eerie, shimmering light.

8 A linking verb agrees with its subject, not the subject complement.

A linking verb such as *is* or *are* should agree with its subject, usually the first element in the sentence, not with the noun or pronoun serving as a subject complement (see pp. 237–38):

The child's sole support is her court-appointed guardians.

Her court-appointed guardians are the child's sole support.

9 *Who, which,* and *that* take verbs that agree with their antecedents.

When used as subjects, *who, which,* and *that* refer to another word in the sentence, called the **antecedent.** The verb agrees with the antecedent:

Mayor Garber ought to listen to the people who work for her.

Bardini is the only aide who has her ear.

CULTURE LANGUAGE

REMINDER

Remind students that phrases like *one of* also require *the* before the noun: *Bardini is one of the aides* [not *one of aides*] *who work unpaid.*

RESOURCES AND IDEAS

Kolln, Martha. "Everyone's Right to Their Own Language." *College Composition and Communication* 37.1 (1986): 100–02. Print. The frequency with which students treat indefinite pronouns as plural suggests that the widely accepted rules of usage discussed in this section may in some ways conflict with practice. Kolln takes a radical stance, arguing that "dicta that designate all indefinite pronouns as singular have no basis either in actual usage or in the rules of logic" (102).

Sklar, Elizabeth S. "The Tribunal of Use: Agreement in the Indefinite Constructions." *College Composition and Communication* 39.4 (1988): 410–22. Print. Sklar reviews historical and textbook treatments of agreement with indefinites and offers some pragmatic strategies for teachers to use.

COLLABORATIVE LEARNING

Ask students to work together on Exercise 15.1 and then to look for agreement problems in each other's journal writing, drafts, or completed work.

ANSWERS: EXERCISE 15.1

1. Weinstein & Associates <u>is</u> a consulting firm that <u>tries</u> to make businesspeople laugh.
2. Statistics from recent research <u>suggest</u> that humor relieves stress.
3. Reduced stress in businesses in turn <u>reduces</u> illness and absenteeism.

Agreement problems often occur with *who, which,* or *that* when the sentence includes *one of the* or *the only one of the:*

Bardini is one of the aides who work unpaid. [Of the aides who work unpaid, Bardini is one.]

Bardini is the only one of the aides who knows the community. [Of the aides, only one, Bardini, knows the community.]

CULTURE LANGUAGE In phrases like those above beginning with *one of the,* be sure the noun is plural: *Bardini is one of the aides* [not *aide*] *who work unpaid.*

10 Nouns with plural form but singular meaning, such as *news,* take singular verbs.

Some nouns with plural form (that is, ending in *-s*) are usually regarded as singular in meaning. They include *athletics, economics, mathematics, measles, mumps, news, physics, politics,* and *statistics,* as well as place names such as *Athens, Wales,* and *United States.*

After so long a wait, the news has to be good.

Statistics is required of psychology majors.

A few of these words take plural verbs only when they describe individual items rather than whole bodies of activity or knowledge: *The statistics prove him wrong.*

Measurements and figures ending in *-s* may also be singular when the quantity they refer to is a unit:

Three years is a long time to wait.

Three-fourths of the library consists of reference books.

11 Titles and words named as words take singular verbs.

When your sentence subject is the name of a corporation, the title of a work (such as a book), or a word you are defining or describing, the verb should be singular even if the name, title, or word is plural:

Hakada Associates is a new firm.

Dream Days remains a favorite book.

Folks is a down-home word for *people.*

Exercise 15.1 Revising: Subject-verb agreement
Revise the verbs in the following sentences as needed to make subjects and verbs agree in number. If the sentence is already correct as given, mark the number preceding it.

Example:
Each of the job applicants type sixty words per minute.
Each of the job applicants <u>types</u> sixty words per minute.

1. Weinstein & Associates are a consulting firm that try to make businesspeople laugh.
2. Statistics from recent research suggests that humor relieves stress.
3. Reduced stress in businesses in turn reduce illness and absenteeism.
4. Reduced stress can also reduce friction within an employee group, which then work more productively.
5. In special conferences held by one consultant, each of the participants practice making the others laugh.
6. One consultant to many companies suggest cultivating office humor with practical jokes such as a rubber fish in the water cooler.
7. When employees or their manager regularly post cartoons on the bulletin board, office spirit usually picks up.
8. When someone who has seemed too easily distracted is entrusted with updating the cartoons, his or her concentration often improves.
9. In the face of levity, the former sourpuss becomes one of those who hides bad temper.
10. Every one of the consultants caution, however, that humor has no place in life-affecting corporate situations such as employee layoffs.

4. Reduced stress can also reduce friction within an employee group, which then <u>works</u> more productively.
5. In special conferences held by one consultant, each of the participants <u>practices</u> making the others laugh.
6. One consultant to many companies <u>suggests</u> cultivating office humor with practical jokes such as a rubber fish in the water cooler.
7. When the manager or employees regularly <u>post</u> cartoons on the bulletin board, office spirit usually picks up.
8. Sentence correct.
9. In the face of levity, the former sourpuss becomes one of those who <u>hide</u> bad temper.
10. Every one of the consultants <u>cautions</u>, however, that humor has no place <u>in</u> life-affecting corporate situations such as employee layoffs.

| **15b** | Make pronouns and their antecedents agree in person, number, and gender. |

The **antecedent** of a pronoun is the noun or other pronoun to which the pronoun refers.

Homeowners fret over their tax bills.
antecedent   pronoun

Its constant increases make the tax bill a dreaded document.
pronoun   antecedent

Since a pronoun derives its meaning from its antecedent, the two must agree in person, number, and gender.

Person, number, and gender in pronoun-antecedent agreement

Person	Number	
	Singular	*Plural*
First	*I*	*we*
Second	*you*	*you*
Third	*he, she, it,* indefinite pronouns, singular nouns	*they,* plural nouns

(continued)

COLLABORATIVE LEARNING

USING MAGAZINES OR A READER

Using essays from a reader or magazine articles, have students work in groups to find sentence structures often associated with agreement problems. Ask the groups to decide how important these structures are for expository prose and to write out what they consider to be the rules governing agreement within these structures.

Person, number, and gender in pronoun-antecedent agreement

(continued)

Gender

Masculine	*he,* nouns naming males
Feminine	*she,* nouns naming females
Neuter	*it,* all other nouns

Grammar checkers A grammar checker cannot help with agreement between pronoun and antecedent because it cannot recognize the intended relation between the two.

(**CULTURE LANGUAGE**) The gender of a pronoun should match its antecedent, not a noun that the pronoun may modify: *Sara Young invited her* [not *his*] *son to join the company's staff.* Also, nouns in English have only neuter gender unless they specifically refer to males or females. Thus nouns such as *book, table, sun,* and *earth* take the pronoun *it.*

Summary of pronoun-antecedent agreement

■ **Basic pronoun-antecedent agreement:**

antecedent   pronoun
Old Faithful spews its columns of water, each of them over 115 feet high.

■ **Antecedents joined by *and*** (opposite):

Old Faithful and Giant are geysers known for their height.

■ **Antecedents joined by *or* or *nor*** (opposite):

Either Giant or Giantess ejects its column the highest.

■ **Indefinite words as antecedents** (opposite):

Each of the geysers has its own personality.

Each person who visits has his or her favorites.

Some return to their favorites year after year.

■ **Collective nouns as antecedents** (p. 313):

A crowd amuses itself watching Old Faithful.

Afterward the crowd go their separate ways.

1 Antecedents joined by *and* usually take plural pronouns.

Two or more antecedents joined by *and* usually take a plural pronoun, whether one or all of the antecedents are singular:

Mr. Bartos and I cannot settle our dispute.

The dean and my adviser have offered their help.

Exceptions When the compound antecedent refers to a single idea, person, or thing, then the pronoun is singular:

My friend and adviser offered her help.

When the compound antecedent follows *each* or *every,* the pronoun is singular:

Every girl and woman took her seat.

2 When parts of an antecedent are joined by *or* or *nor,* the pronoun agrees with the nearer part.

When the parts of an antecedent are connected by *or* or *nor,* the pronoun should agree with the part closer to it:

Tenants or owners must present their grievances.

Either the tenant or the owner will have her way.

When one subject is plural and the other singular, the sentence will be awkward unless you put the plural one second:

Awkward   Neither the tenants nor the owner has yet made her case.

Revised   Neither the owner nor the tenants have yet made their case.

3 With an indefinite word as antecedent, such as *anyone* or *person,* use a singular or plural pronoun as appropriate.

Indefinite words do not refer to any specific person or thing. They include **indefinite pronouns** such as *anyone, everybody,* and *no one* (see p. 305 for a list). They also include **generic nouns,** or singular nouns that refer to typical members of a group, as in *The individual has rights* or *The job requires a person with computer skills.*

Most indefinite pronouns and all generic nouns are singular in meaning. When they serve as antecedents of pronouns, the pronouns should be singular.

Everyone on the women's team now has her own locker.
indefinite
pronoun

CULTURE LANGUAGE

CONFUSION OVER INDEFINITE PRONOUNS

ESL students may be confused by the indefinite pronouns *everyone, everybody,* and *everything* because they mean *all* of a group but are grammatically singular. Explain to students that the *endings* to these words—*one, body,* and *thing*—cause them to be singular rather than plural.

Every person on the women's team now has her own locker.

generic

noun

Five indefinite pronouns—*all, any, more, most, some*—may be singular or plural in meaning depending on what they refer to:

Few women athletes had changing spaces, so most had to change in their rooms.

Most of the changing space was dismal, its color a drab olive green.

Four indefinite pronouns—*both, few, many, several*—are always plural in meaning:

Few realize how their athletic facilities have changed.

Most agreement problems arise with the singular indefinite words. We often use these words to mean something like "many" or "all" rather than "one" and then refer to them with plural pronouns, as in *Everyone has their own locker* or *A person can padlock their locker*. Often, too, we mean indefinite words to include both masculine and feminine genders and thus resort to *they* instead of the **generic** *he*—the masculine pronoun referring to both genders, as in *Everyone deserves his privacy*. (For more on the generic *he*, which many readers view as sexist, see p. 509.)

see p. 509.

STYLE AND PRONOUNS

Ask students to write some of their own sentences using indefinite words and pronouns and then revise them to make the indefinite word plural (and use the matching plural pronoun). Which sentences are the clearest and most concise?

RESOURCES AND IDEAS

Amare, Nicole. "Where is She? Gender Occurrences in Online Grammar Guides." *Research in the Teaching of English* 42.2 (2007): 163–87. Print. Amare analyzed online grammar guides according to NCTE's "Guidelines for Gender-Fair Use of Language" and found instances of linguistic sexism. She encourages writing teachers to teach students how to eliminate gender bias in their writing.

Ways to correct agreement with indefinite words

■ **Change the indefinite word to a plural, and use a plural pronoun to match:**

Faulty	Every athlete deserves their privacy.
Revised	**Athletes** deserve their privacy.

■ **Rewrite the sentence to omit the pronoun:**

Faulty	Everyone is entitled to their own locker.
Revised	Everyone is entitled to **a** locker.

■ **Use *he or she* (*him or her, his or her*) to refer to the indefinite word:**

Faulty	Now everyone has their private space.
Revised	Now everyone has **his or her** private space.

However, used more than once in several sentences, *he or she* quickly becomes awkward. (Many readers do not accept the alternative *he/she*.) Using the plural or omitting the pronoun will usually correct agreement problems and create more readable sentences.

Although some experts accept *they, them,* and *their* with singular indefinite words, most do not, and many teachers and employers regard the plural as incorrect. To be safe, work for agreement between singular indefinite words and the pronouns that refer to them, using the options in the preceding box.

4 With a collective noun as antecedent, such as *group* or *team,* use a singular or plural pronoun depending on meaning.

Collective nouns such as *army, committee, family, group,* and *team* have singular form but may be referred to by singular or plural pronouns, depending on the meaning intended. When the group acts as a unit, the pronoun is singular:

The committee voted to disband itself.

When the members of the group act separately, the pronoun is plural:

The old group have gone their separate ways.

In the last example, note that the verb and pronoun are consistent in number (see also p. 354).

Inconsistent   The old group has gone their separate ways.
Consistent   The old group have gone their separate ways.

(CULTURE LANGUAGE) In standard American English, collective nouns that are noncount nouns (they don't form plurals) usually take singular pronouns: *The mail sits in its own basket.* A few noncount nouns take plural pronouns, including *clergy, military, people, police, the rich,* and *the poor: The police support their unions.* (See also pp. 306–07.)

Exercise 15.2   Revising: Pronoun-antecedent agreement
Revise the following sentences so that pronouns and their antecedents agree in person and number. Some items have more than one possible answer. Try to avoid the generic *he* (see opposite). If you change the subject of a sentence, be sure to change verbs as necessary for agreement. If the sentence is already correct as given, mark the number preceding it.

Example:
Each of the Boudreaus' children brought their laundry home at Thanksgiving.

All of the Boudreaus' children brought their laundry home at Thanksgiving. *Or:* Each of the Boudreaus' children brought laundry home at Thanksgiving. *Or:* Each of the Boudreaus' children brought his or her laundry home at Thanksgiving.

ANSWERS: EXERCISE 15.2

1. Each girl raised in a Mexican American family in the Rio Grande Valley of Texas hopes that one day she will be given a *quinceañera* party for her fifteenth birthday.

2. Such a celebration is very expensive because it entails a religious service followed by a huge party. *Or:* Such celebrations are very expensive because they entail a religious service followed by a huge party.
3. A girl's immediate family, unless it is wealthy, cannot afford the party by itself.
4. The parents will ask each close friend or relative if he or she can help with the preparations. *Or:* The parents will ask close friends or relatives if they can help with the preparations.
5. Sentence correct.

ANSWERS: EXERCISE 15.3

1. Giant pandas are endangered.
2. Conservationists estimate that fewer than two thousand giant pandas live in central China, their natural habitat, because the bamboo forests are shrinking.
3. Giant pandas eat bamboo and gain most of their nutrition from its leaves and stalks.
4. At the Wolong Wildlife Refuge in China, researchers breed pandas in captivity and release the cubs into the wild when they are old enough to survive on their own.
5. Zoos in the United States wish to raise awareness of the giant panda's plight by breeding pairs of adults and allowing the public to view the adorable cubs while they are young.

ANSWERS: EXERCISE 15.4

The writers Richard Rodriguez and Maxine Hong Kingston, despite their differences, share one characteristic: their parents were immigrants to California. A frequent theme of their writings is the difficulties of growing up with two languages and two cultures.

A child whose first language is not English is often ridiculed because he or she cannot communicate "properly." [*Or:* Children whose first language is not English are often ridiculed because they cannot communicate "properly."] Rodriguez learned Spanish at home, but at school classmates and teachers expected him to use their language, English. He remembers his childish embarrassment because of his parents' poor English. College and graduate school, which usually expand one's knowledge, widened the gap between Rodriguez and his Latino culture. His essays suggest that he lost a part of himself, a loss that continues to bother him.

1. Each girl raised in a Mexican American family in the Rio Grande Valley of Texas hopes that one day they will be given a *quinceañera* party for their fifteenth birthday.
2. Such celebrations are very expensive because it entails a religious service followed by a huge party.
3. A girl's immediate family, unless they are wealthy, cannot afford the party by themselves.
4. The parents will ask each close friend or relative if they can help with the preparations.
5. Surrounded by her family and attended by her friends and their escorts, the *quinceañera* is introduced as a young woman eligible for Mexican American society.

Exercise 15.3 Adjusting for agreement

In the sentences below, subjects agree with verbs and pronouns agree with antecedents. Make the change specified in parentheses after each sentence, and then revise the sentence as necessary to maintain agreement. Some items have more than one possible answer.

Example:

The student attends weekly conferences with her teacher. (*Change The student to Students.*)

Students attend weekly conferences with their teacher.

1. The giant panda is endangered. (*Change The giant panda to Giant pandas.*)
2. A conservationist estimates that fewer than two thousand giant pandas live in central China, their natural habitat, because the bamboo forests there are shrinking. (*Change A conservationist to Conservationists.*)
3. The giant panda eats bamboo and gains most of its nutrition from its leaves and stalks. (*Change The giant panda to Giant pandas.*)
4. At the Wolong Wildlife Refuge in China, researchers breed pandas in captivity and release a cub into the wild when it is old enough to survive on its own. (*Change a cub to the cubs.*)
5. A zoo in the United States wishes to raise awareness of the giant panda's plight by breeding a pair of adults and allowing the public to view the adorable cub while it is young. (*Change A zoo to Zoos, a pair to pairs, and cub to the cubs.*)

Exercise 15.4 Revising: Agreement

Revise the sentences in the following paragraphs to correct errors in agreement between subjects and verbs or between pronouns and their antecedents. Try to avoid the generic *he*.

The writers Richard Rodriguez and Maxine Hong Kingston, despite their differences, shares one characteristic: their parents was immigrants to California. A frequent theme of their writings are the difficulties of growing up with two languages and two cultures.

A child whose first language is not English is often ridiculed because they cannot communicate "properly." Rodriguez learned Spanish at home, but at school everyone expected him to use their language, English. He remembers his childish embarrassment because of his parents' poor English. College and graduate school, which usually expands one's knowledge, widened the gap between Rodriguez and his Latino culture. His essays suggests that he lost a part of himself, a loss that continue to bother him.

Kingston spoke Chinese at home and also learned her first English at school. She sometimes write of these experiences, but more often she write to recover and preserve her Chinese culture. *The Woman Warrior,* which offer a blend of autobiography, family history, and mythic tales, describe the struggle of Kingston's female relatives. *China Men* focus on Kingston's male ancestors; each one traveled to Hawaii or California to make money for their wife back in China. Kingston's work, like Rodriguez's essays, reflect the tension and confusion that the child of immigrants often feel when they try to blend two cultures.

Note See page 327 for an exercise involving agreement along with other aspects of grammar.

Kingston spoke Chinese at home and also learned her first English at school. She sometimes <u>writes</u> of these experiences, but more often she <u>writes</u> to recover and preserve her Chinese culture. *The Woman Warrior,* which <u>offers</u> a blend of autobiography, family history, and mythic tales, <u>describes</u> the struggle of Kingston's female relatives. *China Men* <u>focuses</u> on Kingston's male ancestors; each one traveled to Hawaii or California to make money for <u>his</u> wife back in China. Kingston's work, like Rodriguez's essays, <u>reflects</u> the tension and confusion that the child of immigrants often <u>feels</u> when <u>he or she tries</u> [*or:* that the <u>children</u> of immigrants often feel when they try] to blend two cultures.

16
Adjectives and Adverbs

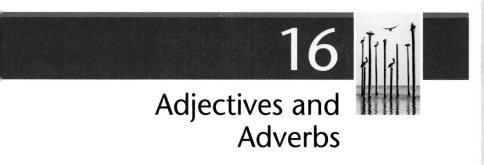

Adjectives and adverbs are modifiers that describe, restrict, or otherwise qualify the words to which they relate.

Functions of adjectives and adverbs

Adjectives modify nouns:	serious student
pronouns:	ordinary one
Adverbs modify verbs:	warmly greet
adjectives:	only three people
adverbs:	quite seriously
phrases:	nearly to the edge of the cliff
clauses:	just when we arrived
sentences:	Fortunately, she is employed.

mycomplab

Visit *mycomplab.com* for more resources and exercises on adjectives and adverbs.

HIGHLIGHTS

Many readers view misuse of adjectives and adverbs as a sign of ignorance or carelessness. You should alert students to the potential effect of errors, of course, and remind them that this text offers helpful advice.

Yet fear of failure can disrupt the writing process and cause students to drop effective phrases and sentences from an essay because they are uncertain about the correct form of a word. This chapter therefore takes a positive approach, showing students the correct way to use adjectives and adverbs rather than emphasizing the *don't*'s. It also offers easily remembered advice to guide writers over trouble spots. The exercises in the chapter ask students not only to recognize errors but also to revise sentences to make sure adjectives and adverbs are used appropriately.

Many of the most common adjectives are familiar one-syllable words such as *bad, strange, large,* and *wrong.* Many others are formed by adding endings such as *-al, -able, -ful, -less, -ish, -ive,* and *-y* to nouns or verbs: *optional, fashionable, beautiful, fruitless, selfish, expressive, dreamy.*

Most adverbs are formed by adding *-ly* to adjectives: *badly, strangely, largely, beautifully.* But note that we cannot depend on *-ly* to identify adverbs, since some adjectives also end in *-ly* (*fatherly, lonely*) and since some common adverbs do not end in *-ly* (*always, here, not, now, often, there*). Thus the only sure way to distinguish between adjectives and adverbs is to determine what they modify.

Grammar checkers A grammar checker will spot some but not all problems with misused adjectives and adverbs. For instance, a checker flagged *Some children suffer bad* and *Chang was the most wisest person in town* and *Jenny did not feel nothing.* But it did not flag *Educating children good is everyone's focus.*

CULTURE LANGUAGE In standard American English an adjective does not change along with the noun it modifies to show plural number: *white* [not *whites*] shoes, *square* [not *squares*] spaces. Only nouns form plurals.

16a Use adjectives only to modify nouns and pronouns.

Adjectives modify only nouns and pronouns. Do not use adjectives instead of adverbs to modify verbs, adverbs, or other adjectives:

Faulty   The groups view family values different.

Revised   The groups view family values differently.

Be especially careful not to use *good* and *bad* in place of *well* and *badly.*

Faulty   Educating children good is everyone's focus.

Revised   Educating children well is everyone's focus.

Faulty   Some children suffer bad.

Revised   Some children suffer badly.

CULTURE LANGUAGE To negate a verb or an adjective, use the adverb *not:*

They are not learning. They are not stupid.

To negate a noun, use the adjective *no:*

No child should fail to read.

16b Use an adjective after a linking verb to modify the subject. Use an adverb to modify a verb.

A **linking verb** is one that links, or connects, a subject and its complement, either a noun (*They are golfers*) or an adjective (*He is lucky*). (See also pp. 237–38.) Linking verbs are forms of *be*, the verbs associated with our five senses (*look, sound, smell, feel, taste*), and a few others (*appear, seem, become, grow, turn, prove, remain, stay*).

Some of these verbs may or may not be linking, depending on their meaning in the sentence. When the word after the verb modifies the subject, the verb is linking and the word should be an adjective: *He feels strong*. When the word modifies the verb, however, it should be an adverb: *He feels strongly about that*.

Two word pairs are especially troublesome in this context. One is *bad* and *badly:*

The weather grew <u>bad</u>.   She felt <u>bad</u>.
   linking adjective   linking adjective
   verb   verb

Flowers grow <u>badly</u> in such soil.
   verb adverb

The other pair is *good* and *well. Good* serves only as an adjective. *Well* may serve as an adverb with a host of meanings or as an adjective meaning only "fit" or "healthy."

Decker trained <u>well</u>.   She felt <u>well</u>.   Her health was <u>good</u>.
  verb adverb   linking adjective   linking adjective
               verb   verb

16c After a direct object, use an adjective to modify the object and an adverb to modify the verb.

After a direct object, an adjective modifies the object, whereas an adverb modifies the verb of the sentence. (See p. 236 for more on direct objects.)

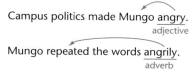

Campus politics made Mungo <u>angry</u>.
               adjective

Mungo repeated the words <u>angrily</u>.
            adverb

You can test whether a modifier should be an adjective or an adverb by trying to separate it from the direct object. If you can separate it, it should be an adverb: *Mungo angrily repeated the words.* If you cannot separate it, it is probably an adjective.

Have students complete Exercise 16.1 in groups. Then, ask each group to revise the original sentences again, this time moving the incorrect adjective or adverb someplace else in the sentence so it is used correctly. For instance, the revised example might read "The announcer warned that slow traffic was moving very" or "The slow announcer warned that traffic was moving very." The sentences might not make as much sense, but the exercise will allow students to demonstrate whether they understand which words adjectives and adverbs can modify.

ANSWERS: EXERCISE 16.1

1. King George III of England declared Samuel Johnson <u>suitable</u> for a pension.
2. Johnson <u>was taken</u> <u>seriously</u> as a critic and dictionary maker.
3. Thinking about his meeting with the king, Johnson felt <u>proud</u>.
4. Sentence correct.
5. After living <u>cheaply</u> for over twenty years, Johnson finally had enough money from the pension to eat and dress <u>well</u>.

SABOTAGING ESSAYS

Give each group a different short essay and have them introduce a number of errors into its adjective and adverb use. (They may want to use correction tape for this task.) Then have students copy the essay so their corrections won't show and give it to a different group, which attempts to find all the changes the first group made. The first group comments on and critiques the "corrected" essay by comparing it to the original version. If students are working in a computer classroom, they can print out the error-ridden version of the essay for the other group.

The instructor considered the student's work <u>thorough</u>. [The adjective can be moved in front of *work* (*student's thorough work*), but it cannot be separated from *work*.]

The instructor considered the student's work <u>thoroughly</u>. [The adverb can be separated from *work*. Compare *The instructor thoroughly considered the student's work.*]

Exercise 16.1 Revising: Adjectives and adverbs

Revise the following sentences so that adjectives and adverbs are used appropriately. If any sentence is already correct as given, mark the number preceding it.

Example:

The announcer warned that traffic was moving very slow.
The announcer warned that traffic was moving very <u>slowly</u>.

1. King George III of England declared Samuel Johnson suitably for a pension.
2. Johnson was taken serious as a critic and dictionary maker.
3. Thinking about his meeting with the king, Johnson felt proudly.
4. Johnson was relieved that he had not behaved badly in the king's presence.
5. After living cheap for over twenty years, Johnson finally had enough money from the pension to eat and dress good.

16d Use the comparative and superlative forms of adjectives and adverbs appropriately.

Adjectives and adverbs can show degrees of quality or amount with the endings *-er* and *-est* or with the words *more* and *most* or *less* and *least*. Most modifiers have three forms:

Positive The basic form listed in the dictionary	**Comparative** A greater or lesser degree of the quality	**Superlative** The greatest or least degree of the quality
Adjectives		
red	redder	reddest
awful	more/less awful	most/least awful
Adverbs		
soon	sooner	soonest
quickly	more/less quickly	most/least quickly

If sound alone does not tell you whether to use *-er/-est* or *more/most,* consult a dictionary. If the endings can be used, the dictionary will list them. Otherwise, use *more* or *most*.

1 Use the correct forms of irregular adjectives and adverbs.

Certain adjectives and adverbs are irregular: they change the spelling of their positive form to show comparative and superlative degrees.

Degrees of irregular adjectives and adverbs

Positive	Comparative	Superlative
Adjectives		
good	better	best
bad	worse	worst
little	littler, less	littlest, least
many		
some	more	most
much		
Adverbs		
well	better	best
badly	worse	worst

2 Use either *-er/-est* or *more/most,* not both.

A double comparative or double superlative combines the *-er* or *-est* ending with the word *more* or *most.* It is redundant.

Chang was the <u>wisest</u> [not <u>most wisest</u>] person in town.
He was <u>smarter</u> [not <u>more smarter</u>] than anyone else.

3 Use the comparative for comparing two things and the superlative for comparing three or more things.

It is the <u>shorter</u> of her two books. [Comparative.]
The Yearling is the <u>most popular</u> of the six books. [Superlative.]

In conversation the superlative form is often used to compare only two things: *When two people argue, the <u>angriest</u> one is usually wrong.* But the distinction between the forms should be observed in writing.

4 Use comparative or superlative forms only for modifiers that can logically be compared.

Some adjectives and adverbs cannot logically be compared—for instance, *perfect, unique, dead, impossible, infinite.* These absolute words can be preceded by adverbs like *nearly* and *almost* that mean "approaching," but they cannot logically be modified by *more*

1. Charlotte was the <u>oldest</u> of the three Brontë sisters, all of whom were novelists.
2. Some readers think Emily Brontë's *Wuthering Heights* is the <u>saddest</u> novel they have ever read.
3. Sentence correct.
4. Critics still argue about whether Charlotte or Emily wrote <u>better</u>.
5. Certainly, <u>this family</u> of women novelists was <u>unique</u>.

Interest in books about the founding of the United States seems to vary with the national mood. Americans show <u>hardly any interest</u> [or <u>little interest</u>] in books about the founders when things are going well in the United States. However, when Americans <u>can barely</u> [or <u>cannot</u>] agree on major issues, sales of books about the Revolutionary War era increase. During such periods, one cannot go to a bookstore without seeing several new volumes about John Adams, Thomas Jefferson, and other founders. When Americans feel they <u>have nothing</u> [or <u>don't have anything</u>] in common, their increased <u>interest</u> in the early leaders may reflect a desire for unity.

or *most* (as in *most perfect*). This distinction is sometimes ignored in speech, but it should always be made in writing:

| Not | He was the <u>most unique</u> teacher we had. |
| But | He was a <u>unique</u> teacher. |

Exercise 16.2 Revising: Comparatives and superlatives

Revise the sentences below so that the comparative and superlative forms of adjectives and adverbs are appropriate for formal usage. Mark the number preceding any sentence that is already correct.

Example:

Attending classes full time and working at two jobs was the most impossible thing I ever did.

Attending classes full time and working at two jobs was <u>impossible</u> [or <u>the hardest thing I ever did</u>].

1. Charlotte was the older of the three Brontë sisters, all of whom were novelists.
2. Some readers think Emily Brontë's *Wuthering Heights* is the most saddest novel they have ever read.
3. Of the other two sisters, Charlotte and Anne, Charlotte was probably the more talented.
4. Critics still argue about whether Charlotte or Emily wrote more better.
5. Certainly this family of women novelists was the most unique.

16e Watch for double negatives.

In a **double negative** two negative words such as *no, not, none, neither, barely, hardly,* or *scarcely* cancel each other out. Some double negatives are intentional: for instance, *She was <u>not unhappy</u>* indicates with understatement that she was indeed happy. But most double negatives say the opposite of what is intended: *Jenny did <u>not</u> feel <u>nothing</u>* asserts that Jenny felt other than nothing, or something. For the opposite meaning, one of the negatives must be eliminated or changed to a positive: *She felt <u>nothing</u>* or *She did <u>not feel anything</u>*.

| Faulty | The IRS <u>cannot hardly</u> audit all tax returns. <u>None</u> of its audits <u>never</u> touch many cheaters. |
| Revised | The IRS <u>cannot</u> audit all tax returns. Its audits <u>never</u> touch many cheaters. |

Exercise 16.3 Revising: Double negatives

Identify and revise the double negatives in the following paragraph. Each error may have more than one correct revision.

Interest in books about the founding of the United States seems to vary with the national mood. Americans show hardly no interest in books about the founders when things are going well in the United

States. However, when Americans can't barely agree on major issues, sales of books about the Revolutionary War era increase. During such periods, one cannot go to no bookstore without seeing several new volumes about John Adams, Thomas Jefferson, and other founders. When Americans feel they don't have nothing in common, their increased interest in the early leaders may reflect a desire for unity.

16f   Use nouns sparingly as modifiers.

We often use one noun to modify another. For example:

child care   flood control   security guard

Such phrases can be both clear and concise, but overuse of noun modifiers can lead to flat, even senseless, writing. To avoid awkwardness or confusion, observe two principles. First, prefer possessives or adjectives as modifiers:

Not	A student takes the state medical board exams to become a dentist technician.
But	A student takes the state medical board's exams to become a dental technician.

Second, use only short nouns as modifiers and use them only in two- or three-word sequences:

Confusing	Minimex maintains a plant employee relations improvement program.
Revised	Minimex maintains a program for improving relations among plant employees.

16g   Distinguish between present and past participles as adjectives.

Both present participles and past participles may serve as adjectives: *a burning building, a burned building.* As in the examples, the two participles usually differ in the time they indicate.

But some present and past participles—those derived from verbs expressing feeling—can have altogether different meanings. The present participle modifies something that causes the feeling: *That was a frightening storm* (the storm frightens). The past participle modifies something that experiences the feeling: *They quieted the frightened horses* (the horses feel fright).

The following participles are among those likely to be confused:

amazing/amazed	astonishing/astonished
amusing/amused	boring/bored
annoying/annoyed	confusing/confused

Present participles generally describe inanimate or nonhuman nouns: *The storm was frightening.* Past participles generally describe animate nouns (since only animate beings experience feelings): *The horses were frightened.*

depressing/depressed   interesting/interested
embarrassing/embarrassed   pleasing/pleased
exciting/excited   satisfying/satisfied
exhausting/exhausted   shocking/shocked
fascinating/fascinated   surprising/surprised
frightening/frightened   tiring/tired
frustrating/frustrated   worrying/worried

Exercise 16.4 Revising: Present and past participles

Revise the adjectives in the following sentences as needed to distinguish between present and past participles. If the sentence is already correct as given, mark the number preceding it.

> *Example:*
> The subject was embarrassed to many people.
> The subject was <u>embarrassing</u> to many people.

1. Several critics found Alice Walker's *The Color Purple* to be a fascinated book.
2. One confused critic wished that Walker had deleted the scenes set in Africa.
3. Another critic argued that although the book contained many depressed episodes, the overall impact was excited.
4. Since other readers found the book annoyed, this critic pointed out its many surprised qualities.
5. In the end most critics agreed that the book was a satisfied novel.

16h Use *a, an, the,* and other determiners appropriately.

Determiners are special kinds of adjectives that mark nouns because they always precede nouns. Some common determiners are *a, an,* and *the* (called **articles**) and *my, their, whose, this, these, those, one, some,* and *any.* They convey information to readers—for instance, by specifying who owns what, which one of two is meant, or whether a subject is familiar or unfamiliar.

Native speakers of standard American English can rely on their intuition when using determiners, but speakers of other languages and dialects often have difficulty with them. In standard English the use of determiners depends on the context they appear in and the kind of noun they precede:

- A **proper noun** names a particular person, place, or thing and begins with a capital letter: *February, Joe Allen, Red River.* Most proper nouns are not preceded by determiners.
- A **count noun** names something that is countable in English and can form a plural: *girl/girls, apple/apples, child/children.* A

ANSWERS: EXERCISE 16.4

1. Several critics found Alice Walker's *The Color Purple* to be a <u>fascinating</u> book.
2. Sentence correct.
3. Another critic argued that although the book contained many <u>depressing</u> episodes, the overall impact was <u>exciting</u>.
4. Since other readers found the book <u>annoying</u>, this critic pointed out its many <u>surprising</u> qualities.
5. In the end most critics agreed that the book was a <u>satisfying</u> novel.

CULTURE LANGUAGE

ARTICLE USE

As the text notes, because other languages use articles differently from English or not at all, even advanced ESL students may find articles difficult; some students may never completely master article use. Refer students who need additional practice with article use to Unit 2 of Len Fox, *Focus on Editing: A Grammar Workbook for Advanced Writers* (White Plains: Longman, 1992), Chapter 10 of Jocelyn Steer and Karen Carlisi, *The Advanced Grammar Book* (Boston: Heinle, 1991), and "Articles and Nouns" in Raymond Murphy's *Grammar in Use: Intermediate* (Cambridge: Cambridge UP, 2000).

singular count noun is always preceded by a determiner; a plural count noun sometimes is.

■ A **noncount noun** names something not usually considered countable in English, and so it does not form a plural. A noncount noun is sometimes preceded by a determiner. Here is a sample of noncount nouns, sorted into groups by meaning:

Abstractions: confidence, democracy, education, equality, evidence, health, information, intelligence, knowledge, luxury, peace, pollution, research, success, supervision, truth, wealth, work

Food and drink: bread, candy, cereal, flour, meat, milk, salt, water, wine

Emotions: anger, courage, happiness, hate, joy, love, respect, satisfaction

Natural events and substances: air, blood, dirt, gasoline, gold, hair, heat, ice, oil, oxygen, rain, silver, smoke, weather, wood

Groups: clergy, clothing, equipment, furniture, garbage, jewelry, junk, legislation, machinery, mail, military, money, police, vocabulary

Fields of study: architecture, accounting, biology, business, chemistry, engineering, literature, psychology, science

A dictionary of English as a second language will tell you whether a noun is a count noun, a noncount noun, or both. (See p. 513 for recommended dictionaries.)

Note Many nouns can be both count and noncount nouns:

The library has a room for readers. [*Room* is a count noun meaning "walled area."]

The library has room for reading. [*Room* is a noncount noun meaning "space."]

Grammar checkers Partly because the same noun may fall into different groups, a grammar checker is an unreliable guide to missing or misused articles and other determiners. For instance, a checker flagged the omitted *a* before *Scientist* in *Scientist developed new processes;* it did not flag the omitted *a* before *new* in *A scientist developed new process;* and it mistakenly flagged the correctly omitted article *the* before *Vegetation* in *Vegetation suffers from drought.*

1 Use *a, an,* and *the* where they are required.

With singular count nouns

A or *an* precedes a singular count noun when the reader does not already know its identity, usually because you have not mentioned it before:

A scientist in the school's chemistry department developed a process to strengthen metals. [*Scientist* and *process* are being introduced for the first time.]

CATEGORIES OF NONCOUNT NOUNS

Refer students who need additional practice with count and noncount nouns to Unit 2 of Len Fox, *Focus on Editing: A Grammar Workbook for Advanced Writers* (White Plains: Longman, 1992), Chapter 1 of Jocelyn Steer and Karen Carlisi, *The Advanced Grammar Book* (Boston: Heinle, 1991), and "Articles and Nouns" in Raymond Murphy's *Grammar in Use: Intermediate* (Cambridge: Cambridge UP, 2000).

The precedes a singular count noun that has a specific identity for the reader, for one of the following reasons:

- **You have mentioned the noun before:**

  A scientist in the school's chemistry department developed a process to strengthen metals. The scientist patented the process. [*Scientist* and *process* were identified in the preceding sentence.]

- **You identify the noun immediately before or after you state it:**

  The most productive laboratory is the research center in the chemistry department. [*Most productive* identifies *laboratory*. *In the chemistry department* identifies *research center*. And *chemistry department* is a shared facility.]

- **The noun names something unique—the only one in existence:**

  The sun rises in the east. [*Sun* and *east* are unique.]

- **The noun names an institution or facility that is shared by the community of readers:**

  Many men and women aspire to the presidency. [*Presidency* is a shared institution.]

  The cell phone has changed communication. [*Cell phone* is a shared facility.]

The is not used before a singular noun that names a general category:

  Sherman said that war is hell. [*War* names a general category.]

  The war in Iraq left many wounded. [*War* names a specific war.]

With plural count nouns

A or *an* never precedes a plural noun. *The* does not precede a plural noun that names a general category. *The* does precede a plural noun that names specific representatives of a category.

  Men and women are different. [*Men* and *women* name general categories.]

  The women formed a team. [*Women* refers to specific people.]

With noncount nouns

A or *an* never precedes a noncount noun. *The* does precede a noncount noun when it names specific representatives of a general category:

  Vegetation suffers from drought. [*Vegetation* names a general category.]

  The vegetation in the park withered or died. [*Vegetation* refers to specific plants.]

With proper nouns

A or *an* never precedes a proper noun. *The* generally does not precede a proper noun:

Garcia lives in Boulder.

There are exceptions, however. For instance, we generally use *the* before plural proper nouns (*the Murphys, the New England Patriots*) and the names of groups and organizations (*the Department of Justice, the Sierra Club*), ships (*the Lusitania*), oceans (*the Pacific*), mountain ranges (*the Alps*), regions (*the Middle East*), rivers (*the Mississippi*), and some countries (*the United States, the Netherlands*).

 Use other determiners appropriately.

The uses of English determiners besides articles also depend on context and kind of noun. The following determiners may be used as indicated with singular count nouns, plural count nouns, or noncount nouns.

With any kind of noun (singular count, plural count, noncount)

my, our, your, his, her, its, their
possessive nouns (*boy's, boys'*)
whose, which(ever), what(ever)
some, any, the other
no

Their account is overdrawn. [Singular count.]
Their funds are low. [Plural count.]
Their money is running out. [Noncount.]

Only with singular nouns (count and noncount)

this, that

This account has some money. [Count.]
That information may help. [Noncount.]

Only with noncount nouns and plural count nouns

most, enough, other, such, all, all of the, a lot of

Most money is needed elsewhere. [Noncount.]
Most funds are committed. [Plural count.]

Only with singular count nouns

one, every, each, either, neither, another

One car must be sold. [Singular count.]

A LOT OF

ESL students tend to use *a lot of* in formal writing because they are unaware that it is an informal, conversational phrase. Give students formal substitutes for *a lot of,* such as *a large amount of* before noncount nouns and *many* before plural count nouns.

ANSWERS: EXERCISE 16.5

From the native American Indians who migrated from Asia 20,000 years ago to the new arrivals who now come by planes, the United States is a nation of foreigners. It is a country of immigrants who are all living under a single flag.

Back in the seventeenth and eighteenth centuries, at least 75 percent of the population came from England. However, between 1820 and 1975 more than 38 million immigrants came to this country from elsewhere in Europe. Many children of the immigrants were self-conscious and denied their heritage; many even refused to learn the native language of their parents and grandparents. They tried to "Americanize" themselves. The so-called Melting Pot theory of social change stressed the importance of blending everyone together into a kind of stew. Each nationality would contribute its own flavor, but the final stew would be something called "American."

This Melting Pot theory was never completely successful. In the last half of the twentieth century, an ethnic revival changed the metaphor. Many people now see American society as a mosaic. Americans are once again proud of their heritage, and ethnic differences make the mosaic colorful and interesting.

Only with plural count nouns

these, those
both, many, few, a few, fewer, fewest, several
two, three, and so forth

Two cars are unnecessary. [Plural count.]

Note *Few* means "not many" or "not enough." *A few* means "some" or "a small but sufficient quantity."

Few committee members came to the meeting.
A few members can keep the committee going.

Do not use *much* with a plural count noun:

Many [not Much] members want to help.

Only with noncount nouns

much, more, little, a little, less, least, a large amount of

Less luxury is in order. [Noncount.]

Note *Little* means "not many" or "not enough." *A little* means "some" or "a small but sufficient quantity."

Little time remains before the conference.
The members need a little help from their colleagues.

Do not use *many* with a noncount noun:

Much [not Many] work remains.

Exercise 16.5 Revising: Articles (CULTURE LANGUAGE)

For each blank below, indicate whether *a, an, the,* or no article should be inserted.

From _____ native American Indians who migrated from _____ Asia 20,000 years ago to _____ new arrivals who now come by _____ planes, _____ United States is _____ nation of foreigners. It is _____ country of immigrants who are all living under _____ single flag.

Back in _____ seventeenth and eighteenth centuries, at least 75 percent of the population came from _____ England. However, between 1820 and 1975 more than 38 million immigrants came to this country from elsewhere in _____ Europe. Many children of _____ immigrants were self-conscious and denied their heritage; many even refused to learn _____ native language of their parents and grandparents. They tried to "Americanize" themselves. The so-called Melting Pot theory of _____ social change stressed _____ importance of blending everyone together into _____ kind of stew. Each nationality would contribute its own flavor, but _____ final stew would be something called "American."

This Melting Pot theory was never completely successful. In the last half of the twentieth century, _____ ethnic revival changed _____ metaphor. Many people now see _____ American society as _____ mosaic. Americans are once again proud of their heritage, and _____ ethnic differences make _____ mosaic colorful and interesting.

Exercise 16.6 Revising: Adjectives and adverbs

Revise the following paragraph so that it conforms to formal usage of adjectives and adverbs.

Americans often argue about which professional sport is better: basketball, football, or baseball. Basketball fans contend that their sport offers more action because the players are constant running and shooting. Because it is played indoors in relative small arenas, basketball allows fans to be more closer to the action than the other sports do. Fans point to how graceful the players fly through the air to the hoop. Football fanatics say they don't hardly stop yelling once the game begins. They cheer when their team executes a real complicated play good. They roar more louder when the defense stops the opponents in a goal-line stand. They yell loudest when a fullback crashes in for a score. In contrast, the supporters of baseball believe that it might be the most perfect sport. It combines the one-on-one duel of pitcher and batter struggling valiant with the tight teamwork of double and triple plays. Because the game is played slow and careful, fans can analyze and discuss the manager's strategy. Besides, they don't never know when they might catch a foul ball as a souvenir. However, no matter what the sport, all fans feel happily only when their team wins.

Exercise on Chapters 13–16 Revising: Grammatical sentences

The following paragraphs contain errors in pronoun case, verb forms, subject-verb agreement, pronoun-antecedent agreement, and the forms of adjectives and adverbs. Revise the paragraphs to correct the errors.

Occasionally, musicians become "crossover artists" whom can perform good in more than one field of music. For example, Wynton and Branford Marsalis was train in jazz by their father, the great pianist Ellis Marsalis. Both of the sons has became successful classical artists. Branford's saxophone captures the richness of pieces by Ravel and Stravinsky. Wynton's albums of classical trumpet music from the Baroque period has brung him many awards. Still, if he was to choose which kind of music he likes best, Wynton would probable choose jazz. In contrast to the Marsalises, violinist Nigel Kennedy growed up studying and performing classical music. In his teens he began playing jazz and even rock music. Today he is known almost as good for his interpretations of Miles Davis and Jimi Hendrix as he is for his classical performances.

Such crossovers are often more harder for vocalists. Each type of music has their own style and feel that is hard to learn. For example, Kiri te Kanawa, one of the great opera sopranos, have sang popular music and folk songs in concerts and on albums. On each occasion, her technique was the most perfect, yet she sounded as if she was simply trying to sing proper. It is even more difficulter for pop or country vocalists to sing opera, as Linda Ronstadt and Gary Morris founded when they appear

---

Using Exercise 16.6 as an example, ask students to write a five- to seven-sentence paragraph using adjectives and adverbs incorrectly. They should be sure to include article and count errors. They can then trade the brief paragraphs with their group members and correct the errors to test their understanding.

ANSWERS: EXERCISE 16.6

Americans often argue about which professional sport is best: basketball, football, or baseball. Basketball fans contend that their sport offers more action because the players are constantly running and shooting. Because it is played indoors in relatively small arenas, basketball allows fans to be closer to the action than the other sports do. Fans point to how gracefully the players fly through the air to the hoop. Football fanatics say they hardly stop yelling once the game begins. They cheer when their team executes a really complicated play well. They roar more loudly when the defense stops the opponents in a goal-line stand. They yell most loudly when a fullback crashes in for a score. In contrast, the supporters of baseball believe that it might be the perfect sport. It combines the one-on-one duel of pitcher and batter struggling valiantly with the tight teamwork of double and triple plays. Because the game is played slowly and carefully, fans can analyze and discuss the manager's strategy. Besides, they never know when they might catch a foul ball as a souvenir. However, no matter what the sport, all fans feel happy only when their team wins.

ANSWERS: EXERCISE ON CHAPTERS 13–16

Occasionally, musicians become "crossover artists" who can perform well in more than one field of music. For example, Wynton and Branford Marsalis were trained in jazz by their father, the great pianist Ellis Marsalis. Both of the sons have become successful classical artists. Branford's saxophone captures the richness of pieces by Ravel and Stravinsky. Wynton's albums of classical trumpet music from the Baroque period have brought him many awards. Still, if he were to choose which kind of music he likes better, Wynton would probably choose jazz. In contrast to the Marsalises, violinist Nigel Kennedy grew up studying and performing classical music. In his teens he began playing jazz and even rock music. Today he is known almost as well for his interpretations of Miles Davis and Jimi Hendrix as he is for his classical performances.

Such crossovers are often harder for vocalists. Each type of music has its own style and feel that are hard to learn. For example, Kiri te Kanawa, one of the great opera sopranos, has sung popular music and folk songs in concerts and on albums. On each occasion, her technique was nearly perfect, yet she sounded as if she were simply trying to sing properly. It is even more difficult for pop or country vocalists to sing opera, as Linda Ronstadt and Gary Morris found when they appeared in *La Bohème*. Each of them has a clear, pure voice, but a few critics said that he and she lacked the vocal power necessary for opera. However, Bobby McFerrin has been successful singing both pop and classical pieces. He won pop Grammy awards, but he is equally able to sing classical pieces *a cappella* (without musical accompaniment). His voice's remarkable range and clarity allow him to imitate many musical instruments.

No matter how successful, all of these musicians have shown great courage by performing in a new field. They are willing to test and stretch their talents, and each of us music fans benefits.

in *La Bohème.* Each of them have a clear, pure voice, but a few critics said that him and her lacked the vocal power necessary for opera. However, Bobby McFerrin been successful singing both pop and classical pieces. He won pop Grammy awards, but he is equal able to sing classical pieces *a cappella* (without musical accompaniment). His voice's remarkable range and clarity allows him to imitate many musical instruments.

No matter how successful, all of these musicians has shown great courage by performing in a new field. They are willing to test and stretch their talents, and each of we music fans benefit.

PART 4

Clear Sentences

17 Sentence Fragments

18 Comma Splices and Fused Sentences

19 Pronoun Reference

20 Shifts

21 Misplaced and Dangling Modifiers

22 Mixed and Incomplete Sentences

HIGHLIGHTS

This chapter opens with a positive approach, showing students how to test sentences for completeness, revise any fragments, and punctuate revised fragments. Following the opening section are discussions of particular structures that are often mispunctuated as complete sentences: subordinate clauses; verbal and prepositional phrases; and other word groups such as appositives, parts of compound predicates, and nouns plus modifiers. The chapter concludes with a discussion of the acceptable uses of incomplete sentences.

RESOURCES AND IDEAS

Harris, Muriel. "Mending the Fragmented Free Modifier." *College Composition and Communication* 32.2 (1981): 175–82. Print. Harris presents strategies for identifying kinds of fragments and correcting them.

Noguchi, Rei R. "Fragments and Beyond." Chapter 5 in *Grammar and the Teaching of Writing: Limits and Possibilities*. Urbana: NCTE, 1991. 84–112. Print. Noguchi outlines a positive approach to teaching students how to recognize, revise, or make use of sentence fragments.

Schuster, Edgar H. "A Fresh Look at Sentence Fragments" *English Journal* 95.5 (2006): 78–83. Print. Using examples from two volumes of *Best American Essays*, Schuster examines the ways in which professional writers use sentence fragments in their work. He then offers a set of guidelines for using sentence fragments for various stylistic purposes.

17

Sentence Fragments

A **sentence fragment** is part of a sentence that is set off as if it were a whole sentence by an initial capital letter and a final period or other end punctuation. Although writers occasionally use fragments deliberately and effectively (see p. 337), readers perceive most fragments as serious errors because, expecting complete sentences, they find partial sentences distracting or confusing. (Before reading further, you may find it helpful to review pp. 231–39 and 250–53 on sentences and clauses.)

Complete sentence versus sentence fragment

A complete sentence or **main clause**

■ contains a subject and a predicate verb (*The wind blows*)

■ and is not a subordinate clause (beginning with a word such as *because* or *who*).

A sentence fragment

■ lacks a predicate verb (*The wind <u>blowing</u>*)

■ or lacks a subject (*And blows*)

■ or is a subordinate clause not attached to a complete sentence (*Because the wind blows*).

Grammar checkers A grammar checker can spot many but not all sentence fragments, and it may flag sentences that are actually correct commands, such as *Continue reading*.

17a Test your sentences for completeness, and revise any fragments.

The following three tests will help you determine whether a word group punctuated as a sentence is actually a complete sentence. If the word group does not pass *all three* tests, it is a fragment and needs to be revised.

mycomplab ▐

Visit *mycomplab.com* for more resources and exercises on sentence fragments.

Tests for complete sentences

Perform *all three* of the following tests to be sure your sentences are complete.

1. Find the predicate verb.
2. Find the subject.
3. Make sure the clause is not subordinate.

Test 1: Find the predicate verb.

Look for a predicate verb in the group of words. Some fragments lack any verb at all:

Fragment	Uncountable numbers of sites on the World Wide Web.
Revised	Uncountable numbers of sites make up the World Wide Web.

Other fragments may include a verb form but not a **finite verb,** one that changes form as indicated below. A verbal does not change; it cannot serve as a predicate verb without the aid of a helping verb.

	Finite verbs in complete sentences	Verbals in sentence fragments
Singular	The network grows.	The network growing.
Plural	Networks grow.	Networks growing.
Present	The network grows.	
Past	The network grew.	The network growing.
Future	The network will grow.	

CULTURE LANGUAGE Some languages allow forms of *be* to be omitted as helping or linking verbs. But English requires stating forms of *be:*

Fragments	The network growing. It much larger than its developers anticipated.
Revised	The network is growing. It is much larger than its developers anticipated.

Test 2: Find the subject.

If you find a finite, predicate verb, look for its subject by asking *who* or *what* performs the action or makes the assertion of the verb. The subject of the sentence will usually come before the verb. If there is no subject, the word group is probably a fragment:

Fragment	And has great popular appeal.
Revised	And the Web has great popular appeal.

In one kind of complete sentence, a command, the subject *you* is understood: [You] *Experiment with the Web.*

FRAGMENTS

Students have been bombarded with so many fragments in advertising and popular prose ("Less filling! Tastes great!") that they may in fact not realize that incomplete sentences are usually unacceptable. Your first job may be to convince them that what is acceptable in speech and informal writing is not always desirable in formal writing.

NEWSCASTERS

The breathless style of radio and television newscasters often includes fragments. Ask students to write down examples from the evening news. Newspapers, especially tabloids, can be a good source, too.

SIZE DOESN'T MATTER!

Remind students that the length of a sentence does not determine its completeness. Sometimes, students think short sentences are unacceptable. However, you might explain that "I go" is a complete sentence, whereas adding "when" or some other subordinating word (see Test 3) actually creates a fragment.

CULTURE LANGUAGE   Some languages allow the omission of the sentence subject, especially when it is a pronoun. But in English, except in commands, the subject is always stated:

Fragments	Web commerce has expanded dramatically. Has hurt traditional stores.
Revised	Web commerce has expanded dramatically. It has hurt traditional stores.

Test 3: Make sure the clause is not subordinate.

A subordinate clause usually begins with a subordinating word:

Subordinating conjunctions			Relative pronouns	
after	once	until	that	who/whom
although	since	when	which	whoever/whomever
as	than	where		whose
because	that	whereas		
if	unless	while		

(See p. 251 for a longer list of subordinating conjunctions.)
Subordinate clauses serve as parts of sentences (as nouns or modifiers), not as whole sentences:

Fragment	When the government devised the Internet.
Revised	The government devised the Internet.
Revised	When the government devised the Internet, <u>no expansive computer network existed</u>.
Fragment	The reason that the government devised the Internet.
Revised	The reason that the government devised the Internet <u>was to provide secure links among departments and defense contractors</u>.

Note Questions beginning with *how, what, when, where, which, who, whom, whose,* and *why* are not sentence fragments: *Who was responsible? When did it happen?*

Revising sentence fragments

Almost all sentence fragments can be corrected in one of the two ways shown in the following box. The choice depends on the importance of the information in the fragment.

Revision of sentence fragments

Option 1
Rewrite the fragment as a complete sentence. This revision gives the information in the fragment the same importance as that in other complete sentences.

Fragment	A major improvement in public health occurred with the widespread use of vaccines. <u>Which protected children against life-threatening diseases.</u>
Revised	A major improvement in public health occurred with the widespread use of vaccines. They protected children against life-threatening diseases.

Two main clauses may be separated by a semicolon instead of a period (p. 445).

Option 2

Combine the fragment with a main clause. This revision subordinates the information in the fragment to the information in the main clause.

Fragment	The polio vaccine eradicated the disease from most of the globe. <u>The first vaccine to be used widely.</u>
Revised	The polio vaccine, the first to be used widely, eradicated the disease from most of the globe.

Punctuating corrected fragments

In the last example in the box, commas separate the inserted phrase from the rest of the sentence because the phrase is not essential to the meaning of any word in the main clause but simply adds information (see p. 427). When a phrase or subordinate clause *is* essential to the meaning of a word in the main clause, a comma or commas do *not* separate the two elements:

Fragment	High school students often use the Web to research colleges. <u>That they might want to visit in person.</u>
Revised	High school students often use the Web to research colleges that they might want to visit in person.

Sometimes a fragment may be combined with the main clause using a colon or a dash (see pp. 469 and 471–72, respectively):

Fragment	Some colleges recruit students from all over the United States. <u>Large cities, suburbs, small towns, and rural areas.</u>
Revised	Some colleges recruit students from all over the United States: large cities, suburbs, small towns, and rural areas.
Fragment	The colleges strive to bring together diverse groups of students. <u>Young people with different backgrounds, experiences, and dreams for the future.</u>
Revised	The colleges strive to bring together diverse groups of students—young people with different backgrounds, experiences, and dreams for the future.

ANSWERS: EXERCISE 17.1

Possible answers

1. Lacks a subject and a verb.
   Complete: An <u>article</u> about vandalism against works of art <u>was</u> interesting.
   Combined: In an interesting article about vandalism against works of art, <u>the author says the vandals' motives vary widely.</u>
2. Lacks a verb.
   Complete: The motives of the vandals <u>vary</u> widely.
   Combined: The motives of the vandals varying widely, <u>researchers can make few generalizations.</u>
3. Complete sentence.
4. Lacks a subject and a verb.
   Complete: But <u>the vandal</u> is not necessarily <u>angry</u> at the artist or the owner.
   Combined: <u>Whoever harms artwork is usually angry,</u> but not necessarily at the artist or the owner.
5. Lacks a verb for the subject <u>man.</u>
   Complete: For instance, a <u>man hammered</u> at Michelangelo's Pietà.
   Combined: For instance, a man who hammered at Michelangelo's Pietà <u>was angry at the Roman Catholic Church.</u>
6. Lacks a subject.
   Complete: And <u>he</u> knocked off the Virgin Mary's nose.
   Combined: <u>A man hammered at Michelangelo's Pietà</u> and knocked off the Virgin Mary's nose.
7. Begins with a subordinating conjunction.
   Complete: He was angry at the Roman Catholic Church.
   Combined: <u>A man hammered at Michelangelo's Pietà</u> because he was angry at the Roman Catholic Church.
8. Begins with *which* but is not a question.
   Complete: <u>The Church</u> knew nothing of his grievance.
   Combined: <u>He was angry at the Roman Catholic Church,</u> which knew nothing of his grievance.
9. Begins with a subordinating conjunction.
   Complete: Many damaged works can be repaired.
   Combined: Although many damaged works can be repaired, <u>even the most skillful repairs are forever visible.</u>
10. Complete sentence.

Exercise 17.1 Identifying and revising sentence fragments

Apply the tests for completeness to each of the following word groups. If a word group is a complete sentence, mark the number preceding it. If it is a sentence fragment, revise it in two ways: by making it a complete sentence, and by combining it with a main clause written from the information given in other items.

> *Example:*
> And could not find his money. [The word group has a verb (*could . . . find*) but no subject.]
> *Revised into a complete sentence:* And <u>he</u> could not find his money.
> *Combined with a new main clause:* <u>He was lost</u> and could not find his money.

1. In an interesting article about vandalism against works of art.
2. The motives of the vandals varying widely.
3. Those who harm artwork are usually angry.
4. But not necessarily at the artist or the owner.
5. For instance, a man who hammered at Michelangelo's *Pietà.*
6. And knocked off the Virgin Mary's nose.
7. Because he was angry at the Roman Catholic Church.
8. Which knew nothing of his grievance.
9. Although many damaged works can be repaired.
10. Usually even the most skillful repairs are forever visible.

17b A subordinate clause is not a complete sentence.

Subordinate clauses contain both subjects and verbs, but they always begin with a subordinating conjunction (*although, if,* and so on) or a relative pronoun (*who, which, that,* and so on). (See pp. 250–51.) Subordinate clauses serve as nouns or modifiers, but they cannot stand alone as complete sentences.

To correct a subordinate clause set off as a sentence, combine it with the main clause or remove or change the subordinating word to create a main clause.

Fragment	Many pine trees bear large cones. <u>Which appear in August.</u>
Revised	Many pine trees bear large cones which appear in August.
Revised	Many pine trees bear large cones. <u>They</u> appear in August.

17c A verbal phrase or a prepositional phrase is not a complete sentence.

A **verbal phrase** consists of an infinitive (*to choose*), a past participle (*chosen*), or a present participle or gerund (*choosing*) together with any objects and modifiers it may have (see p. 247). A verbal phrase is a noun or modifier and cannot serve as the verb in a complete sentence:

Fragment	For many of the elderly, their house is their only asset. <u>Offering some security but no income.</u>
Revised	For many of the elderly, their house is their only asset, offering some security but no income.
Revised	For many of the elderly, their house is their only asset. It offers some security but no income.

A **prepositional phrase** is a modifier consisting of a preposition (such as *in, on, to,* or *with*) together with its object and any modifiers (see pp. 242–43). A prepositional phrase cannot stand alone as a complete sentence:

Fragment	<u>In a squeeze between a valuable asset and little income.</u> Eventually many elderly people sell their homes.
Revised	In a squeeze between a valuable asset and little income, eventually many elderly people sell their homes.
Revised	<u>Many elderly people are in a squeeze between a valuable asset and little income.</u> Eventually they may sell their homes.

⬭ CULTURE LANGUAGE Some English prepositions consist of two or three words: *as well as, along with, in addition to, on top of,* and others. Don't let prepositions of more than one word mislead you into writing sentence fragments.

Fragment	In today's retirement communities, the elderly may have health care, housekeeping, and new friends. <u>As well as financial security.</u>
Revised	In today's retirement communities, the elderly may have health care, housekeeping, and new friends, as well as financial security.

17d Any word group lacking a subject or a verb or both is not a complete sentence.

We often follow a noun with a modifier. No matter how long the noun and its modifier are, they cannot stand alone as a sentence:

Fragments	<u>People waving flags and cheering. Lined the streets for the parade.</u>
Revised	People waving flags and cheering lined the streets for the parade.
Fragment	<u>Veterans who fought in Vietnam.</u> They are finally being honored.
Revised	Veterans who fought in Vietnam are finally being honored.

ANSWERS: EXERCISE 17.2

Possible answers

1. Human beings who perfume themselves are not much different from other animals.
2. Animals as varied as insects and dogs release *pheromones*, chemicals that signal other animals.
3. Human beings have a diminished sense of smell and do not consciously detect most of their own species' pheromones.
4. The human substitute for pheromones may be perfumes, especially musk and other fragrances derived from animal oils.
5. Some sources say that humans began using perfume to cover up the smell of burning flesh during sacrifices to the gods.
6. No sentence fragment.

Appositives are nouns, or nouns and their modifiers, that rename or describe other nouns (see pp. 254–55). They cannot stand alone as sentences:

Fragment	When I was a child, my favorite adult was an old uncle. A retired sea captain who always told me long stories of wild adventures in faraway places.
Revised	When I was a child, my favorite adult was an old uncle, a retired sea captain who always told me long stories of wild adventures in faraway places.

Compound predicates are predicates made up of two or more verbs and their objects, if any (see p. 256). A verb or its object cannot stand alone as a sentence:

Fragment	Uncle Marlon drew out his tales. And embellished them.
Revised	Uncle Marlon drew out his tales and embellished them.
Fragment	He described characters he had met. And storms at sea.
Revised	He described characters he had met and storms at sea.

Note Beginning a sentence with a coordinating conjunction such as *and* or *but* can lead to a sentence fragment. Check every sentence you begin with a coordinating conjunction to be sure it is complete.

Exercise 17.2 Revising: Sentence fragments

Correct any sentence fragment below either by combining it with a main clause or by making it a main clause. If an item contains no sentence fragment, mark the number preceding it.

Example:

Jujitsu is good for self-protection. Because it enables one to overcome an opponent without the use of weapons.

Jujitsu is good for self-protection because it enables one to overcome an opponent without the use of weapons.

1. Human beings who perfume themselves. They are not much different from other animals.
2. Animals as varied as insects and dogs release *pheromones*. Chemicals that signal other animals.
3. Human beings have a diminished sense of smell. And do not consciously detect most of their own species' pheromones.
4. The human substitute for pheromones may be perfumes. Especially musk and other fragrances derived from animal oils.
5. Some sources say that humans began using perfume to cover up the smell of burning flesh. During sacrifices to the gods.
6. Perfumes became religious offerings in their own right. Being expensive to make, they were highly prized.

7. The earliest historical documents from the Middle East record the use of fragrances. Not only in religious ceremonies but on the body.
8. In the nineteenth century chemists began synthesizing perfume oils. Which previously could be made only from natural sources.
9. The most popular animal oil for perfume today is musk. Although some people dislike its heavy, sweet odor.
10. Synthetic musk oil would help conserve a certain species of deer. Whose gland is the source of musk.

17e Be aware of the acceptable uses of incomplete sentences.

A few word groups lacking the usual subject-predicate combination are not sentence fragments because they conform to the expectations of most readers. They include commands (*Move along. Shut the window.*); exclamations (*Oh no!*); questions and answers (*Where next? To Kansas.*); and descriptions in employment résumés (*Weekly volunteer in a soup kitchen.*). Another kind of incomplete sentence, occurring in special situations, is the transitional phrase (*So much for the causes, now for the results. One final point.*).

Experienced writers sometimes use sentence fragments when they want to achieve a special effect. Such fragments appear more in informal than in formal writing. Unless you are experienced and thoroughly secure in your own writing, you should avoid all fragments and concentrate on writing clear, well-formed sentences.

Exercise 17.3 Revising: Sentence fragments

Revise the following paragraph to eliminate sentence fragments by combining them with main clauses or rewriting them as main clauses.

Baby red-eared slider turtles are brightly colored. With bold patterns on their yellowish undershells. Which serve as a warning to predators. The bright colors of skunks and other animals. They signal that the animals will spray nasty chemicals. In contrast, the turtle's colors warn largemouth bass. That the baby turtle will actively defend itself. When a bass gulps down a turtle. The feisty baby claws and bites. Forcing the bass to spit it out. To avoid a similar painful experience. The bass will avoid other baby red-eared slider turtles. The turtle loses its bright colors as it grows too big. For a bass's afternoon snack.

Note See page 376 for an exercise involving sentence fragments along with comma splices, fused sentences, and other sentence errors.

---

7. The earliest historical documents from the Middle East record the use of fragrances, not only in religious ceremonies but on the body.
8. In the nineteenth century chemists began synthesizing perfume oils, which previously could be made only from natural sources.
9. The most popular animal oil for perfume today is musk, although some people dislike its heavy, sweet odor.
10. Synthetic musk oil would help conserve a certain species of deer whose gland is the source of musk.

CREATING PROBLEMS

If students have been assigned Chapter 18, "Comma Splices and Fused Sentences," along with this chapter, ask them to write sample sentences containing fused sentences, comma splices, and fragments. Then have them exchange papers and check to see if the errors have been executed properly. This exercise will help students recognize fused sentences, comma splices, and fragments. (It's much harder to create intentional errors, particularly sentence fragments, than most students will think.)

ANSWERS: EXERCISE 17.3
Possible revision

Baby red-eared slider turtles are brightly colored. Bold patterns on their yellowish undershells serve as a warning to predators. The bright colors of skunks and other animals signal that the animals will spray nasty chemicals. In contrast, the turtle's colors warn largemouth bass that the baby turtle will actively defend itself. When a bass gulps down a turtle, the feisty baby claws and bites, forcing the bass to spit it out. To avoid a similar painful experience, the bass will avoid other baby red-eared slider turtles. The turtle loses its bright colors as it grows too big for a bass's afternoon snack.

HIGHLIGHTS

This chapter begins with a summary of the accepted methods for punctuating consecutive main clauses and follows with advice for recognizing and correcting comma splices and fused sentences. Correction of comma splices and fused sentences may involve strategies that students should employ more frequently in their sentences, particularly subordination and use of the semicolon. To encourage variety in sentence structure along with the avoidance of error, exercises for the chapter ask students to combine sentences following different strategies as well as to recognize and revise comma splices and fused sentences.

It's important to remember that students will naturally commit more of these errors as they struggle to master more complex syntactic patterns. Although you want to point out their mistakes, be careful not to focus too tightly on punctuation errors that occur as they strive for stylistic growth.

RESOURCES AND IDEAS

Teachers and tutors who have little trouble punctuating sentences themselves may find it difficult to understand why some students have such difficulty with punctuation. Beth Rapp Young's "Can You Proofread This?" in Ben Rafoth's *A Tutor's Guide: Helping Writers One-to-One*, 2nd ed. (Portsmouth: Boynton/Cook: 2005) includes appendices that offer numerous suggestions for helping students learn to correct surface errors, such as reading aloud, slowing down, and keeping a personalized checklist of errors. Rei R. Noguchi also offers innovative approaches to these errors in "Run-ons, Comma Splices, and Native-Speaker Abilities" in *Grammar and the Teaching of Writing: Limits and Possibilities* (Urbana: NCTE, 1991, 64–83).

18
Comma Splices and Fused Sentences

A sentence or main clause contains at least a subject and a predicate, which together express a complete thought that can stand alone (see p. 231). When two main clauses fall together, readers need a signal that one clause is ending and another is beginning. The following box shows the ways to provide this signal.

Punctuation of two or more main clauses

■ **Separate main clauses with periods.**

> Main clause **.** Main clause **.**

Hybrid cars are popular with consumers**.** Automakers are releasing new models.

■ **Link main clauses with a coordinating conjunction and a comma.**

> Main clause **,** for and or / so but nor / yet   main clause **.**

Hybrid cars are popular with consumers**,** and automakers are releasing new models.

■ **Link main clauses with a semicolon.**

> Main clause **;** main clause **.**

Hybrid cars are popular with consumers**;** automakers are releasing new models.

---

my**comp**lab

Visit *mycomplab.com* for more resources and exercises on comma splices and fused sentences.

■ **Relate main clauses with a semicolon and a conjunctive adverb or transitional expression.**

Main clause **;** however, for example, etc. **,** main clause **.**

Hybrid cars are popular with consumers**;** as a result**,** automakers are releasing new models.

KNOWING YOUR ERRORS

Writers tend to produce repeated patterns of error (comma splices or sentence fragments, for example) and may struggle to recognize as well as to correct occurrences of those particular patterns of error in their work. It can be extremely helpful for students to learn which errors frequently occur in their work and to keep a list of corrected examples of those errors including appropriate handbook references (page or section numbers) in order to look for those problems in future work.

With a comma splice or a fused sentence, two main clauses run together without one of the signals listed in the box, and readers often must reread for sense. A **comma splice** joins (or splices) main clauses *only* with a comma, not with a coordinating conjunction as well:

Comma splice
The ship was huge, its mast stood eighty feet high.

A **fused sentence** (or **run-on sentence**) joins main clauses with no punctuation at all:

Fused sentence
The ship was huge its mast stood eighty feet high.

Exception Experienced writers sometimes use a comma without a coordinating conjunction between very brief main clauses that are grammatically parallel:

He's not a person, he's a monster.

However, many readers view such punctuation as incorrect. Unless you are certain that your readers will not object to the comma in a sentence like this one, separate the clauses with periods or semicolons, as described in this chapter.

Grammar checkers A grammar checker can detect many comma splices, but it will miss most fused sentences. For example, a checker flagged *Money is tight, we need to spend carefully* but not *Money is tight we need to spend carefully*. A checker may also question sentences that are actually correct, such as *Money being tighter now than before, we need to spend carefully.* Verify that revision is actually needed on any flagged sentence.

CULTURE LANGUAGE An English sentence may not include more than one main clause unless the clauses are separated by a comma and a coordinating conjunction or by a semicolon or colon. If your native language does not have such a rule or has accustomed you to writing long sentences, you may need to edit your English writing especially for comma splices and fused sentences.

Revision of comma splices and fused sentences

1. **Underline the main clauses in your draft.**

    <u>Sailors trained on the ship</u> <u>they learned about wind and sails</u>. <u>Trainees who took the course ranged from high school students to Navy officers</u>. <u>The ship was built in 1910</u>, <u>it had sailed ever since</u>. In almost a century, <u>it had circled the globe forty times</u>. <u>It burned in 2001</u> <u>its cabins and decks were destroyed</u>.

2. **Focus on sentences that contain two or more main clauses.**

3. **If nothing falls between the clauses or only a comma does, revise in one of the following ways.** The choice depends on the relation you want to establish between the clauses, as explained below and opposite.

■ **Separate main clauses with a period.**

Sailors trained on the ship**.** They learned about wind and sails.

■ **Separate main clauses with a comma and a coordinating conjunction.**

The ship was built in 1910**,** and it had sailed ever since.

■ **Separate main clauses with a semicolon.**

The ship was built in 1910**;** it had sailed ever since.

■ **Subordinate one clause to the other,** depending on which clause is more important.

When it burned in 2001**,** its cabins and decks were destroyed.

FANBOYS

A mnemonic that helps students remember the coordinating conjunctions is *fanboys,* which is the first letter of each coordinating conjunction. Put the following chart on the board to illustrate:

	for	
	and	
	nor	
Main clause,	*but*	main clause.
	or	
	yet	
	so	

Remind ESL students that after *nor,* English requires inverted word order.

Comma Splices

18a **Separate two main clauses with a comma *only* when they are joined by a coordinating conjunction.**

A comma cannot separate main clauses unless they are linked by a coordinating conjunction (*and, but, or, nor, for, so, yet*). Readers expect the same main clause to continue after a comma alone. When they find themselves reading a second main clause before they realize they have finished the first, they may have to reread.

You have several options for revising comma splices.

Making separate sentences

Revising a comma splice by making separate sentences from the main clauses will always be correct. The period is not only correct but preferable when the ideas expressed in the two main clauses are only loosely related:

Comma splice	Chemistry has contributed much to our understanding of foods, many foods such as wheat and beans can be produced in the laboratory.
Revised	Chemistry has contributed much to our understanding of foods. Many foods such as wheat and beans can be produced in the laboratory.

CULTURE LANGUAGE Making separate sentences may be the best option if you are used to writing very long sentences in your native language and often write comma splices in English.

Inserting a coordinating conjunction

When the ideas in the main clauses are closely related and equally important, you may correct a comma splice by inserting the appropriate coordinating conjunction immediately after the comma to join the clauses:

Comma splice	Some laboratory-grown foods taste good, they are nutritious.
Revised	Some laboratory-grown foods taste good, and they are nutritious.

Using a semicolon

If the relation between the ideas expressed in the main clauses is very close and obvious without a conjunction, you can separate the clauses with a semicolon.

Comma splice	Good taste is rare in laboratory-grown vegetables, they are usually bland.
Revised	Good taste is rare in laboratory-grown vegetables; they are usually bland.

Subordinating one clause

When the idea in one clause is more important than that in the other, you can express the less important idea in a phrase or a subordinate clause. (See p. 251 for a list of subordinating conjunctions and pp. 391–93 for more on subordination.) Subordination is often more effective than forming separate sentences because it defines the relation between ideas more precisely:

Comma splice	The vitamins are adequate, the flavor is deficient.
Revised	The vitamins are adequate. The flavor is deficient. [Both ideas receive equal weight.]
Improved	Even though the vitamins are adequate, the flavor is deficient. [Emphasis on the second idea.]

18b Separate main clauses related by *however, for example,* and so on.

Two kinds of words that are not conjunctions describe how one main clause relates to another:

- **Conjunctive adverbs,** such as *consequently, finally, hence, however, indeed, therefore,* and *thus.* (See p. 259 for a longer list.)
- Other **transitional expressions,** such as *even so, for example, in fact, of course, to the right,* and *to this end.* (See pp. 88–89 for a longer list.)

When two main clauses are related by a conjunctive adverb or a transitional expression, they must be separated by a period or by a semicolon. The adverb or expression is also generally set off by a comma or commas (see p. 430):

Comma splice	Healthcare costs are higher in the United States than in many other countries, <u>consequently</u> health insurance is also more costly.
Revised	Healthcare costs are higher in the United States than in many other countries. <u>Consequently,</u> health insurance is also more costly.
Revised	Healthcare costs are higher in the United States than in many other countries; <u>consequently,</u> health insurance is also more costly.

Conjunctive adverbs and transitional expressions are different from coordinating conjunctions (*and, but,* and so on) and subordinating conjunctions (*although, because,* and so on):

- **Unlike conjunctions, conjunctive adverbs and transitional expressions do not join two clauses into a grammatical unit.** They merely describe the way two clauses relate in meaning.
- **Unlike conjunctions, conjunctive adverbs and transitional expressions can be moved within a clause** (see also pp. 258–59). No matter where in the clause an adverb or expression falls, though, the clause must be separated from another main clause by a period or semicolon.

Comma splice

The increased time devoted to watching television is not the only cause of the decline in reading ability, <u>however</u>, it is one of the important causes.

Revised with a period

The increased time devoted to watching television is not the only cause of the decline in reading ability. <u>However,</u> it is one of the important causes.

Revised with a semicolon

The increased time devoted to watching television is not the only cause of the decline in reading ability; however, it is one of the important causes.

The increased time devoted to watching television is not the only cause of the decline in reading ability; it is, however, one of the important causes.

Exercise 18.1   Identifying and revising comma splices

Correct each comma splice below in *two* of the ways described on pages 340–41. If an item contains no comma splice, mark the number preceding it.

Example:

Carolyn still had a headache, she could not get the child-proof cap off the aspirin bottle.

Carolyn still had a headache because she could not get the child-proof cap off the aspirin bottle. [Subordination.]

Carolyn still had a headache, for she could not get the child-proof cap off the aspirin bottle. [Coordinating conjunction.]

1. Money has a long history, it goes back at least as far as the earliest records.
2. Many of the earliest records concern financial transactions, indeed, early history must often be inferred from commercial activity.
3. Every known society has had a system of money, though the objects serving as money have varied widely.
4. Sometimes the objects have had real value, in modern times, however, their value has been more abstract.
5. Cattle, fermented beverages, and rare shells have served as money, each one had actual value for the society.

Fused Sentences

| **18c** | Combine two main clauses only with an appropriate conjunction or punctuation mark between them. |

When two main clauses are joined without a word to connect them or a punctuation mark to separate them, the result is a **fused** or **run-on sentence**. Fused sentences can rarely be understood on first reading, and they are never acceptable in standard written English.

Fused   Our foreign policy is not well defined it confuses many countries.

Fused sentences may be corrected in the same ways as comma splices. See pages 340–41.

COLLABORATIVE LEARNING

Ask students to complete Exercises 18.1 and 18.2 independently and compare their responses in small groups. Then ask each group to work together on Exercises 18.3 and 18.4. Finally, have the groups examine each other's work to find and revise examples of comma splices and fused sentences. For students who are having difficulty with these errors, the move from the handbook exercises to their own work can be extremely beneficial.

ANSWERS: EXERCISE 18.1

Possible answers

1. Money has a long history. It goes back at least as far as the earliest records.

   Money has a long history that goes back at least as far as the earliest records.
2. Many of the earliest records concern financial transactions; indeed, early history must often be inferred from commercial activity.

   Many of the earliest records concern financial transactions. Indeed, early history must often be inferred from commercial activity.
3. No comma splice.
4. Sometimes the objects have had real value. In modern times, however, their value has been more abstract.

   Sometimes the objects have had real value; in modern times, however, their value has been more abstract.
5. Cattle, fermented beverages, and rare shells have served as money, and each one had actual value for the society.

   Cattle, fermented beverages, and rare shells have served as money. Each one had actual value for the society.

CREATING PROBLEMS

If students have been assigned Chapter 17, "Sentence Fragments," along with this chapter, ask them to write sample sentences containing comma splices, fused sentences, and fragments. Then have them exchange papers and check to see if the errors have been executed properly. This exercise will help students recognize comma splices, fused sentences, and fragments. (It's much harder to create intentional errors, particularly fused sentences and sentence fragments, than most students will think.)

ANSWERS: EXERCISE 18.2

Possible answers

1. Throughout history money and religion were closely linked <u>because</u> there was little distinction between government and religion.

   Throughout history money and religion were closely linked<u>, for</u> there was little distinction between government and religion.
2. The head of state and the religious leader were often the same person. <u>All</u> power rested in one ruler.

   The head of state and the religious leader were often the same person<u>;</u> all power rested in one ruler.
3. These powerful leaders decided what objects would serve as money<u>, and</u> their backing encouraged public faith in the money.

   These powerful leaders decided what objects would serve as money. <u>Their</u> backing encouraged public faith in the money.
4. <u>When</u> coins were minted of precious metals, the religious overtones of money were strengthened.

   Coins were minted of precious metals. <u>The</u> religious overtones of money were then strengthened.
5. People already believed the precious metals to be divine<u>, so</u> their use in money intensified its allure.

   People already believed the precious metals to be divine; their use in money intensified its allure.

ANSWERS: EXERCISE 18.3

Possible answers

1. The exact origin of paper money is unknown <u>because it</u> has not survived as coins, shells, and other durable objects have.
2. Perhaps goldsmiths were also bankers<u>; thus</u> they held the gold of their wealthy customers.
3. The goldsmiths probably gave customers receipts for their gold<u>, and</u> these receipts were then used in trade.
4. The goldsmiths were something like modern-day bankers<u>;</u> their receipts were something like modern-day money.
5. The goldsmiths became even more like modern-day bankers <u>when they</u> began issuing receipts for more gold than they actually held in their vaults.

Separate sentences

Our foreign policy is not well defined<u>.</u> It confuses many countries.

Comma and coordinating conjunction

Our foreign policy is not well defined<u>,</u> and it confuses many countries.

Semicolon

Our foreign policy is not well defined<u>;</u> it confuses many countries.

Subordinating conjunction

<u>Because</u> our foreign policy is not well defined<u>,</u> it confuses many countries.

Exercise 18.2 Identifying and revising fused sentences

Revise each of the fused sentences below in *two* of the four ways shown above.

Example:

Tim was shy he usually refused invitations.
Tim was shy<u>,</u> so he usually refused invitations.
Tim was shy<u>;</u> he usually refused invitations.

1. Throughout history money and religion were closely linked there was little distinction between government and religion.
2. The head of state and the religious leader were often the same person all power rested in one ruler.
3. These powerful leaders decided what objects would serve as money their backing encouraged public faith in the money.
4. Coins were minted of precious metals the religious overtones of money were then strengthened.
5. People already believed the precious metals to be divine their use in money intensified its allure.

Exercise 18.3 Sentence combining to avoid comma splices and fused sentences

Combine each pair of sentences below into one sentence without creating a comma splice or fused sentence. Combine sentences by (1) supplying a comma and coordinating conjunction, (2) supplying a semicolon, or (3) subordinating one clause to the other. You will have to add, delete, or change words as well as punctuation.

Example:

The sun sank lower in the sky. The colors gradually faded.

As the sun sank lower in the sky<u>,</u> the colors gradually faded. [The first clause is subordinated to the second.]

1. The exact origin of paper money is unknown. It has not survived as coins, shells, and other durable objects have.
2. Perhaps goldsmiths were also bankers. Thus they held the gold of their wealthy customers.
3. The goldsmiths probably gave customers receipts for their gold. These receipts were then used in trade.

4. The goldsmiths were something like modern-day bankers. Their receipts were something like modern-day money.
5. The goldsmiths became even more like modern-day bankers. They began issuing receipts for more gold than they actually held in their vaults.

Exercise 18.4 Revising: Comma splices and fused sentences

Identify and revise the comma splices and fused sentences in the following paragraph.

All those parents who urged their children to eat broccoli were right, the vegetable really is healthful. Broccoli contains sulforaphane, moreover, this mustard oil can be found in kale and Brussels sprouts. Sulforaphane causes the body to make an enzyme that attacks carcinogens, these substances cause cancer. The enzyme speeds up the work of the kidneys then they can flush harmful chemicals out of the body. Other vegetables have similar benefits however, green, leafy vegetables like broccoli are the most efficient. Thus wise people will eat their broccoli it could save their lives.

Note See page 376 for an exercise involving comma splices and fused sentences along with other sentence errors.

19

Pronoun Reference

A **pronoun** such as *it* or *they* derives its meaning from its **antecedent,** the noun it substitutes for. Therefore, a pronoun must refer clearly and unmistakably to its antecedent in order for the meaning to be clear. A sentence such as *Jim told Mark he was not invited* is not clear because the reader does not know whether *he* refers to Jim or to Mark.

One way to make pronoun reference clear is to ensure that the pronoun and antecedent agree in person, number, and gender (see pp. 309–10). The other way is to ensure that the pronoun refers unambiguously to a single, close, specific antecedent.

mycomplab

Visit *mycomplab.com* for more resources and exercises on pronoun reference.

ANSWERS: EXERCISE 18.4

All those parents who urged their children to eat broccoli were right; the vegetable really is healthful. Broccoli contains sulforaphane; moreover, this mustard oil can be found in kale and Brussels sprouts. Sulforaphane causes the body to make an enzyme that attacks carcinogens, <u>substances that</u> cause cancer. The enzyme speeds up the work of the kidneys <u>so that</u> they can flush harmful chemicals out of the <u>body.</u> Other vegetables have similar benefits; however, green, leafy vegetables like broccoli are the most efficient. Thus, wise people will eat their broccoli; it could save their lives.

HIGHLIGHTS

Writers at all levels—advanced or struggling—will be likely to consult this chapter often, for problems with pronoun reference can arise in short, uncomplicated sentences as well as in papers that are ambitious in style and content. The discussion covers a number of particularly troublesome problems: unclear or ambiguous antecedents; broad reference with *this, that, which,* and *it;* indefinite use of *it* and *they;* and inappropriate use of *who, which,* and *that.* In each case, the discussion stresses the need for precision in reference as a way of ensuring that readers can follow the meaning of a passage. The examples and exercises mostly show reference problems within sentences as a way of keeping the discussion as simple and accessible as possible; however, the text points out that reference problems are just as likely to occur between sentences, and the paragraph exercise at the end of the chapter stresses this fact.

Because strings of pronouns are an important device for creating coherence over long stretches of discourse, reference problems between or among sentences can cause considerable misunderstanding. In this sense, pronoun reference errors can point to students' larger conceptual difficulties (such as defining or elaborating on key terms or thinking through a transition). This means that when students learn to recognize their pronoun reference errors, that recognition can provide the occasion for substantive revision and paragraph development.

RETRIEVING SENTENCES

Reverse the process of sentence combining by asking students to reconstruct (or retrieve) the shorter (kernel) sentences that lie behind a long sentence containing a reference error. You may wish to use sentences from the text as a basis for the exercise. This activity will help students spot ambiguity or vague reference in the long sentence. After they have found the shorter sentences, ask students to recombine, this time avoiding the reference problem.

> *Original sentence:* After the van hit John's car, its engine stopped running and its radiator started leaking.
> *Kernels:* The van hit John's car. The van's engine stopped running. The van's radiator started leaking.
> *Recombined sentence:* After the van hit John's car, the van's engine stopped running and its radiator started leaking.

Principal causes of unclear pronoun reference

■ **More than one possible antecedent** (below):

Confusing	To keep birds from eating seeds, soak <u>them</u> in blue food coloring.
Clear	To keep birds from eating seeds, soak <u>the seeds</u> in blue food coloring.

■ **Antecedent too far away** (facing page):

Confusing	Employees should consult with their supervisor <u>who</u> require personal time.
Clear	Employees <u>who</u> require personal time should consult with their supervisor.

■ **Antecedent only implied** (p. 348):

Confusing	Many children begin reading on their own by watching television, but <u>this</u> should probably be discounted in government policy.
Clear	Many children begin reading on their own by watching television, but <u>such self-instruction</u> should probably be discounted in government policy.

See also pages 350–51.

Grammar checkers A grammar checker cannot recognize unclear pronoun reference. For instance, a checker did not spot any of the problems in Exercise 19.2 on page 351.

CULTURE LANGUAGE An English pronoun does need a clear antecedent nearby, but don't use both a pronoun and its antecedent as the subject of the same sentence or clause: *Jim* [not *Jim he*] *told Mark to go alone.* (See also pp. 370–71.)

19a | Make a pronoun refer clearly to one antecedent.

When either of two nouns can be a pronoun's antecedent, the reference will not be clear:

Confusing	Emily Dickinson is sometimes compared with Jane Austen, but <u>she</u> was quite different.

Revise such a sentence in one of two ways:

■ **Replace the pronoun with the appropriate noun:**

Clear	Emily Dickinson is sometimes compared with Jane Austen, but <u>Dickinson</u> [or <u>Austen</u>] was quite different.

■ **Avoid repetition by rewriting the sentence.** If you use the pronoun, make sure it has only one possible antecedent:

Clear   Despite occasional comparison, Emily Dickinson and Jane Austen were quite different.

Clear   Though sometimes compared with her, Emily Dickinson was quite different from Jane Austen.

Sentences that report what someone said, using verbs such as *said* or *told*, often require direct rather than indirect quotation:

Confusing   Juliet Noble told Ann Torre that she was next in line for the job.

Clear   Juliet Noble told Ann Torre, "I am next in line for the job."

Clear   Juliet Noble told Ann Torre, "You are next in line for the job."

Note   Avoid the awkward device of using a pronoun followed by the appropriate noun in parentheses, as in the following example:

Weak   Noble and Torre had both hoped for the job, so she (Noble) was disappointed.

Improved   Noble was disappointed because she and Torre had both hoped for the job.

19b   Place a pronoun close enough to its antecedent to ensure clarity.

A clause beginning *who*, *which*, or *that* generally should fall immediately after the word to which it refers:

Confusing   Jody found a lamp in the attic that her aunt had used.

Clear   In the attic Jody found a lamp that her aunt had used.

Even when only one word could possibly serve as the antecedent of a pronoun, the relationship between the two may still be unclear if they are widely separated:

Confusing   Jane Austen had little formal education but was well educated at home. Far from living an isolated life in the English countryside, the Austens were a large family with a wide circle of friends who provided entertainment and cultural enrichment. They also provided material for her stories.

Clear   Jane Austen had little formal education but was well educated at home. Far from living an isolated life in the English countryside, the Austens were a large family with a wide circle of friends who provided entertainment and cultural enrichment. They also provided material for Jane Austen's stories.

CULTURE LANGUAGE

OMITTED RELATIVE CLAUSE PRONOUNS

Sentences in which the relative clause pronoun is omitted often give ESL students difficulty, and they may make the mistake of adding an extra redundant pronoun. Give them a model sentence to help them remember the rule, such as the following:

We are going to the flea market that we read about in the newspaper.

This can be especially helpful when they are doing sentence-combining exercises, and they may want to keep a few of their own models in a computer file for handy reference. (See also 22a-2 for more on repeated sentence parts.)

ANSWERS: EXERCISE 19.1

POSSIBLE ANSWERS

1. There is a difference between the heroes of the twentieth century and the heroes of earlier times: <u>twentieth-century heroes</u> have flaws in their characters.
2. Sports fans still admire Pete Rose, Babe Ruth, and Joe Namath even though <u>none of these heroes</u> could be perfect.
3. Fans liked Rose for having his young son serve as batboy when <u>Rose</u> was in Cincinnati.
4. The reputation Rose earned as a gambler and tax evader may overshadow his reputation as a ballplayer, but <u>the latter</u> will survive.
5. Rose amassed an unequaled record as a hitter, using his bat to do things no one else has ever done. <u>The record</u> stands even though Rose was banned from baseball.

COLLABORATIVE LEARNING

After students complete Exercise 19.1 individually, have them share their responses to check the clarity of the revised sentences. If they spot ambiguous or remote pronoun references remaining in revised sentences, the group should work together to restructure the sentence again. It can be helpful for students to see many new combinations of the same sentences.

RESOURCES AND IDEAS

Gordon, Karinne. "Personal Voice in Academic Writing." *Ohio Journal of English Language Arts* 47.1 (2007): 44–51. Print. Gordon argues that judicious use of personal pronouns, even in scientific writing, can help students develop their voices.

Moskovit, Leonard. "When Is Broad Reference Clear?" *College Composition and Communication* 34.4 (1983): 454–69. Print. The question of the acceptability of broad reference is a complicated one, as Moskovit points out, and anyone interested in looking at how broad reference operates in sophisticated prose will enjoy his essay.

Nilsen, Alleen Pace. "Why Keep Searching When It's Already *Their*? Reconsidering *Everybody's* Pronoun Problem" *English Journal* 90.4 (2001): 68–73. Print. Nilsen discusses the use

---

Exercise 19.1 Revising: Ambiguous and remote pronoun reference

Rewrite the following sentences to eliminate unclear pronoun reference. If you use a pronoun in your revision, be sure that it refers to only one antecedent and that it falls close enough to its antecedent to ensure clarity.

Example:

Saul found an old gun in the rotting shed that was just as his grandfather had left it.

In the rotting shed Saul found an old <u>gun that</u> was just as his grandfather had left it.

1. There is a difference between the heroes of the twentieth century and the heroes of earlier times: they have flaws in their characters.
2. Sports fans still admire Pete Rose, Babe Ruth, and Joe Namath even though they could not be perfect.
3. Fans liked Rose for having his young son serve as batboy when he was in Cincinnati.
4. The reputation Rose earned as a gambler and tax evader may overshadow his reputation as a ballplayer, but it will survive.
5. Rose amassed an unequaled record as a hitter, using his bat to do things no one else has ever done. It stands even though Rose was banned from baseball.

 19c Make a pronoun refer to a specific antecedent, not an implied one.

A pronoun should refer to a specific noun or other pronoun. The reader can only guess at the meaning of a pronoun when its antecedent is implied by the context, not stated outright.

1 Use *this, that, which,* and *it* cautiously.

The most common kind of implied reference occurs when the pronoun *this, that, which,* or *it* refers to a whole idea or situation described in the preceding clause, sentence, or even paragraph. Such reference, often called **broad reference,** is acceptable only when the pronoun refers clearly to the entire preceding clause. In the following sentence, *which* could not possibly refer to anything but the whole preceding clause:

> I can be kind and civil to people, <u>which</u> is more than you can.
> —George Bernard Shaw

But if a pronoun might confuse a reader, you should avoid using it or provide an appropriate noun:

Confusing The British knew little of the American countryside, and they had no experience with the colonists' guerilla tactics. This gave the colonists an advantage.

Clear The British knew little of the American countryside, and they had no experience with the colonists' guerrilla tactics. This ignorance and inexperience gave the colonists an advantage.

2 *It* and *they* should have definite antecedents.

Although common in speech, using *it* and *they* to refer to indefinite antecedents is inappropriate in writing.

Confusing In Chapter 4 of this book, it describes the early flights of the Wright brothers.

Clear Chapter 4 of this book describes the early flights of the Wright brothers.

Confusing Even in reality TV shows, they present a false picture of life.

Clear Even reality TV shows present a false picture of life.

3 Implied nouns are not clear antecedents.

A noun may be implied in some other word or phrase, as *happiness* is implied in *happy*, *driver* is implied in *drive*, and *mother* is implied in *mother's*. But a pronoun cannot refer clearly to an implied noun, only to a specific, stated one:

Confusing Cohen's report brought her a lawsuit.

Clear Cohen was sued over her report.

Confusing Her reports on psychological development generally go unnoticed outside it.

Clear Her reports on psychological development generally go unnoticed outside the field.

4 Titles of papers are not clear antecedents.

The title of a paper is entirely separate from the paper itself, so a pronoun should not be used in the opening sentence of a paper to refer to the title:

of "they" in spoken English in place of "he or she" or other gender-neutral pronouns. She argues for the eventual acceptance of this practice in writing as well because changes in spoken English are often precursors to changes in written English.

CORRECTING A NARRATIVE

Find or write a brief narrative containing several events and more than one character. Introduce enough reference problems so that readers have difficulty unraveling the events. If you wish, include dialogue in the narrative in such a way that the reference problems make it hard to identify the speakers. (Using *He said* as a tag when there are two men in the narrative is one possibility.) Ask students to work in groups to untangle the problems in the narrative and to rewrite it, removing vague and ambiguous references.

IT, *WHICH*, AND *THEY*

Distribute copies of a student paper that uses *it*, *which*, *they*, and other pronouns in sentences without supplying clear antecedents in preceding sentences. Ask students to work in groups to revise the reference problems. In each case ask the group to consider whether the revision simply involves correcting the error or whether it calls for the writer to clarify and develop his or her transition between sentences or paragraphs.

Title	How to Row a Boat
Confusing	This is not as easy as it looks.
Revised	Rowing a boat is not as easy as it looks.

 Use *you* only to mean "you, the reader."

You should clearly mean "you, the reader." The context must be appropriate for such a meaning:

Inappropriate	In the fourteenth century you had to struggle simply to survive.
Revised	In the fourteenth century one [or a person] had to struggle simply to survive.

Writers sometimes drift into *you* because *one, a person, the individual*, or a similar indefinite word can be difficult to sustain. Sentence after sentence, the indefinite word may sound stuffy, and it requires the sexist *he* or the awkward *he or she* for pronoun-antecedent agreement (see pp. 311–13). To avoid these difficulties, try using plural nouns and pronouns:

Original	In the fourteenth century one had to struggle simply to survive.
Revised	In the fourteenth century people had to struggle simply to survive.

 Use the pronoun *it* only one way in a sentence.

We use *it* idiomatically in expressions such as *It is raining.* We use *it* to postpone the subject in sentences such as *It is true that more jobs are available to women today.* And we use *it* as a personal pronoun in sentences such as *Nicole wanted the book, but she couldn't find it.* All these uses are standard, but two of them in the same passage can confuse the reader:

Confusing	It is true that the Constitution sets limits, but it is also flexible.
Clear	The Constitution does set limits, but it is also flexible.

 Use *who, which,* and *that* for appropriate antecedents.

The relative pronouns *who, which,* and *that* commonly refer to persons, animals, or things. *Who* refers most often to persons but may also refer to animals that have names:

COLLABORATIVE LEARNING

DIFFERENTIATING BETWEEN USES OF "IT"

Ask each group to generate three sentences using "it" idiomatically and three using "it" as a personal pronoun. Have them pair up the sentences, selecting one from each group. Students should then combine each pair, revising as needed to ensure that "it" is used only one way in each combined sentence. You might have each group present to the class one original pair of sentences and the subsequent revision.

USE OF *THAT* OR *WHICH*

Students are often confused about whether to use *which, who,* or *that* because they misunderstand essential and nonessential elements. Students who suffer from this confusion should also consult Chapter 28 and *that/which* in the Glossary of Usage.

Dorothy is the girl <u>who</u> visits Oz.
Her dog, Toto, <u>who</u> accompanies her, gives her courage.

Which refers to animals and things:

The Orinoco River, <u>which</u> is 1600 miles long, flows through Venezuela into the Atlantic Ocean.

That refers to animals and things and occasionally to persons when they are collective or anonymous:

The rocket <u>that</u> failed cost millions.
Infants <u>that</u> walk need constant tending.

(See also p. 429 for the use of *which* and *that* in nonessential and essential clauses.)

The possessive *whose* generally refers to people but may refer to animals and things to avoid awkward and wordy *of which* constructions:

The book <u>whose</u> binding broke was rare. [Compare *The book <u>of which</u> the binding broke was rare.*]

Exercise 19.2 Revising: Indefinite and inappropriate pronoun reference

Many of the pronouns in the following sentences do not refer to specific, appropriate antecedents. Revise the sentences as necessary to make them clear.

Example:

In Glacier National Park, they have moose, elk, and wolves.
<u>Moose, elk, and wolves live</u> in Glacier National Park.

1. "Life begins at forty" is a cliché many people live by, and this may well be true.
2. When she was forty, Pearl Buck's novel *The Good Earth* won the Pulitzer Prize.
3. Buck was a novelist which wrote primarily about China.
4. In *The Good Earth* you have to struggle, but fortitude is rewarded.
5. Buck received much critical praise and earned over $7 million, but she was very modest about it.
6. Kenneth Kaunda, past president of Zambia, was elected to it in 1964, at age forty.
7. When Catherine I became empress of Russia at age forty, they feared more than loved her.
8. At forty, Paul Revere made his famous ride to warn American revolutionary leaders that the British were going to arrest them. This gave the colonists time to prepare for battle.
9. In the British House of Commons they did not welcome forty-year-old Nancy Astor as the first female member when she entered in 1919.
10. In 610 CE, Muhammad, age forty, began to have a series of visions that became the foundation of the Muslim faith. Since then, millions of people have become one.

ANSWERS: EXERCISE 19.2

Possible answers

1. "Life begins at forty" is a cliché many people live by, and this <u>saying</u> may well be true.
2. When <u>Pearl Buck</u> was forty, her novel *The Good Earth* won the Pulitzer Prize.
3. Buck was a novelist <u>who</u> wrote primarily about China.
4. In *The Good Earth* <u>the characters</u> have to struggle, but fortitude is rewarded.
5. Buck received much critical praise and earned over $7 million, but she was very modest about <u>her success</u> [*or* <u>the praise</u> *or* <u>the money</u>].
6. Kenneth Kaunda was elected to the <u>presidency of Zambia</u> in 1964, at age forty.
7. When Catherine I became empress of Russia at age forty, <u>the Russians</u> feared more than loved her.
8. At forty, Paul Revere made his famous ride to warn American revolutionary leaders that the British were going to arrest them. <u>His warning</u> gave the colonists time to prepare for battle.
9. <u>The members of the British House of Commons</u> did not welcome forty-year-old Nancy Astor as the first female member when she entered in 1919.
10. In 610 CE, Muhammad, age forty, began to have a series of visions that became the foundation of the Muslim faith. Since then, millions of people have become <u>Muslims</u>.

ANSWERS: EXERCISE 19.3

Possible revision

In Charlotte Brontë's *Jane Eyre*, <u>Jane</u> is a shy young woman <u>who</u> takes a job as governess. Her employer is a rude, brooding man named Rochester. He lives in a mysterious mansion on the English moors, <u>and both the mansion and the moors</u> contribute an eerie quality to Jane's experience. Eerier still are the fires, strange noises, and other unexplained happenings in the house; but Rochester refuses to discuss <u>them.</u> Eventually, <u>Jane and Rochester</u> fall in love. On the day they are to be married, however, <u>Jane</u> learns that <u>Rochester</u> has a wife hidden in the house. <u>The wife</u> is hopelessly insane and violent and must be guarded at all times, <u>circumstances that explain Rochester's</u> strange behavior. Heartbroken, Jane leaves the moors, and many years pass before <u>she and Rochester</u> are reunited.

HIGHLIGHTS

Shifts in person and number, in tense and mood, in subject and voice, or between direct and indirect quotation can be irritating to readers and occasionally make it hard to follow the meaning of a passage. Often, however, students are not fully aware of the shifts or their effect on a reader. This chapter describes in detail and illustrates the various shifts so that students can learn to identify the problems in their own writing. The exercises ask students to revise sentences and a longer passage, much as they will need to do in revising their own work.

Exercise 19.3   Revising: Pronoun reference

Revise the following paragraph so that each pronoun refers clearly to a single specific and appropriate antecedent.

In Charlotte Brontë's *Jane Eyre*, she is a shy young woman that takes a job as governess. Her employer is a rude, brooding man named Rochester. He lives in a mysterious mansion on the English moors, which contributes an eerie quality to Jane's experience. Eerier still are the fires, strange noises, and other unexplained happenings in the house; but Rochester refuses to discuss this. Eventually, they fall in love. On the day they are to be married, however, she learns that he has a wife hidden in the house. She is hopelessly insane and violent and must be guarded at all times, which explains his strange behavior. Heartbroken, Jane leaves the moors, and many years pass before they are reunited.

Note See page 376 for an exercise involving unclear pronoun reference along with sentence fragments, comma splices, and other sentence errors.

20
Shifts

Inconsistencies in grammatical elements will confuse your readers and distort your meaning. The box on the facing page shows ways to correct inconsistencies, or **shifts,** in nouns, pronouns, and verbs.

Shifts are likely to occur while you are trying to piece together meaning during drafting. But during editing you should make the grammatical elements of your sentences consistent.

Grammar checkers A grammar checker cannot recognize most shifts in sentences. Proofread your work on your own, looking carefully for inconsistencies.

mycomplab

Visit *mycomplab.com* for more resources and exercises on shifts.

Ways to correct shifts

First draft

A [bank] [owes] more to its customers than [is held] in — Shift in verb voice

reserve. [It] [kept] enough assets to meet reasonable — Shift in verb tense

withdrawals, but panicked [customers] may demand — Shift in number

all their deposits. Then demands will exceed sup-

plies, and [banks] will fail. These days, a [person's] — Shifts in number and person

losses are not likely to be great because the govern-

ment insures [your] deposits.

Revised

A bank **owes** more to its customers than **it holds** in reserve. It **keeps** enough assets to meet reasonable withdrawals, but panicked **customers** may demand all their deposits. Then demands will exceed supplies, and **the bank** will fail. These days, the losses of **customers** are not likely to be great because the government insures **their** deposits.

20a | **Keep a sentence or related sentences consistent in person and number.**

Person in grammar refers to the distinction among the person talking (first person), the person spoken to (second person), and the person, object, or concept being talked about (third person). **Number** refers to the distinction between one (singular) and more than one (plural).

Shifts in person

Most shifts in person occur because we can refer to people in general, including our readers, either in the third person (*a person, one; people, they*) or in the second person (*you*):

People should not drive when they have been drinking.
One should not drive when he or she has been drinking.
You should not drive when you have been drinking.

Although any one of these possibilities is acceptable in an appropriate context, a mixture of them is inconsistent:

Inconsistent	If a person works hard, you can gain satisfaction.
Revised	If you work hard, you can gain satisfaction.
Revised	If a person works hard, he or she can gain satisfaction.
Better	If people work hard, they can gain satisfaction.

Ask students to complete Exercise 20.1 together with their group members. Once they have finished this exercise, have them review one another's drafts for shifts in person and number. This activity helps them apply the concepts from the lesson to their own writing.

ANSWERS: EXERCISE 20.1

1. When a taxpayer is waiting to receive a tax refund from the Internal Revenue Service, he or she begins to notice what time the mail carrier arrives. *Or:* When taxpayers are waiting to receive tax refunds ... , they begin to notice what time the mail carrier arrives.
2. If the taxpayer does not receive a refund check within six weeks of filing a return, he or she may not have followed the rules of the IRS. *Or:* If taxpayers do not receive refund checks within six weeks of filing a return, they may not have followed the rules of the IRS.
3. If taxpayers do not include their Social Security numbers on returns, they will have to wait for refunds. *Or:* A taxpayer who does not include a Social Security number on a return will have to wait for a refund.
4. When taxpayers do not file their returns early, they will not get refunds quickly.
5. If taxpayers make errors on the tax forms, they might even be audited, thereby delaying refunds even longer. *Or:* If one has made errors on the tax form, he or she might even be audited, thereby delaying a refund even longer.

Shifts in number

Inconsistency in number occurs most often between a pronoun and its antecedent (see p. 309):

Inconsistent	If a student does not understand a problem, they should consult the instructor.
Revised	If a student does not understand a problem, he or she should consult the instructor.
Better	If students do not understand a problem, they should consult the instructor.
Or	A student who does not understand a problem should consult the instructor.

Note Generic nouns and most indefinite pronouns take singular pronouns with a definite gender: *he, she,* or *it.* When we use a generic noun like *student* or *person* or an indefinite pronoun like *everyone* or *each,* we often mean to include both males and females. To indicate this meaning, use *he or she* rather than *he* (as in the first of the preceding revisions) or, better still, rewrite in the plural or rewrite to avoid the inconsistent pronoun (as in the second and third of the revisions). See pages 311–13 for more discussion and examples.

Inconsistency in number can also occur between other words (usually nouns) that relate to each other in meaning.

Inconsistent	All the boys have a good reputation.
Revised	All the boys have good reputations.

The consistency in the revised sentence is called **logical agreement** because the nouns are consistent (the *boys* have *reputations,* not a single *reputation*).

Exercise 20.1   Revising: Shifts in person and number

Revise the following sentences to make them consistent in person and number.

Example:
A plumber will fix burst pipes, but they won't repair waterlogged appliances.

Plumbers will fix burst pipes, but they won't repair waterlogged appliances.

1. When a taxpayer is waiting to receive a tax refund from the Internal Revenue Service, you begin to notice what time the mail carrier arrives.
2. If the taxpayer does not receive a refund check within six weeks of filing a return, they may not have followed the rules of the IRS.
3. If a taxpayer does not include a Social Security number on a return, you will have to wait for a refund.

4. When taxpayers do not file their return early, they will not get a refund quickly.
5. If one makes errors on the tax form, they might even be audited, thereby delaying a refund even longer.

20b Keep a sentence or related sentences consistent in tense and mood.

Shifts in tense

Within a sentence or from one sentence to another, certain changes in tense may be required to indicate changes in actual or relative time (see pp. 292–93). The following changes are necessary:

Ramon <u>will graduate</u> from college thirty-one years after his father <u>arrived</u> in the United States.

But changes that are not required by meaning distract readers. Unnecessary shifts between past and present in passages narrating a series of events are particularly confusing:

Inconsistent   Immediately after Booth <u>shot</u> Lincoln, Major Rathbone <u>threw</u> himself upon the assassin. But Booth <u>pulls</u> a knife and <u>plunges</u> it into the major's arm.

Revised   Immediately after Booth <u>shot</u> Lincoln, Major Rathbone <u>threw</u> himself upon the assassin. But Booth <u>pulled</u> a knife and <u>plunged</u> it into the major's arm.

Use the present tense consistently to describe what an author has written, including the action in literature or a film:

Inconsistent   The main character in the novel <u>suffers</u> psychologically because he <u>has</u> a clubfoot, but he eventually <u>triumphed</u> over his disability.

Revised   The main character in the novel <u>suffers</u> psychologically because he <u>has</u> a clubfoot, but he eventually <u>triumphs</u> over his disability.

Shifts in mood

Shifts in the mood of verbs occur most frequently in directions when the writer moves between the imperative mood (*Unplug the appliance*) and the indicative mood (*You should unplug the appliance*). (See p. 296.) Directions are usually clearer and more concise in the imperative, as long as its use is consistent:

Inconsistent   <u>Cook</u> the mixture slowly, and <u>you should stir</u> it until the sugar is dissolved.

Revised   <u>Cook</u> the mixture slowly, and <u>stir</u> it until the sugar is dissolved.

CULTURE · LANGUAGE

TENSE SEQUENCING AND SHIFTS

ESL students may be particularly confused about how to tell the difference between correct tense sequencing and incorrect tense shifting. You might need to include a review of section 14h when you are teaching this topic.

ANSWERS: EXERCISE 20.2

1. When your cholesterol count is too high, adjusting your diet and exercise level <u>reduces</u> it.
2. After you <u>lower</u> your cholesterol rate, you decrease the chances of heart attack and stroke.
3. First eliminate saturated fats from your diet; then <u>consume</u> more whole grains and raw vegetables.
4. To avoid saturated fats, substitute turkey and chicken for beef, and <u>use</u> cholesterol-free salad dressing and cooking oil.
5. A regular program of aerobic exercise, such as walking or swimming, improves your cholesterol rate and <u>makes</u> you feel much healthier.

CLASS READING

Use the passage below, or find or write another that contains several kinds of shifts. Distribute copies to the class and read through the passage with students, asking them to identify the problems. This exercise will help make students aware of the different kinds of shifts as they appear in the context of an essay.

As soon as the avalanche was over, Jim pulls himself out of the snowbank and yells, "Where's everybody?" and were we still alive. As each of us in turn started digging out, you could see the damage the huge wall of snow had caused. The snow had destroyed the lodge and cars were swept away.

ANSWERS: EXERCISE 20.3

1. If students learn how to study efficiently, <u>they will make</u> much better grades on tests.
2. Conscientious students begin to prepare for tests immediately after <u>they attend</u> the first class.

Exercise 20.2   Revising: Shifts in tense and mood

Revise each of the following sentences to make it consistent in tense and mood.

Example:

Jenna ran to first, rounded the base, and keeps running until she slides into second.

Jenna ran to first, rounded the base, and <u>kept</u> running until she <u>slid</u> into second.

1. When your cholesterol count is too high, adjusting your diet and exercise level reduced it.
2. After you lowered your cholesterol rate, you decrease the chances of heart attack and stroke.
3. First eliminate saturated fats from your diet; then you should consume more whole grains and raw vegetables.
4. To avoid saturated fats, substitute turkey and chicken for beef, and you should use cholesterol-free salad dressing and cooking oil.
5. A regular program of aerobic exercise, such as walking or swimming, improves your cholesterol rate and made you feel much healthier.

20c   Keep a sentence or related sentences consistent in subject and voice.

When a verb is in the **active voice,** the subject names the actor: *Linda passed the peas.* When a verb is in the **passive voice,** the subject names the receiver of the action: *The peas were passed* [*by Linda*]. (See pp. 298–300.)

A shift in voice may sometimes help focus the reader's attention on a single subject, as in *The candidate campaigned vigorously and was nominated on the first ballot.* However, most shifts in voice also involve shifts in subject. They are unnecessary and confusing.

| Inconsistent | Internet blogs cover an enormous range of topics. Opportunities for people to discuss pet issues are provided on these sites. |
| Revised | Internet blogs cover an enormous range of topics and provide opportunities for people to discuss pet issues. |

Exercise 20.3   Revising: Shifts in subject and voice

Make the following sentences consistent in subject and voice.

Example:

At the reunion they ate hot dogs and volleyball was played.
At the reunion they ate hot dogs and <u>played volleyball.</u>

1. If students learn how to study efficiently, much better grades will be made on tests.
2. Conscientious students begin to prepare for tests immediately after the first class is attended.
3. Before each class all reading assignments are completed, and the students outline the material and answer any study questions.
4. In class they listen carefully and good notes are taken.
5. Questions are asked by the students when they do not understand the professor.

3. Before each class <u>the students complete</u> all reading assignments, outline the material, and answer any study questions.
4. In class they listen carefully and <u>take</u> good notes.
5. The students <u>ask questions</u> when they do not understand the professor.

20d   Keep a quotation or a question consistently direct or indirect.

Direct quotations or questions report the exact words of a quotation or question:

"I am the greatest," bragged Muhammad Ali.
<u>In his day few people asked</u>, "Is he right?"

Indirect quotations or questions report that someone said or asked something, but not in the exact words:

Muhammad Ali bragged <u>that he was the greatest</u>.
In his day few people asked <u>whether he was right</u>.

Shifts between direct and indirect quotations or questions are difficult to follow.

Shift in quotation	Kapek reported that the rats avoided the maze and "as of this writing, none responds to conditioning."
Revised (indirect)	Kapek reported that the rats avoided the maze and <u>that as of his writing none responded to conditioning</u>.
Revised (direct)	Kapek reported, "<u>The rats avoid the maze</u>. As of this writing, none responds to conditioning."
Shift in question	The reader wonders whether the experiment failed or did it perhaps succeed?
Revised (indirect)	The reader wonders whether the experiment failed or <u>whether it perhaps succeeded</u>.
Revised (direct)	<u>Did the experiment fail?</u> Or did it perhaps succeed?

For more on quotations, see pages 436–38 (commas with signal phrases such as *she said*), 459–66 (quotation marks), and 620–25 (integrating quotations into your writing). For more on questions, see pages 419–20.

DIRECT VERSUS INDIRECT QUOTATIONS IN NARRATIVES

Particularly in narrative writing, students might incorporate a great deal of dialogue. If they are working with this type of assignment, at this point, ask them to consider the differing impact of direct versus indirect quotations. For instance, direct quotations can aid in describing someone as they relay the speaker's specific language. Direct quotations are also more immediate, making readers feel like they can "hear" the speaker. Indirect quotations are good for summarizing the gist of what was said when the specific wording isn't as significant. Remind students that whether they opt to use direct or indirect quotations, they must be consistent.

COLLABORATIVE LEARNING

Students can create their own examples of direct and indirect quotations and questions, using the models provided in Exercise 20.4. Ask students to work through Exercise 20.4 in small groups and then to create two or three additional examples.

Alternatively, you might ask students to compare their independent responses to Exercises 20.1–20.4, then work in small groups to revise the paragraph in Exercise 20.5. This gives students the opportunity to help each other recognize shifts and to discuss the effects of unnecessary shifts. You might have each group present their responses to one or two sentences of the paragraph in Exercise 20.5 and encourage the presenters to foreground the group's questions and comments.

ANSWERS: EXERCISE 20.4

1. *Direct:* One anthropologist says, "The functions of marriage have changed, nowhere more dramatically than in industrialized cultures."
Indirect: One anthropologist says that the functions of marriage have changed, most dramatically in industrialized cultures.
2. *Direct:* May siblings marry? Would the union be immoral?
Indirect: The question even arises of whether siblings may marry and whether the union would be immoral.
3. *Direct:* The author points out, "Sibling marriage is still illegal everywhere in the United States, and people are still prosecuted under the law."
Indirect: The author points out that sibling marriage is still illegal everywhere in the United States and that people are still prosecuted under the law.
4. *Direct:* She says, "Incest could be considered a universal taboo. The questions asked about the taboo vary widely."
Indirect: She says that incest could be considered a universal taboo and that the questions asked about the taboo vary widely.
5. *Direct:* Is the taboo a way of protecting the family? Might it be instinctive?
Indirect: Some ask whether the taboo is a way of protecting the family or whether it may be instinctive.

ANSWERS: EXERCISE 20.5

Possible revision

Driving in snow need not be dangerous if you practice a few simple rules. First, <u>avoid</u> fast starts, which prevent the wheels from gaining traction and may result in the car's getting stuck. Second, drive more slowly than usual, and <u>pay</u> attention to the feel of the car: if the steering <u>seems</u> unusually loose or the wheels <u>do</u> not seem to be grabbing the road, slow down. Third, avoid fast stops, which lead to skids. <u>Be alert</u> for other cars and intersections that <u>may</u> necessitate <u>applying the brakes</u> suddenly. If you need to slow down, <u>reduce the car's momentum</u> by downshifting as well as by applying the brakes. When braking, press the pedal to the floor only if you have antilock brakes; otherwise, <u>pump the pedal</u> in short bursts. If you feel the car skidding, <u>release</u>

Exercise 20.4 Revising: Shifts in direct and indirect quotations and questions

Revise each of the following sentences twice, once to make it consistently direct, once to make it consistently indirect. You will have to guess at the exact wording of direct quotations and questions that are now stated indirectly.

Example:
We all wonder what the next decade will bring and will we thrive or not?
Direct: <u>What will the next decade bring?</u> Will we thrive or not?
Indirect: We all wonder what the next decade will bring and <u>whether we will thrive or not.</u>

1. One anthropologist says that the functions of marriage have changed and "nowhere more dramatically than in industrialized cultures."
2. The question even arises of whether siblings may marry and would the union be immoral?
3. The author points out, "Sibling marriage is still illegal everywhere in the United States" and that people are still prosecuted under the law.
4. She says that incest could be considered a universal taboo and "the questions asked about the taboo vary widely."
5. Some ask is the taboo a way of protecting the family or whether it may be instinctive.

Exercise 20.5 Revising: Shifts

Revise the following paragraph to eliminate unnecessary shifts in person, number, tense, mood, and voice.

Driving in snow need not be dangerous if you practice a few rules. First, one should avoid fast starts, which prevent the wheels from gaining traction and may result in the car's getting stuck. Second, drive more slowly than usual, and you should pay attention to the feel of the car: if the steering seemed unusually loose or the wheels did not seem to be grabbing the road, slow down. Third, avoid fast stops, which lead to skids. One should be alert for other cars and intersections that may necessitate that the brakes be applied suddenly. If you need to slow down, the car's momentum can be reduced by downshifting as well as by applying the brakes. When braking, press the pedal to the floor only if you have antilock brakes; otherwise, the pedal should be pumped in short bursts. If you feel the car skidding, the brakes should be released and the wheel should be turned into the direction of the skid, and then the brakes should be pressed or pumped again. If one repeated these motions, the skid would be stopped and the speed of the car would be reduced.

Note See page 376 for an exercise involving shifts along with sentence fragments, comma splices, and other sentence errors.

21

Misplaced and Dangling Modifiers

When reading a sentence in English, we depend principally on the arrangement of the words to tell us how they are related. In writing, we may create confusion if we fail to connect modifiers to the words they modify.

Grammar checkers A grammar checker cannot recognize most problems with modifiers. For instance, a checker failed to flag the misplaced modifiers in *Gasoline high prices affect usually car sales* or the dangling modifier in *The vandalism was visible passing the building*.

Misplaced Modifiers

A modifier is **misplaced** if readers can't easily relate it to the word it modifies. Misplaced modifiers may be awkward, confusing, or even unintentionally funny.

21a Place modifiers where they will clearly modify the words intended.

Readers tend to link a modifying word, phrase, or clause to the nearest word it could modify: *I saw a man in a green hat*. Thus the writer must place the phrase so that it clearly modifies the intended word and not some other.

Confusing   He served steak to the men on paper plates.

Revised   He served the men steak on paper plates.

Confusing   Many dogs are killed by cars and trucks roaming unleashed.

Revised   Many dogs roaming unleashed are killed by cars and trucks.

> mycomplab
>
> Visit *mycomplab.com* for more resources and exercises on misplaced and dangling modifiers.

the brakes, turn the wheel into the direction of the skid, and then press or pump the brakes again. Repeating these motions will stop the skid and reduce the speed of the car.

HIGHLIGHTS

Misplaced and dangling modifiers often interest students because the faulty constructions can be amusing. To tie together all the different problems discussed in the chapter, however, you may want to point out that they all illustrate the importance of position and arrangement in sentences. Split constructions (21d and 21e) conveniently emphasize the need to keep the parts of related syntactic groups clearly unified. Yet both standard speech and formal writing provide frequent examples of freely placed limiting modifiers and of split infinitives. Part of our difficulty in teaching composition is in giving students effective advice about when freedom is constructive and when it is confusing. As in all such matters, the advice of the handbook is largely conservative; you may therefore want to modify it somewhat.

Ways to revise misplaced modifiers

■ **Place modifiers clearly** (previous page and below).

Confusing   Listening to music can cause hearing loss <u>at high levels</u>.

Revised   Listening to music <u>at high levels</u> can cause hearing loss.

■ **Place limiting modifiers carefully** (facing page).

Confusing   The women <u>only</u> reached the summit on their last climb.

Revised   The women reached the summit <u>only</u> on their last climb.

■ **Make each modifier refer to only one grammatical unit** (facing page).

Confusing   Students who fail to complete assignments <u>often</u> receive poor grades.

Revised   Students who <u>often</u> fail to complete assignments receive poor grades.

Revised   Students who fail to complete assignments receive poor grades <u>often</u>.

■ **Keep grammatical units together** (pp. 362–63).

Awkward   The owner ordered the dog <u>to not bark</u>.

Revised   The owner ordered the dog <u>not **to bark**</u>.

■ **Place adverbs and adjectives conventionally** (pp. 364–65).

Awkward   Once endangered, bald eagles were spotted <u>seldom</u> in the eastern United States.

Revised   Once endangered, bald eagles were <u>seldom</u> spotted in the eastern United States.

Confusing   This is the only chocolate chip cookie in a bag that tastes like Mom's. [Actual advertisement.]

Revised   This is the only <u>bagged</u> [or <u>packaged</u>] chocolate chip cookie that tastes like Mom's.

Exercise 21.1   Revising: Misplaced phrases and clauses

Revise the following sentences so that phrases and clauses clearly modify the appropriate words.

Example:

I came to enjoy flying over time.
<u>Over time</u> I came to enjoy flying.

1. Women have contributed much to knowledge and culture of great value.

ANSWERS: EXERCISE 21.1

1. Women have contributed much <u>of great value</u> to knowledge and culture.
2. <u>In 1821</u> Emma Willard founded the Troy Female Seminary, the first institution to provide a college-level education for women.

2. Emma Willard founded the Troy Female Seminary, the first institution to provide a college-level education for women in 1821.
3. Sixteen years later Mary Lyon founded Mount Holyoke Female Seminary, the first true women's college with directors and a campus who would sustain the college even after Lyon's death.
4. *Una* was the first US newspaper, which was founded by Pauline Wright Davis in 1853, that was dedicated to gaining women's rights.
5. Mitchell's Comet was discovered in 1847, which was named for Maria Mitchell.

21b   Place limiting modifiers carefully.

Limiting modifiers include *almost, even, exactly, hardly, just, merely, nearly, only, scarcely,* and *simply.* In speech these modifiers often occur before the verb, regardless of the words they are intended to modify. In writing, however, these modifiers should fall immediately before the word or word group they modify to avoid any ambiguity:

Unclear   She only found that fossil on her last dig.

Revised   She found only that fossil on her last dig.

Revised   She found that fossil only on her last dig.

Exercise 21.2   Using limiting modifiers

Use each of the following limiting modifiers in two versions of the same sentence.

Example:
only
He is the only one I like. He is the one only I like.

1. almost   3. hardly   5. nearly
2. even   4. simply

21c   Make each modifier refer to only one grammatical element.

A modifier can modify only *one* element in a sentence—the subject, the verb, or some other element. A **squinting modifier** seems confusingly to refer to either of two words:

Squinting   Snipers who fired on the soldiers often escaped capture.

Clear   Snipers who often fired on the soldiers escaped capture.

Clear   Snipers who fired on the soldiers escaped capture often.

3. Sixteen years later Mary Lyon founded Mount Holyoke Female Seminary, the first true women's college with a campus and directors who would sustain the college even after Lyon's death.
4. *Una,* which was founded by Pauline Wright Davis in 1853, was the first US newspaper that was dedicated to gaining women's rights.
5. Mitchell's Comet, which was named for Maria Mitchell, was discovered in 1847.

MOVING ONLY

Ask students to create sentences whose meaning changes as a modifier like *only* moves from place to place:

Only students were asked to bring gym shorts and running shoes.
Students were *only* asked to bring gym shorts and running shoes.
Students were asked *only* to bring gym shorts and running shoes.
Students were asked to bring *only* gym shorts and running shoes.

COLLABORATIVE LEARNING

LIMITING AND SQUINTING MODIFIERS

Students can work productively together (in pairs or small groups) on Exercises 21.2 and 21.3. This collaborative effort can be particularly useful when students are asked to create more than one possible revision.

ANSWERS: EXERCISE 21.2

Possible answers

1. Almost everybody hates him.
   Everybody almost hates him.
2. Even now I remember the details of the event.
   Now I remember even the details of the event.
3. We hardly heard him call our names.
   We heard him hardly call our names.
4. Write simply.
   Simply write.
5. I nearly missed the performance that was booed off the stage.

I missed the performance that was <u>nearly</u> booed off the stage.

ANSWERS: EXERCISE 21.3

1. People who <u>often</u> sunbathe can damage their skin. *Or:* People who sunbathe can <u>often</u> damage their skin.
2. Sunbathers who <u>frequently</u> apply a sunscreen block some of the sun's harmful rays. *Or:* <u>Frequently</u>, sunbathers who apply a sunscreen block some of the sun's harmful rays.
3. Men and women who <u>often</u> lie out in the sun have leathery, dry skin. *Or:* <u>Often</u> men and women who lie out in the sun have leathery, dry skin.
4. Doctors tell sunbathers they risk skin cancer <u>when they are older</u>. *Or:* Doctors tell <u>older</u> sunbathers they risk skin cancer.
5. People who <u>usually</u> stay out of the sun will have better skin and fewer chances of skin cancer. *Or:* People who stay out of the sun will <u>usually</u> have better skin and fewer chances of skin cancer.

THE MEDIA

Radio and television newscasts are rich sources of dangling and misplaced modifiers, perhaps because reporters have little time to pay attention to the structure of their sentences. Have students listen to newscasts and record errors: doing so will help them to understand the perspective of a reader who comes across similar errors in an essay. Newspaper headlines and public announcements are also rich sources; from time to time, magazine articles and paperback books appear with collections of particularly humorous errors. But students will be able to find many on their own by looking at the newspaper for headlines like *Young man slain with flowers.*

HOME-GROWN STAR REPORTERS

Ask students to form groups in order to write their own newscasts filled with the kinds of errors they might spot through the activity above. The newscasts (and the errors) should be plausible in style and content, though the content will probably have to be the product of students' imaginations. Having heard many newscasts, however,

When an adverb modifies an entire main clause, as in the last example, it can usually be moved to the beginning of the sentence: *Often, snipers who fired on the soldiers escaped capture.*

> **Exercise 21.3 Revising: Squinting modifiers**
> Revise each sentence twice so that the squinting modifier applies clearly first to one element and then to the other.
>
> *Example:*
> The work that he hoped would satisfy him completely frustrated him.
> The work that he hoped would <u>completely</u> satisfy him frustrated him.
> The work that he hoped would <u>satisfy him</u> frustrated him <u>completely</u>.
>
> 1. People who sunbathe often can damage their skin.
> 2. Sunbathers who apply a sunscreen frequently block some of the sun's harmful ultraviolet rays.
> 3. Men and women who lie out in the sun often have leathery, dry skin.
> 4. Doctors tell sunbathers when they are older they risk skin cancer.
> 5. People who stay out of the sun usually will have better skin and fewer chances of skin cancer.

21d | Keep subjects, verbs, and objects together.

English sentences tend to move from subject to verb to object. The movement is so familiar that modifiers between these elements can be awkward.

A subject and verb may be separated by an adjective that modifies the subject: *The hurricane, which hit the city with ferocious winds, damaged many homes and public buildings.* But an adverb of more than a word usually stops the flow of the sentence:

        subject ⎯⎯ adverb ⎯⎯ verb
Awkward   The city, <u>after the hurricane</u>, began massive rebuilding.

       ⎯ adverb ⎯ subject verb
Revised   <u>After the hurricane</u>, the city began massive rebuilding.

Even a one-word adverb will be awkward between a verb and its object:

        ⎯ verb ⎯ adverb   object
Awkward   The hurricane had damaged <u>badly</u> many homes in the city.

        ⎯ verb ⎯   object
Revised   The hurricane had <u>badly</u> damaged many homes in the city.
          adverb

21e | Keep parts of infinitives or verb phrases together.

An **infinitive** consists of the marker *to* plus the plain form of a verb: *to produce, to enjoy.* The two words in an infinitive are widely regarded as a grammatical unit that should not be split apart by a modifier:

Awkward   The weather service expected temperatures to not rise.
(infinitive marking over "not rise")

Revised   The weather service expected temperatures not to rise.
(infinitive marking over "to rise")

A split infinitive may sometimes be natural and preferable, though it may still bother some readers:

Several US industries expect to more than triple their use of robots.
(infinitive marking over "more than")

Here the split infinitive is more economical than the alternatives, such as *Several US industries expect to increase their use of robots by more than three times.*

A **verb phrase** consists of a helping verb plus a main verb, as in *will call, was going, had been writing* (see p. 274). A single-word adverb may be inserted after the helping verb in a verb phrase (or the first helping verb if more than one): *Scientists have lately been using spacecraft to study the sun.* But when longer adverbs interrupt verb phrases, the result is almost always awkward:

Awkward   People who have osteoporosis can, by increasing their daily
(helping verb — adverb)

intake of calcium and vitamin D, improve their bone density.
(main verb)

Revised   By increasing their daily intake of calcium and vitamin D,
(adverb)

people who have osteoporosis can improve their bone density.
(verb phrase)

CULTURE LANGUAGE   In an English question, place a one-word adverb after the first helping verb and the subject:

(helping verb   subject   adverb   rest of verb phrase)
Will spacecraft ever be able to leave the solar system?

Exercise 21.4   Revising: Separated sentence parts

Revise the following sentences to connect separated parts (subject-predicate, verb-object, verb phrase, infinitive).

Example:

Most children have by the time they are seven lost a tooth.
By the time they are seven, most children have lost a tooth.

1. Myra Bradwell founded in 1868 the *Chicago Legal News.*
2. Bradwell was later denied, although she had qualified, admission to the Illinois Bar Association.
3. In an attempt to finally gain admission to the bar, she carried the case to the Supreme Court, but the justices decided against her.
4. Bradwell was determined that no other woman would, if she were qualified, be denied entrance to a profession.

students will probably have little trouble parodying them in form and matter.

TO SPLIT OR NOT TO SPLIT?

Students may be familiar with *Star Trek*'s famous split infinitive, "to boldly go." Ask them to find examples of other split infinitives published in print or in the media. If you are presenting a conservative view of grammar, ask students to correct their examples. If you are presenting a less conservative approach to grammar, ask students to share their examples and speculate about each writer's intentions. Are the writers deliberately splitting the infinitive for stylistic purposes or are they simply unfamiliar with this rule?

ANSWERS: EXERCISE 21.4

1. In 1868 Myra Bradwell founded the *Chicago Legal News.*
2. Although she had qualified, Bradwell was later denied admission to the Illinois Bar Association.
3. In an attempt finally to gain admission to the bar, she carried the case to the Supreme Court, but the justices decided against her.
4. Bradwell was determined that no other woman would be denied entrance to a profession if she were qualified.
5. In response to Bradwell's persuasion, the Illinois legislature finally passed a bill ensuring that no one would be restricted from a profession on the basis of gender.

5. The Illinois legislature finally passed, in response to Bradwell's persuasion, a bill ensuring that no one on the basis of gender would be restricted from a profession.

21f   Position adverbs with care.

A few adverbs are subject to conventions that can trouble non-native speakers of English.

Adverbs of frequency

Adverbs of frequency include *always, never, often, rarely, seldom, sometimes,* and *usually.* They appear at the beginning of a sentence, before a one-word verb, or after the helping verb in a verb phrase:

Awkward	Robots have put <u>sometimes</u> humans out of work.

(verb phrase / adverb)

| **Revised** | Robots have <u>sometimes</u> put humans out of work. |

(helping verb / adverb / main verb)

| **Revised** | <u>Sometimes</u> robots have put humans out of work. |

(adverb / verb phrase)

Adverbs of frequency always follow the verb *be:*

| **Awkward** | Robots <u>often</u> are helpful to workers. |

(adverb verb)

| **Revised** | Robots are <u>often</u> helpful to workers. |

(verb adverb)

Adverbs of degree

Adverbs of degree include *absolutely, almost, certainly, completely, especially, extremely, hardly,* and *only.* They fall just before the word modified (an adjective, another adverb, sometimes a verb).

| **Awkward** | Robots have been useful <u>especially</u> in making cars. |

(adjective adverb)

| **Revised** | Robots have been <u>especially</u> useful in making cars. |

(adverb adjective)

Adverbs of manner

Adverbs of manner include *badly, sweetly, tightly,* and others that describe how something is done. They usually fall after the verb:

| **Awkward** | Robots <u>smoothly</u> work on assembly lines. |

(adverb verb)

| **Revised** | Robots work <u>smoothly</u> on assembly lines. |

(verb adverb)

The adverb *not*

When the adverb *not* modifies a verb, place it after the helping verb (or the first helping verb if more than one):

helping main
verb verb
Awkward Robots do think <u>not</u>.

helping main
verb verb
Revised Robots do <u>not</u> think.

Place *not* after a form of *be: Robots are <u>not</u> thinkers.*

When *not* modifies another adverb or an adjective, place it before the other modifier: *Robots are <u>not</u> sleek machines.*

 Arrange adjectives appropriately.

English follows distinctive rules for arranging two or three adjectives before a noun. (A string of more than three adjectives before a noun is rare.) The order depends on the meaning of the adjectives, as indicated in the following table:

Determiner	Opinion	Size or shape	Color	Origin	Material	Noun used as adjective	Noun
many						state	**laws**
	striking		green	Thai			**birds**
a	fine			German			**camera**
this		square			wooden		**table**
all						business	**reports**
the			blue		litmus		**paper**

See pages 433–34 on punctuating adjectives before a noun.

Exercise 21.5 Revising: Placement of adverbs and adjectives

Revise the sentences below to correct the positions of adverbs or adjectives. If a sentence is already correct as given, mark the number preceding it.

Example:
Gasoline high prices affect usually car sales.
<u>High</u> gasoline prices <u>usually</u> affect car sales.

1. Some years ago Detroit cars often were praised.
2. Luxury large cars especially were prized.
3. Then a serious oil shortage led drivers to value small foreign cars that got good mileage.
4. When gasoline ample supplies returned, consumers bought again American large cars and trucks.
5. Consumers not were loyal to the big vehicles when gasoline prices dramatically rose.

Dangling Modifiers

21h Relate dangling modifiers to their sentences.

A **dangling modifier** does not sensibly modify anything in its sentence:

Dangling   Passing the building, the vandalism became visible.

Dangling modifiers usually introduce sentences, contain a verb form, and imply but do not name a subject. In the preceding example, the implied subject is the someone or something passing the building. Readers assume that this implied subject is the same as the subject of the sentence (*vandalism* in the example), but vandalism does not pass buildings. The modifier "dangles" because it does not connect sensibly to the rest of the sentence.

Certain kinds of modifiers are the most likely to dangle:

■ **Participial phrases:**

Dangling   Passing the building, the vandalism became visible.
Revised   As we passed the building, the vandalism became visible.

■ **Infinitive phrases:**

Dangling   To understand the causes, vandalism has been studied.
Revised   To understand the causes, researchers have studied vandalism.

■ **Prepositional phrases in which the object of the preposition is a gerund:**

Dangling   After studying the problem, vandals are now thought to share certain characteristics.
Revised   After studying the problem, researchers think that vandals share certain characteristics.

■ **Elliptical clauses in which the subject and perhaps the verb are omitted:**

Dangling   When destructive, researchers have learned that vandals are more likely to be in groups.
Revised   When vandals are destructive, researchers have learned, they are more likely to be in groups.

Dangling modifiers are especially likely when the verb in the main clause is in the **passive voice** instead of the **active voice,** as in *vandalism has been investigated* and *vandals are thought.* (See pp. 298–300 for more on the passive voice.)

Identifying and revising dangling modifiers

- **Identify the modifier's subject.** If the modifier lacks a stated subject (as *when in diapers* does), identify what the modifier describes.
- **Compare the subject of the modifier and the subject of the sentence.** Verify that what the modifier describes is in fact the subject of the main clause. If it is not, the modifier probably dangles.
- **Revise as needed.** Either (*a*) recast the dangling modifier with a stated subject of its own, or (*b*) change the subject of the main clause to be what the modifier describes.

	┌─── modifier ───┐ subject
Dangling	When in diapers, my mother remarried.
Revision *a*	When I was in diapers, my mother remarried.
Revision *b*	When in diapers, I attended my mother's second wedding.

Note A modifier may be dangling even when the sentence elsewhere contains a word the modifier might seem to describe, such as *vandals* below:

Dangling   When destructive, researchers have learned that vandals are more likely to be in groups.

In addition, a dangling modifier may fall at the end of a sentence:

Dangling   The vandalism was visible passing the building.

Revising dangling modifiers

Revise most dangling modifiers in one of two ways, depending on what you want to emphasize in the sentence.

- **Change the subject of the main clause to a word the modifier properly describes:**

  Dangling   To express themselves, graffiti decorate walls.
  Revised   To express themselves, some youths decorate walls with graffiti.

- **Rewrite the dangling modifier as a complete clause with its own stated subject and verb:**

  Revised   Because some youths need to express themselves, they decorate walls with graffiti.

Exercise 21.6   Revising: Dangling modifiers

Revise the following sentences to eliminate any dangling modifiers. Each item has more than one possible answer.

ANSWERS: EXERCISE 21.6
Possible answers

1. After Andrew Jackson had accomplished many deeds of valor, his fame led to his election to the presidency in 1828 and 1832.

2. <u>By the time Jackson was fourteen</u>, both of <u>his</u> parents had died.
3. To aid the American Revolution, <u>Jackson chose service</u> as a mounted courier.
4. Though not well educated, <u>Jackson proved his ability</u> in a successful career as a lawyer and judge.
5. <u>Because Jackson won</u> many military battles, the American public believed in his leadership.

SENTENCE COMBINING

Exercise 21.7 requires students to combine pairs of sentences whose content and structure make them likely causes of misplaced or dangling modifiers. Extend this activity by having students create their own sentences that would be easy to miscombine. Choose the best pairs, copy them, and have the class work on them for an exercise. This activity leads to considerable discussion and some imaginative and amusing results when the students work in groups.

ANSWERS: EXERCISE 21.7

Possible answers

1. <u>As evening falls in the Central American rain forests</u>, the tungara frogs begin their croaking chorus.
2. <u>Croaking loudly at night</u>, male tungara frogs sing "songs" designed to attract female frogs.
3. But predators, <u>also hearing the croaking</u>, gather to feast on the frogs.
4. <u>Lured by their croaking dinners</u>, the predators include bullfrogs, snakes, bats, and opossums.
5. <u>Although the frogs hope to mate</u>, their nightly chorus can result in death instead.

ANSWERS: EXERCISE 21.8

Possible revision

<u>Several nights a week</u>, Central American tungara frogs silence their mating croaks. When not croaking, <u>they reduce</u> the chance that they will be eaten by predators. The frogs seem <u>to believe fully</u> in "safety in numbers." <u>More than likely</u>, they will croak along with a large group rather than by themselves. By forgoing croaking on some nights, <u>the frogs</u> prevent the species from "croaking."

Example:
Driving north, the vegetation became increasingly sparse.

Driving north, <u>we noticed that</u> the vegetation became increasingly sparse.

<u>As we drove north</u>, the vegetation became increasingly sparse.

1. After accomplishing many deeds of valor, Andrew Jackson's fame led to his election to the presidency in 1828 and 1832.
2. By the age of fourteen, both of Jackson's parents had died.
3. To aid the American Revolution, service as a mounted courier was chosen by Jackson.
4. Though not well educated, a successful career as a lawyer and judge proved Jackson's ability.
5. Winning many military battles, the American public believed in Jackson's leadership.

Exercise 21.7 Sentence combining: Placing modifiers

Combine each pair of sentences below into a single sentence by rewriting one as a modifier. Make sure the modifier applies clearly to the appropriate word. You will have to add, delete, and rearrange words, and you may find that more than one answer is possible in each case.

Example:
Bob demanded a hearing from the faculty. Bob wanted to appeal the decision.

<u>Wanting to appeal the decision</u>, Bob demanded a hearing from the faculty.

1. Evening falls in the Central American rain forests. The tungara frogs begin their croaking chorus.
2. Male tungara frogs croak loudly at night. The "songs" they sing are designed to attract female frogs.
3. But predators also hear the croaking. They gather to feast on the frogs.
4. The predators are lured by their croaking dinners. The predators include bullfrogs, snakes, bats, and opossums.
5. The frogs hope to mate. Their nightly chorus can result in death instead.

Exercise 21.8 Revising: Misplaced and dangling modifiers

Revise the following paragraph to eliminate any misplaced or dangling modifiers.

Central American tungara frogs silence several nights a week their mating croaks. When not croaking, the chance that the frogs will be eaten by predators is reduced. The frogs seem to fully believe in "safety in numbers." They more than likely will croak along with a large group rather than by themselves. By forgoing croaking on some nights, the frogs' behavior prevents the species from "croaking."

Note See page 376 for an exercise involving misplaced and dangling modifiers along with other sentence errors.

22
Mixed and Incomplete Sentences

Mixed Sentences

A **mixed sentence** contains two or more parts that are incompatible—that is, the parts do not fit together. The misfit may be in grammar or in meaning.

Grammar checkers A grammar checker may recognize a simple mixed construction such as *reason is because*, but it will fail to flag most mixed sentences.

22a Untangle sentences that are mixed in grammar.

Sentences mixed in grammar combine two or more incompatible grammatical structures.

1 Make sure subject and verb fit together grammatically.

A mixed sentence may occur when you start a sentence with one plan and end it with another:

	┌─── modifier (prepositional phrase) ───┐ verb
Mixed	By paying more attention to impressions than facts leads us to misjudge others.
	┌─── modifier (prepositional phrase) ───┐ subject + verb
Revised	By paying more attention to impressions than facts, <u>we misjudge</u> others.
	┌─── subject (gerund phrase) ───┐ verb
Revised	<u>Paying</u> more attention to impressions than facts <u>leads</u> us to misjudge others.

Constructions that use *Just because* clauses as subjects are common in speech but should be avoided in writing.

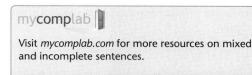

mycomplab

Visit *mycomplab.com* for more resources on mixed and incomplete sentences.

HIGHLIGHTS

The first two sections of Chapter 22 treat sentences whose subjects and predicates are incompatible. The tangled sentences in some student writing have more complex causes than this brief discussion of mixed sentences can address. But the two most common problems do seem to be subjects and predicates that are incompatible in grammar and in meaning.

The third section deals with compound constructions that are grammatically or idiomatically incomplete. Ill-prepared students seem to encounter this problem less often than better-prepared students do, perhaps because only the latter use such constructions. On the other hand, incomplete comparisons (22d) are common, and you may wish to call particular attention to them.

The final section, covering omission of needed words, is designed primarily as an aid to grading papers. Instructors who notice words missing in a student essay can call attention to the problem by using the number-and-letter code to refer students to this section.

USING STUDENT WRITING

Because the mixed and incomplete sentences in student writing have complicated causes and because the problems in one student's essay are likely to differ widely from those in another student's paper, most instructors choose simply to discuss the chapter and use some of the exercises rather than elaborate with classroom activities and assignments. In working with individual students, however, most instructors are able to devise activities that suit individual needs. Instructors who wish to alert students to the problem of incomplete compound constructions, incomplete comparisons, and omission of needed words can draw from a student paper or write a passage containing these problems and then ask students to work with the passage, perhaps in small groups, proofreading it and correcting the errors. Students' journals and error logs are excellent sources of material as well as good places to practice revision strategies. Encourage students to keep a log of the patterns of error that tend to recur in their work, along with corrected examples. That log can provide a good resource for future revision and editing sessions.

RESOURCES AND IDEAS

Krishna, Valerie. "The Syntax of Error." *Journal of Basic Writing* 1.1 (1975): 43–9. Print. The author views problems like mixed constructions and shifts as the result of a weak sentence core, and she encourages teachers to pay attention to this underlying problem in helping students avoid such errors.

Shuman, R. Baird. "Grammar for Writers: How Much Is Enough?" *The Place of Grammar in Writing Instruction: Past, Present, Future.* Ed. Susan Hunter and Ray Wallace. Portsmouth: Boynton, 1995. 114–28. Print. Shuman offers simplified strategies for presenting sentence structure as a meaningful concept in an effort to prevent some student errors.

Weaver, Constance, Jonathan Bush, Jeff Anderson, and Patricia Bills. "Grammar Intertwined throughout the Writing Process: An 'inch wide and a mile deep.'" *English Teaching: Practice and Critique* 5.1 (2006): 77–101. Print. The authors discuss how to incorporate grammar, including parallelism and other sentence-level skills, in the context of students' own writing.

Mixed	┌─── modifier (subordinate clause) ───┐┌─ verb ─┐ Just because no one is watching doesn't mean we have license to break the law.
Revised	┌─── modifier (subordinate clause) ───┐ subject + verb Even when no one is watching, we don't have license to break the law.

In some mixed sentences the grammar is so jumbled that the writer has little choice but to start over:

Mixed	My long-range goal is through law school and government work I hope to help people deal with those problems we all deal with more effectively.
Revised	My long-range goal is to go to law school and then work in government so that I can help people deal more effectively with problems we all face.

A mixed sentence is especially likely when you are working on a computer and connect parts of two sentences or rewrite half a sentence but not the other half. A mixed sentence may also occur when you don't make the subject and the predicate verb carry the principal meaning. (See pp. 378–80.) If you need help identifying the subject and predicate, see pages 231–34.

2 State parts of sentences, such as subjects, only once. (CULTURE LANGUAGE)

In some languages other than English, certain parts of sentences may be repeated. These include the subject in any kind of clause and an object or adverb in an adjective clause. In English, however, these parts are stated only once in a clause.

Repetition of subject

You may be tempted to restate a subject as a pronoun before the verb. But the subject needs stating only once in its clause.

Faulty	The liquid it reached a temperature of 180°F.
Revised	The liquid reached a temperature of 180°F.

Faulty	Gases in the liquid they escaped.
Revised	Gases in the liquid escaped.

Repetition in an adjective clause

Adjective clauses begin with *who, whom, whose, which, that, where,* and *when* (see p. 252). The beginning word replaces another word: the subject (*He is the person who called*), an object of a verb or preposition (*He is the person whom I mentioned*), or a preposition and pronoun (*He knows the office where [in which] the conference will occur*).

Do not state the word that *who, whom,* and so on replace in an adjective clause:

Faulty   The technician *whom* the test depended on her was burned. [*Whom* should replace *her.*]

Revised   The technician *whom* the test depended on was burned.

Adjective clauses beginning with *where* or *when* do not need an adverb such as *there* or *then:*

Faulty   Gases escaped at a moment when the technician was unprepared then.

Revised   Gases escaped at a moment when the technician was unprepared.

 22b | Match subjects and predicates in meaning.

In a sentence with mixed meaning, the subject is said to be or do something illogical. Such a mixture is sometimes called **faulty predication** because the predicate conflicts with the subject.

Illogical equation with *be*

When a form of *be* connects a subject and a word that describes the subject (a complement), the subject and complement must be logically related:

Mixed   A compromise between the city and the country would be the ideal place to live.

Revised   A community that offered the best qualities of both city and country would be the ideal place to live.

Is when, is where

Definitions require nouns on both sides of *be.* Definition clauses beginning with *when* or *where* are common in speech but should be avoided in writing:

Mixed   An examination is when you are tested on what you know.

Revised   An examination is a test of what you know.

Reason is because

The commonly heard construction *reason is because* is redundant since *because* means "for the reason that":

Mixed   The reason the temple requests donations is because the school needs expansion.

Revised   The <u>reason</u> the temple requests donations <u>is that</u> the school needs expansion.

Revised   The temple requests donations <u>because</u> the school needs expansion.

Other mixed meanings

Mismatched subjects and predicates are not confined to sentences with *be:*

Mixed   The <u>use</u> of emission controls <u>was created</u> to reduce air pollution.

Revised   Emission <u>controls were created</u> to reduce air pollution.

Exercise 22.1   Revising: Sentences mixed in grammar or meaning

Revise the following sentences so that their parts fit together both in grammar and in meaning. Each item has more than one possible answer.

Example:

When they found out how expensive pianos are is why they were discouraged.

They were discouraged <u>because</u> they found out how expensive pianos are.

When they found out how expensive pianos are, <u>they</u> were discouraged.

1. A hurricane is when the winds in a tropical depression rotate counterclockwise at more than seventy-four miles per hour.
2. Because hurricanes can destroy so many lives and so much property is why people fear them.
3. Through high winds, storm surge, floods, and tornadoes is how a hurricane can kill thousands of people.
4. Many scientists observe that hurricanes in recent years they have become more ferocious and destructive.
5. However, in the last half-century, with improved communications systems and weather satellites have made hurricanes less deadly.

Exercise 22.2   Revising: Repeated sentence parts   (CULTURE LANGUAGE)

Revise the following sentences to eliminate any unnecessary repetition of sentence parts.

Example:

Over 87 percent of Americans they have heard of global warming.

Over 87 percent of <u>Americans have</u> heard of global warming.

1. Global warming it is caused by the gradual erosion of the ozone layer that protects the earth from the sun.
2. Scientists who study this problem they say that the primary causes of erosion are the use of fossil fuels and the reduction of forests.
3. Many nonscientists they mistakenly believe that aerosol spray cans are the primary cause of erosion.

ANSWERS: EXERCISE 22.1

Possible answers

1. A hurricane <u>occurs</u> when the winds in a tropical depression rotate counterclockwise at more than seventy-four miles per hour.
2. Because hurricanes can destroy so many lives and so much proper<u>ty, p</u>eople fear them.
3. Through high winds, storm surge, floods, and tornadoe<u>s, a</u> hurricane can kill thousands of people.
4. Many scientists observe that hurricanes in recent <u>years have</u> become more ferocious and destructive.
5. However, in the last <u>half-century, improved</u> communications systems and weather satellites have made hurricanes less deadly.

ANSWERS: EXERCISE 22.2

1. <u>Global warming is</u> caused by the gradual erosion of the ozone layer that protects the earth from the sun.
2. Scientists who study this <u>problem say</u> that the primary causes of erosion are the use of fossil fuels and the reduction of forests.
3. Many <u>nonscientists mistakenly</u> believe that aerosol spray cans are the primary cause of erosion.
4. One scientist whom others <u>respect argues</u> that Americans have effectively reduced their use of aerosol sprays.
5. He argues that we will stop global warming only when the public learns the real cause<u>s.</u>

4. One scientist whom others respect him argues that Americans have effectively reduced their use of aerosol sprays.
5. He argues that we will stop global warming only when the public learns the real causes then.

———— Incomplete Sentences ————

The most serious kind of incomplete sentence is the fragment (see Chapter 17). But sentences are also incomplete when they omit one or more words needed for clarity.

Grammar checkers A grammar checker will not flag most kinds of incomplete sentences discussed in this section.

22c	**Omissions from compound constructions should be consistent with grammar and idiom.**

In both speech and writing, we commonly omit words not necessary for meaning, such as those bracketed in the examples below. Notice that all the sentences contain compound constructions (see p. 256):

By 2015 automobile-emission standards will be tougher, and by 2020 [automobile-emission standards will be] tougher still.

Some cars run on electricity and some [run] on methane or another alternative fuel.

Environmentalists have hopes for alternative fuels and [for] public transportation.

Such omissions are possible only when you omit words that are common to all the parts of a compound construction. When the parts differ in either grammar or idiom, all words must be included in all parts:

One new car <u>gets</u> eighty miles per gallon of gasoline; some old cars <u>get</u> as little as five miles per gallon. [One verb is singular, the other plural.]

Environmentalists <u>were</u> invited to submit proposals and <u>were</u> eager to do so. [Each *were* has a different grammatical function: the first is a helping verb; the second is a linking verb.]

They believe <u>in</u> and work <u>for</u> fuel conservation. [Idiom requires different prepositions with *believe* and *work*.]

In the sentence *My brother and friend moved to Dallas*, the omission of *my* before *friend* indicates that *brother* and *friend* are the same person. If two different persons are meant, the modifier or article must be repeated: *My brother and my friend moved to Dallas*.

(See pp. 518–19 for a list of English idioms with prepositions and pp. 398–401 for a discussion of grammatical parallelism.)

22d All comparisons should be complete and logical.

Comparisons make statements about the relation between two or more things, as in *Dogs are more intelligent than cats.*

1 State a comparison fully enough to ensure clarity.

Unclear   Automakers worry about their industry more than environmentalists.

Clear   Automakers worry about their industry more than environmentalists <u>do</u>.

Clear   Automakers worry about their industry more than <u>they worry about</u> environmentalists.

2 The items being compared should in fact be comparable.

Illogical   The cost of a hybrid car can be greater than a gasoline-powered car. [Illogically compares a cost and a car.]

Revised   The cost of a hybrid car can be greater than <u>the cost of</u> [or <u>that of</u>] a gasoline-powered car.

3 Use *any* or *any other* appropriately in comparisons.

Comparing a person or thing with all others in the same group creates two units: (1) the individual person or thing and (2) all *other* persons or things in the group. The two units need to be distinguished:

Illogical   Los Angeles is larger than <u>any</u> city in California. [The sentence seems to say that Los Angeles is larger than itself.]

Logical   Los Angeles is larger than <u>any other</u> city in California.

Comparing a person or thing with the members of a *different* group assumes separate units to begin with. The two units do not need to be distinguished with *other:*

Illogical   Los Angeles is larger than <u>any other</u> city in Canada. [Canadian cities are a group to which Los Angeles does not belong.]

Logical   Los Angeles is larger than <u>any</u> city in Canada.

4 Comparisons should state what is being compared.

Brand X gets clothes <u>whiter</u>. [Whiter than what?]

Brand Y is so much <u>better</u>. [Better than what?]

22e Include all needed prepositions, articles, and other words.

In haste or carelessness we sometimes omit small words such as prepositions and articles that are needed for clarity:

Incomplete   Regular payroll deductions are a type painless savings. You hardly notice missing amounts, and after period of years the contributions can add a large total.

Revised   Regular payroll deductions are a type of painless savings. You hardly notice the missing amounts, and after a period of years the contributions can add up to a large total.

Be careful not to omit *that* when the omission is confusing:

Incomplete   The personnel director expects many employees will benefit from the plan. [*Many employees* seems to be the object of *expects.*]

Revised   The personnel director expects that many employees will benefit from the plan.

Attentive proofreading is the best insurance against the kinds of omissions described in this section. *Proofread all your papers carefully.* See page 66 for tips.

⟨CULTURE LANGUAGE⟩ If your native language or dialect is not standard American English, you may have difficulty knowing when to use the English articles *a, an,* and *the.* For guidelines on using articles, see pages 322–25.

Exercise 22.3   Revising: Incomplete sentences

Revise the following sentences so that they are complete, logical, and clear. Some items have more than one possible answer.

Example:
Our house is closer to the bank than the subway stop.
Our house is closer to the bank than it is to the subway stop.
Our house is closer to the bank than the subway stop is.

1. The first ice cream, eaten in China in about 2000 BC, was more lumpy than the modern era.
2. The Chinese made their ice cream of milk, spices, and overcooked rice and packed in snow to solidify.
3. In the fourteenth century ice milk and fruit ices appeared in Italy and the tables of the wealthy.
4. At her wedding in 1533 to the king of France, Catherine de Médicis offered more flavors of fruit ices than any hostess offered.
5. Modern sherbets resemble her ices; modern ice cream her soft dessert of thick, sweetened cream.

Exercise 22.4   Revising: Mixed and incomplete sentences

Revise the following paragraph to eliminate mixed or incomplete constructions.

The Hancock Tower in Boston is thin mirror-glass slab that rises almost eight hundred feet. When it was being constructed was when its windows began cracking, and some fell crashing to the ground. In order to minimize risks is why the architects and owners replaced over a third

Exercises 22.3 and 22.4 work well as an extended group project. Encourage groups to experiment with alternate responses, and ask each group to present any problem points they encountered as well as their successful responses to one or more sections.

ANSWERS: EXERCISE 22.3
Possible answers

1. The first ice cream, eaten in China in about 2000 BC, was more lumpy than ice cream in [*or* that in] the modern era.
2. The Chinese made their ice cream of milk, spices, and overcooked rice and packed it in snow to solidify.
3. In the fourteenth century ice milk and fruit ices appeared in Italy and on the tables of the wealthy.
4. At her wedding in 1533 to the King of France, Catherine de Médicis offered more flavors of fruit ices than any other hostess offered.
5. Modern sherbets resemble her ices; modern ice cream resembles her soft dessert of thick, sweetened cream.

ANSWERS: EXERCISE 22.4
Possible answers

The Hancock Tower in Boston is a thin mirror-glass slab that rises almost eight hundred feet. When it was being constructed, its windows began cracking, and some fell crashing to the ground. In order to minimize risks, the architects and owners replaced over a third of the huge windows with plywood until the problem could be found and solved. With its plywood sheath, the building was homelier than any other skyscraper, the butt of many jokes. Eventually, however, it was discovered that the windows cracked because the joint between the double panes of glass was too rigid. Thicker single-pane windows were installed, and the silly plywood building crystallized into a reflective jewel.

ANSWERS: EXERCISE ON CHAPTERS 17–22

Possible answers

Many people who are physically challenged <u>have</u> accomplished much, which proves that they are not "handicapped." Confined to wheelchairs, Bob Sampson and Stephen Hawking <u>forged</u> <u>successful careers</u>. Despite <u>his</u> muscular dystrophy, <u>Sampson</u> earned a law degree. He also worked for United Airlines for more than thirty years. Stephen Hawking <u>is</u> most famous for his book *A Brief History of Time*. <u>Hawking is</u> unable to speak, <u>but his</u> voice synthesizer allows him to dictate <u>his</u> books, conduct public lectures, <u>and</u> teach mathematics classes at Cambridge University.

Franklin D. Roosevelt, Ann Adams, and Itzhak Perlman all refused <u>to</u> let polio destroy their lives. Indeed, <u>as President</u>, Roosevelt led the United States during two of the worst periods of its history: the Great Depression and World War II. Roosevelt inspired hope and determination in the American people, <u>reassuring them with his</u> <u>strong, clear voice</u>. Ann Adams, who was talented in art before polio paralyzed her, knew she had to continue to be <u>an artist</u>. Having retrained herself to draw with a pencil grasped in her teeth, <u>she</u> produced sketches of children and pets. <u>These</u> <u>drawings</u> were turned into greeting cards <u>whose</u> <u>profits</u> sustained her. Roosevelt and Adams were stricken with polio when they were adults; Itzhak Perlman <u>was stricken</u> when <u>he was</u> a child. He was unable to play sports; instead, he studied the violin. <u>Now</u> many think he is greater than any other violinist in the world.

Like Perlman, many physically challenged individuals turn to the arts. Perhaps <u>they do so be</u>cause [*or:* the reason is that] the <u>joy of artistic</u> achievement compensates for other pleasures they cannot experience. Stevie Wonder, José Feliciano, and Andrea Bocelli all express <u>their souls</u> <u>through their music</u>. Although <u>they are</u> unable to see physically, their music reveals how well they <u>truly</u> see. Hearing impairment struck Ludwig van Beethoven and Marlee Matlin, <u>but</u> it did not stop them from developing their talents. Already a successful composer, <u>Beethoven wrote</u> many of his most powerful pieces after he became deaf. Similarly, Matlin has had excellent acting roles in movies, plays, and television programs; indeed, she won an Oscar for *Children of a Lesser God*. She encourages others to develop their abilities, and <u>she has inspired</u> many hearing-impaired actors.

the huge windows with plywood until the problem could be found and solved. With its plywood sheath, the building was homelier than any skyscraper, the butt of many jokes. Eventually, however, it was discovered that the reason the windows cracked was because joint between the double panes of glass was too rigid. The solution of thicker single-pane windows was installed, and the silly plywood building crystallized into reflective jewel.

Exercise on Chapters 17–22   Revising: Clear sentences

Clarify meaning in the following paragraphs by revising sentence fragments, comma splices, fused sentences, problems with pronoun reference, awkward shifts, misplaced and dangling modifiers, and mixed and incomplete sentences. Most errors can be corrected in more than one way.

Many people who are physically challenged. They have accomplished much. Which proves that they are not "handicapped." Confined to wheelchairs, successful careers were forged by Bob Sampson and Stephen Hawking. Despite Sampson's muscular dystrophy, he earned a law degree he also worked for United Airlines for more than thirty years. Stephen Hawking most famous for his book *A Brief History of Time*. Unable to speak, Hawking's voice synthesizer allows him to dictate his books and conduct public lectures. And teach mathematics classes at Cambridge University.

Franklin D. Roosevelt, Ann Adams, and Itzhak Perlman all refused let polio destroy their lives. Indeed, Roosevelt led the United States during two of the worst periods of its history as President. The Great Depression and World War II. Reassured by his strong, firm voice, Roosevelt inspired hope and determination in the American people. Ann Adams, who was talented in art before polio paralyzed her, knew she had to continue to be one. Having retrained herself to draw with a pencil grasped in her teeth. She produces sketches of children and pets. That were turned into greeting cards. The profits from the cards sustained her. Roosevelt and Adams were stricken with polio when they were adults; Itzhak Perlman when a child. He was unable to play sports, instead he studied the violin, now many think he is greater than any violinist in the world.

Like Perlman, many physically challenged individuals turn to the arts. Perhaps the reason is because the joy of artistic achievement compensates for other pleasures they cannot experience. Stevie Wonder, José Feliciano, and Andrea Bocelli all express, through their music, their souls. Although unable to see physically, their music reveals truly how well they see. Hearing impairment struck Ludwig van Beethoven and Marlee Matlin it did not stop them from developing their talents. Already a successful composer, many of Beethoven's most powerful pieces were written after he became deaf. Similarly, Matlin has had excellent acting roles in movies, plays, and television programs, indeed she won an Oscar for *Children of a Lesser God*. She encourages others to develop their ability, and many hearing-impaired actors have been inspired by her.

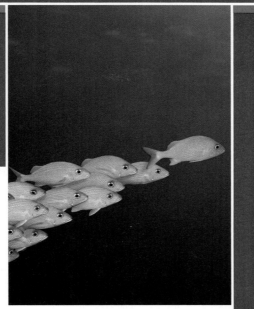

PART **5**

Effective Sentences

23 Emphasizing Ideas

24 Using Coordination and Subordination

25 Using Parallelism

26 Achieving Variety

This chapter looks at two ways to achieve emphasis within sentences: by the distribution of information and by the choice of strategies to create specific effects. The opening sections consider subjects and verbs as the heart of sentences and the importance of beginnings and endings. Additional special features of the chapter include its treatment of cumulative and periodic sentences and discussions that stress the rhetorical effect of each sentence pattern. The exercises are designed to help students feel comfortable using these patterns in their writing. Most students benefit from some work with these basic ways of controlling emphasis as well as from discussion of conciseness (23f). Students who have problems with sentence structure, however, may have more difficulty with the effective uses of repetition (23d) and separation (23e) for emphasis.

23
Emphasizing Ideas

When you emphasize the main ideas in your sentences, you hold and channel readers' attention.

Grammar checkers A grammar checker may spot some problems with emphasis, such as nouns made from verbs, passive voice, wordy phrases, and long sentences that may also be flabby and unemphatic. However, no checker can help you identify the important ideas in your sentences or determine whether those ideas receive appropriate emphasis.

Ways to emphasize ideas

- Use the subjects and verbs of sentences to state key actors and actions (below).
- Use the beginnings and endings of sentences to pace and stress information (p. 380).
- Arrange series items in order of increasing importance (p. 383).
- Use an occasional balanced sentence (p. 383).
- Carefully repeat key words and phrases (p. 384).
- Set off important ideas with punctuation (p. 385).
- Write concisely (p. 386).

23a | Using subjects and verbs effectively

The heart of every sentence is its subject, which usually names the actor, and its predicate verb, which usually specifies the subject's action: *Children* [subject] *grow* [verb]. When these elements do not identify the sentence's key actor and action, readers must find that information elsewhere and the sentence may be wordy and unemphatic.

In the following sentences, the subjects and verbs are underlined.

mycomplab

Visit *mycomplab.com* for more resources and exercises on emphasis.

| Unemphatic | The <u>intention</u> of the company <u>was</u> to expand its workforce. A <u>proposal</u> <u>was</u> also <u>made</u> to diversify the backgrounds and abilities of employees. |

These sentences are unemphatic because their key ideas do not appear in their subjects and verbs. Revised, the sentences are not only clearer but more concise:

| Revised | The <u>company</u> <u>intended</u> to expand its workforce. It also <u>proposed</u> to diversify the backgrounds and abilities of employees. |

The constructions below usually drain meaning from a sentence's subject and verb.

Nouns made from verbs

Nouns made from verbs can obscure the key actions of sentences and add words. These nouns include *intention* (from *intend*), *proposal* (from *propose*), *decision* (from *decide*), *expectation* (from *expect*), *persistence* (from *persist*), *argument* (from *argue*), and *inclusion* (from *include*).

| Unemphatic | After the company made a <u>decision</u> to hire more workers with disabilities, its next <u>step</u> was the <u>construction</u> of wheelchair ramps and other facilities. |
| Revised | After the company <u>decided</u> to hire more workers with disabilities, it next <u>constructed</u> wheelchair ramps and other facilities. |

Weak verbs

Weak verbs, such as *made* and *was* in the unemphatic sentence above, tend to stall sentences just where they should be moving and often bury key actions:

| Unemphatic | The company <u>is</u> now the leader among businesses in complying with the 1990 Americans with Disabilities Act. Its officers <u>make</u> speeches on the act to business groups. |
| Revised | The company now <u>leads</u> other businesses in complying with the 1990 Americans with Disabilities Act. Its officers <u>speak</u> on the act to business groups. |

Passive voice

Verbs in the passive voice state actions received by, not performed by, their subjects. Thus the passive de-emphasizes the true actor of the sentence, sometimes omitting it entirely. Generally, prefer the active voice, in which the subject performs the verb's action. (See also pp. 298–300.)

RESOURCES AND IDEAS

An understanding of the roles of topics and comments and of the possible relationships of old and new information can be very useful for writers seeking greater clarity and more effective emphasis in their writing. To supplement the discussion in this section of the handbook you may wish to turn to several excellent texts:

Kolln, Martha J. *Rhetorical Grammar: Grammatical Choices, Rhetorical Effects.* 5th ed. New York: Longman, 2007. Print. Kolln discusses many grammar issues and the rhetorical impact they have on writing.

Lanham, Richard. *Analyzing Prose.* 2nd ed. London: Continuum, 2003. Print. Lanham offers extensive advice on revising for stylistic effect.

Micciche, Laura R. "Making a Case for Rhetorical Grammar." *College Composition and Communication* 55.4 (2004): 716–37. Print. Micciche attempts to reconcile liberatory pedagogy, which usually ignores or downplays the importance of grammar, with the teaching of grammar. She argues for teaching grammar by discussing the rhetorical impact of sentence-level choices.

Vande Koppel, William J. *Clear and Coherent Prose.* Glenview: Scott Foresman, 1989. Print.

Williams, Joseph M. *Style: Lessons in Clarity and Grace.* 9th ed. New York: Longman, 2007. Print.

Unemphatic	The 1990 <u>law is seen</u> by most businesses as fair, but the costs of complying <u>have</u> sometimes <u>been objected to.</u>
Revised	Most <u>businesses see</u> the 1990 law as fair, but <u>some have objected to</u> the costs of complying.

ANSWERS: EXERCISE 23.1

Possible answers

1. <u>Many heroes helped</u> to emancipate the slaves.
2. <u>Harriet Tubman</u>, an escaped slave herself, <u>guided</u> hundreds of other slaves to freedom on the Underground Railroad.
3. <u>Tubman risked</u> a return to slavery or possible death.
4. During the Civil War <u>she</u> also <u>carried</u> information from the South to the North.
5. After the war <u>Tubman helped</u> needy former slaves by raising money for refugees.

COLLABORATIVE LEARNING

EMPHASIS IN CONTEXT

After completing Exercise 23.1 either individually or in groups, ask students to review a piece of each other's writing for sentences in which their noun or verb choices may obscure key actors and actions. Writers should then revise the selected sentences and share their revisions with the group to receive further suggestions.

Exercise 23.1 Revising: Emphasis of subjects and verbs

Rewrite the following sentences so that their subjects and verbs identify their key actors and actions.

Example:

The issue of students making a competition over grades is a reason why their focus on learning may be lost.

<u>Students</u> who compete over grades <u>may lose</u> their focus on learning.

1. The work of many heroes was crucial in helping to emancipate the slaves.
2. The contribution of Harriet Tubman, an escaped slave herself, included the guidance of hundreds of other slaves to freedom on the Underground Railroad.
3. A return to slavery was risked by Tubman or possibly death.
4. During the Civil War she was also a carrier of information from the South to the North.
5. After the war needy former slaves were helped by Tubman's raising of money for refugees.

23b Using sentence beginnings and endings

Readers automatically seek a writer's principal meaning in the main clause of a sentence—essentially, in the subject that names the actor and the verb that usually specifies the action (see the preceding pages). Thus you can help readers understand your intended meaning by controlling the information in your subjects and the relation of the main clause to any modifiers attached to it.

Old and new information

Generally, readers expect the beginning of a sentence to contain information that they already know or that you have already introduced. They then look to the sentence ending for new information. In the unemphatic passage below, the second and third sentences both begin with new topics, while the old topics appear at the ends of the sentences. The pattern of the passage is A→B. C→B. D→A.

Unemphatic	$\overset{A}{\underline{Education}}$ often means $\overset{B}{\underline{controversy}}$ these days, with rising costs and constant complaints about its inadequacies. But the $\overset{C}{\underline{value}}$ of schooling should not be obscured by the

controversy. The single best <u>means</u> of economic advancement, despite its shortcomings, remains <u>education</u>.

In the more emphatic revision, old information begins each sentence and new information ends the sentence. The passage follows
the pattern A→B. B→C. A→D.

> Revised   <u>Education</u> often means <u>controversy</u> these days, with rising
> costs and constant complaints about its inadequacies.
> But the <u>controversy</u> should not obscure the <u>value</u> of
> schooling. <u>Education</u> remains, despite its shortcomings,
> the single best means of economic <u>advancement</u>.

Cumulative and periodic sentences

You can call attention to information by placing it first or last
in a sentence, reserving the middle for incidentals:

> Unemphatic   Education remains the single best means of economic
> advancement, despite its shortcomings. [Emphasizes
> shortcomings.]
>
> Revised   Despite its shortcomings, education remains the single
> best means of economic advancement. [Emphasizes ad-
> vancement more than shortcomings.]
>
> Revised   Education remains, despite its shortcomings, the single
> best means of economic advancement. [De-emphasizes
> shortcomings.]

Many sentences begin with the main clause and then add modifiers to explain, amplify, or illustrate it. Such sentences are called
cumulative (because they accumulate information as they proceed)
or **loose** (because they are not tightly structured). They parallel the
way we naturally think.

> Cumulative   Education has no equal in opening minds, instilling val-
> ues, and creating opportunities.
>
> Cumulative   Most of the Great American Desert is made up of bare
> rock, rugged cliffs, mesas, canyons, mountains, sepa-
> rated from one another by broad flat basins covered with
> sunbaked mud and alkali, supporting a sparse and mea-
> sured growth of sagebrush or creosote or saltbush, de-
> pending on location and elevation.
>
> —Edward Abbey

The opposite kind of sentence, called **periodic,** saves the main
clause until just before the end (the period) of the sentence. Everything before the main clause points toward it.

**MEMORY AID: THINKING ABOUT
CUMULATIVE AND PERIODIC SENTENCES**

The following examples may help students
remember how to formulate and how to distinguish between cumulative and periodic sentences:

1. *Cumulative sentences:* A cumulative sentence is created much like a portrait, detail by detail. The diver (for example) paused at the end of
the board, gazing down at the smooth, greenish-
blue water meters below, his arms stretched out
in front, his legs trembling slightly with anticipation and tension, drops of water falling from his
fingertips into the swirling wind filled with mur-
murs from the crowd below and behind his solitary figure.

2. *Periodic sentences:* In a form that parallels
the dramatic movement of a tragedy, the meaning of a periodic sentence is built from words and
phrases preceding the main clause. In Shakespeare's play *Othello*, step by step, with slowly
gathering force and filled with increasing tension
and foreboding, the opening scenes create a situation that makes the tragic events inevitable.

RESOURCES AND IDEAS

Christensen, Francis. "A Generative Rhetoric of the Sentence." *Notes Toward a New Rhetoric: Nine Essays for Teachers*. Ed. Francis Christensen and Bonniejean Christensen. 3rd ed. Bangor: Booklocker.com, 2007, 19–38. Print. Christensen demonstrates how to analyze the levels of generality in sentences and discusses and illustrates the structure of the cumulative sentence.

COLLABORATIVE LEARNING

Ask students to complete Exercise 23.2 individually and then to compare and revise their responses in groups. Have each group present one of their responses to the class, and encourage the other groups to call attention to places where they created an alternative response.

ANSWERS: EXERCISE 23.2

Possible answers

1. Pat Taylor strode into the packed room, greeting students called "Taylor's Kids" and nodding to their parents and teachers.
2. This wealthy Louisiana oilman had promised his "Kids" free college educations because he was determined to make higher education available to all qualified but disadvantaged students.
3. The students welcomed Taylor, their voices singing "You Are the Wind Beneath My Wings," their faces flashing with self-confidence.
4. They had thought a college education was beyond their dreams, seeming too costly and too demanding.
5. To help ease the costs and demands of getting to college, Taylor created a bold plan of scholarships, tutoring, and counseling.

Periodic	In opening minds, instilling values, and creating opportunities, education has no equal.
Periodic	With people from all over the world—Korean doctors, Jamaican cricket players, Vietnamese engineers, Haitian cabdrivers, Chinese athletes, Indian grocers—the American mosaic is continually changing.

The periodic sentence creates suspense for readers by reserving important information for the end. But readers should already have an idea of the sentence's subject—because it was discussed or introduced in the preceding sentence—so that they know what the opening modifiers describe. A variation of the periodic sentence names the subject at the beginning, follows it with a modifier, and then completes the main clause:

Dick Hayne, who works in jeans and loafers and likes to let a question cure in the air for a while before answering it, bears all the markings of what his generation used to call a laid-back kind of guy.

　　　　　　　　　　　　　　　　　—George Rush

Exercise 23.2　Sentence combining: Beginnings and endings

Locate the main idea in each group of sentences below. Then combine each group into a single sentence that emphasizes that idea by placing it at the beginning or the end. For sentences 2–5, determine the position of the main idea by considering its relation to the previous sentences: if the main idea picks up a topic that's already been introduced, place it at the beginning; if it adds new information, place it at the end.

Example:

The storm blew roofs off buildings. It caused extensive damage. It knocked down trees. It severed power lines.

Main idea at beginning: The storm caused extensive damage, blowing roofs off buildings, knocking down trees, and severing power lines.

Main idea at end: Blowing roofs off buildings, knocking down trees, and severing power lines, the storm caused extensive damage.

1. Pat Taylor strode into the room. The room was packed. He greeted students called "Taylor's Kids." He nodded to their parents and teachers.
2. This was a wealthy Louisiana oilman. He had promised his "Kids" free college educations. He was determined to make higher education available to all qualified but disadvantaged students.
3. The students welcomed Taylor. Their voices joined in singing. They sang "You Are the Wind Beneath My Wings." Their faces beamed with hope. Their eyes flashed with self-confidence.
4. The students had thought a college education was beyond their dreams. It seemed too costly. It seemed too demanding.

5. Taylor had to ease the costs and the demands of getting to college. He created a bold plan. The plan consisted of scholarships, tutoring, and counseling.

 23c Arranging parallel elements effectively

Series

With parallelism, you use similar grammatical structures for ideas linked by *and, but,* and similar words: *Blustery winds and upturned leaves often signal thunderstorms.* (See Chapter 25.) In addition, you should arrange the parallel ideas in order of their importance:

Unemphatic	The storm ripped the roofs off several buildings, killed ten people, and knocked down many trees in town. [Buries the most serious damage—deaths—in the middle.]
Emphatic	The storm knocked down many trees in town, ripped the roofs off several buildings, and killed ten people. [Arranges items in order of increasing importance.]

You may want to use an unexpected item at the end of a series for humor or for another special effect:

Early to bed and early to rise makes a man healthy, wealthy, and dead.
—James Thurber

But be careful when creating such a series. The following series seems thoughtlessly random rather than intentionally humorous:

Unemphatic	The painting has subdued tone, intense feeling, and a height of about three feet.
Emphatic	The painting, about three feet high, has subdued tone and intense feeling.

Balanced sentences

A sentence is **balanced** when its clauses are parallel—that is, matched in grammatical structure (Chapter 25). When used carefully, balanced sentences can be especially effective in alerting readers to a strong comparison between two ideas. Read the following examples aloud to hear their rhythm.

The fickleness of the women I love is equalled only by the infernal constancy of the women who love me. —George Bernard Shaw

In a pure balanced sentence two main clauses are exactly parallel: they match item for item.

Scratch a lover, and find a foe. —Dorothy Parker

ANSWERS: EXERCISE 23.3

Possible answers

1. Remembering her days as a "conductor" on the Underground Railroad made Harriet Tubman proud, but <u>remembering her years as a slave made her angry</u>.
2. Tubman wanted freedom regardless of personal danger, whereas <u>her husband, John, wanted personal safety regardless of freedom</u>.
3. Tubman proved her fearlessness in many ways: <u>she disobeyed John's order not to run away</u>, she was a spy for the North during the Civil War, <u>and she led hundreds of other slaves to freedom</u>.
4. To conduct slaves north to freedom, Tubman risked <u>being caught by Southern patrollers, being returned to slavery, and being hanged for a huge reward</u>.
5. After the war Tubman worked tirelessly for civil rights and women's suffrage; <u>she also raised money for homes for needy former slaves</u>.

But the term is commonly applied to sentences that are only approximately parallel or that have only some parallel parts:

> If thought corrupts language, language can also corrupt thought.
> —George Orwell

> As the traveler who has once been from home is wiser than he who has never left his own doorstep, so a knowledge of one other culture should sharpen our ability to scrutinize more steadily, to appreciate more lovingly, our own.
> —Margaret Mead

Exercise 23.3 Revising: Series and balanced elements

Revise the following sentences so that elements in a series or balanced elements are arranged to give maximum emphasis to main ideas.

Example:

The campers were stranded without matches, without food or water, and without a tent.

The campers were stranded without matches, without a tent, and without food or water.

1. Remembering her days as a "conductor" on the Underground Railroad made Harriet Tubman proud, but she got angry when she remembered her years as a slave.
2. Tubman wanted freedom regardless of personal danger, whereas for her husband, John, personal safety was more important than freedom.
3. Tubman proved her fearlessness in many ways: she led hundreds of other slaves to freedom, she was a spy for the North during the Civil War, and she disobeyed John's order not to run away.
4. To conduct slaves north to freedom, Tubman risked being returned to slavery, being hanged for a huge reward, and being caught by Southern patrollers.
5. After the war Tubman worked tirelessly for civil rights and women's suffrage; raising money for homes for needy former slaves was something else she did.

23d Repeating ideas

Repetition of words and phrases often clutters and weakens sentences, as discussed on pages 527–28. But carefully planned repetition can be an effective means of emphasis. Such repetition often combines with parallelism. It may occur in a series of sentences (see p. 85) or in a series of words, phrases, or clauses within a sentence, as in the following examples:

> There is something uneasy in the Los Angeles air this afternoon, some unnatural stillness, some tension.
> —Joan Didion

> We have the tools, all the tools—we are suffocating in tools—but we cannot find the actual wood to work or even the actual hand to work it.
> —Archibald MacLeish

23e Separating ideas

When you save important information for the end of a sentence, you can emphasize it even more by setting it off from the rest of the sentence, as in the second example below:

> Mothers and housewives are the only workers who do not have regular time off, so they are the great vacationless class.

> Mothers and housewives are the only workers who do not have regular time off. They are the great vacationless class.
> —Anne Morrow Lindbergh

You can vary the degree of emphasis by varying the extent to which you separate one idea from the others. A semicolon provides more separation than a comma, and a period provides still more separation. Compare the following sentences:

> Most of the reading which is praised for itself is neither literary nor intellectual, but narcotic.

> Most of the reading which is praised for itself is neither literary nor intellectual; it is narcotic.

> Most of the reading which is praised for itself is neither literary nor intellectual. It is narcotic.   —Donald Hall

Sometimes a dash or a pair of dashes will isolate and thus emphasize a part of a statement (see also pp. 470–71):

> His schemes were always elaborate, ingenious, and exciting—and wholly impractical.

> Athletics—that is, winning athletics—has become a profitable university operation.

Exercise 23.4 Emphasizing with repetition or separation

Emphasize the main idea in each of the following sentences or groups of sentences by following the instructions in parentheses: either combine sentences so that parallelism and repetition stress the main idea, or place the main idea in a separate sentence. Each item has more than one possible answer.

Example:

> I try to listen to other people's opinions. When my mind is closed, I find that other opinions open it. And they can change my mind when it is wrong. (*Parallelism and repetition.*)

> I try to listen to other people's opinions, for they can open my mind when it is closed and they can change my mind when it is wrong.

1. One of the few worthwhile habits is daily reading. One can read for information. One can read for entertainment. Reading can give one a broader view of the world. (*Parallelism and repetition.*)

CLEAR THE CONFUSION

Choose a particularly confusing or unemphatic passage from a student essay, give it to student groups, and ask them to decide what devices covered in the chapter could be used to improve the passage. Ask them to make the changes as a group, and have a representative of each group write the revised passage on the board so that the class as a whole can compare the various revisions. This exercise works well in a wired classroom where responses can be posted to the course Web site for general discussion.

PRACTICE REVISING FOR CONCISENESS

Distribute to students a paragraph, possibly from a student paper or a Web site, that needs to be tightened. In their groups, have students revise the paragraph for conciseness using the tips in the "Ways to achieve conciseness" box. As a class, compare revised paragraphs either by reading the revisions aloud or by posting them on the course Web site.

2. Reading introduces new words. One encounters unfamiliar styles of expression through reading. (*Parallelism and repetition.*)
3. Students who read a great deal will more likely write vividly, coherently, and grammatically, for they will have learned from other authors. (*Separation.*)
4. Reading gives knowledge. One gets knowledge about other cultures. One will know about history and current events. One gains information about human nature. (*Parallelism and repetition.*)
5. As a result of reading, writers have more resources and more flexibility, and thus reading creates better writers. (*Separation.*)

23f Being concise

Conciseness—brevity of expression—aids emphasis no matter what the sentence structure. Unnecessary words detract from necessary words. They clutter sentences and obscure ideas.

Weak   In my opinion the competition in the area of grades is distracting. It distracts many students from their goal, which is to obtain an education that is good. There seems to be a belief among a few students that grades are more important than what is measured by them.

Emphatic   The competition for grades distracts many students from their goal of obtaining a good education. A few students seem to believe that grades are more important than what they measure.

Techniques for tightening sentences are listed in the following box. Some of these techniques appear earlier in this chapter. All of them are covered in Chapter 39 on writing concisely.

Ways to achieve conciseness

■ **Make the subject and verb of each sentence identify its actor and action** (pp. 378, 524):

Avoid nouns made from verbs.
Use strong verbs.
Rewrite the passive voice as active.

■ **Cut or shorten empty words or phrases** (p. 525):

Shorten filler phrases, such as *by virtue of the fact that.*
Cut all-purpose words, such as *area, factor.*
Cut unneeded qualifiers, such as *in my opinion, for the most part.*

■ **Cut unnecessary repetition** (p. 527).
■ **Reduce clauses to phrases and phrases to single words** (p. 528).

- **Avoid constructions beginning with** *there is, here is,* **or** *it is* (p. 529).
- **Combine sentences** (p. 529).
- **Cut or rewrite jargon** (p. 529).

Exercise 23.5 Revising: Conciseness

Revise the following sentences to make them more emphatic by eliminating wordiness.

Example:

The problem in this particular situation is that we owe more money than we can afford under present circumstances.

The problem is that we owe more money than we can afford.

1. As far as I am concerned, customers who are dining out in restaurants in our country must be wary of suggestive selling, so to speak.
2. In suggestive selling, diners are asked by the waiter to buy additional menu selections in addition to what was ordered by them.
3. For each item on the menu, there is another food that will naturally complement it.
4. For example, customers will be presented with the question of whether they want to order french fries along with a sandwich or whether they want to order a salad along with a steak dinner.
5. Due to the fact that customers often give in to suggestive selling, they often find that their restaurant meals are more costly than they had intended to pay.

Exercise 23.6 Revising: Emphasizing ideas

Drawing on the advice in this chapter, rewrite the following paragraph to emphasize main ideas and to de-emphasize less important information.

In preparing pasta, there is a requirement for common sense and imagination rather than for complicated recipes. The key to success in this area is fresh ingredients for the sauce and perfectly cooked pasta. The sauce may be made with just about any fresh fish, meat, cheese, herb, or vegetable. As for the pasta itself, it may be dried or fresh, although fresh pasta is usually more delicate and flavorful, as many experienced cooks find. Dried pasta is fine with zesty sauces; with light oil and cream sauces fresh pasta is the best choice. There is a difference in the cooking time for dried and fresh pasta, with dried pasta taking longer. It is important that the cook follow the package directions and that the pasta be tested before the cooking time is up. The pasta is done when the texture is neither tough nor mushy but *al dente,* or "firm to the bite," according to the Italians, who ought to know.

Note See page 413 for an exercise involving emphasis along with parallelism and other techniques for effective sentences.

Ask students to complete Exercise 23.5 in small groups and to present their most effective responses to the class.

ANSWERS: EXERCISE 23.5

Possible answers

1. <u>Customers in restaurants</u> must be wary of suggestive selling.
2. In suggestive selling, <u>the waiter asks diners</u> to <u>buy menu</u> selections <u>besides</u> what <u>they ordered.</u>
3. For each item on the menu, <u>another food will</u> naturally complement it.
4. For example, customers will <u>be asked</u> whether they <u>want french fries with</u> a sandwich <u>or a salad with</u> a steak dinner.
5. <u>Customers who</u> give in to suggestive <u>selling often</u> find that their restaurant meals <u>cost more</u> than they had intended to pay.

Have students work in groups to revise the paragraph in Exercise 23.6. Encourage each group to discuss various possible responses and to make a case for the effectiveness of their revision. Then have each group present their revised paragraph to the class either by writing on the blackboard or by posting them to the course Web site.

ANSWERS: EXERCISE 23.6

Possible revision

<u>Preparing pasta requires</u> common sense and imagination rather <u>than complicated</u> recipes. The key to <u>success is</u> fresh ingredients for the sauce and perfectly cooked pasta. The sauce <u>may contain</u> just about any fresh fish, meat, cheese, herb, or vegetable. <u>The pasta itself may</u> be dried or fresh, although <u>many experienced cooks find fresh pasta</u> more delicate and flavorful. Dried pasta is fine with zesty sauces; <u>fresh pasta is best</u> with light oil and cream sauces. <u>Dried pasta takes longer</u> to cook than fresh pasta does. <u>The cook should follow</u> the package directions <u>and should test</u> the pasta before the cooking time is up. <u>According to the Italians, who ought to know,</u> the pasta is done when the texture is neither tough nor mushy but *al dente,* or "firm to the bite."

HIGHLIGHTS

The material in this chapter emphasizes how writers can use coordination and subordination to relate ideas and distinguish central ideas from less important material. The opening section illustrates how coordination relates facts and ideas and then goes on to address the problems of excessive and faulty coordination. The second section follows a parallel pattern in discussing subordination, focusing on subordinate clauses. But since effective writing depends on a writer's ability to work with the whole range of subordinate structures, the uses of single words, appositives, and prepositional, verbal, and absolute phrases are also illustrated. The final section cautions briefly against the often unclear and misused connectors *like*, *while*, and *as*.

Included in this chapter are subsections on punctuating coordinated and subordinated elements, designed to help students not only punctuate correctly but also see punctuation as an instrument and extension of effective sentence structure. Coordination and subordination are strategies that can be enhanced by practicing sentence-combining techniques. Such practices work best if students are encouraged to work on them over the course of a semester, as this handbook recommends, rather than just in one unit or lesson. The exercises in this chapter ask students to revise sentences and longer passages and to combine sentences in ways that implement the range of strategies introduced in the chapter.

COLLABORATIVE LEARNING

COORDINATING FOR FUN

Have each small group write a paragraph or two made up of short declarative sentences. (Students often enjoy the opportunity to create humorously short sentences on a topic of their choice.) Groups then trade exercises and revise them using the sentence-combining techniques they have learned in this section.

24

Using Coordination and Subordination

When clearly written, your sentences show the relations between ideas and stress the more important ideas over the lesser ones. Two techniques can help you achieve such clarity:

- *Coordination* **shows that two or more elements in a sentence are equally important in meaning.** You signal coordination with words such as *and*, *but*, and *or*.

  equally important
  Car insurance is costly, but health insurance seems a luxury.

- *Subordination* **shows that some elements in a sentence are less important than other elements for your meaning.** Usually, the main idea appears in the main clause, and supporting information appears in single words, phrases, and subordinate clauses.

  less important (subordinate clause)   more important (main clause)
  Because accidents and thefts occur frequently, car insurance is costly.

Grammar checkers A grammar checker may spot some errors in punctuating coordinated and subordinated elements, and it can usually flag long sentences that may contain excessive coordination or subordination. But otherwise it can provide little help because it cannot recognize the relations among ideas in sentences.

24a Coordinating to relate equal ideas

By linking equally important information, you can emphasize the relations for readers. Compare the following passages:

String of simple sentences
We should not rely so heavily on oil. Coal and uranium are also overused. We have a substantial energy resource in the moving waters of our rivers.

---

mycomplab

Visit *mycomplab.com* for more resources and exercises on coordination and subordination.

Ways to coordinate information in sentences

- **Link main clauses with a comma and a coordinating conjunction:** *and, but, or, nor, for, so, yet* (p. 422).

  Independence Hall in Philadelphia is faithfully restored **,** but many years ago it was in bad shape.

- **Relate main clauses with a semicolon alone or a semicolon and a conjunctive adverb:** *however, indeed, thus,* etc. (pp. 445, 446).

  The building was standing **;** however, it suffered from neglect.

- **Within clauses, link words and phrases with a coordinating conjunction:** *and, but, or, nor* (pp. 256–57).

  The people and officials of the nation were indifferent to Independence Hall or took it for granted.

- **Link main clauses, words, or phrases with a correlative conjunction:** *both . . . and, not only . . . but also,* etc. (p. 257).

  People not only took the building for granted but also neglected it.

Smaller streams add to the total volume of water. The resource renews itself. Oil and coal are irreplaceable. Uranium is also irreplaceable. The cost of water does not increase much over time. The costs of coal, oil, and uranium rise dramatically.

Ideas coordinated

We should not rely so heavily on oil, coal, and uranium, for we have a substantial energy resource in the moving waters of our rivers and streams. Oil, coal, and uranium are irreplaceable and thus subject to dramatic cost increases; water, however, is self-renewing and more stable in cost.

The second passage is shorter and considerably easier to understand because it links coordinate ideas with the underlined words.

Punctuating coordinated words, phrases, and clauses

Most coordinated words, phrases, and subordinate clauses are not punctuated with commas (see pp. 439–40). The exceptions are items in a series and coordinate adjectives:

We rely heavily on coal, oil, and uranium. [A series; see p. 433.]
Dirty, unhealthy air is one result. [Coordinate adjectives; see pp. 433–34.]

In a sentence consisting of two main clauses, punctuation depends on whether a coordinating conjunction, a conjunctive adverb, or no connecting word links the clauses:

Oil is irreplaceable, but water is self-renewing. [See pp. 422–24.]
Oil is irreplaceable; however, water is self-renewing. [See p. 446.]
Oil is irreplaceable; water is self-renewing. [See p. 445.]

I'VE GOT A LITTLE LIST

You may wish to remind students that section 12d of the handbook contains a detailed discussion of coordinating conjunctions. If students make a simple list of the conjunctions and keep it on their computer where it is handy, they may find themselves becoming more aware of the words and their functions as they read and write:

and	or	for	yet
but	nor	so	

Another Little List

Section 12d of the handbook also contains a detailed discussion of conjunctive adverbs. You can help create awareness of conjunctive adverbs by asking students to make a list of the words and keep it in a convenient place on their computer. As they read and write later, students may pay greater attention to the conjunctive adverbs and their functions:

also	namely	anyway
next	besides	now
certainly	otherwise	finally
similarly	further	still
however	then	indeed
therefore	likewise	thus
meanwhile	undoubtedly	

MACRO PUNCTUATION

Many people (not just students) do not know that they must in some instances precede "however" with a semicolon rather than a comma. If your students make this mistake frequently, they can create a "macro" command in their word processor containing the keystrokes "; however" and press the macro function key instead of typing out the word "however." They will still need to check to see whether or not their sentence is properly punctuated.

COMPUTER ACTIVITY

MISSING INFORMATION

Have each student create a sentence using coordination. The sentence should have one piece of necessary information *omitted* so that the resulting coordination is illogical. Ask the student to send it around by e-mail or post it; the rest of the class can try to guess what information needs to be filled in.

CONJUNCTIVE MAD LIBS

Give one student in each group a short piece of writing from which all the conjunctive adverbs have been removed and replaced by blanks. That student asks other group members to supply conjunctive adverbs. As in the game "Mad Libs," the other students do not look at the page, so their choices are made randomly. After all the blanks have been filled, the first student reads the resulting, faulty essay aloud, and students collapse with laughter.

COLLABORATIVE LEARNING

Ask students to complete Exercises 24.1 and 24.2 individually and then to compare and revise their responses in small groups. You might ask each group to present a successful combination to the class and to discuss why it seems more effective.

ANSWERS: EXERCISE 24.1

Possible revisions

1. Many chronic misspellers do not have the time or the motivation to master spelling rules. They may rely on dictionaries to catch misspellings, but most dictionaries list words under their correct spellings. One kind of dictionary is designed for chronic misspellers. It lists each word under its common *mis*spellings and then provides the correct spelling and definition.

2. Henry Hudson was an English explorer, but he captained ships for the Dutch East India Company. On a voyage in 1610 he passed Greenland and sailed into a great bay in today's northern Canada. He thought he and his sailors could winter there, but the cold was terrible and food ran out. The sailors mutinied and cast Hudson and eight others adrift in a small boat. Hudson and his companions perished.

---

1 Using coordination effectively

A string of coordinated elements—especially main clauses—creates the same effect as a string of simple sentences: it obscures the relative importance of ideas and details.

Excessive coordination	The weeks leading up to the resignation of President Richard Nixon were eventful, and the Supreme Court and the Congress closed in on him, and the Senate Judiciary Committee voted to begin impeachment proceedings, and finally the President resigned on August 9, 1974.

Such a passage needs editing to stress the important points (underlined below) and to de-emphasize the less important information:

Revised	The weeks leading up to the resignation of President Richard Nixon were eventful, as the Supreme Court and the Congress closed in on him and the Senate Judiciary Committee voted to begin impeachment proceedings. Finally, the President resigned on August 9, 1974.

2 Coordinating logically

Coordinated sentence elements should be logically equal and related, and the relation between them should be the one expressed by the connecting word. If either principle is violated, the result is **faulty coordination.**

Faulty	John Stuart Mill was a nineteenth-century utilitarian, and he believed that actions should be judged by their usefulness or by the happiness they cause. [The two clauses are not separate and equal: the second expands on the first by explaining what a utilitarian such as Mill believed.]
Revised	John Stuart Mill, a nineteenth-century utilitarian, believed that actions should be judged by their usefulness or by the happiness they cause.
Faulty	Mill is recognized as a utilitarian, and he did not found the utilitarian school of philosophy. [The two clauses seem to contrast, requiring *but* or *yet* between them.]
Revised	Mill is recognized as a utilitarian, but he did not found the utilitarian school of philosophy.

Exercise 24.1 Sentence combining: Coordination

Combine sentences in the following passages to coordinate related ideas in the ways that seem most effective to you. You will have to supply coordinating conjunctions or conjunctive adverbs and the appropriate punctuation.

1. Many chronic misspellers do not have the time to master spelling rules. They may not have the motivation. They may rely on dictionaries to catch misspellings. Most dictionaries list words under their correct spellings. One kind of dictionary is designed for chronic

misspellers. It lists each word under its common *miss*spellings. It then provides the correct spelling. It also provides the definition.

2. Henry Hudson was an English explorer. He captained ships for the Dutch East India Company. On a voyage in 1610 he passed by Greenland. He sailed into a great bay in today's northern Canada. He thought he and his sailors could winter there. The cold was terrible. Food ran out. The sailors mutinied. The sailors cast Hudson adrift in a small boat. Eight others were also in the boat. Hudson and his companions perished.

Exercise 24.2 Revising: Excessive or faulty coordination

Revise the following sentences to eliminate excessive or faulty coordination. Relate ideas effectively by adding or subordinating information or by forming more than one sentence. Each item has more than one possible answer.

Example:

My dog barks, and I have to move out of my apartment.

Because my dog's barking <u>disturbs my neighbors</u>, I have to move out of my apartment.

1. Often soldiers admired their commanding officers, and they gave them nicknames, and these names frequently contained the word "old," but not all of the commanders were old.
2. General Thomas "Stonewall" Jackson was also called "Old Jack," and he was not yet forty years old.
3. Another Southern general in the Civil War was called "Old Pete," and his full name was James Longstreet.
4. The Union general Henry W. Halleck had a reputation as a good military strategist, and he was an expert on the work of a French military authority, Henri Jomini, and Halleck was called "Old Brains."
5. General William Henry Harrison won the Battle of Tippecanoe, and he received the nickname "Old Tippecanoe," and he used the name in his presidential campaign slogan "Tippecanoe and Tyler, Too," and he won the election in 1840, but he died of pneumonia a month after taking office.

24b Subordinating to distinguish main ideas

With **subordination** you use words or word groups to indicate that some ideas in a sentence are less important than the idea in the main clause. In the following sentence, it is difficult to tell what is most important:

| Excessive coordination | Computer prices have dropped, and production costs have dropped more slowly, and computer manufacturers have had to contend with shrinking profits. |

The following revision places the point of the sentence (shrinking profits) in the main clause and reduces the rest of the information to a modifier (underlined):

USING STUDENT WRITING

Ask students to share a paragraph or two from their drafts with the other members of their group. Group members should comment on the use of coordination and subordination and suggest places where more or less of either might aid the writer in achieving her or his purpose.

AVOIDING EXCESSIVE SUBORDINATION

Choose paragraphs from student essays that demonstrate overuse or faulty use of subordination, and distribute them to the class. Have students rewrite the paragraphs and then compare their versions in small groups to determine which are the most clear and effective revisions.

ANSWERS: EXERCISE 24.2

Possible answers

1. <u>Because</u> soldiers admired their commanding officers, <u>they often</u> gave them nicknames <u>containing</u> the word "old," <u>even though</u> not all of the commanders were old.
2. General Thomas "Stonewall" Jackson was also called "Old Jack," <u>although</u> he was not yet forty years old.
3. Another Southern general, <u>whose full name was James Longstreet</u>, was called "Old Pete."
4. The Union General Henry W. Halleck had a reputation as a good military strategist, and he was an expert on the work of a French military authority, Henri Jomini. <u>Therefore</u>, Halleck was called "Old Brains."
5. <u>After</u> General William Henry Harrison won a victory at the Battle of Tippecanoe, <u>he</u> received the nickname "Old Tippecanoe." <u>He</u> used the name in his presidential campaign slogan "Tippecanoe and Tyler, Too." <u>Although</u> he won the election in 1840, <u>he</u> died of pneumonia a month after taking office.

SCAVENGER HUNT

Ask students to hunt around on the Web for one example of each kind of subordinating structure (space or time, cause or effect, condition, concession, purpose, and identification). If your classroom is wired, you can do this exercise as a race during a class period, and have students post their examples (and the links to where they found them) to the rest of the class.

DISTINCTIONS BETWEEN SUBORDINATING WORDS

Some ESL students may understand the conceptual differences among words that subordinate according to space or time, cause or effect, condition, concession, purpose, and identification (see the list on p. 389). However, within each category, they may have a harder time knowing which word to use; so, for instance, they may use *although, as if, even though, though, despite, except for,* and *in spite of* interchangeably. Ask them to collect examples of proper use of each of these terms from their reading, and then discuss why each one works in its particular context.

RESOURCES AND IDEAS

On sentence combining

Connors, Robert J. "The Erasure of the Sentence." *College Composition and Communication* 52.1 (2001): 96–128. Print. Connors suggests that sentence combining and imitation exercises, which fell out of favor after the paradigm shift in composition theory, remain useful for improving student writing.

Crowhurst, Marion. "Sentence Combining: Maintaining Realistic Expectations." *College Composition and Communication* 34.1 (1983): 62–72. Print. Crowhurst offers pragmatic suggestions about what teachers should and should not expect when introducing sentence combining into their classrooms.

Daiker, Donald, Andrew Kerek, and Max Morenberg. *Sentence Combining: A Rhetorical Perspective.* Carbondale: Southern Illinois UP, 1985. Print.

Myers, Sharon A. "ReMembering the Sentence." *College Composition and Communication* 54.4 (2003): 610–28. Print. Myers echoes Robert Connors's call for a return to sentence-based methods of instruction. She answers critics of sentence combining by providing both theoretical and pedagogical perspectives on sentence-based instruction.

O'Hare, Frank. *Sentence-Combining: Improving Student Writing without Formal Grammar Instruction.* Urbana: NCTE. 1973. Print. O'Hare demonstrates the improvements that can be effected when students practice sentence combining.

Revised   Because production costs have dropped more slowly than prices, computer manufacturers have had to contend with shrinking profits.

No rules can specify what information in a sentence you should make primary and what you should subordinate; the decision will depend on your meaning. But, in general, you should consider using subordinate structures for details of time, cause, condition, concession, purpose, and identification (size, location, and the like). You can subordinate information with the structures listed in the box opposite.

In general, the shorter a subordinate structure is, the less emphasis it has. The following examples show how subordinate structures may convey various meanings with various weights. (Some appropriate subordinating words for each meaning appear in parentheses.)

Space or time (*after, before, since, until, when, while; at, in, on, until*)
The mine explosion killed six workers. The owners adopted safety measures.
After the mine explosion killed six workers, the owners adopted safety measures. [Subordinate clause.]
After six deaths in a mine explosion, the owners adopted safety measures. [Prepositional phrases.]

Cause or effect (*as, because, since, so that; because of, due to*)
Jones had been without work for six months. He was having trouble paying his bills.
Because Jones had been without work for six months, he was having trouble paying his bills. [Subordinate clause.]
Having been jobless for six months, Jones could not pay his bills. [Verbal phrase.]

Condition (*if, provided, since, unless, whenever; with, without*)
Forecasters predict a mild winter. Farmers hope for an early spring.
Whenever forecasters predict a mild winter, farmers hope for an early spring. [Subordinate clause.]
With forecasts for a mild winter, farmers hope for an early spring. [Prepositional phrase.]

Concession (*although, as if, even though, though; despite, except for, in spite of*)
The horse looked gentle. It proved hard to manage.
Although the horse looked gentle, it proved hard to manage. [Subordinate clause.]
The horse, a gentle-looking animal, proved hard to manage. [Appositive.]
The gentle-looking horse proved hard to manage. [Single word.]

Purpose (*in order that, so that, that; for, toward*)
Congress passed new immigration laws. Many Vietnamese refugees could enter the United States.

Ways to subordinate information in sentences

- **Use a subordinate clause beginning with a subordinating conjunction:** *although, because, if, whereas,* etc. (p. 251).

  Although some citizens had tried to rescue Independence Hall, they had not gained substantial public support.

- **Use a subordinate clause beginning with a relative pronoun:** *who, whoever, which, that* (p. 251).

  The first strong step was taken by the federal government, which made the building a national monument.

- **Use a phrase** (p. 242).

  Like most national monuments, Independence Hall is protected by the National Park Service. [Prepositional phrase.]

  Protecting many popular tourist sites, the service is a highly visible government agency. [Verbal phrase.]

- **Use an appositive** (p. 254).

  The National Park Service, a branch of the Department of Interior, also runs Yosemite and other wilderness parks.

- **Use a short modifier.**

  At the red brick Independence Hall, park rangers give guided tours and protect the irreplaceable building from vandalism.

Congress passed new immigration laws so that many Vietnamese refugees could enter the United States. [Subordinate clause.]
Congress passed new immigration laws, permitting many Vietnamese refugees to enter the United States. [Verbal phrase.]

Identification (*that, when, where, which, who; by, from, of*)
Old barns are common in New England. They are often painted red.
Old barns, which are often painted red, are common in New England. [Subordinate clause.]
Old barns, often painted red, are common in New England. [Verbal phrase.]
Old red barns are common in New England. [Single word.]

Punctuating subordinate constructions

A modifying word, phrase, or clause that introduces a sentence is usually set off from the rest of the sentence with a comma (see pp. 425–26):

Unfortunately, the bank failed.
In a little over six months, the bank became insolvent.
When the bank failed, many reporters investigated.

Strong, William. *Sentence Combining: A Composing Book*. 3rd ed. New York: McGraw-Hill, 1994. Print. Strong gives exercises to practice sentence combining at varying levels of complexity.

Williams, James D. *Preparing to Teach Writing*. 2nd ed. Mahwah: Lawrence Erlbaum Associates, 1998. Print. See the section on "Style and Sentence Combining," which explores the connections between syntactic and developmental maturity in teaching sentence combining (166–170).

On improving sentence style

Lanham, Richard. *Analyzing Prose*. 2nd ed. London: Continuum, 2003. Print. Lanham offers extensive advice on revising for stylistic effect.

Morenberg, Max, and Jeff Sommers. *The Writer's Options: Lessons in Style and Arrangement*. 8th ed. New York: Longman, 2008. Print. This text includes numerous exercises to aid in learning sentence-combining techniques as part of the writing process.

Soles, Derek. "An Analysis of the Style of Exemplary First-Year Writing." *Teaching English in the Two-Year College* 33.1 (September 2005): 38–49. Print. Using Corbett's prose style matrix, Soles analyzes the style of exemplary freshman essays and concludes that there is an identifiable, hence teachable style valued by freshman writing instructors.

Williams, Joseph. *Style: Lessons in Clarity and Grace*. 8th ed. New York: Longman, 2005. Print. Williams's how-to manual for improving style at the sentence and word level is especially strong in discussing coordination and subordination.

SWITCHING SUBORDINATION

Ask students either individually or in groups to write five sentences using subordination, with one sentence to illustrate each of the points in the "Ways to subordinate information" box. Then, have them switch the order of the sentences to emphasize the information that has been subordinated. Have students share these sentences either in groups or with the class as a whole to see how changing the subordinated information changes meaning.

A modifier that interrupts or concludes a main clause is *not* set off with punctuation when it is essential to the meaning of a word or words in the clause (see p. 427):

> One article about the bank failure won a prize.
> The article that won the prize appeared in the local newspaper.
> The reporter wrote the article because the bank failure affected many residents of the town.

When an interrupting or concluding modifier is *not* essential to meaning, but simply adds information to the sentence, it *is* set off with punctuation, usually a comma or commas (see p. 427):

> The bank, over forty years old, never reopened after its doors were closed.
> The bank managers, who were cleared of any wrongdoing, all found new jobs.
> Some customers of the bank never recovered all their money, though most of them tried to do so.

Like a modifier, an appositive is set off with punctuation (usually a comma or commas) only when it is *not* essential to the meaning of the word it refers to (see p. 429):

> The bank, First City, was the oldest in town.
> Our newspaper, the *Chronicle*, was one of several reporting the story.

A dash or dashes may also be used to set off a nonessential appositive, particularly when it contains commas (see p. 471). A concluding appositive is sometimes set off with a colon (see p. 469).

1 Subordinating logically

Use subordination only for the less important information in a sentence. **Faulty subordination** reverses the dependent relation the reader expects:

Faulty	Ms. Angelo was in her first year of teaching, although she was a better instructor than others with many years of experience. [The sentence suggests that Angelo's inexperience is the main idea, whereas the writer meant to stress her skill *despite* her inexperience.]
Revised	Although Ms. Angelo was in her first year of teaching, she was a better instructor than others with many years of experience.

2 Using subordination effectively

Subordination can do much to organize and emphasize information. But it loses that power when you try to cram too much loosely related detail into one long sentence:

Overloaded   The boats that were moored at the dock when the hurricane, which was one of the worst in three decades, struck were ripped from their moorings, because the owners had not been adequately prepared, since the weather service had predicted that the storm would blow out to sea, which storms do at this time of year.

Such sentences usually have more than one idea that deserves a main clause, so they are best revised by sorting their details into more than one sentence:

Revised   Struck by one of the worst hurricanes in three decades, <u>the boats at the dock were ripped from their moorings</u>. <u>The owners were unprepared</u> because the weather service had said that storms at this time of year blow out to sea.

A common form of excessive subordination occurs with a string of adjective clauses, each beginning with *which, who,* or *that:*

Stringy   The company opened a new plant outside Louisville, which is in Kentucky and which is on the Ohio River, which forms the border between Kentucky and Ohio.

To revise such sentences, recast some of the subordinate clauses as other kinds of modifying structures:

Revised   The company opened a new plant outside Louisville, <u>Kentucky</u>, <u>a city across the Ohio River from Ohio</u>.

Exercise 24.3   Sentence combining: Subordination

Combine each of the following pairs of sentences twice, each time using one of the subordinate structures in parentheses to make a single sentence. You will have to add, delete, change, and rearrange words.

Example:
During the late eighteenth century, workers carried beverages in brightly colored bottles. The bottles had cork stoppers. (*Clause beginning that. Phrase beginning with.*)
During the late eighteenth century, workers carried beverages in brightly colored bottles <u>that had cork stoppers</u>.
During the late eighteenth century, workers carried beverages in brightly colored bottles <u>with cork stoppers</u>.

1. The bombardier beetle sees an enemy. It shoots out a jet of chemicals to protect itself. (*Clause beginning when. Phrase beginning seeing.*)
2. The beetle's spray is very potent. It consists of hot and irritating chemicals. (*Phrase beginning consisting. Phrase beginning of.*)
3. The spray's two chemicals are stored separately in the beetle's body and mixed in the spraying gland. The chemicals resemble a nerve-gas weapon. (*Phrase beginning stored. Clause beginning which.*)

ANSWERS: EXERCISE 24.3
Possible answers

1. <u>When the bombardier beetle sees an enemy</u>, it shoots out a jet of chemicals to protect itself.
<u>Seeing an enemy</u>, the bombardier beetle shoots out a jet of chemicals to protect itself.
2. <u>Consisting of hot and irritating chemicals</u>, the beetle's spray is very potent.
The beetle's spray <u>of hot and irritating chemicals</u> is very potent.
3. <u>Stored separately in the beetle's body and mixed in the spraying gland</u>, the spray's two chemicals resemble a nerve-gas weapon.
The spray's two chemicals, <u>which are stored separately in the beetle's body and mixed in the spraying gland</u>, resemble a nerve-gas weapon.
4. <u>Revolving like a turret on a World War II bomber</u>, the tip of the beetle's abdomen sprays the chemicals.
<u>Spraying the chemicals</u>, the tip of the beetle's abdomen revolves like a turret on a World War II bomber.
5. <u>Although the beetle defeats most of its enemies</u>, it is still eaten by spiders and birds.
The beetle defeats most of its enemies <u>except spiders and birds</u>.

ANSWERS: EXERCISE 24.4

Possible revision

Fewer students today are majoring in the liberal arts—that is, in such subjects as history, English, and the social sciences. Although students think a liberal arts degree will not help them get jobs, they are wrong. They may not get practical, job-related experience from the liberal arts, but they will get a broad education that will never again be available to them. Many employers look for more than a technical, professional education because they think such an education can make an employee's views too narrow. Instead, they want open-minded employees who can think about problems from many angles. Such flexibility—vital to the health of our society—is just what the liberal arts curriculum instills.

ANSWERS: EXERCISE 24.5

Possible answers

1. Genaro González is a successful writer whose stories and novels have been published to critical acclaim.
2. Although he loves to write, he has also earned a doctorate in psychology.
3. His first story, which is titled "Un Hijo del Sol," reflects his consciousness of his Aztec heritage and place in the world.
4. González writes equally well in English and Spanish. He received a large fellowship, enabling him to take a leave of absence from the University of Texas–Pan American, where he teaches psychology. He could write without worrying about an income.
5. González wrote the first version of "Un Hijo del Sol" while he was a sophomore at Pan American. The university is in the Rio Grande valley of southern Texas, which González calls "el Valle" in the story.

REWRITING AN ESSAY

Give students a passage from a student or professional essay (posted to your class Web site or sent as an e-mail attachment) and ask them to rewrite it following a specified strategy: adding subordination, using different subordinators, or adding coordination. They can use one color script for subordination revisions, and another color script for coordination revisions. This exercise can be extended by having students rewrite the passage to change its emphasis.

4. The tip of the beetle's abdomen sprays the chemicals. The tip revolves like a turret on a World War II bomber. (*Phrase beginning re-volving. Phrase beginning spraying.*)
5. The beetle defeats most of its enemies. It is still eaten by spiders and birds. (*Clause beginning although. Phrase beginning except.*)

Exercise 24.4 Revising: Subordination

Rewrite the following paragraph in the way you think most effective to subordinate the less important ideas to the more important ones. Use subordinate clauses, phrases, and single words as you think appropriate.

Fewer students today are majoring in the liberal arts. I mean by "liberal arts" such subjects as history, English, and the social sciences. Students think a liberal arts degree will not help them get jobs. They are wrong. They may not get practical, job-related experience from the liberal arts, but they will get a broad education, and it will never again be available to them. Many employers look for more than a technical, professional education. They think such an education can make an employee's views too narrow. The employers want openminded employees. They want employees to think about problems from many angles. The liberal arts curriculum instills such flexibility. The flexibility is vital to the health of our society.

Exercise 24.5 Revising: Faulty or excessive subordination

Revise the following sentences to eliminate faulty or excessive subordination. Correct faulty subordination by reversing main and subordinate structures. Correct excessive subordination by coordinating equal ideas or by making separate sentences.

Example:
Terrified to return home, he had driven his mother's car into a cornfield.

Having driven his mother's car into a cornfield, he was terrified to return home.

1. Genaro González is a successful writer, which means that his stories and novels have been published to critical acclaim.
2. He loves to write, although he has also earned a doctorate in psychology.
3. His first story, which reflects his consciousness of his Aztec heritage and place in the world, is titled "Un Hijo del Sol."
4. González, who writes equally well in English and Spanish, received a large fellowship that enabled him to take a leave of absence from the University of Texas–Pan American, where he teaches psychology, so that he could write without worrying about an income.
5. González wrote the first version of "Un Hijo del Sol" while he was a sophomore at Pan American, which is in the Rio Grande valley of southern Texas, which González calls "el Valle" in the story.

24c Choosing clear connectors

Most connecting words signal specific and unambiguous relations; for instance, *but* clearly indicates contrast, and *because* clearly indicates cause. A few connectors, however, require careful use, either because they are ambiguous in many contexts or because they are often misused.

1 Using *as* and *while* clearly

The subordinating conjunction *as* can indicate several relations, including comparison and time:

Comparison	The technicians work quickly, as they are required to do.
Time	One shift starts as the other stops.

Avoid using *as* to indicate cause. It is unclear.

Unclear	As the experiment was occurring, the laboratory was sealed. [Time or cause intended?]
Revised	When the experiment was occurring, the laboratory was sealed. [Time.]
Revised	Because the experiment was occurring, the laboratory was sealed. [Cause.]

The subordinating conjunction *while* can indicate either time or concession. Unless the context makes the meaning of *while* unmistakably clear, choose a more exact connector:

Unclear	While technicians work in the next room, they cannot hear the noise. [Time or concession intended?]
Revised	When technicians work in the next room, they cannot hear the noise. [Time.]
Revised	Although technicians work in the next room, they cannot hear the noise. [Concession.]

2 Using *as* and *like* correctly

The use of *as* as a substitute for *whether* or *that* is considered nonstandard (it does not conform to spoken and written standard English):

Nonstandard	They are not sure as the study succeeded.
Revised	They are not sure whether [or that] the study succeeded.

Although the preposition *like* is often used as a conjunction in informal speech and in advertising (*Dirt-Away works like a soap should*), writing generally requires the conjunction *as, as if, as though,* or *that*:

Speech	It seemed like it did succeed.
Writing	It seemed as if [or as though or that] it did succeed.

ANSWERS: EXERCISE 24.6

Possible revision

Sir Walter Raleigh personified the Elizabethan <u>Age, the</u> period of Elizabeth I's rule of <u>England, in</u> the last half of the sixteenth century. Raleigh was a courtier, a poet, an explorer, and an entrepreneur. Supposedly, he gained Queen Elizabeth's <u>favor by</u> throwing his cloak beneath her feet at the right moment, <u>just as she was</u> about to step over a puddle. <u>Although</u> there is no evidence for this <u>story, it</u> illustrates Raleigh's dramatic and dynamic personality. His energy drew others to <u>him, and</u> he was one of Elizabeth's favorites. She supported <u>him and</u> dispensed favors to him. However, he lost his queen's <u>goodwill</u> <u>when without</u> her permission he <u>seduced and</u> <u>eventually married</u> one of her maids of honor. <u>After Elizabeth died</u>, her successor, <u>James I</u>, imprisoned Raleigh in the Tower of London <u>on false</u> <u>charges of treason</u>. Raleigh was released after thirteen <u>years but</u> arrested again two years later on the old treason charges. At the age of sixty-six he was beheaded.

HIGHLIGHTS

This discussion of parallelism is divided into two sections, and it moves from correctness to effective style. The opening section addresses the obligatory use of parallelism in coordinate constructions—those linked by coordinating conjunctions and correlative conjunctions; those in comparisons and contrasts; and those in lists, outlines, and the like. The second section examines how parallelism can be used within and among sentences to increase coherence, emphasize meaning, and heighten the effect. For some students you may wish to emphasize the items in the opening section. But students who have no trouble maintaining obligatory parallelism can often profit by working more creatively with parallelism to tighten and clarify their writing. Exercise 25.3, a sentence-combining exercise, is designed to give students a chance to explore the options for expression that

Exercise 24.6   **Revising: Coordination and subordination**

The following paragraph consists entirely of simple sentences. Use coordination and subordination to combine sentences in the ways you think most effective to emphasize main ideas.

Sir Walter Raleigh personified the Elizabethan Age. That was the period of Elizabeth I's rule of England. The period occurred in the last half of the sixteenth century. Raleigh was a courtier and poet. He was also an explorer and entrepreneur. Supposedly, he gained Queen Elizabeth's favor. He did this by throwing his cloak beneath her feet at the right moment. She was just about to step over a puddle. There is no evidence for this story. It does illustrate Raleigh's dramatic and dynamic personality. His energy drew others to him. He was one of Elizabeth's favorites. She supported him. She also dispensed favors to him. However, he lost his queen's goodwill. Without her permission he seduced one of her maids of honor. He eventually married the maid of honor. Elizabeth died. Then her successor imprisoned Raleigh in the Tower of London. Her successor was James I. The king falsely charged Raleigh with treason. Raleigh was released after thirteen years. He was arrested again two years later on the old treason charges. At the age of sixty-six he was beheaded.

Note See page 413 for an exercise involving coordination and subordination along with parallelism and other techniques for effective sentences.

25

Using Parallelism

Parallelism gives similar grammatical form to sentence elements that have similar function and importance.

The air is dirtied by ‖ factories belching smoke
and ‖ cars spewing exhaust.

Parallel structure reinforces and highlights a close relation between compound sentence elements, whether words, phrases, or clauses.

mycomplab

Visit *mycomplab.com* for more resources and exercises on parallelism.

The principle underlying parallelism is that form should reflect meaning: since the parts of compound constructions have the same function and importance, they should have the same grammatical form.

Grammar checkers A grammar checker cannot recognize problems with parallelism because it cannot recognize the relations among ideas.

25a Using parallelism for coordinate elements

Use parallelism in all the situations illustrated in the box on the next page.

Note Parallel elements match each other in structure, but they do not always match word for word:

The pioneers passed ‖ through the town
                  and ‖ into the vast, unpopulated desert.

1 Using parallelism for elements linked by coordinating conjunctions

The coordinating conjunctions *and, but, or, nor,* and *yet* always signal a need for parallelism:

The industrial base was <u>shifting</u> and <u>shrinking</u>.
Politicians rarely <u>acknowledged the problem</u> or <u>proposed alternatives</u>.
Industrial workers were understandably disturbed <u>that they were losing their jobs</u> and <u>that no one seemed to care</u>.

If sentence elements linked by coordinating conjunctions are not parallel in structure, the resulting sentence will be awkward and distracting:

Nonparallel	Three reasons why steel companies kept losing money were <u>that their plants were inefficient</u>, <u>high labor costs</u>, and <u>foreign competition was increasing</u>.
Revised	Three reasons why steel companies kept losing money were <u>inefficient plants</u>, high labor costs, and <u>increasing foreign competition</u>.

All the words required by idiom or grammar must be stated in compound constructions (see also p. 256).

Nonparallel	Given training, workers can acquire the <u>skills</u> and <u>interest</u> in other jobs. [*Skills* and *interest* require different prepositions, so both must be stated.]
Revised	Given training, workers can acquire the skills <u>for</u> and interest in other jobs.

parallelism provides. The exercise is likely to be most effective when students are given a chance to (1) discuss with one another the impact of various combinations or (2) work collaboratively in exploring various sentence-combining options.

RESOURCES AND IDEAS

Brooks, Phyllis. "Mimesis: Grammar and the Echoing Voice." *College English* 35.2 (1973): 161–68. Print. Brooks suggests the writing of paragraphs that imitate the style of a writer but use different content. She indicates that the practice helps students learn to use a variety of structures, including parenthetical expressions, appositives and modifiers, and parallelism plus reference.

Cook, Claire Kehrwald. "Ill-Matched Partners." *Line by Line: How to Edit Your Own Writing.* Boston: Houghton-Mifflin, 1985. 54–74. Print. Cook provides advice and examples for making work parallel and clear, focusing on sentence-level revisions.

Graves, Richard L. "Symmetrical Form and the Rhetoric of the Sentence." *Rhetoric and Composition: A Sourcebook for Teachers.* Upper Montclair: Boynton/Cook, 1984. 119–27. Print. Graves argues that since comparison is a natural way for humans to organize information, parallelism is an effective way of helping readers acquire and interpret information.

Kolln, Martha J. *Rhetorical Grammar: Grammatical Choices, Rhetorical Effects.* 5th ed. New York: Longman, 2007. Print. Kolln discusses many grammar issues and the rhetorical impact they have on writing. See the section on "Parallelism."

Walker, Robert L. "The Common Writer: A Case for Parallel Structure." *College Composition and Communication* 21.5 (1970): 373–79. Print. Walker believes that students should be encouraged to use a variety of sentence structures and parallelism, which he considers important features of mature sentences.

Williams, Joseph M. "The Phenomenology of Error." *College Composition and Communication* 32.2 (1981): 152–68. Print. Williams describes parallelism problems from the point of view of a writer's stylistic choices.

Patterns of parallelism

■ **Use parallel structures for elements connected by coordinating conjunctions** (*and, but, or,* etc.) **or correlative conjunctions** (*both . . . and, neither . . . nor,* etc.):

In 1988 a Greek cyclist, backed up by ‖ engineers,
physiologists,
and ‖ athletes,

broke the world's record for human flight
with neither ‖ a boost
nor ‖ a motor.

■ **Use parallel structures for elements being compared or contrasted:**

‖ Pedal power
rather than ‖ horse power
propelled the plane.

■ **Use parallel structures for lists, outlines, or headings:**

The four-hour flight was successful because
‖ (1) the cyclist was very fit,
‖ (2) he flew a straight course over water,
and ‖ (3) he kept the aircraft near the water's surface.

SAMPLE ESSAYS

Journal entries and student drafts, along with essays from a reader or a similar source, provide a gold mine of material on which to practice. Ask students to look for parallelism in essays from a reader or a similar source. If the students are working in groups, ask them not only to reach consensus on which elements are parallel but also to decide what functions the parallelism performs.

ADDING PARALLELISM

Take a loose-jointed student essay or a professional essay and distribute it to students (working individually or in groups), asking them to make the sentences denser by adding parallelism wherever possible. Have them also decide when the parallelism adds to the essay and when it detracts.

Often, a word must be repeated to avoid confusion:

Confusing   Thoreau stood up for his principles <u>by not paying</u> his taxes and <u>spending</u> a night in jail. [Did he spend a night in jail or not?]

Revised   Thoreau stood up for his principles by not paying his taxes and <u>by</u> spending a night in jail.

Be sure that clauses beginning *who* or *which* are coordinated only with other *who* or *which* clauses, even when the pronoun is not repeated:

Nonparallel   Thoreau is the nineteenth-century essayist <u>who retired</u> to the woods and <u>he wrote</u> about nature.

Revised   Thoreau is the nineteenth-century essayist who retired to the woods and [<u>who</u>] <u>wrote</u> about nature.

2 Using parallelism for elements linked by correlative conjunctions

Correlative conjunctions are pairs of connectors. For example:

both . . . and   neither . . . nor   not only . . . but also
either . . . or   not . . . but   whether . . . or

Correlative conjunctions stress equality and balance and thus emphasize the relation between elements, even long phrases and clauses. The elements should be parallel to confirm their relation:

> It is not a tax bill but a tax relief bill, providing relief not for the needy but for the greedy. —Franklin Delano Roosevelt

> At the end of the novel, Huck Finn both rejects society's values by turning down money and a home and affirms his own values by setting out for "the territory."

Most errors in parallelism with correlative conjunctions occur when the element after the second connector does not match the element after the first connector.

Nonparallel	Mark Twain refused either to ignore the moral blindness of his society or spare the reader's sensibilities. [*To* follows *either,* so it must also follow *or.*]
Revised	Mark Twain refused either to ignore the moral blindness of his society or to spare the reader's sensibilities.
Nonparallel	Huck Finn learns not only that human beings have an enormous capacity for folly but also enormous dignity. [The first element includes *that human beings have;* the second element does not.]
Revised	Huck Finn learns that human beings have not only an enormous capacity for folly but also enormous dignity.

3 **Using parallelism for elements being compared or contrasted**

Elements being compared or contrasted should ordinarily be cast in the same grammatical form.

> It is better to live rich than to die rich. —Samuel Johnson

Weak	The study found that most welfare recipients wanted to work rather than handouts.
Revised	The study found that most welfare recipients wanted work rather than handouts.
Revised	The study found that most welfare recipients wanted to work rather than to accept handouts.

4 **Using parallelism for lists, outlines, and headings**

The elements of a list or outline that divides a larger subject are coordinate and should be parallel in structure. Parallelism is essential in the headings that divide a paper into sections (see p. 120) and in a formal topic outline (see p. 39).

(see p. 120) ... (see p. 39)

COLLABORATIVE LEARNING

PATTERNS FOR PARALLELISM

Ask students to write three sentences on a topic of their choice (or to revise three sentences from a work in progress), using a different pattern of parallelism in each sentence. Then have students compare their work in groups or as a class. In a networked class, responses can be posted and critiqued on the class Web site. If students have difficulty generating or revising sentences individually, ask them instead to write the sentences in groups. As part of the assignment, ask students to vary the sentences as much as they can in content and in use of parallelism. Then ask the groups to judge each other's work for originality, clarity, and effectiveness.

COLLECTING (AND CORRECTING) NONPARALLEL COMPARISONS

Ask students to review their own essays, journals, or others' blogs to find examples of non-parallel comparison or contrast. Once each group has collected three to five examples to work on, they should correct the error. Remind students that sometimes the whole sentence may need to be revised for clarity in addition to making the compared or contrasted elements parallel.

ANSWERS: EXERCISE 25.1

1. The two sets of parallel phrases (*an automatic or an everyday affair; on solemn occasions and for a special treat*) and the parallel main clauses (*... has not always been ... has tended to be*) emphasize the differences between then and now.
2. The parallel verbs (*rolled out ... cooked ... tended ... marked*) stress the number and variety of the women's responsibilities.
3. Supporting *pleasantest* is a wealth of detail expressed in five parallel absolute phrases: *exhaustion ... in; the sated mosquitoes ... off; the room ... garments; the vines ... day; and the air conditioner ... mosquitoes.* The phrases convey no action, emphasizing the stillness of the scene.
4. The limiting effects of aging are emphasized by the increasingly narrow parallel verbs—*paints, lies, imprisons*—and the parallel objects—*every action, every movement, every thought.*

Faulty	Improved
Changes in Renaissance England	Changes in Renaissance England
1. Extension of trade routes	1. Extension of trade routes
2. Merchant class became more powerful	2. Increased power of the merchant class
3. The death of feudalism	3. Death of feudalism
4. Upsurging of the arts	4. Upsurge of the arts
5. The sciences were encouraged	5. Encouragement of the sciences
6. Religious quarrels began	6. Rise of religious quarrels

Exercise 25.1 Identifying parallel elements

Identify the parallel elements in the following sentences. How does parallelism contribute to the effectiveness of each sentence?

1. Eating an animal has not always been an automatic or an everyday affair; it has tended to be done on solemn occasions and for a special treat.
                                                —Margaret Visser
2. They [pioneer women] rolled out dough on the wagon seats, cooked with fires made out of buffalo chips, tended the sick, and marked the graves of their children, their husbands and each other.
                                                —Ellen Goodman
3. The mornings are the pleasantest times in the apartment, exhaustion having set in, the sated mosquitoes at rest on ceiling and walls, sleeping it off, the room a swirl of tortured bedclothes and abandoned garments, the vines in their full leafiness filtering the hard light of day, the air conditioner silent at last, like the mosquitoes.
                                                —E. B. White
4. Aging paints every action gray, lies heavy on every movement, imprisons every thought.   —Sharon Curtin

Exercise 25.2 Revising: Parallelism

Revise the following sentences to make coordinate, compared, or listed elements parallel in structure. Add or delete words or rephrase as necessary.

Example:

After emptying her bag, searching the apartment, and she called the library, Emma realized she had lost the book.

After emptying her bag, searching the apartment, and <u>calling</u> the library, Emma realized she had lost the book.

1. The ancient Greeks celebrated four athletic contests: the Olympic Games at Olympia, the Isthmian Games were held near Corinth, at Delphi the Pythian Games, and the Nemean Games were sponsored by the people of Cleonae.
2. Each day of the games consisted of either athletic events or holding ceremonies and sacrifices to the gods.

3. In the years between the games, competitors were taught wrestling, javelin throwing, and how to box.
4. Competitors participated in running sprints, spectacular chariot and horse races, and running long distances while wearing full armor.
5. The purpose of such events was developing physical strength, demonstrating skill and endurance, and to sharpen the skills needed for war.
6. Events were held for both men and for boys.
7. At the Olympic Games the spectators cheered their favorites to victory, attended sacrifices to the gods, and they feasted on the meat not burned in offerings.
8. The athletes competed less to achieve great wealth than for gaining honor both for themselves and their cities.
9. Of course, exceptional athletes received financial support from patrons, poems and statues by admiring artists, and they even got lavish living quarters from their sponsoring cities.
10. With the medal counts and flag ceremonies, today's Olympians sometimes seem to be proving their countries' superiority more than to demonstrate individual talent.

25b Using parallelism to increase coherence

Effective parallelism will enable you to combine in a single, well-ordered sentence related ideas that you might have expressed in separate sentences. Compare the following three sentences with the original single sentence written by H. L. Mencken:

> Slang originates in the effort of ingenious individuals to make the language more pungent and picturesque. They increase the store of terse and striking words or widen the boundaries of metaphor. Thus a vocabulary for new shades and differences in meaning is provided by slang.

> Slang originates in the effort of ingenious individuals to make the language more pungent and picturesque—to increase the store of terse and striking words, to widen the boundaries of metaphor, and to provide a vocabulary for new shades and differences in meaning.   —H. L. Mencken

Parallel structure works as well to emphasize the connections among related sentences in a paragraph:

> Lewis Mumford stands high in the company of [twentieth-century] sages. A scholar of cosmic cultural reach and conspicuous public conscience, a distinguished critic of life, arts, and letters, an unequaled observer of cities and civilizations, he is secure in the modern pantheon of great men. He is also an enigma and an anachronism. A legend of epic proportions in intellectual and academic circles, he is surprisingly little known to the public.   —Ada Louise Huxtable

Here, Huxtable tightly binds her sentences with two layers of parallelism: the subject-verb patterns of all four sentences (italic and

ANSWERS: EXERCISE 25.2

Possible answers

1. The ancient Greeks celebrated four athletic contests: the Olympic Games at Olympia, the Isthmian Games near Corinth, the Pythian Games at Delphi, and the Nemean Games at Cleonae.
2. Each day of the games consisted of either athletic events or ceremonies and sacrifices to the gods.
3. In the years between the games, competitors were taught wrestling, javelin throwing, and boxing.
4. Competitors ran sprints, participated in spectacular chariot and horse races, and ran long distances while wearing full armor.
5. The purpose of such events was developing physical strength, demonstrating skill and endurance, and sharpening the skills needed for war.
6. Events were held both for men and for boys.
7. At the Olympic Games the spectators cheered their favorites to victory, attended sacrifices to the gods, and feasted on the meat not burned in offerings.
8. The athletes competed less to achieve great wealth than to gain honor for both themselves and their cities.
9. Of course, exceptional athletes received financial support from patrons, poems and statues by admiring artists, and even lavish living quarters from their sponsoring cities.
10. With the medal counts and flag ceremonies, today's Olympians sometimes seem to be proving their countries' superiority more than demonstrating individual talent.

Ask students to complete Exercise 25.3 individually and work together to compare and revise their responses. Then have each group create a response to Exercise 25.4 and present it to the class. In a wired classroom you might ask groups to post their revised paragraphs for the class to compare and discuss.

ANSWERS: EXERCISE 25.3

Possible answers

1. People can develop post-traumatic stress disorder (PTSD) after experiencing a dangerous situation and fearing for their survival.
2. The disorder can be triggered by a wide variety of events, such as combat, a natural disaster, or a hostage situation.
3. PTSD can occur immediately after the stressful incident or not until many years later.
4. Sometimes people with PTSD will act irrationally and angrily.
5. Other symptoms include dreaming that one is reliving the experience, hallucinating that one is back in the terrifying place, and imagining that strangers are actually one's former torturers.

ANSWERS: EXERCISE 25.4

Possible revision

The great white shark has an undeserved bad reputation. Many people consider the great white not only swift and powerful but also a cunning and cruel predator on humans. However, scientists claim that the great white attacks humans not by choice but by chance. To a shark, our behavior in the water is similar to that of porpoises, seals, and sea lions—the shark's favorite foods. These sea mammals are both agile enough and fast enough to evade the shark. Thus the shark must attack swiftly and noiselessly to surprise the prey and give it little chance to escape. Humans become the shark's victims not because the shark has any preference for or hatred of humans but because humans can neither outswim nor outmaneuver the shark. If the fish were truly a cruel human-eater, it would prolong the terror of its attacks, perhaps by circling or bumping into its intended victims before attacking them.

underlined) and the appositives of the second and fourth sentences (underlined). (See pp. 85–86 for another illustration of parallelism among sentences.)

Exercise 25.3 Sentence combining: Parallelism

Combine each group of sentences below into one concise sentence in which parallel elements appear in parallel structures. You will have to add, delete, change, and rearrange words. Each item has more than one possible answer.

> *Example:*
> The new process works smoothly. It is efficient, too.
> The new process works smoothly and efficiently.

1. People can develop post-traumatic stress disorder (PTSD). They develop it after experiencing a dangerous situation. They will also have felt fear for their survival.
2. The disorder can be triggered by a wide variety of events. Combat is a typical cause. Similarly, natural disasters can result in PTSD. Some people experience PTSD after a hostage situation.
3. PTSD can occur immediately after the stressful incident. Or it may not appear until many years later.
4. Sometimes people with PTSD will act irrationally. Moreover, they often become angry.
5. Other symptoms include dreaming that one is reliving the experience. They include hallucinating that one is back in the terrifying place. In another symptom one imagines that strangers are actually one's former torturers.

Exercise 25.4 Revising: Parallelism

Revise the following paragraph to create parallelism wherever it is required for grammar or for coherence.

The great white shark has an undeserved bad reputation. Many people consider the great white not only swift and powerful but also to be a cunning and cruel predator on humans. However, scientists claim that the great white attacks humans not by choice but as a result of chance. To a shark, our behavior in the water is similar to that of porpoises, seals, and sea lions—the shark's favorite foods. These sea mammals are both agile enough and can move fast enough to evade the shark. Thus the shark must attack with swiftness and noiselessly to surprise the prey and giving it little chance to escape. Humans become the shark's victims not because the shark has any preference or hatred of humans but because humans can neither outswim nor can they outmaneuver the shark. If the fish were truly a cruel human-eater, it would prolong the terror of its attacks, perhaps by circling or bumping into its intended victims before they were attacked.

Note See page 413 for an exercise involving parallelism along with other techniques for effective sentences.

26

Achieving Variety

In a paragraph or an essay, each sentence stands in relation to those before and after it. To make sentences work together effectively, you need to vary their length, structure, and word order to reflect the importance and complexity of ideas. Variety sometimes takes care of itself, but you can practice established techniques for achieving varied sentences:

Ways to achieve variety among sentences

- Vary the length and structure of sentences so that important ideas stand out (next page).
- Vary the beginnings of sentences with modifiers, transitional words and expressions, and occasional expletive constructions (p. 408).
- Occasionally, invert the normal order of subject, verb, and object or complement (p. 411).
- Occasionally, use a command, question, or exclamation (p. 411).

A series of similar sentences will prove monotonous and ineffective, as the following passage illustrates.

> Ulysses S. Grant and Robert E. Lee met on April 9, 1865. Their meeting place was the parlor of a modest house at Appomattox Court House, Virginia. They met to work out the terms for the surrender of Lee's Army of Northern Virginia. One great chapter of American life ended with their meeting, and another began. Grant and Lee were bringing the Civil War to its virtual finish. Other armies still had to surrender, and the fugitive Confederate government would struggle desperately and vainly. It would try to find some way to go on living with its chief support gone. Grant and Lee had signed the papers, however, and it was all over in effect.

These eight sentences are all between twelve and sixteen words long (counting initials and dates), they are about equally detailed, and they all begin with the subject. We get a sense of names, dates, and

Visit *mycomplab.com* for more resources and exercises on sentence variety.

HIGHLIGHTS

This chapter asks students to think of sentences not as single units but as a sequence of ideas working together. Emphasis, coordination, subordination, and parallelism—topics covered in the preceding chapters—all come into play in the examples in this chapter. You will probably want to direct attention to the introduction to this chapter and to the first two sections, covering strategies for varying the length and structure of sentences and for varying sentence beginnings. You may have to decide, though, how much time to devote to the last two sections, which cover the occasional uses of inverted sentence order and of minor sentence types such as questions and commands.

RESOURCES AND IDEAS

Lanham, Richard. *Analyzing Prose.* 2nd ed. London: Continuum, 2003. Print. Lanham offers extensive advice on revising for stylistic effect.

Rubin, Donald, and Kathryn Greene. "Gender-Typical Style in Written Language." *Research in the Teaching of English* 26.1 (1992): 7–40. Print. The authors catalog stylistic and syntactic variations that fall along gender lines.

ADDITIONAL ACTIVITIES

Many of the student activities described for Chapters 23 and 24 can be easily adapted for this chapter.

COMPUTER ACTIVITY

USING STYLE CHECKERS

Style checkers are now widely available; however, the quality of the advice they offer varies considerably. These programs are based on standardized readability tests and are not particularly sensitive to writers' purposes or the levels of sophistication of their audiences. (Try feeding the "Gettysburg Address" or "A Letter from Birmingham Jail" into such a program; the advice the style checkers provide for "improving" these essays will shock and amuse you and your students.)

COLLABORATIVE LEARNING

SIMPLE SENTENCES

Take a professional or student essay, reduce it to simple sentences, and ask students to rewrite it, adding variety. Then ask them to work in groups to compare their versions with the original, analyze the differences, and decide as a group which versions are more effective and why.

LONG SENTENCES

Take a passage from a professional or student essay and combine existing sentences to make them so lengthy they are challenging to read. Have students work in groups to revise the long sentences to add variety. Then have them compare their revisions with the original text, discuss the differences, and determine which versions are more effective and why.

VISUAL ANALYSIS

Students may wish to make bar charts showing sentence lengths to see the average lengths of sentences they use and to target the variations in length they might want to consider.

events but no immediate sense of how they relate or what is most important.

Now compare the preceding passage with the actual passage written by Bruce Catton. Here the four sentences range from eleven to fifty-five words, and only one sentence begins with its subject:

> When Ulysses S. Grant and Robert E. Lee met in the parlor of a modest house at Appomattox Court House, Virginia, on April 9, 1865, to work out the terms for the surrender of Lee's Army of Northern Virginia, a great chapter in American life came to a close, and a great new chapter began.

Suspenseful periodic sentence (pp. 381–82) focuses attention on meeting; details of place, time, and cause are in opening subordinate clause

> These men were bringing the Civil War to its virtual finish.

Short sentence sums up

> To be sure, other armies had yet to surrender, and for a few days the fugitive Confederate government would struggle desperately and vainly, trying to find some way to go on living now that its chief support was gone.

Cumulative sentence (p. 381) reflects lingering obstacles to peace

> But in effect it was all over when Grant and Lee signed the papers.

Short final sentence indicates futility of further struggle

> —Bruce Catton, "Grant and Lee"

The rest of this chapter suggests how you can vary your sentences for the kind of interest and clarity that Catton achieves in this passage.

Grammar checkers Some grammar checkers will flag long sentences, and you can check for appropriate variety in a series of such sentences. But generally these programs cannot help you see where variety may be needed because they cannot recognize the relative importance and complexity of your ideas.

26a Varying sentence length and structure

The sentences of a stylistically effective essay will vary most obviously in their length and the arrangement of main clauses and modifiers. The variation in length and structure makes writing both readable and clear.

1 Varying length

In most contemporary writing, sentences vary from about ten to about forty words. When sentences are all at one extreme or the other, readers may have difficulty focusing on main ideas and seeing the relations among them:

- **Long sentences.** If most of your sentences contain thirty-five words or more, your main ideas may not stand out from the details that support them. Break some of the long sentences into shorter, simpler ones.

- **Short sentences.** If most of your sentences contain fewer than ten or fifteen words, all your ideas may seem equally important and the links between them may not be clear. Try combining them with coordination (p. 388) and subordination (p. 391) to show relationships and to stress main ideas over supporting information.

2 Rewriting strings of brief and simple sentences

A series of brief and simple sentences is both monotonous and hard to understand because it forces the reader to sort out relations among ideas. If you find that you depend on brief, simple sentences, work to increase variety by combining some of them into longer units that emphasize and link important ideas while de-emphasizing incidental information. (See Chapter 24.)

The following examples show how a string of simple sentences can be revised into an effective piece of writing:

Monotonous   The moon is now drifting away from the earth. It moves away at the rate of about one inch a year. This movement is lengthening our days. They increase a thousandth of a second every century. Forty-seven of our present days will someday make up a month. We might eventually lose the moon altogether. Such great planetary movement rightly concerns astronomers, but it need not worry us. It will take 50 million years.

Revised   The moon is now drifting away from the earth about one inch a year. At a thousandth of a second every century, this movement is lengthening our days. Forty-seven of our present days will someday make up a month, if we don't eventually lose the moon altogether. Such great planetary movement rightly concerns astronomers, but it need not worry us. It will take 50 million years.

In the revision, underlining indicates subordinate structures that were simple sentences in the original. With five sentences instead of the original eight, the revision emphasizes the moon's movement, our lengthening days, and the enormous span of time involved.

3 Rewriting strings of compound sentences

Compound sentences are usually just simple sentences linked with conjunctions. Thus a series of them will be as weak as a series of brief, simple sentences, especially if the clauses of the compound sentences are all about the same length:

RESOURCES AND IDEAS

Walpole, Jane R. "The Vigorous Pursuit of Grace and Style." *The Writing Instructor* 1 (1982): 163–69. Print. Walpole offers a number of exercises for developing students' "ear" for style, with particular emphasis on simple sentences.

Williams, Joseph. *Style: Lessons in Clarity and Grace.* 9th ed. New York: Longman, 2007. Print. Williams provides an excellent how-to manual for improving style at the sentence and word level.

Have students work in groups to create responses to Exercise 26.1. Encourage each group to discuss various possible revisions and ask them to present their responses to the class. This exercise works well in a wired classroom where each group's responses can be posted for comparison and general discussion.

ANSWERS: EXERCISE 26.1

Possible revision

Charlotte Perkins Gilman was a leading intellectual in the women's movement during the first decades of the twentieth century. <u>Her book</u> <u>*Women and Economics* challenged</u> Victorian assumptions about the differences between the sexes <u>and</u> explored the economic roots of women's oppression. Gilman wrote little about gaining the vote for women, <u>the issue that then</u> <u>preoccupied feminists and that</u> historians have since focused their analyses on. As a result, Gilman's contribution to today's women's movement has often been overlooked.

Monotonous	Physical illness may involve more than the body, for the mind may also be affected. Disorientation is common among sick people, but they are often unaware of it. They may reason abnormally, or they may behave immaturely.
Revised	Physical illness may involve the mind <u>as well as the body.</u> <u>Though often unaware of it</u>, sick people are commonly disoriented. They may reason abnormally <u>or behave immaturely.</u>

The first passage creates a seesaw effect. The revision, with some main clauses shortened or changed into modifiers (underlined), is both clearer and more emphatic. (See p. 390 for more on avoiding excessive coordination.)

> **Exercise 26.1 Revising: Varied sentence structures**
>
> Rewrite the following paragraph to increase variety so that important ideas receive greater emphasis than supporting information does. You will have to change some main clauses into modifiers and then combine and reposition the modifiers and the remaining main clauses.
>
> Charlotte Perkins Gilman was a leading intellectual in the women's movement during the first decades of the twentieth century. She wrote *Women and Economics.* This book challenged Victorian assumptions about differences between the sexes, and it explored the economic roots of women's oppression. Gilman wrote little about gaining the vote for women, but many feminists were then preoccupied with this issue, and historians have since focused their analyses on this issue. As a result, Gilman's contribution to today's women's movement has often been overlooked.

26b Varying sentence beginnings

An English sentence often begins with its subject, which generally captures old information from a preceding sentence (see pp. 380–81):

> The defendant's <u>lawyer</u> was determined to break the prosecution's witness. <u>She</u> relentlessly cross-examined the stubborn witness for a week.

However, an unbroken sequence of sentences beginning with the subject quickly becomes monotonous, as shown by the unvaried passage on Grant and Lee that opened this chapter (p. 405). You can vary this subject-first pattern by adding modifiers or other elements before the subject.

Note The final arrangement of sentence elements should always depend on two concerns: the relation of a sentence to those preceding and following it and the emphasis required by your meaning.

Adverb modifiers

Adverbs modify verbs, adjectives, other adverbs, and whole clauses. They can often fall in a variety of spots in a sentence. Consider these different emphases:

> <u>For a week</u>, the defendant's lawyer <u>relentlessly</u> cross-examined the stubborn witness.

> <u>Relentlessly</u>, the defendant's lawyer cross-examined the stubborn witness <u>for a week</u>.

> <u>Relentlessly</u>, <u>for a week</u>, the defendant's lawyer cross-examined the stubborn witness.

Notice that the last sentence, with both modifiers at the beginning, is periodic and thus highly emphatic (see pp. 381–82).

CULTURE / LANGUAGE In standard American English, placing certain adverb modifiers at the beginning of a sentence requires you to change the normal subject-verb order as well. The most common of these modifiers are negatives, including *seldom, rarely, in no case, not since,* and *not until.*

Faulty adverb   subject verb phrase
Seldom <u>a witness</u> <u>has held</u> the stand for so long.

Revised helping
adverb verb subject main verb
Seldom <u>has</u> <u>a witness</u> <u>held</u> the stand for so long.

Adjective modifiers

Adjectives, modifying nouns and pronouns, may include participles and participial phrases, as in *flying geese* or *money well spent* (see pp. 245–47). These modifiers may sometimes fall at the beginning of a sentence to postpone the subject:

> The witness was exhausted from his testimony, and he did not cooperate.

> <u>Exhausted from his testimony</u>, the witness did not cooperate.

Coordinating conjunctions and transitional expressions

When the relation between two successive sentences demands, you may begin the second with a coordinating conjunction such as *and* or *but* (p. 257) or with a transitional expression such as *first, for instance, however,* or *therefore* (pp. 88–89).

> The witness had expected to be dismissed after his first long day of cross-examination. <u>But</u> he was not.

> The price of a college education has risen astronomically. <u>For example</u>, tuition at one state university climbed from $4500 to $7000 in just four years.

CULTURE / LANGUAGE

SENTENCE LENGTH AND VARIETY

ESL students may replicate the sentence length and sentence variety conventions of their first language when creating sentences in English. It may require considerable practice before they develop an ear for the rhythm and variety of sentences according to English conventions. The same may hold true for native English speakers if they are unfamiliar with the conventions of a particular genre of English writing. The first two paragraphs of Jane Austen's *Pride and Prejudice* are a good example of long sentences used effectively:

> It is a truth universally acknowledged, that a single man in possession of a good fortune, must be in want of a wife.

> However little known the feelings or views of such a man may be on his first entering a neighbourhood, this truth is so well fixed in the minds of the surrounding families, that he is considered as the rightful property of some one or other of their daughters.

Contrast these paragraphs with an excerpt from Ralph Ellison's *Invisible Man*, in which Ellison uses both short and long sentences to accentuate the content of the story he is telling:

> Once I saw a prizefighter boxing a yokel. The fighter was swift and amazingly scientific. His body was one violent flow of rapid rhythmic action. He hit the yokel a hundred times while the yokel held up his arms in stunned surprise. But suddenly the yokel, rolling about in the gale of boxing gloves, struck one blow and knocked science, speed and footwork as cold as a well-digger's posterior. The smart money hit the canvas. The long shot got the nod.

Invite your students to become attuned to sentence variety in their reading. Reading assignments for your course or their other courses can be plumbed for examples, and your class can make a collection of examples from various genres and forms of writing. This exercise may be especially helpful to students who are just beginning to develop an ear for rhythm and variety in sentence patterns.

EXPLETIVE EDITING

Inexperienced writers often pepper their work with expletive constructions. Ask students to review an essay or journal entry to find every use of *it/there* and a *be* verb in the work. Circle or highlight each instance. Students should then consider each construction individually. Those with specific purposes can be left alone. Those sentences with expletive constructions that do not have stylistic purposes, however, should be rewritten to remove the construction.

COLLABORATIVE LEARNING

Have students complete Exercise 26.2 in small groups and present one or two of their responses to the class. During the group presentations, encourage a general discussion of the relative effectiveness of various responses. This may help students to focus on the connection between stylistic changes and sentence content.

ANSWERS: EXERCISE 26.2

Possible answers

1. Some people are champion procrastinators. Consequently, they seldom complete their work on time.
2. If procrastinators fear criticism or rejection, they will delay completing an assignment.
3. Procrastinators often desire to please a boss or a teacher. Yet they fear failure so much that they cannot do the work.
4. Although procrastination seems a hopeless habit, it is conquerable.
5. Helpfully encouraging procrastinators, teachers or employers can give them the confidence to do good work on time.

ANSWERS: EXERCISE 26.3

Possible revision

When scientists in Egypt dug up 40-million-year-old fossil bones, they had evidence of primitive whales. Called mesonychids, the whale ancestors were small, furry land mammals with four legs. These limbs were complete with kneecaps, ankles, and little toes. In contrast, gigantic modern whales have tiny hind legs inside their bodies and flippers instead of front legs. But scientists are certain that these two very different creatures share the same family tree.

Occasional expletive constructions

An expletive construction—*it, there,* or *here* plus a form of *be*—may occasionally be useful to delay and thus emphasize the subject of the sentence:

His judgment seems questionable, not his desire.
<u>It is</u> his judgment that seems questionable, not his desire.

However, expletive constructions are more likely to flatten writing by adding extra words. You should use them rarely, only when you can justify doing so. (See also p. 529.)

Exercise 26.2 Revising: Varied sentence beginnings

Follow the instructions in parentheses to revise each group of sentences below: either create a single sentence that begins with an adverb or adjective modifier, or make one sentence begin with an appropriate connector.

> *Example:*
> The *Seabird* took first place. It moved quickly in the wind. (*One sentence with adjective modifier beginning <u>Moving</u>.*)
> <u>Moving quickly in the wind</u>, the *Seabird* took first place.

1. Some people are champion procrastinators. They seldom complete their work on time. (*Two sentences with transitional expression.*)
2. Procrastinators may fear criticism. They may fear rejection. They will delay completing an assignment. (*One sentence with adverb modifier beginning <u>If</u>.*)
3. Procrastinators often desire to please a boss or a teacher. They fear failure so much that they cannot do the work. (*Two sentences with coordinating conjunction.*)
4. Procrastination seems a hopeless habit. It is conquerable. (*One sentence with adverb modifier beginning <u>Although</u>.*)
5. Teachers or employers can be helpful. They can encourage procrastinators. They can give procrastinators the confidence to do good work on time. (*One sentence with adjective modifier beginning <u>Helpfully encouraging</u>.*)

Exercise 26.3 Revising: Varied sentence beginnings

Revise the following paragraph to vary sentence beginnings by using each of the following at least once: an adverb modifier, an adjective modifier, a coordinating conjunction, and a transitional expression.

Scientists in Egypt dug up 40-million-year-old fossil bones. They had evidence of primitive whales. The whale ancestors are called mesonychids. They were small, furry land mammals with four legs. These limbs were complete with kneecaps, ankles, and little toes. Gigantic modern whales have tiny hind legs inside their bodies and flippers instead of front legs. Scientists are certain that these two very different creatures share the same family tree.

26c | Inverting the normal word order

The word order of subject, verb, and object or complement is strongly fixed in English (see pp. 236–39). Thus an inverted sentence can be emphatic:

Voters once had some faith in politicians, and they were fond of incumbents. But now <u>all politicians</u>, especially incumbents, <u>voters seem to detest</u>. [The object *all politicians* precedes the verb *detests*.]

Inverting the normal order of subject, verb, and complement can be useful in two successive sentences when the second expands on the first:

Critics have not been kind to Presidents who have tried to apply the ways of private business to public affairs. Particularly <u>explicit was the curt verdict</u> of one critic of President Hoover: Mr. Hoover was never President of the United States; he was four years chairman of the board.
—Adapted from Emmet John Hughes, "The Presidency vs. Jimmy Carter"

Inverted sentences used without need are artificial. Avoid descriptive sentences such as *Up came Ben and down went Katie's spirits.*

26d | Mixing types of sentences

Most written sentences make statements. Occasionally, however, you may want to use questions, commands, or exclamations to enhance variety.

Questions may set the direction of a paragraph, as in *What does a detective do?* or *How is the percentage of unemployed workers calculated?* More often, though, the questions used in exposition or argument do not require answers but simply emphasize ideas that readers can be expected to agree with. Such **rhetorical questions** are illustrated in the following passage:

Another word that has ceased to have meaning due to overuse is *attractive. Attractive* has become verbal chaff. Who, by some stretch of language and imagination, cannot be described as attractive? And just what is it that attractive individuals are attracting? —Diane White

Commands occur frequently in an explanation of a process, particularly in directions, as this passage on freewriting illustrates:

The idea is simply to write for ten minutes (later on, perhaps fifteen or twenty). Don't stop for anything. Go quickly, without rushing. Never stop to look back, to cross something out, to wonder how to spell something, to wonder what word or thought to use, or to think about what you are doing. —Peter Elbow

Have students create individual responses to Exercise 26.4, then ask them to discuss their responses in small groups and create revisions. In a computer classroom, students might trade seats in order to read and comment on each other's work (in each case the commentator can add revision suggestions using a different font). Students can print out and share responses, or post them to the course Web site in a wired classroom.

ANSWERS: EXERCISE 26.4

Possible answers

1. How many cars are registered on this campus?
2. Try to find a parking space on this campus any weekday morning after nine o'clock.
3. What an unexpected pleasure to find a parking space within two blocks of the library!
4. Can the frustration caused by the parking problem be healthy for students? They drive round and round the campus, the minutes of lost study or class time ticking away. Tension builds. As they pass filled row upon filled row in one lot after another, drivers begin to tremble, sweat, and swear. And the anger and panic, instead of abating when finally the car is safely stowed, stays with the students throughout the day.

Have students complete Exercise 26.5 individually and then discuss their responses in small groups. Encourage students to debate the effects of sentence variety in the passage and to use detailed evidence from the passage to support their claims. You might follow up this group activity by leading a general discussion in which you invite groups to report back on the debates they have generated.

ANSWERS: EXERCISE 26.5

Possible answers

The longest sentence is the first one, a cumulative sentence that establishes a story-telling tone. The following question focuses the para-

---

Notice that the authors of these examples use questions and commands to achieve some special purpose. Variety occurs because a particular sentence type is effective for the context, not because the writer set out to achieve variety for its own sake.

Exercise 26.4   Writing varied sentences

Imagine that you are writing an essay on a transportation problem at your school. Practice varying your sentences by composing a sentence or passage to serve each purpose listed below.

1. Write a question that could open the essay.
2. Write a command that could open the essay.
3. Write an exclamation that could open the essay.
4. For the body of the essay, write an appropriately varied paragraph of at least five sentences, including at least one short and one long sentence beginning with the subject; at least one sentence beginning with an adverb modifier; at least one sentence beginning with a coordinating conjunction or transitional expression; and one rhetorical question or command.

Exercise 26.5   Analyzing variety

Examine the following paragraph for sentence variety. By analyzing your own response to each sentence, try to explain why the author wrote each short or long sentence, each cumulative or periodic sentence, each sentence beginning with its subject or beginning some other way, and each question.

My earliest memory of learning to read is sitting with my grandmother on her livingroom sofa as her finger underlined the words of *Go, Dog. Go!* and I struggled to decipher them. Why did she spend so much time with me when she knew I would have every opportunity to finish high school and go to college? She listened patiently because she didn't take my education—or anyone's—for granted. The only one of her ten siblings to graduate from college, she had beaten the odds. She finished high school at the top of her class, held a full-time job while commuting to her college classes, and graduated with honors. Then she then took a job at a public high school where she taught for more than thirty years. She knew that I was unaware of my opportunities, and she did not assume that I would succeed as she had. In her years of teaching, she had seen enough students struggle and drop out to know that failure often comes more easily than success. She was determined that I would be one of the successes—indeed, that I would soar. And soar I did.

Exercise 26.6   Revising: Variety

The following paragraph consists entirely of simple sentences that begin with their subjects. As appropriate, use the techniques discussed in this chapter to vary sentences. Your goal is to make the paragraph more readable and make its important ideas stand out clearly. You will have to delete, add, change, and rearrange words.

> The Italian volcano Vesuvius had been dormant for many years. It then exploded on August 24 in the year AD 79. The ash, pumice, and mud from the volcano buried two busy towns. Herculaneum is one. The more famous is Pompeii. Both towns lay undiscovered for many centuries. Herculaneum and Pompeii were discovered in 1709 and 1748, respectively. The excavation of Pompeii was the more systematic. It was the occasion for initiating modern methods of conservation and restoration. Herculaneum was simply looted of its most valuable finds. It was then left to disintegrate. Pompeii appears much as it did before the eruption. A luxurious house opens onto a lush central garden. An election poster decorates a wall. A dining table is set for breakfast.

Exercise on Chapters 23–26   Revising: Effective sentences

Revise the paragraphs below to emphasize main ideas, de-emphasize supporting information, and achieve a pleasing, clear variety in sentences. As appropriate, employ the techniques discussed in Chapters 23–26, such as using subjects and verbs effectively, subordinating and coordinating, creating parallelism, and varying sentence beginnings. Edit the finished product for punctuation.

> Modern Americans owe many debts to Native Americans. Several pleasures are among the debts. Native Americans originated two fine junk foods. They discovered popcorn. Potato chips were also one of their contributions.
>
> The introduction of popcorn to the European settlers came from Native Americans. Massasoit provided popcorn at the first Thanksgiving feast. The Aztecs offered popcorn to the Spanish explorer Hernando Cortés. The Aztecs wore popcorn necklaces. So did the natives of the West Indies. There were three ways that the Native Americans popped the corn. First, they roasted an ear over fire. The ear was skewered on a stick. They ate only some of the popcorn. They ate the corn that fell outside the flames. Second, they scraped the corn off the cob. The kernels would be thrown into the fire. Of course, the fire had to be low. Then the popped kernels that did not fall into the fire were eaten. The third method was the most sophisticated. It involved a shallow pottery vessel. It contained sand. The vessel was heated. The sand soon got hot. Corn kernels were stirred in. They popped to the surface of the sand and were eaten.
>
> A Native American chef was responsible for devising the crunchy potato chip. His name was George Crum. In 1853 Crum was cooking at Moon Lake Lodge. The lodge was in Saratoga Springs, New York. Complaints were sent in by a customer. The man thought Crum's french-fried potatoes were too thick. Crum tried a thinner batch. These were also unsuitable. Crum became frustrated. He deliberately made the potatoes thin and crisp. They could not be cut with a knife and fork. Crum's joke backfired. The customer raved about the potato chips. The chips were

graph on the grandmother's purpose. The next longest sentence, 5, details and stresses the grandmother's accomplishments. Several sentences begin with modifiers, thus avoiding the monotony of starting every sentence with *She* and creating a periodic sentence for emphasis (4), clarifying sequence (6), and putting the grandmother's views in the context of her teaching experience (8). The shortest sentence, the last one, emphasizes the grandmother's success as a teacher, and its inverted word order also emphasizes the verb *soar*.

COLLABORATIVE LEARNING

Ask students to complete Exercise 26.6 individually and then discuss their responses in groups in preparation for revising them. You might choose several of the revised responses to photocopy and hand out in order to generate discussion of the effects of variety. In a wired classroom, you might ask several student volunteers to post their revised responses in order to provide the basis for discussion.

ANSWERS: EXERCISE 26.6
Possible revision

> After being dormant for many years, the Italian volcano Vesuvius exploded on August 24 in the year AD 79. The ash, pumice, and mud from the volcano buried two towns—Herculaneum and the more famous Pompeii—which lay undiscovered until 1709 and 1748, respectively. The excavation of Pompeii was the more systematic, the occasion for initiating modern methods of conservation and restoration. Whereas Herculaneum was simply looted of its most valuable finds and then left to disintegrate, Pompeii appears much as it did during the eruption. A luxurious house opens onto a lush central garden. An election poster decorates a wall. And a dining table is set for breakfast.

ANSWERS: EXERCISE ON CHAPTERS 23–26

Possible revision

Modern Americans owe many debts to Native Americans, including several pleasures. Native Americans originated two fine junk foods: popcorn and potato chips.

Native Americans introduced popcorn to the European settlers, Massasoit providing popcorn at the first Thanksgiving feast and the Aztecs offering popcorn to the Spanish explorer Hernando Cortés. The Aztecs and natives of the West Indies wore popcorn necklaces. Native Americans popped the corn in three ways. First, they roasted an ear skewered on a stick over fire and ate the corn that fell outside the flames. Second, they scraped the corn off the cob, threw the kernels into a low fire, and ate the popped kernels that did not fall into the fire. Third and most sophisticated, they heated a shallow pottery vessel containing sand, stirred corn kernels into the hot sand, and ate what popped up to the surface.

A Native American chef named George Crum devised the crunchy potato chip. In 1853 Crum was cooking at Moon Lake Lodge in Saratoga Springs, New York. A customer complained that Crum's french-fried potatoes were too thick. Crum tried a thinner batch, but these were also unsuitable. Frustrated, Crum deliberately made the potatoes so thin and crisp that they could not be cut with a knife and fork. Crum's joke backfired, for the customer raved about the potato chips. Soon these Saratoga Chips appeared on the lodge's menu and throughout New England. Crum later opened his own restaurant, of course offering potato chips.

Now all Americans munch popcorn in movies, crunch potato chips at parties, and gorge on both when alone and bored. They can be grateful to Native Americans for these guilty pleasures.

named Saratoga Chips. Soon they appeared on the lodge's menu. They also appeared throughout New England. Crum later opened his own restaurant. Of course, he offered potato chips.

Now all Americans munch popcorn in movies. They crunch potato chips at parties. They gorge on both when alone and bored. They can be grateful to Native Americans for these guilty pleasures.

PART 6

Punctuation

27 End Punctuation

28 The Comma

29 The Semicolon

30 The Apostrophe

31 Quotation Marks

32 Other Punctuation Marks

Commas, semicolons, colons, dashes, parentheses

(For explanations, consult the pages in parentheses.)

Sentences with two main clauses

The bus stopped, but no one got off. (p. 422)
The bus stopped; no one got off. (p. 445)
The bus stopped; however, no one got off. (p. 446)
The mechanic replaced the battery, the distributor cap, and the starter;
    but still the car would not start. (p. 448)
Her duty was clear: she had to locate the problem. (p. 468)

Introductory elements

Modifiers (p. 425)

After the argument was over, we laughed at ourselves.
Racing over the plain, the gazelle escaped the lion.
To dance in the contest, he had to tape his knee.
Suddenly, the door flew open.
With 125 passengers aboard, the plane was half full.
In 1983 he won the Nobel Prize.

Absolute phrases (p. 432)

Its wing broken, the bird hopped around on the ground.

Interrupting and concluding elements

Nonessential modifiers (p. 427)

Jim's car, which barely runs, has been impounded.
We consulted the dean, who had promised to help us.
The boy, like his sister, wants to be a pilot.
They moved across the desert, shielding their eyes from the sun.
The men do not speak to each other, although they share a car.

Nonessential appositives

Bergen's only daughter, Candice, became an actress. (p. 429)
The residents of three counties—Suffolk, Springfield, and Morrison—
    were urged to evacuate. (p. 471)
My father demanded one promise: that we not lie to him. (p. 468)

Essential modifiers (p. 427)

The car that hit mine was uninsured.
We consulted a teacher who had promised to help us.
The boy in the black hat is my cousin.
They were surprised to find the desert teeming with life.
The men do not speak to each other because they are feuding.

Essential appositives (p. 429)

Shaw's play *Saint Joan* was performed last year.

Their sons Tony, William, and Steve all chose military careers, leaving only Matthew to run the family business.

Transitional or parenthetical expressions

We suspect, however, that he will not come. (p. 430)

Jessica is respected by many people—including me. (p. 471)

George Balanchine (1904–83) was a brilliant choreographer of classical ballet. (p. 472)

Absolute phrases (p. 432)

The bird, its wing broken, hopped about on the ground.

The bird hopped about on the ground, its wing broken.

Phrases expressing contrast (p. 432)

The humidity, not just the heat, gives me headaches.

My headaches are caused by the humidity, not just the heat.

Concluding summaries and explanations

The movie opened to bad notices: the characters were judged shallow and unrealistic. (p. 468)

We had gumbo and jambalaya for dinner—a Cajun feast. (p. 471)

Items in a series

Three or more items

Chimpanzees, gorillas, orangutans, and gibbons are all apes. (p. 433)

The cities singled out for praise were Birmingham, Alabama; Lincoln, Nebraska; Austin, Texas; and Troy, New York. (p. 448)

Two or more adjectives before a noun (p. 433)

Dingy, smelly clothes decorated their room.

Dessert consisted of one tiny scoop of ice cream.

Introductory series (p. 471)

Appropriateness, accuracy, and necessity—these criteria should govern your selection of words.

Concluding series

Every word should be appropriate, accurate, and necessary. (p. 439)

Every word should meet three criteria: appropriateness, accuracy, and necessity. (p. 468)

Pay attention to your words—to their appropriateness, their accuracy, and their necessity. (p. 471)

HIGHLIGHTS

This chapter discusses the three marks of punctuation used to end sentences: periods, question marks, and exclamation points. Encourage students to see that these are not just physical boundaries but important parts of the meaning of sentences—and that they therefore deserve careful consideration.

RESOURCES AND IDEAS

Dawkins, John. "Teaching Punctuation as a Rhetorical Tool." *College Composition and Communication* 46.4 (1995): 533–48. Print. Dawkins makes a case for teaching the rhetorical thinking processes that accompany decisions about punctuation marks.

Mann, Nancy. "Teaching Punctuation as Information Management." *College Composition and Communication* 54.3 (2003): 359–93. Print. Mann discusses the evolution of punctuation. She describes a system of teaching punctuation that emphasizes not terminology but the relationships between different words and phrases in writing.

27
End Punctuation

End punctuation marks—the period, the question mark, and the exclamation point—signal the ends of sentences.

Grammar checkers A grammar checker may flag missing question marks after direct questions or incorrect combinations of marks (such as a question mark and a period at the end of a sentence), but it cannot do much else.

27a Use periods after most sentences and with some abbreviations.

1 Use a period to end a statement, mild command, or indirect question.

Statements
These are exciting and trying times.
The airline went bankrupt.

Mild commands
Please do not smoke.
Think of the possibilities.

If you are unsure whether to use an exclamation point or a period after a command, use a period. The exclamation point should be used only rarely (see p. 421).

An **indirect question** reports what someone has asked but not in the form or the exact words of the original:

Indirect questions
Students sometimes wonder whether their teachers read the papers they write.

Abused children eventually stop asking why they are being punished.

 CULTURE LANGUAGE In standard American English, an indirect question uses the wording and subject-verb order of a

---

mycomplab

Visit *mycomplab.com* for more resources and exercises on end punctuation.

statement: *The reporter asked why the negotiations failed*, not *why did the negotiations fail*.

2 Use periods with some abbreviations.

Use periods with abbreviations that consist of or end in small letters. Otherwise, omit periods from abbreviations.

Dr.	Mr., Mrs.	e.g.	Feb.	ft.
St.	Ms.	i.e.	p.	a.m., p.m.
PhD	BC, BCE	USA	IBM	AM, PM
BA	AD, CE	US	USMC	AIDS

Note When a sentence ends in an abbreviation with a period, don't add a second period: *My first class is at 8 a.m.*
See also pages 492–95 on uses of abbreviations in writing.

Exercise 27.1 Revising: Periods

Revise the following sentences so that periods are used correctly.

> *Example:*
> Several times I wrote to ask when my subscription ended?
> Several times I wrote to ask when my subscription ended.

1. The instructor asked when Plato wrote *The Republic*?
2. Give the date within one century
3. The exact date is not known, but it is estimated at 370 BCE
4. Dr Arn will lecture on Plato at 7:30 p.m..
5. The area of the lecture hall is only 1600 sq ft

27b Use question marks after direct questions and sometimes to indicate doubt.

1 Use a question mark with a direct question.

What is the difference between these two people**?**
Will economists ever really understand the economy**?**

After an indirect question, use a period: *The senator asked why the bill had passed.* (See opposite.)
Questions in a series are each followed by a question mark:

The officer asked how many times the suspect had been arrested. Three times**?** Four times**?** More than that**?**

The use of capital letters for questions in a series is optional (see p. 483).

Note Question marks are never combined with other question marks, exclamation points, periods, or commas:

POLITE DEMANDS

Students often question the punctuation of polite demands, such as "Would you please send me your catalog." These sentences are used frequently for requests that the writer expects to be granted. In business use they are punctuated with periods; however, it's never wrong to use a question mark if the writer is in doubt.

COLLABORATIVE LEARNING

PEER EDITING FOR PERIODS AND QUESTION MARKS

In groups, have students complete Exercises 27.1 and 27.2 to review proper use and placement of periods and question marks. Then, ask them to select an essay either in-progress or graded for peer editing. Readers should check their group members' papers for period and question mark use and placement.

ANSWERS: EXERCISE 27.1

1. The instructor asked when Plato wrote *The Republic*.
2. Give the date within one century.
3. The exact date is not known, but it is estimated at 370 BCE.
4. Dr. Arn will lecture on Plato at 7:30 p.m.
5. The area of the lecture hall is only 1600 sq. ft.

COLLABORATIVE LEARNING

ADDING END PUNCTUATION

Write or locate a short text (five to seven sentences) that includes abbreviations and questions. Remove all end punctuation and capitalizations that would indicate where sentences begin and end. Ask students to add periods and question marks as needed. Groups should then compare their answers both with one another and to the original text. In a wired classroom, each group can post the revised version on the class Web site.

Faulty	"What is the point?," readers ask.
Revised	"What is the point**?**" readers ask.

2 **Use a question mark within parentheses to indicate doubt about a number or date.**

The Greek philosopher Socrates was born in 470 (**?**) BC and died in 399 BC from drinking poison after having been condemned to death.

Note Don't use a question mark within parentheses to express sarcasm or irony. Express these attitudes through sentence structure and word choice. (See Chapters 23 and 38.)

Faulty	Stern's friendliness (?) bothered Crane.
Revised	Stern's <u>insincerity</u> bothered Crane.

Exercise 27.2   Revising: Question marks

Revise the following sentences so that question marks (along with other punctuation marks) are used correctly.

> *Example:*
> "Why should I vote for you?," the woman asked the candidate.
> "Why should I vote for you**?**" the woman asked the candidate.

1. In Homer's *Odyssey,* Odysseus took seven years to travel from Troy to Ithaca. Or was it eight years. Or more?
2. Odysseus must have wondered whether he would ever make it home?
3. "What man are you and whence?," asks Odysseus's wife, Penelope.
4. Why does Penelope ask, "Where is your city? Your family?"?
5. Penelope does not recognize Odysseus and asks who this stranger is?

 27c **Use an exclamation point after an emphatic statement, interjection, or command.**

No**!** We must not lose this election**!**
Come here immediately**!**

Follow mild interjections and commands with commas or periods, as appropriate:

No**,** the response was not terrific**.**
To prolong your car's life, change its oil regularly**.**

Use exclamation points sparingly, not to express sarcasm, irony, or amazement. Rely on sentence structure and word choice to express these attitudes. (See Chapters 23 and 38.)

Faulty	After traveling 4.4 billion miles through space, *Voyager 2* was off-target by 21 miles (!).
Revised	After traveling 4.4 billion miles through space, *Voyager 2* was off-target by <u>a mere</u> 21 miles.

Relying on the exclamation point for emphasis is like crying wolf: the mark loses its power to impress the reader. Frequent exclamation points can also make writing sound overemotional:

Overused exclamation points

Our city government is a mess! After just six months in office, the mayor has had to fire four city officials! In the same period the city councilors have done nothing but argue! And city services decline with each passing day!

Note Exclamation points are never combined with other exclamation points, question marks, periods, or commas:

Faulty	"This will not be endured!," he roared.
Revised	"This will not be endured**!**" he roared.

Exercise 27.3   Revising: Exclamation points

Revise the following sentences so that exclamation points (along with other punctuation marks) are used correctly. If a sentence is punctuated correctly as given, mark the number preceding it.

Example:
"Well, now!," he said loudly.
"Well, now**!**" he said loudly.

1. As the firefighters moved their equipment into place, the police shouted, "Move back!".
2. A child's cries could be heard from above: "Help me. Help."
3. When the child was rescued, the crowd called, "Hooray."
4. The rescue was the most exciting event of the day!
5. Let me tell you about it.

Exercise 27.4   Revising: End punctuation

Insert appropriate punctuation (periods, question marks, or exclamation points) where needed in the following paragraph.

When visitors first arrive in Hawaii, they often encounter an unexpected language barrier Standard English is the language of business and government, but many of the people speak Pidgin English Instead of an excited "Aloha" the visitors may be greeted with an excited Pidgin "Howzit" or asked if they know "how fo' find one good hotel" Many Hawaiians question whether Pidgin will hold children back because it prevents communication with the *haoles,* or Caucasians, who run businesses Yet many others feel that Pidgin is a last defense of ethnic diversity on the islands To those who want to make standard English the official language of the state, these Hawaiians may respond, "Just 'cause I speak Pidgin no mean I dumb" They may ask, "Why you no listen" or, in standard English, "Why don't you listen"

Note See page 479 for a punctuation exercise combining periods with other marks of punctuation.

ANSWERS: EXERCISE 27.3

1. As the firefighters moved their equipment into place, the police shouted, "Move back!"
2. A child's cries could be heard from above: "Help me! Help!"
3. When the child was rescued, the crowd called, "Hooray!"
4. The rescue was the most exciting event of the day.
5. Sentence correct.

COLLABORATIVE LEARNING

END PUNCTUATION

Have students complete Exercise 27.4 individually and compare their responses in small groups. Then ask each group to review the punctuation of paragraphs from their own work and help each other to locate and revise punctuation errors. Ask each student to keep a list of the errors that commonly recur in his or her work (along with revised examples) and to use that list in future proofreading tasks.

ANSWERS: EXERCISE 27.4

When visitors first arrive in Hawaii, they often encounter an unexpected language barrier. Standard English is the language of business and government, but many of the people speak Pidgin English. Instead of an excited "Aloha!" the visitors may be greeted with an excited Pidgin "Howzit!" or asked if they know "how fo' find one good hotel." Many Hawaiians question whether Pidgin will hold children back because it prevents communication with the *haoles,* or Caucasians, who run businesses. Yet many others feel that Pidgin is a last defense of ethnic diversity on the islands. To those who want to make standard English the official language of the state, these Hawaiians may respond, "Just 'cause I speak Pidgin no mean I dumb." They may ask, "Why you no listen?" or, in standard English, "Why don't you listen?"

HIGHLIGHTS

The comma probably causes more anguish for apprentice writers than any other punctuation mark. There's no magic formula for accurate use of the comma. Most uses are conventional, but a few require judgment calls—and writers can develop the necessary judgment only through lots of reading and writing. For example, the problem of whether to use commas with essential and nonessential modifiers is probably not a punctuation problem but a matter of understanding what these modifiers do. Commas, or their absence, are just a graphic way of reinforcing the meaning of the modifier. The text's discussion of how context determines a modifier's role in a sentence can help students see this point.

Forcing students to memorize these rules may not make them more accurate writers. Students need to learn how to take the generalizations conveyed by these rules and apply them to specific situations; that means helping them understand the rules, not just getting them to memorize.

A WRITER'S PERSPECTIVE

It is highly important to put [commas] in place as you go along. If you try to come back after doing a paragraph and stick them in the various spots that tempt you you will discover that they tend to swarm like minnows into all sorts of crevices whose existence you hadn't realized and before you know it the whole long sentence becomes immobilized and lashed up squirming in commas. Better to use them sparingly, and with affection, precisely when the need for one arises, nicely, by itself.
—Lewis Thomas, "Notes on Punctuation"

COLLABORATIVE LEARNING

COMMA MYTHS

More than any other piece of punctuation, confusion and myths seem to surround the use of the comma. Ask students in groups to make a list of comma "rules" they have been taught in the past. They should discuss any contradictory advice they might have received. Each group should then present their list of "rules" to the rest of the class. You might direct students to sections in this chapter where their comma rules are addressed, either to affirm or to clarify them.

28
The Comma

Commas usually function within sentences to separate elements (see the box on the next page). Omitting needed commas or inserting needless ones can confuse the reader:

Comma needed	Though very tall Abraham Lincoln was not an overbearing man.
Revised	Though very tall, Abraham Lincoln was not an overbearing man.
Unneeded commas	The hectic pace of Beirut, broke suddenly into frightening chaos when the city became, the focus of civil war.
Revised	The hectic pace of Beirut broke suddenly into frightening chaos when the city became the focus of civil war.

Grammar checkers A grammar checker will ignore many comma errors. For example, a checker failed to catch the missing commas in *The boat ran aground and we were stranded* and in *We cooked lasagna spinach and apple pie.* At the same time the checker overlooked the misused commas in *The trip was short but, the weather was perfect* and *The travelers were tempted by, the many shops, and varied restaurants.*

28a Use a comma before *and, but,* or another coordinating conjunction linking main clauses.

The coordinating conjunctions are *and, but, or, nor, for, so,* and *yet.* When one of them links words or phrases, do not use a comma: *Dugain plays and sings Irish and English folk songs.* However, *do* use a comma when a coordinating conjunction joins main clauses. A **main clause** has a subject and a predicate (but no subordinating word at the beginning) and makes a complete statement (see p. 250).

Visit *mycomplab.com* for more resources and exercises on the comma.

Principal uses of the comma

■ **Separate main clauses linked by a coordinating conjunction** (opposite and next page):

Main clause **,** for and or / so but nor / yet   main clause **.**

The building is finished**,** but it has no tenants.

■ **Set off most introductory elements** (p. 425):

Introductory element **,** main clause **.**

Unfortunately**,** the only tenant pulled out.

■ **Set off nonessential elements** (p. 427):

Main clause **,** nonessential element **.**

The empty building symbolizes a weak local economy**,** which affects everyone.

Beginning of main clause **,** nonessential element **,** end of main clause **.**

The primary cause**,** the decline of local industry**,** is not news.

■ **Separate items in a series** (p. 433):

• • • item 1 **,** item 2 **,** and / or   item 3 • • •

The city needs healthier businesses**,** new schools**,** and improved housing.

■ **Separate coordinate adjectives** (p. 433):

• • • first adjective **,** second adjective   word modified • • •

A tall**,** sleek skyscraper is not needed.

Other uses of the comma:

Set off absolute phrases (p. 432).
Set off phrases expressing contrast (p. 432).
Separate parts of dates, addresses, long numbers (p. 435).
Separate quotations and signal phrases (p. 436).
Prevent misreading (p. 438).

See also page 439 for when *not* to use the comma.

RESOURCES AND IDEAS

Punctuation

Dawkins, John. "Teaching Meaning-Based Punctuation." *Teaching English in the Two-Year College* 31.2 (2003): 154–62. Print. Dawkins explains his hierarchy of punctuation and advocates that instructors employ this theory to help students learn to "use meaning as a basis for decision making" (155).

---. "Teaching Punctuation as a Rhetorical Tool." *College Composition and Communication* 46.4 (1995): 533–48. Print. Dawkins makes a case for teaching the rhetorical thinking processes that accompany decisions about punctuation marks.

Mann, Nancy. "Teaching Punctuation as Information Management." *College Composition and Communication* 54.3 (2003): 359–93. Print. Mann discusses the evolution of punctuation. She describes a system of teaching punctuation that emphasizes the relationships between different words and phrases in writing, and not just terminology.

Meyer, Emily, and Louise Z. Smith, "Punctuation." Print. *The Practical Tutor*. New York: Oxford UP, 1989. Print. The authors offer detailed advice for the often frustrating task of helping students develop effective punctuation skills.

Commas

Meyer, Charles F. "Teaching Punctuation to Advanced Writers." *Journal of Advanced Composition* 6.1 (1985–86): 117–29. Print. Meyer offers a number of strategies that can be used in any classroom.

Shaughnessy, Mina P. *Errors and Expectations: A Guide for the Teacher of Basic Writing*. New York: Oxford UP, 1977. 14–43. Print. Shaughnessy explains teaching punctuation in the context of understanding students' hypotheses about their texts.

Thomas, Lewis. "Notes on Punctuation." *New England Journal of Medicine* 296.19 (1977): 1103–05. Reprinted in *The Medusa and the Snail: More Notes of a Biology Watcher*. New York: Viking, 1979. Print. An experienced scientist and writer explores how punctuation use can affect the meaning of texts.

COMMA POWER

Though writing instructors often treat commas and other marks of punctuation as if they were primarily cues to grammatical structures, these marks also function legitimately as stylistic cues, as indicators of the writer's voice—or so argues Wallace Chafe in "What Good Is Punctuation?" (*The Quarterly of the National Writing Project and the Center for the Study of Writing* 10.1 [1988]: 8–11). Chafe supports his argument with examples from the work of Herman Melville and James Agee and concludes with some useful advice for teaching:

> Students, in addition to being sensitized to their inner voices, will benefit from knowing the range of punctuating options that are available, and from being shown, through examples, what is most appropriate to one style and another. They can learn from practice in writing advertising copy as well as the more academic kinds of exposition, and from experimenting with fiction that mimics the very different punctuation styles of, say, Melville and Agee. At the same time, developing writers need to know that there are certain specific rules for punctuating that violate the prosody of their inner voices and that simply have to be learned. These arbitrary rules are few in number and well defined, and to learn them need be no burden ... The bottom line is that punctuation contributes substantially to the effectiveness of a piece of writing, and that its successful use calls for an awareness of something that is, for this and other reasons, essential to good writing; a sensitivity to the sound of written language.

"In Praise of the Humble Comma," a short and amusing paean to the power of punctuation to affect meaning, might also be handed out to students as a useful reminder of the connections between grammar and content. (Pico Iyer, *Time*, June 13, 1988: 348).

ANSWERS: EXERCISE 28.1

1. Parents once automatically gave their children the father's surname, but some no longer do.
2. Instead, they bestow the mother's name, for they believe that the mother's importance should be recognized.
3. The child's surname may be just the mother's, or it may link the mother's and the father's with a hyphen.

Caffeine can keep coffee drinkers alert, and it may elevate their mood.

Caffeine was once thought to be safe, but now researchers warn of harmful effects.

Coffee drinkers may suffer sleeplessness, for the drug acts as a stimulant to the nervous system.

Note Do not add a comma *after* a coordinating conjunction between main clauses (see also pp. 439–40):

Not   Caffeine increases the heart rate, and, it constricts blood vessels.
But   Caffeine increases the heart rate, and it constricts blood vessels.

Exceptions When the main clauses in a sentence are very long or grammatically complicated, or when they contain internal punctuation, a semicolon before the coordinating conjunction will clarify the division between clauses (see p. 448):

Caffeine may increase alertness, elevate mood, and provide energy; but it may also cause irritability, anxiety, stomach pains, and other ills.

When main clauses are very short and closely related in meaning, you may omit the comma between them as long as the resulting sentence is clear:

Caffeine helps but it also hurts.

If you are in doubt about whether to use a comma in such a sentence, use it. It will always be correct.

Exercise 28.1   Punctuating linked main clauses

Insert a comma before each coordinating conjunction that links main clauses in the following sentences.

> *Example:*
> I would have attended the concert and the reception but I had to baby-sit for my niece.
> I would have attended the concert and the reception, but I had to baby-sit for my niece.

1. Parents once automatically gave their children the father's surname but some no longer do.
2. Instead, they bestow the mother's name for they believe that the mother's importance should be recognized.
3. The child's surname may be just the mother's or it may link the mother's and the father's with a hyphen.
4. Sometimes the first and third children will have the mother's surname and the second child will have the father's.
5. Occasionally the mother and father combine parts of their names and a new hybrid surname is born.

Exercise 28.2 Sentence combining: Linked main clauses

Combine each group of sentences below into one sentence that contains only two main clauses connected by the coordinating conjunction in parentheses. Separate the main clauses with a comma. You will have to add, delete, and rearrange words.

Example:

The circus had come to town. The children wanted to see it. Their parents wanted to see it. (*and*)

The circus had come to town, and the children and their parents wanted to see it.

1. Parents were once legally required to bestow the father's surname on their children. These laws have been contested in court. They have been found invalid. (*but*)
2. Parents may now give their children any surname they choose. The arguments for bestowing the mother's surname are often strong. They are often convincing. (*and*)
3. Critics sometimes question the effects of unusual surnames on children. They wonder how confusing the new surnames will be. They wonder how fleeting the surnames will be. (*or*)
4. Children with surnames different from their parents' may suffer embarrassment. They may suffer identity problems. Giving children their father's surname is still very much the norm. (*for*)
5. Hyphenated names are awkward. They are also difficult to pass on. Some observers think they will die out in the next generation. Or they may die out before. (*so*)

28b **Use a comma to set off most introductory elements.**

An introductory element modifies a word or words in the main clause that follows. These elements are usually set off from the rest of the sentence with a comma:

Subordinate clause (p. 250)

Even when identical twins are raised apart, they grow up very like each other.

Because they are similar, such twins interest scientists.

Verbal or verbal phrase (p. 245)

Explaining the similarity, some researchers claim that one's genes are one's destiny.

Concerned, other researchers deny the claim.

Prepositional phrase (p. 242)

In a debate that has lasted centuries, scientists use identical twins to argue for or against genetic destiny.

---

4. Sometimes the first and third children will have the mother's surname, and the second child will have the father's.
5. Occasionally the mother and father combine parts of their names, and a new hybrid surname is born.

Ask students to complete Exercise 28.2 individually and then discuss their responses in small groups. Have each group discuss the effect of alternative answers and then present one or two of the most successful responses.

ANSWERS: EXERCISE 28.2

Possible answers

1. Parents were once legally required to bestow the father's surname on their children, but these laws have been contested in court and found invalid.
2. Parents may now give their children any surname they choose, and the arguments for bestowing the mother's surname are often strong and convincing.
3. Critics sometimes question the effects of unusual surnames on children, or they wonder how confusing or fleeting the new surnames will be.
4. Children with surnames different from their parents' may suffer embarrassment or identity problems, for giving children their father's surname is still very much the norm.
5. Hyphenated names are awkward and difficult to pass on, so some observers think they will die out in the next generation or before.

COURT REPORTER

To help students understand how commas affect understanding, have them play "court reporter." Ask one or two students to read a passage from their papers or some reading for the class while the other students try to write what they say. Then have the reporters prepare a transcript of what they heard, inserting punctuation where they think it is needed. Each group should compare the reporters' versions with the originals and solve any disputes over comma use by referring to the appropriate sections of this chapter.

Have students complete Exercise 28.3 individually and then compare their responses in small groups. This allows students to debate different kinds of comma usage in a nonintimidating setting.

ANSWERS: EXERCISE 28.3

1. Sentence correct.
2. Because it is sudden and apparently well coordinated, the movement of flocks and schools has seemed to be directed by a leader.
3. However, new studies have discovered that flocks and schools are leaderless.
4. When each bird or fish senses a predator, it follows individual rules for fleeing.
5. Multiplied over hundreds of individuals, these responses look as if they have been choreographed.

Ask students to complete Exercise 28.4 individually and then compare responses in small groups. You might then have each group create one or two sentences of their own involving introductory clauses set off by commas.

Transitional or parenthetical expression (pp. 88–89)
Of course, scientists can now look directly at the genes themselves.

The comma may be omitted after short introductory elements if its omission does not create confusion. (If you are in doubt, however, the comma is always correct.)

Clear	In a hundred years genetics may no longer be a mystery.
Confusing	Despite intensive research scientists still have more questions than answers.
Clear	Despite intensive research, scientists still have more questions than answers.

Commas may also be omitted after some transitional expressions when they start sentences. (See p. 430.)

Thus the debate continues.

Note Take care to distinguish -*ing* words used as modifiers from -*ing* words used as subjects, as shown in the following examples. The former almost always take a comma; the latter never do.

modifier   subject   verb
Studying identical twins, geneticists learn about inheritance.

subject   verb
Studying identical twins helps geneticists learn about inheritance.

Exercise 28.3 Punctuating introductory elements

Insert commas where needed after introductory elements in the following sentences. If a sentence is punctuated correctly as given, mark the number preceding it.

Example:
After the new library opened the old one became a student union.
After the new library opened, the old one became a student union.

1. Moving in a fluid mass is typical of flocks of birds and schools of fish.
2. Because it is sudden and apparently well coordinated the movement of flocks and schools has seemed to be directed by a leader.
3. However new studies have discovered that flocks and schools are leaderless.
4. When each bird or fish senses a predator it follows individual rules for fleeing.
5. Multiplied over hundreds of individuals these responses look as if they have been choreographed.

Exercise 28.4 Sentence combining: Introductory elements

Combine each pair of sentences below into one sentence that begins with an introductory phrase or clause as specified in parentheses. Follow the introductory element with a comma. You will have to add, delete, change, and rearrange words.

Example:

The girl was humming to herself. She walked upstairs. (*Phrase beginning Humming*.)

<u>Humming to herself</u>, the girl walked upstairs.

1. Scientists have made an effort to explain the mysteries of flocks and schools. They have proposed bizarre magnetic fields and telepathy. (*Phrase beginning In*.)
2. Scientists developed computer models. They have abandoned earlier explanations. (*Clause beginning Since*.)
3. The movement of a flock or school starts with each individual. It is rapidly and perhaps automatically coordinated among individuals. (*Phrase beginning Starting*.)
4. One zoologist observes that human beings seek coherent patterns. He suggests that investigators saw purpose in the movement of flocks and schools where none existed. (*Phrase beginning Observing*.)
5. One may want to study the movement of flocks or schools. Then one must abandon a search for purpose or design. (*Phrase beginning To*.)

28c Use a comma or commas to set off nonessential elements.

Commas around part of a sentence often signal that the element is not essential to the meaning of the sentence:

Nonessential element

The company, which is located in Oklahoma, has a good reputation.

This **nonessential element** may modify or rename the word it refers to (*company* in the example), but it does not limit the word to a particular individual or group. (Because it does not restrict meaning, a nonessential element is also called a **nonrestrictive element.**) Nonessential elements are *not* essential, but punctuation *is*.

In contrast, an **essential** (or **restrictive**) element *does* limit the word it refers to:

Essential element

The company rewards employees <u>who work hard</u>.

In this example the underlined essential element cannot be omitted without leaving the meaning of *employees* too general. Because it is essential, such an element is *not* set off with commas. The element *is* essential, but punctuation is *not*.

Meaning and context

The same element in the same sentence may be essential or nonessential depending on your intended meaning and the context in which the sentence appears. For example, look at the second sentence in each of the following passages:

RECOGNIZING NONESSENTIAL ELEMENTS

For students who are still uncertain about whether elements are nonessential or essential, emphasize that nonessential elements *require* punctuation and *follow* these types of items:

1. One of a kind (including proper nouns): *Secretariat, a beautiful chestnut colt, won the Triple Crown in 1973.*
2. All of a kind: *United States senators, who serve six-year terms, face constant pressure to raise campaign funds.*
3. Previously mentioned: *Animal rights activists have been known to stage outrageous demonstrations. The activists, who seek media attention, are prepared to risk criticism to promote their cause.*

Essential

Not all the bands were equally well received, however. The band playing old music held the audience's attention. The other groups created much less excitement. [*Playing old music* identifies a particular band.]

Nonessential

A new band called Fats made its debut on Saturday night. The band, playing old music, held the audience's attention. If this performance is typical, the group has a bright future. [*Playing old music* adds information about a band already named.]

Punctuation of interrupting nonessential elements

When a nonessential element falls in the middle of a sentence, be sure to set it off with a pair of commas, one *before* and one *after* the element. Dashes or parentheses may also set off nonessential elements (see pp. 470 and 472).

1 Use a comma or commas to set off nonessential clauses and phrases.

Clauses and phrases serving as adjectives and adverbs may be either nonessential or essential. In the following examples the underlined clauses and phrases are nonessential: they could be omitted without changing the meaning of the words they modify.

Nonessential

Elizabeth Blackwell was the first woman to graduate from an American medical school, in 1849.

A test for essential and nonessential elements

1. **Identify the element.**

   Hai Nguyen who emigrated from Vietnam lives in Denver.
   Those who emigrated with him live elsewhere.

2. **Remove the element. Does the fundamental meaning of the sentence change?**

   Hai Nguyen lives in Denver. *No.*
   Those live elsewhere. *Yes.* [Who are *Those?*]

3. **If *no*, the element is *nonessential* and should be set off with punctuation.**

   Hai Nguyen, who emigrated from Vietnam, lives in Denver.

   If *yes*, the element is *essential* and should *not* be set off with punctuation.

   Those who emigrated with him live elsewhere.

She was a medical pioneer, <u>helping to found the first medical college for women</u>.

She taught at the school, <u>which was affiliated with the New York Infirmary</u>.

Blackwell, <u>who published books and papers on medicine,</u> practiced pediatrics and gynecology.

She moved to England in 1869, <u>when she was forty-eight</u>.

Note Most adverb clauses are essential because they describe conditions necessary to the main clause. They are set off by a comma only when they introduce sentences (see p. 425) and when they are truly nonessential, adding incidental information (as in the last example above) or expressing a contrast beginning *although, even though, though, whereas,* and the like.

In the following sentences, the underlined elements limit the meaning of the words they modify. Removing the elements would leave the meaning too general.

Essential

The history <u>of aspirin</u> began <u>with the ancient Greeks</u>.

Physicians <u>who sought to relieve their patients' pains</u> recommended chewing willow bark.

Willow bark contains a chemical <u>that is similar to aspirin</u>.

Note Whereas both nonessential and essential clauses may begin with *which,* only essential clauses begin with *that.* Some writers prefer *that* exclusively for essential clauses and *which* exclusively for nonessential clauses. See the Glossary of Usage, page 879, for advice on the use of *that* and *which.*

2 Use a comma or commas to set off nonessential appositives.

An **appositive** is a noun or noun substitute that renames another noun just before it. (See p. 254.) Many appositives are nonessential; thus they are set off, usually with commas.

Nonessential

Toni Morrison's fifth novel, *Beloved,* won the Pulitzer Prize in 1988.

Morrison, <u>a native of Ohio,</u> won the Nobel Prize in 1993.

Take care *not* to set off essential appositives; like other essential elements, they limit or define the word to which they refer.

Essential

Morrison's novel <u>The Bluest Eye</u> is about an African American girl who longs for blue eyes.

The critic <u>Michiko Kakutani</u> says that Morrison's work "stands radiantly on its own as an American epic."

COLLABORATIVE LEARNING

WORD PUZZLES

Divide the class into small groups and give them word puzzles like the following. Each of these puzzles can be solved only if the reader knows how essential and nonessential phrases are punctuated.

1. You are a CIA agent whose job is to keep track of all the Russian spies in Melopolia. One day you receive this message from Washington: "All the Russian spies, formerly residing in the Russian embassy, have been sent home."

Is there anyone left for you to watch?

2. After a long and successful season the university basketball team played its cross-state rival for the conference championship. Pandemonium broke out when a long shot dropped in at the buzzer to give the university the victory. Parties were held all over campus.

When Professor Kean arrived at class the next morning, the students, who had celebrated long into the night, were fast asleep at their desks.

Can you tell what portion of the class was asleep?

3. A severe electrical storm swept through town just after noon. Lightning struck several buildings, including the computer center. Technicians repairing damage there found that the computers which were not equipped with electrical surge protectors needed to have their circuit boards replaced.

Are any of the computers still usable?

COMMAS AND PARENTHESES

Students who know math will appreciate that the commas around parenthetical expressions are like the parentheses in a mathematical equation; if you use one to open the expression, you must have one to close it, or it can't be "solved" properly.

RESOURCES AND IDEAS

Christensen, Francis. "Restrictive and Nonrestrictive Modifiers Again." *Notes Toward a New Rhetoric: Nine Essays for Teachers.* 3rd ed. Ed. Francis Christensen and Bonniejean Christensen. Bangor: Booklocker.com, 2007. 100–12. Print. Christensen discusses and illustrates uses of the comma with a variety of modifying elements.

3 Use a comma or commas to set off transitional or parenthetical expressions.

Transitional expressions

Transitional expressions form links between ideas. They include conjunctive adverbs such as *however* and *moreover* as well as other words or phrases such as *for example* and *of course*. (See pp. 88–89 for a list of transitional words and phrases.) Transitional expressions are nonessential, and most of them are set off with a comma or commas:

> US workers, for example, receive fewer holidays than European workers do.

When a transitional expression links main clauses, precede it with a semicolon and follow it with a comma. (See p. 446.)

> European workers often have long paid vacations; indeed, they may receive a full month.

Exceptions The conjunctions *and, but,* and *yet* are sometimes used as transitional expressions but are never followed by commas (see p. 441). Usage varies with some other transitional expressions, depending on the expression and the writer's judgment. Many writers omit commas with expressions that we read without pauses, such as *also, hence, next, now, then,* and *thus.* The same applies to *therefore* and *instead* when they fall inside or at the ends of clauses.

> US workers therefore put in more work days. But the days themselves may be shorter.
> Then the total hours worked come out roughly the same.

Parenthetical expressions

Parenthetical expressions provide comments, explanations, digressions, or other supplementary information not essential to meaning—for example, *fortunately, unfortunately, all things considered, to be frank, in other words.* Like transitional expressions, most parenthetical expressions are set off, sometimes with commas:

> Surprisingly, the most celebrated holiday in the world is New Year's Day.

Dashes and parentheses may also set off parenthetical expressions. (See pp. 470 and 472, respectively.)

4 Use a comma or commas to set off *yes* and *no,* tag questions, words of direct address, and mild interjections.

Yes and *no*
Yes, the editorial did have a point.
No, that can never be.

Tag questions

They don't stop to consider others, do they?
Jones should be allowed to vote, shouldn't he?

Direct address

Cody, please bring me the newspaper.
With all due respect, sir, I will not do that.

Mild interjections

Well, you will never know who did it.
Oh, they forgot all about the baby.

(You may want to use an exclamation point to set off a forceful interjection. See p. 420.)

Exercise 28.5 Punctuating essential and nonessential elements

Insert commas in the following sentences to set off nonessential elements, and delete any commas that incorrectly set off essential elements. If a sentence is correct as given, mark the number preceding it.

Example:

Our language has adopted the words, *garage* and *fanfare,* from the French.

Our language has adopted the words *garage* and *fanfare* from the French.

1. Italians insist that Marco Polo the thirteenth-century explorer did not import pasta from China.
2. Pasta which consists of flour and water and often egg existed in Italy long before Marco Polo left for his travels.
3. A historian who studied pasta says that it originated in the Middle East in the fifth century.
4. Most Italians dispute this account although their evidence is shaky.
5. Wherever pasta originated, the Italians are now the undisputed masters, in making and cooking it.
6. Marcella Hazan, who has written several books on Italian cooking, insists that homemade and hand-rolled pasta is the best.
7. Most cooks must buy dried pasta lacking the time to make their own.
8. The finest pasta is made from semolina, a flour from hard durum wheat.
9. Pasta manufacturers choose hard durum wheat, because it makes firmer cooked pasta than common wheat does.
10. Pasta, made from common wheat, tends to get soggy in boiling water.

Exercise 28.6 Sentence combining: Essential and nonessential elements

Combine each pair of sentences below into one sentence that uses the element described in parentheses. Insert commas as appropriate. You will have to add, delete, change, and rearrange words. Some items have more than one possible answer.

ANSWERS: EXERCISE 28.5

1. Italians insist that Marco Polo, the thirteenth-century explorer, did not import pasta from China.
2. Pasta, which consists of flour and water and often egg, existed in Italy long before Marco Polo left for his travels.
3. Sentence correct.
4. Most Italians dispute this account, although their evidence is shaky.
5. Wherever pasta originated, the Italians are now the undisputed masters in making and cooking it.
6. Sentence correct.
7. Most cooks must buy dried pasta, lacking the time to make their own.
8. Sentence correct.
9. Pasta manufacturers choose hard durum wheat because it makes firmer cooked pasta than common wheat does.
10. Pasta made from common wheat tends to get soggy in boiling water.

ANSWERS: EXERCISE 28.6

Possible answers

1. American colonists first imported pasta from the English, <u>who discovered it as tourists in Italy</u>.
2. The English <u>returning from their grand tours of Italy</u> were called macaronis because of their fancy airs.
3. A hair style <u>with elaborate curls</u> was also called *macaroni*.
4. The song "Yankee Doodle" refers to this hairdo <u>when it reports that Yankee Doodle "stuck a feather in his cap and called it macaroni."</u>
5. The song<u>, a creation of the English,</u> was actually intended to poke fun at unrefined American colonists.

ANSWERS: EXERCISE 28.7

1. Prices having risen rapidly<u>,</u> the government debated a price freeze.
2. A price freeze<u>,</u> unlike a rise in interest rates<u>,</u> seemed a sure solution.
3. The President would have to persuade businesses to accept a price freeze<u>,</u> his methods depending on their resistance.
4. No doubt the President<u>,</u> his advisers having urged it<u>,</u> would first try a patriotic appeal.
5. The President<u>,</u> not his advisers<u>,</u> insisted on negotiations with businesses.

Example:

> Mr. Ward's oldest sister helped keep him alive. She was a nurse in the hospital. (*Nonessential clause beginning who.*)
>
> Mr. Ward's oldest sister<u>, who was a nurse in the hospital,</u> helped keep him alive.

1. American colonists first imported pasta from the English. The English had discovered it as tourists in Italy. (*Nonessential clause beginning who.*)
2. The English returned from their grand tours of Italy. They were called macaronis because of their fancy airs. (*Essential phrase beginning returning.*)
3. A hair style was also called *macaroni*. It had elaborate curls. (*Essential phrase beginning with.*)
4. The song "Yankee Doodle" refers to this hairdo. It reports that Yankee Doodle "stuck a feather in his cap and called it macaroni." (*Essential clause beginning when.*)
5. The song was actually intended to poke fun at unrefined American colonists. It was a creation of the English. (*Nonessential appositive beginning a creation.*)

28d Use a comma or commas to set off absolute phrases.

An **absolute phrase** modifies a whole main clause rather than any word in the clause, and it usually consists of at least a participle (such as *done* or *having torn*) and its subject (a noun or pronoun). (See p. 249.) Absolute phrases can occur at almost any point in the sentence, and they are always set off by a comma or commas:

> Household recycling having succeeded<u>,</u> the city now wants to extend the program to businesses.
>
> Many businesses<u>,</u> their profits already squeezed<u>,</u> resist recycling.

28e Use a comma or commas to set off phrases expressing contrast.

> The essay needs less wit<u>,</u> more pith.
> The substance<u>,</u> not the style<u>,</u> is important.
> Substance<u>,</u> unlike style<u>,</u> cannot be faked.

Note Writers often omit commas around contrasting phrases beginning with *but: A fullbut hazy moon shone down.*

Exercise 28.7 Punctuating absolute phrases and phrases of contrast

Insert commas in the following sentences to set off absolute phrases and phrases of contrast.

Example:

The recording contract was canceled the band having broken up.
The recording contract was canceled**,** the band having broken up.

1. Prices having risen rapidly the government debated a price freeze.
2. A price freeze unlike a rise in interest rates seemed a sure solution.
3. The President would have to persuade businesses to accept a price freeze his methods depending on their resistance.
4. No doubt the President his advisers having urged it would first try a patriotic appeal.
5. The President not his advisers insisted on negotiations with businesses.

28f Use commas between items in a series and between coordinate adjectives.

1 Use commas between words, phrases, or clauses forming a series.

Place commas between all elements of a **series**—that is, three or more items of equal importance:

Anna Spingle married at the age of seventeen**,** had three children by twenty-one**,** and divorced at twenty-two.

She worked as a cook**,** a baby-sitter**,** and a crossing guard.

Some writers omit the comma before the coordinating conjunction in a series (*Breakfast consisted of coffee, eggs and kippers*). But the final comma is never wrong, and it always helps the reader see the last two items as separate:

Confusing	Spingle's new job involves typing, filing and answering correspondence.
Clear	Spingle's new job involves typing, filing**,** and answering correspondence.

Exception When items in a series are long and grammatically complicated, they may be separated by semicolons. When the items contain commas, they must be separated by semicolons. (See p. 448.)

2 Use commas between two or more adjectives that equally modify the same words.

When two or more adjectives modify the same word equally, they are said to be **coordinate**. The adjectives may be separated either by *and* or by a comma, as in the following examples:

Spingle's scratched and dented car is old, but it gets her to work.
She has dreams of a sleek**,** shiny car.

Punctuating two or more adjectives

1. **Identify the adjectives.**

   She was a faithful sincere friend.
   They are dedicated medical students.

2. **Can the adjectives be reversed without changing meaning?**

   She was a sincere faithful friend. *Yes.*
   They are medical dedicated students. *No.*

3. **Can the word *and* be sensibly inserted between the adjectives?**

   She was a faithful and sincere friend. *Yes.*
   They are dedicated and medical students. *No.*

4. **If *yes* to both questions, the adjectives *are* coordinate and *should* be separated by a comma.**

   She was a faithful, sincere friend.

   If *no* to both questions, the adjectives are *not* coordinate and should *not* be separated by a comma.

   They are dedicated medical students.

Adjectives are not coordinate—and should *not* be separated by commas—when the one nearer the noun is more closely related to the noun in meaning. In each of the next examples, the second adjective and the noun form a unit that is modified by the first adjective:

> Spingle's children work at various part-time jobs.
> They all expect to go to a nearby community college.

See the box above for a test to use in punctuating adjectives.
    Note Numbers are not coordinate with other adjectives:

Faulty	Spingle has three, teenaged children.
Revised	Spingle has three teenaged children.

Do not use a comma between the final adjective and the noun:

Faulty	The children hope to achieve good, well-paying, jobs.
Revised	The children hope to achieve good, well-paying jobs.

Exercise 28.8 Punctuating series and coordinate adjectives

Insert commas in the following sentences to separate elements in series and coordinate adjectives. Mark the number preceding any sentence whose punctuation is already correct.

Example:
Quiet by day, the club became a noisy smoky dive at night.
Quiet by day, the club became a noisy, smoky dive at night.

ANSWERS: EXERCISE 28.8

1. Shoes with high heels originated to protect feet from the mud, garbage, and animal waste in the streets.
2. Sentence correct.
3. The heels were worn by men and made of colorful silk brocades, soft suedes, or smooth leathers.
4. High-heeled shoes received a boost when the short, powerful King Louis XIV of France began wearing them.
5. Eventually only wealthy, fashionable French women wore high heels.

1. Shoes with high heels originated to protect feet from the mud garbage and animal waste in the streets.
2. The first known high heels worn strictly for fashion appeared in the sixteenth century.
3. The heels were worn by men and made of colorful silk brocades soft suedes or smooth leathers.
4. High-heeled shoes received a boost when the short powerful King Louis XIV of France began wearing them.
5. Eventually only wealthy fashionable French women wore high heels.

28g Use commas according to convention in dates, addresses, place names, and long numbers.

Use commas to separate most parts of dates, addresses, and place names: *June 20, 1950; 24 Fifth Avenue, Suite 601; Cairo, Illinois*. Within a sentence, any element preceded by a comma should be followed by a comma as well, as in the examples below:

Dates

July 4, 1776, is the date the Declaration of Independence was signed.

The bombing of Pearl Harbor on Sunday, December 7, 1941, prompted American entry into World War II.

Do not use commas between the parts of a date in inverted order: *Their anniversary on 15 December 2005 was their fiftieth.* You need not use commas in dates consisting of a month or season and a year: *For the United States the war ended in August 1945.*

Addresses and place names

Columbus, Ohio, is the state capital and the location of Ohio State University.

The population of Garden City, Long Island, New York, is 30,000.

Use the address 220 Cornell Road, Woodside, California 94062, for all correspondence.

Do not use a comma between a state and a zip code.

Long numbers

Use the comma to separate the figures in long numbers into groups of three, counting from the right. With numbers of four digits, the comma is optional.

A kilometer is 3,281 feet [*or* 3281 feet].
The new assembly plant cost $7,535,000 to design and build.

CULTURE LANGUAGE Usage in American English differs from that in some other languages and dialects, which use a period, not a comma, to separate the figures in long numbers.

COMPUTER ACTIVITY

US POSTAL REGULATIONS

In addresses on envelopes, the United States Postal Service now asks that the city name be written in block capitals with no comma, followed by the state abbreviation, one space, and the zip code, as in the following example: BERKELEY CA 94720. This format enables their automatic sorting devices to process mail more effectively. See the sample envelope on p. 843.

Students using word-processing or mail-merge programs may find that the computer automatically puts addresses into this format. However, writers still use the format shown in these examples when writing town and state names in the body of their texts. (See 55a for a sample envelope that illustrates the format recommended by the Postal Service.)

ANSWERS: EXERCISE 28.9

1. The festival will hold a benefit dinner and performance on March 10, 2009, in Asheville.
2. The organizers hope to raise more than $100,000 from donations and ticket sales.
3. Performers are expected from as far away as Milan, Italy, and Kyoto, Japan.
4. All inquiries sent to Mozart Festival, PO Box 725, Asheville, North Carolina 28803, will receive a quick response.
5. The deadline for ordering tickets by mail is Monday, December 3, 2008.

AUDIENCE EXPECTATIONS

Discuss the notion of audience expectations when students say, "My biology teacher says to do this," and remind students that being consistent within a document and meeting the expectations of one's readers are the most important considerations in deciding how to use particular punctuation marks. Part 10 lists style guides for various disciplines, which offer students additional information in making the punctuation decisions expected by various communities of readers.

Exercise 28.9 Punctuating dates, addresses, place names, numbers

Insert commas as needed in the following sentences.

Example:
The house cost $27000 thirty years ago.
The house cost $27,000 thirty years ago.

1. The festival will hold a benefit dinner and performance on March 10 2009 in Asheville.
2. The organizers hope to raise more than $100000 from donations and ticket sales.
3. Performers are expected from as far away as Milan Italy and Kyoto Japan.
4. All inquiries sent to Mozart Festival PO Box 725 Asheville North Carolina 28803 will receive a quick response.
5. The deadline for ordering tickets by mail is Monday December 3 2008.

28h Use commas with quotations according to standard practice.

The words *he said, she writes,* and so on identify the source of a quotation. These **signal phrases** may come before, after, or in the middle of the quotation. A signal phrase must always be separated from the quotation by punctuation, usually a comma or commas.

Note Additional issues with quotations are discussed elsewhere in this book:

- **Using quotation marks conventionally,** pages 459–66.
- **Choosing and transcribing quotations from sources,** pages 615–17.
- **Integrating source material into your text,** pages 620–25.
- **Acknowledging the sources of quotations to avoid plagiarism,** pages 630–31 and 634–35.
- **Formatting long prose quotations and poetry quotations** in MLA style, pages 690–91; Chicago style, page 772; and APA style, page 801.

1 Ordinarily, use a comma with a signal phrase before or after a quotation.

Eleanor Roosevelt said, "You must do the thing you think you cannot do."
"Knowledge is power," writes Francis Bacon.

Exceptions Do not use a comma when a signal phrase follows a quotation ending in an exclamation point or a question mark:

"Claude**!**" Mrs. Harrison called.
"Why must I come home**?**" he asked.

Do not use commas with a quotation introduced by *that* or with a quotation that is integrated into your sentence structure:

> James Baldwin insists that "one must never, in one's life, accept . . . injustices as commonplace."

> Baldwin thought that the violence of a riot "had been devised as a corrective" to his own violence.

Use a colon instead of a comma between a signal phrase and a quotation when the signal phrase is actually a complete sentence, with its own subject and predicate:

> The Bill of Rights is unambiguous**:** "Congress shall make no law respecting an establishment of religion, or prohibiting the free exercise thereof."

2 With an interrupted quotation, precede the signal phrase with a comma and follow it with the punctuation required by the quotation.

Original quotation
"The shore has a dual nature, changing with the swing of the tides."

Signal phrase interrupts at comma, ends with comma
"The shore has a dual nature**,**" observes Rachel Carson**,** "changing with the swing of the tides."

Original quotation
"However mean your life is, meet it and live it; do not shun it and call it hard names."

Signal phrase interrupts at semicolon, ends with semicolon
"However mean your life is, meet it and live it**,**" Thoreau advises in *Walden***;** "do not shun it and call it hard names."

Original quotation
"This is the faith with which I return to the South. With this new faith we will be able to hew out of the mountain of despair a stone of hope."

Signal phrase interrupts at end of sentence, ends with period
"This is the faith with which I return to the South**,**" Martin Luther King, Jr., proclaimed**.** "With this new faith we will be able to hew out of the mountain of despair a stone of hope."

Note Using a comma instead of a semicolon or a period after the Thoreau and King signal phrases would result in the error called a comma splice: two main clauses separated only by a comma. (See pp. 340–43.)

1. Sentence correct.
2. "I think of the open-ended writing process as a voyage in two stages," Elbow says.
3. "The sea voyage is a process of divergence, branching, proliferation, and confusion," Elbow continues; "the coming to land is a process of convergence, pruning, centralizing, and clarifying."
4. "Keep up one session of writing long enough to get loosened up and tired," advises Elbow, "long enough in fact to make a bit of a voyage."
5. "In coming to new land," Elbow says, "you develop a new conception of what you are writing about."

COLLABORATIVE LEARNING

Ask students to complete Exercise 28.11 individually and then have them compare their responses in small groups. Encourage the groups to consider the effect of varied comma placement on the meaning of each sentence. As a follow-up exercise you might ask each student to bring in a sentence taken from a magazine or newspaper in which the removal or addition of a comma creates a noticeable change in meaning.

3 Place commas that follow quotations within quotation marks.

"Death is not the greatest loss in life**,**" claims Norman Cousins.
"The greatest loss**,**" Cousins says, "is what dies inside us while we live."

Exercise 28.10 Punctuating quotations

Insert commas or semicolons in the following sentences to correct punctuation with quotations. Mark the number preceding any sentence whose punctuation is already correct.

Example:
The shoplifter declared "I didn't steal anything."
The shoplifter declared**,** "I didn't steal anything."

1. The writer and writing teacher Peter Elbow proposes an "open-ended writing process" that "can change you, not just your words."
2. "I think of the open-ended writing process as a voyage in two stages" Elbow says.
3. "The sea voyage is a process of divergence, branching, proliferation, and confusion" Elbow continues "the coming to land is a process of convergence, pruning, centralizing, and clarifying."
4. "Keep up one session of writing long enough to get loosened up and tired" advises Elbow "long enough in fact to make a bit of a voyage."
5. "In coming to new land" Elbow says "you develop a new conception of what you are writing about."

28i   Use commas to prevent misreading.

In some sentences words may run together in unintended and confusing ways unless a comma separates them:

Confusing   Soon after the business closed its doors.
Clear   Soon after**,** the business closed its doors.

Always check whether a comma added to prevent misreading might cause some other confusion or error. In the first example below, the comma prevents *pasta* and *places* from running into each other as *pasta places*, but it separates the subject (*historian*) and the verb (*places*). The revision solves both problems.

Faulty   A historian who studied pasta, places its origin in the Middle East.
Revised   A historian who studied pasta says that it originated in the Middle East.

Exercise 28.11 Punctuating to prevent misreading

Insert commas in the following sentences to prevent misreading.

Example:
To Laura Ann symbolized decadence.
To Laura, Ann symbolized decadence.

1. Though happy people still have moments of self-doubt.
2. In research subjects have reported themselves to be generally happy people.
3. Among those who have life has included sufferings as well as joys.
4. Of fifty eight subjects reported bouts of serious depression.
5. For half the preceding year had included at least one personal crisis.

28j Use commas only where required.

Commas can make sentences choppy and even confusing if they are used more often than needed. The main misuses of commas are summarized in the box on the next page.

1 Delete any comma after a subject or a verb.

Commas interrupt the movement from subject to verb to object or complement, as in the following faulty examples.

Faulty	The returning soldiers, received a warmer welcome than they expected. [Separation of subject and verb.]
Revised	The returning soldiers received a warmer welcome than they expected.
Faulty	They had chosen, to fight for their country. [Separation of verb *chosen* and object *to fight.*]
Revised	They had chosen to fight for their country.

Exception Use commas between subject, verb, and object or complement only when other words between these elements require punctuation:

Americans, who are preoccupied with other sports, have only recently developed an interest in professional soccer. [Commas set off a nonessential clause.]

2 Delete any comma that separates a pair of words, phrases, or subordinate clauses joined by a coordinating conjunction.

When linking elements with *and, or,* or another coordinating conjunction, do not use a comma unless the elements are main clauses (see p. 422):

Faulty	Banks could, and should help older people manage their money. [Compound helping verb.]
Revised	Banks could and should help older people manage their money.

COMPUTER ACTIVITY

GRAMMAR CHECKERS

If students are using grammar checkers, they may find that the computer challenges punctuation that follows the rules in this book. (Commas in a series are particular targets.) Warn students that such programs may follow slightly different rules, and tell them which rules you want them to follow if such conflicts arise. As a useful case in point you might choose a paragraph of student work with errors and have students run it through various grammar checkers and then display the results for general discussion. While such a display of contradictory "rules" of grammar might seem unnecessarily confusing, it's important to keep in mind that students will be able to use punctuation more effectively when they understand the various reasons behind the rules.

LOGGING MISUSES OF COMMAS

If students are keeping logs of common patterns of errors, direct them to this box to check for erroneous comma usage, being mindful of patterns of error in previous assignments. In addition to noting this section in the text, you might ask students to add to their logs examples of the error from their own writing as well as corrected versions. This exercise can help students apply the comma usage rules they learn in the book to their own writing.

COLLABORATIVE LEARNING

REPUNCTUATING

Take an essay from a reader or a similar source, remove the punctuation you wish to emphasize, make copies of the essay, and ask students to work in groups in order to reach consensus about how it should be punctuated. Tell them not to look at the handbook but to decide on their own the best way to serve the reader's needs through punctuation. When the students have finished, they can compare their work with the original and, using the handbook as a reference, decide which punctuation they think best serves the needs of the essay and the reader. If they decide to disagree with the advice given in the handbook, ask them to write out their own punctuation rules.

Have students practice proofreading, first on articles taken from local newspapers or papers written by members of other classes, and then on their own papers. Discuss why it is more difficult to find mistakes in their own papers than in the writings of others. For many, the difficulty arises because they are looking for what they wanted to write, or thought they wrote, not what they actually put on the page. Advise students to wait several hours between writing and proofreading so that their short-term memories clear and they can see what they've actually written instead of what they wanted to write.

Principal misuses of the comma

■ **Don't use a comma after a subject or verb:**

Faulty   Anyone with breathing problems, should not exercise during smog alerts.

Revised   Anyone with breathing problems should not exercise during smog alerts.

■ **Don't separate a pair of words, phrases, or subordinate clauses joined by *and, or,* or *nor:***

Faulty   Asthmatics are affected by ozone, and sulfur oxides.

Revised   Asthmatics are affected by ozone and sulfur oxides.

■ **Don't use a comma after *and, but, although, because,* or another conjunction:**

Faulty   Smog is dangerous and, sometimes even fatal.

Revised   Smog is dangerous and sometimes even fatal.

■ **Don't set off essential elements:**

Faulty   Even people, who are healthy, should be careful.

Revised   Even people who are healthy should be careful.

Faulty   Bruce Springsteen's song, "Born in the USA," is an anthem.

Revised   Bruce Springsteen's song "Born in the USA" is an anthem.

■ **Don't set off a series:**

Faulty   Cars, factories, and even bakeries, contribute to smog.

Revised   Cars, factories, and even bakeries contribute to smog.

■ **Don't set off an indirect quotation:**

Faulty   Experts say, that the pollutant ozone is especially damaging.

Revised   Experts say that the pollutant ozone is especially damaging.

Faulty   Older people need special assistance because they live on fixed incomes, and because they are not familiar with new accounts, and rates. [Compound subordinate clauses *because . . . because* and compound object of preposition *with.*]

Revised   Older people need special assistance because they live on fixed incomes and because they are not familiar with new accounts and rates.

Faulty   Banks, and community groups can assist the elderly, and eliminate the confusion they often feel. [Compound subject and compound predicate.]

Revised   Banks and community groups can assist the elderly and eliminate the confusion they often feel.

3 Delete any comma after a conjunction.

The coordinating conjunctions (*and, but,* and so on) and the subordinating conjunctions (*although, because,* and so on) are not followed by commas:

Faulty	Parents of adolescents notice increased conflict at puberty, and, they complain of bickering.
Revised	Parents of adolescents notice increased conflict at puberty, and they complain of bickering.
Faulty	Although, other primates leave the family at adolescence, humans do not.
Revised	Although other primates leave the family at adolescence, humans do not.

4 Delete any commas that set off essential elements.

Commas do not set off an essential element, which limits the meaning of the word to which it refers (see p. 427):

Faulty	Hawthorne's work, *The Scarlet Letter,* was the first major American novel. [The title is essential to distinguish the novel from the rest of Hawthorne's work.]
Revised	Hawthorne's work *The Scarlet Letter* was the first major American novel.
Faulty	The symbols, that Hawthorne uses, have influenced other novelists. [The clause identifies which symbols have been influential.]
Revised	The symbols that Hawthorne uses have influenced other novelists.

Quoted or italicized words are essential appositives when they limit the word they refer to (see p. 429). Do not use commas around an essential appositive:

Faulty	James Joyce's short story, "The Dead," was made into an affecting film. [The commas imply wrongly that Joyce wrote only one story.]
Revised	James Joyce's short story "The Dead" was made into an affecting film.
Faulty	The word, *open,* can be either a verb or an adjective.
Revised	The word *open* can be either a verb or an adjective.

The following sentence requires commas because the quoted title is a nonessential appositive:

Her only poem about death, "Mourning," was printed in *The New Yorker.*

no ^

RESOURCES AND IDEAS

Young, Beth Rapp. "Can You Proofread This?" *A Tutor's Guide: Helping Writers One-to-One.* 2nd ed. Ed. Ben Rafoth. Portsmouth: Boynton/Cook: 2005. 111-26. Print. Young's chapter includes appendices that offer numerous suggestions for helping students learn to correct surface errors, such as reading aloud, slowing down, and keeping a personalized checklist of errors.

COLLABORATIVE LEARNING

Ask students to complete Exercise 28.12 individually and to compare their responses in small groups. Then have each group complete Exercise 28.13 as a collaborative project, encouraging each group to debate the placement and elimination of commas.

ANSWERS: EXERCISE 28.12

1. Nearly 32 million US residents speak a first language other than English.
2. After English the languages most commonly spoken in the United States are Spanish, French, and German.
3. Almost 75 percent of the people who speak foreign languages used the words "good" or "very good" when judging their proficiency in English.
4. Sentence correct.
5. The states with the highest proportion of foreign language speakers are New Mexico and California.

---

5 Delete any comma before or after a series unless a rule requires it.

Commas separate the items *within* a series (p. 433) but do not separate the series from the rest of the sentence:

Faulty   The skills of, hunting, herding, and agriculture, sustained the Native Americans.

Revised   The skills of hunting, herding, and agriculture sustained the Native Americans.

In the sentence below, the commas around the series are appropriate because the series is a nonessential appositive (p. 429):

The four major broadcast networks, ABC, CBS, Fox, and NBC, face fierce competition from the cable and satellite networks.

However, many writers prefer to use dashes rather than commas to set off series functioning as appositives (see p. 471).

6 Delete any comma setting off an indirect quotation.

Faulty   The report concluded, that dieting could be more dangerous than overeating.

Revised   The report concluded that dieting could be more dangerous than overeating.

Exercise 28.12   Revising: Needless or misused commas

Revise the following sentences to eliminate needless or misused commas. Mark the number preceding any sentence that is already punctuated correctly.

Example:

The portrait of the founder, that hung in the dining hall, was stolen by pranksters.

The portrait of the founder that hung in the dining hall was stolen by pranksters.

1. Nearly 32 million US residents, speak a first language other than English.
2. After English the languages most commonly spoken in the United States are, Spanish, French, and German.
3. Almost 75 percent of the people, who speak foreign languages, used the words, "good" or "very good," when judging their proficiency in English.
4. Recent immigrants, especially those speaking Spanish, Chinese, and Korean, tended to judge their English more harshly.
5. The states with the highest proportion of foreign language speakers, are New Mexico, and California.

Exercise 28.13 Revising: Commas

Insert commas in the following paragraphs wherever they are needed, and eliminate any misused or needless commas.

Ellis Island New York reopened for business in 1990 but now the customers are tourists not immigrants. This spot which lies in New York Harbor was the first American soil seen, or touched by many of the nation's immigrants. Though other places also served as ports of entry for foreigners none has the symbolic power of, Ellis Island. Between its opening in 1892 and its closing in 1954, over 20 million people about two-thirds of all immigrants were detained there before taking up their new lives in the United States. Ellis Island processed over 2000 newcomers a day when immigration was at its peak between 1900 and 1920.

As the end of a long voyage and the introduction to the New World Ellis Island must have left something to be desired. The "huddled masses" as the Statue of Liberty calls them indeed were huddled. New arrivals were herded about kept standing in lines for hours or days yelled at and abused. Assigned numbers they submitted their bodies to the pokings and proddings of the silent nurses and doctors, who were charged with ferreting out the slightest sign of sickness, disability or insanity. That test having been passed the immigrants faced interrogation by an official through an interpreter. Those, with names deemed inconveniently long or difficult to pronounce, often found themselves permanently labeled with abbreviations, of their names, or with the names, of their hometowns. But, millions survived the examination humiliation and confusion, to take the last short boat ride to New York City. For many of them and especially for their descendants Ellis Island eventually became not a nightmare but the place where life began.

Note See page 479 for a punctuation exercise combining commas with other marks of punctuation.

29
The Semicolon

The semicolon separates equal and balanced sentence elements, usually main clauses (pp. 445–48), sometimes items in series (p. 448).

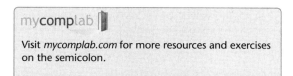

mycomplab

Visit *mycomplab.com* for more resources and exercises on the semicolon.

ANSWERS: EXERCISE 28.13

Ellis Island, New York, reopened for business in 1990, but now the customers are tourists, not immigrants. This spot, which lies in New York Harbor, was the first American soil seen or touched by many of the nation's immigrants. Though other places also served as ports of entry for foreigners, none has the symbolic power of Ellis Island. Between its opening in 1892 and its closing in 1954, over 20 million people, about two-thirds of all immigrants, were detained there before taking up their new lives in the United States. Ellis Island processed over 2000 [*or* 2,000] newcomers a day when immigration was at its peak between 1900 and 1920.

As the end of a long voyage and the introduction to the New World, Ellis Island must have left something to be desired. The "huddled masses," as the Statue of Liberty calls them, indeed were huddled. New arrivals were herded about, kept standing in lines for hours or days, yelled at, and abused. Assigned numbers, they submitted their bodies to the pokings and proddings of the silent nurses and doctors who were charged with ferreting out the slightest sign of sickness, disability, or insanity. That test having been passed, the immigrants faced interrogation by an official through an interpreter. Those with names deemed inconveniently long or difficult to pronounce often found themselves permanently labeled with abbreviations of their names or with the names of their hometowns. But millions survived the examination, humiliation, and confusion to take the last short boat ride to New York City. For many of them and especially for their descendants, Ellis Island eventually became, not a nightmare, but the place where life began.

HIGHLIGHTS

Many inexperienced writers are hesitant to use the semicolon. They may be unfamiliar with the purposes of the mark and therefore reluctant to use it. This chapter should help students understand the four main uses of the semicolon: to separate main clauses not joined by a coordinating conjunction; to separate main clauses joined by a conjunctive adverb; to separate main clauses if they are very long and complex, even when they are joined by a coordinating conjunction; and to separate items in a series if they are long or contain commas. The chapter also covers the places where the semicolon can be misused. When students take risks in using the semicolon, positive reinforcement from you will help encourage them to add this useful punctuation mark to their repertoire.

Grammar checkers A grammar checker can spot a few errors in the use of semicolons. For example, a checker suggested using a semicolon after *perfect* in *The set was perfect, the director had planned every detail,* thus correcting a comma splice. But it missed the incorrect semicolon in *The set was perfect; deserted streets, dark houses, and gloomy mist* (a colon would be correct; see pp. 468–69).

Distinguishing the comma, the semicolon, and the colon

Comma
The *comma* chiefly separates both equal and unequal sentence elements.

- **It separates main clauses when they are linked by a coordinating conjunction** (p. 422):

  An airline once tried to boost sales by advertising the tense alertness of its crews, but nervous fliers did not want to hear about pilots' sweaty palms.

- **It separates subordinate information that is part of or attached to a main clause,** such as an introductory element or a nonessential modifier (pp. 425, 427):

  Although the airline campaign failed, many advertising agencies, including some clever ones, copied its underlying message.

Semicolon
The *semicolon* chiefly separates equal and balanced sentence elements. Often the first clause creates an expectation, and the second clause fulfills the expectation.

- **It separates complementary main clauses that are *not* linked by a coordinating conjunction** (facing page):

  The airline campaign had highlighted only half the story; the other half was buried in the copy.

- **It separates complementary main clauses that are related by a conjunctive adverb or other transitional expression** (p. 446):

  The campaign should not have stressed the pilots' insecurity; instead, the campaign should have stressed the improved performance resulting from that insecurity.

Colon
The *colon* chiefly separates unequal sentence elements.

- **It separates a main clause from a following explanation or summary,** which may or may not be a main clause (pp. 467–68):

  Many successful advertising campaigns have used this message: the anxious seller is harder working and smarter than the competitor.

29a Use a semicolon between main clauses not joined by *and, but,* or another coordinating conjunction.

Main clauses contain a subject and a predicate and do not begin with a subordinating word (see p. 250). When you join two main clauses in a sentence, you have two primary options for separating them:

- **Insert a comma and a coordinating conjunction:** *and, but, or, nor, for, so, yet.* (See p. 422.)

  The drug does little to relieve symptoms, and it can have side effects.

- **Insert a semicolon:**

  The side effects are not minor; some leave the patient quite ill.

Note If you do not link main clauses with a coordinating conjunction and you separate them only with a comma or with no punctuation at all, you will produce a comma splice or a fused sentence. (See Chapter 18.)

Exercise 29.1   Punctuating between main clauses

Insert semicolons to separate main clauses in the following sentences.

> *Example:*
> One man at the auction bid prudently another spent his bank account.
> One man at the auction bid prudently; another spent his bank account.

1. More and more musicians are playing computerized instruments more and more listeners are worrying about the future of acoustic instruments.
2. The computer is not the first new technology in music the pipe organ and saxophone were also technological breakthroughs in their day.
3. Musicians have always experimented with new technology audiences have always resisted the experiments.
4. Most computer musicians are not merely following the latest fad they are discovering new sounds and new ways to manipulate sound.
5. Few musicians have abandoned acoustic instruments most value acoustic sounds as much as electronic sounds.

Exercise 29.2   Sentence combining: Related main clauses

Combine each set of three sentences below into one sentence containing only two main clauses, and insert a semicolon between the clauses. You will have to add, delete, change, and rearrange words. Most items have more than one possible answer.

SEMICOLONS IN CONTEXT

Have students select a work in which they have used few or no semicolons. Then have them locate three or four places in the paper where they might use semicolons. Students should use semicolons for least two of the listed functions, rather than for the same function several times. You might have students turn in both the original sentences and their revisions as an exercise on learning punctuation in context. Remind students that they do not necessarily need to make those changes permanently to the paper, as they must guard against overused semicolons.

ANSWERS: EXERCISE 29.1

1. More and more musicians are playing computerized instruments; more and more listeners are worrying about the future of acoustic instruments.
2. The computer is not the first new technology in music; the pipe organ and saxophone were also technological breakthroughs in their day.
3. Musicians have always experimented with new technology; audiences have always resisted the experiments.
4. Most computer musicians are not merely following the latest fad; they are discovering new sounds and new ways to manipulate sound.
5. Few musicians have abandoned acoustic instruments; most value acoustic sounds as much as electronic sounds.

COLLABORATIVE LEARNING

Ask students to complete Exercise 29.2 individually and then to compare their responses in small groups. Encourage group members to discuss their varying responses and to consider the effects of those differences on the meaning of each sentence. Then have each group present one of their responses to the class and explain the reasons for their sentence-combining choices.

ANSWERS: EXERCISE 29.2

Possible answers

1. Electronic instruments are prevalent in jazz and rock music; they are less common in classical music.
2. Jazz and rock change rapidly; they nourish experimentation and improvisation.
3. Traditional classical music does not change; its notes and instrumentation were established by a composer writing decades or centuries ago.
4. Contemporary classical music not only can draw on tradition; it also can respond to innovations such as jazz rhythms and electronic sounds.
5. Much contemporary electronic music is more than just jazz, rock, or classical; it is a fusion of all three.

RESOURCES AND IDEAS

Petit, Angela. "Stylish Semicolon: Teaching Punctuation as Rhetorical Choice." *English Journal* 92.3 (2003): 66–72. Print. Using the semicolon as her example, Petit argues that punctuation is best taught in the context of lessons on style.

Example:

The painter Andrew Wyeth is widely admired. He is not universally admired. Some critics view his work as sentimental.

The painter Andrew Wyeth is widely but not universally admired; some critics view his work as sentimental.

1. Electronic instruments are prevalent in jazz. They are also prevalent in rock music. They are less common in classical music.
2. Jazz and rock change rapidly. They nourish experimentation. They nourish improvisation.
3. Traditional classical music does not change. Its notes and instrumentation were established by a composer. The composer was writing decades or centuries ago.
4. Contemporary classical music can not only draw on tradition. It can also respond to innovations. These are innovations such as jazz rhythms and electronic sounds.
5. Much contemporary electronic music is more than just one type of music. It is more than just jazz, rock, or classical. It is a fusion of all three.

29b Use a semicolon between main clauses related by *however, for example,* and so on.

Two kinds of words can relate main clauses: **conjunctive adverbs,** such as *consequently, hence, however, indeed,* and *thus* (see p. 259), and other **transitional expressions,** such as *even so, for example,* and *of course* (see pp. 88–89). When either of these connects two main clauses, the clauses should be separated by a semicolon:

An American immigrant, Levi Strauss, invented blue jeans in the 1860s; eventually, his product clothed working men throughout the West.

The position of the semicolon between main clauses never changes, but the conjunctive adverb or transitional expression may move around within a clause. The adverb or expression is usually set off with a comma or commas (see p. 428):

Blue jeans have become fashionable all over the world; however, the American originators still wear more jeans than anyone else.

Blue jeans have become fashionable all over the world; the American originators, however, still wear more jeans than anyone else.

Its mobility distinguishes a conjunctive adverb or transitional expression from other connecting words, such as coordinating and subordinating conjunctions. See pages 258–59 on this distinction.

Note If you use a comma or no punctuation at all between main clauses connected by a conjunctive adverb or transitional expression, you will produce a comma splice or a fused sentence. (See Chapter 18.)

Exercise 29.3   **Punctuating main clauses related by conjunctive adverbs or transitional expressions**

Insert a semicolon in each of the following sentences to separate main clauses related by a conjunctive adverb or transitional expression. Also insert a comma or commas where needed to set off the adverb or expression.

Example:

He knew that tickets for the concert would sell quickly therefore he arrived at the box office hours before it opened.

He knew that tickets for the concert would sell quickly**;** therefore**,** he arrived at the box office hours before it opened.

1. Music is a form of communication like language the basic elements however are not letters but notes.
2. Computers can process any information that can be represented numerically as a result they can process musical information.
3. A computer's ability to process music depends on what software it can run it must moreover be connected to a system that converts electrical vibration into sound.
4. Computers and their sound systems can produce many different sounds indeed the number of possible sounds is infinite.
5. The powerful music computers are very expensive therefore they are used only by professional musicians.

Exercise 29.4   **Sentence combining: Main clauses related by conjunctive adverbs or transitional expressions**

Combine each set of three sentences below into one sentence containing only two main clauses. Connect the clauses with the conjunctive adverb or transitional expression in parentheses, and separate them with a semicolon. Be sure the adverbs and expressions are punctuated appropriately. You will have to add, delete, change, and rearrange words. Each item has more than one possible answer.

Example:

The Albanians censored their news. We got little news from them. And what we got was unreliable. (*therefore*)

The Albanians censored their news**;** <u>therefore</u>**,** the little news we got from them was unreliable.

1. Most music computers are too expensive for the average consumer. Digital keyboard instruments can be inexpensive. They are widely available. (*however*)
2. Inside the keyboard is a small computer. The computer controls a sound synthesizer. The instrument can both process and produce music. (*consequently*)
3. The person playing the keyboard presses keys or manipulates other controls. The computer and synthesizer convert these signals. The signals are converted into vibrations and sounds. (*immediately*)
4. The inexpensive keyboards can perform only a few functions. To the novice computer musician, the range is exciting. The range includes drum rhythms and simulated instruments. (*still*)

ANSWERS: EXERCISE 29.3

1. Music is a form of communication like language; the basic elements, however, are not letters but notes.
2. Computers can process any information that can be represented numerically; as a result, they can process musical information.
3. A computer's ability to process music depends on what software it can run; it must, moreover, be connected to a system that converts electrical vibration into sound.
4. Computers and their sound systems can produce many different sounds; indeed, the number of possible sounds is infinite.
5. The powerful music computers are very expensive; therefore, they are used only by professional musicians.

ANSWERS: EXERCISE 29.4

Possible answers

1. Most music computers are too expensive for the average consumer; <u>however,</u> digital keyboard instruments can be inexpensive and are widely available.
2. Inside the keyboard is a small computer that controls a sound synthesizer; <u>consequently,</u> the instrument can both process and produce music.
3. The person playing the keyboard presses keys or other controls; <u>immediately,</u> the computer and synthesizer convert these signals into vibrations and sounds.
4. The inexpensive keyboards can perform only a few functions; <u>still,</u> to the novice computer musician the range of drum rhythms and simulated instruments is exciting.
5. Would-be musicians can orchestrate whole songs from just the melody lines; <u>thus</u> [*or* <u>thus,</u>] they need never again play "Chopsticks."

5. Would-be musicians can orchestrate whole songs. They start from just the melody lines. They need never again play "Chopsticks." (*thus*)

 29c Use a semicolon to separate main clauses when they are long or contain commas, even with a coordinating conjunction.

We normally use a comma with a coordinating conjunction such as *and* or *but* between main clauses (see p. 422). But a semicolon makes a sentence easier to read when the main clauses are long and complicated or contain commas:

> By a conscious effort of the mind, we can stand aloof from actions and their consequences; and all things, good and bad, go by us like a torrent.
> —Henry David Thoreau

> I doubt if the texture of Southern life is any more grotesque than that of the rest of the nation, but it does seem evident that the Southern writer is particularly adept at recognizing the grotesque; and to recognize the grotesque, you have to have some notion of what is not grotesque and why.
> —Flannery O'Connor

29d Use semicolons to separate items in a series when they are long or contain commas.

We normally use commas to separate items in a series (see p. 433). But when the items are long or contain commas, semicolons help readers identify the items:

> The custody case involved Amy Dalton, the child; Ellen and Mark Dalton, the parents; and Ruth and Hal Blum, the grandparents.

> One may even reasonably advance the claim that the sort of communication that really counts, and is therefore embodied into permanent records, is primarily written; that "words fly away, but written messages endure," as the Latin saying put it two thousand years ago; and that there is no basic significance to at least fifty percent of the oral interchange that goes on among all sorts of persons, high and low.
> —Mario Pei

Exercise 29.5 Punctuating long main clauses and series items

Substitute semicolons for commas in the following sentences to separate main clauses or series items that are long or contain commas.

Example:
After graduation he debated whether to settle in San Francisco, which was temperate but far from his parents, New York City, which was exciting but expensive, or Atlanta, which was close to home but already familiar.

After graduation he debated whether to settle in San Francisco, which was temperate but far from his parents; New York City, which was exciting but expensive; or Atlanta, which was close to home but already familiar.

1. The Indian subcontinent is separated from the rest of the world by clear barriers: the Bay of Bengal and the Arabian Sea to the east and west, respectively, the Indian Ocean to the south, and 1600 miles of mountain ranges to the north.
2. In the north of India are the world's highest mountains, the Himalayas, and farther south are fertile farmlands, unpopulated deserts, and rain forests.
3. India is a nation of ethnic and linguistic diversity, with numerous religions, including Hinduism, Islam, and Christianity, with distinct castes and ethnic groups, and with sixteen languages, including the official Hindi and the "associate official" English.
4. Between the seventeenth and nineteenth centuries, the British colonized most of India, taking control of government, the bureaucracy, and industry, and they assumed a social position above all Indians.
5. During British rule the Indians' own unresolved differences and their frustrations with the British erupted in violent incidents such as the Sepoy Mutiny, which began on February 26, 1857, and lasted two years, the Amritsar Massacre on April 13, 1919, and violence between Hindus and Muslims during World War II that resulted in the separation of Pakistan from India.

29e Use the semicolon only where required.

Semicolons do not separate unequal sentence elements and should not be overused.

1 Delete or replace any semicolon that separates a subordinate clause or a phrase from a main clause.

The semicolon does not separate subordinate clauses from main clauses or phrases from main clauses:

Faulty	Pygmies are in danger of extinction; because of encroaching development.
Revised	Pygmies are in danger of extinction because of encroaching development.
Faulty	According to African authorities; only about 35,000 Pygmies exist today.
Revised	According to African authorities, only about 35,000 Pygmies exist today.

Note Many readers regard a phrase or subordinate clause set off with a semicolon as a kind of sentence fragment. (See Chapter 17.)

ANSWERS: EXERCISE 29.5

1. The Indian subcontinent is separated from the rest of the world by clear barriers: the Bay of Bengal and the Arabian Sea to the east and west, respectively; the Indian Ocean to the south; and 1600 miles of mountain ranges to the north.
2. In the north of India are the world's highest mountains, the Himalayas; and farther south are fertile farmlands, unpopulated deserts, and rain forests.
3. India is a nation of ethnic and linguistic diversity, with numerous religions, including Hinduism, Islam, and Christianity; with distinct castes and ethnic groups; and with sixteen languages, including the official Hindi and the "associate official" English.
4. Between the seventeenth and nineteenth centuries, the British colonized most of India, taking control of government, the bureaucracy, and industry; and they assumed a social position above all Indians.
5. During British rule the Indians' own unresolved differences and their frustrations with the British erupted in violent incidents such as the Sepoy Mutiny, which began on February 26, 1857, and lasted two years; the Amritsar Massacre on April 13, 1919; and violence between Hindus and Muslims during World War II that resulted in the separation of Pakistan from India.

MEMORY AID

Introduce students to this brief list of ways *not* to use the semicolon.

Do not use a semicolon to separate a subordinate clause from a main clause.

Do not use a semicolon to introduce a series.

Do not overuse a semicolon.

COLLABORATIVE LEARNING

OVERUSED SEMICOLONS

Particularly when students have recently mastered correct semicolon use, they might be tempted to overuse them. Select an excerpt of student writing or an example from a reader and revise it to combine many sentences using semicolons. If possible, also use semicolons in a list for which they are not required. Ask students in groups to determine which are the best uses of the semicolon and why. Groups should re-punctuate the selection and defend their decisions to the rest of the class. In a wired classroom, each group can post its revision to the course Web site for review by other groups.

Ask students to complete Exercise 29.6 individually and to compare their responses in small groups. Then ask each group to work collaboratively on Exercise 29.7, encouraging them to debate the effectiveness of each change in punctuation.

ANSWERS: EXERCISE 29.6

1. The main religion in India is Hinduism, a way of life as well as a theology and philosophy.
2. Unlike Christianity and Judaism, Hinduism is a polytheistic religion, with deities numbering in the hundreds.
3. *Possible revision:* Unlike many other religions, Hinduism allows its creeds and practices to vary widely from place to place and person to person. Whereas other religions have churches and principal prophets and

2 **Delete or replace any semicolon that introduces a series or explanation.**

Colons and dashes, not semicolons, introduce series, explanations, and so forth. (See pp. 468 and 471.)

Faulty	Teachers have heard all sorts of reasons why students do poorly; <u>psychological problems, family illness, too much work, too little time.</u>
Revised	Teachers have heard all sorts of reasons why students do poorly**:** psychological problems, family illness, too much work, too little time.
Revised	Teachers have heard all sorts of reasons why students do poorly**—**psychological problems, family illness, too much work, too little time.

3 **Use the semicolon sparingly.**

Use the semicolon only occasionally. Many semicolons in a passage, even when they are required by rule, often indicate repetitive sentence structure. To revise a passage with too many semicolons, you'll need to restructure your sentences, not just remove the semicolons. (See Chapter 26 for tips on varying sentences.)

Semicolon overused

The Make-a-Wish Foundation helps sick children; it grants the wishes of children who are terminally ill. The foundation learns of a child's wish; the information usually comes from parents, friends, or hospital staff; the wish may be for a special toy, a trip to the circus, or a visit to Disneyland. The foundation grants some wishes with its own funds; for other wishes it appeals to those who have what the child desires.

Revised

The Make-a-Wish Foundation grants the wishes of children who are terminally ill. From parents, friends, or hospital staff, the foundation learns of a child's wish for a special toy, a trip to the circus, or a visit to Disneyland. It grants some wishes with its own funds; for other wishes it appeals to those who have what the child desires.

Exercise 29.6   Revising: Misused or overused semicolons

Revise the following sentences to eliminate misused or overused semicolons, substituting other punctuation as appropriate.

Example:
The doctor gave everyone the same advice; get exercise.
The doctor gave everyone the same advice**:** get exercise.

1. The main religion in India is Hinduism; a way of life as well as a theology and philosophy.
2. Unlike Christianity and Judaism; Hinduism is a polytheistic religion; with deities numbering in the hundreds.
3. Hinduism is unlike many other religions; it allows its creeds and prac-

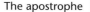

tices to vary widely from place to place and person to person. Other religions have churches; Hinduism does not. Other religions have principal prophets and holy books; Hinduism does not. Other religions center on specially trained priests or other leaders; Hinduism promotes the individual as his or her own priest.

4. In Hindu belief there are four types of people; reflective, emotional, active, and experimental.
5. Each type of person has a different technique for realizing the true, immortal self; which has infinite existence, infinite knowledge, and infinite joy.

Exercise 29.7 Revising: Semicolons

Insert semicolons in the following paragraph wherever they are needed. Eliminate any misused or needless semicolons, substituting other punctuation as appropriate.

The set, sounds, and actors in the movie captured the essence of horror films. The set was ideal; dark, deserted streets, trees dipping their branches over the sidewalks, mist hugging the ground and creeping up to meet the trees, looming shadows of unlighted, turreted houses. The sounds, too, were appropriate, especially terrifying was the hard, hollow sound of footsteps echoing throughout the film. But the best feature of the movie was its actors; all of them tall, pale, and thin to the point of emaciation. With one exception, they were dressed uniformly in gray and had gray hair. The exception was an actress who dressed only in black; as if to set off her pale yellow, nearly white, long hair; the only color in the film. The glinting black eyes of another actor stole almost every scene, indeed, they were the source of all the film's mischief.

Note See page 479 for a punctuation exercise combining semicolons with other marks of punctuation.

holy books, Hinduism does not. And whereas other religions center on specially trained priests or other leaders, Hinduism promotes the individual as his or her own priest.

4. In Hindu belief there are four types of people: reflective, emotional, active, and experimental.
5. Each type of person has a different technique for realizing the true, immortal self, which has infinite existence, infinite knowledge, and infinite joy.

ANSWERS: EXERCISE 29.7

The set, sounds, and actors in the movie captured the essence of horror films. The set was ideal: dark, deserted streets; trees dipping their branches over the sidewalks; mist hugging the ground and creeping up to meet the trees; looming shadows of unlighted, turreted houses. The sounds, too, were appropriate; especially terrifying was the hard, hollow sound of footsteps echoing throughout the film. But the best feature of the movie was its actors, all of them tall, pale, and thin to the point of emaciation. With one exception, they were dressed uniformly in gray and had gray hair. The exception was an actress who dressed only in black, as if to set off her pale yellow, nearly white, long hair, the only color in the film. The glinting black eyes of another actor stole almost every scene; indeed, they were the source of all the film's mischief.

30
The Apostrophe

Unlike other punctuation marks, which separate words, the apostrophe (') appears as *part* of a word to indicate possession or the omission of one or more letters.

my**comp**lab

Visit *mycomplab.com* for more resources and exercises on the apostrophe.

HIGHLIGHTS

This chapter deals with the three reasons to use an apostrophe: to show possession; to indicate a contraction; or to form the plural of letters, numbers, and words named as words. It also explains when the apostrophe should not be used. The chapter focuses on the trouble spots writers are most likely to face and on the strategies they can use to avoid such problems.

Uses and misuses of the apostrophe

Uses of the apostrophe

■ **Use an apostrophe to form the possessives of nouns and indefinite pronouns** (opposite).

Singular	Plural
Ms. Park's	the Parks'
lawyer's	lawyers'
everyone's	two weeks'

■ **Use an apostrophe to form contractions** (p. 456).

it's a girl	shouldn't
you're	won't

■ **The apostrophe is optional for plurals of abbreviations, dates, and words or characters named as words** (p. 458).

MAs or MA's	Cs or C's
1960s or 1960's	*if*s or *if*'s

Misuses of the apostrophe

■ **Do not use an apostrophe plus *-s* to form the possessives of plural nouns ending in *-s*** (p. 454). Instead, use an apostrophe alone after the *-s* that forms the plural.

Not	But
the Kim's car	the Kims' car
boy's fathers	boys' fathers
babie's care	babies' care

■ **Do not use an apostrophe to form plurals of nouns** (p. 455).

Not	But
book's are	books are
the Freed's	the Freeds

■ **Do not use an apostrophe with verbs ending in *-s*** (p. 455).

Not	But
swim's	swims

■ **Do not use an apostrophe to form the possessives of personal pronouns** (p. 456).

Not	But
it's toes	its toes
your's	yours

Grammar checkers A grammar checker usually has mixed results in recognizing apostrophe errors. For instance, it may flag missing apostrophes in contractions (as in *isnt*) but may not distinguish between *its* and *it's*, *their* and *they're*, *your* and *you're*, *whose* and *who's*. A checker may identify some apostrophe errors in possessives but overlook others, and it may flag correct plurals. Instead of relying on your checker, try using your computer's Search or Find function to hunt for all words you have ended in *-s*. Then check each one to ensure that you have used apostrophes correctly.

30a Use the apostrophe to show possession.

In English the **possessive case** shows ownership or possession of one person or thing by another. For nouns and indefinite pronouns, possession may be shown with an *of* phrase (*the hair of the dog, the interest of everyone*), or it may be shown with the addition of an apostrophe and, usually, an *-s* (*the dog's hair, everyone's interest*). Only personal pronouns such as *hers* and *its* do not use apostrophes for possession (p. 456).

Note Apostrophes are easy to misuse. Always check your drafts to ensure the following:

- **Every word ending in *-s* neither omits a needed apostrophe nor adds an unneeded one.**
- **The apostrophe or apostrophe-plus-*s* is an *addition*.** Before this addition, always spell the name of the owner or owners without dropping or adding letters: *girls* becomes *girls'*, not *girl's*.

1 Add *-'s* to singular nouns and indefinite pronouns.

Bill Boughton**'s** skillful card tricks amaze children.

Anyone**'s** eyes would widen. [Indefinite pronoun.]

Most tricks will pique an adult**'s** curiosity, too.

Add *-'s* as well to singular nouns that end in *-s:*

Henry James**'s** novels reward the patient reader.

Los Angeles**'s** weather is mostly warm.

The business**'s** customers filed suit.

Exception We often do not pronounce the possessive *-s* of a few singular nouns ending in an *s* or *z* sound: names with more than one *s* sound (*Moses*), names that sound like plurals (*Rivers, Bridges*), and nouns followed by a word beginning in *s*. In these cases, many writers add only the apostrophe to show possession.

Moses**'** mother concealed him in the bulrushes.

COMPUTER ACTIVITY

SPELLING CHECKERS

Spelling checkers vary; some require both an apostrophe and an *s* after words ending in *s*, while others don't.

RESOURCES AND IDEAS

Bobkoff, Michael. "Apostrophobia: One Therapy." *Teaching English in the Two-Year College* 34.1 (2006): 92–3. Print. Bobkoff suggests using a motivational tool (in his case, the "Master of the Apostrophe" degree students can earn by performing well on an apostrophe test) to help students learn how to use apostrophes correctly.

Hashimoto, Irvin. "Pain and Suffering: Apostrophes and Academic Life." *Journal of Basic Writing* 7.2 (1988): 91–98. Print. Hashimoto reviews, in often humorous fashion, some of the problems students have with apostrophe use.

Wiener, Harvey S. *The Writing Room: A Resource Book for Teachers of English.* New York: Oxford UP, 1981. 175–80. Print. Wiener offers advice on explaining possession to students and describes several exercises designed to help them master the possessive forms of words.

ADD APOSTROPHE PROBLEMS TO PROOF-READING LISTS

Remind students with patterns of apostrophe errors to add this problem to their error log (or "fix-it list") for customized proofreading assistance. They should include examples of the types of apostrophe errors they make (do they often confuse *its* versus *it's*, for example?) from their own writing along with the necessary revisions. They should also note the appropriate section of the text for reference as needed.

COLLABORATIVE LEARNING

YELLOW PAGES

The apostrophe is a messy punctuation mark and is frequently misused. Help students see how popular use is changing the perception of apostrophes by asking students in groups to examine sections of the Yellow Pages or the advertisements in the local newspaper to find examples where expected apostrophes are missing (for instance, "Karins Kurtains" or "Farmers Market"). Encourage them to notice such misuses and bring them to the class's attention.

Joan Rivers' jokes offend many people.

For conscience' sake she confessed her lie.

However, usage varies widely, and the final *-s* is not wrong with words like these (*Moses's*, *Rivers's*, *conscience's*).

2 Add *-'s* to plural nouns not ending in *-s*.

The bill establishes children's rights.

Publicity grabbed the media's attention.

3 Add only an apostrophe to plural nouns ending in *-s*.

Workers' incomes have not risen much over the past decade.

Many students benefit from several years' work after high school.

The Jameses' talents are extraordinary.

Note the difference in the possessives of singular and plural words ending in *-s*. The singular form usually takes the apostrophe and *-s: James's*. The plural takes only the apostrophe: *Jameses'*.

4 Add *-'s* only to the last word of compound words or word groups.

The council president's speech was a bore.

The brother-in-law's business failed.

Taxes are always somebody else's fault.

5 With two or more words, add *-'s* to one or both depending on meaning.

Individual possession

Zimbale's and Mason's comedy techniques are similar. [Each comedian has his own technique.]

Joint possession

The child recovered despite her mother and father's neglect. [The mother and father were jointly neglectful.]

Exercise 30.1 Forming possessives

Form the possessive case of each word or word group in brackets.

Example:

The [men] blood pressures were higher than the [women].

The men's blood pressures were higher than the women's.

1. In the myths of the ancient Greeks, the [goddesses] roles vary widely.
2. [Demeter] responsibility is the fruitfulness of the earth.
3. [Athena] role is to guard the city of Athens.

4. [Artemis] function is to care for wild animals and small children.
5. [Athena and Artemis] father, Zeus, is the king of the gods.
6. Even a single [goddess] responsibilities are often varied.
7. Over several [centuries] time, Athena changes from a [mariner] goddess to the patron of crafts.
8. Athena is also concerned with fertility and with [children] well-being, since [Athens] strength depended on a large and healthy population.
9. Athena often changes into [birds] forms.
10. In [Homer] *Odyssey* she assumes a [sea eagle] form.
11. In ancient Athens the myths of Athena were part of [everyone] knowledge and life.
12. A cherished myth tells how Athena fights to retain possession of her [people] land when the god Poseidon wants it.
13. [Athena and Poseidon] skills are different, and each promises a special gift to the Athenians.
14. At the [contest] conclusion, Poseidon has given water and Athena has given an olive tree, for sustenance.
15. The other gods decide that the [Athenians] lives depend more on Athena than on Poseidon.

30b Delete or replace any apostrophe in a plural noun, a singular verb, or a possessive personal pronoun.

Not all words ending in *-s* take an apostrophe. Three kinds of words are especially likely to attract unneeded apostrophes.

Plural nouns

Form most plural nouns by adding *-s* or *-es* (*boys*, *Smiths*, *families*, *Joneses*). Never add an apostrophe to form the plural:

| Faulty | The unleashed dog's began traveling in a pack. |
| Revised | The unleashed dogs began traveling in a pack. |

| Faulty | The Jones' and Bass' were feuding. |
| Revised | The Jones**es** and Bass**es** were feuding. |

Singular verbs

Do not add an apostrophe to present-tense verbs used with *he*, *she*, *it*, and other third-person singular subjects. These verbs always end in *-s* but *never* with an apostrophe:

| Faulty | The subway break's down less often now. |
| Revised | The subway breaks down less often now. |

| Faulty | It run's more reliably. |
| Revised | It runs more reliably. |

IT'S HUNTING

The most troublesome possessive is *its,* which many students confuse with the contraction *it's.* Ask students to keep a list in their journals of places where they see these words confused, including published work and other students' writing. *It's* hunting makes students learn the *its/it's* rule and become more aware of how they use these words in their own writing.

ANSWERS: EXERCISE 30.2

1. Demeter may be the oldest of the Greek <u>gods,</u> older than Zeus.
2. Many prehistoric <u>cultures</u> had earth <u>goddesses</u> like Demeter.
3. In myth she is the earth mother, which means that the responsibility for the fertility of both <u>animals</u> and <u>plants</u> is <u>hers.</u>
4. The <u>goddess's</u> festival came at harvest time, with <u>its</u> celebration of bounty.
5. The <u>people's prayers</u> to Demeter thanked her for grain and other <u>gifts.</u>

CONTRACTIONS

Some students may have been prohibited from using contractions in high school writing and remain unwilling to use such forms, for any audiences. Discuss with your classes the appropriate places for using contracted words. Explain to students that for some formal academic writing they probably will not use contractions, whereas in less formal writing (such as narrative essays, Web sites, or e-mails) they might. Remind them that if they are in doubt about the level of formality expected of them, they should ask instructors about their preferences.

Possessive personal pronouns

His, hers, its, ours, yours, theirs, and *whose* are possessive forms of the pronouns *he, she, it, we, you, they,* and *who.* They do not take apostrophes:

Faulty	The credit is <u>her's</u> not <u>their's.</u>
Revised	The credit is <u>hers,</u> not <u>theirs.</u>

The personal pronouns are often confused with contractions, such as *it's, you're,* and *who's.* See below.

Exercise 30.2 Distinguishing between plurals and possessives

Supply the appropriate form—possessive or plural—of each word given in brackets. Some answers require apostrophes, and some do not.

Example:

A dozen Hawaiian [shirt], each with [it] own loud design, hung in the window.

A dozen Hawaiian <u>shirts</u>, each with <u>its</u> own loud design, hung in the window.

1. Demeter may be the oldest of the Greek [god], older than Zeus.
2. Many prehistoric [culture] had earth [goddess] like Demeter.
3. In myth she is the earth mother, which means that the responsibility for the fertility of both [animal] and [plant] is [she].
4. The [goddess] festival came at harvest time, with [it] celebration of bounty.
5. The [people] [prayer] to Demeter thanked her for grain and other [gift].

30c Use an apostrophe to indicate the omission in a standard contraction.

it is, it has	it's	let us	let's
he is	he's	does not	doesn't
she is	she's	were not	weren't
they are	they're	class of 2009	class of '09
you are	you're	of the clock	o'clock
who is, who has	who's	madam	ma'am

Contractions are common in speech and in informal writing. They may also be used to relax style in more formal kinds of writing, as they are in this handbook. But be aware that many people disapprove of contractions in any kind of formal writing.

Note Contractions are easily confused with the possessive personal pronouns:

Contraction	Possessive pronoun
it's	its
they're	their
you're	your
who's	whose

Faulty   Legislators know their going to have to cut the budget to eliminate it's deficit.

Revised   Legislators know they're going to have to cut the budget to eliminate its deficit.

If you tend to confuse these forms, search for both spellings throughout your drafts. Then test for correctness:

- **Use an apostrophe when you intend the word to contain the sentence verb is, are, or has,** as in *It is [It's] a shame, It has [It's] happened, They are [They're] to blame, You are [You're] right, Who is [Who's] coming? Who has [Who's] responded?*
- **Don't use an apostrophe when you intend the word to indicate possession,** as in *Its tail was wagging, Their car broke down, Your eyes are blue, Whose book is that?*

Exercise 30.3   Forming contractions

Form contractions from each set of words below. Use each contraction in a complete sentence.

Example:
we are: we're
We're open to ideas.

1. she would
2. could not
3. they are
4. he is
5. do not

6. she will
7. hurricane of 1962
8. is not
9. it is
10. will not

Exercise 30.4   Revising: Contractions and personal pronouns

Revise the following sentences to correct mistakes in the use of contractions and personal pronouns. Mark the number preceding any sentence that is already correct.

Example:
The agencies give they're employees they're birthdays off.
The agencies give their employees their birthdays off.

1. In Greek myth the goddess Demeter has a special fondness for Eleusis, near Athens, and it's people.
2. She finds rest among the people and is touched by their kindness.
3. Demeter rewards the Eleusians with the secret for making they're land fruitful.

ANSWERS: EXERCISE 30.3

Possible answers

1. She'd rather be dancing.
2. He couldn't see her in the crowd.
3. They're at the front door now.
4. He's my brother.
5. We don't like the beach.
6. She'll speak her mind.
7. The recent storm was nearly as bad as the hurricane of '62.
8. Isn't that your cousin?
9. It's a fact.
10. The door won't budge.

ANSWERS: EXERCISE 30.4

1. In Greek myth the goddess Demeter has a special fondness for Eleusis, near Athens, and its people.
2. Sentence correct.
3. Demeter rewards the Eleusians with the secret for making their land fruitful.
4. The Eleusians begin a cult in honor of Demeter, who's worshiped in secret ceremonies.
5. It's unknown what happened in the ceremonies, for no participant ever revealed their [correct] rituals.

4. The Eleusians begin a cult in honor of Demeter, whose worshiped in secret ceremonies.
5. Its unknown what happened in the ceremonies, for no participant ever revealed their rituals.

30d The apostrophe is optional to mark plural abbreviations, dates, and words or characters named as words.

You'll sometimes see apostrophes used to form the plurals of abbreviations (BA's), dates (1900's), and words or characters named as words (*but*'s). However, most current style guides do not recommend the apostrophe in these cases.

BAs   PhDs
1990s   2000s

The sentence has too many *but*s.
Two *3*s end the zip code.

Note Italicize or underline a word or character named as a word (see p. 490), but not the added *-s*.

Exercise 30.5   Revising: Apostrophes

In the following paragraph correct any mistakes in the use of the apostrophe or any confusion between contractions and possessive personal pronouns.

   People who's online experiences include blogging, Web cams, and social-networking sites are often used to seeing the details of other peoples private lives. Many are also comfortable sharing they're own opinions, photographs, and videos with family, friend's, and even stranger's. However, they need to realize that employers and even the government can see they're information, too. Employers commonly put applicants names through social-networking Web sites such as *MySpace* and *Facebook*. Many large companies read their employees outbound e-mail. People can take steps to protect their personal information by adjusting the privacy settings on their social-networking pages. They can avoid posting photos of themselves that they wouldnt want an employer to see. They can avoid sending personal e-mail while their at work. Its the individuals responsibility to keep certain information private.

Note See page 479 for a punctuation exercise involving apostrophes along with other marks of punctuation.

COLLABORATIVE LEARNING

Have students complete Exercise 30.5 individually and then compare their responses in groups. Then ask the groups to review paragraphs from each student's work in order to check apostrophe usage. It's important that students make the connection between the handbook exercises and correct apostrophe usage in their own work.

ANSWERS: EXERCISE 30.5

People <u>whose</u> online experiences include blogging, Web cams, and social-networking sites are often used to seeing the details of other <u>peo-ple's</u> private lives. Many are also comfortable sharing <u>their</u> own opinions, photographs, and videos with family, <u>friends</u>, and even <u>strangers</u>. However, they need to realize that employers and even the government can see <u>their</u> information, too. Employers commonly put <u>applicants'</u> names through social-networking Web sites such as *MySpace* and *Facebook*. Many large companies read their <u>employees'</u> outbound e-mail. People can take steps to protect their personal information by adjusting the privacy settings on their social-networking pages. They can avoid posting photos of themselves that they <u>wouldn't</u> want an employer to see. They can avoid sending personal e-mail while <u>they're</u> at work. <u>It's</u> the <u>individual's</u> responsibility to keep certain information private.

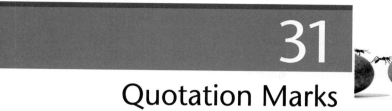

31

Quotation Marks

Quotation marks—either double (" ") or single (' ')—mainly enclose direct quotations from speech and from writing. The box on the next two pages summarizes this use and the combination of quotation marks with commas, semicolons, ellipsis marks, and other punctuation. Additional information on using quotations appears elsewhere in this book:

- **Using commas with signal phrases introducing quotations,** pages 436–38.
- **Using brackets and the ellipsis mark to indicate changes in quotations,** pages 474–77.
- **Quoting sources versus paraphrasing or summarizing them,** pages 611–18.
- **Integrating quotations into your text,** pages 620–25.
- **Acknowledging the sources of quotations to avoid plagiarism,** pages 630–31 and 634–35.
- **Formatting long prose quotations and poetry quotations** in MLA style, pages 690–91; Chicago style, page 772; and APA style, page 801.

Note Always use quotation marks in pairs, one at the beginning of a quotation and one at the end.

Grammar checkers A grammar checker will help you use quotation marks in pairs by flagging a lone mark. It may also look for punctuation inside or outside quotation marks (see p. 465), but it may still fail to detect some errors.

31a Use double quotation marks to enclose direct quotations.

Direct quotations report what someone has said or written in the exact words of the original. Always enclose direct quotations in quotation marks.

mycomp**lab**

Visit *mycomplab.com* for more resources and exercises on quotation marks.

HIGHLIGHTS

The two most common problems students have with quotation marks are failing to close the quotation (see the special cautionary note in the chapter's introduction) and misplacing other punctuation marks inside or outside quotation marks. Take time to review these rules and encourage students to double-check their use of quotation marks. Both practices may save you a great deal of time in marking papers, especially when the students are preparing papers that require the use of cited material.

INDENTED QUOTATIONS AND POETRY

MLA style for double-spacing indented quotations of poetry or prose is new to some students, who may have been taught to single-space such quotations in high school and who see them single spaced in published works. If you are conducting draft-review workshops, ask students to check the spacing of such quotations in their drafts. Particularly in a wired classroom, you might take this opportunity to show students how to use the *increase/decrease indent* and *line spacing* features in your word processing program.

Handling quotations from speech or writing

Direct and indirect quotation

Direct quotation

According to Lewis Thomas, "We are, perhaps uniquely among the earth's creatures, the worrying animal. We worry away our lives."

   Note Do not use quotation marks with a direct quotation that is set off from your text. See pages 690–91 (MLA style), 772 (Chicago style), and 801 (APA style).

Quotation within quotation

Quoting a phrase by Lewis Thomas, the author adds, "We are 'the worrying animal.'"

Indirect quotation

Lewis Thomas says that human beings are unique among animals in their worrying.

Quotation marks with other punctuation marks

Commas and periods

Human beings are the "worrying animal," says Thomas.
Thomas calls human beings "the worrying animal."

Semicolons and colons

Machiavelli says that "the majority of men live content"; in contrast, Thomas calls us "the worrying animal."

Thomas believes that we are "the worrying animal": we spend our lives afraid and restless.

Question marks, exclamation points, dashes

When part of your own sentence:

Who said that human beings are "the worrying animal"?
Imagine saying that we human beings "worry away our lives"!
Thomas's phrase—"the worrying animal"—seems too narrow.

When part of the original quotation:

"Will you discuss this with me?" she asked.
"I demand that you discuss this with me!" she yelled.
"Please, won't you—" She paused.

Altering quotations

Brackets for additions

"We [human beings] worry away our lives," says Thomas.

Brackets for altered capitalization

"[T]he worrying animal" is what Thomas calls us. He says that "[w]e worry away our lives."

Ellipsis marks for omissions

"We are . . . the worrying animal," says Thomas.

Worrying places us "uniquely among the earth's creatures. . . . We worry away our lives."

Punctuating signal phrases with quotations

Introductory signal phrase

He says, "We worry away our lives."

An answer is in these words by Lewis Thomas: "We are, perhaps uniquely among the earth's creatures, the worrying animal."

Thomas says that "the worrying animal" is afraid and restless.

Concluding signal phrase

We are "the worrying animal," says Thomas.

"Who says?" she demanded.

"I do!" he shouted.

Interrupting signal phrase

"We are," says Thomas, "perhaps uniquely among the earth's creatures, the worrying animal."

"I do not like the idea," she said; "however, I agree with it."

Human beings are "the worrying animal," says Thomas. "We worry away our lives."

"Fortunately," said the psychoanalyst Karen Horney, "analysis is not the only way to resolve inner conflicts. Life itself still remains a very effective therapist."

Indirect quotations report what has been said or written, but not in the exact words of the person being quoted. Indirect quotations are *not* enclosed in quotation marks:

The psychoanalyst Karen Horney remarked that analysis is but one solution to personal problems, for life is a good therapist.

(See also pp. 612–15 on paraphrasing quotations.)

31b Use single quotation marks to enclose a quotation within a quotation.

When you quote a writer or speaker, use double quotation marks. When the material you quote contains yet another quotation, distinguish the two by enclosing the second one in single quotation marks:

"In formulating any philosophy," Woody Allen writes, "the first consideration must always be: What can we know? Descartes hinted at the problem when he wrote, 'My mind can never know my body, although it has become quite friendly with my leg.'"

Notice that two different quotation marks appear at the end of the sentence—one single (to finish the interior quotation) and one double (to finish the main quotation).

Exercise 31.1 Using double and single quotation marks

Insert double and single quotation marks as needed in the following sentences. Mark the number preceding any sentence that is already correct.

> *Example:*
> The purpose of this book, explains the preface, is to examine the meaning of the expression Dance is poetry.
>
> "The purpose of this book," explains the preface, "is to examine the meaning of the expression 'Dance is poetry.'"

1. Why, the lecturer asked, do we say Bless you! or something else when people sneeze but not acknowledge coughs, hiccups, and other eruptions?
2. She said that sneezes have always been regarded differently.
3. Sneezes feel more uncontrollable than some other eruptions, she said.
4. Unlike coughs and hiccups, she explained, sneezes feel as if they come from inside the head.
5. She concluded, People thus wish to recognize a sneeze, if only with a Gosh.

31c Set off quotations of dialog according to standard practice.

When quoting conversations, begin a new paragraph for each speaker:

> "What shall I call you? Your name?" Andrews whispered rapidly, as with a high squeak the latch of the door rose.
> "Elizabeth," she said. "Elizabeth."
> —Graham Greene, *The Man Within*

When you quote a single speaker for more than one paragraph, put quotation marks at the beginning of each paragraph but at the end of only the last paragraph. The absence of quotation marks at the end of a paragraph tells readers that the speech is continuing.

Note Quotation marks are optional for quoting unspoken thoughts or imagined dialog:

> I asked myself, "How can we solve this?"
> I asked myself, How can we solve this?

ANSWERS: EXERCISE 31.1

1. "Why," the lecturer asked, "do we say 'Bless you!' or something else when people sneeze but not acknowledge coughs, hiccups, and other eruptions?"
2. Sentence correct.
3. "Sneezes feel more uncontrollable than some other eruptions," she said.
4. "Unlike coughs and hiccups," she explained, "sneezes feel as if they come from inside the head."
5. She concluded, "People thus wish to recognize a sneeze, if only with a 'Gosh.'"

31d Put quotation marks around the titles of works that are parts of other works.

Use quotation marks to enclose the titles of works that are published or released within larger works: see the box below. As in the second article title in the box, use single quotation marks for a quotation within a quoted title, and enclose all punctuation in the title within the quotation marks. Use italics or underlining for all other titles, such as books, plays, periodicals, and movies. (See p. 489.)

Titles to be enclosed in quotation marks

Other titles should be italicized or underlined. (See p. 489.)

Songs
"Lucy in the Sky with
    Diamonds"
"America the Beautiful"

Short poems
"Stopping by Woods on a
    Snowy Evening"
"Sunday Morning"

Articles in periodicals
"Comedy and Tragedy
    Transposed"
"Does 'Scaring' Work?"

Essays
"Politics and the English
    Language"
"Joey: A 'Mechanical Boy'"

Short stories
"The Battler"
"The Gift of the Magi"

**Page or document on a
Web site**
"Readers' Page" (on site
    Friends of Prufrock)

**Episodes of television and
radio programs**
"The Mexican Connection"
    (on *60 Minutes*)
"Cooking with Clams"
    (on *Eating In*)

Subdivisions of books
"Voyage to the Houyhnhnms"
    (Part IV of *Gulliver's Travels*)
"The Mast Head" (Chapter 35
    of *Moby-Dick*)

Note Some academic disciplines do not require quotation marks for titles within source citations. See pages 784–85 (APA style) and 813–14 (CSE style).

Exercise 31.2 Quoting titles

Insert quotation marks as needed for titles in the following sentences. If quotation marks should be used instead of italics, insert them.

Example:
She published an article titled Marriage in Grace Paley's An Interest in Life.

She published an article titled "Marriage in Grace Paley's 'An Interest in Life.'"

ANSWERS: EXERCISE 31.2

1. In Chapter 8, titled "How to Be Interesting," the author explains the art of conversation.
2. The Beatles' song "Let It Be" reminds Martin of his uncle.
3. The article that appeared in *Mental Health* [correct] was titled "Children of Divorce Ask, 'Why?'"
4. In the encyclopedia the discussion under "Modern Art" fills less than a column.
5. One prizewinning essay, "Cowgirls on Wall Street," first appeared in *Entrepreneur* [correct] magazine.

1. In Chapter 8, titled *How to Be Interesting,* the author explains the art of conversation.
2. The Beatles' song Let It Be reminds Martin of his uncle.
3. The article that appeared in *Mental Health* was titled *Children of Divorce Ask, "Why?"*
4. In the encyclopedia the discussion under Modern Art fills less than a column.
5. One prizewinning essay, *Cowgirls on Wall Street,* first appeared in *Entrepreneur* magazine.

31e Quotation marks may be used to enclose words used in a special sense.

On movie sets movable "wild walls" make a one-walled room seem four-walled on film.

Writers often put quotation marks around a word they are using with irony—that is, with a different or even opposite meaning than usual:

With all the "compassion" it could muster, the agency turned away two-thirds of those seeking help. —Joan Simonson

Readers quickly tire of such irony, though, so use it sparingly. Prefer language that expresses your meaning exactly. (See Chapter 38.)

Note For words you are defining, use italics or underlining. (See p. 490.)

31f Use quotation marks only where they are required.

Don't use quotation marks in the titles of your papers unless they contain or are themselves direct quotations:

Not "The Death Wish in One Poem by Robert Frost"
But The Death Wish in One Poem by Robert Frost
Or The Death Wish in "Stopping by Woods on a Snowy Evening"

Don't use quotation marks to enclose common nicknames or technical terms that are not being defined:

Not As President, "Jimmy" Carter preferred to use his nickname.
But As President, Jimmy Carter preferred to use his nickname.

Not "Mitosis" in a cell is fascinating to watch.
But Mitosis in a cell is fascinating to watch.

Don't use quotation marks in an attempt to justify or apologize for slang and trite expressions that are inappropriate to your writing. If slang is appropriate, use it without quotation marks.

Not   We should support the President in his "hour of need" rather than "wimp out" on him.

But   We should give the President the support he needs rather than turn away like cowards.

(See pp. 505 and 522 for more on slang and trite expressions.)

31g Place other punctuation marks inside or outside quotation marks according to standard practice.

The position of another punctuation mark inside or outside a closing quotation mark depends on what the other mark is, whether it appears in the quotation, and whether a source citation immediately follows the quotation.

1 Place commas and periods inside quotation marks.

Commas or periods fall *inside* closing quotation marks, even when (as in the third example) single and double quotation marks are combined:

Swift uses irony in his essay "A Modest Proposal."

Many first-time readers are shocked to see infants described as "delicious."

"'A Modest Proposal,'" writes one critic, "is so outrageous that it cannot be believed."

(See pp. 436–38 for the use of commas, as in the preceding example, to separate a quotation from a signal phrase such as *writes one critic*.)

Exception When a parenthetical source citation immediately follows a quotation, place any period or comma *after* the citation:

One critic calls the essay "outrageous" (Olms 26).

Partly because of "the cool calculation of its delivery" (Olms 27), Swift's satire still chills a modern reader.

See page 651 for more on placing parenthetical citations.

2 Place colons and semicolons outside quotation marks.

Some years ago the slogan in elementary education was "learning by playing"; now educators are concerned with basic skills.

We all know what is meant by "inflation": more money buys less.

3 Place dashes, question marks, and exclamation points inside quotation marks only if they belong to the quotation.

When a dash, question mark, or exclamation point is part of the quotation, put it *inside* quotation marks. Don't use any other punctuation such as a period or comma:

NOTE

Students should note that this rule applies even when closing quotation marks are both single and double. Example: "The author of the article pointed out that the rock group The Police coined the word 'synchronicity.'"

ADDING OTHER PUNCTUATION TO QUOTATIONS

Select a quotation-laden excerpt from a student paper or reader selection. Remove all punctuation except the quotation marks. Ask students to work in groups to re-punctuate the selection correctly. Groups should then compare their version to the original text. In a wired classroom, both the groups' versions and the original can be posted to the course Web site for comparison.

Ask students to complete Exercise 31.3 individually and to compare their responses in small groups. Then have the groups work through Exercise 31.4 as a collaborative project and present their conclusions to the class.

ANSWERS: EXERCISE 31.3

1. In the title essay of her book *The Death of the Moth" and Other Essays*, Virginia Woolf describes the last moments of a "frail and diminutive body." [Italics are correct for book title, but essay title within it quoted.]
2. An insect's death may seem insignificant, but the moth is, in Woolf's words, "life, a pure bead."
3. The moth's struggle against death, "indifferent, impersonal," is heroic.
4. Where else but in such a bit of life could one see a protest so "superb"?
5. At the end Woolf sees the moth lying "most decently and uncomplainingly composed"; in death it finds dignity.

ANSWERS: EXERCISE 31.4

In one class we talked about a passage from "I Have a Dream," the speech delivered by Martin Luther King, Jr., on the steps of the Lincoln Memorial on August 28, 1963:

> When the architects of our republic wrote the magnificent words of the Constitution and the Declaration of Independence, they were signing a promissory note to which every American was to fall heir. This note was a promise that all men would be guaranteed the unalienable rights of life, liberty, and the pursuit of happiness.

"What did Dr. King mean by this statement?" the teacher asked. "Perhaps we should define 'promissory note' first." Then she explained that a person who signs such a note agrees to pay a

---

"But must you——" Marcia hesitated, afraid of the answer.

"Go away!" I yelled.

Did you say, "Who is she?" [When both your sentence and the quotation would end in a question mark or exclamation point, use only the mark in the quotation.]

When a dash, question mark, or exclamation point applies only to the larger sentence, not to the quotation, place it *outside* quotation marks—again, with no other punctuation:

One evocative line in English poetry——"After many a summer dies the swan"——comes from Alfred, Lord Tennyson.

Who said, "Now cracks a noble heart"?

The woman called me "stupid"!

Exercise 31.3   Revising: Quotation marks

The italic words in the following sentences are titles or direct quotations. Insert quotation marks where italics should not be used. Be sure that other marks of punctuation are correctly placed inside or outside the quotation marks.

> *Example:*
> The award-winning essay is *Science and Values.*
> The award-winning essay is "Science and Values."

1. In the title essay of her book *The Death of the Moth and Other Essays,* Virginia Woolf describes the last moments of a *frail and diminutive body.*
2. An insect's death may seem insignificant, but the moth is, in Woolf's words, *life, a pure bead.*
3. The moth's struggle against death, *indifferent, impersonal,* is heroic.
4. Where else but in such a bit of life could one see a protest so *superb*?
5. At the end Woolf sees the moth lying *most decently and uncomplainingly composed*; in death it finds dignity.

Exercise 31.4   Revising: Quotation marks

Insert quotation marks as needed in the following paragraph.

In one class we talked about a passage from I Have a Dream, the speech delivered by Martin Luther King, Jr., on the steps of the Lincoln Memorial on August 28, 1963:

> When the architects of our republic wrote the magnificent words of the Constitution and the Declaration of Independence, they were signing a promissory note to which every American was to fall heir. This note was a promise that all men would be guaranteed the unalienable rights of life, liberty, and the pursuit of happiness.

What did Dr. King mean by this statement? the teacher asked. Perhaps we should define promissory note first. Then she explained that a person who signs such a note agrees to pay a specific sum of money on a particular date or on demand by the holder of the note. One student suggested, Maybe Dr. King meant that the writers of the Constitution and Declaration promised that all people in America should be equal. He and over 200,000 people had gathered in Washington, DC, added another student. Maybe their purpose was to demand payment, to demand those rights for African Americans. The whole discussion was an eye opener for those of us (including me) who had never considered that those documents make promises that we should expect our country to fulfill.

Note See page 479 for a punctuation exercise involving quotation marks along with other marks of punctuation.

32

Other Punctuation Marks

This chapter covers the colon (below), the dash (p. 470), parentheses (p. 472), brackets (p. 474), the ellipsis mark (p. 475), and the slash (p. 478).

Grammar checkers A grammar checker may flag a lone parenthesis or bracket so that you can match it with another parenthesis or bracket. But most checkers cannot recognize other misuses of the marks covered here and instead simply ignore the marks.

32a | Use the colon to introduce and to separate.

The colon is mainly a mark of introduction: it signals that the words following will explain or amplify. The colon also has several conventional uses, such as in expressions of time.

In its main use as an introducer, a colon is *always* preceded by a complete **main clause**—a word group that can stand alone as a

mycomplab

Visit *mycomplab.com* for more resources and exercises on the colon, the dash, parentheses, brackets, the ellipsis mark, and the slash.

specific sum of money on a particular date or on demand by the holder of the note. One student suggested, "Maybe Dr. King meant that the writers of the Constitution and Declaration promised that all people in america should be equal." "He and over 200,000 people had gathered in washington, DC," added another student. "Maybe their purpose was to demand payment, to demand those rights for African Americans." The whole discussion was an eye opener for those of us (including me) who had never considered that those documents make promises that we should expect our country to fulfill.

HIGHLIGHTS

Chapter 32 covers the marks of punctuation not treated in the preceding chapters (27–31): the colon, the dash, parentheses, brackets, the ellipsis mark, and the slash. In addition to exercises for these marks of punctuation, an exercise at the end of the part (p. 479) asks students to practice using most of the punctuation marks covered in Chapters 27–32.

A WRITER'S PERSPECTIVE _____

Q. What is the purpose of the colon?

A. The colon forms a barrier alerting the reader not to go any farther in the sentence.
—Dave Barry

Distinguishing the colon and the semicolon

Colon

The colon is a mark of introduction that separates elements of *unequal* importance, such as statements and explanations or introductions and quotations. The first element must be a complete main clause; the second element need not be.

The business school caters to working students**:** it offers special evening courses in business writing, finance, and management.

The school has one goal**:** to train students to be responsible, competent businesspeople.

Semicolon

The semicolon separates elements of *equal* importance, almost always complete main clauses. (See p. 443.)

Few enrolling students know exactly what they want from the school**;** most hope generally for a managerial career.

---

sentence because it contains a subject and a predicate and does not start with a subordinating word (see p. 250 for more on main clauses). A colon may or may not be followed by a main clause. This is one way the colon differs from the semicolon (see the box above). The colon is interchangeable with the dash, though the dash is more informal and more abrupt (see p. 470).

Note Don't use a colon more than once in a sentence. The sentence should end with the element introduced by the colon.

1 Use a colon to introduce a concluding explanation, a series, an appositive, and some quotations.

Depending on your preference, a complete sentence *after* the colon may begin with a capital letter or a small letter. Just be consistent throughout an essay.

Explanation

Soul food is a varied cuisine**:** it includes spicy gumbos, black-eyed peas, and collard greens.

Soul food has a deceptively simple definition**:** the ethnic cooking of African Americans.

Sometimes a concluding explanation is preceded by *the following* or *as follows* and a colon:

A more precise definition might be the following**:** soul food draws on ingredients, cooking methods, and dishes that originated in Africa, were brought to the New World by slaves, and were modified or supplemented in the Caribbean and the American South.

Series (p. 433)

At least three soul food dishes are familiar to most Americans: fried chicken, barbecued spareribs, and sweet potato pie.

Appositive (p. 254)

Soul food has one disadvantage: fat.

Certain expressions commonly introduce appositives, such as *namely* and *that is*. These expressions should *follow* the colon: *Soul food has one disadvantage: namely, fat.*

Quotation

The comma generally separates a signal phrase from a quotation (see p. 436). But when you introduce a quotation with a complete sentence, use a colon instead:

One soul food chef has a solution: "Soul food doesn't have to be greasy to taste good. Instead of using ham hocks to flavor beans, I use smoked turkey wings. The soulful, smoky taste remains, but without all the fat of pork."

2 Use a colon to separate titles and subtitles and the subdivisions of time.

Titles and subtitles	Time
Charles Dickens: An Introduction to His Novels	1:30 AM
Eros and Civilization: An Inquiry into Freud	12:26 PM

3 Use the colon only where required.

Use the colon only at the *end* of a main clause. Do not use it directly after a verb or preposition.

Not Two critically acclaimed movies directed by Steven Spielberg are: *Schindler's List* and *Saving Private Ryan*.

But Two critically acclaimed movies directed by Steven Spielberg are *Schindler's List* and *Saving Private Ryan*.

Not Shakespeare had the qualities of a Renaissance thinker, such as: humanism and an interest in Greek and Roman literature.

But Shakespeare had the qualities of a Renaissance thinker, such as humanism and an interest in Greek and Roman literature.

Exercise 32.1 Revising: Colons

Insert colons as needed in the following sentences, or delete colons that are misused.

Example:

Mix the ingredients as follows sift the flour and salt together, add the milk, and slowly beat in the egg yolk.

COLONS WITH LISTS

In business and professional writing, colons often end phrases or subordinate clauses that precede lists formatted vertically:

The software has the requirements:
- Pentium ®
- 2.99 GH$_2$
- 1GB RAM
- Microsoft Windows XP

SPOTTING MISUSED COLONS

One common misuse of the colon is to introduce a list not preceded by an independent clause (as in the examples in 32a-3). Ask students to watch for published examples of this type of error in newspapers, advertising, and Web sites. After collecting examples for a week or so, students can compile a list of errors they found. In groups, they might correct a select number of these erroneous examples of colon use.

ANSWERS: EXERCISE 32.1

1. In remote areas of many developing countries, simple signs mark human habitation: a dirt path, a few huts, smoke from a campfire.
2. In the built-up sections of industrialized countries, nature is all but obliterated by signs of human life, such as houses, factories, skyscrapers, and highways.
3. The spectacle makes many question the words of Ecclesiastes 1.4: "One generation passeth away, and another generation cometh; but the earth abideth forever."
4. Yet many scientists see the future differently: they hold that human beings have all the technology necessary to clean up the earth and restore the cycles of nature.
5. All that is needed is a change in the attitudes of those who use technology.

Mix the ingredients as follows**:** sift the flour and salt together, add the milk, and slowly beat in the egg yolk.

1. In remote areas of many developing countries, simple signs mark human habitation a dirt path, a few huts, smoke from a campfire.
2. In the built-up sections of industrialized countries, nature is all but obliterated by signs of human life, such as: houses, factories, skyscrapers, and highways.
3. The spectacle makes many question the words of Ecclesiastes 1.4 "One generation passeth away, and another cometh; but the earth abideth forever."
4. Yet many scientists see the future differently they hold that human beings have all the technology necessary to clean up the earth and restore the cycles of nature.
5. All that is needed is: a change in the attitudes of those who use technology.

32b Use a dash to indicate shifts in tone or thought and to set off some sentence elements.

The dash is mainly a mark of interruption: it signals an insertion or break.

Note In your papers, form a dash with two hyphens (--) or use the character called an em dash on your word processor. Do not add extra space around or between the hyphens or around the em dash.

1 Use a dash or dashes to indicate shifts and hesitations.

Shift in tone

The novel—if one can call it that—appeared in 2007.

Unfinished thought

If the book had a plot—but a plot would be conventional.

Hesitation in dialog

"I was worried you might think I had stayed away because I was influenced by—" He stopped and lowered his eyes.
Astonished, Howe said, "Influenced by what?"
"Well, by—" Blackburn hesitated and for an answer pointed to the table.   —Lionel Trilling

2 Use a dash or dashes to emphasize nonessential elements.

Dashes may be used in place of commas or parentheses to set off and emphasize nonessential elements. (See the box on the facing page.) Dashes are especially useful when these elements are internally punctuated. Be sure to use a pair of dashes when the element interrupts a main clause.

Distinguishing dashes, commas, and parentheses

Dashes, commas, and parentheses may all set off nonessential elements.

Dashes
Dashes give the information the greatest emphasis (facing page):

Many students—including some employed by the college—disapprove of the new work rules.

Commas
Commas are less emphatic (p. 435):

Many students, including some employed by the college, disapprove of the new work rules.

Parentheses
Parentheses are the least emphatic, signaling that the information is just worth a mention (next page):

Many students (including some employed by the college) disapprove of the new work rules.

Appositive (p. 454)
The qualities Monet painted—bright sunlight, rich shadows, deep colors—abounded near the rivers and gardens he used as subjects.

Modifier
Though they are close together—separated by only a few blocks—the two neighborhoods could be in different countries.

Parenthetical expression (p. 472)
At any given time there exists an inventory of undiscovered embezzlement in—or more precisely not in—the country's businesses and banks.
—John Kenneth Galbraith

3 **Use a dash to set off introductory series and concluding series and explanations.**

Introductory series
Shortness of breath, skin discoloration or the sudden appearance of moles, persistent indigestion, the presence of small lumps—all these may signify cancer.

A dash sets off concluding series and explanations more informally and more abruptly than a colon does (see p. 468):

Concluding series
The patient undergoes a battery of tests—MRI, bronchoscopy, perhaps even biopsy.

Concluding explanation
Many patients are disturbed by the MRI——by the need to keep still for long periods in an exceedingly small space.

4 **Use the dash only where needed.**

Don't use the dash when commas, semicolons, and periods are more appropriate. And don't use too many dashes. They can create a jumpy or breathy quality in writing.

Not   In all his life—eighty-seven years—my great-grandfather never allowed his picture to be taken—not even once. He claimed the "black box"—the camera—would steal his soul.

But   In all his eighty-seven years my great-grandfather did not allow his picture to be taken even once. He claimed the "black box"—the camera—would steal his soul.

Exercise 32.2 Revising: Dashes

Insert dashes as needed in the following sentences.

Example:
What would we do if someone like Adolf Hitler that monster appeared among us?

What would we do if someone like Adolf Hitlerthat monsterappeared among us?

1. The movie-theater business is undergoing dramatic changes changes that may affect what movies are made and shown.
2. The closing of independent theaters, the control of theaters by fewer and fewer owners, and the increasing ownership of theaters by movie studios and distributors these changes may reduce the availability of noncommercial films.
3. Yet at the same time the number of movie screens is increasing primarily in multiscreen complexes so that smaller films may find more outlets.
4. The number of active movie screens that is, screens showing films or booked to do so is higher now than at any time since World War II.
5. The biggest theater complexes seem to be something else as well art galleries, amusement arcades, restaurants, spectacles.

32c | Use parentheses to enclose parenthetical expressions and labels for lists within sentences.

Parentheses *always* come in pairs: one before and one after the punctuated material.

1 Use parentheses to enclose parenthetical expressions.

Parenthetical expressions include explanations, digressions, and examples that may be helpful or interesting but are not essen-

---

ANSWERS: EXERCISE 32.2

1. The movie-theater business is undergoing dramatic changes—changes that may affect what movies are made and shown.
2. The closing of independent theaters, the control of theaters by fewer and fewer owners, and the increasing ownership of theaters by movie studios and distributors—these changes may reduce the availability of non-commercial films.
3. Yet at the same time the number of movie screens is increasing—primarily in multi-screen complexes—so that smaller films may find more outlets.
4. The number of active movie screens—that is, screens showing films or booked to do so—is higher now than at any time since World War II.
5. The biggest theater complexes seem to be something else as well—art galleries, amusement arcades, restaurants, spectacles.

ALTERNATIVE EXAMPLE

When you are enclosing a complete sentence within another complete sentence, you need not start the sentence in parentheses with a capital letter nor end it with a punctuation mark. For example:

I spent the weekend buried in books (this is my usual practice) and emerged on Monday in time to go to the library.

tial to meaning. They are emphasized least when set off with a pair of parentheses instead of commas or dashes. (See the box on p. 471.)

> The population of Philadelphia (now about 1.5 million) has declined since 1950.
>
> *Ariel* (published in 1965) contains Sylvia Plath's last poems.

Note Don't put a comma before a parenthetical expression enclosed in parentheses:

> **Not** The population of Philadelphia compares with that of Phoenix, (just over 1.5 million).
>
> **But** The population of Philadelphia compares with that of Phoenix (just over 1.5 million).

If you use a comma, semicolon, or period after a parenthetical expression, place the mark *outside* the closing parenthesis:

> Philadelphia has a larger African American population (over 40 percent), while Phoenix has a larger Latino population (over 40 percent).

If you enclose a complete sentence in parentheses, capitalize the sentence and place the closing period *inside* the closing parenthesis:

> In general, coaches will tell you that scouts are just guys who can't coach. (But then, so are brain surgeons.)
> —Roy Blount

2 **Use parentheses to enclose labels for lists within sentences.**

> Outside the Middle East, the countries with the largest oil reserves are (1) Venezuela (63 billion barrels), (2) Russia (57 billion barrels), and (3) Mexico (51 billion barrels).

When you set a list off from your text, do not enclose such labels in parentheses.

Exercise 32.3 Revising: Parentheses

Insert parentheses as needed in the following sentences.

> *Example:*
> Students can find good-quality, inexpensive furniture for example, desks, tables, chairs, sofas, even beds in junk stores.
> Students can find good-quality, inexpensive furniture (for example, desks, tables, chairs, sofas, even beds) in junk stores.

1. Many of those involved in the movie business agree that multiscreen complexes are good for two reasons: 1 they cut the costs of exhibitors, and 2 they offer more choices to audiences.
2. Those who produce and distribute films and not just the big studios argue that the multiscreen theaters give exhibitors too much power.

RESOURCES AND IDEAS

Palacas, Arthur L. "Parenthetics and Personal Voice." *Written Communication* 6.4 (1989): 506–28. Print. Palacas argues that the use of parenthetical expressions (including those punctuated by parentheses, commas, and dashes) is an important factor in developing a personal style.

ANSWERS: EXERCISE 32.3

1. Many of those involved in the movie business agree that multiscreen complexes are good for two reasons: (1) they cut the costs of exhibitors, and (2) they offer more choices to audiences.
2. Those who produce and distribute films (and not just the big studios) argue that the multiscreen theaters give exhibitors too much power.
3. The major studios are buying movie theaters to gain control over important parts of the distribution process (what gets shown and for how much money).
4. For twelve years (1938–50) the federal government forced the studios to sell all their movie theaters.
5. But because they now have more competition (television and DVD players, for instance), the studios are permitted to own theaters.

3. The major studios are buying movie theaters to gain control over important parts of the distribution process what gets shown and for how much money.
4. For twelve years 1938–50 the federal government forced the studios to sell all their movie theaters.
5. But because they now have more competition television and DVD players, for instance, the studios are permitted to own theaters.

 32d | Use brackets within quotations to indicate your own comments or changes.

Brackets have specialized uses in mathematical equations, but their main use for all kinds of writing is to indicate that you have altered a quotation. If you need to explain, clarify, or correct the words of the writer you quote, place your additions in a pair of brackets:

> "That Texaco station [just outside Chicago] is one of the busiest in the nation," said a company spokesperson.

Use brackets if you need to alter the capitalization of a quotation so that it will fit into your sentence. (See also p. 483.)

> "[O]ne of the busiest in the nation" is how a company spokesperson described the station.

You may also use a bracketed word or words to substitute for parts of a quotation that would otherwise be unclear. In the following sentence, the bracketed word substitutes for *they* in the original:

> "Despite considerable achievements in other areas, [humans] still cannot control the weather and probably will never be able to do so."

See page 621 for additional examples of using brackets with quotations.

The word *sic* (Latin for "in this manner") in brackets indicates that an error in the quotation appeared in the original and was not made by you. When following MLA style, do not italicize *sic* in brackets. Most other styles—including Chicago, APA, and CSE—do italicize *sic*.

> According to the newspaper report, "The car slammed thru [sic] the railing and into oncoming traffic."

Don't use *sic* to make fun of a writer or to note errors in a passage that is clearly nonstandard or illiterate.

Note Always acknowledge the sources of quotations in order to avoid plagiarism. (See pp. 630–31 and 634–35.)

32e Use the ellipsis mark to indicate omissions from quotations and pauses in speech.

The **ellipsis mark** consists of three periods separated by space (. . .). The ellipsis mark usually indicates an omission from a quotation, although it may also show an interruption in dialog.

Note Additional issues with quotations are discussed elsewhere in this book:

- **Choosing and editing quotations,** pages 615–18.
- **Integrating source material into your text,** pages 620–25.
- **Acknowledging the sources of quotations to avoid plagiarism,** pages 630–31 and 634–35. See also example 3 below.

1 The ellipsis mark substitutes for omissions from quotations.

When you omit a part of a quotation, show the omission with an ellipsis mark. All the following examples quote from the passage below about environmentalism.

Original quotation

"At the heart of the environmentalist world view is the conviction that human physical and spiritual health depends on sustaining the planet in a relatively unaltered state. Earth is our home in the full, genetic sense, where humanity and its ancestors existed for all the millions of years of their evolution. Natural ecosystems—forests, coral reefs, marine blue waters—maintain the world exactly as we would wish it to be maintained. When we debase the global environment and extinguish the variety of life, we are dismantling a support system that is too complex to understand, let alone replace, in the foreseeable future." —Edward O. Wilson, "Is Humanity Suicidal?"

1. Omission of the middle of a sentence

"Natural ecosystems . . . maintain the world exactly as we would wish it to be maintained."

2. Omission of the end of a sentence, without source citation

"Earth is our home. . . ." [The sentence period, closed up to the last word, precedes the ellipsis mark.]

3. Omission of the end of a sentence, with source citation

"Earth is our home . . ." (Wilson 27). [The sentence period follows the source citation.]

4. Omission of parts of two or more sentences

Wilson writes, "At the heart of the environmentalist world view is the conviction that human physical and spiritual health depends on sustaining the planet . . . where humanity and its ancestors existed for all the millions of years of their evolution."

RESOURCES AND IDEAS

Grant-Davie, Keith. "Functional Redundancy and Ellipsis as Strategies in Reading and Writing." *Journal of Advanced Composition* 15.3 (1995): 455–69. Print. Grant-Davie looks at the differences between functional and needless redundancy in relation to the use of ellipses, particularly in the field of technical writing.

COLLABORATIVE LEARNING

SPOTTING ELLIPSIS

For a week or so, have students collect examples of the use of ellipsis marks in newspapers, Web sites, blogs, advertising, and other types of published writing. As a class, compile a list of examples. Then, in groups, students should review an assigned portion of the list. For each example, students should determine: (1) whether the ellipsis mark is used correctly, and (2) if it is used correctly, which of the uses discussed in 32e the example illustrates.

5. Omission of one or more sentences

As Wilson puts it, "At the heart of the environmentalist world view is the conviction that human physical and spiritual health depends on sustaining the planet in a relatively unaltered state. . . . When we debase the global environment and extinguish the variety of life, we are dismantling a support system that is too complex to understand, let alone replace, in the foreseeable future."

6. Omission from the middle of a sentence through the end of another sentence

"Earth is our home. . . . When we debase the global environment and extinguish the variety of life, we are dismantling a support system that is too complex to understand, let alone replace, in the foreseeable future."

7. Omission of the beginning of a sentence, leaving a complete sentence

a. Bracketed capital letter

"[H]uman physical and spiritual health," Wilson writes, "depends on sustaining the planet in a relatively unaltered state." [No ellipsis mark is needed because the brackets around the *H* indicate that the letter was not capitalized originally and thus that the beginning of the sentence has been omitted.]

b. Small letter

According to Wilson, "human physical and spiritual health depends on sustaining the planet in a relatively unaltered state." [No ellipsis mark is needed because the small *h* indicates that the beginning of the sentence has been omitted.]

c. Capital letter from the original

Hami comments, ". . . Wilson argues eloquently for the environmentalist world view." [An ellipsis mark is needed because the quoted part of the sentence begins with a capital letter and it is not clear that the beginning of the original sentence has been omitted.]

8. Use of a word or phrase

Wilson describes the earth as "our home." [No ellipsis mark needed.]

Note the following features of the examples:

- **Use an ellipsis mark when it is not otherwise clear that you have left out material from the source,** as when you omit one or more sentences (examples 5 and 6) or when the words you quote form a complete sentence that is different in the original (examples 1–4 and 7c).
- **You don't need an ellipsis mark when it is obvious that you have omitted something,** such as when a bracketed letter or a small letter indicates omission (example 7b) or when a phrase clearly comes from a larger sentence (example 8).

■ **Place an ellipsis mark after a sentence period *except* when a parenthetical source citation follows the quotation,** as in example 3. Then the sentence period falls after the citation.

If you omit one or more lines of poetry or paragraphs of prose from a quotation, use a separate line of ellipsis marks across the full width of the quotation to show the omission:

> In "Song: Love Armed" from 1676, Aphra Behn contrasts two lovers' experiences of a romance:
>
> > Love in fantastic triumph sate,
> >
> > Whilst bleeding hearts around him flowed,
> >
> > . . . .
> >
> > But my poor heart alone is harmed,
> >
> > Whilst thine the victor is, and free. (lines 1-2, 15-16)

(See pp. 690–91 for the format of displayed quotations like this one. And see p. 650 on the source-citation form illustrated here.)

2 **The ellipsis mark indicates pauses or unfinished statements.**

When writing dialog or when writing informally (not in academic writing), you can show hesitation or interruption with an ellipsis mark instead of a dash (p. 470).

> "I wish **. . .**" His voice trailed off.

Exercise 32.4   Using ellipsis marks

Use ellipsis marks and any other needed punctuation to follow the numbered instructions for quoting from the following paragraph.

> Women in the sixteenth and seventeenth centuries were educated in the home and, in some cases, in boarding schools. Men were educated at home, in grammar schools, and at the universities. The universities were closed to female students. For women, "learning the Bible," as Elizabeth Joceline puts it, was an impetus to learning to read. To be able to read the Bible in the vernacular was a liberating experience that freed the reader from hearing only the set passages read in the church and interpreted by the church. A Protestant woman was expected to read the scriptures daily, to meditate on them, and to memorize portions of them. In addition, a woman was expected to instruct her entire household in "learning the Bible" by holding instructional and devotional times each day for all household members, including the servants.
>
> —Charlotte F. Otten, *English Women's Voices, 1540–1700*

1. Quote the fifth sentence, but omit everything from *that freed the reader* to the end.

ANSWERS: EXERCISE 32.4

1. "To be able to read the Bible in the vernacular was a liberating experience. . . ."
2. "To be able to read the Bible in the vernacular . . . freed the reader from hearing only the set passages read in the church and interpreted by the church."
3. "Women in the sixteenth and seventeenth centuries were educated in the home and, in some cases, in boarding schools. . . . A Protestant woman was expected to read the scriptures daily, to meditate on them, and to memorize portions of them."

SLASHING

The rules governing when to put spaces around the slash confuse many students; it's worth a moment's time to review them. In addition, warn students that justifying (aligning) the right margins of text may add or remove spaces around slashes. Generally, they should left-justify documents to preserve the spacing.

COLLABORATIVE LEARNING

Ask students to work individually or in pairs to complete Exercise 32.5, then have them work in small groups to compare and discuss their responses. In asking the groups to report on their findings, encourage students to debate the effect of each punctuation mark.

ANSWERS: EXERCISE 32.5

"Let all the learned say what they can, / 'Tis ready money makes the man." These two lines of poetry by the Englishman William Somerville (1645–1742) may apply to a current American economic problem. Non-American investors with "ready money" pour some of it—as much as $1.3 trillion in recent years—into the United States. The investments of foreigners are varied: stocks and bonds, savings deposits, service companies, factories, art works, even the campaigns of political candidates. Proponents of foreign investment argue that it revives industry, strengthens the economy, creates jobs (more than 3 million, they say), and encourages free trade among nations. Opponents discuss the risks of heavy foreign investment: it makes the American economy vulnerable to outsiders, sucks profits from the country, and gives foreigners an influence in govern-mental decision making. On both sides, it seems, "the learned say . . . / 'Tis ready money makes the man [or country]." The question is, whose money?

COLLABORATIVE LEARNING

REVISING PUNCTUATION

Have students work in small groups to complete the following punctuation exercise. Encourage group members to debate the effect of each punctuation mark, and ask them to present some portion of the passage for class discussion.

2. Quote the fifth sentence, but omit the words *was a liberating experience that.*
3. Quote the first and sixth sentences.

32f | Use the slash between options, between lines of poetry, and in electronic addresses.

Option
I don't know why some teachers oppose pass/fail courses.

Between options, the slash is not surrounded by extra space.
Note The options *and/or* and *he/she* should be avoided. (See the Glossary of Usage, pp. 866 and 872.)

Poetry
Many readers have sensed a reluctant turn away from death in Frost's lines "The woods are lovely, dark and deep, / But I have promises to keep" (13–14).

When you run lines of poetry into your text, separate them with a slash surrounded by space. (See pp. 690–91 for more on quoting poetry.)

Electronic address
http://www.stanford.edu/depts/spc/spc.html

Exercise 32.5 Revising: Colons, dashes, parentheses, brackets, ellipsis marks, slashes

Insert colons, dashes, parentheses, brackets, ellipsis marks, or slashes as needed in the following paragraph. When different marks would be appropriate in the same place, be able to defend the choice you make.

"Let all the learned say what they can, 'Tis ready money makes the man." These two lines of poetry by the Englishman William Somerville 1645–1742 may apply to a current American economic problem. Non-American investors with "ready money" pour some of it as much as $1.3 trillion in recent years into the United States. The investments of foreigners are varied stocks and bonds, savings deposits, service companies, factories, art works, even the campaigns of political candidates. Proponents of foreign investment argue that it revives industry, strengthens the economy, creates jobs more than 3 million, they say, and encourages free trade among nations. Opponents discuss the risks of heavy foreign investment it makes the American economy vulnerable to outsiders, sucks profits from the country, and gives foreigners an influence in governmental decision making. On both sides, it seems, "the learned say 'Tis ready money makes the man or country." The question is, whose money?

Exercise on Chapters 27–32 Revising: Punctuation

The following paragraphs are unpunctuated except for end-of-sentence periods. Insert periods, commas, semicolons, apostrophes, quotation marks, colons, dashes, or parentheses where they are required. When different marks would be appropriate in the same place, be able to defend the choice you make.

Brewed coffee is the most widely consumed beverage in the world. The trade in coffee beans alone amounts to well over $6000000000 a year and the total volume of beans traded exceeds 4250000 tons a year. Its believed that the beverage was introduced into Arabia in the fifteenth century CE probably by Ethiopians. By the middle or late sixteenth century the Arabs had introduced the beverage to the Europeans who at first resisted it because of its strong flavor and effect as a mild stimulant. The French Italians and other Europeans incorporated coffee into their diets by the seventeenth century the English however preferred tea which they were then importing from India. Since America was colonized primarily by the English Americans also preferred tea. Only after the Boston Tea Party 1773 did Americans begin drinking coffee in large quantities. Now though the US is one of the top coffee-consuming countries consumption having been spurred on by familiar advertising claims Good till the last drop Rich hearty aroma Always rich never bitter and by ubiquitous coffee bars.

Produced from the fruit of an evergreen tree coffee is grown primarily in Latin America southern Asia and Africa. Coffee trees require a hot climate high humidity rich soil with good drainage and partial shade consequently they thrive on the east or west slopes of tropical volcanic mountains where the soil is laced with potash and drains easily. The coffee beans actually seeds grow inside bright red berries. The berries are picked by hand and the beans are extracted by machine leaving a pulpy fruit residue that can be used for fertilizer. The beans are usually roasted in ovens a chemical process that releases the beans essential oil caffeol which gives coffee its distinctive aroma. Over a hundred different varieties of beans are produced in the world each with a different flavor attributable to three factors the species of plant *Coffea arabica* and *Coffea robusta* are the most common and the soil and climate where the variety was grown.

ANSWERS: EXERCISE ON CHAPTERS 27– 32

Brewed coffee is the most widely consumed beverage in the world. The trade in coffee beans alone amounts to well over $6,000,000,000 a year, and the total volume of beans traded exceeds 4,250,000 tons a year. It's believed that the beverage was introduced into Arabia in the fifteenth century CE [correct; or C.E.], probably by Ethiopians. By the middle or late sixteenth century, the Arabs had introduced the beverage to the Europeans, who at first resisted it because of its strong flavor and effect as a mild stimulant. The French, Italians, and other Europeans incorporated coffee into their diets by the seventeenth century; the English, however, preferred tea, which they were then importing from India. Since America was colonized primarily by the English, Americans also preferred tea. Only after the Boston Tea Party (1773) did Americans begin drinking coffee in large quantities. Now, though, the US [correct; *or* U.S.] is one of the top coffee-consuming countries, consumption having been spurred on by familiar advertising claims—"Good till the last drop"; "Rich, hearty aroma"; "Always rich, never bitter"— and by ubiquitous coffee bars.

Produced from the fruit of an evergreen tree, coffee is grown primarily in Latin America, southern Asia, and Africa. Coffee trees require a hot climate, high humidity, rich soil with good drainage, and partial shade; consequently, they thrive on the east or west slopes of tropical volcanic mountains, where the soil is laced with potash and drains easily. The coffee beans—actually seeds—grow inside bright red berries. The berries are picked by hand, and the beans are extracted by machine, leaving a pulpy fruit residue that can be used for fertilizer. The beans are usually roasted in ovens, a chemical process that releases the beans' essential oil (caffeol), which gives coffee its distinctive aroma. Over a hundred different varieties of beans are produced in the world, each with a different flavor attributable to three factors: the species of plant (*Coffea arabica* and *Coffea robusta* are the most common) and the soil and climate where the variety was grown.

PART 7

Mechanics

33 Capitals

34 Italics or Underlining

35 Abbreviations

36 Numbers

HIGHLIGHTS

Capitalization at the beginning of sentences will probably not trouble most native speakers of English; however, capitalization within sentences, and in acronyms, can be a challenge for all writers. If your campus has a writing center, check to see if it has special instructional modules that students who have problems with capitalization can use for review.

RESOURCES AND IDEAS

Relatively little has been written about the teaching of capitalization, and most teachers probably assume that rules and drills are the only available instructional strategies. In *The Writing Room: A Resource Book for Teachers of English* (New York: Oxford UP, 1981, 172–74), however, Harvey S. Wiener looks at the sources of capitalization problems for many basic writers—particularly problems of misunderstanding the rules governing sentence boundaries, of confusion over the capitalization of *I* and other personal pronouns, and of difficulty with the sometimes inexact categories of words that are to be treated as proper nouns. Wiener suggests looking for patterns of error in a student's writing, creating groups of words illustrating a particular rule, and asking a student to prepare sentences that demonstrate his or her grasp of a particular convention. These strategies can be used for more skilled writers as well.

The increasing popularity of instant messages, text messages, and e-mail, which are generally more lax in terms of formal correctness about areas such as capitalization, has made some students less careful and clear about the rules. A recent survey found that 50% of teenagers admitted using this informal writing style in their work for school. (See "Teens sometimes 4get when 2 write formally" in *What Works in Teaching and Learning* 4.11; June 2008: 11.) Remind students that writing an instant message to a friend differs in terms of genre and audience expectations from writing an academic essay. It can be helpful to compare and contrast the rules of capitalization in academic writing with the rules (or lack thereof) in these less formal forms.

33

Capitals

Generally, capitalize a word only when a dictionary or conventional use says you must. Consult one of the style guides listed on pages 779–80 and 811 for special uses of capitals in the social, natural, and applied sciences.

Grammar checkers A grammar checker will flag overused capital letters and missing capitals at the beginnings of sentences. It will also spot missing capitals at the beginnings of proper nouns and adjectives—*if* the nouns and adjectives are in the checker's dictionary. For example, a checker caught *christianity* and *europe* but not *china* (for the country) or *Stephen king*.

CULTURE·LANGUAGE Conventions of capitalization vary from language to language. English, for instance, is the only language to capitalize the first-person singular pronoun (*I*), and its practice of capitalizing proper nouns but not most common nouns also distinguishes it from some other languages.

33a Capitalize the first word of every sentence.

> Every writer should own a good dictionary.
> Will inflation be curbed?
> Watch out!

When quoting other writers, you must either reproduce the capital letters beginning their sentences or indicate with brackets that you have altered the source. Whenever possible, integrate the quotation into your own sentence so that its capital letters coincide with your own:

> "Psychotherapists often overlook the benefits of self-deception," the author argues.

> The author argues that "the benefits of self-deception" are not always recognized by psychotherapists.

mycomplab

Visit *mycomplab.com* for more resources and exercises on capital letters.

If you need to alter the capitalization in the source, indicate the change with brackets (see p. 474):

> "[T]he benefits of self-deception" are not always recognized by psychotherapists, the author argues.
>
> The author argues that "[p]sychotherapists often overlook the benefits of self-deception."

Note Capitalization of questions in a series is optional. Both examples below are correct:

> Is the population a hundred? Two hundred? More?
> Is the population a hundred? two hundred? more?

Also optional is capitalization of the first word in a complete sentence after a colon (see p. 467).

33b Capitalize most words in titles and subtitles of works.

Within your text, capitalize all the words in a title *except* the following: articles (*a, an, the*), *to* in infinitives, and connecting words (prepositions and coordinating and subordinating conjunctions) of fewer than five letters. Capitalize even these short words when they are the first or last word in a title or when they fall after a colon or semicolon.

The Sound and the Fury	*Management: A New Theory*
"Courtship Through the Ages"	"Once More to the Lake"
A Diamond Is Forever	*An End to Live For*
"Knowing Whom to Ask"	"Power: How to Get It"
Learning from Las Vegas	*File Under Architecture*
"The Truth About AIDS"	*Only when I Laugh*

Always capitalize the prefix or first word in a hyphenated word within a title. Capitalize the second word only if it is a noun or an adjective or is as important as the first word.

"Applying Stage Make-up"	*Through the Looking-Glass*
The Pre-Raphaelites	

Note The style guides of the academic disciplines have their own rules for capitals in titles. For instance, MLA style for English and some other humanities capitalizes all subordinating conjunctions but no prepositions. In addition, APA style for the social sciences and CSE style for the sciences capitalize only the first word and proper names in book and article titles within source citations. See pages 784–85 (APA) and 812–13 (CSE).

33c Always capitalize the pronoun *I* and the interjection *O*. Capitalize *oh* only when it begins a sentence.

I love to stay up at night, but, oh, I hate to get up in the morning.
He who thinks himself wise, O heavens, is a great fool.   —Voltaire

33d Capitalize proper nouns, proper adjectives, and words used as essential parts of proper nouns.

Proper nouns name specific persons, places, and things: *Shakespeare, California, World War I.* **Proper adjectives** are formed from some proper nouns: *Shakespearean, Californian.*

1 Capitalize proper nouns and proper adjectives.

Capitalize all proper nouns and proper adjectives but not the articles (*a, an, the*) that precede them.

PROPER NOUNS IN OTHER LANGUAGES

Not all languages capitalize proper adjectives and proper nouns used as adjectives. Remind students that in English such words are always capitalized: *Swahili culture,* not *swahili culture.*

Proper nouns and adjectives to be capitalized

Specific persons and things

Stephen King	the Leaning Tower of Pisa
Napoleon Bonaparte	Boulder Dam
Doris Lessing	the Empire State Building

Specific places and geographical regions

New York City	the Mediterranean Sea
China	Lake Victoria
Europe	the Northeast, the South
North America	the Rocky Mountains

But: northeast of the city, going south

Days of the week, months, holidays

Monday	Yom Kippur
May	Christmas
Thanksgiving	Columbus Day

Historical events, documents, periods, movements

World War II	the Middle Ages
the Vietnam War	the Age of Reason
the Boston Tea Party	the Renaissance
the Treaty of Ghent	the Great Depression
the Constitution	the Romantic Movement
the Bill of Rights	the Cultural Revolution

Government offices or departments and institutions

House of Representatives	Polk Municipal Court
Department of Defense	Warren County Hospital
Appropriations Committee	Northeast High School
Sequoia Hospital	Central State College

Political, social, athletic, and other organizations and associations and their members

Democratic Party, Democrats	Rotary Club, Rotarians
Sierra Club	League of Women Voters
Girl Scouts of America, Scout	Boston Celtics
B'nai B'rith	Chicago Symphony Orchestra

Races, nationalities, and their languages

Native American	Germans
African American	Swahili
Caucasian	Italian

But: blacks, whites

Religions and their followers

Christianity, Christians	Judaism, Orthodox Jews
Protestantism, Protestants	Hinduism, Hindus
Catholicism, Catholics	Islam, Muslims

Religious terms for the sacred

God	Buddha
Allah	the Bible [**but** biblical]
Christ	the Koran, the Qur'an

Note Follow your own preference in capitalizing *he, his,* or *him* when referring to God or Allah.

2 **Capitalize common nouns used as essential parts of proper nouns.**

Common nouns name general classes of persons, places, or things, and they usually are not capitalized. However, capitalize common nouns such as *street, avenue, park, river, ocean, lake, company, college, county,* and *memorial* when they are part of proper nouns naming specific places or institutions:

Main Street	Crum Creek
Park Avenue	Lake Superior
Garland Place	Ford Motor Company
Central Park	Madison College
Mississippi River	San Mateo County
Pacific Ocean	George Washington Memorial

EXTRA EXAMPLES

Capitalizing compound words:

un-American
post-Victorian

NOTE

You may wish to point out that when a generic term occurs with a proper name, the generic term is capitalized (the Congo *River*), but when the generic term occurs with two or more proper names, it is usually capitalized when it precedes the proper names but lowercased when it succeeds them (*Lakes* Superior and Ontario; the Congo and Amazon *rivers*).

3 Capitalize trade names.

Trade names identify individual brands of certain products. When a trade name loses its association with a brand and comes to refer to a product in general, it is not capitalized. Refer to a dictionary for current usage when you are in doubt about a name.

Scotch tape	Xerox
Chevrolet	Bunsen burner

But: nylon, thermos

 Capitalize most titles of persons only when they precede proper names.

Professor Otto Osborne	Otto Osborne, a professor of English
Doctor Jane Covington	Jane Covington, a medical doctor
Governor Ella Moore	Ella Moore, the governor

Not   The <u>S</u>enator supported the bill.

But   The <u>s</u>enator supported the bill.

Or   <u>S</u>enator Carmine supported the bill.

Exception Many writers capitalize a title denoting very high rank even when it follows a proper name or is used alone:

Ronald Reagan, past <u>President</u> of the United States, died in 2004.
John Roberts is <u>Chief Justice</u> of the United States.

33f Avoid common misuses of capital letters.

1 Use small letters for common nouns replacing proper nouns.

Not   I am determined to take an <u>Economics</u> course before I graduate from <u>College</u>.

But   I am determined to take an <u>economics</u> course before I graduate from <u>college</u>.

Or   I am determined to take <u>Economics 101</u> before I graduate from <u>Madison College</u>.

2 Capitalize compass directions only when they refer to specific geographical areas

The storm blew in from the <u>northeast</u> and then veered <u>south</u> along the coast. [Here *northeast* and *south* refer to general directions.]

Students from the <u>South</u> have trouble adjusting to the <u>Northeast's</u> bitter winters. [Here *South* and *Northeast* refer to specific regions.]

3 Use small letters for the names of seasons and the names of academic years and terms.

spring	autumn	senior year
summer	fall quarter	winter term

4 Capitalize the names of relationships only when they form part of or substitute for proper names.

my <u>mother</u>	the <u>father</u> of my friend
my <u>uncle</u> Brad	Brad's <u>brother</u>

I remember how <u>Dad</u> scolded us.
<u>Aunt</u> Annie and <u>Uncle</u> Jake died within two months of each other.

5 Use capitals according to convention in online communication.

Online messages written in all-capital letters or with no capital letters are difficult to read. Further, messages in all-capital letters may be considered rude. Use capital letters according to rules 33a–33f in all your online communication.

Exercise 33.1 Revising: Capitals

Capitalize words as necessary in the following sentences, or substitute small letters for unnecessary capitals. Consult a dictionary if you are in doubt. If the capitalization in a sentence is already correct, mark the number preceding the sentence.

Example:

The first book on the reading list is mark twain's *a connecticut yankee in king arthur's court.*

The first book on the reading list is Mark Twain's *A Connecticut Yankee in King Arthur's Court.*

1. San Antonio, texas, is a thriving city in the southwest.
2. The city has always offered much to tourists interested in the roots of spanish settlement of the new world.
3. The alamo is one of five Catholic Missions built by Priests to convert native americans and to maintain spain's claims in the area.
4. But the alamo is more famous for being the site of an 1836 battle that helped to create the republic of Texas.
5. Many of the nearby Streets, such as Crockett street, are named for men who gave their lives in that Battle.
6. The Hemisfair plaza and the San Antonio river link new tourist and convention facilities developed during mayor Cisneros's terms.
7. Restaurants, Hotels, and shops line the River. the haunting melodies of "Una paloma blanca" and "malagueña" lure passing tourists into Casa rio and other excellent mexican restaurants.
8. The university of Texas at San Antonio has expanded, and a Medical Center has been developed in the Northwest part of the city.

ANSWERS: EXERCISE 33.1

1. San Antonio, <u>T</u>exas, is a thriving city in the <u>S</u>outhwest.
2. The city has always offered much to tourists interested in the roots of <u>S</u>panish settlement of the <u>N</u>ew <u>W</u>orld.
3. The <u>A</u>lamo is one of five Catholic <u>m</u>issions built by <u>p</u>riests to convert <u>N</u>ative <u>A</u>mericans and to maintain <u>S</u>pain's claims in the area.
4. But the <u>A</u>lamo is more famous for being the site of an 1836 battle that helped to create the <u>R</u>epublic of Texas.
5. Many of the nearby <u>s</u>treets, such as Crockett <u>S</u>treet, are named for men who gave their lives in that battle.
6. The Hemisfair <u>P</u>laza and the San Antonio <u>R</u>iver link new tourist and convention facilities developed during <u>M</u>ayor Cisneros's terms.
7. Restaurants, <u>h</u>otels, and shops line the river. <u>T</u>he haunting melodies of "Una <u>P</u>aloma <u>B</u>lanca" and "<u>M</u>alagueña" lure passing tourists into Casa <u>R</u>io and other excellent <u>M</u>exican restaurants.
8. The <u>U</u>niversity of Texas at San Antonio has expanded, and a <u>m</u>edical <u>c</u>enter has been developed in the <u>n</u>orthwest part of the city.
9. Sentence correct.
10. The <u>c</u>ity has attracted high-tech industry, creating a corridor of economic growth between <u>S</u>an <u>A</u>ntonio and <u>A</u>ustin and contributing to the <u>T</u>exas economy.

9. Sea World, on the west side of San Antonio, entertains grandparents, fathers and mothers, and children with the antics of dolphins and seals.
10. The City has attracted high-tech industry, creating a corridor of economic growth between san antonio and austin and contributing to the texas economy.

Note See page 498 for an exercise involving capitals along with italics or underlining and other mechanics.

34

Italics or Underlining

Italic type and underlining indicate the same thing: the word or words are being distinguished or emphasized. Italic type is now used almost universally in academic and business writing, and it has recently become the preferred style of the Modern Language Association. Some instructors recommend underlining, so ask your instructor for his or her preference.

Always use either italics or underlining consistently throughout a document in both text and source citations. If you are using italics, make sure that the italic characters are clearly distinct from the regular type. If you are using underlining and you underline two or more words in a row, underline the space between the words, too: Criminal Statistics: Misuses of Numbers.

Grammar checkers A grammar checker cannot recognize problems with italics or underlining. Use the guidelines in this chapter to edit your work.

34a Italicize or underline the titles of works that appear independently.

Within your text, italicize or underline the titles of works that are published, released, or produced separately from other works (see the box opposite). Use quotation marks for all other titles (see p. 463).

mycomplab

Visit *mycomplab.com* for more resources and exercises on italics and underlining.

Titles to be italicized or underlined

Other titles should be placed in quotation marks. (See p. 463.)

Books
War and Peace
Psychology: An Introduction

Plays
Hamlet
The Phantom of the Opera

Computer software
Microsoft Internet Explorer
Acrobat Reader

Web sites
Google
Friends of Prufrock

Pamphlets
The Truth About Alcoholism
Plants of the Desert

Long musical works
Tchaikovsky's *Swan Lake*
The Beatles' *Revolver*
But: Symphony in C

Television and radio programs
All Things Considered
NBC Sports Hour

Long poems
Beowulf
Paradise Lost

Periodicals
Time
Boston Globe
Yale Law Review

Published speeches
Lincoln's *Gettysburg Address*
Pericles's *Funeral Oration*

Movies, DVDs, and videos
Schindler's List
How to Relax

Works of visual art
Michelangelo's *David*
Picasso's *Guernica*

Note Italicize or underline a mark of punctuation only when it is part of the title. In newspaper titles, highlight the name of the city only when it is part of the title. And for all periodical titles, do not capitalize or highlight the article *the* when it begins the title.

Who is the publisher of the Manchester *Guardian***?**

The national edition of the *New York Times* often differs substantially from the late edition.

Exceptions Legal documents, the Bible, the Koran, and their parts are generally not italicized or underlined.

Not   They registered their *deed*.
But   They registered their deed.

Not   We studied the *Book of Revelation* in the *Bible*.
But   We studied the Book of Revelation in the Bible.

Many sciences do not use italics or underlining for some or all titles within source citations. (See pp. 812–13 on CSE style.)

Italicize or underline the names of ships, aircraft, spacecraft, and trains.

Queen Elizabeth 2	*Orient Express*	*Apollo XI*
Challenger	*Spirit of St. Louis*	*Montrealer*

 Italicize or underline foreign words and phrases that have not been absorbed into English.

English has adopted many foreign words and phrases—such as the French "bon voyage"—and they need not be italicized or underlined. Do italicize or underline words considered foreign, consulting a dictionary if needed.

The scientific name for the brown trout is *Salmo trutta*. [The Latin scientific names for plants and animals are always italicized or underlined.]

What a life he led! He was a true *bon vivant*.

The Latin *De gustibus non est disputandum* translates roughly as "There's no accounting for taste."

34d **Italicize or underline words or characters named as words.**

Use italics or underlining to indicate that you are citing a character or word as a word rather than using it for its meaning. Words you are defining fall under this convention:

The word *syzygy* refers to a straight line formed by three celestial bodies, as in the alignment of the earth, sun, and moon.

Some people say *th,* as in *thought,* with a faint *s* or *f* sound.

Carved into the column, twenty feet up, was a mysterious *7*.

 Occasionally, italics or underlining may be used for emphasis.

Italics or underlining can stress an important word or phrase, especially in reporting how someone said something:

"Why on earth would *you* do that?" she cried.

But use such emphasis very rarely. Excessive underlining or italics will make your writing sound immature or hysterical:

The settlers had *no* firewood and *no* food. Many of them *starved* or *froze to death* that first winter.

34f In online communication, use alternatives for italics or underlining.

Some forms of online communication do not allow italics or underlining for the purposes described in this chapter. On Web sites, for instance, underlining often indicates a link to another site.

To distinguish elements that usually require italics or underlining, type an underscore before and after the element: *Measurements coincide with those in _Joule's Handbook_.* You can also emphasize words with asterisks: *I *will not* be able to attend.*

Avoid using all-capital letters for emphasis. (See also p. 487.)

Exercise 34.1 Revising: Italics or underlining

In the following sentences, circle (1) the words and phrases that need highlighting with italics or underlining and (2) the words and phrases that are highlighted unnecessarily. Note that some highlighting is correct as given.

Example:

Of Hitchcock's movies, Psycho is the scariest.
Of Hitchcock's movies, *Psycho* is the scariest.

1. Of the many Vietnam veterans who are writers, Oliver Stone is perhaps the most famous for writing and directing the films Platoon and Born on the Fourth of July.
2. Tim O'Brien has written short stories for Esquire, GQ, and Massachusetts Review.
3. Going After Cacciato is O'Brien's dreamlike novel about the horrors of combat.
4. The word Vietnam is technically two words (*Viet* and *Nam*), but most American writers spell it as *one* word.
5. American writers use words or phrases borrowed from Vietnamese, such as di di mau ("go quickly") or dinky dau ("crazy").
6. Philip Caputo's *gripping* account of his service in Vietnam appears in the book A Rumor of War.
7. Caputo's book was made into a television movie, also titled *A Rumor of War.*
8. David Rabe's plays—including The Basic Training of Pavlo Hummel, Streamers, and Sticks and Bones—depict the effects of the war *not only* on the soldiers *but also* on their families.
9. Called the *poet laureate of the Vietnam war,* Steve Mason has published two collections of poems: Johnny's Song and Warrior for Peace.
10. The Washington Post published *rave* reviews of Veteran's Day, an autobiography by Rod Kane.

Note See page 498 for an exercise involving italics or underlining along with capitals and other mechanics.

ANSWERS: EXERCISE 34.1

1. Of the many Vietnam veterans who are writers, Oliver Stone is perhaps the most famous for writing and directing the films (*Platoon*) and (*Born on the Fourth of July*).
2. Tim O'Brien has written short stories for (*Esquire*), (*GQ*), and (*Massachusetts Review*).
3. (*Going After Cacciato*) is O'Brien's dreamlike novel about the horrors of combat.
4. The word (*Vietnam*) is technically two words (*Viet* and *Nam*), but most American writers spell it as (*one*) word. [*Viet* and *Nam* were correctly italicized.]
5. American writers use words or phrases borrowed from Vietnamese, such as (*di di mau*) ("go quickly") or (*dinky dau*) ("crazy").
6. Philip Caputo's (*gripping*) account of his service in Vietnam appears in the book *A Rumor of War.*
7. Sentence correct.
8. David Rabe's plays—including (*The Basic Training of Pavlo Hummel*), (*Streamers*), and (*Sticks and Bones*)—depict the effects of the war (*not only*) on the soldiers (*but also*) on their families.
9. Called ("the poet laureate of the Vietnam war,") Steve Mason has published two collections of poems: (*Johnny's Song*) and (*Warrior for Peace*).
10. (*The Washington Post*) published (*rave*) reviews of *Veteran's Day,* an autobiography by Rod Kane.

35

Abbreviations

The following guidelines on abbreviations pertain to the text of a nontechnical document. All academic disciplines use abbreviations in source citations, and much technical writing, such as in the sciences and engineering, uses many abbreviations in the document text. For the requirements of the discipline you are writing in, consult one of the style guides listed on pages 760 (humanities), 779–80 (social sciences), and 811 (natural and applied sciences).

Usage varies, but writers increasingly omit periods from abbreviations that consist of or end in capital letters: *US, BA, USMC, PhD.* See page 419 on punctuating abbreviations.

Grammar and spelling checkers A grammar checker may flag some abbreviations, such as *ft.* (for *foot*) and *st.* (for *street*). A spelling checker will flag abbreviations it does not recognize. But neither checker can tell you whether an abbreviation is appropriate for your writing situation or will be clear to your readers.

35a Use standard abbreviations for titles immediately before and after proper names.

Before the name	After the name
Dr. James Hsu	James Hsu, MD
Mr., Mrs., Ms., Hon., St., Rev., Msgr., Gen.	DDS, DVM, PhD, EdD, OSB, SJ, Sr., Jr.

Use abbreviations such as *Rev., Hon., Prof., Rep., Sen., Dr.,* and *St.* (for *Saint*) only if they appear before a proper name. Spell them out in the absence of a proper name:

Not   We learned to trust the Dr.

But   We learned to trust the doctor.

Or   We learned to trust Dr. Kaplan.

The abbreviations for academic degrees—*PhD, MA, BA,* and the like—may be used without a proper name: *My brother took*

 mycomplab

Visit *mycomplab.com* for more resources and exercises on abbreviations.

Abbreviations for nontechnical writing

- Titles before or after proper names: *Dr. Jorge Rodriguez; Jorge Rodriguez, PhD.*
- Familiar abbreviations and acronyms: *USA, AIDS.*
- *BC, BCE, AD, CE, AM, PM, no.,* and $ with dates and numbers.
- *I.e., e.g.,* and other Latin abbreviations within parentheses and in source citations.
- *Inc., Bros., Co.,* and & with names of business firms.

seven years to get his <u>PhD</u>. *It will probably take me just as long to earn my* <u>BA</u>.

35b Familiar abbreviations and acronyms are acceptable in most writing.

An **acronym** is an abbreviation that spells a pronounceable word, such as WHO, NATO, and AIDS. These and other abbreviations that use initials are acceptable in most writing as long as they are familiar to readers. Abbreviations of two or more words written in all capital letters may be written without periods (see p. 419):

Institutions	LSU, UCLA, TCU
Organizations	CIA, FBI, YMCA, AFL-CIO
Corporations	IBM, CBS, ITT
People	JFK, LBJ, FDR
Countries	US, USA

Note If a name or term (such as *operating room*) appears often in a piece of writing, then its abbreviation (*OR*) can cut down on extra words. Spell out the full term at its first appearance, give its abbreviation in parentheses, and use the abbreviation from then on.

35c Use *BC, BCE, AD, CE, AM, PM, no.,* and $ only with specific dates and numbers.

44 BC	AD 1492	8:05 PM (*or* p.m.)	no. 36 (*or* No. 36)
44 BCE	1492 CE	11:26 AM (*or* a.m.)	$7.41

Not	Hospital routine is easier to follow in the <u>AM</u> than in the <u>PM</u>.
But	Hospital routine is easier to follow in the <u>morning</u> than in the <u>afternoon or evening</u>.

Note The abbreviation BC ("before Christ") always follows a date, whereas AD (*anno Domini*, Latin for "in the year of the Lord")

CULTURE LANGUAGE

ABBREVIATIONS AND ARTICLES

Abbreviations can be particularly challenging for nonnative writers; for instance, when do we use words like *a, an,* or *the* (the *FBI* but *NATO*)? Encourage ESL students to build a word list of abbreviations and acronyms and sort them by the use (or nonuse) of such markers.

IBID. AND *OP. CIT.*

Many students are unsure about how to use scholarly abbreviations like *ibid.* ("in the same place") or *op. cit.* ("in the work cited"). These Latin abbreviations are no longer used in the citation styles of the Modern Language Association, American Psychological Association, or Council of Science Editors. *The Chicago Manual of Style* still sanctions the use of *ibid.* in some circumstances; see Chapter 51.

precedes a date. Increasingly, these abbreviations are being replaced by BCE ("before the common era") and CE ("common era"), respectively. Both follow the date.

 35d Generally, reserve Latin abbreviations for source citations and comments in parentheses.

The following common Latin abbreviations are generally not italicized or underlined.

i.e.	*id est:* that is
cf.	*confer:* compare
e.g.	*exempli gratia:* for example
et al.	*et alii:* and others
etc.	*et cetera:* and so forth
NB	*nota bene:* note well

He said he would be gone a fortnight (i.e., two weeks).
Trees, too, are susceptible to disease (e.g., Dutch elm disease).
Bloom et al., editors, *Anthology of Light Verse*

Some writers avoid these abbreviations in formal writing, even within parentheses.

 35e Use *Inc., Bros., Co.,* or *&* (for *and*) only in official names of business firms.

Not	The Santini <u>bros.</u> operate a large moving firm in New York City.
But	The Santini <u>brothers</u> operate a large moving firm in New York City.
Or	Santini <u>Bros.</u> is a large moving firm in New York City.
Not	We read about the Hardy Boys <u>&</u> Nancy Drew.
But	We read about the Hardy Boys <u>and</u> Nancy Drew.

 35f Spell out most units of measurement and names of places, calendar designations, people, and courses.

In most academic, general, and business writing, certain words should always be spelled out. (In source citations and technical writing, however, these words are more often abbreviated.)

Units of measurement
The dog is thirty <u>inches</u> [not <u>in.</u>] high.
The building is 150 <u>feet</u> [not <u>ft.</u>] tall.

Exception Long phrases such as *miles per hour* (*m.p.h.*) or *cycles per second* (*c.p.s.*) are usually abbreviated, with or without periods: *The speed limit on that road was once 75 m.p.h.* [or *mph*].

Geographical names

The publisher is in Massachusetts [not Mass. or MA].
He came from Auckland, New Zealand [not NZ].
She lived on Morrissey Boulevard [not Blvd.].

Exceptions The United States is often referred to as the USA or the US. In writing of the US capital, use the abbreviation DC for District of Columbia when it follows the city's name: Washington, DC.

Names of days, months, and holidays

The truce was signed on Tuesday [not Tues.], April [not Apr.] 16.
The Christmas [not Xmas] holidays were uneventful.

Names of people

Virginia [not Va.] Woolf was British.
Robert [not Robt.] Frost wrote accessible poems.

Courses of instruction

I'm majoring in political science [not poli. sci.].
Economics [not Econ.] is a difficult course.

Exercise 35.1   Revising: Abbreviations

Revise the following sentences as needed to correct inappropriate use of abbreviations for nontechnical writing. Mark the number preceding any sentence in which abbreviations are appropriate as written.

Example:
One prof. lectured for five hrs.
One professor lectured for five hours.

1. In the Sept. 17, 2003, issue of *Science* magazine, Virgil L. Sharpton discusses a theory that could help explain the extinction of dinosaurs.
2. About 65 mill. yrs. ago, a comet or asteroid crashed into the earth.
3. The result was a huge crater about 10 km. (6.2 mi.) deep in the Gulf of Mex.
4. Sharpton's new measurements suggest that the crater is 50 pct. larger than scientists previously believed.
5. Indeed, 20-yr.-old drilling cores reveal that the crater is about 186 mi. wide, roughly the size of Conn.
6. The space object was traveling more than 100,000 m.p.h. and hit earth with the impact of 100 to 300 million megatons of TNT.
7. On impact, 200,000 cubic km. of rock and soil were vaporized or thrown into the air.
8. That's the equivalent of 2.34 bill. cubic ft. of matter.
9. The impact would have created 400-ft. tidal waves across the Atl. Ocean, temps. higher than 20,000 degs., and powerful earthquakes.

ANSWERS: EXERCISE 35.1

1. In the September 17, 2003, issue of *Science* magazine, Virgil L. Sharpton discusses a theory that could help explain the extinction of dinosaurs.
2. About 65 million years ago, a comet or asteroid crashed into the earth.
3. The result was a huge crater about 10 kilometers (6.2 miles) deep in the Gulf of Mexico.
4. Sharpton's new measurements suggest that the crater is 50 percent larger than scientists previously believed.
5. Indeed, 20-year-old drilling cores reveal that the crater is about 186 miles wide, roughly the size of Connecticut.
6. Sentence correct.
7. On impact, 200,000 cubic kilometers of rock and soil were vaporized or thrown into the air.
8. That's the equivalent of 2.34 billion cubic feet of matter.
9. The impact would have created 400-foot tidal waves across the Atlantic Ocean, temperatures higher than 20,000 degrees, and powerful earthquakes.
10. Sharpton theorizes that the dust, vapor, and smoke from this impact blocked the sun's rays for months, cooled the earth, and thus resulted in the death of the dinosaurs.

10. Sharpton theorizes that the dust, vapor, and smoke from this impact blocked the sun's rays for mos., cooled the earth, and thus resulted in the death of the dinosaurs.

Note See page 498 for an exercise involving abbreviations along with capitals and other mechanics.

36
Numbers

This chapter addresses the use of numbers (numerals versus words) in the text of a document. All disciplines use many more numerals in source citations.

Grammar checkers A grammar checker will flag numerals beginning sentences and can be customized to ignore or to look for numerals (see p. 64). But it can't tell you whether numerals or spelled-out numbers are appropriate for your writing situation.

36a Use numerals according to standard practice in the field you are writing in.

Always use numerals for numbers that require more than two words to spell out:

> The leap year has 366 days.
> The population of Minot, North Dakota, is about 36,500.

In nontechnical academic writing, spell out numbers of one or two words:

> Twelve nations signed the treaty.
> The ball game drew forty-two thousand people. [A hyphenated number may be considered one word.]

Visit *mycomplab.com* for more resources and exercises on numbers.

HIGHLIGHTS

The representation of numbers in general writing is the subject of this chapter. The rules for when to use figures for numbers and when to write out numbers are few and easily memorized.

USING NUMBERS

Audience expectations dictate whether or not numbers are spelled out. As the text notes, audiences that routinely use numerical data, like engineers or accountants, generally prefer figures. Other audiences, including other academic readers and general readers, follow the guidelines discussed here. Remind students to apply whatever guidelines they follow consistently throughout a document.

In much business writing, use numerals for all numbers over ten (*five reasons, 11 participants*). In technical academic and business writing, such as in science and engineering, use numerals for all numbers over ten, and use numerals for zero through nine when they refer to exact measurements (*2 liters, 1 hour*). (Consult one of the style guides listed on pp. 779–80 and 811 for more details.)

Note Use a combination of numerals and words for round numbers over a million: *26 million, 2.45 billion.* And use either all numerals or all words when several numbers appear together in a passage, even if convention would require a mixture:

Inconsistent	The satellite Galatea is about twenty-six thousand miles from Neptune. It is 110 miles in diameter and orbits Neptune in just over ten hours.
Revised	The satellite Galatea is about 26,000 miles from Neptune. It is 110 miles in diameter and orbits Neptune in just over 10 hours.

(CULTURE LANGUAGE) In American English a comma separates the numerals in long numbers (*26,000*), and a period functions as a decimal point (*2.06*).

36b Use numerals according to convention for dates, addresses, and other information.

Even when a number requires one or two words to spell out, we conventionally use numerals in the following situations:

Days and years
June 18, 2000   AD 12   456 BCE   1999

Exception The day of a month may be expressed in words when it is not followed by a year (*June fifth; October first*).

Pages, chapters, volumes, acts, scenes, lines
Chapter 9, page 123
Hamlet, act 5, scene 3, lines 35–40

Decimals, percentages, and fractions
22.5
48% (*or* 48 percent)
3½

Addresses
RD 2
419 Stonewall Street
Washington, DC 20036

Scores and statistics
21 to 7
a mean of 26
a ratio of 8 to 1

Exact amounts of money
$4.50
$3.5 million (*or* $3,500,000)

The time of day
9:00 AM
2:30 PM

ADDITIONAL EXAMPLES
Biblical reference
2 Kings 3.6

Measurements
55 miles per hour
2 liters
1 tablespoon
9 × 12-inch paper or 9" × 12" paper

DRAMATIC REFERENCES
The MLA recommends the numbers alone, separated by periods, for acts, scenes, and lines: *Hamlet* 5.1.35.

ANSWERS: EXERCISE 36.1

1. The planet Saturn is <u>900</u> million miles, or nearly <u>1.5 billion</u> kilometers, from the sun.
2. Sentence correct.
3. Thus, Saturn orbits the sun only <u>2.4</u> times during the average human life span.
4. It travels in its orbit at about <u>21,600</u> miles per hour.
5. <u>Fifteen</u> to <u>twenty</u> times denser than Earth's core, Saturn's core measures <u>seventeen thousand</u> miles across.
6. The temperature at Saturn's cloud tops is <u>–170</u> degrees Fahrenheit.
7. In <u>1933</u>, astronomers found on Saturn's surface a huge white spot <u>two</u> times the size of Earth and <u>seven</u> times the size of Mercury.
8. Saturn's famous rings reflect almost <u>70</u> percent of the sunlight that approaches the planet.
9. The ring system is almost <u>40,000</u> miles wide, beginning 8800 miles from the planet's visible surface and ending <u>47,000</u> miles from that surface.
10. Saturn generates about <u>130</u> trillion kilowatts of electricity.

Exceptions Round dollar or cent amounts of only a few words may be expressed in words: *seventeen dollars; fifteen hundred dollars; sixty cents.* When the word *o'clock* is used for the time of day, also express the number in words: *two o'clock* (not *2 o'clock*).

36c | **Always spell out numbers that begin sentences.**

For clarity, spell out any number that begins a sentence. If the number requires more than two words, reword the sentence so that the number falls later and can be expressed as a numeral:

Not | 3.9 billion people live in Asia.
But | The population of Asia is <u>3.9 billion</u>.

Exercise 36.1 Revising: Numbers

Revise the following sentences so that numbers are used appropriately for nontechnical writing. Mark the number preceding any sentence in which numbers are already used appropriately.

> *Example:*
> Charlie paid two hundred five dollars for used scuba gear.
> Charlie paid <u>$205</u> for used scuba gear.

1. The planet Saturn is nine hundred million miles, or nearly one billion five hundred million kilometers, from the sun.
2. A year on Saturn equals almost thirty of our years.
3. Thus, Saturn orbits the sun only two and four-tenths times during the average human life span.
4. It travels in its orbit at about twenty-one thousand six hundred miles per hour.
5. 15 to 20 times denser than Earth's core, Saturn's core measures 17,000 miles across.
6. The temperature at Saturn's cloud tops is minus one hundred seventy degrees Fahrenheit.
7. In nineteen hundred thirty-three, astronomers found on Saturn's surface a huge white spot 2 times the size of Earth and 7 times the size of Mercury.
8. Saturn's famous rings reflect almost seventy percent of the sunlight that approaches the planet.
9. The ring system is almost forty thousand miles wide, beginning 8800 miles from the planet's visible surface and ending forty-seven thousand miles from that surface.
10. Saturn generates about one hundred thirty trillion kilowatts of electricity.

Exercise on Chapters 33–36 Revising: Mechanics

Revise the following paragraphs to correct any errors in the use of capital letters, italics or underlining, abbreviations, and numbers. (For abbreviations and numbers, follow standard practice for nontechnical writing.) Consult a dictionary as needed.

According to many sources—e.g., the Cambridge Ancient History and Gardiner's Egypt of the Pharaohs—the ancient egyptians devoted much attention to making Life more convenient and pleasurable for themselves.

Our word pharaoh for the ancient egyptian rulers comes from the egyptian word pr'o, meaning "great house." Indeed, the egyptians placed great emphasis on family residences, adding small bedrms. as early as 3500 yrs. bce. By 3000 bce, the egyptians made ice through evaporation of water at night and then used it to cool their homes. About the same time they used fans made of palm fronds or papyrus to cool themselves in the day. To light their homes, the egyptians abandoned the animal-fat lamps Humans had used for 50 thousand yrs. Instead, around 1300 bce the people of Egt. devised the 1st oil lamps.

egyptians found great pleasure in playing games. Four thousand three hundred yrs. ago or so they created one of the oldest board games known. the game involved racing ivory or stone pieces across a papyrus playing board. By three thousand bce, egyptian children played marbles with semi-precious stones, some of which have been found in gravesites at nagada, EG. Around one thousand three hundred sixty bce, small children played with clay rattles covered in silk and shaped like animals.

To play the game of love, egyptian men and women experimented with cosmetics applied to skin and eyelids. kohl, history's first eyeliner, was used by both sexes to ward off evil. 5000 yrs. ago egyptians wore wigs made of vegetable fibers or human hair. In 9 hundred bce, queen Isimkheb wore a wig so heavy that she needed assistance in walking. To adjust their make-up and wigs, egyptians adapted the simple metal mirrors devised by the sumerians in the bronze age, ornamenting them with carved handles of ivory, gold, or wood. Feeling that only those who smelled sweet could be attractive, the egyptians made deodorants from perfumed oils, e.g., cinnamon and citrus.

ANSWERS: EXERCISE ON CHAPTERS 33–36

According to many sources—for example, the *Cambridge Ancient History* and Gardiner's *Egypt of the Pharaohs* [titles italicized]—the ancient Egyptians devoted much attention to making life more convenient and pleasurable for themselves.

Our word *pharaoh* [defined word italicized] for the ancient Egyptian rulers comes from the Egyptian word *pr'o* [forgeign word italicized], meaning "great house." Indeed, the Egyptian placed great emphasis on family residences, adding small bedrooms as early as 3500 BCE. By 3000 BCE, the Egyptians made ice through evaporation of water at night and then used it to cool their homes. About the same time they used fans made of palm fronds or papyrus to cool themselves in the day. To light their homes, the Egyptians abandoned the animal-fat lamps humans had used for fifty thousand years. Instead, around 1300 BCE the people of Egypt devised the first oil lamps.

Egyptians found great pleasure in playing games. Around 4300 years ago they created one of the oldest board games known. The game involved racing ivory or stone pieces across a papyrus playing board. By 3000 BCE, Egyptian children played marbles with semiprecious stones, some of which have been found in gravesites at Nagada, Egypt. Around 1360 BCE, small children played with clay rattles covered in silk and shaped like animals.

To play the game of love, Egyptian men and women experimented with cosmetics applied to skin and eyelids. Kohl, history's first eyeliner, was used by both sexes to ward off evil. Five thousand years ago Egyptians wore wigs made of vegetable fibers or human hair. In 900 BCE, Queen Isimkheb wore a wig so heavy that she needed assistance in walking. To adjust their make-up and wigs, Egyptians adapted the simple metal mirrors devised by the Sumerians in the Bronze Age, ornamenting them with carved handles of ivory, gold, or wood. Feeling that only those who smelled sweet could be attractive, the Egyptians made deodorants from perfumed oils, for example, cinnamon and citrus.

PART **8**

Effective Words

37 Using Appropriate Language

38 Using Exact Language

39 Writing Concisely

40 Spelling and the Hyphen

HIGHLIGHTS

There's no substitute for experience when it comes to choosing the right words, and students with limited experience in reading and writing, or whose first language is not English, may find learning to use proper diction a formidable hurdle. Time, encouragement, and careful explanations can help them gain confidence. If your campus has a writing center, check to see if it offers drills or instructional materials to help students improve their resources in language.

This chapter covers types of diction to be avoided or used with care in formal standard American English: dialect; nonstandard grammar, punctuation, capitalization, abbreviations, and spelling common in online communication; slang; colloquialisms; regionalisms; neologisms; technical language; pretentious language; sexist or biased language; and labels. The chart on "Eliminating sexist language" (pp. 508–09) should be particularly helpful for students who have had little or spotty exposure to standards of inclusive, nonsexist language.

A WRITER'S PERSPECTIVE

Proper words in proper places make the true definition of a style.
—JONATHAN SWIFT, "Letter to a Young Clergyman"

RESOURCES AND IDEAS

On vocabulary building

Harklau, Linda. "From the 'Good Kids' to the 'Worst': Representation of English Language Learners across Educational Settings." *TESOL Quarterly* 34.1 (2000): 35–67. Print. Harklau shows how the institutional image of language minority students changes in negative ways as these students transition from nurturing high school to indifferent college.

Minchew, Sue S., and Peggy F. Hopper. "Techniques for Using Humor and Fun in the Language Arts Classroom." *Clearing House: A Journal of Educational Strategies, Issues, and Ideas* 81.5 (2008): 232–36. Print. The authors suggest numerous fun activities to help students improve their vocabulary and overall word awareness using diverse sources includ-

37

Using Appropriate Language

Appropriate language suits your writing situation—your subject, purpose, and audience. Like everyone, you vary your words depending on the context in which you are speaking and writing. Look, for example, at the underlined words in these two sentences:

> Some patients decide to <u>bag</u> counseling because their <u>shrinks</u> seem <u>strung out</u>.

> Some patients decide to <u>abandon</u> counseling because their <u>therapists</u> seem <u>disturbed</u>.

The first sentence might be addressed to friends in casual conversation. The second is more suitable for an academic audience.

The more formal language of the second example is typical of **standard American English.** This is the dialect of English normally expected and used in school, business, government, the professions, and the communications media. (For more on its role in academic writing, see pp. 168–70.)

The vocabulary of standard American English is huge, allowing expression of an infinite range of ideas and feelings; but it does exclude words that only some groups of people use, understand, or find inoffensive. Some of those more limited vocabularies should be avoided altogether; others should be used cautiously and in special situations, as when aiming for a special effect with an audience you know will appreciate it. Whenever you doubt a word's status, consult a dictionary (see p. 512).

Grammar checkers A grammar checker can often be set to flag potentially inappropriate words, such as nonstandard dialect, slang, colloquialisms, and gender-specific terms (*manmade, mailman*). However, the checker can flag only words listed in its dictionary of questionable words. For example, a checker flagged *businessman* as potentially sexist in *A successful businessman puts clients first,* but the checker did not flag *his* in *A successful businessperson lis-*

mycomplab

Visit *mycomplab.com* for more resources and exercises on appropriate language.

Appropriate language in academic writing

■ **Use standard American English,** the dialect recommended by this handbook. Slang, colloquial language, and other vocabularies are sometimes appropriate in academic writing. Nonstandard dialect, online shortcuts, and pretentious writing are rarely or never appropriate. (See below and pp. 504–07.)

Inappropriate	With a little help, <u>Web-shy folks</u> can <u>get to be hotshot surfers.</u>
Revised	With a little help, people reluctant to explore the Web can become capable users.

■ **Avoid stereotypes.** (See pp. 507–08.)

Stereotype	<u>Football players</u> need tutors and counselors.
Revised	Football players with poor grades need tutors and counselors.

■ **Avoid sexist language.** (See pp. 508–10.)

Sexist	<u>Teenage girls</u> are ideal babysitters.
Revised	Teenagers who enjoy young children are ideal babysitters.

■ **Be sensitive when labeling groups.** (See p. 510.)

Inappropriate	The <u>hurricane victims</u> needed immediate help.
Revised	The people affected by the hurricane needed immediate help.

tens to his clients. If you use a checker to review your language, you'll need to determine whether a flagged word is or is not appropriate for your writing situation. (See p. 64 for tips on customizing a grammar checker.)

 37a Revising nonstandard dialect

Like many countries, the United States consists of scores of regional, social, and ethnic groups with their own distinct dialects, or versions of English. Standard American English is one of these dialects, and so are Black English, Appalachian English, Creole, and the English of coastal Maine. All the dialects of English share many features, but each also has its own vocabulary, pronunciation, and grammar.

If you speak a dialect of English besides standard American English, be careful about using your dialect in situations where standard English is the norm, such as in academic or public writing. Dialects are not wrong in themselves, but forms imported from

ing Internet jokes, Johnny Carson routines, and William Safire's *Fumble Rules*.

Simpson, Mary Scott. "Teaching Writing: Beginning with the Word." *College English* 39.8 (1978): 934–39. Print. The author describes class activities and readings designed to develop sensitivity to words and build vocabulary.

PUNDITS' PERSPECTIVES

Students may have heard of popular usage commentators like William Safire, John Simon, or James Kilpatrick; ask students to review books or articles by these commentators in the library, see what diction issues they consider most important, and consider whether they agree. A good counterpoint to such commentators is Harvey A. Daniels's *Famous Last Words: The American Language Crisis Reconsidered* (Urbana: NCTE, 1983). See also, Bill Bryson's *Made in America: An Informal History of the English Language in the United States* (New York: Morrow, 1994) for an appealing historical overview of shifts in usage.

HUCK FINN

You may wish to make the following examples the subject of class discussion. Students usually find them quite interesting.

In his explanatory note at the beginning of *The Adventures of Huckleberry Finn*, Mark Twain explains one of the difficulties with using nonstandard language:

> In this book a number of dialects are used, to wit: the Missouri negro dialect; the extremist form of the backwoods Southwestern dialect; the ordinary "Pike County" dialect; and four modified varieties of this last. The shadings have not been done in a haphazard fashion, or by guesswork; but painstakingly, and with the trustworthy guidance and support of personal familiarity with these several forms of speech. I make this explanation for the reason that without it many readers would suppose that all these characters were trying to talk alike and not succeeding.
>
> —THE AUTHOR

From the opening lines of *The Adventures of Huckleberry Finn:*

You don't know about me without you have read a book by the name of *The Adventures of Tom Sawyer;* but that ain't no matter. That book was made by Mr. Mark Twain, and he told the truth, mainly. There was things which he stretched; but mainly he told the truth. That is nothing. I never seen anybody but lied one time or another, without it was Aunt Polly, or the widow, or maybe Mary. Aunt Polly—Tom's Aunt Polly, she is—and Mary, and the widow Douglas is all told about in that book, which is mostly a true book, with some stretchers, as I said before.

RESOURCES AND IDEAS

The influence of digital media has been a popular topic of discussion among scholars in recent years. For an overview of the topic, you might look at David Buckingham's *Youth, Identity, and Digital Media* (Cambridge: MIT Press, 2008), a collection of essays exploring the impact on young people of immersion in new media. David Crystal's works *Language and the Internet* (2nd ed. New York: Cambridge UP, 2006) and *Txtng: The Gr8 Db8* (New York: Oxford UP, 2008) discuss specifically the impact of the Internet and text messaging on language.

Because many students spend times engage in online communication that uses shortcuts (text messaging, instant messaging, etc.), they might find that language creeping into more formal academic writing. Here are some activities to help students edit for such abbreviations in their writing:

- Remind students that their audience for an academic essay likely differs from their online audience. Have them write a brief analysis of the expectations their essay's audience has regarding shortcuts—and remind them that you are a member of that audience.
- During peer review sessions, have students edit one another's papers for inappropriate shorthand.
- Ask students to create a list of commonly used text shortcuts. Then, have them "translate" the abbreviation into language appropriate for an academic paper. Distrib-

one dialect into another may still be perceived as unclear or incorrect. When you know standard English is expected in your writing, edit to eliminate expressions in your dialect that you know (or have been told) differ from standard English. These expressions may include *theirselves, hisn, them books,* and others labeled "nonstandard" by a dictionary. They may also include certain verb forms, as discussed on pages 275–88. For help identifying and editing nonstandard language, see "⟨CULTURE LANGUAGE⟩ Guide" inside the back cover of this book.

Your participation in the community of standard English does not require you to abandon your own dialect. You may want to use it in writing you do for yourself, such as journals, notes, and drafts, which should be composed as freely as possible. You may want to quote it in an academic paper, as when analyzing or reporting conversation in dialect. And, of course, you will want to use it with others who speak it.

37b Revising the shortcuts of online communication

Rapid communication by e-mail and text or instant messaging encourages some informalities that are inappropriate for academic writing. If you use these media frequently, you may need to proofread your academic papers especially to identify and revise errors such as the following:

- **Sentence fragments.** Make sure every sentence has a subject and a predicate. Avoid fragments such as *Observing the results* and *After the meeting.* For more on fragments, see pages 330–36.
- **Missing punctuation.** Between and within sentences, use standard punctuation marks. Check especially for missing commas within sentences and missing apostrophes in possessives and contractions. See pages 422–38 and 452–57.
- **Missing capital letters.** Use capital letters at the beginnings of sentences, for proper nouns and adjectives, and in titles. See pages 482–86.
- **Nonstandard abbreviations and spellings.** Avoid forms such as *2* for *to* or *too, b4* for *before, bc* for *because, ur* for *you are* or *you're,* and + or & for *and.* See pages 538–44.

37c Using slang only when appropriate

All groups of people—from musicians and computer scientists to vegetarians and golfers—create novel and colorful expressions called **slang.** The following quotation, for instance, is from an essay on the slang of "skaters" (skateboarders):

> Curtis slashed ultra-punk crunchers on his longboard, while the Rubeman flailed his usual Gumbyness on tweaked frontsides and lofty fakie ollies.
> —Miles Orkin, "Mucho Slingage by the Pool"

Among those who understand it, slang may be vivid and forceful. It often occurs in dialog, and an occasional slang expression can enliven an informal essay. Some slang, such as *dropout* (*She was a high school dropout*), has proved so useful that it has passed into the general vocabulary.

But most slang is too flippant and imprecise for effective communication, and it is generally inappropriate for college or business writing. Notice the gain in seriousness and precision achieved in the following revision:

| Slang | Many students start out <u>pretty together</u> but then <u>get weird</u>. |
| Revised | Many students start out <u>with clear goals</u> but then <u>lose their direction</u>. |

37d Using colloquial language only when appropriate

Colloquial language designates the words and expressions appropriate to everyday spoken language. Regardless of our backgrounds and how we live, we all try to *get along with* each other. We play with *kids*, *go crazy* for something, and in our worst moments try to *get back at* someone who has made us do the *dirty work*.

When you write informally, colloquial language may be appropriate to achieve the casual, relaxed effect of conversation. An occasional colloquial word dropped into otherwise more formal writing can also help you achieve a desired emphasis. But colloquial language does not provide the exactness needed in more formal college, public, and professional writing. In such writing you should generally avoid any words and expressions labeled "informal" or "colloquial" in your dictionary. Take special care to avoid **mixed diction,** a combination of standard and colloquial words:

| Mixed diction | According to a Native American myth, the Great Creator <u>had a dog hanging around with him</u> when he created the earth. |
| Revised | According to a Native American myth, the Great Creator <u>was accompanied by a dog</u> when he created the earth. |

ute copies to students, or in a wired classroom, post the translations for students to consult during editing.

COMPUTER ACTIVITY

FIELD RESEARCH

Have students work in teams as "anthropologists" to collect examples of Internet (text and instant messaging) shorthand. They can compare their research with guides available online such as *noslang.com* or *internetslang.com*. See also *A Concise Collection of College Students' Slang* by Xin-An Lu and David W. Graf, Jr. (Lincoln: Universe, 2004). Other topics for research reports might be the languages of rap or rock music, of some activity (skateboarding or football), or of some social group (fraternities, volunteer firefighters).

CULTURE LANGUAGE

THEORETICAL PERSPECTIVE ON DIALECT

If your students are interested in the matter of what ought to be done about language variation, you could share a theoretical perspective from linguistics. Linguists have identified three different philosophies about how to resolve the problem of language variation. One philosophy is that of *eradication*, which holds that language variations should be completely eliminated. A second philosophy is that of *appreciation*, which holds that dialects ought to be celebrated as reflections of our diverse cultural traditions. A third philosophy is that of *biloquialism* or *bidialectalism*, which holds that people should learn more than one language variety so that they can express themselves in multiple situations without giving up their ways of relating in the multiple communities to which they belong. A class discussion on the relative merits of these three approaches might be a lively one.

TECHNICAL JARGON

Using technical language is appropriate when both writers and readers understand the specialized body of knowledge to which the technical language refers. Have students practice translating between technical and nontechnical language to gain experience in deciding what level of language might be appropriate for particular situations. For a study of the sources of academic and newspaper jargon see Walter Nash's *Jargon: Its Uses and Abuses* (Oxford: Blackwell, 1993).

COLLABORATIVE LEARNING

EUPHEMISTICALLY SPEAKING

Have small groups of students find examples of pretentious or euphemistic language in political or other public speeches or advertising. Groups can compare notes in class and decide which examples are the most silly and which are the most duplicitous.

 37e **Using regionalisms only when appropriate**

Regionalisms are expressions or pronunciations peculiar to a particular area. Southerners may say they *reckon*, meaning "think" or "suppose." People in Maine invite their Boston friends to come *down* rather than *up* (north) to visit. New Yorkers stand *on* rather than *in* line for a movie.

Regional expressions are appropriate in writing addressed to local readers and may lend realism to regional description, but they should be avoided in writing intended for a general audience.

37f **Revising neologisms**

Neologisms are words created (or coined) so recently that they have not come into established use. An example is *prequel* (made up of *pre-*, meaning "before," and the ending of *sequel*), a movie or book that takes the story of an existing movie or book back in time. Some neologisms do become accepted as part of our general vocabulary—*motel*, coined from *motor* and *hotel*, is an example. But most neologisms pass quickly from the language. Unless such words serve a special purpose in your writing and are sure to be understood by your readers, you should avoid them.

37g **Using technical words with care**

All disciplines and professions rely on special words or give common words special meanings. Chemists speak of *esters* and *phosphatides*, geographers and mapmakers refer to *isobars* and *isotherms*, and literary critics write about *motifs* and *subtexts*. Such technical language allows specialists to communicate precisely and economically with other specialists who share their vocabulary. But without explanation these words are meaningless to nonspecialists. When you are writing for nonspecialists, avoid unnecessary technical terms and carefully define terms you must use.

37h **Revising indirect or pretentious writing**

In most writing, small, plain, and direct words are preferable to big, showy, or evasive words. Avoid euphemisms, double talk, and pretentious writing.

A **euphemism** is a presumably inoffensive word that a writer or speaker substitutes for a word deemed potentially offensive or too blunt, such as *passed away* for "died." Euphemisms appear whenever a writer or speaker wants to soften the truth, as when a governor mentions the *negative growth* (meaning "decline") in her state. Use euphemisms only when you know that blunt, truthful words would needlessly hurt or offend members of your audience.

A kind of euphemism that deliberately evades the truth is **double talk** (also called **doublespeak** or **weasel words**): language intended to confuse or to be misunderstood. Today double talk is unfortunately common in politics and advertising—the *revenue enhancement* that is really a tax, the *biodegradable* bags that last decades. Double talk has no place in honest writing.

Euphemism and sometimes double talk seem to keep company with fancy writing. Any writing that is more elaborate than its subject requires will sound **pretentious**—that is, excessively showy. Choose your words for their exactness and economy. The big, ornate word may be tempting, but pass it up. Your readers will be grateful.

Pretentious	To perpetuate our endeavor of providing funds for our elderly citizens as we do at the present moment, we will face the exigency of enhanced contributions from all our citizens.
Revised	We cannot continue to fund Social Security and Medicare for the elderly unless we raise taxes.

37i Revising sexist and other biased language

Even when we do not mean it to, our language can reflect and perpetuate hurtful prejudices toward groups of people, especially racial, ethnic, religious, age, and sexual groups. Such biased language can be obvious—words such as *nigger, whitey, mick, kike, fag, dyke,* and *broad*. But it can also be subtle, generalizing about groups in ways that may be familiar but that are also inaccurate or unfair. For instance, people with physical disabilities are as varied a group as any other: the only thing they have in common is some form of impairment. To assume that people with disabilities share certain attitudes (shyness, helplessness, victimization, whatever) is to disregard the uniqueness of each person.

Biased language reflects poorly on the user, not on the person or persons whom it mischaracterizes or insults. Unbiased language does not submit to false generalizations. It treats people as individuals and labels groups as they wish to be labeled.

1 Avoiding stereotypes of race, ethnicity, religion, age, and other characteristics

A **stereotype** is a generalization based on poor evidence, a kind of formula for understanding and judging people simply because of their membership in a group:

RESOURCES AND IDEAS

On sexism in language

Amare, Nicole. "Where is She? Gender Occurrences in Online Grammar Guides." *Research in the Teaching of English* 42.2 (2007): 163–87. Print. Amare analyzed online grammar guides according to NCTE's "Guidelines for Gender-Fair Use of Language" and found instances of linguistic sexism. She encourages writing teachers to teach students how to eliminate gender bias in their writing.

Goueffic, Louise. *Breaking the Patriarchal Code: The Linguistic Basis of Sexual Bias.* Manchester: Knowledge, Ideas and Trends, 1996. Print. Goueffic argues for the relationship between biased language and discriminatory social practices.

Hayes, Christopher G. "A Brief Writing Assignment for Introducing Non-Sexist Pronoun Usage." *Teaching English in the Two-Year College* 28.1 (2000): 74–77. Print. Hayes describes an in-class writing activity that asks students to write a narrative in which they assign genders to characters from specific professions (a nurse, a physician, etc.). He uses the results, which tend to reinforce gender stereotypes, to start a discussion about the negative impact of gender bias in writing.

Maggio, Rosalie. *The Bias-Free Word Finder.* Boston: Beacon, 1992. Print. Originally published as *The Dictionary of Bias-Free Usage: A Guide to Nondiscriminatory Language.* Phoenix: Oryx, 1991. Print. Maggio provides a thesaurus of bias-free synonyms for gendered terms.

Miller, Casey, and Kate Swift. *The Handbook of Nonsexist Writing for Writers, Editors, and Speakers.* 2nd ed. New York: HarperCollins, 1988. Print. Miller and Swift's book is the standard handbook for people concerned with avoiding linguistic sexism.

Men are uncommunicative.
Women are emotional.
Liberals want to raise taxes.
Conservatives are affluent.

At best, stereotypes betray an uncritical writer, one who is not thinking beyond notions received from others. Worse, they betray a writer who does not mind hurting others or even *wants* to hurt others.

In your writing, be alert for any general statements about people based on only one or a few characteristics. Be especially cautious about substituting such statements for the evidence you should be providing instead.

Stereotype   Elderly drivers should have their licenses limited to daytime driving. [Implies that all elderly people are poor night drivers.]

Revised   Drivers with impaired night vision should have their licenses limited to daytime driving.

Some stereotypes have become part of the language, but they are still potentially offensive.

Stereotype   The administrators are too blind to see the need for a new gymnasium. [Equates vision disability and lack of understanding.]

Revised   The administrators do not understand the need for a new gymnasium.

2 | Avoiding sexist language

Among the most subtle and persistent biased language is that expressing narrow ideas about men's and women's roles, position, and value in society. This **sexist language** distinguishes needlessly between men and women in such matters as occupation, ability, behavior, temperament, and maturity. Like other stereotypes, it can wound or irritate readers, and it indicates the writer's thoughtlessness or unfairness. The following box suggests ways of eliminating sexist language.

Eliminating sexist language

- **Avoid demeaning and patronizing language**—for instance, identifying women and men differently or trivializing either gender:

Sexist   Dr. Keith Kim and Lydia Hawkins wrote the article.
Revised   Dr. Keith Kim and Dr. Lydia Hawkins wrote the article.
Revised   Keith Kim and Lydia Hawkins wrote the article.

Sexist   Ladies are entering formerly male occupations.
Revised   Women are entering formerly male occupations.

■ **Avoid occupational or social stereotypes,** assuming that a role or profession is exclusively male or female:

Sexist   The considerate doctor commends a nurse when <u>she</u> provides <u>his</u> patients with good care.

Revised   The considerate doctor commends a nurse <u>who provides good care for patients.</u>

■ **Avoid referring needlessly to gender:**

Sexist   Marie Curie, <u>a woman chemist</u>, discovered radium.
Revised   Marie Curie, <u>a chemist</u>, discovered radium.

Sexist   The patients were tended by <u>a male nurse</u>.
Revised   The patients were tended by <u>a nurse</u>.

■ **Avoid using *man* or words containing *man* to refer to all human beings.** Here are a few alternatives:

businessman	businessperson
chairman	chair, chairperson
congressman	representative in Congress, legislator
craftsman	craftsperson, artisan
layman	layperson
mankind	humankind, humanity, human beings, people
policeman	police officer
salesman	salesperson

Sexist   <u>Man</u> has not reached the limits of social justice.
Revised   <u>Humankind [or Humanity]</u> has not reached the limits of social justice.

Sexist   The furniture consists of <u>manmade</u> materials.
Revised   The furniture consists of <u>synthetic</u> materials.

■ **Avoid the generic *he,*** the male pronoun used to refer to both genders. (See also pp. 311–13.)

Sexist   The newborn child explores <u>his</u> world.
Revised   Newborn <u>children</u> explore <u>their</u> world. [Use the plural for the pronoun and the word it refers to.]
Revised   The newborn child explores <u>the</u> world. [Avoid the pronoun altogether.]
Revised   The newborn child explores <u>his or her</u> world. [Substitute male and female pronouns.]

Use the last option sparingly—only once in a group of sentences and only to stress the singular individual.

(CULTURE LANGUAGE) Forms of address vary widely from culture to culture. In some cultures, for instance, one shows respect by referring to all older women as if they were married, using

LISTING ONE'S OWN LABELS

Ask students to list labels for groups to which they belong (for example, Christian, white, student, woman). Then, ask students to consider pejorative or biased terms they wouldn't want applied to themselves (*Bible-thumper* for Christians, or *chick* for women, for example). Discussing the stereotypical terms that might be applied to them and why those terms might be offensive can help students better understand that following bias-free language guidelines is not simply "political correctness," but rather a way of creating rapport with and showing respect for readers.

Ask students to complete Exercise 37.1 individually, with the aid of their own dictionaries. Then have students work in small groups to compare their responses and debate the appropriateness of each member's substitutions. This exercise can often provide the basis for a class-wide discussion on the correlation between word choice and context.

ANSWERS: EXERCISE 37.1

Possible answers

1. Acquired immune deficiency syndrome (AIDS) is a <u>serious threat</u> all over the world.
2. The disease <u>is transmitted</u> primarily by sexual intercourse, exchange of bodily fluids, shared needles, and blood transfusions.
3. Those who think the disease is limited to <u>homosexuals</u>, <u>drug users</u>, and foreigners are quite mistaken.
4. <u>Statistics</u> suggest that in the United States one in every five hundred college <u>students</u> carries the virus.

the equivalent of the title *Mrs.* Usage in the United States is changing toward making no assumptions about marital status, rank, or other characteristics—for instance, using the title *Ms.* for a woman unless she is known to prefer *Mrs.* or *Miss.*

3 Using appropriate labels

We often need to label groups: *swimmers, politicians, mothers, Christians, westerners, students.* But labels can be shorthand stereotypes that slight the person labeled and ignore the preferences of the group members themselves. Showing sensitivity when applying labels reveals you to be alert to readers' needs and concerns. Although sometimes dismissed as "political correctness," such sensitivity hurts no one and helps gain your readers' trust and respect.

- **Avoid labels that (intentionally or not) disparage the person or group you refer to.** A person with emotional problems is not a *mental patient.* A person with cancer is not a *cancer victim.* A person using a wheelchair is not *wheelchair-bound.*
- **Use names for racial, ethnic, and other groups that reflect the preferences of each group's members,** or at least many of them. Examples of current preferences include *African American* or *black, latino/latina* (for Americans and American immigrants of Spanish-speaking descent), and *people with disabilities* (rather than *the handicapped*). But labels change often. To learn how a group's members wish to be labeled, ask them directly, attend to usage in reputable periodicals, or check a recent dictionary.
- **Identify a person's group only when it is relevant to the point you're making.** Consider the context of the label: Is it a necessary piece of information? If not, don't use it.

A helpful reference for appropriate labels is *Guidelines for Bias-Free Writing*, by Marilyn Schwartz and the Task Force on Bias-Free Language of the Association of American University Presses.

> **Exercise 37.1 Revising: Appropriate words**
> Rewrite the following sentences as needed for standard American English. Consult a dictionary to determine whether particular words are appropriate and to find suitable substitutes.
>
> *Example:*
> If negotiators get hyper during contract discussions, they may mess up chances for a settlement.
>
> If negotiators <u>become excited or upset</u> during contract discussions, they may <u>harm</u> chances for a settlement.
>
> 1. Acquired immune deficiency syndrome (AIDS) is a major deal all over the world.
> 2. The disease gets around primarily by sexual intercourse, exchange of bodily fluids, shared needles, and blood transfusions.

3. Those who think the disease is limited to homos, druggies, and foreigners are quite mistaken.
4. Stats suggest that in the United States one in every five hundred college kids carries the virus.
5. A person with AIDS does not deserve to be subjected to exclusionary behavior or callousness on the part of his fellow citizens. Instead, he has the necessity for all the compassion, medical care, and financial assistance due those who are in the extremity of illness.
6. An AIDS victim often sees a team of doctors or a single doctor with a specialized practice.
7. The doctor may help his patients by obtaining social services for them as well as by providing medical care.
8. The AIDS sufferer who loses his job may need public assistance.
9. For someone who is very ill, a full-time nurse may be necessary. She can administer medications and make the sick person as comfortable as possible.
10. Some people with AIDS have insurance, but others lack the bread for premiums.

5. <u>People</u> with AIDS do not deserve <u>others' exclusion</u> or callousness. Instead, <u>they need</u> all the compassion, medical care, and financial assistance due the seriously ill.
6. A <u>person with AIDS</u> often sees a team of doctors or a single doctor with a specialized practice.
7. The doctor may <u>help patients</u> by obtaining social services for them as well as providing medical care.
8. The <u>person with AIDS</u> who loses <u>his or her</u> job may need public assistance.
9. For someone who is very ill, a full-time nurse may be necessary. <u>The nurse</u> can administer medications and <u>make</u> the sick person as comfortable as possible.
10. Some people with AIDS have insurance, but others lack the <u>money</u> for premiums.

38

Using Exact Language

To write clearly and effectively, you will want to find the words that fit your meaning exactly and convey your attitude precisely. Don't worry too much about choosing exact words while you are drafting an essay. If the right word doesn't come to you, leave a blank. Revision (p. 50) or editing (p. 59) is the stage to consider tone, specificity, and precision.

Grammar checkers A grammar checker can provide some help with inexact language. For instance, you can set it to flag commonly confused words (such as *continuous/continual*), misused prepositions in idioms (such as *accuse for* instead of *accuse of*), and clichés. (See p. 64 on setting a checker.) But the checker can flag only words stored in its dictionary. It can't help you at all with inappropriate connotation, excessive abstraction, or other problems discussed in this chapter.

HIGHLIGHTS

Chapter 38 helps students understand the value of precision in word choice. It begins with a discussion of widely-used desk and ESL dictionaries and explains a typical entry from an abridged dictionary. Next, it describes the difference between denotative and connotative meanings and the necessity of knowing both kinds of meanings when choosing a word. The third section explains why maintaining balance between abstract and concrete terms, and between general and specific terms, is an important element of good writing. Next, the chapter treats idiomatic language. This section contains a useful chart listing idioms and the prepositions they take, which will be helpful for ESL students and native speakers alike. The chapter closes with sections on figurative language and clichés. The exercises in this chapter will be easier to complete if students use a dictionary.

Visit *mycomplab.com* for more resources on exact language.

A WRITER'S PERSPECTIVE _____

Whenever we come upon one of those intensely right words . . . the resulting effect is physical as well as spiritual, and electrically prompt.
—MARK TWAIN, "William Dean Howells"

RESOURCES AND IDEAS

Crovitz, Darren, and Jessica A. Miller. "Register and Charge: Using Synonym Maps to Explore Connotation." *English Journal* 97.4 (2008): 49–55. Print. The authors describe an innovative system mapping numerous synonyms for a single term, placing each synonym on a matrix. Each word is placed by its degree of positive or negative connotation and level of informality or formality.

Dong, Yu Ren. "Don't Keep Them in the Dark! Teaching Metaphors to English Language Learners." *English Journal* 93.4 (2004): 29–35. Print. The author discusses the problems metaphorical language presents to ESL students and offers some strategies for teaching metaphors.

Skorczewski, Dawn. "'Everybody Has Their Own Ideas': Responding to Cliché in Student Writing." *College Composition and Communication* 52.2 (2000): 220–39. Print. Skorczewski argues that students' use of clichés, rather than indicating lack of critical thinking, may also demonstrate their grappling with new ideas.

Williams, Joseph M. *Style: Lessons in Clarity and Grace.* 9th ed. New York: Longman, 2007. Print. Williams offers practical and relevant advice for achieving a clear, readable writing style.

CULTURE
LANGUAGE

USAGE EXPERTS

Some dictionary publishers ask panels of usage experts about the acceptability of certain terms. Though the recommendations are usually helpful, students should understand that these are still opinions, and they may not apply to the situations in the student's own writing. Some dictionaries also censor the terms they include, omitting vulgar words and other offensive terms.

Avoiding common mistakes in word choice

- **Make sure words have the meanings you intend.** Check the meanings of words whose meanings you aren't sure of. (See below for more on dictionaries.)

| Incorrect | Increased global temperatures will <u>effect</u> everyone. |
| Revised | Increased global temperatures will affect everyone. |

- **Make sure that any word suggested by a spelling checker is the one you mean.** (See p. 63 for more on spelling checkers.)

| Incorrect | The results were <u>defiant</u>: the experiment was a failure. |
| Revised | The results were definite: the experiment was a failure. |

- **Use idioms correctly.** (See p. 518 for more on idioms.)

| Incorrect | The planners <u>agreed over</u> the details of the evacuation plan. |
| Revised | The planners agreed **on** the details of the evacuation plan. |

38a Using a dictionary and a thesaurus

For writing exactly, a dictionary is essential and a thesaurus can be helpful.

1 Using a desk dictionary

A desk dictionary defines about 150,000 to 200,000 words and provides pronunciation, grammatical functions, etymology (word history), and other information. The sample below is from *Merriam-Webster's Collegiate Dictionary.*

Dictionary entry for *reckon*

Spelling and word division

Pronunciation

reck·on \'re-kən\ *vb* reck·oned; reck·on·ing \'re-kə-niŋ, 'rek-niŋ\ [ME *rekenen,* fr. OE -*recenian* (as in *gerecenian* to narrate); akin to OE *reccan*] *vt* (13c) **1 a** : COUNT ⟨~ the days till Christmas⟩ **b** : ESTIMATE, COMPUTE ⟨~ the height of a building⟩ **c** : to determine by reference to a fixed basis ⟨the existence of the U.S. is ~ed from the Declaration of Independence⟩ **2** : to regard or think of as: CONSIDER **3** *chiefly dial* : THINK, SUPPOSE ⟨I ~ I've outlived my time —Ellen Glasgow⟩ ~ *vi* **1** : to settle accounts **2** : to make a calculation **3 a** : JUDGE **b** *chiefly dial* : SUPPOSE, THINK **4** : to accept something as certain / place reliance ⟨I ~ on your promise to help⟩ — **reckon with** to take into consideration — **reckon without** : to fail to consider : IGNORE

Etymology

Meanings

Quotation and source

Idioms

Grammatical functions and forms

Label

Synonym

Good desk dictionaries, in addition to *Merriam-Webster's*, include the *American Heritage College Dictionary*, the *Random House Webster's College Dictionary*, and *Webster's New World Dictionary*. Most of these dictionaries are available in both print and electronic form (CD-ROM or online). In addition, several Web sites provide online dictionaries or links to online dictionaries. *Dictionary.com* allows you to search for word meanings in more than a dozen general and specialized dictionaries, including *American Heritage*.

(CULTURE LANGUAGE) If English is not your native language, you probably should have a dictionary prepared especially for students using English as a second language (ESL). Such a dictionary contains special information on prepositions, count versus noncount nouns, and many other matters. Reliable ESL dictionaries include *COBUILD English Language Dictionary*, *Longman Dictionary of Contemporary English*, and *Oxford Advanced Learner's Dictionary*.

2 Using a thesaurus

To find a word with the exact shade of meaning you intend, you may want to consult a thesaurus, or book of **synonyms**—words with approximately the same meaning. A thesaurus such as *Roget's International Thesaurus* lists most imaginable synonyms for thousands of words. The word *news*, for instance, has half a page of synonyms in *Roget's International*, including *tidings, dispatch, gossip,* and *journalism.*

Since a thesaurus aims to open up possibilities, its lists of synonyms include approximate as well as precise matches. The thesaurus does not define synonyms or distinguish among them, however, so you need a dictionary to discover exact meanings. In general, don't use a word from a thesaurus—even one you like the sound of—until you are sure of its appropriateness for your meaning.

Note Many Web sites, such as *Thesaurus.com*, provide tools for finding synonyms. Your word processor may also include a thesaurus, making it easy to look up synonyms and insert the chosen word into your text. But still you should consult a dictionary unless you are certain of the word's meaning.

Exercise 38.1 Using a dictionary

Consult your dictionary on five of the following words. For each word, write down (*a*) the division into syllables, (*b*) the pronunciation, (*c*) the grammatical functions and forms, (*d*) the etymology, (*e*) each meaning, and (*f*) any special uses indicated by labels. Finally, use the word in at least two sentences of your own.

1. depreciation	4. manifest	7. potlatch	10. toxic
2. secretary	5. assassin	8. plain (*adj.*)	11. steal
3. grammar	6. astrology	9. ceremony	12. obelisk

COLLABORATIVE LEARNING

Assign each group a common word (*nice, happy,* or *bad,* for example). They should then consult a thesaurus and generate a list of at least five synonyms. Along with each synonym, students should include an explanation of the connotation of the synonym and an example of each synonym used correctly in a sentence. (For example, *ecstatic* means extremely happy or thrilled: *Linda was ecstatic when she won the lottery.*) As a class, discuss some of the more interesting or obscure synonyms students find.

Ask students to complete Exercise 38.1 individually, assigning the same five words to everyone. Then, in groups, students can compare their responses. They should discuss the strengths and weaknesses of the particular dictionaries they used. Finally, they should review one another's sentences for correct usage of the assigned words.

ANSWERS: EXERCISE 38.1

The answers to this exercise will depend on the dictionary being consulted. Each one uses a different notation system, and in some cases they disagree over syllable division. Thus, no answers are provided.

Using the right word for your meaning

Precisely expressing your meaning requires understanding both the denotations and the connotations of words. A word's **denotation** is the thing or idea it refers to, the meaning listed in the dictionary without reference to the emotional associations it may arouse in a reader. Using words according to their established denotations is essential if readers are to grasp your meaning. Here are a few guidelines:

■ **Consult a dictionary whenever you are unsure of a word's meaning.**

■ **Distinguish between similar-sounding words that have widely different denotations:**

Inexact   Older people often suffer <u>infirmaries</u> [places for the sick].

Exact   Older people often suffer <u>infirmities</u> [disabilities].

Some words, called **homonyms** (from the Greek meaning "same name"), sound exactly alike but differ in meaning: for example, *principal/principle* and *rain/reign/rein.* (See pp. 532–33 for a list of commonly confused homonyms.)

■ **Distinguish between words with related but distinct denotations:**

Inexact   Television commercials <u>continuously</u> [unceasingly] interrupt programming.

Exact   Television commercials <u>continually</u> [regularly] interrupt programming.

In addition to their emotion-free denotations, many words carry related meanings that evoke specific feelings. These **connotations** can shape readers' responses and are thus a powerful tool for writers. (At the same time they are a potential snare for readers. See p. 186.) Some connotations are personal: the word *dog,* for instance, may have negative connotations for the letter carrier who has been bitten three times. Usually, though, people agree about connotations. The following word pairs are just a few of many that have related denotations but very different connotations:

pride: sense of self-worth
vanity: excessive regard for oneself

firm: steady, unchanging, unyielding
stubborn: unreasonable, bullheaded

enthusiasm: excitement
mania: excessive interest or desire

Understanding connotation is especially important in choosing among synonyms, or words with approximately the same meanings. For instance, *cry* and *weep* both denote the shedding of tears, but *cry* more than *weep* connotes a sobbing sound accompanying the tears. *Sob* itself connotes broken, gasping crying, with tears, whereas *wail* connotes sustained sound, perhaps without tears.

Exercise 38.2 Revising: Denotation

Revise any underlined word below that is not used according to its established denotation. Circle any word used correctly. Consult a dictionary if you are uncertain of a word's precise meaning.

Example:

Sam and Dave are going to Bermuda and Hauppauge, <u>respectfully</u>, for spring vacation.

Sam and Dave are going to Bermuda and Hauppauge, <u>respectively</u>, for spring vacation.

1. Maxine Hong Kingston was <u>rewarded</u> many prizes for her first two books, *The Woman Warrior* and *China Men*.
2. Kingston <u>sites</u> her mother's tales about ancestors and ancient Chinese customs as the sources of these memoirs.
3. In her childhood Kingston was greatly <u>effected</u> by her mother's tale about a pregnant aunt who was <u>ostracized</u> by villagers.
4. The aunt gained <u>avengeance</u> by drowning herself in the village's water supply.
5. Kingston decided to make her nameless relative <u>infamous</u> by giving her <u>immortality</u> in *The Woman Warrior*.

Exercise 38.3 Considering the connotations of words

Fill the blank in each sentence below with the most appropriate word from the list in parentheses. Consult a dictionary to be sure of your choice.

Example:

Channel 5 _____ Oshu the winner before the polls closed. (*advertised, declared, broadcast, promulgated*)

Channel 5 <u>declared</u> Oshu the winner before the polls closed.

1. AIDS is a serious health _____. (*problem, worry, difficulty, plight*)
2. Once the virus has entered the blood system, it _____ T-cells. (*murders, destroys, slaughters, executes*)
3. The _____ of T-cells is to combat infections. (*ambition, function, aim, goal*)
4. Without enough T-cells, the body is nearly _____ against infections. (*defenseless, hopeless, desperate*)
5. To prevent exposure to the disease, one should be especially _____ in sexual relationships. (*chary, circumspect, cautious, calculating*)

ANSWERS: EXERCISE 38.2

1. Maxine Hong Kingston was <u>awarded</u> many prizes for her first two books, *The Woman Warrior* and *China Men*.
2. Kingston <u>cites</u> her mother's tales about ancestors and ancient Chinese customs as the sources of these memoirs.
3. In her childhood Kingston was greatly <u>affected</u> by her mother's tale about a pregnant aunt who was ostracized by villagers. [*Ostracized* correct.]
4. The aunt gained <u>vengeance</u> by drowning herself in the village's water supply.
5. Kingston decided to make her nameless relative <u>famous</u> by giving her immortality in *The Woman Warrior*. [*Immortality* correct.]

ANSWERS: EXERCISE 38.3

1. AIDS is a serious health <u>problem</u>.
2. Once the virus has entered the blood system, it <u>destroys</u> T-cells.
3. The <u>function</u> of T-cells is to combat infections.
4. Without enough T-cells, the body is nearly <u>defenseless</u> against infections.
5. To prevent exposure to the disease, one should be especially <u>cautious</u> in sexual relationships.

38c Balancing the abstract and concrete, the general and specific

To understand a subject as you understand it, your readers need ample guidance from your words. When you describe a building as *beautiful* and nothing more, you force readers to provide their own ideas of what makes a building beautiful. If readers bother (and they may not), they surely will not conjure up the image you had in mind. Use words to tell readers what you want them to know, that the beautiful building is *a sleek, silver skyscraper with blue-tinted windows,* for instance, or *a Victorian brick courthouse with tall, arched windows.*

Clear, exact writing balances abstract and general words, which outline ideas and objects, with concrete and specific words, which sharpen and solidify.

- **Abstract words** name ideas: *beauty, inflation, management, culture, liberal.* **Concrete words** name qualities and things we can know by our five senses of sight, hearing, touch, taste, and smell: *sleek, humming, rough, salty, musty.*
- **General words** name classes or groups of things, such as *buildings, weather,* and *birds,* and include all the varieties of the class. **Specific words** limit a general class, such as *buildings,* by naming a variety, such as *skyscraper, Victorian courthouse,* or *hut.*

Note that *general* and *specific* are relative terms: the same word may be more general than some words but more specific than others.

	General	
weather	↑	bird
rain		parrot
downpour		cockatoo
sudden downpour	↓	my pet cockatoo Moyshe
	Specific	

Abstract and general words are useful in the broad statements that set the course for your writing:

The wild horse in America has a romantic history.

We must be free from government interference in our affairs.

Relations between the sexes today are only a little more relaxed than they were in the past.

But the sentences following these would have to develop the ideas with concrete and specific details. When your meaning calls for an abstract or general word, make sure you define it, explain it, and narrow it. Look at how concrete and specific information turns vague sentences into exact ones in the following examples:

Vague	The size of his hands made his smallness real. [How big were his hands? How small was he?]
Exact	Not until I saw his delicate, doll-like hands did I realize that he stood a full head shorter than most other men.
Vague	The long flood caused a lot of awful destruction in the town. [How long did the flood last? What destruction did it cause? Why was the destruction awful?]
Exact	The flood waters, which rose swiftly and then stayed stubbornly high for days, killed at least six townspeople and made life a misery for the hundreds who had to evacuate their ruined homes and stores.

Note You can use your computer's Find function to help you find and revise abstract and general words that you tend to overuse. Examples of such words might include *nice, interesting, things, very, good, a lot, a little,* and *some.*

Exercise 38.4 Revising: Concrete and specific words

Make the following paragraph vivid by expanding the sentences with appropriate details of your own choosing. Substitute concrete and specific words for the abstract and general ones that are underlined.

I remember <u>clearly</u> how <u>awful</u> I felt the first time I <u>attended</u> Mrs. Murphy's second-grade class. I had <u>recently</u> moved from a <u>small</u> town in Missouri to a <u>crowded</u> suburb of Chicago. My new school looked <u>big</u> from the outside and seemed <u>dark</u> inside as I <u>walked</u> down the <u>long</u> corridor toward the classroom. The class was <u>noisy</u> as I neared the door; but when I <u>entered</u>, <u>everyone</u> became <u>quiet</u> and <u>looked</u> at me. I felt <u>uncomfortable</u> and <u>wanted</u> a place to hide. However, in a <u>loud</u> voice Mrs. Murphy <u>directed</u> me to the front of the room to introduce myself.

Exercise 38.5 Using concrete and specific words

For each abstract or general word below, give at least two other words or phrases that illustrate increasing specificity or concreteness. Consult a dictionary as needed. Use the most specific or concrete word from each group in a sentence of your own.

Example:
awake, <u>watchful</u>, <u>vigilant</u>
<u>Vigilant</u> guards patrol the buildings.

1. fabric
2. delicious
3. car
4. narrow-minded
5. reach (*verb*)
6. green
7. walk (*verb*)
8. flower
9. serious
10. pretty
11. teacher
12. nice
13. virtue
14. angry
15. crime

ANSWERS: EXERCISE 38.5

Possible answers

1. fabric, upholstery fabric, velvet
   She chose a wine-colored <u>velvet</u> for backing the pillow.
2. delicious, tart, lemony
   He made a meringue pie, <u>lemony</u> and delicately brown.
3. car, foreign car, <u>Volvo station wagon</u>
   He bought a 1973 Volvo station wagon.
4. narrow-minded, prejudiced, sexist
   My uncle's <u>sexist</u> attitudes cause many arguments in our family.
5. reach, stretch, lunge
   Each child <u>lunged</u> for the prize thrown by the clown.
6. green, dark green, bilious green
   The algae covered the surface with a <u>bilious green</u> scum.
7. walk, march, goose-step
   The soldiers <u>goose-stepped</u> menacingly.
8. flower, daisy, ox-eyed daisy
   Some people call <u>the ox-eyed daisy</u> a "brown-eyed Susan."
9. serious, solemn, grim
   His <u>grim</u> expression frightened us.
10. pretty; with small, regular features; with a button nose and a tiny, smiling mouth
    The infant, <u>with a button nose and a tiny, smiling mouth,</u> was a perfect model for baby products.
11. teacher, history teacher, American history teacher
    My <u>American history teacher</u> requires three research papers.
12. nice, considerate, sympathetic
    I need a <u>sympathetic</u> friend.
13. virtue, honesty, frankness
    His <u>frankness</u> was refreshing after I had heard so much flattery.
14. angry, furious, raging
    <u>Raging</u> uncontrollably, Andy insulted everyone around him.
15. crime, theft, armed robbery
    Drug addicts sometimes commit <u>armed robbery</u> to pay for their habits.

COMPUTER ACTIVITY

RARE SPECIMENS

Establish a "gallery" of interesting idioms on your class Web site. As students come across interesting or unusual examples of idioms they can post them to the site. They should check a dictionary of idioms and report on what they find about their specimen.

CULTURE LANGUAGE

IDIOMS

Idioms are particularly challenging for nonnative speakers of English, and even native speakers may find some idioms impenetrable. Asking students to add to the lists in this chapter, or to examine dictionaries of idioms, may yield interesting discussions and paper topics.

38d Using idioms

Idioms are expressions in any language whose meanings cannot be determined simply from the words in them or whose component words cannot be predicted by any rule of grammar; often, they violate conventional grammar. Examples of English idioms include *put up with, plug away at,* and *make off with.*

Idioms involving prepositions can be especially confusing for both native and nonnative speakers of English. A number of these idioms appear in the box below.

Idioms with prepositions

abide <u>by</u> a rule
    <u>in</u> a place or state
accords <u>with</u>
according <u>to</u>
accuse <u>of</u> a crime
adapt <u>from</u> a source
    <u>to</u> a situation
afraid <u>of</u>
agree <u>on</u> a plan as a group
    <u>to</u> someone else's plan
    <u>with</u> a person
angry <u>with</u>
aware <u>of</u>
based <u>on</u>
capable <u>of</u>
certain <u>of</u>
charge <u>for</u> a purchase
    <u>with</u> a crime
concur <u>in</u> an opinion
    <u>with</u> a person
contend <u>for</u> a principle or prize
    <u>with</u> an obstacle
dependent <u>on</u>
differ <u>about</u> or <u>over</u> a question
    <u>from</u> in some quality
    <u>with</u> a person
disappointed <u>by</u> or <u>in</u> a person
    <u>in</u> or <u>with</u> a thing

familiar <u>with</u>
identical <u>with</u> or <u>to</u>
impatient <u>for</u> a raise
    <u>with</u> a person
independent <u>of</u>
infer <u>from</u>
inferior <u>to</u>
involved <u>in</u> a task
    <u>with</u> a person
oblivious <u>of</u> or <u>to</u> one's surroundings
    <u>of</u> something forgotten
occupied <u>by</u> a person
    <u>in</u> study
    <u>with</u> a thing
opposed <u>to</u>
part <u>from</u> a person
    <u>with</u> a possession
prior <u>to</u>
proud <u>of</u>
related <u>to</u>
rewarded <u>by</u> the judge
    <u>for</u> something done
    <u>with</u> a gift
similar <u>to</u>
superior <u>to</u>
wait <u>at</u> a place
    <u>for</u> a train, a person
    <u>on</u> a customer

CULTURE LANGUAGE If you are learning standard American English, you are justified in stumbling over its prepositions: their meanings can shift depending on context, and they have many idiomatic uses. In mastering the prepositions of standard English, you probably can't avoid memorization. But you can help yourself by memorizing related groups, such as those below for the very common *at, in, on, for,* and *since.*

At, in, or *on* in expressions of time
- Use *at* before actual clock time: *at 8:30.*
- Use *in* before a month, year, century, or period: *in April, in 2007, in the twenty-first century, in the next month.*
- Use *on* before a day or date: *on Tuesday, on August 3, on Labor Day.*

At, in, or *on* in expressions of place
- Use *at* before a specific place or address: *at the school, at 511 Iris Street.*
- Use *in* before a place with limits or before a city, state, country, or continent: *in the house, in a box, in Oklahoma City, in China, in Asia.*
- Use *on* to mean "supported by" or "touching the surface of": *on the table, on Iris Street, on page 150.*

For or *since* in expressions of time
- Use *for* before a period of time: *for an hour, for two years.*
- Use *since* before a specific point in time: *since 1999, since Friday.*

A dictionary of English as a second language is the best source for the meanings of prepositions; see the recommendations on page 513. In addition, some reference works focus on prepositions. See, for instance, volume 1 (*Verbs with Prepositions and Particles*) of the *Oxford Dictionary of Current Idiomatic English.*

Exercise 38.6   Using prepositions in idioms

Insert the preposition that correctly completes each idiom in the following sentences. Consult the box on the previous page or a dictionary as needed.

Example:

I disagree _____ many feminists who say women should not be homemakers.

I disagree with many feminists who say women should not be homemakers.

1. Children are waiting longer to become independent _____ their parents.
2. According _____ US Census data for young adults ages eighteen to twenty-four, 57 percent of men and 47 percent of women live full-time with their parents.
3. Some of these adult children are dependent _____ their parents financially.

CULTURE LANGUAGE

PREPOSITIONS

As the text notes, prepositions follow few specific rules, and, because of idiomatic usage, they often cannot be translated directly into students' first languages. As a result, even advanced ESL students find prepositions difficult. In addition to consulting an ESL dictionary, as recommended in the text, students who need additional help with prepositions might refer to Unit 6 of Len Fox, *Focus on Editing: A Grammar Workbook for Advanced Writers* (White Plains: Longman, 1992), and Appendix C of Alan Meyers, *Writing with Confidence,* 8th ed. (New York: Longman, 2006).

ANSWERS: EXERCISE 38.6

1. Children are waiting longer to become independent of their parents.
2. According to US Census data for young adults ages eighteen to twenty-four, 57 percent of men and 47 percent of women live full-time with their parents.
3. Some of these adult children are dependent on their parents financially.
4. In other cases, the parents charge their children for housing, food, and other living expenses.
5. Many adult children are financially capable of living independently but prefer to save money rather than contend with high housing costs.

4. In other cases, the parents charge their children _____ housing, food, and other living expenses.
5. Many adult children are financially capable _____ living independently but prefer to save money rather than contend _____ high housing costs.

38e Using figurative language

Figurative language (or a **figure of speech**) departs from the literal meanings (the denotations) of words, usually by comparing very different ideas or objects:

Literal   As I try to write, I can think of nothing to say.

Figurative   As I try to write, my mind is a slab of black slate.

When you use figurative language imaginatively and carefully, it can capture your meaning more precisely and feelingly than literal language.

Figurative language is common in speech. Having *slept like a log*, you may get up to find it *raining cats and dogs*. But the rapid exchange of speech leaves little time for inventiveness, and most figures of daily conversation, like those above, are worn and hackneyed. Writing gives you time to reject the tired figure and to search out fresh, concrete words and phrases.

The two most common figures of speech are the simile and the metaphor. Both compare two things of different classes, often one abstract and the other concrete. A **simile** makes the comparison explicit and usually begins with *like* or *as:*

Whenever we grow, we tend to feel it, as a young seed must feel the weight and inertia of the earth when it seeks to break out of its shell on its way to becoming a plant.   —Alice Walker

To hold America in one's thoughts is like holding a love letter in one's hand—it has so special a meaning.   —E. B. White

Instead of stating a comparison, a **metaphor** implies it, omitting such words as *like* or *as:*

I cannot and will not cut my conscience to fit this year's fashions.   —Lillian Hellman

A school is a hopper into which children are heaved while they are young and tender; therein they are pressed into certain standard shapes and covered from head to heels with official rubber stamps.   —H. L. Mencken

Two other figures of speech are personification and hyperbole. **Personification** treats ideas and objects as if they were human:

COLLABORATIVE LEARNING

FIGURATIVE CLICHES

Have students brainstorm commonplace figures of speech like those listed in the text (others might include "I was sick as a dog," "you lie like a rug," "he eats like a horse") and list them on the board. Ask students to work in small groups to identify the figurative connection implied in each saying, and then to substitute a fresher or more accurate image to convey a similar idea.

The economy consumes my money and gives me little in return.
I could hear the whisper of snowflakes, nudging each other as they fell.

Hyperbole deliberately exaggerates:

She appeared in a mile of billowing chiffon, flashing a rhinestone as big as an ostrich egg.
He yelled so loud that his voice carried to the next county.

To be successful, figurative language must be fresh and unstrained, calling attention not to itself but to the writer's meaning. One kind of figurative language gone wrong is the **mixed metaphor**, in which the writer combines two or more incompatible figures. Since metaphors often generate visual images in the reader's mind, a mixed metaphor can be laughable:

| Mixed | Various thorny problems that we try to sweep under the rug continue to bob up all the same. |

To revise a mixed metaphor, follow through consistently with just one image:

| Improved | Various thorny problems that we try to weed out continue to thrive all the same. |

Exercise 38.7 Analyzing figurative language

Identify each figure of speech in the following sentences as a simile or a metaphor, and analyze how it adds to the writer's meaning.

1. A distant airplane, a delta wing out of nightmare, made a gliding shadow on the creek's bottom that looked like a stingray crossing upstream. —Annie Dillard
2. Her roots ran deep into the earth, and from those roots she drew strength enough to hold still against all the forces of chance and disorder. —N. Scott Momaday
3. As a member of the winning team (the graduating class of 1940) I had outdistanced unpleasant sensations by miles. I was headed for the freedom of open fields. —Maya Angelou
4. All artists quiver under the lash of adverse criticism. —Catherine Drinker Bowen
5. Every writer, in a roomful of writers, wants to be the best, and the judge, or umpire, or referee is soon overwhelmed and shouted down like a chickadee trying to take charge of a caucus of crows. —James Thurber

Exercise 38.8 Using figurative language

Invent appropriate figurative language of your own (simile, metaphor, hyperbole, or personification) to describe each of the following scenes or qualities, and use each figure in a sentence.

ANSWERS: EXERCISE 38.7

1. *A delta wing out of nightmare* is a metaphor. *Like a stingray crossing upstream* is a simile. Both convey the menace of an airplane and its shadow.
2. *Her roots ran deep into the earth* and *from those roots she drew strength* are both metaphors establishing the person's indomitability.
3. *Outdistanced unpleasant sensations* and *headed for the freedom of open fields* are both metaphors equating Angelou's sense of release with the runner's freedom.
4. *Lash of adverse criticism* is a metaphor that makes clear the power of words to hurt.
5. The judge is like a *chickadee* and the roomful of writers is like a *caucus of crows*—two similes that convey the judge's powerlessness in the face of the writers' bombast.

ANSWERS: EXERCISE 38.8

Individual response.

Example:
The attraction of a lake on a hot day
The small waves like fingers beckoned us irresistibly.

1. The sound of a kindergarten classroom
2. People waiting in line to buy tickets to a rock concert
3. The politeness of strangers meeting for the first time
4. A streetlight seen through dense fog
5. The effect of watching television for ten hours straight

38f Using fresh, not trite, expressions

Trite expressions, or **clichés,** are phrases so old and so often repeated that they have become stale. They include the following:

acid test	ladder of success
add insult to injury	moving experience
better late than never	needle in a haystack
beyond the shadow of a doubt	point with pride
brought back to reality	ripe old age
cold, hard facts	shoulder the burden
cool as a cucumber	smart as a whip
crushing blow	sneaking suspicion
easier said than done	sober as a judge
face the music	stand in awe
flat as a pancake	strong as an ox
green with envy	thin as a rail
hard as a rock	tired but happy
heavy as lead	tried and true
hit the nail on the head	untimely death
hour of need	wise as an owl

Besides these old phrases, stale writing may also depend on fashionable words that are losing their effect: for instance, *lifestyle, enhance, awesome, fantastic,* and *caring.*

Many of these expressions were once fresh and forceful, but constant use has dulled them. They, in turn, will dull your writing by suggesting that you have not thought about what you are saying and have resorted to the easiest phrase.

Clichés may slide into your drafts while you are trying to express your meaning. In editing, then, be wary of any expression you have heard or used before. Substitute fresh words of your own or restate the idea in plain language.

Trite	A healthful lifestyle enhances your ability to go for the gold, allows you to enjoy life to the fullest, and helps you live to a ripe old age.
Revised	Living healthfully helps you perform well, enjoy life thoroughly, and live long.

Exercise 38.9 Revising: Trite expressions

Revise the following sentences to eliminate trite expressions.

Example:

The basketball team had almost seized victory, but it faced the test of truth in the last quarter of the game.

The basketball team seemed about to win, but the real test came in the last quarter of the game.

1. The disastrous consequences of the war have shaken the small nation to its roots.
2. Prices for food have shot sky high, and citizens have sneaking suspicions that others are making a killing on the black market.
3. Medical supplies are so few and far between that even civilians who are as sick as dogs cannot get treatment.
4. With most men fighting or injured or killed, women have had to bite the bullet and bear the men's burden in farming and manufacturing.
5. Last but not least, the war's heavy drain on the nation's pocketbook has left the economy in a shambles.

39
Writing Concisely

Concise writing makes every word count. Conciseness is not the same as mere brevity: detail and originality should not be cut along with needless words. Rather, the length of an expression should be appropriate to the thought.

You may find yourself writing wordily when you are unsure of your subject or when your thoughts are tangled. It's fine, even necessary, to stumble and grope while drafting. But you should straighten out your ideas and eliminate wordiness during revision and editing.

mycomplab

Visit *mycomplab.com* for more resources and exercises on writing concisely.

ANSWERS: EXERCISE 38.9

Possible answers

1. These <u>disasters</u> of the war have shaken the small <u>nation</u> <u>severely</u>.
2. Prices for food have <u>risen markedly</u>, and citizens <u>suspect</u> that others are <u>profiting</u> on the black market.
3. Medical supplies are so <u>scarce</u> that even <u>very sick</u> civilians cannot get treatment.
4. With most men fighting or injured or killed, women have had to <u>take the men's places</u> in farming and manufacturing.
5. <u>Finally</u>, the war's <u>high cost</u> has <u>destroyed the nation's economy</u>.

HIGHLIGHTS

Eliminating unnecessary words is a task almost as difficult as choosing the right word. Students often revert to very simple sentence structures when they begin to cut flab from their sentences. You'll have to help them see that lean sentences can still be complex sentences. This chapter can help show your students techniques to achieve conciseness: strengthening subjects and verbs; cutting empty words; cutting excess repetition; reducing or combining sentences, clauses, and phrases; eliminating expletives; and rewriting jargon.

A WRITER'S PERSPECTIVE

A good word is like a good tree whose roots are firmly fixed and whose top is in the sky.
—THE KORAN 14.24

RESOURCES AND IDEAS

Connors, Robert J. "The Erasure of the Sentence." *College Composition and Communication* 52.1 (2001): 96–128. Print. Argues for the efficacy of pedagogy that uses sentence-based rhetorics.

Sloane, Brenda. "Say It Straight: Teaching Conciseness." *Teaching English in the Two-Year College* 30.4 (2003): 429–33. Print. Sloane offers a series of assignments, including a challenging 100-word autobiographical essay, which she uses to explain, model, and reinforce concise writing.

COLLABORATIVE LEARNING

CUTTING WORDS

Before your students hand in their essays, ask them to cut a specific number of words (ten to fifteen for a start) without harming the meaning. This approach can work with paragraphs as well and makes a good small-group activity.

COMPUTER ACTIVITY

THE LARD FACTOR

Richard Lanham in *Revising Prose* (5th ed., New York: Longman, 2007) uses this equation to calculate the "lard factor" of unnecessary words in any piece of writing:

# of words cut from original ÷
# of words in original =
% of lard in original

Lanham argues that as much as 40 percent of any piece of writing may be lard; this estimate emphasizes the need to revise for unnecessary words. Ask students to revise sample passages of published writing or one another's work and calculate the lard factor to test this argument. Students working on computers can use the Word Count function of their word processor to estimate the "lard factor" in a longer piece.

Ways to achieve conciseness

Wordy (87 words)

The highly pressured nature of critical-care nursing is due to the fact that the patients have life-threatening illnesses. Critical-care nurses must have possession of steady nerves to care for patients who are critically ill and very sick. The nurses must also have possession of interpersonal skills. They must also have medical skills. It is considered by most health-care professionals that these nurses are essential if there is to be improvement of patients who are now in critical care from that status to the status of intermediate care.

Focus on subject and verb, and cut or shorten empty words and phrases.
Avoid nouns made from verbs.
Cut unneeded repetition.
Combine sentences.
Change passive voice to active voice.
Revise *there is* constructions.
Cut unneeded repetition, and reduce clauses and phrases.

Concise (37 words)

Critical-care nursing is highly pressured because the patients have life-threatening illnesses. Critical-care nurses must possess steady nerves and interpersonal and medical skills. Most health-care professionals consider these nurses essential if patients are to improve to intermediate care.

Grammar checkers Any grammar checker will identify at least some wordy structures, such as repeated words, weak verbs, passive voice, and *there is* and *it is* constructions. But a checker can't identify all potentially wordy structures, nor can it tell you whether a structure is appropriate for your ideas.

CULTURE LANGUAGE As you'll see in the examples that follow, wordiness is not a problem of incorrect grammar. A sentence may be perfectly grammatical but still contain unneeded words that interfere with your idea.

39a Focusing on the subject and verb

Using the subjects and verbs of your sentences for the key actors and actions will reduce words and emphasize important ideas. (See pp. 378–80 for more on this topic.)

Wordy	The <u>reason</u> why most of the country shifts to daylight time <u>is</u> that <u>winter</u> days are much shorter than summer days.
Concise	Most of the <u>country</u> <u>shifts</u> to daylight time because winter days are much shorter than summer days.

Focusing on subjects and verbs will also help you avoid several other causes of wordiness (also discussed further on pp. 378–80):

Nouns made from verbs

Wordy	The <u>occurrence</u> of the winter solstice, the shortest day of the year, <u>is</u> an event occurring about December 22.
Concise	The winter <u>solstice</u>, the shortest day of the year, <u>occurs</u> about December 22.

Weak verbs

Wordy	The earth's axis <u>has</u> a tilt as the planet <u>is</u> in orbit around the sun so that the northern and southern hemispheres <u>are</u> alternately in alignment toward the sun.
Concise	The earth's axis <u>tilts</u> as the planet <u>orbits</u> the sun so that the northern and southern hemispheres alternately <u>align</u> toward the sun.

Passive voice

Wordy	During its winter the northern hemisphere <u>is tilted</u> farthest away from the sun, so the nights <u>are made</u> longer and the days <u>are made</u> shorter.
Concise	During its winter the northern hemisphere <u>tilts</u> away from the sun, <u>making</u> the nights longer and the days shorter.

See also pages 298–99 on changing the passive voice to the active voice, as in the example above.

39b Cutting or shortening empty words and phrases

Empty words and phrases walk in place, gaining little or nothing in meaning. When you cut or shorten them, your writing will move faster and work harder.

Many empty phrases can be cut entirely:

all things considered	in a manner of speaking
as far as I'm concerned	in my opinion
for all intents and purposes	last but not least
for the most part	more or less

Wordy	<u>In my opinion</u>, the council's proposal to improve the city center is inadequate, <u>all things considered</u>.
Revised	The council's proposal to improve the city center is inadequate.

Other empty words can be cut along with some words around them:

angle	character	kind	situation
area	element	manner	thing
aspect	factor	nature	type
case	field		

Wordy   The <u>type</u> of large expenditures on advertising that manufacturers must make is a very important <u>aspect</u> of the cost of detergents.

Concise   Manufacturers' large advertising expenditures increase the cost of detergents.

Still other empty phrases can be reduced from several words to a single word:

For	Substitute
at all times	always
at the present time	now
at this point in time	now
in today's society	now
in the nature of	like
for the purpose of	for
in order to	to
until such time as	until
for the reason that	because
due to the fact that	because
because of the fact that	because
by virtue of the fact that	because
despite the fact that	although
in the event that	if
by means of	by
in the final analysis	finally

Wordy   <u>At this point in time</u>, the software is expensive <u>due to the fact that</u> it has no competition.

Revised   The software is expensive <u>now</u> <u>because</u> it has no competition.

Exercise 39.1   Revising: Subjects and verbs; empty words and phrases

Revise the following sentences to achieve conciseness by focusing on subjects and verbs and by cutting or reducing empty words and phrases. See also page 380 for an additional exercise in focusing on subjects and verbs.

Example:

I made college my destination because of many factors, but most of all because of the fact that I want a career in medicine.

I <u>came</u> to college <u>mainly because</u> I want a career in medicine.

1. *Gerrymandering* refers to a situation in which the lines of a voting district are redrawn so that a particular party or ethnic group has benefits.
2. The name is a reference to the fact that Elbridge Gerry, the governor of Massachusetts in 1812, redrew voting districts in Essex County.
3. On the map one new district was seen to resemble something in the nature of a salamander.
4. Upon seeing the map, a man who was for all intents and purposes a critic of Governor Gerry's administration cried out, "Gerrymander!"
5. At the present time, changes may be made in the character of a district's voting pattern by a political group by gerrymandering to achieve the exclusion of rival groups' supporters.

39c Cutting unnecessary repetition

Planned repetition and restatement can make writing more coherent (p. 85) or emphatic (p. 384). But unnecessary repetition weakens sentences:

Wordy	Many unskilled workers without training in a particular job are unemployed and do not have any work.
Concise	Many unskilled workers are unemployed.

The use of one word two different ways within a sentence is confusing:

Confusing	Preschool instructors play a role in the child's understanding of male and female roles.
Clear	Preschool instructors contribute to the child's understanding of male and female roles.

The simplest kind of useless repetition is the phrase that says the same thing twice. In the following examples, the unneeded words are underlined:

biography of his life	habitual custom
circle around	important [basic] essentials
consensus of opinion	large in size
continue on	puzzling in nature
cooperate together	repeat again
few in number	return again
final completion	revert back
frank and honest exchange	square [round] in shape
the future to come	surrounding circumstances

CULTURE LANGUAGE Phrases like those above are redundant because the main word already implies the underlined word or words. The repetition is not emphatic but tedious. A dictionary will tell you what meanings a word implies. *Assassinate,* for

---

ANSWERS: EXERCISE 39.1

Possible answers

1. *Gerrymandering* means redrawing the lines of a voting district to benefit a particular party or ethnic group.
2. The name refers to Elbridge Gerry, who as governor of Massachusetts in 1812 redrew voting districts in Essex County.
3. On the map one new district looked like a salamander.
4. Upon seeing the map, a critic of Governor Gerry's administration cried out, "Gerrymander!"
5. Now a political group may try to change a district's voting pattern by gerrymandering to exclude rival groups' supporters.

LEGAL BILINGUALISM

Sometimes, particularly in legal language, phrases contain paired synonyms like *last will and testament*. These go back to the time immediately after the Norman Conquest of England in 1066, when English law proceedings were conducted in both French and English, and the words had to be clear to speakers of either language.

CULTURE LANGUAGE

DISCURSIVE VERSUS CONCISE STYLES

ESL students may have difficulty being concise if their native language is more discursive, or if repetition is encouraged in their native language. Reinforce with these students that English is an extremely compact language compared to many. Remind them as well that as their English vocabulary increases, they will have more words at their disposal to use in place of longer, more descriptive phrases.

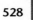

When students have completed Exercise 39.2 individually, have them compare their responses in small groups and discuss the effects of their varying strategies.

ANSWERS: EXERCISE 39.2

Possible answers

1. <u>After their tours of duty</u>, some Vietnam veterans had problems <u>readjusting to</u> life in America.
2. Afflicted with post-traumatic stress disorder, some veterans <u>had trouble</u> holding jobs and maintaining relationships.
3. Some who <u>used drugs</u> in Vietnam could not break <u>their habits</u> after they <u>returned to</u> the United States.
4. The few veterans who committed crimes and violent acts gained so much <u>notoriety that</u> many Americans thought all veterans were <u>crazy</u>.
5. As a result of such <u>stereotyping</u>, Vietnam-era veterans <u>are protected by</u> antidiscrimination laws.

instance, means "murder someone well known," so the following sentence is redundant: *Julius Caesar was* <u>*assassinated and killed*</u>.

Exercise 39.2   Revising: Unnecessary repetition

Revise the following sentences to achieve conciseness. Concentrate on eliminating repetition and redundancy.

Example:

Because the circumstances surrounding the cancellation of classes were murky and unclear, the editor of the student newspaper assigned a staff reporter to investigate and file a report on the circumstances.

Because the circumstances <u>leading to</u> the cancellation of classes were <u>unclear</u>, the editor of the student newspaper assigned a <u>staffer</u> to investigate and <u>report the story</u>.

1. Some Vietnam veterans coming back to the United States after their tours of duty in Vietnam had problems readjusting again to life in America.
2. Afflicted with post-traumatic stress disorder, a psychological disorder that sometimes arises after a trauma, some veterans had psychological problems that caused them to have trouble holding jobs and maintaining relationships.
3. Some who used to use drugs in Vietnam could not break their drug habits after they returned back to the United States.
4. The few veterans who committed crimes and violent acts gained so much notoriety and fame that many Americans thought all veterans were crazy, insane maniacs.
5. As a result of such stereotyping of Vietnam-era veterans, veterans are included in the same antidiscrimination laws that protect other victims of discrimination.

39d Reducing clauses to phrases, phrases to single words

Modifiers—subordinate clauses, phrases, and single words—can be expanded or contracted depending on the emphasis you want to achieve. (See pp. 242–55 on phrases and clauses and 391–93 on working with modifiers.) When editing your sentences, consider whether any modifiers can be reduced without loss of emphasis or clarity:

Wordy   The Channel Tunnel, <u>which runs between Britain and France</u>, bores through <u>a bed of solid chalk that is twenty-three miles across</u>.

Concise   The Channel Tunnel <u>between Britain and France</u> bores through <u>twenty-three miles of solid chalk</u>.

39e Revising *there is, here is,* and *it is* constructions

You can postpone the sentence subject with the words *there, here,* and *it: There are three points made in the text. Here is the main problem. It was not fair that only seniors could vote.* (See p. 261.) These constructions can be useful to emphasize the subject (as when introducing it for the first time) or to indicate a change in direction. But often they just add words and create limp substitutes for more vigorous sentences:

Wordy	There were delays and cost overruns that plagued construction of the Channel Tunnel. It had been the expectation of investors that they would see earnings soon after there were trains passing through the tunnel, but profits took years to materialize.
Concise	Delays and cost overruns plagued construction of the Channel Tunnel. Investors had expected to see earnings soon after trains began passing through the tunnel, but profits took years to materialize.

39f Combining sentences

Often the information in two or more sentences can be combined into one tight sentence:

Wordy	An unexpected problem with the Channel Tunnel is stowaways. The stowaways are mostly illegal immigrants. They are trying to smuggle themselves into England. They cling to train roofs and undercarriages.
Concise	An unexpected problem with the Channel Tunnel is stowaways, mostly illegal immigrants who are trying to smuggle themselves into England by clinging to train roofs and undercarriages.

A number of exercises in this handbook give you practice in sentence combining. For a list, see "Sentence combining" in the book's index.

39g Rewriting jargon

Jargon can refer to the special vocabulary of any discipline or profession (see p. 506). But it has also come to describe vague, inflated language that is overcomplicated, even incomprehensible. When it comes from government or business, we call it *bureaucratese.*

ANSWERS: EXERCISE 39.3

Possible answers

1. The Mexican general Antonio López de Santa Anna introduced chewing gum to the United States.
2. After his defeat by the Texans in 1845, the exiled general chose to settle in New York.
3. In his baggage the general had stashed a piece of chicle, the dried milky sap of the Mexican sapodilla tree.
4. Santa Anna's friend Thomas Adams brought more of this resin into the country, planning to make rubber.
5. When the plan failed, Adams got a much more successful idea from the way General Santa Anna used the resin, as a gum for chewing.

COLLABORATIVE LEARNING

When students have completed Exercise 39.4 individually, have them discuss their responses in pairs, noting places where they used different strategies to achieve conciseness. As a follow-up to this exercise you might use several student revisions as the basis for a general discussion of the point at which a productive revision for conciseness might become reductive of the meaning of the passage.

ANSWERS: EXERCISE 39.4

Possible answers

After much thought, he concluded that carcinogens could be treated like automobiles. Instead of giving in to a fear of cancer, we should balance the benefits we receive from potential carcinogens (such as plastic and pesticides) against the damage they do. Similarly, instead of responding irrationally to the pollution caused by automobiles, we have decided to live with them and enjoy their benefits while simultaneously working to improve them.

Jargon   The weekly social gatherings stimulate networking by members of management from various divisions, with the aim of developing contacts and maximizing the flow of creative information.

Translation   The weekly parties give managers from different divisions a chance to meet and to share ideas.

Exercise 39.3   Revising: Conciseness

Rewrite each passage below into a single concise sentence, using the techniques described in this chapter.

Example:

He was taking some exercise in the park. Then several thugs were suddenly ahead of him in his path.

He was exercising [or jogging or strolling] in the park when several thugs suddenly loomed in his path.

1. Chewing gum was originally introduced to the United States by Antonio López de Santa Anna. He was the Mexican general.
2. After he had been defeated by the Texans in 1845, the general, who was exiled, made the choice to settle in New York.
3. A piece of chicle had been stashed by the general in his baggage. Chicle is the dried milky sap of the Mexican sapodilla tree.
4. There was more of this resin brought into the country by Santa Anna's friend Thomas Adams. Adams had a plan to make rubber.
5. The plan failed. Then the occasion arose for Adams to get a much more successful idea on the basis of the use to which the resin was put by General Santa Anna. That is, Adams decided to make a gum that could be chewed.

Exercise 39.4   Revising: Conciseness

Make the following passage as concise as possible. Be merciless.

At the end of a lengthy line of reasoning, he came to the conclusion that the situation with carcinogens [cancer-causing substances] should be regarded as similar to the situation with the automobile. Instead of giving in to an irrational fear of cancer, we should consider all aspects of the problem in a balanced and dispassionate frame of mind, making a total of the benefits received from potential carcinogens (plastics, pesticides, and other similar products) and measuring said total against the damage done by such products. This is the nature of most discussions about the automobile. Instead of responding irrationally to the visual, aural, and air pollution caused by automobiles, we have decided to live with them (while simultaneously working to improve on them) for the benefits brought to society as a whole.

40

Spelling and the Hyphen

English spelling is difficult, even for some very experienced and competent writers. You can train yourself to spell better, and this chapter will help you. But you can also improve instantly by acquiring the habits listed in the following box.

Ways to improve your spelling

- **Carefully proofread all your writing.** Use the proofreading tips on page 66 to help you find spelling errors.
- **Check a dictionary** *every time* **you doubt a spelling.** Being suspicious of your spellings and relying on a dictionary will take care of many potential spelling errors.
- **Create a list of your spelling errors.** Keep a record of words you misspell, and check the list every time you write a paper. With experience, you'll learn to recognize and correct the words you typically misspell.
- **Use a spelling checker critically.** A spelling checker can help you find spelling errors in your papers. However, its usefulness is limited because it can't spot the common error of confusing words with similar spellings, such as *now/not, to/too, their/they're/there,* and *principal/principle.* See pages 63–64 for more on spelling checkers.

40a | Recognizing typical spelling problems

Spelling well involves recognizing situations that commonly lead to misspelling: pronunciation can mislead you in several ways; different forms of the same word may have different spellings; and some words have more than one acceptable spelling.

Visit *mycomplab.com* for more resources and exercises on spelling and the hyphen.

HIGHLIGHTS

No quick formula exists for turning poor spellers into good ones. Students with serious spelling problems may need systematic instruction in spelling, which, like systematic instruction in vocabulary, is rarely allowed by course time. You may want to refer such students to a skills center on campus or, if there are no such services, to a good spelling workbook. There are, however, activities and assignments that can help. Most students can improve their spelling markedly by learning and actually applying the limited number of standard rules, by maintaining a record of words that repeatedly cause them trouble, and by faithfully practicing brief groups of words from a spelling list. Such advice, though uninspired and unoriginal, does produce real improvement if a student can be persuaded to follow it, perhaps with the added reminder that lack of confidence in spelling distracts the student from more important matters in writing.

A WRITER'S PERSPECTIVE _____

Everyone misspells occasionally, usually because of carelessness or simple failure to observe closely. Good spelling requires an eye for detail.
—WILLIAM F. IRMSCHER

It's a poor imagination that can only think of one way to spell a word.
—ATTRIBUTED TO MARK TWAIN

COLLABORATIVE LEARNING

HOMONYM HOMEWORK

Sometimes the quickest way to learn distinctions in spelling between words that sound the same is to memorize the words and their definitions. The context in which the word is encountered can also become a kind of mnemonic (in addition to deliberately constructed mnemonics such as "the principal is a pal"). Divide the text's list of homonyms among the class and have students work in groups to create exercise questions by posing one-sentence contexts for several of the words on this list, as for example: "I [*accept/except*] the package from the UPS driver." The compiled exercise questions might be assigned as a quiz either in a subsequent class or on the network.

CLASS-WIDE ERROR LOG

While students will certainly benefit from keeping logs of individual errors, they can also benefit from error logs that are specific to certain assignments or to this particular class. You might start an error log for students, noting common spelling errors you find in their essays and including examples of how to correct each, along with references to the appropriate sections of the handbook. If you teach in a networked classroom, you can share the log via the course Web site and update it as needed.

RESOURCES AND IDEAS

The March 2008 issue of *English Journal* features the theme "Teaching Spelling and Vocabulary in High School." Many of the articles offer practical solutions for helping

---

1 **Being wary of pronunciation**

In English, unlike some other languages, pronunciation of words is an unreliable guide to their spelling. The same letter or combination of letters may have different sounds in different words. (Say aloud these different ways of pronouncing the letters *ough: tough, dough, cough, through, bough.*) In addition, some words contain letters that are not pronounced clearly or at all, such as the *ed* in *asked,* the silent *e* in *swipe,* or the unpronounced *gh* in *tight.*

Pronunciation is a particularly unreliable guide in spelling **homonyms,** words pronounced the same though they have different spellings and meanings: *great/grate, to/too/two.* Some commonly confused homonyms and near-homonyms, such as *accept/except,* are listed below. (See p. 540 for tips on how to use spelling lists.)

Words commonly confused

accept (to receive)
except (other than)
affect (to have an influence on)
effect (a result)
all ready (prepared)
already (by this time)
allude (to refer to indirectly)
elude (to avoid)
allusion (an indirect reference)
illusion (an erroneous belief or
　perception)
ascent (a movement up)
assent (to agree, or an agreement)
bare (unclothed)
bear (to carry, or an animal)
board (a plane of wood)
bored (uninterested)
born (brought into life)
borne (carried)
brake (to stop)
break (to smash)
buy (to purchase)
by (next to)
capital (the seat of a government)
capitol (the building where a
　legislature meets)

cite (to quote an authority)
sight (the ability to see)
site (a place)
desert (to abandon)
dessert (after-dinner course)
discreet (reserved, respectful)
discrete (individual or distinct)
elicit (to bring out)
illicit (illegal)
eminent (well known)
imminent (soon to happen)
fair (average, or lovely)
fare (a fee for transportation)
forth (forward)
fourth (after *third*)
gorilla (a large primate)
guerrilla (a kind of soldier)
hear (to perceive by ear)
here (in this place)
heard (past tense of *hear*)
herd (a group of animals)
hole (an opening)
whole (complete)
its (possessive of *it*)
it's (contraction of *it is* or
　it has)

lead (heavy metal)
led (past tense of *lead*)

lessen (to make less)
lesson (something learned)

meat (flesh)
meet (to encounter, or a competition)

no (the opposite of *yes*)
know (to be certain)

passed (past tense of *pass*)
past (after, or a time gone by)

patience (forbearance)
patients (persons under medical care)

peace (the absence of war)
piece (a portion of something)

persecute (to oppress, to harass)
prosecute (to pursue, to take legal action against)

plain (clear)
plane (a carpenter's tool, or an airborne vehicle)

presence (the state of being at hand)
presents (gifts)

principal (most important, or the head of a school)
principle (a basic truth or law)

rain (precipitation)
reign (to rule)
rein (a strap for controlling an animal)

raise (to build up)
raze (to tear down)

right (correct)
rite (a religious ceremony)
write (to make letters)

road (a surface for driving)
rode (past tense of *ride*)

scene (where an action occurs)
seen (past participle of *see*)

seam (a junction)
seem (to appear)

stationary (unmoving)
stationery (writing paper)

straight (unbending)
strait (a water passageway)

their (possessive of *they*)
there (opposite of *here*)
they're (contraction of *they are*)

to (toward)
too (also)
two (following *one*)

waist (the middle of the body)
waste (discarded material)

weak (not strong)
week (Sunday through Saturday)

weather (climate)
whether (*if*, or introducing a choice)

which (one of a group)
witch (a sorcerer)

who's (contraction of *who is* or *who has*)
whose (possessive of *who*)

your (possessive of *you*)
you're (contraction of *you are*)

students spell. For example, in "Teaching Challenged Spellers in High School English Classrooms" (38–44), Rebecca Bowers Sipe discusses causes of spelling problems and offers a list of approaches to help students improve their spelling.

Other good references on teaching spelling include the following:

Brown, Alan S. "Encountering Misspellings and Spelling Performance: Why Wrong Isn't Right." *Journal of Educational Psychology* 80.4 (1988): 488–94. Print. Brown analyzes the psychology of student misspellings.

Chomsky, Carol. "Reading, Writing, and Phonology." *Harvard Educational Review* 40.2 (1970): 287–309. Print. Chomsky ties problems with spelling and word recognition to problems with hearing and distinguishing certain morphemes.

Clark, Roger, and I. Y. Hashimoto. "A Spelling Program for College Students." *Teaching English in the Two-Year College* 11.1 (1984): 34–38. Print. The authors describe activities to help students improve spelling over the course of a semester.

Dobie, Ann R. "Orthographical Theory and Practice; or, How to Teach Spelling." *Journal of Basic Writing* 5.2 (1986): 41–48. Print. Responses to this article appear in both the 1987 and 1988 volumes of this journal.

Kissell, Brian, and Karen Wood. "Side Trip: The Pearls and Perils of Spell-Checkers." *Voices from the Middle* 15.3 (2008): 31–32. Print. The authors address the impact of spell-checkers on student spelling skills and how they both benefit and hinder these skills.

Sensenbaugh, Roger. "Spelling Instruction and the Use of Word Lists." *Composition Chronicle* 6.3 (1993): 8–9. Print. The author describes techniques for helping students become better spellers.

Sipe, Rebecca Bowers, Dawn Putnam, Karen Reed-Nordwall, Tracy Rosewarne, and Jennifer Walsh. *They Still Can't Spell? Understanding and Supporting Challenged Spellers in Middle and High School.* Portsmouth: Heinemann, 2003. Print. The authors offer strategies for teaching spelling in the context of students' own writing, including keeping an error log and teaching general rules.

2 | **Distinguishing between different forms of the same word**

Spelling problems may occur when forms of the same word have different spellings, as in the following examples.

Verbs and nouns

Verb	Noun	Verb	Noun
advise	advice	enter	entrance
describe	description	marry	marriage
speak	speech	omit	omission

Nouns and adjectives

Noun	Adjective	Noun	Adjective
comedy	comic	height	high
courtesy	courteous	Britain	British
generosity	generous		

Irregular verbs

begin, began, begun	know, knew, known
break, broke, broken	ring, rang, rung

Irregular nouns

child, children	shelf, shelves
goose, geese	tooth, teeth
mouse, mice	woman, women

Other differences

four, forty	thief, theft

3 Using preferred spellings CULTURE LANGUAGE

Many words have variant spellings as well as preferred spellings. Often the variant spellings listed in an American dictionary are British spellings.

American	British
color, humor	colour, humour
theater, center	theatre, centre
canceled, traveled	cancelled, travelled
judgment	judgement
realize	realise

40b Following spelling rules

Misspelling is often a matter of misspelling a syllable rather than the whole word. The following general rules focus on troublesome syllables, with notes for the occasional exceptions.

1 Distinguishing between *ie* and *ei*

Words like *believe* and *receive* sound alike in the second syllable, but the syllable is spelled differently. Use the familiar jingle to distinguish between *ie* and *ei*:

I before *e,* except after *c,* or when pronounced "ay" as in *neighbor* and *weigh.*

i before *e*	believe	bier	hygiene
	grief	thief	friend

ei after *c*	ceiling	conceive	perceive
	receive	deceit	conceit
ei sounded	neighbor	weight	eight
as "ay"	sleigh	freight	vein

Exceptions In some words an *ei* combination neither follows *c* nor is pronounced "ay." These words include *either, neither, foreign, forfeit, height, leisure, weird, seize,* and *seizure.* This sentence might help you remember some of them: *The weird foreigner neither seizes leisure nor forfeits height.*

Exercise 40.1 Distinguishing between *ie* and *ei*

Insert *ie* or *ei* in the words below. Check doubtful spellings in a dictionary.

1. br__f
2. dec__ve
3. rec__pt
4. s__ze
5. for__gn
6. pr__st
7. gr__vance
8. f__nd
9. l__surely
10. ach__ve
11. pat__nce
12. p__rce
13. h__ght
14. fr__ght
15. f__nt
16. s__ve

2 Keeping or dropping a final *e*

Many words end with an unpronounced or silent *e: move, brave, late, rinse.* Drop the final *e* when adding an ending that begins with a vowel:

advise + able = advisable
force + ible = forcible

surprise + ing = surprising
guide + ance = guidance

Keep the final, silent *e* when adding an ending that begins with a consonant:

battle + ment = battlement
accurate + ly = accurately

care + ful = careful
like + ness = likeness

Exceptions The silent *e* is sometimes retained before an ending beginning with a vowel. It is kept when *dye* becomes *dyeing,* to avoid confusion with *dying.* It is kept to prevent mispronunciation of words like *shoeing* (not *shoing*) and *mileage* (not *milage*). And the final *e* is often retained after a soft *c* or *g,* to keep the sound of the consonant soft rather than hard:

courageous
outrageous

changeable
manageable

noticeable
embraceable

The silent *e* is also sometimes *dropped* before an ending beginning with a consonant, when the *e* is preceded by another vowel:

argue + ment = argument
due + ly = duly
true + ly = truly

ANSWERS: EXERCISE 40.1

1. brief
2. deceive
3. receipt
4. seize
5. foreign
6. priest
7. grievance
8. fiend
9. leisurely
10. achieve
11. patience
12. pierce
13. height
14. freight
15. feint
16. sieve

ANSWERS: EXERCISE 40.2

1. malicious
2. lovable *or* loveable
3. serviceable
4. retirement
5. suing
6. virtuous
7. notable
8. battling
9. suspension

Exercise 40.2 Keeping or dropping a final *e*

Combine the following words and endings, keeping or dropping a final *e* as necessary to make correctly spelled words. Check doubtful spellings in a dictionary.

1. malice + ious
2. love + able
3. service + able
4. retire + ment
5. sue + ing
6. virtue + ous
7. note + able
8. battle + ing
9. suspense + ion

3 Keeping or dropping a final *y*

Words ending in *y* often change their spelling when an ending is added to them. Change the final *y* to an *i* when it follows a consonant:

| beauty, beauties | worry, worried | supply, supplies |
| folly, follies | merry, merrier | deputy, deputize |

But keep the *y* when it follows a vowel, when the ending is *-ing*, or when it ends a proper name:

| day, days | cry, crying | May, Mays |
| obey, obeyed | study, studying | Minsky, Minskys |

Exercise 40.3 Keeping or dropping a final *y*

Combine the following words and endings, changing or keeping a final *y* as necessary to make correctly spelled words. Check doubtful spellings in a dictionary.

1. imply + s
2. messy + er
3. apply + ing
4. delay + ing
5. defy + ance
6. say + s
7. solidify + s
8. Murphy + s
9. supply + ed

ANSWERS: EXERCISE 40.3

1. implies
2. messier
3. applying
4. delaying
5. defiance
6. says
7. solidifies
8. Murphys
9. supplied

4 Doubling consonants

Whether to double a word's final consonant depends first on the number of syllables in the word. In one-syllable words, double the final consonant when a single vowel precedes the final consonant. Otherwise, don't double the consonant.

| slap, slapping | pair, paired |
| tip, tipping | park, parking |

In words of more than one syllable, double the final consonant when a single vowel precedes the final consonant *and* the consonant ends a stressed syllable once the ending is added. Otherwise, don't double the consonant.

refer, referring	refer, reference
begin, beginning	relent, relented
occur, occurrence	despair, despairing

Exercise 40.4 Doubling consonants

Combine the following words and endings, doubling final consonants as necessary to make correctly spelled words. Check doubtful spellings in a dictionary.

1. repair + ing
2. admit + ance
3. benefit + ed
4. shop + ed
5. conceal + ed
6. allot + ed
7. drip + ing
8. declaim + ed
9. parallel + ing

5 Attaching prefixes

Adding a prefix such as *dis*, *mis*, and *un* does not change the spelling of a word. When adding a prefix, do not drop a letter from or add a letter to the original word:

uneasy	anti-intellectual	defuse	misstate
unnecessary	disappoint	de-emphasize	misspell
antifreeze	dissatisfied	misinform	

(See also p. 545 for when to use hyphens with prefixes: *prehistory* versus *ex-student*.)

6 Forming plurals

Nouns

Most nouns form plurals by adding *s* to the singular form:

boy, boys	table, tables
carnival, carnivals	Murphy, Murphys

Some nouns ending in *f* or *fe* form the plural by changing the ending to *ve* before adding *s:*

leaf, leaves	wife, wives
life, lives	yourself, yourselves

Singular nouns ending in *s*, *sh*, *ch*, or *x* form the plural by adding *es:*

kiss, kisses	church, churches
wish, wishes	Jones, Joneses

(Notice that verbs ending in *s*, *sh*, *ch*, or *x* form the third-person singular in the same way. *Taxes* and *lurches* are examples.)

Nouns ending in *o* preceded by a vowel usually form the plural by adding *s:*

ratio, ratios	zoo, zoos

Nouns ending in *o* preceded by a consonant usually form the plural by adding *es:*

hero, heroes	tomato, tomatoes

IRREGULAR PLURALS

There are a few irregular plurals in English; most survive from Anglo-Saxon (for example, *child/children*) or are borrowed from other languages (*alumnus/alumni*). All native English nouns added since the Norman Conquest of England in 1066 have been regular, using the *-s* or *-es* suffixes to form the plural.

Exceptions Some very common nouns form irregular plurals:

child, children   man, men
mouse, mice   woman, women

Some English nouns that were originally Italian, Greek, Latin, or French form the plural according to their original language:

analysis, analyses   datum, data
basis, bases   medium, media
beau, beaux   phenomenon, phenomena
crisis, crises   piano, pianos
criterion, criteria   thesis, theses

A few such nouns may form irregular or regular plurals: for instance, *index, indices, indexes; curriculum, curricula, curriculums*. The regular plural is more contemporary.

CULTURE LANGUAGE Noncount nouns do not form plurals, either regularly (with an added *s*) or irregularly. Examples of noncount nouns include *equipment, courage,* and *wealth*. (See p. 323.)

Compound nouns

Form plurals of compound nouns in one of two ways. Add *s* to the last word when the component words are roughly equal in importance, whether or not they are hyphenated:

city-states   breakthroughs
painter-sculptors   bucket seats

Add *s* to a noun combined with other parts of speech:

fathers-in-law   passersby

Note, however, that most modern dictionaries give the plural of *spoonful* as *spoonfuls*.

Exercise 40.5 Forming plurals
Make the correct plural of each of the following singular words. Check doubtful spellings in a dictionary.

1. pile
2. donkey
3. beach
4. summary
5. mile per hour
6. box
7. switch
8. sister-in-law
9. Bales
10. cupful
11. libretto
12. video
13. thief
14. goose
15. hiss
16. appendix

40c Developing spelling skills

The following techniques can help you improve your spelling. In addition, do not overrely on your computer's spelling checker (see pp. 63–64).

1 Editing and proofreading carefully

If spelling is a problem for you, give it high priority while editing your writing (p. 59) and again while proofreading, your last chance to catch misspelled words (p. 65). Reading a draft backward, word by word, can help you spot mistakes such as switched or omitted letters in words you know. Because the procedure forces you to consider each word in isolation, it can also highlight spellings you may be less sure of. A sense of uncertainty is crucial in spotting and correcting spelling errors, even for good spellers who make relatively few errors. Listen to your own uncertainty, and let it lead you to the dictionary.

2 Using a dictionary

How can you look up a word you can't spell? Start by guessing at the spelling and looking up your guess. If that doesn't work, pronounce the word aloud to come up with other possible spellings, and look them up. Unless the word is too specialized to be included in your dictionary, trial and error will eventually pay off.

If you're using a spelling checker, it may do the guessing for you by providing several choices for misspelled words. But you may still need to check a dictionary to verify your choice.

3 Pronouncing carefully

Careful pronunciation is not always a reliable guide to spelling (see p. 532), but it can keep you from misspelling words that are often mispronounced. For example:

athletics (*not* atheletics)
disastrous (*not* disasterous)
environment (*not* envirnment)
frustrate (*not* fustrate)
government (*not* goverment)
height (*not* heighth)
history (*not* histry)
irrelevant (*not* irrevelant)

laboratory (*not* labratory)
library (*not* libary)
lightning (*not* lightening)
mischievous (*not* mischievious)
nuclear (*not* nucular)
recognize (*not* reconize)
representative (*not* representive)
strictly (*not* stricly)

4 Tracking and analyzing your errors

Keep a list of the words marked "misspelled" or "spelling" or "sp" in your papers. This list will contain hints about your particular spelling problems, such as confusing *affect* and *effect* or forming plurals incorrectly. (If you need help analyzing the list, consult your writing instructor.) The list will also provide a personalized study guide, a focus for your efforts to spell better.

CAREFUL PROOFREADING

Many of the errors made with spelling can be avoided through careful proofreading. Three proofreading techniques that force the writer to read more slowly and carefully are (1) reading the essay aloud, (2) reading the essay backward, from the last sentence to the first, and (3) reading the essay one word at a time, using a notecard or ruler to block out upcoming text.

MAKING WORDS YOUR OWN

One way to help students remember words they look up in a dictionary is to have them highlight the word, jot it down on an ongoing list, and then use it in a sentence of their own. At a later date, students should go back to their "dictionary list" and try to use each word in a one-sentence context. If students keep up this practice throughout a semester they will have added those words to their working vocabularies.

SPELLING LOGS

Most students benefit from keeping lists, or logbooks, of their spelling problems. After a few weeks of recording data, they may be able to see patterns of difficulty emerge. Students should add misspelled words found using a computer spelling checker to their spelling logs for those times when they are away from their machines or the computer is down. Some good examples of pattern recognition are found in Kristene F. Anderson, "Using a Spelling Survey to Develop Basic Writers' Linguistic Awareness," *Journal of Basic Writing* 16.2 (1987): 72–78 and *They Still Can't Spell?* by Rebecca Bowers Sipe et al.

SEPARATING THE -*SEDES*

Students may learn to distinguish whether -*sede*, -*ceed*, or -*cede* should be planted at the end of a word by memorizing the words *proceed, exceed, succeed,* and *supersede. Proceed, exceed,* and *succeed* are the only words ending in -*ceed. Supersede* is the only word ending in -*sede*. All the remaining -*cede* words end in -*cede*.

SPELLING BEE

Ask students to submit lists of words they have trouble with. Circulate all the lists to give student teams time to memorize them; then hold an old-fashioned spelling bee in class.

5 Using mnemonics

Mnemonics (pronounced with an initial *n* sound) are techniques for assisting your memory. The *er* in *letter* and *paper* can remind you that *stationery* (meaning "writing paper") has an *er* near the end; *stationary* with an *a* means "standing in place." Or the word *dome* with its long *o* sound can remind you that the building in which the legislature meets is spelled *capitol,* with an *o*. The *capital* city is spelled with *al* like *Albany,* the capital of New York. If you identify the words you have trouble spelling, you can think of your own mnemonics, which may work better for you than someone else's.

6 Studying spelling lists

Learning to spell commonly misspelled words will reduce your spelling errors. For general improvement, work with the following list of commonly misspelled words. Study only six or seven words at a time. If you are unsure of the meaning of a word, look it up in a dictionary and try using it in a sentence. Pronounce the word out loud, syllable by syllable, and write the word out. (The list of similar-sounding words on pp. 532–33 should be considered an extension of the following list.)

absence	aggressive	appropriate
abundance	all right	approximately
acceptable	all together	argument
accessible	allegiance	arrest
accidentally	almost	ascend
accommodate	a lot	assassinate
accomplish	already	assimilation
accumulate	although	assistance
accuracy	altogether	associate
accustomed	amateur	atheist
achieve	among	athlete
acknowledge	amount	attendance
acquire	analysis	audience
across	analyze	average
actually	angel	
address	annual	bargain
admission	answer	basically
adolescent	apology	because
advice	apparent	beginning
advising	appearance	belief
against	appetite	believe
aggravate	appreciate	beneficial

benefited
boundary
breath
Britain
bureaucracy
business

calculator
calendar
caricature
carrying
cede
ceiling
cello
cemetery
certain
changeable
changing
characteristic
chief
chocolate
choose
chose
climbed
coarse
column
coming
commercial
commitment
committed
committee
competent
competition
complement
compliment
conceive
concentrate
concert
condemn
conquer
conscience
conscious
consistency
consistent
continuous

controlled
controversial
convenience
convenient
coolly
course
courteous
criticism
criticize
crowd
cruelty
curiosity
curious
curriculum

deceive
deception
decide
decision
deductible
definitely
degree
dependent
descend
descendant
describe
description
desirable
despair
desperate
destroy
determine
develop
device
devise
dictionary
difference
dining
disagree
disappear
disappoint
disapprove
disastrous
discipline
discriminate

discussion
disease
disgusted
dissatisfied
distinction
divide
divine
division
doctor
drawer

easily
ecstasy
efficiency
efficient
eighth
either
eligible
embarrass
emphasize
empty
enemy
entirely
entrepreneur
environment
equipped
especially
essential
every
exaggerate
exceed
excellent
exercise
exhaust
exhilarate
existence
expense
experience
experiment
explanation
extremely

familiar
fascinate
favorite

February
fiery
finally
forcibly
foreign
foresee
forty
forward
friend
frightening
fulfill

gauge
generally
ghost
government
grammar
grief
guarantee
guard
guidance

happily
harass
height
heroes
hideous
humorous
hungry
hurriedly
hurrying
hypocrisy
hypocrite

ideally
illogical
imaginary
imagine
imitation
immediately
immigrant
incidentally
incredible
independence
independent
individually

inevitably
influential
initiate
innocuous
inoculate
insistent
integrate
intelligence
interest
interference
interpret
irrelevant
irresistible
irritable
island

jealousy
judgment

kindergarten
knowledge

laboratory
leisure
length
library
license
lieutenant
lightning
likelihood
literally
livelihood
loneliness
loose
lose
luxury
lying

magazine
maintenance
manageable
marriage
mathematics
meant
medicine
miniature

minor
minutes
mirror
mischievous
missile
misspelled
morale
morals
mortgage
mournful
muscle
mysterious

naturally
necessary
neighbor
neither
nickel
niece
ninety
ninth
noticeable
nuclear
nuisance
numerous

obstacle
occasion
occasionally
occur
occurrence
official
omission
omit
omitted
opinion
opponent
opportunity
opposite
ordinary
originally

paid
panicky
paralleled
parliament

particularly
peaceable
peculiar
pedal
perceive
perception
performance
permanent
permissible
persistence
personnel
perspiration
persuade
persuasion
physical
physiology
physique
pitiful
planning
playwright
pleasant
poison
politician
pollute
possession
possibly
practically
practice
prairie
precede
preference
preferred
prejudice
preparation
prevalent
primitive
privilege
probably
procedure
proceed
process
professor
prominent
pronunciation
psychology
purpose

pursue
pursuit

quandary
quantity
quarter
questionnaire
quiet
quizzes

realistically
realize
really
rebel
rebelled
recede
receipt
receive
recognize
recommend
reference
referred
relief
relieve
religious
remembrance
reminisce
renown
repetition
representative
resemblance
resistance
restaurant
rhyme
rhythm
ridiculous
roommate

sacrifice
sacrilegious
safety
satellite
scarcity
schedule
science
secretary

seize
separate
sergeant
several
sheriff
shining
shoulder
siege
significance
similar
sincerely
sophomore
source
speak
specimen
speech
sponsor
strategy
strength
strenuous
stretch
strict
strictly
studying
succeed
successful
sufficient
summary
superintendent
supersede
suppress
surely
surprise
suspicious

teammate
technical
technique
temperature
tendency
than
then
thorough
though
throughout
together

tomatoes	unnecessary	weather
tomorrow	until	Wednesday
tragedy	usable	weird
transferred	usually	wherever
truly		whether
twelfth		wholly
tyranny	vacuum	woman
	vegetable	women
	vengeance	writing
unanimous	vicious	
unconscious	villain	
undoubtedly	visible	yacht

40d Using the hyphen to form or divide words

The hyphen (-) is a mark of punctuation used either to form words or to divide them at the ends of lines.

1 Forming compound adjectives

When two or more words serve together as a single modifier before a noun, a hyphen or hyphens form the modifying words clearly into a unit:

> She is a well-known actor.
> The conclusions are based on out-of-date statistics.
> Some Spanish-speaking students work as translators.

When the same compound adjectives follow the noun, hyphens are unnecessary and are usually left out.

> The actor is well known.
> The statistics were out of date.
> Many students are Spanish speaking.

Hyphens are also unnecessary in compound modifiers containing an *-ly* adverb, even when the modifiers fall before the noun: *clearly defined terms; swiftly moving train.*

When part of a compound adjective appears only once in two or more parallel compound adjectives, hyphens indicate which words the reader should mentally join with the missing part:

> School-aged children should have eight- or nine-o'clock bedtimes.

2 Writing fractions and compound numbers

Hyphens join the numerator and denominator of fractions and the parts of the whole numbers twenty-one to ninety-nine:

three-fourths   twenty-four
one-half   eighty-seven

3 Forming coined compounds

Writers sometimes create (coin) temporary compounds and join the words with hyphens:

Muhammad Ali gave his opponent a come-and-get-me look.

4 Attaching some prefixes and suffixes

Do not use hyphens with prefixes except as follows:

- **With the prefixes *self-*, *all-*, and *ex-*:** *self-control, all-inclusive, ex-student.*
- **With a prefix before a capitalized word:** *un-American.*
- **With a capital letter before a word:** *T-shirt.*
- **To prevent misreading:** *de-emphasize, anti-intellectual.*

The only suffix that regularly requires a hyphen is *-elect,* as in *president-elect.*

5 Eliminating confusion

Hyphens can prevent possible confusion:

Confusing   Doonesbury is a comic strip character. [Is Doonesbury a comic (funny) character who strips or a character in a comic strip?]
Clear   Doonesbury is a comic-strip character.

Hyphens can also clarify words with added prefixes. For example, *recreation* (*creation* with the prefix *re-*) could mean either "a new creation" or "diverting, pleasurable activity." The use of a hyphen, *re-creation,* limits the word to the first meaning. Without a hyphen the word suggests the second meaning.

6 Dividing words at the ends of lines

You can avoid occasional short lines in your documents by dividing some words between the end of one line and the beginning of the next. On a word processor, you can set the program to divide words automatically at appropriate breaks (in the Tools menu, select Language and then Hyphenation). To divide words manually, follow these guidelines:

- **Divide words only between syllables**—for instance, *win-dows,* not *wi-ndows.* Check a dictionary for correct syllable breaks.

- Never divide a one-syllable word.
- **Leave at least two letters on the first line and three on the second line.** If a word cannot be divided to follow this rule (for instance, *a-bus-er*), don't divide it.
- **Break an electronic address only after a slash.** Do not hyphenate, because readers may perceive any added hyphens as part of the address.

Exercise 40.6 Using hyphens in compound words

Insert hyphens as needed in the following compounds. Mark all compounds that are correct as given. Consult a dictionary as needed.

1. reimburse
2. deescalate
3. forty odd soldiers
4. little known bar
5. seven eighths
6. seventy eight
7. happy go lucky
8. preexisting
9. senator elect
10. postwar
11. two and six person cars
12. ex songwriter
13. V shaped
14. reeducate

ANSWERS: EXERCISE 40.6

1. Correct
2. de-escalate
3. forty-odd soldiers
4. little-known bar
5. seven-eighths
6. seventy-eight
7. happy-go-lucky
8. pre-existing
9. senator-elect
10. Correct
11. two- and six-person cars
12. ex-songwriter
13. V-shaped
14. re-educate

PART **9**

Research Writing

41 Planning a Research Project

42 Finding Sources

43 Working with Sources

44 Avoiding Plagiarism and Documenting Sources

45 Writing the Paper

46 Using MLA Documentation and Format

47 Two Research Papers in MLA Style

HIGHLIGHTS

Many students actively dislike or fear writing research papers—either because of misconceptions about the purpose of such assignments or because of previous unpleasant or purely mechanistic experiences with research writing. As a result, you may find that some students resist this type of writing. The chapters in Part 9 show students not only how valuable and interesting research writing can be, but also that it is an extension of the critical thinking, reading, and writing skills stressed in the handbook.

Part 9 offers a detailed overview of research writing, from finding information (using both electronic and print resources) to shaping it, documenting it, and presenting it according to a consistent set of standards. It includes a discussion of online research and standard reference sources and a chapter-length treatment of plagiarism.

A special feature of Part 9 is its use of the research and writing process of two students (Justin Malik and Vanessa Haley) as examples. Following Malik's and Haley's progress from beginning to end of their research process will give your students a better sense of how the strategies discussed in the handbook might be applied in actual first-year college writing projects.

Chapter 41 presents research gathering as a strategic task and offers a series of descriptions and suggestions to help students move through a research project effectively, including how to annotate a working bibliography.

A WRITER'S PERSPECTIVE

> Not the least part of discovery is asking the right questions.
>
> —St. Augustine

RESOURCES AND IDEAS

English Journal's March 2006 (95.4) issue focuses on the theme "Reading, Writing, and Re-Presenting Research" and includes articles on Web-based research, multi-genre projects, and incorporating research into creative writing.

Ballenger, Bruce. *Beyond Note Cards: Rethinking the Freshman Research Paper*. Portsmouth: Boynton/Cook, 1999. Print. Ballenger offers a theoretically based approach to research writing that focuses on making intellectual inquiry the driving force behind these projects.

41

Planning a Research Project

If you've ever watched a TV or movie detective pursue a culprit, you know that research can be exciting. When an investigator has a goal in sight, the seemingly mundane work of digging through files, interviewing witnesses, and piecing together clues becomes a concentrated and enthusiastic search.

This same excitement can be yours when you conduct research in college. Honest and inquisitive research writing does demand close attention to details, but the work will be rewarding as you see the details steadily contributing to your own ideas and to the ideas of others. Through your research, synthesis, and writing, you will gain significant, in-depth understanding of a subject that you may not have known much about when you started, and you will add to the body of knowledge about the subject. You will become an expert in your own right.

Like most of the writing you do in college, research writing is a process that involves stages. Generally, you will pass through and return to the following stages during the course of a research project:

- **Choosing a subject**
- **Finding information about the subject**
- **Evaluating source information and synthesizing the ideas of others with your own**
- **Integrating source information into your writing**
- **Documenting the ideas of others in source citations**
- **Drafting, revising, and editing the project**

These topics and others are covered throughout Chapters 41–45.

The kind of paper or project you produce will be influenced by whether you are expected to report, to interpret, or to analyze sources.

- In **reporting**, you survey, organize, and objectively present the available evidence about a topic.

mycomplab

Visit *mycomplab.com* for more resources and exercises on planning a research project.

■ In **interpreting**, you examine a range of views on a topic and argue your own conclusion about it.

■ In **analyzing**, you argue for the solution to a problem or the answer to a question based on your critical thinking about texts such as scholarly or literary works. (In this context, *analysis* stands for the entire process of critical reading and writing. See pp. 138–52.)

No matter what kind of paper you write, always focus on developing your own ideas, using sources as support. Avoid the temptation to seek a "silver bullet"—that is, to locate two or three perfect sources that already say everything you want to say about your subject. Instead of merely repeating others' ideas, read and synthesize many sources so that you develop your own ideas.

Throughout Chapters 41–45, we will follow the development of research papers by two students, Justin Malik and Vanessa Haley. Malik's work, emphasizing interpretation, receives somewhat more attention; Haley's work, emphasizing analysis, enters the discussion whenever her process differed significantly from Malik's. Both students' final papers appear in Chapter 47.

41a   Starting out

With its diverse and overlapping activities, research writing demands more planning than other kinds of writing. A thoughtful plan and systematic procedures will help you anticipate your needs, schedule your time, and complete the work successfully.

1 Preparing a schedule

As soon as you receive an assignment for a research project, you can begin developing a strategy for completing it. The first step should be making a schedule that apportions the available time to the necessary work. A possible schedule appears on the next page. In it the research-writing process corresponds to the general writing process discussed in Chapters 1–3: planning or developing (steps 1–9), drafting (step 10), and revising and editing (step 11), plus the additional important stage of documenting the sources you use (steps 12–13).

2 Keeping a research journal

To keep track of your activities and ideas during research, maintain a research journal throughout the process. (See pp. 19 and 143 on journal keeping.) Make your journal portable so that you can carry it with you conveniently. Many researchers use paper notebooks or handheld or notebook computers. Some schools offer students blog space for recording research and other learning activities.

He includes exercises and assignments, and addresses how to use a double-entry journal.

Ford, James E., ed. *Teaching the Research Paper: From Theory to Practice, From Research to Writing.* Metuchen: Scarecrow Press, 1995. Print. These essays address the value of teaching research papers in composition classes; models of research units and practical suggestions are included.

Moulton, Margaret, and Vicki Homes. "The Research Paper: A Historical Perspective." *Teaching English in the Two-Year College* 30.4 (2003): 365–73. Print. The authors present a fascinating historical account, from the 1870s to the present, of the value and relevance of the research paper assignment.

Nelson, Jennie. "The Research Paper: A 'Rhetoric of Doing' or a 'Rhetoric of the Finished Word'?" *Composition Studies* 22.2 (1994): 65–75. Print. Nelson argues that the research paper does not serve any useful educational purpose unless students understand it as a learning process.

Pelham, Fran O'Byrne. "The Research Journal: Integrating Reading, Writing, and Research." *Composition Chronicle* 6.3 (1993): 4–5. Print. Pelham recommends using a journal to supplement typical research activities and to allow students to "research, reflect, write, and then attend recursively to these events."

Roen, Duane, Veronica Pantoja, Lauren Yena, Susan K. Miller, and Eric Waggoner, eds. "Teaching Research Skills." *Strategies for Teaching First-Year Composition.* Urbana: NCTE, 2002. 569–612. Print. This chapter includes five pieces, each offering a different approach to research writing, including introducing students to academic discourse and using proposals in a composition class.

Wilson, Matthew. "Research, Expressivism and Silence." *Journal of Advanced Composition* 15.2 (1995): 241–60. Print. A thought-provoking analysis of the challenges that teachers face in defining research papers, and that students face in writing them.

Zemliansky, Pavel, and Wendy Bishop, eds. *Research Writing Revisited: A Sourcebook for Teachers.* Portsmouth: Boynton/Cook, 2004. Print. This collection offers perspectives and advice on teaching many varieties of research writing, including ethnography, I-search papers, and service learning projects.

SUPPORT FOR THE RESEARCH-PHOBIC

Some students, especially those who have never done a research project before, may have significant anxiety about their ability to undertake a research project, manage all the phases, and end up with a decent final product. It may be helpful for students to share anxieties in small groups as a way of overcoming them. Such discussions work only if there is mutual trust among members of the group, so this activity would work best with a group that has been working together regularly for a while and has had a chance to build trust.

SMART SCHEDULING

Beginning college students need help in establishing a realistic schedule. Emphasize strongly that each of the four segments in the "Scheduling steps" chart on this page truly will take about a quarter of the time. Share with them the schedule for a writing project you've recently completed, and point out the kinds of places where delays are likely to occur.

PUT IT ON THE CALENDAR

If students have calendar or scheduling software, they can put their research schedule in calendar format and keep it handy for easy reference. Revising the schedule becomes a matter of a few keystrokes.

COMPUTER JOURNAL

The advantage to keeping a hard copy journal is that the student can write in it anywhere at any time. However, some students may find it easier to keep an electronic journal, particularly if they are doing a lot of their searching and source consultation on computers. Students can carry a floppy disk with their journal file and load the file whenever they want to make a journal entry.

Scheduling steps in research writing
(See the pages in parentheses for discussion of the steps.)

Complete
by:

_____ 1. Setting a schedule and beginning a research journal (previous page)
_____ 2. Finding a researchable subject and question (below)
_____ 3. Developing a research strategy (p. 554)
_____ 4. Finding sources, both print and electronic (p. 561), and making a working bibliography (p. 557)

_____ 5. Evaluating and synthesizing sources (pp. 590, 604)
_____ 6. Mining and interacting with sources (p. 607), often using summary, paraphrase, and direct quotation (p. 611)
_____ 7. Taking steps to avoid plagiarism (p. 626)
_____ 8. Developing a thesis statement (p. 636)

_____ 9. Creating a structure (p. 637)
_____ 10. Drafting the paper (p. 640), integrating summaries, paraphrases, and direct quotations into your ideas (p. 620)

_____ 11. Revising and editing the paper (p. 641)
_____ 12. Citing sources in your text (p. 634)
_____ 13. Preparing the list of works cited (p. 634)
_____ 14. Preparing and proofreading the final manuscript (p. 643)

_____ Final paper due

Each segment marked off by a horizontal line will occupy *roughly* one-fourth of the total time. The most unpredictable segments are the first two, so get started early enough to accommodate the unexpected.

In the research journal's dated entries, you can write about the sources you consult, the leads you want to pursue, and any difficulties you encounter. Most important, you can record your thoughts about sources, leads, dead ends, new directions, relationships, and anything else that strikes you. The very act of writing in your journal can expand and clarify your thinking.

Note The research journal is the place to track and develop your own ideas. To avoid mixing up your thoughts and those of others, keep separate notes on what your sources actually say, using one of the methods discussed on pages 608–11.

 Finding a researchable subject and question

Before reading this section, review the suggestions given on pages 6–9 for finding and limiting an essay subject. Generally, the same procedure applies to writing any kind of research paper: begin with an assigned subject or one that interests you (perhaps one you've already written about without benefit of research), and then narrow the subject to manageable size by asking questions about it. However, selecting and limiting a subject for a research paper can present special opportunities and problems.

1 | Choosing an appropriate subject

A subject for a research paper has four primary requirements, each with corresponding pitfalls:

1. **Ample sources of information are available on the subject.** Other researchers should have had a chance to produce evidence on the subject, weigh the evidence, and publish their conclusions. And the sources should be accessible.

   Avoid very recent subjects, such as a new medical discovery or a breaking story in today's newspaper.

2. **The subject encourages research in the kinds and number of sources required by the assignment.**

   Avoid (*a*) subjects that depend entirely on personal opinion and experience, such as the virtues of your hobby; and (*b*) subjects that require research in only one source, such as a straight factual biography or a how-to like "Making Lenses for Eyeglasses." (An exception to *b* is a paper in which you analyze a single work such as a novel or painting.)

3. **The subject will lead you to an assessment of sources and to defensible conclusions.** Even when a research paper is intended to persuade, the success of the argument will depend on the balanced presentation of all significant points of view.

   Avoid controversial subjects that rest entirely on belief or prejudice, such as when human life begins or why women (or men) are superior. These subjects may certainly be disputed; however, your own views could slant your research or conclusions, and your readers are unlikely to be swayed from their own beliefs.

Checklist for a good research subject

1. **Published sources are ample:** the subject is not so recent that other researchers will still be discovering it.
2. **Sources are diverse:** the subject is neither wholly personal nor wholly factual.
3. **Sources can be assessed objectively:** the subject is not solely a matter of belief or prejudice.
4. **Sources can be examined thoroughly** in the assigned time and length: the subject is not too broad.

TRADING SCHEDULES

After students have drafted schedules for their research projects individually, have them show their schedule to a partner, who can help to evaluate the feasibility of the project and consider how to adjust the schedule if necessary.

LIBRARIANS AS ALLIES

It's useful to work with the research librarians at your school throughout the process of planning and implementing a research course. In particular, you might consult with the librarians before students begin to generate subjects for their research papers. The librarians can tell you which subjects may have limited resources available or describe new materials they've recently acquired. This will help you guide your students in selecting workable subjects. Many librarians will offer in-class workshops to help students become familiar with the library's resources. Scheduling such a presentation also allows students to connect with a librarian so they will be more willing to ask for research assistance in the future.

NOTEKEEPING

Note cards or notebooks are fairly easy tools for inexperienced writers to use. However, some students just aren't comfortable with cards, and their research actually may suffer if they are forced to use them. If students have great trouble keeping cards, suggest that they keep their notes in their journal or in a word processing document; the greater space may give them more freedom to compose effectively.

COMPUTER ACTIVITY

SCOPE ASSESSMENT

Beginning researchers often have difficulty assessing the scope of the subject they have chosen. Ask all students to post their subject ideas to the class Web site. Then, have an online class discussion in which everyone helps to evaluate the scope of each student's subject. This can also work well as a collaborative activity. Write students' proposed topics on the board or overhead, and they can discuss the scope of each subject as a class.

4. **The subject suits the length of paper assigned and the time given for research and writing.**

Avoid broad subjects that have too many sources to survey adequately, such as a major event in history or the collected works of a poet.

2 │ Posing a research question

Asking a question about your subject can give direction to your research by focusing your thinking on a particular approach. You can even begin asking questions before you find your specific subject, as a way of opening avenues you may not have considered.

The students Justin Malik and Vanessa Haley both wrote on environmental topics, but they arrived at their research questions by slightly different paths. For a composition course, Malik's instructor assigned an interpretation with a persuasive purpose but left the selection of the subject to the student. Malik had recently read newspaper articles on a subject that intrigued him: how big businesses are trying to improve their environmental records. Taking the broad subject of business and the environment as his starting point, he used clustering (see pp. 23–24) to pursue some ideas. While generating the cluster opposite, Malik found himself giving the most thought to green products—consumer goods that are promoted as friendly to the environment. Malik posed questions until he hit on a question that seemed interesting and significant: *Can buying green products make a real difference for the environment?*

In developing a topic and question for an analysis paper assigned in a composition course, Vanessa Haley followed a somewhat different procedure. Instead of starting with a general subject, as Malik did, Haley began by looking for an unresolved question, an interesting problem, or a disagreement among the experts in some field of study. She had recently been reading an anthology of writings on the environment, and she had been disturbed by how many naturalists and environmentalists view human beings not as part of "nature" but as something separate from it, usually as its destroyer. In her journal, Haley wrote this entry:

> Many writers see nature as a place for humans to retreat to, or a wonderful thing that humans are ruining. Humans aren't considered natural themselves—human civilization isn't considered natural. Human civ. is "anti-natural." Isn't such a separation unrealistic and damaging? We *are* natural. We're here to stay, and we're not going back to the Stone Age, so we'd better focus on the connections between "us" and "it" (nature) rather than just the differences. Dillard seems to do this—seems to connect human and natural worlds. People are neither better nor worse than nature but just bound up in it. "Nature is as careless as it is bountiful, and . . . with that extravagance goes a crushing waste that will one day include our own cheap lives" ("Fecundity").

Clustering for a research question

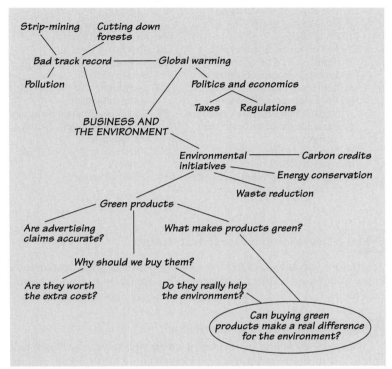

At the end of her journal entry, Haley refers to and quotes the writer Annie Dillard, one of the authors represented in the anthology. Haley decided to explore Dillard's views further by reading and analyzing more of her work. Haley's opening question for investigation, then, was *How does Annie Dillard see the place of humanity in nature?*

Exercise 41.1 Finding a topic and question

Choose three of the following subjects (or three subjects of your own), and narrow each one to at least one subject and question suitable for beginning work on a research paper. (This exercise can be the first step in a research-writing project that continues through Chapters 41–45.)

1. Bilingual education
2. National security and civil rights
3. Distribution of music by conventional versus electronic means
4. Dance in America
5. The history of women's suffrage
6. Genetically modified foods
7. Immigrants in the United States

RESOURCES AND IDEAS

Capossela, Toni-Lee. "Students as Sociolinguists: Getting Real Research from Freshman Writers." *College Composition and Communication* 42.1 (1991): 75–79. Print. Capossela uses students' command of their own language to engage in real-world issues and write research papers.

Davis, Robert, and Mark Shadle. "'Building a Mystery': Alternative Research Writing and the Academic Act of Seeking." *College Composition and Communication* 51.3 (2000): 417–66. Print. The authors urge us to expand our definition of the research paper and allow students to write personal research papers and compose multi-genre/media/disciplinary/cultural research papers.

Strickland, James. "Just the FAQs: An Alternative to Teaching the Research Paper." *English Journal* 94.1 (2004): 23–28. Print. Strickland proposes moving away from thesis-driven research papers. He proposes an alternative assignment, an FAQ, in order to help students use technology to apply their research and more clearly envision their audience.

Taylor, Tim N. "The Research Paper as an Act of Citizenship: Possibilities and Pragmatism." *Teaching English in the Two-Year College* 33.1 (2005): 50–61. Print. Taylor argues that students should focus on local issues as a form of civic engagement.

8. Space exploration
9. Business espionage
10. The effect of television on professional sports
11. Child abuse
12. African Americans and civil rights
13. Successes in cancer research
14. Computer piracy
15. The European exploration of North America before Columbus
16. Hazardous substances in the workplace
17. Television evangelism
18. Science fiction
19. Treatment or prevention of AIDS in the United States or Africa
20. Water pollution
21. Women writers
22. Campaign financing
23. Comic film actors
24. An unsolved crime
25. Alternative fuels
26. Male and female heroes in modern fiction
27. Computers and the privacy of the individual
28. Gothic or romance novels in the nineteenth and twenty-first centuries
29. The social responsibility of business
30. Stem-cell research

41c Developing a research strategy

Before you start looking for sources, consider what you already know about your subject and where you are likely to find information on it.

1 Tapping into your own knowledge

Discovering what you already know about your subject will guide you in discovering what you don't know. Take some time to spell out facts you have learned, opinions you have heard or read elsewhere, and of course your own opinions. Use one of the discovery techniques discussed in Chapter 2 to explore and develop your ideas: keeping a journal, observing your surroundings, freewriting, list making, clustering, asking the journalist's questions, using the patterns of development, or thinking critically.

When you've explored your thoughts, make a list of questions for which you don't have answers, whether factual (*How much do Americans spend on green products?*) or more open-ended (*Are they worth the higher prices?*). These questions will give you clues about the sources you need to look for first.

2 Setting goals for sources

For many research projects, you'll want to consult a mix of sources, as described on the following pages. You may start by seeking the outlines of your topic—the range and depth of opinions about it—in reference works and articles in popular periodicals or through a Web search. Then, as you refine your views and your research question, you'll move on to more specialized sources, such as scholarly books and periodicals and your own interviews or surveys. (See pp. 565–88 for more on each kind of source.)

The mix of sources you choose depends heavily on your subject. For example, Justin Malik's paper on green consumerism required the use of very recent sources because environmentally friendly products are fairly new to the marketplace. Your mix of sources may also be specified by your instructor or limited by the requirements of your assignment.

Library and Internet sources

The print and electronic sources available through your library—mainly reference works, periodicals, and books—have two big advantages over most of what you'll find on the open Web: they are cataloged and indexed for easy retrieval; and they are generally reliable, having been screened first by their publishers and then by the library's staff. In contrast, the Internet's retrieval systems are more difficult to use effectively, and Internet sources tend to be less reliable because most do not pass through any screening before being posted. (There are many exceptions, such as online scholarly journals and reference works. But these sources are generally available through your library's Web site as well.)

Most instructors expect research writers to consult sources found in and through the library, including print sources. But most will accept Internet sources, too, if you have used them judiciously. Even with its disadvantages, the Internet can be a valuable resource for primary sources, current information, and a diversity of views. For guidelines on evaluating both library and Internet sources, see pages 590–603.

Primary and secondary sources

Use **primary sources** when they are available or are required by your assignment. These sources are firsthand accounts, such as historical documents (letters, speeches, and so on), eyewitness reports (including articles by journalists who are on location), works of literature, reports on experiments or surveys conducted by the writer, and your own interviews, experiments, observations, or correspondence.

Many assignments will allow you to use **secondary sources**, which report and analyze information drawn from other sources, often primary ones. Examples include a reporter's summary of a controversial issue, a historian's account of a battle, a critic's reading of a poem, and a psychologist's evaluation of several studies. Secondary sources may contain helpful summaries and interpretations that direct, support, and extend your own thinking. However, most research-writing assignments expect your own ideas to go beyond those in such sources.

Scholarly and popular sources

The scholarship of acknowledged experts is essential for depth, authority, and specificity. Most instructors expect students to emphasize scholarly sources in their research. But the general-interest views and information of popular sources can help you apply more scholarly approaches to daily life.

- **Check the title.** Is it technical, or does it use a general vocabulary?
- **Check the publisher.** Is it a scholarly journal (such as *Cultural Geographies*) or a publisher of scholarly books (such as Harvard University Press), or is it a popular magazine (such as *Consumer Reports* or *Newsweek*) or a publisher of popular books (such as Little, Brown)?
- **Check the length of periodical articles.** Scholarly articles are generally much longer than magazine and newspaper articles.
- **Check the author.** Have you seen the name elsewhere, which might suggest that the author is an expert?
- **Check the electronic address.** Addresses, or URLs, for Internet sources often include an abbreviation that tells you something about the origin of the source: scholarly sources usually end in *edu, org* or *gov,* while popular sources usually end in *com.* See pages 596–97 for more on types of online sources.

Older and newer sources

- **Check the publication date.** For most subjects a combination of older, established sources (such as books) and current sources (such as newspaper articles, interviews, and Web sites) will provide both background and up-to-date information. Only historical subjects or very current subjects (such as social-networking Web sites) require an emphasis on one extreme or another.

Impartial and biased sources

Seek a range of viewpoints. Sources that attempt to be impartial can offer trustworthy facts and an overview of your subject. Sources with clear biases can offer a diversity of opinion. Of course, to discover bias, you may have to read the source carefully (see p. 591); but you can infer quite a bit just from a bibliographical listing.

- **Check the title.** It may reveal something about point of view. (Consider these contrasting titles uncovered by Justin Malik: "Go for the Green" versus "Where the Green Is: Examining the Paradox of Environmentally Conscious Consumption.")
- **Check the author.** You may have heard of the author before as a respected researcher (thus more likely to be objective) or as a leading proponent of a certain view (less likely to be objective).

Note Internet sources must be approached with particular care. See pages 593–603.

Sources with helpful features

Depending on your topic and how far along your research is, you may want to look for sources with features such as illustrations (which can clarify important concepts), bibliographies (which can direct you to other sources), and indexes (which can help you develop keywords for electronic searches; see pp. 563–65).

> **Exercise 41.2 Developing a research strategy**
> Following the suggestions on page 554, write what you already know about the topic you selected in Exercise 41.1 (pp. 553–54), and then frame some questions for which you'll need to find answers. Also in writing, consider the kinds of sources you'll probably need to consult, using the categories given on the preceding pages.

41d Making a working, annotated bibliography

When you begin searching for sources, it may be tempting to pursue each possibility as you come across it. But that approach would prove inefficient and probably ineffective. Instead, you'll want to find out the *full range* of sources available—from scholarly and popular articles to books and Web sites—and then decide on a good number to consult. For a paper of 1800 to 2500 words, try for ten to thirty promising titles as a start.

To keep track of where sources are, compile a **working bibliography** as you uncover possibilities. Record the information for a source as soon as you think you may want to use it, following the guidelines on the next three pages. Then you'll be able to find the source when you're ready to consult it, and you'll have the information needed to cite the source in your paper.

Many instructors ask students to prepare an annotated bibliography that records not only *where* sources are but also *what* they are. Suggestions for compiling an annotated bibliography appear on pages 560 and 590.

1 Tracking source information

You have several options for making a working bibliography:

- **Copy source information by hand on note cards** (usually 3" × 5"), one source to a card. With this system, you can record source information no matter where you are, as long as you have a pen or pencil, and you can easily add, delete, and rearrange sources. Some instructors require that a working bibliography be submitted on note cards.

KEEP AN EYE ON YOUR MATERIALS

A student's research project can be ruined when unattended notes are lost or stolen in the library. Remind students to keep an eye on their materials while they work.

If students have access to bibliographic software, they can use it to record and keep track of their working bibliographies. One of the advantages of using bibliographic software is that students can quickly produce lists of citations arranged alphabetically, chronologically, or by subject. This way, they can quickly evaluate whether they rely too much on works by one particular author; how many sources they have on a particular aspect of their subject; and whether their sources are mostly outdated or whether they have sufficient recent titles.

- **Create the working bibliography on your word processor or handheld computer,** either typing the information yourself or downloading it from online indexes, catalogs, and other sources. You'll be able to sort sources by subject or by author and to copy bibliographic data into your paper when you prepare final source citations.
- **Combine the two systems:** print and cut up computer-generated source listings, and then paste or tape each source on a note card.

Whatever system you use, be sure to record all the information you will need. A downloaded listing, for instance, may look complete but lack the name of the database and other crucial information.

The two records below come from Justin Malik's working bibliography. The first, for a book, Malik handwrote in his research notebook. The second, for a magazine article, Malik downloaded from an online database, printed out, and then annotated with information he knew he would need.

Basic entries for a working bibliography

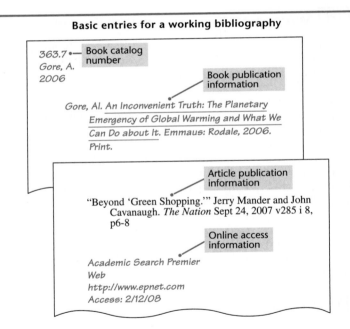

2 Recording source information

When you turn in your paper, you will be expected to attach a list of the sources you have used. So that readers can check or follow up on your sources, your list must include all the information needed to find the sources, in a format readers can understand. The following box shows the information you should record for each type of source so that you will not have to retrace your steps later. See later pages for illustrations of how to locate this information for printed journal articles (659), newspaper articles (661), and books (664) and for Web sites (673), Web journal articles (681), and sources in online databases (682).

Information for a working bibliography

For books

Library call number
Name(s) of author(s), editor(s), translator(s), or others listed
Title and subtitle
Publication data:
  Place of publication
  Publisher's name
  Date of publication
Other important data, such as edition or volume number
Medium (print, Web, etc.)

For periodical articles

Name(s) of author(s)
Title and subtitle of article
Title of periodical
Publication data:
  Volume number and issue number (if any) in which article appears
  Date of issue
  Page numbers on which article appears
Medium (print, Web, etc.)

For electronic sources

Name(s) of author(s)
Title and subtitle of source
Title of Web site, periodical, or other larger work
Publication data, such as data listed above for a book or

article; the publisher or sponsor of a Web site; and the date of release, revision, or online posting
Any publication data for the source in another medium (print, film, etc.)
Format of online source (Web site or page, podcast, e-mail, etc.)
Date you consulted the source
Title of any database used to reach the source
Complete URL (but see the note below)
Digital Object Identifier, if any (for APA style)
Medium (Web, CD-ROM, etc.)

For other sources

Name(s) of author(s), creator(s), or others listed, such as a government department, recording artist, or photographer
Title of work
Format, such as unpublished letter, live performance, or photograph
Publication or production data:
  Publication title
  Publisher's or producer's name
  Date of publication, release, or production
Identifying numbers (if any)
Medium (print, typescript, etc.)

Note MLA documentation style does not require URLs for citations of most electronic sources; other styles do require them. Recording URLs will ensure that you have them if you need them and will make it easy to track down sources if you want to consult them again. For sources you reach through databases, record URLs only if they are usable by others outside your school. Most database URLs are unique to the search or the subscriber.

RESOURCES AND IDEAS

Adler-Kassner, Linda, and Heidi Estrem. "Rethinking Research Writing: Public Literacy in the Composition Classroom." *WPA: Writing Program Administration* 26.3 (2003): 119–31. Print. The authors discuss implementing an inquiry-driven approach to research writing, such as those of Bruce Ballenger, Ken Macrorie, and Bonnie Sunstein and Elizabeth Chiseri-Strater in their ethnographic *FieldWorking* text (3rd ed. Boston: Bedford/St. Martin's, 2007).

Chappell, Virginia A., Randall Hensley, and Elizabeth Simmons-O'Neill. "Beyond Information Retrieval: Transforming Research Assignments into Genuine Inquiry." *Journal of Teaching Writing* 13.2 (1994): 209–24. Print. Describes techniques for teaching students to evaluate sources, develop research questions, and analyze data within a range of disciplinary contexts.

Macrorie, Ken. *The I-Search Paper: Revised Edition of Searching Writing.* Portsmouth: Boynton/Cook, 1988. Print. Macrorie teaches students to conduct "I-search," personally motivated and inspired research using primary sources as well as library work.

Randall, Sally N. "Information Charts: A Strategy for Organizing Student Research." *Journal of Adolescent and Adult Literacy* 39.7 (1996): 536–43. Print. Randall suggests methods for helping students to organize information and plan further research strategies.

Roessig, Lesley. "Making Research Matter." *English Journal* 96.4 (2007): 50–55. Print. Roessig describes an assignment in which she asks students to compile short research pieces to be published for the class on topics related to the novels they read. She argues that context makes research more significant.

Whenever possible, record source information in the correct format for the documentation style you will be using. Then you will be less likely to omit needed information or to confuse dates, numbers, and other data when it's time to write your citations. This book describes four styles: MLA (p. 644), Chicago (p. 760), APA (p. 779), and CSE (p. 811). For others, consult one of the guides listed on pages 779–80 and 811. (Malik's first source record on p. 558 follows MLA style.) See also page 635 for tips on using bibliography software to format source information.

3 Annotating your bibliography

Annotating a working bibliography converts a simple list into a tool for assessing sources. When you discover a possible source, record not only its publication information but also the following:

■ **What you know about the source's content.** Periodical databases and book catalogs generally include abstracts or summaries of sources that can help you with this part of the annotation.

■ **How you think the source may be helpful in your research.** Does it offer expert opinion, statistics, an important example, or a range of views? Does it place your subject in a historical, social, or economic context?

Taking time to prepare thorough annotations can help you discover gaps that may remain in your sources and will later help you decide which sources to pursue in depth. Justin Malik annotated a bibliography entry on his computer with a summary and a note on the source features he thought would be most useful to him:

Entry for an annotated working bibliography

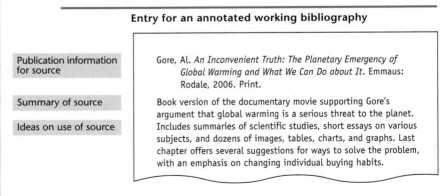

Publication information for source

Gore, Al. *An Inconvenient Truth: The Planetary Emergency of Global Warming and What We Can Do about It.* Emmaus: Rodale, 2006. Print.

Summary of source

Ideas on use of source

Book version of the documentary movie supporting Gore's argument that global warming is a serious threat to the planet. Includes summaries of scientific studies, short essays on various subjects, and dozens of images, tables, charts, and graphs. Last chapter offers several suggestions for ways to solve the problem, with an emphasis on changing individual buying habits.

As you become more familiar with your sources, you can use your initial annotated bibliography to record your evaluation of them and more detailed thoughts on how they fit into your research. See page 590 on this later stage.

Exercise 41.3   Compiling an annotated working bibliography

Prepare an annotated working bibliography of at least ten sources for a research paper on one of the following people or on someone of your own choosing. Begin by limiting the subject to a manageable size, posing a question about a particular characteristic or achievement of the person. Then consult reference works, periodical indexes, the library's book catalog, and the Web. (See pp. 565–88 for more on these resources.) For each source, record complete publication information as well as a summary and a note on the source's potential use.

1. Steven Jobs (a founder of Apple Computer), or another business entrepreneur
2. Ruth Bader Ginsburg, or another Supreme Court justice
3. Emily Dickinson, or another writer
4. Shaquille O'Neal, or another sports figure
5. Isamu Noguchi, or another artist

42

Finding Sources

Once you have discovered a research subject and question, have developed a research strategy, and know how to make an annotated working bibliography, you're ready to find sources. This chapter discusses electronic searches and the kinds of sources, both print and electronic, that are available to you.

Note If you require sources that are not available from your own library, you may be able to obtain them from another library by mail, fax, or computer. Ask your librarian for help, and plan ahead: interlibrary loans can take a week or longer.

42a   Starting with your library's Web site

As you conduct research, the Web will be your gateway to ideas and information. Always start with the Web site of your library, not

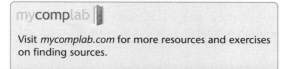

Visit *mycomplab.com* for more resources and exercises on finding sources.

GETTING THE BEST SOURCES

If your students are going to have a library instruction session covering online searching, you might reconnoiter with the reference librarian before your class meets. Give the librarian a list of your students' research questions, so that when class meets, the librarian can help point your students to the most useful sources and search tools.

COMPARING SEARCHES

Ask students to enter the same search phrase into Google and one or more other search engines. Then ask them to compare the source links each search yields.

THE LIBRARY AS OFFICE

If space and library regulations permit, consider holding office hours in the library while students are conducting their research there. Your presence will encourage more consultation between you and your students. This practice is especially useful in conjunction with whatever library orientation programs your school offers first-year students.

MAKING THE LIBRARY ACCESSIBLE

Students are often confused when the library provides both an electronic catalog of its own books and access to online subscription services. They may think that every source they find on a subscription service is in the library, or that searching the library catalog is the same as searching the other databases. Make sure that students understand what kind of information is available from each source.

Also keep in mind that learning to use a new cataloging system (electronic or print) can be frustrating and slow and may involve a series of baffling dead ends. To help students through this process, you might implement a combination of the following:

Plan frequent trips to the library (or allow for ongoing work with research databases in your own electronic classroom).

Assign students to ongoing research teams, partnering students who are more skilled

---

A tip for researchers

Take advantage of two valuable resources offered by your library:

■ **An orientation,** which introduces the library's resources and explains how to reach and use the Web site and the print holdings.
■ **Reference librarians,** whose job it is to help you and others navigate the library's resources. Even very experienced researchers often consult reference librarians.

---

with a public search engine such as *Google*. (*Google Scholar*, a tool that searches for scholarly articles, is discussed on p. 573.) The library's site will lead you to vast resources, including books, periodical articles, and reference works that aren't available on the open Web. More important, unlike many sources you can find using a public search engine, every source you find on the library's site will have passed through filters to ensure its value. A scholarly journal article, for instance, undergoes at least three successive reviews: first, subject-matter experts deem it worth publishing in the journal; next, a database vendor deems the journal worth including in the database; and finally, your school's librarians deem the database worth subscribing to.

Google and other search engines may seem more user-friendly than the library's Web site and may seem to return plenty of sources for you to work with. Many of the sources may indeed be reliable and relevant to your research, but many more will not be. In the end, a library Web search will be more efficient and more effective than a direct Web search. (For help with evaluating sources from any resource, see pp. 590–603.)

Note Start with your library's Web site, but don't stop there. Many books, periodicals, and other excellent sources are available only on library shelves, not online, and most instructors expect research papers to be built to some extent on these resources. When you spot promising print sources while browsing a library's online databases, make records of them and then look them up at the library. You can also browse the bookshelves to discover sources (see p. 570).

42b Searching electronically

Searching electronically requires planning. A too-casual search can miss helpful sources while returning hundreds, even thousands, of irrelevant sources. Become familiar with the kinds of electronic sources available to you and with the different search strategies for each (below). And take time early in your research to develop **keywords** that name your subject for databases and Web search engines (p. 564).

 Anticipating the kinds of electronic sources

Your school's library, its Web site, and the open Web offer several kinds of electronic resources that are suitable for academic research.

- **The library's catalog of holdings** is a database that lists all the resources that the library owns or subscribes to: books, journals, magazines, newspapers, reference works, and more. The catalog may also include the holdings of other school libraries nearby or in your state.
- **Online databases** include indexes, bibliographies, and other reference works. They are your main route to articles in periodicals, providing publication information, summaries, and often full text (see below). Your library subscribes to the databases and makes them available through its Web site. (You may also discover databases directly on the Web, but, again, the library is the more productive starting place.)
- **Databases on CD-ROM** include the same information as online databases, but they must be read at a library computer terminal. Increasingly, libraries are moving away from CD-ROMs in favor of online databases.
- **Full-text resources** contain the entire contents of articles, book chapters, even whole books. The library's databases provide access to the full text of many listed sources. In addition, many Web sites, such as those for government agencies, offer the full text of articles, reports, and other publications.

2 **Searching databases and the open Web**

To develop keywords it helps to understand an important difference in how library databases and the open Web work:

- **A database indexes sources by authors, titles, publication years, and its own subject headings.** The subject headings reflect the database's directory of terms and are assigned by people who have read the sources. You can find these subject headings by using your own keywords until you locate a promising source. The information for the source will list the headings under which the database indexes the source and others like it. (See p. 575 for an illustration.) You can then use those headings for further searches.
- **A Web search engine seeks your keywords in the titles and texts of sites.** The process is entirely electronic, so the results

with computers in mentoring relationships with those who are tackling the electronic medium for the first time.

Demonstrate (or ask your research librarian to demonstrate) common dead ends, such as keyword searches that generate plentiful sources in one database and no sources in another.

Frequently direct the students to bring their research journals to class and to report their progress and their setbacks, so that they understand that they are sharing a learning process.

Remind students to vary electronic information with material found in print sources (for example, the bibliography of one good article can often yield several more productive sources and start the student off on a new set of electronic searches).

KEYWORD BRAINSTORMING

Have students work together to brainstorm keywords that might work for each student's subject.

HANDS-ON LEARNING

The barrage of information about various types of sources available through the library can be overwhelming to your students, and they may not retain it unless they have a chance to use the databases, search engines, and catalogs themselves. If you have time, consider an experiential approach rather than a long lecture about sources and how to use them. Create a worksheet of questions for students to answer, working in groups. The students will be the detectives, and will have to discover sources and figure out how to use them in order to complete the worksheet. You can give strategic hints along the way, and at the end of the exercise ask them to report on what they have discovered.

TO WORKS CITED

If your students have bibliographic software, they may be able to e-mail source citations to themselves in a compatible format, so that they can get the information into their bibliographies without retyping. Remind them to double-check citations for corrections before turning in finished work, however.

KEYWORD LISTS

Have students meet you in the library or the electronic classroom with individual lists of keywords in their areas of interest. Have students try their keywords in several databases, noting subheadings of interest and revising the keywords in places where a database or search engine works from a different system of subject headings. The goal of the exercise is not only for students to generate the variations on keywords that may be needed for different databases but also to narrow and define their topics further.

RESOURCES AND IDEAS

Anderson, Daniel, Bret Benjamin, Christopher Busiel, and Bill Paredes-Holt. *Teaching Online: Internet Research, Conversation, and Composition.* New York: Longman, 1998. Print. A useful and practical guide to electronic research; in particular, see Chapter 5, "The Electronic Library."

Eagleton, Maya, and Elizabeth Dobler. *Reading the Web: Strategies for Internet Inquiry.* New York: Guilford, 2007. Print. The authors draw on theory and current research to outline a plan for Web literacy and offer clear suggestions on how to teach students to use the Internet effectively.

Helms-Park, Rena, and Paul Stapleton. "How the Views of Faculty Can Inform Undergraduate Web-Based Research: Implications for Academic Writing." *Computers and Composition* 23.4 (2006): 444–61. Print. The authors study how faculty assess the credibility of Web sources and discuss the implications for students. They also include checklists students can use when evaluating Web sources.

Mark, Beth L., and Trudi E. Jacobson. "Teaching Anxious Students Skills for the Electronic Li-

from a search engine will depend on how well your keywords describe your subject and anticipate the words used in sources. If you describe your subject too broadly or describe it specifically but don't match the vocabulary in relevant sources, your search will turn up few relevant sources and probably many that aren't relevant.

3 Refining keywords

Every database and search engine provides a system that you can use to refine your keywords for a productive search. The basic operations appear in the box below, but resources do differ. For instance, some assume that *AND* should link two or more keywords, while others provide options specifying "Must contain all the words" and other equivalents for the operations in the box. You can learn a search engine's system by consulting its Advanced Search page.

Ways to refine keywords

Most databases and many search engines work with **Boolean operators**, terms or symbols that allow you to expand or limit your keywords and thus your search.

■ Use *AND* or + to narrow the search by including only sources that use all the given words. The keywords *green AND products* request only the sources in the shaded area:

■ Use *NOT* or – ("minus") to narrow the search by excluding irrelevant words. *Green AND products NOT guide* excludes sources that use the word *guide:*

■ Use *OR* to broaden the search by giving alternate keywords. *Green AND products OR goods* allows for sources that use a synonym for *products:*

- **Use parentheses or quotation marks to form search phrases.** For instance, *(green products)* requests the exact phrase, not the separate words. Only sources using *green products* would turn up.
- **Use wild cards to permit different versions of the same word.** In *consum**, for instance, the wild card * indicates that sources may include *consume, consumer, consumerism,* and *consumption* as well as *consumptive, consumedly,* and *consummate.* The example suggests that you have to consider all the variations allowed by a wild card and whether it opens up your search too much. If you seek only two or three from many variations, you may be better off using *OR: consumption OR consumerism.* (Note that some systems use ?, :, or + for a wild card instead of *.)
- **Be sure to spell your keywords correctly.** Some search tools will look for close matches or approximations, but correct spelling gives you the best chance of finding relevant sources.

Note You will probably have to use trial and error in developing your keywords. Because different databases have different directories and many search tools have no directory at all, you should count on occasionally running dry (turning up few or no sources) or hitting uncontrollable gushers (turning up hundreds or thousands of mostly irrelevant sources). But the process is not busywork —far from it. Besides leading you eventually to worthwhile sources, it can also teach you a great deal about your subject: how you can or should narrow it, how it is and is not described by others, what others consider interesting or debatable about it, and what the major arguments are.

42c | Finding reference works

Reference works, often available online, include encyclopedias, dictionaries, digests, bibliographies, indexes, atlases, and handbooks. Your research *must* go beyond reference works; indeed, many instructors discourage students from relying on such sources for ideas and information in final papers. But reference works can help you get started:

- They can help you decide whether your subject interests you and meets the requirements for a research paper (pp. 551–52).

brary." *College Teaching* 43.1 (1995): 28–31. Print. Suggests do's and don't's when introducing students to electronic library databases.

Selfe, Cynthia L., and Richard J. Selfe, Jr. "The Politics of the Interface: Power and Its Exercise in Electronic Contact Zones." *College Composition and Communication* 45.4 (1994): 480–504. Print. The authors probe some of the larger cultural issues surrounding technological innovations such as the World Wide Web, including their political and ideological ramifications for education.

Sidler, Michelle. "Web Research and Genres in Online Databases: When the Glossy Page Disappears." *Computers & Composition* 19.1 (2002): 57–70. Print. Sidler discusses the difficulties students often face identifying genres and evaluating the credibility of sources from online databases. She suggests metaphors to help students distinguish among types of sources.

Guide to research sources

Reference works: helpful for summaries of topics and information for further research

- General encyclopedias *567*
- Specialized encyclopedias, dictionaries, bibliographies *567*
- Unabridged dictionaries and special dictionaries on language *568*
- Biographical reference works *568*
- Atlases and gazetteers *569*
- Almanacs and yearbooks *569*

General books: literary works, nonfiction surveys, in-depth studies, and other materials, available for circulation

- The library catalog *569*
- Search strategy *570*
- References to books *571*

Periodicals: magazines, journals, and newspapers, containing detailed and current information

- Periodical databases *572*
- Abstracts *576*
- Helpful databases *576*
- Locating articles *577*

The Web: access to your school's library holdings and databases, other libraries, publications, organizations, governments, and individuals

- Search engines *578*
- Sample search *580*

Other online sources:

- E-mail *582*
- Blogs *582*
- Discussion lists *582*
- Web forums and newsgroups *583*

Government publications: practical advice, raw data, reports, and other information *583*

Images, audio, and video: photographs, paintings, graphs, speeches, interviews, performances, news footage, and more *584*

Your own sources: interviews, observations, surveys, and other primary sources you create *586*

- They can direct you to more detailed sources on your subject.
- They can help you refine keywords for electronic searches, giving you the terminology of the field you're researching.
- They can identify the main debates in a field and the proponents of each side.

Justin Malik's use of reference works illustrates how helpful such sources can be as a starting point, even for a topic as current as green products. Malik first consulted *Dictionary of Environment and Development* (to get some background on environmental issues) and *Encyclopedia of Advertising* (to explore the recent history of promotional campaigns for green products).

The following lists give the types of reference works. Ask a reference librarian if you're unsure of where to start. The librarian can also advise you which sources are available through the library's Web site, in print at the library, or directly via the Web.

General encyclopedias

General encyclopedias give brief overviews and bibliographies. Covering all fields, they are convenient but very limited.

Encyclopedia Americana
Encyclopaedia Britannica
Random House Encyclopedia

Note The Web-based encyclopedia *Wikipedia* (found at *wikipedia.org*) is one of the largest reference sites on the Internet. Like any encyclopedia, *Wikipedia* can provide background information for research on a topic; but unlike other encyclopedias, *Wikipedia* is a **wiki,** a kind of Web site that can be contributed to or edited by anyone, not just reliable experts. Ask your instructor whether *Wikipedia* is an acceptable source before you use it. If you do use it, you must carefully evaluate any information you find, using the guidelines on pages 596–600.

Specialized encyclopedias, dictionaries, bibliographies

A specialized encyclopedia, dictionary, or bibliography generally covers a single field or subject. These works will give you more detailed and more technical information than a general reference work will, and many of them (especially bibliographies) will direct you to particular books and articles on your subject. For information on specialized reference works in various disciplines, consult lists elsewhere in this book:

- **Literature** (p. 741)
- **Other humanities,** including history, the arts, philosophy, and religion (p. 757)
- **Social sciences,** such as business and economics, criminal justice, education, and psychology (p. 777)
- **Natural and applied sciences,** such as biology, engineering, mathematics, and physics (p. 808)

Several databases allow you to search for reference entries across many specialized sources:

COMPARING ENCYCLOPEDIAS

Working with a partner, students can look up a subject in both a general encyclopedia and a specialized encyclopedia. They will quickly discover differences in scope and depth of coverage.

REVIEWING WIKIPEDIA ENTRIES

Assemble students in their research groups and assign each group a topic. Have them find and review the relevant Wikipedia entry for their topic. Then, ask each group to consult one or two other (non-wiki) sources about their topic. Try to guide them toward credible, authoritative sources. Have them compare the Wikipedia entry to the other sources. Are there differences in the entries in terms of degree of coverage or attitude toward the topic? Is any significant information left out of the Wikipedia entry? Each group should report their findings to the class. This exercise can demonstrate to students that Wikipedia can be a valuable starting point for research, but it isn't always a credible, objective source.

QUICK ACCESS DICTIONARIES

Some dictionaries can be accessed online for free, or your library may hold a subscription. Your students may find it helpful to bookmark a dictionary Web site and use it when they need to look up a word.

CHECK PUBLICATION DATES

Reference books are expensive, and few college libraries can afford to update all the references in their collections all the time. Remind students to check the editions and publication dates of the reference sources they use; the information in older works may need to be updated or supplemented. Online versions of reference works may be updated more frequently.

Essay and General Literature Index. Lists tens of thousands of articles and essays that appear in books (rather than periodicals) and that might not be listed elsewhere.

Oxford Reference Online. A compilation of general and specialized dictionaries, encyclopedias, and other sources.

Reference Universe. Searches the indexes and article titles in subject encyclopedias and other reference sources in a variety of disciplines.

Unabridged dictionaries and special dictionaries on language

Unabridged dictionaries are more comprehensive than college or abridged dictionaries. Special dictionaries give authoritative information on aspects of language. (See Chapter 38 for more on the kinds of dictionaries and how to use them.)

Unabridged dictionaries

A Dictionary of American English on Historical Principles
The Oxford English Dictionary
Webster's Third New International Dictionary of the English Language

Special dictionaries

R. W. Burchfield, ed., *The New Fowler's Modern English Usage*
Frederic G. Cassidy et al., eds., *Dictionary of American Regional English*
Robert L. Chapman, ed., *Roget's International Thesaurus*
Bryan A. Garner, *A Dictionary of Modern American Usage*
J. E. Lighter, ed., *Historical Dictionary of American Slang*
Charles T. Onions et al., eds., *The Oxford Dictionary of English Etymology*

Biographical reference works

If you want to learn about someone's life, achievements, credentials, or position, or if you want to learn the significance of a name you've come across, consult one of the following reference works:

American Men and Women of Science
American National Biography
Biography and Genealogy Master Index (citations of biographical entries in more than 3000 reference works)
Contemporary Authors
Current Biography
Dictionary of American Biography
Dictionary of American Negro Biography
Dictionary of Literary Biography
Dictionary of National Biography (British)
Dictionary of Scientific Biography
Marquis Who's Who (nearly twenty publications organized by geography, profession, and other categories)
Notable American Women
Webster's New Biographical Dictionary
World Authors

Atlases and gazetteers

Atlases are bound collections of maps; gazetteers are geographical dictionaries.

Britannica World Atlas
National Atlas of the United States of America
National Geographic Atlas of the World
Times Atlas of the World
Times Atlas of World History
Webster's New Geographical Dictionary

Almanacs and yearbooks

Both almanacs and yearbooks are annual compilations of facts. Yearbooks record information about the previous year in a country, field, or other subject. Almanacs give facts about a variety of fields.

Americana Annual
Britannica Book of the Year
Facts on File Yearbook
Time Almanac
US Bureau of the Census, *Statistical Abstract of the United States*
World Almanac and Book of Facts

42d   Finding books

Books can provide background information, subject surveys, popular views of culture, statements of scholarly theory, research results—in short, a broad range of secondary and primary sources (see p. 555).

1   Using the library catalog

Your library's catalog is searchable at terminals in the library and via the library's Web site. With *WorldCat*, available through most libraries, you can also search for specific books in the catalogs of tens of thousands of libraries worldwide. You may be able to borrow books from another library in your area. Ask a librarian for assistance with remote searches and loans. And allow time for a book to be sent after your request.

All book catalogs contain similar information, though it may be organized differently from one library to the next. By far the most widely used format derives from the Library of Congress cataloging system and includes author, title, publisher, date of publication, description (number of pages, size, and other data), subject headings the book is listed under, and the library's call number (which directs you to the book's location in the stacks). See page 571 for a complete book record showing all this information.

COMPUTER ACTIVITY

BROWSING NEARBY BOOKS

Once your students have located a book relevant to their topics, they might try browsing the nearby shelves for additional titles. Some library e-catalogs will allow you to do this onscreen.

2 Using a search strategy

Unless you seek a specific author or title, you'll want to find books with a subject or keyword search of the library's catalog. In a subject search, you start with headings found in *Library of Congress Subject Headings* (*LCSH*), the massive directory under which the Library of Congress catalogs books. In a keyword search, you start with your own description of your subject as a way of locating appropriate *LCSH* headings.

The keyword approach is illustrated here by part of Justin Malik's catalog search. In his initial keyword search (screen 1), Malik used *environmentalism and products*. The search produced a number of promising books (screen 2), including the first one, *Building the Green Economy*. The complete record for this book (screen 3) showed that it was indexed under three *LCSH* subject headings: *Sustainable development—Citizen participation; Environmentalism—Economic aspects;* and *Green products*. Malik then used these headings to search the catalog further.

Note In addition to searching the book catalog, you can also browse the library shelves. The first part of the call number for a promising title (*HC79.E5* in the full record opposite) will lead you to other books on the same subject that a catalog search might miss.

---

1. Initial keyword search of a book catalog

| Easy Search | **Books** | Journals | Reserves | Media | Other |

FIND BOOKS IN THE LIBRARY AND ON THE WEB

environmentalism and products • | Keyword ⬍ | (Go) **More Options**
Find items by keyword, title, or author. → Keywords

---

2. Book catalog search results

#	Full Title	Date
☐ 1	Building the green economy : success stories from the grassroots / Kevin Danaher, Shannon Biggs, Jason Mark.	2007
	Library Location: Undergrad reserves Call Number: HC79.E5 D3532	
☐ 2	Design e² [videorecording] : the economies of being environmentally conscious / director, Tad Fettig ; series producer, Elizabeth Westrate ; narration writers, Mark Decena, John Kenney ; produced by kontentreal, LLC.	2006
	Library Location: Architecture & Art Vault [non-circulating] Call Number: NA2542.36 .D48	
☐ 3	Environmental marketing : strategies, practice, theory, and research / Michael Jay Polonsky, Alma T. Mintu-Wimsatt, editors.	1995
	Library Location: Business & Economics Call Number: HF5413 .E58	

3. Book catalog full record

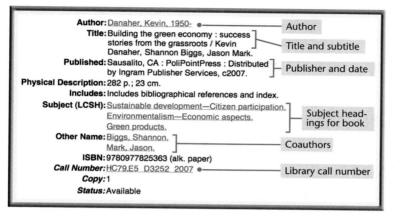

Author: Danaher, Kevin, 1950- — Author
Title: Building the green economy : success stories from the grassroots / Kevin Danaher, Shannon Biggs, Jason Mark. — Title and subtitle
Published: Sausalito, CA : PoliPointPress : Distributed by Ingram Publisher Services, c2007. — Publisher and date
Physical Description: 282 p. ; 23 cm.
Includes: Includes bibliographical references and index.
Subject (LCSH): Sustainable development—Citizen participation. Environmentalism—Economic aspects. Green products. — Subject headings for book
Other Name: Biggs, Shannon. Mark, Jason. — Coauthors
ISBN: 9780977825363 (alk. paper)
Call Number: HC79.E5 D3252 2007 — Library call number
Copy: 1
Status: Available

3 Using references to books

The following can help you identify books that have information about your topic:

- *WorldCat*, mentioned earlier, allows you to conduct subject, author, title, and keyword searches of library catalogs around the world. You might, for example, want to know if the author of an encyclopedia article has published any relevant books since the date of the encyclopedia. You could search for the author's name on *WorldCat* to find out.
- **Review indexes** list published reviews of books and can help you evaluate whether a book is relevant to your subject:

  Book Review Digest Plus. Summarizes and indexes reviews of books.
  Book Review Index

  For specialized review indexes, see pages 778 (social sciences) and 809 (natural and applied sciences).

42e Finding periodicals

Periodicals include newspapers, journals, and magazines. Newspapers, the easiest to recognize, are useful for detailed accounts of past and current events. Journals and magazines can be harder to distinguish, but their differences are important. Most college instructors expect students' research to rely more on journals than on magazines.

Journals	Magazines
Examples	
American Anthropologist, Journal of Black Studies, Journal of Chemical Education	*The New Yorker, Time, Rolling Stone, People*
Availability	
Mainly through college and university libraries	Public libraries, newsstands, and bookstores
Purpose	
Advance knowledge in a particular field	Express opinion, inform, or entertain
Authors	
Specialists in the field	May or may not be specialists in their subjects
Readers	
Often specialists in the field	Members of the general public or a subgroup with a particular interest
Source citations	
Source citations always included	Source citations rarely included
Length of articles	
Usually long, ten pages or more	Usually short, fewer than ten pages
Appearance	
Bland, with black-only type, little or no decoration, and only illustrations that directly amplify the text, such as graphs	Generally lively, with color, decoration (headings, sidebars, and other elements), and illustrations (drawings, photographs)
Frequency of publication	
Quarterly or less often	Weekly, biweekly, or monthly
Pagination of issues	
May be paged separately (like a magazine) or may be paged sequentially throughout an annual volume, so that issue number 3 (the third issue of the year) could open on page 327.	Paged separately, each beginning on page 1

1 Using periodical databases

Periodical databases index the articles in journals, magazines, and newspapers. Often these databases include abstracts, or summaries, of the articles, and they may offer the full texts of the articles as well. Your library subscribes to many periodical databases and to services that offer multiple databases. (See p. 576 for a list.)

Most databases and services will be searchable through the library's Web site.

Note The search engine *Google* is developing *Google Scholar*, a search engine at *scholar.google.com* that seeks out scholarly articles. It is particularly useful for subjects that range across disciplines, for which discipline-specific databases can be too limited. *Google Scholar* can connect to your library's holdings if you tell it to do so under Scholar Preferences. Keep in mind, however, that *Google Scholar*'s searches are not as yet exhaustive. Your library probably subscribes to most of the periodicals searched by *Google Scholar*, so begin there.

Selection of databases

To decide which databases to consult, you'll need to consider what you're looking for:

- **How broadly and deeply should you search?** Periodical databases vary widely in what they index. Some, such as *ProQuest Research Library*, cover many subjects but don't index the full range of periodicals in each subject. Others, such as *Historical Abstracts*, cover a single subject but then include most of the available periodicals and other resources as well. If your subject ranges across disciplines—as Justin Malik's subject of green consumerism does—then start with a broad database. If your subject focuses on a particular discipline, then start with a narrower database.

- **Which databases most likely include the kinds of resources you need?** The Web sites of most libraries allow you to narrow a database search to a particular kind of periodical (such as newspapers or journals) or to a particular discipline. You can then discover each database's focus by checking the description of the database (sometimes labeled "Help" or "Guide") or the list of indexed resources (sometimes labeled "Publications" or "Index"). The description will also tell you the time period the database covers, so you'll know whether you also need to consult older print indexes at the library.

Database searches

When you first search a database, use your own keywords to locate sources. The general procedure is discussed on pages 564–65. Your goal is to find at least one source that seems just right for your subject, so that you can then see what subject headings the database itself uses for such sources. Using one or more of those headings will focus and speed your search.

Justin Malik first searched *EBSCOhost Academic Search Premier*, a broad database covering more than 4500 periodicals. His keywords *green and products* returned more than 7000 articles, and none on the first page dealt with his subject. He then tried *green AND products AND environment,* getting fewer returns but still nothing usable on the first page. He stopped there to brainstorm other terms that might work better, some of them synonyms and some narrower:

green	products	environment
responsible	shopping	environmentalism
conscious	consumption	pollution
eco-friendly	advertising	waste
sustainable	economics	
	business	

The three screen shots here show Malik's use of one combination of these terms, *conscious AND consumption AND environment.* The first three returns (screen 2) included one source clearly related to Malik's subject. The full record for the source (screen 3) provided an abstract of the source along with the database's headings for the article. Malik had seen one of these headings, *consumerism,* in his background research, but he had thought the term might be too specialized to produce good results. Now he tried it on *Academic Search Premier* and found dozens of additional source possibilities. To broaden his search, he also tried some of the subject headings for these other sources, such as *Environmental economics and sustainable development—citizen participation.* When he thought he had found a good range of possible sources, including government publications as well as scholarly and popular articles, he moved on to other databases.

1. Initial keyword search of a periodical database

2. Partial keyword search results

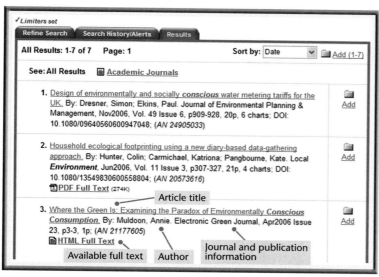

3. Full article record with abstract

Title: Where the Green Is: Examining the Paradox of Environmentally *Conscious Consumption.* — Article title [Find More Like This]

Authors: Muldoon, Annie *goinggreenottawa@yahoo.ca* — Author

Source: Electronic Green Journal; Apr2006 Issue 23, p3-3, 1p — Journal and publication information

Document Type: Article

Subject Terms: *GREEN marketing
*CONSUMERISM
*GREEN products
*ENVIRONMENTAL economics
*CONSUMER protection
*RECYCLED products
*CONSUMER goods
*NATURAL products
*MARKETING — Database subject headings

Abstract — Abstract
The article discusses issues related to green consumerism. It also examines the merits and shortcomings of green consumerism. Green consumerism is defined as the purchasing and non-purchasing decisions made by consumers, based at least partly on environmental or social criteria. There is much debate about the value of green consumerism. Critics claim that environmentally conscientious shopping has negligible effects, does not address wider issues relating to the creation of needs and capitalism, and has been co-opted by advertisers as a *marketing* technique. One of the problems with green consumption, according to its detractors, is that it supports the corporate ideal that places environmental responsibility on the shoulders of individuals. Government regulation needs to be a part of the green consumerism movement. One way for this to happen is for governments to gradually increase the prices of natural resources, until they begin to reflect their full cost. Another possibility is government certified eco-labelling for products that are proven to exert less of a strain on the natural *environment.*

Persistent link to this record: http://search.ebscohost.com/login.aspx?direct=true&db=aph&AN=21177605&site=ehost-live

Database: Academic Search Premier — Database

Many databases allow you to limit your search to so-called peer-reviewed or refereed journals—that is, scholarly journals whose articles have been reviewed before publication by experts in the field and then revised by the author. (Malik's initial search on *EBSCOhost Academic Search Premier* included this limitation, as shown in screen 1, p. 574.) Limiting your search to peer-reviewed journals can help you navigate huge databases that might otherwise return scores of unusable articles from other kinds of periodicals.

Note As you follow leads in online indexes, it's easy to lose track of what database you're using. You'll need this information for any article you obtain online, so make sure you have it. If you print search records or e-mail them to yourself, the database information will appear on the record along with other bibliographic information (see screen 3 on the previous page).

The use of abstracts

The full article record on the previous page shows a key feature of many databases' periodical listings: an abstract that summarizes the article. Describing research methods, conclusions, and other information, an abstract can tell you whether you want to pursue an article and thus save you time. However, the abstract cannot replace the actual article. If you want to use the work as a source, you must consult the full text, as described opposite.

Helpful databases

The list below includes databases to which academic libraries commonly subscribe. Some of these databases—for instance, *ProQuest Research Library* and *EBSCOhost Academic Search*—cover much the same material, so your library may not subscribe to all of them.

Note More specific lists of indexes for academic disciplines appear later in this book: see pages 741 (literature), 759 (other humanities), 778 (social sciences), and 809 (natural and applied sciences).

> *EBSCOhost Academic Search.* A periodical index covering magazines and journals in the social sciences, sciences, arts, and humanities. Many articles are available full-text.
>
> *InfoTrac Expanded Academic.* The Gale Group's general periodical index covering the social sciences, sciences, arts, and humanities as well as national news periodicals. It includes full-text articles.
>
> *LexisNexis Academic.* An index of news and business, legal, and reference information, with full-text articles. *LexisNexis* includes international, national, and regional newspapers, newsmagazines, legal and business publications, and court cases.
>
> *ProQuest Research Library.* A periodical index covering the sciences, social sciences, arts, and humanities, including many full-text articles.

While using databases like these, you may want to consult a **citation index** to see what has been written *about* an article or a book, as when one scholar comments on the work of another. The three main citation indexes are *Arts and Humanities Citation Index, Social Science Citation Index,* and *Science Citation Index.* All three are available on the database *ISI Web of Science,* which many libraries subscribe to.

2 Locating the articles in periodicals

Many article listings you find will include or link directly to the full text of the article, which you'll be able to read online and print or e-mail to yourself. If the full text is not available online, you'll need to consult the periodical itself. Usually the article listing will also say whether the periodical is available in your library. If you don't see this information, then consult the library's list of periodicals (often called *serials*) either in the main catalog or in a separate catalog.

Your library probably holds recent issues of print periodicals in the periodicals room. Back issues are usually stored elsewhere, in one of three forms:

- **In bound volumes**
- **On** *microfilm,* a filmstrip showing pages side by side
- **On** *microfiche,* a sheet of film with pages arranged in rows and columns.

Consulting periodicals stored on microfilm or microfiche requires using a special machine, or "reader," with which you locate the page and project it on a screen. (Some readers are also attached to scanners or photocopiers.) Any member of the library's staff will show you how to operate the reader.

If the periodical you seek is not available in your library, you may be able to obtain the article by interlibrary loan. The article may arrive online, by mail, or by fax, and there may be a fee for the service. Even electronic loans can sometimes take a week or more, so place your order early.

Note Many periodicals are available both online and in print, and most documentation styles require you to specify which version you consulted. For scholarly journals, the two versions are likely to be identical in content though not in format: for instance, the online version may not include the print version's page breaks and numbers. (However, a full-text version in PDF format reproduces the actual pages of the print journal. To open PDF files, you may need to download a program called *Acrobat Reader.*) For newspapers and magazines, the two versions often differ more: for instance, the online version may be shorter or longer than the print version, may contain fewer illustrations, or may include links to other resources.

42f Finding sources on the Web

As an academic researcher, you enter the Web in two ways: through your library's Web site, and through public search engines such as *Yahoo!* and *Google.* The library entrance, covered in the preceding sections, is your main path to the books and periodicals that, for most subjects, should make up most of your sources. The public entrance, discussed here, can lead to a wealth of information and ideas, but it also has a number of disadvantages:

- **The Web is a wide-open network.** Anyone with the right hardware and software can place information on the Internet, and even a carefully conceived search can turn up sources with widely varying reliability: journal articles, government documents, scholarly data, term papers written by high school students, sales pitches masked as objective reports, wild theories. You must be especially diligent about evaluating Internet sources (see pp. 593–603).
- **The Web changes constantly.** No search engine can keep up with the Web's daily additions and deletions, and a source you find today may be different or gone tomorrow. You should not put off consulting an online source that you think you may want to use. If it seems appropriate for your needs, take notes from it or (if the source allows) download it to your own computer. Be sure to record complete source information at the same time (see p. 559 for a list of what to record).
- **The Web provides limited information on the past.** Sources dating from before the 1980s or even more recently probably will not appear on the Web.
- **The Web is not all-inclusive.** Most books and many periodicals are available only via the library, not directly via the Web.

Clearly, the Web warrants cautious use. It should not be the only resource you work with.

Note Open-source wikis, such as *Wikipedia* and *SourceWatch,* are Web sites that can be contributed to and edited by anyone. Ask your instructor whether wikis are acceptable sources before using one, and evaluate any information you find on a wiki using the guidelines on pages 593–600.

1 Using a search engine

To find sources on the Web, you use a **search engine** that catalogs Web sites in a series of directories and conducts keyword searches. Generally, use a directory when you haven't yet refined your topic or you want a general overview. Use keywords when you have refined your topic and you seek specific information.

Current search engines

Dozens of search engines are available. The box below lists the currently most popular engines. (To reach any of them, enter its URL in the Address or Location field of your Web browser.)

Web search engines

The features of search engines change often, and new ones appear constantly. For the latest on search engines, see the links collected by *Easy Searcher* at *www.easysearcher.com.*

Directories that review sites

BUBL Link (bubl.ac.uk)
Internet Public Library (ipl.org/div/subject)
Internet Scout Project (scout.wisc.edu/archives)
Librarians' Internet Index (lii.org)

Search engines

AlltheWeb (alltheweb.com)
AltaVista (altavista.com)
Ask.com (ask.com)
Dogpile (dogpile.com)
Google (google.com)
Livesearch (livesearch.com)
MetaCrawler (metacrawler.com)
Yahoo! (yahoo.com)

Note For a good range of reliable sources, try out more than a single search engine, perhaps as many as four or five. No search engine can catalog the entire Web—indeed, even the most powerful engine may not include half the sites available at any given time, and most engines include only a fifth or less. In addition, most search engines accept paid placements, giving higher billing to sites that pay a fee. These so-called sponsored links are usually marked as such, but they can compromise a search engine's method for arranging sites in response to your keywords.

Customized searches

The home page of a search engine includes a field for you to type your keywords into. Generally, it will also include an Advanced Search link that you can use to customize your search. For instance, you may be able to select a range of dates, a language, or a number of results to see. Advanced Search will also explain how to use operators such as *AND* and *NOT* to limit or expand your search.

COMPUTER ACTIVITY

FINDING GOOD SEARCH TERMS

Have your students conduct a search on their own research topics. They might begin by brainstorming some search terms. Like Justin Malik, they may find it necessary to modify their search strategies, so remind them to try different search engines and to look for likely search terms as they go. The assignment ends with a report to you on how they conducted the search and what they found.

RESOURCES AND IDEAS

Carbone, Nick. *Writing Online: A Student's Guide to the Internet and World Wide Web.* 3rd ed. New York: Houghton, 2000. Print. This guide covers many aspects of online research including finding and evaluating sources and documenting Web materials.

Davis, Chris. "The I-Search Paper Goes Global: Using the Internet as a Research Tool." *English Journal* 84.6 (1995): 27–33. Print. Davis shows how the Internet enhances students' abilities to develop and follow through on their own research interests.

Helms-Park, Rena, Pavlina Radia, and Paul Stapleton. "A Preliminary Assessment of *Google Scholar* as a Source of EAP Students' Research Materials." *The Internet and Higher Education* 10.1 (2007): 65–76. Print. The authors facilitated an independent rating of sources compiled by L2 learners using various search methods. They found that sources located using *Google Scholar* did not differ in quality from those found using the library's electronic resources, whereas sources found using *Google* and many electronic sources were qualitatively different.

Jones, John. "Patterns of Revision in Online Writing: A Study of Wikipedia's Featured Articles." *Written Communication* 25.2 (2008): 262–89. Print. Jones discusses theories of revision and applies them to Wikipedia articles, analyzing the types of changes made to articles.

Search records

Your Web browser includes functions that allow you to keep track of Web sources and your search:

■ **Use *Favorites* or *Bookmarks* to save site addresses as links.** Click one of these terms near the top of the browser screen to add a site you want to return to. A favorite or bookmark remains on file until you delete it.

■ **Use *History* to locate sites you have visited before.** The browser records sites for a certain period, such as a day, a week, or a month. (You can set the period in the browser's Tools menu.) If you forgot to bookmark a site, click History or Go to recover the site from the search history.

Note If you do Web research on a public computer, such as in a lab at school, your favorites and history probably will not be saved from one day to the next. To track sources that you may want to return to, copy the site URLs and e-mail them to yourself.

2 Following a sample Web search

For his initial search of the Web, Justin Malik started on *Google* with the keywords *green consumption*. But the search returned more than 3.4 *million* items, as shown on screen 1 opposite. Although some sources on the first page looked promising, Malik realized he had to alter his strategy to get more focused results. Following the same procedure he had used with a periodical database, Malik experimented with combinations of synonyms and narrower terms. The keywords *"green consumption" "environmental issues"* did refine the search but still produced 2400 results.

From *Google*'s Advanced Search help, Malik learned that he could specify what he wanted to see in the URLs of sources. Adding *site:.org* limited the results to nonprofit organizations, whose URLs end in *.org*. With *"green consumption" "environmental issues" site:.org*, Malik received 387 results (see screen 2). Although the number was still large, the nonprofit origin combined with *Google*'s criteria for ranking sources gave Malik confidence that the first fifty or so would serve his needs. He continued to limit the search by replacing *site:.org* with *site:.gov* (government publications), *site:.edu* (educational institutions), and *site:.com* (commercial organizations).

Knowing that no search engine catalogs every Web site, Malik also tried his successful keywords on two other engines, *AlltheWeb* and *Dogpile*. The *AlltheWeb* search turned up an additional promising site among the first thirty. The *Dogpile* search, which worked through multiple search engines, returned about sixty more items, including many irrelevant ones but also one more possible source.

Malik's Web search illustrates the trial-and-error approach required to refine keywords so that they locate worthwhile sources. Almost any Web search will require similar persistence and patience.

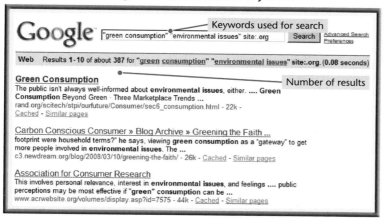

1. First *Google* search results

2. *Google* results with refined keywords

42g Finding other online sources

Several online sources can put you directly in touch with experts and others whose ideas and information may inform your research. Because these sources, like Web sites, are unfiltered, you must always evaluate them carefully. (See pp. 600–03.)

1 Using e-mail

As a research tool, e-mail allows you to communicate with others who are interested in your topic. You might, for instance, carry on an e-mail conversation with a teacher at your school or interview an expert in another state to follow up on a scholarly article he or she published. (See pp. 829–31 on writing e-mail.)

2 Using blogs

Blogs (Web logs) are personal sites on which an author posts time-stamped comments, generally centering on a common theme, in a format that allows readers to respond to the author or to one another. You can find directories of blogs at *blogcatalog.com*. See also pages 832–33 for a discussion and example of communicating via blogs.

Like all other online media discussed in this section, blogs consulted as potential sources must be evaluated carefully. Some are reliable sources of opinion, news, or evolving scholarship, and many refer to worthy books, articles, Web sites, and other resources. But lots of blogs are little more than outlets for their authors' gripes and prejudices. See pages 600–03 for tips on telling the good from the bad.

3 Using discussion lists

A **discussion list** (sometimes called a **listserv** or just a **list**) uses e-mail to connect individuals who are interested in a common subject, often with a scholarly or technical focus. By sending a question to an appropriate list, you may be able to reach scores of people who know something about your topic. For an index of discussion lists, see *tile.net/lists*.

When conducting research on a discussion list, follow the guidelines for writing e-mail on pages 829–31 as well as these tips:

- *Lurk* for a while—reading without posting messages. Make sure the discussion is relevant to your topic, and get a sense of how the group interacts.
- **Consult the list's archive.** Your question may already have been answered.
- **Don't ask for information you can find elsewhere.** Most list members are glad to help with legitimate questions but resent messages that rehash familiar debates or that ask them to do someone else's work.
- **Evaluate messages carefully.** Many list subscribers are passionate experts with fair-minded approaches to their topics, but almost anyone with an Internet connection can post a message to a list. See pages 600–03 on evaluating online sources.

4 Using Web forums and newsgroups

Web forums and newsgroups are more open and less scholarly than discussion lists, so their messages require even more diligent evaluation. **Web forums** allow participants to join a conversation simply by selecting a link on a Web page. For a directory of forums, see *delphiforums.com*. **Newsgroups** are organized under subject headings such as *soc* for social issues and *biz* for business. For a directory of newsgroups, see *groups.google.com*.

42h Finding government publications

Government publications provide a vast array of data compilations, reports, policy statements, public records, and other historical and contemporary information. For US government publications, by far the most numerous, consult the Government Printing Office's *GPO Access* at *www.gpoaccess.gov*. Also helpful is *Google US Government Search* (*google.com/ig/usgov*) because it returns *.gov* (government) and *.mil* (military) documents and its ranking system emphasizes the most useful documents. Many federal, state, and local government agencies post important publications—legislation, reports, press releases—on their own Web sites. You can find lists of sites for various federal agencies by using the keywords *United States federal government* with any search engine. Justin Malik took this approach to find statistics from the Environmental Protection Agency on the volume of municipal solid waste (MSW) produced in the United States (see the screen shot below).

Graph from a government publication

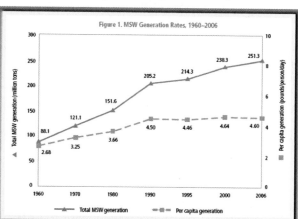

Government Web sites can be sources for data, policy, consumer advice, and other information.

BREAKING THE ICE

After your students have spent a little time lurking on a discussion list, blog, or group relevant to their topic, tell them to submit a posting asking for information on their topic and then report to you about the responses they receive.

ONLINE VS. PRINT CATALOGS

Some online catalogs cover material dating only from the years since online databases and the Web became popularized, so for older data your students may have to consult a print version of the catalog. For instance, the online *Catalog of United States Government Publications* (which is updated daily) goes back to 1994. Information predating 1994 can be found in the print version, the *Monthly Catalog of United States Government Publications*.

Besides what's available online, your library will have a large collection of printed government publications only if it is a depository library (that is, designated to receive such documents). If yours is a depository library, ask a librarian to help you locate the documents you seek.

42i Finding images, audio, and video

Images, audio, and video can be used as both primary and secondary sources in a research project. A painting, an advertisement, or a video of a speech might be the subject of a paper and thus a primary source. A podcast of a radio interview with an expert on your subject or a college lecture might serve as a secondary source. Because many of these sources are unfiltered—they can be posted by anyone—you must always evaluate them as carefully as you would any source you find on the open Web. (See pp. 600–03.)

Note You must also cite every image, audio, and video source fully in your paper, just as you cite text sources, with author, title, and publication information. In addition, some sources will require that you seek permission from the copyright holder, either the source itself or a third party such as a photographer or the creator of a video. Permission is especially likely to be required if you are submitting your paper on the public Web. See pages 632–34 for more about online publication.

1 Finding images

Pages 223–26 discuss the use of images to support an argument. To find images, you have a number of options:

- **Scout for images while reading print or online sources.** Your sources may include charts, graphs, photographs, and other images that can support your ideas. When you find an image you may want to use, photocopy or download it so you'll have it available later.
- **Create your own images,** such as photographs or charts. See pages 121–25 for suggestions on creating images.
- **Use an image search engine.** *Google, Yahoo!, AlltheWeb,* and some other search engines conduct specialized image searches. They can find scores of images, but the results may be inaccurate or incomplete because the sources surveyed often do not include descriptions of the images. (The engines search file names and any text accompanying the images.)
- **Use a public image database.** The following sites generally conduct accurate searches because their images are filed with

information such as a description of the image, the artist's name, and the image's date:

Adflip (*adflip.com*). Historical and contemporary print advertisements.

Duke University, *Ad*Access* (*library.duke.edu/digitalcollections/adaccess*). Print advertisements spanning 1911–55.

Library of Congress, *American Memory* (*memory.loc.gov/ammem*). Maps, photographs, and prints documenting the American experience.

Library of Congress, *Prints and Photographs Online Catalog* (*loc.gov/rr/ print/catalog.html*). Images from the library's collection, including those available through *American Memory*.

New York Public Library Digital Gallery (*digitalgallery.nypl.org/nypldigital*). Maps, drawings, photographs, and paintings from the library's collection.

Political Cartoons (*politicalcartoons.com*). Cartoons on contemporary issues and events.

■ **Use a public image directory.** The following sites collect links to image sources:

Art Source (*ilpi.com/artsource/general.html*). Sources on art and architecture.

Museum Computer Network (*mcn.edu/resources/index.asp*). Museum collections.

MuseumLink's Museum of Museums (*museumlink.com*). Links to museums all over the world.

Washington State University, *Popular Culture: Resources for Critical Analysis* (*wsu.edu/~amerstu/pop*). Sources on advertising, fashion, magazines, toys, and other artifacts of popular culture.

Yale University Arts Library, *Image Resources* (*www.library.yale.edu/art*). Sources on the visual and performing arts.

■ **Use a subscription database.** Your library may subscribe to the following resources:

ARTstor. Museum collections and a database of images typically used in art history courses.

Associated Press, *AccuNet/AP Multimedia Archives.* Historical and contemporary news images.

Grove Art Online. Art images and links to museum sites.

Many images you find will be available at no charge for copying or downloading, but some sources do charge a fee for use. Before paying for an image, check with a librarian to see if it is available elsewhere for free.

2 | Finding audio and video

Audio and video, widely available on the Web and on CD-ROM, can provide you and your readers with the experience of "being there." For example, if you are researching the media response to Martin Luther King's famous "I Have a Dream" speech and you are publishing your paper electronically, you might insert links to the speech and to TV and radio coverage of it.

- ■ **Audio files** such as podcasts, Webcasts, and CDs record radio programs, interviews, speeches, lectures, and music. They are available on the Web and through your library. Online sources of audio include the Library of Congress's *American Memory* (see the previous page) and podcasts at *www.podcastdirectory.com.*
- ■ **Video files** capture performances, public presentations and speeches, news events, and other activities. They are available on the Web and through your library on DVD. Online sources of video include the Library of Congress's *American Memory* (see the previous page); *YouTube*, which includes commercials, historical footage, current events, and much more (*youtube.com*); and search engines such as *Google* (*video.google.com*).

42j Generating your own sources

Some academic writing assignments will require you to consult primary sources and to conduct primary research for information of your own. In many papers this primary research will be the sole basis for your writing, as when you analyze a poem or report on an experiment you conducted. In other papers you will be expected to use primary research to support, extend, or refute the ideas of others. Three common forms of primary research are observation, personal interviews, and surveys.

1 Observing

Observation can be an effective way to gather fresh information on your subject. You may observe in a controlled setting—for instance, watching children playing in a child-development lab. Or you may observe in a more open setting—for instance, watching the interactions among students at a cafeteria on your campus. Be sure your observation has a well-defined purpose that relates to your research project. Throughout the observation, take careful notes, either on paper or on a handheld computer, and always record the date, time, and location for each session.

2 Conducting personal interviews

A personal interview with an expert on the topic you are researching can provide the kind of information you won't find in books, articles, or Web documents. Because of the give-and-take of an interview, you can ask questions precisely geared to your topic and follow up on points of confusion and unexpected leads. In addition, quotations and paraphrases from an interview can give your paper immediacy and authority.

You can conduct an interview in person, over the telephone, or online. A personal interview is preferable if you can arrange it because you can see the person's expressions and gestures as well as hear his or her tone. But telephone and online interviews allow you to consult someone who resists a personal interview or who lives far away from you, while still retaining most advantages of interaction.

A few precautions will help you get the maximum information from an interview with the minimum disruption to the person you are interviewing:

- **Choose your interviewee carefully.** If you do not already know whom to consult for an interview, ask a teacher in the field or do some telephone or library research. Likely sources, depending on your topic, are those who have written about your topic or something closely related, officials in government, businesspeople, even a relative, if he or she is an expert in your topic because of experience, scholarship, or both.
- **Call or write for an appointment.** Tell the person exactly why you are calling, what you want to discuss, and how long you expect the interview to take. Be true to your word on all points.
- **Prepare a list of open-ended questions to ask**—perhaps ten or twelve for a one-hour interview. Plan on doing some research for these questions to discover background on the issues and your subject's published views on the issues.
- **Pay attention to your subject's answers** so that you can ask appropriate follow-up questions. Take care in interpreting answers, especially if you are online and thus can't depend on facial expressions, gestures, and tone of voice to convey the subject's attitudes. Ask for clarification when you need it.
- **Keep thorough notes.** Take notes during an in-person or telephone interview, or record the interview, if you have the equipment and your subject agrees. For online interviews, save the discussion in a file of its own.
- **Verify quotations.** Before you quote your subject in your paper, check with him or her to ensure that the quotations are accurate.
- **Send a thank-you note immediately after the interview.** Promise your subject a copy of your finished paper, and send the paper promptly.

3 Conducting surveys

Asking questions of a defined group of people can provide information about respondents' attitudes, behavior, backgrounds, and expectations. Use the following tips to plan and conduct a survey:

RESOURCES AND IDEAS

Bishop, Wendy. *Ethnographic Writing Research: Writing It Down, Writing It Up, and Reading It.* Portsmouth: Boynton/Cook, 1999. Print. Bishop defines ethnographic research and helps walk readers through the potential problems and possibilities presented by this type of work.

Heath, Shirley Brice. *Ways with Words: Language, Life, and Work in Communities.* New York: Cambridge UP, 1983. Print. Heath provides a thorough and accessible demonstration of how to conduct ethnographic research, illustrated by her study of the communities of Roadville and Trackton.

Sinor, Jennifer, and Michael Huston. "The Role of Ethnography in the Post-Process Classroom." *Teaching English in the Two-Year College* 31.4 (2004): 369–82. Print. The authors provide an overview of the rise in ethnographic work in composition courses and discuss how ethnographic writing helps make students aware of "how writing functions in society and the social context that surrounds all acts of communication" (380).

Tryzna, Thomas N. "Research Outside the Library: Learning a Field." *College Composition and Communication* 37.2 (1986): 217–23. Print. Tryzna shows how to begin a research project outside the library and find valuable primary sources.

COLLABORATIVE ACTIVITY

SURVEYS ABOUT SURVEYS

If students are planning to use surveys as part of their research, have them share drafts of their surveys in groups or pairs. Using the guidelines in the "Conducting surveys" section, readers can provide feedback on the writer's hypothesis, population, and questions. Students can then revise their surveys if necessary prior to administering them.

- **Decide what you want to find out.** The questions you ask should be dictated by your purpose. Formulating a **hypothesis** about your subject—a generalization that can be tested—will help you refine your purpose.
- **Define your population.** Think about the kinds of people your hypothesis is about—for instance, college men or preschool children. Plan to sample this population so that your findings will be representative.
- **Write your questions.** Surveys may contain closed questions that direct the respondent's answers (checklists and multiple-choice, true/false, or yes/no questions) or open-ended questions that allow brief, descriptive answers. Avoid loaded questions that reveal your own biases or make assumptions about subjects' answers, such as "Do you want the United States to support democracy in China?" or "How much more money does your father make than your mother?"
- **Test your questions.** Use a few respondents with whom you can discuss the answers. Eliminate or recast questions that respondents find unclear, discomforting, or unanswerable.
- **Tally the results.** Count the actual numbers of answers, including any nonanswers.
- **Seek patterns in the raw data.** Such patterns may confirm or contradict your hypothesis. Revise the hypothesis or conduct additional research if necessary.

Exercise 42.1 Using the library

To become familiar with the research sources available through your library, visit both the library and its Web site for answers to the following questions. Ask a librarian for help whenever necessary.

1. Which resources does the library include on its Web site? Which resources require a visit to the library?
2. Where are reference books stored in the library? How are they cataloged and arranged? Which ones are available through the Web site? Where and in what format(s) are (*a*) *Contemporary Authors,* (*b*) *Encyclopaedia Britannica,* and (*c*) *MLA International Bibliography of Books and Articles on the Modern Languages and Literatures?*
3. Where is the catalog of the library's periodicals? Where and in what format(s) does the library have current and back issues of the following periodicals: (*a*) the *New York Times,* (*b*) *Harper's* magazine, and (*c*) *Journal of Social Psychology?*
4. What tools does the library's Web site offer for finding periodical databases that are appropriate for a particular research subject?
5. Research the focus and indexed publications of two periodical databases, such as *Academic Search Premier, JSTOR, LexisNexis, PAIS,* or *ProQuest Research Library.* What disciplines does each database seem most suited for?
6. Does the book catalog cover all of the library's book holdings? If not, which books are not included, and where are they cataloged?

7. What are the library call numbers of the following books: (*a*) *The Power Broker,* by Robert Caro; (*b*) *Heart of Darkness,* by Joseph Conrad; and (*c*) *The Hero with a Thousand Faces,* by Joseph Campbell?

Exercise 42.2 Finding library sources

Locate at least six promising articles and books for the subject you began working on in the previous chapter (Exercise 41.1, p. 553, and Exercise 41.2, p. 557). Consider the sources "promising" if they seem directly to address your central research question. Following the guidelines on pages 557–60, make an annotated working bibliography of the sources. Be sure to include all the information you will need to acknowledge the sources in your final paper.

Exercise 42.3 Finding Web sources

Use at least two Web search engines to locate six or seven promising sources for your research project. Begin by developing a list of keywords that can be used to query one of the search engines (see pp. 564–65). Then try your keywords on the other search engine as well. How do the results differ? What keyword strategies worked best for finding relevant information? Add promising sources to your annotated working bibliography.

43
Working with Sources

The previous chapters helped you lay the groundwork for a research project. This chapter takes you into the most personal, most intensive, and most rewarding part of research writing: using the sources you've found to extend and support your own ideas, to make your subject your own. As before, the work of Justin Malik (on green consumerism) and Vanessa Haley (on the work of Annie Dillard) will illustrate the activity and thought that go into research writing.

CULTURE LANGUAGE Making a subject your own requires thinking critically about sources and developing independent ideas. These goals may at first be uncomfortable if your native culture emphasizes understanding and respecting established authority more

mycomplab

Visit *mycomplab.com* for more resources and exercises on working with sources.

HIGHLIGHTS

This chapter tackles one of the most difficult aspects of research writing. Students unskilled in research or with comparatively undeveloped critical thinking skills may not know what to do with the sources they find. Students will follow Justin Malik's and Vanessa Haley's research-in-progress and observe how these students work with sources. New to this edition of the handbook is an expanded discussion of how to evaluate library sources, Web sites, and blogs and other online sources with annotated examples of each (43a).

Subsequent sections focus on how students may respond to and interact with the sources they find, including detailed coverage of methods of gathering and organizing information. Section 43d, which covers summary, paraphrase, and quotation, includes new, paired examples of plagiarized and unplagiarized versions of sources for students to compare. The final section covers methods of introducing source material into the text of a research paper. The chapter's exercises provide practice in all aspects of handling sources.

than questioning and enlarging it. This chapter offers guidance in working with sources so that you can become an expert in your own right and convincingly convey your expertise to others.

43a Evaluating sources

1 Gaining an overview

Once you have a satisfactory working bibliography, you want to get a sense of your sources' usefulness and value.

- **Look first at sources that seem most likely to define your subject.** Justin Malik started with a scholarly review of the literature on green consumption. Vanessa Haley turned first to a book by Annie Dillard, Haley's subject. (For a paper like Haley's that analyzes a writer's work, always begin with that work.)
- **Scan sources to gauge the kind and extent of their ideas and information.** Don't get bogged down collecting information at this point. Instead, ensure that your sources are appropriately detailed and cover the full range of your subject—that together they promise to help you answer your research question.
- **Update your annotated bibliography with assessments of sources.** As you take the measure of sources, add your evaluations to your working bibliography. The writing will help you differentiate sources and start you on building connections among them. In each annotation, summarize the purpose, main

Annotated bibliography entry with assessment

Publication information for source	Gore, Al. *An Inconvenient Truth: The Planetary Emergency of Global Warming and What We Can Do about It*. Emmaus: Rodale, 2006. Print.
Summary of source (from working bibliography)	Book version of the documentary movie supporting Gore's argument that global warming is a serious threat to the planet. Includes summaries of scientific studies, short essays on various subjects, and dozens of images, tables, charts, and graphs. Last chapter offers several suggestions for ways to solve the problem, with an emphasis on changing individual buying habits.
Assessment of source	Urgent and alarming argument, with lots of data that seem thorough and convincing. But book is aimed at a general audience and doesn't have formal source citations. Can use book for broad concepts, but for data I'd have to track down Gore's scholarly sources.

argument, and any apparent bias of the source. Also note any questions you have about it. The example on the facing page from Justin Malik's evolving bibliography adds to the entry on page 560.

2 | **Judging relevance and reliability**

Not all the sources you find will prove worthwhile: some may be irrelevant to your subject, and others may be unreliable. Gauging the relevance and reliability of sources is the essential task of evaluating them. If you haven't already done so, read this book's Chapters 7 and 9 on critical reading. They provide a foundation for answering the questions in the box below.

Questions for evaluating sources

For online sources, supplement these questions with those on pages 593 and 600–01.

Relevance

■ **Does the source devote some attention to your subject?** Does it focus on your subject or cover it marginally? How does it compare to other sources you've found?

■ **Is the source appropriately specialized for your needs?** Check the source's treatment of a topic you know something about, to ensure that it is neither too superficial nor too technical.

■ **Is the source up to date enough for your subject?** When was it published? If your subject is current, your sources should be, too.

Reliability

■ **Where does the source come from?** Did you find it through your library or directly through the Internet? (If the latter, see the following pages.) Is it popular or scholarly?

■ **Is the author an expert in the field?** Check the author's credentials in a biography (if the source includes one), in a biographical reference (see p. 568), or by a keyword search of the Web.

■ **What is the author's bias?** How do the author's ideas relate to those in other sources? What areas does the author emphasize, ignore, or dismiss?

■ **Is the source fair, reasonable, and well-written?** Does it provide sound reasoning and a fair picture of opposing views? Is the tone calm and objective? Is the source logically organized and error-free?

■ **Are the author's claims well supported?** Does the author provide accurate, relevant, representative, and adequate evidence to back up his or her claims? Does the author cite sources, and if so are they reliable?

COLLABORATIVE LEARNING

Individually, ask students to evaluate a printed source they are considering using for their research project using the "Questions for evaluating sources" box. They should bring a copy of the source to class along with their evaluation. In small groups or pairs, ask another group member to evaluate the same source also using the "Questions for evaluating sources" box. Then ask students to compare their evaluations. Overall, do they agree with each other about the source's suitability for the topic and assignment? Why or why not?

Note In evaluating sources, you need to consider how they came to you. The sources you find through the library, both in print and on the Web, have been previewed for you by their publishers and by the library's staff. They still require your critical reading, but you can have some confidence in the information they contain. With online sources you reach directly, however, you cannot assume similar previewing, so your critical reading must be especially rigorous. Special tips for evaluating Web sites and other online sources appear on the following pages.

3 Evaluating library sources

To evaluate sources you find through your library, either in print or on the library's Web site, look at dates, titles, summaries, introductions, headings, author biographies, and any source notes. The following criteria expand on the most important tips in the box on the previous page. On pages 594–95 you can see how Justin Malik applied these criteria to two print sources, a magazine article and a journal article, that he consulted during his research into green consumerism.

Identify the origin of the source.

Check whether a library source is popular or scholarly. Scholarly sources, such as refereed journals and university press books, are generally deeper and more reliable, though some popular sources, such as first-hand newspaper accounts and books for a general audience, are often appropriate for research projects.

Check the author's expertise.

The authors of scholarly publications tend to be experts whose authority can be verified. Check the source to see whether it contains a biographical note about the author, check a biographical reference (see p. 568), or check the author's name in a keyword search of the Web. Look for other publications by the author and for his or her job and any affiliation, such as teacher at a university, researcher with a nonprofit organization, author of general-interest books, or writer for popular magazines.

Identify the author's bias.

Every author has a point of view that influences the selection and interpretation of evidence. You may be able to learn about an author's bias from biographies, review indexes (p. 571), and citation indexes (p. 577). But also look at the source itself. How do the author's ideas relate to those in other sources? What areas does the author emphasize, ignore, or dismiss? When you're aware of sources' biases, you can attempt to balance them.

Determine whether the source is fair, reasonable, and well written.

Even a strongly biased work should present solid reasoning and give balanced coverage to opposing views—all in an objective tone. View with suspicion any source that is not organized logically and written in clear, error-free sentences.

Analyze support for the author's claims.

Evidence should be accurate, relevant to the argument, representative of its context, and adequate for the point being made (see pp. 183–85). The author's sources should themselves be reliable.

4 Evaluating Web sites

To a great extent, the same critical reading that helps you evaluate library sources will help you evaluate Web sites that you reach directly. But most Web sites have not undergone prior screening by editors and librarians. On your own, you must distinguish scholarship from corporate promotion, valid data from invented statistics, well-founded opinion from clever propaganda.

The strategy summarized in the box below can help you make such distinctions. On pages 598–99 you can see how Justin Malik applied the strategy to two Web sites he found during his research into green consumerism.

Questions for evaluating Web sites

Supplement these questions with those on page 591.

- **What type of site are you viewing?** What does the type lead you to expect about the site's purpose and content?
- **Who is the author or sponsor?** How credible is the person or group responsible for the site?
- **What is the purpose of the site?** What does the site's author or sponsor intend to achieve?
- **What does context tell you?** What do you already know about the site's subject that can inform your evaluation? What kinds of support or other information do the site's links provide?
- **What does presentation tell you?** Is the site's design well thought out and effective? Is the writing clear and error-free?
- **How worthwhile is the content?** Are the site's claims well supported by evidence? Is the evidence from reliable sources? When was the site last updated?

(continued on p. 596)

COMPUTER ACTIVITIES

WEB CLUES

Since electronic sources pose special problems, particularly for determining reliability, it will be helpful to conduct additional in-class evaluations of such sources. In a wired classroom, you might run through a short Web search and then ask students to help you evaluate the reliability of the sources you find, using the criteria provided by the handbook. Then ask students to work in pairs to evaluate one or two of their Web site sources and to report their findings to the class. In each case, encourage students to recount (and to keep journal records of) the methods they used to determine a source's reliability and relevance.

DISINGENUOUS SITES

Some Web sites, particularly those sponsored by some kinds of activist organizations, attempt to appear nonbiased when in fact they have a very strong bias. They may post pseudo-scholarship on their sites in an attempt to look research-based and academic. If you come across such sites, they can be excellent teaching tools. Students will be eager to develop the savvy to uncover the true bias underlying a Web site, and you can point out to them that intelligent readers use the same methods of analysis to evaluate all texts, including student research papers.

COLLABORATIVE LEARNING

WEB SOURCE EVALUATION

Since sources found on the Web are sometimes difficult to evaluate, you might devote class time to helping students analyze sample sources. Begin by reviewing a sample item in class: What clues are there about whether the material is primary or secondary, scholarly or popular? Is it dated? Did the material come from an individual's home page, an institutional archive? Is the author named? Has that author published additional work found in print? Is the material referenced in a scholarly bibliography? Does the author cite other sources; does the piece include a bibliography of its own sources? Then have each student bring in a printout of material gleaned from the Web along with a record of the search procedures he or she used to find it (in an electronic classroom you might have students work directly from the screen). Ask students to work in small groups to evaluate their sources and to report their findings on one source to the class.

Evaluating library sources

Opposite are sample pages from two library sources that Justin Malik considered for his paper on green consumerism. Malik evaluated the sources using the questions in the box on page 591 and the guidelines on pages 592–93.

Makower	Jackson
Origin	
Interview with Joel Makower published in *Vegetarian Times*, a popular magazine.	Article by Tim Jackson published in *Journal of Industrial Ecology*, a scholarly journal sponsored by two reputable universities: MIT and Yale.
Author	
Gives Makower's credentials at the beginning of the interview: the author of a book on green products and of a monthly newsletter on green businesses. Quotes another source that calls Makower the "guru of green business practice."	Includes a biography at the end of the article that describes Jackson as a professor at the University of Surrey (UK) and lists his professional activities related to the environment.
Bias	
Describes and promotes green products. Concludes with an endorsement of a for-profit Web site that tracks and sells green products.	Presents multiple views of green consumerism. Argues that a solution to environmental problems will involve green products and less consumption but in different ways than currently proposed.
Reasonableness and writing	
Presents Makower's data and perspective on distinguishing good from bad green products, using conversational writing in an informal presentation.	Presents and cites opposing views objectively, using formal academic writing.
Source citations	
Lacks source citations for claims and data.	Includes more than three pages of source citations, many of scholarly and government sources and all cited within the article.
Assessment	
Probably unreliable: Despite Makower's reputation, the article comes from a nonscholarly source, takes a one-sided approach to consumption, and depends on statistics credited only to Makower.	**Probably reliable:** The article comes from a scholarly journal, the author is an expert in the field, he discusses many views and concedes some, and his source citations confirm evidence from reliable sources.

First and last pages of
an interview with Joel
Makower, published
in *Vegetarian Times*

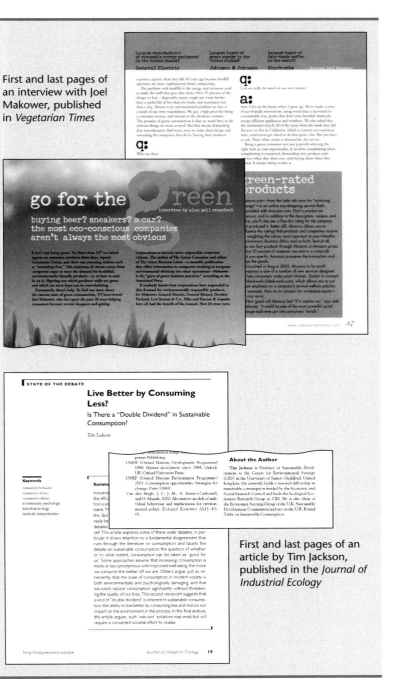

First and last pages of an
article by Tim Jackson,
published in the *Journal
of Industrial Ecology*

(continued from p. 593)

Note To evaluate a Web document, you'll often need to travel to the site's home page to discover the author or sponsor, date of publication, and other relevant information. The page you're reading may include a link to the home page. If it doesn't, you can find it by editing the URL in the Address or Location field of your browser. Working backward, delete the end of the URL up to the last slash and hit Enter. Repeat this step until you reach the home page. There you may also find a menu option, often labeled "About," that will lead you to a description of the site's author or sponsor.

Determine the type of site.

When you search the Web, you're likely to encounter various types of sites. Although they overlap—a primarily informational site may include scholarship as well—the types can usually be identified by their content and purposes. Here are the main types:

- **Scholarly sites:** These sites have a knowledge-building interest and include research reports with supporting data and extensive documentation of scholarly sources. The URLs of the sites generally end in *edu* (originating from an educational institution), *org* (a nonprofit organization), or *gov* (a government department or agency). Such sites are more likely to be reliable than the others described below.
- **Informational sites:** Individuals, nonprofit organizations, corporations, schools, and government bodies all produce sites intended to centralize information on subjects as diverse as astronomy, hip-hop music, and zoo design. The sites' URLs may end in *edu, org, gov,* or *com* (originating from a commercial organization). Such sites generally do not have the knowledge-building focus of scholarly sites and may omit supporting data and documentation, but they can provide useful information and often include links to scholarly and other sources.
- **Advocacy sites:** Many sites present the views of individuals or organizations that promote certain policies or actions. Their URLs usually end in *org,* but they may end in *edu* or *com.* Some advocacy sites include serious, well-documented research to support their positions, but others select or distort evidence.
- **Commercial sites:** Corporations and other businesses maintain Web sites to explain themselves, promote themselves, or sell goods and services. The URLs of commercial sites end in *com.* Although the information on such a site furthers the sponsor's profit-making purpose, it can include reliable data.
- **Personal sites:** The sites maintained by individuals range from diaries of a family's travels to opinions on political issues to reports on evolving scholarship. The sites' URLs usually end in

---

TRYING OUT SITES

Ask students to provide you with an example of these five types of sites (scholarly, informational, advocacy, commercial, and personal) on their research topic. Then ask them to outline a research paragraph based on each site to get a better understanding of how useful (or useless) each kind of site is for their purposes.

com or *edu*. Personal sites are only as reliable as their authors, but some do provide valuable eyewitness accounts, links to worthy sources, and other usable information. A particular kind of personal site, the blog, is discussed on pages 600–03.

Note Informational sites called **wikis** allow anyone to contribute and edit information. Older entries on reputable wikis, such as *Wikipedia*, tend to be reliable because they have been reviewed and edited by experts, but recent entries may contain errors and even misinformation. Ask your instructor whether wikis are acceptable sources. If so, evaluate them carefully against other, more reliable sources using the guidelines in the box on page 595 and below.

Identify the author and sponsor.

A reputable site will list its authors, will name the group responsible for the site, and will provide information or a link for contacting the author and the sponsor. If none of this information is provided, you should not use the source. If you have only the author's or the sponsor's name, you may be able to discover more in a biographical dictionary, through a keyword search, or in your other sources. Make sure the author and the sponsor have expertise on the subject they're presenting: if an author is a doctor, for instance, what is he or she a doctor of?

Gauge purpose and bias.

A Web site's purpose determines what ideas and information it offers. Inferring that purpose tells you how to interpret what you see on the site. If a site is intended to sell a product or an opinion, it will likely emphasize favorable ideas and information while ignoring or even distorting what is unfavorable. In contrast, if a site is intended to build knowledge—for instance, a scholarly project or journal—it will likely acknowledge diverse views and evidence.

Determining the purpose of a site often requires looking beyond the first page and beneath the surface of words and images. To start, read what the site says about itself, usually found on a page labeled "About." Be suspicious of any site that doesn't provide information about itself and its goals.

Consider context.

Your evaluation of a Web site should be informed by considerations outside the site itself. Chief among these is your own knowledge. What do you already know about the site's subject and the prevailing views of it? Where does this site seem to fit into that picture? What can you learn from this site that you don't already know?

(continued on p. 600)

Evaluating Web sites

Opposite are screen shots from two Web sites that Justin Malik consulted for his paper on green consumerism. Malik evaluated the sources using the questions in the boxes on pages 591 and 593.

We Can Solve the Climate Crisis	*Nature Reports: Climate Change*
Author and sponsor	
Author of article is not listed. Site sponsor is the Alliance for Climate Protection, a nonprofit organization founded by former vice president Al Gore.	Listed authors are scientists, experts on climate change. (Biographies appear at the end of the article.) Site sponsor is the Nature Publishing Group, which also publishes the reputable science journal *Nature*.
Purpose and bias	
Advocacy site with self-stated purpose of "educating people in the US and around the world that the climate crisis is both urgent and solvable." Urges site visitors to register and become active in efforts to stop global warming.	Informational site with the self-stated purpose of providing "authoritative, in-depth reporting on climate change and its wider implications for policy, society and the economy." Article expresses bias toward reducing pollution to stop climate change.
Context	
One of many sites enlisting readers in action against climate change.	One of many sites publishing current research on climate issues.
Presentation	
Inviting, professionally designed site with error-free writing.	Clean, professionally designed site with error-free writing.
Content	
Site looks new, but it and the article are undated. Article clearly explains the science of climate change but without references or links to scholarly research. Other pages on the site feature video clips of individuals making personal appeals to viewers.	Article is current (date above the title) and clearly explains the science of climate change with references and links to scholarly sources. Other links connect to hundreds of articles elsewhere on the site about climate-related topics.
Assessment	
Probably unreliable: Despite the reputation of the site sponsor, the article lacks the source citations needed for credibility about climate change. It's ok that an advocacy site is biased, but it should be more substantial to serve as a source.	**Probably reliable:** The article has an explicit bias toward stopping climate change, but the site sponsor has a scholarly reputation, the authors are climate-change experts, and the references cite many scholarly and government sources.

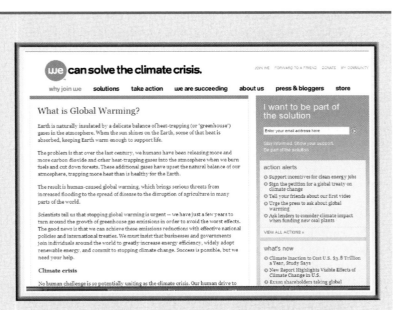

Article published on the Web site *We Can Solve the Climate Crisis*

Article published on the Web site *Nature Reports: Climate Change*

(continued from p. 597)

In addition, you can follow some of the site's links to see how they support, or don't support, the site's credibility. For instance, links to scholarly sources lend authority to a site—but *only* if the scholarly sources actually relate to and back up the site's claims.

Look at presentation.

Considering both the look of a site and the way it's written can illuminate its intentions and reliability. Are the site's elements all functional and well integrated, or is the site cluttered with irrelevant material and graphics? Does the site seem carefully constructed and well maintained, or is it sloppy? Does the design reflect the apparent purpose of the site, or does it undercut or conceal that purpose in some way? Is the text clearly written, or is it difficult to understand? Is it error-free, or does it contain typos and grammatical errors?

Analyze content.

With information about a site's author, purpose, and context, you're in a position to evaluate its content. Are the ideas and information current, or are they dated? (Check the publication date.) Are they slanted and, if so, in what direction? Are the views and data authoritative, or do you need to balance them—or even reject them? Are claims made on the site supported by evidence drawn from reliable sources? These questions require close reading of both the text and its sources.

5 | Evaluating other online sources

Blogs, online discussions, and online images, video, and audio require the same critical scrutiny as Web sites do. Blogs and discussion groups can be sources of reliable data and opinions, but you will also encounter wrong or misleading data and skewed opinions. One podcast may provide an interview with a recognized expert while another claims authority that it doesn't deserve. A *YouTube* search using "I have a dream" brings up videos of Martin Luther King, Jr., delivering his famous speech as well as videos of people speaking hatefully about King and the speech.

Use the following strategy for evaluating such online sources. See pages 602–03 for Justin Malik's use of this strategy with a blog he found while researching green consumerism.

Questions for evaluating blogs, online discussions, images, video, and audio

Supplement these questions with those on page 591.

- **Who is the author or creator?** How credible is he or she?
- **What is the author's or creator's purpose?** What can you tell about why the author or creator is publishing the work?

- **What does the context reveal?** What do other responses to the work, including responses to a blog posting or the other messages in a discussion thread, indicate about the source's balance and reliability?
- **How worthwhile is the content?** Are the claims made by the author or creator supported by evidence? Is the evidence from reliable sources?
- **How does the source compare with other sources?** Do the claims made by the author or creator seem accurate and fair, given what you've seen in sources you know to be reliable?

Identify the author or creator.

Checking out the author or creator of a blog, online posting, video file, or podcast can help you judge its reliability. If the author or creator uses a screen name, write directly to him or her requesting full name and credentials. Do not use the source if you don't get a response. Once you know the person's name, you may be able to obtain background information from a keyword search of the Web or a biographical dictionary.

You can also get a sense of the interests and biases of an author or creator by tracking down his or her other publications. For a blog, check whether the author cites or links to other publications. For a discussion-group posting, look for an archive or other feature that allows you to find additional messages by the same author. For multimedia sources, try to gain an overview of the creator's work.

Analyze the author's or creator's purpose.

What can you tell about *why* the author or creator is publishing the work? Look for claims, use (or not) of evidence, and treatment of opposing views. All these convey the person's stand on the subject and general fairness, and they will help you position the source among your other sources.

Consider the context.

Blogs, discussion-group postings, and multimedia sources are often difficult to evaluate in isolation. Looking beyond a particular contribution to the responses of others will give you a sense of how the author or creator is regarded. On a blog, look at the comments others have posted. Do the same with postings, going back to the initial posting in the discussion thread and reading forward.

Analyze content.

A reliable source will offer evidence for claims and sources for evidence. If you don't see such supporting information, ask the author or creator for it. (If he or she fails to respond, don't use the source.) Then verify the sources with your own research: are they reputable?

Evaluating a blog

Opposite is a screen shot from a blog that Justin Malik consulted for his paper on green consumerism. Malik evaluated the blog using the questions in the boxes on pages 591 and 600–01.

Author and sponsor

Listed author is a climate scientist. (A link provides her credentials.) Blog sponsor is the Environmental Defense Fund, a nonprofit organization operating for more than forty years.

Purpose and bias

Advocacy site and blog with self-stated purpose of drawing on "science, economics, and law to create . . . solutions to society's most urgent environmental problems." Urges site visitors to join the organization and donate money to support its work. Posting assumes readers are somewhat familiar with the science of climate change.

Context

One of many blogs advocating and enlisting readers in action against climate change.

Presentation

Clean, professionally designed site with error-free writing.

Content

Posting is current (date under the title) and clearly explains recent findings with links to government and scholarly sources.

Assessment

Probably reliable: The site sponsor has a bias toward environmental causes, but it has a strong reputation, the author of the blog posting is an expert, and the posting cites reliable sources.

The tone of writing can also be a clue to its purpose and reliability. Blogs, online discussions, and some podcasts tend to be more informal and often more heated than other kinds of dialog, but look askance at writing that's contemptuous, dismissive, or shrill.

Compare with other sources.

Always consider blogs, postings, and multimedia sources in comparison to other sources so that you can distinguish singular, untested views from more mainstream views that have been subject to verification. Don't assume that a blog author's information and opinions are reliable just because you see them on other blogs. The technology allows content to be picked up instantly by other blogs, so widespread distribution indicates only popularity, not reliability.

Be wary of blogs or postings that reproduce periodical articles, reports, or other publications. Try to locate the original version of the publication to be sure it has been reproduced fully and accurately, not quoted selectively or distorted. If you can't locate the original version, don't use the publication as a source.

Posting on the blog *Climate 411*, sponsored by the
Environmental Defense Fund

Exercise 43.1 Evaluating a source

Imagine that you are researching a paper on the advertising techniques
that are designed to persuade consumers to buy products. You have
listed the following book in your working bibliography:

Vance Packard, *The Hidden Persuaders,* revised edition, 1981.

On your own or with your classmates (as your instructor wishes), obtain
this book from a library and evaluate it as a source for your paper. Use
the guidelines on page 591.

Exercise 43.2 Evaluating Web sites

Find and evaluate two Web sites: a commercial site, such as Microsoft's
or Apple's, and a site for a nonprofit organization, such as the American
Medical Association or Greenpeace. What do you know or can you infer
about each site's sponsor or author? What seems to be the site's purpose
or purposes? What do the site's links contribute? How effective is the
site's design? How reliable do you judge the site's information to be?
How do the two sites differ in these respects?

Exercise 43.1 works well as a group project,
particularly since the library may contain limited
copies of Packard's book. You might consider
putting this book on reserve so that each group
can examine it for a limited amount of time. Have
each group present its findings to the class, paying particular attention to the methods the students used to evaluate the book. As the groups
give their presentations, you might have students
keep a running list of those methods on the blackboard, on the overhead, or on the class Web site.

As a variation on Exercise 43.1 (or a follow-
up to it) you might have one group work with
Packard and other groups work with additional
authors who have varying approaches to advertising (such as Michael Schudson, Mark Crispin
Miller, or Stuart Ewen). This task will encourage
students to identify differences in arguments and
approaches.

ANSWERS: EXERCISE 43.1

Responses will vary. Packard's book is fa-
mously critical of advertising methods. Students
should recognize Packard's bias while also valuing his expertise and evidence.

ANSWERS: EXERCISE 43.2

Individual response.

COLLABORATIVE LEARNING

In a wired classroom, you could do Exercises 43.3 and 43.4 as a class. Look at the postings together and discuss them, using the chart for evaluating blogs, online discussions, images, audio, and video on pages 600–01. Or have students e-mail their evaluation paragraphs to the rest of the class or post them on your class Web site. As a class, you can develop your own annotated list of online and multimedia sources.

ANSWERS: EXERCISE 43.3

Individual response.

ANSWERS: EXERCISE 43.4

Individual response.

RESOURCES AND IDEAS

Two issues of *English Journal* have featured research-related themes: The March 2006 issue (95.4) "Reading, Writing, and Re-Presenting Research" and the September 1999 issue (89.1) "Research Revisited." The September 1999 issue features helpful articles on evaluating Web sources, including Kathryn A. Johnston's "A Librarian's Approach to Research" (99–106) and Susan A. Gardner, Hiltraut H. Benham, and Bridget M. Newell's "Oh, What a Tangled Web We've Woven! Helping Students Evaluate Sources" (39–44).

Bishop, Wendy, and Pavel Zemliansky, eds. *The Subject Is Research: Processes and Practices.* Portsmouth: Boynton/Cook, 2001. Print. This collection provides a number of ideas for helping students research and use sources more effectively, including how to maintain one's own voice when using source material, locating primary sources, and using the Internet.

Higgens, Lorraine. "Reading to Argue: Helping Students Transform Source Texts." *Hearing Ourselves Think: Cognitive Research in the College Writing Classroom.* Ed. Ann M. Penrose and Barbara M. Sitko. New York, Oxford: Oxford UP, 1993. 70–101. Print. Higgens explores strategies through which students learn to use their sources, and debates between their sources, as the basis for developing their own arguments.

Exercise 43.3   Evaluating a blog

Visit *bloglines.com* or *blogcatalog.com* to find a blog on a controversial subject such as stem-cell research or online sharing of music files. Who is responsible for the blog? What can you tell about its purpose? How reliable do you judge its ideas and information to be?

Exercise 43.4   Evaluating an online discussion

Using *groups.google.com,* locate a newsgroup on a subject that interests you. (If you already participate in an online discussion group, you can use it instead.) Pick one series of at least ten related messages on a single topic. Write a brief summary of each message (see pp. 134–35 on summarizing). Then analyze and synthesize the messages to develop a one- or two-paragraph evaluation of the discussion. Which messages seem reliable? Which don't? Why?

43b   Synthesizing sources

When you begin to locate the differences and similarities among sources, you move into the most significant part of research writing: forging relationships for your own purpose. This **synthesis,** an essential step in critical reading (pp. 150–51), continues through the drafting and revision of a research paper. As you read, take notes, and infer connections—say, between one writer's ideas and another's or between two works by the same author—you create new knowledge.

All kinds of connections may occur to you as you work with sources. Justin Malik, researching the environmental impacts of green consumption, found data in one study to support another source's assertions about the personal benefits of buying less. He also uncovered a central disagreement among sources over whether changing individual consumer behavior would make a significant difference on a global scale. Vanessa Haley, writing about Annie Dillard, sought and found similarities in Dillard's ideas about the place of humanity in nature, ideas expressed in varying contexts throughout Dillard's best-known book. Haley also discovered that her view of Dillard was partly supported by some of the critics she consulted but not supported by others. She knew she would have to take account of these divergent views in her paper.

Your synthesis of sources will grow more detailed and sophisticated as you proceed through the process of working with sources described in the balance of this chapter: mining and interacting with sources (pp. 607–11), deciding whether to summarize, paraphrase, or quote directly from sources (pp. 611–19), and integrating sources into your sentences (pp. 620–25). Unless, like Vanessa Haley, you are analyzing primary sources such as the works of a writer, read your sources quickly and selectively at first to obtain an overview of your subject and a sense of how the sources approach it. Instead of taking detailed notes about what sources say, record your own ideas about the sources in your research journal (p. 549) or your annotated bibliography (p. 590).

Respond to sources.

Write down what your sources make you think. Do you agree or disagree with the author? Do you find his or her views narrow, or do they open up new approaches for you? Is there anything in the source that you need to research further before you can understand it? Does the source prompt questions that you should keep in mind while reading other sources?

Connect sources.

When you notice a link between sources, jot it down. Do two sources differ in their theories or their interpretations of facts? Does one source illuminate another—perhaps commenting or clarifying or supplying additional data? Do two or more sources report studies that support a theory you've read about or an idea of your own?

Heed your insights.

Apart from ideas prompted by your sources, you are sure to come up with independent thoughts: a conviction, a point of confusion that suddenly becomes clear, a question you haven't seen anyone else ask. These insights may occur at unexpected times, so it's good practice to keep a notebook or computer handy to record them.

Draw your own conclusions.

As your research proceeds, the responses, connections, and insights you form through synthesis will lead you to answer your starting research question with a statement of your thesis (see p. 636). They will also lead you to the main ideas supporting your thesis—conclusions you have drawn from your synthesis of sources, forming the main divisions of your paper.

Use sources to support your conclusions.

Effective synthesis requires careful handling of evidence from sources so that it meshes smoothly into your sentences and yet is clearly distinct from your own ideas. When drafting your paper, make sure that each paragraph focuses on an idea of your own, with the support for the idea coming from your sources. Generally, open each paragraph with your own idea, provide evidence from a source or sources with appropriate citations, and close with an interpretation of the evidence. (Avoid ending a paragraph with a

Spivey, Nancy Nelson. "The Shaping of Meaning: Options in Writing the Comparison." *Research in the Teaching of English* 25.4 (1991): 390–418. Print. Spivey shows that the use of sources can affect students' processes of invention, arrangement, and style.

COLLABORATIVE LEARNING

UNDERSTANDING THE DEBATES

Students often experience some difficulty in identifying connections among their sources. To help them develop a better sense of the debates surrounding their topic and the major authors involved in these debates, ask your students to look through the bibliographies and footnotes (or endnotes) of their principal sources for additional sources to read. Likely prospects include titles or authors that are more frequently cited than others. As a follow-up exercise, you might have students work in groups to give oral presentations about the connections and debates as developed among three of their sources. You might also have students turn in a one-page analysis of the crucial connections among those three sources.

As a preliminary activity to Exercise 43.5, have students work in groups to debate the similarities and differences among the three authors and their approaches. Encourage students to support their views with evidence from the three passages. Then have each student create the paragraph specified by Exercise 43.4 and share it with his or her group. The collaborative approach will enrich students' interpretive responses to the passages, and will help make them aware that their own views on the topic are not self-evident but must be argued on the basis of evidence.

source citation; instead, end with your own idea.) In this way, your paper will synthesize others' work into something wholly your own. For more on structuring paragraphs in academic writing, see pages 163–64.

ANSWERS: EXERCISE 43.5

The key similarities and differences are these:

Similarities: Nadelmann and Posey agree that crackdowns or penalties do not stop the drug trade. Nadelmann and Runkle agree that the drug trade affects the young, who are most impressionable.

Differences: Nadelmann maintains that the illegal drug trade does more to entice youths to drugs than do the drugs themselves, whereas Runkle maintains that the illegality discourages youths from using prohibited drugs. Posey, in contrast to Runkle, claims that penalties do nothing to discourage drug abusers.

Students' paragraphs will depend on their views, but here is a sample response:

Posey seems to invalidate the whole debate over drug legalization: nothing, he says from experience, will stop drug abuse. But such a futile view, whatever its truth, cannot stop the search for a solution. We have tried the prohibition favored by Runkle. Even if, as she claims, students are using fewer illegal drugs, prohibition has not worked. It may be time to try the admittedly risky approach proposed by Nadelmann, legalizing drugs to "drive the drug-dealing business off the streets."

COMPUTER ACTIVITY

SOUNDING BOARDS

If you are teaching a distance education course, your students may miss out on the opportunity to have a sounding board for their impressions of a source. Let pairs or small groups read the same source and then have an open-ended discussion about the source online, using e-mail or your class Web site.

Exercise 43.5 Synthesizing sources

The following three passages address the same issue, the legalization of drugs. What similarities do you see in the authors' ideas? What differences? Write a paragraph of your own in which you use these authors' views as a point of departure for your own view about drug legalization.

Perhaps the most unfortunate victims of drug prohibition laws have been the residents of America's ghettos. These laws have proved largely futile in deterring ghetto-dwellers from becoming drug abusers, but they do account for much of what ghetto residents identify as the drug problem. Aggressive, gun-toting drug dealers often upset law-abiding residents far more than do addicts nodding out in doorways. Meanwhile other residents perceive the drug dealers as heroes and successful role models. They're symbols of success to children who see no other options. At the same time the increasingly harsh criminal penalties imposed on adult drug dealers have led drug traffickers to recruit juveniles. Where once children started dealing drugs only after they had been using them for a few years, today the sequence is often reversed. Many children start using drugs only after working for older drug dealers for a while. Legalization of drugs, like legalization of alcohol in the early 1930s, would drive the drug-dealing business off the streets and out of apartment buildings and into government-regulated, tax-paying stores. It also would force many of the gun-toting dealers out of the business and convert others into legitimate businessmen.

—Ethan A. Nadelmann, "Shooting Up"

Statistics argue against legalization. The University of Michigan conducts an annual survey of twelfth graders, asking the students about their drug consumption. In 1980, 56.4 percent of those polled said they had used marijuana in the past twelve months, whereas in 2007 only 41.7 percent had done so. Cocaine use was even more reduced in the same period (22.6 percent to 7.8 percent). At the same time, twelve-month use of legally available drugs—alcohol and nicotine-containing cigarettes—remained fairly steady around 72 percent and 55 percent, respectively. The numbers of illegal drug users haven't declined nearly enough: those teenaged marijuana and cocaine users are still vulnerable to addiction and even death, and they threaten to infect their impressionable peers. But clearly the prohibition of illegal drugs has helped, while the legal status of alcohol and cigarettes has not made them less popular.

—Sylvia Runkle, "The Case Against Legalization"

I have to laugh at the debate over what to do about the drug problem. Everyone is running around offering solutions—from making drug use a more serious criminal offense to legalizing it. But there isn't a real solution. I know that. I used and abused drugs, and people, and society, for two decades. Nothing worked to get me to stop all that behavior except just plain being sick and tired. Nothing. Not threats, not ten-plus years in prison, not anything that was said to me. I used until I got through. Period. And that's when you'll win the war. When all the dope fiends are done. Not a minute before.

—Michael W. Posey, "I Did Drugs Until They Wore Me Out. Then I Stopped."

Exercise 43.6 Evaluating and synthesizing sources

Look up the sources in the working bibliography you made in Exercises 42.2 and 42.3 (p. 589). Evaluate the sources for their relevance and reliability. If the sources seem unreliable or don't seem to give you what you need, expand your working bibliography and evaluate the new sources. In your research journal or annotated bibliography, write down your responses to sources, the connections you perceive among sources, and other original ideas that occur to you.

43c Mining and interacting with sources

When you have decided which sources to pursue, you may be ready to gather and synthesize information, or you may want to step back and get your bearings. Your choice will depend mainly on how familiar you are with the main issues of your subject and whether you have formed a central idea about it.

- **When you know what you're looking for, proceed with information gathering.** If you've formed a good idea of your thesis and a sense of the topics you will cover, you'll have a framework in which to start finding and synthesizing the information in your sources.
- **When you're uncertain of your direction, stop to draft a thesis statement and create an outline.** These steps (discussed on pp. 636–40) can help when you're attracted to several different theses or when you don't see how the various areas of your subject relate.

The following sections discuss a way of reading sources and methods of gathering and organizing information from sources.

1 Skimming and then reading

The most efficient method of reading secondary sources during research is **skimming**, reading quickly to look for pertinent information. (Primary sources usually need to be read more carefully, especially when they are the focus of your paper.) Follow these guidelines for skimming:

- **Read with a specific question in mind,** not randomly in hopes of hitting something worthwhile.
- **Consult reference aids**—tables of contents, menus, indexes, or headings—to find what you want.
- **Concentrate on headings and main ideas,** skipping material unrelated to the specific question you are researching.

When you find something relevant, read slowly and carefully to achieve a clear understanding of what the author is saying and to interpret and evaluate the material in the context of your own and others' opinions.

2 Gathering and organizing information

Before you begin mining your sources, decide on categories into which your subject can be divided. (If you have previously outlined your preliminary ideas, use outline headings for these categories.) Justin Malik, for instance, divided his general subject of green consumption into these categories:

> Environmental crisis
> Business opportunities
> Advertising messages
> Benefits of green products
> Environmental consequences of consumption
> Activist perspectives (economic, social, and political issues)
> Alternative solutions

Headings for your categories will go at the top of each of your source notes to cue you about its content.

Researchers vary in their methods for working with sources, but all methods share the same goals:

- **Keep accurate records of what sources say.** Accuracy helps prevent misrepresentation and plagiarism.
- **Keep accurate records of how to find sources.** These records are essential for retracing steps and for citing sources in the final paper. (See pp. 557–60 on recording information in a working bibliography.)
- **Synthesize sources.** Information gathering is not a mechanical process but a critical one, leading to an understanding of sources, the relationships among them and your own ideas, and their support for your ideas.

You can accomplish these goals by taking handwritten notes, typing notes into a computer, annotating photocopies or printouts of sources, or annotating downloaded documents. On any given project, you may use all the methods. Each has advantages and disadvantages.

Note Whichever method you use, take two steps with every note, photocopy, printout, or downloaded document:

- **Key the material to your outline** so that you know where it belongs.
- **Record the source's complete publication information,** or use the author's name as a shorthand reference to a list where you keep complete publication information. With printouts and downloads, always record sources' URLs, even if you won't need them in your final source citations, so that you can return to the sites if needed. Use Copy and Paste to record URLs accurately.

Handwritten notes

Writing notes by hand, either in a research notebook or on 4" × 6" cards, will prove useful when you come across a source with no computer or photocopier handy or when you need to record something brief. Handwritten notes can be risky, though. It's easy to introduce errors as you work from source to paper. And it's possible to copy source language and then later mistake and use it as your own, thus plagiarizing the source. Always take care to make accurate notes and to place big quotation marks around any passage you quote. Some researchers reduce the risk of plagiarism by summarizing or paraphrasing sources on notes instead of quoting them, as described on pages 611–17. Other researchers delay this step until drafting because it increases the risk of error.

Notes on computer

Taking notes on a computer can streamline the path of source to note to your paper because you can import the notes into your draft as you write. If you label your files carefully, you can sort notes much as you would on note cards. (The examples on pages 612–18 illustrate one way of labeling computer notes.)

Computer notes have the same disadvantages as handwritten notes: the risk of introducing errors and the risk of plagiarizing. As with handwritten notes, be a stickler for accuracy and use quotation marks for quotations.

Photocopies and printouts

Photocopying from print sources or printing out online sources each has distinct advantages for researchers:

- **Both methods are convenient,** particularly when sources must remain in the library (for instance, bound periodicals and reference works) or when you find sources online (for instance, full-text articles or trustworthy Web pages).

- **Both methods may be safer than handwritten or computer notes.** Many researchers and teachers believe that photocopying or printing out sources reduces the risks of error and plagiarism. Each method requires manipulating source material only once, not twice, to use it in your paper. And with each method you see exactly what's quoted as you work the source material into your draft.

But photocopies and printouts have disadvantages, too:

- **They can discourage synthesis** by substituting busywork for thinking. You must read, question, and draw meaning from photocopies and printouts as critically as you would any other sources. Highlight or annotate the relevant passages with underlining, circles, and marginal notes about their significance for your subject. (See the example below.)
- **Source records can get lost.** You must take special care to note the publication information for sources directly on a printout or photocopy. If you don't have this information for your final paper, you can't use the source.
- **Photocopies and printouts can encourage unselective quotation.** When drafting from a complete source rather than notes on the source, you may be tempted to import whole blocks rather than the bits that advance and support your ideas. See page 616 for guidelines on judicious use of quotations.

Source printout with annotations

Environmental consequences of consumption

EPA, *Municipal Solid Waste* . . . *http://www.epa.gov/epaoswer/non-hw/muncpl/pubs/msw06.pdf*

The breakdown, by weight, of waste generated in 2006 by product category is shown in Figure 6. Containers and packaging made up the largest portion of waste generated, 31.7 percent or 80 million tons. The second largest portion came from nondurable goods, which amounted to 25.5 percent or 64 million tons. Durable goods make up the third largest segment, accounting for 16 percent or 40 million tons.

Packaging causes almost 1/3 of all waste . . .

The generation and recovery of materials in the product categories, by weight and recovery as a percent of generation, are shown in Table 2. The table shows that the recovery of containers and packaging was the highest of the four product categories, with about 40 percent of the generated materials recycled. Steel, paper products, and aluminum were the most recycled materials by percentage in this category.

. . . and less than half of it is recycled.

Downloads

Researching online, you can usually download full-text articles, Web pages, discussion-group messages, and other materials onto your computer. If you also take notes on your computer, you can use it to organize much or all of your research and then, while drafting, import source information from one file into another.

These advantages of downloading are offset by clear disadvantages:

- **Copying downloaded source material into your paper creates a high risk of plagiarism.** You must keep clear boundaries between your own ideas and words and those of others—perhaps by using distinctive type fonts or colors. And make sure to record publication information as part of every downloaded document.
- **Downloading can discourage synthesis.** Even more than with photocopies and printouts, you must make an effort to understand, analyze, and interact with sources. Many researchers print out downloaded sources and mark up paper copies. Alternatively, you can use your word processor's Comment and Highlight functions to annotate the electronic file or simply type your own comments into the source. (But use a different color or font!)

43d   Using summary, paraphrase, and quotation

Deciding whether to summarize, paraphrase, or quote directly from sources is an important step in synthesizing the sources' ideas and your own. You engage in synthesis when you use your own words to summarize an author's argument or paraphrase a significant example or when you select a significant passage to quote. Choosing summary, paraphrase, or quotation should depend on why you are using a source.

Note Summaries, paraphrases, and quotations all require source citations. A summary or paraphrase without a source citation or a quotation without quotation marks and a source citation is plagiarism. (See pp. 626–34 for more on plagiarism.)

1   Summarizing

When you **summarize**, you condense an extended idea or argument into a sentence or more in your own words. A full discussion of summary appears on pages 134–35, and you should read that section if you have not already done so.

Summary is most useful when you want to record the gist of an author's idea without the background or supporting evidence. Justin Malik summarized the following quotation from one of his sources—the introduction by Thomas Princen, Michael Maniates, and Ken Conca to their anthology *Confronting Consumption*, page 4:

> Such intuition is even making its way, albeit slowly, into scholarly circles, where recognition is mounting that ever-increasing pressures on

RESOURCES AND IDEAS

Kennedy, Mary Lynch. "The Composing Process of College Students Writing from Sources." *Written Communication* 2.4 (1985): 434–56. Print. Kennedy's research shows that "fluent" readers and writers take more notes, do more planning, and reread more frequently than do less effective readers.

McGinley, William. "The Role of Reading and Writing while Composing from Sources." *Reading Research Quarterly* 27.3 (1992): 227–48. Print. McGinley demonstrates that students writing from sources use highly recursive nonlinear as well as linear reading, writing, and reasoning processes.

Shirley, Sue. "The Art of Paraphrase." *Teaching English in the Two-Year College* 32.2 (2004): 186–88. Print. Shirley offers a series of six exercises designed to teach students how to paraphrase source material appropriately.

Wakefield, Sarah. "Using Music Sampling to Teach Research Skills." *Teaching English in the Two-Year College* 33.4 (2006): 357–60. Print. Wakefield discusses how using examples of musical sampling, as in the work of Sean "P. Diddy" Combs, can help students to understand quoting, paraphrasing, and summarizing.

COLLABORATIVE LEARNING

SKILLS DRILL

Pick an essay or article to use in class, and practice taking notes from it with your students. If they all summarize, paraphrase, and quote from the same article and discuss their results in groups, they may gain confidence when moving on to their own research materials.

SUMMARIES AND ADD

Students who have attention deficit disorder (ADD or ADHD) often have difficulty summarizing texts. They may benefit from working on summarizing assignments with their learning specialist.

ecosystems, life-supporting environmental services, and critical natural cycles are driven not only by the sheer number of resource users and the inefficiencies of their resource use, but also by the patterns of resource use themselves. In global environmental policymaking arenas, it is becoming more and more difficult to ignore the fact that overdeveloped countries must restrain their consumption if they expect underdeveloped countries to embrace a more sustainable trajectory. And while global population growth still remains a huge issue in many regions around the world—both rich and poor—per-capita growth in consumption is, for many resources, expanding eight to twelve times faster than population growth.

In the following one-sentence summary, Malik picks out the kernel of the authors' passage and expresses it in his own words:

Summary of source

Environmental consequences of consumption

Princen, Maniates, and Conca 4

Overconsumption may be a more significant cause of environmental problems than increasing population is.

Notice how Malik records the authors' names and the page number in his note to avoid accidentally plagiarizing the authors' idea in his paper.

The examples below show the preceding summary in the context of a draft, the first lacking proper citation and the second with proper citation (in MLA style).

Summary with no citation (plagiarized)

Always seeking newer and better things, we consume without regard for the resources we use or the waste we leave behind. In fact, overconsumption may be a more significant cause of environmental problems than increasing population is.

Summary with proper citation (not plagiarized)

Always seeking newer and better things, we consume without regard for the resources we use or the waste we leave behind. In fact, according to Thomas Princen, Michael Maniates, and Ken Conca, overconsumption may be a more significant cause of environmental problems than increasing population is (4).

See page 631 for more examples of plagiarism and revision.

2 Paraphrasing

When you **paraphrase,** you follow much more closely the author's original presentation, but you restate it using your own words and

A MNEMONIC FOR PARAPHRASING

A useful mnemonic that helps students remember how to paraphrase effectively is "New words and new word order." The emphasis on syntactic change in the mnemonic helps prevent mere synonym substitution.

sentence structures. Paraphrase when you want to present or examine an author's line of reasoning but you don't feel the original words merit direct quotation. Generally, a paraphrase is briefer than the original quotation and omits examples and other details.

The note below shows how Malik might have paraphrased the passage by Princen, Maniates, and Conca given on pages 611–12. Notice the record of the authors' names and the page number, which would help Malik avoid confusing the paraphrase with his own ideas and then inadvertently plagiarizing the source in his paper.

Complete paraphrase of source

Environmental consequences of consumption

Princen, Maniates, and Conca 4

Scholars are coming to believe that consumption is partly to blame for changes in ecosystems, reduction of essential natural resources, and changes in natural cycles. Policy makers increasingly see that wealthy nations have to start consuming less if they want developing nations to adopt practices that reduce pollution and waste. Rising population around the world does cause significant stress on the environment, but consumption is increasing even more rapidly than population.

This paraphrase uses simpler sentences and more common terms than the original passage, in effect translating it as shown below. Only words that lack satisfactory synonyms—such as *ecosystems, natural, cycles,* and *population*—remain the same.

Source authors' words	Malik's paraphrase
Such intuition is even making its way, albeit slowly, into scholarly circles, where recognition is mounting that	Scholars are coming to believe that
ever-increasing pressures on ecosystems, life-supporting environmental services, and critical natural cycles are driven not only by the sheer number of resource users and the inefficiencies of their resource use, but also by the patterns of resource use themselves.	overconsumption is partly to blame for changes in ecosystems, reduction of essential natural resources, and changes in natural cycles.
In global environmental policy-making arenas, it is becoming more and more difficult to ignore the fact that	Policy makers increasingly see that

MALIK'S EXAMPLE

The trickiest aspect of paraphrasing is changing the language without changing the meaning. Note for your students that Malik's paraphrase uses very few words from the original (you might want to have your students count them). Note that he does not merely replace words with synonyms, but changes sentence structure as well.

COLLABORATIVE LEARNING

Distribute a short article to students in class. Assign each group a section to paraphrase. Have students first paraphrase their assigned section individually, and then compare their paraphrases with others in the group. They should check one another's work to ensure that word choices and sentence structure are changed, while the original meaning is retained. Each group should then create a definitive paraphrase of the section that they can share with the class.

Source authors' words	Malik's paraphrase
overdeveloped countries must restrain their consumption if they expect underdeveloped countries to embrace a more sustainable trajectory.	wealthy nations have to start consuming less if they want developing nations to adopt practices that reduce pollution and waste.
And while global population growth still remains a huge issue in many regions around the world—both rich and poor—	Rising population around the world does cause significant stress on the environment,
per-capita growth in consumption is, for many resources, expanding eight to twelve times faster than population growth.	but consumption is increasing even more rapidly than population.

Follow these guidelines when paraphrasing:

- **Read the material several times to be sure you understand it.**
- **Restate the main ideas in your own words and sentence structures.** You do not have to follow the organization of the original or restate all of it. Select and restate only what you need. If complete sentences seem too detailed or cumbersome, use phrases. Justin Malik might have written the following briefer paraphrase of the quotation by Princen, Maniates, and Conca.

Abbreviated paraphrase of source

Environmental consequences of consumption

Princen, Maniates, and Conca 4

Overconsumption is increasing more rapidly than population + contributing to major ecological crises. Wealthy nations have to start consuming less.

- **Be careful not to distort meaning.** Don't change the source's emphasis or omit connecting words, qualifiers, and other material whose absence will confuse you later or cause you to misrepresent the source. (See also p. 618.)
- **Be careful not to plagiarize the source.** Use your own words and sentence structures, and always provide a citation in your notes.

The following examples show the preceding abbreviated paraphrase in the context of a draft, the first lacking proper citation and the second with proper citation (in MLA style).

Paraphrase with no citation (plagiarized)

Always seeking newer and better things, we consume without regard for the resources we use or the waste we leave behind. In fact, overconsumption is increasing more rapidly than population and contributing to major ecological crises. Wealthy nations have to start consuming less.

Paraphrase with proper citation (not plagiarized)

Always seeking newer and better things, we consume without regard for the resources we use or the waste we leave behind. In fact, according to Thomas Princen, Michael Maniates, and Ken Conca, overconsumption is increasing more rapidly than population and contributing to major ecological crises. Wealthy nations have to start consuming less (4).

See page 631 for more examples of plagiarism and revision.

CULTURE LANGUAGE If English is not your native language and you have difficulty paraphrasing the ideas in sources, try this: Before attempting a paraphrase, read the original passage several times. Then, instead of "translating" line by line, try to state the gist of the passage without looking at it. Check your effort against the original to be sure you have captured the source author's meaning and emphasis without using his or her words and sentence structures. If you need a synonym for a word, look it up in a dictionary.

3   Quoting

When you **quote** a source, you reproduce the author's exact words. Choose quotations carefully, making sure that they work for, not replace, your ideas.

Deciding when to quote

Your notes from sources may include many quotations, especially if you rely on photocopies, printouts, or downloads. Whether to use a quotation in your draft, instead of a summary or paraphrase, depends on whether the source is primary or secondary and on how important the exact words are.

- **Quote extensively only when you are analyzing primary sources,** such as literary works and historical documents. The quotations will often be both the target of your analysis and the chief support for your ideas. You may need to quote many brief passages, integrated into your sentences, and then comment on the quotations to clarify your analysis and win readers' agreement with it. For examples, see Vanessa Haley's analysis of Annie Dillard's writing (p. 720) and the three literary analyses in Chapter 49 (pp. 746, 750, and 752).
- **Quote selectively when you are drawing on secondary sources**—reports or analyses of other sources, such as a critic's

view of a poem or a historian's synthesis of several eyewitness reports. Favor summaries and paraphrases over quotations, and put every quotation to each test in the box below. Most papers of ten or so pages should not need more than two or three quotations that are longer than a few lines each.

Tests for direct quotations from secondary sources

The author's original satisfies one of these requirements:

- The language is unusually vivid, bold, or inventive.
- The quotation cannot be paraphrased without distortion or loss of meaning.
- The words themselves are at issue in your interpretation.
- The quotation represents and emphasizes a body of opinion or the view of an important expert.
- The quotation emphatically reinforces your own idea.
- The quotation is an illustration, such as a graph, diagram, or table.

The quotation is as short as possible:

- It includes only material relevant to your point.
- It is edited to eliminate examples and other unneeded material. (For editing quotations, see the bulleted list below.)

Transcribing and using quotations

When you quote a source, either in your notes or in your draft, take precautions to avoid plagiarism or misrepresentation of the source:

- **Copy the material carefully.** Take down the author's exact wording, spelling, capitalization, and punctuation.
- **Proofread every direct quotation at least twice.**
- **Use quotation marks around the quotation** so that later you won't confuse it with a paraphrase or summary. Be sure to transfer the quotation marks into your draft as well, unless the quotation is long. See later pages for handling long quotations in MLA style (690–91), Chicago style (772), and APA style (801).
- **Use brackets** to add words for clarity or to change the capitalization of letters (see pp. 474, 483).
- **Use ellipsis marks** to omit irrelevant words or sentences (see p. 475).
- **Cite the source of the quotation in your draft.** See pages 634–35 on documenting sources.

For a summary of conventions regarding quotations, see the chart on pages 460–61.

The note below shows how Justin Malik might have quoted part of the passage on pages 611–12 by Princen, Maniates, and Conca, using brackets and ellipsis marks to make the quotation more concise. Notice the record of the authors' names and the page number as well as the quotation marks around the authors' exact words—all of which would help Malik avoid plagiarizing the source in his paper.

Quotation of source

Environmental consequences of consumption

Princen, Maniates, and Conca 4

"[E]ver-increasing pressures on ecosystems, life-supporting environmental services, and critical natural cycles are driven not only by the sheer number of resource users . . . but also by the patterns of resource use themselves."

The following examples show the preceding quotation in the context of a draft, the first lacking appropriate punctuation and proper citation and the second corrected (in MLA style).

Quotation lacking quotation marks, an ellipsis mark, and a citation (plagiarized)
Increasing consumption may be as much of a threat to the environment as increasing population. In fact, ever-increasing pressures on ecosystems, life-supporting environmental services, and critical natural cycles are driven not only by the sheer number of resource users but also by the patterns of resource use themselves.

Quotation with quotation marks, an ellipsis mark, and proper citation (not plagiarized)
Increasing consumption may be as much of a threat to the environment as increasing population. According to Thomas Princen, Michael Maniates, and Ken Conca, "ever-increasing pressures on ecosystems, life-supporting environmental services, and critical natural cycles are driven not only by the sheer number of resource users . . . but also by the patterns of resource use themselves" (4).

See pages 630–31 for more examples of plagiarism and revision.

4 | Combining quotation, summary, and paraphrase

Using quotation in combination with summary or paraphrase can help you shape the material to suit your purposes (although you must be careful not to distort the author's meaning). The note on the next page shows how Justin Malik might have used a combination of quotation and paraphrase to record the statement by Princen, Maniates, and Conca. Notice the record of the authors' names and the page number as well as the quotation marks around the

RESPONSIBLE USE

Students can learn a great deal about the ethics of responsible summary, paraphrase, and quotation by practicing on each other. Have each student e-mail an abstract of his or her paper-in-progress to a partner in the class. Ask the partner to quote directly from the abstract, to paraphrase part of the abstract, and then to summarize the other person's project. Have each student check the accuracy of his or her partner's quotation, paraphrase, and summary.

IRRESPONSIBLE USE

As a follow-up to the previous exercise you might ask each student's partner to misquote deliberately or to paraphrase or summarize in a way that misrepresents the project. Then ask the student authors to identify the particular ways in which their work has been misrepresented.

authors' exact words—all of which would help Malik avoid plagiarizing the source in his paper.

Combined paraphrase and quotation of source

> Environmental consequences of consumption
>
> Princen, Maniates, and Conca 4
>
> Scholars are coming to believe that consumption as much as rising population is to blame for "ever-increasing pressures on ecosystems, life-supporting environmental services, and critical natural cycles."

The examples below show the combined paraphrase and quotation in the context of a draft. The first example cites the source but passes off the quoted language as part of the paraphrase. The second example includes the needed quotation marks.

Combined paraphrase and quotation without quotation marks (plagiarized)

Always seeking newer and better things, we consume without regard for the resources we use or the waste we leave behind. According to Thomas Princen, Michael Maniates, and Ken Conca, scholars are coming to believe that consumption as much as rising population is to blame for ever-increasing pressures on ecosystems, life-supporting environmental services, and critical natural cycles (4).

Combined paraphrase and quotation with quotation marks (not plagiarized)

Always seeking newer and better things, we consume without regard for the resources we use or the waste we leave behind. According to Thomas Princen, Michael Maniates, and Ken Conca, scholars are coming to believe that overconsumption as much as rising population is to blame for "ever-increasing pressures on ecosystems, life-supporting environmental services, and critical natural cycles" (4).

See pages 630–31 for more examples of plagiarism and revision.

5 | Using sources accurately and fairly

When borrowing from sources, you must represent the author's meaning exactly, without distorting it. In the inaccurate summary on the facing page, the writer has stated a meaning exactly opposite that of the original. The original quotation, from the artist Henri Matisse, appears in Jack D. Flam, *Matisse on Art*, page 148.

Original   For the artist creation begins with vision. To see is itself a creative operation, requiring an effort. Everything that we see in our daily life is more or less distorted by acquired habits, and this is perhaps more evident in an age like ours when cinema posters and magazines present us every day with a flood of ready-made images which are to the eye what prejudices are to the mind.

Inaccurate summary   Matisse said that the artist can learn how to see creatively by looking at posters and magazines (qtd. in Flam 148).

The revision below combines summary and quotation to represent the author's meaning exactly:

Accurate summary   Matisse said that the artist must overcome visual "habits" and "prejudices," particularly those developed in response to images of popular culture (qtd. in Flam 148).

Exercise 43.7 Summarizing and paraphrasing

Prepare two source notes, one summarizing the entire following paragraph and the other paraphrasing the first four sentences (ending with the word *autonomy*). Use the note format illustrated in the preceding section, omitting only the subject heading.

> Federal organization [of the United States] has made it possible for the different states to deal with the same problems in many different ways. One consequence of federalism, then, has been that people are treated differently, by law, from state to state. The great strength of this system is that differences from state to state in cultural preferences, moral standards, and levels of wealth can be accommodated. In contrast to a unitary system in which the central government makes all important decisions (as in France), federalism is a powerful arrangement for maximizing regional freedom and autonomy. The great weakness of our federal system, however, is that people in some states receive less than the best or the most advanced or the least expensive services and policies that government can offer. The federal dilemma does not invite easy solutions, for the costs and benefits of the arrangement have tended to balance out.
>
> —Peter K. Eisinger et al., *American Politics*, page 44

Exercise 43.8 Combining summary, paraphrase, and direct quotation

Prepare a source note that combines paraphrase or summary and direct quotation to state the main idea of the following passage. Use the note format illustrated in the preceding section, omitting only the subject heading.

> Most speakers unconsciously duel even during seemingly casual conversations, as can often be observed at social gatherings where they show less concern for exchanging information with other guests than for asserting their own dominance. Their verbal dueling often employs very subtle weapons like mumbling, a hostile act which defeats the listener's desire to understand what the speaker claims he is trying to say (but is really not saying because he is mumbling!). Or the verbal dueler may

ANSWERS: EXERCISE 43.7

Possible summary

Eisinger et al. 44
Federalism, unlike a unitary system, allows the states autonomy. Its strength and its weakness—which are in balance—lie in the regional differences it permits.

Possible paraphrase

Eisinger et al. 44
Under federalism, each state can devise its own ways of handling problems and its own laws. The system's advantage is that a state can operate according to its people's culture, morals, and wealth. A unitary system like that in France does not permit such diversity.

ANSWERS: EXERCISE 43.8

Possible answer

Farb 107
Speakers at parties often "unconsciously duel" in conversations in order to assert "dominance" over others. A speaker may mumble, thus preventing a listener from understanding what is said. Or he or she may continue talking after the listener has moved away, a "challenge to the listener to return and acknowledge the dominance of the speaker."

keep talking after someone has passed out of hearing range—which is
often an aggressive challenge to the listener to return and acknowledge
the dominance of the speaker.
—Peter K. Farb, *Word Play*, page 107

Exercise 43.9 Gathering information from sources

Continuing from Exercise 43.6 (p. 607), as the next step in preparing a
research paper, gather and organize the information from your sources.
Mark every note, photocopy, printout, and download with the source's
publication information and a heading related to your paper. Annotate
relevant passages of photocopies, printouts, and downloads. For handwritten or computer notes, use direct quotation, summary, or paraphrase
as seems appropriate, being careful to avoid inaccuracy and plagiarism.
(If you need help recognizing plagiarism, see Chapter 44.)

43e Integrating sources into your text

Integrating sources into your sentences is key to synthesizing
others' ideas and information with your own. Evidence drawn from
sources should *back up* your conclusions, not *be* your conclusions:
you don't want to let your evidence overwhelm your own voice and
point of view. The point of research writing is to investigate and go
beyond sources, to interpret them and use them to support your
own independent ideas.

Note Integrating borrowed material into your sentences involves several conventions discussed elsewhere in this book:

- **Using commas to punctuate signal phrases,** pages 436–38.
- **Placing other punctuation marks with quotation marks,** pages
  465–66.
- **Using brackets for changes in quotations,** page 474 and oppo-
  site.
- **Using ellipsis marks for omissions from quotations,** pages
  475–77.
- **Punctuating and placing parenthetical citations,** pages 650–52.
- **Setting off long quotations from your text without quotation
  marks,** pages 690–91 (MLA style), 772 (Chicago style), and 801
  (APA style).

1 Introducing borrowed material

When using a summary, a paraphrase, or a quotation, smooth
the transition between your ideas and words and those of your
source.

Note The examples in this and the next section use the MLA
style of source documentation and also present-tense verbs (such as

disagrees). For specific variations in documentation and verb tense within the academic disciplines, see pages 624–25.

Links between borrowed material and your own sentences

Readers will be distracted from your point if borrowed material does not fit into your sentence. In the passage below, the writer has not meshed the structures of her own and her source's sentences:

> **Awkward**   One editor disagrees with this view and "a good reporter does not fail to separate opinions from facts" (Lyman 52).

In the following revision the writer adds words to integrate the quotation into her sentence:

> **Revised**   One editor disagrees with this view, <u>maintaining that</u> "a good reporter does not fail to separate opinions from facts" (Lyman 52).

Alterations of quotations

To mesh your own and your source's words, you may sometimes need to make a substitution or addition to the quotation, signaling your change with brackets:

Words added

"The tabloids [of England] are a journalistic case study in bad reporting," claims Lyman (52).

Verb form changed

A bad reporter, Lyman implies, is one who "[fails] to separate opinions from facts" (52). [The bracketed verb replaces *fail* in the original.]

Capitalization changed

"[T]o separate opinions from facts" is a goal of good reporting (Lyman 52). [In the original, *to* is not capitalized.]

Noun supplied for pronoun

The reliability of a news organization "depends on [reporters'] trustworthiness," says Lyman (52). [The bracketed noun replaces *their* in the original.]

2   Interpreting borrowed material

You need to work borrowed material into your sentences so that readers see without effort how any quotation, paraphrase, or summary contributes to your point. If you merely dump source material into your paper without explaining how you intend it to be understood, readers will have to struggle to understand your sentences and the relationships you are trying to establish. For example, the following passage forces us to figure out for ourselves that the writer's sentence and the quotation state opposite points of view.

> Dumped   Many news editors and reporters maintain that it is impossible to keep personal opinions from influencing the selection and presentation of facts. "True, news reporters, like everyone else, form impressions of what they see and hear. However, a good reporter does not fail to separate opinions from facts" (Lyman 52).

In the revision the underlined additions tell us how to interpret the quotation:

> Revised   Many news editors and reporters maintain that it is impossible to keep personal opinions from influencing the selection and presentation of facts. <u>Yet not all authorities agree with this view. One editor grants that</u> "news reporters, like everyone else, form impressions of what they see and hear." <u>But, he insists,</u> "a good reporter does not fail to separate opinions from facts" (Lyman 52).

Signal phrases

In the revised passage above, the words *One editor grants* and *he insists* are **signal phrases:** they tell readers who the source is and what to expect in the quotations that follow. Signal phrases usually contain (1) the source author's name (or a substitute for it, such as *One editor* and *he*) and (2) a verb that indicates the source author's attitude or approach to what he or she says. In the preceding example, *grants* implies concession and *insists* implies argument. The box on the next page gives a list of verbs that are often used in signal phrases.

Vary your signal phrases to suit your interpretation of borrowed material and also to keep readers' interest. A signal phrase may precede, interrupt, or follow the borrowed material:

Signal phrase precedes
Lyman insists that "a good reporter does not fail to separate opinions from facts" (52).

Signal phrase interrupts
"However," Lyman insists, "a good reporter does not fail to separate opinions from facts" (52).

Signal phrase follows
"[A] good reporter does not fail to separate opinions from facts," Lyman insists (52).

Background information

You can add information to a signal phrase to inform readers why you are using a source. In most cases, provide the author's name in the text, especially if the author is an expert or if readers will recognize the name:

Verbs for signal phrases

Use verbs that convey information about source authors' attitudes or approaches. In the sentence *Smith* _____ *that the flood might have been disastrous,* filling the blank with *observes, finds,* or *insists* would create different meanings.

Note Disciplines vary in the tenses of verbs used within signal phrases. The verbs listed below are in the present tense, which is typical of writing about literature and in other humanities. But in the social and natural sciences, the past tense (*asked*) or present perfect tense (*has asked*) is more common. See page 625.

Author is neutral	Author infers or suggests	Author argues	Author is uneasy or disparaging
comments	analyzes	claims	belittles
describes	asks	contends	bemoans
explains	assesses	defends	complains
illustrates	concludes	disagrees	condemns
notes	finds	holds	deplores
observes	predicts	insists	deprecates
points out	proposes	maintains	derides
records	reveals	**Author agrees**	laments
relates	shows	admits	warns
reports	speculates	agrees	
says	suggests	concedes	
sees	supposes	concurs	
thinks		grants	
writes			

Author named

Harold Lyman grants that "news reporters, like everyone else, form impressions of what they see and hear." But, Lyman insists, "a good reporter does not fail to separate opinions from facts" (52).

If the source title contributes information about the author or the context of the quotation, you can provide it in the text:

Title given

Harold Lyman, in his book *The Conscience of the Journalist*, grants that "news reporters, like everyone else, form impressions of what they see and hear." But, Lyman insists, "a good reporter does not fail to separate opinions from facts" (52).

Finally, if the quoted author's background and experience reinforce or clarify the quotation, you can provide these credentials in the text:

Credentials given

Harold Lyman, a newspaper editor for more than forty years, grants that "news reporters, like everyone else, form impressions of what they see and hear." But, Lyman insists, "a good reporter does not fail to separate opinions from facts" (52).

You need not always name the author, source, or credentials in your text. In fact, such introductions may get in the way when you are simply establishing facts or weaving together facts and opinions from varied sources. In the following passage, the information is more important than the source, so the name of the source is confined to a parenthetical acknowledgment:

> To end the abuses of the British, many colonists were urging three actions: forming a united front, seceding from Britain, and taking control of their own international relations (Wills 325–36).

3 Following discipline styles for integrating sources

The preceding guidelines for introducing and interpreting borrowed material apply generally across academic disciplines, but there are differences in verb tense and documentation style.

English and some other humanities

Writers in English, foreign languages, and related disciplines use MLA style for documenting sources (see Chapter 46) and generally use the present tense of verbs in signal phrases. In discussing sources other than works of literature, the present perfect tense is also sometimes appropriate:

> Lyman insists . . . [present].
> Lyman has insisted . . . [present perfect].

In discussing works of literature, use only the present tense to describe both the work of the author and the action in the work:

> Kate Chopin builds irony into every turn of "The Story of an Hour." For example, Mrs. Mallard, the central character, finds joy in the death of her husband, whom she loves, because she anticipates "the long procession of years that would belong to her absolutely" (23).

Avoid shifting tenses in writing about literature. You can, for instance, shorten quotations to avoid their past-tense verbs:

> Shift   Her freedom elevates her, so that "she carried herself unwittingly like a goddess of victory" (24).
>
> No shift Her freedom elevates her, so that she walks "unwittingly like a goddess of victory" (24).

History and other humanities

Writers in history, art history, philosophy, and related disciplines generally use the present tense or present perfect tense of verbs in signal phrases:

> Lincoln persisted, as Haworth has noted, in "feeling that events controlled him."[3]

What Miller <u>calls</u> Lincoln's "severe self-doubt"[6] undermined the President's effectiveness on at least two occasions.

The raised numbers after the quotations are part of the Chicago documentation style, used in history and other disciplines and discussed on pages 760–61.

Social and natural sciences

Writers in the sciences generally use a verb's present tense just for reporting the results of a study (*The data suggest* . . .). Otherwise, they use a verb's past tense or present perfect tense in a signal phrase, as when introducing an explanation, interpretation, or other commentary. (Thus when you are writing for the sciences, generally convert the list of signal-phrase verbs on p. 623 from the present to the past or present perfect tense.)

> Lin (1999) <u>has suggested</u> that preschooling may significantly affect children's academic performance through high school (pp. 22–23).

> In an exhaustive survey of the literature published between 1990 and 2000, Walker (2001) <u>found</u> "no proof, merely a weak correlation, linking place of residence and rate of illness" (p. 121).

These passages conform to APA documentation style, discussed on pages 779–99. APA style, or one quite similar to it, is also used in sociology, education, nursing, biology, and many other sciences.

Exercise 43.10   Introducing and interpreting borrowed material

Drawing on the ideas in the following paragraph and using examples from your own observations and experiences, write a paragraph about anxiety. Integrate at least one direct quotation and one paraphrase from the following paragraph into your own sentences. In your paragraph identify the author by name and give his credentials: he is a professor of psychiatry and a practicing psychoanalyst.

> There are so many ways in which man is different from all the lower forms of animals, and almost all of them make us uniquely susceptible to feelings of anxiousness. Our imagination and reasoning powers facilitate anxiety; the anxious feeling is precipitated not by an absolute impending threat—such as the worry about an examination, a speech, travel—but rather by the symbolic and often unconscious representations. We do not have to be experiencing a potential danger. We can experience something related to it. We can recall, through our incredible memories, the original symbolic sense of vulnerability in childhood and suffer the feeling attached to that. We can even forget the original memory and still be stuck with the emotion—which is then compounded by its seemingly irrational quality at this time. It is not just the fear of death which pains us, but the anticipation of it; or the anniversary of a specific death; or a street, a hospital, a time of day, a color, a flower, a symbol associated with death.
> —Willard Gaylin, "Feeling Anxious," page 23

ANSWERS: EXERCISE 43.10

Sample paragraph

Why does a woman who is otherwise happy regularly suffer anxiety attacks at the first sign of spring? Why does a man who is otherwise a competent, relaxed driver feel panic whenever he approaches a traffic rotary? According to Willard Gaylin, a professor of psychiatry and a practicing psychoanalyst, such feelings of anxiety are attributable to the uniquely human capacities for remembering, imagining, and forming "symbolic and often unconscious representations" of experiences (23). The feeling of anxiety, Gaylin says, "is . . . compounded by its seemingly irrational quality": it may appear despite the absence of an immediate source of worry or pain (23). The anxious woman is not aware of it, but her father's death twenty years before in April has caused her to equate spring with death. Similarly, the man has forgotten that a terrible accident he witnessed as a child occurred at a rotary. For both people, the anxious feelings are not reduced but heightened because they seem to be unfounded.

44

Avoiding Plagiarism and Documenting Sources

The knowledge building that is the focus of academic writing rests on the integrity of everyone who participates, including students, in using and crediting sources. The work of a writer or creator is his or her intellectual property. You and others may borrow the work's ideas and even its words or an image, but you *must* acknowledge that what you borrowed came from someone else.

When you acknowledge sources in your writing, you are doing more than giving credit to the writer or creator of the work you consulted. You are also showing what your own writing is based on, which in turn gives you credibility as a researcher and writer. Acknowledging sources creates the trust among scholars, students, writers, and readers that knowledge building requires.

Plagiarism (from a Latin word for "kidnapper") is the presentation of someone else's work as your own. Whether deliberate or accidental, plagiarism is a serious offense. It breaks trust, and it undermines or even destroys your credibility as a researcher and writer. In most colleges, a code of academic honesty calls for severe consequences for plagiarism: a reduced or failing grade, suspension from school, or expulsion.

- *Deliberate* plagiarism:
  Copying or downloading a phrase, a sentence, or a longer passage from a source and passing it off as your own by omitting quotation marks and a source citation.
  Summarizing or paraphrasing someone else's ideas without acknowledging your debt in a source citation.
  Handing in as your own work a paper you have bought, copied off the Web, had a friend write, or accepted from another student.

Checklist for avoiding plagiarism

Type of source

Are you using

- your own independent material,
- common knowledge, or
- someone else's independent material?

You must acknowledge someone else's material.

Quotations

- Do all quotations exactly match their sources? Check them.
- Have you inserted quotation marks around quotations that are run into your text?
- Have you shown omissions with ellipsis marks and additions with brackets?
- Does every quotation have a source citation?

Paraphrases and summaries

- Have you used your own words and sentence structures for every paraphrase and summary? If not, use quotation marks around the original author's words.
- Does every paraphrase and summary have a source citation?

The Web

- Have you obtained any necessary permission to use someone else's material on the Web?

Source citations

- Have you acknowledged every use of someone else's material in each place you used it?
- Does your list of works cited include all the sources you have used?

- *Accidental* plagiarism:

    Reading a wide variety of print or Web sources on a subject without taking notes on them, and then not remembering the difference between what you recently learned and what you already knew.

    Forgetting to place quotation marks around another writer's words.

    Carelessly omitting a source citation for a paraphrase.

    Omitting a source citation for another's idea because you are unaware of the need to acknowledge the idea.

The way to avoid plagiarism is to acknowledge your sources by documenting them. This chapter discusses plagiarism and the Internet (next page), shows how to distinguish what doesn't require

INTELLECTUAL PROPERTY AND CULTURE

Ideas about ownership of intellectual property vary among cultures. In some cultures scholarly research consists of finding expert sources and copying information without attribution. ESL students who copy without attribution or too closely paraphrase sources may be following the procedures they have been taught. In their countries plagiarism may be considered less objectionable than in the United States, or perhaps in their culture students are encouraged to use classic works in their own writing. See "Teaching Writing to ESL Students" (p. 62 of this manual) for further discussion of ESL students' attitudes toward plagiarism. Discuss the issue of intellectual ownership with your students, emphasizing that in the United States research and writing are valued for their originality.

acknowledgment from what does (this page through p. 631), covers issues particular to online sources (pp. 632–34), and provides an overview of source documentation (pp. 634–35).

CULTURE LANGUAGE The concept of intellectual property and thus the rules governing plagiarism are not universal. In some other cultures, for instance, students may be encouraged to copy the words of scholars without acknowledgment, in order to demonstrate their mastery of or respect for the scholars' work. In the United States, however, using an author's work without a source citation is considered theft. When in doubt about the guidelines in this chapter, ask your instructor for advice.

44a Committing and detecting plagiarism on the Internet

The Internet has made it easier to plagiarize than ever before, and it has also made plagiarism easier to catch.

Even honest students risk accidental plagiarism by downloading sources and importing portions into their drafts (see p. 610). Dishonest students may take advantage of the downloading process to steal others' work. They may also use the term-paper businesses on the Web, which offer both ready-made research and complete papers, usually for a fee. **Paying for research or a paper does not make it the buyer's work.** Anyone who submits someone else's work as his or her own is a plagiarist.

Students who plagiarize from the Internet deprive themselves of an education in honest research, and they also expose themselves to detection. Teachers can use search engines to find specific phrases or sentences anywhere on the Web, including among scholarly publications, all kinds of Web sites, and term-paper collections. They can search term-paper sites as easily as students can, looking for similarities with papers they've received. They can also use detection software such as *Turnitin* that compares students' work with other work anywhere on the Internet, seeking matches as short as a few words.

Some instructors suggest that their students use plagiarism-detection programs to verify that their own work does not include accidental plagiarism, at least not from the Internet.

44b Knowing what you need not acknowledge

Two kinds of information do not have to be acknowledged in source citations: your own independent material and common knowledge.

1 Using your independent material

Your own independent material includes your thoughts, observations from experience, compilations of facts, or experimental results, expressed in your words or format. For example, you might offer a conclusion about crowd behavior based on watching crowds at concerts or draw a diagram from information you gathered yourself. Though you generally should describe the basis for your conclusions so that readers can evaluate your thinking, you need not cite sources for them.

Note that someone else's ideas and facts are not yours, even when you express them entirely in your own words and sentence structures. The ideas and facts require acknowledgment.

2 Using common knowledge

Common knowledge consists of the standard information of a field of study as well as folk literature and commonsense observations.

- **Standard information** includes the major facts of history, such as the dates during which Charlemagne ruled as emperor of Rome (800–14). It does *not* include interpretations of facts, such as a historian's opinion that Charlemagne was sometimes needlessly cruel in extending his power.
- **Folk literature,** such as the fairy tale "Snow White," is popularly known and cannot be traced to a particular writer. Literature traceable to a writer is *not* folk literature, even if it is very familiar.
- **Commonsense observations** are things most people know, such as that inflation is most troublesome for people with low and fixed incomes. A particular economist's idea about the effects of inflation on Chinese immigrants is *not* a commonsense observation.

As long as you express it in your own words and sentence structures, you may use common knowledge as your own.

The first time you come across an idea or a piece of information that you may want to use, record the publication information for the source. If in wider reading you repeatedly encounter the same idea or information without cited sources, then you may assume it's common knowledge. Don't take unnecessary risks, however: a source citation for common knowledge is not wrong.

44c Knowing what you *must* acknowledge

You must always acknowledge other people's independent material—that is, any facts or ideas that are not common knowledge or

---

your own. The source may be anything, including a book, an article, a movie, an interview, a microfilmed document, a Web page, a newsgroup posting, or an opinion expressed on the radio. You must acknowledge summaries or paraphrases of ideas or facts as well as quotations of the language and format in which ideas or facts appear: wording, sentence structures, arrangement, and special graphics (such as a diagram).

You need to acknowledge another's material no matter how you use it, how much of it you use, or how often you use it. Whether you are quoting a single important word, paraphrasing a single sentence, or summarizing three paragraphs, and whether you are using the source only once or a dozen times, you must acknowledge the original author every time. See pages 634–35 for how to acknowledge sources and pages 650–53 for where to place source citations in relation to cited material.

1 Using copied language: Quotation marks and a source citation

Copied words and sentence structure

The following example baldly plagiarizes the original quotation from Jessica Mitford's *Kind and Usual Punishment*, page 9. Without quotation marks or a source citation, the example matches Mitford's wording (underlined) and closely parallels her sentence structure:

Original (quotation)	"The character and mentality of the keepers may be of more importance in understanding prisons than the character and mentality of the kept."
Plagiarism	But the character of prison officials (the keepers) is of more importance in understanding prisons than the character of prisoners (the kept).

To avoid plagiarism, the writer can paraphrase and cite the source (see the next page) or use Mitford's actual words *in quotation marks and with a source citation* (here, in MLA style):

Revision (quotation)	According to one critic of the penal system, "The character and mentality of the keepers may be of more importance in understanding prisons than the character and mentality of the kept" (Mitford 9).

Changed sentence structure but copied words

Even with a source citation and with a different sentence structure, the next example is still plagiarism because it uses some of Mitford's words (underlined) without quotation marks:

Plagiarism	According to one critic of the penal system, the psychology of <u>the kept</u> may say less about prisons than the psychology of <u>the keepers</u> (Mitford 9).
Revision (quotation)	According to one critic of the penal system, the psychology of "the kept" may say less about prisons than the psychology of "the keepers" (Mitford 9).

2 Using a paraphrase or summary: Your own words and sentence structure and a source citation

Changed sentence structure but copied words

The following example changes the sentence structure of the original Mitford quotation opposite, but it still uses Mitford's words (underlined) without quotation marks or a source citation:

Plagiarism	In <u>understanding prisons</u>, we might focus less on the <u>character and mentality of the kept</u> than on those of <u>the keepers</u>.

To avoid plagiarism, the writer can use quotation marks and cite the source or *use his or her own words* and still *cite the source* (because the idea is Mitford's, not the writer's):

Revision (paraphrase)	Mitford holds that we may be able to learn less about prisons from the psychology of prisoners than from the psychology of prison officials (9).
Revision (paraphrase)	We may understand prisons better if we focus on the personalities and attitudes of the prison workers rather than those of the inmates (Mitford 9).

Changed words but copied sentence structure

In the next example, the writer cites Mitford and does not use her words but still plagiarizes her sentence structure:

Plagiarism	One critic of the penal system maintains that <u>the psychology of prison officials may be more informative about prisons than the psychology of prisoners</u> (Mitford 9).
Revision (paraphrase)	One critic of the penal system maintains that we may be able to learn less from the psychology of prisoners than from the psychology of prison officials (Mitford 9).

Exercise 44.1 Recognizing plagiarism

The following numbered items show various attempts to quote or paraphrase a passage by George E. Vaillant. Carefully compare each attempt with the original passage. Which attempts are plagiarized, inaccurate, or both, and which are acceptable? Why?

COLLABORATIVE LEARNING

Have students complete Exercise 44.1 individually and then discuss their responses in small groups. Encourage groups to debate the accuracy of each attempted quotation or paraphrase, paying particular attention to items on which group members have differing responses. Students learn a great deal from the task of identifying the particular way in which a passage has been plagiarized or accurately represented.

1. Plagiarized: takes phrases directly from the original without quotation marks.
2. Acceptable: acknowledges the source, uses quotation marks around copied words, and uses brackets around an addition to the quotation.
3. Inaccurate and plagiarized: the passage uses phrases from the original without quotation marks and distorts its meaning.
4. Acceptable: acknowledges the source, restates the original in new words and correctly conveys the original's meaning.
5. Inaccurate and plagiarized: fails to acknowledge the source and fails to convey accurately the concepts of "discrimination" and "confusing" outlined in the original.
6. Inaccurate: ellipses are needed to indicate that material was omitted, and brackets must be placed around lowercase *s* to indicate revision. In addition, the editing of the passage omits mention of "psychiatric labeling," the focus of the original.

COLLABORATIVE LEARNING

FAIR-USE JURY

When students are unsure whether they have violated principles of fair use for their online sources, have them submit the material in question to the rest of the class, who can render opinions. This exercise will help to impress upon students that the principles of fair use are ones that reasonable people would agree to.

I would agree with the sociologists that psychiatric labeling is dangerous. Society can inflict terrible wounds by discrimination, and by confusing health with disease and disease with badness.
—George E. Vaillant, *Adaptation to Life,* p. 361

1. According to George Vaillant, society often inflicts wounds by using psychiatric labeling, confusing health, disease, and badness (361).
2. According to George Vaillant, "psychiatric labeling [such as 'homosexual' or 'schizophrenic'] is dangerous. Society can inflict terrible wounds by . . . confusing health with disease and disease with badness" (361).
3. According to George Vaillant, when psychiatric labeling discriminates between health and disease or between disease and badness, it can inflict wounds on those labeled (361).
4. Psychiatric labels can badly hurt those labeled, says George Vaillant, because they fail to distinguish among health, illness, and immorality (361).
5. Labels such as "homosexual" and "schizophrenic" can be hurtful when they fail to distinguish among health, illness, and immorality.
6. "I would agree with the sociologists that society can inflict terrible wounds by discrimination, and by confusing health with disease and disease with badness" (Vaillant 361).

44d Acknowledging online sources

Online sources are so accessible and so easy to download into your own documents that it may seem they are freely available, exempting you from the obligation to acknowledge them. They are not. Acknowledging online sources is somewhat trickier than acknowledging print sources, but no less essential. Further, if you are publishing your work on the Web, you need to take account of sources' copyright restrictions as well.

Note Ask your instructor for advice whenever you are unsure about citing an online source or seeking permission to use copyrighted material.

1 Acknowledging online sources in an unpublished project

When you use material from an online source in a print or online document to be distributed just to your class, your obligation to cite sources does not change: you must acknowledge someone else's independent material in whatever form you find it. With online sources, that obligation can present additional challenges.

- **Record complete publication information each time you consult an online source.** Online sources may change from one day to the next or even disappear entirely. See page 559 for the information to record, such as the electronic address and the publication date. Without the proper information, you *may not* use the source.

- **Acknowledge linked sites.** If you use not only a Web site but also one or more of its linked sites, you must acknowledge the linked sites as well. The fact that one person has used a second person's work does not release you from the responsibility to cite the second work.

- **Seek the author's permission before using an e-mail message, discussion-group posting, or blog contribution.** Obtaining permission advises the author that his or her ideas are about to be distributed more widely and lets the author verify that you have not misrepresented the ideas. (See p. 601 for advice on tracing authors.)

2 **Acknowledging print and online sources in a Web composition**

When you use material from print or online sources in a composition for the Web, you must not only acknowledge your sources, as discussed above, but take the additional precaution of observing copyright restrictions.

A Web site is a medium of publication just as a book or magazine is and so involves the same responsibility to obtain reprint permission from copyright holders. The exception is a password-protected site (such as a course site), which many copyright holders regard as private. You can find information about copyright holders and permissions on the copyright page of a print publication (following the title page) and on a page labeled something like "Terms of Use" on a Web site. If you don't see an explicit release for student use or publication on private Web sites, assume you must seek permission.

The legal convention of **fair use** allows an author to reprint a small portion of copyrighted material without obtaining the copyright holder's permission, as long as the author acknowledges the source. The online standards of fair use differ for print and online sources and are not fixed in either case. The guidelines below are conservative:

- **Print sources:** Quote without permission fewer than fifty words from an article or fewer than three hundred words from a book. You'll need permission to use any longer quotation from an article or book; any quotation at all from a play, poem, or song; and any use of an entire work—such as a photograph, chart, or other illustration.

- **Online sources:** Quote without permission text that represents just a small portion of the whole—say, up to forty words out of three hundred. Follow the preceding print guidelines for plays, poems, songs, and illustrations, adding multimedia elements (audio or video clips) to the list of works that require reprint permission for any use.

■ **Links:** You may need to seek permission to link your site to another one—for instance, if you rely on the linked site to provide substantial evidence for your claims or if you incorporate a linked site's multimedia element (an image or a sound or video clip) into your site.

Note Although most online sources are copyrighted, much valuable material is not: either the creator does not claim copyright, or the copyright has lapsed so that the work is in the public domain. The first category includes most government documents; the second includes most works by authors who have been dead at least fifty years. You do not need permission to reprint from such a source, but *you still must cite the source.*

44e Documenting sources

Every time you borrow the words, facts, or ideas of others, you must **document** the source—that is, supply a reference (or document) telling readers that you borrowed the material and where you borrowed it from.

Editors and teachers in most academic disciplines require special documentation formats (or styles) in their scholarly journals and in students' papers. All the styles use a citation in the text that serves two purposes: it signals that material is borrowed, and it refers readers to detailed information about the source so that they can locate both the source and the place in the source where the borrowed material appears. The detailed source information appears either in footnotes or at the end of the paper.

Aside from these essential similarities, the disciplines' documentation styles differ markedly in citation form, arrangement of source information, and other particulars. Each discipline's style reflects the needs of its practitioners for certain kinds of information presented in certain ways. For instance, the currency of a source is important in the social and natural sciences, where studies build on and correct each other; thus in-text citations in these disciplines usually include a source's date of publication. In the humanities, however, currency is less important, so in-text citations do not include date of publication.

The disciplines' documentation formats are described in style guides listed elsewhere in this book for the humanities (p. 760), the social sciences (pp. 779–80), and the natural and applied sciences (p. 811). This book also discusses and illustrates four common documentation styles:

- **MLA style,** used in English, foreign languages, and some other humanities (pp. 644–48).
- **Chicago style,** used in history, art history, philosophy, religion, and some other humanities (pp. 760–71).
- **APA style,** used in psychology and some other social sciences (pp. 779–99).
- **CSE style,** used in the biological and some other sciences (pp. 811–17).

Ask your instructor which style you should use. If no style is required, use the guide that's most appropriate for the discipline in which you're writing. Do follow one system for citing sources—and one system only—so that you provide all the necessary information in a consistent format.

Note Bibliography software—*Zotero, Refworks, Endnote,* and others—can help you format your source citations in the style of your choice. Always ask your instructors if you may use such software for your papers. The programs prompt you for needed information (author's name, book title, and so on) and then arrange, capitalize, underline, and punctuate the information as required by the style. But no program can anticipate all the varieties of source information, nor can it substitute for your own care and attention in giving your sources complete acknowledgment using the required form.

45
Writing the Paper

Writing a research paper begins when you seek a topic and continues as you evaluate and gather information from your sources. During research, you might even pause to draft paragraphs or sections that pull your sources together to support your ideas. At some point, though, you'll need to turn your attention to the whole paper—ensuring that it has a clear thesis (next page), creating a structure

Visit *mycomplab.com* for more resources and exercises on writing and revising a research paper.

STATED INTENTIONS

Have students complete this sentence in their journals or on a stick-on note they can post at their workplaces: "In this paper I intend to [statement of purpose], so that my audience, [describe intended readers], will [desired result]." This sentence reminds students to consider purpose, audience, and desired results as they write, and it should lead to clearer thesis statements.

COLLABORATIVE LEARNING

THESIS STATEMENT

Have students write their thesis statements on large sheets of paper. Exchange thesis lists among groups, and have each group analyze and suggest revisions for the theses on their lists. The revising group should be prepared to explain its suggestions to the original writers.

In the later stages of their projects have students repeat this exercise as they read one another's drafts. In this case, groups should check to make sure that each student's thesis accurately represents the point of his or her paper.

THE EVOLVING THESIS

Remind students that the thesis of a research paper can change. As they conduct their research and write their papers, they may find that their purpose, opinion, or conception of their audience has shifted. In such circumstances, revising the thesis is not only desirable but necessary to compose an effective paper.

TEMPLATES FOR THESIS STATEMENTS

Sometimes students need assistance boiling down their point into a manageable thesis statement. Come up with some generic thesis statement templates that fit the students' specific assignment. For example, here is a template for an essay proposing a solution to a problem: *[Problem/ condition] could be remedied/fixed/improved by [solution].* Here is a thesis for a critical analysis paper: *[Name work being analyzed] persuades the audience using [technique A], [technique B], and [technique C].* James Zebroski's *Thinking Through Theory: Vygotskian Perspectives on the Teaching of Writing* (Portsmouth: Boynton/Cook, 1994) offers numerous thesis statement templates to use for

(facing page), writing the complete draft (p. 640), revising and editing the paper (p. 641), and preparing the final draft (p. 643). To illustrate these stages, we continue to draw on Justin Malik's and Vanessa Haley's work.

Note This chapter complements and extends the detailed discussion of the writing situation and the writing process in Chapters 1–3, which also include many tips for using a word processor. If you haven't already done so, read Chapters 1–3 before this one.

45a Developing a thesis statement

Perhaps earlier in the research-writing process, but certainly once you have gathered information from your sources, you will want to express your central idea and perspective in a thesis statement of one or two sentences. (See pp. 27–32 if you need guidance on developing a thesis statement.) Drafting a thesis statement will help you see the overall picture and organize your notes.

Justin Malik's and Vanessa Haley's work on their research papers illustrates how a thesis statement evolves to become complete and specific. Before finishing his reading on green consumerism, Malik wrote the following draft of a thesis statement:

Tentative thesis statement

Consumers need to think very carefully before buying products that claim to be green because many of them actually do more harm than good.

This statement captured Malik's preliminary idea that green products may not be as beneficial to the environment as advertised. But after further reading, Malik rethought this idea. Many of his sources quoted the environmentalists' slogan "Reduce, reuse, recycle," and he began to ask whether green products meet these basic goals. That question opened up new questions: How does consumption in general affect the environment, and can green products significantly reduce this effect? With more research, Malik revised his thesis statement:

Revised thesis statement

Although green consumerism can help the environment, consumerism itself is the root of some of the most pressing ecological problems we face. To make a real difference, we must consume less.

For Vanessa Haley, framing a thesis statement for her paper on Annie Dillard required drawing together (synthesizing) Dillard's ideas about humanity and nature into a single statement of Haley's own. The first draft merely conveyed Haley's interest in Dillard:

Tentative thesis statement

Unlike many other nature writers, Dillard does not reinforce the separation between humanity and nature.

The revision stated Haley's synthesis of Dillard's ideas:

Revised thesis statement

In her encounters with nature, Dillard probes a spiritual as well as a physical identity between human beings and nature that could help to heal the rift between them.

Exercise 45.1 Developing a thesis statement

Draft and revise a thesis statement for your developing research paper. Make sure the revised version specifically asserts your main idea.

45b Creating a structure

Before starting to draft your research paper, organize your ideas and information so that you know the main divisions of your paper, the order you'll cover them in, and the important supporting ideas for each division. The goal is to create a structure that presents your ideas in a sensible and persuasive sequence and that supports ideas at each level with enough explanation and evidence. Consult the discussion of organization on pages 33–43 if you need help distinguishing general and specific information, arranging groups of information, or using a computer effectively for developing a structure.

1 Arranging ideas and support

Creating a structure for a research paper involves almost constant synthesis, the forging of relationships among ideas (see p. 604). As you arrange and rearrange source information and your own thoughts, you find connections among ideas and determine which are most important, which are merely supportive, and which are not relevant at all.

To build a structure, follow these guidelines:

- **Arrange your source information in categories** according to the subject headings you attached to each note, photocopy, or printout. Each category should correspond to a main section of your paper: a key idea of your own that supports the thesis along with the evidence for that idea.
- **Review your research journal and annotated bibliography.** Hunt for connections between sources, opinions of sources, and other thoughts that can help you organize your paper.
- **Look objectively at your categories.** If some are skimpy, with little information, consider whether you should drop the categories or conduct more research to fill them out. If most of your information falls into one or two categories, consider whether the categories are too broad and should be divided. (Does any of this rethinking affect your thesis statement? If so, revise it accordingly.)

ethnographic papers. By starting with templates, students can craft tentative thesis statements and then modify them to fit their needs as their drafts evolve.

ANSWER: EXERCISE 45.1

Individual response.

A DOZEN HATS UNUSED

Reassure students that they're not the only researchers who find interesting information that just doesn't fit in their final work. Historian Barbara Tuchman reports that while researching *The Guns of August,* she discovered that Emperor Franz Joseph gave his wife the same birthday present each year: a dozen hats, which he required her to wear. Tuchman says that she moved the note card from stack to stack, trying to fit it in her 500-plus-page book; however, she finally had to relegate it to the stack marked "unused." Tuchman told this story in an essay she wrote a decade after *The Guns of August* was published—it took that long for her to find a place to use it. You might also encourage students to use a word processor's Footnote function to store information that doesn't seem immediately to fit into a draft in progress. When that draft gets printed out complete with footnotes or endnotes, the student has another opportunity to review the material and decide whether it should become a formal footnote or endnote, should be added in, or should be deleted.

■ **Within each category, distinguish between the main idea and the supporting ideas and evidence.** Only the support should come from your sources. The main idea should be your own.

2 Using an outline

An outline can help you shape your research and also discover potential problems, such as inadequate support and overlapping or irrelevant ideas.

Informal outline

For some research projects, you may find an **informal outline** sufficient: you list main points and supporting information in the order you expect to discuss them. Because of its informality, such an outline can help you try out different arrangements of material, even fairly early in the research process.

While examining his sources, Justin Malik experimented with an informal outline to see how his developing ideas might fit together:

> Environmental crisis
>   Global warming
>   Resource use
>   Biodiversity
>   Pollution
>   Waste
>
> Consumerism
>   Rising standards of living causing more waste
>   Ecological effects—American vs. global
>   Inequality
>   Personal issues: expenses, working hours, stress, unhappiness
>   Voluntary simplicity movement
>
> Green products
>   Appeal to consumers
>   Advantages for businesses
>   Environmental benefits
>   Problems caused by manufacturing, shipping, and discarding products, even green products

This informal outline helped Malik decide not to continue researching consumerism (the second section) because he had more than enough to work with and the topic seemed likely to overwhelm his central question of whether buying green products can solve the environmental crisis (the last and first sections).

Formal outline

Unlike an informal outline, a **formal outline** arranges ideas tightly and in considerable detail, with close attention to hierarchy and phrasing. The example below shows the formal outline's format and schematic content:

    I. First main idea
      A. First subordinate idea
        1. First evidence for subordinate idea
          a. First detail of evidence
          b. Second detail of evidence
        2. Second evidence for subordinate idea
      B. Second subordinate idea
    II. Second main idea

In this model, levels of headings correspond to levels of importance or detail in the paper:

- **Main ideas (Roman numerals) are the major divisions of the paper.** Each division covers a part of your thesis statement and will probably take a number of paragraphs to develop.
- **Subordinate ideas (capital letters) are the building blocks.** These ideas are your own and will probably take a paragraph or two to develop. They may serve as the topic sentences of paragraphs.
- **Evidence (Arabic numerals) and its details (small letters) support each idea.** The evidence from one or more sources will occupy much of each body paragraph. (A fourth sublevel, if needed, is labeled with Arabic numerals enclosed in parentheses.)

Each level of the outline is indented farther than the level it supports. (Your word processor may be able to help you with labels and indentions.)

A formal outline can help you decide not only what your main ideas are and how you will arrange them but also how you will support them. Some of this information may not emerge until you are drafting, however, so remain open to revising the outline as you proceed. And consider using a formal outline as a revision tool as well, creating a map of your completed first draft to check and improve the structure (see p. 52).

To be an effective organizer for your thoughts or an effective revision tool, a formal outline should be detailed and should adhere to several principles of logical arrangement, clarity, balance, and completeness. (See pp. 36–39 for examples and more details.)

- **The outline should indicate which ideas are primary and which are subordinate.** A long, undivided list of parallel items probably needs to be subdivided.
- **Parallel headings should represent ideas of equal importance and generality.** They should not overlap one another.
- **Single sublevels should be avoided.** They illogically divide something into only one part.

A formal outline is usually written either in phrases (a **topic outline**) or in sentences (a **sentence outline**). A complete topic outline is illustrated on page 37. A complete sentence outline accompanies Justin Malik's research paper on pages 694–95. Either is suitable for a research paper, though a sentence outline, because it requires complete statements, conveys more information.

> ### Exercise 45.2 Creating a structure
> Continuing from Exercise 45.1 (p. 637), arrange your notes into a structure. As specified by your instructor, make an informal outline or a formal sentence or topic outline to guide the drafting of your paper.

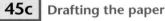 **45c** Drafting the paper

Beginning a draft of what will be a relatively long and complicated paper can be difficult, so it may help to remember that you do not have to proceed methodically from beginning to end.

1 Working section by section

In writing a first draft, remember that a primary reason for doing a research paper is to learn how to interpret and evaluate the evidence in sources, draw your own conclusions from the evidence, and weave the two together in a way that establishes your expertise in your subject. The weaving will be easier if you view each principal idea of your paper (each Roman numeral of your outline) as a unit. Usually these principal ideas require a block of paragraphs to develop.

Compose the units of your paper as if each will stand alone (though of course you will pull the units together before your draft is complete).

- **Begin each unit by stating the idea,** which should be a conclusion you have drawn from reading and responding to your sources.
- **Follow the statement with specific support from your sources:** facts and examples; summaries, paraphrases, or quotations of secondary sources with your analysis; quotations of passages from primary sources with your analysis.
- **Present fairly any disagreements among experts.** Give the evidence that leads you to side with one expert or another.
- **Try to remain open to new interpretations or new arrangements of ideas that occur to you.**

Note Proceeding in this way will help you avoid a common trap of research writing: allowing your sources to control you, rather than vice versa. Make sure each unit of your paper centers on an idea of your own, not someone else's, and that your paragraphs are pointed toward demonstrating that idea, not merely presenting sources.

Tips for drafting a research paper

- **Reread the assignment to review your instructor's criteria.** Make sure you have all the materials you'll need to meet the criteria.
- **Write a quick two- or three-paragraph summary of what the paper will be about.** This writing will get your juices flowing and give you a sense of direction. (Pretend you're writing to a friend if that will help loosen you up.) A version of the material you generate in this way may eventually prove useful for your paper's introduction or conclusion.
- **Start with the section of the paper you feel most confident about.** At first, skip any parts that scare you or give you undue trouble, even the introduction.
- **Work in chunks, one unit or principal idea at a time.** Fit the sections together only after you begin to see the draft take shape.
- **Center each section on an idea of your own.** Use source material to back up the idea.
- **Take great care in working with source material.** Integrate sources into your own ideas (p. 620), and do not plagiarize (p. 626).
- **Insert source citations into the draft as you quote, paraphrase, or summarize.** Use author's names and page numbers.

2 Tracking source citations

As you draft your paper, insert the source of each summary, paraphrase, and quotation in parentheses in the text—for instance, "(Gore 43)," referring to page 43 in a work by Gore. If you are conscientious about inserting these notes and carrying them through successive drafts, you will be less likely to plagiarize accidentally and you will have little difficulty documenting your sources in the final paper.

Exercise 45.3 Drafting your paper

Draft the research paper you have been developing in Chapters 41–44. Before beginning the draft, study your research journal and your source information. While drafting, follow your thesis statement and outline as closely as you need to, but stay open to new ideas, associations, and arrangements.

45d Revising and editing the paper

When you have written a first draft, take a break for at least a day so that you can gain some objectivity about your work and can read the draft critically when you begin to revise.

1 Revising

Always revise your draft first, satisfying yourself with the content and shape of the whole before trying to edit sentences and

ANSWER: EXERCISE 45.3

Individual response.

A WRITER'S PERSPECTIVE

Intelligent, even fastidious revision . . . is, or certainly should be, an art in itself
—JOYCE CAROL OATES

REVISION OUTLINES

Some students will profit by using outlining as a revision strategy. Once students have written one or two drafts of their research papers, have them work in pairs or small groups to outline their drafts, paying particular attention to connections between paragraphs and the presentation of major points.

ELEVENTH-HOUR THESES

Students can panic when it becomes clear in the final revision stages that the paper still lacks a crucial source or a strong thesis. You can prepare students for these moments by helping them to understand that papers often develop beyond the scope or direction of writers' original research, outlines, and planned theses. Taking advantage of these developments by finding an additional source or writing a new thesis statement is often the key to a successful revision.

words. Begin with the advice and checklist on pages 50–56, and supplement with the checklist below.

Checklist for revising a research paper

Assignment

How does the draft satisfy all of the criteria stated in your instructor's assignment?

Thesis statement

How well does your thesis statement describe your subject and your perspective as they emerged during drafting?

Structure

(Outlining your draft as suggested on pp. 638–39 can help you see structure at a glance.)

How consistently does borrowed material illuminate and support—not lead and dominate—your own ideas? How well is the importance of ideas reflected in the emphasis they receive? Will the arrangement of ideas be clear to readers?

Evidence

Where might readers need more evidence in order to accept your ideas? Where might the evidence seem weak or irrelevant?

Reasonableness and clarity

How reasonable will readers find your arguments? (See pp. 199–203.) Where do you need to define terms or concepts that readers may not know or may dispute?

---

2 **Editing**

When you complete your revision—and only then—you are ready to edit. If you do not compose on a computer, copy or retype the new draft if possible so that you have a clean copy to work on. If you do compose on a computer, you can edit directly on screen or print a clean copy. (Some writers find it easier to spot errors on paper than on screen.)

For editing, consult the advice and checklist on pages 59–62. Try to read the paper from the point of view of someone who has not spent hours planning and researching but instead has come fresh to the paper. Look for lapses in sense, awkward passages, wordiness, poor transitions between ideas and evidence, unnecessary repetition, wrong or misspelled words, errors in grammar, punctuation, or mechanics—in short, anything that is likely to interfere with a reader's understanding of your meaning.

3 Completing source citations

Before you prepare your final draft (next section), you must insert final source citations into your text and prepare the list of sources for the end of the paper. See pages 634–35 on documenting sources in various disciplines' styles.

Exercise 45.4 Revising and editing your paper

Using the revision and editing checklists on pages 54–55 and 60–61 and the checklist and pointers here, revise and edit your research paper. Work to improve not only the presentation of ideas but also, if necessary, the ideas themselves. Make sure you have provided an in-text citation for every summary, paraphrase, and direct quotation of a source and that your list of sources is complete.

45e Preparing and proofreading the final draft

Prepare the final draft of your paper when you have edited the text, added the source citations, and written the list of works cited. Most instructors expect research papers to be neatly typed with clear titling, double spacing, standard margins, and minimal handwritten corrections. Your instructor may have additional requirements, suggested by the discipline in which you are writing. This book explains four such document formats:

- **MLA format,** used in English, foreign languages, and some other humanities, pages 653–54 and 689–91. See also Chapter 47 for the sample research papers of Justin Malik and Vanessa Haley.
- **Chicago format,** used in history, art history, religion, philosophy, and some other humanities, pages 760–63 and 771–73.
- **APA format,** used in psychology and other social sciences, pages 783–85 and 799–802.
- **CSE format,** used in the natural and applied sciences, pages 812–13 and 817–18.

In any discipline, you can use a word processor to present your ideas effectively and attractively with readable type fonts, headings, illustrations, and other elements. See Chapter 5 for ideas.

Before you submit your paper, proofread it carefully for typographical errors, misspellings, and other errors. (See p. 66 for proofreading tips.) Unless the errors are very numerous (more than several on a page), you can correct them by whiting out or crossing out (neatly) and inserting the correction (neatly) in ink. Don't let the pressure of a deadline prevent you from proofreading, for even minor errors can impair clarity or annoy readers and thus negate some of the hard work you have put into your project.

Exercise 45.5 Preparing and proofreading your final draft

Prepare the final draft of your research paper, following your instructor's requirements for document format. If your instructor does not specify a format, follow the MLA guidelines on pages 689–91. Proofread and correct the paper before submitting it.

ANSWER: EXERCISE 45.4

Individual response.

COLLABORATIVE LEARNING

Group work can be invaluable in the final stages covered by Exercises 45.4 and 45.5 as students help one another revise, edit, and proofread. They can fine-tune thesis statements, hone arguments, and read drafts aloud to catch errors.

RESOURCES AND IDEAS

Bishop, Wendy, ed. *Acts of Revision: A Guide for Writers*. Portsmouth: Boynton/Cook, 2004. Print. This collection approaches revision as a playful, experimental process and offers specific guidelines on revising research writing (Chapter 4) as well as suggestions for sentence-level concerns.

Harris, Joseph. *Revision: How to Do Things with Texts*. Logan: Utah State UP, 2006. Print. Harris models how students can work with intellectual writing to make it more lively and less static.

Walvoord, B. E., V. J. Anderson, J. R. Breihan, L. P. McCarthy, S. M. Robinson, and A. K. Sherman. "Functions of Outlining Among College Students in Four Disciplines." *Research in the Teaching of English* 29.4 (1995): 390–421. Print. This statistical study of the functions of outlining shows that students who produce successful papers tend to outline at several points in the drafting process.

ANSWER: EXERCISE 45.5

Individual response.

46

Using MLA Documentation and Format

English, foreign languages, and some other humanities use the documentation style of the Modern Language Association, detailed in the *MLA Handbook for Writers of Research Papers* (6th ed., 2003) and substantially updated in the *MLA Style Manual and Guide to Scholarly Publishing* (3rd ed., 2008). This chapter presents the updated citation formats of the *MLA Style Manual*.

MLA documentation style employs brief parenthetical citations within the text that direct readers to a list of works cited at the end of the text. A parenthetical citation might look like this:

Only one article mentions this discrepancy (Wolfe 62).

The name Wolfe directs readers to the article by Wolfe in the list of works cited, and the page number 62 specifies the page in the article on which the cited material appears.

This chapter presents the essentials of MLA style: what to include in a parenthetical citation (below), where to place citations (p. 650), when to use footnotes or endnotes in addition to parenthetical citations (p. 653), how to create the list of works cited (p. 653), and how to format the entire paper (p. 689).

46a Using MLA in-text citations

1 Writing parenthetical text citations

In-text citations of sources must include just enough information for the reader to locate both of the following.

mycomplab

Visit *mycomplab.com* for more resources and exercises on MLA documentation and format.

- The *source* in your list of works cited.
- The *place* in the source where the borrowed material appears.

For any kind of source, you can usually meet both these requirements by providing the author's last name and (if the source uses them) the page numbers where the material appears. The reader can find the source in your list of works cited and find the borrowed material in the source itself.

Note For most sources, you will provide the author's or authors' last names and a page reference. Do not include the title unless you are citing more than one work by exactly the same author(s) or the source has no listed author (models 5 and 6, p. 647). The examples below cite a book to which neither of these exceptions applies:

Incorrect One textbook discusses the "ethical dilemmas in public relations practice" (Wilcox, Ault, and Agee, *Public Relations* 125).

Incorrect One textbook discusses the "ethical dilemmas in public relations practice" (*Public Relations* 125).

Correct One textbook discusses the "ethical dilemmas in public relations practice" (Wilcox, Ault, and Agee 125).

1. Author not named in your text

When you have not already named the author in your sentence, provide the author's last name and the page number(s), with no punctuation between them, in parentheses.

One researcher concludes that "women impose a distinctive construction on moral problems, seeing moral dilemmas in terms of conflicting responsibilities" (Gilligan 105-06).

MLA parenthetical citations

1. Author not named in your text *645*
2. Author named in your text *646*
3. A work with two or three authors *646*
4. A work with more than three authors *646*
5. A work by an author of two or more cited works *647*
6. An anonymous work *647*
7. A work with a corporate author *647*
8. A nonprint source *647*
9. A multivolume work *648*
10. An entire work or a work with no page or other reference numbers *648*
11. A work with numbered paragraphs or sections instead of pages *649*
12. An indirect source *649*
13. A literary work *649*
14. The Bible *650*
15. Two or more works in the same citation *650*

See model 6 for the form to use when the source does not have an author. And see models 10 and 11 for the forms to use when the source does not provide page numbers.

2. Author named in your text

When you have already given the author's name with the material you're citing, do not repeat it in the parenthetical citation. Give just the page number(s).

> Carol Gilligan concludes that "women impose a distinctive construction on moral problems, seeing moral dilemmas in terms of conflicting responsibilities" (105-06).

See model 6 for the form to use when the source does not list an author. And see models 10 and 11 for the forms to use when the source does not provide page numbers.

3. A work with two or three authors

If the source has two or three authors, give all their last names in the text or in the citation. Separate two authors' names with and:

> As Frieden and Sagalyn observe, "The poor and the minorities were the leading victims of highway and renewal programs" (29).

> According to one study, "The poor and the minorities were the leading victims of highway and renewal programs" (Frieden and Sagalyn 29).

With three authors, add commas and also and before the final name:

> The textbook by Wilcox, Ault, and Agee discusses the "ethical dilemmas in public relations practice" (125).

> One textbook discusses the "ethical dilemmas in public relations practice" (Wilcox, Ault, and Agee 125).

4. A work with more than three authors

If the source has more than three authors, you may list all their last names or give only the first author's name followed by et al. (the abbreviation for the Latin *et alii*, "and others"). The choice depends on what you do in your list of works cited (see p. 655).

> Increased competition means that employees of public relations firms may find their loyalty stretched in more than one direction (Cameron et al. 417).

> Increased competition means that employees of public relations firms may find their loyalty stretched in more than one direction (Cameron, Wilcox, Reber, and Shin 417).

5. A work by an author of two or more cited works

If your list of works cited includes two or more works by the same author, then your citation must tell the reader which of the author's works you are referring to. Give the title either in the text or in a parenthetical citation. In a parenthetical citation, give the full title only if it is brief; otherwise, shorten the title to the first one, two, or three main words (excluding *A, An,* or *The*).

> At about age seven, children begin to use appropriate gestures with their stories (Gardner, *Arts* 144-45).

The full title of Gardner's book is *The Arts and Human Development* (see the works-cited entry on p. 655). This shortened title is italicized because the source is a book.

6. An anonymous work

For a work with no named author or editor (whether an individual or an organization), use a full or shortened version of the title, as explained above. In your list of works cited, you alphabetize an anonymous work by the first main word of the title (see p. 658), so the first word of a shortened title should be the same. The following citations refer to an unsigned source titled "The Right to Die." The title appears in quotation marks because the source is a periodical article.

> One article notes that a death-row inmate may demand his own execution to achieve a fleeting notoriety ("Right" 16).

> "The Right to Die" notes that a death-row inmate may demand execution to achieve a fleeting notoriety (16).

If two or more anonymous works have the same title, distinguish them with additional information in the text citation, such as the publication date.

7. A work with a corporate author

Some works list as author a government body, association, committee, company, or other group. Cite such a work by the organization's name. If the name is long, work it into the text to avoid an intrusive parenthetical citation.

> A 2008 report by the Hawaii Department of Education provides evidence of an increase in graduation rates (12).

8. A nonprint source

Cite a nonprint source such as a Web page or a DVD just as you would any other source. If your works-cited entry lists the source under the name of an author or other contributor, use that name in the text citation. The following example cites an authored source that has page numbers.

> Business forecasts for the fourth quarter tended to be optimistic (White 4).

If your works-cited entry lists the work under its title, cite the work by title in your text, as explained in model 6. The next example cites an entire work (a film on DVD) and gives the title in the text, so it omits a parenthetical citation (see model 10).

> Seven decades after its release, *Citizen Kane* is still remarkable for its rich
> black-and-white photography.

9. A multivolume work

If you consulted only one volume of a multivolume work, your list of works cited will say so (see model 30 on p. 667), and you can treat the volume as you would any book.

If you consulted more than one volume of a multivolume work, give the appropriate volume in your text citation.

> After issuing the Emancipation Proclamation, Lincoln said, "What I did, I did
> after very full deliberations, and under a very heavy and solemn sense of responsi-
> bility" (5: 438).

The number 5 indicates the volume from which the quotation was taken; the number 438 indicates the page number in that volume. When the author's name appears in such a citation, place it before the volume number with no punctuation: (Lincoln 5: 438).

If you are referring generally to an entire volume of a multivolume work and are not citing specific page numbers, add the abbreviation vol. before the volume number, as in (vol. 5) or (Lincoln, vol. 5) (note the comma after the author's name). Then readers will not misinterpret the volume number as a page number.

10. An entire work or a work with no page or other reference numbers

When you cite an entire work rather than a part of it, you may omit any page or other reference number. If the work you cite has an author, try to work the author's name into your text. You will not need a parenthetical citation then, but the source still must appear in your list of works cited.

> Boyd deals with the need to acknowledge and come to terms with our fear of
> nuclear technology.

Use the same format when you cite a specific passage from a work with no page, paragraph, or other reference numbers, such as a Web source.

NO PAGE NUMBERS?

Remind students that sometimes a printed copy of a Web-based source might include page numbers that were not included in the original source. Page numbers should only refer to numbering included in the original source material, not those created by the printing software, which can change.

If the author's name does not appear in your text, put it in a parenthetical citation.

Almost 20 percent of commercial banks have been audited for the practice (Friis).

11. A work with numbered paragraphs or sections instead of pages

Some electronic sources number each paragraph or section instead of each page. In citing passages in these sources, give the paragraph or section number(s) and distinguish them from page numbers: after the author's name, put a comma, a space, and par. (one paragraph), pars. (more than one paragraph), sec., or secs.

Twins reared apart report similar feelings (Palfrey, pars. 6-7).

12. An indirect source

When you want to use a quotation that is already in quotation marks—indicating that the author you are reading is quoting someone else—try to find the original source and quote directly from it. If you can't find the original source, then your citation must indicate that your quotation of it is indirect. In the following citation, qtd. in ("quoted in") says that Davino was quoted by Boyd.

George Davino maintains that "even small children have vivid ideas about nuclear energy" (qtd. in Boyd 22).

The list of works cited then includes only Boyd (the work consulted), not Davino.

13. A literary work

Novels, plays, and poems are often available in many editions, so your instructor may ask you to provide information that will help readers find the passage you cite no matter what edition they consult.

■ **Novels:** The page number comes first, followed by a semicolon and then information on the appropriate part or chapter of the work.

Toward the end of James's novel, Maggie suddenly feels "the thick breath of the definite—which was the intimate, the immediate, the familiar, as she hadn't had them for so long" (535; pt. 6, ch. 41).

■ **Poems that are not divided into parts:** You may omit the page number and supply the line number(s) for the quotation. To prevent confusion with page numbers, precede the numbers with line or lines in the first citation; then use just the numbers.

In Shakespeare's Sonnet 73 the speaker identifies with the trees of late autumn, "Bare ruined choirs, where late the sweet birds sang" (line 4). "In me," Shakespeare writes, "thou seest the glowing of such fire / That on the ashes of his youth doth lie . . ." (9-10).

(See pp. 750–51 for a sample paper on a poem.)

■ **Verse plays and poems that are divided into parts:** Omit a page number and cite the appropriate part—act (and scene, if any), canto, book, and so on—plus the line number(s). Use Arabic numerals for parts, including acts and scenes (3.4), unless your instructor specifies Roman numerals (III.iv).

Later in Shakespeare's *King Lear* the disguised Edgar says, "The prince of darkness is a gentleman" (3.4.147).

(See pp. 752–54 for a sample paper on a verse play.)

■ **Prose plays:** Provide the page number followed by the act and scene, if any. See the reference to *Death of a Salesman* on page 652.

14. The Bible

When you cite passages of the Bible in parentheses, abbreviate the title of any book longer than four letters—for instance, Gen. (Genesis), 1 Sam. (1 Samuel), Ps. (Psalms), Prov. (Proverbs), Matt. (Matthew), Rom. (Romans). Then give the chapter and verse(s) in Arabic numerals.

According to the Bible, at Babel God "did . . . confound the language of all the earth" (Gen. 11.9).

15. Two or more works in the same citation

When you refer to more than one work in a single parenthetical citation, separate the references with a semicolon.

Two recent articles point out that a computer badly used can be less efficient than no computer at all (Gough and Hall 201; Richards 162).

Since long citations in the text can distract the reader, you may choose to cite several or more works in an endnote or footnote rather than in the text. See page 653.

2 **Positioning and punctuating parenthetical citations**

The following guidelines will help you place and punctuate text citations to distinguish between your own and your sources' ideas and to make your own text readable. See also pages 620–25 on editing quotations and using signal phrases to integrate source material into your sentences.

Where to place citations

Position text citations to accomplish two goals:

- **Make it clear exactly where your borrowing begins and ends.**
- **Keep the citation as unobtrusive as possible.**

You can accomplish both goals by placing the parenthetical citation at the end of the sentence element containing the borrowed material. This sentence element may be a phrase or a clause, and it may begin, interrupt, or conclude the sentence. Usually, as in the following examples, the element ends with a punctuation mark.

> The inflation rate might climb as high as 30 percent (Kim 164), an increase that could threaten the small nation's stability.

> The inflation rate, which might climb as high as 30 percent (Kim 164), could threaten the small nation's stability.

> The small nation's stability could be threatened by its inflation rate, which, one source predicts, might climb as high as 30 percent (Kim 164).

In the last example the addition of one source predicts clarifies that Kim is responsible only for the inflation-rate prediction, not for the statement about stability.

When your paraphrase or summary of a source runs longer than a sentence, clarify the boundaries by using the author's name in the first sentence and placing the parenthetical citation at the end of the last sentence.

> Juliette Kim studied the effects of acutely high inflation in several South American and African countries since World War II. She discovered that a major change in government accompanied or followed the inflationary period in 56 percent of cases (22-23).

When you cite two or more sources in the same paragraph, position authors' names and parenthetical citations so that readers can see who said what. In the following example, the beginnings and ends of sentences clearly mark the different sources.

> Schools use computers extensively for drill-and-practice exercises, in which students repeat specific skills such as spelling words, using the multiplication facts, or, at a higher level, doing chemistry problems. But many education experts criticize such exercises for boring students and failing to engage their critical thinking and creativity. Jane M. Healy, a noted educational psychologist and teacher, takes issue with "interactive" software for children as well as drill-

and-practice software, arguing that "some of the most popular 'educational' software . . . may be damaging to independent thinking, attention, and motivation" (20). Another education expert, Harold Wenglinsky of the Educational Testing Service, found in a well-regarded 1998 study that fourth and eighth graders who used computers frequently, including for drill and practice, actually did worse on tests than their peers who used computers less often (*Does It Compute?* 21). In a later article, Wenglinsky concludes that "the quantity of use matters far less than the quality of use." In schools, he says, high-quality computer work, involving critical thinking, is still rare ("In Search" 17).

How to punctuate citations

Generally place a parenthetical citation *before* any punctuation required by your sentence. If the borrowed material is a quotation, place the citation *between* the closing quotation mark and the punctuation:

> Spelling argues that during the 1970s American automobile manufacturers met consumer needs "as well as could be expected" (26), but not everyone agrees with him.

The exception is a quotation ending in a question mark or exclamation point. Then use the appropriate punctuation inside the closing quotation mark, and follow the quotation with the text citation and a period.

> "Of what use is genius," Emerson asks, "if the organ . . . cannot find a focal distance within the actual horizon of human life?" ("Experience" 60). Mad genius is no genius.

When a citation appears at the end of a quotation set off from the text, place it one space *after* the punctuation ending the quotation. Do not use additional punctuation with the citation or quotation marks around the quotation.

> In Arthur Miller's *Death of a Salesman*, the most poignant defense of Willie Loman comes from his wife, Linda:
>
>> He's not the finest character that ever lived. But he's a human being, and a terrible thing is happening to him. So attention must be paid. He's not to be allowed to fall into his grave like an old dog. Attention, attention must finally be paid to such a person. (56; act 1)

(This citation of a play includes the act number as well as the page number. See p. 650.)

See the two sample research papers starting on pages 692 and 720 for further examples of placing parenthetical references in relation to summaries, paraphrases, and quotations.

3 Using footnotes or endnotes in special circumstances

Occasionally you may want to use footnotes or endnotes in place of parenthetical citations. If you need to refer to several sources at once, listing them in a long parenthetical citation could be intrusive. In that case, signal the citation with a numeral raised above the appropriate line of text and write a note beginning with the same numeral to cite the sources:

Text   At least five studies have confirmed these results.[1]

Note   1. Abbott and Winger 266-68; Casner 27; Hoyenga 78-79;
        Marino 36; Tripp, Tripp, and Walk 179-83.

You may also use a footnote or endnote to comment on a source or to provide information that does not fit easily in the text:

Text   So far, no one has confirmed these results.[2]

Note   2. Manter tried repeatedly to replicate the experiment, but he
        was never able to produce the high temperatures (616).

Indent a note one-half inch, type the numeral on the text line, and follow the numeral with a period and a space. If the note appears as a footnote, place it at the bottom of the page on which the citation appears, set it off from the text with quadruple spacing, and single-space the note itself. If the note appears as an endnote, place it in numerical order with the other endnotes on a page between the text and the list of works cited. Double-space all the endnotes. (See pp. 714–15 for examples of endnotes and the format for typing a page of endnotes.)

46b Preparing the MLA list of works cited

In MLA documentation style, your in-text parenthetical citations (discussed in 46a) refer the reader to complete information on your sources in a list you title Works Cited and place at the end of your paper. The list should include all the sources you quoted, paraphrased, or summarized in your paper. (If your instructor asks you to include sources you examined but did not cite, title the list Works Consulted.)

Follow this format for the list of works cited:

■ **Arrange your sources in alphabetical order** by the last name of the author. If an author is not given in the source, alphabetize the source by the first main word of the title (excluding *A, An,* or *The*).

■ **Type the entire list double-spaced,** both within and between entries.

MLA works-cited page

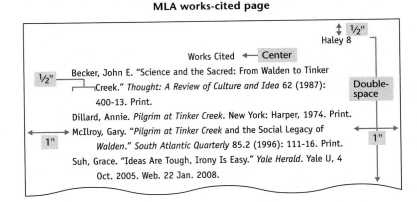

- ■ **Indent the second and subsequent lines of each entry one-half inch from the left.** Your word processor can format this so-called hanging indent automatically.

For complete lists of works cited, see the papers by Justin Malik (pp. 716 and 718) and Vanessa Haley (p. 725).

The box on pages 656–57 directs you to the MLA formats for works-cited entries. Use your best judgment in adapting the models to your particular sources. If you can't find a model that exactly matches a source you used, locate and follow the closest possible match. You will certainly need to combine formats—for instance, drawing on model 2 ("Two or three authors") and model 10 ("An article in a national newspaper") for a national newspaper article with two authors.

Note MLA style now requires that you give the medium for every source you cite, such as print, Web, DVD, or television. For example, if you consulted an article in a print magazine, your works-cited entry should list the medium as Print. If you consulted a book on the Web, your works-cited entry should list the medium as Web. The models here all conform to this standard.

1 | Listing authors

The following models show how to handle authors' names in citing any kind of source.

1. One author

Ehrenreich, Barbara. *Dancing in the Streets: A History of Collective Joy*. New York: Metropolitan-Holt, 2006. Print.

Give the author's full name—last name first, a comma, first name, and any middle name or initial. Omit any title, such as *Dr.* or *PhD*.

End the name with a period. If your source lists an editor as author, see model 22, page 665.

2. Two or three authors

Lifton, Robert Jay, and Greg Mitchell. *Who Owns Death: Capital Punishment, the American Conscience, and the End of Executions*. New York: Morrow, 2000. Print.

Wilcox, Dennis L., Phillip H. Ault, and Warren K. Agee. *Public Relations: Strategies and Tactics*. 8th ed. New York: Irwin, 2006. Print.

Give the authors' names in the order provided on the title page. Reverse the first and last names of the first author *only*, not of any other authors. Separate two authors' names with a comma and and; separate three authors' names with commas and with and before the third name. If your source lists two or three editors as authors, see model 22, page 665.

3. More than three authors

Cameron, Glen T., Dennis L. Wilcox, Bryan H. Reber, and Jae-Hwa Shin. *Public Relations Today: Managing Competition and Conflict*. New York: Pearson, 2007. Print.

Cameron, Glen T., et al. *Public Relations Today: Managing Competition and Conflict*. New York: Pearson, 2007. Print.

You may, but need not, give all authors' names if the work has more than three authors. If you choose not to give all names, provide the name of the first author only, and follow the name with a comma and the abbreviation et al. (for the Latin *et alii*, meaning "and others"). If your source lists more than three editors as authors, see model 22, page 665.

4. The same author(s) for two or more works

Gardner, Howard. *The Arts and Human Development*. New York: Wiley, 1973. Print.

---. *Five Minds for the Future*. Boston: Harvard Business School P, 2007. Print.

Give the author's name only in the first entry. For the second and any subsequent works by the same author, substitute three hyphens for the author's name, followed by a period. Note that the three hyphens stand for *exactly* the same name or names. If the second Gardner source were by Gardner and somebody else, both names would have to be given in full.

Place an entry or entries using three hyphens immediately after the entry that names the author. Within the set of entries by the

(continued on p. 658)

MLA works-cited models

1. Authors

1. One author *654*
2. Two or three authors *655*
3. More than three authors *655*
4. The same author(s) for two or more works *655*
5. A corporate author *658*
6. Author not named (anonymous) *658*

2. Periodical print sources

Articles in scholarly journals

7. An article in a journal with volume and issue numbers *658, 659*
8. An article in a journal with only issue numbers *660*
9. An abstract of a journal article or a dissertation *660*

Articles in newspapers

10. An article in a national newspaper *660, 661*
11. An article in a local newspaper *660*

Articles in magazines

12. An article in a weekly or biweekly magazine *662*
13. An article in a monthly or bimonthly magazine *662*

Reviews, editorials, letters to the editor, interviews

14. A review *662*
15. An editorial *662*
16. A letter to the editor *662*
17. An interview *662*

Articles in series or in special issues

18. An article in a series *663*
19. An article in a special issue *663*

3. Nonperiodical print sources

Books

20. Basic format for a book *663, 664*
21. A second or subsequent edition *665*
22. A book with an editor *665*
23. A book with an author and an editor *665*
24. A book with a translator *665*
25. An anthology *666*
26. A selection from an anthology *666*
27. Two or more selections from the same anthology *666*
28. An article in a reference work *667*
29. An illustrated book or graphic narrative *667*
30. A multivolume work *667*
31. A series *668*
32. A republished book *668*
33. The Bible *668*
34. A book with a title in its title *668*
35. Published proceedings of a conference *669*
36. An introduction, preface, foreword, or afterword *669*
37. A book lacking publication information or pagination *669*

Other nonperiodical print sources

38. A government publication *670*
39. A pamphlet or brochure *670*
40. A dissertation *670*
41. A letter *671*

4. Nonperiodical Web sources

Nonperiodical sources available only on the Web

42. A short work with a title *672, 673*

43. A short work without a title *674*
44. An entire site *674*
45. An article in a newspaper *674*
46. An article in a magazine *675*
47. A government publication *675*
48. An article in a reference work *675*
49. An image *675*
50. A television or radio program *676*
51. A video recording *676*
52. A sound recording *677*
53. A podcast *677*
54. A blog entry *677*
55. A wiki *678*

Nonperiodical Web sources also available in print

56. A short work with print publication information *678*
57. A book with print publication information *678*

Nonperiodical Web sources also available in other media

58. A sound recording with other publication information *679*
59. A film or video recording with other publication information *679*
60. An image with other publication information *679*

Citation of a URL

61. A source requiring citation of the URL *679*

5. Journals on the Web and periodicals in online databases

Web journals consulted directly

62. An article in a scholarly journal *680*
63. An abstract of a journal article *681*

Web periodicals consulted in online databases

64. An article in a scholarly journal *682*
65. An abstract of a journal article *683*
66. An article in a newspaper *683*
67. An article in a magazine *683*

6. Other electronic sources

Publications on CD-ROM or DVD-ROM

68. A nonperiodical CD-ROM or DVD-ROM *683*
69. A periodical CD-ROM or DVD-ROM *684*

E-mail and discussion-group postings

70. An e-mail message *684*
71. A posting to a discussion group *684*

Digital files

72. A text file *684*
73. A media file *685*

7. Other sources

74. A television or radio program *685*
75. A personal or broadcast interview *685*
76. A sound recording *686*
77. A film, DVD, or video recording *686*
78. A painting, photograph, or other work of visual art *686*
79. A personal photograph *687*
80. A map, chart, graph, or diagram *687*
81. A cartoon or comic strip *687*
82. An advertisement *687*
83. A performance *687*
84. A lecture, speech, address, or reading *688*

(continued from p. 655)

same author, arrange the sources alphabetically by the first main word of the title, as in the Gardner examples (*Arts*, then *Five*).

If you cite two or more sources that list as author(s) exactly the same editor(s), follow the hyphens with a comma and ed. or eds. as appropriate. (See model 22, p. 665.)

5. A corporate author

Vault Technologies. *Turnkey Parking Solutions*. Salt Lake City: Mills, 2008. Print.

Corporate authors include associations, committees, institutions, government bodies, companies, and other groups. List the name of the group as author when a source gives only that name and not an individual's name.

6. Author not named (anonymous)

The Dorling Kindersley World Reference Atlas. London: Dorling, 2007. Print.

List a work that names no author—neither an individual nor a group—by its full title. If the work is a book, italicize the title. If the work is a periodical article or other short work, enclose the title in quotation marks:

"Let the Horse Race Begin." *Time* 31 Mar. 2008: 22. Print.

Alphabetize the work by the title's first main word, excluding *A*, *An*, or *The* (*Dorling* in the first example and Let in the second).

2 Listing periodical print sources

Print periodicals include scholarly journals, newspapers, and magazines that are published at regular intervals (quarterly, monthly, weekly, or daily). To cite more than one author, two or more articles by the same author, a corporate author, or an article with no named author, see models 1–6.

Note The treatment of volume and issue numbers and publication dates varies depending on the kind of periodical being cited, as the models indicate. For the distinction between journals and magazines, see page 572.

Articles in scholarly journals

7. An article in a journal with volume and issue numbers (print)

Bee, Robert. "The Importance of Preserving Paper-Based Artifacts in a Digital Age." *Library Quarterly* 78.2 (2008): 174-94. Print.

The facing page shows the basic format for an article in a periodical (a journal) and the location of the required information in the journal. See page 661 for parallel information on a newspaper article.

Format for a print journal article

①
Bee, Robert. "The Importance of Preserving Paper-Based Artifacts in a Digital Age."
②
③   ④   ⑤   ⑥   ⑦
Library Quarterly 78.2 (2008): 179-94. Print.

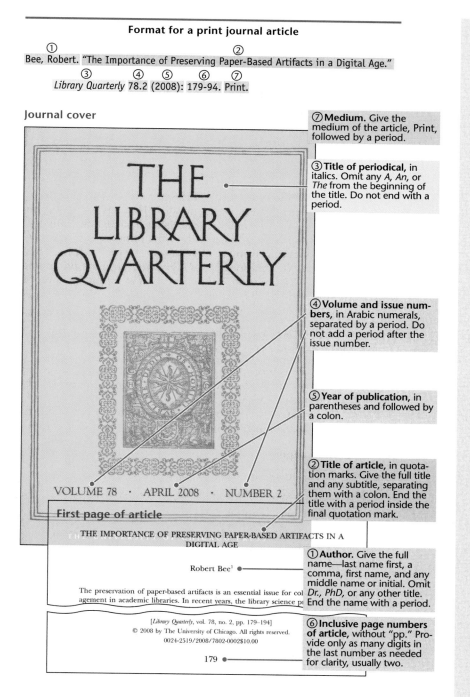

Journal cover

THE LIBRARY QVARTERLY

VOLUME 78 · APRIL 2008 · NUMBER 2

First page of article

THE IMPORTANCE OF PRESERVING PAPER-BASED ARTIFACTS IN A DIGITAL AGE

Robert Bee[1] ●

The preservation of paper-based artifacts is an essential issue for col
agement in academic libraries. In recent years, the library science pr

[*Library Quarterly*, vol. 78, no. 2, pp. 179–194]
© 2008 by The University of Chicago. All rights reserved.
0024-2519/2008/7802-0002$10.00

179 ●

⑦ **Medium.** Give the medium of the article, Print, followed by a period.

③ **Title of periodical,** in italics. Omit any *A, An,* or *The* from the beginning of the title. Do not end with a period.

④ **Volume and issue numbers,** in Arabic numerals, separated by a period. Do not add a period after the issue number.

⑤ **Year of publication,** in parentheses and followed by a colon.

② **Title of article,** in quotation marks. Give the full title and any subtitle, separating them with a colon. End the title with a period inside the final quotation mark.

① **Author.** Give the full name—last name first, a comma, first name, and any middle name or initial. Omit *Dr., PhD,* or any other title. End the name with a period.

⑥ **Inclusive page numbers of article,** without "pp." Provide only as many digits in the last number as needed for clarity, usually two.

8. An article in a journal with only issue numbers (print)

Rymhs, Deena. "David Collier's *Surviving Saskatoon* and New Comics." *Canadian*
Literature 194 (2007): 75-92. Print.

If a scholarly journal numbers only issues, not volumes, give the issue
number alone after the journal title.

9. An abstract of a journal article or a dissertation (print)

Lever, Janet. "Sex Differences in the Games Children Play." *Social Problems*
23.2 (1996): 478-87. *Psychological Abstracts* 63.5 (1996): item 1431.
Print.

For an abstract of a journal article, first provide the publication information for the article, following model 7. Then give the information for the abstract. If the abstract publisher lists abstracts by item
rather than page number, add item before the number.

For an abstract appearing in *Dissertation Abstracts* (*DA*) or *Dis-*
sertation Abstracts International (*DAI*), give the author's name and
the title, Diss. (for "Dissertation"), the institution granting the author's
degree, the date of the dissertation, and the publication information.

Steciw, Steven K. "Alterations to the Pessac Project of Le Corbusier." Diss.
U of Cambridge, England, 1986. *DAI* 46.10 (1986): 565C. Print.

See also model 40 on page 670 (entire dissertation), model 63
on page 681 (abstract on the Web), and model 65 on page 683 (abstract in an online database).

Note Most instructors expect you to consult and cite full articles, not abstracts. See page 576.

Articles in newspapers

10. An article in a national newspaper (print)

Stout, David. "Blind Win Court Ruling on US Currency." *New York Times* 21 May
2008, natl. ed.: A23. Print.

See the facing page for an analysis of this entry and the location of
the required information in the newspaper.

11. An article in a local newspaper (print)

Arntaenius, Linda. "Merwick Rezoning Pushes Senior Housing Debate." *Town*
Topics [Princeton] 21 May 2008: 1+. Print.

If the city of publication does not appear in the title of a local
newspaper, follow the title with the city name, not italicized, in
brackets.

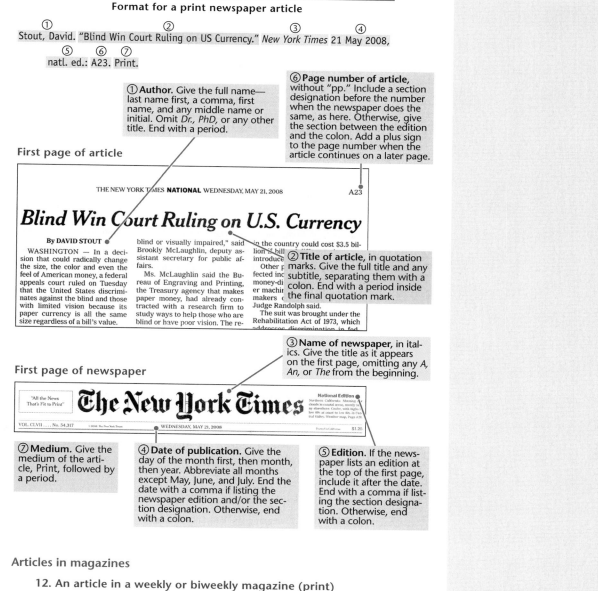

Format for a print newspaper article

① ② ③ ④
Stout, David. "Blind Win Court Ruling on US Currency." *New York Times* 21 May 2008,
⑤ ⑥ ⑦
natl. ed.: A23. Print.

① **Author.** Give the full name— last name first, a comma, first name, and any middle name or initial. Omit *Dr., PhD,* or any other title. End with a period.

⑥ **Page number of article,** without "pp." Include a section designation before the number when the newspaper does the same, as here. Otherwise, give the section between the edition and the colon. Add a plus sign to the page number when the article continues on a later page.

First page of article

THE NEW YORK TIMES **NATIONAL** WEDNESDAY, MAY 21, 2008   A23

Blind Win Court Ruling on U.S. Currency

By DAVID STOUT

WASHINGTON — In a decision that could radically change the size, the color and even the feel of American money, a federal appeals court ruled on Tuesday that the United States discriminates against the blind and those with limited vision because its paper currency is all the same size regardless of a bill's value.

blind or visually impaired," said Brookly McLaughlin, deputy assistant secretary for public affairs.

Ms. McLaughlin said the Bureau of Engraving and Printing, the Treasury agency that makes paper money, had already contracted with a research firm to study ways to help those who are blind or have poor vision. The re-

in the country could cost $3.5 billion

Other p fected inc money-di er machin makers

Judge Randolph said.

The suit was brought under the Rehabilitation Act of 1973, which addresses discrimination in fed

② **Title of article,** in quotation marks. Give the full title and any subtitle, separating them with a colon. End with a period inside the final quotation mark.

③ **Name of newspaper,** in italics. Give the title as it appears on the first page, omitting any *A, An,* or *The* from the beginning.

First page of newspaper

"All the News That's Fit to Print"

The New York Times

National Edition

VOL. CLVII .... No. 54,317   WEDNESDAY, MAY 21, 2008 $1.25

⑦ **Medium.** Give the medium of the article, Print, followed by a period.

④ **Date of publication.** Give the day of the month first, then month, then year. Abbreviate all months except May, June, and July. End the date with a comma if listing the newspaper edition and/or the section designation. Otherwise, end with a colon.

⑤ **Edition.** If the newspaper lists an edition at the top of the first page, include it after the date. End with a comma if listing the section designation. Otherwise, end with a colon.

Articles in magazines

12. An article in a weekly or biweekly magazine (print)

Fortini, Amanda. "Pomegranate Princess." *New Yorker* 31 Mar. 2008: 92-99. Print.

Give the author, title of the article, and title of the magazine. Follow the magazine title with the day, the month, and the year of publication. (Abbreviate all months except May, June, and July.) Don't place the date in parentheses, and don't provide a volume or issue number. Give the page numbers of the article and the medium, Print.

13. An article in a monthly or bimonthly magazine (print)

Douthat, Ross. "The Return of the Paranoid Style." *Atlantic Monthly* Apr. 2008:

52-59. Print.

Follow the magazine title with the month and the year of publication. (Abbreviate all months except May, June, and July.) Don't place the date in parentheses, and don't provide a volume or issue number. Give the page numbers of the article and the medium, Print.

Reviews, editorials, letters to the editor, interviews

14. A review (print)

Glasswell, Kathryn, and George Kamberelis. "Drawing and Redrawing the Map

of Writing Studies." Rev. of *Handbook of Writing Research*, by Charles A.

MacArthur, Steve Graham, and Jill Fitzgerald. *Reading Research Quarterly*

42.2 (2007): 304-23. Print.

Rev. is an abbreviation for "Review." The names of the authors of the work being reviewed follow the title of the work, a comma, and by. If the review has no title of its own, then Rev. of and the title of the reviewed work immediately follow the name of the reviewer.

15. An editorial (print)

"A Global AIDS Campaign Stalled." Editorial. *New York Times* 21 June 2008,

natl. ed.: A18. Print.

For an editorial with no named author, begin with the title and add the word Editorial after the title, as in the example. For an editorial with a named author, start with his or her name and then proceed as in the example.

16. A letter to the editor (print)

McBride, Thad. "Swapping the Suit and Tie." Letter. *Economist* 29 Mar. 2008:

30. Print.

Add the word Letter after the title, if there is one, or after the author's name.

17. An interview (print)

Aloni, Shulamit. Interview. *Palestine-Israel Journal of Politics, Economics, and*

Culture 14.4 (2007): 63-68. Print.

Begin with the name of the person interviewed. If the interview does not have a title (as in the example), add Interview after the name. (Replace this description with the title if there is one.) You may also add the name of the interviewer if you know it—for example, Interview by Benson Wright. See model 75 (p. 685) to cite a broadcast interview or an interview you conduct yourself.

Articles in series or in special issues

18. An article in a series (print)

Kleinfeld, N. R. "Living at an Epicenter of Diabetes, Defiance, and Despair." *New York Times* 10 Jan. 2006, natl. ed.: A1+. Print. Pt. 2 of a series, Bad Blood, begun 9 Jan. 2006.

Cite an article in a series following the appropriate model on pages 658–62 for a scholarly journal, newspaper, or magazine. If you wish, end the entry with a description to indicate that the article is part of a series.

19. An article in a special issue (print)

Rubini, Monica, and Michela Menegatti. "Linguistic Bias in Personnel Selection." *Celebrating Two Decades of Linguistic Bias Research.* Ed. Robbie M. Sutton and Karen M. Douglas. Spec. issue of *Journal of Language and Social Psychology* 27.2 (2008): 168-81. Print.

Cite an article in a special issue of a periodical by starting with the author and title of the article. Follow with the title of the special issue, Ed., and the names of the issue's editor(s). Add Spec. issue of before the periodical title. Conclude with publication information, using the appropriate model on pages 658–62 for a journal or magazine.

3 Listing nonperiodical print sources

Nonperiodical print sources are works that are not published at regular intervals, such as books, government publications, and pamphlets. To cite more than one author, two or more articles by the same author, a corporate author, or a source with no named author, see models 1–6.

Books

20. Basic format for a book (print)

Lahiri, Jhumpa. *Unaccustomed Earth.* New York: Knopf, 2008. Print.

The next page shows the basic format for a book and the location of the required information in the book. When other information is

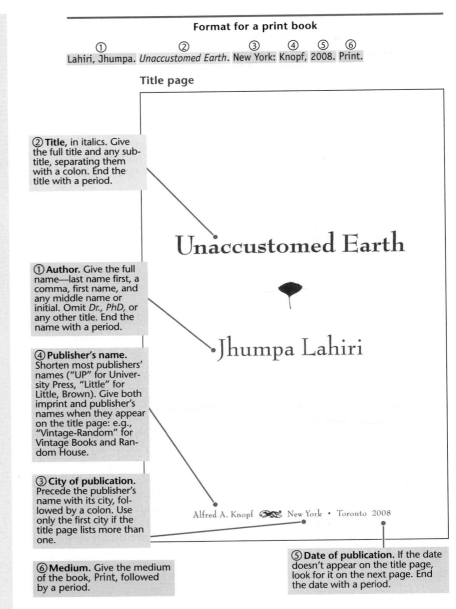

Format for a print book

① ② ③ ④ ⑤ ⑥
Lahiri, Jhumpa. *Unaccustomed Earth*. New York: Knopf, 2008. Print.

Title page

② **Title,** in italics. Give the full title and any sub-title, separating them with a colon. End the title with a period.

Unaccustomed Earth

① **Author.** Give the full name—last name first, a comma, first name, and any middle name or initial. Omit *Dr., PhD,* or any other title. End the name with a period.

Jhumpa Lahiri

④ **Publisher's name.** Shorten most publishers' names ("UP" for University Press, "Little" for Little, Brown). Give both imprint and publisher's names when they appear on the title page: e.g., "Vintage-Random" for Vintage Books and Random House.

③ **City of publication.** Precede the publisher's name with its city, followed by a colon. Use only the first city if the title page lists more than one.

Alfred A. Knopf New York • Toronto 2008

⑥ **Medium.** Give the medium of the book, Print, followed by a period.

⑤ **Date of publication.** If the date doesn't appear on the title page, look for it on the next page. End the date with a period.

required, it usually falls either between the author's name and the title or between the title and the publication information, as in the following models.

21. A second or subsequent edition (print)

Bolinger, Dwight L. *Aspects of Language*. 3rd ed. New York: Harcourt, 1981.
Print.

For any edition after the first, place the edition number after the title. (If an editor's name follows the title, place the edition number after the name. See model 26.) Use the appropriate designation for editions that are named or dated rather than numbered—for instance, Rev. ed. for "Revised edition."

22. A book with an editor (print)

Holland, Merlin, and Rupert Hart-Davis, eds. *The Complete Letters of Oscar
Wilde*. New York: Holt, 2000. Print.

Handle editors' names like authors' names (models 1–4), but add a comma and the abbreviation ed. (one editor) or eds. (two or more editors) after the last editor's name.

23. A book with an author and an editor (print)

Mumford, Lewis. *The City in History*. Ed. Donald L. Miller. New York: Pantheon,
1986. Print.

When citing the work of the author, give his or her name first, and give the editor's name after the title, preceded by Ed. (singular only, meaning "Edited by"). When citing the work of the editor, use model 22 for a book with an editor, adding By and the author's name after the title:

Miller, Donald L., ed. *The City in History*. By Lewis Mumford. New York:
Pantheon, 1986. Print.

24. A book with a translator (print)

Alighieri, Dante. *The Inferno*. Trans. John Ciardi. New York: NAL, 1971. Print.

When citing the work of the author, as in the preceding example, give his or her name first, and give the translator's name after the title, preceded by Trans. ("Translated by").

When citing the work of the translator, give his or her name first, followed by a comma and trans. Follow the title with By and the author's name:

Ciardi, John, trans. *The Inferno*. By Dante Alighieri. New York: NAL, 1971.
Print.

When a book you cite by author has a translator *and* an editor, give the translator's and editor's names in the order used on the book's title page.

25. An anthology (print)

Kennedy, X. J., and Dana Gioia, eds. *Literature: An Introduction to Fiction,*
Poetry, and Drama. 10th ed. New York: Longman, 2007. Print.

Cite an entire anthology only when citing the work of the editor or editors or when your instructor permits cross-referencing like that shown in model 27. Give the name of the editor or editors (followed by ed. or eds.) and then the title of the anthology.

26. A selection from an anthology (print)

Mason, Bobbie Ann. "Shiloh." *Literature: An Introduction to Fiction, Poetry,*
and Drama. Ed. X. J. Kennedy and Dana Gioia. 10th ed. New York: Longman, 2007. 604-13. Print.

This listing adds the following to the anthology entry in model 25: author of selection, title of selection (in quotation marks), and inclusive page numbers for the selection (without the abbreviation "pp."). If you wish, you may also supply the original date of publication for the work you are citing, after its title. See model 32 on page 668.

If the work you cite comes from a collection of works by one author that has no editor, use the following form:

Auden, W. H. "Family Ghosts." *The Collected Poetry of W. H. Auden.* New York:
Random, 1945. 132-33. Print.

If the work you cite is a scholarly article that was previously printed elsewhere, provide the complete information for the earlier publication of the piece, followed by Rpt. in ("Reprinted in") and the information for the source in which you found the piece:

Molloy, Francis C. "The Suburban Vision in John O'Hara's Short Stories."
Critique: Studies in Modern Fiction 25.2 (1984): 101-13. Rpt. in *Short*
Story Criticism: Excerpts from Criticism of the Works of Short Fiction Writ-
ers. Ed. David Segal. Vol. 15. Detroit: Gale, 1989. 287-92. Print.

27. Two or more selections from the same anthology (print)

Erdrich, Louise. "Indian Boarding School: The Runaways." Kennedy and Gioia
1106.

Kennedy, X. J., and Dana Gioia, eds. *Literature: An Introduction to Fiction,*
Poetry, and Drama. 10th ed. New York: Longman, 2007. Print.

Merwin, W. S. "For the Anniversary of My Death." Kennedy and Gioia 877-78.

Stevens, Wallace. "Thirteen Ways of Looking at a Blackbird." Kennedy and
Gioia 880-82.

When you are citing more than one selection from the same source, your instructor may allow you to avoid repetition by giving the source in full (the Kennedy and Gioia entry) and then simply cross-referencing it in entries for the works you used. Thus the Erdrich, Merwin, and Stevens examples replace full publication information with Kennedy and Gioia and the appropriate pages in that book. Note that each entry appears in its proper alphabetical place among other works cited. Because each entry cross-references the Kennedy anthology, the medium is not required.

28. An article in a reference work (print)

"Reckon." *Merriam-Webster's Collegiate Dictionary*. 11th ed. 2008. Print.

Wenner, Manfred W. "Arabia." *The New Encyclopaedia Britannica: Macropaedia*.
    15th ed. 2007. Print.

List an article in a reference work by its title (first example) unless the article is signed (second example). For works with entries arranged alphabetically, you need not include volume or page numbers. For well-known works like those above, you may also omit the editors' names and all publication information except any edition number and the year of publication. For works that are not well known, give full publication information:

"Hungarians in America." *The Ethnic Almanac*. Ed. Stephanie Bernardo Johns.
    6th ed. New York: Doubleday, 2002. 121-23. Print.

See also models 48 (p. 675) and 68 (p. 683), respectively, to cite reference works appearing on the Web or on a CD-ROM or DVD-ROM.

29. An illustrated book or graphic narrative (print)

Wilson, G. Willow. *Cairo*. Illus. M. K. Perker. New York: Vertigo-DC Comics,
    2005. Print.

When citing the work of the writer of a graphic narrative or illustrated book, follow the example above: author's name, title, Illus. ("Illustrated by"), and the illustrator's name. When citing the work of an illustrator, list his or her name first, followed by a comma and illus. ("illustrator"). After the title and By, list the author's name.

Garth Williams, illus. *Charlotte's Web*. By E. B. White. 1952. New York: Harper,
    1999. Print.

30. A multivolume work (print)

Lincoln, Abraham. *The Collected Works of Abraham Lincoln*. Ed. Roy P. Basler.
    Vol. 5. New Brunswick: Rutgers UP, 1953. Print. 8 vols.

If you use only one volume of a multivolume work, give that volume number before the publication information (Vol. 5 in the preceding example). You may add the total number of volumes at the end of the entry (8 vols. in the example).

If you use two or more volumes of a multivolume work, give the work's total number of volumes before the publication information (8 vols. in the following example). Your text citation will indicate which volume you are citing (see p. 648).

> Lincoln, Abraham. *The Collected Works of Abraham Lincoln*. Ed. Roy P. Basler.
> 8 vols. New Brunswick: Rutgers UP, 1953. Print.

If you cite a multivolume work published over a period of years, give the inclusive years as the publication date: for instance, Cambridge: Harvard UP, 1978-90.

31. A series (print)

> Bergman, Ingmar. *The Seventh Seal*. New York: Simon, 1995. Print. Mod. Film
> Scripts Ser. 12.

Place the name of the series (not quoted or italicized) at the end of the entry, followed by a period, a series number (if any), and another period. Abbreviate common words such as *modern* and *series*.

32. A republished book (print)

> James, Henry. *The Bostonians*. 1886. New York: Penguin, 2001. Print.

Republished books include books reissued under new titles and paperbound editions of books originally released in hard covers. Place the original publication date (but not the place of publication or the publisher's name) after the title, and then provide the full publication information for the source you are using. If the book was originally published under a different title, add this title after Rpt. of ("Reprint of") at the end of the entry (after Print) and move the original publication date after the title—for example, Rpt. of *Thomas Hardy: A Life*. 1941.

33. The Bible (print)

> The Bible. Print. King James Vers.
> *The Holy Bible*. Trans. Ronald Youngblood et al. Grand Rapids: Zondervan,
> 1984. Print. New Intl. Vers.

When citing a standard version of the Bible (first example), do not italicize the title or the name of the version at the end. You need not provide publication information. For an edition of the Bible (second example), italicize the title, provide editors' and/or translators' names, give full publication information, and add the version name at the end.

34. A book with a title in its title (print)

> Eco, Umberto. *Postscript to* The Name of the Rose. Trans. William Weaver.
> New York: Harcourt, 1983. Print.

When a book's title contains another book title (here *The Name of the Rose*), do not italicize the second title. When a book's title contains a quotation or the title of a work normally placed in quotation marks, keep the quotation marks and italicize both titles: *Critical Response to Henry James's "The Beast in the Jungle."*

35. Published proceedings of a conference (print)

Stimpson, Bill, ed. *2007 Annual Conference and Exhibition.* Proc. of Amer. Wind
 Energy Assn. Conf., 3-6 June 2007, New York. Red Hook: Curran, 2008.
 Print.

To cite the published proceedings of a conference, use a book model—here, an edited book (model 22). Between the title and the publication data, add information about the conference, such as its name, date, and location. You may omit any of this information that already appears in the source title. Treat a particular presentation at the conference like a selection from an anthology (model 26).

36. An introduction, preface, foreword, or afterword (print)

Donaldson, Norman. Introduction. *The Claverings.* By Anthony Trollope. New
 York: Dover, 1977. vii-xv. Print.

An introduction, foreword, or afterword is often written by someone other than the book's author. When citing such a piece, give its name without quotation marks or italics, as with Introduction above. (If the piece has a title of its own, provide it, in quotation marks, between the name of the author and the name of the book.) Follow the title of the book with By and the book author's name. Give the inclusive page numbers of the part you cite. (In the example above, the small Roman numerals refer to the front matter of the book, before page 1.)

When the author of a preface or introduction is the same as the author of the book, give only the last name after the title:

Gould, Stephen Jay. Prologue. *The Flamingo's Smile: Reflections in Natural
 History.* By Gould. New York: Norton, 1985. 13-20. Print.

37. A book lacking publication information or pagination (print)

Carle, Eric. *The Very Busy Spider.* New York: Philomel, 1984. N. pag. Print.

Some books are not paginated or do not list a publisher or a place of publication. To cite such a book, provide as much information as you can and indicate the missing information with an abbreviation: N.p. if no city of publication, n.p. if no publisher, n.d. if no publication date, and N. pag. if no page numbers.

Other nonperiodical print sources

38. A government publication (print)

United Nations. Dept. of Economic and Social Affairs. *World Youth Report 2007: Young People's Transition to Adulthood—Progress and Challenges.* New York: United Nations, 2008. Print.

United States. Cong. House. Committee on Agriculture, Nutrition, and Forestry. *Food and Energy Act of 2007.* 110th Cong., 1st sess. Washington: GPO, 2007. Print.

Wisconsin. Dept. of Public Instruction. *Bullying Prevention Program: Grades 6-8.* Madison: Wisconsin Dept. of Public Instruction, 2007. Print.

If a government publication does not list a person as author or editor, give the appropriate agency as author, as in the above examples. Provide information in the order illustrated, separating elements with periods: the name of the government, the name of the agency (which may be abbreviated), and the title and publication information. For a congressional publication (second example), give the house and committee involved before the title, and give the number and session of Congress after the title. In this example, GPO stands for the US Government Printing Office.

If a government publication lists a person as author or editor, treat the source as an authored or edited book:

Putko, Michelle. *Women in Combat Compendium.* Carlisle: US Army War Coll., Strategic Studies Inst., 2008. Print.

See model 47 (p. 675) to cite a government publication you find on the Web.

39. A pamphlet or brochure (print)

Understanding Childhood Obesity. Tampa: Obesity Action Coalition, 2008. Print.

Most pamphlets and brochures can be treated as books. In this example, the pamphlet has no listed author, so the title comes first. If your source has an author, give his or her name first, followed by the title and publication information.

40. A dissertation (print)

McFaddin, Marie Oliver. *Adaptive Reuse: An Architectural Solution for Poverty and Homelessness.* Diss. U of Maryland, 2007. Ann Arbor: UMI, 2007. Print.

Treat a published dissertation like a book, but after the title insert Diss. ("Dissertation"), the institution granting the degree, and the year.

For an unpublished dissertation, use quotation marks rather than italics for the title and omit publication information.

Wilson, Stuart M. "John Stuart Mill as a Literary Critic." Diss. U of Michigan, 1990. Print.

41. A letter (print)

Buttolph, Mrs. Laura E. Letter to Rev. and Mrs. C. C. Jones. 20 June 1857. *The Children of Pride: A True Story of Georgia and the Civil War.* Ed. Robert Manson Myers. New Haven: Yale UP, 1972. 334-35. Print.

List a published letter under the writer's name. Specify that the source is a letter and to whom it was addressed, and give the date on which it was written. Treat the remaining information like that for a selection from an anthology (model 26, p. 666). (See also model 16, p. 662, for the format of a letter to the editor of a periodical.)

For an unpublished letter in the collection of a library or archive, specify the writer, recipient, and date, as for a published letter. Then provide the medium, either MS ("manuscript") or TS ("typescript"). End with the name and location of the archive.

James, Jonathan E. Letter to his sister. 16 Apr. 1970. MS. Jonathan E. James Papers. South Dakota State Archive, Pierre.

For a letter you received, give the name of the writer, note the fact that the letter was sent to you, provide the date of the letter, and add the medium, MS or TS.

Wynne, Ava. Letter to the author. 6 Apr. 2008. MS.

To cite an e-mail message or a discussion-group posting, see models 70–71 (p. 684).

4 | Listing nonperiodical Web sources

This section shows how to cite nonperiodical sources that you find on the Web. These sources may be published only once or occasionally, or they may be updated frequently but not regularly. (Most online magazines and newspapers fall into the latter category, even if they relate to printed periodicals, because their content changes often and unpredictably. See models 45 and 46.) Some nonperiodical Web sources are available only on the Web (next page); others are available in other media as well (pp. 678–79). See models 62–67 (pp. 680–83) to cite a scholarly journal that you find on the Web and any periodical that you find in an online database.

The MLA no longer recommends providing a URL (electronic address) in Web source citations because URLs change frequently and because users can search for documents using search engines. However, do include a URL if your source is hard to find without it, if your source could be confused with another one, or if your instructor requires you to include URLs. See model 61 (p. 679) for the form to use when citing a URL.

Note The *MLA Style Manual* does not label its examples of non-periodical Web sources as particular types. For ease of reference, the following models identify and illustrate the kinds of Web sources you are likely to encounter. If you don't see just what you need, consult the index of models on pages 656–57 for a similar source type whose format you can adapt. If your source does not include all of the information needed for a complete citation, find and list what you can.

Nonperiodical sources available only on the Web

Many nonperiodical Web sources are available only online. The following list, adapted from the *MLA Style Manual*, itemizes the possible elements in a nonperiodical Web publication, in order of their appearance in a works-cited entry:

1. **Name of the author or other person responsible for the source,** such as an editor, translator, or performer. See models 1–6 (pp. 654–58) for the handling of authors' names. For other kinds of contributors, see models 22–24 (editors and translators) and models 74, 76–77, and 83 (performers, directors, and so on).

2. **Title of the cited work.** Use quotation marks for titles of articles, blog entries, and other sources that are parts of larger works. Use italics for books, plays, and other sources that are published independently.

3. **Title of the Web site,** in italics.

4. **Version or edition cited,** if any, following model 21 (p. 665)—for example, *Index of History Periodicals*. 2nd ed.

5. **Publisher or sponsor of the site,** followed by a comma. If you cannot find a publisher or sponsor, use N.p. ("No publisher") instead.

6. **Date of electronic publication, latest revision, or posting.** If no date is available, use n.d. ("no date") instead.

7. **Medium of publication:** Web.

8. **Date of your access:** day, month, year.

For some Web sources, you may want to include information that is not on this list, such as the names of both the writer and the performers on a television show.

42. A short work with a title (Web)

Molella, Arthur. "Cultures of Innovation." *The Lemelson Center for the Study of Invention and Innovation*. Smithsonian Inst., Natl. Museum of Amer. Hist., Spring 2005. Web. 3 Aug. 2008.

See the facing page for an analysis of this entry and the location of the required information on the Web site. If the short work you are

Format for a short work on the Web

①   ②   ③
Molella, Arthur. "Cultures of Innovation." *The Lemelson Center for the Study of Inven-*

tion and Innovation. Smithsonian Inst., Natl. Museum of Amer. Hist., Spring
                    ④   ⑤

⑥   ⑦
2005. Web. 3 Aug. 2008.

Top of page

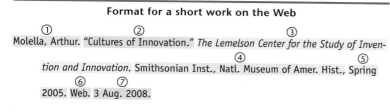

③ **Site title,** italicized and ending with a period.

② **Title of the short work,** in quotation marks. End the title with a period inside the final quotation mark.

① **Author.** Give the full name—last name first, a comma, first name, and any middle name or initial. Omit *Dr., PhD,* or any other title. End the name with a period. If you don't see the author's name at the top of the page, look at the bottom. If no author is listed, begin with the title of the short work.

Bottom of page

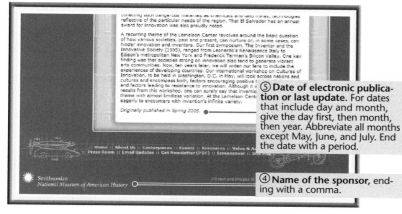

⑤ **Date of electronic publication or last update.** For dates that include day and month, give the day first, then month, then year. Abbreviate all months except May, June, and July. End the date with a period.

④ **Name of the sponsor,** ending with a comma.

⑥ **Medium.** Give the medium of the article, Web, followed by a period.

⑦ **Date of your access.** Give the day first, then month, then year. Abbreviate all months except May, June, and July. End the date with a period. (Since this date does not appear on the site, you'll need to record it separately.)

citing lacks an author, follow model 6 (p. 658) for an anonymous source, starting the entry with the title of the work:

> "Clean Energy." *Union of Concerned Scientists: Citizens and Scientists for Environmental Solutions.* Union of Concerned Scientists, 5 Feb. 2008. Web. 11 Mar. 2008.

To cite a short Web source that also appears in another medium (such as print), see models 56–60 (pp. 678–79). To cite an article from a Web journal or from an online database, see models 62–67 (pp. 680–83).

43. A short work without a title (Web)

> Crane, Gregory, ed. Home page. *The Perseus Digital Library.* Dept. of Classics, Tufts U, n.d. Web. 21 July 2008.

If you are citing an untitled short work from a Web site, such as the home page of a site or a posting to a blog, insert Home page, Online posting, or another descriptive label in place of the title. Do not use quotation marks or italics for this label.

Note that this source lacks a publication date, indicated by n.d. after the sponsor's name.

44. An entire site (Web)

> Cheit, Ross E., ed. *The Recovered Memory Project.* Taubman Center for Public and Amer. Insts., Brown U, July 2007. Web. 8 Oct. 2008.

When citing an entire Web site—for instance, a scholarly project or a foundation site—include the name of the editor, author, or compiler (if available); the title of the site; the sponsor; the date of publication or most recent update; the medium (Web); and your date of access.

If your source lacks a named author or editor, begin with the site title:

> *Union of Concerned Scientists: Citizens and Scientists for Environmental Solutions.* Union of Concerned Scientists, 5 Feb. 2008. Web. 11 Mar. 2008.

If your source lacks a sponsor, use the abbreviation N.p. ("No publisher"). If it lacks a publication date, use the abbreviation n.d. The source below lacks both a sponsor and a publication date:

> Corbett, John. *STARN: Scots Teaching and Resource Network.* N.p., n.d. Web. 26 Nov. 2008.

45. An article in a newspaper (Web)

> Carvajal, Doreen. "High-Tech Crime Is an Online Bubble That Hasn't Burst." *New York Times.* New York Times, 7 Apr. 2008. Web. 8 Apr. 2008.

List the author, article title, and newspaper title, as in model 10 or 11 (pp. 660–61). Then give the publishers's name and the date. End with the medium of publication (Web) and the date of your access. (See model 66 to cite a newspaper article in an online database.)

Use the preceding format to adapt the models for print periodicals if you need to cite a Web newspaper review, editorial, letter to the editor, interview, or article in a series (models 14–18, pp. 662–63).

46. An article in a magazine (Web)

Yabroff, Jennie. "Art Aimed to Shock." *Newsweek*. Newsweek, 26 Apr. 2008. Web. 15 May 2008.

List the author, article title, and magazine title, as in model 12 or 13 (pp. 661–62). Then give the publisher's name and the date. End with the medium (Web) and the date of your access. (See model 67 to cite a magazine article in an online database.)

Use the preceding format to adapt the models for print periodicals if you need to cite a Web magazine review, editorial, letter to the editor, interview, article in a series, or special issue (models 14–19, pp. 662–63).

47. A government publication (Web)

United States. Dept. of Agriculture. "Inside the Pyramid." *MyPyramid.gov*. US Dept. of Agriculture, n.d. Web. 1 Mar. 2008.

See model 38 for examples of government publications in print. Provide the same information for online publications along with the facts of Web publication. The example above includes the names of the government and department; the title of the source, in quotation marks; the title of the Web site, in italics; n.d. (because there is no publication date); the medium (Web); and the date of access.

48. An article in a reference work (Web)

"Yi Dynasty." *Encyclopaedia Britannica Online*. Encyclopaedia Britannica, 2008. Web. 7 Apr. 2008.

This source does not list an author, so the entry begins with the title of the article and then proceeds as for other Web sources. If a reference article has an author, place the name before the article title, as in model 42.

For reference works that you find in print or on CD-ROM or DVD-ROM, see models 28 (p. 667) and 68 (p. 683), respectively.

49. An image (Web)

To cite images that are available only on the Web, give the name of the artist or creator, the title of the work, the date of the work (if any), a word describing the type of image (if not otherwise clear from the image or site title), the title of the Web site, the sponsor, the date of the site, the medium (Web), and your date of access. The following examples show a range of possibilities.

A *work of visual art:*

> Simpson, Rick. *Overload. Museum of Computer Art*. Museum of Computer Art,
>
> 2008. Web. 1 Apr. 2008.

A *photograph:*

> Touboul, Jean. *Desert 1*. 2002. Photograph. *Artmuse.net*. Jean Touboul, 2007.
>
> Web. 14 Nov. 2008.

An *advertisement:*

> United States. Dept. of Educ. Federal Student Aid. Advertisement. *Facebook*.
>
> Facebook, 2008. Web. 6 May 2008.

A *map, chart, graph, or diagram:*

> "Greenhouse Effect." Diagram. *Earthguide*. Scripps Inst. of Oceanography,
>
> 2008. Web. 17 July 2008.

See also model 60 (p. 679) to cite an image that appears both on the Web and in another medium. And see models 78–82 (pp. 686–87) to cite images that aren't on the Web.

50. A television or radio program (Web)

> Seabrook, Andrea, host. *All Things Considered*. Natl. Public Radio, 6 Apr. 2008.
>
> Web. 21 Apr. 2008.

The Web sites of television and radio networks and programs often include both content that was broadcast as part of a show and content that is unique to the site. Cite such material by its title or by the name of the person whose work you cite. Identify the role of anyone but an author (host in the example). Give the site title, the sponsor, the date, the medium (Web), and the date of your access. You may also cite other contributors (and their roles) after the title, as in model 52.

See also model 74 (p. 685) to cite a television or radio program that isn't on the Web.

51. A video recording (Web)

> Green Children Foundation, prod. *The Green Children Visit China. YouTube*.
>
> YouTube, 7 Jan. 2008. Web. 28 June 2008.

Cite a video on the Web either by its title or by the name of the person whose work you are citing—in this example, the foundation that produced the video. Identify the role of anyone but an author (prod. in the example). Give the video title, the site title, the sponsor, the date, the medium (Web), and the date of your access. You may also cite other contributors (and their roles) after the title, as in model 52.

See also model 53 to cite a podcast of a video recording; model 59 (p. 679) to cite a video recording or film that appears both on the Web and in another medium (such as DVD); and model 77 (p. 686) to cite a film, DVD, or video recording that isn't on the Web.

52. A sound recording (Web)

Beglarian, Eve. *Five Things.* Perf. Beglarian et al. *Kalvos and Damian.* N.p., 23
Oct. 2001. Web. 8 Mar. 2008.

Cite a musical sound recording by its title or by the name of the person whose work you are citing—in this example, the composer. (If the composer's name comes after the title, precede it with By. See the next example.) This example also gives the work title, the performers of the work, the site title, the sponsor (here unknown, so replaced with N.p.), the date, the medium (Web), and the date of access.

The same format may be used for a spoken-word recording that you find on the Web:

Wasserstein, Wendy, narr. "Afternoon of a Faun." By Wasserstein. *The Borzoi
Reader Online.* Knopf, 2001. Web. 14 Feb. 2008.

See also the next model to cite a sound podcast; model 58 to cite a sound recording that appears both on the Web and in another medium (such as CD); and model 76 (p. 686) to cite a sound recording that isn't on the Web.

53. A podcast (Web)

Simon, Bob. "Exonerated." *60 Minutes. CBS News.* CBS News, 25 May 2008.
Web. 6 June 2008.

This podcast from a news program lists the author of a story on the show, the title of the story (in quotation marks), and the program (italicized) as well as the site title, sponsor, date, medium (Web), and access date. If a podcast does not list an author or other creator, begin with the title.

54. A blog entry (Web)

Marshall, Joshua Micah. "Asking the Tough Questions." *Talking Points Memo.*
TPM Media, 15 May 2008. Web. 21 May 2008.

To cite an entry from a blog, give the author, the title of the entry, the title of the blog or site, the name of the sponsor (or N.p. if no sponsor is named), the publication date, the medium (Web), and the date of your access. See model 43 (p. 674) to cite a blog entry without a title.

55. A wiki (Web)

"Podcast." *Wikipedia*. Wikimedia, n.d. Web. 20 Nov. 2008.

To cite an entry from a wiki, follow the above example: entry title, site title, sponsor, publication date (here n.d. because the wiki entry is undated), medium (Web), and date of access. Begin with the site title if you are citing the entire wiki.

Nonperiodical Web sources also available in print

Some sources you find on the Web may be books, poems, short stories, and other works that have been scanned from print versions. To cite such a source, generally provide the information for original print publication as well as that for Web publication. Begin your entry as if you were citing the print work, consulting models 20–41 for an appropriate format. Then, instead of giving "Print" as the medium, provide the title of the Web site you used, any version or edition number, the medium you used (Web), and the date of your access.

56. A short work with print publication information (Web)

Wheatley, Phillis. "On Virtue." *Poems on Various Subjects, Religious and Moral*. London, 1773. N. pag. *American Verse Project*. Web. 21 July 2008.

The print information for this poem follows model 26 (p. 666) for a selection from an anthology, but it omits the publisher's name because the anthology was published before 1900. The print information ends with N. pag. because the original source has no page numbers.

57. A book with print publication information (Web)

James, Henry. *The Ambassadors*. 1903. New York: Scribner's, 1909. *Oxford Text Archive*. Web. 5 May 2008.

The print information for this novel follows model 32 (p. 668) for a republished book, so it includes both the original date of publication (1903) and the publication information for the scanned book.

Nonperiodical Web sources also available in other media

Some images, films, and sound recordings that you find on the Web may have been published before in other media and then scanned or digitized for the Web. To cite such a source, generally provide the information for original publication as well as that for

Web publication. Begin your entry as if you were citing the original, consulting models 74–84 (pp. 685–88) for an appropriate format. Then, instead of giving the original medium of publication, provide the title of the Web site you used, the medium you used (Web), and your date of access.

58. A sound recording with other publication information (Web)

"Rioting in Pittsburgh." CBS Radio, 1968. *Vincent Voice Library*. Web.
    7 Dec. 2008.

For Web sound recordings with original publication information, base citations on model 76 (p. 686), adding the information for Web publication.

59. A film or video recording with other publication information (Web)

Coca Cola. Advertisement. Dir. Haskell Wexler. 1971. *American Memory*. Lib. of
    Cong. Web. 8 Apr. 2008.

For Web films or videos with original publication information, base citations on model 77 (p. 686), adding the information for Web publication.

60. An image with other publication information (Web)

Pollock, Jackson. *Lavender Mist: Number 1*. 1950. Natl. Gallery of Art, Washington.
    WebMuseum. Web. 7 Apr. 2008.

Keefe, Mike. "FAA Inspector in a Quandary." Cartoon. *Denver Post* 5 Apr. 2008.
    PoliticalCartoons.com. Web. 7 Apr. 2008.

For Web images with original publication information, base citations on models 78–82 (pp. 686–87), adding the information for Web publication.

Citation of a URL

61. A source requiring citation of the URL

Joss, Rich. "Dispatches from the Ice: The Second Season Begins." *Antarctic*
    Expeditions. Smithsonian Natl. Zoo and Friends of the Natl. Zoo, 26 Oct.
    2007. Web. 26 Sept. 2008. <http://nationalzoo.si.edu/
    ConservationAndScience/AquaticEcosystems/Antarctica/Expedition/
    FieldNew/2-FieldNews.cfm>.

Because a URL does not always provide a convenient or usable route to a source, the MLA no longer recommends including URLs in works-cited entries. However, you should include URLs when your instructor requires them. You should also give a URL when readers may not be able to locate a source without one. For example, using a search engine to find "Dispatches from the Ice" (the title in the example) yields more than ten hits, one of which links to the correct site but the wrong document.

If you need to include a URL, ensure accuracy by using Copy and Paste to duplicate it in a file or an e-mail to yourself. In your list of works cited, give the URL after your date of access and a period. Put angle brackets on both ends of the URL, and end with a period. Break URLs *only* after slashes—do not hyphenate.

5 Listing journals on the Web and periodicals in online databases

This section covers two kinds of periodicals: scholarly journals that you reach directly on the Web (below) and journals, newspapers, and magazines that you reach through online databases (p. 681). Newspapers and magazines that you reach directly on the Web are typically not periodicals (because their content changes often and unpredictably), so they are covered in models 45 and 46 (pp. 674–75).

Citations for Web journals and for periodicals in online databases resemble those for print periodicals, with some changes for the different medium.

Web journals consulted directly

The journals you find directly on the Web may be published only online or may be published in print versions as well. The citation format is the same in either case: begin with an appropriate print model (pp. 658–60), but replace "Print" with Web and add your access date. Because many Web journals are unpaged, you may have to substitute n. pag. for page numbers.

62. An article in a scholarly journal (Web)

Polletta, Francesca. "Just Talk: Public Deliberation after 9/11." *Journal of Public Deliberation* 4.1 (2008): n. pag. Web. 7 Apr. 2008.

See the facing page for an analysis of this entry and the location of the required information in the Web journal. For a journal article reached in an online database, see model 64.

Use the same format to adapt the models for print periodicals if you need to cite a Web journal review, editorial, letter to the editor, interview, article in a series, or special issue (models 14–19, pp. 662–63).

Format for a journal article on the Web

① ② ③
Polletta, Francesca. "Just Talk: Public Deliberation after 9/11." *Journal of Public*
④ ⑤ ⑥ ⑦ ⑧
Deliberation 4.1 (2008): n. pag. Web. 7 Apr. 2008.

⑤ **Year of publication,** in parentheses and followed by a colon.

③ **Title of journal,** in italics. Omit any *A, An,* or *The* from the beginning of the title. Do not end with a period.

⑦ **Medium.** Give the medium of the article, Web, followed by a period.

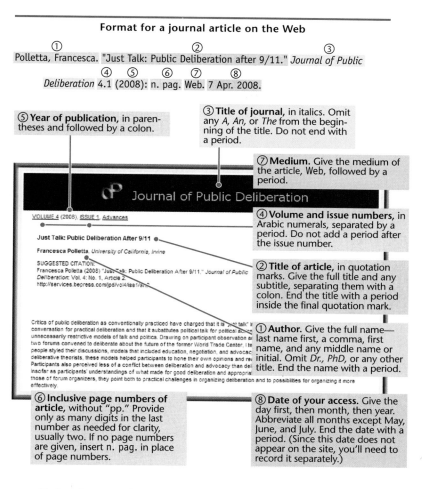

④ **Volume and issue numbers,** in Arabic numerals, separated by a period. Do not add a period after the issue number.

② **Title of article,** in quotation marks. Give the full title and any subtitle, separating them with a colon. End the title with a period inside the final quotation mark.

① **Author.** Give the full name—last name first, a comma, first name, and any middle name or initial. Omit *Dr., PhD,* or any other title. End the name with a period.

⑥ **Inclusive page numbers of article,** without "pp." Provide only as many digits in the last number as needed for clarity, usually two. If no page numbers are given, insert n. pag. in place of page numbers.

⑧ **Date of your access.** Give the day first, then month, then year. Abbreviate all months except May, June, and July. End the date with a period. (Since this date does not appear on the site, you'll need to record it separately.)

63. An abstract of a journal article (Web)

Polletta, Francesca. "Just Talk: Public Deliberation after 9/11." *Journal of Public Deliberation* 4.1 (2008): n. pag. Abstract. Web. 7 Apr. 2008.

Treat a Web abstract like a Web journal article, but add Abstract between the publication information and the medium. (You may omit this label if the journal title clearly indicates that the cited work is an abstract.) See model 65 to cite an abstract in an online database.

Web periodicals consulted in online databases

Many articles in journals, newspapers, and magazines are available in online databases that you reach through your library's Web site, such as *Academic Search Premier, ProQuest,* and *Project Muse.* Follow models 7–19 (pp. 658–63) for print periodicals, but replace "Print" with the title of the database you consulted, the medium (Web), and the date of your access.

64. An article in a scholarly journal (online database)

Gorski, Paul C. "Privilege and Repression in the Digital Era: Rethinking the

Sociopolitics of the Digital Divide." *Race, Gender and Class* 10.4 (2003):

145-76. *Ethnic NewsWatch.* Web. 23 Apr. 2008.

See below for an analysis of the preceding entry and the location of the required information in the database.

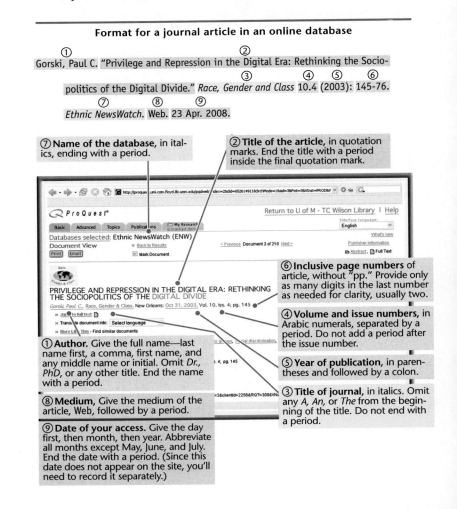

Format for a journal article in an online database

① ②
Gorski, Paul C. "Privilege and Repression in the Digital Era: Rethinking the Socio-
③ ④ ⑤ ⑥
politics of the Digital Divide." *Race, Gender and Class* 10.4 (2003): 145-76.
⑦ ⑧ ⑨
Ethnic NewsWatch. Web. 23 Apr. 2008.

⑦ **Name of the database,** in italics, ending with a period.

② **Title of the article,** in quotation marks. End the title with a period inside the final quotation mark.

⑥ **Inclusive page numbers** of article, without "pp." Provide only as many digits in the last number as needed for clarity, usually two.

④ **Volume and issue numbers,** in Arabic numerals, separated by a period. Do not add a period after the issue number.

⑤ **Year of publication,** in parentheses and followed by a colon.

① **Author.** Give the full name—last name first, a comma, first name, and any middle name or initial. Omit *Dr., PhD,* or any other title. End the name with a period.

③ **Title of journal,** in italics. Omit any *A, An,* or *The* from the beginning of the title. Do not end with a period.

⑧ **Medium,** Give the medium of the article, Web, followed by a period.

⑨ **Date of your access.** Give the day first, then month, then year. Abbreviate all months except May, June, and July. End the date with a period. (Since this date does not appear on the site, you'll need to record it separately.)

65. An abstract of a journal article (online database)

Gorski, Paul C. "Privilege and Repression in the Digital Era: Rethinking the
Sociopolitics of the Digital Divide." *Race, Gender and Class* 10.4 (2003):
145-76. Abstract. *Ethnic NewsWatch.* Web. 23 Apr. 2008.

Treat an abstract in an online database like a journal article in a
database, but add Abstract between the publication information and
the database title. (You may omit this label if the journal title
clearly indicates that the cited work is an abstract.)

66. An article in a newspaper (online database)

Buckman, Rebecca. "Driver Cell Phone Bans Questioned." *Wall Street Journal*
13 May 2008, eastern ed.: D2+. *ProQuest.* Web. 12 Oct. 2008.

Follow model 10 or 11 (p. 660) for citing author, title of article, title
of newspaper, publication date, edition (if any), and page numbers.
Add the title of the database, the medium (Web), and the date of your
access.

67. An article in a magazine (online database)

Brown, Kathryn. "The Skinny on the Environment." *Scientific American* Jan.
2008: 30-37. *Academic Search Premier.* Web. 3 Aug. 2008.

Follow model 12 or 13 (pp. 661–62) for citing author, title of article,
title of magazine, publication date, and page numbers. Add the title
of the database, the medium (Web), and the date of your access.

6 **Listing other electronic sources**

Publications on CD-ROM or DVD-ROM

68. A nonperiodical CD-ROM or DVD-ROM

Nunberg, Geoffrey. "Usage in the Dictionary." *The American Heritage Dictionary
of the English Language.* 4th ed. Boston: Houghton, 2000. CD-ROM.

Single-issue CD-ROMs may be encyclopedias, dictionaries, books,
and other resources that are published just once, like print books.
Follow models 20–37 for print books (pp. 663–69), but replace "Print"
with CD-ROM or DVD-ROM. If the disc has a vendor that differs from the
publisher of the work, add the vendor's place of publication, name,
and publication date after the medium—for instance, Oklahoma City: So-
quest, 2006.

See also models 28 (p. 667) and 48 (p. 675) to cite reference
works in print and on the Web.

69. A periodical CD-ROM or DVD-ROM

Kolata, Gina. "Gauging Body Mass Index in a Changing Body." *New York Times* 28 June 2005, natl. ed.: D1+. CD-ROM. *New York Times Ondisc.* UMI-ProQuest. Sept. 2005.

Databases on CD-ROM or DVD-ROM are issued periodically—for instance, every six months or every year. The journals, newspapers, and other publications included in such a database are generally available in print as well, so your works-cited entry should give the information for both formats. Start with information for the print version, following models 7–19 (pp. 658–63). Then replace "Print" with the medium (CD-ROM or DVD-ROM), the database title, the vendor's name (UMI-ProQuest in the example), and the database publication date.

E-mail and discussion-group postings

70. An e-mail message

Bailey, Elizabeth. "Re: London." Message to the author. 27 Mar. 2008. E-mail.

For e-mail, give the writer's name; the title, if any, from the e-mail's subject heading, in quotation marks; Message to the author (or the name of a recipient besides you); the date of the message; and the medium, E-mail. You do not need to include the date of your access.

71. A posting to a discussion group

Williams, Frederick. "Circles as Primitive." *The Math Forum @ Drexel.* Drexel U, 28 Feb. 2008. E-mail.

Cite a posting to a discussion group like a blog entry (model 54, p. 667). This example for a discussion-list posting includes author's name, title of the posting, title of the discussion list, name of the sponsor, date of the posting, and medium (E-mail). If the posting is untitled, give Online posting instead. You need not add the date of your access.

Digital files

You may want to cite a digital file that is not on the Web or on a disc, such as a PDF document, a JPEG image, or an MP3 sound recording that you downloaded onto your computer. Use the appropriate model for your kind of source (for instance, model 79 for a personal photograph), but replace the medium with the file format you're using. If you don't know the file format, use Digital file.

72. A text file (digital)

Berg, John K. "Estimates of Persons Driving While Intoxicated." *Law Enforcement Today* 17 Apr. 2008. PDF file.

Fernandez, Carlos. "Summers in Spain." 2008. *Microsoft Word* file.

73. A media file (digital)

Springsteen, Bruce. "Empty Sky." *The Rising*. Columbia, 2002. MP3 file.

Boys playing basketball. Personal photograph by Granger Goetz. 2008. JPEG file.

7 │ Listing other sources

The source types covered in this section are not on a computer or, generally, in printed sources. Most of them have parallel citation formats elsewhere in this chapter when you reach them through electronic and print media. See model 17 (p. 662) to cite an interview in print. See models 49–52 (pp. 675–77) to cite images, television and radio programs, video recordings, and sound recordings that are available only on the Web. See models 58–60 (p. 679) to cite such sources when they are available on the Web and in other media. And see model 73 to cite such sources in digital files.

74. A television or radio program

"Piece of My Heart." By Stacy McKee. Dir. Mark Tinker. *Grey's Anatomy*. ABC. KGO, San Francisco, 1 May 2008. Television.

Start with the title unless you are citing the work of a person or persons. The example here cites an episode title (in quotation marks) and the names of the episode's writer and director. By and Dir. identify their roles. Then the entry gives the program title (in italics), the name of the network, the call letters and city of the local station, the date, and the medium (Television). If you list individuals who worked on the entire program rather than an episode, put their names after the program title.

75. A personal or broadcast interview

Paul, William. Personal interview. 6 June 2008.

Diaz, Junot. Interview by Terry Gross. *Fresh Air*. Natl. Public Radio. WGBH, Boston, 18 Oct. 2007. Radio.

Begin with the name of the person interviewed. For an interview you conducted, specify Personal interview or the medium (such as Telephone interview or E-mail interview), and then give the date. For an interview you heard or saw, provide the title if any or Interview if there is no title. Add the name of the interviewer if he or she is identified. Then follow an appropriate model for the kind of source (here, a radio program), and end with the medium (here, Radio).

76. A sound recording

Rubenstein, Artur, perf. Piano Concerto no. 2 in B-flat. By Johannes Brahms.

Cond. Eugene Ormandy. Philadelphia Orch. RCA, 1972. LP.

Springsteen, Bruce. "Empty Sky." *The Rising*. Columbia, 2002. CD.

Begin with the name of the individual whose work you are citing. Unless this person is the composer, identify his or her role, as with perf. ("performer") in the first example. If you're citing a work identified by form, number, and key (first example), do not use quotation marks or italics for the title. If you're citing a song or song lyrics (second example), give the title in quotation marks; then provide the title of the recording in italics. Following the title, identify the composer or author if you haven't already, after By, and name and identify other participants you want to mention. Then provide the manufacturer of the recording, the date of release, and the medium: LP in the first example, CD in the second.

77. A film, DVD, or video recording

A Beautiful Mind. Dir. Ron Howard. Universal, 2001. Film.

Start with the title of the work unless you are citing the work of a person (see the next example). Generally, identify and name the director. You may list other participants (writer, lead performers, and so on) as you judge appropriate. For a film, end with the distributor, date, and medium (Film).

For a DVD or videocassette, include the original release date (if any), the distributor's name, and the medium (DVD or Videocassette).

Balanchine, George, chor. *Serenade*. Perf. San Francisco Ballet. Dir. Hilary

Bean. 1991. PBS Video, 2006. DVD.

78. A painting, photograph, or other work of visual art

Arnold, Leslie. *Seated Woman*. N.d. Oil on canvas. DeYoung Museum, San Francisco.

Sugimoto, Hiroshi. *Pacific Ocean, Mount Tamalpais*. 1994. Photograph.

Private collection.

To cite an actual work of art, name the artist and give the title (in italics) and the date of creation (or N.d. if the date is unknown). Then provide the medium of the work (such as Oil on canvas or Photograph) and the name and location of the owner, if known. (Use Private collection if not.)

For a work you see only in a reproduction, provide the complete publication information for the source you used. Omit the medium of the work itself, and replace it with the medium of the reproduction (Print in the following example). Omit such information only if you examined the actual work.

Hockney, David. *Place Furstenberg, Paris*. 1985. Coll. Art Gallery, New Paltz.
David Hockney: A Retrospective. Ed. Maurice Tuchman and Stephanie
Barron. Los Angeles: Los Angeles County Museum of Art, 1988. 247. Print.

79. A personal photograph

Common milkweed on Lake Michigan shoreline. Personal photograph by the
author. 22 Aug. 2008.

For a personal photograph by you or by someone else, describe the
subject (without quotation marks or italics), say who took the photograph, and add the date.

80. A map, chart, graph, or diagram

"The Sonoran Desert." Map. *Sonoran Desert: An American Deserts Handbook*. By
Rose Houk. Tucson: Western Natl. Parks Assn., 2000. 12. Print.

Unless the creator of an illustration is given on the source, list the
illustration by its title. Put the title in quotation marks if it comes
from another publication or in italics if it is published independently. Then add a description (Map, Chart, and so on), the publication information, and the medium (here, Print).

81. A cartoon or comic strip

Trudeau, Garry. "Doonesbury." Comic strip. *San Francisco Chronicle* 28 Aug.
2008: E6. Print.

Cite a cartoon or comic strip with the artist's name, the title (in quotation marks), the description Cartoon or Comic strip, the publication
information, and the medium (here, Print).

82. An advertisement

Escape Hybrid by Ford. Advertisement. *New Yorker* 10 Dec. 2007: 11. Print.

Cite an advertisement with the name of the product or company advertised, the description Advertisement, the publication information,
and the medium (Print, Television, Radio, and so on).

83. A performance

Levine, James, cond. Boston Symphony Orch. Symphony Hall, Boston. 2 May
2008. Performance.
The New Century. By Paul Rudnick. Dir. Nicholas Martin. Mitzi E. Newhouse
Theater, New York. 6 May 2008. Performance.

For a live performance, generally base your citation on film citations (model 77). Place the title first (second example) unless you

Have students work through Exercise 46.1 individually, and then give them the opportunity to discuss and revise their entries in small groups. This process will allow students to develop specific questions about correct bibliographic form and then address them in a supportive setting.

As a follow-up, have students list their own sources in correct bibliographic form, making note of entries that pose unusual classification or citation challenges. Ask them to send those entries to the rest of the class by e-mail, so that their classmates can see how they resolved the challenge.

ANSWERS: EXERCISE 46.1

The citations below are in MLA style and are alphabetized.

Eggert, Wayne G. "State and Local Sales/Use Tax Simplification." *The Sales Tax in the Twenty-first Century*. Ed. Matthew Murray and William F. Fox. Westport: Praeger, 2004. 67–80. Print.

"The Internet Tax Freedom Act and the Digital Divide." *Center on Budget and Policy Priorities*. Center on Budget and Policy Priorities, 26 Sept. 2007. Web. 2 Nov. 2008.

James, Nora. Interview. 1 Nov. 2008. E-mail.

Novack, Janet. "Point, Click, Pay Tax." *Forbes* 28 Nov. 2007: 56–58. *ProQuest*. Web. 10 Nov. 2008.

Osborne, Sally G. *All's Fair in Internet Commerce, or Is It?* New York: Random, 2004. Print.

United States. Advisory Commission on Electronic Commerce. *Report to Congress*. US Advisory Commission on Electronic Commerce, Apr. 2005. Web. 12 Nov. 2008.

Zimmerman, Malai, and Kent Hoover. "Use of Third Parties to Collect State and Local Taxes on Internet Sales." *The Pacific Business Journal* 5.2 (2004): 45–48. Print.

are citing the work of an individual (first example). After the title, provide relevant information about participants as well as the theater, city, and performance date. Conclude with the medium (Performance).

84. A lecture, speech, address, or reading

Katrib, Ruba. "New Art: South Florida Exhibit." Museum of Contemporary Art. MOCA at Goldman Warehouse, Miami. 4 Sept. 2007. Address.

Give the speaker's name, the title if any (in quotation marks), the title of the meeting if any, the name of the sponsoring organization, the location of the presentation, and the date. End with a description of the type of presentation (Lecture, Speech, Address, Reading).

Although the MLA does not provide a specific style for citing classroom lectures in your courses, you can adapt the preceding format for this purpose.

Cavanaugh, Carol. Class lecture on teaching mentors. Lesley U. 4 Apr. 2008. Lecture.

Exercise 46.1 Writing works-cited entries

Prepare works-cited entries from the following information. Follow the MLA models given in this chapter unless your instructor specifies a different style. Arrange the finished entries in alphabetical order, not numbered.

1. An article titled "Use of Third Parties to Collect State and Local Taxes on Internet Sales," appearing in the print periodical *The Pacific Business Journal,* volume 5, issue 2, in 2004. The authors are Malai Zimmerman and Kent Hoover. The article appears on pages 45 through 48 of the journal.

2. A government publication you consulted on November 12, 2008, on the Web. The author is the Advisory Commission on Electronic Commerce. The commission is an agency of the United States government. The title of the publication is *Report to Congress*. It was published in April 2005.

3. A Web article with no listed author. The title and sponsor of the Web site is Center on Budget and Policy Priorities. The title of the article is "The Internet Tax Freedom Act and the Digital Divide," and the site is dated September 26, 2007. You consulted the site on November 2, 2008.

4. An article in the magazine *Forbes,* published November 28, 2007, on pages 56 through 58. The author is Janet Novack. The title is "Point, Click, Pay Tax." You accessed the source through the database *ProQuest* on November 10, 2008.

5. A print book titled *All's Fair in Internet Commerce, or Is It?* by Sally G. Osborne. The book was published in 2004 by Random House in New York.

6. An e-mail interview you conducted with Nora James on November 1, 2008.
7. An article titled "State and Local Sales/Use Tax Simplification," appearing on pages 67 through 80 of a print anthology, *The Sales Tax in the Twenty-first Century*. The anthology is edited by Matthew N. Murray and William F. Fox. The article is by Wayne G. Eggert. The anthology was published in 2004 by Praeger in Westport, Connecticut.

46c Using MLA document format

The MLA's manual for students, the *MLA Handbook*, provides guidelines for a fairly simple document format, with just a few elements. For guidelines on type fonts, headings, lists, illustrations, and other features that MLA style does not specify, see pages 117–25.

The samples below show the formats for the first page and a later page of a paper. For the format of the list of works cited, see pages 653–54.

First page of MLA paper

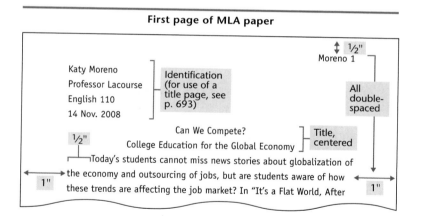

Later page of MLA paper

Margins Use minimum one-inch margins on all sides of every page.

Spacing and indentions Double-space throughout. Indent paragraphs one-half inch. (See below for indention of poetry and long prose quotations.)

Paging Begin numbering on the first page, and number consecutively through the end (including the list of works cited). Use Arabic numerals (1, 2, 3) positioned in the upper right, about one-half inch from the top. Place your last name before the page number in case the pages later become separated.

Identification and title MLA style does not require a title page for a paper. If your instructor asks you to supply a title page, see pages 692–93. Otherwise, follow the sample on the previous page, providing your name, the date, and other information requested by your instructor. Place this identification an inch from the top of the page, aligned with the left margin and double-spaced.

Double-space again, and center the title. Do not highlight the title with underlining, boldface, larger type, or quotation marks. Capitalize the words in the title according to the guidelines on page 483. Double-space the lines of the title and between the title and the text.

Poetry and long prose quotations Treat a single line of poetry like any other quotation, running it into your text and enclosing it in quotation marks. You may run in two or three lines of poetry as well, separating the lines with a slash surrounded by space.

> An example of Robert Frost's incisiveness is in two lines from "Death of the Hired Man": "Home is the place where, when you have to go there / They have to take you in" (119-20).

Always set off from your text a poetry quotation of more than three lines. Use double spacing above and below the quotation and for the quotation itself. Indent the quotation one inch from the left margin. *Do not add quotation marks.*

> Emily Dickinson stripped ideas to their essence, as in this description of "A narrow Fellow in the Grass," a snake:
>
> > I more than once at Noon
> > Have passed, I thought, a Whip lash
> > Unbraiding in the Sun
> > When stopping to secure it
> > It wrinkled, and was gone – (12-16)

Also set off a prose quotation of more than four typed lines. (See p. 615 on when to use such long quotations.) Double-space and indent as with the preceding poetry example. *Do not add quotation marks.*

> In the influential *Talley's Corner* from 1967, Elliot Liebow observes that "unskilled" construction work requires more skill than is generally assumed:
>
> > A healthy, sturdy, active man of good intelligence requires from two to four weeks to break in on a construction job. . . . It frequently happens that his foreman or the craftsman he services is not willing to wait that long for him to get into condition or to learn at a glance the difference in size between a rough 2 x 8 and a finished 2 x 10. (62)

Do not use a paragraph indention for a quotation of a single complete paragraph or a part of a paragraph. Use paragraph indentions of one-quarter inch only for a quotation of two or more complete paragraphs.

47
Two Research Papers in MLA Style

The following pages show the research papers of Justin Malik and Vanessa Haley, whose work we followed in Chapters 41–45. (Malik's paper begins on the next page, Haley's on p. 720.) Both students followed the styles of the *MLA Style Manual* for documenting sources and the *MLA Handbook* for formatting their papers. Accompanying both students' papers are comments on format, source citations, and other matters.

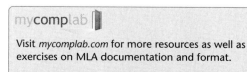

Visit *mycomplab.com* for more resources as well as exercises on MLA documentation and format.

small groups. Students may have strong opinions about these final drafts. Both papers are effective, but neither is perfect, so you can ask your students to reflect upon any aspect of the final drafts that surprised them, how they themselves would have written the paper differently, or what, as readers, they would like to see added, omitted, or changed.

MODELS OF STUDENT WRITING

Justin Malik's paper is an example of a successful student effort at research writing. Malik skillfully balances his argument with the evidence from source material. You may wish to discuss this balance with your students, as writers with less research writing experience may have difficulty determining how much of the paper should be reportage. Some may get so caught up in reporting evidence that they lose track of their arguments; others may produce argument papers based upon insufficient research. You can emphasize for students that Malik's outline sketches the argument, not the evidence, and that using an outline is one way to ensure that a research paper is more than simply a report. You can also point out how Malik's argument evolved from his research.

Another strength of the paper is the deftness of its transitions. Malik connects chunks of research logically. He begins by introducing information on the environmental crisis and connecting that information to the expanding market for green products. He briefly addresses the problems with green products. Then the first major shift occurs on page 2 of his paper (see comment 16), where he begins his argument that overconsumption, not failure to use green products, is the problem. The second shift occurs on page 6 (see comment 33). Here, Malik starts to focus on solutions for reducing consumption.

You can also use this paper to discuss the mechanical issues associated with research writing, from the introduction of quoted material to citation style to page layout. The annotations provide detailed comments on all these features, and a variety of electronic sources for the paper gives students examples of proper citation of such sources.

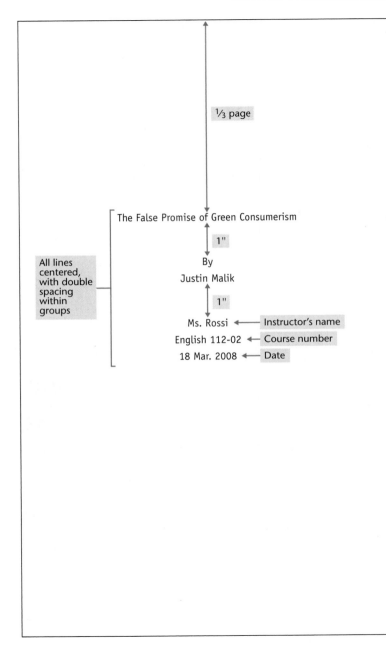

1   **Title page format.** A title page is not required by MLA style but may be required by your instructor. If so, or if you are required to submit an outline with your paper, prepare a title page as shown opposite.

If your instructor does not require a title page for your paper, follow MLA style: place your name, the identifying information, and the date on the first page of the paper. See Vanessa Haley's paper, page 720, for this format.

Next two pages

2   **Outline format.** If your instructor asks you to include your final outline, place it between the title page and the text and number the pages with small Roman numerals (i, ii). Follow the formatting annotations on the next two pages.

3   **Outline content.** Malik includes his final thesis statement as part of his outline so that his instructor can see how the parts relate to the whole. Notice that each main division (numbered with Roman numerals) relates to the thesis statement and that all the subdivisions relate to their main division.

Malik casts his final outline in full sentences. Some instructors request topic outlines, in which ideas appear in phrases instead of in sentences and do not end with periods. (See p. 37 for this format.)

COLLABORATIVE LEARNING

FROM OUTLINE TO ESSAY

In peer review groups, ask students to discuss how Justin Malik's outline evolved into his final paper. Notice how the outline focuses on Malik's ideas and argument, not information from his source material. How did he determine where to place source material? How does he tie the evidence to his own ideas?

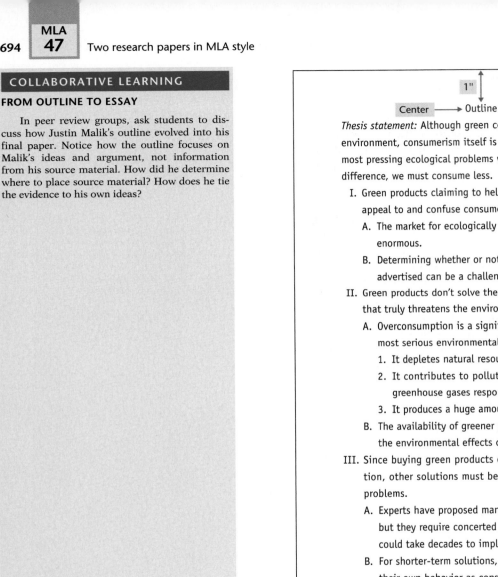

Author's name and page number → Malik i

1"   ½"

Center ——→ Outline

2
3

Thesis statement: Although green consumerism can help the environment, consumerism itself is the root of some of the most pressing ecological problems we face. To make a real difference, we must consume less.

Double-space

I. Green products claiming to help the environment both appeal to and confuse consumers.

   A. The market for ecologically sound products is enormous.

   B. Determining whether or not a product is as green as advertised can be a challenge.

II. Green products don't solve the high rate of consumption that truly threatens the environment.

   A. Overconsumption is a significant cause of three of the most serious environmental problems.

      1. It depletes natural resources.

      2. It contributes to pollution, particularly from the greenhouse gases responsible for global warming.

      3. It produces a huge amount of solid waste.

   B. The availability of greener products has not reduced the environmental effects of consumption.

III. Since buying green products does not reduce consumption, other solutions must be found for environmental problems.

   A. Experts have proposed many far-reaching solutions, but they require concerted government action and could take decades to implement.

   B. For shorter-term solutions, individuals can change their own behavior as consumers.

      1. Precycling may be the greenest behavior that individuals can adopt.

Malik ii

   a. Precycling means avoiding purchase of products that use raw materials and excessive packaging.

   b. More important, precycling means avoiding purchases of new products whenever possible.

2. For unavoidable purchases, individuals can buy green products and influence businesses to embrace ecological goals.

1"

Author's name and page number → Malik 1 ↑ ½"

Title, centered ——→ The False Promise of Green Consumerism

They line the aisles of just about any store. They seem to dominate television and print advertising. Chances are that at least a few of them belong to you. From organic jeans to household cleaners to hybrid cars, products advertised as environmentally friendly are readily available and are so popular they're trendy. It's easy to see why Americans are buying these things in record numbers. The new wave of "green" consumer goods makes an almost irresistible promise: we can save the planet by shopping.

Double-space

Saving the planet does seem to be urgent. Thanks partly to former Vice President Al Gore, who sounded the alarm in 1992 with *Earth in the Balance* and again in 2006 with *An Inconvenient Truth,* the threat of global warming has become a regular feature in the news media and a recurring theme in popular culture.[1] Unfortunately, as Gore himself points out, climate change is just one of many environmental problems competing for our attention: the rainforests are vanishing; our air and our water are dangerously polluted; an alarming number of species are facing extinction; and landfills are overflowing (*Earth* 23-28). All the bad news can be overwhelming, and most people feel powerless to halt the damage. Thus it is reassuring that we may be able to help by making small changes in what we buy—but it is not entirely true. Although green consumerism can help the environment, consumerism itself is the root of some of the most pressing ecological problems we face. To make a real difference, we must consume less.

The market for items perceived as ecologically sound is enormous. Experts estimate that spending on green products already approaches $200 billion a year (Adler et al.). Shoppers respond well to new options, whether the purchase is as minor as a bottle of chemical-free dish soap or as major as a front-

1"

1"

4
5
6
7
8
9
10
11

1"

4 a Title. Malik's title clearly indicates the topic of his paper and previews his main idea. **b Paper format.** Because he provides a title page as requested by his instructor, Malik does not repeat his full name on the first page of the text. For MLA style, which omits a title page, the following would appear in the upper left of this first page:

Justin Malik

Ms. Rossi

English 112-02

18 Mar. 2008

(See Vanessa Haley's paper, p. 720, for an example of a research paper without a title page.) Follow the formatting annotations on the facing page for margins and spacing.

5 Introduction. Malik offers examples of the subject of his paper—green consumer products—and suggests a reason for their popularity. He delays presenting his thesis in order to establish some background about the severity of the environmental problems that the products address.

6 a Omission of a parenthetical citation. Malik does not provide a parenthetical citation for Gore's books because he names the author and titles in the text and refers to the complete works.
b Using an endnote for supplementary information. Here Malik inserts a reference to a note at the end of the paper that gives examples of global warming as a recurring theme in popular culture. Malik signals the note with the raised numeral 1.

7 Citation of a work by an author of two or more works. To clarify which of Gore's two books he is citing, Malik gives a shortened form of the title in the parenthetical citation.

8 Thesis statement. Malik's introduction has led up to this statement, which asserts the claim that he will support in the paper.

9 Relation to outline. This paragraph begins part I of Malik's outline (see p. 694).

10 Selecting supporting evidence. Malik paraphrases and quotes two sources in this paragraph to support his point about the size of the market for green consumer products. The use of signal phrases and the placement of parenthetical citations clarify the sources of the information.

11 a Citation of a source with more than three authors. The Adler citation indicates with et al. ("and others") that Adler was a coauthor with at least three others. See the works-cited entry for this source on page 716. **b Citation of an article without page numbers.** The Adler article, which Malik found in an online database, gave no page or other reference numbers, so the citation includes only the author's name.

Malik 2

loading washing machine. Not surprisingly, businesses are responding by offering as many new eco-products as they can.
Sandra Jones of the *Chicago Tribune* reports that "green product introductions [have] skyrocketed" lately. She cites a market   **12**
research report by the Mintel International Group: in the first
five years of this century, new household products labeled as
green rose from zero to 153, eco-conscious health and beauty
aids increased by more than a thousand percent, and organic
food and beverage options nearly tripled (B1). These new products are offered for sale at stores like Wal-Mart, Target, Home
Depot, Starbucks, and Pottery Barn. It seems clear that green   **13**
consumerism has grown into a mainstream interest.

     Determining whether or not a product is as green as ad-
vertised can be a challenge. Claims vary: a product might be
labeled as organic, biodegradable, energy efficient, recycled,
carbon neutral, renewable, or just about anything that sounds
environmentally positive. However, none of these terms carries a
universally accepted meaning, and no enforceable labeling regulations exist ("It's Not Easy"). Some of the new product options   **14**
offer clear environmental benefits: for instance, compact fluores-
cent light bulbs last ten times as long as regular bulbs and draw
about a third of the electricity (Gore, *Inconvenient* 306), and   **15**
paper made from recycled fibers saves many trees. But other
"green" products just as clearly do little or nothing to help the
environment: a disposable razor made with less plastic is still a
disposable razor, destined for a landfill after only a few uses.

     Distinguishing truly green products from those that are not   **16**
so green merely scratches the surface of a much larger issue. The
products aren't the problem; it's our high rate of consumption
that poses the real threat to the environment. We seek what's
newer and better—whether cars, clothes, phones, computers,
televisions, shoes, or gadgets—and they all require resources to

12 a Adding to a quotation with brackets. Malik adds the word *have* to Jones's sentence so that the quotation will fit the grammar of his own sentence, and he encloses the addition with brackets. **b Mixing quotation and paraphrase.** In addition to quoting Jones, Malik paraphrases statistical information from her article that he had quoted in his original note. **c Use of an indirect source.** Jones cited Mintel International Group, and Malik uses the same information. Mintel International is thus an indirect source. Such sources are appropriate only when the cited material is not available to consult. In this case, Malik could not find a copy of the original Mintel report, so the indirect source is appropriate.

13 Common knowledge. Malik already knew that several major stores stock green products; in fact, he had purchased many of the products he names as examples throughout the paper. Thus he treats the information as common knowledge and does not cite a source. (See p. 629 for more on common knowledge.)

14 Anonymous source. Malik cites a magazine article for which no author is named, so he uses a short version of the title for the citation. Because the article is only one page long and his works-cited list provides full bibliographic information, Malik does not give a page number in the parenthetical citation.

15 a Citation of a paraphrase. Because he does not name Gore in the text, Malik correctly gives the name in the citation. **b Citation of one of two works by the same author.** Malik uses a brief version of Gore's title in the parenthetical citation in order to distinguish the source from another of Gore's books that he also cites. **c Placement of a parenthetical citation.** Malik used Gore's book only for the information on light bulbs, so he places the parenthetical citation directly after the borrowed example. **d Common knowledge and personal experience.** Many sources mentioned the trees saved by recycled paper, so Malik treats the example as common knowledge and omits a source citation. Malik also omits a citation for the razor example, which came from his personal experience.

16 a Relation to outline. This paragraph begins part II of Malik's outline. See page 694. **b Transitional sentences.** The first two sentences of the paragraph shift the emphasis from green products (the previous section of the paper) to the environmental effects of consumption. **c Drawing conclusions.** Malik begins his discussion of the problem of consumption with his own conclusions about what he learned.

Malik 3

make, ship, and use them. Political scientists Thomas Princen, Michael Maniates, and Ken Conca maintain that overconsumption is a leading force behind several ecological crises, warning that

> ever-increasing pressures on ecosystems, life-supporting environmental services, and critical natural cycles are driven not only by the sheer number of resource users . . . but also by the patterns of resource use themselves. (4)

Those patterns of resource use are disturbing. In just the second half of the twentieth century, gross world product (the global output of consumer goods) grew at five times the rate of population growth—a difference explained by a huge rise in consumption per person. (See fig. 1.) Such growth might be good

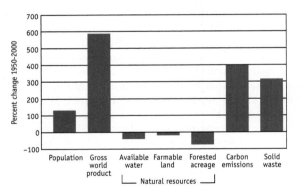

Fig. 1. Global population, consumption, and environmental impacts, 1950-2000. Data from United Nations Development Programme; *Human Development Report: Changing Today's Consumption Patterns—For Tomorrow's Human Development*; New York: Oxford UP; 1998; 4; print; and from Earth Policy Inst.; "Eco-Economy Indicators"; *Earth Policy Institute*; EPI, Feb. 2008; Web; 6 Mar. 2008.

17 **a** **Format of a long quotation.** This quotation exceeds four typed lines, so Malik sets it off from his text without quotation marks, with double spacing throughout, and with an extra indention of ten spaces or one inch. **b** **Omission of an ellipsis mark.** Malik omits the first part of the quoted sentence, but he doesn't use an ellipsis mark because the small *e* in "ever" makes the omission clear. **c** **Use of an ellipsis mark.** Malik uses an ellipsis mark (three spaced periods) to show that he has omitted words from the quotation. **d** **Citation with a displayed quotation.** The parenthetical citation after the quotation falls *outside* the sentence period.

18 **Synthesis of sources.** Here and in the next several paragraphs, Malik integrates information from sources with his own conclusions about the significance of the data and ideas. Signal phrases and source citations clearly distinguish Malik's ideas from sources' information.

19 **Use of a figure.** Malik created a bar chart to show the relative increases in consumption and population and to illustrate the effects of both on the environment. He refers to the figure and elaborates on its meaning in the text.

20 **a** **Figure caption.** Malik captions the figure so that readers know how to interpret it. **b** **Citation of sources for data.** Following MLA style, the caption includes complete information on the two sources for the data. If this were the only use of the sources, Malik would not have to repeat the information in his list of works cited. However, he cites both sources in his text as well, so his works-cited list includes entries for them.

Malik 4

for the economy, but it is bad for the environment. As fig. 1 shows, it is accompanied by the depletion of natural resources, increases in the carbon emissions that cause global warming, and increases in the amount of solid waste disposal.

The first negative effect of overconsumption, the depletion of resources, occurs because the manufacture and distribution of any consumer product depends on the use of water, land, and raw materials such as wood, metal, and oil. Paul **21** Hawken, a respected environmentalist, explains that just in the United States "[i]ndustry moves, mines, extracts, shovels, burns, wastes, pumps, and disposes of *4 million pounds of material* in order to provide one average . . . family's needs for a **22** year" (qtd. in DeGraaf, Wann, and Naylor 85; emphasis added). The United Nations Development Programme's 1998 **23** *Human Development Report* (still the most comprehensive study of the environmental impacts of consumerism) warns that many regions in the world don't have enough water, productive soil, or forests to meet the basic needs of their populations (4). More recent data from the Earth Policy Institute show that as manufacturing and per-person consumption continue to rise, the resources needed for survival continue to decline. Thus heavy consumption poses a threat not only to the environment but also to the well-being of the human race. **24**

In addition to using up scarce natural resources, manufacturing and distributing products harms the earth by spewing pollution into the water, soil, and air. The most worrisome aspect of that pollution may be its link to global warming. As Al Gore ex- **25** plains, the energy needed to power manufacturing and distribution comes primarily from burning fossil fuels, a process that releases carbon dioxide and other greenhouse gases into the air. Those gases build up and trap heat in the earth's atmosphere. The result, most scientists now believe, is increasing global

21 **a** **Integrating source material.** Here and elsewhere, Malik establishes his source's credentials in a signal phrase and effectively integrates paraphrases and quotations into his own sentences. **b** **Editing a quotation with brackets.** By using brackets around the small *i*, Malik indicates that he changed the capitalization of the original source so that it would fit into his own sentence.

22 **a** **Citation of an indirect source.** With the use of qtd. in, Malik indicates correctly that he found the quotation by Hawken (an indirect source) in the book by DeGraaf, Wann, and Naylor (a direct source). **b** **Indirect sources.** Indirect sources are appropriate only when the quoted material is not available to consult. Malik's source, DeGraaf, Wann, and Naylor, gave full bibliographic information for Hawken's book, and Malik should have gone directly to it. **c** **Adding emphasis to a quotation.** Malik italicizes important words in the quotation. He acknowledges this change in the parenthetical citation with emphasis added, separated from the page number by a semicolon. **d** **Punctuation with a parenthetical citation.** The period that ends a sentence containing a quotation comes after the citation.

23 **a** **Citation of a work with a corporate author.** The source Malik cites here does not name individual authors, so he lists the sponsoring organization as author. Naming the organization in the text avoids an awkwardly long parenthetical citation. **b** **Citation when the author is named in your text.** Because Malik names the United Nations Development Programme in his text, he does not repeat the name in the parenthetical citation that follows his paraphrase.

24 **Omission of a parenthetical citation.** The Earth Policy Institute data come from an Internet source that lacks page or other identifying numbers. Since Malik names the author in his text, he doesn't include a parenthetical citation.

25 **a** **Clarifying the boundaries of source material.** The bulk of this paragraph summarizes information from Al Gore's book *An Inconvenient Truth,* surrounded by Malik's interpretation of its implications for his thesis. Malik makes the extent of the summary clear by giving Gore's name at the beginning and a parenthetical citation at the end. **b** **Citing a summary.** Malik condenses information from several sections of Gore's book into one brief sentence. He uses a series of page numbers (next page) to indicate the exact locations of the information in his source.

Malik 5

temperatures that will raise sea levels, expand deserts, and cause more frequent floods and hurricanes (*Inconvenient* 26-27, 81, 118-19, 184). As the preceding bar chart shows, carbon emissions, like production of consumer goods in general, are rising at rates out of proportion with population growth. The more we consume, the more we contribute to global warming.

    As harmful as they are, gradual global warming and the depletion of resources half a world away can be difficult to comprehend or appreciate. A more immediate environmental effect of our buying habits can be seen in the volumes of trash those habits create. The US Environmental Protection Agency found that in a single year (2006), US residents, corporations, and institutions produced 251 million tons of municipal solid waste, amounting to "4.6 pounds per person per day" (1-2). Nearly a third of that trash came just from the wrappers, cans, bottles, and boxes used for shipping consumer goods. (See fig. 2.) Yet the mountains of trash left over from consumption are only a

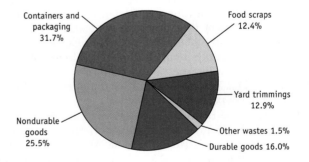

Fig. 2. Sources of municipal solid waste in the United States, 2006. Chart from United States, Environmental Protection Agency, Solid Waste and Emergency Response; *Municipal Solid Waste Generation, Recycling, and Disposal in the United States: Facts and Figures for 2006*; US Environmental Protection Agency, Nov. 2007; Web; 4 Feb. 2008.

26

27

28

29

26 **Synthesis of sources.** Rather than leave it to his readers to interpret the information provided in his chart and the paragraphs surrounding it, Malik offers his own interpretation of what the information means in the context of his thesis.

27 **Revision of a draft.** In his first draft Malik sometimes strung his source information together without interpreting it. In revising he added comments of his own (in blue) to introduce the information in the context of his ideas:

> As harmful as they are, gradual global warming and the depletion of resources half a world away can be difficult to comprehend or appreciate. A more immediate environmental effect of our buying habits can be seen in the volumes of trash those habits create. The US Environmental Protection Agency found that in a single year (2006), US residents, corporations, and institutions produced 251 million tons of municipal solid waste, amounting to "4.6 pounds per person per day" (1-2). Nearly a third of that trash came just from the wrappers, cans, bottles, and boxes used for shipping consumer goods. (See fig. 2.) Yet the mountains of trash left over from consumption are only a part of the problem. In industrial countries overall, 90 percent of waste comes not from what gets thrown out, but from the manufacturing processes of converting natural resources into consumer products (DeGraaf, Wann, and Naylor 192). Nearly everything we buy creates waste in production, comes in packaging that gets discarded immediately, and ultimately ends up in landfills that are already overflowing.

28 **Use of a figure.** Malik uses a pie chart to show that containers and packaging account for the largest portion of solid waste produced in the United States. He refers to the figure in the preceding text.

29 **a** **Figure caption.** Malik captions the figure so that readers know how to interpret it. **b** **Citation of a source for a figure.** Following MLA style, Malik provides a source note indicating where he obtained the figure. The note includes complete information for the source even though Malik also cites the work fully in his list of works cited.

Malik 6

part of the problem. In industrial countries overall, 90 percent of
waste comes not from what gets thrown out, but from the manufacturing processes of converting natural resources into consumer products (DeGraaf, Wann, and Naylor 192). Nearly every-   30
thing we buy creates waste in production, comes in packaging
that gets discarded immediately, and ultimately ends up in landfills that are already overflowing.

Unfortunately, the growing popularity of green products
has not reduced the environmental effects of consumption.
A study conducted by economists Jeff Rubin and Benjamin Tal
for the research firm CIBC World Markets found that while eco-   31
friendly and energy-efficient products have become more available, "consumption is growing by ever-increasing amounts."
The authors give the example of automobiles: in the last generation, cars have become much more energy efficient, but the
average American now drives 2500 more miles a year, for a
net gain in energy use (4-5). At the same time, per-person
waste production in the United States has risen by more than
20 percent (United States 1). Greener products may reduce our   32
cost of consumption and even reduce our guilt about consumption, but they do not reduce consumption and its effects.

If buying green won't solve the problems caused by   33
overconsumption, what will? Politicians, environmentalists,   34
and economists have proposed an array of far-reaching ideas,
including creating a financial market for carbon credits and
offsets, aggressively taxing consumption and pollution, offering financial incentives for environmentally positive behaviors, and even abandoning market capitalism altogether
(Muldoon).[2] However, all of these are "top-down" solutions   35
that require concerted government action. Gaining support
for any one of them, putting it into practice, and getting
results could take decades. In the meantime, the environment

30 **a** **Citation when the author is not named in your text.** Because Malik does not give the three authors' names in his text, he provides the names in the parenthetical citation along with a page number. **b** **Citation of a work with three authors.** Malik gives all three authors' last names, separating them with commas and *and* before the final name.

31 **a** **Mixing quotation and paraphrase.** Malik quotes and paraphrases from Rubin and Tal's article to give readers a good sense of the issue they raise. **b** **Editing a quotation.** Malik had a long quotation by Rubin and Tal, but he selected from it only the words that supported the point he was making. The entire quotation appears in this note:

Consumer behavior

Rubin and Tal 4

"The problem is that energy efficiency is not the final objective—reducing total energy consumption must be the final objective both to the challenges of conventional oil depletion and to greenhouse gas emissions. Despite the huge gains in energy efficiency, that is simply not happening. Instead, energy consumption is growing by ever-increasing amounts. While energy use per unit of US GDP has fallen by almost 50% since 1975, total energy usage in the US economy has risen by more than 40%."

---

c **Punctuation with a quotation.** The period falls inside the closing quotation mark because the quotation is not immediately followed by a parenthetical citation.

32 **Drawing conclusions.** Malik ends his discussion of the environmental effects of consumption with his own conclusion about the popularity of green products as a solution.

33 **a** **Relation to outline.** With this paragraph, Malik begins part III of his outline (see p. 694). **b** **Transitional question.** Malik begins the new section with a question that bridges the previous discussion and the next one.

34 **a** **Summary of sources.** Malik opted to summarize the more far-reaching solutions to overconsumption because he wanted to focus on individuals' actions. **b** **Using an endnote for citation of several sources.** Malik avoids a lengthy and obtrusive parenthetical citation by referring readers to endnote 2, which lists several sources that reinforce Muldoon (see p. 714).

35 **Citation of an article without page numbers.** The Muldoon article, which Malik found directly on the Web, has no page or other reference numbers, so the citation includes only the author's name.

Malik 7

would continue to deteriorate. Clearly, short-term solutions are also essential.

The most promising short-term solution is for individuals to change their own behavior as consumers. The greenest behavior that individuals can adopt may be precycling, the term widely used for avoiding purchases of products that involve the use of raw materials. Precycling includes choosing eco-friendly products made of recycled or nontoxic materials (such as aluminum-free deodorants and fleece made from soda bottles) and avoiding items wrapped in excessive packaging (such as kitchen tools strapped to cardboard and printer cartridges sealed in plastic clamshells). More important, though, precycling means not buying new things in the first place. Renting and borrowing, when possible, saves money and resources; so does keeping possessions in good repair and not replacing them until absolutely necessary. Good-quality used items, from clothing to furniture to electronics, can be obtained for free, or very cheaply, through online communities like *Craigslist* and *Freecycle*, from thrift stores and yard sales, or by trading with friends and relatives. When consumers choose used goods over new, they can help to reduce demand for manufactured products that waste energy and resources, and they can help to keep unwanted items out of the waste stream.

Avoiding unnecessary purchases brings personal benefits as well. Brenda Lin explained in an e-mail interview that frugal living not only saves money but also provides pleasure:

> You'd be amazed at what people throw out or give away: perfectly good computers, oriental rugs, barely used sports equipment, designer clothes, you name it. . . . It's a game for me to find what I need in other people's trash or at Goodwill.

36

37

36 **a** **Common knowledge.** In his reading Malik saw many references to the concept of precycling, so he treats the information in this paragraph as common knowledge and does not cite a source for it. (See p. 629 for more on common knowledge.) **b** **Defining terms.** Because readers might not be familiar with precycling, Malik defines the concept and expands on the definition with four examples. **c** **Omission of parenthetical citations.** The precycling examples and suggestions in this paragraph are Malik's own and so do not require source citations.

37 **a** **Primary source: personal interview.** Malik tested his ideas by conducting an e-mail interview with the producer of a public-access television program about voluntary simplicity. He uses both a paraphrase and a quotation from the interview, with the subject's permission. **b** **Introducing borrowed material.** Malik paraphrases and quotes Lin as an expert, so he should have established her credentials. **c** **Editing a quotation with an ellipsis mark.** Malik uses an ellipsis mark (three spaced periods) and a period to show that he has omitted a full sentence from the quotation. **d** **Omission of a parenthetical citation.** Malik does not provide a parenthetical citation at the end of the quotation on the next page because the source (an interview) has no page or other reference numbers and the necessary information (Lin's name) appears in the text before the quotation.

Malik 8

> You should see the shock on people's faces when
> I tell them where I got my stuff. I get almost as
> much enjoyment from that as from saving
> money and helping the environment at the same
> time.

Lin's experience relates to a study of the personal and social consequences of consumerism by the sociologist Juliet B. Schor. Schor found that the more people buy, the less happy they tend to feel because of the stress of working longer hours to afford their purchases (11-12). Researching the opposite effect, Schor conducted interviews with hundreds of Americans who had drastically reduced their spending so that they would be less dependent on paid work. For these people, she discovered, a deliberately lower standard of living improved quality of life by leaving more time to spend with family and pursue personal interests (136-42). Reducing consumption, it turns out, does not have to translate into sacrifice.

For unavoidable purchases like food and light bulbs, buying green can make a difference by influencing corporate decisions. Some ecologists and economists believe that as more shoppers choose earth-friendly products over their traditional counterparts—or boycott products that are clearly harmful to the environment—more manufacturers and retailers will look for ways to limit the environmental effects of their industrial practices and the goods they sell (Gore, *Earth* 193; Muldoon). Indeed, as environmental business consultant Gregory C. Unruh points out in an article for *Harvard Business Review*, several major companies, among them Wal-Mart, Coca-Cola, General Electric, and Nike, have already taken up sustainability initiatives in response to market pressure. In the process, the companies have discovered that environmentally minded practices tend to raise profits and strengthen

38

39

40

38 **Clarifying the boundaries of source material.** By mentioning Schor's name before he summarizes her findings and citing page numbers for each summary, Malik indicates which ideas are Schor's and which are his own.

39 **Parenthetical citation of more than one work.** Malik found the idea that consumer pressure can affect business behavior in two sources, so he cites both in parentheses, separating the citations with a semicolon. The second source lacked page or other reference numbers, so its citation does not include a number.

40 **Defining terms.** *Sustainability initiatives* might be unfamiliar to readers, so Malik should have defined the term or avoided it. The term refers to actions taken to reduce resource use and pollution in order to preserve the environment.

Malik 9

customer loyalty (111-12). By giving industry solid, bottom-line reasons to embrace ecological goals, consumer demand for earth-friendly products can magnify the effects of individual action.

Careful shopping can help the environment, but green doesn't necessarily mean "Go." All consumption depletes resources, increases the likelihood of global warming, and creates waste, so even eco-friendly products must be used in moderation. As individuals, we can each play a small role in helping the environment—and help ourselves at the same time—by not buying anything we don't really need, even if it seems environmentally sound. Reducing our personal impact on the earth is a small price to pay for preserving a livable planet for future generations.

41
42

43

41 Citation when the author is named in the text. Because Malik names Unruh in his text (previous page of the paper), he does not repeat the name in the parenthetical citation.

42 Drawing a conclusion. Rather than leave it to readers to figure out the significance of the preceding paragraph, Malik offers his own conclusion.

43 Conclusion. In his final paragraph Malik summarizes the main points of his paper to remind readers of both the environmental problems caused by consumption and the benefits of consuming less.

½"
Malik 10

1 space

Notes ← Center

½"

44
45

⌐1. Just a few examples of global warming as a theme in
recent popular culture include the animated films *Happy Feet*
(2006) and *The Simpsons Movie* (2007); Gore's Oscar-winning
documentary *An Inconvenient Truth* (2006); HGTV's programs
Living with Ed (2008) and *Green Home Giveaway* (2008); the
Live Earth concert (2007); special "green" issues of magazines
ranging from *Reader's Digest* (2008) to *Modern Bride* (2008);
and a carbon-emissions module for the computer game
SimCity (2009).

2. See Muldoon for in-depth explanations of these proposals. Additional governmental and institutional solutions
are described in Gore (*Earth* and *Inconvenient*); in DeGraaf,
Wann, and Naylor; in Princen, Maniates, and Conca; and in
United Nations Development Programme.

Double-
space

44 Format of notes. The heading Notes is centered one inch from the top of the page. (The heading would be singular—Note—if Malik had only one note.) Follow the annotations on the facing page for formatting.

45 Endnotes for additional relevant information. Malik uses endnotes for information and sources that are somewhat relevant to his thesis but not essential and that don't fit easily into the text. Note 1 provides several examples to support his comment that global warming has become a recurring theme in popular culture. Note 2 directs readers to a source for more information and cites several additional sources that would be obtrusive in a parenthetical citation. (See p. 653 for more on supplementary notes.)

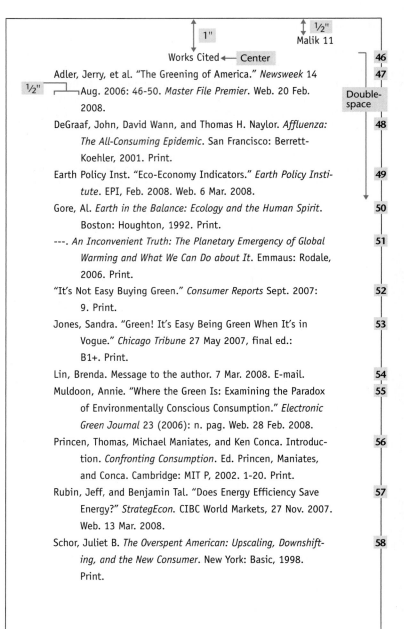

1"

½"
Malik 11

Works Cited ← Center

Adler, Jerry, et al. "The Greening of America." *Newsweek* 14
½" Aug. 2006: 46-50. *Master File Premier*. Web. 20 Feb.
2008.

DeGraaf, John, David Wann, and Thomas H. Naylor. *Affluenza:
The All-Consuming Epidemic*. San Francisco: Berrett-
Koehler, 2001. Print.

Earth Policy Inst. "Eco-Economy Indicators." *Earth Policy Institute*. EPI, Feb. 2008. Web. 6 Mar. 2008.

Gore, Al. *Earth in the Balance: Ecology and the Human Spirit*.
Boston: Houghton, 1992. Print.

---. *An Inconvenient Truth: The Planetary Emergency of Global
Warming and What We Can Do about It*. Emmaus: Rodale,
2006. Print.

"It's Not Easy Buying Green." *Consumer Reports* Sept. 2007:
9. Print.

Jones, Sandra. "Green! It's Easy Being Green When It's in
Vogue." *Chicago Tribune* 27 May 2007, final ed.:
B1+. Print.

Lin, Brenda. Message to the author. 7 Mar. 2008. E-mail.

Muldoon, Annie. "Where the Green Is: Examining the Paradox
of Environmentally Conscious Consumption." *Electronic
Green Journal* 23 (2006): n. pag. Web. 28 Feb. 2008.

Princen, Thomas, Michael Maniates, and Ken Conca. Introduction. *Confronting Consumption*. Ed. Princen, Maniates,
and Conca. Cambridge: MIT P, 2002. 1-20. Print.

Rubin, Jeff, and Benjamin Tal. "Does Energy Efficiency Save
Energy?" *StrategEcon*. CIBC World Markets, 27 Nov. 2007.
Web. 13 Mar. 2008.

Schor, Juliet B. *The Overspent American: Upscaling, Downshifting, and the New Consumer*. New York: Basic, 1998.
Print.

Double-
space

46
47
48
49
50
51
52
53
54
55
56
57
58

46 Format of a list of works cited. The heading Works Cited is centered at the top of the page. The entries are alphabetized by the last name of the first author or (for sources without authors) by the first main word of the title.

47 a Source with more than three authors. A source with more than three authors may be listed with just the first author's name followed by et al. ("and others"). (See p. 655.) Malik's parenthetical citation also uses et al. (p. 696). **b Article in a weekly magazine consulted in an online database.** Here and in all other entries for Web sources, Malik provides the medium of publication, Web, and his date of access.

48 a Source with three authors. Malik reverses the first name and gives the other two in normal order, separated by and. **b Print book.** Here and in all other entries for print sources, Malik provides the medium of publication, Print.

49 a Source with a corporate author. Malik lists and alphabetizes the source by its corporate author. **b Short, titled work on a Web site.** Malik lists the title of the page, the title of the Web site, and the sponsor as well as the publication date, medium, and his date of access. He abbreviates the sponsor's name because it is the same as the author's.

50 Print book with one author.

51 Additional source by the same author. Since the author of the previous entry is also Al Gore, in this entry Malik replaces the name with three hyphens followed by a period.

52 a Source with no listed author. Malik lists and alphabetizes the source by its title. **b Article in a print monthly magazine.**

53 Article in a print newspaper. Malik lists the first page on which the article appears (B1) and uses a plus sign (+) to indicate that the article continues on a later page.

54 Personal interview by e-mail.

55 a Article in a scholarly journal on the Web. b Scholarly journal that uses only issue numbers. The issue number for this source is 23. **c Article with no page numbers.** The abbreviation n. pag. indicates that the journal Malik consulted is unpaginated.

56 a Selection from an anthology. b Introduction to a book. This source is the untitled introduction to an anthology, so Malik inserts Introduction in place of a title. Since the book is also edited by the three authors, he gives only their last names after Ed.

57 a Source with two authors. Malik reverses the first author's name and, after and, gives the second author's name in normal order. **b Short, titled work on a Web site.**

58 Book with one author.

Malik 12

United Nations Development Programme. *Human Development Report 1998: Changing Today's Consumption Patterns—For Tomorrow's Human Development*. New York: Oxford UP, 1998. Print. **59**

United States. Environmental Protection Agency. Solid Waste and Emergency Response. *Municipal Solid Waste Generation, Recycling, and Disposal in the United States: Facts and Figures for 2006*. US Environmental Protection Agency, Nov. 2007. Web. 4 Feb. 2008. **60**

Unruh, Gregory C. "The Biosphere Rules." *Harvard Business Review* 86.2 (2008): 111-17. *Business Source Premier*. Web. 14 Mar. 2008. **61**

59 **Print book with a corporate author.** The source does not list an individual as author, so Malik names the organization as author.

60 **US government source on the Web.** The source does not name an individual as author, so Malik lists as author the organization responsible for the source: first the government, then the agency, then the group within the agency.

61 **a** **Article in a scholarly journal consulted in an online database.** **b** **Scholarly journal that numbers volumes and issues.** The issue and volume numbers for this source are 86.2.

MODELS OF STUDENT WRITING

Vanessa Haley's paper is a good example of a short essay with limited outside research. Students who are new to critical writing often have difficulty establishing their own position in contradistinction to those of other critics. In her paper, Haley has accomplished the delicate task of drawing upon the perspectives of critics while articulating her own unique perspective, and you may want to spend some time discussing this with your students. You could even ask them to read the same outside sources Haley read and then evaluate how successful she was in distinguishing her own point of view from those of the other critics.

This paper also features a sophisticated introduction, in which Haley identifies two reductive and mutually opposed points of view about nature and rejects them both in favor of a third alternative. You can use this paragraph as an example of writing that goes beyond binary thinking. You may also find that your students want to talk about Haley's contention that human civilization is a part of nature—it's an interesting, debatable claim, one that Haley wields well but that may be controversial in your classroom.

COLLABORATIVE LEARNING

CREATING AN OUTLINE

After reading Vanessa Haley's paper, have students work individually to outline her argument, using a similar structure to the outline of Justin Malik's paper. Then, in their groups, have them compare outlines to discuss the structure of the paper. At what points do their individually written outlines differ? Collaboratively, each group should create what they consider to be a definitive outline, which they should then share with the class.

Haley 1

Vanessa Haley

Professor Moisan

English 101

6 Feb. 2008

Annie Dillard's Healing Vision

It is almost a commonplace these days that human arrogance is destroying the environment. Environmentalists, naturalists, and now the man or woman on the street seem to agree: the long-held belief that human beings are separate from nature, destined to rise above its laws and conquer it, has been ruinous.

Unfortunately, the defenders of nature tend to respond to this ruinous belief with harmful myths of their own: nature is pure and harmonious; humanity is corrupt and dangerous. Much writing about nature lacks a recognition that human beings and their civilization are as much a part of nature as trees and whales are, neither better nor worse. Yet without such a recognition, how can humans overcome the damaging sense of separation between themselves and the earth? How can humans develop realistic solutions to environmental problems that will work for humanity *and* the rest of nature?

One nature writer who seems to recognize the naturalness of humanity is Annie Dillard. In her best-known work, the Pulitzer Prize-winning *Pilgrim at Tinker Creek*, she is a solitary person encountering the natural world, and some critics fault her for turning her back on society. But in those encounters with nature, Dillard probes a spiritual as well as a physical identity between human beings and nature that could help to heal the rift between them.

Dillard is not renowned for her sense of involvement with human society. Like Henry David Thoreau, with whom she is often compared, she retreats from rather than confronts human society. The critic Gary McIlroy points out that although

Annotations (left margin of student paper):

Format of heading and title when no title page is required (see also p. 689)

Introduction of environmental theme

Focus on issue to be resolved

Introduction of Dillard to resolve issue

Thesis statement

Acknowledgment of opposing critical view

Haley 2

Thoreau discusses society a great deal in *Walden*, he makes no attempt "to find a middle ground between it and his experiment in the woods" (113). Dillard has been similarly criticized. For instance, the writer Eudora Welty comments that

> Annie Dillard is the only person in her book, substantially the only one in her world; I recall no outside human speech coming to break the long soliloquy of the author. Speaking of the universe very often, she is yet self-surrounded and, beyond that, book-surrounded. Her own book might have taken in more of human life without losing a bit of the wonder she was after. (37)

It is true, as Welty says, that in *Pilgrim* Dillard seems detached from human society. However, she actually was always close to it at Tinker Creek. In a later book, *Teaching a Stone to Talk*, she says of the neighborhood, "This is, mind you, suburbia. It is a five-minute walk in three directions to rows of houses. . . . There's a 55 mph highway at one end of the pond, and a nesting pair of wood ducks at the other" (qtd. in Suh).

Rather than hiding from humanity, Dillard seems to be trying to understand it through nature. In *Pilgrim* she reports buying a goldfish, which she names Ellery Channing. She recalls once seeing through a microscope "red blood cells whip, one by one, through the capillaries" of yet another goldfish (124). Now watching Ellery Channing, she sees the blood in his body as a bond between fish and human being: "Those red blood cells are coursing in Ellery's tail now, too, in just that way, and through his mouth and eyes as well, and through mine" (125). Gary McIlroy observes that this blood, "a symbol of the sanctity of life, is a common bond between Dillard and the fish, between animal and human life in general, and between Dillard and other people" (115).

First response to opposing view

Second response to opposing view

Secondary source's analysis of Dillard

Haley 3

For Dillard, the terror and unpredictability of death unify all life. The most sinister image in *Pilgrim*—one that haunts Dillard—is that of the frog and the water bug. Dillard reports walking along an embankment scaring frogs into the water when one frog refused to budge. As Dillard leaned over to investigate, the frog "slowly crumpled and began to sag. The spirit vanished from his eyes as if snuffed. His skin emptied and dropped; his very skull seemed to collapse and settle like a kicked tent" (6). The frog was the victim of a water bug that injects poisons to "dissolve the victim's muscles and bones and organs" (6). Such events lead Dillard to wonder about a creator who would make all life "power and beauty, grace tangled in a rapture with violence" (8). Human beings no less than frogs and water bugs are implicated in this tangle.

Dillard is equally as disturbed by birth as by death. In a chapter of *Pilgrim* called "Fecundity," she focuses on the undeniable reproductive urge of entire species. Her attitude is far from sentimental:

> I don't know what it is about fecundity that so appalls. I suppose it is the teeming evidence that birth and growth, which we value, are ubiquitous and blind, that life itself is so astonishingly cheap, that nature is as careless as it is bountiful, and that with extravagance goes a crushing waste that will one day include our own cheap lives. (160)

The cheapness and brutality of life are problems Dillard wrestles with, wondering which is "amiss": the world, a "monster," or human beings, with their "excessive emotions" (177-78). No matter how hard she tries to leave human society, Dillard has no choice but to "bring human values to the creek" (179). The violent, seemingly pointless birth and death of all life are, spiritually,

---

Combination of quotation and Haley's own analysis (next four paragraphs) interprets and synthesizes Dillard's ideas

Mixture of summary and quotation provides context and keeps quotations trim

Discussion of physical identity of all creatures: death and birth

Comment on quotation advises reader what to look for

Quotations, including some long ones set off from the text, convey Dillard's voice as well as her ideas

Discussion of spiritual identity of all creatures

Haley 4

two branches of the same creek, the creek that
waters the world. . . . We could have planned
things more mercifully, perhaps, but our plan
would never get off the drawing board until we
agreed to the very compromising terms that are
the only ones that being offers. (180)

For Dillard, accepting the monstrousness as well as the beauty
of "being" is the price all living things pay for freedom.

In "The Waters of Separation," the final chapter of
Pilgrim, Dillard writes about a winged maple key, or seed. At
this point in the book, the critic Sandra Humble Johnson
notes, Dillard "has been humbled and emptied; she can no
longer apply effort to her search for meaning in a parasitic
world" (4). It is the winter solstice—the shortest day of the
year. And then Dillard spies the maple key descending to earth
and germination. "It rose, just before it would have touched a
thistle, and hovered pirouetting in one spot, then twirled on
and finally came to rest" (267). The key moved, says Dillard,
"like a creature muscled and vigorous, or a creature spread
thin to that other wind, the wind of the spirit . . . , a generous, unending breath" (268). Dillard vows to see the maple
key in all of the earth and in herself. "If I am a maple key
falling, at least I can twirl" (268).

According to the critic John Becker, "Annie Dillard does
not walk out on ordinary life in order to bear witness against
it"; instead, she uses the distance from other people "to make
meaning out of the grotesque disjointedness of man and nature" (408). Gary McIlroy says, nonetheless, that Dillard "does
not succeed in encompassing within her vision any but the
most fragmentary consequences for society at large" (116).
Possibly both are correct. In *Pilgrim at Tinker Creek*, Annie
Dillard suggests a vision of identity among all living things

Haley's interpretation of Dillard's ideas

Resolution of Dillard's concerns

Conclusion: ties together divergent critical views, environmental theme, and Dillard's work

COLLABORATIVE LEARNING

ANALYZING THE PAPERS

Break students into four groups and have each group compare one of the following aspects of Malik's and Haley's papers: rhetorical strategy, structure, appropriateness of sources, and introduction of borrowed material.

COMPUTER ACTIVITY

HYPERTEXT COMMENTARY

The numbered comments that go with Malik's paper and the marginal comments on Haley's paper can provide your students with a model of how readers (including you) evaluate papers. They can practice this sort of holistic critique and commentary on one another's papers. Have them trade computer files of their papers with a partner. Have each partner provide commentary on the other's paper, using the commentary in this chapter as a model. They can either insert comments (highlighted or in a different color) directly into the text, or they can use the Comment function of their word processor.

RESOURCES AND IDEAS

Robillard, Amy E. "Young Scholars Affecting Composition: A Challenge to Disciplinary Citation Practices." *College English* 68.3 (2006): 253–70. Print. Robillard discusses the differing functions of citation among academic and student writers. She specifically questions the practice of citing student writing only using a student's first name (or pseudonym).

Soles, Derek. "Grading as a Teaching Strategy." *Teaching English in the Two-Year College* 29.2 (2001): 122–34. Print. Grading supports process instruction when teachers grade drafts, grade with colleagues, comment in a positive and encouraging voice, and share with students their evaluative criteria.

Haley 5

that could inform modern humanity's efforts to thrive in harmony with its environment, but she does not make the leap to practicalities. Life, she says, "is a faint tracing on the surface of a mystery. . . . We must somehow take a wider view, look at the whole landscape, really see it, and describe what's going on here" (9). The description, and acting on it, may take generations. As we proceed, however, we may be guided by Dillard's efforts to mend the disjointedness, to see that human beings and maple keys alike twirl equally.

Haley 6

Works Cited

Becker, John E. "Science and the Sacred: From Walden to
Tinker Creek." *Thought: A Review of Culture and Idea* 62
(1987): 400-13. Print.

Dillard, Annie. *Pilgrim at Tinker Creek*. New York: Harper, 1974.
Print.

Johnson, Sandra Humble. *The Space Between: Literary
Epiphany in the Work of Annie Dillard*. Kent: Kent State
UP, 1992. Print.

McIlroy, Gary. "*Pilgrim at Tinker Creek* and the Social Legacy
of *Walden*." *South Atlantic Quarterly* 85.2 (1996):
111-16. Print.

Suh, Grace. "Ideas Are Tough, Irony Is Easy." *Yale Herald*. Yale
U, 4 Oct. 2005. Web. 22 Jan. 2008.

Welty, Eudora. Rev. of *Pilgrim at Tinker Creek*, by Annie Dillard.
New York Times Book Review 24 Mar. 1974: 36-37.
ProQuest Historical Newspapers. Web. 20 Jan. 2006.

PART 10

Writing in the Academic Disciplines

48 Working with the Goals and Requirements of the Disciplines

49 Reading and Writing About Literature

50 Writing in Other Humanities

51 Writing in the Social Sciences

52 Writing in the Natural and Applied Sciences

48
Working with the Goals and Requirements of the Disciplines

Chapter 8 outlines the general concerns of subject, purpose, and audience that figure in most academic writing situations. The disciplines have more in common as well: methods of gathering evidence, kinds of assignments, scholarly tools, language conventions, and styles for source citations and document formats. This chapter introduces these common goals and requirements. The following chapters then distinguish the disciplines along the same lines, focusing on literature (Chapter 49), other humanities (50), the social sciences (51), and the natural and applied sciences (52).

48a Using methods and evidence

The **methodology** of a discipline is the way its practitioners study their subjects—that is, how they proceed when investigating the answers to questions. Methodology relates to how practitioners analyze evidence and ideas. For instance, a literary critic and a social historian would probably approach Shakespeare's *Hamlet* quite differently: the literary critic might study the play for a theme among its poetic images; the historian might examine the play's relation to Shakespeare's context—England at the turn of the seventeenth century.

Whatever their approach, academic writers do not compose entirely out of their personal experience. Rather, they combine the evidence of their experience with that appropriate to the discipline, drawing well-supported conclusions about their subjects. The evidence of the discipline comes from research like that described in Chapters 41–43—from primary or secondary sources.

---

mycomplab

Visit *mycomplab.com* for more resources as well as exercises on writing in the academic disciplines.

Guidelines for academic writers

- Become familiar with the methodology and the kinds of evidence appropriate for the discipline in which you are writing.
- Analyze the special demands of each assignment. The questions you set out to answer, the assertions you wish to support, will govern how you choose your sources and evidence.
- Become familiar with the discipline's specialized tools and language.
- Use the discipline's style for source citations and document format.

- **Primary sources** are firsthand or original accounts, such as historical documents, works of art, and reports on experiments that the writer has conducted. When you use primary sources, you conduct original research and generate your own evidence. You might use your analysis of a painting as evidence for an interpretation of the painting. Or you might use data from your own survey of students to support your conclusions about students' attitudes.
- **Secondary sources** are books and articles written *about* primary sources. Much academic writing requires that you use such sources to spark, extend, or support your own ideas, as when you review the published opinions on your subject before contributing conclusions from your original research.

48b Understanding writing assignments

For most academic writing, your primary purpose will be either to explain something to your readers or to persuade them to accept your conclusions. To achieve your purpose, you will adapt your writing process to the writing situation, particularly to your readers' likely expectations for evidence and how you use it. Most assignments will contain key words that imply some of these expectations—words such as *compare, define, analyze,* and *illustrate* that express customary ways of thinking about and organizing a vast range of subjects. Pages 93–101 and 824 explore these so-called patterns of development. You should be aware of such keywords and alert to them in the wording of assignments.

48c Using tools and language

When you write in an academic discipline, you use the scholarly tools of that discipline, particularly its periodical indexes. In addition,

Neff, Joyce, and Carl Whithaus. *Writing Across Distances and Disciplines: Research and Pedagogy in Distributed Learning.* Mahwah: Erlbaum, 2007. Print. This collection addresses WAC and WID issues as related to distance education and connections between the corporate and academic spheres.

Walvoord, Barbara E. "The Future of WAC." *College English* 58.1 (1996): 58–79. Print. Walvoord, a long-time WAC program administrator, examines the challenges facing this "movement," including its relationship to other programs and institutions and its role in assessment.

Young, Art. *Teaching Writing Across the Curriculum.* 3rd ed. Upper Saddle River: Prentice, 1999. Web. 11 Nov. 2008. *wac.colostate.edu/ books/young_teaching.* Available online through the WAC Clearinghouse. Young features a number of assignments that can be used to aid in students' using writing to learn or in writing to communicate.

COLLABORATIVE LEARNING

CLARIFYING ASSIGNMENTS

Many students have trouble identifying the primary expectations of some assignments. It is important for students to learn to read assignments carefully and to learn to ask teachers for more information when the assignment is unclear. Have students bring in paper assignments from previous and current courses. Choose a selection of assignments from various disciplines and photocopy them for the class or post them on the class Web site. Then ask students to work in small groups to highlight the primary expectations of each assignment, consider the goal implied by the assignment, and list additional questions that might help clarify each assignment further. As groups present their findings, you might also generate a discussion of the similarities and differences in expectations across the disciplines.

A WRITER'S PERSPECTIVE

Has not every one of us struggled for words, although the connection between "things" was already clear?

—Albert Einstein

DISCIPLINE STYLES

Divide students into groups according to their intended majors (humanities majors, business majors, and so on). Send them to the library to survey professional journals in their intended fields and discover what style(s) of documentation these journals require. (The style is often found in an "Instructions to Authors" section, usually located somewhere near the table of contents.) Ask groups to report their discoveries to the class.

ASK THE EXPERTS

Have students work individually or in discipline-specific groups to identify a faculty member in a specific field to interview. Students should ask the faculty member to discuss the conventions of writing in his/her field, including the expected documentation style. Have students report their findings to the class.

RESOURCES AND IDEAS

Herrington, Anne, and Charles Moran, eds. *Genre Across the Disciplines*. Logan: Utah State UP, 2005. Print. This collection focuses on how genre, which the authors view as determined by situation and context, can inform pedagogy across the curriculum and in first-year composition courses.

McCleod, Susan, and Elaine Maimon. "Clearing the Air: WAC Myths and Realities." *College English* 62.5 (2000): 573–83. Print. The authors provide an excellent summary of why WAC programs fail and discuss model programs.

Peters, Brad, and Julie Fisher Robertson. "Portfolio Partnerships between Faculty and WAC: Lessons from Disciplinary Practice, Reflection, and Transformation." *College Composition and Communication* 59.2 (2007): 206–36. Print. The authors describe a project in which a WAC program partnered with nursing faculty to assess students' portfolios.

Segall, Mary T., and Robert A. Smart. *Direct from the Disciplines: Writing Across the Curriculum*. Portsmouth: Boynton/Cook, 2005. Print. The authors provide suggestions for how to implement and improve a WAC program.

you may use the aids developed by practitioners of the discipline for efficiently and effectively approaching research, conducting it, and recording the findings. Many of these aids, such as a system for recording evidence from sources, are discussed in Chapters 41–43 and can be adapted to any discipline. Other aids are discussed in the following chapters.

Pay close attention to the texts assigned in a course and any materials given out in class, for these items may introduce you to valuable references and other research aids, and they will use the specialized language of the discipline. This specialized language allows practitioners to write to each other both efficiently and precisely. It also furthers certain concerns of the discipline, such as accuracy and objectivity. Scientists, for example, try to interpret their data objectively, so they avoid *undoubtedly, obviously,* and other words that slant conclusions. Some of the language conventions like this one are discussed in the following chapters. As you gain experience in a particular discipline, keep alert for such conventions and train yourself to follow them.

48d Following styles for source citations and document format

Most disciplines publish journals that require authors to use a certain style for source citations and a certain format for documents. In turn, most instructors in a discipline require the same of students writing papers for their courses.

When you cite your sources, you tell readers which ideas and information you borrowed and where they can find your sources. Thus source citations indicate how much knowledge you have and how broad and deep your research was. They also help you avoid **plagiarism,** the serious offense of presenting the words, ideas, and data of others as if they were your own. (See Chapter 44 on avoiding plagiarism.)

Document format specifies such features as margins and the placement of the title. But it also extends to special elements of the manuscript, such as tables or an abstract, that may be required by the discipline.

Chapters 50–52 direct you to the style guides published by different disciplines and outline the requirements of the ones used most often. If your instructor does not require a particular style, use that of the Modern Language Association, which is described and illustrated at length in Chapter 46.

49
Reading and Writing About Literature

By Sylvan Barnet

Why read literature? Let's approach this question indirectly by asking why people *write* literature. A thousand years ago a Japanese writer, Lady Murasaki, offered an answer. Here is one of her characters talking about what motivates a writer:

> Again and again something in one's own life or in the life around one will seem so important that one cannot bear to let it pass into oblivion. There must never come a time, the writer feels, when people do not know about this.

When we read certain works—Murasaki's *The Tale of Genji* is one of them—we share this feeling; we are caught up in the writer's world, whether it is the Denmark of Shakespeare's *Hamlet* or the America of Toni Morrison's *Beloved*. We read literature because it gives us an experience that seems important, usually an experience that is both new and familiar. A common way of putting this is to say that reading broadens us and helps us understand our own experience.

49a Using the methods and evidence of literary analysis

When we read nonliterary writings, it may be enough to get the gist of the argument; in fact, we may have to work through many words to find the heart of the matter—say, three claims on behalf of capital punishment. But when we read a story, a poem, or a play, we must pay extremely close attention to what might be called the feel of the words. For instance, the word *woods* in Robert Frost's "Stopping by Woods on a Snowy Evening" has a rural, folksy quality that *forest* doesn't have, and many such small distinctions contribute to the poem's effect.

Visit *mycomplab.com* for more resources as well as exercises on reading and writing about literature.

HIGHLIGHTS

In classes where literature is studied, there's a temptation to spend more time talking about literature and less time writing about it, which can be counterproductive to the goals of a writing class. To keep students developing positively, this chapter stresses using the processes of critical reading, thinking, and writing skills as a way of analyzing imaginative writing. It also focuses on helping students to transfer the skills they have worked on throughout their writing course to other courses and purposes. The chapter covers different kinds of writing assignments about literature and points students to a wide variety of library and online resources for research. It also takes students through the process of researching and drafting essays about literature and includes sample student essays on works of fiction, poetry, and drama.

RESOURCES AND IDEAS

Bawarshi, Anis. "The Genre Function." *College English* 62.3 (2000): 335–60. Print. Bawarshi explores genre as constitutive of texts, authors, readers, and social identity and argues against the privileging of literary texts by teachers.

Bergmann, Linda S., and Edith M. Baker. *Composition and/or Literature: The End(s) of Education*. Urbana: NCTE, 2006. Print. This collection addresses the differences between composition and literature, and shows how work from each type of course can benefit the other.

Gould, Christopher. "Literature in the Basic Writing Course: A Bibliographic Survey." *College English* 49.5 (1987): 558–74. Print. Gould provides a survey of "easily accessible materials that relate to the use of literature" in introductory courses.

Lindemann, Erika. "Freshman Composition: No Place for Literature." *College English* 55.3 (1993): 311–16. Print. Lindemann warns that using literature in composition classes may lead to a de-emphasis on student writing; she includes useful advice for class design.

Lynn, Steven. *Texts and Contexts: Writing About Literature with Critical Theory.* New York: HarperCollins, 1994. Print. Lynn introduces a number of critical approaches from New Criticism through deconstruction to feminist studies, and he brings all methods to bear on a selected group of texts to demonstrate how they might "open up" texts for students.

Raymond, Richard C. "When Writing Professors Teach Literature: Shaping Questions, Finding Answers, Effecting Change." *College Composition and Communication* 59.3 (2008): 473–502. Print. Advocating "disciplinary unity," Raymond provides an overview of the tensions in the field between literature and composition, and describes how he used literature in the context of teaching composition in an Albanian university.

Tate, Gary. "A Place for Literature in Freshman Composition." *College English* 55.3 (1993): 317–21. Print. Tate argues that using literature makes student writers more aware of the resources implicit in language.

NO "RIGHT" OR "WRONG"

Students tend to have tunnel vision about literary interpretation, believing there's only one "right way" to read a work. In guiding their reading and response, encourage them to see the multiple possibilities implicit in literary works. You might ask them to compose point-counterpoint readings of texts or to use a text like Steven Lynn's *Texts and Contexts* (reference above) to construct a spectrum of responses to the literature they are reading. A consistent use of group workshops in which students discuss their varying responses to a literary text can also help students to recognize the multiplicity of possible responses.

Literary authors are concerned with presenting human experience concretely, with *showing* rather than *telling*. Consider the following proverb and an unmemorable paraphrase of it:

> A rolling stone gathers no moss.
>
> If a rock is always moving around, vegetation won't have a chance to grow on it.

The familiar original offers a small but complete world: hard (stone) and soft (moss), inorganic and organic, at rest and in motion. The original is also shapely: each noun (*stone, moss*) has one syllable, and each word of motion (*rolling, gathers*) has two syllables, with the accent on the first of the two. Such relationships unify the proverb into a pleasing whole that stays in our minds.

1 Reading a work of literature

Reading literature critically involves interacting with a text. The techniques complement those for critically reading any text, so if you haven't read Chapter 7 on such reading, you should do so. Responding critically is a matter not of making negative judgments but of analyzing the parts, interpreting their meanings, seeing how the parts relate, and evaluating significance or quality.

Previewing and responding

You can preview a literary text somewhat as you can preview any other text. You may gauge the length of the text to determine whether you can read it in one sitting, and you may read a biographical note to learn about the author. In a literary text, however, you won't find aids such as section headings or summaries that can make previewing other texts especially informative. You have to dive into the words themselves.

Do write while reading. If you own the book you are reading, don't hesitate to underline or highlight passages that especially interest you for one reason or another. Don't hesitate to annotate the margins, indicating your pleasures, displeasures, and uncertainties with remarks such as *Nice detail* or *Do we need this long description?* or *Not believable*. If you don't own the book, make these notes on separate sheets or on your computer.

An effective way to interact with a text is to keep a **reading journal**. A journal is not a diary in which you record your doings; instead, it is a place to develop and store your reflections on what you read, such as an answer to a question you may have posed in the margin of the text. You could make an entry in the form of a letter to the author or from one character to another. In many literature courses, students collaborate to develop their understanding of a literary work. In such a case, you may want to use your journal to reflect on what other students have said—for instance, why your opinion differs so much from someone else's.

You can keep a reading journal in a notebook or on your computer. Some readers prefer a two-column format like that illustrated on page 143, with summaries, paraphrases, and quotations from the text on the left and with their own responses to these passages on the right. Or you may prefer a less structured format like that illustrated on pages 735–36.

Reading a sample story

Here is a very short story by Kate Chopin (1851–1904). (The last name is pronounced in the French way, something like "show pan.") Following the story are a student's annotations and journal entry on the story.

Kate Chopin

The Story of an Hour

Knowing that Mrs. Mallard was afflicted with a heart trouble, great care was taken to break to her as gently as possible the news of her husband's death.

It was her sister Josephine who told her, in broken sentences, veiled hints that revealed in half concealing. Her husband's friend Richards was there, too, near her. It was he who had been in the newspaper office when intelligence of the railroad disaster was received, with Brently Mallard's name leading the list of "killed." He had only taken the time to assure himself of its truth by a second telegram, and had hastened to forestall any less careful, less tender friend in bearing the sad message.

She did not hear the story as many women have heard the same, with a paralyzed inability to accept its significance. She wept at once with sudden, wild abandonment, in her sister's arms. When the storm of grief had spent itself she went away to her room alone. She would have no one follow her.

There stood, facing the open window, a comfortable, roomy armchair. Into this she sank, pressed down by a physical exhaustion that haunted her body and seemed to reach into her soul.

She could see in the open square before her house the tops of trees that were all aquiver with the new spring life. The delicious breath of rain was in the air. In the street below a peddler was crying his wares. The notes of a distant song which some one was singing reached her faintly, and countless sparrows were twittering in the eaves.

There were patches of blue sky showing here and there through the clouds that had met and piled one above the other in the west facing her window.

She sat with her head thrown back upon the cushion of the chair quite motionless, except when a sob came up into her throat and shook her, as a child who has cried itself to sleep continues to sob in its dreams.

She was young, with a fair, calm face, whose lines bespoke repression and even a certain strength. But now there was a dull stare in her eyes, whose gaze was fixed away off yonder on one of those patches of blue sky. It was not a glance of reflection, but rather indicated a suspension of intelligent thought.

There was something coming to her and she was waiting for it, fearfully. What was it? She did not know; it was too subtle and elusive to name. But she felt it creeping out of the sky, reaching toward her through the sounds, the scents, the color that filled the air.

Now her bosom rose and fell tumultuously. She was beginning to recognize this thing that was approaching to possess her, and she was striving to beat it back with her will—as powerless as her two white slender hands would have been.

When she abandoned herself a little whispered word escaped her slightly parted lips. She said it over and over under her breath: "Free, free, free!" The vacant stare and the look of terror that had followed it went from her eyes. They stayed keen and bright. Her pulses beat fast, and the coursing blood warmed and relaxed every inch of her body.

She did not stop to ask if it were not a monstrous joy that held her. A clear and exalted perception enabled her to dismiss the suggestion as trivial.

She knew that she would weep again when she saw the kind, tender hands folded in death; the face that had never looked save with love upon her, fixed and gray and dead. But she saw beyond that bitter moment a long procession of years to come that would belong to her absolutely. And she opened and spread her arms out to them in welcome.

There would be no one to live for her during those coming years; she would live for herself. There would be no powerful will bending her in the blind persistence with which men and women believe they have a right to impose a private will upon a fellow creature. A kind intention or a cruel intention made the act seem no less a crime as she looked upon it in that brief moment of illumination.

And yet she had loved him—sometimes. Often she had not. What did it matter! What could love, the unsolved mystery, count for in face of this possession of self-assertion which she suddenly recognized as the strongest impulse of her being.

"Free! Body and soul free!" she kept whispering.

Josephine was kneeling before the closed door with her lips to the keyhole, imploring for admission. "Louise, open the door! I beg; open the door—you will make yourself ill. What are you doing, Louise? For heaven's sake open the door."

"Go away. I am not making myself ill." No; she was drinking in the very elixir of life through that open window.

Her fancy was running riot along those days ahead of her. Spring days, and summer days, and all sorts of days that would be her own. She breathed a quick prayer that life might be long. It was only yesterday she had thought with a shudder that life might be long.

She arose at length and opened the door to her sister's importunities. There was a feverish triumph in her eyes, and she carried herself unwittingly like a goddess of Victory. She clasped her sister's waist and together they descended the stairs. Richards stood waiting for them at the bottom.

Some one was opening the front door with a latchkey. It was Brently Mallard who entered, a little travel-stained, composedly carrying his gripsack and umbrella. He had been far from the scene of accident, and did not even know there had been one. He stood amazed at Josephine's piercing cry; at Richards' quick motion to screen him from the view of his wife. But Richards was too late.

When the doctors came they said she had died of heart disease—of joy that kills.

Following a student's work

In this chapter we'll follow the analysis and writing of a student, Janet Vong, to see one approach to Chopin's story. Vong first annotated the story while reading it. The opening five paragraphs, with her notes, appear below:

> Knowing that Mrs. Mallard was afflicted with a <u>heart trouble</u>, great care was taken to break to her as gently as possible the news of her husband's death.
>
> *"heart disease" at end of story*
>
> It was her sister Josephine who told her, in broken sentences, veiled hints that revealed in half concealing. Her husband's friend Richards was there, too, near her. It was he who had been in the newspaper office when intelligence of the railroad disaster was received, with Brently Mallard's name leading the list of "killed." He had only taken the time to assure himself of its truth by a second telegram, and had hastened to forestall any less careful, less tender friend in bearing the sad message.
>
> *Too hasty, it turns out*
>
> *Would men have heard differently? Is au. sexist?*
>
> She did not hear the story <u>as many women have heard the same</u>, with a paralyzed <u>inability to accept its significance</u>. She wept at once with sudden, wild abandonment, in her sister's arms. <u>When the storm of grief had spent itself</u> she went away to her room alone. She would have no one follow her.
>
> *←old-fashioned style*
>
> There stood, facing the open window, a comfortable, roomy armchair. <u>Into this she sank</u>, pressed down by a physical exhaustion that haunted her body and seemed to reach into her soul.
>
> She could see in the open square before her house the tops of trees that were all aquiver with the new spring life. The delicious breath of rain was in the air. In the street below a peddler was crying his wares. The notes of a distant song which some one was singing reached her faintly, and countless sparrows were twittering in the eaves.
>
> *Notices spring: odd in a story of death*

Writing in her journal, Vong posed questions about the story—critical points, curiosities about characters, possible implications:

Title nothing special. What might be a better title?
Could a woman who loved her husband be so heartless? *Is* she heartless? *Did* she love him?
What are (were) Louise's feelings about her husband?
Did she want too much? *What* did she want?
Could this story happen today? Feminist interpretation?

LOOKING BACK

Remind students of the reasons they have been keeping journals throughout your course. You may want to encourage them to review 2a-2 as they begin keeping a reading journal.

COLLABORATIVE LEARNING

FINDING THEMES

Divide the class into several groups and have each group brainstorm about the many themes that occur in a particular work. Choose Kate Chopin's "The Story of an Hour" or another short work from an anthology. Have each group explain its three favorite themes to the rest of the class, supplying evidence for each theme with one or two explicated passages from the piece.

ANALYZING PASSAGES

Have students work in small groups to analyze a key passage from Kate Chopin's "The Story of an Hour." Ask each group to consider the appropriate questions provided by the handbook: Does the passage reveal a significant move in the plot? Does it explore a key development for one of the characters? What evidence of point of view and tone are available in the passage? Does it contain imagery or symbolism? Then have each group give their analysis of the passage. Where student readings differ markedly, encourage those groups to find additional evidence for their readings.

COMPUTER ACTIVITY

CONTINUATIONS

Post the opening paragraph of a published short story on the class Web site and ask students to continue the story, keeping in mind the expectations about plot, character, setting, and tone that have been set up by that opening paragraph. Have students "publish" the resulting stories on the network, and lead a discussion about the different choices that various students made in their continuations, the elements in the original paragraph that they picked up on or discarded, and the extent to which the tone of the original was maintained or parodied. Encourage students to talk about the elements that they noticed in the original paragraph as they created their continuations.

Sister (Josephine)—a busybody?
Tricky ending—but maybe it could be true.
"And yet she had loved him—sometimes. Often she had not." Why does one love someone "sometimes"?
Irony: plot has reversal. Are characters ironic too?

Vong's journal entry illustrates brainstorming—the discovery technique of listing ideas (or questions) however they occur, without editing (see pp. 22–23). Another productive journal technique is focused freewriting—concentrating on a single issue (such as one of Vong's questions) and writing nonstop for a set amount of time, again without editing (p. 22).

2 Analyzing a work of literature

Like any discipline, the study of literature involves particular frameworks of analysis—particular ways of seeing literary works that help determine what parts the critical reader identifies and how he or she interprets them. For instance, some critics look at a literary work mainly as an artifact of the particular time and culture in which it was created, while other critics emphasize the work's effect on its readers.

This chapter emphasizes so-called formalist criticism, which focuses on a literary work primarily as something to be understood in itself. This critical framework engages the reader immediately in the work of literature, without requiring extensive historical or cultural background, and it introduces the conventional elements of literature that all critical approaches discuss, even though they view the elements differently. The box on the next two pages lists these elements—plot, characters, setting, and so on—and offers questions about each one that can help you think constructively and imaginatively about what you read.

One significant attribute of a literary work is its meaning or themes, or what we can interpret to be its themes. Readers may well disagree over the persuasiveness of someone's argument, but they will rarely disagree over its meaning. With literature, however, disagreements over themes occur all the time because (as we have seen) literature *shows* rather than *tells:* it gives us concrete images of imagined human experiences, but it usually does not say how we ought to understand the images.

Further, readers bring to their reading not only different critical views, as noted earlier, but also different personal experiences. A woman who has recently lost her husband may interpret "The Story of an Hour" differently from most other readers. Or a story that bores a reader at age fifteen may deeply move him at twenty-five. The words on the page remain the same, but their meaning changes.

Questions for a literary analysis

See later boxes for specific questions on fiction (pp. 747–48), poetry (p. 749), and drama (pp. 751–52).

Plot

The relationships and patterns of events. Even a poem has a plot, such as a change in mood from bitterness to resignation.

What actions happen?

What conflicts occur?

How do the events connect to each other and to the whole?

Characters

The people the author creates, including the narrator of a story or the speaker of a poem.

Who are the principal people in the work?

How do they interact?

What do their actions, words, and thoughts reveal about their personalities and the personalities of others?

Do the characters stay the same, or do they change? Why?

Point of view

The perspective or attitude of the speaker in a poem or the voice who tells a story. The point of view may be **first person** (a participant, using *I*) or **third person** (an outsider, using *he, she, it, they*). A first-person narrator may be a major or a minor character in the narrative and may be **reliable** or **unreliable** (unable to report events wholly or accurately). A third-person narrator may be **omniscient** (knows what goes on in all characters' minds), **limited** (knows what goes on in the mind of only one or two characters), or **objective** (knows only what is external to the characters).

Who is the narrator (or the speaker of a poem)?

How does the narrator's point of view affect the narrative?

Tone

The narrator's or speaker's attitude, perceived through the words (for instance, joyful, bitter, or confident).

What tone (or tones) do you hear? If there is a change, how do you account for it?

Is there an ironic contrast between the narrator's tone (for instance, confidence) and what you take to be the author's attitude (for instance, pity for human overconfidence)?

Imagery

Word pictures or details involving the senses: sight, sound, touch, smell, taste.

(continued)

RESOURCES AND IDEAS

Biddle, Arthur W., and Toby Fulwiler, eds. *Reading, Writing, and the Study of Literature.* New York: McGraw, 1989. This collection of essays details many ways of introducing students to various methods of literary interpretation; the authors provide extensive bibliographies.

Lentricchia, Frank, and Thomas McLaughlin. *Critical Terms for Literary Study.* 2nd ed. Chicago: U of Chicago P, 1995. Print. The authors have compiled twenty-five cogent essays defining key terms in light of contemporary theory.

Richardson, Mark. "Who Killed Annabel Lee? Writing about Literature in the Composition Classroom." *College English* 66.3 (2004): 278–93. Print. Richardson attempts to reconcile using literature in a writing class with current composition theory and demonstrates how he has used Poe's poem alongside students' knowledge of popular culture to teach writing.

Young, Art, and Toby Fulwiler, ed. *When Writing Teachers Teach Literature: Bringing Writing to Reading.* Portsmouth: Boynton/Cook, 1995. Print. This collection addresses the many ways literature can be used to teach writing.

COLLABORATIVE LEARNING

GROUP ANALYSIS

Using a short story or poem students have read, ask each group to address one aspect of those listed in the "Questions for a literary analysis" box. Every group should discuss "Themes" and "Appeal." Groups can then present their ideas to the class.

Questions for a literary analysis

(continued)

What images does the writer use? What senses do they draw on?

What patterns are evident in the images (for instance, religious or commercial images)?

What is the significance of the imagery?

Symbolism

Concrete things standing for larger and more abstract ideas. For instance, the American flag may symbolize freedom, a tweeting bird may symbolize happiness, a dead flower may symbolize mortality.

What symbols does the author use? What do they seem to signify?

How does the symbolism relate to the other elements of the work, such as character or theme?

Setting

The place where the action happens.

What does the locale contribute to the work?

Are scene shifts significant?

Form

The shape or structure of the work.

What *is* the form? (For example, a story might divide sharply in the middle, moving from happiness to sorrow.)

What parts of the work does the form emphasize, and why?

Themes

The main ideas—conceptions of human experience suggested by the work as a whole. A theme is neither a plot (what happens) nor a subject (such as mourning or marriage). Rather it is what the author says with that plot about that subject.

Can you state each theme in a sentence? Avoid mentioning specific characters or actions; instead, write an observation applicable to humanity in general. For instance, you might state the following about Kate Chopin's "The Story of an Hour": *Happiness depends partly on freedom.*

Do certain words, passages of dialog or description, or situations seem to represent a theme most clearly?

How do the work's elements combine to develop each theme?

Appeal

The degree to which the work pleases you.

What do you especially like or dislike about the work?

Do you think your responses are unique, or would they be common to most readers? Why?

In writing about literature, we can offer only our *interpretation* of meaning rather than *the* meaning. Still, most people agree that there are limits to interpretation: it must be supported by evidence that a reasonable reader finds at least plausible if not totally convincing. For instance, the student who says that in "The Story of an Hour" Mrs. Mallard does not die but merely falls into a deathlike trance goes beyond the permissible limits because the story offers no evidence for such an interpretation.

3 | Using evidence in writing about literature

The evidence for a literary analysis always comes from at least one primary source (the work or works being discussed) and may come from secondary sources (critical and historical works). (See p. 729 for more on primary and secondary sources.) For example, if you were writing about Chopin's "The Story of an Hour," the primary material would be the story itself, and the secondary material (if you used it) might be critical studies of Chopin.

The bulk of your evidence in writing about literature will usually be quotations from the work, although you will occasionally summarize or paraphrase as well (see pp. 611–15). When using quotations, keep in mind the criteria in the box on page 743.

Your instructor will probably tell you if you are expected to consult secondary sources for an assignment. They can help you understand a writer's work, but your primary concern should always be the work itself, not what critics A, B, and C say about it. In general, then, quote or summarize secondary material sparingly. And always cite your sources.

49b | Understanding writing assignments in literature

A literature instructor may ask you to write one or more of the following types of papers. The first two are the most common.

- **A literary analysis paper:** Give your ideas about a work of literature—your interpretation of its meaning, context, or representations based on specific words, characters, and events.
- **A literary research paper:** Combine analysis of a literary work with research about the work and perhaps its author. A literary research paper draws on both primary and secondary sources. For example, you might respond to what scholars have written about the symbolism in a play by Tennessee Williams, or you might research medieval England as a way to understand the context of Chaucer's *Canterbury Tales*.

- **A personal response or reaction paper:** Give your thoughts and feelings about a work of literature. For example, you might compare a novel's description of a city with your experience of the same city.
- **A book review:** Give a summary of a book and a judgment about the book's value. In a review of a novel, for example, you might discuss whether the plot is interesting, the characters are believable, and the writing style is enjoyable. You might also compare the work to other works by the author.
- **A theater review:** Give your reactions to and opinions about a theatrical performance. You might summarize the plot of the play, describe the characters, identify the prominent themes, evaluate the other elements (writing, performances, direction, stage setting), and make a recommendation to potential viewers.

49c Using the tools and language of literary analysis

1 Writing tools

The fundamental tool for writing about literature is reading critically. Asking analytical questions such as those on pages 737–38 can help you focus your ideas. In addition, keeping a reading journal can help you develop your thoughts. Keep careful, well-organized notes on any research materials. Finally, discuss the work with others who have read it. They may offer reactions and insights that will help you shape your own ideas.

2 Language considerations

Use the present tense of verbs to describe both the action in a literary work (*Brently Mallard suddenly appears*) and the writing of an author (*Chopin briefly describes the view* or *In his essay he comments that . . .*). Use the past tense to describe events that actually occurred in the past (*Chopin was born in 1851*).

Some instructors discourage students from using the first-person *I* (as in *I felt sorry for the character*) in writing about literature. At least use *I* sparingly to avoid sounding egotistical. Rephrase sentences to avoid using *I* unnecessarily—for instance, *The character evokes the reader's sympathy.*

3 Research sources

In addition to the following resources on literature, you may also want to consult some on other humanities (pp. 757–60).

THE MYSTIQUE OF LITERATURE

Most students will need to be convinced that critical thinking, reading, and writing skills can be transferred to literature. Students sometimes acquire the attitude that literature is somehow "untouchable," that it is "special," different from other works they read. Work through Janet Vong's critical strategies (pp. 735–36) with your students to help them understand how the skills they've developed will enable them to read and write about literature.

COLLABORATIVE LEARNING

TENSES

Students sometimes have trouble making their prose conform to the conventions of tense usage in critical writing about literature. To get them used to these conventions, have students review each other's drafts and make suggestions for revision of tense usage.

Specialized encyclopedias, dictionaries, and bibliographies

Cambridge Bibliography of English Literature
Cambridge Encyclopedia of Language
Cambridge Guide to Literature in English
Dictionary of Literary Biography
Handbook to Literature
Literary Criticism Index
McGraw-Hill Encyclopedia of World Drama
New Princeton Encyclopedia of Poetry and Poetics
Oxford Companion to American Literature
Oxford Companion to the Theatre
Schomburg Center Guide to Black Literature from the Eighteenth Century to the Present

Library databases and indexes

Abstracts of Folklore Studies
Dissertation Abstracts International (doctoral dissertations)
Early English Books Online
Gale Literary Resource Center
Humanities Index
Literary Criticism Index
Literary Index
Literature Online
MLA International Bibliography of Books and Articles on the Modern Languages and Literatures
World Shakespeare Bibliography

Book reviews

Book Review Digest
Book Review Index

Sources on the open Web

Alex Catalog of Electronic Texts (infomotions.com/alex)
EServer (eserver.org)
Internet Public Library: Online Literary Criticism (ipl.org/div/litcrit)
Literary Resources on the Net (andromeda.rutgers.edu/~jlynch/Lit)
Mr. Shakespeare and the Internet (shakespeare.palomar.edu)
Online Books Page (online books.library.upenn.edu)
Voice of the Shuttle (vos.ucsb.edu)

49d Citing sources and formatting documents in writing about literature

Unless your instructor specifies otherwise, use the documentation style of the Modern Language Association (MLA), detailed in Chapter 46. In this style, parenthetical citations in the text of the paper refer to a list of works cited at the end. Sample papers illustrating this style appear in Chapter 47 as well as in this chapter.

Use MLA format for headings, margins, and other elements, as detailed on pages 689–91.

49e Drafting and revising a literary analysis

The process for writing a literary analysis is similar to that for any other kind of essay: once you've done the reading and thought about it, you need to focus your ideas, gather evidence, draft, and revise.

1 Conceiving a thesis

After reading, rereading, and making notes, you probably will be able to formulate a tentative thesis statement—an assertion of your main point, your argument. (For more on thesis statements, see pp. 27–32.) Clear the air by glancing over your notes and by jotting down a few especially promising ideas—brief statements of what you think your key points may be and their main support. One approach is to seek patterns in the work, such as recurring words, phrases, images, events, symbols, or other elements. (Go back to the work, if necessary, to expand the patterns your notes reveal.) Such patterns can help you see themes both in the work itself and in your ideas about it.

Considering Kate Chopin's "The Story of an Hour," Janet Vong at first explored the idea that Mrs. Mallard, the main character, was unrealistic and thus unconvincing. (See Vong's journal entry on pp. 735–36.) But the more Vong examined the story and her notes, the more she was impressed by a pattern of ironies, or reversals, that actually helped to make Mrs. Mallard believable. In her journal Vong explored the idea that the many small reversals paved the way for Mrs. Mallard's own reversal from grief to joy:

> title? "Ironies in an Hour" (?) "An Hour of Irony" (?) "Kate Chopin's Irony" (?)
> thesis: irony at end is prepared for
> chief irony: Mrs. M. dies just as she is beginning to enjoy life
> smaller ironies:
>   1. "sad message" brings her joy
>   2. Richards is "too late" at end
>   3. Richards is too early at start
>   4. "joy that kills"
>   5. death brings joy and life

From these notes Vong developed her thesis statement:

> The irony of the ending is believable partly because it is consistent with earlier ironies in the story.

This thesis statement asserts a specific idea that can be developed and convincingly argued with evidence from Chopin's story. A good thesis statement will neither assert a fact (*Mrs. Mallard dies soon after hearing that her husband has died*) nor overgeneralize (*The story is an insult to women*).

2 Gathering evidence

In writing about literature, you use mainly evidence gathered from the work itself: quotations and sometimes paraphrases and summaries that support your ideas about the work. You can see examples of quoting and paraphrasing in Janet Vong's final draft on pages 746–47. The box below offers guidelines for using quotations in literary analysis.

Guidelines for using quotations in literary analysis

- **Use quotations to support your assertions, not to pad the paper.** Quote at length only when necessary to your argument.
- **Specify how each quotation relates to your idea.** Introduce the quotation—for example, *At the outset Chopin conveys the sort of person Richards is:* ". . ." Sometimes, comment after the quotation. (See pages 620–25 for more on integrating quotations into your writing.)
- **Reproduce spelling, punctuation, capitalization, and all other features exactly as they appear in the source.** See page 474 for the use of brackets when you need to add something to a quotation, and see page 475 for the use of an ellipsis mark when you need to omit something from a quotation.
- **Document your sources.** See pages 634–35.

You may wonder how much you should summarize the plot of the work. A brief plot summary can be helpful to readers who are unfamiliar with the work. Sometimes plot elements place your ideas in the context of the work or remind readers where your quotations come from. Plot elements may even be used as evidence, as Vong uses the ironic ending of the Chopin story. But plot summary is not literary analysis, and summary alone is not sufficient evidence to support a thesis. Keep any plot summaries brief and to the point.

For a literary research paper, evidence will come from the work itself and from secondary sources such as scholarly works and critical appraisals. The thesis and principal ideas of the paper must still be your own, but you may supplement your reading of the work with the views of respected scholars or critics. Sometimes you may choose to build your own argument in part by disputing others' views. However you draw on secondary sources, remember that they must be clearly identified and documented, even when you use your own words.

Note You can find student essays on the Web that may lead you to other sources or may suggest ideas you hadn't considered. If you want to use another student's paper as a secondary source, you must evaluate it with special care because it will not have passed through a reviewing process, as an article in a scholarly journal does. (See pp. 593–603 on evaluating online sources.) You must also, of course, clearly identify and document the source: borrowing *any* other writer's ideas or words without credit is plagiarism. (See pp. 626–34.)

3 | Writing a draft

Drafting your essay is your opportunity to develop your thesis or to discover it if you haven't already. The draft below was actually Janet Vong's second: she deleted some digressions from her first draft and added more evidence for her points. The numbers in parentheses refer to the pages from which she drew the quotations. (See pp. 644–53 on this form of documentation.) Ask your instructor whether you should always give such citations, especially for a short poem or story like Chopin's.

Ironies in an Hour

After we know how the story turns out, if we reread it we find irony at the very start, as is true of many other stories. Mrs. Mallard's friends assume, mistakenly, that Mrs. Mallard was deeply in love with her husband, Brently Mallard. They take great care to tell her gently of his death. The friends mean well, and in fact they *do* well. They bring her an hour of life, an hour of freedom. They think their news is sad. Mrs. Mallard at first expresses grief when she hears the news, but soon she finds joy in it. So Richards's "sad message" (50), though sad in Richards's eyes, is in fact a happy message.

Among the ironic details is the statement that when Mallard enters the house, Richards tries to conceal him from Mrs. Mallard, but Richards is "too late" (51). This is ironic because earlier Richards has "hastened" (50) to bring his sad message; if he had been too late at the start, Brently Mallard would have arrived at home first, and Mrs. Mallard's life would not end an hour later but would simply go on as before. Yet another irony at the end of the story is the diagnosis of the doctors. The doctors say she died of "heart disease—of joy that kills" (51). In one sense the doctors are right: Mrs. Mallard has experienced a great joy. But of course the doctors totally misunderstand the joy that kills her.

The central irony resides not in the well-intentioned but ironic actions of Richards, or in the unconsciously ironic words of the doctors, but in her own life. She "sometimes" (51) loved her husband, but in a way she has been dead. Now, his apparent death brings her new life. This new life comes to her at the season of the year when "the tops of trees . . . were all aquiver with the new spring life" (50). But, ironically, her new life will last only an hour. She looks forward to "summer days" (51), but she will not see even the end of this spring day. Her years of marriage were ironic. They brought her a sort of living death instead of joy. Her new life is ironic, too. It grows out of her moment of grief for her supposedly dead husband, and her vision of a new life is cut short.

4 | Revising and editing

As in other writing, use at least two drafts to revise and edit, so that you can attend separately to the big structural issues and the smaller surface problems. See pages 54–55 and 60–61 for general revision and editing checklists. The additional checklist below can help you with a literary analysis.

Checklist for revising a literary analysis

- **Title:** Does the title of your essay give the title and author of the work you discuss and also an idea of your approach to the work?
- **Introduction:** Does the introductory paragraph name the author and the title so that readers know exactly what work you are discussing? (Avoid opening sentences such as "In this story. . . .") Does the introduction state and develop your thesis a bit so that readers know where they will be going?
- **Organization:** How effective is the organization? The essay should not dwindle or become anticlimactic; rather, it should build up.
- **Quotations:** What evidence does each quotation provide? Do quotations let readers hear the author's voice?
- **Analysis vs. summary:** Is the essay chiefly devoted to analysis, not to summary? Summarize the plot only briefly and only to further your own ideas. A summary is not an essay.
- **Verb tenses:** Have you used the present tense of verbs to describe both the author's work and the action in the work (for example, *Chopin shows* or *Mrs. Mallard dies*)?
- **Evaluation:** How well will readers understand your evaluation of the work and what it is based on? Your evaluation may be implied (as in Janet Vong's essay on "The Story of an Hour"), or it may be explicit. In either case, give the reasons for judging the work to be effective or not, worth reading or not. It is not enough to express your likes or dislikes; readers need the support of specific evidence from the work.
- **Are all your sources documented in MLA style?**

Janet Vong's final draft appears on the next two pages with annotations that highlight some of its features.

COLLABORATIVE LEARNING

MODELS OF STUDENT WRITING

This final draft of Janet Vong's paper on Kate Chopin's "The Story of an Hour" is a fine model of the short literary analysis, and you may wish to spend some time discussing it with students. It features a creative thesis and a tightly organized, economical development. Students who have little experience writing about literature sometimes organize their papers to match the progression of the text they are analyzing instead of around the development of their thesis statements. If your students have this difficulty, they may find it particularly helpful to see that Vong's paper moves from the least important to the most important of her arguments and that in presenting evidence she moves back and forth from the beginning to the end of Chopin's story.

You might also want to use Chopin's story to talk about irony, a literary device students sometimes have difficulty identifying. Vong does a particularly nice job of discussing how readers may come to a deeper understanding of Chopin's story as its ironic implications sink in.

Author's name and identification in MLA format (p. 689)	Janet Vong Mr. Romano English 102 20 Feb. 2008

Paper title incorporating author and title of analyzed work

Introduction naming author/ title and stating thesis

Ironies of Life in Kate Chopin's
"The Story of an Hour"

Kate Chopin's "The Story of an Hour"—which takes only a few minutes to read—has an ironic ending: Mrs. Mallard dies just when she is beginning to live. On first reading, the ending seems almost too ironic for belief. On rereading the story, however, one sees that the ending is believable partly because it is consistent with other ironies in the story.

Detailing of story's ironies, using quotations and some summary to emphasize the reversals

Irony appears at the very start of the story. Because Mrs. Mallard's friends and her sister assume, mistakenly, that she was deeply in love with her husband, Brently Mallard, they take great care to tell her gently of his death. They mean well, and in fact they *do* well, bringing her an hour of life, an hour of joyous freedom, but it is ironic that they think their news is sad. True, Mrs. Mallard at first expresses grief when she hears the news, but soon (unknown to the others) she finds joy. So Richards's "sad message" (50), though sad in Richards's eyes, is in fact a happy message.

Parenthetical citations in MLA style referring to the work cited at the end of the paper (see p. 644)

Among the small but significant ironic details is the statement near the end of the story that when Mallard enters the house, Richards tries to conceal him from Mrs. Mallard, but Richards is "too late" (51). Almost at the start of the story, in the second paragraph, Richards has "hastened" (50) to bring his sad news. But if Richards had arrived too late at the start, Brently Mallard would have arrived at home first, and Mrs. Mallard's life would not end an hour later but would simply go on as before. Yet another irony at the end of the story is the diagnosis of the doctors. They say she died of "heart disease—of joy that kills" (51). In one sense they are right: Mrs. Mallard has for the last hour experienced a great joy. But of course the doctors totally misunderstand the joy that kills her. It is not joy at seeing her husband alive, but her realization that the great joy she experienced during the last hour is over.

All of these ironic details add richness to the story, but the central irony resides not in the well-intentioned but ironic actions of Richards, or in the unconsciously ironic words of the doctors, but in Mrs. Mallard's own life. She "sometimes" (51) loved her husband, but in a way she has been dead, a body subjected to her husband's will. Now, his apparent death brings her new life. Appropriately, this new life comes to her at the season of the year when "the tops of trees . . . were all aquiver with the new spring life" (50). But, ironically, her new life will last only an hour. She is "Free, free, free" (51)—but only until her husband walks through the doorway. She looks forward to "summer days" (51), but she will not see even the end of this spring day. If her years of marriage were ironic, bringing her a sort of living death instead of joy, her new life is ironic, too, not only because it grows out of her moment of grief for her supposedly dead husband, but also because her vision of "a long procession of years" (51) is cut short within an hour on a spring day.

[New page.]

Work Cited

Chopin, Kate. "The Story of an Hour." *An Introduction to Literature: Fiction, Poetry, and Drama.* Ed. Sylvan Barnet, William Burto, and William E. Cain. 15th ed. New York: Longman, 2008. 50-51. Print.

New page for work cited in MLA style (p. 653)

49f | Writing about fiction, poetry, and drama

A work of literature falls into a category, or **genre**—fiction, poetry, or drama—depending on how it is structured. The different genres of literature require different approaches in writing.

1 | Writing about fiction

The "Questions for a literary analysis" on pages 737–38 will help you think about any work of literature, including a story or novel, and find a topic to write on. The following questions provide additional prompts for thinking about fiction. For an example of writing about fiction, see Janet Vong's essay opposite and above.

Questions for analyzing fiction

- **What happens in the story?** For yourself, summarize the plot (the gist of the happenings). Think about what your summary *leaves out.*
- **Is the story told in chronological order, or are there flashbacks or flashforwards?** On rereading, what foreshadowing (hints of what is to come) do you detect?
- **What conflicts does the work include?**
- **How does the writer develop characters?** Are the characters revealed by explicit comment or through action? With which character(s) do you sympathize? Are the characters plausible? What motivates them? What do minor characters contribute to the work?

(continued)

OPENING PARAGRAPH

Students can learn a great deal about the choices a writer makes in creating a piece of fiction by writing fiction of their own. Ask each student to create a one-paragraph opening for a short story; then have students work in small groups to analyze their fictional paragraphs. What does each opening paragraph reveal about the kind of story being told—will it be comic, tragic, realistic, supernatural? What expectations does the opening set up about the characters and events that will follow? What questions does it raise?

As a follow-up to this exercise, ask each group to turn back to the Kate Chopin story and analyze its one-sentence opening with some of the same questions in mind. Having read the story, students may be surprised to find how much they can deduce from that seemingly simple statement.

RESOURCES AND IDEAS

Barnet, Sylvan, and William Cain. *A Short Guide to Writing About Literature.* 10th ed. New York: Longman, 2006. Print. The authors offer students concise advice about how to read literature and think critically about fiction, poetry, and drama. This guide also provides checklists for students to use in evaluating their own writing about literature.

Rockas, Leo. *Ways In: Analyzing and Responding to Literature.* Upper Montclair: Boynton/Cook, 1984. Print. Chapter 4 offers examples of and exercises for writing about fiction.

Questions for analyzing fiction
(continued)

- **Who tells the story?** Is the narrator a character, or does the narrator stand entirely outside the characters' world? What does the narrator's point of view contribute to the story's theme? (On narrative points of view, see p. 737.)
- **What is the setting?** What do the time and place of the action contribute to the work?
- **Are certain characters, settings, or actions symbolic?** Do they stand for something in addition to themselves?
- **What are the themes?** That is, what does the work add up to? Do the themes reinforce your values, or do they challenge them?
- **Is the title informative?** Did its meaning change for you after you read the work?

A WRITER'S PERSPECTIVE

A poem is a perhaps.
—IVOR WILLIAMS

You can tear a poem apart to see what makes it technically tick, ... but you come back to the mystery of having been moved by words.
—DYLAN THOMAS

2 **Writing about poetry**

Two types of essays on poetry are especially common. One is an analysis of some aspect of the poem in relation to the whole—for instance, the changes in the speaker's tone or the functions of meter and rhyme. The second is an **explication**, a line-by-line (sometimes almost word-by-word) reading that seeks to make explicit everything that is implicit in the poem. Thus an explication of the first line of Robert Frost's "Stopping by Woods on a Snowy Evening" (the line goes "Whose woods these are I think I know") might call attention to the tentativeness of the line ("I think I know") and to the fact that the words are not in the normal order ("I think I know whose woods these are"). These features might support the explanation that the poet is introducing—very quietly—a note of the *un*usual, in preparation for the experience that follows. Although one might conceivably explicate a long poem, the method is so detailed that in practice writers usually confine it to short poems or to short passages from long poems.

The "Questions for a literary analysis" on pages 737–38 will help you think about any work of literature, including a poem, and find a topic to write on. The questions on the facing page provide additional ways to think about poetry.

An essay on poetry with secondary sources

The sample paper on pages 750–51 analyzes the short poem opposite by Gwendolyn Brooks. The paper illustrates a literary analysis that draws not only on the poem itself but also on secondary

Questions for analyzing poetry

■ **What parts of the poem interest or puzzle you?** What words seem especially striking or unusual?

■ **How can you describe the poem's *speaker* (sometimes called the *persona* or the *voice*)?** The speaker may be very different from the author.

■ **What tone or emotion do you detect**—for instance, anger, affection, sarcasm? Does the tone change during the poem?

■ **What is the structure of the poem?** Are there stanzas (groups of lines separated by space)? If so, how is the thought related to the stanzas?

■ **What are the themes of the poem?** What is it about? Are the themes stated or implied?

■ **What images do you find?** Look for evocations of sight, sound, taste, touch, or smell. Is there a surprising pattern of images—say, images of business in a poem about love? What does the poem suggest symbolically as well as literally? (Trust your responses. If you don't sense a symbolic overtone, move on. Don't hunt for symbols.)

sources—that is, critical works *about* the poem. In the opening paragraph, for instance, the writer uses brief quotations from two secondary sources to establish the problem, the topic that he will address. These quotations, like the two later quotations from secondary material, are used to make points, not to pad the essay.

Note In the paper, the parenthetical citations for Brooks's poem give line numbers of the poem, whereas the citations for the secondary sources give page numbers of the sources. See pages 649–50 and 646, respectively, for these two forms of citation.

Gwendolyn Brooks

The Bean Eaters

They eat beans mostly, this old yellow pair.
Dinner is a casual affair.
Plain chipware on a plain and creaking wood,
Tin flatware.

Two who are Mostly Good.   5
Two who have lived their day,
But keep on putting on their clothes
And putting things away.

And remembering . . .
Remembering, with twinklings and twinges,   10
As they lean over the beans in their rented back room that
    is full of beads and receipts and dolls and cloths,
    tobacco crumbs, vases and fringes.

RESOURCES AND IDEAS

Bizzaro, Patrick. *Responding to Student Poems: Applications of Critical Theory.* Urbana: NCTE, 1993. Print. See Chapter 7 in particular for a discussion of having students read and produce poetry as complementary activities (159–91).

Hollander, John. *Rhyme's Reason: A Guide to English Verse.* 3rd ed. New Haven: Yale UP, 2001. Print. Hollander offers a brief guide to poetry analysis, with amusing examples and some innovative analysis strategies.

Rockas, Leo. *Ways In: Analyzing and Responding to Literature.* Upper Montclair: Boynton/ Cook, 1984. Print. Contains examples and exercises for writing about drama and poetry.

Suchet, David. "Caliban in *The Tempest.*" *Players of Shakespeare.* Ed. Philip Brockbank. Cambridge: Cambridge UP, 1985. 167–79. Print. Suchet, an experienced Shakespearean actor, shows how he reads and rereads a drama to find the clues that lead him to create a character.

READING POETRY

To help students get the sound of a poem, have them read it aloud (or you might read a poem aloud to them). Explain to them that there does not need to be a pause at the end of every line, but that they should pause according to the poem's punctuation. It might also be helpful to hear recordings of the poet him/herself or a professional reading the work.

MODELS OF STUDENT WRITING

Gwendolyn Brooks's "The Bean Eaters" may strike students as being so quotidian in its language and subject as to defy interpretation. Particularly if they are new to literary interpretation, students may not be sensitive to the nuances a single word or phrase can carry and may think that Kenneth Scheff and the critics he quotes read too much into poetry. If your students feel this way, try having several of them read the poem aloud in class to see if their readings come across in different ways. Ask them to try to see how much they can affect the meaning of the poem by reading it aloud in as many different ways as possible.

You can also use Scheff's paper to talk about how to incorporate the perspectives of other critics in one's own interpretations. Scheff's paper is strong overall, but you might ask your students if they think he has differentiated his own perspective sufficiently from those of his critics or whether his interpretation is too derivative of those he cites. Ask them to suggest ways Scheff could strengthen his argument.

Kenneth Scheff

Professor MacGregor

English 101A

8 May 2008

Marking Time Versus Enduring in

Gwendolyn Brooks's "The Bean Eaters"

Gwendolyn Brooks's poem "The Bean Eaters" runs only eleven lines. It is written in plain language about very plain people. Yet its meaning is ambiguous. One critic, George E. Kent, says the old couple who eat beans "have had their day and exist now as time-markers" (141). However, another critic, D. H. Melhem, perceives not so much time marking as "endurance" in the old couple (123). The reader must decide whether this poem is a despairing picture of old age or a more positive portrait.

"The Bean Eaters" describes an "old yellow pair" who "eat beans mostly" (line 1) off "Plain chipware" (3) with "Tin flatware" (4) in "their rented back room" (11). Clearly, they are poor. They live alone, not with friends or relatives—children or grandchildren are not mentioned—but with memories and a few possessions (9-11). They are "Mostly Good" (5), words Brooks capitalizes at the end of a line, perhaps to stress the old people's adherence to traditional values as well as their lack of saintliness. They are unexceptional, whatever message they have for readers.

The isolated routine of the couple's life is something Brooks draws attention to with a separate stanza:

> Two who are Mostly Good.
> Two who have lived their day,
> But keep on putting on their clothes
> And putting things away. (5-8)

Brooks emphasizes how isolated the couple is by repeating "Two who." Then she emphasizes how routine their life is by repeating "putting."

A pessimistic reading of this poem seems justified. The critic Harry B. Shaw reads the lines just quoted as perhaps despairing: "they are putting things away as if winding down an operation and readying for withdrawal from activity" (80). However, Shaw observes, the word "But" also indicates that the couple resist slipping away, that they intend to hold on (80). This dual meaning is at the heart of Brooks's poem: the old people live a meager existence, yes, but their will, their self-control, and their connection with another person—their essential humanity—are unharmed.

The truly positive nature of the poem is revealed in the last stanza. In Brooks's words, the old people remember with some "twinges" perhaps, but also with "twinklings" (10), a cheerful image. As Melhem says, these people are "strong in mutual affection and shared memories" (123). And the final line, which is much longer than all the rest and which catalogs the evidence of the couple's long life together, is almost musically affirmative: "As they lean over the beans in their rented back room that is full of beads and receipts and dolls and cloths, tobacco crumbs, vases and fringes" (11).

What these people have is not much, but it is something.

[New page.]

Works Cited

Brooks, Gwendolyn. "The Bean Eaters." *An Introduction to Literature: Fiction,*
  Poetry, and Drama. Ed. Sylvan Barnet, William Burto, and William E. Cain.
  15th ed. New York: Longman, 2008. 922. Print.

Kent, George E. *A Life of Gwendolyn Brooks.* Lexington: UP of Kentucky, 1990. Print.

Melhem, D. H. *Gwendolyn Brooks: Poetry and the Heroic Voice.* Lexington: UP of
  Kentucky, 1987. Print.

Shaw, Harry B. *Gwendolyn Brooks.* Boston: Twayne, 1980. Print. Twayne's United
  States Authors Ser. 395.

3 Writing about drama

Because plays—even some one-act plays—are relatively long, analytic essays on drama usually focus on only one aspect of the play, such as the structure of the play, the function of a single scene, or a character's responsibility for his or her fate. The essay's introduction indicates what the topic is and why it is of some importance, and the introduction may also state the thesis. The conclusion often extends the analysis, showing how a study of the apparently small topic helps to illuminate the play as a whole.

The "Questions for a literary analysis" on pages 737–38 will help you think about any work of literature, including a play, and find a topic to write on. The questions in the following box provide additional prompts for thinking about drama.

Questions for analyzing drama

- **How does the plot (the sequence of happenings) unfold?** Does it seem plausible? If not, is the implausibility a fault? If there is more than one plot, are the plots parallel, or are they related by way of contrast?
- **Are certain happenings recurrent?** If so, how are they significant?
- **What kinds of conflict are in the play**—for instance, between two groups, two characters, or two aspects of a single character? How are the conflicts resolved? Is the resolution satisfying to you?

(continued)

DRAMA ONSTAGE

Many students have only read dramas in literature classes and have never seen them acted. If your campus or local library has DVDs of the dramas you are studying, arrange to show scenes (or even the entire work) to the class. Many students are genuinely shocked to see and hear how performers interpret (i.e., analyze) dramatic works, and their resulting papers often benefit from the insights they gain by watching performances. Showing multiple versions of a single scene can help students see a range of interpretations.

PERFORMING A SCENE

Break the class into small groups and ask each group to perform a scene from a play for their classmates. You can allow students to bring in props or encourage them to make their interpretations through voice and gesture. Then ask the rest of the class to analyze the group's interpretation. What aspects did the group emphasize, and why?

Questions for analyzing drama

(continued)

■ **How does the author develop the characters?** How trustworthy are the characters when they describe themselves or others? Do some characters serve as foils, or contrasts, for other characters, thus helping to define the other characters? Do the characters change as the play proceeds? Are the characters' motivations convincing?

■ **What do the author's stage directions add to your understanding and appreciation of the play?** If there are few stage directions, what do the speeches imply about the characters' manner, tone, and gestures?

■ **What do you make of the setting, or location?** Does it help to reveal characters or themes?

■ **Do certain costumes** (dark suits, flowery shawls, stiff collars) **or properties** (books, pictures, candlesticks) **strike you as symbolic?**

An essay on drama (no secondary sources)

The following essay on William Shakespeare's *Macbeth* focuses on the title character, examining the extent to which he is and is not a tragic hero. Although the writer bases the essay on his personal response to the play, he does not simply state a preference, as if saying he likes vanilla more than chocolate; instead, he argues a case and offers evidence from the play to support his claims.

The writer delays stating his thesis fully until the final paragraph: Macbeth is a hero even though he is a villain. But this thesis is nonetheless evident throughout the essay, from the title through the opening three paragraphs (which establish a context and the case the writer will oppose) through each of the five body paragraphs (which offer five kinds of evidence for the thesis).

Note The parenthetical citations in this essay include act, scene, and line numbers—MLA style for citations of verse plays (see p. 650).

Michael Spinter

Professor Nelson

English 211, sec. 4

8 Oct. 2008

Macbeth as Hero

When people imagine a tragic hero, they probably think of a fundamentally sympathetic person who is entangled in terrifying circumstances and who ultimately dies, leaving the world a diminished place. For instance, Hamlet must avenge his father's murder, and in doing so he performs certain actions that verge on the wrongful, such as behaving cruelly to his beloved Ophelia and his mother and killing Rosencrantz and Guildenstern. But in the end Hamlet seems fundamentally a decent man and Denmark seems the poorer for his death.

Macbeth, however, is different. He kills King Duncan and Duncan's grooms, kills Banquo, attempts to kill Banquo's son, and finally kills Lady Macduff and her children and her servants. True, the only people whom he kills with his own hands are Duncan and the grooms—the other victims are destroyed by hired murderers—but clearly Macbeth is responsible for all of the deaths. He could seem to be an utterly unscrupulous, sneaking butcher rather than a tragic hero for whom a reader can feel sympathy.

Certainly most of the other characters in the play feel no sympathy for Macbeth. Macduff calls him a "hell-kite," or a hellish bird of prey (4.3.217), a "tyrant" (5.7.14), a "hell-hound" (5.8.3), and a "coward" (5.8.23). To Malcolm he is a "tyrant" (4.3.12), "devilish Macbeth" (4.3.117), and a "butcher" (5.8.69). Readers and spectators can hardly deny the truth of these characterizations. And yet Macbeth does not seem merely villainous. It would be going too far to say that Macbeth is always sympathetic, but he is deeply interesting and not to be dismissed as an out-and-out monster. What accounts for his hold on readers' and spectators' feelings? At least five factors play their parts.

Macbeth is appealing because he is an impressive military figure. In the first extended description of Macbeth, the Captain speaks of "brave Macbeth—well he deserves that name" (1.2.16). The Captain tells how Macbeth valiantly fought on behalf of his king, and King Duncan exclaims, "O valiant cousin! Worthy gentleman!" (1.2.2). True, Macbeth sometimes cringes, such as when he denies responsibility for Banquo's death: "Thou canst not say I did it" (3.4.51). But throughout most of the play, he is a bold and courageous soldier.

Of course, Macbeth's ability as a soldier is not enough by itself to explain his appeal. He is at the same time a victim—a victim of his wife's ambition and a victim of the witches. Yes, he ought to see through his wife's schemes, and he ought to resist the witches, just as Banquo resists them, but surely Macbeth is partly tricked into crime. He is responsible, but others can imagine themselves falling as he does, and his status as a victim arouses sympathy.

Also contributing to a sense of Macbeth's humanity is the conscience he retains despite his terrible deeds. For instance, after he murders Duncan he cannot sleep at night. When he tells Lady Macbeth that he has heard a voice saying "Macbeth does murder sleep" (2.2.35), she ridicules him, but the voice is prophetic: he is doomed to sleepless nights. Macbeth's torment over his deed shows that he knows he has done wrong and that he still has some decent human feelings.

MODELS OF STUDENT WRITING

Michael Spinter's paper on *Macbeth* is strong in both argumentation and organization. Spinter makes an excellent case for his claim that Macbeth is heroic. Your students may wish to discuss this claim, and you can ask them whether they find Spinter's arguments persuasive. If they don't think Spinter is persuasive, ask them what he could have done to make his case stronger, or how they would suggest he modify his thesis.

You may also want to use this paper to talk about matters of structure. It takes a skillful writer to make a paper work with a thesis positioned at the end. Ask your students whether they think it works in Michael Spinter's paper or whether he would have been better off putting the thesis at the beginning, and ask them to justify their opinions.

Finally, you might ask students to reflect upon all three sample papers in this chapter (Janet Vong's, Kenneth Scheff's, and Michael Spinter's) and to compare and contrast their respective strengths and weaknesses.

Macbeth eventually loses all of his allies, even his wife, and he then claims sympathy as a lonely, guilt-haunted figure. On this point, scene 2 of act 3 is especially significant. When Lady Macbeth asks Macbeth why he keeps to himself (line 8), he confides something of the mental stress that he is undergoing. But when she asks, "What's to be done?" (44), he cannot bring himself to tell her that he is plotting the deaths of Banquo and Fleance. Instead of further involving his wife, the only person with whom he might still have a human connection, Macbeth says, "Be innocent of the knowledge, dearest chuck . . ." (45). The word *chuck*, an affectionate form of *chick*, shows warmth and intimacy that are touching, but his refusal or his inability to confide in his wife and former partner in crime shows how fully isolated he is from all human contact. Readers and spectators cannot help feeling some sympathy for him.

Finally, Macbeth is appealing, rather than disgusting, because he speaks so eloquently. The greatness of his language compels rapt attention. Some speeches are very familiar, such as "My way of life / Is fall'n into the sear, the yellow leaf . . ." (5.3.23-24) and "Tomorrow and tomorrow and tomorrow / Creeps in this petty pace from day to day . . ." (5.5.19-20). But almost every speech Macbeth utters is equally memorable, from his first, "So foul and fair a day I have not seen" (1.3.38), to his last:

> Before my body
> I throw my warlike shield. Lay on, Macduff:
> And damned be him that first cries, "Hold, enough!" (5.8.32-34)

If readers and spectators judge Macbeth only by what he does, of course they will see a foul murderer. But if they give due weight to his bravery, his role as a victim, his tormented conscience, his isolation, and especially his moving language, then they will not simply judge Macbeth. Rather, they will see that this villain is not merely awful but awesome.

[New page.]

Work Cited

Shakespeare, William. *The Tragedy of Macbeth*. Ed. Sylvan Barnet. Rev. ed. New York: NAL, 1987. Print.

50
Writing in Other Humanities

The humanities include literature, the visual arts, music, film, dance, history, philosophy, and religion. The preceding chapter discusses the particular requirements of reading and writing about literature. This chapter concentrates on history. Although the arts, religion, and other humanities have their own concerns, they share many important goals and methods with literature and history.

50a Using the methods and evidence of the humanities

Writers in the humanities record and speculate about the growth, ideas, and emotions of human beings. Based on the evidence of written words, artworks, and other human traces and creations, humanities writers explain, interpret, analyze, and reconstruct the human experience.

The discipline of history focuses particularly on reconstructing the past. In Greek the word for history means "to inquire": historians inquire into the past to understand the events of the past. Then they report, explain, analyze, and evaluate those events in their context, asking such questions as what happened before or after the events or how the events were related to then existing political and social structures.

Historians' reconstructions of the past—their conclusions about what happened and why—are always supported with reference to the written record. The evidence of history is mainly primary sources, such as eyewitness accounts and contemporary documents, letters, commercial records, and the like. For history papers, you might also be asked to support your conclusions with those in secondary sources.

Visit *mycomplab.com* for more resources on writing in history, the visual arts, and other humanities.

MacNealy, Mary Sue. *Strategies for Empirical Research in Writing.* Needham Heights: Allyn & Bacon, 1999. An introduction to research methods in the humanities, geared for students but useful to teachers as well.

Monroe, Jonathan, ed. *Local Knowledges, Local Practices: Writing in the Disciplines at Cornell.* Pittsburgh: U of Pittsburgh P, 2003. Print. This collection discusses how writing is used in many fields at Cornell, including foreign language, religion, and philosophy.

Thelin, William H. "Understanding Problems in Critical Classrooms." *College Composition and Communication* 57.1 (2005): 114–41. Print. The author offers a defense of critical pedagogy in the face of mounting criticism against it.

Tuchman, Barbara. *Practicing History: Selected Essays.* New York: Knopf, 1981. Print. Tuchman demonstrates and gives practical recommendations for analytic writing in history.

Weisser, Christian. *Moving Beyond Academic Discourse: Composition Studies and the Public Sphere.* Carbondale: Southern Illinois UP, 2002. Print. Weisser argues that student writing will improve if students do more nonacademic writing for specific audiences.

ADDITIONAL RESOURCES FOR STUDENTS

If your students need more help in writing for the humanities, you might refer them to the following:

Barnet, Sylvan. *A Short Guide to Writing About Art.* 9th ed. New York: Prentice, 2008. Print.

Bellman, Jonathan. *A Short Guide to Writing About Music.* 2nd ed. New York: Longman, 2007. Print.

Corrigan, Timothy. *A Short Guide to Writing About Film.* 6th ed. New York: Longman, 2007. Print.

Marius, Richard and Melvin E. Page. *A Short Guide to Writing About History.* 6th ed. New York: Longman, 2007. Print.

Storey, William Kelleher. *Writing History: A Guide for Students.* 3rd ed. New York: Oxford UP, 2008. Print. This guide includes information on researching historical topics both in

In reading historical sources, you need to weigh and evaluate their evidence. If, for example, you find conflicting accounts of the same event, you need to consider the possible biases of the authors. In general, the more a historian's conclusions are supported by public records such as deeds, marriage licenses, and newspaper accounts, the more reliable the conclusions are likely to be.

50b Understanding writing assignments in the humanities

Papers in the humanities generally perform one or more of the following operations:

- **Explanation:** for instance, showing how a painter developed a particular technique or clarifying a general's role in a historical battle.
- **Analysis:** examining the elements of a philosophical argument or breaking down the causes of a historical event.
- **Interpretation:** inferring the meaning of a film from its images or the significance of a historical event from contemporary accounts of it.
- **Synthesis:** finding a pattern in a historical period or in a composer's works.
- **Evaluation:** judging the quality of an architect's design or a historian's conclusions.

Most likely, you will use these operations in combination—say, interpreting and explaining the meaning of a painting and then evaluating it. (These operations are discussed in more detail in Chapter 7.)

50c Using the tools and language of the humanities

The tools and language of the humanities vary according to the discipline. Major reference works in each field, such as those listed on the next four pages, can clarify specific tools you need and language you should use.

1 Writing tools

A useful tool for the arts is to ask a series of questions to analyze and evaluate a work. (A list of such questions for reading literature appears on pp. 737–38.) In any humanities discipline, a journal—a log of questions, reactions, and insights—can help you discover and record your thoughts. (See pp. 141 and 559.)

In history the tools are those of any thorough and efficient researcher, as discussed in Chapters 41–43: a system for finding and tracking sources; a methodical examination of sources, including evaluating and synthesizing them; a system for gathering source information; and a separate system, such as a research journal, for tracking one's own evolving thoughts.

2 Language considerations

Historians strive for precision and logic. They do not guess about what happened or speculate about "what if." They avoid trying to influence readers' opinions with words having strongly negative or positive connotations, such as *stupid* or *brilliant*. Instead, historians show the evidence and draw conclusions from that. Generally, they avoid using *I* because it tends to draw attention away from the evidence and toward the writer.

Writing about history demands some attention to the tenses of verbs to maintain consistency. Generally, historians use the past tense to refer to events that occurred in the past. They reserve the present tense only for statements about the present or statements of general truths. For example:

> Franklin Delano Roosevelt <u>died</u> in 1945. Many of Roosevelt's economic reforms <u>persist</u> in programs such as Social Security, unemployment compensation, and farm subsidies.

3 Research sources

The following lists give resources in the humanities. (Resources for literature appear on pp. 740–41.)

Specialized encyclopedias, dictionaries, and bibliographies

The arts

Architecture: From Prehistory to Post-modernity
Baker Biographical Dictionary of Music
Dictionary of Art
Encyclopedia of World Art
Film Literature Index
Film Review Index
Garland Encyclopedia of World Music
Guide to the Literature of Art History 2
Guinness Encyclopedia of Popular Music
International Encyclopedia of Dance
International Television and Video Almanac
MLA International Bibliography of Books and Articles on the Modern Languages and Literatures
New Grove Dictionary of Music and Musicians

print and online and writing about them, including information on peer review.

WRITING ASSIGNMENTS

Ask students to bring in examples of writing assignments from their other humanities courses and to classify them according to the list on this page. Which are most and least frequently used? Students might also interview professors from their other courses, individually or in teams, to learn which writing strategies are most important for success in those courses.

TENSES

Students sometimes have trouble making judgments about which tense to use in historical writing. To get them used to conventions of tense usage, have students review each other's drafts and suggest revisions.

SOURCES

To help students become familiar with the humanities research sources listed in the text (pp. 757–60), have each student look up one source (either a library source or a Web source) and make a brief presentation on it in class.

MAKE LIBRARIANS YOUR ALLIES, AGAIN

If students need information about writing in specific disciplines, you might consider inviting your library's subject-area librarian (if you have one) to discuss resources available in that field, either in the library or in your classroom. In a networked classroom, you might arrange a classroom visit, so students can do hands-on research.

New Grove Dictionary of Opera
Oxford Companion to Twentieth-Century Art

History

Afro-American Reference
American Decades
American Indian Studies: A Bibliographic Guide
Dictionary of American History
Dictionary of the Middle Ages
Encyclopedia of American History
Encyclopedia of Latin American History and Culture
Encyclopedia of Russian History
Encyclopedia of World History
Harvard Guide to American History
History: Illustrated Search Strategy and Sources
Middle East Abstracts and Index
New Cambridge Modern History
Oxford Classical Dictionary

Philosophy and religion

Anchor Bible Dictionary
Catholic Encyclopedia
Dictionary of the History of Ideas
Encyclopedia Judaica
Encyclopedia of Asian Philosophy
Encyclopedia of Ethics
Encyclopedia of Philosophy
Encyclopedia of Religion
Oxford Dictionary of Islam
Oxford Dictionary of the Christian Church

Library databases and indexes

America: History and Life
Art Index
Arts and Humanities Citation Index
ARTStor
ATLA Religion Database
Avery Index to Architectural Periodicals
Dissertation Abstracts International (doctoral dissertations)
Film Literature Index
Historical Abstracts
Humanities Index
Index Islamicus
JSTOR
MLA International Bibliography
Music Index
Nineteenth-Century Masterfile
Philosopher's Index

Book reviews

Book Review Digest
Book Review Index

Sources on the open Web

General

Arts and Humanities Data Service (ahds.ac.uk)
BUBL LINK (bubl.ac.uk)
EDSITEment (edsitement.neh.gov)
Internet Public Library (ipl.org/div/subject/browse/hum00.00.00)
Intute: Arts and Humanities (www.intute.ac.uk/artsandhumanities)
*Librarians Internet Index: Arts and Humanities (search.lii.org/
    index.jsp?more=SubTopic)*
Voice of the Shuttle Humanities (vos.ucsb.edu)

Art

Art History Resources on the Web (witcombe.sbc.edu/ARTHLinks.html)
Artnet (artnet.com)
ArtSource (www.ilpi.com/artsource/welcome.html)
BUBL LINK: The Arts (bubl.ac.uk/link/linkbrowse.cfm?menuid=9847)
World Wide Arts Resources (wwar.com/browse.html)

Dance

Artslynx International Dance Resources (www.artslynx.org/dance)
BUBL LINK: Dance (bubl.ac.uk/link/d/dance.htm)

Film

CinemaSpot (cinemaspot.com)
*Film Studies on the Internet (www.library.ualberta.ca/subject/film/websites/
    index.cfm)*
Internet Movie Database (imdb.com)

History

*History: North America (www.libraries.rutgers.edu/rul/rr_gateway/
    research_ guides/history_us/history_us.shtml)*
Best of History Web Sites (besthistorysites.net)
National Women's History Project (nwhp.org)

Music

American Music Resource (amrhome.net)
MusicMoz (musicmoz.org)
Music Theory Online (societymusictheory.org/mto)
Web Resources for Research in Music (www.music.ucc.ie/wrrm)

Philosophy

Philosophy Documentation Center (pdcnet.org)
P-Search (philosophy.hku.hk/psearch/info.php)
*Social Science Information Gateway: Philosophy (www.intute.ac.uk/
    artsandhumanities/philosophy)*

Stanford Encyclopedia of Philosophy (plato.stanford.edu)
Voice of the Shuttle: Philosophy (vos.ucsb.edu/browse.asp?id=2724)

Religion
Academic Info: Religion Gateway (academicinfo.net/religindex.html)
Pluralism Project (pluralism.org/directory/index.php)
Religious Studies Web Guide (www.acs.ucalgary.ca/~lipton)
Religious Worlds (www.religiousworlds.com/index.html)
Virtual Religion Index (virtualreligion.net/vri)

Theater
McCoy's Brief Guide to Internet Resources in Theater and Performance Studies
    (www2.stetson.edu/csata/thr_guid.html)
Theater Connections (uncc.edu/jvanoate/theater)
TheatreHistory.com (theatrehistory.com)

50d Citing sources in Chicago style

Writers in the humanities generally rely on one of the following guides for source-citation style:

The Chicago Manual of Style, 15th ed., 2003
A Manual for Writers of Research Papers, Theses, and Dissertations, by Kate L. Turabian, 7th ed., rev. Wayne C. Booth, Gregory G. Colomb, and Joseph M. Williams, 2007
MLA Handbook for Writers of Research Papers, 6th ed., by Joseph Gibaldi, 2003
MLA Style Manual and Guide to Scholarly Publishing, 3rd ed., 2008

The recommendations of the *MLA Style Manual* and *MLA Handbook* are discussed and illustrated in Chapter 46. Unless your instructor specifies otherwise, use these recommendations for papers in English and foreign languages. In history, art history, and many other disciplines, however, writers rely on *The Chicago Manual of Style* or the student reference adapted from it, *A Manual for Writers.* (Kate Turabian)

 Both books detail two documentation styles. One, used mainly by scientists and social scientists, closely resembles the style of the American Psychological Association, covered in Chapter 51. The other style, used more in the humanities, calls for footnotes or endnotes and an optional bibliography. This style is described below.

1 Using Chicago notes and a list of works cited

In the Chicago note style, a raised numeral in the text refers the reader to source information in an endnote or a footnote. In these notes, the first citation of each source contains all the information readers need to find the source. Thus your instructor may consider a list of works cited optional because it provides much the same information. Ask your instructor whether you should use footnotes or endnotes and whether you should include a list of works cited.

Whether you are providing footnotes or endnotes, use single spacing for each note and double spacing between notes, as shown in the samples below. Separate footnotes from the text with a short line. Place endnotes directly after the text, beginning on a new page. For a list of sources at the end of the paper, use the format on the following page. Arrange the sources alphabetically by the authors' last names.

Chicago footnotes

Chicago endnotes

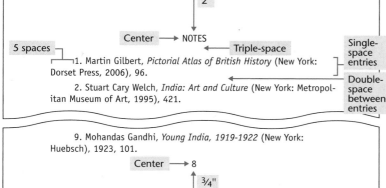

Chicago list of works cited

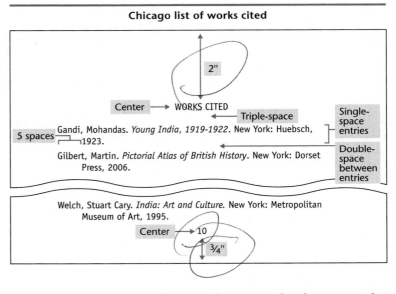

The examples below illustrate the essentials of a note and a works-cited entry.

Note

6. Martin Gilbert, *Pictorial Atlas of British History* (New York: Dorset Press, 2006), 96.

Works-cited entry

Gilbert, Martin. *Pictorial Atlas of British History*. New York: Dorset Press, 2006.

Treat some features of notes and works-cited entries the same:

- Single-space each note or entry, and double-space between them.
- Italicize or underline the titles of books and periodicals. Ask your instructor for his or her preference.
- Enclose in quotation marks the titles of parts of books or articles in periodicals.
- Do not abbreviate publishers' names, but omit "Inc.," "Co.," and similar abbreviations.
- Do not use "p." or "pp." before page numbers.

Treat other features of notes and works-cited entries differently:

Note	Works-cited entry
Start with a number that corresponds to the note number in the text.	Do not begin with a number.

Indent the first line five spaces.	Indent the second and subsequent lines five spaces.
Give the author's name in normal order.	Begin with the author's last name.
Use commas between elements such as author's name and title.	Use periods between elements.
Enclose publication information in parentheses, with no preceding punctuation	Precede the publication information with a period, and don't use parentheses.
Include the specific page number(s) you borrowed from, omitting "p." or "pp."	Omit page numbers except for parts of books or articles in periodicals.

You can instruct your computer to position footnotes at the bottoms of appropriate pages. It will also automatically number notes and renumber them if you add or delete one or more.

2 Following Chicago models

The Chicago models for common sources are indexed on the next page. The models show notes and works-cited entries together for easy reference. Be sure to use the numbered note form for notes and the unnumbered works-cited form for works-cited entries.

Listing authors

1. One, two, or three authors

1. Carol Gilligan, *In a Different Voice: Psychological Theory and Women's Development* (Cambridge: Harvard University Press, 1982), 27.

Gilligan, Carol. *In a Different Voice: Psychological Theory and Women's Development*. Cambridge: Harvard University Press, 1982.

1. Dennis L. Wilcox, Phillip H. Ault, and Warren K. Agee, *Public Relations: Strategies and Tactics,* 6th ed. (New York: Irwin, 2005), 182.

Wilcox, Dennis L., Phillip H. Ault, and Warren K. Agee. *Public Relations: Strategies and Tactics*. 6th ed. New York: Irwin, 2005.

2. More than three authors

2. Geraldo Lopez and others, *China and the West* (Boston: Little, Brown, 2004), 461.

Lopez, Geraldo, Judith P. Salt, Anne Ming, and Henry Reisen. *China and the West*. Boston: Little, Brown, 2004.

3. Author not named (anonymous)

6. *The Dorling Kindersley World Reference Atlas* (London: Dorling Kindersley, 2005), 150-51.

The Dorling Kindersley World Reference Atlas. London: Dorling Kindersley, 2005.

Chicago note and works-cited models

Authors

1. One, two, or three authors *763*
2. More than three authors *763*
3. Author not named (anonymous) *763*

Print periodicals

4. An article in a journal *764*
5. An article in a newspaper *765*
6. An article in a magazine *765*
7. A review *765*

Print books

8. Basic format for a book *765*
9. A book with an editor *765*
10. A book with an author and an editor *765*
11. A translation *766*
12. A later edition *766*
13. A work in more than one volume *766*
14. A selection from an anthology *766*
15. A work in a series *766*
16. An article in a reference work *766*

Web and other electronic sources

17. An article in a journal *767*
18. An article in a magazine *767*

19. An article in a newspaper *767*
20. An article in an online database *767*
21. A book *768*
22. An article in a reference work *768*
23. An audio or visual source *768*
24. A message posted to a blog or discussion group *769*
25. Electronic mail *769*
26. A work on CD-ROM or DVD-ROM *769*

Other sources

27. A government publication *769*
28. A published letter *769*
29. A published or broadcast interview *770*
30. A personal letter or interview *770*
31. A work of art *770*
32. A film, DVD, or video recording *770*
33. A sound recording *770*

Shortened notes *771*

Listing print periodicals: Journals, newspapers, magazines

4. An article in a journal (print)

4. Janet Lever, "Sex Differences in the Games Children Play," *Social Problems* 23 (1996): 482.

Lever, Janet. "Sex Differences in the Games Children Play." *Social Problems* 23 (1996): 478-87.

Provide the issue number if the journal numbers issues, as shown below. Note that the issue number is required for any journal that pages each issue separately or that numbers only issues, not volumes.

4. Robert Bee, "The Importance of Preserving Paper-Based Artifacts in a Digital Age," *The Library Quarterly* 78, no. 2 (2008): 176.

Bee, Robert. "The Importance of Preserving Paper-Based Artifacts in a Digital Age." *The Library Quarterly* 78, no. 2 (2008): 174-194.

5. An article in a newspaper (print)

5. David Stout, "Blind Win Court Ruling on US Currency," *New York Times,* May 21, 2008, national edition, A23.

Stout, David. "Blind Win Court Ruling on US Currency." *New York Times,* May 21, 2008, national edition, A23.

Chicago style does not require page numbers for newspaper articles, whether in notes or in works-cited entries. Thus A23 could be omitted from the above examples.

6. An article in a magazine (print)

6. Amanda Fortini, "Pomegranate Princess," *New Yorker,* March 31, 2008, 94.

Fortini, Amanda. "Pomegranate Princess." *New Yorker,* March 31, 2008, 92-99.

Chicago works-cited style does not require inclusive page numbers for magazine articles, so 92-99 could be omitted from the preceding example.

7. A review (print)

7. John Gregory Dunne, "The Secret of Danny Santiago," review of *Famous All over Town,* by Danny Santiago, *New York Review of Books,* August 16, 1994, 25.

Dunne, John Gregory. "The Secret of Danny Santiago." Review of *Famous All over Town,* by Danny Santiago. *New York Review of Books,* August 16, 1994, 17-27.

Listing print books

8. Basic format for a book (print)

8. Barbara Ehrenreich, *Dancing in the Streets: A History of Collective Joy* (New York: Henry Holt, 2006), 97-117.

Ehrenreich, Barbara. *Dancing in the Streets: A History of Collective Joy.* New York: Henry Holt, 2006.

9. A book with an editor (print)

9. Hendrick Ruitenbeek, ed., *Freud as We Knew Him* (Detroit: Wayne State University Press, 1973), 64.

Ruitenbeek, Hendrick, ed. *Freud as We Knew Him.* Detroit: Wayne State University Press, 1973.

10. A book with an author and an editor (print)

10. Lewis Mumford, *The City in History,* ed. Donald L. Miller (New York: Pantheon, 1986), 216-17.

Mumford, Lewis. *The City in History.* Edited by Donald L. Miller. New York: Pantheon, 1986.

11. A translation (print)

11. Dante Alighieri, *The Inferno,* trans. John Ciardi (New York: New American Library, 1971), 51.

Alighieri, Dante. *The Inferno*. Translated by John Ciardi. New York: New American Library, 1971.

12. A later edition (print)

12. Dwight L. Bolinger, *Aspects of Language,* 3rd ed. (New York: Harcourt Brace Jovanovich, 1981), 20.

Bolinger, Dwight L. *Aspects of Language*. 3rd ed. New York: Harcourt Brace Jovanovich, 1981.

13. A work in more than one volume (print)

Citation of one volume without a title:

13. Abraham Lincoln, *The Collected Works of Abraham Lincoln,* ed. Roy P. Basler (New Brunswick: Rutgers University Press, 1953), 5:426-28.

Lincoln, Abraham. *The Collected Works of Abraham Lincoln*. Edited by Roy P. Basler. Vol. 5. New Brunswick: Rutgers University Press, 1953.

Citation of one volume with a title:

13. Linda B. Welkin, *The Age of Balanchine,* vol. 3 of *The History of Ballet* (New York: Columbia University Press, 1999), 56.

Welkin, Linda B. *The Age of Balanchine*. Vol. 3 of *The History of Ballet*. New York: Columbia University Press, 1999.

14. A selection from an anthology (print)

14. Rosetta Brooks, "Streetwise," in *The New Urban Landscape,* ed. Richard Martin (New York: Rizzoli, 2005), 38-39.

Brooks, Rosetta. "Streetwise." In *The New Urban Landscape,* ed. Richard Martin, 37-60. New York: Rizzoli, 2005.

15. A work in a series (print)

15. Ingmar Bergman, *The Seventh Seal,* Modern Film Scripts 12 (New York: Simon and Schuster, 1995), 27.

Bergman, Ingmar. *The Seventh Seal*. Modern Film Scripts 12. New York: Simon and Schuster, 1995.

16. An article in a reference work (print)

16. *Merriam-Webster's Collegiate Dictionary,* 11th ed., s.v. "reckon."

Merriam-Webster's Collegiate Dictionary. 11th ed. S.v. "reckon."

As in the example, use the abbreviation s.v. (Latin *sub verbo,* "under the word") for reference works that are alphabetically arranged. Well-known works like the one listed here do not need publication information except for edition number. Chicago style generally recommends notes only, not works-cited entries, for reference works; a works-cited model is given here in case your instructor requires such entries.

Listing Web and other electronic sources

The Chicago Manual's models for documenting electronic sources derive mainly from those for print sources, with the addition of an electronic address (URL) or other indication of the medium along with any other information that may help readers locate the source. Chicago requires the date of your access to an online source only if the source could change significantly (for instance, a blog). However, your instructor may require access dates for a broader range of online sources, so they are included in the following models (in parentheses at the end).

Note Chicago style allows many ways to break URLs between the end of one line and the beginning of the next: after slashes, before most punctuation marks (periods, commas, question marks, and so on), and before or after equal signs and ampersands (&). *Do not* break after a hyphen or add any hyphens.

17. An article in a journal (Web)

17. Andrew Palfrey, "Choice of Mates in Identical Twins," *Modern Psychology* 4, no. 1 (2003): 28, http://www.liasu/edu/modpsy/palfrey4(1).htm (accessed February 25, 2008).

Palfrey, Andrew. "Choice of Mates in Identical Twins." *Modern Psychology* 4, no. 1 (2003): 26-40. http://www.liasu/edu/modpsy/palfrey4(1).htm (accessed February 25, 2008).

18. An article in a magazine (Web)

18. Nina Shen Rastogi, "Peacekeepers on Trial," *Slate,* May 28, 2008, http://www.slate.com/id/2192272 (accessed June 20, 2008).

Rastogi, Nina Shen. "Peacekeepers on Trial." *Slate,* May 28, 2008. http://www.slate.com/id/2192272 (accessed June 20, 2008).

19. An article in a newspaper (Web)

19. Elissa Gootman, "Gifted Programs in the City Are Less Diverse," *New York Times,* June 19, 2008, http://www.nytimes.com/2008/06/19/nyregion/19gifted.html (accessed August 17, 2008).

Gootman, Elissa. "Gifted Programs in the City Are Less Diverse." *New York Times,* June 19, 2008. http://www.nytimes.com/2008/06/19/nyregion/19gifted.html (accessed August 17, 2008).

20. An article in an online database (Web)

20. Irina Netchaeva, "E-Government and E-Democracy," *International Journal for Communication Studies* 64 (2002): 470-71, http://www.epnet.com (accessed June 20, 2008).

Netchaeva, Irina. "E-Government and E-Democracy." *International Journal for Communication Studies* 64 (2002): 467-78. http://www.epnet.com (accessed June 20, 2008).

For news and journal databases, including those to which your library subscribes, you may omit the name of the database. Give its main URL (as in the examples) unless the work has a usable URL of its own.

21. A book (Web)

21. Jane Austen, *Emma*, ed. R. W. Chapman (1816; Oxford: Clarendon, 1926; Oxford Text Archive, 2004), chap. 1, http://ota.ahds.ac.uk/Austen/Emma.1519 (accessed July 15, 2008).

Austen, Jane. *Emma*. Edited by R. W. Chapman. 1816. Oxford: Clarendon, 1926. Oxford Text Archive, 2004. http://ota.ahds.ac.uk/Austen/Emma.1519 (accessed July 15, 2008).

Provide print publication information, if any.

22. An article in a reference work (Web)

22. *Encyclopaedia Britannica Online*, s.v. "Wu-ti," http://www.eb.com:80 (accessed September 23, 2008).

Encyclopaedia Britannica Online. S.v. "Wu-ti." http://www.eb.com:80 (accessed September 23, 2008).

23. An audio or visual source (Web)

A work of art:

23. Jackson Pollock, *Shimmering Substance,* 1946, Museum of Modern Art, New York, http://moma.org/collection/conservation/pollock/shimmering_substance.html (accessed March 12, 2008).

Pollock, Jackson. *Shimmering Substance*. 1946. Museum of Modern Art, New York. http://moma.org/collection/conservation/pollock/shimmering_substance.html (accessed March 12, 2008).

See also model 30 to cite a work of art that you view in person.

A sound recording:

23. Ronald W. Reagan, State of the Union Address, January 26, 1982, Vincent Voice Library, Digital and Multimedia Center, University of Michigan, http://www.lib.msu.edu/vincent/presidents/reagan.html (accessed May 6, 2008).

Reagan, Ronald W. State of the Union Address. January 26, 1982. Vincent Voice Library. Digital and Multimedia Center, University of Michigan. http://www.lib.msu.edu/vincent/presidents/reagan.html (accessed May 6, 2008).

A film or film clip:

23. Leslie J. Stewart, *96 Ranch Rodeo and Barbecue* (1951); 16mm; from Library of Congress, *Buckaroos in Paradise: Ranching Culture in Northern Nevada, 1945-1982,* MPEG, http://memory.loc.gov/cgi-bin/query (accessed January 7, 2008).

Stewart, Leslie J. 96 *Ranch Rodeo and Barbecue*. 1951; 16 mm. From Library of Congress, *Buckaroos in Paradise: Ranching Culture in Northern Nevada, 1945-1982*. MPEG, http://memory.loc.gov/cgi-bin/query (accessed January 7, 2008).

24. A message posted to a blog or discussion group (Web)

24. Chris Horner, "EU Emissions," Cooler Heads Blog, June 18, 2008, http://www.globalwarming.org/node/2362 (accessed July 2, 2008).

Horner, Chris. "EU Emissions." Cooler Heads Blog. June 18, 2008. http://www .globalwarming.org/node/2362 (accessed July 2, 2008).

24. Michael Tourville, "European Currency Reform," e-mail to International Finance discussion list, January 6, 2008, http://www.weg.isu .edu/finance-dl/archive/46732 (accessed January 12, 2008).

Tourville, Michael. "European Currency Reform." E-mail to International Finance discussion list. January 6, 2008. http://www.weg.isu.edu/ finance-dl/archive/46732 (accessed January 12, 2008).

25. Electronic mail

25. Elizabeth Bailey, "Re: London," e-mail message to author, May 4, 2008.

Bailey, Elizabeth. "Re: London." E-mail message to author. May 4, 2008.

26. A work on CD-ROM or DVD-ROM

26. *The American Heritage Dictionary of the English Language,* 4th ed. (Boston: Houghton Mifflin, 2000), CD-ROM.

The American Heritage Dictionary of the English Language. 4th ed. Boston: Houghton Mifflin, 2000. CD-ROM.

Listing other sources

27. A government publication (print)

27. House Committee on Ways and Means, *Medicare Payment for Outpatient Physical and Occupational Therapy Services,* 110th Cong., 1st sess., 2007, H. Doc. 772, 18-19.

U.S. Congress. House. Committee on Ways and Means. *Medicare Payment for Outpatient Physical and Occupational Therapy Services*. 110th Cong., 1st sess., 2007. H. Doc. 772.

27. Hawaii Department of Education, *Kauai District Schools, Profile 2007-08* (Honolulu, 2008), 38.

Hawaii. Department of Education. *Kauai District Schools, Profile 2007-08*. Honolulu, 2008.

28. A published letter (print)

28. Mrs. Laura E. Buttolph to Rev. and Mrs. C. C. Jones, June 20, 1857, in *The Children of Pride: A True Story of Georgia and the Civil War,* ed. Robert Manson Myers (New Haven, CT: Yale University Press, 1972), 334.

Buttolph, Laura E. Mrs. Laura E. Buttolph to Rev. and Mrs. C. C. Jones, June 20, 1857. In *The Children of Pride: A True Story of Georgia and the Civil War,* edited by Robert Manson Myers. New Haven, CT: Yale University Press, 1972.

29. A published or broadcast interview

29. Junot Diaz, interview by Terry Gross, *Fresh Air,* NPR, October 18, 2007.

Diaz, Junot. Interview by Terry Gross. *Fresh Air.* NPR. October 18, 2007.

30. A personal letter or interview

30. Ann E. Packer, letter to author, June 15, 2008.

Packer, Ann E. Letter to author. June 15, 2008.

30. William Paul, interview by author, December 19, 2005.

Paul, William. Interview by author. December 19, 2005.

31. A work of art

31. John Singer Sargent, *In Switzerland,* 1908, Metropolitan Museum of Art, New York.

Sargent, John Singer. *In Switzerland.* 1908. Metropolitan Museum of Art, New York.

32. A film, DVD, or video recording

32. George Balanchine, *Serenade,* DVD, San Francisco Ballet (New York: PBS Video, 2006).

Balanchine, George. *Serenade.* DVD. San Francisco Ballet. New York: PBS Video, 2006.

33. A sound recording

33. Johannes Brahms, *Piano Concerto no. 2 in B-flat,* Artur Rubinstein, Philadelphia Orchestra, Eugene Ormandy, compact disc, RCA BRC4-6731.

Brahms, Johannes. *Piano Concerto no. 2 in B-flat.* Artur Rubinstein. Philadelphia Orchestra. Eugene Ormandy. Compact disc. RCA BRC4-6731.

Using shortened notes

To streamline documentation, Chicago style recommends shortened notes for sources that are fully cited elsewhere, either in a complete list of works cited or in previous notes. Ask your instructor whether your paper should include a list of works cited and, if so, whether you may use shortened notes for first references to sources as well as for subsequent references.

A shortened note contains the author's last name, the work's title (minus any initial *A, An,* or *The*), and the page number. Reduce long titles to four or fewer key words.

Complete note

4. Janet Lever, "Sex Differences in the Games Children Play," *Social Problems* 23 (1996): 482.

Complete works-cited entry

Lever, Janet. "Sex Differences in the Games Children Play." *Social Problems* 23 (1996): 478-87.

Shortened note

12. Lever, "Sex Differences," 483.

You may use the Latin abbreviation ibid. (meaning "in the same place") to refer to the same source cited in the preceding note. Give a page number if it differs from that in the preceding note.

12. Lever, "Sex Differences," 483.

13. Gilligan, *In a Different Voice,* 92.

14. Ibid., 93.

15. Lever, "Sex Differences," 483.

Chicago style allows for in-text parenthetical citations when you cite one or more works repeatedly. In the following example, the raised number 2 refers to the source information in a note; the number in parentheses is a page number in the same source.

British rule, observes Stuart Cary Welch, "seemed as permanent as Mount Everest."[2] Most Indians submitted, willingly or not, to British influence in every facet of life (42).

50e Formatting documents in Chicago style

The following guidelines for document format come mainly from Turabian's *Manual for Writers,* which offers more specific advice than *The Chicago Manual* on the format of students' papers. See pages 761–62 for the format of footnotes, endnotes, and a list of works cited. And see pages 117–26 for advice on type fonts, lists, illustrations, and other elements of document design.

Margins and spacing Use minimum one-inch margins on all pages of the body. (The first page of endnotes or works cited begins two inches from the top; see pp. 761–62.) Double-space your own text and between notes and works-cited entries; single-space displayed quotations (see the next page) and each note and works-cited entry.

Paging Number pages consecutively from the first text page through the end (endnotes or works cited). Use Arabic numerals

First page of Chicago paper

World War I was a transformative event for every participant, not least for faraway India. Though at first it was unified strongly behind

resented were the Rowlatt Acts of 1919, by which the British Parliament withdrew juries from the trials of agitators. This action was seen

(1, 2, 3) in the upper right corner of all pages except the first page of endnotes and first page of works cited. On those pages, the number falls at the foot of the page (see pp. 761–62).

Title page On an unnumbered title page provide the title of the paper, your name, the course title, your instructor's name, and the date. Use all capital letters only for the paper's title, and center everything horizontally. Single-space between adjacent lines, and add extra space as shown opposite.

Poetry and long prose quotations Display certain quotations separately from your text: three or more lines of poetry and two or more sentences of prose. Indent a displayed quotation four spaces from the left, single-space the quotation, and double-space both above it and below it. *Do not add quotation marks.*

Gandhi articulated the principles of his movement in 1922:

> I discovered that pursuit of truth did not permit violence being inflicted on one's opponent, but that he must be weaned from error by patience and sympathy. For what appears to be truth to one may appear to be error to the other. And patience means self-suffering.[9]

Chicago title page

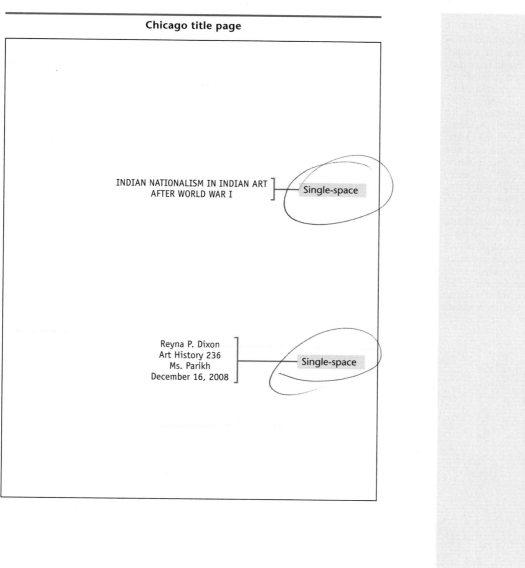

INDIAN NATIONALISM IN INDIAN ART
AFTER WORLD WAR I ⎤
                    Single-space

Reyna P. Dixon ⎤
Art History 236
Ms. Parikh
December 16, 2008 ⎦
                    Single-space

HIGHLIGHTS

Chapter 51 begins by introducing students to research methods in the social sciences, including observation, interviewing, survey conducting, and experimentation. It also covers the distinction between quantitative and qualitative data, types of social science assignments, writing tools, and language conventions. Updated resources for research in the various disciplines, including both print and online resources, are listed in 51c. Section 51d explains to students how to cite sources in the social sciences according to American Psychological Association (APA) standards. It includes annotated samples of print and online journal articles that show students how to find key source information as well as expanded coverage of how to document online and media sources based on the *APA Style Guide to Electronic References* (2007). Color highlighting on every parenthical citation and model reference makes important elements easy to locate. Section 51e shows students how to format documents using APA style. The chapter concludes with excerpts from a sample student paper for a sociology course.

51

Writing in the Social Sciences

The social sciences—including anthropology, economics, education, management, political science, psychology, and sociology—focus on the study of human behavior. As the name implies, the social sciences examine the way human beings relate to themselves, to their environment, and to one another.

51a Using the methods and evidence of the social sciences

Researchers in the social sciences systematically pose a question, formulate a hypothesis (a generalization that can be tested), collect data, analyze those data, and draw conclusions to support, refine, or disprove their hypothesis. This is the scientific method developed in the natural sciences (see p. 806).

Social scientists gather data in several ways:

- They make **firsthand observations of human behavior,** recording the observations in writing or electronically.
- They **interview subjects about their attitudes and behavior,** recording responses in writing or electronically. (See pp. 586–87 for guidelines on conducting an interview.)
- They **conduct broader surveys using questionnaires,** asking people about their attitudes and behavior. (See pp. 587–88 for guidelines on conducting a survey.)
- They **conduct controlled experiments,** structuring an environment in which to encourage and measure a specific behavior.

In their writing, social scientists explain their own research or analyze and evaluate others' research.

---

mycomplab

Visit *mycomplab.com* for more resources as well as exercises on writing in the social sciences.

Social science research methods generate two kinds of data:

- *Quantitative data* are numerical, such as statistical evidence based on surveys, polls, tests, and experiments. When public-opinion pollsters announce that 47 percent of US citizens polled approve of the President's leadership, they are offering quantitative data gained from a survey. Social science writers present quantitative data in graphs, charts, and other illustrations that accompany their text.
- *Qualitative data* are not numerical but more subjective: they are based on interviews, firsthand observations, and inferences, taking into account the subjective nature of human experience. Examples include an anthropologist's description of the initiation rites in a culture she is studying or a psychologist's interpretation of interviews he conducted with a group of adolescents.

51b Understanding writing assignments in the social sciences

Depending on what social science courses you take, you may be asked to complete a variety of assignments:

- A **summary** or **review of research** reports on the available research literature on a subject, such as infants' perception of color.
- A **case analysis** explains the components of a phenomenon, such as a factory closing.
- A **problem-solving analysis** explains the components of a problem, such as unreported child abuse, and suggests ways to solve it.
- A **research paper** interprets and sometimes analyzes and evaluates the writings of other social scientists about a subject, such as the effect of national appeals in advertising. An example appears in Chapter 47, pages 692–719.
- A **research report** explains the author's own original research or the author's attempt to replicate someone else's research. A research report begins on page 802.

Many social science disciplines have special requirements for the content and organization of each kind of paper. The requirements appear in the style guides of the disciplines, listed on pages 779–80. For instance, the American Psychological Association specifies the outline for research reports that is illustrated on pages 802–05. Because of the differences among disciplines and even among different kinds of papers in the same discipline, you should always ask your instructor what he or she requires for an assignment.

QUALITATIVE AND QUANTITATIVE DATA

To help your students become more familiar with the two kinds of data, have them conduct a brief study of a topical conversation while lurking on an online discussion (but not a synchronous one). Ask them to choose a collection of postings from the discussion (a day's worth, perhaps) and to gather some statistical data about the conversation (for instance, the number of participants, the number of times a word or phrase is mentioned, or the number of participants adhering to each opinion stated). After amassing the data, they can graph it and post the graph to your class Web site. Then ask them to go back over the same collection of postings and write a qualitative description of them in the style of one of the social science disciplines.

LINKS TO EXAMPLES

Go online to locate good published examples of each of the kinds of papers listed in 51b: a research summary, a case analysis, a problem-solving analysis, a research paper, and a research report. Download them or post links on your class Web site so that students can have models easily available to them.

CLASSIFYING SAMPLES

Ask students to bring in examples of writing assignments from their social-science courses and to classify them according to the list on page 775. They might also work in teams to interview professors from their other courses about which writing strategies are most important for success in those courses.

FURTHER READING FOR STUDENTS

If your students need more help in writing for the social sciences, you might refer them to some of the following:

Bazerman, Charles. *The Informed Writer: Using Sources in the Disciplines.* 5th ed. Boston: Houghton, 1995. Print.

Becker, Howard S., et al. *Writing for Social Scientists: How to Start and Finish Your Thesis, Book, or Article.* 2nd ed. Chicago: U of Chicago P, 2007. Print.

Cuba, Lee. *A Short Guide to Writing About Social Science.* 4th ed. New York: Longman, 2002. Print.

Dunn, Dana. *A Short Guide to Writing About Psychology.* New York: Longman, 2004. Print.

Holland, Kenneth, and Arthur W. Biddle. *Writer's Guide: Political Science.* Lexington: Heath, 1987. Print.

McCloskey, Donald. *The Writing of Economics.* New York: Macmillan, 1987. Print.

Sociology Writing Group. *A Guide to Writing Sociology Papers.* 5th ed. New York: Worth, 2001. Print.

Staines, Gail M., Katherine Johnson, and Mark Bonacci. *Social Sciences Research: Research, Writing, and Presentation Strategies for Students.* 2nd ed. Lanham: Scarecrow P, 2007. Print.

COLLABORATIVE LEARNING

SMART QUESTIONS

Framing questions is one of the most important aspects of good social-science research, and students will need to apply their skills in critical thinking and writing to the task of composing research questions and survey questions. Have your students practice question writing by conceiving a research question and then carrying out a small survey among the members of the class. Then have them work in small groups to look at survey results and evaluate each student's research and survey questions.

RESEARCH LOGS

Encourage any student considering a career in research to keep a research log. Almost every company that employs researchers will require those workers to document each day's activities in a log in order to record and protect potentially patent-worthy research.

 51c Using the tools and language of the social sciences

The following guidelines for tools and language apply to most social sciences. However, the particular discipline you are writing in, or an instructor in a particular course, may have additional requirements. Many of the research sources listed on the next several pages can tell you more about your discipline's conventions.

1 Writing tools

Many social scientists rely on a **research journal or log,** in which they record their ideas throughout the research-writing process. Even if a research journal is not required in your courses, you may want to use one. As you begin formulating a hypothesis, you can record preliminary questions. Then when you are in the field conducting research, you can use the journal to react to the evidence you are collecting, to record changes in your perceptions and ideas, and to assess your progress. (See pp. 141 and 559 for more on journals.)

To avoid confusing your reflections on the evidence with the evidence itself, keep records of actual data—notes from interviews, observations, surveys, and experiments—separately from the journal.

2 Language considerations

Each social science discipline has specialized terminology for concepts basic to the discipline. In sociology, for example, the words *mechanism, identity,* and *deviance* have specific meanings different from those of everyday usage. And *identity* means something different in sociology, where it applies to groups of people, than in psychology, where it applies to the individual. Social scientists also use precise terms to describe or interpret research. For instance, they say *The subject expressed a feeling of* rather than *The subject felt* because human feelings are not knowable for certain; or they say *These studies indicate* rather than *These studies prove* because conclusions are only tentative.

Just as social scientists strive for objectivity in their research, they also strive to demonstrate their objectivity through language in their writing. They avoid expressions such as *I think* in order to focus attention on what the evidence shows, not the researcher's opinions. (However, many social scientists prefer *I* to *the researcher* when they refer to their own actions, as in *I then interviewed the subjects.* Ask your instructor for his or her preferences.) Social scientists also avoid direct or indirect expression of their personal biases or emotions, either in discussions of other researchers' work or in descriptions of research subjects. Thus one social scientist does not call another's work *sloppy* or *immaculate* and does not refer to his or her own subjects as *drunks* or *innocent victims*. Instead, the writer uses neutral language and ties conclusions strictly to the data.

3 Research sources

The following lists give resources in social sciences.

Specialized encyclopedias, dictionaries, and bibliographies

General
International Bibliography of the Social Sciences
International Encyclopedia of the Social and Behavioral Sciences
Dictionary of the Social Sciences

Business and economics
Advertising Age Encyclopedia of Advertising
Blackwell Encyclopedia of Management
Dictionary of Business and Management
Encyclopedia of Banking and Finance
Encyclopedia of Business Information Sources
McGraw-Hill Encyclopedia of Economics
The MIT Dictionary of Modern Economics
The New Palgrave Dictionary of Economics and the Law

Education
Encyclopedia of American Education
Encyclopedia of Education
Encyclopedia of Educational Research
The Philosophy of Education: An Encyclopedia

Political science and law
Black's Law Dictionary
Encyclopedia of Government and Politics
Information Sources of Political Science
Oxford Companion to American Law
West's Encyclopedia of American Law

Psychology, sociology, and anthropology
APA Dictionary of Psychology
Blackwell Dictionary of Sociology
Countries and Their Culture
Encyclopedia of Anthropology
Encyclopedia of Crime and Justice
Encyclopedia of North American Indians
Encyclopedia of Psychology
Encyclopedia of Sociology
Handbook of Psychology
Macmillan Dictionary of Anthropology
Race and Ethnic Relations
Sage Handbook of Sociology

Monroe, Jonathan, ed. *Local Knowledges, Local Practices: Writing in the Disciplines at Cornell.* Pittsburgh: U of Pittsburgh P, 2003. Print. This collection discusses how writing is used in many fields at Cornell, including anthropology and sociology.

Monroe, Jonathan, ed. *Writing and Revising in the Disciplines.* Ithaca: Cornell UP, 2002. Print. Part Two, "The Social Sciences," of this collection features essays from experts discussing their experiences with writing in their fields.

Shamoon, Linda K., and Robert A. Schwegler. "Sociologists Reading Student Texts: Expectations and Perceptions." *The Writing Instructor* 7.2 (1988): 71–81. Print. The authors argue that the way sociologists perceive the features of a student paper differ considerably from the way composition instructors often perceive the features. Sociologists look first of all for a line of sociological reasoning carried through-out a paper, supported by evidence acceptable to sociologists and made clear by indicators such as topic sentences.

Young, Art. "Writing Across and Against the Curriculum." *College Composition and Communication.* 54.3 (2003): 472–85. Print. Young discusses how literature can be used in non-English courses to help students engage with the material. Specifically, he addresses the use of poetry in a psychology class.

Library databases and indexes

ABI/INFORM (business)
Abstracts in Anthropology
Anthropology Plus
AnthroSource
Business Periodicals Index
Business Source Premier
Communication and Mass Media Complete
Criminal Justice Periodicals
— *Dissertation Abstracts International* (doctoral dissertations)
EconLit
— *Education Index*
— *Educational Resources Information Center* (ERIC)
Hispanic American Periodicals Index
Human Resources Abstracts
Index to Legal Periodicals
International Political Science Abstracts
LexisNexis Academic Universe (legal publications and news sources)
PAIS International (government publications and political science journals)
PsychInfo
Social Sciences Index
Sociological Abstracts
Urban Affairs Abstracts
Wilson Business Abstracts
Worldwide Political Science Abstracts

Book reviews

Index to Book Reviews in the Social Sciences

Sources on the open Web

General
Data on the Net (*3stages.org/idata*)
Social Science Information Gateway (*sosig.ac.uk*)
WWW Virtual Library: Social and Behavorial Sciences (*vlib.org/SocialSciences*)

Anthropology
American Anthropological Association (*aaanet.org*)
American Folklife Center (*loc.gov/folklife*)
Anthro.Net (*home1.gte.net/ericjw1/index.html*)
Anthropology Review Database (*wings.buffalo.edu/anthropology/ARD*)
National Anthropological Archives (*www.nmnh.si.edu/naa/index.htm*)

Business and economics
Academic Info: Business Administration (*academicinfo.net/bus.html*)
Biz/ed (*www.bized.co.uk*)
Resources for Economists on the Internet (*rfe.org*)
Virtual International Business and Economic Sources (*library.uncc.edu/ display/?dept=reference&format=open&page=68*)

Education
Educator's Reference Desk (*eduref.org*)
Gateway to Educational Materials (*thegateway.org*)
Learner.org (*learner.org*)
Social Science Information Gateway: Education (*sosig.ac.uk/roads/ subject-listing/World/educ.html*)
US Department of Education (*ed.gov*)

Ethnic and gender studies
Diversity and Ethnic Studies (*public.iastate.edu/~savega/divweb2.htm*)
Gender Inn (*www.uni-koeln.de/phil-fak/englisch/datenbank/e_index.htm*)
National Women's History Project Resource Center (*www.nwhp.org/ resourcecenter/index.php*)
Voice of the Shuttle: Gender Studies (*vos.ucsb.edu/browse.asp?id=2711*)

Political science and law
Legal Information Institute (*www.law.cornell.edu*)
Librarians' Index to the Internet: Law (*search.lii.org/ index.jsp?more=SubTopic3*)
Oyez: US Supreme Court Multimedia (*www.oyez.org*)
Political Science Resources (*www.psr.keele.ac.uk*)
Thomas Legislative Information on the Internet (*thomas.loc.gov*)
Ultimate Political Science Links (*www.rvc.cc.il.us/faclink/pruckman/ PSLinks.htm*)

Psychology
Encyclopedia of Psychology (*www.psychology.org*)
National Institute of Mental Health (*www.nimh.nih.gov*)
Psychology: Online Resource Central (*psych-central.com*)
Psych Web (*psywww.com*)

Sociology
Social Science Information Gateway: Sociology (*sosig.ac.uk/roads/ subject-listing/World/sociol.html*)
SocioSite (*www2.fmg.uva.nl/sociosite*)
SocioWeb (*socioweb.com*)
WWW Virtual Library: Sociology (*socserv2.socsci.mcmaster.ca/w3virtsoclib*)

51d Citing sources in APA style

Some of the social sciences publish style guides that advise practitioners how to organize, document, and type papers in those fields. The following is a partial list:

American Anthropological Association, *AAA Style Guide*, 2003 (*www .aaanet.org/publications/guidelines.cfm*)
American Political Science Association, *Style Manual for Political Science*, 2006

COMPUTER ACTIVITY

REUSABLE SOURCES

Students may want to bookmark one or more of the general Web sources listed on this page, if those sources are ones students will reuse. You can also ask students to write a brief annotation of any source they find especially helpful. Annotations can be posted to your class Web site and your class can create its own annotated list of sources.

American Psychological Association, *Publication Manual of the American Psychological Association,* 5th ed., 2001, and *APA Style Guide to Electronic References,* 2007

American Sociological Association, *ASA Style Guide,* 3rd ed., 2007

Linguistic Society of America, "LSA Style Sheet," published every December in *LSA Bulletin*

A Uniform System of Citation (law), 18th ed., 2005

By far the most widely used style is that of the American Psychological Association (APA), so we detail it here. Always ask your instructor in any discipline what style you should use.

1 Using APA parenthetical text citations

In APA documentation style, parenthetical citations within the text refer the reader to a list of sources at the end of the text. A parenthetical citation contains the author's last name, the date of publication, and sometimes the page number from which material is borrowed.

1. Author not named in your text

One critic of Milgram's experiments insisted that the subjects "should have been fully informed of the possible effects on them" (Baumrind, 1988, p. 34).

When you do not name the author in your text, place in parentheses the author's last name and the date of the source. Separate the elements with commas. Position the reference so that it is clear what material is being documented *and* so that the reference fits as smoothly as possible into your sentence structure. (See pp. 650–52 for guidelines.) The following would also be correct:

In the view of one critic of Milgram's experiments (Baumrind, 1988), the subjects "should have been fully informed of the possible effects on them" (p. 34).

APA parenthetical text citations

1. Author not named in your text *780*
2. Author named in your text *781*
3. A work with two authors *781*
4. A work with three to five authors *781*
5. A work with six or more authors *782*
6. A work with a group author *782*
7. A work with no author or an anonymous work *782*
8. One of two or more works by the same author(s) *782*
9. Two or more works by different authors *783*
10. An indirect source *783*
11. An electronic source *783*

Unless none is available, the APA requires a page or other identifying number for a direct quotation (as in the preceding examples) and recommends an identifying number for a paraphrase. Use an appropriate abbreviation or symbol before the number—for instance, p. for *page* and ¶ for *paragraph* (or para. if you do not have the symbol). The identifying number may fall with the author and date (first example) or by itself in a separate pair of parentheses (second example). See also model 11, page 783.

2. Author named in your text

Baumrind (1988) insisted that the subjects in Milgram's study "should have been fully informed of the possible effects on them" (p. 34).

When you use the author's name in the text, do not repeat it in the reference. Place the source date in parentheses after the author's name. Place any page or paragraph reference either after the borrowed material (as in the example) or with the date: (1988, p. 34). If you cite the same source again in the paragraph, you need not repeat the reference as long as it is clear that you are using the same source and the page number (if any) is the same. Here is a later sentence from the same paragraph containing the example above:

Baumrind also criticized the experimenters' rationale.

3. A work with two authors

Pepinsky and DeStefano (1997) demonstrated that a teacher's language often reveals hidden biases.

One study (Pepinsky & DeStefano, 1997) demonstrated the hidden biases often revealed in a teacher's language.

When given in the text, two authors' names are connected by and. In a parenthetical citation, they are connected by an ampersand, &.

4. A work with three to five authors

Pepinsky, Dunn, Rentl, and Corson (1999) further demonstrated the biases evident in gestures.

In the first citation of a work with three to five authors, name all the authors.

In the second and subsequent references to a work with three to five authors, generally give only the first author's name, followed by et al. (Latin abbreviation for "and others"):

In the work of Pepinsky et al. (1999), the loaded gestures included head shakes and eye contact.

However, two or more sources published in the same year could shorten to the same form—for instance, two references shortening to Pepinsky et al., 1999. In that case, cite the last names of as many authors as you need to distinguish the sources, and then give et al.: for instance, (Pepinsky, Dunn, et al., 1999) and (Pepinsky, Bradley, et al., 1999).

5. A work with six or more authors

One study (Rutter et al., 2003) attempted to explain these geographical differences in adolescent experience.

For six or more authors, even in the first citation of the work, give only the first author's name, followed by et al. If two or more sources published in the same year shorten to the same form, give additional names as explained with model 4.

6. A work with a group author

The group's later work improved significantly (Lenschow Research, 2008).

For a work that lists an institution, agency, corporation, or other group as author, treat the name of the group as if it were one person's name. If the name is long and has a familiar abbreviation, you may use the abbreviation in the second and subsequent citations. For example, you might abbreviate American Psychological Association as APA.

7. A work with no author or an anonymous work

One article ("Right to Die," 1996) noted that a death-row inmate may crave notoriety.

For a work with no named author, use the first two or three words of the title in place of an author's name, excluding an initial *The*, *A*, or *An*. Italicize book and journal titles, place quotation marks around article titles, and capitalize the significant words in all titles cited in the text. (In the reference list, however, do not use quotation marks for article titles, and capitalize only the first word in all but periodical titles. See p. 785.)

For a work that lists "Anonymous" as the author, use that word in the citation: (Anonymous, 2007).

8. One of two or more works by the same author(s)

At about age seven, most children begin to use appropriate gestures to reinforce their stories (Gardner, 1973a).

When you cite one of two or more works by the same author(s), the date will tell readers which source you mean—as long as your reference list includes only one source published by the author(s) in that year. If your reference list includes two or more works published by the same author(s) *in the same year*, the works should be lettered in the reference list (see p. 787). Then your parenthetical citation should include the appropriate letter with the date: 1973a in the example.

9. Two or more works by different authors

Two studies (Marconi & Hamblen, 1999; Torrence, 2007) found that monthly safety meetings can dramatically reduce workplace injuries.

List the sources in alphabetical order by their authors' names. Insert a semicolon between sources.

10. An indirect source

Supporting data appeared in a study by Chang (cited in Torrence, 2007).

The phrase cited in indicates that the reference to Chang's study was found in Torrence. Only Torrence then appears in the list of references.

11. An electronic source

Ferguson and Hawkins (2006) did not anticipate the "evident hostility" of participants (¶ 6).

Electronic sources can be cited like printed sources, usually with the author's last name and the publication date. When quoting or paraphrasing electronic sources that number paragraphs instead of pages, provide the paragraph number preceded by the symbol ¶ if you have it, or by para. Even if the source does not number its paragraphs, you can still direct readers to a specific location by listing the heading under which the quotation appears and then (counting paragraphs yourself) the number of the paragraph in which the quotation appears—for example, (Endter & Decker, 2008, Method section, ¶ 3). When the source does not number pages or paragraphs or provide frequent headings, omit any reference number.

2 Using an APA reference list

In APA style, the in-text parenthetical citations refer to the list of sources at the end of the text. This list, titled References, includes full publication information on every source cited in the paper. The list falls at the end of the paper, numbered in sequence with the preceding pages.

The following sample shows the format of the first page of the APA reference list:

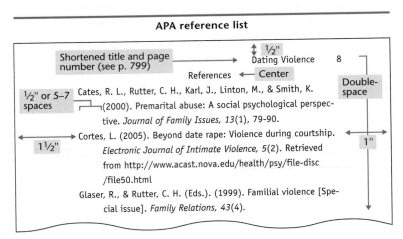

APA reference list

Shortened title and page number (see p. 799)

½"
Dating Violence   8

References ← Center

Double-space

½" or 5–7 spaces Cates, R. L., Rutter, C. H., Karl, J., Linton, M., & Smith, K. (2000). Premarital abuse: A social psychological perspective. *Journal of Family Issues, 13*(1), 79-90.

Cortes, L. (2005). Beyond date rape: Violence during courtship. *Electronic Journal of Intimate Violence, 5*(2). Retrieved from http://www.acast.nova.edu/health/psy/file-disc /file50.html

1½"

1"

Glaser, R., & Rutter, C. H. (Eds.). (1999). Familial violence [Special issue]. *Family Relations, 43*(4).

Arrangement Arrange sources alphabetically by the author's last name. If there is no author, alphabetize by the first main word of the title.

Spacing Double-space everything in the references, as shown in the sample, unless your instructor requests single spacing. (If you do single-space the entries themselves, always double-space *between* them.)

Indention As illustrated in the sample, begin each entry at the left margin, and indent the second and subsequent lines five to seven spaces or one-half inch. Your word processor can create this so-called hanging indent automatically.

Punctuation Separate the parts of the reference (author, date, title, and publication information) with a period and one space. Do not use a final period in references to electronic sources when they conclude with a DOI or URL (see p. 793).

Authors For works with up to six authors, list all authors with last name first, separating names and parts of names with commas. Use initials for first and middle names even when names are listed fully on the source itself. Use an ampersand (&) before the last author's name. See model 3, page 786, for the treatment of seven or more authors.

Publication date Place the publication date in parentheses after the author's or authors' names, followed by a period. Generally, this date is the year only, though for some sources (such as magazine and newspaper articles) it includes month and sometimes day as well.

Titles In titles of books and articles, capitalize only the first word of the title, the first word of the subtitle, and proper nouns; all other words begin with small letters. In titles of journals, capitalize all significant words (see p. 483 for guidelines). Italicize the titles of books and journals. Do not italicize or use quotation marks around the titles of articles.

City of publication For sources that are not periodicals (such as books or government publications), give the city of publication. The following US cities do not require state names as well: Baltimore, Boston, Chicago, Los Angeles, New York, Philadelphia, and San Francisco. Follow their names with a colon. For most other cities, add a comma after the city name, give the two-letter postal abbreviation of the state, and then add a colon. (You may omit the state if the publisher is a university whose name includes the state name, such as University of Arizona.)

Publisher's name Also for nonperiodical sources, give the publisher's name after the place of publication and a colon. Shorten names of many publishers (such as Morrow for William Morrow), and omit *Co., Inc.,* and *Publishers*. However, give full names for associations, corporations, and university presses (such as Harvard University Press), and do not omit *Books* or *Press* from a publisher's name.

Page numbers Use the abbreviation p. or pp. before page numbers in books and in newspapers. Do *not* use the abbreviation for journals and magazines. For inclusive page numbers, include all figures: 667-668.

See the next page for an index to APA reference-list models. If you don't see a model for a kind of source you used, try to find one that comes close, and provide ample information so that readers can trace the source. Often you will have to combine models to cite a source accurately.

Listing authors

1. One author

Rodriguez, R. (1982). *A hunger of memory: The education of Richard Rodriguez.* Boston: Godine.

The initial R. appears instead of the author's first name, even though the author's full first name appears on the source. In this book title, only the first words of the title and subtitle and the proper name are capitalized.

2. Two to six authors

Nesselroade, J. R., & Baltes, P. B. (1999). *Longitudinal research in behavioral studies.* New York: Academic Press.

APA reference-list models

Authors

1. One author *785*
2. Two to six authors *785*
3. Seven or more authors *786*
4. A group author *787*
5. Author not named (anonymous) *787*
6. Two or more works by the same author(s) published in the same year *787*

Print periodicals

7. An article in a journal *788, 789*
8. An abstract of a journal article *788*
9. An article in a newspaper *788*
10. An article in a magazine *788*
11. A review *788*

Print books

12. Basic format for a book *790*
13. A book with an editor *790*
14. A book with a translator *790*
15. A later edition *790*
16. A work in more than one volume *790*
17. An article or a chapter in an edited book *791*

Web and other electronic sources

18. A journal article with a Digital Object Identifier (DOI) *791, 792*
19. A journal article without a DOI *793*
20. A journal article in an online database *793*
21. An abstract of a journal article *793*
22. An article in a newspaper *793*
23. An article in a magazine *794*
24. Newspaper or magazine content exclusive to the Web *794*
25. A review *794*
26. A report or other material from the Web site of an organization or government *794*
27. A book *795*
28. An article in a reference work *795*
29. An article in a wiki *795*
30. A dissertation *795*
31. A podcast *796*
32. A film or video recording *796*
33. An image *796*
34. A message posted to a blog or discussion group *796*
35. E-mail or a nonretrievable online posting *796*

Other sources

36. A report *796*
37. A government publication *797*
38. A dissertation *797*
39. An interview *797*
40. A motion picture *798*
41. A musical recording *798*
42. A television series or episode *798*

With two to six authors, separate author's names with commas and use an ampersand (&) before the last author's name.

3. Seven or more authors

Wimple, P. B., Van Eijk, M., Potts, C. A., Hayes, J., Obergau, W. R., Zimmer, S., et al. (2001). *Case studies in moral decision making among adolescents.* San Francisco: Jossey-Bass.

With seven or more authors, substitute et al. (Latin abbreviation for "and others") for all authors' names after the first six.

4. A group author

Lenschow Research. (2008). *Trends in secondary curriculum.* Baltimore: Arrow Books.

For a work with a group author—such as a research group, a committe, a government agency, or a corporation—begin the entry with the group name. In the reference list, alphabetize the work as if the first main word (excluding *The, A,* and *An*) were an author's last name.

5. Author not named (anonymous)

Merriam-Webster's collegiate dictionary (11th ed.). (2008). Springfield, MA: Merriam-Webster.

Let the horse race begin. (2008, March 31). *Time, 171,* 22.

When no author is named, list the work under its title and alphabetize it by the first main word (excluding *The, A, An*).

For a work whose author is actually given as "Anonymous," use that word in place of the author's name and alphabetize it as if it were a name.

Anonymous. (2006). *Teaching research, researching teaching.* New York: Alpine Press.

6. Two or more works by the same author(s) published in the same year

Gardner, H. (1973a). *The arts and human development.* New York: Wiley.

Gardner, H. (1973b). *The quest for mind: Piaget, Lévi-Strauss, and the structuralist movement.* New York: Knopf.

When citing two or more works by exactly the same author(s), published in the same year, arrange them alphabetically by the first main word of the title and distinguish the sources by adding a letter to the date. Both the date and the letter are used in citing the source in your text (see p. 782).

When citing two or more works by exactly the same author(s) but *not* published in the same year, arrange the sources in order of their publication dates, earliest first.

Listing print periodicals: Journals, newspapers, magazines

7. An article in a journal (print)

Selwyn, N. (2005). The social processes of learning to use computers. *Social Science Computer Review, 23*(1), 122-135.

The facing page shows the basic format for a print journal article and the location of the required information in the journal.

Note The APA *Publication Manual* requires a journal's issue number in a reference citation only when the annual volume is not paged consecutively. However, the 2007 APA update, *APA Style Guide to Electronic References*, changed the format to require the citation of both volume and issue numbers if they are available.

8. An abstract of a journal article (print)

Emery, R. E. (2006). Marital turmoil: Interpersonal conflict and the children of discord and divorce. *Psychological Bulletin, 92*(12), 310-330. Abstract obtained from *Psychological Abstracts*, 2007, *69*(3), Item 1320.

When you cite the abstract of an article rather than the article itself, give full publication information for the article, followed by Abstract obtained from and the information for the collection of abstracts, including title, date, volume and issue numbers, and either page number or other reference number (Item 1320 in the example).

9. An article in a newspaper (print)

Stout, D. (2008, May 28). Blind win court ruling on U.S. currency. *The New York Times*, p. A23.

Give month *and* day along with year of publication. Use *The* in the newspaper name if the paper itself does. Precede the page number(s) with p. or pp.

10. An article in a magazine (print)

Wilkinson, A. (2008, June 2). Crime fighting of the future. *The New Yorker*, 26-33.

Give the full date of the issue: year, followed by a comma, month, and day (if any). Give all page numbers even when the article appears on discontinuous pages, without "pp." If a magazine has a volume number, provide it as in model 5.

11. A review (print)

Dinnage, R. (1987, November 29). Against the master and his men [Review of the book *A mind of her own: The life of Karen Horney*]. *The New York Times Book Review*, 10-11.

Format for a print journal article

① ② ③ ④
Selwyn, N. (2005). The social processes of learning to use computers. *Social Science*

⑤ ⑥
Computer Review, 23(1), 122-135.

Journal cover

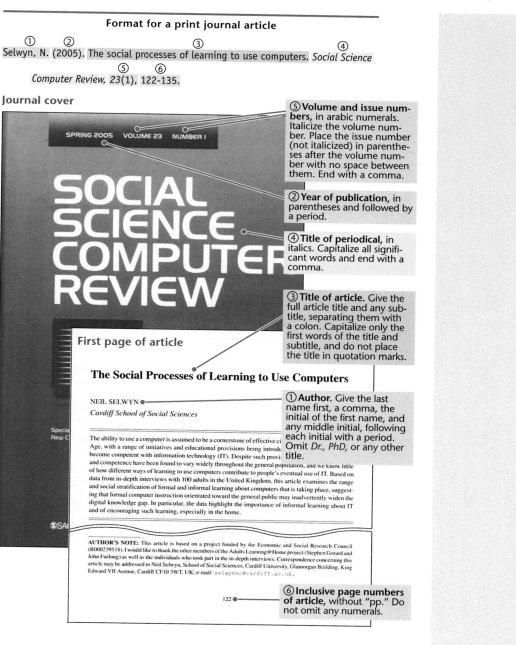

⑤ **Volume and issue numbers,** in arabic numerals. Italicize the volume number. Place the issue number (not italicized) in parentheses after the volume number with no space between them. End with a comma.

② **Year of publication,** in parentheses and followed by a period.

④ **Title of periodical,** in italics. Capitalize all significant words and end with a comma.

③ **Title of article.** Give the full article title and any subtitle, separating them with a colon. Capitalize only the first words of the title and subtitle, and do not place the title in quotation marks.

First page of article

The Social Processes of Learning to Use Computers

NEIL SELWYN
Cardiff School of Social Sciences

The ability to use a computer is assumed to be a cornerstone of effective ci... Age, with a range of initiatives and educational provisions being introdu... become competent with information technology (IT). Despite such provi... and competence have been found to vary widely throughout the general population, and we know little of how different ways of learning to use computers contribute to people's eventual use of IT. Based on data from in-depth interviews with 100 adults in the United Kingdom, this article examines the range and social stratification of formal and informal learning about computers that is taking place, suggesting that formal computer instruction orientated toward the general public may inadvertently widen the digital knowledge gap. In particular, the data highlight the importance of informal learning about IT and of encouraging such learning, especially in the home.

AUTHOR'S NOTE: This article is based on a project funded by the Economic and Social Research Council (R000239518). I would like to thank the other members of the Adults Learning@Home project (Stephen Gorard and John Furlong) as well as the individuals who took part in the in-depth interviews. Correspondence concerning this article may be addressed to Neil Selwyn, School of Social Sciences, Cardiff University, Glamorgan Building, King Edward VII Avenue, Cardiff CF10 3WT, UK; e-mail: selwynnc@cardiff.ac.uk.

122

① **Author.** Give the last name first, a comma, the initial of the first name, and any middle initial, following each initial with a period. Omit *Dr., PhD,* or any other title.

⑥ **Inclusive page numbers of article,** without "pp." Do not omit any numerals.

If the review is not titled, use the bracketed information as the title, keeping the brackets.

Listing print books

12. Basic format for a book (print)

Ehrenreich, B. (2007). *Dancing in the streets: A history of collective joy.* New York: Holt.

Give the author's or authors' names, following models 1–4. Then give the complete title, including any subtitle. Italicize the title, and capitalize only the first words of the title and subtitle. End the entry with the city of publication and the publisher's name. (See p. 785 for how to treat these elements.)

13. A book with an editor (print)

Dohrenwend, B. S., & Dohrenwend, B. P. (Eds.). (1999). *Stressful life events: Their nature and effects.* New York: Wiley.

List the editors' names as if they were authors, but follow the last name with (Eds.).—or (Ed.), with only one editor. Note the periods inside and outside the final parenthesis.

14. A book with a translator (print)

Trajan, P. D. (1927). *Psychology of animals* (H. Simone, Trans.). Washington, DC: Halperin.

The name of the translator appears in parentheses after the title, followed by a comma, Trans. and a closing parenthesis, and a final period. Note also the absence of periods in DC.

15. A later edition (print)

Bolinger, D. L. (1981). *Aspects of language* (3rd ed.). New York: Harcourt Brace Jovanovich.

The edition number in parentheses follows the title and is followed by a period.

16. A work in more than one volume (print)

Lincoln, A. (1953). *The collected works of Abraham Lincoln* (R. P. Basler, Ed.). (Vol. 5). New Brunswick, NJ: Rutgers University Press.

Lincoln, A. (1953). *The collected works of Abraham Lincoln* (R. P. Basler, Ed.). (Vols. 1-8). New Brunswick, NJ: Rutgers University Press.

The first entry cites a single volume (5) in the eight-volume set. The second cites all eight volumes. Use the abbreviation Vol. or Vols. in parentheses and follow the closing parenthesis with a period. In the absence of an editor's name, the description of volumes would follow the title directly: *The collected works of Abraham Lincoln* (Vol. 5).

17. An article or a chapter in an edited book (print)

Paykel, E. S. (1999). Life stress and psychiatric disorder: Applications of the clinical approach. In B. S. Dohrenwend & B. P. Dohrenwend (Eds.), *Stressful life events: Their nature and effects* (pp. 239-264). New York: Wiley.

Give the publication date of the collection (1999 here) as the publication date of the article or chapter. After the article or chapter title and a period, say In and then provide the editors' names (in normal order), (Eds.) and a comma, the title of the collection, and the page numbers of the article in parentheses.

Listing Web and other electronic sources

In 2007 the APA updated its *Publication Manual* with the *APA Style Guide for Electronic References*. Most electronic references begin as those for print references do: author, date, title. Then you add information on how to retrieve the source, generally giving either a DOI (see model 18) or a URL (see model 19). In addition, note the following:

- APA does not require your access date if the source is unlikely to change or if it has a publication date or edition or version number. See models 26 and 28 for use of an access date.
- When you need to divide a URL or DOI from one line to the next, APA calls for breaking before punctuation such as a period or slash. (But break after the two slashes in http://.) Do not hyphenate a URL or a DOI.

If you don't see a model for your particular electronic source, consult the index of models on page 786 for a similar source type whose format you can adapt. If your source does not include all of the information needed for a complete citation, find and list what you can.

18. A journal article with a Digital Object Identifier (DOI) (Web)

Cunningham, J. A., & Selby, P. (2007). Relighting cigarettes: How common is it? *Nicotine and Tobacco Research, 9*(5), 621-623. doi:10.1080 /14622200701239688

The illustration below shows the basic format for a periodical article that you access either directly online or through an online database as well as the location of the required information on the source.

Format for a journal article on the Web

① ② ③
Cunningham, J. A., & Selby, P. (2007). Relighting cigarettes: How common is it?

④ ⑤ ⑥ ⑦
Nicotine and Tobacco Research, 9(5), 621-623. doi:10.1080

/14622200701239688

④ **Title of periodical,** in italics. Capitalize all significant words and end with a comma.

⑤ **Volume and issue numbers,** in arabic numerals. Italicize the volume number. Enclose the issue number (not italicized) in parentheses after the volume number with no space between them. End with a comma.

Top of page

② **Year of publication,** in parentheses and followed by a period.

⑥ **Inclusive page numbers of article,** without "pp." Do not omit any numerals.

③ **Title of article.** Give the full article title and any subtitle, separating them with a colon. Capitalize only the first words of the title and subtitle, and do not place the title in quotation marks.

① **Authors.** Give each author's last name, first initial, and any middle initial. Separate names from initials with commas, and use & before the last author's name. Omit *Dr., PhD,* or any other title. See models 1–4 (pp. 785–87) to cite single and multiple authors.

Bottom of page

⑦ **Retrieval information,** either a DOI (shown here) or a URL (model 19). See model 20 for how to cite an article without a DOI that you retrieve from a database.

Because URLs change often, many publishers now assign a *Uniform Resource Locator* Digital Object Identifier (DOI) to journal articles and other documents. A DOI functions as a unique identifier and a link to the text. When a DOI is available, include it instead of a URL or a database name. (The DOI may be evident on the source, or it may be found by clicking on "Article" or "Cross-Ref.") Do not add a period at the end of the DOI.

19. A journal article without a DOI (Web)

Polletta, F. (2008). Just talk: Public deliberation after 9/11. *Journal of Public Deliberation, 4*(1). Retrieved from http://services.bepress.com/jpd /vol4/iss1/art2

When a journal article does not have a DOI, give its URL instead in a statement beginning Retrieved from. Do not add a period at the end of the URL. If the journal is available only by subscription, give the URL of the journal's home page.

20. A journal article in an online database (Web)

Many reference works and periodicals are available full-text from electronic databases to which your library subscribes, such as ProQuest Direct or LexisNexis. If a database article has a DOI, use model 18. You need not give the database name, as the DOI will lead readers directly to the source.

The APA does not show how to cite an online-database article that lacks a DOI and lacks a URL that others can use. (Many database URLs are not usable because they are unique to the search and/or to the subscribing institution.) Unless your instructor suggests otherwise, give the database name in the retrieval statement, after Retrieved from. Omit any URL.

Rosen, I. M., Maurer, D. M., & Darnall, C. R. (2008). Reducing tobacco use in adolescents. *American Family Physician, 77*(4), 483-490. Retrieved from EBSCOhost Academic Search Premier database.

21. An abstract of a journal article (Web)

Polletta, F. (2008). Just talk: Public deliberation after 9/11. *Journal of Public Deliberation, 4*(1). Abstract retrieved from http://services.bepress.com /jpd/vol4/iss1/art2

22. An article in a newspaper (Web)

Gootman, E. (2008, June 19). Gifted programs in the city are less diverse. *The New York Times*. Retrieved from http://www.nytimes.com

If you consulted a newspaper article on the open Web, give a retrieval statement that includes the URL of the newspaper's home page, as in the example. If you found the article in an online database and the article has an unusable URL, give the name of the database, as in model 23.

23. An article in a magazine (Web)

Young, E. (2008, April 12). Beneath the waves. *New Scientist, 198*, 34-37. Retrieved from Academic Search Elite database.

If you found a magazine article in an online database and the article has an unusable URL, give the name of the database in the retrieval statement, as above. If you consulted a magazine article on the open Web, give the complete URL of the article.

24. Newspaper or magazine content exclusive to the Web (Web)

Gawande, A. (2008, June 30). Can't stop [Online exclusive]. *The New Yorker.* Retrieved from http://www.newyorker.com/online/2008/06/30 /080630on_audio_gawande/

If you cite material from a newspaper's or magazine's Web site that is not included in the print version of the publication, add [Online exclusive] after the title and give the complete URL.

25. A review (Web)

Alvarez, A. (2008, May 29). On the edge [Review of the book *A treatise of civil power*]. *The New York Review of Books, 55*, 27-39. Retrieved from Academic Search Premier database.

Cite an online review like a print review (model 11, p. 788), concluding with retrieval information (here, a database name because the URL is unusable and there is no DOI).

26. A report or other material from the Web site of an organization or government (Web)

Ellerman, D., & Joskow, P. L. (2008, May). *The European Union's emissions trading system in perspective.* Retrieved from the Pew Center on Global Climate Change: http://www.pewclimate.org/eu-ets

McConnell, L. M., Koenig, B. A., Greeley, H. T., & Raffin, T. A. (2004, August 17). *Genetic testing and Alzheimer's disease: Has the time come?* Retrieved from Stanford University, Project in Genomics, Ethics, and Society: http://scbe.stanford.edu/pges

Treat the title of an independent Web document like the title of a book. Provide the name of the sponsoring organization as part of the retrieval statement if the name of the publisher isn't clear from the author's name, the title, or the URL.

If the document you cite has no named author, begin with the title and place the publication date after the title:

> *Clean vehicles.* (2008, April 24). Retrieved from the Union of Concerned Scientists: http://www.ucsusa.org/clean_vehicles

If the document you cite is undated, use the abbreviation n.d. in place of the publication date and give the date of your access in the retrieval statement:

> U.S. Department of Agriculture. (n.d.). *Inside the Pyramid.* Retrieved April 23, 2008, from http://www.mypyramid.gov/pyramid/index.html

27. A book (Web)

> Hernandez, L. M., & Munthali, A. W. (Eds.). (2007). *Training physicians for public health careers.* Retrieved from National Academies Press: http://books.nap.edu/catalog.php?record_id=11915

See models 14–17 (pp. 790–91) to cite variations in book entries: a translator, a later edition, a book in more than one volume, and an article or a chapter in a book.

28. An article in a reference work (Web)

> Perception. (2008). In *Encyclopaedia Britannica Online.* Retrieved September 1, 2008, from http://www.britannica.com

Because the most recent change or update may not be clear from the entry, include the date of your access in the retrieval statement. APA requires only the home page or index page URL for reference works.

29. An article in a wiki (Web)

> Clinical neuropsychology. (2008, January 27). Retrieved from Wikipedia: http://en.wikipedia.org/wiki/Clinical_neuropsychology

If the most recent change or update to the wiki is not clear from the entry, give your date of retrieval.

30. A dissertation (Web)

> McFaddin, M. O. (2007). *Adaptive reuse: An architectural solution for poverty and homelessness.* Retrieved from ProQuest Digital Dissertations. (AAT 1378764)

See also model 38 opposite for examples of print dissertations.

31. A podcast (Web)

Ferracca, J. (Producer). (2008, June 11). Who owns antiquities? *Here on earth: Radio without borders.* Podcast retrieved from http://www.wpr.org /hereonearth/archive_080611k.cfm

32. A film or video recording (Web)

Green Children Foundation (Producer). (2008, January 7). *The green children visit China* [Video file]. Retrieved from http://youtube.com /watch?v=uD4xfLTxCsY

33. An image (Web)

United Nations Population Fund. (2005). *Percent of population living on less than $1/day* [Map]. Retrieved from http://www.unfpa.org/profile /images/map1.jpg

34. A message posted to a blog or discussion group (Web)

Munger, D. (2008, June 19). Does music help us learn language? Message posted to Cognitive Daily blog: http://scienceblogs.com /cognitivedaily/2008/06/does_music_help_us_learn_langu.php

Tourville, M. (2006, January 6). European currency reform. Message posted to International Finance electronic mailing list, archived at http:// www.isu.edu/finance-dl/46732

Include postings to blogs and discussion groups in your list of references *only* if they are retrievable by others. The sources here are retrievable at the addresses given.

35. E-mail or a nonretrievable online posting (text citation)

At least one member of the research team has expressed reservations about the design of the study (L. Kogod, personal communication, February 6, 2006).

Personal e-mail and other online postings that are not retrievable by others should be cited only in your text, as here, not in your list of references.

Listing other sources

36. A report (print)

Gerald, K. (2003). *Medico-moral problems in obstetric care* (Report No. NP-71). St. Louis, MO: Catholic Hospital Association.

Treat the report like a book, but provide any report number in parentheses immediately after the title, with no punctuation between them.

For a report from the Educational Resources Information Center (ERIC), provide the ERIC document number in parentheses at the end of the entry:

> Jolson, M. K. (2001). *Music education for preschoolers* (Report No. TC-622). New York: Teachers College, Columbia University. (ERIC Document Reproduction Service No. ED264488)

37. A government publication (print)

> Hawaii. Department of Education. (2008). *Kauai district schools, profile 2007-08*. Honolulu, HI: Author.

> Stiller, A. (2002). *Historic preservation and tax incentives*. Washington, DC: U.S. Department of the Interior.

> U.S. House. Committee on Ways and Means. (2007). *Medicare payment for outpatient physical and occupational therapy services*. 110th Cong., 1st Sess. Washington, DC: U.S. Government Printing Office.

If no person is named as the author, list the publication under the name of the sponsoring agency. When the agency is both the author and the publisher, use Author in place of the publisher's name, as in the first example.

38. A dissertation (print)

A dissertation abstracted in DAI and obtained from UMI: ⊃ UMI

> Steciw, S. K. (1986). Alterations to the Pessac project of Le Corbusier. *Dissertation Abstracts International, 46*(6), 5650. (UMI No. 6216202)

A dissertation abstracted in DAI and obtained from the university:

> Chang, J. K. (2003). Therapeutic intervention in treatment of injuries to the hand and wrist (Doctoral dissertation, University of Michigan, 2003). *Dissertation Abstracts International, 50*(3), 162.

An unpublished dissertation:

> Holcomb, C. M. (2008). *Dance as therapy for reducing anxiety in elementary-age children: Case studies in grades 1 through 6*. Unpublished doctoral dissertation, University of Washington.

39. An interview (print)

> Schenker, H. (2007). No peace without third-party intervention [Interview with Shulamit Aloni]. *Palestine-Israel Journal of Politics, Economics, and Culture, 14*(4), 63-68.

List a published interview under the interviewer's name, and provide the title, if any, without italics or quotation marks. If there is no title, or if the title does not indicate the interview format or the interviewee (as in the example), add a bracketed explanation. End with the publication information for the kind of source the interview appears in (here, a journal).

An interview you conduct yourself should not be included in the list of references. Instead, use an in-text parenthetical citation, as shown in model 35 (p. 796) for a nonretrievable online posting.

40. A motion picture

American Psychological Association (Producer). (2001). *Ethnocultural psychotherapy* [Motion picture]. (Available from the American Psychological Association, 750 First Street, NE, Washington, DC 20002-4242, or online from http://www.apa.org/videos/4310240.html)

Howard, R. (Director). (2001). *A beautiful mind* [Motion picture]. United States: Universal.

A motion picture may be a film, DVD, or video. Depending on whose work you are citing, begin with the name or names of the creator, director, producer, or primary contributor, followed by the function in parentheses. (The second example would begin with the producer's name if you were citing the motion picture as a whole, not specifically the work of the director.) Add [Motion picture] after the title. For a motion picture in wide circulation (second example), give the country of origin and the name of the organization that released the picture. For a motion picture that is not widely circulated (first example), give the distributor's name and address in parentheses.

41. A musical recording

Springsteen, B. (2002). Empty sky. On *The rising* [CD]. New York: Columbia.

Begin with the name of the writer or composer. (If you cite another artist's recording of the work, provide this information after the title of the work—for example, [Recorded by E. Davila].) Give the medium in brackets ([CD], [LP], and so on). Finish with the city and name of the recording label.

42. A television series or episode

Rhimes, S. (Executive Producer). (2008). *Grey's anatomy* [Television series]. San Francisco: CBS.

McKee S. (Writer), & Tinker, M. (Director). (2008). Piece of my heart [Television series episode]. In S. Rhimes (Executive Producer), *Grey's anatomy*. San Francisco: CBS.

For a television series, begin with the producers' names and identify their function in parentheses. Add [Television series] after the series title, and give the city and name of the network. For an episode, begin with the writer and then the director, identifying the function of each in parentheses, and add [Television series episode] after the episode title. Then provide the series information, beginning with In and the producers' names and function, giving the series title, and ending with the city and name of the network.

51e Formatting documents in APA style

The APA *Publication Manual* distinguishes between documents intended for publication (which will be set in type) and those submitted by students (which are the final copy). The following guidelines apply to most undergraduate papers. Check with your instructor for any modifications to this format.

Note See pages 783–85 for the APA format of a reference list. And see pages 117–26 for guidelines on type fonts, lists, tables and figures, and other elements of document design.

Margins Use one-inch margins on the top, bottom, and right side. Add another half-inch on the left to accommodate a binder.

Spacing and indentions Double-space your text and references. (See p. 801 for spacing of displayed quotations.) Indent paragraphs and displayed quotations one-half inch or five to seven spaces.

Paging Begin numbering on the title page, and number consecutively through the end (including the reference list). Type Arabic numerals (1, 2, 3) in the upper right, about half an inch from the top.

Place a shortened version of your title five spaces to the left of the page number.

Title page Include the full title, your name, the course title, the instructor's name, and the date. (See the next page.) Type the title on the top half of the page, followed by the identifying information, all centered horizontally and double-spaced. Include a shortened form of the title along with the page number at the top of this and all other pages.

Abstract Summarize (in a maximum of 120 words) your subject, research method, findings, and conclusions. (See the next page.) Put the abstract on a page by itself.

Body Begin with a restatement of the paper's title and then an introduction (not labeled). (See the next page.) The introduction presents the problem you researched, your method, the relevant background (such as related studies), and the purpose of your research.

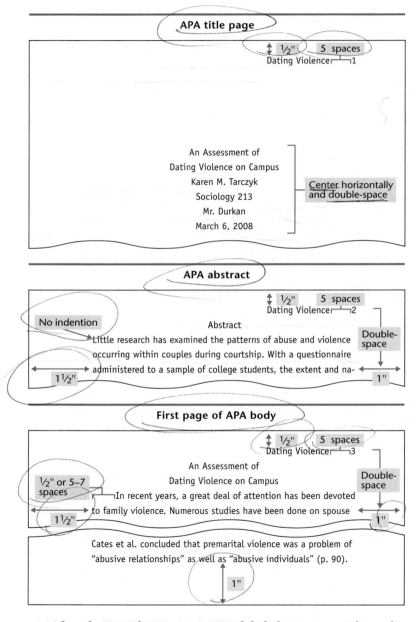

APA title page

½"   5 spaces
Dating Violence ⌐ 1

An Assessment of
Dating Violence on Campus
Karen M. Tarczyk
Sociology 213
Mr. Durkan
March 6, 2008

Center horizontally
and double-space

APA abstract

½"   5 spaces
Dating Violence ⌐ 2

No indention

Abstract

Double-space

Little research has examined the patterns of abuse and violence occurring within couples during courtship. With a questionnaire administered to a sample of college students, the extent and na-

1½"

1"

First page of APA body

½"   5 spaces
Dating Violence ⌐ 3

An Assessment of
Dating Violence on Campus

½" or 5–7
spaces

In recent years, a great deal of attention has been devoted to family violence. Numerous studies have been done on spouse

Double-space

1½"

1"

Cates et al. concluded that premarital violence was a problem of "abusive relationships" as well as "abusive individuals" (p. 90).

1"

After the introduction, a section labeled Method provides a detailed discussion of how you conducted your research, including a description of the research subjects, any materials or tools you used (such as questionnaires), and the procedure you followed. In the illustration below, the label Method is a <u>first-level heading</u> and the label *Sample* is a second-level heading.

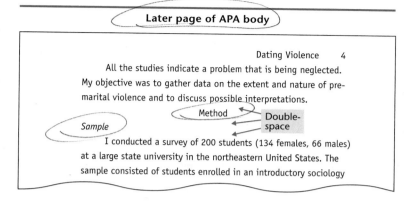

Later page of APA body

Dating Violence   4

All the studies indicate a problem that is being neglected. My objective was to gather data on the extent and nature of pre-marital violence and to discuss possible interpretations.

Method ← Double-space

Sample

I conducted a survey of 200 students (134 females, 66 males) at a large state university in the northeastern United States. The sample consisted of students enrolled in an introductory sociology

Format headings (including a third level, if needed) as follows:

First-Level Heading

Second-Level Heading

Third-level heading. Run this heading into the text paragraph with a standard paragraph indention.

The Results section (labeled with a <u>first-level heading</u>) summarizes the data you collected, explains how you analyzed them, and presents them in detail, often in tables, graphs, or charts.

The Discussion section (labeled with a <u>first-level heading</u>) interprets the data and presents your conclusions. (When the discussion is brief, you may combine it with the previous section under the heading Results and Discussion.)

The References section, beginning a new page, includes all your sources. See pages 783–85 for an explanation and sample.

Long quotations Run into your text all quotations of forty words or less, and enclose them in quotation marks. For quotations of more than forty words, set them off from your text by indenting all lines one-half inch or five spaces, double-spacing above and below. For student papers, the APA allows single-spacing of displayed quotations:

Echoing the opinions of other Europeans at the time, Freud (1961) had a poor view of Americans:

> The Americans are really too bad. . . . Competition is much more pungent with them, not succeeding means civil death to every one, and they have no private resources apart from their profession, no hobby, games, love or other interests of a cultured person. And success means money. (p. 86)

Do not use quotation marks around a quotation displayed in this way.

Illustrations Present data in tables, graphs, or charts, as appropriate. (See the sample on p. 804 for a clear table format to follow.) Begin each illustration on a separate page. Number each kind of illustration consecutively and separately from the other (Table 1, Table 2, etc., and Figure 1, Figure 2, etc.). Refer to all illustrations in your text—for instance, (see Figure 3). Generally, place illustrations immediately after the text references to them. (See pp. 121–25 for more on illustrations.)

51f Examining a sample social science paper

Below and on the following pages are excerpts from a sociology paper. The student followed the organization described on the preceding pages both in establishing the background for her study and in explaining her own research. She also followed the APA style of source citation and document format, although page borders and running heads are omitted here and only the required page breaks are indicated.

Excerpts from a research report

[Title page.]

An Assessment of

Dating Violence on Campus

Karen M. Tarczyk

Sociology 213

Mr. Durkan

March 6, 2008

[New page.]

Abstract

Little research has examined the patterns of abuse and violence occurring within couples during courtship. With a questionnaire administered to a sample of college students, the extent and nature of such abuse and violence were investigated. The results, some interpretations, and implications for further research are discussed.

[New page.]

An Assessment of Dating

Violence on Campus

In recent years, a great deal of attention has been devoted to family violence. Numerous studies have been done on spouse and child abuse. However, violent behavior occurs in dating relationships as well, yet the problem of dating violence has been relatively ignored by sociological research. It should be examined

---

further since the premarital relationship is one context in which individuals learn and adopt behaviors that surface later in marriage.

The sociologist James Makepeace (1989) contended that courtship violence is a "potential mediating link" between violence in one's family of orientation and violence in one's later family of procreation (p. 103). Studying dating behaviors at Bemidji State University in Minnesota, Makepeace reported that one-fifth of the respondents had had at least one encounter with dating violence. He then extended these percentages to students nationwide, suggesting the existence of a major hidden social problem.

More recent research supports Makepeace's. Cates, Rutter, Karl, Linton, and Smith (2000) found that 22.3% of respondents at Oregon State University had been either the victim or the perpetrator of premarital violence. Another study (Cortes, 2005) found that so-called date rape, while much more publicized and discussed, was reported by many fewer woman respondents (2%) than was other violence during courtship (21%).

[The introduction continues.]

All these studies indicate a problem that is being neglected. My objective was to gather data on the extent and nature of premarital violence and to discuss possible interpretations.

Method

Sample

I conducted a survey of 200 students (134 females, 66 males) at a large state university in the northeastern United States. The sample consisted of students enrolled in an introductory sociology course.

[The explanation of method continues.]

The Questionnaire

A questionnaire exploring the personal dynamics of relationships was distributed during regularly scheduled class. Questions were answered anonymously in a 30-minute time period. The survey consisted of three sections.

[The explanation of method continues.]

Section 3 required participants to provide information about their current dating relationships. Levels of stress and frustration, communication between partners, and patterns of decision making were examined. These variables were expected to influence the amount of violence in a relationship. The next part of the survey was adopted from Murray Strauss's Conflict Tactics Scales (1992). These scales contain 19 items designed to measure conflict and the means of conflict resolution, including reasoning, verbal aggression, and actual violence.

Results

The questionnaire revealed significant levels of verbal aggression and threatened and actual violence among dating couples. A high number of students, 50% (62 of 123 subjects), reported that they had been the victim of verbal abuse. In addition, almost 14% (17 of 123) of respondents admitted being threatened with some type of violence, and more than 14% (18 of 123) reported being pushed, grabbed, or shoved. (See Table 1.)

[The explanation of results continues.]

[Table on a page by itself.]

Table 1

Incidence of Courtship Violence

Type of violence	Number of students reporting	Percentage of sample
Insulted or swore	62	50.4
Threatened to hit or throw something	17	13.8
Threw something	8	6.5
Pushed, grabbed, or shoved	18	14.6
Slapped	8	6.5
Kicked, bit, or hit with fist	7	5.7
Hit or tried to hit with something	2	1.6
Threatened with a knife or gun	1	0.8
Used a knife or gun	1	0.8

Discussion

Violence within premarital relationships has been relatively ignored. The results of the present study indicate that abuse and force do occur in dating relationships. Although the percentages are small, so was the sample. Extending them to the entire campus population would mean significant numbers. For example, if the nearly 6% incidence of being kicked, bitten, or hit with a fist is typical, then 300 students of a 5,000-member student body might have experienced this type of violence.

[The discussion continues.]

If the courtship period is characterized by abuse and violence, what accounts for it? The other sections of the survey examined some variables that appear to influence the relationship. Level of stress and frustration, both within the relationship and in the respondent's life, was one such variable. The communication level between partners, both the frequency of discussion and the frequency of agreement, was another.

[The discussion continues.]

The method of analyzing the data in this study, utilizing frequency distributions, provided a clear overview. However, more tests of significance and correlation and a closer look at the social and individual variables affecting the relationship are warranted. The courtship period may set the stage for patterns of married life. It merits more attention.

[New page.]

References

Cates, R. L., Rutter, C. H., Karl, J., Linton, M., & Smith, K. (2000). Premarital abuse: A social psychological perspective. *Journal of Family Issues, 13*(1), 79-90.

Cortes, L. (2005). Beyond date rape: Violence during courtship. *Electronic Journal of Intimate Violence, 5*(2). Retrieved from http://www.acast.nova.edu/health /psy/file-disc/file50.html

Glaser, R., & Rutter, C. H. (Eds.). (1999). Familial violence [Special issue]. *Family Relations, 43*(4).

Makepeace, J. M. (1989). Courtship violence among college students. *Family Relations, 28*(6), 97-103.

Strauss, M. L. (1992). *Conflict Tactics Scales.* New York: Sociological Tests.

52

Writing in the Natural and Applied Sciences

The natural and applied sciences include biology, chemistry, physics, mathematics, engineering, computer science, and their branches. Their purpose is to understand natural and technological phenomena. (A *phenomenon* is a fact or event that can be known by the senses.) Scientists conduct experiments and write to explain the step-by-step processes in their methods of inquiry and discovery.

Visit *mycomplab.com* for more resources on writing in the natural and applied sciences.

HIGHLIGHTS

Chapter 52 introduces students to the essentials of writing in the natural and applied sciences. A brief discussion of the scientific method and empirical evidence begins the chapter, followed by discussions of types of science assignments (summaries, critiques, lab reports, research reports, and research proposals), writing tools, and language conventions. Library and online resources for research are listed, and there are sections on how to cite sources and format documents in the natural and applied sciences according to *Scientific Style and Format, The CSE Manual for Authors, Editors, and Publishers*. 7th ed. (2006). The chapter concludes with excerpts from a sample student lab report for a biology course.

RESOURCES AND IDEAS

Carter, Michael. "Ways of Knowing, Doing, and Writing in the Disciplines." *College Composition and Communication* 58.3 (2007): 385–418. Print. Carter uses genre theory to offer a way for WID professionals to engage more meaningfully with faculty. The appendix includes sample outcome statements for zoology, psychology, and textiles engineering departments.

Greenway, William. "Imaginary Gardens with Real Toads: Nature Writing in the Curriculum." *Teaching English in the Two-Year College* 17.3 (1990): 189–92. Print. Greenway demonstrates that nature writing, such as Annie Dillard's personal essays and Wordsworth's poetry, can help prepare students to write scientific research papers.

Hamilton, David. "Writing Science." *College English* 40.1 (1978): 32–40. Print. Hamilton argues that instruction in science writing should emphasize writing not simply as a tool for scientists but as an essential and creative part of the scientific act.

Vargas, Marjorie Fink. "Writing Skills for Science Labs." *The Science Teacher* 53.8 (1986): 29–33. Print. The author describes a fifty-minute class activity that helps students understand choices of person and voice dictated by the stylistic conventions of lab reports.

Winsor, Dorothy A. "Engineering Writing/Writing Engineering." *College Composition and Communication* 41.1 (1990): 58–70. Print. Winsor uses "contemporary views about the textual shaping of knowledge" to examine engineers' writing and their "domain-specific" knowledge.

Zimmet, Nancy. "Engaging the Disaffected: Collaborative Writing across the Curriculum Projects." *English Journal* 90.1 (2000): 102–06. Print. Zimmet describes a collaboration between high school science teachers and the science faculty at a local university, and describes how writing was used.

52a Using the methods and evidence of the sciences

Scientists investigate phenomena by the **scientific method**, a process of continual testing and refinement.

The scientific method

- **Observe carefully.** Accurately note all details of the phenomenon being researched.
- **Ask questions about the observations.**
- **Formulate a** *hypothesis,* or preliminary generalization, that explains the observed facts.
- **Test the hypothesis** with additional observation or controlled experiments.
- **If the hypothesis proves accurate, formulate a** *theory,* or unified model, that explains *why.*
- **If the hypothesis is disproved, revise it or start anew.**

Scientific evidence is almost always quantitative—that is, it consists of numerical data obtained from the measurement of phenomena. These data are called **empirical** (from a Greek word for "experience"); they result from observation and experience, generally in a controlled laboratory setting but also (as sometimes in astronomy or biology) in the natural world. Often the empirical evidence for scientific writing comes from library research into other people's reports of their investigations. Surveys of known data or existing literature are common in scientific writing.

52b Understanding writing assignments in the sciences

No matter what your assignment, you will be expected to document and explain your evidence carefully so that anyone reading can check your sources and replicate your research. It is important for your reader to know the context of your research—both the previous experimentation and research on your particular subject (acknowledged in the survey of the literature) and the physical conditions and other variables surrounding your own work.

Assignments in the natural and applied sciences include the following:

- **A summary** distills a research article to its essence in brief, concise form. (Summary is discussed in detail on pp. 134–35.)
- **A critique** summarizes and critically evaluates a scientific report.

■ **A laboratory report** explains the procedure and results of an experiment conducted by the writer. (See p. 818 for an example.)
■ **A research report** explains the experimental research of other scientists and the writer's own methods, findings, and conclusions.
■ **A research proposal** reviews the relevant literature and explains a plan for further research.

A laboratory report has four or five major sections:

1. **"Abstract"**: a summary of the report.
2. **"Introduction" or "Objective"**: a review of why the study was undertaken, a summary of the background of the study, and a statement of the problem being studied.
3. **"Method" or "Procedure"**: a detailed explanation of how the study was conducted, including any statistical analysis.
4. **"Results"**: an explanation of the major findings (including unexpected results) and a summary of the data presented in graphs and tables.
5. **"Discussion"**: an interpretation of the results and an explanation of how they relate to the goals of the experiment. This section also describes new hypotheses that might be tested as a result of the experiment. If the section is brief, it may be combined with the previous section in a single section labeled "Conclusions."

In addition, laboratory or research reports may include a list of references (if other sources were consulted). They almost always include tables and figures (graphs and charts) containing the data from the research (see p. 819).

52c Using the tools and language of the sciences

Tools and language concerns vary from discipline to discipline in the sciences. Consult your instructor for specifics about the field in which you are writing. You can also discover much about a discipline's tools and language from the research sources listed on the next three pages.

1 Writing tools

In the sciences a **lab notebook** or **scientific journal** is almost indispensable for accurately recording the empirical data from observations and experiments. Use such a notebook or journal for these purposes:

■ **Record observations** from reading, from class, or from the lab.
■ **Ask questions and refine hypotheses.**

■ **Record procedures.**
■ **Record results.**
■ **Keep an ongoing record of ideas and findings** and how they change as data accumulate.
■ **Sequence and organize your material** as you compile your findings and write your report.

Make sure that your records of data are clearly separate from your reflections on the data so that you don't mistakenly confuse the two in drawing your conclusions.

2 Language considerations

Science writers prefer to use objective language that removes the writer as a character in the situation and events being explained, except as the impersonal agent of change, the experimenter. Although usage is changing, scientists still rarely use *I* in their reports and evaluations, and they often resort to the passive voice of verbs, as in *The mixture was then subjected to centrifugal force.* This conscious objectivity focuses attention (including the writer's) on the empirical data and what they show. It discourages the writer from, say, ascribing motives and will to animals and plants. For instance, instead of asserting that the sea tortoise *evolved* its hard shell *to protect* its body, a scientist would write only what could be observed: that the hard shell *covers and thus protects* the tortoise's body.

Science writers typically change verb tenses to distinguish between established information and their own research. For established information, such as that found in journals and other reliable sources, use the present tense: *Baroreceptors monitor blood pressure.* For your own and others' research, use the past tense: *The bacteria died within three hours. Marti reported some success.*

Each discipline in the natural and applied sciences has a specialized vocabulary that permits precise, accurate, and efficient communication. Some of these terms, such as *pressure* in physics, have different meanings in the common language and must be handled carefully in science writing. Others, such as *enthalpy* in chemistry, have no meanings in the common language and must simply be learned and used correctly.

3 Research sources

The following lists give resources in the sciences.

Specialized encyclopedias, dictionaries, and bibliographies

American Medical Association Encyclopedia of Medicine
Concise Encyclopedia of Computer Science

Concise Oxford Dictionary of Mathematics
Dorland's Illustrated Medical Dictionary
Encyclopedia of Astronomy and Astrophysics
Encyclopedia of Bioethics
Encyclopedia of Chemistry
Encyclopedia of Electronics
Encyclopedia of Environmental Science
Encyclopedia of Geology
Encyclopedia of Physics
Grzimek's Animal Life Encyclopedia
Introduction to Reference Sources in Health Sciences
McGraw-Hill Encyclopedia of Science and Technology
Science and Technology in World History
Space Almanac
Van Nostrand's Scientific Encyclopedia
Wiley Encyclopedia of Electrical and Electronics Engineering
World Resources (environment)

Library databases and indexes

ACM Digital Library
Aerospace and High Technology Database
Applied Science and Technology Index
Biological Abstracts
Biological and Agricultural Index
Chemical Abstracts
CINAHL: Cumulative Index to Nursing and Allied Health Literature
Compendex Engineering Index
Computer Abstracts
Dissertation Abstracts International
Ecology Abstracts
GeoRef
Inspec
MathSciNet: Mathematical Reviews
Medline
Pollution Abstracts
Science Citation Index
Toxline

Book reviews

Technical Book Review Index

Sources on the open Web

General

BUBL LINK: Natural Sciences and Mathematics (*bubl.ac.uk/linkbrowse
.cfm?menuid=6402*)
Google Directory: Science (*directory.google.com/Top/Science*)
Intute: Science, Engineering and Technology (*www.intute.ac.uk/sciences*)
Librarians' Internet Index: Science (*search.lii.org/index.jsp?more=SubTopic13*)

RESOURCES AND IDEAS

Ambron, Joanna. "Writing to Improve Learning in Biology." *Journal of College Science Teaching* 16.4 (1987): 263–66. Print. Ambron shows how using journal entries, freewriting, and short ungraded essays contribute to improved analytical skills.

Coghill, Anne M., and Lorrin R. Garson, eds.. *The ACS Style Guide: Effective Communication of Scientific Information.* 3rd ed. Washington: ACS, 2006. Print.

Dorroh, John. "Reflections on Expressive Writing in the Science Class." *The Quarterly of the National Writing Project and the Center for the Study of Writing and Literacy* 15.3 (1993): 28–30. Print. Dorroh describes use of an "expressive mode" notebook, portfolio grading, and writing-based instruction to improve student performance.

Gardner, Susan, and Toby Fulwiler. *The Journal Book: For Teachers in Technical and Professional Programs.* Portsmouth: Boynton/Cook, 1998. Print. This collection offers numerous ways to incorporate journals and letter writing into courses in fields outside liberal arts, including engineering, nursing, and medicine.

Goodman, W. Daniel, and John C. Bean. "A Chemistry Laboratory Project to Develop Thinking and Writing Skills." *Journal of Chemical Education* 60.6 (1983): 483–84. Print. The authors outline "a method for conducting an undergraduate chemistry laboratory, in this case sophomore organic chemistry, that integrates a project laboratory with a writing task involving peer group interaction." The method requires "students to carry out an independent investigation of the synthesis of one or more aliphatic esters and to present their research in the form of professional papers."

Johnstone, Anne C., et al. *Uses for Journal-Keeping: An Ethnography of Writing in a University Science Class.* Norwood: Ablex, 1994. Print. Johnstone offers an ethnographic study of the uses of different writing activities in learning science.

Killingsworth, M. Jimmie, and Michael K. Gilbertson. *Signs, Genres, and Communities in Technical Communication.* Amityville: Baywood,

1992. Print. An examination of reports, manuals, and proposals characterizes them as "crystals of social action" within particular discourse communities.

Monroe, Jonathan, ed. *Local Knowledges, Local Practices: Writing in the Disciplines at Cornell.* Pittsburgh: U of Pittsburgh P, 2003. Print. This collection discusses how writing is used in many fields at Cornell, including animal science and neurobiology.

Moskovitz, Cary, and David Kellogg. "Primary Science Communication in the First-Year Writing Course." *College Composition and Communication* 57.2 (2005): 307–34. Print. Noting the recent expansion of texts both studied and produced in composition courses, the authors argue "that scientific literature be treated equally with other texts when instructors and program administrators think about what *might* be included in writing courses" (329).

Wilkinson, A. M. "Jargon and the Passive Voice: Prescriptions and Proscriptions for Scientific Writing." *Journal of Technical Writing and Communication* 22.3 (1992): 319–25. Print. The author reviews circumstances under which scientific writers should use the passive voice and warns against sweeping prohibitions of this strategy.

Young, Art, and Toby Fulwiler. *Writing Across the Disciplines: Research into Practice.* Upper Montclair: Boynton/Cook, 1986. Print. This collection contains a number of essays demonstrating writing assignments in the sciences.

The National Academies: Science, Engineering, and Medicine (nas.edu)
The Public Library of Science (www.plos.org)
WWW Virtual Library: Natural Sciences and Mathematics (vlib.org/Science.html)

Biology
Biology.Arizona.Edu (biology.arizona.edu)
National Biological Information Infrastructure (www.nbii.gov)

Chemistry
Chemistry.org (chemistry.org/portal/a/c/s/1/home.html)
ChemSpy (www.chemspy.com)
ChemWeb (www.chemweb.com)
WWW Virtual Library: Links for Chemists (liv.ac.uk/Chemistry/Links/links.html)

Computer science
IEEE Computer Society (computer.org)
University of Texas Virtual Computer Library (utexas.edu/computer/vcl)
WWW Virtual Library: Computing and Computer Science (vlib.org/Computing)

Engineering
National Academy of Engineering (nae.edu)
TechXtra: Engineering, Mathematics, and Computing (www.techxtra.ac.uk)

Environmental science
Center for International Earth Science Information Network (ciesin.org)
EE-Link: Environmental Education on the Internet (eelink.net)
EnviroLink (envirolink.org)
Environment Directory (webdirectory.com)

Geology
American Geological Institute (www.agiweb.org)
Digital Library for Earth System Education (dlese.org)
Geosource (www.library.uu.nl/geosource)
US Geological Survey Library (library.usgs.gov)

Health sciences
American Medical Association (ama-assn.org)
Centers for Disease Control and Prevention (www.cdc.gov)
Hardin MD (www.lib.uiowa.edu/hardin/md)
PubMed (www.ncbi.nlm.nih.gov/sites/entrez)
World Health Organization (who.int/en)

Mathematics
Internet Mathematics Library (mathforum.org/library)
Mathematical Atlas (math-atlas.org)

Physics and astronomy
American Institute of Physics (aip.org)
Astronomy Links (astronomylinks.com)
PhysicsWeb (physicsweb.org)
Science@NASA (science.hq.nasa.gov/index.html)

52d Citing sources in CSE style

Within the natural and applied sciences, practitioners use one of two styles of documentation, varying slightly from discipline to discipline. Following are some of the style guides most often consulted:

American Chemical Society, *ACS Style Guide: A Manual for Authors and Editors*, 3rd ed., 2006

American Institute of Physics, *Style Manual for Guidance in the Preparation of Papers*, 4th ed., 1997

American Medical Association Manual of Style, 10th ed., 2007

Council of Science Editors, *Scientific Style and Format: The CSE Manual for Authors, Editors, and Publishers*, 7th ed., 2006

The most thorough and widely used of these guides is the last one, *Scientific Style and Format*, which details both styles of scientific documentation: one using author and date and one using numbers. Both types of text citation refer to a list of references at the end of the paper (see the next page). Ask your instructor which style you should use.

1 Using CSE name-year text citations

In the CSE name-year style, parenthetical text citations provide the last name of the author being cited and the source's year of publication. At the end of the paper, a list of references, arranged alphabetically by authors' last names, provides complete information on each source.

The CSE name-year style closely resembles the APA name-year style detailed on pages 779–99. You can follow the APA examples for in-text citations, making several notable changes for CSE:

- **Do not use a comma to separate the author's name and the date:** (Baumrind 1968, p. 34).
- **Separate two authors' names with and (not "&"):** (Pepinsky and DeStefano 1997).
- **For sources with three or more authors, use et al. (Latin abbreviation for "and others") after the first author's name:** (Rutter et al. 1996).

2 Using CSE numbered text citations

In the CSE number style, raised numbers in the text refer to a numbered list of references at the end of the paper.

Two standard references[1,2] use this term.

These forms of immunity have been extensively researched.[3]

Hepburn and Tatin[2] do not discuss this project.

Assignment of numbers The number for each source is based on the order in which you cite the source in the text: the first cited source is 1, the second is 2, and so on.

Reuse of numbers When you cite a source you have already cited and numbered, use the original number again (see the last example on the previous page, which reuses the number 2 from the first example).

This reuse is the key difference between the CSE numbered citations and numbered references to footnotes or endnotes. In the CSE style, each source has only one number, determined by the order in which the source is cited. With notes, in contrast, the numbering proceeds in sequence, so that each source has as many numbers as it has citations in the text.

Citation of two or more sources When you cite two or more sources at once, arrange their numbers in sequence and separate them with a comma and no space, as in the first example on the previous page.

3 Using a CSE reference list

For both the name-year and the number styles of in-text citation, provide a list, titled References, of all sources you have cited. Format the page as shown for APA references on page 784, except that CSE entries are single-spaced.

The following examples show the differences and similarities between the name-year and number styles:

Name-year style

Hepburn PX, Tatin JM. 2005. Human physiology. New York (NY): Columbia University Press.

Number style

2. Hepburn PX, Tatin JM. Human physiology. New York (NY): Columbia University Press; 2005.

Spacing In both styles, single-space each entry and double-space between entries.

Arrangement In the name-year style, arrange entries alphabetically by authors' last names. In the number style, arrange entries in numerical order—that is, in order of their citation in the text.

Format In both styles, begin the first line of each entry at the left margin and indent subsequent lines.

Authors In both styles, list each author's name with the last name first, followed by initials for first and middle names. Do not use a comma between an author's last name and initials, and do not use periods or spaces with the initials. Do use a comma to separate authors' names.

Placement of dates In the name-year style, the date follows the author's or authors' names. In the number style, the date follows the publication information (for a book) or the periodical title (for a journal, magazine, or newspaper).

Journal titles In both styles, do not italicize or underline journal titles. For titles of two or more words, abbreviate words of six or more letters (without periods) and omit most prepositions, articles, and conjunctions. Capitalize each word. For example, *Journal of Chemical and Biochemical Studies* becomes J Chem Biochem Stud.

Book and article titles In both styles, do not italicize, underline, or use quotation marks around a book or an article title. Capitalize only the first word and any proper nouns.

Publication information for journal articles The name-year and number styles differ in the placement of the publication date (see opposite). However, both styles end with the journal's volume number, any issue number in parentheses, a colon, and the inclusive page numbers of the article, run together without space: 28:329-30 or 62(2):26-40.

The following box indexes the CSE models. The models include examples of both a name-year reference and a number reference for each type of source.

CSE reference-list models

Authors
1. One author *814*
2. Two to ten authors *814*
3. More than ten authors *814*
4. Author not named *814*
5. Two or more cited works by the same author(s) published in the same year *814*

Print periodicals
6. An article in a journal *814*
7. An article in a newspaper *814*
8. An article in a magazine *815*

Print books
9. Basic format for a book *815*
10. A book with an editor *815*
11. A selection from a book *815*

Web and other electronic sources
12. An article in a journal *815*
13. An article in a database *815*
14. A book *816*
15. A Web site *816*
16. A message posted to a discussion list *816*
17. A personal online communication *817*
18. A document on CD-ROM or DVD-ROM *817*

Other sources
19. A report written and published by the same organization *817*
20. A report written and published by different organizations *817*
21. An audio or visual recording *817*

Listing authors

1. One author

Gould SJ. 1987. Time's arrow, time's cycle. Cambridge (MA): Harvard University Press.

1. Gould SJ. Time's arrow, time's cycle. Cambridge (MA): Harvard University Press; 1987.

2. Two to ten authors

Hepburn PX, Tatin JM, Tatin JP. 2008. Human physiology. New York (NY): Columbia University Press.

2. Hepburn PX, Tatin JM, Tatin JP. Human physiology. New York (NY): Columbia University Press; 2008.

3. More than ten authors

Evans RW, Bowditch L, Dana KL, Drumond A, Wildovitch WP, Young SL, Mills P, Mills RR, Livak SR, Lisi OL, et al. 2004. Organ transplants: ethical issues. Ann Arbor (MI): University of Michigan Press.

3. Evans RW, Bowditch L, Dana KL, Drummond A, Wildovitch WP, Young SL, Mills P, Mills RR, Livak SR, Lisi OL, et al. Organ transplants: ethical issues. Ann Arbor (MI): University of Michigan Press; 2004.

4. Author not named

Health care for children with diabetes. 2008. New York (NY): US Health Care.

4. Health care for children with diabetes. New York (NY): US Health Care; 2008.

5. Two or more cited works by the same author(s) published in the same year

Gardner H. 1973a. The arts and human development. New York (NY): Wiley.

Gardner H. 1973b. The quest for mind: Piaget, Lévi-Strauss, and the structuralist movement. New York (NY): Knopf.

(The number style does not require such forms.)

Listing print periodicals: Journals, newspapers, magazines

6. An article in a journal (print)

Kim P. 2006. Medical decision making for the dying. Milbank Quar. 64(2):26-40.

6. Kim P. Medical decision making for the dying. Milbank Quar. 2006;64(2):26-40.

If a journal article has a Digital Object Identifier (DOI), you may include the number at the end of the entry for readers' convenience. (See p. 793 for more on DOIs.)

7. An article in a newspaper (print)

Stout D. 2008 May 28. Blind win court ruling on US currency. New York Times (National Ed.). Sect. A:23 (col. 3).

7. Stout, D. Blind win court ruling on US currency. New York Times (National Ed.). 2008 May 28;Sect. A:23 (col. 3).

8. An article in a magazine (print)

Wilkinson A. 2008 June 2. Crime fighting of the future. New Yorker. 26-33.

8. Wilkinson A. Crime fighting of the future. New Yorker. 2008 June 2:26-33.

Listing print books

9. Basic format for a book (print)

Wilson EO. 2004. On human nature. Cambridge (MA): Harvard University Press.

9. Wilson EO. On human nature. Cambridge (MA): Harvard University Press; 2004.

10. A book with an editor (print)

Jonson P, editor. 2008. Anatomy yearbook 2008. Los Angeles (CA): Anatco.

10. Jonson P, editor. Anatomy yearbook 2008. Los Angeles (CA): Anatco; 2008.

11. A selection from a book (print)

Krigel R, Laubenstein L, Muggia F. 2005. Kaposi's sarcoma. In: Ebbeson P, Biggar RS, Melbye M, editors. AIDS: a basic guide for clinicians. 2nd ed. Philadelphia (PA): Saunders. p. 100-26.

11. Kriegel R. Laubenstein L, Muggia F. Kaposi's sarcoma. In: Ebbeson P, Biggar RS, Melbye M, editors. AIDS: a basic guide for clinicians. 2nd ed. Philadelphia (PA): Saunders; 2005. p. 100-26.

Listing Web and other electronic sources

Do not add a period after a URL at the end of an entry. If you must break a URL from one line to the next, do so only after a slash, and do not hyphenate.

12. An article in a journal (Web)

Grady GF. 2007. The here and now of hepatitis B immunization. Today's Med [Internet]. [cited 2007 Dec 7]; 6(2):39-41. Available from: http://www.fmrt.org/todayamedicine/Grady050293.pdf6

12. Grady GF. The here and now of hepatitis B immunization, Today's Med [Internet]. 2007 [cited 2007 Dec 7]; 6(2):39-41. Available from: http://www.fmrt.org/todaysmedicine/Grady050293.pdf6

Give the date of your access, preceded by "cited," in brackets: [cited 2007 Dec 7] in the examples. If the article has no reference numbers (pages, paragraphs, and so on), give your calculation of its length in brackets—for instance, [about 15 p.] or [20 paragraphs]. If the article has a Digital Object Identifier (DOI), you may include the number for readers' convenience. Add it to the end of the entry after a space. (See p. 793 for more on DOIs.)

13. An article in a database (Web)

McAskill MR, Anderson TJ, Jones RD. 2005. Saccadic adaptation in neurological disorders. Prog Brain Res. 140:417-431. PubMed [database on the Internet]. Bethesda (MD): National Library of Medicine; [cited 2007 Mar 6]. Available from: http://www.ncbi.nlm.nih.gov/PubMed

13. McAskill MR, Anderson TJ, Jones RD. Saccadic adaptation in neurological disorders. Prog Brain Res. 2005;140:417-431. PubMed [database on the Internet]. Bethesda (MD): National Library of Medicine; [cited 2007 Mar 6]. Available from: http://www.ncbi.nlm.nih.gov/PubMed

Provide information on the database: title, [database on the Internet], place of publication, and publisher. (If the database author is different from the publisher, give the author's name before the title.) If you see a date of publication or a copyright date for the database, give it after the publisher's name. Add the date of your access, preceded by cited, in brackets. If the article has a Digital Object Identifier (DOI), you may include the number for readers' convenience. Add it to the end of the entry after a space. (See p. 793 for more on DOIs.)

14. A book (Web)

Ruch BJ, Ruch DB. 2007. Homeopathy and medicine: resolving the conflict [Internet]. New York (NY): Albert Einstein College of Medicine [cited 2008 Jan 28]. Available from: http://www.einstein.edu/medicine/books/ruch.html

14. Ruch BJ, Ruch DB. Homeopathy and medicine: resolving the conflict [Internet]. New York (NY): Albert Einstein College of Medicine; 2007 [cited 2008 Jan 28]. Available from: http://www.einstein.edu/medicine/books/ruch.html

As with an online journal article, give the date of your access, preceded by cited, in brackets.

15. A Web site

American Medical Association [Internet]. 2008. Chicago (IL): American Medical Association; [cited 2008 Nov 26]. Available from: http://ama-assn.org

15. American Medical Association [Internet]. Chicago (IL): American Medical Association; 2008 [cited 2008 Nov 26]. Available from: http://ama-assn.org

16. A message posted to a discussion list

Stalinsky Q. 2007 Aug 16. Reconsidering the hormone-replacement study. Woman Physicians Congress [discussion list on the Internet]. Chicago (IL): American Medical Association; [cited 2008 Aug 17]. Available from: ama-wpc@ama-assn.org

16. Stalinsky Q. Reconsidering the hormone-replacement study. Woman Physicians Congress [discussion list on the Internet]. Chicago (IL): American Medical Association; 2007 Aug 16 [cited 2008 Aug 17]. Available from: ama-wpc@ama-assn.org

17. A personal online communication (text citation)

One member of the research team has expressed reservation about the study design (personal communication from L. Kogod, 2008 Feb 6; unreferenced).

A personal letter or e-mail message should be cited in your text, not in your reference list. The format is the same for both the name-year and the number styles.

18. A document on CD-ROM or DVD-ROM

Reich WT, editor. 2008. Encyclopedia of bioethics [DVD-ROM]. New York (NY): Co-Health.

18. Reich WT editor. Encyclopedia of bioethics [DVD-ROM]. New York (NY): Co-Health; 2008.

Listing other sources

19. A report written and published by the same organization

Warnock M. 2006. Report of the Committee on Fertilization and Embryology. Waco (TX): Baylor University Department of Embryology. Report No.: BU/DE.4261.

19. Warnock M. Report of the Committee on Fertilization and Embryology. Waco (TX): Baylor University Department of Embryology; 2006. Report No.: BU/DE.4261.

20. A report written and published by different organizations

Hackney, JD (Rancho Los Amigos Hospital, Downey, CA). 2007. Effect of atmospheric pollutants on human physiologic function. Washington (DC): Environmental Protection Agency (US). Report No.: R-801396.

20. Hackney, JD (Rancho Los Amigos Hospital, Downey, CA). Effect of atmospheric pollutants on human physiologic function. Washington (DC): Environmental Protection Agency (US); 2007. Report No.: R-801396.

21. An audio or visual recording

Cell mitosis [DVD–ROM]. 2008. White Plains (NY): Teaching Media.

21. Cell mitosis [DVD-ROM]. White Plains (NY): Teaching Media; 2008.

52e Formatting documents in CSE style

Scientific Style and Format is not specific about margins, spacing for headings, and other elements of document format. Unless your instructor specifies otherwise, you can use the format of the APA (pp. 799–802). The CSE exception to this style is the list of references, which is described on pages 812–13.

The most troublesome aspects of manuscript preparation in the sciences are equations or formulas, tables, and figures. When typing equations or formulas, be careful to reproduce alignments, indentions, underlining, and characters accurately. If your word processor lacks special characters, leave space for them and write them in by hand.

Because you will be expected to share your data with your readers, most of your writing for the sciences is likely to require illustrations to present the data in concise, readable form. Tables usually summarize raw data (see opposite for an example), whereas figures (mainly charts, graphs, and diagrams) recast the data to show noteworthy comparisons or changes. Follow the guidelines on pages 121–25 for preparing tables and figures.

52f Examining a sample science paper

The following biology paper illustrates the CSE number style for documenting sources. On page 820, passages from the paper and a reformatted list of references show the name-year style. Except for the citations and the references, the paper is formatted in APA style because CSE does not specify a format.

A laboratory report: CSE number style

[Title page.]

Exercise and Blood Pressure

Liz Garson

Biology 161

Ms. Traversa

December 13, 2007

[New page.]

Abstract

The transient elevation of blood pressure following exercise was demonstrated by pressure measurements of twenty human subjects before and after exercise.

[New page.]

Exercise and Blood Pressure

Introduction

The purpose of this experiment was to verify the changes in blood pressure that accompany exercise, as commonly reported.[1,2] A certain blood pressure is necessary for the blood to supply nutrients to the body tissues. Baroreceptors near the heart monitor pressure by determining the degree to which blood stretches the wall of the blood vessel.

[The introduction continues.]

During exercise, the metabolic needs of the muscles override the influence of the baroreceptors and result in an increase in blood pressure. This increase in blood pres-

---

sure is observed uniformly (irrespective of sex or race), although men demonstrate a higher absolute systolic pressure than do women.[3] During strenuous exercise, blood pressure can rise to 40 percent above baseline.[1]

Method

The subjects for this experiment were twenty volunteers from laboratory classes, ten men and ten women. All pressure measurements were performed using a standard sphygmomanometer, which was tested for accuracy. To ensure consistency, the same sphygmomanometer was used to take all readings. In addition, all measurements were taken by the same person to avoid discrepancies in method or interpretation.

The first pressure reading was taken prior to exercise as the subject sat in a chair. This pressure was considered the baseline for each subject. All subsequent readings were interpreted relative to this baseline.

In the experiment, the subjects ran up and down stairs for fifteen minutes. Immediately after exercising, the subjects returned to the laboratory to have their pressure measured. Thirty minutes later, the pressure was measured for the final time.

[Table on a page by itself.]

Table 1. Blood pressure measurements for all subjects (mmHg)

Subject	Baseline[a]	Post-exercise	30-minute reading
Male			
1	110/75	135/80	115/75
2	125/80	140/90	135/85
3	125/70	125/70	125/70
4	130/85	170/100	140/90
5	120/80	125/95	120/80
6	115/70	135/80	125/75
7	125/70	150/80	130/70
8	130/80	145/85	130/80
9	140/75	180/85	155/80
10	110/85	135/95	115/80
Female			
11	110/60	140/85	115/60
12	130/75	180/85	130/75
13	125/80	140/90	130/80
14	90/60	90/60	90/60
15	115/65	145/70	125/65
16	100/50	130/65	110/50
17	120/80	140/80	130/80
18	110/70	135/80	120/75
19	120/80	140/90	130/80
20	110/80	145/90	120/80

[a]Normal blood pressure at rest: males, 110-130/60-90; females, 110-120/50-80.

Results

Table 1 contains the blood pressure measurements for the male and female subjects. With the exception of subjects 3 and 14, all subjects demonstrated the expected post-exercise increase in blood pressure, with a decline to baseline or near baseline thirty minutes after exercise. The data for subjects 3 and 14 were invalid because the subjects did not perform the experiment as directed.

Discussion

As expected, most of the subjects demonstrated an increase in blood pressure immediately after exercise and a decline to near baseline levels thirty minutes after exercise. The usual pressure increase was 20-40 mmHg for the systolic pressure and 5-10 mmHg for the diastolic pressure.

In the two cases in which blood pressure did not elevate with exercise (subjects 3 and 14), the subjects simply left the laboratory and returned fifteen minutes later without having exercised. The experimental design was flawed in not assigning someone to observe the subjects as they exercised.

[New page.]

References

1. Guyton AC. Textbook of medical physiology. Philadelphia (PA): Saunders; 2006.

2. Rowell LB. Blood pressure regulation during exercise. Ann Med. 2004;28:329-33.

3. Gleim GW, Stachenfeld NS. Gender differences in the systolic blood pressure response to exercise. Am Heart J. 2001;121:524-30.

A laboratory report: CSE name-year style

These excerpts from the preceding paper show documentation in CSE name-year style:

The purpose of this experiment was to verify the changes in blood pressure that accompany exercise, as commonly reported (Guyton 2006; Rowell 2004).

This increase in blood pressure is observed uniformly (irrespective of sex or race), although men demonstrate a higher absolute systolic pressure than do women (Gleim and Stachenfeld 2001). During strenuous exercise, blood pressure can rise to 40 percent above baseline (Guyton 2006).

References

Gleim GW, Stachenfeld NS. 2001. Gender differences in the systolic blood pressure response to exercise. Am Heart J. 121:524-30.

Guyton AC. 2006. Textbook of medical physiology. Philadelphia (PA): Saunders.

Rowell LB. 2004. Blood pressure regulation during exercise. Ann Med. 28:329-33.

PART 11

Special Writing Situations

53 Essay Examinations

54 Writing Online

55 Public Writing

56 Oral Presentations

53
Essay Examinations

In writing an essay for an examination, you summarize or analyze a topic, usually in several paragraphs or more and usually within a time limit. An essay question not only tests your knowledge of a subject (as short-answer and objective questions do) but also tests your ability to think critically about what you have learned. If you have not already done so, read pages 136–38 on preparing for exams and Chapter 7 on critical thinking and reading.

53a Preparing for an essay examination

To do well on an essay exam, you will need to understand the course content, not only the facts but also the interpretation of them and the relations between them.

- **Take careful lecture notes.**
- **Thoughtfully, critically read the assigned texts or articles.**
- **Review regularly.** Give the material time to sink in and stimulate your thinking.
- **Create summaries.** Recast others' ideas in your own words, and extract the meaning from notes and texts. (See pp. 134–35 for instructions on summarizing.)
- **Prepare notes or outlines to reorganize the course material around key topics or issues.** One technique is to create and answer likely essay questions. For instance, in a business course you might focus on the advantages and disadvantages of several approaches to management. In a short-story course you might locate a theme running through all the stories you have read by a certain author or from a certain period. In a psychology course you might outline various theorists' views of what causes a disorder such as schizophrenia. Working through such topics can help you anticipate questions, master the material, and estimate your time during the actual exam.

mycomplab

Visit *mycomplab.com* for more resources as well as exercises on essay exams.

53b Planning your time and your answer

When you first receive an examination, take a few minutes to get your bearings and plan an approach. The time will not be wasted.

- **Read the exam all the way through at least once.** Don't start answering any questions until you've seen them all.
- **Weigh the questions.** Determine which questions seem most important, which ones are going to be most difficult for you, and approximately how much time you'll need for each question. (Your instructor may help by assigning a point value to each question as a guide to its importance or by suggesting an amount of time for you to spend on each question.)

Planning continues when you turn to an individual essay question. Resist the temptation to rush right into an answer without some planning, for a few minutes can save you time later and help you produce a stronger essay.

- **Read the question at least twice.** You will be more likely to stick to the question and answer it fully.
- **Examine the words in the question and consider their implications.** Look especially for words such as *describe, define, explain, summarize, analyze, evaluate,* and *interpret,* each of which requires a different kind of response. Here, for example, is an essay question whose key term is *explain:*

Question

Given humans' natural and historical curiosity about themselves, why did a scientific discipline of anthropology not arise until the 20th century? Explain, citing specific details.

See the box on the next page and consult earlier discussions of such terms on pages 25–26 and 93–101.

- **Make a brief outline of the main ideas you want to cover.** Use the back of the exam sheet or booklet for scratch paper. In the brief outline below, a student planned her answer to the anthropology question above.

Outline

1. Unscientific motivations behind 19th-c anthro.
   Imperialist/colonialist govts.
   Practical goals
   Nonobjective and unscientific (Herodotus, Cushing)
2. 19th-c ethnocentricity (vs. cultural relativism)
3. 19th-c anthro. = object collecting
   20th-c shift from museum to univ.
   Anthro. becomes acad. disc. and professional (Boas, Malinowski)

COMPUTER ACTIVITY

Ask students to create a list of test-related verbs and give a brief description of what each requires in an answer. For example, *compare* means to list similarities and *contrast* means to list differences. Compile all student responses on the course Web site so students have a glossary of test terms.

Sample instructions for essay examinations

Sample instructions	Key terms	Strategies for answers	Examples of wrong answers
Define *dyslexia* and compare and contrast it with two other learning disabilities.	Define	Specify the meaning of *dyslexia*—distinctive characteristics, ways the impairment works, etc.	Feelings of children with dyslexia. Causes of dyslexia.
	Compare and contrast	Analyze similarities and differences (severity, causes, treatments, etc.).	Similarities without differences, or vice versa.
Analyze the role of Horatio in *Hamlet*.	Analyze	Break Horatio's role into its elements (speeches, relations with other characters, etc.).	Plot summary of *Hamlet*. Description of Horatio's personality.
Explain the effects of the drug Thorazine.	Explain	Set forth the facts and theories objectively.	Argument for or against Thorazine.
	Effects	Analyze the consequences.	Reasons for prescribing Thorazine.
Discuss term limits for elected officials.	Discuss	Explain and compare the main points of view on the issue.	Analysis of one view. Argument for or against one view.
Summarize the process that resulted in the Grand Canyon.	Summarize	Distill the subject to its main points, elements, or steps.	Detailed description of the Grand Canyon.
How do you evaluate the Laffer curve as a predictor of economic growth?	Evaluate	Provide your opinion of significance or value, supported with evidence.	Explanation of the Laffer curve, without evaluation. Comparison of the Laffer curve and another predictor, without evaluation.

A WRITER'S PERSPECTIVE

*The papers they had written lay
in piles of blue and white
But though they wrote it all by rote
they did not write it right*

—ANONYMOUS

■ **Write a thesis statement for your essay that responds directly to the question and represents your view of the topic.** (If you are unsure of how to write a thesis statement, see pp. 27–32.) Include key phrases that you can expand with supporting evidence for your view. The thesis statement of the student whose outline appears above concisely previews a three-part answer to the sample question:

Thesis statement

Anthropology did not emerge as a scientific discipline until the 20th century because of the practical and political motivations behind 19th-century ethnographic studies, the ethnocentric bias of Western researchers, and a conception of culture that was strictly material.

53c | Starting the essay

An essay exam does not require a smooth and inviting opening. Instead, begin by stating your thesis immediately and giving an overview of the rest of your essay. Such a capsule version of your answer tells your reader (and grader) generally how much command you have and also how you plan to develop your answer. It also gets you off to a good start.

The opening statement should address the question directly and exactly, as it does in the successful essay answer beginning on the next page. In contrast, the opening of the unsuccessful essay (p. 827) restates the question but does not answer it, nor does the opening provide any sense of the writer's thesis.

53d | Developing the essay

Develop your essay as you would develop any piece of sound academic writing:

■ **Observe the methods, terms, or other special requirements of the discipline in which you are writing.**
■ **Support your thesis statement with solid generalizations,** each one perhaps the topic sentence of a paragraph.
■ **Support each generalization with specific, relevant evidence.**

If you observe a few *don't*s as well, your essay will have more substance:

■ **Avoid filling out the essay by repeating yourself.**
■ **Avoid other kinds of wordiness that pad and confuse,** whether intentionally or not. (See pp. 523–30.)

■ **Avoid resorting to purely subjective feelings.** Keep focused on analysis, or whatever is asked of you. (It may help to abolish the word *I* from the essay.)

The following essays illustrate a successful and an unsuccessful answer to the sample essay question on page 823 about anthropology. Both answers were written in the allotted time of forty minutes. Marginal comments on each essay highlight their effective and ineffective elements.

WHAT WORKS AND WHAT DOESN'T

Comparing these sample "successful" and "unsuccessful" essay exam answers should help students get a better idea of what to strive for in their own essay exam answers. The successful answer is direct, substantive, and well structured. You may also want to have students take a closer look at the use of transitions in the successful essay; they provide coherence within and among paragraphs, giving the reader essential information about how the various pieces of information in the essay are interrelated.

ACHIEVABLE STANDARDS

Both of the sample essay answers here (successful and unsuccessful) are clearly written and correct in grammar and usage. Your students may think they set a standard impossible to achieve. You can reinforce the idea that content and structure are the most important elements in a good essay exam answer and that they should not waste valuable exam time trying to perfect grammar, sentence structure, or mechanics. If they leave time at the end they can do a quick clean-up to catch any egregious errors.

Successful essay answer

Introduction stating thesis	Anthropology did not emerge as a scientific discipline until the 20th century because of the practical and political motivations behind 19th-century ethnographic studies, the ethnocentric bias of Western researchers, and a conception of culture that was strictly material.
Direct answer to question and preview of three-part response	
First main point: practical aims	Before the 20th century, ethnographic studies were almost always used for practical goals. The study of human culture can be traced back at least as far as Herodotus's investigations of the
Example	Mediterranean peoples. Herodotus was like many pre-20th-century "anthropologists" in that he was employed by a government that needed information about its neighbors, just as the colonial nations in the 19th century needed information about their newly conquered subjects. The early politically motivated ethnographic studies that the colonial nations sponsored tended to be isolated projects, and they aimed less to advance general knowledge than to
Example	solve a specific problem. Frank Hamilton Cushing, who was employed by the American government to study the Zuni tribe of New Mexico, and who is considered one of the pioneers of anthropology, didn't even publish his findings. The political and practical aims of anthropologists and the nature of their research prevented their work from being a scholarly discipline in its own right.
Second main point: ethnocentricity	Anthropologists of the 19th century also fell short of the standards of objectivity needed for truly scientific study. This partly had to do with anthropologists' close connection to imperialist governments. But even independent researchers were hampered by the prevailing assumption that Western cultures were inherently superior. While the modern anthropologist believes that a culture must be studied in terms of its own values, early ethnographers were ethnocentric: they judged "primitive" cultures by their own "civilized" values. "Primitive" peoples were seen as uninteresting in their own right. The reasons to study them, ultimately, were to satisfy curiosity, to exploit them, or to prove their inferiority. There was even some debate as to whether so-called savage peoples were human.
Third main point (with transition *Finally*): focus on objects	Finally, the 19th century tended to conceive of culture in narrow, material terms, often reducing it to a collection of artifacts. When not working for a government, early ethnographers usually worked for a museum. The enormous collections of exotica still found in many museums today are the legacy of this 19th-century object-oriented conception of anthropology, which ignored the myths, symbols, and rituals the objects related to. It was only when

the museum tradition was broadened to include all aspects of a culture that anthropology could come into existence as a scientific discipline. When anthropologists like Franz Boas and Bronislaw Malinowski began to publish their findings for others to read and criticize and began to move from the museum to the university, the discipline gained stature and momentum.

In brief, anthropology required a whole series of ideological shifts to become modern. Once it broke free of its purely practical bent, the cultural prejudices of its practitioners, and the narrow conception that limited it to a collection of objects, anthropology could grow into a science.

Examples

Conclusion, restating thesis supported by essay

Unsuccessful essay answer

The discipline of anthropology, the study of humans and their cultures, actually began in the early 20th century and was strengthened by the Darwinian revolution, but the discipline did not begin to take shape until people like Franz Boas and Alfred Kroeber began doing scientific research among nonindustrialized cultures. (Boas, who was born in Germany but emigrated to the US, is the father of the idea of historical particularism.)

Introduction, not answering question

No thesis statement or sense of direction

Irrelevant information

Since the dawn of time, humans have always had a natural curiosity about themselves. Art and literature have always reflected this need to understand human emotions, thought, and behavior. Anthropology is yet another reflection of this need. Anthropologists have a different way of looking at human societies than artists or writers. Whereas the latter paint an individualistic, impressionistic portrait of the world they see, anthropologists study cultures systematically, scientifically. They are thus closer to biologists. They are *social scientists*, with the emphasis on both words.

Cliché added to language of question without answering question

Wheel spinning, positioning contemporary anthropology as a scientific discipline

Another reason why anthropology did not develop until the 20th century is that people in the past did not travel very much. The expansion of the automobile and the airplane has played a major role in the expansion of the discipline.

Not Another reason *but the first reason given*

Assertion without support

Cushing's important work among the Zuni Indians in New Mexico is a good example of the transition between 19th-century and 20th-century approaches to anthropology. Cushing was one of the first to develop the method of *participant observation*. Instead of merely coming in as an outsider, taking notes, and leaving, Cushing actually lived among the Zuni, dressing like them and following their customs. In this way, he was able to build a relationship of trust with his informants, learning much more than someone who would have been seen as an outsider.

Next three paragraphs: discussion of pioneers showing familiarity with their work but not answering question

Franz Boas, as mentioned earlier, was another anthropology pioneer. A German immigrant, Boas proposed the idea of *historical particularism* as a response to the prevailing theory of *cultural evolution*. Cultural evolution is the idea that cultures gradually evolve toward higher levels of efficiency and complexity. Historical particularism is the idea that every culture is unique and develops differently. Boas developed his theory to counter those who believed in cultural evolution. Working with the Kwakiutl Indians, he was also one of the first anthropologists to use a native assistant to help him gain access to the culture under study.

Padding with repletion

Irrelevant information

ONLINE EXAMS

If your students are going to compose and submit their essay exams using a computer, have them do a dry run with a practice document to make sure they know how to save, format, and submit it according to your specifications.

Vague assertion without support

Irrelevant and empty conclusion

A third pioneer in anthropology was Malinowski, who developed a theory of *functionalism*—that culture responds to biological, psychological, and other needs. Malinowski's work is extremely important and still influential today.

Anthropologists have made great contributions to society over the course of the past century. One can only hope that they will continue the great strides they have made, building on the past to contribute to a bright new future.

53e Rereading the essay

The time limit on an essay examination does not allow for the careful rethinking and revision you would give an essay or research paper. You need to write clearly and concisely the first time. But try to leave yourself a few minutes after finishing the entire exam for rereading the essay (or essays) and doing touch-ups.

- **Correct mistakes:** illegible passages, misspellings, grammatical errors, and accidental omissions.
- **Verify that your thesis is accurate**—that it is, in fact, what you ended up writing about.
- **Ensure that you have supported all your generalizations.** Cross out irrelevant ideas and details, and add any information that now seems important. (Write on another page, if necessary, keying the addition to the page on which it belongs.)

54

Writing Online

Both in and out of college, you will write extensively online. Many forms of online writing expand your options as a writer, but they also present distinctive challenges, both conceptual and technical. This

mycomplab

Visit *mycomplab.com* for more resources as well as exercises on e-mail, online collaboration, and Web composition.

chapter discusses some of the options and challenges of e-mail (below), online collaboration (p. 831), and Web composition (p. 834).

54a Writing effective e-mail

To use e-mail productively for college work, pause to weigh each element of the message. Consider especially your audience and purpose and how your tone will come across to readers. In the message shown below, the writer knows the recipients well and yet has serious information to convey to them, so he writes informally but states his points and concerns carefully. Writing to the corporation mentioned in the message, the writer would be more formal in both tone and approach. Although e-mail is typically more casual than printed correspondence, in academic settings a crafted message is more likely to achieve the intended purpose. Proofread all but the most informal messages for errors in grammar, punctuation, and spelling.

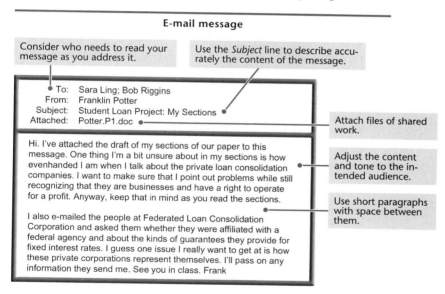

E-mail message

Consider who needs to read your message as you address it.

Use the *Subject* line to describe accurately the content of the message.

To: Sara Ling; Bob Riggins
From: Franklin Potter
Subject: Student Loan Project: My Sections
Attached: Potter.P1.doc

Attach files of shared work.

Hi. I've attached the draft of my sections of our paper to this message. One thing I'm a bit unsure about in my sections is how evenhanded I am when I talk about the private loan consolidation companies. I want to make sure that I point out problems while still recognizing that they are businesses and have a right to operate for a profit. Anyway, keep that in mind as you read the sections.

Adjust the content and tone to the intended audience.

I also e-mailed the people at Federated Loan Consolidation Corporation and asked them whether they were affiliated with a federal agency and about the kinds of guarantees they provide for fixed interest rates. I guess one issue I really want to get at is how these private corporations represent themselves. I'll pass on any information they send me. See you in class. Frank

Use short paragraphs with space between them.

For more on using e-mail to interact with the other students in a course, see pages 832–33. For more on using e-mail as a research tool, see page 582.

1 Addressing messages

Send a message only to the people who need to read it. As a general rule, avoid sending messages to many recipients at once—all the students in a course, say, or all the participants in a discussion

Students are first introduced to e-mail composition. Next, they are taught about two methods of online collaboration they are likely to use in their courses: online discussions and peer review of document drafts.

The second half of the chapter discusses how to create an original Web site. Topics covered include structure and content development, how to achieve good flow and ease of navigation, and the use of images, video, and sound on Web sites.

RESOURCES AND IDEAS

Breuch, Lee-Ann Kastman. *Virtual Peer Review: Teaching and Learning about Writing in Online Environments.* Albany: State U of New York P, 2004. Print. Breuch explores how technology affects the peer review process and discusses theoretical implications of the interaction of composition and technology.

Crow, Angela. "What's Age Got to Do with It? Teaching Older Students in Computer-Aided Classrooms." *Teaching English in the Two-Year College* 27.4 (2000): 400–06. Print. Crow offers suggestions for helping returning college students succeed: expect those students to learn more slowly, don't overload them with information, and scaffold assignments to reinforce new skills.

Golub, Jeffrey N., ed. *More Ways to Handle the Paper Load: On Paper and Online.* Urbana: NCTE, 2006. Golub offers practical advice for handling assignments both on paper and in electronic form.

Reiss, Donna, et al., eds. *Electronic Communication Across the Curriculum.* Urbana: NCTE, 1998. Written from a range of disciplinary perspectives, these essays discuss how teachers have used electronic communication to create communities within and across disciplines.

Takayoshi, Pamela, and Brian A. Huot, eds. *Teaching Writing with Computers: An Introduction.* 3rd ed. Boston: Houghton, 2002. Print. This collection of essays provides both historical perspective on technology's role in composition pedagogy and also includes more forward-looking works.

Tornow, Joan. *Link/Age: Composing in the Online Classroom.* Logan: Utah State UP, 1997. Print. An ethnographical study of how students use language online and the implications for teaching composition.

Yohon, Teresa, and Don Zimmerman. "Strategies for Online Critiquing of Student Assignments." *Journal of Business and Technical Communication* 18.2 (2004): 220–32. Print. The authors discuss how to use the features such as *Track Changes* and *Comment* in word processing programs to respond to student work.

PROFESSIONALISM IN E-MAIL

Remind students that e-mails to their instructors should not be written like messages to friends. They should capitalize and punctuate correctly, use full words rather than text abbreviations, and include a greeting and a closure. These more formal messages are good practice for professional use of e-mail.

COMPUTER ACTIVITIES

STRATEGIES FOR NOVICES

Students new to e-mail and/or the Web may find it difficult to master the technology, focus on a project, and fine-tune their writing all at once. You might want to give them a purely social topic the first time they send e-mail or chat messages, so that they can focus on getting comfortable with the environment. Then they can begin working on group dynamics and writing collaborations.

FILING MAIL

Most e-mail programs allow users to make folders or mailboxes in which to store messages. Students might want to set up e-mail folders in which to keep incoming and outgoing mail on different topics or regarding different class projects.

group—unless what you have to say applies to all of them. Occasionally, you may indeed have a worthwhile idea or important information that everyone on the list will want to know. But spamming—flooding entire lists with irrelevant messages—is rude and irritating.

Similarly, avoid sending frivolous messages to all the members of a group. Instead of dashing off "I agree" and distributing the two-word message widely, put some time into composing a thoughtful response and send it only to those who will be interested.

2 Composing messages

The messages you send are going to people, not merely inboxes, so craft your messages with the recipients in mind.

- **Don't say or do anything you wouldn't say or do face to face.**
- **Use names.** In the body of your message, address your reader(s) by name if possible and sign off with your own name and information on how to contact you. Your own name is especially important if your e-mail address does not spell it out.
- **Pay careful attention to tone.** Refrain from flaming, or attacking, correspondents. Don't use all capital letters, which SHOUT. And use irony or sarcasm only cautiously: in the absence of facial expressions, either one can lead to misunderstanding. To indicate irony and emotions, you can use an emoticon such as the smiley :-). These sideways faces can easily be overused, though, and they should not substitute for thoughtfully worded opinions.
- **Avoid saying anything in e-mail that you would not say in a printed document such as a letter or memo.** E-mail can usually be retrieved from the server, and in business and academic settings it may well be retrieved in disputes over contracts, grades, and other matters.

3 Reading and responding to messages

When you read and respond to messages, again consider the people behind them.

- **Be a forgiving reader.** Avoid nitpicking over spelling or other surface errors. And because attitudes are sometimes difficult to convey, give authors an initial benefit of the doubt: a writer who at first seems hostile may simply have tried too hard to be concise; a writer who at first seems unserious may simply have failed at injecting humor into a worthwhile message.
- **Consider who will read your response.** The Reply function will automatically address the person who wrote you, whereas the Reply All function will address others who may have been sent copies of the original message. Before you send the message, choose the readers who need to see the message.

E-mail response

To: Franklin Potter
From: Bob Riggins
Subject: Re: Student Loan Project: My Sections

Franklin Potter wrote:

I also e-mailed the people at Federated Loan Consolidation Corporation and asked them whether they were affiliated with a federal agency and about the kinds of guarantees they provide for fixed interest rates. I guess one issue I really want to get at is how these private corporations represent themselves. I'll pass on any information they send me. See you in class. Frank

Hey Frank. I might be able to help with the Fed Loan Corporation. My sister just graduated and consolidated her student loans. She has a lot of information. I'll ask her if she has ever heard of them.

Bob

Make sure the To *field addresses the appropriate person or people.*

Use the subject of the original message unless you are changing or expanding it.

When quoting the original message, select only the parts you are responding to and delete the rest.

- **Respect others' privacy.** Forward messages only with permission or only if you know that the author of the message won't mind. If you add more recipients to your response, make sure not to pass on previous private messages by mistake.
- **Avoid participating in flame "wars,"** overheated dialogs that contribute little or no information or understanding. If a war breaks out in a discussion, ignore it: don't rush to defend someone who is being attacked, and don't respond even if you are under attack yourself.

54b Collaborating online

Writing often involves collaborating with others as much as it does working in solitude. Indeed, many teachers and businesses expect writers to collaborate on generating ideas and producing and revising drafts. Computers have vastly expanded the options for collaboration, ranging from simple e-mail exchanges to video conferencing and virtual environments.

In this section we look at strategies for online collaboration in your courses. Your instructors or your school's technology advisers will introduce you to the system and help set you up. Here we focus on nontechnical matters of participating in discussions and working on drafts.

1 Participating in discussions

Many instructors use online conversations for discussing class readings and other topics and to help students generate ideas for

E-MAIL AND COMMUNITY

Some teachers find that e-mail is an excellent tool for developing a sense of community and fostering dialogue among the members of their classes. Each small group can function as a study group and can stay in touch by e-mail. Larger conversations might include all the members of one class, or even members of different class sections.

COMPOSED MESSAGES

If your students are using e-mail to request access to information from outside sources (institutions, archives, individuals, etc.) you may want to have them draft a polite e-mail request and circulate it to the class for comment before sending it out.

DISCRETION AND THE GROUP ADDRESS

It can be helpful to create a nickname the group members can all use to send mail to one another, with the complete list of e-mail addresses linked to the nickname in each student's electronic address book. But if groups use this shortcut method, they should be reminded to keep their electronic address books up to date: if a student drops out of the group, all other members should delete that student's address from the nickname list. New members of the group must be added to each member's electronic address book to ensure they receive all group mailings.

E-MAIL AND COURTESY

It might be interesting for your students to think about why people incline to discourtesy online, either in their e-mail or when posting to electronic discussion groups. This topic might be especially helpful when you teach audience, tone, or rhetorical stance. Ask students to bring in examples of discourteous discussion postings and suggest revisions that would change the tone of those postings.

COLLABORATIVE LEARNING

KEEP IT SMALL

Students can experience shyness online just as they do in person, and you may find some voices dominating while others are always silent. Working in very small groups can help reticent students feel more comfortable about adding their voices to the conversation.

BACKUP CLASS PLAN

If you have to cancel a class, you can still hold class discussion. Create a discussion topic and start several discussion threads. If you wish to have a live chat, you can set it up for the time your class would normally meet. Alternatively, you can have a delayed discussion and ask students to contribute to at least one thread before class meets again.

COLLABORATIVE LEARNING

ONLINE COMMUNITY I

Ask students to have an online chat in which they brainstorm ideas for a study of community, anonymity, and identity online. Give them a time limit for their session (try 10 minutes) and have them save the transcript and then review later when they meet in person. Ask them to pick the best ideas from the transcript and present them to the class.

ONLINE COMMUNITY II

As a follow up to the first "Online community" exercise, have students participate in one or more groups or blogs with national or international membership in order to conduct their own research on the topic of anonymity, identity, and community online.

ONLINE COMMUNITY III

Ask your students to collect clippings from the blog they explored in the "Online community II." Have them share their clipping files with the rest of their small group, and have group members respond with comments.

writing. There are two basic types of online conversation: delayed conversation, such as that occurring by e-mail, blog, or wiki; and real-time chat, which occurs immediately, like a telephone conversation.

Delayed conversation

E-mail, Web discussion groups, blogs, and wikis allow detailed, thoughtful messages and responses, so they are good places to try out ideas, explore assignments, and respond to others' work. When writing in such media, observe the guidelines for composing and responding to messages on pages 830–31.

The screen shots on these pages show part of a discussion thread on *Blackboard* courseware and a query and responses on a course blog. The writing is casual but also thoughtful and specific. In the *Blackboard* examples, notice that the second writer actually challenges the first writer's assumption but frames the challenge productively in the context of the issue being discussed. Disagreements are bound to occur in online conversation, but they need not be unpleasant.

Discussion on *Blackboard*

Author: Sara Ling
Subject: Internet Identity

Hi everyone. I'm hoping you can give me some advice about my topic and maybe share some of your experiences. I disagree with Kadi's argument that the Internet will lead to more fragmentation, not community. On the snowboarding forum that I sometimes participate in, I received a lot of hostile responses when I logged on as a woman. But another member of the group wrote to tell me that when she logged on as a man, she was welcomed into the group. It made me realize that the anonymity of the Internet could be used to bring people together, not split them apart.

Have any of you had similar experiences when you've been online? Do you think that anonymity can bring people together?

Sara

Author: Franklin Potter
Subject: Re: Internet Identity

I think you have a point about the names used on the Internet having a lot to do with how people relate. But I'm not sure that your experience totally challenges what Kadi is saying. When I've been online, I've found that people who are a lot alike tend to hang out and encourage each other. Even if the other woman on the snowboarding forum was able to change her identity, she still ended up confiding in you. I guess I would just be careful about claiming that anonymity will automatically bring different kinds of people together. Hope this helps.

Frank

Discussion on a course blog

English 1201
Writing in the World

Tuesday, 9/13/08

Service-learning projects

Some of you have asked for names of groups needing help from students, especially groups that will really *use* students. I've got some ideas, but maybe other students do, too. Suggestions?   9:24 AM

Comments

Try the Neighborhood Hunger Program (326-1135). I'm going to be working with them on a project to increase food and furniture donations from the community. It'll involve a lot of writing, I think. The group also needs help organizing the warehouse and reaching out to needy families in the community.
Posted by Jessica C 9/13/08 11:03 AM

I'm talking to ReadingWorks at the Springfield VA Hospital. They teach reading and writing to veterans. They always need volunteer tutors, but I don't think I'm ready for that yet, so I hope to do some publicity for them. The director is open to my involvement, but she's very busy and worried about supervising such work. Maybe if three or four of us presented a team proposal and proved we could work independently, she'd be encouraged. Anyone want to join in?
Posted by AlexRamirez 9/13/08 5:46 PM

Online chat

You may be familiar with chat conversations from using instant messaging with friends and family. In academic settings, chat will likely occur with courseware such as *WebCT* or *Blackboard*.

Collaborating via chat discussions will be more productive if you take a few tips:

- **Use the chat space for brainstorming topics and exchanging impressions.** The pace of online chat rarely allows lengthy consideration and articulation of messages.
- **Focus on a thread or common topic.** Online chat can be the electronic equivalent of a party, with different conversations occurring in the same space. If you have trouble tracking all the messages, concentrate on the ones that relate to your interest.
- **Write as quickly and fluidly as possible.** Don't worry about producing perfect prose.

2 Working on drafts

In writing and other courses, you and your fellow students may be invited to exchange and respond to one another's projects by e-mail or over the Web. To guide your reading of others' work, use the revision checklist on pages 54–55 and the collaboration tips on pages 68–71. Focus on the deep issues in others' drafts, especially early drafts: thesis, purpose, audience, organization, and support for the thesis. Hold comments on style, grammar, punctuation, and other surface matters until you're reviewing later drafts, if indeed you are expected to comment on them at all.

Exchanging drafts online generally requires a file-naming system that identifies each project's writer, title, and version. Your instructor may establish such a system, or you and your classmates can develop one. See pages 55–56 for tips.

COMPUTER ACTIVITY

SAVING ALL THE VERSIONS

Tell students to keep each draft of their paper, including those that include the comments of their peer groups, in a separate file so that they can have a record of the progression of their writing process. Later, they can look back over the drafts and discuss their writing process with you.

RESOURCES AND IDEAS

Bass, Randy. "Story and Archive in the Twenty-First Century." *College English* 61.6 (1999): 659–70. Print. Bass discusses the impact of hypertext and electronic media on English Studies.

Hocks, Mary E. "Understanding Visual Rhetoric in Digital Writing Environments." *College Composition and Communication* 54.4 (2003): 629–56. Print. Hocks discusses visual rhetoric in two works created for the Web and argues for teaching design as part of writing pedagogy.

Westbrook, Steve. "Visual Rhetoric in a Culture of Fear: Impediments to Multimedia Production." *College English* 68.5 (2006): 457–80. Print. Westbrook discusses how institutional forces, including copyright laws, can limit the distribution of student multimedia work.

Wysocki, Anne Frances, Johndan Johnson-Eilola, Cynthia L. Selfe, and Geoffrey Sirc. *Writing New Media: Theory and Applications for Expanding the Teaching of Composition.* Logan: Utah State UP, 2004. Print. This collection weaves together theory with practical classroom exercises and assignments for writing. It also includes an extensive bibliography of print materials.

54c Creating effective Web compositions

Creating a Web page or site is sometimes as simple as saving a document in a different format, but more often it means thinking in a new way.

The diagrams on the facing page show a key difference between traditional printed documents and Web sites. Most traditional documents are meant to be read in sequence from start to finish. In contrast, most Web sites are so-called hypertexts: they are intended to be examined in whatever order readers choose as they follow links to pages within the site and to other sites.

When you create a composition for the Web, it will likely fall into one of two categories discussed in this section: pages such as class papers that resemble printed documents in being linear and text-heavy and that call for familiar ways of writing and reading; or "native" hypertext documents that you build from scratch, which call for screen-oriented writing and reading.

These general guidelines will help you create effective Web sites:

- **Plan the site carefully.** A hypertext can disorient readers as they scroll up and down and pursue various links. Page length, links, menus, and other cues should work to keep readers oriented.
- **Anticipate what readers may see on their screens.** Each reader's screen frames and organizes the experience of a Web composition. Screen space is limited, and it varies from one computer to another. Text and visual elements should be managed for maximum clarity and effectiveness on a variety of screens.
- **Integrate visual and sound elements into the text.** Web compositions can include not only tables, charts, and photographs (which printed documents may also have) but also video (such as animation or film clips) and audio (such as music or excerpts from speeches). However, any visual or sound elements should

Traditional print document

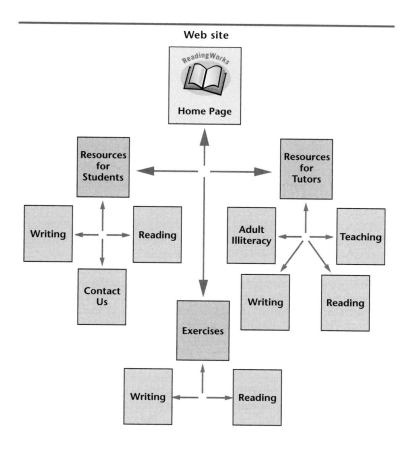

Web site

HARD COPY HYPERTEXT

Your students are probably already familiar with hypertext documents. You can point out to them that a hard copy of a paper-in-progress becomes a hypertext document when it includes any of the following: peer review comments, instructor's comments, the author's notes for revision, or the next draft of the paper.

SPATIAL LEARNERS

Some students will excel at creating architectural diagrams of their Web sites like the one shown on this page. For students with comparatively weak writing skills, the knowledge that they have strengths in visual skills may boost their confidence and suggest how they can best approach prewriting.

CITE THE SITE

Students should be reminded that borrowing text from the Web sites of others is a form of plagiarism unless they give attribution. They should use proper quotation, paraphrase, and summary technique, and they may want to include links to the original sites from which they have borrowed material.

RECOMMENDED HTML EDITORS

Ask your students to locate some online reviews of different HTML editors. On the basis of what they read, they can compose and send a memo to the rest of the class in which they discuss the various software packages and make a recommendation about which one class members should use.

CHECKING THE TRANSLATION

Students should remember to look at their papers after saving them as HTML documents but before posting them to your class Web site. They should not assume that their software is a flawless translator. It's always important for human eyes to check the work of the computer. They also should check their documents in various Web browsers.

not merely embellish the text but contribute substantially to it. In addition, you should find out whether your readers' equipment will likely be able to handle multimedia elements and whether readers themselves may have disabilities that prevent their seeing or hearing such elements (see the note below).

- **Acknowledge your sources.** It's easy to incorporate material from other sources into a Web site, but you have the same obligation to cite your sources as you do in a printed document (see pp. 626–31). Further, your Web site is a form of publication, like a magazine or a book. Unless the material you are using explicitly allows copying without permission, you may need to seek the copyright holder's permission, just as print publishers do. (See pp. 632–34 for more on copyright.)

Note If you anticipate that some of your readers may have visual, hearing, or reading disabilities, you'll need to consider their needs while designing Web sites. Some of these considerations are covered under document design on page 126, and others are fundamental to any effective Web design, as discussed in this section. In addition, avoid any content that relies exclusively on images or sound, instead supplementing such elements with text descriptions. At the same time, try to provide key concepts in words as well as in images and sound. For more on Web design for readers with disabilities, visit the American Council for the Blind at *acb.org/ accessible-formats.html* and the World Wide Web Consortium at *www.w3.org/ WAI.*

1 Using HTML

Most Web pages are created using hypertext markup language, or HTML, and an HTML editor. The HTML editing program inserts command codes into your document that achieve the effects you want when the material appears on the Web.

From the user's point of view, most HTML editors work much as word processors do, with similar options for sizing, formatting, and highlighting copy and with a display that shows what you will see in the final version. Indeed, you can compose a Web page without bothering at all about the behind-the-scenes HTML coding. As you gain experience with Web building, however, you may want to create more sophisticated pages by editing the codes themselves.

2 Creating online papers

When an instructor asks you to post a paper to a Web site, you can compose it on your word processor and then use the Save As HTML function available on most programs to translate it into a Web page. After translating the paper, your word processor should allow you to modify some of the elements on the page, or you can open the translated document in an HTML editor. The illustration below shows the opening screen of a student's project for a composition course.

Paper submitted on the Web

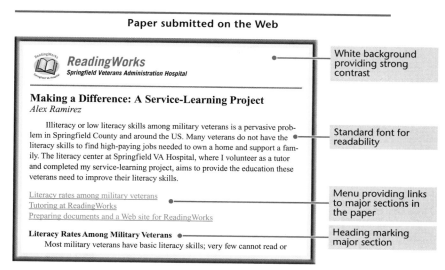

ReadingWorks
Springfield Veterans Administration Hospital

Making a Difference: A Service-Learning Project
Alex Ramirez

Illiteracy or low literacy skills among military veterans is a pervasive problem in Springfield County and around the US. Many veterans do not have the literacy skills to find high-paying jobs needed to own a home and support a family. The literacy center at Springfield VA Hospital, where I volunteer as a tutor and completed my service-learning project, aims to provide the education these veterans need to improve their literacy skills.

Literacy rates among military veterans
Tutoring at ReadingWorks
Preparing documents and a Web site for ReadingWorks

Literacy Rates Among Military Veterans
Most military veterans have basic literacy skills; very few cannot read or

— White background providing strong contrast

— Standard font for readability

— Menu providing links to major sections in the paper

— Heading marking major section

3 Creating original sites

When you create an original Web site, you need to be aware that Web readers generally alternate between skimming pages for highlights and focusing intently on sections of text. To facilitate this kind of reading, you'll want to consider the guidelines on pages 834–36 for handling text and also your site's structure and content, flow, ease of navigation, and use of images, video, and sound.

Structure and content

Organize your site so that it efficiently arranges your content and also orients readers:

- **Sketch possible site plans before getting started.** (See p. 835 for an example.) Your aim is to develop a sense of the major components of your project and to create a logical space for each component.

- **Consider how menus on the site's pages can provide overviews of the organization as well as direct access to the pages.** The Web site on the next page includes a menu on the left side of the page.

- **Treat the first few sentences of any page as a get-acquainted space for you and your readers.** In the sample on the next page, the text hooks readers with questions and orients them with general information.

■ **Distill your text so that it includes only essential information.** Concise prose is essential in any writing situation, of course. But Web readers expect to scan text quickly and, in any event, have difficulty following long text passages on a computer screen.

Original Web site

Banner identifying sponsoring organization

Introductory text appealing to readers' interests

Menu providing overview of the site's organization and content

Invitation to use the site menu

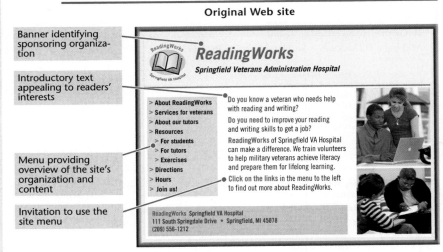

Flow

Beginning Web authors sometimes start at the top of the page and then add element upon element until information proceeds down the screen much as it would in a printed document. However, by thinking about how information will flow on a page, you can take better advantage of the Web's visual nature:

■ **Standardize elements of your design to create expectations in readers and to fulfill those expectations.** For instance, develop a uniform style for the main headings of pages, for headings within pages, and for menus.

■ **Make scanning easy for readers.** Focus readers on crucial text by adding space around it. Add headings to break up text and to highlight content. Use lists to reinforce the parallel importance of items. (See pp. 117–21 for more on all these design elements.)

Easy navigation

A Web site of more than a few pages requires a menu on every page so that readers can navigate the site. Like the table of contents in a book, a menu lists the features of the site, giving its plan at a glance. By clicking on any item in the list, readers can go directly to a page that interests them.

You can embed a menu at the top, side, or bottom of a page. Menus at the top or side are best on short pages because they will not scroll off the screen as readers move down the page. On longer pages, menus at the bottom prevent readers from dead-ending—that is, reaching a point where they can't easily move forward or backward. You can also use a combination of menus.

In designing a menu, keep it simple: many different type fonts and colors will overwhelm readers instead of orienting them. And make the menus look the same from one page to the next so that readers recognize them easily.

Images, video, and sound

Exploring the Web, you'll see that site designers have taken advantage of the Web's ability to handle multimedia elements—images, video, and sound. Most Web readers expect at least some enhancement of text.

Note See pages 633–34 on observing copyright restrictions with images, video, and sound.

Images

Several guidelines can help you use images effectively in your Web compositions:

- **Use visual elements for a purpose.** They should supplement or replace text, highlight important features, and direct the flow of information. Don't use them for their own sake, as mere decoration.
- **Compose descriptions of images that relate them to your text.** Don't ask the elements to convey your meaning by themselves.
- **Provide alternative descriptions of images** to give a sense of them to readers with vision loss or readers whose Web browsers can't display them.

Video and sound

Video and sound files can provide information that is simply unavailable in printed documents. For instance, as part of a film review you might place a short clip from the film on your Web page and then provide a close reading of the clip. Or as part of a project on a controversial issue you might provide links to sound files containing political speeches.

Before you incorporate video and sound into your Web compositions, make certain that they have a legitimate purpose. They should add essential information that can't be provided in any other medium, and they should be well integrated with the rest of your composition.

CAPTIONING PHOTOS

Have students bring in photos (not of themselves) that they are considering for inclusion on their Web pages. Collect all the photos, shuffle them, and pass them out to the members of the class. Ask each student to write a caption for the photograph he or she receives. Finally, have students read their captions and ask each photo's owner to identify what it really is. The discrepancies can be hilarious, and this will help students understand the importance of clarity in identifying the images on their Web pages.

COMPUTER ACTIVITIES

VIRTUAL GALLERY

To give students practice in the technical side of putting images on their Web sites, establish a gallery page on your class Web site. Ask each student to select or create a photo or drawing on a theme of your choice, scan it, and post it to your class Web site.

VIRTUAL CINEMA

To give students practice in the technical side of putting video clips on their Web sites, have a film festival on your class Web site. Each student can find or create a one-minute video on a topic of your choice. If you choose a humorous topic, you can have a lot of fun with this activity.

VIRTUAL CONCERT HALL

To give students practice in the technical side of putting sound recordings on their Web sites, establish a concert hall on your class Web site. Students can post sound recordings. You might want to establish a topical theme, such as "songs about peace," or see how many versions of a single song (John Lennon's "Imagine," for instance) your students can locate.

Sources

For the multimedia elements in a Web composition, you can use your own or obtain them from other sources:

- **Create your own graphs, diagrams, and other illustrations using a graphics program.** See pages 121–25 for tips on creating effective images.
- **Incorporate your own artwork, photographs, video clips, and sound recordings.** You may be able to find the needed equipment and software at your campus computer lab.
- **Obtain icons, photographs, video, and other multimedia elements from other electronic sources.** Be sure to acknowledge your sources and to obtain reprint permission if needed (see pp. 632–34).

55
Public Writing

Writing outside of school, such as for business or for community work, resembles academic writing in many ways. It usually involves the same basic writing process, discussed in Part 1: assessing the writing situation, developing what you want to say, freely working out your meaning in a draft, and editing and revising so that your writing will achieve your purpose with readers. It often involves research, as discussed in Part 9. And it involves the standards of conciseness, appropriate and exact language, and correct grammar and usage discussed in Parts 3–8.

But public writing has its own conventions, too. They vary widely depending on what you're writing and why, whether it is a proposal for your job or a flyer announcing a dinner for a community group. This chapter covers several types of public writing: business letters and memos (next page); job applications (p. 847); business reports

HIGHLIGHTS

This chapter focuses on multiple forms of public writing, including business letters and memos, job applications, reports and proposals, and a section on writing for community work. The proliferation of service learning curricula in colleges and universities means that students may find themselves needing to write on behalf of a community organization. They may also need to write about their experience for their service learning course. Section 55d, "Writing for community work," includes samples of a flyer, a newsletter, and a brochure for a nonprofit organization.

Public writing should be a subject of considerable interest to your students, for almost all of them can imagine a future in which it plays an important role. Although people in business and nonprofit organizations generally write under strict time constraints, they use the same critical thinking, reading, and writing skills presented throughout the handbook to analyze their audiences, plan their strategies, and compose their work. Professionals who write documents that represent their company or organization need to put a high value on correctness and clarity. Job

mycomplab

Visit *mycomplab.com* for more resources as well as exercises on job applications, business reports, and other kinds of public writing.

and proposals (p. 850); and flyers, newsletters, and brochures for community work (p. 852).

Note Chapter 5 discusses type fonts, headings, illustrations, and other elements of document design. In addition, a word processor's wizards or templates can help you format documents such as letters, résumés, and brochures. Before using such a tool, be sure the format is appropriate for your writing situation. And remember that a formatting tool can do nothing to help you express your ideas effectively.

CULTURE LANGUAGE Public writing in the United States, especially in business, favors efficiency. If you are accustomed to public writing in another culture, the US style may seem abrupt or impolite. A business letter elsewhere may be expected to begin with polite questions about the addressee or with compliments for the addressee's company, whereas US business letters are expected to get right to the point. (See the sample letters in this chapter for examples.)

55a Writing business letters and memos

When you write in business, you are addressing busy people who want to see quickly why you are writing and how they should respond to you. A wordy letter or a memo with grammatical errors may prevent you from getting what you want, either because the reader cannot understand your wish or because you present yourself poorly.

In all business writing, follow these general guidelines:

- **State your purpose right at the start.**
- **Be straightforward, clear, concise, objective, and courteous.**
- **Observe conventions of grammar and usage,** which make your writing clear and impress your reader with your care.

The formats of business letters and memos are fairly standardized and are thus expected by your correspondents.

1 Using a standard format for letters

Use either unlined white paper measuring 8½" × 11" or what is called letterhead stationery with your address printed at the top of the sheet. Type the letter single-spaced, with double space between elements, on only one side of a sheet.

The two most common forms for business letters—the full block and the modified block—are illustrated on the next page and on page 847, respectively. Annotations on the samples indicate spacing, margins, and other aspects of format.

applicants and laypeople writing business correspondence have similar needs for clarity and accuracy. This chapter emphasizes those virtues in all public writing situations.

RESOURCES AND IDEAS

Blackburn-Brockman, Elizabeth, and Kelly Belanger. "One Page or Two?: A National Study of CPA Recruiters' Preference for Résumé Length." *Journal of Business Communication* 38.1 (2001): 29–57. Print. The authors found that recruiters preferred two-page résumés for entry-level positions.

Conn, Cynthia. "Integrating Writing Skills and Ethics Training in Business Communication Pedagogy: A Résumé Case Study Exemplar." *Business Communication Quarterly* 71.2 (2008): 138–51. Print. The author discusses how to teach both résumé writing skills and the ethics of such writing.

Elgin, Peter, and Maria Clapham. "Attributes Associated with the Submission of Electronic Versus Paper Résumés." *Computers in Human Behavior* 20.4 (2004): 535–50. Print. The authors studied how electronic and paper résumés are perceived by recruiters, and they found that paper résumé applicants were perceived as more friendly, while the electronic résumé applicants appeared "more intelligent, more technologically advanced, and possessing better overall qualifications."

Fugere, Brian, Chelsea Hardaway, and Jon Warshawsky. *Why Business People Speak Like Idiots: A Bullfighter's Guide.* New York: Free P, 2005. Print. Despite the silly title, this book takes a hard look at inane business jargon.

Hafer, Gary R. "Computer-Assisted Illustration and Instructional Documents in Technical Writing Classes." *Computers and Composition* 13.1 (1996): 49–56. Print. Hafer argues for the advantages of teaching technical writing in the electronic classroom and offers practical advice on how to create instructional teams and design assignments.

Lanham, Richard. *Revising Business Prose.* 4th ed. New York: Macmillan, 1999. Print. Lanham offers strategies for recognizing and eliminating "businessese" from professional writing.

Mendelson, Michael. "Business Prose and the Nature of the Plain Style." *Journal of Business*

Communication 24.2 (1987): 3–18. Print. Mendelson demonstrates how various stylistic possibilities afford students different persuasive strategies.

Odell, Lee, and Dixie Goswami, eds. *Writing in Nonacademic Settings.* New York: Guilford, 1985. Print. This essay collection encompasses the theory and practice of writing in the workplace, with heavy emphasis on ethnographic studies of "real" writers at work.

Rogers, Priscilla S. and Jone Rymer. "Analytical Tools to Facilitate Transitions Into New Writing Contexts: A Communicative Perspective." *Journal of Business Communication* 38.2 (2001): 112–50. Print. The authors studied the writing of business students and developed a matrix for assessing and overcoming deficiencies.

MODELS OF STUDENT WRITING

Janet Marley's letter of complaint is at once direct, concise, firm, and unemotional, and students may want to discuss exactly how Marley achieves this balance in the tone of her letter. Be prepared for your students to differ in their assessments of Marley's letter: some may think it quite daring while others may think it insufficiently forceful. They probably have their own ideas about how to write a letter of complaint, so you might want to let them revise the letter according to their own predilections. Then pass the revisions around the room and let the class assess the effectiveness of each student's revisions. If students pretend that they are the recipient when they read one another's versions of the letter, they may find it easier to imagine how a circulation supervisor of a magazine would be likely to respond.

Students may find it helpful to use this letter as a model when formatting their own letters.

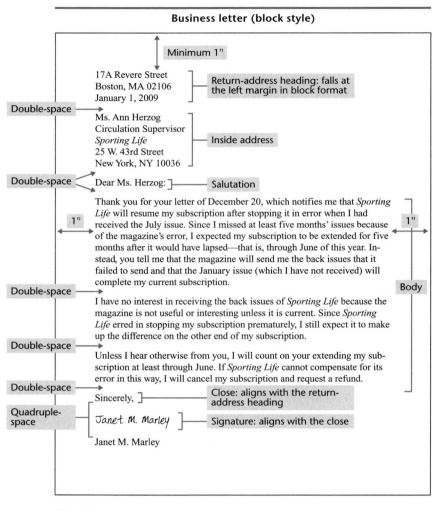

Business letter (block style)

Minimum 1"

17A Revere Street
Boston, MA 02106
January 1, 2009

Return-address heading: falls at the left margin in block format

Double-space

Ms. Ann Herzog
Circulation Supervisor
Sporting Life
25 W. 43rd Street
New York, NY 10036

Inside address

Double-space

Dear Ms. Herzog:

Salutation

1"

Thank you for your letter of December 20, which notifies me that *Sporting Life* will resume my subscription after stopping it in error when I had received the July issue. Since I missed at least five months' issues because of the magazine's error, I expected my subscription to be extended for five months after it would have lapsed—that is, through June of this year. Instead, you tell me that the magazine will send me the back issues that it failed to send and that the January issue (which I have not received) will complete my current subscription.

1"

Double-space

I have no interest in receiving the back issues of *Sporting Life* because the magazine is not useful or interesting unless it is current. Since *Sporting Life* erred in stopping my subscription prematurely, I still expect it to make up the difference on the other end of my subscription.

Body

Double-space

Unless I hear otherwise from you, I will count on your extending my subscription at least through June. If *Sporting Life* cannot compensate for its error in this way, I will cancel my subscription and request a refund.

Double-space

Sincerely,

Close: aligns with the return-address heading

Quadruple-space

Janet M. Marley

Signature: aligns with the close

Janet M. Marley

The letter

Return-address heading Unless you're using letterhead stationery, the return-address heading of the letter gives your address (but not your name) and the date. If you are using letterhead, you need add only the date.

Inside address The inside address shows the name, title, and complete address of the person you are writing to. (See p. 844 for abbreviations of state names.)

Salutation The salutation greets the addressee. Whenever possible, address your letter to a specific person. (Call the company or department to ask whom to address.) If you can't find a person's name, then use a job title (*Dear Human Resources Manager, Dear Customer Service Manager*) or use a general salutation (*Dear Smythe Shoes*). Use *Ms.* as the title for a woman when she has no other title, when you don't know how she prefers to be addressed, or when you know that she prefers to be addressed as *Ms.* If you know a woman prefers to be addressed as *Mrs.* or *Miss*, use the appropriate title.

Body The body of the letter, containing its substance, begins at the left margin in both letter styles. Instead of indenting the first line of each paragraph, place an extra line of space between paragraphs so that they are readily visible.

Close The letter's close should reflect the level of formality in the salutation. For formal letters, *Cordially, Yours truly*, and *Sincerely* are common closes. For less formal letters, you may choose to use *Regards, Best wishes*, or the like. Only the first word of the close is capitalized, and the close is followed by a comma.

Signature The signature of a business letter falls below the close and has two parts. One is your name typed on the fourth line below the close. The other is your handwritten signature, which fills the space between the close and your typed name. The signature should consist only of your name, as you sign checks and other documents.

Other information Below the signature at the left margin, you may want to include additional information such as *Enc. 3* (indicating that there are three enclosures with the letter) or *cc: Margaret Newton* (indicating that a copy is being sent to the person named).

The envelope

The envelope should accommodate the letter once it is folded horizontally in thirds. The next page shows the common Postal Service abbreviations for addresses.

Envelope for a business letter

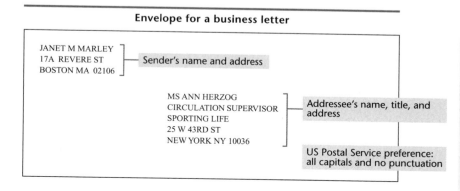

Street names

Avenue	AVE	Expressway	EXPY	Road	RD
Boulevard	BLVD	Freeway	FWY	Square	SQ
Circle	CIR	Lane	LN	Street	ST
Court	CT	Parkway	PKY	Turnpike	TPKE

Compass points

North	N	West	W	Southwest	SW
East	E	Northeast	NE	Northwest	NW

State names

Alabama	AL	Kentucky	KY	North Dakota	ND
Alaska	AK	Louisiana	LA	Ohio	OH
Arizona	AZ	Maine	ME	Oklahoma	OK
Arkansas	AR	Maryland	MD	Oregon	OR
California	CA	Massachusetts	MA	Pennsylvania	PA
Colorado	CO	Michigan	MI	Puerto Rico	PR
Connecticut	CT	Minnesota	MN	Rhode Island	RI
Delaware	DE	Mississippi	MS	South Carolina	SC
District of		Missouri	MO	South Dakota	SD
Columbia	DC	Montana	MT	Tennessee	TN
Florida	FL	Nebraska	NE	Texas	TX
Georgia	GA	Nevada	NV	Utah	UT
Hawaii	HI	New		Vermont	VT
Idaho	ID	Hampshire	NH	Virginia	VA
Illinois	IL	New Jersey	NJ	Washington	WA
Indiana	IN	New Mexico	NM	West Virginia	WV
Iowa	IA	New York	NY	Wisconsin	WI
Kansas	KS	North Carolina	NC	Wyoming	WY

2 **Writing requests and complaints**

Letters requesting something—for instance, a pamphlet, information about a product, a T-shirt advertised in a magazine—must be specific and accurate about the item you are requesting. The letter should describe the item completely and, if applicable, include a copy or description of the advertisement or other source that prompted your request.

Letters complaining about a product or a service (such as a wrong billing from the telephone company) should be written in a reasonable but firm tone. (See the sample letter on p. 842.) Assume that the addressee is willing to resolve the problem when he or she has the relevant information. In the first sentence of the letter, say what you are writing about. Then provide as much background as needed, including any relevant details from past correspondence (as in the sample letter). Describe exactly what you see as the problem, sticking to facts and avoiding discourse on the company's social responsibility or your low opinion of its management. In the clearest and fewest possible words and sentences, proceed directly from one point to the next without repeating yourself. Always include your opinion of how the problem can be solved. Many companies are required by law to establish a specific procedure for complaints about products and services. If you know of such a procedure, be sure to follow it.

3 **Writing business memos**

Unlike business letters, which address people in other organizations, business memorandums (memos, for short) address people within the same organization. A memo can be quite long, but more often it deals briefly with a specific topic, such as an answer to a

---

Business memo

Bigelow Wax Company

TO: Aileen Rosen, Director of Sales
FROM: Patricia Phillips, Territory 12   *PP*
DATE: March 17, 2008
SUBJECT: 2007 sales of Quick Wax in Territory 12

> Heading: company's name, addressee's name, writer's name and initials, date, and subject description

Since it was introduced in January 2007, Quick Wax has been unsuccessful in Territory 12 and has not affected the sales of our Easy Shine. Discussions with customers and my own analysis of Quick Wax suggest three reasons for its failure to compete with our product.

> Body: single-spaced with double spacing between paragraphs; paragraphs not indented

1. Quick Wax has not received the promotion necessary for a new product. Advertising—primarily on radio—has been sporadic and has not developed a clear, consistent image for the product. In addition, the Quick Wax sales representative in Territory 12 is new and inexperienced; he is not known to customers, and his sales pitch (which I once overheard) is weak. As far as I can tell, his efforts are not supported by phone calls or mailings from his home office.

2. When Quick Wax does make it to the store shelves, buyers do not choose it over our product. Though priced competitively with our product, Quick Wax is poorly packaged. The container seems smaller than ours, though in fact it holds the same eight ounces. The lettering on the Quick Wax package (red on blue) is difficult to read, in contrast to the white-on-green lettering on the Easy Shine package.

3. Our special purchase offers and my increased efforts to serve existing customers have had the intended effect of keeping customers satisfied with our product and reducing their inclination to stock something new.

Copies: L. Mendes, Director of Marketing
J. MacGregor, Customer Service Manager

> People receiving copies

MEMO SHARING

Encourage students to bring in memos from their current or previous places of business if they have received permission to share them. Photocopy or post to the course Web site a set of five to ten memos and ask students to work in groups to identify indications of purpose and audience, and to evaluate the clarity and effectiveness of each memo.

A STRONG LEAD

The first paragraph of a memo is the most important one. Have your students practice drafting the first paragraph of a memo, in which they present a solution, make a recommendation, provide an answer, or give an evaluation. They can circulate their drafts in small groups and as a group pick the entry that is clearest and most succinct.

MODELS OF STUDENT WRITING

Patricia Phillips's memo is a fine example that might prompt a class discussion on how purpose for writing and audience can vary widely in business writing. Each of the other models of writing in this chapter (the letter of complaint on p. 842, the application letter on p. 847, and the résumés on pp. 849 and 850) asks for something significant and is addressed to readers who may be disinclined to do what the writer asks. Those situations demand that the writer pay extra attention to tone. Memo writers, in contrast, usually want to write as quickly and efficiently as possible, and unless they are writing about a very sensitive matter, they do not need to fine-tune their tone or presentation. Ask your students to evaluate Phillips's purpose and audience in order to see why directness is appropriate in her memo.

question, a progress report, or an evaluation. Both the content and the format of a memo aim to get to the point and dispose of it quickly. See the sample on the preceding page for the format of a memo. Use the following tips to make a memo's content effective:

- **State your reason for writing in the first sentence.** You might outline a problem, make a request, refer to a request that prompted the memo, or briefly summarize new findings. Do not, however, waste words with expressions like *The purpose of this memo is. . . .*
- **Devote the first paragraph to a succinct presentation of your solution, recommendation, answer, or evaluation.** The first paragraph should be short, and by its end your reader should know precisely what to expect from the rest of the memo: the details and reasoning that support your conclusion.
- **Deliver the support in the body of the memo.** The paragraphs may be numbered or bulleted so that the main divisions of your message are easy to see. In a long memo, you may need headings (see p. 120).
- **Suit your style and tone to your audience.** For instance, you'll want to address your boss or a large group of readers more formally than you would a coworker who is also a friend.
- **Write concisely.** Keep your sentences short and your language simple, using technical terms only when your readers will understand them. Say only what readers need to know.

4 Communicating electronically

Electronic communication—mainly e-mail and faxes—adds a few twists to business writing. E-mail plays such a prominent role in communication of all sorts that we discuss it extensively as part of writing online (see pp. 829–31). Generally, the standards for business e-mail are the same as for other business correspondence.

Faxes follow closely the formats of print documents, but there are some unique concerns:

- **Consider legibility.** Small type, photographs, horizontal lines, and other elements that look fine on your copy may not be legible to the addressee.
- **Include a cover sheet.** Most faxes require a cover sheet with the addressee's name, company, and fax number; the date, time, and subject; your own name and fax and telephone numbers; and the total number of pages (including the cover sheet) in the fax.
- **Advise your addressee to expect a fax.** The advice is essential if the fax is confidential, because the machine is often shared.
- **Consider urgency.** Transmission by fax can imply that the correspondence is urgent. If yours isn't, you may want to use the mail instead.

55b Writing a job application

In applying for a job or requesting a job interview, send both a résumé and a cover letter. If you need to submit your application electronically, see pages 848–49.

1 Writing the cover letter

The cover letter should be formatted in block style (p. 842) or modified block style (below). In composing the letter, use the sample below and the guidelines on the next page.

Job-application letter (modified block style)

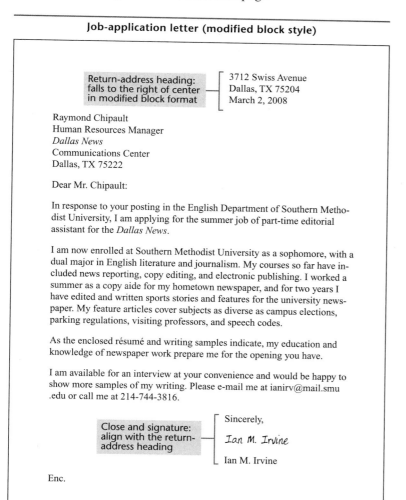

Return-address heading: falls to the right of center in modified block format —
3712 Swiss Avenue
Dallas, TX 75204
March 2, 2008

Raymond Chipault
Human Resources Manager
Dallas News
Communications Center
Dallas, TX 75222

Dear Mr. Chipault:

In response to your posting in the English Department of Southern Methodist University, I am applying for the summer job of part-time editorial assistant for the *Dallas News*.

I am now enrolled at Southern Methodist University as a sophomore, with a dual major in English literature and journalism. My courses so far have included news reporting, copy editing, and electronic publishing. I worked a summer as a copy aide for my hometown newspaper, and for two years I have edited and written sports stories and features for the university newspaper. My feature articles cover subjects as diverse as campus elections, parking regulations, visiting professors, and speech codes.

As the enclosed résumé and writing samples indicate, my education and knowledge of newspaper work prepare me for the opening you have.

I am available for an interview at your convenience and would be happy to show more samples of my writing. Please e-mail me at ianirv@mail.smu.edu or call me at 214-744-3816.

Close and signature: align with the return-address heading —
Sincerely,

Ian M. Irvine

Ian M. Irvine

Enc.

ADDITIONAL TIPS FOR WRITING THE COVER LETTER

Remind students not to rehash their résumés in a cover letter. The cover letter should build a bridge between the employer's needs and the job seeker's qualifications. To ensure that they address the employer's needs, students might consider writing the cover letter with the job description in front of them, being sure to refer to core competencies required and using the same terminology as the employer.

MODELS OF STUDENT WRITING

Students (and job applicants in general) often have a hard time writing reader-based letters of application. Some have difficulty selling their skills strongly enough; some focus on why they need or want the job more than on what they have to offer. Ian Irvine presents his qualifications succinctly and organizes his information well. Your students may disagree, however, about the effectiveness of his letter: some may think it lacks pizzazz; others may like the formality and professionalism of its tone.

Irvine's letter (and the two versions of Irvine's résumé on pp. 849 and 850) may make for a good class discussion. Begin by asking your students to imagine they are Raymond Chipault at the *Dallas News*. Have them read Irvine's letter and decide whether it makes them want to read his résumé. Have them give justifications for their decisions and make any suggestions for revision they deem appropriate. Finally, ask them to read one of the résumés and decide whether they would want to interview Irvine. Again, they should justify their decisions and make suggestions for revision.

Have students work in groups to critique each other's résumés and cover letters. Encourage the groups to ask each candidate about information that seems inconsistent or unclear as well as to check for errors. You might even have the group members pretend to be employers and conduct mock interviews based upon the applicant's materials.

Students may be able to take advantage of several commercially prepared résumé-formatting packages. Although these programs are useful, remind students that hiring officers at companies may see literally thousands of these cookie-cutter résumés each year. The time students spend individualizing their own résumés may result in documents that better catch and keep a reader's attention.

Remind students to make sure that they use a new or nearly new ink cartridge when printing out their résumés, in order to guarantee the clearest, sharpest copy possible. (This is especially important if the résumé will be photocopied or electronically scanned.)

Ask each student to e-mail an electronic résumé (as an attachment) to a partner in the class. Have the partner read the résumé both onscreen and in printout form and give feedback on design and keywords. The partner should attempt to open the attachment using as many different word-processing programs as possible, in order to verify that the document can be translated with its formatting intact.

- **Interpret your résumé for the particular job.** Don't detail your entire résumé, reciting your job history. Instead, highlight and reshape only the relevant parts.
- **Announce at the outset what job you seek and how you heard about it.**
- **Include any special reason you have for applying,** such as a specific career goal.
- **Summarize your qualifications for this particular job,** including relevant facts about education and employment and emphasizing notable accomplishments. Mention that additional information appears in an accompanying résumé.
- **Describe your availability.** At the end of the letter, mention that you are free for an interview at the convenience of the addressee, or specify when you will be available (for instance, when your current job or classes leave you free).

2 Writing and formatting the résumé

The résumé that accompanies your letter of application should provide information in table format that allows a potential employer to evaluate your qualifications. The résumé should include your name and address, a career objective, your education and employment history, special skills or awards, and information about how to obtain your references. All the information should fit on one uncrowded page unless your education and experience are extensive. See the sample on the next page for writing and formatting guidelines for a résumé that you submit in print.

Employers may ask for an electronic version of your résumé so that they can add it to a computerized database of applicants. The employers may scan your printed résumé to convert it to an electronic file, which they can then store in an appropriate database. Or they may ask you to provide the résumé electronically, either attaching it to or embedding it in an e-mail message. If an employer requests a scannable or electronic résumé, use the following guidelines and consult the sample on page 850.

- **Keep the design simple for accurate scanning or electronic transmittal.** Avoid images, unusual type, more than one column, vertical or horizontal lines, italics, and underlining.
- **Use concise, specific words to describe your skills and experience.** The employer's computer may use keywords (often nouns) to identify the résumés of suitable job candidates, and you want to ensure that your résumé includes the appropriate keywords. Name your specific skills—for example, the computer programs you can operate—and write concretely with words like *manager* (not *person with responsibility for*) and *reporter* (not *staff member*

Résumé (print)

Ian M. Irvine   3712 Swiss Avenue
                                     Dallas, TX 75204
                                     214-744-3816
                                     ianirv@mail.smu.edu

Position desired	Part-time editorial assistant.
Education	*Southern Methodist University*, 2006 to present. Current standing: sophomore. Major: English literature and journalism. Journalism courses: news reporting, copy editing, electronic publishing, communication arts, broadcast journalism.
	Abilene (Texas) Senior High School, 2002-06. Graduated with academic, college-preparatory degree.
Employment history	2006 to present. Reporter, *Daily Campus*, student newspaper of Southern Methodist University. Write regular coverage of baseball, track, and soccer teams. Write feature stories on campus policies and events. Edit sports news, campus listings, features.
	Summer 2007. Copy aide, *Abilene Reporter-News*. Assisted reporters with copy routing and research.
	Summer 2006. Painter, Longhorn Painters, Abilene. Prepared and painted exteriors and interiors of houses.
Special skills	Fluent in Spanish. Proficient in Internet research and word processing.
References	Available on request: Placement Office Southern Methodist University Dallas, TX 75275

Annotations (right margin):
- Name and contact information
- Career objective stated simply and clearly
- Education before work experience for most college students
- Headings marking sections, set off with space and highlighting
- Conventional use of capital letters: yes for proper nouns and after periods; no for job titles, course names, department names, and so on
- Standard, consistent type font

who reports). Look for likely keywords in the employer's description of the job you seek.

55c Writing business reports and proposals

Reports and proposals are text-heavy documents, sometimes lengthy, that convey information such as the results of research, a plan for action, or a recommendation for change. As with other busi-

Résumé (scannable or electronic)

Ian M. Irvine
3712 Swiss Avenue
Dallas, TX 75204
214-744-3816
ianirv@mail.smu.edu

KEYWORDS: Editor, editorial assistant, publishing, electronic publishing.

OBJECTIVE
Part-time editorial assistant.

EDUCATION
Southern Methodist University, 2006 to present.
Major: English literature and journalism.
Journalism courses: news reporting, copy editing, electronic publishing, communication arts, broadcast journalism.

Abilene (Texas) Senior High School, 2002-06.
Academic, college preparatory degree.

EMPLOYMENT HISTORY
Reporter, Daily Campus, Southern Methodist University, 2006 to present.
Writer of articles for student newspaper on sports teams, campus policies, and local events. Editor of sports news, campus listings, and features.

Copy aide, Abilene Reporter-News, Abilene, summer 2007.
Assistant to reporters, routing copy and doing research.

Painter, Longhorn Painters, Abilene, summer 2006.
Preparation and painting of exteriors and interiors of houses.

SPECIAL SKILLS
Fluent in Spanish.
Proficient in Internet research and word processing.

REFERENCES
Available on request:
Placement Office
Southern Methodist University
Dallas, TX 75275

Accurate keywords, allowing the employer to place the résumé into an appropriate database

Simple design, avoiding unusual type, italics, multiple columns, decorative lines, and images

Standard font easily read by scanners

Every line aligning at left margin

ness correspondence, you will prepare a report or proposal for a specific purpose, and you will be addressing interested but busy readers.

Reports and proposals usually divide into sections. The sections vary depending on purpose, but often they include a summary, which tells the reader what the document is about; a statement of the problem or need, which justifies the report or proposal; a statement of the plan or solution, which responds to the problem or need; and a recommendation or evaluation. Consider the following guidelines and the samples opposite and on page 852.

- **Do your research.** The standard formats of reports and proposals require you to be well informed, so be alert to where you have enough information or where you don't.
- **Focus on the purpose of each section.** Stick to the point of each section, saying only what you need to say, even if you have additional information. Each section should accomplish its purpose and contribute to the whole.
- **Follow an appropriate format.** In many businesses, reports and proposals have specific formatting requirements. If you are unsure about the requirements, ask your supervisor.

Report

Canada Geese at ABC Institute: An Environmental Problem

Summary

The flock of Canada geese on and around ABC Institute's grounds has grown dramatically in recent years to become a nuisance and an environmental problem. This report reviews the problem, considers possible solutions, and proposes that ABC Institute and the US Fish and Wildlife Service cooperate to reduce the flock by humane means.

The Problem

Canada geese began living at Taylor Lake next to ABC Institute when they were relocated there in 1985 by the state game department. As a nonmigratory flock, the geese are present year-round, with the highest population each year occurring in early spring. In recent years the flock has grown dramatically. The Audubon Society's annual Christmas bird census shows a thirty-fold increase from the 37 geese counted in 1986 to the 1125 counted in 2008.

The principal environmental problem caused by the geese is pollution of grass and water by defecation. Geese droppings cover the ABC Institute's grounds as well as the park's picnicking areas. The runoff from these droppings into Taylor Lake has substantially affected the quality of the lake's water, so that local authorities have twice (2007 and 2008) issued warnings against swimming.

Possible Solutions

The goose overpopulation and resulting environmental problems have several possible solutions:

- Harass the geese with dogs and audiovisual effects (light and noise) so that the geese choose to leave. This solution is inhumane to the geese and unpleasant for human neighbors.
- Feed the geese a chemical that will weaken the shells of their eggs and thus reduce growth of the flock. This solution is inhumane to the geese and also impractical, because geese are long-lived.
- Kill adult geese. This solution is, obviously, inhumane to the geese.
- Thin the goose population by trapping and removing many geese (perhaps 600) to areas less populated by humans, such as wildlife preserves.

Though costly (see figures below), the last solution is the most humane. It would be harmless to the geese, provided that sizable netted enclosures are used for traps. [Discussion of solution and "Recommendations" section follow.]

Descriptive title conveying report's contents

Standard format: summary, statement of the problem, solutions, and (not shown) recommendations

Major sections delineated by headings

Formal tone, appropriate to a business-writing situation

Single spacing with double spacing between paragraphs and around the list

Bulleted list emphasizing alternative solutions

Internal proposal

Memo format for internal proposal (p. 845)

Springfield Veterans Administration Hospital

To: Jefferson Green, Director, Finance and Operations
From: Kate Goodman, Director, ReadingWorks   *KG*
Date: March 5, 2008
Subject: Budget proposal for ReadingWorks Awards Dinner

"Overview": statement of proposal

OVERVIEW

ReadingWorks requests funding for an awards dinner.

"Need": justification for the request

NEED

ReadingWorks, the literacy center operated by Springfield VA Hospital, has for 6 years served between 50 and 70 patients/students a year with a small paid staff and a corps of dedicated volunteers. In the past year the center's paid staff and 20 volunteers provided more than 1260 hours of literacy tutoring to 67 students, an increase of 14 students over last year. I want to recognize the efforts and accomplishments of our students and tutors by holding an awards dinner for them and their families.

Formal tone appropriate for a proposal

"Plan": explanation of request

PLAN

I propose the following event for Friday, May 23, 7:30 to 10:30 PM: dinner and nonalcoholic beverages for approximately 135 students, tutors, and their guests; entertainment; and certificates for approximately 20 students and tutors. I request the use of Suite 42 because it can accommodate as many as 200 people as well as caterers and a DJ. Hospital staff will need to have the room ready by 6:00 PM on May 23.

"Budget" and "Personnel": details on the proposal's requirements

BUDGET

Dinner and beverages for about 135 attendees	$2700
Music for two hours	200
Certificates	50
TOTAL	$2950

Bids from local businesses are attached.

Single spacing with double spacing between sections

PERSONNEL

Five hospital employees will be needed to set up, take down, and clean Suite 42 before and after the dinner.

 55d | Writing for community work

At some point in your life, you're likely to volunteer for a community organization such as a soup kitchen, a daycare center, a literacy program, or a tutoring center for immigrants learning English. Many college courses involve service learning, in which you do such volunteer work, write about the experience for your course, and write *for* the organization you're helping.

Flyer

FIRST ANNUAL AWARDS DINNER

ReadingWorks
Springfield VA Hospital

WHEN
Friday night
May 23
7:30 to 10:30

WHERE
Suite 42
Springfield VA Hospital

WHO
Students, tutors, and their families are invited to join us for an evening of food and music as we celebrate their efforts and accomplishments.

ReadingWorks of Springfield Veterans Administration Hospital
111 South Springdale Drive
Springfield, MI 45078

For information
contact ReadingWorks
209-556-1212

Large type and color focusing a distant reader's attention on important information: what's happening, when, where, and who is invited

White space drawing viewers' eyes to main message and creating flow among elements

Color highlighting only key information

Less important information set in smaller type

PRESENTING DOCUMENTS

Ask students to bring in a written document from an organization for which they volunteer or would like to volunteer. Each student can pass the document around and explain what its purpose is, whether they think it is a good example of its kind, and what they might do to improve it.

SURVEYING THE LITERATURE

Assign students to attend their student activities fair and observe which flyers or handouts seem to them the most appealing, clear, and effective.

REAL-WORLD ASSIGNMENTS

If your students are in a service learning course and need to write a document for an organization, you could allow them to work on that document as an assignment for your course as well. The principles of good writing and document design you are teaching will have an immediate and real-world significance to your students.

The writing you do for a community group may range from flyers (above) to newsletters and brochures (next two pages). Two guidelines in particular will help you prepare effective projects:

■ **Craft each document for its purpose and audience.** You are trying to achieve a specific aim with your readers, and the approach and tone you use will influence their responses. If, for example, you are writing letters to local businesses to raise funds for a homeless shelter, bring to mind the people who will read your letter. How can you best persuade those readers to donate money?

CLASS NEWSLETTER

As a class, take on a small service project, such as organizing contributions to World Hunger Day on campus. Have students work together to create two versions of a flyer, a print version to be posted around campus and an electronic version to be sent to students by e-mail.

■ **Expect to work with others.** Much public writing is the work of more than one person. Even if you draft the document on your own, others will review the content, tone, and design. Such collaboration is rewarding, but it sometimes requires patience and goodwill. See pages 68–71 and 831–34 for advice on collaborating.

The illustrations in this section show documents prepared for ReadingWorks, a literacy program. See also pages 841–46 and 849–52 on business letters, memos, and proposals, as well as pages 861–63 on *PowerPoint* presentations.

Newsletter

Multicolumn format allowing room for headings, articles, and other elements on a single page

Two-column heading emphasizing the main article

Elements helping readers skim for highlights: spacing, varied font sizes, lines, and a bulleted list

Color focusing readers' attention on banner, headlines, and table of contents

Lively but uncluttered overall appearance

Box in the first column highlighting table of contents

 ReadingWorks

Springfield Veterans Administration Hospital **SUMMER 2008**

From the director

Can you help? With more and more learners in the ReadingWorks program, we need more and more tutors. You may know people who would be interested in participating in the program, if only they knew about it.

Those of you who have been tutoring VA patients in reading and writing know both the great need you fulfill and the great benefits you bring to the students. New tutors need no special skills—we'll provide the training—only patience and an interest in helping others.

We've scheduled an orientation meeting for Friday, September 12, at 6:30 PM. Please come and bring a friend who is willing to contribute a couple of hours a week to our work.

Thanks,
Kate Goodman

IN THIS ISSUE

First Annual Awards Dinner	1
New Guidelines on PTSD	1
Textbooks	2
Lesson Planning	2
Dyslexia Workshop	2
Support for Tutors	3
Writing by Students	3
Calendar of Events	4

FIRST ANNUAL AWARDS DINNER

A festive night for students and tutors

The first annual Reading-Works Awards Dinner on May 23rd was a great success. Springfield's own Golden Fork provided tasty food and Amber Allen supplied lively music. The students decorated Suite 42 on the theme of books and reading. In all, 127 people attended.

The highlight of the night was the awards ceremony. Nine students, recommended by their tutors, received certificates recognizing their efforts and special accomplishments in learning to read and write:

Ramon Berva
Edward Byar
David Dunbar
Tony Garnier
Chris Guigni
Akili Haynes
Josh Livingston
Alex Obeld
B. J. Resnansky

In addition, nine tutors received certificates commemorating five years of service to ReadingWorks:

Anita Crumpton
Felix Cruz-Rivera
Bette Elgen
Kayleah Bortoluzzi
Harriotte Henderson
Ben Obiso
Meggie Puente
Max Smith
Sara Villante

Congratulations to all!

PTSD: New Guidelines

Most of us are working with veterans who have been diagnosed with post-traumatic stress disorder. Because this disorder is often complicated by alcoholism, depression, anxiety, and other problems, the National Center for PTSD has issued some guidelines for helping PTSD patients in ways that reduce their stress.

• The hospital must know your tutoring schedule, and you need to sign in and out before and after each tutoring session.

• To protect patients' privacy, meet them only in designated visiting and tutoring areas, never in their rooms.

• Treat patients with dignity and respect, even when (as sometimes happens) they grow frustrated and angry. Seek help from a nurse or orderly if you need it.

Brochure

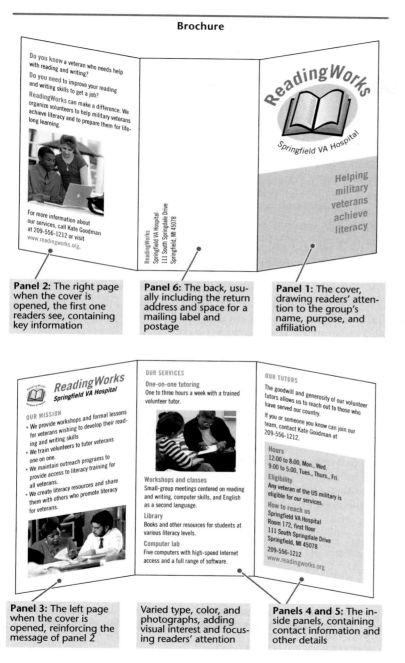

Do you know a veteran who needs help with reading and writing?

Do you need to improve your reading and writing skills to get a job?

ReadingWorks can make a difference. We organize volunteers to help military veterans achieve literacy and to prepare them for life-long learning.

For more information about our services, call Kate Goodman at 209-556-1212 or visit www.readingworks.org.

ReadingWorks
Springfield VA Hospital
111 South Springdale Drive
Springfield, MI 45078

ReadingWorks
Springfield VA Hospital

Helping
military
veterans
achieve
literacy

Panel 2: The right page when the cover is opened, the first one readers see, containing key information

Panel 6: The back, usually including the return address and space for a mailing label and postage

Panel 1: The cover, drawing readers' attention to the group's name, purpose, and affiliation

ReadingWorks
Springfield VA Hospital

OUR MISSION
- We provide workshops and formal lessons for veterans wishing to develop their reading and writing skills
- We train volunteers to tutor veterans one on one.
- We maintain outreach programs to provide access to literacy training for all veterans.
- We create literacy resources and share them with others who promote literacy for veterans.

OUR SERVICES
One-on-one tutoring
One to three hours a week with a trained volunteer tutor.

Workshops and classes
Small-group meetings centered on reading and writing, computer skills, and English as a second language.

Library
Books and other resources for students at various literacy levels.

Computer lab
Five computers with high-speed Internet access and a full range of software.

OUR TUTORS
The goodwill and generosity of our volunteer tutors allows us to reach out to those who have served our country.

If you or someone you know can join our team, contact Kate Goodman at 209-556-1212.

Hours
12:00 to 8:00, Mon., Wed.
9:00 to 5:00, Tues., Thurs., Fri.
Eligibility
Any veteran of the US military is eligible for our services.
How to reach us
Springfield VA Hospital
Room 172, first floor
111 South Springdale Drive
Springfield, MI 45078
209-556-1212
www.readingworks.org

Panel 3: The left page when the cover is opened, reinforcing the message of panel 2

Varied type, color, and photographs, adding visual interest and focusing readers' attention

Panels 4 and 5: The inside panels, containing contact information and other details

56
Oral Presentations

At some point during your education or your work, you will probably be called on to speak to a group. Oral presentation can be anxiety producing, even for those who are experienced at it. This chapter shows you how you can apply your experiences as a writer to public speaking, and it offers some techniques that are uniquely appropriate for effective oral presentations.

56a   Writing and speaking

Writing and speechmaking have much in common: both require careful consideration of your subject, purpose, and audience. Thus the mental and physical activities that go into the writing process can also help you prepare and deliver a successful oral presentation.

Despite many similarities, however, writing for readers is not the same as speaking to listeners. Whereas a reader can go back and reread a written message, a listener cannot stop a speech to rehear a section. Several studies have reported that immediately after hearing a short talk, most listeners cannot recall half of what was said.

Effective speakers adapt to their audience's listening ability by reinforcing their ideas through repetition and restatement. They use simple words, short sentences, personal pronouns, contractions, and colloquial expressions. In formal writing, these strategies might seem redundant and too informal; but in speaking, they improve listeners' comprehension.

56b   Considering purpose and audience

The most important step in developing an oral presentation is to identify your purpose: what do you want your audience to know or do as a result of your speech? Topic and purpose are *not* the

Checklist for an oral presentation

■ **Purpose:** What do you want your audience to know or do as a result of your presentation? How can you achieve your purpose in the time and setting you've been given? (See the previous page and below.)

■ **Audience:** What do you know about the characteristics and opinions of your audience? How can this information help you adapt your presentation to your audience's interests, needs, and opinions? (See below and the next page.)

■ **Organization and content:** How are your ideas arranged? Where might listeners have difficulty following you? What functions do your introduction and conclusion perform? How relevant and interesting is your supporting material for your topic and your audience? (See the next page.)

■ **Method of delivery:** What method of delivery do you plan: extemporaneous? reading from a text? memorized? a mixture? How does your method suit the purpose, setting, and occasion of your presentation? (See pp. 860–61.)

■ **Vocal and physical delivery:** In rehearsing your presentation, what do you perceive as your strengths and weaknesses? Is your voice suitably loud for the setting? Are you speaking clearly? Are you able to move your eyes around the room so that you'll be making eye contact during the presentation? Is your posture straight but not stiff? Do your gestures reinforce your ideas? Do you use visual aids appropriately? (See pp. 861–62.)

■ **Confidence and credibility:** What techniques will you use to overcome the inevitable anxiety about speaking? How will you project your confidence and competence? (See pp. 863–64.)

same thing. Asking *What am I talking about?* is not the same as asking *Why am I speaking?*

In school and work settings, oral presentations may include anything from a five-minute report before a few peers to an hour-long address before a hundred people. Whatever the situation, you're likely to be speaking for the same reasons that you write in school or at work: to explain something to listeners or to persuade listeners to accept your opinion or take an action. See pages 9–11 for more on these purposes.

Adapting to your audience is a critical task in public speaking as well as in writing. You'll want to consider the questions about audience on page 13. But a listening audience requires additional considerations as well:

■ **Why is your audience assembled?** Listeners who attend because they want to hear you and your ideas may be easier to interest and motivate than listeners who are required to attend.

GLOBAL WARMING PRESENTATION II

To help students get practice presenting to a specific audience, ask them to work in groups to outline a presentation on global warming for three different audiences: an elementary-school science class; a campaign fund-raiser for a political candidate; and an association of automobile executives. They should aim to keep their central argument the same for each version but decide how they will tailor the presentation appropriately for each audience.

GOOD FIRST IMPRESSIONS ON A BORING TOPIC

In small groups, have students outline an introduction to a presentation on driving etiquette for the campus student body. They can brainstorm different ways of making this potentially boring topic interesting to listeners.

GLOBAL WARMING PRESENTATION III

Choose one or more of the outlines created by groups of students in the "Global Warming II" exercise and post it to your class Web site. Then ask students to surf the Web looking for apt quotations, images, or stories to support the presentation. They can post their findings for the rest of the class to review.

- **How large is your audience?** With a small group you can be informal. If you are speaking to a hundred or more people, you may need a public address system, a lectern, special lighting, and audiovisual equipment.
- **Where will you speak?** Your approach should match the setting—more casual for a small classroom, more formal for an auditorium.
- **How long are you scheduled to speak?** Whatever the time limit, stick to it. Audiences lose patience with someone who speaks longer than expected.

When speaking, unlike when writing, you can see and hear your audience's responses during your presentation. If you sense that an audience is bored, try to spice up your presentation. If an audience is restless, consult your watch to make sure you have not gone over your time. If you sense resistance, try to make midspeech adjustments to respond to that resistance.

56c | Organizing the presentation

An effective oral presentation, like an effective essay, has a recognizable shape. The advice in Chapter 2 for organizing and outlining an essay serves the speechmaker as well as the writer (see pp. 33–43). Here are additional considerations for the introduction, conclusion, and supporting material.

1 | The introduction

First impressions count. A strong beginning establishes an important relationship among three elements in an oral presentation: you, your topic, and your audience. More specifically, the beginning of an oral presentation should try to accomplish three goals:

- **Gain the audience's attention and interest.** Begin with a question, an unusual example or statistic, or a short, relevant story.
- **Put yourself in the speech.** If you demonstrate your expertise, experience, or concern, your audience will be more interested in what you say and more trusting of you.
- **Introduce and preview your topic and purpose.** By the time your introduction is over, listeners should know what your topic is and the direction in which you wish to take them as you develop your ideas.

In addition to these guidelines for beginning a speech, there are some important pitfalls to avoid:

- **Don't try to cram too much into your introduction.** Focus on engaging the audience and quickly previewing your talk.
- **Don't begin with an apology.** A statement such as *I wish I'd been given more time to get ready for this presentation* will only undermine your listeners' confidence in you.
- **Don't begin with *My speech is about.* . . .** The statement is dull, and it does little to clarify purpose.

2 Supporting material

Just as you do when writing, you can and should use facts, statistics, examples, and expert opinions to support spoken arguments (see pp. 181–83). In addition, as a speaker you can draw on other kinds of supporting material:

- **Use vivid description.** Paint a mental image of a scene, a concept, an event, or a person.
- **Use well-chosen quotations.** They can add an emotional or humorous moment to your speech.
- **Use true or fictional stories.** A memorable narrative can rivet the audience's attention and illustrate your point.
- **Use analogies.** Comparisons between essentially unlike things, such as a politician and a tightrope walker, link concepts memorably. (For more on analogy, see p. 99.)

Use a variety of supporting material in your speech. A presentation that consists of nothing but statistics can bore an audience. Nonstop storytelling may interest listeners but fail to achieve your purpose.

3 The conclusion

Last impressions count as much as first impressions. You may hope that listeners will remember every detail of your speech, but they are more likely to leave with a general impression and a few ideas about you and your message. You want your conclusion to be clear, of course, but you also want it to be memorable. Remind listeners of how your topic and main idea connect to their needs and interests.

56d Delivering the presentation

Writing and speaking differ most obviously in the form of delivery: the writer is represented in print; the speaker is represented in person. This section describes the methods and techniques of oral presentation as well as some ways of coping with stage fright.

COLLABORATIVE LEARNING

GLOBAL WARMING PRESENTATION IV

Have students do a dry run of their global warming presentation with a partner or their small group. Rehearsing is an effective way to reduce anxiety about public speaking and to learn to adapt to a live audience.

1 | Methods of delivery

An oral presentation may be delivered impromptu, extemporaneously, from a text, or from memory. No one technique is best for all speeches; indeed, a single speech may include two or more forms or even all four—perhaps a memorized introduction, an extemporaneous body in which quotations are read from a text, and impromptu responses to audience questions during or after the speech.

Speaking impromptu

Impromptu means "without preparation": an impromptu presentation is one you deliver off-the-cuff, with no planning or practice. You may be called on in a class to express your opinion or to summarize something you've written. You may speak up at a neighborhood meeting. An audience member may ask you a question at the end of an oral presentation. The only way to prepare for such incidents is to be well prepared in general—to be caught up on course reading, for instance, or to know the facts in a debate.

Speaking extemporaneously

Extemporaneous speaking—that done with some preparation, but without reading from a text—is the most common form of presentation, typical of class lectures and business briefings. With extemporaneous speaking, you have time to prepare and practice in advance. Then, instead of following a script of every word, you speak from notes that guide you through the presentation.

Speaking from a text

Delivering a presentation from a text involves writing the text out in advance and then reading aloud from it. With a text in front of you, you're unlikely to lose your way. However, a reading speaker can be dull for an audience. Try to avoid this form of delivery for an entire presentation.

If you do use a text, write it so that it sounds spoken (less formal) rather than written (more formal): for instance, the sentence *Although costs rose, profits remained steady* would sound fine in writing but stiff and awkward in speech because in conversation we rarely use such a structure. In addition, rehearse thoroughly so that you can read with expression and can look up frequently to make eye contact with listeners (see opposite).

Speaking from memory

A memorized presentation has a distinct advantage: complete freedom from notes or a text. That means you can look at your audience every minute and can move away from a lectern and even into the audience. However, you may be like most speakers in seeming less relaxed, not more relaxed, when presenting from memory: your mind is too busy retrieving the next words to attend to the responses of the audience. Further, you risk forgetting your place or a whole passage.

For these reasons, many experts discourage memorization. At least reserve the method for the introduction, perhaps, or some other part with which you want to make a strong impression. Rehearse not only to memorize the words but, beyond that, to deliver the words fresh, as if for the first time.

2 Vocal delivery

The sound of your voice will influence how your listeners receive you. When rehearsing, consider volume, speed, and articulation.

- **Speak loudly.** In a meeting with five other people, you can speak in a normal volume. As your audience grows in size, so should your volume. Most speakers can project to as many as a hundred people, but a larger audience may require a microphone.
- **Speak slowly enough to be understandable.**
- **Speak clearly and correctly.** To avoid mumbling or slurring words, practice articulating. Sometimes it helps to open your mouth a little wider than usual.

3 Physical delivery

You are more than your spoken words when you make an oral presentation. Your face and body also play a role in how your speech is received.

- **Make eye contact with listeners.** Move your gaze around the entire room, settle on someone, and establish direct eye contact; then move on to someone else.
- **Stand up.** Always stand for a presentation, unless it takes place in a small room where standing would be inappropriate. You can see more audience members when you stand, and they in turn can hear your voice and see your gestures more clearly.
- **Stand straight, and move around.** Turn your body toward one side of the room and then the other, step out from behind any lectern or desk, and gesture appropriately, as you would in conversation.

4 Visual aids

You can supplement an oral presentation with visual aids such as posters, models, slides, videos, or presentation software such as *PowerPoint*. Visual aids can emphasize key points, organize related material (images, statistics, quotations) on *Power-Point*. They might even choose to display an outline of their main arguments onscreen.

POWERPOINT TRYOUT

Students can try out different feature options (such as backgrounds, colors, and fonts) in drafts of their presentation. Peer groups can provide quick assessments of the effectiveness of various feature choices to help each writer know what revisions to make.

POWERPOINT PROBLEMS

Ask students to discuss in groups the biggest problems they see (or have experienced) with using *PowerPoint*. For example, speakers read off the slides and fail to engage with the audience, or speakers crowd the slides with too much information, making the text hard to read. Then, as a class, use their discussions to create a list of *PowerPoint* do's and don'ts.

PRACTICING IN SMALL GROUPS

Have students practice their speeches in front of their groups first, using their visuals and standing as if presenting to the class. Ask group members to critique students' work. This exercise will allow students to receive feedback on their work before delivering it to the class, as well as giving them additional practice in front of a small, receptive audience.

concepts, and illustrate complex procedures. They can gain the attention of listeners and improve their understanding and memory.

The following guidelines can help you create effective and appropriate visual aids:

- **Use visual aids to underscore your points.** Short lists of key ideas, illustrations such as graphs or photographs, or objects such as models can make your presentation more interesting and memorable. But use visual aids judiciously: a constant flow of illustrations or objects will bury your message.
- **Match visual aids and setting.** An audience of five people may be able to see a photograph and share a chart; an audience of a hundred will need projected images. *large word*
- **Coordinate visual aids with your message.** Time each visual aid to reinforce a point you're making. Tell listeners what they're looking at—what they should be getting from the aid. Give them enough viewing time so they don't mind turning their attention back to you.
- **Show visual aids only while they're needed.** To regain your audience's attention, remove or turn off any aid as soon as you have finished with it.

Many speakers use *PowerPoint* or other software to project visual aids. (See the sample slides on the next page.) Screens of brief points supported by data, images, or video can help listeners follow your main points. To use *PowerPoint* or other software effectively, follow the guidelines above and also the following:

- **Don't put your whole presentation on screen.** Select key points, and distill them to as few words as possible. Think of the slides as quick, easy-to-remember summaries.
- **Use a simple design.** Avoid turning your presentation into a show about the software's many capabilities.
- **Use a consistent design.** For optimal flow through the presentation, each slide should be formatted similarly.
- **Add only relevant illustrations.** Avoid loading the presentation with mere decoration.

5 Practice

Practicing an oral presentation is the equivalent of editing and proofreading a written text. You won't gain much by practicing silently in your head; instead, you need to rehearse out loud, with the notes you will be using. For your initial rehearsals, you can gauge your performance by making an audio- or videotape of yourself or by practicing in front of a mirror. A recording will let you hear mumbling, too-rapid delivery, grammatical errors, mispro-

PowerPoint slides

Making a Difference?

A Service-Learning Project at ReadingWorks

Springfield Veterans Administration Hospital

ReadingWorks

Springfield VA Hospital

Jessica Cho
Nathan Hall
Alex Ramirez

FALL 2008

First slide, introducing the project and presentation

Simple, consistent slide design focusing viewers' attention on information, not *PowerPoint* features

Semester goals

- **Tutor military veterans**
- **Research adult literacy**
- **Keep a journal**
- **Collaborate on documents for ReadingWorks**
- **Report experiences and findings**

Later slide, using brief, bulleted points to be explained by the speaker

Photographs reinforcing the project's activities

nounced words, and unclear concepts. A mirror or video will reveal your stance, your gestures, and your eye contact. Any of these practice techniques will tell you if your presentation is running too long or too short.

If you plan to use visual aids, you'll need to practice with them, too, preferably in the room where you'll make the presentation and certainly with the help of anyone who will be assisting you. Your goal is to eliminate hitches (upside-down slides, missing charts) and to weave the visuals seamlessly into your presentation.

6 Stage fright

Many people report that speaking in front of an audience is their number-one fear. Even many experienced and polished speakers have some anxiety about delivering an oral presentation, but they use

RESOURCES AND IDEAS

Baker, William. "Visual Communication: Integrating Visual Instruction into Business Communication Courses." *Business Communication Quarterly* 69.4 (2006): 403–07. Print. Baker discusses how to use *PowerPoint* and *Publisher* to teach elements of visual communication, including how to use balance, color, and repetition.

Beason, Larry. "Ethos and Error: How Business People React to Errors." *College Composition and Communication* 53.1 (2001): 33–64. Print. Beason's study suggests that business leaders see errors in business communication as a sign of carelessness and faulty thinking and would be reluctant to hire applicants who commit such errors.

Felske, Claudia Klein. "Beyond the Page: Students as Actor-Readers." *English Journal* 95.1 (2005): 58–63. Print. The author explains a method she uses to help students understand Shakespeare and develop their oral language skills.

George, Don. "Peer Support in Speech Preparation." *Speech Communication Teacher* 7.3 (1993): 4–5. Print. A brief piece describing exercises for cultivating a team approach to public speaking using debating club strategies.

Henry, Jim. *Writing Workplace Cultures: An Archaeology of Professional Writing.* Carbondale: Southern Illinois UP, 2000. Print. Henry describes a fascinating study of workplace cultures and of how such cultures shape discourse.

Lucas, Stephen E. *The Art of Public Speaking.* 9th ed. New York: McGraw Hill, 2001. Print. This is a standard speech communication textbook that can be used to integrate a speechmaking component onto the writing classroom. See also Lucas's videotaped collection, *Speeches for Analysis and Discussion* (New York: Random, 1989).

Mackiewicz, Jo. "Comparing PowerPoint Experts' and University Students' Opinions about *PowerPoint* Presentations." *Journal of Technical Writing and Communication* 38.2 (2008): 149–65. Print. Mackiewicz compares expert advice on creating effective *PowerPoint* presentations with students' opinions; she found that they agree in most respects, but that students are more open to the judicious use of animation.

Menzel, Kent E., and Lori J. Carrell. "The Relationship Between Preparation and Performance in Public Speaking." *Communication Education* 43.1 (1994): 17–26. Print. Explores the effects of factors like anxiety level, preparation time, and scholastic ability on the quality of oral presentations. The authors show, for example, that time spent on preparing visual aids adds to an effective delivery, partly because of the motivational and anxiety-reducing effects.

Rowan, Katherine E. "A New Pedagogy for Explanatory Public Speaking: Why Arrangement Should Not Substitute for Invention." *Communication Education* 44.3 (1995): 236–50. Print. Rowan makes the case against current speech communication textbooks that focus on the organization of definitions, examples, and visual aids without recognizing the process of critical thinking through which students develop the content of the speech in relation to effective modes of presentation.

Sullivan, Gwendolyn F. "Improving Delivery Skills: The Practice Impromptu." *Speech Communication Teacher* 11.2 (1997): 5–6. Print. This short piece describes group activities and preparatory exercises (such as inviting a guest speaker) that help students learn to deliver impromptu speeches.

this nervous energy to their advantage, letting it propel them into working hard on each presentation, and rehearsing until they're satisfied with their delivery. They know that the symptoms of anxiety are usually imperceptible to listeners, who cannot see or hear a racing heart, upset stomach, cold hands, and worried thoughts.

Several techniques can help you reduce your level of anxiety:

- **Use simple relaxation exercises.** Deep breathing or tensing and relaxing your stomach muscles can ease some of the physical symptoms of speech anxiety.
- **Think positively.** Instead of worrying about the mistakes you might make, concentrate on how well you've prepared and practiced your presentation and how significant your ideas are.
- **Don't avoid opportunities to speak in public.** Practice and experience build speaking skills and offer the best insurance for success.

Glossary of Usage

This glossary provides notes on words or phrases that often cause problems for writers. The recommendations for standard American English are based on current dictionaries and usage guides such as the ones listed on pp. 512–13. Items labeled **nonstandard** should be avoided in academic and business settings. Those labeled **colloquial** and **slang** occur in speech and in some informal writing but are best avoided in formal college and business writing. (Words and phrases labeled *colloquial* include those labeled by many dictionaries with the equivalent term *informal*.) See Chapters 37 and 38 for further discussion of word choice and for exercises in usage. See p. 512 for a description of dictionary labels. Also see pp. 532–33 for a list of commonly confused words that are pronounced the same or similarly.

The glossary is necessarily brief. Keep a dictionary handy for all your writing, and make a habit of referring to it whenever you doubt the appropriateness of a word or phrase.

a, an   Use *a* before words beginning with consonant sounds, including those spelled with an initial pronounced *h* and those spelled with vowels that are sounded as consonants: *a* historian, *a one-o'clock class, a university.* Use an before words that begin with vowel sounds, including those spelled with an initial silent *h: an organism, an L, an honor.*

The article before an abbreviation depends on how the abbreviation is read: *She was once an AEC undersecretary* (AEC is read as three separate letters); *Many Americans opposed a SALT treaty* (SALT is read as one word, *salt*).

For the use of *a/an* versus *the,* see pp. 322–25.

accept, except   *Accept* is a verb meaning "receive." *Except* is usually a preposition or conjunction meaning "but for" or "other than"; when it is used as a verb, it means "leave out." *I can accept all your suggestions except the last one. I'm sorry you excepted my last suggestion from your list.*

adverse, averse   *Adverse* and *averse* both mean "opposed" or "hostile." But *averse* describes the subject's opposition to something, whereas *adverse* describes something opposed to the subject: *The President was averse to adverse criticism.*

advice, advise   *Advice* is a noun, and *advise* is a verb: *Take my advice; do as I advise you.*

affect, effect   Usually *affect* is a verb, meaning "to influence," and *effect* is a noun, meaning "result": *The drug did not affect his driving; in fact, it seemed to have no effect at all.* But *effect* occasionally is used as a verb meaning "to bring about": *Her efforts effected a change.* And *affect* is used in psychology as a noun meaning "feeling or emotion": *One can infer much about affect from behavior.*

aggravate   *Aggravate* should not be used in its colloquial meaning of "irritate" or "exasperate" (for example, *We were aggravated by her constant arguing*). *Aggravate* means "make worse": *The President was irritated by the Senate's indecision because he feared any delay might aggravate the unrest in the Middle East.*

agree to, agree with   *Agree to* means "consent to," and *agree with* means "be in accord with": *How can they agree to a treaty when they don't agree with each other about the terms?*

ain't   Nonstandard for *am not, isn't,* or *aren't.*

all, all of   Usually *all* is sufficient to modify a noun: *all my loving, all the things you are.* Before a pronoun or proper noun, *all of* is usually appropriate: *all of me, in all of France.*

all ready, already   *All ready* means "completely prepared," and *already* means "by now" or "before now": *We were all ready to go to the movie, but it had already started.*

all right   *All right* is always two words. *Alright* is a common error.

all together, altogether   *All together* means "in unison" or "gathered in one place." *Altogether* means "entirely." *It's not altogether true that our family never spends vacations all together.*

allusion, illusion   An *allusion* is an indirect reference, and an *illusion* is a deceptive appearance: *Paul's constant allusions to Shakespeare created the illusion that he was an intellectual.*

almost, most   *Almost* means "nearly"; *most* means "the greater number (or part) of." In formal writing, *most* should not be used as a substitute for *almost: We see each other almost* [not *most*] *every day.*

a lot   *A lot* is always two words, used informally to mean "many." *Alot* is a common misspelling.

among, between   Use *among* for relationships involving more than two people or things. Use *between* for relationships involving only two or for comparing one thing to a group to which it belongs. *The four of them agreed among themselves that the choice was between New York and Los Angeles.*

amongst   Although common in British English, in American English *amongst* is an overrefined substitute for *among.*

amount, number   Use *amount* with a singular noun that names something not countable (a noncount noun): *The amount of food varies.* Use *number* with a plural noun that names more than one of something countable (a plural count noun): *The number of calories must stay the same.*

an, and   *An* is an article (see *a, an*). *And* is a coordinating conjunction.

and etc.   *Et cetera (etc.)* means "and the rest"; *and etc.* therefore is redundant. See also *et al., etc.*

and/or   *And/or* indicates three options: one or the other or both (*The decision is made by the mayor and/or the council*). If you mean all three options, *and/or* is appropriate. Otherwise, use *and* if you mean both, *or* if you mean either.

and which, and who *And which* or *and who* is correct only when used to introduce a second clause beginning with the same relative pronoun: *Jill is my cousin who goes to school here and who calls me constantly.* Otherwise, *and* is not needed: *WCAS is my favorite AM radio station, which* [not *and which*] *I listen to every morning.*

ante-, anti- The prefix *ante-* means "before" (*antedate, antebellum*); *anti-* means "against" (*antiwar, antinuclear*). Before a capital letter or *i, anti-* takes a hyphen: *anti-Freudian, anti-isolationist.*

anxious, eager *Anxious* means "nervous" or "worried" and is usually followed by *about. Eager* means "looking forward" and is usually followed by *to. I've been anxious about getting blisters. I'm eager* [not *anxious*] *to get new running shoes.*

anybody, any body; anyone, any one *Anybody* and *anyone* are indefinite pronouns; *any body* is a noun modified by *any; any one* is a pronoun or adjective modified by *any. How can anybody communicate with any body of government? Can anyone help Amy? She has more work than any one person can handle.*

any more, anymore *Any more* means "no more"; *anymore* means "now." Both are used in negative constructions: *He doesn't want any more. She doesn't live here anymore.*

anyplace Colloquial for *anywhere.*

anyways, anywheres Nonstandard for *anyway* and *anywhere.*

apt, liable, likely *Apt* and *likely* are interchangeable. Strictly speaking, though, *apt* means "having a tendency to": *Horace is apt to forget his lunch in the morning. Likely* means "probably going to": *Horace is leaving so early today that he's likely to catch the first bus.*

 Liable normally means "in danger of" and should be confined to situations with undesirable consequences: *Horace is liable to trip over that hose.* Strictly, *liable* means "responsible" or "exposed to": *The owner will be liable for Horace's injuries.*

are, is Use *are* with a plural subject (*books are*), *is* with a singular subject (*book is*).

as *As* may be vague or ambiguous when it substitutes for *because, since,* or *while*: *As the researchers asked more questions, their money ran out.* (Does *as* mean "while" or "because"?) *As* should never be used as a substitute for *whether* or *who. I'm not sure whether* [not *as*] *we can make it. That's the man who* [not *as*] *gave me directions.*

as, like See *like, as.*

as, than In comparisons, *as* and *than* precede a subjective-case pronoun when the pronoun is a subject: *I love you more than he* [*loves you*]. *As* and *than* precede an objective-case pronoun when the pronoun is an object: *I love you as much as* [*I love*] *him.* (See also p. 268.)

assure, ensure, insure *Assure* means "to promise": *He assured us that we would miss the traffic. Ensure* and *insure* often are used interchangeably to mean "make certain," but some reserve *insure* for matters of legal and financial protection and use *ensure* for more general meanings: *We left early to ensure that we would miss the traffic. It's expensive to insure yourself against floods.*

as to A stuffy substitute for *about: The suspect was questioned about* [not *as to*] *her actions.*

at The use of *at* after *where* is wordy and should be avoided: *Where are you meeting him?* is preferable to *Where are you meeting him at?*

at this point in time Wordy for *now, at this point,* or *at this time.*

averse, adverse See *adverse, averse.*

awful, awfully Strictly speaking, *awful* means "awe-inspiring." As intensifiers meaning "very" or "extremely" (*He tried awfully hard*), *awful* and *awfully* should be avoided in formal speech or writing.

a while, awhile *Awhile* is an adverb; *a while* is an article and a noun. Thus *awhile* can modify a verb but cannot serve as the object of a preposition, and *a while* is just the opposite: *I will be gone awhile* [not *a while*]. *I will be gone for a while* [not *awhile*].

bad, badly In formal speech and writing, *bad* should be used only as an adjective; the adverb is *badly. He felt bad because his tooth ached badly.* In *He felt bad,* the verb *felt* is a linking verb and the adjective *bad* is a subject complement. (See also pp. 318–19.)

being as, being that Colloquial for *because,* the preferable word in formal speech or writing: *Because* [not *Being as*] *the world is round, Columbus never did fall off the edge.*

beside, besides *Beside* is a preposition meaning "next to." *Besides* is a preposition meaning "except" or "in addition to" as well as an adverb meaning "in addition." *Besides, several other people besides you want to sit beside Dr. Christensen.*

better, had better *Had better* (meaning "ought to") is a verb modified by an adverb. The verb is necessary and should not be omitted: *You had better* [not just *better*] *go.*

between, among See *among, between.*

bring, take Use *bring* only for movement from a farther place to a nearer one and *take* for any other movement. *First, take these books to the library for renewal, then take them to Mr. Daniels. Bring them back to me when he's finished.*

bunch In formal speech and writing, *bunch* (as a noun) should be used only to refer to clusters of things growing or fastened together, such as bananas and grapes. Its use to mean a group of items or people is colloquial; *crowd* or *group* is preferable.

burst, bursted; bust, busted *Burst* is a standard verb form meaning "to fly apart suddenly." Its main forms are *burst, burst, burst;* the form *bursted* is nonstandard. The verb *bust* (*busted*) is slang.

but, hardly, scarcely These words are negative in their own right; using *not* with any of them produces a double negative (see p. 320). *We have but* [not *haven't got but*] *an hour before our plane leaves. I could hardly* [not *couldn't hardly*] *make out her face.*

but, however, yet Each of these words is adequate to express contrast. Don't combine them. *He had finished, yet* [not *but yet*] *he continued.*

but that, but what These wordy substitutes for *that* and *what* should be avoided: *I don't doubt that* [not *but that*] *you are right.*

calculate, figure, reckon As substitutes for *expect* or *imagine* (*I figure I'll go*), these words are colloquial.

can, may Strictly, *can* indicates capacity or ability, and *may* indicates permission: *If I may talk with you a moment, I believe I can solve your problem. May* also indicates possibility: *You may like what you hear.*

can't help but This idiom is common but redundant. Either *I can't help wishing* or the more formal *I cannot but wish* is preferable to *I can't help but wish.*

case, instance, line Expressions such as *in the case of, in the instance of,* and *along the lines of* are usually padding and should be avoided.

censor, censure To *censor* is to edit or remove from public view on moral or some other grounds; to *censure* is to give a formal scolding. *The lieutenant was censured by Major Taylor for censoring the letters her soldiers wrote home from boot camp.*

center around *Center on* is more logical than, and preferable to, *center around.*

climatic, climactic *Climatic* comes from *climate* and refers to weather: *Recent droughts may indicate a climatic change. Climactic* comes from *climax* and refers to a dramatic high point: *During the climactic duel between Hamlet and Laertes, Gertrude drinks poisoned wine.*

complement, compliment To *complement* something is to add to, complete, or reinforce it: *Her yellow blouse complemented her black hair.* To *compliment* something is to make a flattering remark about it: *He complimented her on her hair. Compliment* also functions as a noun: *She thanked him for the compliment.* The adjective *complimentary* can also mean "free": *complimentary tickets.*

compose, comprise *Compose* means "to make up": *The parts compose the whole. Comprise* means "to consist of": *The whole comprises the parts.* Thus, *The band comprises* [not *is comprised of*] *twelve musicians. Twelve musicians compose* [not *comprise*] *the band.*

conscience, conscious *Conscience* is a noun meaning "a sense of right and wrong"; *conscious* is an adjective meaning "aware" or "awake." *Though I was barely conscious, my conscience nagged me.*

contact Often used imprecisely as a verb instead of a more exact word such as *consult, talk with, telephone,* or *write to.*

continual, continuous *Continual* means "constantly recurring": *Most movies on television are continually interrupted by commercials. Continuous* means "unceasing": *Some cable channels present movies continuously without commercials.*

convince, persuade In the strictest sense, to *convince* someone means to change his or her opinion; to *persuade* someone means to move him or her to action. *Convince* is thus properly followed by *of* or *that,* whereas *persuade* is followed by *to: Once he had convinced Othello of Desdemona's infidelity, Iago easily persuaded him to kill her.*

could care less The expression is *could not* [*couldn't*] *care less. Could care less* indicates some care, the opposite of what is intended.

could of See *have, of.*

couple of   Used colloquially to mean "a few" or "several."

credible, creditable, credulous   *Credible* means "believable": *It's a strange story, but it seems credible to me. Creditable* means "deserving of credit" or "worthy": *Steve gave a creditable performance. Credulous* means "gullible": *The credulous Claire believed Tim's lies.* See also *incredible, incredulous.*

criteria   The plural of *criterion* (meaning "standard for judgment"): *Our criteria are strict. The most important criterion is a sense of humor.*

data   The plural of *datum* (meaning "fact"): *Out of all the data generated by these experiments, not one datum supports our hypothesis.* Usually, a more common term such as *fact, result,* or *figure* is preferred to *datum.* Though *data* is often used with a singular verb, many readers prefer the plural verb and it is always correct: *The data fail* [not *fails*] *to support the hypothesis.*

device, devise   *Device* is the noun, and *devise* is the verb: *Can you devise some device for getting his attention?*

different from, different than   *Different from* is preferred: *His purpose is different from mine.* But *different than* is widely accepted when a construction using *from* would be wordy: *I'm a different person now than I used to be* is preferable to *I'm a different person now from the person I used to be.*

differ from, differ with   To *differ from* is to be unlike: *The twins differ from each other only in their hairstyles.* To *differ with* is to disagree with: *I have to differ with you on that point.*

discreet, discrete   *Discreet* (noun form *discretion*) means "tactful": *What's a discreet way of telling Maud to be quiet? Discrete* (noun form *discreteness*) means "separate and distinct": *Within a computer's memory are millions of discrete bits of information.*

disinterested, uninterested   *Disinterested* means "impartial": *We chose Pete, as a disinterested third party, to decide who was right. Uninterested* means "bored" or "lacking interest": *Unfortunately, Pete was completely uninterested in the question.*

don't   *Don't* is the contraction for *do not,* not for *does not: I don't care, you don't care,* and *he doesn't* [not *don't*] *care.*

due to   *Due* is an adjective or noun; thus *due to* is always acceptable as a subject complement: *His gray hairs were due to age.* Many object to *due to* as a preposition meaning "because of" (*Due to the holiday, class was canceled*). A rule of thumb is that *due to* is always correct after a form of the verb *be* but questionable otherwise.

due to the fact that   Wordy for *because.*

each and every   Wordy for *each* or *every.* Write *each one of us* or *every one of us,* not *each and every one of us.*

eager, anxious   See *anxious, eager.*

effect   See *affect, effect.*

elicit, illicit   *Elicit* is a verb meaning "bring out" or "call forth." *Illicit* is an adjective meaning "unlawful." *The crime elicited an outcry against illicit drugs.*

emigrate, immigrate *Emigrate* means "to leave one place and move to another" (the Latin prefix *e-* means "out of": "migrate out of"): *The Chus emigrated from Korea. Immigrate* means "to move into a place where one was not born" (the Latin prefix *im-* means "into": "migrate into"): *They immigrated to the United States.*

ensure See *assure, ensure, insure.*

enthused Used colloquially as an adjective meaning "showing enthusiasm." The preferred adjective is *enthusiastic: The coach was enthusiastic* [not *enthused*] *about the team's victory.*

especially, specially *Especially* means "particularly" or "more than other things"; *specially* means "for a specific reason." *I especially treasure my boots. They were made specially for me.*

et al., etc. Use *et al.*, the Latin abbreviation for "and other people," only in source citations: *Jones et al.* Avoid *etc.*, the Latin abbreviation for "and other things," in formal writing, and do not use it to refer to people or to substitute for precision, as in *The government provides health care, etc.* See also *and etc.*

everybody, every body; everyone, every one *Everybody* and *everyone* are indefinite pronouns: *Everybody* [or *Everyone*] *knows Tom steals. Every one* is a pronoun modified by *every*, and *every body* is a noun modified by *every*. Both refer to each thing or person of a specific group and are typically followed by *of: The game commissioner has stocked every body of fresh water in the state with fish, and now every one of our rivers is a potential trout stream.*

everyday, every day *Everyday* is an adjective meaning "used daily" or "common"; *every day* is a noun modified by *every: Everyday problems tend to arise every day.*

everywheres Nonstandard for *everywhere.*

except See *accept, except.*

except for the fact that Wordy for *except that.*

explicit, implicit *Explicit* means "stated outright": *I left explicit instructions. He explicitly consented. Implicit* means "implied, unstated": *We had an implicit understanding. I trust Marcia implicitly.*

farther, further *Farther* refers to additional distance (*How much farther is it to the beach?*), and *further* refers to additional time, amount, or other abstract matters (*I don't want to discuss this any further*).

feel Avoid this word in place of *think* or *believe: She thinks* [not *feels*] *that the law should be changed.*

fewer, less *Fewer* refers to individual countable items (a plural count noun), *less* to general amounts (a noncount noun, always singular): *Skim milk has fewer calories than whole milk. We have less milk left than I thought.*

field The phrase *the field of* is wordy and generally unnecessary: *Margaret plans to specialize in* [not *in the field of*] *family medicine.*

figure See *calculate, figure, reckon.*

fixing to Avoid this colloquial substitute for "intend to": *The school intends* [not *is fixing*] *to build a new library.*

flaunt, flout *Flaunt* means "show off": *If you have style, flaunt it. Flout* means "scorn" or "defy": *Hester Prynne flouted convention and paid the price.*

flunk A colloquial substitute for *fail.*

former, latter *Former* refers to the first-named of two things, *latter* to the second-named: *I like both skiing and swimming, the former in the winter and the latter all year round.* To refer to the first- or last-named of three or more things, say *first* or *last: I like jogging, swimming, and hang gliding, but the last is inconvenient in the city.*

fun As an adjective, *fun* is colloquial and should be avoided in most writing: *It was a pleasurable* [not *fun*] *evening.*

further See *farther, further.*

get This common verb is used in many slang and colloquial expressions: *get lost, that really gets me, getting on. Get* is easy to overuse; watch out for it in expressions such as *it's getting better* (substitute *improving*) and *we got done* (substitute *finished*).

go As a substitute for *say* or *reply, go* is colloquial: *He says* [not *goes*], *"How do you do, madam?"*

good, well *Good* is an adjective, and *well* is nearly always an adverb: *Larry's a good dancer. He and Linda dance well together. Well* is properly used as an adjective only to refer to health: *You look well.* (*You look good,* in contrast, means "Your appearance is pleasing.")

good and Colloquial for "very": *I was very* [not *good and*] *tired.*

had better See *better, had better.*

had ought The *had* is unnecessary and should be omitted: *He ought* [not *had ought*] *to listen to his mother.*

half Either *half a* or *a half* is appropriate usage, but *a half a* is redundant: *Half a loaf* [not *A half a loaf*] *is better than none. I'd like a half-gallon* [not *a half a gallon*] *of mineral water, please.*

hanged, hung Though both are past-tense forms of *hang, hanged* is used to refer to executions and *hung* is used for all other meanings: *Tom Dooley was hanged* [not *hung*] *from a white oak tree. I hung* [not *hanged*] *the picture you gave me.*

hardly See *but, hardly, scarcely.*

have, of Use *have,* not *of,* after helping verbs such as *could, should, would, may,* and *might: You should have* [not *should of*] *told me.*

he, she; he/she Convention has allowed the use of *he* to mean "he or she": *After the infant learns to creep, he progresses to crawling.* However, many writers today consider this usage inaccurate and unfair because it seems to exclude females. The construction *he/she,* one substitute for *he,* is awkward and objectionable to most readers. The better choice is to make the pronoun plural, to rephrase, or, sparingly, to use *he or she.* For instance: *After infants learn to creep, they progress to crawling. After learning to creep, the infant progresses to crawling. After the infant learns to creep, he or she progresses to crawling.* (See also pp. 311–13 and 508–10.)

herself, himself   See *myself, herself, himself, yourself.*

hisself   Nonstandard for *himself.*

hopefully   *Hopefully* means "with hope": *Freddy waited hopefully for a glimpse of Eliza.* The use of *hopefully* to mean "it is to be hoped," "I hope," or "let's hope" is now very common; but since many readers continue to object strongly to the usage, you should avoid it. *I hope* [not *Hopefully*] *the law will pass.*

idea, ideal   An *idea* is a thought or conception. An *ideal* (noun) is a model of perfection or a goal. *Ideal* should not be used in place of *idea*: *The idea* [not *ideal*] *of the play is that our ideals often sustain us.*

if, whether   For clarity, use *whether* rather than *if* when you are expressing an alternative: *If I laugh hard, people can't tell whether I'm crying.*

illicit   See *elicit, illicit.*

illusion   See *allusion, illusion.*

immigrate, emigrate   See *emigrate, immigrate.*

impact   Both the noun and the verb *impact* connote forceful or even violent collision. Avoid the increasingly common diluted meanings of *impact*: "an effect" (noun) or "to have an effect on" (verb). The diluted verb (*The budget cuts impacted social science research*) is bureaucratic jargon.

implicit   See *explicit, implicit.*

imply, infer   Writers or speakers *imply*, meaning "suggest": *Jim's letter implies he's having a good time.* Readers or listeners *infer*, meaning "conclude": *From Jim's letter I infer he's having a good time.*

in, into   *In* indicates location or condition: *He was in the garage. She was in a coma. Into* indicates movement or a change in condition: *He went into the garage. She fell into a coma.* Generally avoid the slang sense of *into* meaning "interested in" or "involved in": *I am into Zen.*

in . . .   A number of phrases beginning with *in* are needlessly wordy and should be avoided: *in the event that* (for *if*); *in the neighborhood of* (for *approximately* or *about*); *in this day and age* (for *now* or *nowadays*); *in spite of the fact that* (for *although* or *even though*); and *in view of the fact that* (for *because* or *considering that*). Certain other *in* phrases are nothing but padding and can be omitted entirely: *in nature, in number, in reality,* and *in a very real sense.* (See also pp. 525–26.)

incredible, incredulous   *Incredible* means "unbelievable"; *incredulous* means "unbelieving": *When Nancy heard Dennis's incredible story, she was frankly incredulous.* See also *credible, creditable, credulous.*

individual, person, party   *Individual* should refer to a single human being in contrast to a group or should stress uniqueness: *The US Constitution places strong emphasis on the rights of the individual.* For other meanings *person* is preferable: *What person* [not *individual*] *wouldn't want the security promised in that advertisement? Party* means "group" (*Can you seat a party of four for dinner?*) and should not be used to refer to an individual except in legal documents. See also *people, persons.*

infer   See *imply, infer.*

in regards to   Nonstandard for *in regard to, as regards,* or *regarding.* See also *regarding.*

inside of, outside of   The *of* is unnecessary when *inside* and *outside* are used as prepositions: *Stay inside* [not *inside of*] *the house. The decision is outside* [not *outside of*] *my authority. Inside of* may refer colloquially to time, though in formal English *within* is preferred: *The law was passed within* [not *inside of*] *a year.*

instance   See *case, instance, line.*

insure   See *assure, ensure, insure.*

irregardless   Nonstandard for *regardless.*

is, are   See *are, is.*

is because   See *reason is because.*

is when, is where   These are faulty constructions in sentences that define: *Adolescence is a stage* [not *is when a person is*] *between childhood and adulthood. Socialism is a system in which* [not *is where*] *government owns the means of production.* (See also p. 371.)

its, it's   *Its* is the pronoun *it* in the possessive case: *That plant is losing its leaves. It's* is a contraction for *it is* or *it has: It's* [*It is*] *likely to die. It's* [*It has*] *got a fungus.* Many people confuse *it's* and *its* because possessives are most often formed with *-'s;* but the possessive *its,* like *his* and *hers,* never takes an apostrophe.

-ize, -wise   The suffix *-ize* changes a noun or adjective into a verb: *revolutionize, immunize.* The suffix *-wise* changes a noun or adjective into an adverb: *clockwise, otherwise, likewise.* Avoid the two suffixes except in established words: *The two nations are ready to settle on* [not *finalize*] *an agreement. I'm highly sensitive* [not *sensitized*] *to that kind of criticism. Financially* [not *Moneywise*], *it's a good time to buy land.*

kind of, sort of, type of   In formal speech and writing, avoid using *kind of* or *sort of* to mean "somewhat": *He was rather* [not *kind of*] *tall.*

Kind, sort, and *type* are singular and take singular modifiers and verbs: *This kind of dog is easily trained.* Agreement errors often occur when these singular nouns are combined with the plural adjectives *these* and *those: These kinds* [not *kind*] *of dogs are easily trained. Kind, sort,* and *type* should be followed by *of* but not by *a: I don't know what type of* [not *type* or *type of a*] *dog that is.*

Use *kind of, sort of,* or *type of* only when the word *kind, sort,* or *type* is important: *That was a strange* [not *strange sort of*] *statement.*

later, latter   *Later* refers to time; *latter* refers to the second-named of two items. See also *former, latter.*

lay, lie   *Lay* means "put" or "place" and takes a direct object: *We could lay the tablecloth in the sun.* Its main forms are *lay, laid, laid. Lie* means "recline" or "be situated" and does not take an object: *I lie awake at night. The town lies east of the river.* Its main forms are *lie, lay, lain.* (See also p. 278.)

leave, let   *Leave* and *let* are interchangeable only when followed by *alone; leave me alone* is the same as *let me alone.* Otherwise, *leave* means "depart" and *let* means "allow": *Julia would not let Susan leave.*

less   See *fewer, less.*

let   See *leave, let.*

liable   See *apt, liable, likely.*

lie, lay   See *lay, lie.*

like, as   In formal speech and writing, *like* should not introduce a full clause (with a subject and a verb) because it is a preposition. The preferred choice is *as* or *as if: The plan succeeded as* [not *like*] *we hoped. It seemed as if* [not *like*] *it might fail. Other plans like it have failed.*

When *as* serves as a preposition, the distinction between *as* and *like* depends on meaning. *As* suggests that the subject is equivalent or identical to the description: *She was hired as an engineer. Like* suggests resemblance but not identity: *People like her do well in such jobs.* See also *like, such as.*

like, such as   Strictly, *such as* precedes an example that represents a larger subject, whereas *like* indicates that two subjects are comparable. *Steve has recordings of many great saxophonists such as Ben Webster and Lee Konitz. Steve wants to be a great jazz saxophonist like Ben Webster and Lee Konitz.*

Many writers prefer to keep *such* and *as* together: *Steve admires saxophonists such as* . . . rather than *Steve admires such saxophonists as.* . . .

likely   See *apt, liable, likely.*

line   See *case, instance, line.*

literally   This word means "actually" or "just as the words say," and it should not be used to qualify or intensify expressions whose words are not to be taken at face value. The sentence *He was literally climbing the walls* describes a person behaving like an insect, not a person who is restless or anxious. For the latter meaning, *literally* should be omitted.

lose, loose   *Lose* means "mislay": *Did you lose a brown glove? Loose* means "unrestrained" or "not tight": *Ann's canary got loose. Loose* can also function as a verb meaning "let loose": *They loose the dogs as soon as they spot the bear.*

lots, lots of   Colloquial substitutes for *very many, a great many,* or *much.* Avoid *lots* and *lots of* in college or business writing. When you use either one informally, be careful to maintain subject-verb agreement: *There are* [not *is*] *lots of fish in the pond.*

may, can   See *can, may.*

may be, maybe   *May be* is a verb, and *maybe* is an adverb meaning "perhaps": *Tuesday may be a legal holiday. Maybe we won't have classes.*

may of   See *have, of.*

media   *Media* is the plural of *medium* and takes a plural verb: *All the news media are increasingly visual.* The singular verb is common, even in the media, but many readers prefer the plural verb and it is always correct.

might of   See *have, of.*

moral, morale   As a noun, *moral* means "ethical conclusion" or "lesson": *The moral of the story escapes me. Morale* means "spirit" or "state of mind": *Victory improved the team's morale.*

most, almost See *almost, most.*

must of See *have, of.*

myself, herself, himself, yourself The *-self* pronouns refer to or inten-sify another word or words: *Paul helped himself; Jill herself said so.* The *-self* pronouns are often used colloquially in place of personal pronouns, but that use should be avoided in formal speech and writing: *No one except me* [not *myself*] *saw the accident. Our delegates will be Susan and you* [not *yourself*]. See also p. 266 on the unchanging forms of the *-self* pronouns in standard American English.

nohow Nonstandard for *in no way* or *in any way.*

nothing like, nowhere near These colloquial substitutes for *not nearly* are best avoided in formal speech and writing: *That program is not nearly* [not *nowhere near*] *as expensive.*

nowheres Nonstandard for *nowhere.*

number See *amount, number.*

of, have See *have, of.*

off of *Of* is unnecessary. Use *off* or *from* rather than *off of: He jumped off* [or *from,* not *off of*] *the roof.*

OK, O.K., okay All three spellings are acceptable, but avoid this collo-quial term in formal speech and writing.

on, upon In modern English, *upon* is usually just a stuffy way of saying *on.* Unless you need a formal effect, use *on: We decided on* [not *upon*] *a location for our next meeting.*

on account of Wordy for *because of.*

on the other hand This transitional expression of contrast should be preceded by its mate, *on the one hand: On the one hand, we hoped for snow. On the other hand, we feared that it would harm the animals.* How-ever, the two combined can be unwieldy, and a simple *but, however, yet,* or *in contrast* often suffices: *We hoped for snow. Yet we feared that it would harm the animals.*

outside of See *inside of, outside of.*

owing to the fact that Wordy for *because.*

party See *individual, person, party.*

people, persons In formal usage, *people* refers to a general group: *We the people of the United States. . . . Persons* refers to a collection of individ-uals: *Will the person or persons who saw the accident please notify. . . .* Except when emphasizing individuals, prefer *people* to *persons.* See also *individual, person, party.*

per Except in technical writing, an English equivalent is usually pref-erable to the Latin *per: $10 an* [not *per*] *hour; sent by* [not *per*] *parcel post; requested in* [not *per* or *as per*] *your letter.*

percent (per cent), percentage Both of these terms refer to fractions of one hundred. *Percent* always follows a number (*40 percent of the voters*), and the word should be used instead of the symbol (%) in general writing. *Percentage* stands alone (*the percentage of votes*) or follows an adjective (*a high percentage*).

person   See *individual, person, party.*

persons   See *people, persons.*

persuade   See *convince, persuade.*

phenomena   The plural of *phenomenon* (meaning "perceivable fact" or "unusual occurrence"): *Many phenomena are not recorded. One phenomenon is attracting attention.*

plenty   A colloquial substitute for *very: The reaction occurred very* [not *plenty*] *fast.*

plus   *Plus* is standard as a preposition meaning *in addition to: His income plus mine is sufficient.* But *plus* is colloquial as a conjunctive adverb: *Our organization is larger than theirs; moreover* [not *plus*], *we have more money.*

practicable, practical   *Practicable* means "capable of being put into practice"; *practical* means "useful" or "sensible": *We figured out a practical new design for our kitchen, but it was too expensive to be practicable.*

precede, proceed   The verb *precede* means "come before": *My name precedes yours in the alphabet.* The verb *proceed* means "move on": *We were told to proceed to the waiting room.*

prejudice, prejudiced   *Prejudice* is a noun; *prejudiced* is an adjective. Do not drop the *-d* from *prejudiced: I knew that my parents were prejudiced* [not *prejudice*].

pretty   Overworked as an adverb meaning "rather" or "somewhat": *He was somewhat* [not *pretty*] *irked at the suggestion.*

previous to, prior to   Wordy for *before.*

principal, principle   *Principal* is an adjective meaning "foremost" or "major," a noun meaning "chief official," or, in finance, a noun meaning "capital sum." *Principle* is a noun only, meaning "rule" or "axiom." *Her principal reasons for confessing were her principles of right and wrong.*

proceed, precede   See *precede, proceed.*

provided, providing   *Provided* may serve as a subordinating conjunction meaning "on the condition (that)"; *providing* may not. *The grocer will begin providing food for the soup kitchen provided* [not *providing*] *we find a suitable space.*

question of whether, question as to whether   Wordy substitutes for *whether.*

raise, rise   *Raise* means "lift" or "bring up" and takes a direct object: *The Kirks raise cattle.* Its main forms are *raise, raised, raised. Rise* means "get up" and does not take an object: *They must rise at dawn.* Its main forms are *rise, rose, risen.* (See also p. 278.)

real, really   In formal speech and writing, *real* should not be used as an adverb; *really* is the adverb and *real* an adjective. *Popular reaction to the announcement was really* [not *real*] *enthusiastic.*

reason is because   Although colloquially common, this expression should be avoided in formal speech and writing. Use a *that* clause after *reason is: The reason he is absent is that* [not *is because*] *he is sick.* Or: *He is absent because he is sick.*

reckon See *calculate, figure, reckon.*

regarding, in regard to, with regard to, relating to, relative to, with respect to, respecting Stuffy substitutes for *on, about,* or *concerning: Mr. McGee spoke about* [not *with regard to*] *the plans for the merger.*

respectful, respective *Respectful* means "full of (or showing) respect": *Be respectful of other people. Respective* means "separate": *The French and the Germans occupied their respective trenches.*

rise, raise See *raise, rise.*

scarcely See *but, hardly, scarcely.*

sensual, sensuous *Sensual* suggests sexuality; *sensuous* means "pleasing to the senses." *Stirred by the sensuous scent of meadow grass and flowers, Cheryl and Paul found their thoughts growing increasingly sensual.*

set, sit *Set* means "put" or "place" and takes a direct object: *He sets the pitcher down.* Its main forms are *set, set, set. Sit* means "be seated" and does not take an object: *She sits on the sofa.* Its main forms are *sit, sat, sat.* (See also p. 278.)

shall, will *Will* is the future-tense helping verb for all persons: *I will go, you will go, they will go.* The main use of *shall* is for first-person questions requesting an opinion or consent: *Shall I order a pizza? Shall we dance?* (Questions that merely inquire about the future use *will: When will I see you again?*) *Shall* can also be used for the first person when a formal effect is desired (*I shall expect you around three*), and it is occasionally used with the second or third person to express the speaker's determination (*You shall do as I say*).

should, would *Should* expresses obligation: *I should fix dinner. You should set the table. Jack should wash the dishes. Would* expresses a wish or hypothetical condition: *I would do it. Wouldn't you?* When the context is formal, however, *should* is sometimes used instead of *would* in the first person: *We should be delighted to accept.*

should of See *have, of.*

since *Since* mainly relates to time: *I've been waiting since noon.* But *since* is also often used to mean "because": *Since you ask, I'll tell you.* Revise sentences in which the word could have either meaning, such as *Since I studied physics, I have been planning to major in engineering.*

sit, set See *set, sit.*

situation Often unnecessary, as in *The situation is that we have to get some help* (revise to *We have to get some help*) or *The team was faced with a punting situation* (revise to *The team was faced with punting* or *The team had to punt*).

so Avoid using *so* alone as a vague intensifier: *He was so late. So* needs to be followed by *that* and a clause that states a result: *He was so late that I left without him.*

some *Some* is colloquial as an adverb meaning "somewhat" or "to some extent" and as an adjective meaning "remarkable": *We'll have to hurry somewhat* [not *some*] *to get there in time. Those are remarkable* [not *some*] *photographs.*

somebody, some body; someone, some one *Somebody* and *someone* are indefinite pronouns; *some body* is a noun modified by *some;* and *some one* is a pronoun or an adjective modified by *some*. *Somebody ought to invent a shampoo that will give hair some body. Someone told Janine she should choose some one plan and stick with it.*

someplace Informal for *somewhere*.

sometime, sometimes, some time *Sometime* means "at an indefinite time in the future": *Why don't you come up and see me sometime? Sometimes* means "now and then": *I still see my old friend Joe sometimes. Some time* means "a span of time": *I need some time to make the payments.*

somewheres Nonstandard for *somewhere*.

sort of, sort of a See *kind of, sort of, type of.*

specially See *especially, specially.*

such Avoid using *such* as a vague intensifier: *It was such a cold winter. Such* should be followed by *that* and a clause that states a result: *It was such a cold winter that Napoleon's troops had to turn back.*

such as See *like, such as.*

supposed to, used to In both of these expressions, the *-d* is essential: *I used to* [not *use to*] *think so. He's supposed to* [not *suppose to*] *meet us.*

sure Colloquial when used as an adverb meaning *surely: James Madison sure was right about the need for the Bill of Rights.* If you merely want to be emphatic, use *certainly: Madison certainly was right.* If your goal is to convince a possibly reluctant reader, use *surely: Madison surely was right. Surely Madison was right.*

sure and, sure to; try and, try to *Sure to* and *try to* are the correct forms: *Be sure to* [not *sure and*] *vote. Try to* [not *Try and*] *vote early to avoid a line.*

take, bring See *bring, take.*

than, as See *as, than.*

than, then *Than* is a conjunction used in comparisons, *then* an adverb indicating time: *Holmes knew then that Moriarty was wilier than he had thought.*

that, which *That* always introduces an essential clause: *We should use the lettuce that Susan bought* (*that Susan bought* limits *lettuce* to a particular lettuce). *Which* can introduce both essential and nonessential clauses, but many writers reserve *which* only for nonessential clauses: *The leftover lettuce, which is in the refrigerator, would make a good salad* (*which is in the refrigerator* simply provides more information about the lettuce we already know of). Essential clauses (with *that* or *which*) are not set off by commas; nonessential clauses (with *which*) are. (See also pp. 428–29.)

that, who, which Use *that* to refer to most animals and to things: *The animals that escaped included a zebra. The rocket that failed cost millions.* Use *who* to refer to people and to animals with names: *Dorothy is the girl who visits Oz. Her dog, Toto, who accompanies her, gives her courage.* Use *which* only to refer to animals and things: *The river, which runs more than a thousand miles, empties into the Indian Ocean.* (See also pp. 350–51.)

their, there, they're   *Their* is the possessive form of *they: Give them their money. There* indicates place (*I saw her standing there*) or functions to postpone the sentence subject (*There is a hole behind you*). *They're* is a contraction for *they are: They're going fast.*

theirselves   Nonstandard for *themselves.*

them   In standard American English, *them* does not serve as an adjective: *Those* [not *Them*] *people want to know.*

then, than   See *than, then.*

these kind, these sort, these type, those kind   See *kind of, sort of, type of.*

this, these   *This* is singular: *this car* or *This is the reason I left. These* is plural: *these cars* or *These are not valid reasons.*

this here, these here, that there, them there   Nonstandard for *this, these, that,* and *those.*

thru   A colloquial spelling of *through* that should be avoided in all academic and business writing.

thusly   A mistaken form of *thus.*

till, until, 'til   *Till* and *until* have the same meaning; either is acceptable. *'Til,* a contraction of *until,* is an old form that has been replaced by *till.*

time period   Since a *period* is an interval of time, the expression is redundant: *They did not see each other for a long time* [not *time period*]. *Six accidents occurred in a three-week period* [not *time period*].

to, too, two   *To* is a preposition; *too* is an adverb meaning "also" or "excessively"; and *two* is a number. *I too have been to Europe two times.*

too   Avoid using *too* as a vague intensifier: *Monkeys are too mean.* When you do use *too,* explain the consequences of the excessive quality: *Monkeys are too mean to make good pets.*

toward, towards   Both are acceptable, though *toward* is preferred. Use one or the other consistently.

try and, try to   See *sure and, sure to; try and, try to.*

type of   See *kind of, sort of, type of.* Don't use *type* without *of: It was a family type of* [not *type*] *restaurant.* Or, better: *It was a family restaurant.*

uninterested   See *disinterested, uninterested.*

unique   *Unique* means "the only one of its kind" and so cannot sensibly be modified with words such as *very* or *most: That was a unique* [not *a very unique* or *the most unique*] *movie.*

until   See *till, until, 'til.*

upon, on   See *on, upon.*

usage, use   *Usage* refers to conventions, most often those of a language: *Is "hadn't ought" proper usage? Usage* is often misused in place of the noun *use: Wise use* [not *usage*] *of insulation can save fuel.*

use, utilize   *Utilize* can be used to mean "make good use of": *Many teachers utilize computers for instruction.* But for all other senses of "place in service" or "employ," prefer *use.*

used to   See *supposed to, used to.*

wait for, wait on   In formal speech and writing, *wait for* means "await" (*I'm waiting for Paul*), and *wait on* means "serve" (*The owner of the store herself waited on us*).

ways   Colloquial as a substitute for *way: We have only a little way* [not *ways*] *to go.*

well   See *good, well.*

whether, if   See *if, whether.*

which, that   See *that, which.*

which, who, that   See *that, who, which.*

who, whom   *Who* is the subject of a sentence or clause (*We don't know who will come*). *Whom* is the object of a verb or preposition (*We do not know whom we invited*). (See also pp. 269–70.)

who's, whose   *Who's* is the contraction of *who is* or *who has: Who's [Who is] at the door? Jim is the only one who's [who has] passed. Whose* is the possessive form of *who: Whose book is that?*

will, shall   See *shall, will.*

wise   See *-ize, -wise.*

with regard to, with respect to   See *regarding.*

would   See *should, would.*

would be   Often used instead of *is* or *are* to soften statements needlessly: *One example is* [not *would be*] *gun-control laws. Would* can combine with other verbs for the same unassertive effect: *would ask, would seem, would suggest,* and so on.

would have   Avoid this construction in place of *had* in clauses that begin *if* and state a condition contrary to fact: *If the tree had* [not *would have*] *withstood the fire, it would have been the oldest in the state.* (See also p. 297.)

would of   See *have, of.*

you   In all but very formal writing, *you* is generally appropriate as long as it means "you, the reader." In all writing, avoid indefinite uses of *you,* such as *In one ancient tribe your first loyalty was to your parents.* (See also p. 350.)

your, you're   *Your* is the possessive form of *you: Your dinner is ready. You're* is the contraction of *you are: You're bound to be late.*

yourself   See *myself, herself, himself, yourself.*

Glossary of Terms

This glossary defines terms of grammar, rhetoric, literary analysis, research, and other aspects of writing. Page numbers in parentheses refer you to sections of the text where the term is explained more fully.

absolute phrase   A phrase consisting of a noun or pronoun plus the *-ing* or *-ed* form of a verb (a participle): *Our accommodations arranged, we set out on our journey. They will hire a local person, other things being equal.* An absolute phrase modifies a whole clause or sentence (rather than a single word), and it is not joined to the rest of the sentence by a connector. (See p. 249.)

abstract and concrete   Two kinds of language. **Abstract** words refer to ideas, qualities, attitudes, and conditions that can't be perceived with the senses: *beauty, guilty, victory.* **Concrete** words refer to objects, persons, places, or conditions that can be perceived with the senses: *Abilene, scratchy, toolbox.* See also *general and specific.* (See pp. 516–17.)

acronym   A pronounceable word formed from the initial letter or letters of each word in an organization's title: for example, NATO (North Atlantic Treaty Organization).

active voice   See *verb voice.*

adjectival   A term sometimes used to describe any word or word group, other than an adjective, that is used to modify a noun. Common adjectivals include nouns (*wagon train, railroad ties*), phrases (*fool on the hill*), and clauses (*the man that I used to be*).

adjective   A word used to modify a noun (*beautiful morning*) or a pronoun (*ordinary one*). (See Chapter 16.) Nouns, some verb forms, phrases, and clauses may also serve as adjectives: *book sale; a used book; sale of old books; the sale, which occurs annually.* (See *clauses, prepositional phrases,* and *verbals and verbal phrases.*)

Adjectives come in several classes:

- A **descriptive adjective** names some quality of a noun: *beautiful morning, dark horse.*
- A **limiting adjective** narrows the scope of a noun. It may be a **possessive** (*my, their*); a **demonstrative adjective** (*this train, these days*); an **interrogative adjective** (*what time? whose body?*); or a number (*two boys*).
- A **proper adjective** is derived from a proper noun: *French language, Machiavellian scheme.*

Adjectives can also be classified according to position:

- An **attributive adjective** appears next to the noun it modifies: *full moon.*
- A **predicate adjective** is connected to its noun by a linking verb: *The moon is full.* See also *complement.*

adjective clause   See *adjective.*

adjective phrase   See *adjective.*

adverb   A word used to modify a verb (*warmly greet*), an adjective (*only three people*), another adverb (*quite seriously*), or a whole sentence (*Fortunately, she is employed*). (See Chapter 16.) Some verb forms, phrases, and clauses may also serve as adverbs: *easy to stop, drove by a farm, plowed the fields when the earth thawed.* (See *clause, prepositional phrase,* and *verbals and verbal phrases.*)

adverb clause   See *adverb.*

adverbial   A term sometimes used to describe any word or word group, other than an adverb, that is used to modify a verb, an adjective, another adverb, or a whole sentence. Common adverbials include nouns (*This little piggy stayed home*), phrases (*This little piggy went to market*), and clauses (*This little piggy went wherever he wanted*).

adverbial conjunction   See *conjunctive adverb.*

adverb phrase   See *adverb.*

agreement   The correspondence of one word to another in person, number, or gender. A verb must agree with its subject (*The chef orders egg sandwiches*), a pronoun must agree with its antecedent (*The chef surveys her breakfast*), and a demonstrative adjective must agree with its noun (*She likes these kinds of sandwiches*). (See Chapter 15.)

   Logical agreement requires consistency in number between other related words, usually nouns: *The students brought their books* [not *book*]. (See p. 354.)

analogy   A comparison between members of different classes, such as a nursery school and a barnyard or a molecule and a pair of dancers. Usually, the purpose is to explain something unfamiliar to readers through something familiar. (See p. 99.)

analysis   The separation of a subject into its elements. Sometimes called **division,** analysis is fundamental to critical thinking, reading, and writing (pp. 147–48, 156–58) and is a useful tool for developing essays (p. 25) and paragraphs (pp. 96–97).

antecedent   The word to which a pronoun refers: *Jonah, who is not yet ten, has already chosen the college he will attend* (*Jonah* is the antecedent of the pronouns *who* and *he*). (See pp. 309–13.)

APA style   The style of documentation recommended by the American Psychological Association and used in many of the social sciences. (For discussion and examples, see pp. 779–802.)

appeals   Attempts to engage and persuade readers. An **emotional appeal** touches readers' feelings, beliefs, and values. An **ethical appeal** presents the writer as competent, sincere, and fair. A **rational appeal** engages readers' powers of reasoning. (See pp. 205–07.)

appositive   A word or phrase appearing next to a noun or pronoun that renames or identifies it and is equivalent to it: *My brother Michael, the best horn player in town, won the state competition* (*Michael* identifies which brother is being referred to; *the best horn player in town* renames *Michael*). (See pp. 254–55.)

argument Writing whose primary purpose is to convince readers of an idea or persuade them to act. (See Chapters 9–11.)

article The word *a, an,* or *the.* Articles are sometimes called **determiners** because they always signal that a noun follows. (See pp. 322–25 for when to use *a/an* versus *the.* See p. 865 for when to use *a* versus *an.*)

assertion See *claim.*

assumption A stated or unstated belief or opinion. Uncovering assumptions is part of critical thinking, reading, and writing (see pp. 148–50, 160). In argument, assumptions connect claims and evidence (see pp. 185–86).

audience The intended readers of a piece of writing. Knowledge of the audience's needs and expectations helps a writer shape writing so that it is clear, interesting, and convincing. (See pp. 12–15, 166.)

auxiliary verb See *helping verb.*

balanced sentence A sentence consisting of two clauses with parallel constructions: *Do as I say, not as I do. Befriend all animals; exploit none.* Their balance makes such sentences highly emphatic. (See p. 383.)

belief A conviction based on morality, values, or faith. Statements of belief often serve as assumptions and sometimes as evidence, but they are not arguable and so cannot serve as the thesis in an argument. (See p. 180.)

blog A Web site, often created and maintained by a person or small group of people, with regular, dated entries of commentary or descriptions of events.

body In a piece of writing, the large central part where ideas supporting the thesis are presented and developed. See also *conclusion* and *introduction.*

brainstorming A technique for generating ideas about a subject: concentrating on the subject for a fixed time (say, fifteen minutes), you list every idea and detail that comes to mind. (See pp. 22–23.)

cardinal number The type of number that shows amount: *two, sixty, ninety-seven.* Contrast *ordinal number* (such as *second, ninety-seventh*).

case The form of a noun or pronoun that indicates its function in the sentence. Most pronouns have three cases:

- The **subjective case** (*I, she*) for the subject of a verb or for a subject complement.
- The **objective case** (*me, her*) for the object of a verb, verbal, or preposition.
- The **possessive case** to indicate ownership, used either as an adjective (*my, her*) or as a noun (*mine, hers*).

(See p. 265 for a list of the forms of personal and relative pronouns.)

Nouns use the subjective form (*dog, America*) for all cases except the possessive (*dog's, America's*).

cause-and-effect analysis The determination of why something happened or what its consequences were or will be. (See pp. 26 and 99–100.)

characters The people in a literary work, including the narrator of a story or the speaker of a poem. (See p. 737.)

Chicago style   A style of documentation recommended by *The Chicago Manual of Style* and used in history, art, and some other humanities. (For discussion and examples, see pp. 760–73.)

chronological organization   The arrangement of events as they occurred in time, usually from first to last. (See pp. 40, 82.)

citation   In research writing, the way of acknowledging material borrowed from sources. Most systems of citation are basically similar: a number or brief parenthetical reference in the text indicates that particular material is borrowed and directs the reader to information on the source at the end of the work. The systems do differ, however. (See pp. 644–91 for MLA style, pp. 760–63 for Chicago style, pp. 779–802 for APA style, and pp. 811–18 for CSE style.)

claim   A positive statement or assertion that requires support. Claims are the backbone of any argument. (See pp. 178–81.)

classification   The sorting of many elements into groups based on their similarities. (See pp. 26 and 97–98.)

clause   A group of related words containing a subject and a predicate. A **main (independent) clause** can stand by itself as a sentence. A **subordinate (dependent) clause** serves as a single part of speech and so cannot stand by itself as a sentence.

> Main clause   We can go to the movies.
> Subordinate clause   We can go if Julie gets back on time.

A subordinate clause may function as an adjective (*The car that hit Fred was speeding*), an adverb (*The car hit Fred when it ran a red light*), or a noun (*Whoever was driving should be arrested*). (See p. 252.)

clichés   See *trite expressions.*

climactic organization   The arrangement of material in order of increasing drama or interest, leading to a climax. (See pp. 42, 84.)

clustering   A technique for generating ideas about a subject: drawing and writing, you branch outward from a center point (the subject) to pursue the implications of ideas. (See pp. 23–24.)

coherence   The quality of an effective essay or paragraph that helps readers see relations among ideas and move easily from one idea to the next. (See pp. 42–43, 79–90.)

collaborative learning   Students working together in groups to help each other become better writers and readers. (See pp. 68–71, 831–34.)

collective noun   See *noun.*

colloquial language   The words and expressions of everyday speech. Colloquial language can enliven informal writing but is generally inappropriate in formal academic or business writing. See also *formal and informal.* (See p. 505.)

comma splice   A sentence error in which two main clauses are separated by a comma with no coordinating conjunction. (See Chapter 18.)

> Comma splice   The book was long, it contained useful data.
> Revised   The book was long; it contained useful data.
> Revised   The book was long, and it contained useful data.

common noun   See *noun.*

comparative   See *comparison.*

comparison   The form of an adverb or adjective that shows its degree of quality or amount.

- The **positive degree** is the simple, uncompared form: *gross, shyly.*
- The **comparative degree** compares the thing modified to at least one other thing: *grosser, more shyly.*
- The **superlative degree** indicates that the thing modified exceeds all other things to which it is being compared: *grossest, most shyly.*

The comparative and superlative degrees are formed either with the endings *-er/-est* or with the words *more/most, less/least.* (See pp. 318–19.)

comparison and contrast   The identification of similarities (comparison) and differences (contrast) between two or more subjects. (See pp. 26, 98–99.)

complement   A word or word group that completes the sense of a subject, an object, or a verb. (See pp. 236–39.)

- A **subject complement** follows a linking verb and renames or describes the subject. It may be an adjective, noun, or pronoun. *I am a lion tamer, but I am not yet experienced* (the noun *lion tamer* and the adjective *experienced* complement the subject *I*). Adjective complements are also called **predicate adjectives.** Noun complements are also called **predicate nouns** or **predicate nominatives.**
- An **object complement** follows and modifies or refers to a direct object. The complement may be an adjective or a noun. *If you elect me president, I'll keep the students satisfied* (the noun *president* complements the direct object *me,* and the adjective *satisfied* complements the direct object *students*).
- A **verb complement** is a direct or indirect object of a verb. It may be a noun or pronoun. *Don't give the chimp that peanut* (*chimp* is the indirect object and *peanut* is the direct object of the verb *give;* both objects are verb complements).

complete predicate   See *predicate.*

complete subject   See *subject.*

complex sentence   See *sentence.*

compound construction   Two or more words or word groups serving the same function, such as a **compound subject** (*Harriet and Peter poled their barge down the river*), **compound predicate** (*The scout watched and waited*) or parts of a predicate (*She grew tired and hungry*), and **compound sentence** (*He smiled, and I laughed*). (See p. 256.) **Compound words** include nouns (*featherbrain, strip-mining*) and adjectives (*two-year-old, downtrodden*).

compound-complex sentence   See *sentence.*

compound predicate   See *compound construction.*

compound sentence   See *sentence.*

compound subject   See *compound construction.*

conciseness   Use of the fewest and freshest words to express meaning clearly and achieve the desired effect with readers. (See Chapter 39.)

conclusion   The closing of an essay, tying off the writer's thoughts and leaving readers with a sense of completion. (See pp. 107–09 for suggestions.)

A *conclusion* is also the result of deductive reasoning. See *deductive reasoning* and *syllogism*.

concrete   See *abstract and concrete*.

conditional statement   A statement expressing a condition contrary to fact and using the subjunctive mood of the verb: *If she were mayor, the unions would cooperate.* See also *mood*.

conjugation   A list of the forms of a verb showing tense, voice, mood, person, and number. The conjugation of the verb *know* in present tense, active voice, indicative mood is *I know, you know, he/she/it knows, we know, you know, they know.* (See p. 290 for a fuller conjugation.)

conjunction   A word that links and relates parts of a sentence.

- **Coordinating conjunctions** (*and, but, or, nor, for, so, yet*) connect words or word groups of equal grammatical rank: *The lights went out, but the doctors and nurses kept caring for patients.* (See p. 257.)
- **Correlative conjunctions** or correlatives (such as *either . . . or, not only . . . but also*) are two or more connecting words that work together: *He was certain that either his parents or his brother would help him.* (See p. 257.)
- **Subordinating conjunctions** (*after, although, as if, because, if, when,* and so on) begin subordinate clauses and link them to main clauses: *The seven dwarfs whistle while they work.* (See p. 251.)

conjunctive adverb (adverbial conjunction)   An adverb (such as *besides, consequently, however, indeed,* or *therefore*) that relates two main clauses in a sentence: *We had hoped to own a house by now; however, housing costs have risen too fast.* (See p. 259.) The error known as a comma splice results when two main clauses related by a conjunctive adverb are separated only by a comma. (See pp. 342–43.)

connector (connective)   Any word or phrase that links words, phrases, clauses, or sentences. Common connectors include coordinating, correlative, and subordinating conjunctions; conjunctive adverbs; and prepositions.

connotation   An association called up by a word, beyond its dictionary definition. Contrast *denotation*. (See pp. 514–15.)

construction   Any group of grammatically related words, such as a phrase, a clause, or a sentence.

contraction   A condensation of an expression, with an apostrophe replacing the missing letters: for example, *doesn't* (for *does not*), *we'll* (for *we will*). (See pp. 456–57.)

contrast   See *comparison and contrast*.

coordinate adjectives   Two or more adjectives that equally modify the same noun or pronoun: *The camera panned the vast, empty desert.* (See pp. 433–34.)

coordinating conjunction   See *conjunction*.

coordination   The linking of words, phrases, or clauses that are of equal importance, usually with a coordinating conjunction: *He and I laughed, but she was not amused.* Contrast *subordination*. (See pp. 388–90.)

correlative conjunction (correlative) See *conjunction*.

count noun See *noun*.

critical thinking, reading, and writing Looking beneath the surface of words and images to discern meaning and relationships and to build knowledge. (See Chapter 7.)

CSE style Either of two styles of documenting sources recommended by the Council of Science Editors and frequently used in the natural and applied sciences and in mathematics. (For discussion and examples, see pp. 811–18.)

cumulative (loose) sentence A sentence in which modifiers follow the subject and verb: *Ducks waddled by, their tails swaying and their quacks rising to heaven.* Contrast *periodic sentence*. (See pp. 366–67.)

dangling modifier A modifier that does not sensibly describe anything in its sentence. (See pp. 366–67.)

> **Dangling** <u>Having arrived late</u>, the concert was underway.
>
> **Revised** <u>Having arrived late</u>, <u>we found that</u> the concert was underway.

data In argument, a term used for *evidence*. See *evidence*.

database A collection and organization of information (data). A database may be printed, but the term is most often used for electronic sources.

declension A list of the forms of a noun or pronoun, showing inflections for person (for pronouns), number, and case. See p. 265 for a declension of the personal and relative pronouns.

deductive reasoning Applying a generalization to specific circumstances in order to reach a conclusion. See also *syllogism*. Contrast *inductive reasoning*. (See pp. 200–03.)

definition Specifying the characteristics of something to establish what it is and is not. (See pp. 25, 95–96, 181.)

degree See *comparison*.

demonstrative adjective See *adjective*.

demonstrative pronoun See *pronoun*.

denotation The main or dictionary definition of a word. Contrast *connotation*. (See pp. 514–15.)

dependent clause See *clause*.

derivational suffix See *suffix*.

description Detailing the sensory qualities of a thing, person, place, or feeling. (See pp. 25 and 94.)

descriptive adjective See *adjective*.

descriptor See *keyword(s)*.

determiner A word that marks and precedes a noun: for example, *a, an, the, my, your.* See also *article*. (See pp. 322–26 for the uses of determiners before nouns.)

developing (planning) The stage of the writing process when one finds a subject, explores ideas, gathers information, focuses on a central thesis, and organizes material. Compare *drafting* and *revising*. (See Chapters 1–2.)

dialect A variety of a language used by a specific group or in a specific region. A dialect may be distinguished by its pronunciation, vocabulary, and grammar. (See pp. 168–70 and 503–04.)

diction The choice and use of words. (See Chapters 37–39.)

dictionary form See *plain form*.

direct address A construction in which a word or phrase indicates the person or group spoken to: *Have you finished, John? Farmers, unite.*

direct object See *object*.

direct question A sentence asking a question and concluding with a question mark: *Do they know we are watching?* Contrast *indirect question*.

direct quotation (direct discourse) See *quotation*.

discussion list A mailing list of subscribers who use e-mail to converse on a particular subject.

division See *analysis*.

documentation In research writing, supplying citations that legitimate the use of borrowed material and support claims about its origins. Contrast *plagiarism*. (See pp. 634–35.)

document design The control of a document's elements to achieve the flow, spacing, grouping, emphasis, and standardization that are appropriate for the writing situation. (See Chapter 5.)

domain The part of a Web address (or URL) that gives the organization sponsoring the site.

double negative A generally nonstandard form consisting of two negative words used in the same construction so that they effectively cancel each other: *I don't have no money.* Rephrase as *I have no money* or *I don't have any money.* (See p. 320.)

double possessive A possessive using both the ending -'s and the preposition *of: That is a favorite expression of Mark's.*

double talk (doublespeak) Language intended to confuse or to be misunderstood. (See p. 507.)

drafting The stage of the writing process when ideas are expressed in connected sentences and paragraphs. Compare *developing (planning)* and *revising*. (See pp. 46–48.)

editing A distinct step in revising a written work, focusing on clarity, tone, and correctness. Compare *revising*. (See pp. 59–62.)

ellipsis The omission of a word or words from a quotation, indicated by the three spaced periods of an **ellipsis mark**: *"that all . . . are created equal."*

elliptical clause A clause omitting a word or words whose meaning is understood from the rest of the clause: *David likes Minneapolis better than* [*he likes*] *Chicago.* (See p. 253.)

emotional appeal See *appeals*.

emphasis   The manipulation of words, sentences, and paragraphs to stress important ideas. (See Chapter 23.)

essay   A nonfiction composition of multiple paragraphs, focused on a single subject and with a central idea or thesis.

essential element   A word or word group that is necessary to the meaning of a sentence because it limits the thing it refers to: removing it would leave the meaning unclear or too general. Also called a **restrictive element,** an essential element is not set off by punctuation: *The keys to the car are on the table. That man who called about the apartment said he'd try again tonight.* Contrast *nonessential element.* (See pp. 427–31, 441.)

ethical appeal   See *appeals.*

etymology   The history of a word's meanings and forms.

euphemism   A presumably inoffensive word that a writer or speaker substitutes for a word deemed possibly offensive or too blunt—for example, *passed away* for "died." (See pp. 506–07.)

evaluation   A judgment of the quality, value, currency, bias, or other aspects of a work. (See pp. 151–52, 161, 590–603.)

evidence   The facts, examples, expert opinions, and other information that support the claims in an argument. (See pp. 181–85, 204–05.)

expletive   A sentence that postpones the subject by beginning with *there, here,* or *it* and a form of the verb *be: It is impossible to get a ticket. There should be more seats available. Here are our options.* (See p. 261.)

exposition   Writing whose primary purpose is to explain something about a subject.

fallacies   Errors in reasoning. Some evade the issue of the argument; others oversimplify the argument. (See pp. 190–95.)

faulty predication   A sentence error in which the meanings of subject and predicate conflict, so that the subject is said to be or do something illogical: *The installation of air bags takes up space in a car's steering wheel and dashboard.* (See pp. 371–72.)

figurative language (figures of speech)   Expressions that suggest meanings different from their literal meanings in order to achieve special effects. (See pp. 520–21.) Some common figures:

- **Hyperbole,** deliberate exaggeration: *The bag weighed a ton.*
- **Metaphor,** an implied comparison between two unlike things: *The wind stabbed through our clothes.*
- **Personification,** the attribution of human qualities to a thing or idea: *The water beckoned seductively.*
- **Simile,** an explicit comparison, using *like* or *as,* between two unlike things: *The sky glowered like an angry parent.*

A **mixed metaphor** is a confusing or ludicrous combination of incompatible figures: *The wind stabbed through our clothes and shook our bones.*

finite verb   Any verb that makes an assertion or expresses a state of being and can stand as the main verb of a sentence or clause: *The moose eats the leaves.* (See p. 245.) Contrast *verbal,* which is formed from a finite verb but is unable to stand alone as the main verb of a sentence: *I saw the moose eating the leaves.*

first person   See *person*.

foil   A character in a literary work who contrasts with another character and thus helps to define that other character. (See p. 752.)

formal and informal   Levels of usage achieved through word choice and sentence structure. More informal writing, as in a letter to an acquaintance or a personal essay, resembles some speech in its colloquial language, contractions, and short, fairly simple sentences. More formal writing, as in academic papers and business reports, avoids these attributes of speech and tends to rely on longer and more complicated sentences.

format   In a document such as an academic paper or a business letter, the arrangement and spacing of elements on the page. See also *document design*.

fragment   See *sentence fragment*.

freewriting   A technique for generating ideas: in a fixed amount of time (say, fifteen minutes), you write continuously without stopping to reread. (See pp. 21–22.)

function word   A word, such as an article, conjunction, or preposition, that serves primarily to clarify the roles of and relations between other words in a sentence: *We chased the goat for an hour but finally caught it.* Contrast *lexical word*.

fused sentence (run-on sentence)   A sentence error in which two main clauses are joined with no punctuation or connecting word between them. (See p. 339.)

> **Fused**   I heard his lecture it was dull.
>
> **Revised**   I heard his lecture; it was dull.

future perfect tense   See *tense*.

future tense   See *tense*.

gender   The classification of nouns or pronouns as masculine (*he, boy, handyman*), feminine (*she, woman, actress*), or neuter (*it, typewriter, dog*).

general and specific   Terms designating the relative number of instances or objects included in a group signified by a word. The following list moves from most **general** (including the most objects) to most **specific** (including the fewest objects): *vehicle, four-wheeled vehicle, automobile, sedan, Ford Taurus, blue Ford Taurus, my sister's blue Ford Taurus named Hank.* See also *abstract and concrete*. (See pp. 516–17.)

generalization   A claim inferred from evidence. See also *inductive reasoning*.

generic he   *He* used to mean *he or she*. For ways to avoid *he* when you intend either or both genders, see pp. 311–13 and 509.

generic noun   A noun that refers to a typical member of a group rather than to a specific person or thing: *Any person may come. A student needs good work habits. A school with financial problems may shortchange its students.* A singular generic noun takes a singular pronoun (*he, she,* or *it*). (See pp. 311–13.)

genitive case   Another term for possessive case. See *case*.

genre   A type of writing, such as case study, research report, essay, or poem.

gerund A verbal that ends in *-ing* and functions as a noun: *Working is all right for killing time* (*working* is the subject of the verb *is*; *killing* is the object of the preposition *for*). See also *verbals and verbal phrases*. (See p. 246.)

gerund phrase A word group consisting of a gerund plus any modifiers or objects. See also *verbals and verbal phrases*.

grammar A description of how a language works.

grounds A term used for *evidence* in argument. See *evidence*.

helping verb (auxiliary verb) A verb used with another verb to convey time, obligation, and other meanings: *You should write a letter. You have written other letters.* The **modals** include *can, could, may, might, must, ought, shall, should, will, would.* The other helping verbs are forms of *be, have,* and *do.* (See pp. 274, 280–84.)

homonyms Words that are pronounced the same but have different spellings and meanings, such as *heard/herd* and *to/too/two.* (See pp. 532–33 for a list.)

HTML (hypertext markup language) A computer language used for creating Web pages. An **HTML editor** is a program for coding documents in HTML. (See p. 836.)

hyperbole See *figurative language*.

hypertext Text such as that on the Web that provides links allowing users to move easily and variously within and among documents. Contrast *linear text*.

idiom An expression that is peculiar to a language and that may not make sense if taken literally: for example, *bide your time,* and *by and large.* See pp. 518–19 for a list of idioms involving prepositions, such as *agree with them* and *agree to the contract.*

illustration or support Examples or reasons that develop an idea. (See pp. 25 and 94–95.)

imagery A word or phrase that draws on the sense of sight, hearing, touch, taste, or smell to describe an object or feeling, as in *she wrapped the shaking child in her spindly arms, thundering waves beat the beach,* or *his smooth skin suggested a life lived indoors.*

imperative See *mood*.

indefinite pronoun See *pronoun*.

independent clause See *clause*.

indicative See *mood*.

indirect object See *object*.

indirect question A sentence reporting a question, usually in a subordinate clause, and ending with a period: *The student asked when the paper was due.* Contrast *direct question*.

indirect quotation (indirect discourse) See *quotation*.

inductive reasoning Inferring a generalization from specific evidence. Contrast *deductive reasoning*. (See pp. 199–200.)

infinitive A verbal formed from the plain form of the verb plus the **infinitive marker** *to: to swim, to write.* Infinitives and infinitive phrases may function as nouns, adjectives, or adverbs. See also *verbals and verbal phrases.* (See p. 247.)

infinitive marker See *infinitive.*

infinitive phrase A word group consisting of an infinitive plus any subject, objects, or modifiers. See also *verbals and verbal phrases.*

inflection The variation in the form of a word that indicates its function in a particular context. See *declension,* the inflection of nouns and pronouns; *conjugation,* the inflection of verbs; and *comparison,* the inflection of adjectives and adverbs.

inflectional suffix See *suffix.*

informal See *formal and informal.*

intensifier A modifier that adds emphasis to the word(s) it modifies: for example, <u>very</u> slow, <u>so</u> angry.

intensive pronoun See *pronoun.*

interjection A word standing by itself or inserted in a construction to exclaim or command attention: <u>Hey!</u> <u>Ouch!</u> What <u>the heck</u> did you do that for?

interpretation The determination of meaning or significance—for instance, in a work such as a poem or photograph or in the literature on some issue such as job discrimination. (See pp. 148–50, 160.)

interrogative Functioning as or involving a question.

interrogative adjective See *adjective.*

interrogative pronoun See *pronoun.*

intransitive verb A verb that does not take a direct object: *The woman <u>laughed</u>.* (See p. 236.)

introduction The opening of an essay, a transition for readers between their world and the writer's. The introduction often contains a statement of the writer's thesis. (See pp. 104–07 for suggestions.)

invention The discovery and exploration of ideas, usually occurring most intensively in the early stages of the writing process. (See pp. 16–26 for invention techniques.)

inversion A reversal of the usual word order in a sentence, as when a verb precedes its subject or an object precedes its verb: *Down swooped the hawk. Our aims we stated clearly.*

irony The use of words to suggest a meaning different from what the words say literally: *What a happy face!* (said to someone scowling miserably); *With that kind of planning, prices are sure to go down* (written with the expectation that prices will rise).

irregular verb A verb that forms its past tense and past participle in some other way than by the addition of *-d* or *-ed* to the plain form: for example, *go, went, gone; give, gave, given.* Contrast *regular verb.* (See pp. 276–77 for a list of irregular verbs.)

jargon In one sense, jargon is the specialized language of any group, such as doctors or baseball players. In another sense, jargon is vague, pretentious, wordy, and ultimately unclear writing such as that found in some academic, business, and government publications. (See pp. 529–30.)

journal A personal record of observations, reactions, ideas, and other thoughts. Besides providing a private place to think in writing, a journal is useful for making notes about reading (pp. 141–42, 143–44, 154–56, 732–33), discovering ideas for essays (pp. 19–20), and keeping track of research (pp. 549, 732–33, 776, 807).

journalist's questions A set of questions useful for probing a subject to discover ideas about it. (See pp. 24–25.)

keyword(s) A word or words that define a subject, used for searching databases such as library catalogs and periodical indexes and for searching the Web. (See pp. 563–65.)

lexical word A word, such as a noun, verb, or modifier, that carries part of the meaning of language. Contrast *function word.*

linear text Text such as a conventional printed document that is intended to be read in sequence. Contrast *hypertext.* (See pp. 836–37.)

linking verb A verb that relates a subject to its complement: *Julie is a Democrat. He looks harmless. The boy became a man.* Common linking verbs are the forms of *be;* the verbs relating to the senses, such as *look* and *smell;* and the verbs *become, appear,* and *seem.* (See p. 237.)

listserv See *discussion list.*

logical agreement See *agreement.*

logical fallacies See *fallacies.*

main clause See *clause.*

main verb The part of a verb phrase that carries the principal meaning: *had been walking, could happen, was chilled.* See also *verb phrase.*

mass noun Another term for noncount noun. See *noun.*

mechanics The use of capital letters, italics or underlining, abbreviations, numbers, and divided words. (See Chapters 33–36.)

metaphor See *figurative language.*

misplaced modifier A modifier so far from the term it modifies or so close to another term it could modify that its relation to the rest of the sentence is unclear. (See Chapter 21.)

Misplaced	The boys played with firecrackers that they bought illegally in the field.
Revised	The boys played in the field with firecrackers that they bought illegally.

A **squinting modifier** could modify the words on either side of it: *The plan we considered seriously worries me.*

mixed construction A sentence containing two or more parts that do not fit together in grammar or in meaning. (See pp. 369–72.)

mixed metaphor See *figurative language.*

MLA style The style of documenting sources recommended by the Modern Language Association and used in many of the humanities, including English. (For explanation and examples, see Chapter 46.)

modal See *helping verb.*

modifier Any word or word group that limits or qualifies the meaning of another word or word group. Modifiers include adjectives and adverbs as well as words, phrases, and clauses that act as adjectives and adverbs.

mood   The form of a verb that shows how the speaker or writer views the action. (See pp. 296–97.)

- The **indicative mood,** the most common, is used to make statements or ask questions: *The play will be performed Saturday. Did you get the tickets?*
- The **imperative mood** gives a command: *Please get good seats.*
- The **subjunctive mood** expresses a wish, a condition contrary to fact, a recommendation, or a request: *I wish George were coming with us. Did you suggest that he join us?*

narration   Recounting a sequence of events, usually in the order of their occurrence. (See pp. 25 and 93–94.) Literary narration tells a story. (See Chapter 49.)

narrator   The speaker in a poem or the voice who tells a story. (See pp. 737, 748, 749.)

neologism   A word coined recently and not in established use. (See p. 506.)

newsgroup   An Internet discussion group with a common site where all postings are recorded. (See p. 583.)

nominal   A noun, a pronoun, or a word or word group used as a noun: *Joan and I talked. The rich owe a debt to the poor* (adjectives acting as subject and object). *Baby-sitting can be exhausting* (gerund acting as subject). *I like to play with children* (infinitive phrase acting as object).

nominative   Another term for subjective case. See *case.*

noncount noun   See *noun.*

nonessential element   A word or word group that does not limit the term or construction it refers to and thus is not essential to the meaning of the sentence. Also called a **nonrestrictive element,** a nonessential element is set off by punctuation, usually commas: *The new apartment building, in shades of tan and gray, will house fifty people* (nonessential adjective phrase). *Sleep, which we all need, occupies a third of our lives* (nonessential adjective clause). *His wife, Patricia, is a chemist* (nonessential appositive). Contrast *essential element.* (See pp. 427–31.)

nonfinite verb   See *verbals and verbal phrases.*

nonrestrictive element   See *nonessential element.*

nonstandard   Words and grammatical forms not conforming to standard American English. (See pp. 503–04.)

noun   A word that names a person, place, thing, quality, or idea: *Maggie, Alabama, clarinet, satisfaction, socialism.* Nouns normally form the possessive case by adding *-'s* (*Maggie's*) and the plural by adding *-s* or *-es* (*clarinets, messes*), although there are exceptions (*men, women, children*). The forms of nouns depend partly on where they fit in certain overlapping groups:

- **Common nouns** name general classes and are not capitalized: *book, government, music.*

- **Proper nouns** name specific people, places, and things and are capitalized: *Susan, Athens, Fenway Park.*
- **Count nouns** name things considered countable in English (they form plurals): *ounce/ounces, camera/cameras, person/people.*
- **Noncount nouns** name things not considered countable in English (they don't form plurals): *chaos, fortitude, silver, earth, information.*
- **Collective nouns** are singular in form but name groups: *team, class, family.*

noun clause   A word group containing a subject and a verb and functioning as a subject, object, or complement: *Everyone wondered how the door opened. Whoever opened it had left.*

number   The form of a noun, pronoun, demonstrative adjective, or verb that indicates whether it is singular or plural: *woman, women; I, we; this, these; runs, run.*

object   A noun, pronoun, or word group that receives the action of or is influenced by a transitive verb, a verbal, or a preposition.

- A **direct object** receives the action of a verb or verbal and frequently follows it in a sentence: *We sat watching the stars. Emily caught whatever it was you had.* (See p. 236.)
- An **indirect object** tells for or to whom something is done: *I lent Stan my car. Reiner bought us all champagne.* (See p. 238.)
- An **object of a preposition** usually follows a preposition and is linked by it to the rest of the sentence: *They are going to Rhode Island for the blues festival.* (See p. 243.)

object complement   See *complement.*

objective   See *case.*

opinion   A conclusion based on facts; an arguable, potentially changeable claim. Claims of opinion form the backbone of any argument. (See p. 179.)

ordinal number   The type of number that shows order: *first, eleventh, twenty-fifth.* Contrast *cardinal number* (such as *one, twenty-five*).

paragraph   Generally, a group of sentences set off by a beginning indention and developing a single idea. That idea is often stated in a **topic sentence.** (See Chapter 4.)

parallelism   Similarity of grammatical form between two or more coordinated elements: *Rising prices and declining incomes left many people in bad debt and worse despair.* (See Chapter 25.)

paraphrase   The restatement of source material in one's own words and sentence structures, useful for borrowing the original author's line of reasoning but not his or her exact words. Paraphrases must always be acknowledged in source citations. (See pp. 612–15.)

parenthetical citation   In the text of a paper, a brief reference, enclosed in parentheses, indicating that material is borrowed and directing the reader to the source of the material. See also *citation.*

parenthetical expression   A word or construction that interrupts a sentence and is not part of its main structure, called *parenthetical* because it could (or does) appear in parentheses: *Childe Hassam (1859–1935) was an American painter. The book, incidentally, is terrible.* (See pp. 472–73.)

participial phrase A word group consisting of a participle plus any objects or modifiers. See also *verbals and verbal phrases*.

participle A verbal showing continuing or completed action, used as an adjective or part of a verb phrase but never as the main verb of a sentence or clause. (See p. 246.)

- A **present participle** ends in *-ing*: *My heart is breaking* (part of verb phrase). *I like to watch the rolling waves* (adjective).
- A **past participle** most commonly ends in *-d, -ed, -n,* or *-en* (*wished, shown, given*) but sometimes changes the spelling of the verb (*sung, done, slept*): *Jeff has broken his own record* (part of verb phrase). *The closed door beckoned* (adjective).

See also *verbals and verbal phrases*.

particle A preposition or adverb in a two-word verb: *look up, catch on.* (See pp. 287–88.)

parts of speech The classes into which words are commonly grouped according to their form, function, and meaning: nouns, pronouns, verbs, adjectives, adverbs, conjunctions, prepositions, and interjections. See separate entries for each part of speech.

passive voice See *verb voice*.

past participle See *participle*.

past perfect tense See *tense*.

past tense See *tense*.

patterns of development Ways of thinking that can help you develop and organize ideas in essays and paragraphs. (See pp. 25–26 and 92–101.)

perfect tenses See *tense*.

periodic sentence A suspenseful sentence in which modifiers precede the main clause, which falls at the end: *Postponing decisions about family while striving to establish themselves in careers, many young adults are falsely accused of greed.* Contrast *cumulative sentence*. (See pp. 381–82.)

person The form of a verb or pronoun that indicates whether the subject is speaking, spoken to, or spoken about. In English only personal pronouns and verbs change form to indicate difference in person. In the **first person**, the subject is speaking: *I am* [or *We are*] *planning a party*. In the **second person**, the subject is being spoken to: *Are you coming?* In the **third person**, the subject is being spoken about: *She was* [or *They were*] *going*.

personal pronoun See *pronoun*.

personification See *figurative language*.

phrase A group of related words that lacks a subject or a predicate or both and that acts as a single part of speech. See *absolute phrase, prepositional phrase, verbals and verbal phrases,* and *verb phrase*.

plagiarism The presentation of someone else's ideas or words as if they were one's own. Whether accidental or deliberate, plagiarism is a serious and often punishable offense. (See pp. 626–34.)

plain case Another term for the subjective case of nouns. See *case*.

plain form The dictionary form of a verb: *make, run, swivel.* See also *verb forms.*

planning See *developing (planning).*

plot The pattern of events in a work of literature. (See p. 737.)

plural More than one. See *number.*

point of view The perspective or attitude of the narrator or speaker in a work of literature. See also *person.* (See p. 737.)

positive degree See *comparison.*

possessive See *case.*

predicate The part of a sentence that makes an assertion about the subject. A predicate must contain a finite verb and may contain modifiers, objects of the verb, and complements. The **simple predicate** consists of the verb and its helping verbs: *A wiser person would have made a different decision.* The **complete predicate** includes the simple predicate and any modifiers, objects, and complements: *A wiser person would have made a different decision.* See also *intransitive verb, linking verb,* and *transitive verb.* (See pp. 231–32, 236–39.)

predicate adjective See *complement.*

predicate noun (predicate nominative) See *complement.*

prefix A letter or group of letters (such as *sub, in, dis, pre*) that can be added at the beginning of a root or word to create a new word: *sub + marine = submarine; dis + grace = disgrace.* Contrast *suffix.*

premise Generally, a claim or assumption basic to an argument. In a deductive syllogism, one premise applied to another leads logically to a conclusion. See also *syllogism.* (See pp. 201–03.)

preposition A word that forms a noun or pronoun (plus any modifiers) into a prepositional phrase: *about love, down the steep stairs.* The common prepositions include these as well as *after, before, by, for, from, in, on, to,* and many others. (See p. 242.)

prepositional phrase A word group consisting of a preposition and its object, plus any modifiers. A prepositional phrase usually functions as an adjective (*The boy in green stood up*) or as an adverb (*He walked to the speaker's platform*). (See pp. 242–44.)

present participle See *participle.*

present perfect tense See *tense.*

present tense See *tense.*

pretentious writing Writing that is more elaborate than the situation requires, usually full of fancy phrases and showy words. (See pp. 506–07.)

primary source Firsthand information, such as an eyewitness account of events; a diary, speech, or other historical document; a work of literature or art; a report of a survey or experiment; and one's own interview, observation, or correspondence. Contrast *secondary source.* (See p. 555.)

principal clause A main or independent clause. See *clause.*

principal parts The plain form, past-tense form, and past participle of a verb. See *verb forms.* (See pp. 272–74.)

problem-solution organization   The arrangement of material to state and explain a problem and then to propose and explain a solution. (See pp. 42, 83–84.)

process analysis   The explanation of how something works or how to do something. (See pp. 26, 100–01.)

progressive tense   See *tense.*

pronoun   A word used in place of a noun. There are eight types of pronouns:

- **Personal pronouns** refer to a specific individual or to individuals: *I, you, he, she, it, we, they.* (See p. 265.)
- **Indefinite pronouns,** such as *everybody* and *some,* do not refer to specific nouns (*Everybody speaks*). (See pp. 305–06.)
- **Relative pronouns**—*who, whoever, which, that*—relate groups of words to nouns or pronouns (*The book that won is a novel*). (See pp. 251, 265.)
- **Interrogative pronouns**—*who, whom, whose, which, what*—introduce questions (*Who will contribute?*).
- **Intensive pronouns**—personal pronouns plus *-self* or *-selves*—emphasize a noun or other pronoun (*He himself asked that question*). (See pp. 266, 876.)
- **Reflexive pronouns** have the same form as intensive pronouns. They indicate that the sentence subject also receives the action of the verb (*They injured themselves*). (See p. 266.)
- **Demonstrative pronouns** such as *this, that,* and *such* identify or point to nouns (*This is the problem*).
- **Reciprocal pronouns**—*each other* and *one another*—are used as objects of verbs when the subjects are plural (*They loved each other*).

proofreading   Reading and correcting a final draft for misspellings, typographical errors, and other mistakes. (See pp. 65–66.)

proper adjective   See *adjective.*

proper noun   See *noun.*

purpose   For a writer, the chief reason for communicating something about a subject to a particular audience. Purposes are both general (usually explanation or persuasion) and specific (taking into account the subject and desired outcome). (See pp. 9–11.)

quotation   Repetition of what someone has written or spoken. In **direct quotation (direct discourse)**, the person's words are duplicated exactly and enclosed in quotation marks: *Polonius told his son, Laertes, "Neither a borrower nor a lender be."* An **indirect quotation (indirect discourse)** reports what someone said or wrote but not in the exact words and not in quotation marks: *Polonius advised his son, Laertes, not to borrow or lend.*

rational appeal   See *appeals.*

reciprocal pronoun   See *pronoun.*

reflexive pronoun   See *pronoun.*

regional language   Expressions common to the people in a particular geographical area. (See p. 506.)

regular verb   A verb that forms its past tense and past participle by adding -*d* or -*ed* to the plain form: *love, loved, loved; open, opened, opened.* Contrast *irregular verb.* (See p. 275.)

relative clause   A subordinate clause beginning with a relative pronoun such as *who* or *that* and functioning as an adjective.

relative pronoun   See *pronoun.*

restrictive element   See *essential element.*

revising   The stage of the writing process in which one considers and improves the meaning and underlying structure of a draft. Compare *developing (planning)* and *drafting.* (See pp. 50–56.)

rhetoric   The principles for finding and arranging ideas and for using language in speech or writing to achieve the writer's purpose in addressing his or her audience.

rhetorical question   A question asked for effect, with no answer expected. The person asking the question either intends to provide the answer or assumes it is obvious: *If we let one factory pollute the river, what does that say to other factories that want to dump wastes there?*

run-on sentence   See *fused sentence.*

sans serif   See *serifs.*

secondary source   A source reporting or analyzing information in other sources, such as a critic's view of a work of art, a historian's report on eyewitness accounts, or a sociologist's summary of others' studies. Contrast *primary source.* (See p. 555.)

second person   See *person.*

sentence   A complete unit of thought, consisting of at least a subject and a predicate that are not introduced by a subordinating word. Sentences can be classed by structure in four ways. A **simple sentence** contains one main clause: *I'm leaving.* A **compound sentence** contains at least two main clauses: *I'd like to stay, but I'm leaving.* A **complex sentence** contains one main clause and at least one subordinate clause: *If you let me go now, you'll be sorry.* A **compound-complex sentence** contains at least two main clauses and at least one subordinate clause: *I'm leaving because you want me to, but I'd rather stay.* (See pp. 262–63.)

sentence fragment   A sentence error in which a group of words is set off as a sentence even though it begins with a subordinating word or lacks a subject or a predicate or both. (See Chapter 17.)

Fragment	She lost the race. Because she was injured. [*Because*, a subordinating conjunction, makes the underlined clause subordinate.]
Revised	She lost the race because she was injured.
Fragment	He could not light a fire. Thus could not warm the room. [The underlined word group lacks a subject.]
Revised	He could not light a fire. Thus he could not warm the room.

sentence modifier   An adverb or a word or word group acting as an adverb that modifies the idea of the whole sentence in which it appears rather than any specific word: *In fact, people will always complain.*

series   A sequence of three or more items of equal importance: *The children are named John, Hallie, and Nancy.* The items in a series are separated with commas. (See p. 433.)

serifs   Small lines on the characters in type fonts, such as those at the bottom of this A. **Sans serif** type, such as Arial, does not have serifs. (See p. 118.)

setting   The place where the action of a literary work happens. (See p. 738.)

sexist language   Language expressing narrow ideas about men's and women's roles, positions, capabilities, or value. (See pp. 507–10.)

signal phrase   Words that indicate who is being quoted: *"In the future," said Andy Warhol, "everyone will be world-famous for fifteen minutes."* (For punctuating signal phrases, see pp. 436–37. For using signal phrases to integrate quotations, see pp. 622–23.)

simile   See *figurative language.*

simple predicate   See *predicate.*

simple sentence   See *sentence.*

simple subject   See *subject.*

simple tense   See *tense.*

singular   One. See *number.*

slang   Expressions used by the members of a group to create bonds and sometimes exclude others. Most slang is too vague, short-lived, and narrowly understood to be used in any but very informal writing. (See pp. 504–05.)

spatial organization   In a description of a person, place, or thing, the arrangement of details as they would be scanned by a viewer—for instance, from top to bottom or near to far. (See pp. 40 and 82.)

specific   See *general and specific.*

split infinitive   The often awkward interruption of an infinitive and its marker *to* by an adverb: *Management decided to immediately introduce the new product.* (See pp. 362–63.)

squinting modifier   See *misplaced modifier.*

standard American English   The dialect of English used and expected by educated writers and readers in colleges and universities, businesses, and professions. (See pp. 168–70, 503–04.)

subject   In grammar, the part of a sentence that names something and about which an assertion is made in the predicate. The **simple subject** consists of the noun alone: *The quick brown fox jumps over the lazy dog.* The **complete subject** includes the simple subject and its modifiers: *The quick brown fox jumps over the lazy dog.* (See pp. 231–32.)

subject complement   See *complement.*

subjective   See *case.*

subjunctive   See *mood.*

subordinate clause   See *clause.*

subordinating conjunction See *conjunction*.

subordination The use of grammatical constructions to de-emphasize one element in a sentence by making it dependent on rather than equal to another element: *Although I left six messages for him*, the doctor failed to call. Contrast *coordination*. (See pp. 391–95.)

substantive A word or word group used as a noun.

suffix A **derivational suffix** is a letter or group of letters that can be added to the end of a root word to make a new word, often a different part of speech: *child, childish; shrewd, shrewdly; visual, visualize*. An **inflectional suffix** adapts a word to different grammatical relations: *boy, boys; fast, faster; tack, tacked*.

summary A condensation and restatement of source material in one's own words and sentence structures, useful in reading for comprehending the material (see pp. 134–35) and in research writing for presenting the gist of the original author's idea (pp. 611–12). Summaries appearing in a paper must always be acknowledged in source citations.

superlative See *comparison*.

syllogism A form of deductive reasoning in which two premises stating generalizations or assumptions together lead to a conclusion. *Premise:* Hot stoves can burn me. *Premise:* This stove is hot. *Conclusion:* This stove can burn me. See also *deductive reasoning*. (See pp. 201–02.)

symbolism The use of a concrete thing to suggest something larger and more abstract, as a red rose may symbolize passion. (See p. 738.)

synonyms Words with approximately but not exactly the same meanings, such as *snicker, giggle,* and *chortle*. (See p. 512.)

syntax In sentences, the grammatical relations among words and the ways those relations are indicated.

synthesis Drawing one's own conclusions about the elements within a work (such as the images in a poem) or entire works (entire poems). Synthesis is an essential skill in critical thinking and reading (pp. 150–51, 160–61), in academic writing (pp. 164–65), and in research writing (pp. 604–06).

tag question A question attached to the end of a statement and consisting of a pronoun, a helping verb, and sometimes the word *not: It isn't raining, is it? It is sunny, isn't it?*

tense The form of a verb that expresses the time of its action, usually indicated by the verb's inflection and by helping verbs.

- The **simple tenses** are the **present** (*I race, you go*), the **past** (*I raced, you went*), and the **future,** formed with the helping verb *will* (*I will race, you will go*).
- The **perfect tenses,** formed with the helping verbs *have* and *had,* indicate completed action. They are the **present perfect** (*I have raced, you have gone*), the **past perfect** (*I had raced, you had gone*), and the **future perfect** (*I will have raced, you will have gone*).
- The **progressive tenses,** formed with the helping verb *be* plus the present participle, indicate continuing action. They include the **present progressive** (*I am racing, you are going*), the **past progres-**

sive (*I was racing, you were going*), and the **future progressive** (*I will be racing, you will be going*).

(See p. 290 for a list of tenses with examples.)

theme   The main idea of a work of literature. (See p. 738.)

thesis   The central, controlling idea of an essay, to which all assertions and details relate. (See p. 27.)

thesis statement   A sentence or more that asserts the central, controlling idea of an essay and perhaps previews the essay's organization. (See pp. 27–32.)

third person   See *person*.

tone   The sense of a writer's attitudes toward self, subject, and readers revealed by words and sentence structures as well as by content. (See pp. 14, 186–87, 206–07, 737.)

topic   The subject of an essay or paragraph.

topic sentence   See *paragraph*.

transitional expression   A word or phrase, such as *thus* or *for example*, that links sentences and shows the relations between them. (See pp. 87–89 for a list.) The error known as a comma splice occurs when two main clauses related by a transitional expression are separated only by a comma. (See pp. 342–43.)

transitive verb   A verb that requires a direct object to complete its meaning. (See pp. 236–37.)

trite expressions (clichés)   Stale expressions that dull writing and suggest that the writer is careless or lazy. (See p. 522.)

two-word verb   A verb plus a preposition or adverb that affects the meaning of the verb: *jump off, put away, help out*. (See pp. 287–88.)

unity   The quality of an effective essay or paragraph in which all parts relate to the central idea and to each other. (See pp. 42–43 and 74–77.)

URL (uniform resource locator)   An address for a document on the Web.

variety   Among connected sentences, changes in length, structure, and word order that help readers see the importance and complexity of ideas. (See Chapter 26.)

verb   A word or group of words indicating the action or state of being of a subject. The inflection of a verb and the use of helping verbs with it indicate its tense, mood, voice, number, and sometimes person. See separate listings for each aspect and for *predicate*. (See Chapter 14.)

verbals and verbal phrases   **Verbals** are verb forms used as adjectives (*swimming children*), adverbs (*designed to succeed*), or nouns (*addicted to running*). The verbals in the preceding examples are a participle, an infinitive, and a gerund, respectively. (See separate entries for each type.) Verbal phrases consist of verbals plus objects or modifiers: *Swimming fast, the children reached the raft. Willem tried to unlatch the gate. Running in the park is his only recreation.* (See pp. 245–47.)

A verbal is a **nonfinite verb:** it cannot serve as the only verb in the predicate of a sentence. For that, it requires a helping verb. (See p. 245.)

verb forms Verbs have five distinctive forms. The first three are the verb's **principal parts:**

- The **plain form** is the dictionary form: *live, swim.*
- The **past-tense form** adds *-d* or *-ed* to the plain form if the verb is regular: *live, lived.* If the verb is irregular, the plain form changes in some other way, such as *swim, swam.*
- The **past participle** is the same as the past-tense form for regular verbs. For irregular verbs, the past participle may differ (*swum*).
- The **present participle** adds *-ing* to the plain form: *living, swimming.*
- The **-s form** adds *-s* or *-es* to the plain form: *lives, swims.*

verb phrase A verb consisting of a helping verb and a main verb: *has started, will have been invited.* A verb phrase can serve as the predicate of a clause: *The movie has started.*

verb voice The form of a verb that tells whether the sentence subject performs the action or is acted upon. In the active voice the subject acts: *We made the decision.* In the passive voice the subject is acted upon: *The decision was made by us.* (See pp. 298–99.)

voice The sense of oneself projected in one's writing through selection of information, role played in relation to readers, and tone. (See pp. 14–15.)

warrant A term used for *assumption* in argument. See *assumption.*

Web forum A discussion group on the Web, open to everyone and organized around subjects.

wiki A Web site that can be contributed to or modified by anyone who registers to use the site.

word order The arrangement of the words in a sentence, which plays a large part in determining the grammatical relation among words in English.

writing process The activities involved in producing a finished piece of writing. The overlapping stages of the process—developing or planning, drafting, and revising—vary among writers and even for the same writer in different writing situations. (See Chapters 1–3.)

writing situation The unique combination of writer, subject, audience, purpose, and other elements that defines an assignment or occasion and helps direct the writer's choices. (See pp. 4–5.)

Credits

Text and Illustrations

Bogdanovich, Peter. *Pieces in Time*. New York: Arbor House Publishing Company, 1973.

Britt, Suzanne. "That Lean and Hungry Look." *Newsweek,* October 9, 1978.

Brooks, Gwendolyn. "The Bean Eaters" by Gwendolyn Brooks, 1991. Reprinted by Consent of Brooks Permissions.

Butler, John A. *CyberSearch*. New York: Penguin Reference, 1998.

Campbell, Neil A., and Jane B. Reece. *Biology,* 7th edition. Glenview: Benjamin Cummings, 2005, p. 47.

Catton, Bruce. "Grant and Lee: A Study in Contrasts" by Bruce Catton, 1956. Copyright U.S. Capitol Historical Society. All rights reserved. Reprinted by permission.

Cunningham, John A., and Peter Selby. "Relighting Cigarettes: How Common Is It?" by John A. Cunningham and Peter Selby, *Nicotine and Tobacco Research*, 9 (5), 621–623, 2007, reprinted by permission of Taylor & Francis Ltd., www.tandf.co.uk/journals.

Davies, Antony. "Unemployment Rates of High School Graduates and College Graduates, 1984–2004," from *The Economics of College Tuition* by Antony Davies. Copyright © 2005. Reprinted by permission.

Devoe, Alan. "Nature's Utmost" by Alan Devoe.

Dyson, Freeman J. From *Disturbing the Universe* by Freeman J. Dyson. Copyright © 1979 by Freeman J. Dyson. Reprinted by permission of Basic Books, a member of Perseus Books Group.

Ferris, Timothy. *Coming of Age in the Milky Way*. New York: HarperCollins, 2003.

Friedman, Thomas L. "It's a Flat World After All." *The New York Times,* April 3, 2005.

Gates, Jr., Henry Louis. Excerpt from "Two Nations . . . Both Black, Social and Economic Division in the Black Community" by Henry Louis Gates, Jr. Copyright © 1992 by Henry Louis Gates, Jr. Originally published in *Forbes*. Reprinted by permission of the author.

Goreau, Angeline. "Hers: Worthy Women Revisited" by Angeline Goreau. Copyright © 1986 by Angeline Goreau. Originally appeared in *The New York Times*, December 11, 1986. Reprinted by permission of Georges Borchardt, Inc., for the author.

Ik, Kim Yong. Excerpt from "A Book-Writing Venture" by Kim Yong Ik. Originally published in *The Writer*, October 1965. Copyright © Kim Yong Ik. Reprinted by permission of Faith M. Leigh.

Jeffrey, Mac. "Does Rx Spell Rip-Off?" *The New York Times,* April 7, 1978.

Kuralt, Charles. From *Dateline America* by Charles Kuralt. Text copyright © 1979 by CBS, Inc. Reprinted by permission of Harcourt Inc.

Mayer, Lawrence. "The Confounding Enemy of Sleep." *Fortune,* June 1974.

Ornstein, Robert. From "A Letter to the Director" by Robert Ornstein, *Human Nature*, August 1978.

Ouchi, William G. *Theory Z*. Reading: Addison-Wesley, 1981.

Reston, Jr., James. "You Cannot Refine It." *The New Yorker,* 1985.

Rose, Phyllis. "On Shopping" in *Never Say Goodbye* by Phyllis Rose. New York: Doubleday, 1986.

Rosen, Ruth. "Search for Yesterday" by Ruth Rosen, from *Watching Television*, edited by Todd Gitlin. New York: Pantheon Books, 1986.

Sale, Kirkpatrick. "The Environmental Crisis Is Not Our Fault" by Kirkpatrick Sale, *The Nation*, April 30, 1990. Reprinted by permission of *The Nation*.

Selwyn, Neil. "The Social Processes of Learning to Use Computers" by Neil Selwyn from *Social Science Computer Review*, 2005, 23, (1), p. 122. Copyright © 2005 by Sage Publications Inc. Journals. Reproduced with permission of Sage Publications Inc. Journals in the format Textbook via Copyright Clearance Center.

Sowell, Thomas. "Student Loans" from *Is Reality Optional? and Other Essays* by Thomas Sowell, 1993. Reprinted by permission of Thomas Sowell and Creators Syndicate, Inc.

Staples, Brent. Excerpt from "Black Men and Public Space" by Brent Staples, *Harper's*, December 1986. Copyright © 1986 by Brent Staples. Reprinted by permission of the author.

Tan, Amy. "The Language of Discretion" by Amy Tan. Copyright © 1990 by Amy Tan. First appeared in *State of the Language*. Reprinted by permission of the author and the Sandra Dijkstra Literary Agency.

Tuchman, Barbara. "The Decline of Quality" by Barbara Tuchman, *The New York Times*, November 2, 1980. Reprinted by the permission of Russell & Volkening as agents for the author. Copyright © 1980 by Barbara Tuchman.

UNFPA. "AIDS Clock" from the UNFPA Web site, *www.unfpa.org*, 2008. Produced by UNFPA, the United Nations Population Fund, using data provided by UNAIDS. Design by Allysson Lucca. Reprinted by permission.

Wax, Judith. *Starting in the Middle*. New York: Holt, Rinehart, and Winston, 1979.

Woolf, Virginia. *The Waves*. New York: Harcourt, 1931.

Zinsser, William. *The Lunacy Boom*. New York: Harper & Row, 1970.

Photos

Title page, clockwise from top left: David Fischer/Digital Vision/Getty; Stone/Getty; Jamie Grill/Iconica/Getty; The Image Source/Getty; Andersen Ross/Blend Images/Getty; **1:** Image Source/Getty; **125:** NASA; **127:** Blend Images/Getty; **155:** *Boostup.org*; **158:** Steve Simon; **174:** *Boostup.org*; **212:** Michael Foujols/Corbis; **213:** Lydia Kibiuk/Society for Neuroscience December 2001; **214:** UNICEF; **222:** Big Brothers Big Sisters of America; **224:** Getty; **226:** Michael Foujols/Corbis; **229:** The Image Bank/Getty; **329:** Sabah Arar/AFP/Getty; **377:** Photographer's Choice/Getty; **415:** Stone/Getty; **481:** Neo Vision/Getty; **501:** Joe Schilling/Time Life Pictures/Getty; **547:** Digital Vision/Getty; **727:** Stone/Getty; **821:** Stockbyte/Getty.

Index

A

a, an
 capitalization in titles, 483
 choosing between, 865
 vs. *the*, 323–25
Abbreviations, 492–95
 a vs. *an* with, 865
 for academic degrees, 492–93
 common Latin, 493–94
 for courses of instruction, 495
 for dates and numbers, 493–94
 for days, months, and holidays,
  495
 for frequently used terms, 493
 for geographical names, 495
 Inc., Bros., Co., and *&,* 494
 for names of people, 493, 495
 in nontechnical writing, 492–95
 in online communication, 504
 for organizations, 419, 493
 periods with, 419, 492–95
 plurals of, 458
 Postal Service, 844
 for titles with names, 492–93
 for units of measurement, 494
abide by, in, 518
about, as preposition, 243
above, as preposition, 243
Absolute phrases
 defined, 249, 432, 882
 punctuation of, 249, 432
Absolute statements, 191, 194
Abstract and concrete words
 in argument, 181
 defined, 516, 882
 and exactness, 516–17
Abstract language, grammar
  checkers for, 511
Abstracts
 on computerized databases, 741
 documenting: APA style, 788,
  793, 797; MLA style, 660, 681,
  683
 in one's own papers, 799, 818
 as research sources, 576, 758,
  778, 809
Academic integrity, 626–35
Academic sites, MLA style, 674

Academic skills, 128–38
 exam preparation, 136–38
 listening and note taking, 130–31
 reading comprehension, 131–35
 time management, 129–30
Academic terms or years, capitalization of, 487
Academic writing, 162–75
 audience for, 12–15, 166
 content and structure for, 39–42,
  167–68
 designing, 112–13
 discipline styles in, 136
 documentation styles for, 624–25
 and e-mail, 829
 essay examinations, 136–38
 goals and requirements of, 728–30
 guidelines for, 167–68
 in humanities, 731–73
 language in, 168–70
 about literature, 731–54
 in natural and applied sciences,
  805–20
 plagiarism in, 136
 purpose of, 165–66
 in response to texts, 162–65
 revising and editing in, 136
 in social sciences, 774–805
 sources, acknowledging in, 136
 synthesis in, 136, 164–65, 604–06
 voice in, 169–70
 thesis, developing, 136
 writing situation for, 135
accept, except, 532, 865
accordingly
 as conjunctive adverb, 259
 punctuation with, 430, 446
according to, accords with, 518
according to, as preposition, 243
Accuracy, for preventing plagiarism,
  608
Accurate evidence, 184
accuse of, 518
Acknowledgment of sources
 necessity for, 626–35
 using APA style, 779–99
 using Chicago style, 760–71
 using CSE style, 812–17
 using MLA style, 644–91

IAE INDEX

The marginal index covers material found only in
the Instructor's Annotated Edition: the six introductory chapters headed "Designing and Teaching Composition Courses" and the authors of resources listed next to the students' text.

A

Abbott, Robert D., IAE-45
Academic writing, IAE-4, IAE-14–IAE-15
Ackerman, John M., 151
Adler-Kassner, Linda, 560
Alexander, Jonathan, IAE-60
Allal, Linda, 54
Amare, Nicole, 312, 508
Ambron, Joanna, 809
Anderson, Daniel, 564
Anderson, Jeff, 370
Anderson, Kristene F., 540
Anderson, Virginia Johnson, 42, 643
Anson, Chris M., 145
Answer Key, IAE-16
Applebee, Arthur N., IAE-9, IAE-19
Austen, Jane, 409
Austin, Marlisa, 243

B

Bacon, Nora, 12
Baker, Edith M., 731
Baker, William, 863
Ball, Kevin, 4
Ballenger, Bruce, 548, 560
Barnet, Sylvan, 747, 756
Barrett, Edward, IAE-37, IAE-45
Bartholomae, David, IAE-4, IAE-5, IAE-19,
  IAE-23, IAE-33, 4, 48, 233, 728
Bass, Randy, 834
Bawarshi, Anis, 731, 755
Bazerman, Charles, 775
Beall, Herbert, 807
Bean, John C., 809
Beason, Larry, 233, 863
Beavis, Catherine, IAE-60
Beck, James P., 56
Becker, Alton L., IAE-3, IAE-7, 79
Becker, Howard S., 776
Belanger, Kelly, 841
Belanoff, Pat, IAE-31, IAE-33, IAE-45
Bellman, Jonathan, 756
Benham, Hiltraut H., 604
Benjamin, Bret, 564
Bergmann, Linda S., 731

Berkenkotter, Carol, IAE-3, IAE-5
Berlin, James A., IAE-4, IAE-5, 4
Berthoff, Ann E., IAE-3, IAE-5, 150
Berzsenyi, Christyne A., 57
Beyer, Barry K., 755
Biddle, Arthur W., 737, 776
Bills, Patricia, 370
Birkenstein, Cathy, 640
Bishop, Wendy, IAE-45, 54, 549, 587, 604, 643
Bizzaro, Patrick, IAE-45, 748
Bizzell, Patricia, IAE-4, IAE-5, IAE-9
Blaauw-Hara, Mark, 231
Black, Laurel Johnson, IAE-31, IAE-33
Blackburn-Brockman, Elizabeth, 23, 841
Blakeslee, Ann M., 4
Bloom, Lynn Z., IAE-5, 4, 48
Bobkoff, Michael, 454
Bolter, Jay David, IAE-60
Bonacci, Mark, 776
Braine, George, IAE-69
Brammer, Charlotte, IAE-37, IAE-45
Brannon, Lil, IAE-22, IAE-33
Breihan, John R., 42, 643
Brent, Doug, 177
Breuch, Lee-Ann Kastman, IAE-60, 69, 829
Britton, James, IAE-3, IAE-5
Broad, Bob, IAE-33
Brook, Robert, IAE-36, IAE-45
Brooke, Rupert, 6
Brookfield, Stephen D., 146
Brooks, Phyllis, 399
Brostoff, Anita, 85
Brown, Alan S., 533
Brown, Carol Smullen, IAE-33
Bruffee, Kenneth, IAE-4, IAE-5, IAE-35, IAE-45
Brunk-Chavez, Beth L., 178, 200
Bryson, Bill, 503
Buckingham, David, 504
Buffamanti, Suzanne, 146
Bush, Jonathan, 370
Bushman, Donald, 242
Busiel, Christopher, 564

C

Cain, William, 747
Capossela, Toni-Lee, 554
Carbone, Nick, 580
Carlisi, Karen, IAE-68, IAE-70, 237, 285, 291, 299, 323
Carrell, Lori J., 864
Carroll, Lee Ann, 162

Acronyms
    a vs. *an* with, 865
    defined, 493, 882
    punctuation for, 419, 493
across, as preposition, 243
Active reading, 141
Active voice
    converting passive to, 298
    dangling modifiers and, 366
    defined, 261, 298, 904
    effectiveness of, 379–80, 525
    vs. passive, 261
    shifts between passive and, 356
    tenses of regular verb in, 290
AD, BC, 493–94
adapt from, to, 518
Address (electronic). *See* Digital
    Object Identifier (DOI); URL
    (uniform resource locator)
Address (street, city, and state)
    in business letters, 842, 847
    commas in, 435
    numbers in, 497
    Postal Service, 844
Address, direct
    commas to set off, 431
    defined, 889
Address, forms of (*Miss, Mrs.,* etc.),
    509–10, 843
Address, public. *See also* Oral pre-
    sentations; Speeches
    MLA style, 688
Adequate evidence, 185, 218–19
Ad hominem argument, 191, 193
Adjectival, defined, 882
Adjective clauses
    defined, 252, 882
    nonessential vs. essential, 428–29
    punctuation of, 253, 428–29
    repetition in, 370–71
Adjective complements. *See* Subject
    complements
Adjective phrases, 247–48, 882
Adjectives, 315–26
    absolute, 319–20
    vs. adverbs, 240, 316–18
    appropriate use of, 315–26
    attributive, 882
    at beginning of sentence, 409
    comparative form of, 240, 318–20, 886
    compound, 544
    coordinate: commas with, 258, 389, 433–34; defined, 433, 888; tests for, 434
    defined, 233, 240, 315, 882

    degree of, 240, 318–20, 886
    demonstrative, 882
    descriptive, 882
    after direct objects, 317–18
    formation of, 316
    infinitives and infinitive phrases
        as, 247
    interrogative, 882
    irregular, 319
    limiting, 882
    after linking verbs, 317
    negating, 316
    nouns as, 241, 321
    as object complements, 239
    order of, 365
    positive form of, 240, 318–20, 886
    possessives as, 882
    predicate, 882, 886
    prepositional phrases as, 243
    present vs. past participle as,
        321–22
    proper, 484–85, 882
    punctuation with, 433–34
    as subject complements, 237, 317
    subordinate clauses as, 252
    superlative form of, 240, 318–20, 886
    types of, 882
    verbals and verbal phrases as,
        247–48
Ad populum argument, 191, 193
Advanced Search option, 579, 580–81
Adverb clauses
    defined, 252, 883
    nonessential vs. essential, 428–29
    punctuation of, 253, 428–29
Adverbial, defined, 883
Adverbial conjunctions. *See* Con-
    junctive adverbs
Adverb phrases, 883
Adverbs, 315–26. *See also* Conjunc-
    tive adverbs
    absolute, 319–20
    vs. adjectives, 240, 316–18
    appropriate use of, 315–26
    at beginning of sentence, 409
    comparative form of, 240, 318–20,
        886
    defined, 233, 240, 315, 883
    degree of, 240, 318–20
    after direct objects, 317–18
    formation of, 316
    infinitives and infinitive phrases
        as, 247
    irregular, 319
    after linking verbs, 317

placement of, 361, 362–63
positive form of, 240, 318–20, 886
prepositional phrases as, 243
subordinate clauses as, 252
superlative form of, 240, 318–20, 886
in two-word verbs, 287–88
verbals and verbal phrases as, 247
adverse, averse, 865
Advertisements. *See* Illustrations and artworks
advice, advise, 865
a few, few, 326
affect, effect, 532, 865
afraid of, 518
after
  as preposition, 243, 259, 392
  as subordinating conjunction, 251, 259, 392
Afterword, MLA style, 669
against, as preposition, 243
aggravate, 866
Agreement, logical, 354, 883
Agreement of demonstrative adjectives and nouns, 883
Agreement of pronouns and antecedents, 309–13
  with antecedents joined by *and,* 311
  with antecedents joined by *or* or *nor,* 311
  with collective nouns, 313
  defined, 301, 883
  in gender, 309–10
  grammar checkers for, 310
  with indefinite words, 305–06
Agreement of subjects and verbs, 301–08
  with collective nouns, 306–07
  defined, 883
  grammar checkers for, 302
  with indefinite pronouns, 305–06
  with intervening words, 304
  with linking verbs, 307
  with measurements or figures ending in *-s,* 308
  with singular nouns ending in *-s,* 308
  with subjects joined by *and,* 304–05
  with subjects joined by *or* or *nor,* 305
  with titles of works, 308
  with *who, which, that,* 307–08
  with words being defined, 308
agree on, to, with, 518, 866

ain't, 866
all
  pronouns with, 312
  verbs with, 305–06
all, all of, 866
Allah and God, capitalization of terms representing, 485
all ready, already, 532, 866
all right, 866
AlltheWeb, 579, 580
all together, altogether, 866
allude, elude, 532
allusion, illusion, 532, 866
Almanacs
  list of, 569
  MLA style, 667
almost, most, 866
along, as preposition, 243
along with
  as preposition, 243
  subject-verb agreement with, 304
a lot, 866
already, all ready, 532
also
  as conjunctive adverb, 259
  punctuation with, 430, 446
AltaVista, 579
although, as subordinating conjunction, 251, 392
AM, PM, 419, 493
American Memory, 585
American Psychological Association. *See* APA style
American vs. British spelling, 534
among, as preposition, 243
among, between, 866
amongst, 866
amount, number, 866
an, a. See a, an
an, and, 866
Analogy
  defined, 99, 195, 883
  in essay development, 26
  false, 195
  in paragraph development, 99
Analysis
  in critical thinking and reading, 25–26, 147–48
  defined, 96–97, 147, 883
  of drama, 751–52
  in essay development, 25
  of fiction, 747–48
  guidelines for, 147
  of illustrations, 156–60
  of literature, 731–54, 756
  in paragraph development, 96–97

Carson, Joan G., IAE-70
Carter, Duncan, 151
Carter, Michael, 806
Caruso, Isabella, IAE-68, IAE-70
Celce-Murcia, Marianne, IAE-68, IAE-69, 285
Chafe, Wallace, 424
Chaika, Elaine, 366
Chambers, Marilyn J., 147, 184
Chanquoi, Lucile, 54
Chappell, Virginia A., 560
Cheville, Julie, 174
Chicago, Judy, 220
Chidsley, Dickson, 204
Chiseri-Strater, Elizabeth, 560
Chomsky, Carol, 533
Christensen, Bonniejean, 430
Christensen, Francis, 382, 430
Clapham, Maria, 841
Clark, Beverly Lyon, IAE-45
Clark, Irene L., IAE-45
Clark, Roger, 533
Clary-Lemon, Jennifer, IAE-6
Clemens, Samuel, 503
Coe, Richard M., 8, 85
Coghill, Anne M., 809
Cognitive process, writing as, IAE-3
Cohan, Carol, 103
Cole, Kirsti, 852
Coles, William E., Jr., IAE-2, IAE-5
Collaborative learning, IAE-35–IAE-44
  computers in, IAE-48, IAE-50
  customizing materials for, IAE-37
  developing skills in, IAE-36–IAE-37
  with ESL students, IAE-64
  forming groups for, IAE-35–IAE-36
  worksheets for, IAE-38–IAE-44
College Composition and Communication, 777
Comment sheets, IAE-27
Comments, written, IAE-25
Committee on Classroom Practices, IAE-33, IAE-45
Composition course. See Writing course
Computer-aided learning, IAE-47–IAE-59
  access to computers and, IAE-48–IAE-49
  collaborative, IAE-48, IAE-50
  distractions in, IAE-49
  document design in, IAE-50
  editing in, IAE-50
  electronic documents in, IAE-50–IAE-51
  grammar checkers in, IAE-51
  Handbook in, IAE-49–IAE-50
  Handbook ancillaries in, IAE-50–IAE-51

Computer-aided learning *(continued)*
  institutional culture and, IAE-49
  instructional applications of, IAE-47–IAE-48
  Internet resources for, IAE-50–IAE-51
  online communication in, IAE-50–IAE-51, IAE-51
  online tutorials in, IAE-51
  print resources in, IAE-49–IAE-50
  research-based writing in, IAE-50
  sample schedule for, IAE-58–IAE-60
  skills and training for, IAE-49, IAE-50
  software for, IAE-50–IAE-51
  spell checkers in, IAE-50
  style checkers in, IAE-50, IAE-51
  time demands of, IAE-49
Conferences, IAE-32
Conn, Cynthia, 841
Conners, David, 777
Connor, Ulla, IAE-70
Connors, Robert J., IAE-4, IAE-5, IAE-33, 113, 231, 392, 524
Conrad, Susan M., IAE-70
Coogan, David, IAE-60
Cook, Claire Kehrwald, 399
Cook, Devan, 67
Cooper, Charles R., IAE-33
Cooper, Marilyn M., 201
Corbett, Edward P.J., IAE-5
Corder, Jim W., IAE-45
Correction code/symbols, IAE-23–IAE-24, IAE-26
Corrigan, Dagmar Stuehrk, 204
Corrigan, Timothy, 756
CourseSmart, IAE-51
Cowie, Neil, IAE-70
Creel, Gill, 70
Cross-cultural issues, IAE-63–IAE-65.
    See also ESL students
Cross-curricular writing, IAE-4, IAE-14–IAE-16
  by ESL students, IAE-68
  readers in, IAE-15–IAE-16
Crovitz, Darren, 512
Crow, Angela, IAE-60, 70, 829
Crowhurst, Marion, 392
Crystal, David, 492, 504
Cuba, Lee, 776
Currie, Pat, IAE-70

D

Daemmrich, Ingrid, 777
Daiker, Donald A., IAE-5, 4, 255, 392
Daniels, Harvey A., 503

Analysis *(continued)*
  of poetry, 748–51
  as type of research paper, 549
and
  and agreement: of pronouns, 311; of verbs, 304–05
  ampersand (&) for, 494, 786
  beginning sentences with, 336
  as coordinating conjunction, 257, 399–400
  linking words, phrases, and subordinate clauses, 439–41
  between main clauses, 257, 422–24
  punctuation with, 257–58, 422–24, 430, 433, 439–41, 448
  and sentence fragments, 336
  as transitional expression, 430
and etc., 866
and/or, 866
and which, and who, 867
angry with, 518
Annotated bibliographies
  adding assessments to, 590–91
  creating, 557–60
Annotation
  of images, 153–54, 155–56
  marginal, 70
  of text, 131–32, 133, 141–44, 735
Anonymous or unsigned works
  APA style: parenthetical citations, 782; reference list, 787, 795
  Chicago style, 763
  CSE style, 814
  MLA style: parenthetical citations, 647; works cited, 658, 662, 674
ante-, anti-, 867
Antecedents
  agreement of pronouns with, 301, 309–13, 883
  collective nouns as, 313
  compound, 311
  defined, 301, 307, 309, 883
  generic nouns as, 311–12
  grammar checkers for, 310, 346
  implied, 349
  indefinite pronouns as, 311–13
  placement for clarity, 347
  reference of pronouns to, 345–51
  of relative pronouns, 307–08, 347, 351–52
Anthologies, documenting
  APA style, 790–91
  Chicago style, 766
  CSE style, 815
  MLA style, 666

Anthropology, research sources on, 777, 778
anxious, eager, 867
any
  in comparisons, 374
  as determiner, 322, 325
  pronouns with, 311–12
  verbs with, 305–06
anybody
  pronouns with, 311–12
  verbs with, 305–06
anybody, any body; anyone, any one, 867
any more, anymore, 867
anyone
  pronouns with, 311–12
  verbs with, 305–06
any other, in comparisons, 374
anyplace, 867
anything
  pronouns with, 311–12
  verbs with, 305–06
anyways, anywheres, 867
APA style
  defined, 883
  for document format, 799–802
  indexes to documentation models: parenthetical citations, 780; reference list, 786
  parenthetical citations: index to, 780; models of, 780–83
  reference list: guidelines for, 783–99; index to, 786; models of, 785–99
  sample paper in, 802–05
Apostrophes, 451–58
  to form contractions, 456–57
  to form plural abbreviations, dates, or words or characters named as words, 458
  to form possessives, 265, 452–54
  grammar checkers for, 452–53
  misuse of: with plural nouns, 455; with possessive personal pronouns, 453, 456; with singular verbs, 455
  space with, in documents, 119
Appeals to readers
  beliefs or needs and, 183
  defined, 205, 883
  emotional, 192–93, 205–06, 226, 883
  ethical, 206–07, 226, 883
  inappropriate, 191, 192–93
  rational, 205–06, 225–26, 883
  in visual arguments, 225–26

appear, as linking verb, 237
Appositives
    case of pronoun in, 267–68
    defined, 254, 336, 883
    nonessential vs. essential, 255,
      429
    punctuation of: colon for, 255,
      469; commas for, 255, 394, 429,
      441; dashes for, 255, 394, 471
    as sentence fragment, 255, 336
    subordination with, 393, 394
Appropriate language. *See* Words
apt, liable, likely, 867
are, is, 867
Argument, 176–95
    answering opposing views in,
      207–08
    anticipating objections in, 207–08
    appealing to readers in, 192–93,
      205–07
    assumptions in, 178, 185–86,
      199–205
    claims in, 178–81, 199–205
    common ground, finding, 208–10
    critical reading of, 176–95
    deductive reasoning in, 200–03,
      888
    defined, 10, 884
    developing, 196–210
    elements of, 177–78
    emotional appeals in, 205–06, 226
    ethical appeals in, 206–07, 226
    evaluating, 187
    evidence in, 177–78, 181–85,
      199–205
    examples of, 211–15
    fallacies in, 190–95
    inductive reasoning in, 199–200,
      892
    organization of, 209–10
    rational appeals in, 205–06,
      225–26
    reasoning effectively in, 199–205
    revision of, 210–11
    Rogerian, 208–10
    sample of, 212–15
    subjects for, 196–97
    Toulmin scheme for, 177–78,
      199
    visual, 216–26
around, as preposition, 243
Art, research sources on, 758, 759.
    See also Illustrations and art-
    works
Articles *(a, an, the)*
    a vs. *an,* 865

capitalization in titles, 483
    careless omission of, 374–75
    defined, 884
    grammar checkers for, 323
    with nouns, 234
    uses of, 322–25
Articles in periodicals
    databases/indexes of: general,
      576–77; in humanities, 758; in
      literature, 741; in natural and
      applied sciences, 808–09; in
      social sciences, 778
    documenting: APA style, 788–90,
      791–94; Chicago style, 764–65,
      767–68; CSE style, 814–16;
      MLA style, 658–63, 674–75,
      680–83, 684
    finding bibliographic information
      for, 659, 661, 681
    indexes of, 576–77, 758, 778
    in online databases, 563, 572–77,
      681–83
    posted on blogs, 602
    print vs. online format, 577
    as research sources, 571–77
    titles of, quotation marks for,
      463
    working bibliography information
      for, 559
Artworks. *See* Illustrations and
    artworks
as
    case of pronouns after, 268
    as connector, 397
    defined, 867
    misuse of, 397
    as preposition, 243
    as subordinating conjunction,
      251, 392
as . . . as, as correlative conjunction,
    257
as, like, 875
as, than, 867
as a result
    as conjunctive adverb, 259
    punctuation with, 430, 446
ascent, assent, 532
as for, as preposition, 243
aside from, as preposition, 243
as if, as subordinating conjunction,
    251, 392
Ask.com, 579
as long as, as subordinating
    conjunction, 251
assent, ascent, 532
Assertions. *See* Claims

Daniels, Henry, 279
David, Denise, 146
Davis, Chris, 580
Davis, Robert, IAE-45, 554
Dawkins, John, IAE-19, 263, 418
Day, Robert, 807
Deans, Thomas, IAE-5, 852
Deen, Rosemary, IAE-20
Dejoy, Nancy, IAE-5, 151, 852
DeLuca, Geraldine, IAE-19
Demming, Mary P., 162
DeSena, Laura Hennessey, 627
Diagnostic and Editing Tests and Exercises,
    IAE-17
Dickson, Marcia, IAE-31, IAE-33, IAE-60
Dickson, Randi, 204
Dishner, Ernest K., 150
Dixon, Chris Jennings, IAE-19
Dobie, Ann R., 533
Dobler, Elizabeth, 564
Documents, electronic, IAE-50–IAE-51
Dong, Yu Ren, 512
Dornsife, Robert S., Jr., 55
Dorroh, John, 809
Doss, Van, 125
Downs, Douglas, IAE-5
Drafting, IAE-2, IAE-8
    evaluation and, IAE-28–IAE-29
Draga, Sam, 125
Duncan, Mike, 42, 74
Dunn, Dana, 776
Dunn, Patricia, 23

E

Eagleton, Maya, 564, 607
Eble, Kenneth E., IAE-19
Ede, Lisa, IAE-46, 12, 13, 56
Eden, Rick, 103
Editing
    computer-aided, IAE-50
    evaluation of, IAE-28–IAE-29
    vs. revising, IAE-28
Elbow, Peter, IAE-2, IAE-5, IAE-45, 12, 23, 24,
    42, 54, 147
Elgin, Peter, 841
Ellison, Ralph, 409
Emig, Janet, IAE-3, IAE-5, 150
English Journal, 548, 604
Enos, Teresa, 232
Ervin, Elizabeth, 242
ESL students, IAE-62–IAE-69
    approach to learning, IAE-63–IAE-64

ESL students *(continued)*
attitudes toward errors, IAE-66
attitudes toward plagiarism, IAE-65
in collaborative learning, IAE-64
contrastive rhetoric and, IAE-64
cross-cultural issues and, IAE-63–IAE-65
evaluation for, IAE-67–IAE-68
expectations of professors, IAE-64
feedback for, IAE-66–IAE-67
fossilization and, IAE-66
Generation 1.5, IAE-63
international, IAE-62
levels of support and specificity and, IAE-64–IAE-65
permanent resident, IAE-62–IAE-63
process vs. product approach and, IAE-65–IAE-66
profile of, IAE-62–IAE-63
reader- vs. writer-responsible languages and, IAE-64–IAE-65
sentence-level errors by, IAE-68–IAE-69
teaching techniques for, IAE-66–IAE-67
topic selection by, IAE-65
Estrem, Heidi, 560
Evaluation, IAE-21–IAE-33
cans and can'ts in, IAE-32–IAE-33
collaboration in, IAE-32
comment sheets in, IAE-27
composing comments in, IAE-22–IAE-23
conferences in, IAE-32
coping with paper load in, IAE-29–IAE-32
correction code/symbols in, IAE-23–IAE-24, IAE-26
discussing with students, IAE-26
for ESL students, IAE-67–IAE-68
of final drafts, IAE-21–IAE-22
grading in, IAE-26–IAE-28, IAE-29–IAE-30, IAE-32
of papers in progress, IAE-21
portfolios in, IAE-31
praise and criticism in, IAE-22–IAE-23
priority setting in, IAE-25–IAE-26
for revision, IAE-28–IAE-29
student-set standards in, IAE-32
written comments in, IAE-25
Evans, Rick, IAE-36, IAE-45, 6
Expressionistic theory, IAE-2–IAE-3
Expressive process, writing as, IAE-2–IAE-3

F

Fagan, Deirdre, 470
Faigley, Lester, IAE-5, 43, 86, 103

Assignments, writing
finding and adapting subjects of, 4, 6–9
in humanities, 739–40, 756
in literature, 739–40
in natural and applied sciences, 806–07
in social sciences, 775
Assumptions
connecting evidence to claims with, 185–86, 199–205
defined, 148, 178, 884
discovering and interpreting, 148–50, 160–61, 185–86
faulty, 149–50
in visual arguments, 219–20
assure, ensure, insure, 867
Asterisk, as alternative for italics or underlining, 491
as though, as subordinating conjunction, 251
as to, 867
Astronomy, research sources on, 810
as well as, subject-verb agreement with, 304
at
vs. *in* and *on,* 519
as preposition, 243, 392
with *where,* 867
Atlases, 569
at this point in time, 867
Attributive adjectives, 882
Audience
for academic writing, 12, 166
analyzing, 12–15
anticipating objections of, 207–08
appealing to, 205–07
appropriate role and tone for, 12, 14–15
defined, 884
developing argument for, 198–99
disabilities, designing for, 126, 836, 839
for e-mail communications, 829–30
identifying, 12
for images, 154
instructor as, 12, 166
needs of, 5, 12–15, 198–99
online, 829–30
for oral presentations, 856–58
purpose and, 5, 9–11
questions about, 5, 13
using specific information for, 12, 14–15
vision loss, designing for, 126

Audiovisual works. *See* Films, DVDs, and video recordings; illustrations and artworks; Sound recordings
Authors
APA style: parenthetical citations, 780–83; reference list, 785–99
Chicago style: endnotes or footnotes, 760–71; list of works cited, 760–71
CSE style: name-year text citations, 811; numbered text citations, 811–12; reference list, 812–13, 812–17
determining in online sources, 597–98, 601
MLA style: list of works cited, 654–88; notes, 653; parenthetical citations, 644–53
Auxiliary verbs. *See* Helping verbs (auxiliary verbs)
averse, adverse, 865
aware of, 518
awful, awfully, 867
a while, awhile, 867

B

Background information, 622–24
bad, badly, 316, 867
Balanced sentences, 383–84, 884
Bandwagon approach, 191, 192–93
Bar charts. *See* Illustrations and artworks
bare, bear, 532
based on, 518
BC, AD, 419, 493–94
BCE, CE, with dates, 493–94
be
forms of, 274
as helping verb, 274, 281–82
as linking verb, 237, 317
in mixed constructions, 371
principal parts, 276
in subjunctive mood, 297
be able to, as helping verb, 274, 283
bear, bare, 532
because
avoiding after *reason is,* 371–72
as subordinating conjunction, 251, 392
because of
vs. *on account of,* 876
as preposition, 243, 392
become, as linking verb, 237

before
  as preposition, 243, 259
  as subordinating conjunction,
    251, 259, 392
Begging the question, 191, 193
Beginnings of sentences
  and or *but* in, 336
  avoiding *here is/are, there is/are* in,
    410
  numbers in, 498
  use for emphasis, 380–82, 408–10
  varying, 89, 408–10
behind
  as adverb, 259
  as preposition, 243, 259
being as, being that, 867
Belief, 180, 183, 884
below, as preposition, 243
beneath, as preposition, 243
beside, as preposition, 243
beside, besides, 867
besides
  as conjunctive adverb, 259
  punctuation with, 430, 446
be supposed to, as helping verb, 274,
  283
better, had better, 867
between, among, 866
between, as preposition, 243
beyond, as preposition, 243
Biased language, 187, 507–10
Bible, MLA style
  list of works cited, 668
  parenthetical citation, 650
Bibliographies. *See also* APA style;
  Chicago style; CSE style; MLA
  style
  annotated, 557–60
  guides to preparation of, 635, 760,
    779–80, 811
  as reference source, 571, 741,
    757–58, 777, 808–09
  software for creating, 635
  working: compiling, 557–60; in-
    formation for, 559; sources for,
    557–60; word processors for,
    558
Biographical reference works, 568
Biology, research sources on, 810
Blackboard, 832
Block quotations
  APA style, 801
  Chicago style, 772
  MLA style, 690–91
Blogs
  collaboration using, 832–33

defined, 884
documenting: APA style, 796;
  Chicago style, 769; MLA style,
  674, 677–78
evaluating, 582, 600–02
permission for use of, 633
as research sources, 582,
  600–02
board, bored, 532
Body
  of argument, 209
  of business letter, 843
  of business memo, 845–46
  defined, 884
  of essay, 39–42
Boldface type, 118–19
Bookmarks/Favorites, 580
Book reviews
  digests of, 571
  documenting: APA style, 788, 790,
    794; Chicago style, 765; MLA
    style, 662, 674–75, 680
  as research sources, 741, 759,
    778, 809
  as writing assignments, 740
Books
  annotated bibliography informa-
    tion for, 559
  computerized catalogs for, 563,
    569–71
  documenting: APA style, 785–87,
    790–91, 795; Chicago style,
    763–67, 768; CSE style, 814–15,
    816; MLA style, 663–69, 678,
    683
  finding bibliographic information
    for, 664
  guides to, 569–71
  subdivisions of, 463
  titles of: capitalization of, 483;
    italics or underlining for,
    489
  working bibliography information
    for, 559
Boolean operators with keywords,
  564–65, 579
bored, board, 532
born, borne, 532
both
  as determiner, 326
  as indefinite pronoun, 305–06,
    311–12
  pronouns with, 311–12
  verbs with, 305–06
both . . . and, as correlative conjunction, 257, 400–01

Farr, Marcia, 279
Feagin, Caley O'Dwyer, IAE-37, IAE-46
Feedback. *See* Evaluation
Feldman, Ann M., IAE-5, 155, 755, 852
Felske, Claudia Klein, 863
Ferris, Dana R., 178
Fife, Jane Mathison, IAE-33
Figgins, Margo A., 279
Final drafts, response to, IAE-21–IAE-22.
  See also Evaluation
Fishman, Stephen M., IAE-19
Fiske, John, 147
Flaherty, Alice, 48
Flammia, Madelyn, 113
Fleck, Catherine, IAE-68, IAE-70
Flower, Linda S., IAE-3, IAE-5, IAE-6, 4, 6, 21
Fontaine, Sheryl I., IAE-19
Ford, James E., 549
Foreign students. *See* ESL students
Forman, Janis, IAE-45
Fossilized errors, IAE-66
Foster, David, IAE-19
Fox, Len, 302, 323, 519
Freedman, Sarah Warshauer, IAE-33
Freire, Paolo, IAE-4
Frye, Bob, 24
Fugere, Brian, 841
Fulkerson, Richard, IAE-4, IAE-5, 5, 107
Fulwiler, Toby, IAE-4, IAE-5, 18, 52, 54, 728,
  737, 809, 810

G

Gage, John T., 204
Gannett, Cinthia, 18
Gardner, Susan, 18, 604, 809
Gardner, Traci, IAE-19
Garrison, Roger, IAE-33
Garson, Lorrin R., 809
Gastel, Barbara, 807
Geisler, Cheryl, 204
Generation 1.5 ESL students, IAE-63
George, Diana, IAE-19, 113, 156, 201, 204
George, Don, 863
Gere, Anne Ruggles, IAE-33, IAE-45, 56
Gergits, Julia M., IAE-35, IAE-45
Gilbert, Judith, IAE-31, IAE-33
Gilbertson, Michael K., 809
Gill, Ken, IAE-31, IAE-33
Glazer, Susan Mandel, IAE-31, IAE-33
Goldfine, Ruth, 6
Goldstein, Lynn M., IAE-70
Golub, Jeffrey, IAE-33, IAE-45, 6, 147, 829

Gonzalez, Casey, IAE-45
Goodburn, Amy, 4
Goodman, W. Daniel, 809
Gordon, Karinne, 348
Gorrell, Donna, 260, 341
Goswami, Dixie, 842
Goueffic, Louise, 508
Gould, Christopher, 731
Grading, IAE-26–IAE-28, IAE-29–IAE-30,
    IAE-32
    of ESL students, IAE-68
Graf, David W., Jr., 504
Graff, Gerald, 640
Grammar checkers, IAE-50, IAE-51
Grant-Davies, Keith, 475
Graves, Richard L., IAE-19, 399
Greene, Kathryn, 405
Greene, Stuart, 151
Greenway, William, 806
Grimm, Nancy, IAE-37, IAE-45, 70
Grusin, Richard, IAE-60
Guinee, Kathleen, 607

H

Hafer, Gary R., 841
Hairston, Maxine, IAE-4, IAE-6, IAE-9
Hamilton, David, 806
Hanks, Christine, 155
Hardaway, Chelsea, 841
Haring-Smith, Tori, IAE-45
Harklau, Linda, 502
Harrington, Jane, 67
Harris, Jeanette, IAE-45, 67
Harris, Joseph, IAE-45, 54, 643
Harris, Muriel, IAE-34, IAE-45, 54, 330
Hartman, Kathleen A., 155
Hashimoto, Irvin Y., 242, 454, 533
Hawisher, Gail, IAE-60
Hayes, Christopher G., 508
Hayes, John R., IAE-3, IAE-5, IAE-6, 4, 6, 21
Heath, Shirley Brice, 279, 587
Hecker, Linda, 25
Heller, Rafael, IAE-35, IAE-45
Helms-Park, Rena, 564, 580
Hemmeter, Thomas, 777
Henry, Jim, 863
Henry, Matthew, 113
Hensley, Randall, 560
Herriman, Jennifer, 242
Herrington, Anne, 174, 242, 263, 728, 730
Herzberg, Bruce, IAE-19
Higgens, Lorraine, 604

Brackets
    for altered capitalization in quo-
        tations, 460, 474, 482–83
    for changes in quotations, 460,
        474, 482–83, 616
    forming, in document, 119
    grammar checkers for, 467
Brainstorming, 22–23, 735–36, 884
brake, break, 532
bring, take, 867
British vs. American spelling, 534
Broad reference, 348–49
Brochures. *See also* Pamphlets
    designing, 853–55
    documenting, MLA style, 670
Bros., 494
Browser, 580
BUBL Link, 579
Bulleted lists, 116, 119
Bulletin boards, electronic. *See* Dis-
    cussion groups, online
bunch, 867
burst, bursted; bust, busted, 867
Business and economics, research
    sources on, 777, 778
Business letters and memos, 841–46
Business writing. *See* Public writing
but
    beginning sentences with, 336
    in contrasting phrases, 432
    as coordinating conjunction, 257,
        399–400
    linking words, phrases, and sub-
        ordinate clauses, 439–41
    between main clauses, 422–24
    punctuation with, 257–58,
        422–24, 430, 441, 448
    and sentence fragments, 336
but, hardly, scarcely, 867
but, however, yet, 867
but that, but what, 867
buy, by, 532
by, as preposition, 243, 393

C

calculate, figure, reckon, 869
Campus know-how, 128
can, as helping verb, 274, 283–84
can, may, 869
can't help but, 869
capable of, 518
capital, capitol, 532
Capitalization, 482–87
    avoiding unnecessary, 486–87
    brackets for altered, 474, 482–83

after colons, 468, 483
of compass directions, 486
of days of week, months, and hol-
    idays, 484
of first word of sentence, 482–83
of geographical names, 484
of governments and institutions,
    485
grammar checkers for, 482
of historical events, etc., 484
of hyphenated words, 483
of *I* and *O,* 484
in online communication, 487,
    504, 830
with personal names, 486
of persons and things, 484, 486
of political and other groups, 485
of product trade names, 486
of pronouns for God and Allah,
    485
of proper nouns and adjectives,
    484–85
of questions in series, 419, 483
in quoted material, 482–83
of races, nationalities, and lan-
    guages, 485
of relationships, 487
of religions and religious terms,
    485
in résumés, 849
of seasons or academic years, 487
of titles of persons, 486
of titles of works: APA style, 785;
    CSE style, 813; general guide-
    lines for, 483
Captions of images, 154, 225
Card catalogs, 563, 569–71
Cardinal numbers, 884
Cartoons. *See* Illustrations and art-
    works
Case, 264–71
    in appositives, 267–68
    after *as* or *than,* 268
    in compound objects, 267
    in compound subjects, 266
    defined, 264, 884
    genitive, 891
    before gerunds, 271
    grammar checkers for, 265–66
    with infinitives, 268
    of nouns, 265, 271, 452–54
    objective, 265, 267, 884
    plain, 897
    possessive, 265, 452–54, 884
    of pronouns, 264–71
    in subject complements, 266

subjective, 264, 266, 884
we vs. *us* before noun, 267
who vs. *whom*, 269–70
case, instance, line, 869
Case analysis, 775
Catalog, library, 563, 569–71
Cause-and-effect analysis
defined, 884
in essay development, 26
in paragraph development, 99–100
transitional expressions for, 89
CD-ROMs
documenting: APA style, 798; Chicago style, 769; CSE style, 817; MLA style, 667, 683–84
reference works on, 513
searching, 563, 564–65
CE, BCE, with dates, 493–94
censor, censure, 869
center around, 869
Central idea
of essay, 27–32
of paragraph, 75
certainly
as conjunctive adverb, 259
punctuation with, 430, 446
certain of, 518
Characters (literary), 737, 884
Characters (letters, numbers), used as words, 490
charge for, with, 518
Charts. *See* Illustrations and artworks
Chat (online), 833
Checkers. *See* grammar checkers *under specific issues;* Grammar/style checkers; Spelling checkers
Checklists
arguments, revising, 211
editing, 60–61
evaluating sources, 591, 593, 600–01
fallacies, 191
inductive and deductive reasoning, 203
literary analysis, revising, 745
oral presentations, 857
plagiarism, avoiding, 627
research papers, revising, 642
revision, 54–55
thesis statements, revising, 31
Chemistry, research sources on, 810
Chicago Manual of Style, The. See Chicago style

Chicago style
defined, 885
document format, 760–63, 771–73
index to documentation models, 764
list of works cited: format of, 760–71; index to, 764; models of, 763–71
notes: format of, 760–71; index to, 764; models of, 763–71
for poetry and long prose quotations, 772
Chronological organization
defined, 885
of essay, 40
of paragraph, 82
Citation indexes, 577, 741, 758
Citation of sources
defined, 885
in drafting process, 641
for images, 223, 630
necessity for, 626–35
in revision process, 642–43
using APA style, 779–99
using Chicago style, 760–71
using CSE style, 812–17
using MLA style, 644–91
Citations, parenthetical. *See* Parenthetical citations
cite, sight, site, 532
Claims
balancing in synthesis of texts, 164–65
defined, 177, 216, 885
in images, 216–17
kinds of, 178–81
linked to evidence by assumptions, 178, 199–205
supporting with evidence, 181–85
testing, 178–81, 216–17
Clarity, achieving, 299
Classification
defined, 885
in essay development, 26
in paragraph development, 97–98
Clauses
adjective. *See* Adjective clauses
adverb. *See* Adverb clauses
conjunctive adverbs with, 258–59, 342–43, 444, 446
coordinating conjunctions with, 256–59, 340–41, 422–42
defined, 242, 250, 885
dependent. *See* Subordinate (dependent) clauses
elliptical, 253, 366, 889

Highburg, Nels P., IAE-46
Hilligoss, Susan, 55
Hillocks, George, Jr., IAE-34, IAE-45, 6
Hobson, Eric H., IAE-60, 231
Hocks, Mary E., IAE-60, 224, 834
Holland, Kenneth, 776
Hollander, John, 748
Homes, Vicki, 549
Hopper, Peggy, 502
Horner, Bruce, 67, 233
Howard, Rebecca Moore, 627
Hum, Sue, IAE-60
Hunt, Kellogg, IAE-17, IAE-19
Hunter, Susan, 21, 231
Huntley, David, 155
Huot, Brian, IAE-34, IAE-60, 829
Huston, Michael, 587
Hyland, Fiona, IAE-70
Hyland, Ken, IAE-70

I

Information technology. *See* Computer-aided learning
Inman, James, IAE-60
Instructor's Resource Manual, IAE-16
International students. *See* ESL students
Internet resources, IAE-16, IAE-50–IAE-51. *See also* Computer-aided learning
Irmscher, William, IAE-19
Iyer, Pico, 424

J

Jacobson, Trudy E., 565
James, William, 304
Janik, Allan, 150, 179
Jarratt, Susan C., IAE-6
Jenseth, Richard, 147
Johnson, Cheryl, 207
Johnson, Karen E., 255
Johnson, Katherine, 776
Johnson, Paul J., 148
Johnson, T.R., 70
Johnson, Walter H., 243
Johnson-Eilola, Johndan, IAE-7, IAE-61, 156, 834
Johnston, Kathryn A., 604
Johnstone, Anne C., 809
Jones, Billie J., 174
Jones, John, 581
Jones, Libby Falk, 148

K

Kail, Harvey, IAE-45
Kantz, Margaret, 607
Kasterly, James L., 200
Katula, Richard A., 178
Katz, Steven B., 807
Kearns, Edward, 67
Kellogg, David, 810
Kendricks, Michelle R., 224
Kennedy, Mary Lynch, 611
Kent, Thomas, IAE-6
Kerek, Andrew, 255
Killingsworth, M. Jimmie, 155, 809
Kim, Loel, 70
Kirsch, Gesa, 13
Kissell, Brian, 533
Kline, Nancy, 149
Kneupper, Charles W., 25, 200
Knoblauch, C.H., IAE-22, IAE-33, 74
Koerber, Amy, 174
Kolln, Martha, 308, 379, 399
Krishna, Valerie, 370
Kuhne, Michael, 70

L

Lakey, Kris, 22
Lamb, Catherine, 200
Lambert, Judith R., 155
Landow, George, IAE-60
Langrehr, Don, 224
Languages, reader- vs. writer-responsible, IAE-64–IAE-65
Lanham, Richard, 103, 379, 393, 405, 524, 841
Largy, Pierre, 54
Larsen, Richard B., 255
Larsen-Freeman, Diane, IAE-68, IAE-69, 285
Larson, Bruce, IAE-34
Leder, Nevin, IAE-68, IAE-70
Lee, Amy, IAE-19
Leki, Ilona, IAE-64, IAE-70
Lent, Robin, 174
Lentricchia, Frank, 737
Leonard, James S., IAE-45
Lindemann, Erika, IAE-19, 5, 731
Lindquist, Julie, IAE-6
Liszka, Thomas R., 32
Literature-based courses, IAE-14
Little, Brown Handbook
  ancillary publications for, IAE-16–IAE-17
  assumptions shaping, IAE-8–IAE-9
  in computer-aided learning, IAE-49–IAE-50
  familiarizing students with, IAE-10

Clauses *(continued)*
  independent. *See* Main (independent) clauses
  introductory, punctuation of, 425–26
  main. *See* Main (independent) clauses
  nonessential vs. essential, 428–29
  noun, 252, 896
  punctuating, 425–26, 428–29, 439–40, 443–48
  reducing to phrases, 528
  relative, 900
  as sentence fragments, 334
  subordinate. *See* Subordinate (dependent) clauses
Clichés
  avoiding, 522
  common, 522
  defined, 522, 903
  grammar checkers for, 511
  no quotation marks for, 464–65
Climactic organization
  defined, 885
  for essays, 42
  for paragraphs, 84
climatic, climactic, 869
Close of business letter, 843
Closing paragraph, of essay, 107–09
Clustering, 23–24, 885
Co., 494
Coherence. *See also* Unity
  combining devices to achieve, 90
  defined, 43, 79, 885
  of essays, 42–44, 111
  of paragraphs, 79–90
  parallelism for, 85–86, 383–84, 403–04
  sample essay, 43–44
  of sentences, 383–84
  of Web pages, 44
Collaboration
  benefiting from, 70–71
  commenting during, 68–71
  courseware for, 832
  defined, 68, 885
  guidelines for, 68–71, 831–34
  online, 831–34
  peer reviews, 52, 68–71
  using computers, 831–34
  working well during, 832
Collective nouns
  agreement of pronouns with, 313
  agreement of verbs with, 306–07
  defined, 313, 896
  plural, 313

Colloquial language
  appropriate uses of, 505
  defined, 865, 885
  grammar checkers for, 502–03
Colons, 467–69
  with appositives, 255, 469
  in business letter salutations, 842
  capitalization after, 468, 483
  vs. comma, 444
  vs. dash, 468, 471
  to introduce quotations, series, etc., 437, 468–69
  misuse of, 469
  preceded by complete main clause, 468
  with quotation marks, 465, 469
  vs. semicolon, 444, 450, 468
  before subtitles, 469
  in time of day, 469
Color
  considering for readers with vision loss, 126
  in document design, 118–19, 120–21
  on Web pages, 839
Combining sentences. *See* Sentence combining, to achieve conciseness
Comic strips. *See* Illustrations and artworks
Commands
  formation of, 261, 296, 331
  punctuation after, 418, 420
  for variety, 411–12
Commas, 422–42. *See also* Commas, misuse of
  with absolute phrases, 432
  in addresses, 435
  with appositives, 255, 394, 429
  for clarity, 438
  with conjunctive adverbs, 259, 342–43, 446
  with coordinate adjectives, 389, 433–34
  vs. dashes, 430, 471
  in dates, 435
  grammar checkers for, 422
  with introductory elements, 425–26
  between items in series, 258, 389, 433
  in long numerals, 497
  with main clauses linked by coordinating conjunctions, 340–41, 422–42
  with mild interjections, 431

misuse or overuse of. *See* Commas, misuse of
with nonessential elements, 427–31
in numbers, 435
vs. parentheses, 430, 471
with parentheses, 473
with parenthetical expressions, 430, 471
with phrases of contrast, 432
with place names, 435
with prepositional phrases, 244, 425, 428–29
to prevent misreading, 438
with quotation marks, 436–38, 460, 465
vs. semicolon, 444–45
between short main clauses, 339, 424
with signal phrases, 436–38
with subordinate clauses, 253, 393–94, 428–29
with tag questions, 431
with transitional expressions, 90, 342–43, 426, 430, 446
with verbals and verbal phrases, 248
with words of direct address, 431
with *yes* and *no*, 430
Commas, misuse of, 439–42. *See also* Comma splices
after *and, but,* or *yet,* 430, 441
in comma splices. *See* Comma splices
between compound words, phrases, or subordinate clauses, 439–40
after a coordinating conjunction, 441
with direct quotations, 436–37
with essential appositives, 429, 441
with essential elements, 430
with exclamation points or question marks, 421
between final coordinate adjective and noun, 434
grammar checkers for, 422
with indirect quotations, 442
before a parenthesis, 473
to separate verb or preposition from object, 439–40
before or after series, 442
to set off single quoted words, 441
after a subject or verb, 439

after a subordinating conjunction, 441
Comma splices
causes of, 258
with conjunctive adverbs and transitional expressions, 259, 342–43
correction of, 340–43, 437
defined, 339, 885
grammar checkers for, 339
with main clauses and no coordinating conjunction, 342–43
in quotation interrupted by signal phrase, 437
Comments
adding on a word processor, 34, 70
benefiting from, 70–71
collaborative learning and, 68–71
giving and receiving, 68–71
Common knowledge, 629
Commonly confused words, grammar checkers for, 511
Common nouns, 485, 895
Community work, writing for, 852–55
Comparative degree
appropriate use of, 318–20
defined, 240, 318, 886
formation of, 318–20
of irregular adjectives and adverbs, 318
Comparison and contrast. *See also* Comparisons; Contrasts
defined, 886
in essay development, 26
organizing, 98–99
in paragraph development, 98–99
Comparisons. *See also* Comparison and contrast
completeness of, 374
degrees of, 318–20
double, 319
as essay introductions, 106–07
illogical, 319–20, 374
parallelism in, 400, 401
pronoun case in, 268
transitional expressions for, 88
Complaint letters, 844–45
complement, compliment, 869
Complements
object, 238–39, 886
subject: adjectives as, 238, 317; defined, 237–38, 886; nouns as, 238; pronouns as, 266
verb, 886. *See also* Direct objects; Indirect objects

Little, Brown Handbook
guidelines for using, IAE-8–IAE-18
new features of, IAE-9–IAE-10
in organizing composition course, IAE-10–IAE-15
quiz for users, IAE-10
sentence combining with, IAE-17
tutoring with, IAE-17–IAE-18
use with other texts, IAE-15
Little, Brown Handbook Answer Key, IAE-16
Little, Brown Workbook, IAE-16
Lotto, Edward, 42
Lu, Xin-An, 504
Lucas, Stephen E., 863
Lunsford, Andrea, IAE-4, IAE-5, IAE-33, IAE-46, 13, 56
Lyman, Huntington, 279
Lynch, Dennis A., 201
Lynn, Steven, 732

M

Mackiewicz, Jo, 863
MacNealy, Mary Sue, 756
Macrorie, Ken, IAE-2, IAE-6, 560
Madden-Simpson, Janet, IAE-46
Madraso, Jan, 113
Maggio, Rosalie, 508
Maimon, Elaine, 730
Mann, Nancy, 418, 423
Marginal comments, IAE-25
Marius, Richard, 756
Mark, Beth L., 565
Markels, Robin Bell, 85
Marzano, Robert J., 149
Matsuda, Paul, IAE-70
Matthiessen, F.O., 140
Maxley, John M., 178
McCarthy, Lucille Parkinson, IAE-19, 42, 643
McCleod, Susan H., 149, 730
McClish, Glen, 107
McCloskey, Donald, 776
McComiskey, Bruce, IAE-6, 5
McCormick, Kathleen, 184
McCrary, Donald, IAE-20
McCrimmon, Miles, IAE-20
McDonald, W.U., Jr., IAE-34
McDonnell, Kathryn E., IAE-71
McGinley, William, 611
McLaughlin, Thomas, 737
McLaughlin, Timothy, 14
Meehan, Ryan, IAE-36, IAE-46

Mellen, Cheryl, 57
Mendelson, Michael, 841
Menzel, Kent E., 864
Meyer, Charles F., 423
Meyer, Emily, 423
Meyers, Alan, 244, 302, 323, 519
Micciche, Laura R., 379
Miller, Casey, 508
Miller, Jessica, 512
Miller, Susan, IAE-6, 549
Minchew, Sue S., 502
Mirskin, Jerry, 149
Mirtz, Ruth, IAE-36, IAE-45, 6
Mitchell, Ruth, 103
MLA Style Manual and Guide to Scholarly Publishing, 644
Mlynarczyk, Rebecca Williams, IAE-70
Modern Language Association (MLA), 644
Moffett, James, IAE-6
Moneysmith, Jayne, 207
Monroe, Jonathan, 756, 777, 778, 810
Moore, Vincent, 193
Moran, Charles, 174, 728, 730
Morenberg, Max, 255, 393
Morris, Richard, IAE-60, 55
Morris, Robert, 146
Moskovit, Leonard, 348
Moskovitz, Cary, 810
Moss, Beverly, IAE-46
Moulton, Margaret, 549
Moxley, Joe, IAE-37, IAE-46
Murphy, Raymond, 285, 323, 365
Murray, Donald M., IAE-2, IAE-6
MyCompLab, IAE-16, IAE-51–IAE-58
Myers, Sharon A., 232, 392

N

Nash, Walter, 505
National Council of Writing Program Administrators, 691
NCTE Committee on Classroom Practices, 147
Neff, Joyce, 729
Nelson, Gayle L., IAE-70
Nelson, Jennie, 549
Newell, Bridget M., 604
Newkirk, Thomas, IAE-6, 5
Newman, Michael, 232
Nilsen, Alleen Pace, 348
Noguchi, Rei, 232, 330, 338
Norton, Robert, 113

Complete predicate, 231–32, 898
Complete subject, 231–32, 901
Complexity
    essay organization by, 42
    paragraph organization by, 84–85
Complex sentences, 263, 900
compose, comprise, 869
Compound adjectives, 544
Compound antecedents, agreement of pronoun with, 311
Compound-complex sentences, 263, 900
Compound constructions
    case in, 266
    with conjunctive adverbs, 258–59, 389
    with coordinating conjunctions, 256–59, 389
    defined, 256, 886
    omissions from, 373
    punctuation of, 422–24, 433, 439–42
    with semicolons, 443–50
Compound nouns, forming plurals of, 538
Compound numbers, hyphenation of, 544–45
Compound object, pronouns in, 267
Compound predicate, 231, 336, 886
Compound sentences
    avoiding series of, 407–08
    with conjunctive adverbs, 259, 389
    with coordinating conjunctions, 256–59, 389
    defined, 262–63, 886, 900
    semicolons in, 443–50
Compound subject
    agreement of pronoun with, 311
    agreement of verb with, 304–05
    case of pronouns in, 266
    defined, 231, 886
    sample, 256
Compound words
    defined, 886
    forming plurals of, 538
    forming possessives of, 454
    hyphenation of, 544
    comprise, compose, 869
Computerized databases. *See* Databases, electronic
Computerized library catalogs, 563, 569–71
Computerized sources. *See* Electronic sources

Computers
    AutoSummarize function, 135
    bibliography software, 635
    brainstorming on, 23
    bulleted lists, creating, 119
    collaborating on, 831–34
    Comment function, 70, 611
    designing documents on, 112–26
    drafting on, 48, 643
    editing on, 52–53, 63
    file management on, 55–56
    finding overused words with, 517
    formatting source citations with, 635, 763
    freewriting on, 22
    grammar and style checkers, 63–65
    graphics programs, 121, 840
    HTML editors, 836, 892
    hypertext documents on, 834–40
    hyphenation with, 545
    invisible writing on, 22, 23
    journals on, 19, 141
    for keeping notes, 130–31, 141, 609
    research with. *See* Research writing
    revising on, 52–53
    saving and backing up documents on, 48, 55
    sources on, 561–65
    spelling checkers on, 63–64, 531, 538, 539
    text highlighting, 75
    Track Changes function, 56
    using the Web on, 563–64, 578–81
Computer science, research sources on, 810
Computer service. *See* Databases, electronic
Computer software
    to create bibliographies, 635
    italics or underlining for titles of, 489
concerning, as preposition, 243
Conciseness, achieving, 523–30
    avoiding redundancy, 527–28
    in business letters, 844–45
    in business memos, 846
    combining sentences, 529
    cutting empty words and phrases, 525–26
    cutting repetition, 527–28
    defined, 386, 886
    eliminating expletives, 529
    for emphasis, 386–87

reducing clauses and phrases, 528
in résumés, 848–49
rewriting jargon, 529–30
using active voice, 386–87, 525
using strong verbs, 386–87,
524–25
Conclusion
of argument, 209–10
defined, 887
of essay, 39, 107–09
of oral presentation, 859
of research paper, 712
of syllogism, 200–03
transitional expressions for, 89
Concrete and abstract words
in argument, 181
defined, 516, 882
and exactness, 516–17
concur in, with, 518
Conditional sentences
defined, 294, 887
and subjunctive mood, 296
and verb tense sequence, 294–95
Conference proceedings, MLA style,
669
Conjugation, 280–84, 887
Conjunctions
adverbial. *See* Conjunctive adverbs
capitalization in titles, 483
coordinating. *See* Coordinating
conjunctions
correlative. *See* Correlative conjunctions
defined, 233, 887
subordinating. *See* Subordinating
conjunctions
Conjunctive adverbs
and comma splices, 259, 342–43,
446
comma with, 259, 342, 430, 446
vs. coordinating and subordinating conjunctions, 258–59,
342–43
defined, 342, 887
list of, 259
position in clause, 258–59,
342–43, 446
semicolon with main clauses related by, 258–59, 343, 446
Connectors (connectives), 397, 887
Connotation
defined, 887
grammar checkers for, 511
of synonyms, 514–15
and tone, 186–87
conscience, conscious, 869

consequently
as conjunctive adverb, 259
punctuation with, 430, 446
consequently, as transitional expression, 89
Consistency. *See also* Agreement of
pronouns and antecedents;
Agreement of subjects and
verbs
for coherent paragraphs, 86
in person and number, 353–55
in subject and voice, 356
in tense and mood, 355
on Web pages, 839
Construction, defined, 887
contact, 869
contend for, with, 518
Context
determining in evaluating Web
sites, 597–600
of images, 157, 160–61
of visual evidence, 219
and word meanings, 427–28
of writing situation, 4
continual, continuous, 869
Contractions
apostrophes in, 456–57
defined, 887
vs. possessive personal pronouns,
456–57
use of, 456–57
Contrary-to-fact clauses
subjunctive for, 296
and tense sequence, 294–95
Contrasts. *See also* Comparison and
contrast
commas with phrases expressing,
432
parallelism in, 400, 401
transitional expressions for, 88
convince, persuade, 869
Coordinate adjectives
commas with, 258, 389, 433–34
defined, 433, 887
tests for, 434
Coordinating conjunctions
beginning sentences with, 336,
409
and compound constructions,
256–59
vs. conjunctive adverbs, 258–59,
342–43
with coordinate adjectives,
433–34
for correcting comma splices or
fused sentences, 340–41

O

Odell, Lee, IAE-33, 149, 842
O'Hare, Frank, IAE-17, IAE-20, 392
O'Neill, Peggy, IAE-33
Ong, Walter J., 12
Online communication, IAE-51. *See also*
Computer-aided learning
Online resources, IAE-16, IAE-50–IAE-51
Online Writing Center of the University of
Wisconsin at Madison, 232
Overman, Elizabeth Smith, IAE-60, 55

P

Page, Melvin E., 756
Palacas, Arthur L., 473
Pantoja, Veronica, 549
Paredes-Holt, Bill, 564
Park, Douglas B., 14
Passmore, John, IAE-20
Pechenik, Jan, 807
Pederson, Don, 184
Pelham, Fran O'Bryne, 549, 607
Penrod, Diane, IAE-60, 113
Penrose, Ann M., 807
Perdeu, Virginia, 42
Perelman, Les, IAE-6
Perl, Sondra, IAE-3, IAE-6
Perrin, Robert, 22
Peters, Brad, 730
Petit, Angela, 446
Petraglia, Joseph, IAE-4, IAE-6
Petrosky, Anthony, IAE-4, IAE-19
Pettersen, Nancy-Laurel, 243
Pike, Kenneth L., IAE-3, IAE-7
Pixton, William H., 366
Plagiarism, IAE-65
Platz, Judith, 107
Podis, JoAnne M., 77
Podis, Leonard A., 25, 77
Polio, Charlene, IAE-68, IAE-70
Ponsot, Marie, IAE-20
Porter, James E., IAE-60
Porter, Jeffrey, 204
Portfolios, IAE-31
Porush, David, 807
Prewriting, IAE-2
Price, Gayle B., 24, 151
Price, Margaret, 627
Process-oriented writing, IAE-12–IAE-13
computers in, IAE-47
for ESL students, IAE-65

Process-oriented writing *(continued)*
 vs. product-oriented writing, IAE-65–IAE-66
Purdue Online Writing Lab (OWL), 232
Putnam, Dawn, 533

Q

Qualley, Donna, 22, 149

R

Radia, Pavlina, 580
Raimes, Ann, IAE-68, IAE-70
Randall, Sally N., 560
Rankin, Elizabeth, IAE-20
Rapkins, Angela A., 178, 193
Raymond, Richard S., 732
Readence, John E., 150
Reader- *vs.* writer-responsible languages, IAE-64–IAE-65
Readers, IAE-15–IAE-16
Redfern, Richard K., 265
Reed-Nordwall, Karen, 533
Rees, Mary, IAE-37, IAE-45
Refugee students. *See* ESL students
Reid, Joy M., IAE-70
Reiff, Mary Jo, 14
Reiss, Donna, IAE-60, 829
Reither, James A., IAE-6, IAE-9, IAE-46
Research, computer-aided, IAE-50. *See also*
 Computer-aided learning
Response to student writing. *See* Evaluation
Revision, IAE-2
 computer-aided, IAE-50
 vs. editing, IAE-28
 evaluation of, IAE-28–IAE-29
Reynolds, Mark, 24
Reynolds, Tom, 70
Rhetoric
 contrastive, IAE-64
 courses emphasizing, IAE-12
Rhetorical readers, IAE-15–IAE-16
Rhetorics, IAE-16
Rice, Jeff, 22
Richardson, Mark, 737
Rico, Gabrielle Lusser, 24
Rieke, Richard, 150, 179
Riis, Jacob, 218
Robbins, Sarah, 852
Roberge, Mark, IAE-70
Roberts-Miller, Patricia, IAE-6, 178
Robertson, Julie Fisher, 149, 730
Robillard, Amy E., 724

Coordinating conjunctions
 (continued)
 defined, 233, 887
 list of, 257
 parallelism with, 399–400
 punctuation with, 340–41, 389, 433, 439–42
Coordination
 defined, 388, 887–88
 excessive, 390, 391–92
 faulty, 390
 grammar checkers for, 388
 parallelism and, 399–400
 punctuation with, 389
 to relate equal ideas, 390
 use of, 388–90
Copyright, Web compositions and, 633–34, 836
Corporate or group author
 APA style: parenthetical citations, 782; reference list, 787
 MLA style: list of works cited, 658; parenthetical citations, 647
Correlative conjunctions
 defined, 233, 257, 400–01, 887
 list of, 257
 parallelism with, 400–01
Correspondence. *See* Letters (correspondence)
could, as helping verb, 274, 283–84
could care less, 869
could have vs. *had*, 297
could of, 872
Council of Science Editors. *See* CSE style
Count nouns
 defined, 322–23, 896
 and use of *a, an,* or *the,* 322–25
 and use of other determiners, 325–26
couple of, 870
Courseware, 832
Cover letters for job application, 847–48
Creativity, 139
credible, creditable, credulous, 870
criteria, 870
Critical thinking and reading, 138–215
 and academic integrity, 162
 and academic writing, 162–65
 analysis in, 96–97, 147–48, 156–60
 annotating text during, 133, 141
 of arguments, 176–226
 defined, 888

in developing essay topic, 18–19, 162–63
evaluation in, 151–52, 161, 589–625
first reading and, 132–33
goals of, 138–39
with illustrations, 153–61
interpretation in, 148–50, 160
with online sources, 593, 596–602
previewing material for, 142, 732
reading journal for, 141
rereadings for, 133
with research sources, 589–625
skimming for, 142
summarizing and, 134–35, 145–46
synthesis in, 150–51, 160–61, 604–06
techniques for, 25–26, 138–61
of visual arguments, 216–26
for Web sites and pages, 593, 596–600
Critical writing. *See also* Critical thinking and reading; Research writing
in academic situations, 162–75
approaches to, 163–64
audience for, 166
language in, 168–70
purpose in, 165–66
in research writing, 611–25
in response to images, 173–75
in response to texts, 162–65, 171–73
sample essays, 171–75
structure and content of, 167–68
synthesis in, 164–65, 604–06, 607–11, 620–25
voice in, 14–15, 167, 169–70
Critique
 defined, 138–39
 of an image, 173–75
 as research paper, 806
 of a text, 171–72
CSE style
 vs. APA style, 811
 defined, 888
 document format, 817–20
 for documenting sources, 811–17
 indexes to documentation models, 813
 laboratory reports, 817–20
 reference list: index of models, 813; name-year style, 812–17; number style, 812–17
 sample paper in, 818–20

text citations: name-year style, 811; number style, 811–12
Culture-language issues. *See also inside back cover*
a, an vs. the, 323–25
academic writing, 170
adjective clauses, repetition in, 370–71
adjectives: negating, 316; no plurals of, 316; order of, 365; present vs. past participle, 321–22
adverbs: placement of, 363, 364–65, 409; in two-word verbs, 287–88
argument, 177, 197
articles (a, an, the), 323–25, 375
at vs. in vs. on, 519
audience: critical reading and, 69, 141; direct approach with, 104, 177, 841; establishing personal connection with, 40; expectations of, 29, 40
auxiliary (helping) verbs, 280–84
be, omission of, 331
beginnings of sentences, varying, 89
capitalization, 482
collaboration, 69
collective nouns, 306–07, 313
commas in long numerals, 497
comma splices, 339, 341
conciseness, achieving by avoiding redundancy, 527–28
conditional sentences and verb tense sequence, 294–95
content and structure of papers, 29, 40
contrary-to-fact clauses and tense sequence, 294–95
count nouns: defined, 322–23, 896; and use of a, an, or the, 322–25; and use of other determiners, 325–26
critical reading, 141
determiners: a, an, the, 323–25; defined, 322–23, 888; other, 325–26; uses of, 322–26
dictionaries, 513
discovering ideas, 17
evaluating sources, 589–90
expert opinions, 183
expletives, omitted there, here, or it, 261
few, a few, 326

forms of address (Mrs., Miss, etc.), 509–10
for vs. since, 291–92, 519
for or to after verb, 238
fused sentences, 339
gender, pronoun-antecedent agreement in, 310
gerunds: vs. infinitives, after verbs, 285–87; after prepositions, 246
helping verbs, 280–84
ideas, developing, 589–90
idioms: dictionaries for, 519; with prepositions, 243, 518–19
indirect questions, 418–19
infinitives with verb, 285–87
intellectual property and, 628
intransitive verbs vs. transitive verbs, 237
introductions, 104
invisible writing, 22
irregular verbs, 275
journal writing, 20
little, a little, 326
many, much, 326
modals, as helping verbs, 283–84
noncount nouns, 233–34, 306–07, 313, 322–26, 538
no vs. not, 316
and nonstandard dialect, 275, 503–04
noun plurals, forming, 233–34, 538
numbers, punctuation with, 435, 497
omitted helping verbs, 281
paragraphing, 74
paraphrasing, 615
participles, past vs. present, 321–22
passive voice, 282, 298
perfect tenses, 291–92
plagiarism, avoiding, 628
plural noun after one of the, 308
plurals, 233–34, 538
prepositions, 243, 287–88, 335, 518–19
progressive tenses, 281–82, 292
pronoun-antecedent agreement, 310, 313, 346
pronouns: omitting, 332; redundant with sentence subject, 346, 370–71
public writing, 841
questions, 363
redundant phrases, 527–28

Robinson, Susan Miller, 42, 643
Robinson, William S., 298
Rockas, Leo, 747, 748
Roen, Duane H., IAE-20, 13, 549
Roessig, Lesley, 560
Rogers, Priscilla S., 842
Rohman, D. Gordon, IAE-2, IAE-6
Romantic theory, IAE-2
Ronald, Kate, IAE-20
Rose, Mike, IAE-6, 48
Rose, Shirley K., 162
Rosewarne, Tracy, 533
Roskelly, Hephzibah, IAE-20, IAE-46
Roth, Richard W., 178
Rowan, Katherine E., 864
Rubin, Donald L., 184, 405
Russell, David P., IAE-6
Rutz, Carol, IAE-34
Rymer, Jone, 842

S

Saltz, Laura, IAE-20, IAE-68
Salvatori, Mariolina, 174
Sams, Lynn, 232
Santos, Tony, IAE-68, IAE-70
Schmid, Dawn, IAE-68, IAE-70
Schramer, James J., IAE-35, IAE-45
Schultz, Marcia, 178
Schuster, Edgar H., 330
Schwegler, Robert A., 778
Seabury, Marcia Bundy, 8
Segall, Mary T., 730
Selber, Stuart, IAE-60
Self, Dickie, IAE-60
Selfe, Cynthia, IAE-7, IAE-60, IAE-61, 55, 156, 565, 834
Selfe, Richard J., Jr., 565
Sellen, Mary, 224
Sensenbaugh, Roger, 533
Sentence combining, IAE-17
Seppänen, Aimo, 242
Shadle, Mark, 554
Shamoon, Linda K., 778
Shaughnessy, Mina, IAE-20, IAE-22–IAE-23, IAE-34, 150, 233, 423
Shaw, Margaret L., IAE-34
Sherman, A. Kimbrough, 42, 643
Sherrard, Carol, 155, 620
Shipka, Jody, 8
Shirley, Sue, 611
Shor, Ira, 150
Shuman, R. Baird, 370

Sidler, Michelle, IAE-60, 55, 565
Simmons, Jay, 14
Simmons-O'Neill, Elizabeth, 560
Simpson, Mary Scott, 503
Singer, Jonathan, IAE-37, IAE-46
Sinor, Jennifer, 587
Sipe, Rebecca Bowers, 533, 540
Sirc, Geoffrey, IAE-7, IAE-61, 70, 156, 834
Skeen, Thomas, 852
Sklar, Elizabeth S., 308
Skorczewski, Dawn, 512
Sloan, Gary, 42, 85
Sloane, Brenda, 524
Smart, Robert A., 730
Smit, David W., IAE-4, IAE-6, IAE-46
Smith, Louise Z., 423
Smith, Rochelle, 42, 85
Smitherman, Geneva, 279
Snair, Scott, 151
Snyder, Ilana, IAE-60
Social process, writing as, IAE-4–IAE-5
Sociology Writing Group, 776
Software, IAE-16, IAE-50–IAE-51. See also
    Computer-aided learning
Soleil, Naome, 156
Soles, Derek, 393, 724
Solomon, Martha, 255
Sommers, Jeffrey, IAE-34, 57, 393
Sommers, Nancy, IAE-3, IAE-6, IAE-20, IAE-22,
    IAE-34, 54, 57
Song, Bailin, IAE-68, IAE-70
Spalter, Anne Morgan, 156
Spear, Karen, IAE-46
Speck, Bruce, IAE-34, IAE-46
Spell checkers, IAE-50
Spellmeyer, Kurt, IAE-46
Sperling, Melanie, IAE-33, 71
Spigelman, Candace, IAE-46, 7
Spivey, Nancy Nelson, 605
Spooner, Michael, IAE-46
Staines, Gail M., 776
Stapleton, Paul, 564, 580
Steer, Jocelyn, IAE-68, IAE-70, 237, 285, 291,
    299, 323
Stern, Arthur A., 74
Stern, Susan Ryan, IAE-34
Sternglass, Marilyn, IAE-6
Stevens, Robert, IAE-33, IAE-45
Stewart, Donald, IAE-4, IAE-6, IAE-46
Stewart, Ruth, 151
Stewart, Thomas, 155
Storey, William Kelleher, 756
Straub, Richard, IAE-22, IAE-34, 57

Culture-language issues (continued)
    repeated sentence parts, 346,
        370–71
    -s and -ed verb endings, 279
    -self pronouns, 266
    sentence fragments, 335
    sources, evaluating, 589–90
    spelling, 534
    and standard American English,
        503–4
    subject of sentence, 231, 332, 346,
        370–71
    subjects for writing, 197
    subject-verb agreement, 302–04,
        306–07, 308
    subordinating conjunctions, 251
    thesis statement, 29
    titles for women, 509–10
    transitional expressions, 89
    transitive vs. intransitive verbs,
        237
    transitive verbs in passive voice,
        282, 298
    verbs: helping, 280–84; negating,
        316; and noncount noun agree-
        ment, 306–07; tenses of, 289;
        transitive, 282; two-word,
        287–88, 903
    wordiness, avoiding, 524
    word order in sentences, 236, 363,
        364–65, 409
Cumulative (loose) sentences, 381,
    888

D

-d. See -ed, -d verb endings
Dance, research sources on, 759
Dangling modifiers
    defined, 366–67, 888
    grammar checkers for, 359
    revision of, 367
Dashes, 470–72
    with appositives, 255, 394, 471
    for changes in tone, 470
    vs. colon, 468, 471
    vs. comma, 430, 471
    for concluding explanation, 472
    for concluding series, 472
    for emphasis, 385
    forming and spacing, 119, 470
    for hesitation in dialog, 470
    for introductory series, 450, 471
    misuse or overuse of, 472
    for nonessential elements, 430,
        470–71

    vs. parentheses, 471
    for parenthetical expressions,
        430, 471
    with quotation marks, 460,
        465–66
    vs. semicolon, 450
    for unfinished thoughts, 470
Data. See also Evidence
    defined, 177–78, 888
    empirical, 806
    qualitative vs. quantitative, 775
data, 870
Databases, electronic
    on CD-ROMs, 563
    defined, 888
    documenting sources from: APA
        style, 791–94; Chicago style,
        767–68; CSE style, 816; MLA
        style, 681–83, 684
    finding bibliographic information
        for, 575–76, 681–83
    kinds of, 563
    library catalog, 563, 569–71
    list of, 576–77
    online, 563, 572–77
    of online images, 584–85
    for periodicals: general, 576–77;
        in humanities, 758; in litera-
        ture, 741; in natural and ap-
        plied sciences, 808–09; in social
        sciences, 778
    résumés on, 848–50
    vs. search engines, 563–64
    searching, 563–65, 573–76
    selection of, 573
    subscription via library, 572,
        576–77, 681–82
Date of access
    APA style, 791
    Chicago style, 767
    CSE style, 815–16
    MLA style, 680
Dates
    BC and AD with, 419, 493–94
    BCE and CE with, 493–94
    commas in, 435
    doubtful, indicating, 420
    numerals vs. words for, 497
    publication, 556
Days of the week
    abbreviations for, 495
    capitalization of, 484
Deadlines, 5
Declension, 265, 888
Deductive reasoning, 200–03,
    888

Defined terms
  in argument, 181
  italics or underlining for, 490
  singular verb with, 308
Definition
  defined, 888
  in essay development, 25
  in paragraph development, 95–96
  of terms, in argument, 181
Degree for adjectives and adverbs, 318–20, 886
Demonstrative adjectives, 882
Demonstrative pronouns, 899
Denotation, 514, 888
Dependent clauses. *See* Subordinate (dependent) clauses
dependent on, 518
Depository libraries, 584
Derivational suffix, 902
Description
  defined, 888
  in essay development, 25
  objective vs. subjective, 94
  in paragraph development, 94
Descriptive adjectives, 882
Descriptive title, 53
Descriptors. *See* Keywords
desert, dessert, 532
Design of documents. *See* Document design and format
despite, as preposition, 243, 392
Details
  in argument, 181–85
  in essay development, 5, 12, 14
  in paragraph development, 92–93
Determiners
  a, an, the, 234, 323–25
  defined, 322, 888
  grammar checkers for, 323
  other determiners, 325–26
  uses of, 322–26
Developing (planning), 16–44, 548–60, 833–34, 837, 889
Development of essay topic, 16–44
  audience needs and, 5, 12–15
  brainstorming for, 22–23
  clustering for, 23–24
  critical thinking for, 25–26
  freewriting for, 21–22
  journalist's questions for, 24–25
  keeping a journal for, 19–21
  list making for, 22–23
  observing surroundings for, 21
  patterns for, 25–26. *See also* individual patterns
  reading for, 18–19

Development of paragraphs, 92–102
  combining methods for, 101
  defined, 92
  patterns for, 93–101. *See also* individual patterns
  specific information in, 92–93
device, devise, 870
Diagrams. *See* Illustrations and artworks
Dialect. *See also* Culture-language issues
  defined, 503–04, 889
  grammar checkers for, 502
  nonstandard, 503–04
  standard American English as, 168, 503–04
Dialog
  hesitations in, 470
  paragraphing for, 110, 462
  quotation marks for, 462
Diction, 502–22, 889. *See also* specific topics under Words
Dictionaries
  documenting: Chicago style, 769; MLA style, 667, 675, 683
  electronic, 513
  ESL, 513
  list of, 513
  for meanings, 512–13
  sample entry, 513
  special, 568
  specialized, in research, 741, 757–58, 809
  vs. thesaurus, 512–13
  types of, 568
  unabridged, 568
Dictionary form of verbs. *See* Plain form of verbs
differ about, from, over, with, 518
different from, different than, 870
differ from, differ with, 870
Digests of books, 571
Digital Object Identifier (DOI)
  APA style, 791–93
  CSE style, 815, 816
Direct address
  commas with, 431
  defined, 889
Direct discourse. *See* Quotations, direct
Direct objects. *See also* Objects
  adjective vs. adverb after, 317–18
  case form for, 265
  defined, 236, 896
  separation from verb, 362
  after transitive verb, 236–37, 278

Strenski, Ellen, IAE-37, IAE-46
Strickland, James, 554
Strong, William, IAE-20, 256, 393
Stroupe, Craig, 224
Student evaluation. *See* Evaluation
Stygall, Gail, IAE-46
Style checkers, IAE-50, IAE-51
Suchet, David, 749
Sullivan, Gwendolen F., IAE-4, 864
Sullivan, Patricia A., IAE-6, IAE-60
Sunstein, Bonnie, 560
Swift, Kate, 508
Syllabus, sample, IAE-18–IAE-19
Szotstak, Donna Rane, 149

T

Tagemics theory, IAE-3
Takayoshi, Pamela, IAE-60, 829
Tate, Gary, IAE-19, 732
Taylor, Tim N., 8, 554
Taylor, Todd W., IAE-61
Tedlock, David, 7
Thelin, William H., 756
Thematic courses, IAE-13–IAE-14
Thematic readers, IAE-15–IAE-16
Thomas, Katherine M., 243
Thomas, Lewis, 423
Tichenor, Stuart, 14
Tierney, Robert J., 150
Tingle, Nick, 162
Tobin, Lad, IAE-20, IAE-46, 5
Tornow, Joan, 829
Toulmin, Stephen, 150, 179
Trimbur, John, IAE-46, 14, 56, 807
Tripp, Ellen L., 150
Tryzna, Thomas N., 587
Tuchman, Barbara, 637, 756
Tucker, Amy, 8
Tutorials, online, IAE-51
Tutoring, IAE-17–IAE-18
Tuzi, Frank, 175
Twain, Mark, 503

V

Valentine, Kathryn, 691
Valerie-Gold, Maria, 162
Van Dam, Andries, 156
Vande Koppel, William J., 379
Vandenberg, Peter, IAE-6
VangoNotes, IAE-17
Vargas, Marjorie Fink, 806

Viera, Carroll, 233
Villanueva, Victor, IAE-7
Vipond, Douglas, IAE-46

W

Waggoner, Eric, 549
Wakefield, Sarah, 611
Walker, Robert L., 399
Wallace, David, 8
Wallace, Ray, 231
Walpole, Jane R., 407
Walsh, Jennifer, 533
Walsh, John A., 151
Walter, Jeffrey, 204
Walvoord, Barbara, IAE-4, IAE-7, 42, 643, 729
Ward, Irene, IAE-61
Wardle, Elizabeth, IAE-5
Warshawsky, Jon, 841
Washington, Eugene, 25
Weaver, Christopher C., IAE-34
Weaver, Constance, 243, 370
Web site(s), IAE-50–IAE-51. *See also* Computer-aided learning
Webb, Patricia, 852
Weiser, Irwin, IAE-31, IAE-34, 72
Weissberg, Bob, 71
Weisser, Christian, 756
Welch, Nancy, 55, 71, 852
Wells, Susan, 14
Werner, Stuart, IAE-45
Wesley, Kimberly, 22
Westbrook, Steve, IAE-61, 224, 834
Wharton, Christine E., IAE-45
Whitaker, Elaine E., 627
White, Edward M., IAE-5, IAE-34, 4, 71
White, Fred D., 18
Whitehill, Sharon, 18
Whithaus, Carl, 729
Wickliff, Greg, 156
Wiebe, Russel, 55
Wiener, Harvey S., IAE-46, 79, 454, 482
Wilcox, Lance, 25
Wilkinson, A.M., 810
Williams, James D., 155, 393
Williams, Joseph, 275, 379, 393, 399, 407, 512
Williams, Robin, 125
Wilson, Matthew, 549
Wilson, Smokey, 175
Winder, Barbara E., 208
Winsor, Dorothy A., 806

Direct questions
    defined, 889
    forming, 260
    vs. indirect questions, 357
    question mark with, 418–19
    shifts between indirect questions and, 357
Direct quotations. *See* Quotations, direct
Disabilities, considerations in Web documents, 836, 839. *See also* Vision loss
disappointed by, in, with, 518
Disciplines. *See* Academic writing
Discourse, direct and indirect. *See* Indirect quotations; Quotations, direct
Discovery. *See* Development of essay topic
discreet, discrete, 532, 870
Discussion groups, online
    author's permission for use of, 633
    collaboration via, 831–32
    defined, 580, 889
    discussion lists, e-mail, 889
    documenting: APA style, 796; Chicago style, 769; CSE style, 816; MLA style, 684
    evaluating, 582, 600–02
    lists or listservs, 889
    newsgroups, 583, 895
    for opposing views in argument, 207
    permission to reuse material, 633
    as research source, 582, 600–02
    Web forums, 583, 904
disinterested, uninterested, 870
Dissertation Abstracts, 660, 797
Dissertations
    APA style, 795, 797
    MLA style, 660, 670–71
Division. *See* Analysis
Division of words, 545–46
do, does, did as helping verbs, 274, 283
Documentation of sources
    and avoiding plagiarism, 626–35
    computer software for, 635
    defined, 634, 889
    disciplines: APA style, 779–99; Chicago style, 760–71; CSE style, 811–20; MLA style, 644–88
    guides for the humanities, 760
    guides for the natural and applied sciences, 811

    guides for the social sciences, 779–80
    necessity for, 634–35
    programs for citation styles, 635
    styles of, 634–35. *See also* APA style; Chicago style; CSE style; MLA style
Document design and format
    for academic papers, 112–13
    APA style: document format, 799–802; reference-list format, 779–99
    for brochures, 853–55
    for business letters, 841–44
    for business memos, 845–46
    charts, 123–24
    Chicago style: document format, 771–73; works-cited format, 760–71
    color in, 120–21
    on computer, 112–26
    CSE style: document format, 817–18; reference-list format, 811–17
    defined, 889, 891
    diagrams, 124–25
    effective vs. ineffective, 113–17
    elements of, 117–20
    for fax transmissions, 846
    figures, 122, 123–25
    for flyers, 853–54
    graphs, 124
    headings, 120
    identification, 690
    illustrations, 121–26
    for job-application letters, 847–48
    lists, 119
    for literary analysis, 741–42
    margins, 117
    MLA style: document format, 689–91; works-cited format, 653–88
    for newsletters, 853–54
    photographs, 124–25
    for *PowerPoint* slides, 862–63
    principles of, 113–17
    for proposals, 849–52
    for readers with disabilities, 836, 839
    for readers with vision loss, 126
    for reports, 849–51
    for research papers, 643
    for résumés, 848–50
    tables, 122
    text, 117–19
    type styles and sizes, 118

using photos in, 121
Web compositions, 834–40
white space, 113, 115–16
Documents
format of. *See* Document design and format
government. *See* Government publications
hypertext, 834–40, 892
Dogpile, 579, 580
DOI. *See* Digital Object Identifier (DOI)
Dollar sign *($)*, 493, 497–98
Domain, 889
don't, 870
don't, doesn't, 870
Double comparatives, 319
Double negatives, 320, 889
Double possessives, 889
Doublespeak, 507, 889
Double superlatives, 319
Double talk, 507, 889
down, as preposition, 243
Downloading research sources
obtaining permission to use, 840
pros and cons, 610–11
retaining citation information, 141
Drafting
collaboration in, 833–34
defined, 47, 889
of essays, 46–50
of literary analysis, 744–45
of research papers, 640–41
of thesis statements, 29–32
Drama. *See* Plays
due to
appropriate use of, 870
as preposition, 392
due to the fact that, 870
during, as preposition, 243
DVDs. *See* Films, DVDs, and video recordings

E

each
pronouns with, 311–12
verbs with, 304–06
each and every, 870
eager, anxious, 867
EBSCOhost Academic Search, 573–76
-ed, -d verb endings
grammar checkers for, 279

for past tense and past participle, 230, 234, 273, 275, 279
Edited works
APA style, 790
Chicago style, 765
CSE style, 815
MLA style, 665
Editing
checklist for, 60–61
defined, 889
of essays, 59–65
of literary analyses, 745–47
of research papers, 642
vs. revision, 52–53
for spelling, 539
Editions, later
APA style, 790
Chicago style, 766
MLA style, 665
Editorials, MLA style, 662, 674–75, 680
Education, research sources on, 777, 779
effect, affect, 532, 865
either
pronouns with, 311–12
verbs with, 305–06
either . . . or, as correlative conjunction, 257, 400–01
Either/or fallacy, 191, 194–95
Electronic addresses. *See* Digital Object Identifier (DOI); URL (uniform resource locator)
Electronic communication. *See also* E-mail (electronic mail); Instant messaging; Internet; Text messaging; Web sites
for collaboration, 831–34
faxes, 846
Electronic mail. *See* E-mail (electronic mail)
Electronic résumés, 848–50
Electronic sources
acknowledging, 632–34
avoiding plagiarism with, 628, 632–34
blogs, 582, 600–02
discussion groups, 582, 600–02
documenting: APA style: parenthetical citations, 783; reference list, 791–96; Chicago style, 767–69; CSE style, 815–17; MLA style: list of works cited, 671–83; parenthetical citations, 647–48
downloading, 141, 610–11, 840

Winter, Dave, 852
Winterowd, W. Ross, IAE-34, 86
Witte, Stephen P., 43, 86, 103
Wlecke, Albert O., IAE-2, IAE-6
Wolff, Janice M., IAE-7
Wood, Karen, 533
Worsham, Lynn, IAE-6
Writer- *vs.* reader-responsible languages, IAE-64–IAE-65
Writing course
emphasizing academic writing, IAE-14–IAE-15
emphasizing content and ideas, IAE-13–IAE-14
emphasizing patterns of development, IAE-12
emphasizing patterns of expression and thought, IAE-11
emphasizing rhetoric, IAE-12
emphasizing writing about literature, IAE-14
emphasizing writing process, IAE-12–IAE-13
organization of, IAE-10–IAE-15
sample syllabi for, IAE-18–IAE-19
Writing process, IAE-1–IAE-5. *See also* Process-oriented writing
courses emphasizing, IAE-12–IAE-13
Writing-across-the-curriculum, IAE-4, IAE-14–IAE-16
by ESL students, IAE-68
readers in, IAE-15–IAE-16
Wu, Su-Yueh, 184
Wysocki, Anne, IAE-4, IAE-7, IAE-61, 156, 834

Y

Yagelski, Robert P., 5
Yancey, Kathleen Blake, IAE-4, IAE-7, IAE-20, IAE-31, IAE-34, IAE-46, 71, 72, 156
Yena, Lauren, 549
Yoder, Rhoda Byler, 273
Yohon, Teresa, 830
York, Lorraine, IAE-46
Young, Art, IAE-5, IAE-60, 728, 729, 737, 778, 810
Young, Beth Rapp, 338, 442
Young, Richard E., IAE-3, IAE-7

Z

Zak, Frances, IAE-34
Zamel, Vivian, IAE-70

Zebroski, James, 637
Zeller, Robert, 161
Zemliansky, Pavel, 549, 604
Zimmerman, Don, 830
Zimmet, Nancy, 806

Electronic sources *(continued)*
  evaluating, 589–625
  gathering information from, 141,
    610–11
  library Web site vs. search en-
    gines, 561–62
  plagiarism with, 628
  reference works, 513
  in research, 561–65
  research strategy for, 561–65,
    578–81
  search engines vs. library Web
    sites, 561–62
  searching, 561–65, 578–81
  types of, 563
  Web sites or pages, 578–81, 593,
    596–600
  working bibliography information
    from, 559
elicit, illicit, 532, 870
Ellipsis marks
  defined, 889
  forming and spacing, 119, 475
  to indicate omissions from quota-
    tions, 461, 475–77, 616
  for pauses and unfinished state-
    ments, 477
Elliptical clauses, 253, 366, 889
elude, allude, 532
E-mail (electronic mail), 829–31
  in academic settings, 829
  addressing, 829–30
  alternatives for italics or under-
    lining in, 491
  author's permission for use of,
    633
  capitalization in, 487, 830
  collaboration via, 832
  composing, 830
  documenting: APA style, 796;
    Chicago style, 769; CSE style,
    817; MLA style, 684
  interviews through, 587
  as research source, 580, 587
  responding to, 830–31
  revising shortcuts of, 504
Em dashes, 119, 470–72
emigrate, immigrate, 871
eminent, imminent, 532
Emoticons, 830
Emotional appeals, 192–93, 205–06,
  226, 883
Emphasis, 378–87
  active voice for, 379–80
  balanced sentences for, 383–84
  conciseness for, 386–87

cumulative sentences for, 381
  defined, 890
  in document design, 116–17
  effective subjects and verbs for,
    378–80
  grammar checkers for, 378
  inverted word order for, 261
  italics or underlining for, 490
  organizing for, 41–42, 82–85
  parallelism for, 383–84
  periodic sentences for, 381–82
  punctuation for, 385, 420–21,
    470–71
  repetition for, 384
  sentence beginnings and endings
    for, 380–82, 408–10
  separation of ideas for, 385
  in series, 383
  short paragraph for, 109
  strong verbs for, 378–80
  there is, here is, or *it is* for, 261,
    410
Empty words and phrases, 525–26
Encyclopedias
  documenting: APA style, 795;
    Chicago style, 768; MLA style,
    667, 675, 683
  as research sources, 565–69, 741,
    757–58, 777, 808–09
Endings of sentences, emphasis in,
  380–82
Endnote, 635
Endnotes. *See* Footnotes or endnotes
End punctuation marks, 418–21
Engineering, research sources on,
  810
English (discipline). *See also* Literary analysis; MLA style
  integrating borrowed material in,
    624
  sources in, 741
English as a second language (ESL).
  See Culture-language issues
ensure, assure, insure, 867
enthused, 871
Envelopes, for business letters,
  843–44
Environmental science, research
  sources on, 810
-er, -est, as endings of adjectives and
  adverbs, 318
ERIC, APA style, 797
-es. See -s, -es
ESL. *See* Culture-language issues
especially, specially, 871

Essay examinations, 136–38
  outlines as study aids for, 822,
    823
  reading questions for, 823
  sample responses, 826–28
  thesis statements for, 825
Essays
  audience for, 5, 12–15
  comments on, 68–71
  conclusion of, 107–09
  creating title for, 53
  defined, 890
  developing argument for, 196–210
  developing subject for, 16–44
  drafting, 46–50
  editing, 59–65
  final draft of, 66–68
  introduction to, 104–07
  organization of, 33–34, 209–10
  outline for, 34–39
  paragraphs in, linking, 111
  purpose of, 5, 9–11
  research for, 5
  revising, 50–56
  subject of, 4, 6–9
  thesis of, 27–32
  title of. *See* Title of paper
  tone of, 14–15
  types of, 10
  unity and coherence of, 42–44
Essential elements
  appositives, 429, 441
  clauses and phrases, 428–29, 441
  defined, 427, 890
  misuse of commas with, 427, 429,
    441
  vs. nonessential elements, 427
  punctuating, 427, 441
  test for, 428
  that vs. *which* for clauses, 429,
    879
-est, -er, as endings of adjectives and
    adverbs, 318
et al., 494, 646, 655, 811
et al., etc., 871
etc., 494, 871
Ethical appeals, 206–07, 226, 883
Ethnic studies, research sources on,
    779
Etymology, 890
Euphemisms, 187, 506–07, 890
Evaluation
  of blog postings, 600–02
  in critical thinking, 146, 151–52,
    161
  defined, 151, 890

  of discussion-group messages,
    600–02
  guidelines for, 152, 591, 593,
    600–01
  of illustrations, 161, 600–02
  of library sources, 592–95
  of multimedia sources, 600–02
  of online sources, 593, 596–602
  of research sources, 582, 589–625
  of Web sources, 582, 593,
    596–600
  as writing assignment, 756
Evasions, recognizing, 190–93, 220
even if, as subordinating conjunc-
    tion, 251
even so, as transitional expression,
    88
even though, as subordinating con-
    junction, 251, 392
every, agreement of verb with sub-
    ject preceded by, 304
everybody
  pronouns with, 311–12
  verbs with, 305–06
*everybody, every body; everyone,
    every one,* 871
everyday, every day, 871
everyone
  pronouns with, 311–12
  verbs with, 305–06
everything
  pronouns with, 311–12
  verbs with, 305–06, 311–12
everywheres, 871
Evidence
  accuracy of, 184, 218
  adequacy of, 185, 218–19
  appeals to beliefs or needs, 183,
    218
  in arguments, 181–85, 199–205,
    218–19
  context of, 219
  defined, 177–78, 890
  distortion of, 184
  examples as, 182, 218
  expert opinions as, 182–83, 218
  facts as, 182, 218
  in history, 755–56
  interpreting and integrating,
    163–65
  kinds of, 181–85, 218
  for literary analysis, 739, 743–44
  in the natural and applied sci-
    ences, 806
  related to claims and assump-
    tions, 177–78, 199–205

Evidence *(continued)*
  relevance of, 184, 591–92
  reliability of, 183–85, 218–19
  representativeness of, 184–85
  responsible use of, 204–05
  in the social sciences, 774–75
  in visual arguments, 218–19
Exact language. *See* Words
Examinations
  preparing for, 136–38
  taking essay, 822–28
Examples
  in developing paragraphs, 94–95
  in research sources, 560
  to support claims, 182
  transitional expressions for,
    88–89
except, accept, 532, 865
except, as preposition, 243
except for, as preposition, 243, 392
except for the fact that, 871
excepting, as preposition, 243
Exclamation point
  misuse of, 418, 420–21
  with other punctuation, 421,
    465–66
  use of, 420–21
Expert opinion, 182–83, 560
Explanation
  as purpose for writing, 10
  as writing assignment, 756
Expletives
  defined, 261, 890
  for emphasis, 386–87, 410
  grammar checkers for, 524
  omitted *there, here,* or *it* from,
    261
  subject-verb agreement with, 307
  wordiness of, 261, 529
explicit, implicit, 871
Exposition, 10, 890

F

Facts, 182
fair, fare, 532
Fair use, 633–34
Fallacies
  checklist of, 191
  defined, 190, 890
  in visual arguments, 220–21
  in written arguments, 190–95
False analogy, 191, 195
False authority, 191, 192
False dilemma (either/or fallacy),
    191, 194–95

Familiarity
  essay organization by, 42
  paragraph organization by,
    84–85
familiar with, 518
fare, fair, 532
farther, further, 871
Faulty predication, 371–72, 890
Faulty reasoning, 190–95, 202
Faulty subordination, 394
Favorites/Bookmarks, 580
Fax transmissions, 846
feel
  appropriate use of, 871
  as linking verb, 237
few
  as determiner, 326
  pronouns with, 312
  verbs with, 305–06
few, a few, 326
fewer, less, 871
Fiction, analyzing and writing
    about, 747–48
field, 871
Figurative language, 520–21, 890
figure, calculate, reckon, 869
Figures. *See also* Illustrations and
    artworks; Numbers
  format in document, 122–25
Figures of speech, 520–21, 890
Files, computer
  commenting on, 70
  managing, 55–56
  naming, 55, 834
  sharing, 834
  tracking changes in, 56
  working with, 48, 55–56
Films, DVDs, and video recordings
  documenting: APA style, 796, 798;
    Chicago style, 768–69, 770; CSE
    style, 817; MLA style, 676–77,
    679, 683–84, 686
  evaluating, 600–02
  as research sources, 600–02
  research sources on, 759
  titles of, italics or underlining for,
    489
  in Web compositions, 834, 835,
    839
Final drafts, 66–68, 643, 745–47
finally
  as conjunctive adverb, 259
  as transitional expression, 88
Finite verbs, 245, 331, 890
First drafts, 46–50, 640–41,
    744–45

First person
  in academic writing, 169, 740, 757, 776, 808
  defined, 897
  and grammatical agreement, 302
  point of view, in literature, 737
fixing to, 871
Flaming, 831
Flattery, 191, 193
flaunt, flout, 872
Flow
  in designing documents, 114–15, 116
  in Web documents, 838
flunk, 872
Flyers, 853–54
Focused freewriting, 21–22
Foil (in literary analysis), 752, 891
Fonts
  in document design, 118
  for readers with vision loss, 126
  in Web pages, 839
Footnotes or endnotes
  Chicago style: format of, 760–61; vs. list of works cited, 760–63; models of, 763–71
  MLA style, format of, 653, 714
for
  as coordinating conjunction, 257
  as preposition, 243, 392
  punctuation with, 257–58, 422–42, 445, 448
  vs. *since,* 291–92, 519
  after verb, 237
Foreign words and phrases
  italics or underlining for, 490
  plurals of, 538
Foreword, MLA style, 669
for example
  punctuation with, 342–43, 430, 446
  as transitional expression, 88
Form, of literary work, 738
Formalist criticism, 736
Formal outlines
  constructing, 36–39, 638–40
  for revision, 36–39
  sentence, 39, 640, 693–95
  topic, 38, 640
Formal vs. informal usage
  in academic writing, 168–70, 502, 504–05, 891
  in business writing, 502, 504–05, 891
  in e-mail, 829
  in this handbook, vii

Format, document. *See* Document design and format
former, latter, 872
Form of images, 155
forth, fourth, 532
Fractions
  hyphenation of, 544–45
  numerals vs. words for, 497
Fragments. *See* Sentence fragments
Freewriting
  defined, 21, 891
  focused, 21–22
  invisible, 22
  in literary analysis, 736
from, as preposition, 243, 393
Full-text resources, 563, 575, 577, 610–11
fun, 872
Function words, 251, 891
Funnel introductions, 104–05
further
  as conjunctive adverb, 259
  punctuation with, 430, 446
further, farther, 871
furthermore
  as conjunctive adverb, 259
  punctuation with, 430, 446
Fused sentences (run-on sentences)
  correction of, 340, 343–44
  defined, 339, 343, 891
  grammar checkers for, 339
Future perfect progressive tense, 290, 292
Future perfect tense, 290, 291, 902
Future progressive tense, 290, 292, 903
Future tense, 290, 902

G

Gathering information. *See* Information gathering
Gazetteers, 569
Gender
  defined, 891
  pronoun-antecedent agreement in, 309–13
  sexist language and, 187, 312, 508–10, 901
Gender-specific terms, grammar checkers for, 502–03
Gender studies, research sources on, 779
Generalization
  defined, 199, 891
  hasty, 191, 193

Generalization *(continued)*
  in inductive and deductive reasoning, 200–03
  sweeping, 191, 193–94
General-to-specific organization
  for essays, 41
  for paragraphs, 82–83
General vs. specific, 33–34, 516–17, 891
Generic *he*, 312, 354, 509, 891. *See also* Sexist language
Generic nouns
  defined, 311, 891
  pronouns with, 311–12, 354
Genitive case, 891. *See also* Possessive case
Genres, 162, 891
Geographical names
  abbreviation of, 495, 844
  capitalization of, 484, 486
  commas with, 435
Geology, research sources on, 810
Gerunds and gerund phrases
  defined, 246, 285, 892
  grammar checkers for, 285
  vs. infinitives, after verbs, 285–87
  as nouns, 246
  possessives before, 271
  after prepositions, 246
  vs. present participles, 246, 271, 426
  punctuating, 248
get, 872
go, 872
God and Allah, capitalization of terms representing, 485
good, well, 317, 872
good and, 872
Google, 562, 579, 580–81
Google Scholar, 573
Google US Government Search, 583
gorilla, guerrilla, 532
Government offices, capitalization of, 485
Government publications
  documenting: APA style, 794–95, 797; Chicago style, 769; CSE style, 817; MLA style, 647, 658, 670, 675
  as research sources, 583–84
GPO Access, 583
Grammar, defined, 230, 892
Grammar/style checkers, 63–65. *See also* grammar checkers *under specific issues*

Graphic art. *See* Illustrations and artworks
Graphic narrative works, MLA style, 667
Graphs. *See* Illustrations and artworks
Grounds, in argument, 177–78, 892. *See also* Evidence
Group dynamics in online collaboration, 831–34
Grouping, in document design, 116
Group or corporate author
  APA style: parenthetical citation, 782; reference list, 787
  MLA style: list of works cited, 658; parenthetical citation, 647
Group work. *See* Collaboration
grow, as linking verb, 237
guerrilla, gorilla, 532

H

had better, as helping verb, 274, 284
had better, better, 868
had ought, 872
had vs. *could have* or *would have*, 297
half, 872
Handwritten research notes, pros and cons, 609
hanged, hung, 872
Hanging indents
  in APA reference list, 784
  in Chicago works-cited list, 763
  creating, on word processor, 654
  in CSE reference list, 812
  in MLA works-cited list, 654
hardly, scarcely, but, 867
Hasty generalizations, 191, 193
have
  as helping verb, 274, 282
  principal parts of, 276
have, has, 282
have, of, 872
have to, as helping verb, 274, 283
he
  case of, 265
  generic, 312, 354, 509, 891
  vs. *him*, 266
  with indefinite antecedent, 312–13
  as personal pronoun, 235
  and sexist language, 312, 509
he, she, he/she, 312, 478, 872
Headings
  in APA style, 801
  in business memos, 846

as design elements, 116, 120
and page breaks, 120
parallelism in, 120, 401–02
in résumés, 849
uses of, 120
Health sciences, research sources
on, 810
hear, here, 532
heard, herd, 532
Helping verbs (auxiliary verbs)
combined with main verbs,
280–84
defined, 234, 274, 892
grammar checkers for, 280
list of, 274
modals, 283–84
uses of, 274, 280–84
hence
comma with, 430
as conjunctive adverb, 259
as transitional expression, 89
he or she, 312
her
as determiner, 325
vs. *she,* 266
herd, heard, 532
here, hear, 532
here is, here are
and agreement of verb, 307
eliminating for conciseness, 261,
524, 529
as expletive construction, 261,
410, 529, 890
necessity of *here* in, 261
herself, himself, myself, yourself, 876
Highlighting of text, 118–19
his
as determiner, 325
vs. *he,* 266
hisself, 873
Historical Abstracts, 573
Historical events and periods, capitalization of, 484
History. *See also* Humanities
integrating borrowed material in,
624–25
research sources on, 758, 759
writing about, 755–56
hole, whole, 532
Holidays
abbreviation of, 495
capitalization of, 484
Home pages. *See* Web sites
Homonyms
defined, 514, 532, 892
list of common, 532–33

hopefully, 873
how, in noun clauses, 252
however
as conjunctive adverb, 258–59
punctuation with, 430, 446
as transitional expression, 88
however, yet, but, 868
HTML (hypertext markup language), 836, 892
Humanities, 755–73
assignments in: literature,
739–40; other disciplines, 756
documentation: Chicago style,
760–71; MLA style, 644–725
document formats: Chicago style,
771–73; MLA style, 689–91
integrating borrowed material in,
624–25
methods and evidence in: literature, 731–39; other disciplines,
755–56
research sources on: literature,
741; other disciplines, 757–60
style guides in, 760
tools and language in: literature,
741; other disciplines, 756–60
hung, hanged, 872
Hyperbole, 521, 890
Hypertext documents, 834–40, 892.
See also Web sites
Hyphenated words
capitalization in titles, 483
forming, 544–45
Hyphens
to attach prefixes and suffixes,
545
with capitalized words, 483, 545
in coined compounds, 545
in compound words, 544–45
in forming dashes, 119, 470
in fractions, 544–45
in modifiers, 545
in numbers, 496, 544–45
in URLs (electronic addresses),
546, 680, 767, 791, 815
in word division, 545–46
Hypothesis, 774, 806

I

I
capitalization of, 484
case of, 265
vs. *me,* 266
as personal pronoun, 235
in writing about literature, 740

ibid., 771
idea, ideal, 873
Ideas
    discovering, 16–44
    emphasizing, 378–87
    organizing, 33–34
identical with, to, 518
Idioms
    common, with prepositions, 518
    defined, 518, 892
    grammar checkers for, 511
    omissions from, 373
if
    subjunctive after, 296–97
    as subordinating conjunction,
        251, 392
if, whether, 873
if only, as subordinating conjunc-
        tion, 251
illicit, elicit, 532, 870
Illogical comparisons, 319–20,
        374
illusion, allusion, 532, 866
Illustrated books, MLA style,
        667
Illustration or support. *See also*
        Examples
    defined, 892
    in essay development, 25
    in paragraph development, 94–95
Illustrations and artworks
    acknowledging sources of,
        121–22, 125, 584, 633–34
    advertisements, MLA style,
        675–76, 687
    allusions in, 157
    as arguments, 216–26
    arrangement in, 157
    audience for, 154
    captions of, 154, 225
    cartoons, MLA style, 687
    characterization in, 157
    charts: in document design,
        123–24; MLA style, 675–76, 687
    color in, 157
    comic strips, MLA style, 687
    content of, 155
    context for, 153–61
    copyrights of, 173, 634
    creating, 121, 840
    critical reading of, 153–61,
        173–75
    diagrams: in document design,
        125; MLA style, 675–76, 687
    in document design, 121–25,
        223–26

document format: APA style, 802;
    MLA style, 121–26, 212–15, 700,
    704
documenting: APA style, 796;
    Chicago style, 768–69, 770;
    MLA style, 667, 675–76, 679,
    684–85, 686–87
elements of, 156–57
emphasis in, 156
evaluating, 600–02
as evidence for arguments,
    224–25
form of, 155
graphs: in document design,
    123–24; MLA style, 675–76, 687
images: APA style, 796; MLA
    style, 675–76, 679, 684–85
maps, MLA style, 675–76, 687
narration in, 156
in natural and applied sciences,
    818
in oral presentations, 861–63
paintings: Chicago style, 768, 770;
    MLA style, 686–87
permission for using, 584, 633–34
photographs: in document design,
    124–25; documenting, MLA
    style, 675–76, 685, 686, 687
point of view in, 156
purpose of, 154
as research source, 600–02
in social sciences, 802
sources of, 125, 584–85
tables: in document design, 122;
    APA style, 804; CSE style, 819;
    MLA style, 122
tension in, 157
titles of, italics or underlining for,
    489
types of, 121–25
using, 121–25, 584–85
viewing critically, 153–61, 216–21
visual arguments with, 223–26
in Web compositions, 633–34,
    834, 835, 839–40
Imagery, in literature, 737–38, 892
Images (photographs, paintings,
    etc.). *See* Illustrations and art-
    works
immigrate, emigrate, 871
imminent, eminent, 532
impact, 873
impatient for, with, 518
Imperative mood
    defined, 296, 895
    shifts between indicative and, 355

implicit, explicit, 871
imply, infer, 873
in
  as adverb, 259
  vs. *at* and *on,* 519
  as preposition, 243, 259, 392
  in wordy phrases, 873
in, into, 873
in addition
  as conjunctive adverb, 259
  punctuation with, 430, 446
in addition to
  as preposition, 243
  subject-verb agreement with, 304
Inc., 494
incidentally
  as conjunctive adverb, 259
  punctuation with, 430, 446
in comparison
  as conjunctive adverb, 259
  punctuation with, 259
Incomplete sentences. *See also* Sentence fragments
  grammar checkers for, 373
  types of, 373–75
in contrast, as conjunctive adverb, 259
incredible, incredulous, 873
indeed
  as conjunctive adverb, 259
  punctuation with, 430, 446
  as transitional expression, 88
Indefinite pronouns
  alternatives to *he* with, 312–13
  case of, 265
  defined, 305, 899
  list of, 305
  possessive case of, 453
  pronoun agreement with, 311–13
  verb agreement with, 305–06
Independent clauses. *See* Main (independent) clauses
independent of, 518
Indexes to periodicals. *See* Databases, electronic
Indicative mood
  defined, 296, 895
  shifts between imperative and, 355
Indirect discourse. *See* Indirect quotations
Indirect objects, 238, 896. *See also* Objects
Indirect questions
  defined, 418, 892
  vs. direct questions, 357

  punctuation of, 418–19
  shift between direct questions and, 357
Indirect quotations. *See also* Quotations, direct
  defined, 461, 899
  vs. direct quotations, 357
  no commas with, 442, 460
  no quotation marks with, 460
  shift between direct quotations and, 357
Indirect sources
  appropriate use of, 702, 721
  parenthetical citation of: APA style, 783; MLA style, 649
individual, person, party, 873
Individual possession, possessive case to indicate, 452–54
Inductive reasoning, 199–200, 892
in fact
  as conjunctive adverb, 259
  punctuation with, 430, 446
  as transitional expression, 88
infer, imply, 873
Inference
  defined, 148
  faulty, 149–50
infer from, 518
inferior to, 518
Infinitive marker *(to),* 247, 892–93
Infinitives and infinitive phrases
  as adjectives, 247
  as adverbs, 247
  capitalization of *to* in titles, 483
  case of pronouns with, 268
  as dangling modifiers, 366
  defined, 247, 285, 892–93
  functions of, 247
  vs. gerunds, after verbs, 285–87
  grammar checkers for, 285
  as nouns, 247
  omission of *to* before, 247
  punctuating, 248
  split, 362–63
  subjects or objects of, 268
  tense sequence and, 292–93
Inflection, 893
Inflectional suffix, 902
Informal outlines, 34–35, 638
Informal usage. *See* Formal vs. informal usage
Information gathering
  accurate record keeping in, 608
  direct quotation in, 616
  downloading for, 610–11
  in first reading, 132–33

Information gathering *(continued)*
in interviews, 586–87
note taking for, 609
paraphrasing in, 612–15, 617–18
photocopying for, 609–10
reading for, 18–19, 608–11
in rereading, 133
in research process, 607–19
risk of plagiarism during, 609–11, 616–17
for studying, 130–31
summarizing in, 134–35, 611–12, 617–18
using computers for, 141, 563, 609
Information services. *See* Databases, electronic
InfoTrac Expanded Academic, 576
-ing
in gerund, 246, 426
in present participle, 246, 273, 426
in progressive tenses, 282, 290, 292
in order that, as subordinating conjunction, 251, 392
in regards to, 874
inside, as preposition, 243
Inside address, 842, 847
inside of, as preposition, 243
inside of, outside of, 874
in spite of, as preposition, 243, 392
instance, line, case, 869
Instant messaging
for collaborative work, 833
revising shortcuts of, 504
instead
as conjunctive adverb, 259
punctuation with, 430, 446
instead of, as preposition, 243
insure, ensure, assure, 867
Integrating borrowed material, 620–25
in English and some other humanities, 624
in history and some other humanities, 624–25
interpretation and, 621–24
introduction and, 620–21
with signal phrases, 622–25
in social and natural sciences, 625
Integrity in academic writing, 626–35
Intellectual property
necessity for documenting, 626, 629–30
obtaining permission to use, 632–34
and plagiarism, 626–35
Intensifiers, 893
Intensive pronoun, 899
Interjections
defined, 233, 893
punctuating, 420, 431
Interlibrary loans, 561, 569, 577
Internet, 578–81. *See also* Blogs; Electronic sources; Web sites
acknowledging sources from, 608–11, 633–34
addresses. *See* URL (uniform resource locator)
advantages and disadvantages of, for research, 561–62
collaborating via, 831–34
discussion groups. *See* Discussion groups, online
e-mail. *See* E-mail (electronic mail)
online collaboration and, 831–34
Internet Public Library, 579
Internet Scout Project, 579
Interpretation
of borrowed material, 621–24
in critical thinking and reading, 148–50, 160
defined, 148, 893
guidelines for, 147
of illustrations, 160
as kind of research paper, 549, 756
Interrogative, 893
Interrogative adjectives, 882
Interrogative pronouns, 265, 899
Interviews
conducting, 586–87
documenting: APA style, 797–98; Chicago style, 770; MLA style, 662–63, 674–75, 680, 685
as primary sources, 586–87
into, as preposition, 243
Intransitive verbs
defined, 236, 278, 893
vs. transitive verbs, 238
Introducing borrowed material (quotations, paraphrases, summaries), techniques for, 620–25
Introduction
of argument, 209
defined, 893
of essay, 39, 104–07
of oral presentation, 858–59
of research source, MLA style, 669

Introductory sentence elements
colon with, 467–68
comma with, 425–26
dash with, to set off series, 471
variety in, 408–10
Invention, 16–26, 893. *See also*
Development of essay topic
Inversion, 893
Inverted word order
defined, 893
for emphasis, 411
subject-verb agreement and, 307
types of sentences, 260–61
Invisible writing, 22, 23
involved in, with, 518
Irony, 186, 464, 830, 893
irregardless, 874
Irregular verbs
defined, 275, 893
forms of, 275–77
grammar checkers for, 275
list of common, 275–77
nonstandard forms of, 275
spelling, 534
is, are, 867
is because, 371–72, 877
is when, is where, 371, 874
it
case of, 265
definite antecedent for, 349
as expletive, 261, 307, 386–87,
410
omitted from expletive, 261
as personal pronoun, 235
reference of, 349
specific antecedent for, 349
used one way in a sentence,
350
Italics and underlining, 488–91
comparing, 118, 488
for definitions, 490
for emphasis, 490
for foreign words, 490
grammar checkers for, 488
for names of ships, aircraft,
spacecraft, and trains, 490
for titles of works, 489
for words or characters named as
words, 490
it is, as expletive construction, 261,
410, 524, 529, 890
it is, it has, as contraction *it's,* 456,
874
its, as determiner, 325
its, it's
grammar checkers for, 452–53

possessive vs. contraction, 457,
532, 874
-ize, -wise, 874

J

Jargon, 529–30, 893
Job-application letters and résumés,
847–49
Joint possession, possessive case to
indicate, 454
Journalist's questions, 24–25, 893
Journals, personal
advantages of, 19–20
on computer, 19, 141
defined, 893
for fluency and experimentation,
20
reading, 141, 549–50, 732–33
research, 549–50, 757, 776,
807–08
uses of, 20–21
Journals, scholarly. *See* Periodicals
Jumping to a conclusion, 191, 193
just because, in mixed sentences,
369–70

K

Keywords
Boolean operators in, 563–65
brainstorming, 573–76
for catalog searches, 563–65, 570
for database searches, 563–65,
570, 573–76
vs. database subject headings,
563–64, 569–71, 573–76
defined, 563, 893
developing, 563–65
devices in, 564–65
refining, 564–65, 569–71, 573–76,
580–81
in résumés, 848–50
sample searches using, 573–75,
580–81
for Web searches, 563–65, 578–81
kind of, sort of, type of, 874
know, no, 533

L

Labels
in dictionaries, 865
in lists and outlines, 37–38, 473
for people, and biased language,
187, 510

Lab notebooks, 807–08
Laboratory reports
    sample, 818–20
    as writing assignment, 807
Language. *See also* Culture-lan-
    guage issues; Words
    of academic writing, 168–70
    appropriate, 502–10
    capitalization of names of, 485
    colloquial, 885
    exact, 514–15
    figurative, 520–21, 890
    formal vs. informal, 502, 504–05
    nonstandard. *See* Culture-lan-
        guage issues
    standard. *See* Standard American
        English
    writing vs. speech, 502–06, 856
later, latter, 874
Latin
    common abbreviations of, 494
    italics or underlining for, 490
    roots from, 538
latter, former, 872
Law, research sources on, 777, 779
lay, lie, 278, 874
lead, led, 533
least, as determiner, 326
leave, let, 874
Lectures. *See also* Oral presenta-
    tions; Speeches
    MLA style, 688
Legal documents, italics or under-
    lining for, 489
less, as determiner, 326
less, fewer, 871
lessen, lesson, 533
let, leave, 874
Letters (correspondence)
    for business, 841–44
    documenting: APA style, 796;
        Chicago style, 769–70; CSE
        style, 817; MLA style, 671
    faxes, 846
    job application, 847–48
    requests and complaints, 844–45
Letters (of alphabet)
    apostrophe for omission of, 458
    forming plurals of, 458
    italics or underlining for, 490
    for labeling lists and outlines,
        37–38, 473
    used as words, 490
Letter writing. *See* Business letters
    and memos; Letters (correspon-
    dence); Public writing

Lexical word, 893
LexisNexis Academic, 576
liable, apt, likely, 867
Librarians' Internet Index, 579
Libraries
    book catalogs in, 563, 569–71
    catalogs of holdings, 563
    computer access to, 561–62
    databases in, 563, 565–69, 572–77
    depository, 584
    electronic sources via, 561–62,
        569–71, 572–77
    evaluating sources from, 592–95
    government publications in, 584
    loans between, 569, 577
    online databases via, 561–62,
        569–71, 572–77
    periodicals and indexes in, 571–77
    printed material, 561–62
    reference librarians in, 562
    reference works in, 565–69
    vs. search engines, 561–62, 578
    Web access to holdings, 561–62
    Web sites of, 561–62, 578
*Library of Congress Subject Head-
    ings,* 570
lie, lay, 276, 278, 874
like
    misuse of, 397, 875
    as preposition, 243
like, as, 875
like, such as, 875
likely, apt, liable, 867
likewise
    as conjunctive adverb, 259
    punctuation with, 430, 446
    as transitional expression, 88
Limited narrator, in literature, 737
Limiting adjective, 882
Limiting modifiers, 361
line, case, instance, 869
Linear text, 834, 893
Line breaks, 119
Line graphs
    documenting, MLA style, 687
    using and reading. *See* Illustra-
        tions and artworks
Line spacing, 117–18
Linking verbs
    adjectives, not adverbs, after, 317
    agreement with subjects, 307
    defined, 237, 317, 893
    list of, 237
    pronouns after, 266
    with subject complements,
        237–38

List making, 22–23
List of works cited. *See also* APA
    style; CSE style
    Chicago style, 760–71
    MLA style, 653–88
Lists. *See also* Series
    design of, 119
    numbers or letters for, 473
    parallelism in, 400, 401–02
    on Web pages, 838
Listservs. *See* Discussion groups,
    online
literally, 875
Literary analysis, 731–54
    approaches to, 731–33
    documentation in, MLA style,
        649–50, 678, 747, 751
    document format for, 746–47
    drafting, 744–45
    of drama, 751–52
    of fiction, 747–48
    format of quotations in: Chicago
        style, 772; MLA style, 690–91
    integrating borrowed material in,
        624
    language in, 520–21, 890
    methods and evidence of, 731–39
    of poetry, 748–51
    questions for, 737–38
    reading literature for, 732–36
    revising and editing, 745–47
    sample papers: drama, 752–54;
        poetry, 748–51; short story,
        746–47
    sources for, 741
    vs. summary, 743, 745
    thesis in, 742–43
    tools and language in, 741
    use of present tense in, 291, 740
    use of quotations in, 739, 743–45
    writing assignments for, 739–40
Literary research, 739
little, a little, 326
Livesearch, 579
Logic. *See* Reasoning
Logical agreement, 354, 883
Logical comparisons, 319–20, 374
Logical fallacies. *See* Fallacies
Long quotations, formatting
    in APA style, 801
    in Chicago style, 772
    in MLA style, 691
look, as linking verb, 237
Loose sentences, 381, 888
lose, loose, 875
lots, lots of, 875

Lurking, 582
-ly
    adjectives and adverbs ending in,
        240, 316
    superlative and comparative with,
        318

M

Magazines. *See* Periodicals
Main (independent) clauses
    colon with, 444, 467–68
    comma splice with, avoiding,
        342–43
    defined, 250, 885
    fused, avoiding, 340, 343–44
    joined by coordinating conjunc-
        tions, 257, 389, 422–42, 448
    punctuation between, 258, 259,
        338–44, 422–42, 443–50
    related by conjunctive adverbs or
        transitional expressions,
        258–59, 342–43, 446
    vs. subordinate clause, 250
Main verbs
    defined, 274, 894
    grammar checkers for, 280
*Manual for Writers of Term Papers,
    Theses, and Dissertations, A*
    (Turabian). *See* Chicago style
Manuscripts. *See* Document design
    and format
many
    as determiner, 326
    pronouns with, 312
    verbs with, 305–06
many, much, 326
Maps. *See* Illustrations and artworks
Margins and spacing
    in business correspondence,
        839–40, 845
    in documents, 117, 690, 799
Mass noun. *See* Noncount nouns
Mathematics, research sources on,
    810
may, as helping verb, 274, 283–84
may, can, 869
may be, maybe, 875
may of, 872
Meaning, in literature, 736–39
Meanings of words
    connotative, 514–15
    denotative, 514
meanwhile
    as conjunctive adverb, 259
    punctuation with, 430, 446

Measurements, units of
   abbreviations for, 494
   numbers with, 497
   verb agreement with, 308
meat, meet, 533
Mechanics, 482–98, 894
media, 875
Media files, MLA style, 685
Medium of publication, documenting
   APA style, 798–99
   Chicago style, 767
   CSE style, 817
   MLA style, 654, 672, 675, 679, 717
Memos, business, 845–46
Menus on Web pages, 838–39
Message forums, 832
MetaCrawler, 579
Metaphors, 520, 890
Methodology, 728–29
me vs. *I,* 266–67
Microfiche and microfilm, 577
might, as helping verb, 274, 283
might of, 872
Misplaced modifiers, 359–65
   defined, 359, 894
   grammar checkers for, 359
   limiting, 361
   and position of adverbs and ad-
      jectives, 364–65
   squinting, 361–62, 894
   between subject and verb, 362
   within verb phrase or infinitive,
      362–63
Miss, Mrs., Ms., 509–10, 843
Mixed constructions, 369–72, 894
Mixed diction, 505
Mixed metaphors, 521, 890
Mixed sentences
   defined, 369
   in grammar, 369–72
   grammar checkers for, 369
   in meaning, 371–72
*MLA Handbook for Writers of Re-
      search Papers. See* MLA style
MLA style
   defined, 894
   document format, 653–54, 689–91
   footnotes or endnotes to supple-
      ment parenthetical citations,
      653
   indexes to documentation mod-
      els: parenthetical citations, 645;
      works cited, 656–57
   list of works cited: format of,
      653–54, 716–19, 725; index to,
      656–57; models of, 654–88

   parenthetical citations: index to,
      645; models of, 644–50;
      placing, 651–52; punctuation
      with, 652
   for poetry and long prose quota-
      tions, 690–91
   sample papers in, 691–725
*MLA Style Manual and Guide to
      Scholarly Publishing. See* MLA
      style
Mnemonics, for spelling, 540
Modal verbs. *See also* Helping verbs
      (auxiliary verbs)
   defined, 892
   uses of, 283–84
Modern Language Association. *See*
      MLA style
Modifiers
   adjectives and adverbs, 240,
      315–26
   as antecedents, 361
   at beginning of sentence, 409
   dangling, 366–67, 888
   defined, 240, 894–95
   grammar checkers for, 359
   limiting, 361
   misplaced, 359–65, 894
   nonessential vs. essential,
      427–28
   nouns as, 241, 321
   phrases as, 242–49
   placement for emphasis, 409
   prepositional phrases as, 243
   punctuating, 425–31, 433–34
   sentence, 900
   squinting, 361–62, 894
   subordinate clauses as, 252–53
   verbals and verbal phrases as,
      247–48
Money amounts
   dollar signs with, 493, 497–98
   numerals vs. words for, 497–98
Months of the year
   abbreviations for, 495
   capitalization of, 484
Mood. *See also* Imperative mood;
      Indicative mood; Subjunctive
      mood
   defined, 296, 895
   shifts in, 355
moral, morale, 875
more
   in comparatives, 318–20
   as determiner, 326
   pronouns with, 311–12
   verbs with, 305–06

moreover
    as conjunctive adverb, 259
    punctuation with, 430, 446
most
    as determiner, 325
    pronouns with, 311–12
    in superlatives, 318–20
    verbs with, 305–06
most, almost, 866
Motion pictures or movies. *See*
    Films, DVDs, and video record-
    ings
Mrs., Miss, Ms., 419, 492, 509–10,
    843
Ms., Miss, Mrs., 419, 492, 509–10,
    843
much
    as determiner, 326
    pronouns with, 311–12
    verbs with, 305–06
much, many, 326
Multilingual writers, tips for. *See*
    Culture-language issues
Multimedia sources. *See also* Films,
    DVDs, and video recordings;
    Illustrations and artworks;
    Sound recordings; Web sites
    acknowledging, 634
    creating and using, 121–22,
    223–26, 839–40
    documenting: APA style, 796, 798;
    Chicago style, 768, 770; CSE
    style, 817; MLA style, 684–86
    evaluating, 216–21, 600–02
    as research sources, 584–86
    in Web compositions, 633–34,
    834, 835, 839–40
Multivolume works
    APA style, 790–91
    Chicago style, 766
    MLA style: list of works cited,
    667–68; parenthetical citation,
    648
Musical works. *See also* Sound
    recordings
    documenting: APA style, 798;
    Chicago style, 770; MLA style,
    677, 679, 684–85, 686
    research sources on, 759
    titles of: italics or underlining for
    long works, 489; quotation
    marks for songs, 463
must, as helping verb, 274, 283
must of, 872
my, as determiner, 322, 325
myself, herself, himself, yourself, 876

N

Names
    abbreviation of, 493
    abbreviation of titles with,
    492–93
    capitalization of, 484
Narration
    defined, 895
    in essay development, 25
    in literary works, 737, 895
    in paragraph development, 93–94
    personal, as evidence in argu-
    ment, 182, 204
Narrator, in literature, 737, 748
Nationalities, capitalization of, 485
Navigation on Web sites and pages,
    838–39
n.d. (no date)
    APA style, 795
    MLA style, 678
near, as preposition, 243
Negatives, double, 320
neither
    pronouns with, 311–12
    verbs with, 305–06, 311
neither . . . nor, as correlative con-
    junction, 257, 400–01
Neologisms, 506, 895
nevertheless
    as conjunctive adverb, 259
    punctuation with, 430, 446
Newsgroups. *See* Discussion groups,
    online
Newsletters, 852–54
Newspapers. *See* Periodicals
next
    as conjunctive adverb, 259
    punctuation with, 430, 446
next to, as preposition, 243
Nicknames, 464
no. (number), 493
no, commas with, 430
no, know, 533
nobody
    pronouns with, 311–12
    verbs with, 305–06
No date. *See n.d.* (no date)
nohow, 876
Nominal, 895
Nominative, 895
Noncount nouns
    agreement of pronoun with, 313
    agreement of verb with, 307
    defined, 323, 896
    list of, 323

Noncount nouns *(continued)*
  no plurals of, 538
  and use of *a, an,* or *the,* 323
  and use of other determiners,
    325–26
none
  pronouns with, 311–12
  verbs with, 305–06
Nonessential elements
  appositives, 429
  clauses and phrases, 427–31
  defined, 427, 895
  vs. essential elements, 427–28
  punctuating, 427–31, 442, 470–71
  test for, 428
  which, for clauses, 429, 879
nonetheless
  as conjunctive adverb, 259
  punctuation with, 430, 446
Nonfinite verbs, 245–46, 331. *See*
  also Verbals and verbal phrases
Nonperiodical sources, documenting
  APA style, 790–91, 795–98
  Chicago style, 765–66, 768–70
  CSE style, 815, 816–17
  MLA style, 663–80, 683, 684–88
Nonprint sources
  APA style, 791–99
  Chicago style, 767–70
  CSE style, 815–17
  MLA style, 647–48, 672–88
Nonrestrictive elements. *See*
  Nonessential elements
Non sequitur, 190–91
Nonstandard usage, 895. *See also*
  Culture-language issues; Stan-
  dard American English
no one
  pronouns with, 311–12
  verbs with, 305–06
No pagination. *See n. pag.* (no page)
nor
  and agreement: of pronouns, 311;
    of verbs, 305–06
  as coordinating conjunction, 257,
    399–400
  punctuation with, 257–58,
    422–24, 430, 439–41, 445, 448
not . . . but, as correlative conjunction, 257, 400–01
not, position of, 364–65
Notes. *See* Footnotes or endnotes
Note taking
  in class, 130–31
  for information gathering,
    609

nothing
  pronouns with, 311–12
  verbs with, 305–06
nothing like, nowhere near, 876
not only . . . but also, as correlative
  conjunction, 257, 400–01
Noun clauses, 252, 896
Noun complements, 237–38
Noun phrases, 247–48
Nouns
  a, an, the with, 322–25
  abstract, 516–17
  case of, 264–71, 453–54
  collective, 313, 896
  common, 485, 895
  concrete, 516–17
  count, 322–26, 896
  declension of, 265, 888
  defined, 233, 895–96
  determiners with, 322–26
  forming plurals of, 233–34, 455,
    537–38
  forming possessives of, 233,
    453–54
  generic, 311–12, 354, 891
  gerunds and gerund phrases as,
    246
  implied, 349
  infinitives and infinitive phrases
    as, 247
  as modifiers, 241, 321
  negating with *no,* 316
  noncount, 323–25, 538, 896
  plural, 455
  with plural form but singular
    meaning, 308
  predicate, 231
  proper, 322, 323–25, 484–85,
    896
  as subject complements, 237–38
  subordinate clauses as, 252
  types of, 895–96
now
  as conjunctive adverb, 259
  punctuation with, 430, 446
nowhere near, nothing like, 876
nowheres, 876
now that, as subordinating conjunction, 251
n.p. (no city of publication), MLA
  style, 669, 677–78
n. pag. (no page)
  APA style, 783
  MLA style, 648–49, 669, 678
Number (singular, plural)
  defined, 273, 353, 896

pronoun-antecedent agreement
in, 309–13
shifts in, 86–87, 353–55
subject-verb agreement in, 301–08
number, amount, 866
Numbered lists, 119, 401–02
Numbers
abbreviations for, 493
at beginning of sentence, 498
cardinal, 884
commas with, 435
compound, 544–45
contractions of, 458
as determiners, 325–26
doubtful, indicating, 420
grammar checkers for, 496
for labeling figures, 225
for labeling outlines, 37–38, 473,
639
numerals vs. words for, 496–98
ordinal, 896
with other adjectives, 434
plurals of, 458
Numerals. *See* Numbers

O

O, oh, capitalization of, 484
Object complements, 238–39, 886
Objections to argument, anticipation of, 207–08
Objective case
defined, 265, 884
forms for, 265
uses of, 265, 267
Objective description, 94
Objective narrator, in literature, 737
Objects
appositives identifying, 267–68
case of, 265
compound, 267
defined, 236, 239, 243, 896
direct, 236, 265, 317–18, 362, 896
indirect, 238, 896
of infinitives, 268
of prepositions, 242–43, 265, 896
of verbals, 247, 268
of verbs, 236–39, 265, 267
oblivious of, to, 518
Observation
in developing essay subject, 21
as primary source in research,
586
weighing evidence obtained by,
218
occupied by, in, with, 518

of, as preposition, 243, 393
of, have, 872
of course, as transitional expression,
88, 430
off, as preposition, 243
off of, 876
oh, O, capitalization of, 484
OK, O.K., okay, 876
Omissions
from comparisons, 374
from compound constructions,
373, 399–400
from contractions, 456
from direct quotations, 461, 616,
743
of necessary words, 374–75
Omniscient narrator, 737
on
vs. *at* and *in,* 519
as preposition, 243, 392
on, upon, 876
on account of
vs. *because of,* 876
as preposition, 243
once, as subordinating conjunction,
251
one
as determiner, 322, 325
pronouns with, 311–12
verbs with, 305–06
vs. *you,* 350
one of the, 308
Online papers, posted via the Web,
836–37
Online sources. *See* Electronic
sources
on the other hand, 876
onto, as preposition, 243
on top of, as preposition, 243
Opening paragraph, of essay,
104–07
Opinion
as claim in argument, 179
defined, 179, 896
as essay introduction, 106
expert, 182–83
opposed to, 518
Opposing views to argument, acknowledging, 207–08, 209
or
and agreement: of pronouns, 311;
of verbs, 305–06
as coordinating conjunction, 257,
399–400
linking words, phrases, and subordinate clauses, 439–41

or (continued)
    between main clauses, 257, 422–24
    punctuation with, 422–24, 430,
        433, 439–41, 448
Oral presentations, 856–64. *See also*
        Speeches
    checklist for, 857
    delivering, 859–64
    MLA style, 688
    organization of, 858–59
    PowerPoint in, 861–63
    purpose and audience for, 856–58
    writing vs. speaking, 856
Order of ideas. *See* Organization
Ordinal numbers, 896
Organization
    of argument, 209–10
    for emphasis, 41–42, 82–85
    of essay, 33–34
    of literary analysis, 745
    of oral presentation, 858–59
    of paragraphs, 81–85
    of research paper, 637–40
    of science paper, 807
    of social science paper, 775
    by space or time, 40, 81–82
    of Web pages, 837
Organizations, names of
    abbreviations for, 419, 493, 494
    capitalization of, 485
otherwise
    as conjunctive adverb, 259
    punctuation with, 430, 446
ought to, as helping verb, 274, 284
our, as determiner, 325
out, as preposition, 243
Outlines
    creating headings from, 120
    for essay exams, 822, 823
    of essays, 34–39
    formal, 36–39, 638–40
    format for, 34–39, 638–40, 693–95
    informal, 34–35, 638
    parallelism in, 39, 400, 401–02
    preliminary, 23
    principles for constructing,
        36–39, 638–40
    of research papers, 638–40,
        693–95
    for revising, 52
    sample, 37–39, 694–95
    scratch, 34–35
    sentence vs. topic, 39, 640
    for studying, 130–31
    tree diagrams, 35–36
out of, as preposition, 243

outside, as preposition, 243
outside of, inside of, 874
over, as preposition, 243
Oversimplification, 191, 193–95,
    221
owing to the fact that, 876

P

p., pp., 785
Page breaks and headings, 120
Page numbers, documenting
    APA style, 781, 785
    Chicago style, 762–63
    CSE style, 813
    MLA style, 645, 658–63, 666, 669,
        671, 683
Pagination
    of journals, 572
    none, documentation of: APA
        style, 783; CSE style, 815; MLA
        style, 648–49, 669, 678, 681
    in one's own papers: APA style,
        799; Chicago style, 771–72; CSE
        style, 817–18; MLA style, 690
    in periodicals: APA style, 788–89;
        Chicago style, 762; CSE style,
        814–15; MLA style, 659
Paintings. *See* Illustrations and
        artworks
Pamphlets. *See also* Brochures
    MLA style, 670
    titles of, italics or underlining for,
        489
par., para., or pars. (paragraph)
    APA style, 781, 783
    CSE style, 815
    MLA style, 649
Paragraph numbers, documenting
    APA style, 781, 783
    CSE style, 815
    MLA style, 649
Paragraphs, 72–111
    central idea in, 75
    coherence of, 79–90
    concluding, 107–09
    consistency in, 86–87
    defined, 72, 896
    development of, 92–102
    for dialog, 110, 462
    emphatic, 109
    indention of, 72
    introductory, 104–07
    length of, 102
    linked, in essays, 111
    organization of, 81–85

parallel structures in, 85–86
pronouns in, 86
repetition in, 86
topic sentence in, 74–77, 896
transitional, 110
transitional expressions in, 87–90
unity of, 74–77
uses of, 72–73
Parallelism, 398–404
for coherence, 85–86, 383, 403–04
for coordinate elements, 399–402
with coordinating conjunctions, 399–400
with correlative conjunctions, 400–01
defined, 398, 896
for emphasis, 383
grammar checkers for, 399
in headings, 120, 400, 401–02
in lists and outlines, 39, 400, 401–02
in paragraphs, 85–86
in series, 383
Paraphrases
avoiding plagiarism with, 627, 631
defined, 612–13, 896
documentation of, 627, 631
examples of, 613–14, 631
guidelines for, 614
introducing, in a paper, 620–25
vs. summaries and direct quotations, 611–18, 631
vs. translation, 613–14
verbs for introducing, 623
Parentheses, 472–73
vs. commas, 430, 473
with complete sentence, 473
vs. dashes, 471, 473
grammar checkers for, 467
for labels of lists or outlines, 473
with other punctuation, 473
for parenthetical expressions, 430, 473
question mark in, 420
Parenthetical citations
APA style: index to, 780; models of, 780–83
Chicago style, 771
CSE style, 813
defined, 896
MLA style: index to, 645; models of, 644–50; notes with, 653; placement and punctuation of, 650–52

Parenthetical expressions
commas with, 430, 473
dashes with, 471, 473
defined, 430, 472–73, 896
parentheses with, 472–73
Parenthetical references. *See* Parenthetical citations
part from, with, 518
Participles and participial phrases. *See also* Past participle; Present participle
as adjectives, 246
as dangling modifiers, 366
defined, 246, 897
distinguishing between present and past, 321–22
nonessential vs. essential, 428–29
present participle vs. gerund, 246, 271, 426
punctuating, 248, 426
tense sequence and, 293
Particles, 287–88, 897
Parts of speech, 233, 897
party, individual, person, 873
passed, past, 533
Passive voice
avoiding, 299, 379–80, 525
converting between active voice and, 298–99
dangling modifiers and, 366
defined, 261, 282, 298, 904
formation of, 282, 298–99
grammar checkers for, 300, 524
in science writing, 300, 808
shifts between active and, 356
transitive verbs for, 282, 298
uses of, 300, 525
past, as preposition, 243
Past participle
as adjective, 246, 321–22
defined, 246, 273, 897, 904
formation of, 273
with forms of *be,* 282
with forms of *have,* 282
irregular, 275–77
in passive voice, 282
vs. present participle, 321–22
and tense sequence, 293
Past perfect progressive tense, 290, 292
Past perfect tense, 290, 291–92, 902
Past progressive tense, 281–82, 290, 292, 902–03
Past tense
in academic writing, 623, 625, 757, 808

Past tense (continued)
defined, 273, 290, 902
formation of, 273, 290, 904
irregular, 275–77
and tense sequence, 293
patience, patients, 533
Patterns of development. See also
individual patterns
defined, 897
in essay development, 25–26
in paragraph development,
93–101
peace, piece, 533
Peer editing. See Collaboration
Peer-reviewed journals, 576
people, persons, 876
per, 876
percent (per cent), percentage, 876
Perfect infinitive, and tense sequence, 292–93
Perfect tenses, 282, 290, 291–92,
902
Performances, MLA style, 687–88
Periodical databases. See Databases,
electronic; Periodicals
Periodical indexes. See Databases,
electronic
Periodicals
databases of: general, 576–77; in
humanities, 758; in literature,
741; in natural and applied sciences, 808–09; in social sciences, 778
database searches for, 572–77
defined, 571
documentation of. See Articles in
periodicals
finding and using, 571–77
journals vs. magazines, 571–72
kinds of, 571–72
pagination of, 572, 659, 762,
788–89, 814–15
peer-reviewed or refereed, 576
quotation marks for titles of articles in, 463
titles of, italics or underlining for,
489
Periodic sentences, 381–82, 409, 897
Periods
correcting comma splice with,
338, 340–42, 437
correcting fused sentence with,
342
vs. dash, 472
ending sentences with, 418–19
parentheses with, 473

with quotation marks, 460, 465
vs. semicolon, 385
with signal phrases, 437
with some abbreviations, 419,
492–95
space with, in documents, 119
Permission, obtaining
for material used in a Web composition, 633–34
for postings on e-mail, discussion
groups, or blogs, 633, 831
persecute, prosecute, 533
Person
in academic writing, 169, 740,
757, 776, 808
defined, 273, 353, 897
pronoun-antecedent agreement
in, 309–13
shifts in, 87, 353
subject-verb agreement in, 302
person, party, individual, 873
Personal pronouns
in academic writing, 169, 740,
757, 776, 808
agreement with antecedents, 301,
309–13
cases of, 264–71
defined, 235, 899
list of, 235, 265
no apostrophe with possessive,
453, 457
reference of, 345–51
Personification, 520–21, 890
persons, people, 876
person vs. you, 350
persuade, convince, 869
phenomena, 877
Phenomena, in scientific research,
806
Philosophy, research sources on,
758, 759–60
Photocopying research sources,
pros and cons, 609–10
Photographs. See Illustrations and
artworks
Phrases
absolute, 249, 432, 882
adjective, 246, 247, 882
coordinate, 256–57, 439–40
defined, 242, 897
as modifiers, 242–49
nonessential vs. essential, 428–29
prepositional, 242–44, 425
punctuation of, 244, 248, 249,
432, 439–40
reducing to single words, 528

redundant, 527–28
verb, 274, 363
verbal, 247–48, 425. *See also*
    Verbals and verbal phrases
Physics, research sources on, 810
Pie charts. *See* Illustrations and art-
    works
Place names. *See* Geographical
    names
Plagiarism
    vs. academic integrity, 626–35
    accidental, 627
    avoiding, 146, 611, 626–35
    checklist for avoiding, 627
    consequences of, 626
    defined, 626, 897
    deliberate, 626
    detecting, on the Internet, 628
    with downloaded sources, 610–11
    during information gathering,
        609–11
    and intellectual property,
        626–35
    with online sources, 628, 632–34,
        836
    with paraphrases, 612–15, 631
    and public domain works, 634
    with quotations, 611, 616–17,
        630–31
    in sentence structure, 630–31
    with summaries, 611, 631
    Turnitin to detect, 628
    vs. using common knowledge,
        629
    vs. using your own independent
        material., 629
plain, plane, 533
Plain case, 897
Plain form of verbs
    defined, 272–73, 898, 904
    in forming tenses, 290
    with helping verbs, 274
Planning. *See* Developing (planning)
Plays
    acts and scenes of, 650, 652
    MLA style: list of works cited,
        687–88; parenthetical citations,
        650, 652
    research sources on, 760
    reviews of, as writing assign-
        ments, 740
    titles of, italics or underlining for,
        489
    writing about, 751–52
plenty, 877
Plot, in literature, 737, 898

Plurals. *See also* Agreement of pro-
    nouns and antecedents; Agree-
    ment of subjects and verbs
    of abbreviations, 458
    apostrophe with possessives of,
        454
    of compound nouns, 538
    defined, 233–34, 898
    grammar checkers for, 452–53
    irregular, 234, 538
    of letters and numbers, 458
    misuse of apostrophe to form,
        455
    of nouns, 233–34, 302, 537–38
plus, 877
PM, 493
Podcasts
    documentation: APA style, 796;
        MLA style, 677
    evaluating, 600–02
    as research sources, 559, 584,
        586, 600, 601
Poetry
    analyzing, 748–51
    documenting, MLA style: lists of
        works-cited, 678; parenthetical
        citations, 649–50
    ellipsis marks with, 477
    format of quotations from:
        Chicago style, 772; MLA style,
        690
    slash between lines of, 478, 690
    titles of: italics or underlining for
        long, 489; quotation marks for
        short, 463
    writing about, 748–51
Point-by-point organization, in
    comparison and contrast, 98–99
Point of view, in literature, 737, 898
Political science, research sources
    on, 777, 779
Portfolio, writing, 71–72
Position of modifiers. *See* Word
    order
Positive degree, 240, 318–20, 886
Possessive case
    apostrophes to indicate, 265,
        453–54
    defined, 265, 453, 884
    double, 889
    forms for, 265, 453–54
    of nouns, 233, 265, 453–54
    with *of* (double possessive), 889
    of pronouns, 265, 453, 456
    uses of, 265, 453–54
Post hoc fallacy, 191, 194

PowerPoint, for oral presentations, 861–63
practicable, practical, 877
precede, proceed, 877
Predicate adjectives, 882, 886. *See also* Subject complements
Predicate nouns (predicate nominatives), 886. *See also* Subject complements
Predicates. *See also* Complements; Objects; Verbs
　agreement with subject, 301–08
　in basic sentence patterns, 236–39
　complete, 898
　components of, 236–39
　compound, 336, 886
　defined, 231, 898
　in sentences with mixed grammar, 369–72
　in sentences with mixed meaning (faulty predication), 371–72, 890
　simple, 231–32, 898
Predication, faulty, 371–72, 890
Preface, MLA style, 669
Prefixes
　with capitalized words, 545
　defined, 898
　hyphenation of, 545
　spelling with, 537
Prejudice, in argument, 180
prejudice, prejudiced, 877
Premise of argument, 200–03, 898
Prepositional phrases
　as adjectives or adverbs, 243
　as dangling modifiers, 366
　defined, 243, 898
　functions of, 243
　punctuation of, 244, 425
　as sentence fragments, 244, 335
　subordination with, 392–93
Prepositions
　at, in, on, 519
　defined, 233, 242, 898
　dictionary of, 519
　for, since, 291–92, 519
　grammar checkers for, 511
　idioms with, 518
　list of, 243
　object of, 243, 265, 267, 896
　omission of, 374–75
　position of, 244
　in two-word verbs, 287–88
presence, presents, 533
Present infinitive, and tense sequence, 292–93

Present participle
　as adjective, 246, 321–22
　defined, 246, 273, 897, 904
　vs. gerund, 246, 271, 426
　vs. past participle, 321–22
　in progressive tense, 281–82
　and tense sequence, 293
Present perfect participle, 293
Present perfect progressive tense, 290, 292
Present perfect tense
　in academic writing, 623, 624–25
　defined, 290, 902
Present progressive tense, 281–82, 290, 292, 902
Present tense
　in academic writing, 623, 740, 757, 808
　defined, 290, 902
　special uses of, 291
　in writing about literature, 291, 740
Pretentious writing, 507, 898
pretty, 877
Previewing material
　for reading texts, 132, 732
　for viewing images, 154
previous to, prior to, 877
Primary sources
　defined, 555, 729, 898
　in literary analysis, 739, 743
　one's own research as, 586–87, 629
　quotations from, 615, 621
　reading, 607–08
　as research sources, 555, 640, 729
　vs. secondary sources, 555, 607, 615–16, 729
principal, principle, 533, 877
Principal clause, 898. *See also* Main (independent) clauses
Principal parts of verbs, 272–73, 898, 904
Printing out research sources, pros and cons, 609–10
Print sources, documenting
　APA style, 789–91, 796–97
　Chicago style, 764–66, 769–70
　CSE style, 814–15, 817
　MLA style, 658–71, 687
prior to, 518
Problem-solution organization
　defined, 899
　for essay, 42
　for paragraph, 83–84
　sample report, 851

proceed, precede, 877
Proceedings, MLA style, 669
Process
    critical reading of images, 153–61
    critical reading of texts, 140–52
    reading and writing about literature, 731–54
    reading for comprehension, 131–35
    research writing, 549–50
    writing, 2–72
Process analysis
    defined, 899
    in essay development, 26
    in paragraph development, 100–01
Progressive tenses
    be in forming, 281–82
    defined, 292, 902–03
    forms of, 290
    uses of, 281–82
Pronoun-antecedent agreement. *See* Agreement of pronouns and antecedents
Pronouns. *See also* Indefinite pronouns; Personal pronouns; Relative pronouns
    agreement with antecedents, 301, 309–13
    case of, 264–71
    defined, 233, 235, 899
    demonstrative, 899
    gender of, 309–10
    grammar checkers for, 265–66, 346
    indefinite, 265, 899
    intensive, 899
    interrogative, 265, 899
    after linking verbs, 266
    objective forms of, 265
    for paragraph coherence, 86
    personal, 899
    possessive forms of, 265, 456
    reciprocal, 899
    reference of, 345–51
    reflexive, 899
    relative, 265, 899
    subjective forms of, 265
    types of, 899
Pronunciation, as guide to spelling, 532, 539
Proofreading
    defined, 899
    of final draft, 643
    for omissions, 375
    for spelling, 539
    techniques for, 65–66

Proper nouns and adjectives
    a, an, or *the* with, 323–25
    capitalization of, 484–85
    defined, 484, 882, 896
Proposals, 849–52
ProQuest Research Library, 573, 576
Prose, formatting long quotations from
    APA style, 801
    Chicago style, 772
    MLA style, 691
prosecute, persecute, 533
proud of, 518
prove, as linking verb, 237
provided, as subordinating conjunction, 251, 392
provided, providing, 877
Psychology, research sources on, 777, 779
Publication Manual of the American Psychological Association. See APA style
Publications, government. *See* Government publications
Public writing, 840–55
    brochures, 853–55
    for community work, 852–55
    fax transmissions, 846
    flyers, 853–54
    letters, 841–44
    memos, 845–46
    newsletters, 852–54
    proposals, 849–52
    reports, 849–51
    résumés, 848–50
Punctuation. *See also individual marks*
    of absolute phrases, 249, 432
    apostrophe, 451–58
    of appositives. *See* Appositives
    brackets, 474
    charts of, 416–17, 460–61
    colon, 467–69
    comma, 422–42
    with conjunctive adverbs, 259, 342–43, 446
    of coordinate elements, 257–58, 389, 422–24, 433–34, 439–41
    dash, 470–72
    ellipsis mark, 475–77
    of essential and nonessential elements, 427–41
    exclamation point, 420–21
    hyphen, 544–46
    of linked main clauses, 340–44, 422–42, 443–50

Punctuation *(continued)*
  in online communication, 504
  parentheses, 472–73
  with parenthetical citations, 652
  of parenthetical expressions, 430,
    472–73
  period, 418–19
  of prepositional phrases, 244,
    425, 427–29
  question mark, 419–20
  quotation marks, 436–38, 459–66
  semicolon, 443–50
  slash, 478
  of subordinate clauses, 253,
    425–26, 427–29
  of subordinate elements, 393–94
  with titles, 463
  with transitional expressions, 90,
    342–43, 430, 446
  of verbals and verbal phrases,
    248, 425, 427–29
Purpose
  of academic writing, 165–66
  of argument, 198–99
  of critical reading, 138–39
  defined, 899
  defining one's own, 9–11
  determining, in evaluating Web
    sources, 593, 597
  in e-mail communications, 829
  of essay, 5, 9–11
  of images, 154
  of oral presentation, 856–58
  of research paper, 548–49

Q

Qualitative evidence, 775
Quantitative evidence, 775, 806
Question mark
  after direct questions, 419–20
  with other punctuation, 420,
    465–66
*question of whether, question as to
    whether,* 877
Questions
  for analysis in critical reading, 147
  about audience, 5, 13
  critical reading of arguments, 178
  developing a thesis statement
    from, 29–32
  direct, 260, 357, 419–20, 889
  on essay examinations, 823–25
  in essay introductions, 106
  for evaluating blogs and online
    discussions, 600–01

  for evaluating sources, 591, 593,
    600–01
  for evaluating Web sites, 593
  formation of, 260
  indirect, 357, 418–19, 892
  journalist's, 24–25, 893
  for previewing images, 154
  for previewing text, 142
  for refining a writing subject, 4–5,
    7–9, 552–53
  for research, 552–53
  rhetorical, 411, 900
  series of, capitalization for, 419,
    483
  shift in form of, 357
  about subject, 4, 7–9
  tag, 431, 902
  who vs. *whom* in, 269
Quotation marks, 459–66
  avoiding unnecessary, 464–65
  chart of uses, 460
  for dialog, 462
  for direct quotations, 460–61
  double, 459–61
  grammar checkers for, 459
  in information gathering, 616
  for language copied from source,
    630–31
  with other punctuation, 437, 465
  with poetry, 690
  for quotation within a quotation,
    460, 461–62
  single, 461–62
  space with, in documents, 119
  for titles, 463
  for words used in a special sense,
    464
Quotations, direct
  accuracy of, 460–61, 618–19
  avoiding plagiarism with, 626–35
  brackets for changes in, 460, 474,
    482–83
  capitalization in, 482–83
  colons with, 460, 465, 469
  commas with, 436–38, 465
  conventions for handling, 460, 621
  and copyrights, 633–34
  dashes with, 465–66
  defined, 459, 899
  of dialog, 110, 462
  displayed separately from text:
    APA style, 801; Chicago style,
    772; MLA style, 690–91
  documentation of, 627, 630–31
  ellipsis marks in, 461, 475–77
  in essay introductions, 105–06

exclamation points with, 465–66
fair use of, 633–34
guide to handling, 460
vs. indirect quotation, 357. *See
 also* Indirect quotations
in information gathering, 615–17
integrating, into sentences and
 papers, 620–21
interpreting, in a paper, 621–24
introducing, in a paper, 620–21
in literary analysis, 739, 743
long quotations, format of: APA
 style, 801; Chicago style, 772;
 MLA style, 691
omissions from, 461, 475–77
vs. paraphrase and summary,
 615–16
periods with, 437
plagiarism with, avoiding, 627,
 630–31
of poetry: Chicago style, 772;
 MLA style, 690
punctuating, 460
question marks with, 419–20
within quotation, 460, 461–62
quotation marks for, 460–61
semicolons with, 437
shifts between indirect quotations
 and, 357
sic in, 474
signal phrases with: punctuating,
 436–38; using, 622–25
when to use, 460, 739
Quotations, indirect. *See* Indirect
 quotations

R

Races of people, capitalization of,
 485
Racist language
 avoiding, 507–08
 detecting, 187
Radio programs. *See* Television and
 radio programs
rain, reign, rein, 533
raise, raze, 533
raise, rise, 278, 877
rather than, as subordinating conjunction, 251
Rational appeals, 205–06, 225–26,
 884
Readers. *See* Audience
Reading
 for comprehension, 131–35
 critical, 138–46

for developing essay topic,
 140–44
for discovering subject, 18–19
literature, 732–36
for research paper, 589–625
Readings (lectures). *See also* Oral
 presentations; Speeches
MLA style, 688
real, really, 877
Reasonableness, 187
Reasoning
 connecting evidence to claims
 with, 199–205
 deductive, 200–03, 888
 with evidence, 199–206
 faulty, 190–95
 inductive, 199–200, 892
 reason is because, 371–72, 877
Reciprocal pronouns, 899
reckon, calculate, figure, 869
Recursive writing process
 defined, 2–3
 for developing and shaping ideas,
 17
 for drafting, 47
 for revising, 51
Red herring, 191–92
Reductive fallacy, 191, 194
Redundant phrases, 527–28
Refereed journals, 576
Reference list. *See also* Chicago
 style; MLA style
APA style, 779–99
CSE style, 811–17
Reference of pronouns, 345–51
 ambiguous, 345–50
 appropriate *who, which, that*,
 351–52
 appropriate *you*, 350
 broad, 348–49
 to clear antecedents, 345–50
 definite *it, they*, 349
 to implied nouns, 349
 remote, 347
 single meaning for *it*, 350
 to specific antecedents, 349
 to titles of papers, 349–50
 unclear *this, that, which, it*, 348–49
References, parenthetical. *See*
 Parenthetical citations
Reference works, 565–69
 almanacs and yearbooks, 569
 atlases and gazetteers, 569
 biographical, 568
 defined, 565–67
 dictionaries, 568

Reference works *(continued)*
  documenting: APA style, 795;
    Chicago style, 766–67, 768, 769;
    MLA style, 667, 675
  electronic, 513, 561–62, 565–69
  encyclopedias, 567–68
  government publications, 583–84
  guides to books, 565–69, 571
  guides to sources, 566
  for the humanities, 757–60
  indexes to periodicals, 572–77
  for literature, 741
  for the natural and applied
    sciences, 808–10
  online and print, 565–69
  periodical databases, 572–77
  for the social sciences, 777–79
  using, 565–69
Reflexive pronouns, 899
Refworks, 635
regarding, as preposition, 243
*regarding, in regard to, with regard
  to, relating to, relative to, with
  respect to, respecting*, 878
regardless of, as preposition, 243
Regionalisms (regional language),
  506, 899
Regular verbs
  defined, 275, 900
  forms of, 275
  tenses of, 290
related to, 518
Relationships, capitalization of
  names of, 487
Relative clauses, 900
Relative pronouns
  case of: listed, 265; in questions,
    269; in subordinate clauses,
    269–70
  defined, 235, 251, 899
  list of, 251, 332
  reference of, 351–52
  and sentence fragments, 334
  subordination with, 269–70
  verb agreement with, 307–08
Relevance and reliability, in evaluating sources, 591–92
Relevance of evidence, 183–85
Reliable narrator, in literature, 737
Religion, research sources on, 758,
  760
Religious groups and terms, capitalization of, 485
remain, as linking verb, 237
Repetition
  for emphasis, 384

in redundant phrases, 527–28
  of sentence parts, 370–71
  transitional expressions for, 89
  unnecessary, 527–28
Reports
  documenting: APA style, 794–95,
    796–97; CSE style, 817
  as kind of research paper, 548,
    775, 807
  sample, 851
Representative evidence, 184–85
Research journals, 549–50, 776
Research proposals, 807
Research questions, 552–53, 636–37
Research writing
  analysis, 549
  annotated bibliography for,
    557–60
  APA style: document format,
    799–802; parenthetical cita-
    tions, 780–83; reference list,
    783–99
  avoiding plagiarism in, 626–35
  bibliography for. *See subentries
    here for individual styles*
  blogs for, 582
  books for, 569–71
  Chicago style: document format,
    771–73; notes and list of works
    cited, 760–71
  citing sources in, 634–35
  CSE style: document format,
    817–18; name-year text
    citations, 811; numbered text
    citations, 811–12; reference list,
    812–17
  defined, 548–49
  discussion groups for, 582
  drafting, 640–41
  electronic searches for, 561–65
  electronic sources for, 565–69
  e-mail for, 582
  evaluating sources for, 589–625
  examples of: APA style, 802–05;
    CSE style, 818–20; MLA style,
    691–725
  government publications for,
    583–84
  in humanities, 731–54, 755–73
  images for, 584–85
  integrating summaries, para-
    phrases, and quotations in,
    620–25
  interpretation, 549
  journals, 549–50
  keywords for, 563–65

library for, 561–64, 565–77, 584
about literature, 731–54
MLA style: document format,
653–54, 689–91; list of works
cited, 653–88; parenthetical
citations, 644–53
multimedia sources for, 584–86
in natural and applied sciences,
805–20
outline for, 638–40
paraphrasing sources in, 612–15,
617–18
periodicals for, 571–77
planning, 548–60
primary sources for, 555, 586–88,
729
quoting sources in, 615–18
reading for, 589–625
reference works for, 565–69
report, 548
revising, 641–42
scheduling, 549, 550
secondary sources for, 555, 729
in social sciences, 774–805
sources for, 565–88
strategies for, 554–57
subjects for, 551–52
summarizing sources in, 611–12,
617–18
synthesizing sources for, 604–06
thesis statement for, 636–37
types of, 548–49
Web for, 578–81
working bibliography for, 557–60
respectful, respective, 878
Responding to texts. *See* Critical
writing
Restrictive elements. *See* Essential
elements
Résumés, 848–50
Return-address heading, 842, 847
Reviews
digests of, 571
documenting: APA style, 788, 790,
794; Chicago style, 765; MLA
style, 662, 674–75, 680
as research sources, 759, 778
as writing assignments, 740
Revision
of argument, 210–11
checklists for, 54–55, 74, 211, 642,
745
and collaboration, 68–71
computers and, 55–56
defined, 50–51, 900
vs. editing, 52–53

of essay, 50–56
file management and, 55–56
of literary analysis, 745–47
outlines for, 37
of paragraphs, 74
of research paper, 641–42
sample, 56–59
of sentence fragments, 332–33
of thesis statement, 29–32
rewarded by, for, with, 518
Rhetoric, 900
Rhetorical questions, 411, 900
right, rite, write, 533
rise, raise, 278, 877
rite, write, right, 533
road, rode, 533
Rogerian argument, 208, 210
Role of essay writer, 14–15
Run-on sentences, 891. *See also*
Fused sentences (run-on
sentences)

S

-s, -es
grammar checkers for, 279,
452–53
for plural nouns, 230, 302, 537–38
possessives of words ending in,
454
for regular verbs, 234, 274, 279,
302, 904
and subject-verb agreement, 302
-'s
for plurals of words and characters used as words, 458
for possessives, 453–54
Salutation, business letter, 842–43
Sample documents
APA-style paper, 802–05
argument, 212–15
brochure, 855
critique of an image, 174–75
critique of a text, 171–73
CSE-style paper, 818–20
final draft, 66–68
flyer, 853
illustrations, 123–25
laboratory report, 818–20
MLA style: argument, 212–15;
critiques, 171–73, 174–75; literary analysis, drama, 752–54;
literary analysis, poetry,
750–51; literary analysis, short
story, 746–47; research papers,
691–725

Sample documents *(continued)*
newsletter, 854
outline, 37–39, 694–95
PowerPoint slides, 863
problem-solution report, 851
proposal, 852
report, 851
revision, 56–59
unified and coherent essay,
43–44, 111
Sans serif type fonts, 118, 901
scarcely, but, hardly, 867
scene, seen, 533
Scheduling
research writing, 549–50
study time, 135–37
Scholarly project, MLA style, 674
Sciences, natural and applied,
805–20
assignments in, 806–07
CSE documentation style: name-
year text citations, 811;
numbered text citations,
811–12; reference list, 812–17
CSE document format, 817–18
integrating borrowed material in,
625
methods and evidence in, 806
research sources on, 808–10
sample paper in, 818–20
style guides in, 811
tools and language in, 807–10
Sciences, social. *See* Social sciences
Scientific method, 806
*Scientific Style and Format: The CSE
Manual for Authors, Editors,
and Publishers. See* CSE style
Scratch outline, 34–35
seam, seem, 533
Search engines
Advanced Search options, 579,
580–81
defined, 578
for finding images, 584
keyword searches of, 563–65,
578–81
list of, 579
sample search, 580–81
using, 578–81
Searches, keyword. *See* Keywords
Search histories, 580
Search strategy for sources, 554–57,
569–71
Seasons, capitalization of, 487
Secondary sources
defined, 555, 729, 900

in literary analysis, 739, 743–44
vs. primary sources, 555, 607, 729
quotations from, 555
reading, 607–08
as research sources, 555, 640, 729
Second person, 169, 302, 897
seem, as linking verb, 237
seen, scene, 533
-self pronouns, 266, 876
Semicolons, 443–50
vs. colon, 444, 450, 468
vs. comma, 444, 448
with conjunctive adverbs and
transitional expressions, 259,
343, 446
correcting comma splices with,
341, 343, 437
correcting fused sentences with,
343–44
vs. dash, 450
grammar checkers for, 444
misuse or overuse of, 449–50
with parentheses, 473
vs. period, 385
with quotation marks, 460, 465
sentence fragments with, 449
to separate main clauses, 259,
341, 443–48
in series, 258, 448, 450
with signal phrases, 437
sensual, sensuous, 878
Sentence combining, to achieve
conciseness, 524
Sentence-combining exercises
absolute phrases, 250
appositives, 256
beginnings and endings, 382–83
comma splices and fused sentences, 344–45
compound constructions, 260
coordination, 390–91
essential and nonessential elements, 431–32
introductory elements, 426–27
linked main clauses, 425
main clauses with conjunctive adverbs or transitional expressions, 447–48
parallelism, 404
placing modifiers, 368
prepositional phrases, 245
related main clauses, 445–46
sentence structures, 264
single-word modifiers, 241–42
subordinate clauses, 254
subordination, 395–96

verbals and verbal phrases, 248–49
who vs. *whom*, 270–71
Sentence fragments, 330–37
  acceptable uses of, 337
  appositive as, 255, 336
  vs. complete sentences, 230, 281
  compound predicate as, 336
  defined, 281, 900
  grammar checkers for, 330
  noun plus modifier as, 336
  in online communication, 504
  prepositional phrase as, 244
  revision of, 332–33
  with semicolon, 449
  subordinate clause as, 332, 334
  tests for completeness, 331
  verbal phrase as, 245–48, 334–35
Sentence modifiers, 900. *See also* Modifiers
Sentence outlines, 39, 640
Sentences. *See also* Sentence fragments
  balanced, 383–84, 884
  beginnings of: for emphasis, 380–82; varying, 408–10
  capitalization of first word of, 468, 482–83
  changing word order of, 260–61, 307
  complex, 263, 900
  compound, 262–63, 886, 900
  compound-complex, 263, 900
  conditional, 294–95
  cumulative (loose), 381, 888
  defined, 231, 900
  elements of, 231–39
  endings of, for emphasis, 381–82
  end punctuation for, 418–21
  fused. *See* Fused sentences (run-on sentences)
  incomplete, 373–75
  length of, 406–07
  mixed, 369–72
  passive, 298–99, 525
  patterns of, 236–39
  periodic, 381–82, 409, 897
  repeated parts of, 370–71
  run-on. *See* Fused sentences (run-on sentences)
  simple, 262, 407, 900
  thesis. *See* Thesis and thesis statement
  topic. *See* Topic sentence
  transitional, 111

types of, 262–63
variety in, 405–10, 903
Sequence of tenses
  in conditional sentences, 294–95
  with infinitives, 292–93
  with participles, 293
  with past and past perfect tense, 293
Series
  capitalization of questions in, 419, 483
  colon to introduce, 450, 469
  commas around, 442
  commas in, 433
  dashes with, 442, 471
  defined, 433, 901
  documenting: Chicago style, 766; MLA style, 663, 668
  emphasis in, 383
  parallelism in, 383
  semicolons in, 258, 448, 450
Serif typefaces, 118, 901
Service learning, 852–55
set, sit, 278, 878
Setting, in literature, 738, 901
several
  pronouns with, 312
  verbs with, 305–06
Sexist language
  avoiding, 187, 312, 508–10
  defined, 508, 901
  pronoun use and, 312, 509
shall, as helping verb, 274, 284
shall, will, 878
she
  case of, 265
  function in sentence, 235
  vs. *her,* 266
  with indefinite antecedent, 312
she, he; he/she, 312, 478, 872
Shifts, 352–57
  dashes to indicate, 470
  in direct and indirect questions, 357
  in direct and indirect quotations, 357
  grammar checkers for, 87
  in number, 86–87, 353–55
  and paragraph coherence, 87
  in person, 87, 353
  in subject or voice, 356
  in tense or mood, 86–87, 355
Short stories, quotation marks for titles of, 463

should, as helping verb, 274, 284
should, would, 878
should have, as helping verb, 284
should of, 872
sic, use of, 474
sight, site, cite, 532
Signal phrases
   commas with, 436–38, 461
   concluding, 461
   defined, 436, 901
   for integrating borrowed
      material, 622–25
   interrupting quotations with,
      436–38, 461
Signatures
   in business letters, 842, 843
   in e-mail, 830
similarly
   as conjunctive adverb, 259
   punctuation with, 430, 446
   as transitional expression, 88
similar to, 518
Similes, 520, 890
Simple predicate, 231, 898
Simple sentence, 262, 407, 900
Simple subject, 231–32, 900
Simple tenses, 290, 902
Simplicity, on Web pages, 839
since
   vs. *for,* 291–92, 519
   as preposition, 243
   as subordinating conjunction,
      251, 392
   unclear use of, 878
Singular, 233–34, 901
sit, set, 278, 878
site, cite, sight, 532
situation, 878
Size
   as design element, 116–17
   of type, 118
Skimming, 132, 607–08
Slang
   defined, 504–05, 901
   dictionary labels for, 865
   grammar checkers for, 502
   no quotation marks for, 464–65
   uses of, 504–05
Slashes
   between options, 478
   to separate lines of poetry, 478,
      690
   in URLs (electronic addresses),
      546, 680, 767, 791, 815
smell, as linking verb, 237
Snob appeal, 191, 192, 220

so
   as coordinating conjunction, 257
   as intensifier, 878
   punctuation with, 257–58,
      422–24, 445, 448
Social sciences, 774–805
   APA documentation style: paren-
      thetical citations, 780–83; refer-
      ence list, 783–99
   APA document format, 799–802
   assignments in, 775
   integrating borrowed material in,
      625
   methods and evidence in, 774–75
   research sources on, 777–79
   sample paper in, 802–05
   style guides in, 779–80
   tools and language in, 776–79
Sociology, research sources on, 777,
   779
Software. *See* Computer software
some
   as determiner, 322, 325
   pronouns with, 311–12
   usage of, 878
   verbs with, 305–06
somebody
   pronouns with, 311–12
   verbs with, 305–06
*somebody, some body; someone,
   some one,* 879
someone
   pronouns with, 311–12
   verbs with, 305–06
someplace, 879
something
   pronouns with, 311–12
   verbs with, 305–06
sometime, sometimes, some time,
   879
somewheres, 879
Songs. *See* Musical works
sort of, type of, kind of, 874
so that, as subordinating conjunction, 251, 392–93
sound, as linking verb, 237
Sound recordings. *See also* Musical
   works
   acknowledging, 633–34
   documenting: APA style, 798;
      Chicago style, 768, 770; CSE
      style, 817; MLA style, 677, 679,
      684–85, 686
   evaluating, 600–02
   as research sources, 559, 586,
      600–02

titles of: italics or underlining for long works, 489; quotation marks for songs, 463
use in Web compositions, 633–34, 834, 836, 839–40
Sources. *See also* Electronic sources; Primary sources; Secondary sources
acknowledgment of: APA style, 779–99; Chicago style, 760–71; CSE style, 812–17; MLA style, 644–91
in annotated bibliography, 557–60, 590–91
blogs, 582
books, 569–71
citing to avoid plagiarism, 626–35
discussion groups, 582
electronic, 565–69
electronic searches for, 561–65
e-mail, 582
evaluating, 589–625
gathering information from, 561–88, 607–11
government publications, 583–84
guides to, 566
with helpful features, 557
in humanities, 741, 757–60
for images, 584–85
impartial or biased, 556
integrating into text, 620–25
keeping accurate records on, 608, 609–10
keywords for finding, 563–65, 569–71
kinds of, 554–57, 566
library, 561–64, 565–69, 584
library vs. Internet, 561–62, 564–65, 591–94
in literature, 741
in natural and applied sciences, 808–10
older vs. newer, 556
periodicals, 571–77
permission for use of, 633–34
reference works, 565–69
scholarly vs. popular, 556
setting goals for, 554–57
synthesizing, 604–06
tapping into own knowledge, 554
tracking, 557–60, 576
types of, 561–62
Web, 578–81
in working bibliography, 557–60
Spatial organization
defined, 901

of essay, 40
of paragraph, 81–82
specially, especially, 871
Specific information
for audience, 12
in paragraph development, 92–93
Specific-to-general organization
of essay, 41
of paragraph, 83
Specific vs. general, 33–34, 516–17, 891
Speeches. *See also* Oral presentations
MLA style, 688
italics or underlining for titles of, 489
Speech vs. writing, 502–06, 856
Spelling, 531–44
American vs. British, 534
of commonly misspelled words, 540–44
of compound words, 545
for different forms of same word, 533–34
of homonyms, 514, 532–33
irregular, 534
mnemonics for, 540
in online communication, 504
pronunciation as guide to, 532
rules for, 534–38
Spelling checkers, 63–64, 512, 531, 539
Split infinitives, 362–63, 901
Spoken vs. written language, 502–06, 856
Squinting modifiers, 361–62, 894
Standard American English
in academic writing, 168–70, 502
defined, 168, 502, 901
grammar checkers for, 502
vs. other dialects and languages, 168, 170, 503–04, 865
Standardizing
elements in document design, 116
elements in Web design, 838
State names. *See* Geographical names
stationary, stationery, 533
Statistics
as evidence, 182
numerals vs. words for, 497
in research sources, 560
stay, as linking verb, 237
Stereotypes
avoiding, 507–08
as fallacy in argument, 191, 194

still
  as conjunctive adverb, 259
  punctuation with, 430, 446
Stories
  quotation marks for titles of, 463
  writing about, 747–48
straight, strait, 533
Study skills. *See* Academic skills
Style, writing
  appropriate words for, 502–10
  effective sentences for, 378–412
  exact words for, 511–22
  tone for, 14
  voice for, 14
Style/grammar checkers, 64–65. *See
    also* grammar checkers *under
    specific issues*
Style guides
  humanities, 643, 760
  natural and applied sciences, 811
  social sciences, 779–80
Subject-by-subject organization, in
    comparison and contrast, 98–99
Subject complements
  adjectives or nouns as, 237–38,
    317
  defined, 237–38, 886
  with linking verbs, 237–38
  subjective case for pronouns as,
    266
Subject directories in Web searches,
    578
Subjective case
  defined, 264, 884
  forms for, 266
  uses of, 264, 266
Subjective description, 94
Subject of infinitive, 268
Subject of paper
  for argument, 196–97
  broad vs. specific, 7–9
  choosing and limiting, 4, 6–9
  developing, 16–44
  for oral presentation, 856
  refining by questioning, 4, 7–9,
    552–53
  for research paper, 551–52
Subject of sentence
  agreement with verb, 301–08
  case of, 266
  complete, 231–32, 901
  compound, 266, 311, 886
  consistency in, 356
  defined, 231, 901
  effective use for emphasis, 378–80
  finding, 331–32

and mixed grammar, 369–72
and mixed meaning (faulty predi-
    cation), 371–72
omitted, 331–32
postponed, 260–61
repeated, 370–71
separated from verb, 362
simple, 231–32, 901
Subject-verb agreement. *See* Agree-
    ment of subjects and verbs
Subjunctive mood
  defined, 296, 895
  grammar checkers for, 297
  use of, 296–97
Subordinate (dependent) clauses
  as adjectives or adverbs, 252
  commas with, 428–29, 441
  correcting comma splices with,
    341
  correcting fused sentences with,
    343–44
  defined, 250, 885
  elliptical, 253, 366, 889
  as introductory element, 425–26
  vs. main (independent) clause,
    250
  misuse of semicolon with, 449–50
  as modifiers, 231
  as nouns, 252
  punctuation of, 253, 393–94,
    425–26, 428–29, 441
  as sentence fragment, 334
  verb tense in, 294–95
Subordinating conjunctions
  vs. conjunctive adverbs, 258–59,
    342–43
  correcting comma splices with,
    341
  correcting fused sentences with,
    343–44
  defined, 233, 251, 887
  list of, 251, 332, 392–93
  misused, 397
  no comma after, 441
  other function words with, 251
  and sentence fragments, 334
Subordination, 391–97
  defined, 388, 902
  to distinguish main ideas, 391–95
  excessive, 394–95
  faulty, 394
  grammar checkers for, 388
  punctuation with, 393–94
  use of, 393
Subscription services. *See* Data-
    bases, electronic

finding bibliographic information
for, 682
as research sources, 572–77
Substantive, 902
Subtitles, colons with, 469
such
as determiner, 325
as vague intensifier, 879
such as, like, 875
Suffixes
defined, 902
derivational, 902
hyphens with, 545
inflectional, 902
Suggestive title, 53
Summaries
as aid to critical reading, 145–46
as aid to reading comprehension,
134–35
avoiding plagiarism with, 627,
631
colon before, 450, 468
vs. critical writing, 171, 743, 745
defined, 134, 611, 902
draft, 135
for essay exams, 822
examples of, 134–35, 611–12
in information gathering, 611–12,
617–18
introducing, in a paper, 620–21
vs. literary analysis, 743, 745
vs. paraphrases and direct quotations, 611–18, 631
as research paper, 806
in responding to texts, 163
revised, 135
techniques for writing, 134–35
transitional expressions for, 89
verbs for introducing, 623
Summary or review of research reports, 775
Superfluous commas. *See* Commas,
misuse of
superior to, 518
Superlative degree
appropriate use of, 318–20
defined, 240, 318, 886
formation of, 318–20
of irregular adjectives and adverbs, 319
supposed to, used to, 879
sure, 879
sure and, sure to; try and, try to, 879
Surveys
for gathering quantitative and
qualitative data, 775

as primary sources in research,
587–88, 729
Sweeping generalization, 191,
193–94
Syllogism
deductive reasoning with, 201–03
defined, 201, 902
Symbolism, in literature, 738, 902
Synonyms
defined, 515, 902
dictionaries and thesauruses of,
513
Syntax, 902
Synthesis
in academic writing, 164–65,
604–06
in critical thinking and reading,
150–51, 160–61, 604–06
defined, 150, 902
guidelines for, 147
in research writing, 604–06, 756
in responding to texts, 162–65,
604–06
in viewing illustrations, 160–61

T

Tables
APA style, 804
CSE style, 819
MLA style, 122
uses and design of, 122
Tag questions, 431, 902
take, bring, 867
Taking notes. *See* Information gathering
taste, as linking verb, 237
Technical terms
no quotation marks with, 464
use of, 506
Technical writing
abbreviations in, 492, 494–95
brackets in, 474
capital letters in, 482
documentation in, 811–20
illustrations in, 817–18
numbers in, 497
terms in, 464, 506
Telephone interviews, 587
Television and radio programs
documenting: APA style, 798–99;
MLA style, 676, 685
titles: italics or underlining for
programs, 489; quotation
marks for episodes, 463
Templates, word processing, 117

Tenses of verbs, 289–95
  in conditional sentences, 294–95
  defined, 289, 902–03
  in humanities, 624–25, 757
  of infinitives, 292–93
  list and forms of, 290
  in literary analysis, 624, 740
  in natural and applied sciences,
    625, 808
  perfect, 290, 291–92, 902
  present, 291
  progressive, 281–82, 292, 902–03
  sequence of, 292–93
  shifts in, 86–87, 355
  simple, 902
  in social sciences, 625
  use of appropriate, 289–95
Term papers. *See* Research writing
Terms, defined. *See* Defined terms
Text files, MLA style, 684–85
Text messaging, revising shortcuts
    of, 504
than
  case of pronoun after, 268
  as subordinating conjunction, 251
than, as, 867
than, then, 879
that
  in adjective clauses, 252, 370–71
  case of, 265
  with clauses that demand, re-
    quest, or recommend, 297
  close antecedent for, 347
  as determiner, 325
  in essential clause, 429, 879
  and excessive subordination, 395
  no comma with, before direct or
    indirect quotation, 437, 441
  in noun clauses, 252
  omission of, 375
  quotation introduced by, 437
  reference of, 347, 348–49, 351–52
  as relative pronoun, 235, 251,
    351–52, 393
  specific antecedent for, 348–49
  as subordinating conjunction, 251
  subordination with, 392–93
  verbs with, 307–08
  vs. *which,* 429, 879
  vs. *who* and *which,* 351–52, 879
the
  vs. *a, an,* 323–25
  capitalization in titles, 483
Theater. *See* Plays
their, as determiner, 322, 325
their, there, they're, 533, 880

theirselves, 880
them
  not as adjective, 880
  vs. *they,* 266
Theme, in literature, 738, 903
then
  as conjunctive adverb, 259
  punctuation with, 430, 446
then, than, 879
the only one of the, agreement prob-
    lems with, 308
there, they're, their, 457, 533, 880
thereafter
  as conjunctive adverb, 259
  punctuation with, 430, 446
therefore
  as conjunctive adverb, 259
  punctuation with, 430, 446
  as transitional expression, 89
there is, there are
  and agreement of verb, 307
  eliminating for conciseness, 261,
    524, 529
  as expletive construction, 261,
    410, 529, 890
  grammar checkers for, 524
  necessity of *there* in, 261
  uses of, 261, 410, 529
Thesauruses, 513
these, as determiner, 322, 326
these, this, 880
these kind, these sort, these type,
    those kind, 880
Theses. *See* Dissertations
Thesis and thesis statement
  argumentative, 28–29, 179
  conceiving, 27–29
  defined, 27, 198, 903
  developing from questions, 29–32
  drafting and revising, 29–32
  of essay, 27–32, 104–07
  in essay examination, 825
  in essay introduction, 104–07
  explanatory, 28–29
  functions of, 28
  of literary analysis, 742–43
  of research paper, 636–37
  in responding to texts, 163
they
  to avoid generic *he,* 313, 353–55
  case of, 265
  definite antecedent for, 349
  as personal pronoun, 235
  reference of, 349
  shifts in person and, 353
  vs. *them,* 266

they're, their, there, 533, 880
Third person
    in academic writing, 169, 740,
        757, 776, 808
    defined, 897
    and grammatical agreement, 302
    point of view, in literature, 737
this
    as determiner, 322, 325
    reference of, 348–49
    specific antecedent for, 348–49
this, these, 880
*this here, these here, that there, them
        there,* 880
those, as determiner, 322, 326
though, as subordinating conjunc-
        tion, 251, 392
Threads, in online chat, 833
through, as preposition, 243
throughout, as preposition, 243
thru, 880
thus
    as conjunctive adverb, 259
    punctuation with, 430, 446
    as transitional expression, 89
thusly, 880
till
    as preposition, 243
    as subordinating conjunction, 251
till, until, 'til, 880
Time
    AM or *PM* with, 493
    at, in, or *on* in expressions of,
        519
    colon used to punctuate, 469
    for or *since* in expressions of,
        291–92, 519
    management for studying, 29–30
    numerals vs. words for, 497
    organization by: of essay, 40; of
        paragraph, 82
    transitional expressions for, 89
time period, 880
Title of paper
    capitalization of, 483
    creating, 53
    descriptive, 53
    format for, 689
    no quotation marks for, 464
    reference of pronoun to, 349–50
    suggestive, 53
Title page
    APA style, 799
    Chicago style, 773
    MLA style, adaptation for, 689,
        692–93

Titles of persons
    abbreviations for, 492–93
    in business letters, 843
    capitalization of, 486
    Ms. vs. *Mrs.* or *Miss,* 509–10, 843
Titles of works. *See also* Title of
        paper
    agreement of verb with, 308
    APA style, 785
    articles in periodicals, 463
    books, 463
    capitalization in, 483
    Chicago style, 762
    colon before subtitle in, 469
    computer software, 489
    CSE style, 813
    essays, 463
    italics or underlining for, 463, 489
    long musical works, 489
    MLA style, 659, 664
    movies, 463, 489
    pamphlets, 489
    periodicals, 463
    plays, 463, 489
    poems: long, 489; short, 463
    quotation marks for, 463
    short stories, 463
    songs, 463
    speeches, published, 489
    subdivisions of books, 463
    television and radio: episodes,
        463; programs, 489
    visual art, 489
    Web: entire sites, 489; pages or
        documents, 463
Titles within titles, MLA style, 668–69
to
    as infinitive marker, 247, 892–93
    no capital for, in titles, 483
    omission from infinitive, 247
    as preposition, 243
    after verb, 238
to, too, two, 533, 880
together with, subject-verb agree-
        ment with, 304
Tone of writing
    in business memos, 846
    dashes to indicate shifts in, 470
    defined, 14, 186, 903
    determining appropriate, 14–15,
        186–87
    in e-mail, 830
    in literature, 737
    in online discussion lists, 602
    reading critically, in argument,
        186–87

too, as vague intensifier, 880
too, two, to, 533, 880
Topic of paper. *See* Subject of paper
Topic outlines, 38, 640
Topic sentence
    defined, 74, 896
    focusing on, 75
    position in paragraph, 75–77
    unstated, 77
to this end, as transitional expression, 89
Toulmin, Stephen, 177–78, 199
toward, as preposition or subordinating conjunction, 243, 392
toward, towards, 880
Track Changes function, on word processor, 56
Trade names, capitalization of, 486
Transitional expressions
    at beginning of sentence, 409
    for coherence, 87–90
    and comma splices, 342–43
    defined, 87, 903
    list of, 88–89
    overuse and placement of, 89
    in paragraphs, 87–90
    position in clause, 342–43
    punctuation with, 90, 342–43, 426, 430, 446
Transitions. *See also* Transitional expressions
    for coherence, 87–90, 111
    list of expressions for, 88–89
    between paragraphs, 111
    paragraphs for, 110
Transitive verbs
    defined, 236, 278, 903
    vs. intransitive verbs, 236–37
    in passive voice, 282, 298
Translated works
    APA style, 790
    Chicago style, 766
    MLA style, 665
Tree diagrams, for organizing, 35–36
Trite expressions (clichés), 464–65, 522, 903
Truth, of syllogisms, 201–03
try and, try to, 879
Turabian, *A Manual for Writers of Term Papers, Theses, and Dissertations. See* Chicago style
Turnitin, 628
two, too, to, 533, 880
Two-word verbs
    defined, 287, 903
    grammar checkers for, 288
    lists of, 287–88
    separable vs. inseparable, 287–88
Type fonts
    point sizes, 118
    serif and sans serif, 118, 901
type of, 880
type of, sort of, kind of, 874

U

under, as preposition, 243
Underlining. *See* Italics and underlining
underneath, as preposition, 243
undoubtedly
    as conjunctive adverb, 259
    punctuation with, 430, 446
Uniform Resource Locator. *See* URL (uniform resource locator)
uninterested, disinterested, 870
unique, 319–20, 880
Unity. *See also* Coherence
    defined, 42–43, 903
    of essays, 42–43
    of paragraphs, 74–77
    sample essay, 43–44, 111
    on Web pages, 44
unless, as subordinating conjunction, 251, 393
unlike, as preposition, 243
Unpublished dissertations or theses. *See* Dissertations
Unreliable narrator, in literature, 737
Unstated premise, 202
until
    as preposition, 243, 259, 393
    as subordinating conjunction, 251, 259, 393
until, till, 'til, 880
up, as preposition, 243
upon, as preposition, 243
upon, on, 876
URL (uniform resource locator)
    breaking: APA style, 791; Chicago style, 767; CSE style, 815; MLA style, 680; no hyphenation, 546
    defined, 903
    documenting: APA style, 791, 793–96, 798; Chicago style, 767–69; CSE style, 815; MLA style, 671, 679–80
    in evaluating sources, 596–97
    recording as research source, 609
    slashes in, 478
    and Web sources, 671, 679–80
    in working bibliography, 559

us
case of, 265
vs. *we*, with noun, 267
Usage
in academic writing, 168–70,
502–06, 891
in business writing, 502–06, 891
in e-mail, 829, 830
formal vs. informal, 168–70,
502–06, 891
glossary of, 865–81
nonstandard, 503–04, 895
spoken vs. written, 502–06
standard American English,
168–70, 503–04
in this handbook, vii
usage, use, 880
use, utilize, 880
used to, as helping verb, 274, 284
used to, supposed to, 879
Usenet newsgroups. *See* Discussion
groups, online

V

Validity, of syllogism, 201–03
Variety in sentences, 405–10
defined, 405, 903
grammar checkers for, 406
inverting word order for, 411
length and, 406–07
mixing sentence types for,
411–12
sentence beginnings for, 408–10
with signal phrases, 622–25
Verbals and verbal phrases
as adjectives, 247–48
as adverbs, 247
defined, 245, 247, 903
as nonfinite verbs, 245–46, 331,
903
as nouns, 247–48
objects of, 247–48, 268
punctuating, 248, 425
as sentence fragments, 245–48,
334–35
subordination with, 393
types of, 334–35
uses of, 245–48
Verb complements, 886. *See also* Direct objects; Indirect objects
Verb phrases
defined, 274, 903
separating parts of, 363
Verbs. *See also* Predicates
agreement with subjects, 301–08

auxiliary (helping), 234, 274,
280–84
defined, 233, 903
and disciplines' styles, 624–25
effective use for emphasis, 378–80
finite vs. nonfinite, 245–46, 331,
890, 903
forms of, 234, 272–88, 904
with gerund or infinitive, 285–87
grammar checkers for: gerunds
and infinitives, 285; incorrect
main verbs, 280; irregular
verbs, 275; omitted helping
verbs, 280; omitted -*s* and -*d*
endings, 279; passive voice,
300; subjunctive mood, 297;
tenses and tense sequences,
289; two-word verbs, 288
helping, 234, 274, 280–84, 892
infinitive. *See* Infinitives and infinitive phrases
intransitive, 236, 893
for introducing summaries, paraphrases, and quotations, 623,
624–25
irregular, 234, 275–77, 893
linking, 237–38, 266, 307, 317,
894
main, 274, 894
mood of, 273, 296–97, 355
negating, 316
nonfinite vs. finite, 245–46, 331,
890, 903
number of, 273
object of, 238, 265, 267
omitted, 281
person of, 273
phrase, 274, 363
principal parts of, 272–73, 898, 904
regular, 275, 290, 900
in science writing, 625, 808
separation from subject, object,
or complement, 362
in signal phrases, 623, 624–25
strong vs. weak, 378–80, 525
tenses of, 273, 289–95, 355
transitive, 236–37, 282, 903
two-word, 287–88, 903
voice of, 273, 298–300, 379–80,
525
Video recordings. *See* Films, DVDs,
and video recordings
Vision loss
considering when designing documents, 126
font choices to accommodate, 118

Vision loss *(continued)*
    using verbal descriptions for im-
        ages, 839
    Web designs for, 836
Visual arguments
    reading critically, 216–21
    using, 223–26
Visual art, works of. *See* Illustra-
    tions and artworks
Visual literacy, 153–61, 216–26
Visuals. *See* Illustrations and art-
    works
Vocabulary. *See* Words
Voice (of verbs)
    active vs. passive, 261, 282,
        298–300, 366
    avoiding passive, 300, 379–80, 525
    converting active to passive, 299
    converting passive to active, 298
    defined, 273, 298, 904
    shifts in, 356
Voice (of writer)
    in academic writing, 169–70
    defined, 14, 904
    in responding to texts, 164–65
    for specific audience, 14–15
Volumes
    books: APA style, 790–91; Chicago
        style, 766; MLA style, 648,
        667–68
    periodicals: APA style, 788–89;
        Chicago style, 764; CSE style,
        813; MLA style, 659

W

waist, waste, 533
wait at, for, on, 518, 881
Warrant, 178, 904. *See also*
    Assumptions
ways, 881
we
    case of, 265, 267
    as personal pronoun, 235
    vs. *us,* with noun, 267
weak, week, 533
Weasel words, 507
weather, whether, 533
Web. *See* Web sites
Webcasts, 584, 586
WebCT, 833
Web logs. *See* Blogs
Web pages. *See* Web sites
Web sites. *See also* Electronic
        sources; Internet
    accessibility of, 839
    achieving flow in, 838
    acknowledging sources from,
        632–34
    addresses. *See* URL (uniform
        resource locator)
    browser search history of, 580
    coherence in, 44
    color use in, 120–21, 839
    consistent elements in, 838
    copyright and, 633–34, 836
    creating hypertext documents for,
        834–40
    vs. databases, 564–65
    design and content of, 834–40
    disadvantages of as research
        sources, 555, 564–65, 578
    documenting sources found on:
        APA style, 791–96; Chicago
        style, 767–69; CSE style,
        815–17; MLA style, 671–83
    downloading material from, 142,
        608, 632–34
    evaluating sources on, 593,
        596–600
    finding bibliographic information
        for, 673
    fonts for, 839
    headings on, 120
    HTML for, 836
    hypertext documents on, 834–40
    illustrations on, 839–40
    keyword searches of, 563–65,
        580–81
    library catalogs and databases on,
        563, 569–71, 572–77
    library vs. search engine for
        access, 561–62
    lists in, 838
    menus for, 837, 839
    navigation of, 839
    original sites, 837–40
    papers posted on, 836–37
    paragraphing conventions for,
        73–74
    permission for use of, 633
    plagiarism and, 628, 632–34
    printed documents vs., 834
    saving search results, 578
    search engines, 563–65, 578–81
    searching, 578–81
    simplicity in, 839
    as sources for research, 578–81
    standardizing appearance of,
        839
    structure and content of,
        837–38

titles of: italics for entire sites, 489; quotation marks for pages or documents, 463
unity and coherence of, 44
visual elements in, 839–40
Web sources. *See* Web sites
well, good, 317, 872
what
    as determiner, 325
    as interrogative pronoun, 899
    in noun clauses, 252
    as relative pronoun, 251
whatever
    in noun clauses, 252
    as relative pronoun, 251
when
    in adjective clauses, 252, 370–71
    in noun clauses, 252
    as subordinating conjunction, 251, 393
whenever, as subordinating conjunction, 251, 393
where
    in adjective clauses, 252, 370–71
    in noun clauses, 252
    as subordinating conjunction, 251, 393
whereas, as subordinating conjunction, 251
wherever, as subordinating conjunction, 251
whether
    in noun clauses, 252
    as subordinating conjunction, 251
whether . . . or, as correlative conjunction, 257, 400–01
whether, if, 873
whether, weather, 533
which
    in adjective clauses, 252, 370–71
    case of, 265
    close antecedent for, 347
    as determiner, 325
    with essential and nonessential clauses, 429, 879
    and excessive subordination, 395
    as interrogative pronoun, 899
    omission of, 370–71
    parallelism of clauses with, 400
    reference of, 347, 348–49, 351–52
    as relative pronoun, 235, 251, 393
    specific antecedent for, 348–49
    vs. *that,* 429, 879
    vs. *that* and *who,* 351–52, 879
    verbs with, 307–08
which, witch, 533

while
    as connector, 397
    misuse of, 397
    as subordinating conjunction, 251, 393, 397
who
    in adjective clauses, 252, 370–71
    case forms of, 265, 269–70
    close antecedent for, 347
    and excessive subordination, 395
    as interrogative pronoun, 899
    in noun clauses, 252
    omission of, 370–71
    parallelism of clauses with, 400
    reference of, 347, 351–52
    as relative pronoun, 235, 251, 393
    vs. *that* and *which,* 351–52, 879
    verbs with, 307–08
    vs. *whom,* 269–70, 881
whoever
    case of, 265
    in noun clauses, 252
    as relative pronoun, 251
    vs. *whomever,* 269–70
who is, who has, as contraction *who's,* 456–57, 881
whole, hole, 532
whom
    in adjective clauses, 252, 370–71
    case of, 265
    in noun clauses, 252
    omission of, 370–71
    as relative pronoun, 251
    vs. *who,* 269–70, 881
whomever
    case of, 265
    in noun clauses, 252
    as relative pronoun, 251
    vs. *whoever,* 269–70
who's, whose
    contraction vs. possessive, 457, 533, 881
    grammar checkers for, 452–53
whose
    in adjective clauses, 252, 370–71
    as determiner, 322, 325
    reference of, 351–52
    as relative pronoun, 251
    vs. *who's,* 457, 533, 881
why, in noun clauses, 252
Wikipedia
    MLA style, 678
    as research source, 567, 578, 597

Wikis
    defined, 904
    documenting: APA style, 795;
        MLA style, 678
    as research source, 567, 578, 597
will, as helping verb, 274, 284
will, shall, 878
-wise, -ize, 874
with, 243, 392
within, 243
without, 243, 393
with regard to, with respect to, 878
Wizards and templates, 117
Word classes, 233
Word division, 545–46
Word groups, expanding sentences
    with, 242–55
Wordiness, avoiding, 523–30
    avoiding nouns made from verbs,
        524, 525
    combining sentences, 524
    cutting empty words and phrases,
        525–26
    cutting repetition, 527–28
    eliminating *there is, here is*, and *it
        is* constructions, 261, 529
    for emphasis, 386–87
    focusing on subject and verb,
        524–25
    grammar checkers for, 524
    reducing clauses and phrases, 528
    rewriting jargon, 529–30
    simplifying, 525–29
    using active voice, 524–25
    using strong verbs, 525
Word order
    defined, 904
    English vs. other languages, 236
    inverted, 260–61, 307, 411, 893
    with modifiers, 359–65
    normal, 236–39, 411
    subject-verb agreement and, 307
Words, 502–22
    abstract vs. concrete words,
        516–17
    appropriate language, 502–10
    biased language, 507–10
    clichés, 522
    colloquial language, 505
    commonly confused, 532–33
    compound, 886
    conciseness, 523–30
    connotation, 186–87, 514–15, 887
    denotation, 514, 888
    double talk (doublespeak), 507,
        889

euphemisms, 506–07
    exact language, 514–15
    figurative language, 520–21, 890
    formal vs. informal language, 502,
        504–05
    general vs. specific words, 516–17
    idioms, 373, 518, 892
    jargon, 529–30, 893
    neologisms, 506
    nonstandard. *See* Culture-lan-
        guage issues
    pretentious writing, 507
    regionalisms, 506, 899
    sexist language, 312, 508–10
    slang, 464–65, 504–05, 865, 901
    standard. *See* Standard American
        English
    technical words, 506
    trite expressions, 464–65, 522, 903
    used as words: forming plurals of,
        458; italics or underlining for,
        490; quotation marks for, 464
    weasel words, 507
    wordiness, avoiding, 523–30
Word spacing, 119
Words used as words
    forming plurals of, 458
    italics and underlining for, 490
    quotation marks for, 464
Working bibliographies
    annotated, 557–60
    information for, 557–60
Works cited. *See also* APA style;
        CSE style
    Chicago style, 760–71
    MLA style, 653–88
Works of art. *See* Illustrations and
        artworks
World Wide Web. *See* Blogs; Elec-
        tronic sources; Internet; Web
        sites
would, as helping verb, 274, 284
would, should, 878
would be, 881
would have vs. *had*, 297, 881
would of, 872
write, right, rite, 533
Writing process, 2–72
    audience in, 12–15
    collaborating in, 68–71, 831–34
    critical approach to, 25–26,
        171–75
    defined, 2, 904
    developing or planning, 16–44
    drafting, 46–50
    invisible writing in, 22

portfolio as result of, 71–72
purpose in, 9–11
recursiveness of. *See* Recursive
  writing process
revising, 50–56
stages of, 2–3
strategies for, 25–26
subject in, 6–9
Writing situation
  analyzing, 4–5
  checklist for, 4–5
  context for, 4
  defined, 4–5, 904
Written vs. spoken language,
  502–06, 856

 Y

Yahoo!, 579
Yearbooks, 569
yes, commas with, 430
yet
  as coordinating conjunction, 257

punctuation with, 257–58,
  422–42, 445, 448
yet, but, however, 868
you
  in academic writing, 169
  appropriate use of, 350, 881
  case of, 265
  deletion in commands, 261,
    331
  as personal pronoun, 235
  shifts in person and, 353
your, as determiner, 325
your, you're
  contraction vs. possessive, 457,
    533, 881
  grammar checkers for, 452–53
yourself, herself, himself, myself,
  876

Z

Zip codes, 435
Zotero, 635

Useful Lists and Summaries

Abbreviations, 493
Academic skills
  developing, 128–29
  exams, 136–38, 822–28
  note taking in class, 131
  reading, 131–33, 140
  time management, 129–31
Academic writing
  responding to texts, 163–64
  tips for, 135–36
Agreement
  pronoun-antecedent, 310
  subject-verb, 304
Apostrophes, 454
Arguments
  critically reading, 178
  fallacies in, 191
  organizing, 210
  revising, 211
  visual, 216–26
Articles (a, an, the), uses of, 322–25
Assignments, responding to, 6–9
Audience, questions about, 13
Capital letters
  proper nouns and adjectives, 484–85
  titles of persons, 486
  titles of works, 483
Collaboration, 69–71, 831–34
Comma splices, revision of, 340
Conjunctions
  coordinating, 257
  correlative, 257
  subordinating, 251
Conjunctive adverbs, 259
Document design, elements of, 117–25
Drafting, tips for, 46–48
Editing checklist, 60–61
Fused sentences, revision of, 340
Glossary of Terms, 882–904
Glossary of Usage, 865–81
Job application, 847–50
Oral presentations, checklist for, 857
Paragraphs
  closing, 107–10
  opening, 104–07
  revising, 74
Paraphrasing, 612–15
Plagiarism, avoiding, 627
Prepositions
  idioms with, 518
  list of, 243
Pronouns
  case forms of, 265
  indefinite, 305
  personal, 265

  relative, 251
Proofreading, tips for, 66
Punctuation, conventions and options, 416–17
Quotations
  editing and punctuating, 460–61
  using and introducing, 620–25
Reading critically
  images, 153–61
  texts, 140–52
Reading for comprehension
  previewing, 132–33
  summarizing, 134–35
  understanding, 133
Research writing
  avoiding plagiarism in, 626–34
  citation of sources in: APA, 779–802; Chicago, 760–71; CSE, 811–18; MLA, 644–88
  evaluating sources for, 591, 593, 600–01
  keyword searches for, 564–65
  kinds of sources for, 566
  scheduling, 550
  subjects for, 551
  working bibliography for, 559
Revision checklist, 54–55
Sentence fragments
  revision of, 332–333
  tests for, 331
Sentence patterns, 237
Sexist language, eliminating, 508–09
Spelling rules, 534–38
Subordination, methods of, 393
Summarizing, 134–35, 145–46, 611–12
Thesis statement, 27–32
Titles of works
  capital letters for, 483
  quotation marks for, 463
  italics or underlining for, 489
Titling an essay, 53
Transitional expressions, 88–89
Verbs and verbals
  helping verbs, 280
  irregular verbs, 275–77
  tense forms and uses, 290
  test for verbs and verbals, 245–46
  voice (active vs. passive), 299
Wordiness, avoiding, 524
Words
  common mistakes in choosing, 512
  commonly confused, 532
  commonly misspelled, 540–44
  in academic writing, 168–70, 503
Writing situation, checklist for, 4–5

Editing Symbols

Boldface numbers and letters refer to chapters and sections of the handbook.

ab	Faulty abbreviation, **35**		*p*	Error in punctuation, **27–32**
ad	Misused adjective or adverb, **16**		*. ? !*	Period, question mark, exclamation point, **27**
agr	Error in agreement, **15**			
ap	Apostrophe needed or misused, **30**		$\hat{,}$	Comma, **28**
			;	Semicolon, **29**
appr	Inappropriate language, **37**		$\check{v}$	Apostrophe, **30**
arg	Faulty argument, **9–11**		" "	Quotation marks, **31**
awk	Awkward construction		: — ( ) [ ] . . . /	Colon, dash, parentheses, brackets, ellipsis mark, slash, **32**
case	Error in case form, **13**			
cap	Use capital letter, **33**			
cit	Missing source citation or error in form of citation, **44**		*par,* ¶	Start new paragraph, **4**
			¶ *coh*	Paragraph not coherent, **4b**
coh	Coherence lacking, **2c-4, 4b**		¶ *dev*	Paragraph not developed, **4c**
con	Be more concise, **39**		¶ *un*	Paragraph not unified, **4a**
coord	Coordination needed or faulty, **24a**		*pass*	Ineffective passive voice, **14j**
			pn agr	Error in pronoun-antecedent agreement, **15b**
cs	Comma splice, **18a–b**			
d	Ineffective diction (word choice), **37–39**		*ref*	Error in pronoun reference, **19**
			rep	Unnecessary repetition, **39c**
des	Ineffective or incorrect document design, **5**		*rev*	Revise or proofread, **3**
			shift	Inconsistency, **20**
det	Error in use of determiner, **16h**		*sp*	Misspelled word, **40**
dev	Inadequate development, **2, 4c**		*sub*	Subordination needed or faulty, **24b**
div	Incorrect word division, **40d**			
dm	Dangling modifier, **21h**		*t*	Error in verb tense, **14g–h**
eff	Ineffective sentence(s), **23–26**		*t seq*	Error in tense sequence, **14h**
emph	Emphasis lacking or faulty, **23**		*trans*	Transition needed, **4b-6, 4e**
exact	Inexact language, **39**		*und*	Underline or italicize, **34**
fp	Faulty predication, **22b**		*usage*	See Glossary of Usage, p. 865
frag	Sentence fragment, **17**		*var*	Vary sentence structure, **26**
fs	Fused sentence, **18c**		*vb*	Error in verb form, **14a–f**
gram	Error in grammar, **12–16**		*vb agr*	Error in subject-verb agreement, **15a**
hyph	Error in use of hyphen, **40d**			
inc	Incomplete construction, **22c–e**		*w*	Wordy, **39**
ital	Italicize or underline, **34**		*ww*	Wrong word, **38b**
k	Awkward construction		*//*	Faulty parallelism, **25**
lc	Use lowercase (small) letter, **33f**		*#*	Separate with a space
log	Faulty logic, **9g, 10d**		$\bigcirc$	Close up the space
mech	Error in mechanics, **33–36**		✍	Delete
mixed	Mixed construction, **22a–b**		t͟h͟e͟	Capitalize, **33**
mm	Misplaced modifier, **21a–g**		T̷he	Use a small letter, **33**
mng	Meaning unclear		t⦣e⦣h	Transpose letters or words
no cap	Unnecessary capital letter, **33f**		X	Obvious error
no $\hat{,}$	Comma not needed, **28j**		^	Something missing, **22e**
no ¶	No new paragraph needed, **4**		??	Document illegible or meaning unclear
num	Error in use of numbers, **36**			

Throughout this handbook, the symbol **CULTURE LANGUAGE** signals topics for students whose first language or dialect is not standard American English. These topics can be tricky because they arise from rules in standard English that are quite different in other languages and dialects. Many of the topics involve significant cultural assumptions as well.

No matter what your language background, as a college student you are learning the culture of US higher education and the language that is used and shaped by that culture. The process is challenging, even for native speakers of standard American English. It requires not just writing clearly and correctly but also mastering conventions of developing, presenting, and supporting ideas. The challenge is greater if, in addition, you are trying to learn standard American English and are accustomed to other conventions. Several habits can help you succeed:

- **Read.** Besides course assignments, read newspapers, magazines, and books in English. The more you read, the more fluently and accurately you'll write.
- **Write.** Keep a journal in which you practice writing in English every day.
- **Talk and listen.** Take advantage of opportunities to hear and use English.
- **Ask questions.** Your instructors, tutors in the writing lab, and fellow students can clarify assignments and help you identify and solve writing problems.
- **Don't try for perfection.** No one writes perfectly, and the effort to do so can prevent you from expressing yourself fluently. View mistakes not as failures but as opportunities to learn.
- **Revise first; then edit.** Focus on each essay's ideas, support, and organization before attending to grammar and vocabulary. See the revision and editing checklists on pages 54–55 and 60–61.
- **Set editing priorities.** Concentrate first on any errors that interfere with clarity, such as problems with word order or subject-verb agreement.

The following index leads you to text discussions of writing topics that you may need help with. The pages marked * include exercises for self-testing.

Academic writing, 168, *170, 503–04
Adjective(s)
   clauses, repetition in, 370–71,*372
   no, with a noun, 316
   no plurals for, 316
   order of, 365, *365
   participles as, 321–22, *322
Adverb(s)
   introductory, word order after, 409
   not, with a verb or adjective, 316, 364
   position of, 364–65, *365, 409

Argument
   expert opinion as evidence in, 183, 628
   subjects for, 197
   taking a position in, 177
Articles (*a, an, the*), 322–25, *326
Audience, 29, 40, 69, 104, 168, 177
Business writing, 841
Capital letters, 482
Collaboration, 69

18 cs / fs
Comma Splices, Fused Sentences 338
a Main clauses without *and, but,* etc.
b Main clauses with *however, for example,* etc.
c Main clauses with no conjunction or punctuation

19 ref
Pronoun Reference 345
a Clear reference
b Close reference
c Specific reference
d Appropriate *you*
e Clear *it*
f Appropriate *who, which, that*

20 shift
Shifts 352
a Person and number
b Tense and mood
c Subject and voice
d Indirect and direct quotations and questions

21 mm / dm
Misplaced and Dangling Modifiers 359
a Clear placement
b Limiting modifiers (*only,* etc.)
c Squinting modifiers
d Separated subject-verb-object
e Separated infinitive or verb phrase
f Position of adverbs
g Order of adjectives
h Dangling modifiers

22 mixed / inc
Mixed and Incomplete Sentences 369
a Mixed grammar
b Mixed meaning (faulty predication)
c Incomplete compounds
d Incomplete comparisons
e Careless omissions

5 Effective Sentences

23 emph
Emphasis 378
a Subjects and verbs
b Sentence beginnings and endings
c Parallel elements
d Repetition
e Separation
f Conciseness

24 coord / sub
Coordination and Subordination 388
a Coordination
b Subordination
c Clear connectors (*as, while, like*)

25 //
Parallelism 398
a With *and, both . . . and,* etc.
b For coherence

26 var
Variety 405
a Sentence length and structure
b Sentence beginnings
c Inverted word order
d Mixed sentence types

6 Punctuation

Chart 416–17

27 . ? !
End Punctuation 418
a Period
b Question mark
c Exclamation point

28 ⌃
Comma 422
a Main clauses with *and, but,* etc.
b Introductory elements
c Nonessential elements
d Absolute phrases
e Phrases of contrast
f Series; two or more adjectives
g Dates, addresses, etc.
h *He said,* etc., with quotations
i To prevent misreading
j Misuse and overuse
  1 After subject or verb
  2 Compound subject, predicate, etc.
  3 After *and, although,* etc.
  4 Around essential elements
  5 Around series
  6 Indirect quotation

29 ;
Semicolon 443
a Main clauses without *and, but,* etc.
b Main clauses with *however, for example,* etc.
c Main clauses that are long or contain commas
d Series items that are long or contain commas
e Misuse and overuse

30 ⌄
Apostrophe 451
a Possession
b Misuses: plurals, verbs, pronouns
c Contractions
d Plural abbreviations, dates, etc.

31 " "
Quotation Marks 459
Chart 460–61
a Direct quotations
b Within a quotation
c Dialog
d Titles of songs, stories, etc.
e Words used in a special sense
f Overuse
g With other punctuation

32 : — ( ) [ ] . . . /
Other Marks 467
a Colon
b Dash
c Parentheses
d Brackets
e Ellipsis mark
f Slash

7 Mechanics

33 cap
Capitals 482
a First word of sentence
b Titles of works
c *I* and *O*
d Proper nouns and adjectives
e Titles of persons
f Misuses

34 ital / und
Italics or Underlining 488
a Titles of books, movies, etc.
b Names of vehicles
c Foreign words
d Words or characters named as words
e Emphasis
f Online communication

35 ab
Abbreviations 492
a Titles with proper names
b Familiar abbreviations
c *BC, BCE, AD, CE, AM, PM, no., $*
d Latin abbreviations
e *Inc., Bros., Co., &*
f Misuses

36 num
Numbers 496
a Numerals vs. words
b Dates, addresses, etc.
c Beginning sentences

8 Effective Words

37 appr
Appropriate Language 502
a Nonstandard dialect
b Online shortcuts
c Slang
d Colloquialisms
e Regionalisms
f Neologisms
g Technical language
h Indirect or pretentious writing
i Sexist and other biased language

CONTINUED ON REVERSE ⟶

Plan of the Book

38 exact
Exact Language *511*
a Dictionary and thesaurus
b Right word for meaning
c Concrete, specific words
d Idioms
e Figurative language
f Fresh, not trite, expressions

39 w
Writing Concisely *523*
a Focusing on subject and verb
b Cutting empty words
c Cutting repetition
d Reducing clauses and phrases
e Revising *there is, here is, it is*
f Combining sentences
g Rewriting jargon

40 sp
Spelling and the Hyphen *531*
a Spelling problems
b Spelling rules
c Spelling skills
d Hyphen to form or divide words

9 Research Writing

41
Planning a Research Project *548*
a Starting out
b Researchable subject and question
c Research strategy
d Working, annotated bibliography

42
Finding Sources *561*
a Your library's Web site
b Searching electronically
c Reference works
d Books
e Periodicals
f The Web
g Other online sources
h Government publications
i Images, audio, video
j Your own sources

43
Working with Sources *589*
a Evaluating sources
b Synthesizing sources
c Mining and interacting with sources
d Using summary, paraphrase, and direct quotation
e Integrating sources into your text

44 plag
Avoiding Plagiarism and Documenting Sources *626*
a Plagiarism and the Internet
b What you need not acknowledge
c What you *must* acknowledge
d Acknowledging online sources
e Documenting sources

45
Writing the Paper *635*
a Thesis statement
b Structure
c Drafting
d Revising and editing
e Final draft

46 MLA
MLA Documentation and Format *644*
a MLA IN-TEXT CITATIONS
b MLA LIST OF WORKS CITED
c MLA DOCUMENT FORMAT

47 MLA
Two Research Papers in MLA Style *691*
"THE FALSE PROMISE OF GREEN CONSUMERISM" *692*
"ANNIE DILLARD'S HEALING VISION" *720*

10 Writing in the Disciplines

48
Goals and Requirements of the Disciplines *728*
a Methods and evidence
b Writing assignments
c Tools and language
d Source citations and document format

49
Literature *731*
a Methods and evidence
b Writing assignments
c Tools and language
d Source citations and document format
e Drafting and revising
SAMPLE ANALYSIS OF A SHORT STORY *746*
f Fiction, poetry, and drama
SAMPLE ANALYSIS OF A POEM *750*
SAMPLE ANALYSIS OF A PLAY *752*

50
Other Humanities *755*
a Methods and evidence
b Writing assignments
c Tools and language
d CHICAGO SOURCE CITATIONS
e CHICAGO DOCUMENT FORMAT

51
The Social Sciences *774*
a Methods and evidence
b Writing assignments
c Tools and language
d APA SOURCE CITATIONS
e APA DOCUMENT FORMAT
f SAMPLE APA PAPER *802*

52
The Natural and Applied Sciences *805*
a Methods and evidence
b Writing assignments
c Tools and language
d CSE SOURCE CITATIONS
e CSE DOCUMENT FORMAT
f SAMPLE CSE PAPER *818*

11 Special Writing Situations

53
Essay Exams *822*
a Preparing
b Planning
c Starting
d Developing
SAMPLE ESSAY EXAMS *826*
e Rereading

54
Writing Online *828*
a E-mail
b Online collaboration
c Web compositions

55
Public Writing *840*
a Letters and memos
SAMPLE LETTER AND MEMO *842, 845*
b Job applications
SAMPLE LETTER AND RESUMES *847, 849–50*
c Reports and proposals
SAMPLE REPORT AND PROPOSAL *851–52*
d Community work
SAMPLE FLYER, NEWSLETTER, AND BROCHURE *853–55*

56
Oral Presentations *856*
a Writing and speaking
b Purpose and audience
c Organization
d Delivery

usage
Glossary of Usage *865*

terms
Glossary of Terms *882*

Index *907*

CULTURE LANGUAGE Guide
(inside back cover)